INTERMEDIATE ACCOUNTING

Lane A. Daley

University of Alberta

Robert L. Vigeland

Texas Christian University

COLLEGE DIVISION   South-Western Publishing Co.

Cincinnati, Ohio

Sponsoring Editor:	David L. Shaut
Developmental Editor:	Minta S. Berry
Production Editor:	Sharon L. Smith
Production House:	Berry Publication Services
Cover Design:	Annette Ross/Bruce Design
Internal Design:	Lesiak/Crampton Design
Cover Photographer:	Frank Miller
Marketing Manager:	Michael O'Brien

Library of Congress Cataloging-in-Publication Data

Daley, Lane, 1953–
    Intermediate accounting / Lane A. Daley, Robert L. Vigeland.
       p.   cm.
    Includes index.
    ISBN 0-538-82935-4
    1. Accounting.   I. Vigeland, Robert L., 1949–   . II. Title.
HF5635.D173   1993
657'.046—dc20   93-38260
                                  CIP

1 2 3 4 5 6 7 K 9 8 7 6 5 4 3

Printed in the United States of America

I (T) P

International Thomson Publishing
South-Western Publishing Co. is an ITP Company. The ITP trademark is used under license.

Material from the Uniform CPA Examination Questions and Unofficial Answers, Copyright © 1977–1988 by the American Institute of Certified Public Accountants, Inc., is reprinted or adapted with permission.

 This book is printed on acid-free paper that meets Environmental Protection Agency standards for recycled paper.

Preface

Intermediate accounting courses are fundamentally important in undergraduate and graduate accounting programs. In most programs, an intermediate course is the first accounting course a student takes after declaring the accounting major. Intermediate accounting provides a foundation for the coursework that follows by exposing the student to the core of generally accepted accounting principles. Until recently, the prevailing wisdom has been that this foundation should consist primarily of strong technical skills and detailed familiarity with authoritative pronouncements from the accounting standard setters. With the proliferation of authoritative pronouncements in the last two decades, such an approach has led to encyclopedic intermediate accounting texts and courses that stress only technical issues.

Our view is that such an approach to intermediate accounting is unfortunate for several reasons. As a practical matter, intermediate accounting students are, in most cases, several years away from opportunities to practice the technical skills that they acquire in their intermediate courses. The complexity of today's accounting standards ensures that much of the technical expertise gained in intermediate accounting courses will almost certainly disappear before the student has an opportunity to apply it.

At a more fundamental level, we believe that accounting students require more than technical preparation to succeed in their careers. Not only must accounting professionals understand how to prepare financial statements in accordance with generally accepted accounting principles, but they must also understand the role of financial statements in our economy, the economic attributes of firms that are captured by financial statements, and the economic and political forces that shape accounting practice and accounting standard setting. How can financial statements continue to serve the needs of society if accountants themselves lack this fundamental understanding? How can accountants exercise the judgment their profession requires without this fundamental understanding?

This text aims to provide students with a better understanding of the context of financial accounting and reporting. How do financial statements reflect economic events and transactions of interest to observers of a firm? What political and economic forces have shaped the development of accounting practice? To what extent do financial accounting standards and practice influence managerial decisions? How is this influence exerted? These are some of the questions addressed in this book. When technical considerations are discussed within the appropriate economic and political context, they become more understandable, more relevant, and more easily retained.

To help students gain this contextual understanding, we try to make sure that before any accounting issues are addressed, students first understand the nature of the complex business transactions that are captured in a firm's financial statements. For instance, what is the nature of a capital lease and how does it differ from other long-term lease contracts? Why are there so many ways of compensating employees? How do the various types of compensation such as stock options, stock appreciation rights, profit sharing plans, pensions, post-retirement benefits plans, and bonuses operate? If students cannot answer these questions adequately, then they cannot hope to understand the accounting treatments applied to these transactions.

In the process of developing an appreciation for the complexities of financial reporting issues, we use numerous references from the various accounting standards and from corporate annual reports. To highlight these references throughout the text, we have inserted the symbols shown here.

Accounting Standards

Annual Reports

The book also includes carefully selected cases that are far more substantial than those usually found in intermediate accounting books. These cases, most of which are drawn from actual corporate financial statements, not only help to illustrate various accounting practices, but they also permit students to see the effects of accounting decisions and understand the context of financial reporting.

This text is designed to appeal to faculty at both graduate and undergraduate institutions where there is an appreciation of the need for technical, conceptual, and contextual understanding in an intermediate level financial accounting course. We want the students using our book to understand fully that financial accounting involves far more than just an application of rules to solve problems. Our hope is that students using this book will be prepared to exercise professional judgment, discuss and explain controversial and complex accounting and reporting issues, and, eventually, take an active role in accounting policy formulation.

ACKNOWLEDGMENTS

Throughout the textbook, relevant professional statements of the Financial Accounting Standards Board and other authoritative publications are discussed, quoted, paraphrased, or footnoted. We are indebted to the American Institute of Certified Public Accountants and the Financial Accounting Standards Board for material from their publications.

As this book has been under development, numerous individuals have contributed to it. The input of editors and reviewers has been valuable as we have written and revised the manuscript of this text. We thank the following reviewers for their insightful comments during the development of the manuscript:

Diana L. Adcox
University of North Florida

Matthew Anderson
Michigan State University

Craig Bain
Northern Arizona University

Dennis Bline
University of Texas-San Antonio

Bruce Bublitz
University of Kansas

Gregory Bushong
University of Kentucky

Allen Frank
The University of West Florida

Dan Givoly
Northwestern University

Trevor Harris
Columbia University

Bart P. Hartman
Louisiana State University

Thomas Hoar
Houston Community College

Scott I. Jerris
West Virginia University

Raymond D. King
New York University

William Kross
Purdue University

David F. Larcker
University of Pennsylvania

Ronald M. Mano
Weber State College

Richard J. Murdock
The Ohio State University

Thomas R. Nunamaker
Washington State University

A. George Petrie
University of Texas-Pan American

Susan Pourciau
Florida State University

Byung T. Ro
Purdue University

Brian Shapiro
The University of Arizona

Wayne H. Shaw
University of Colorado at Boulder

Mary Stone
University of Alabama

Donald Tang
Portland State University

Ralph E. Welton, Jr.
Clemson University

James Worthington
Auburn University

We also appreciate the professionals we have worked with at South-Western Publishing Co. It has been a pleasure working with them.

We welcome your comments and suggestions as you use this book.

Lane A. Daley
Robert L. Vigeland

About the Authors

Lane A. Daley joined the faculty of the University of Alberta as the Chartered Accountant's Chair of Accountancy in 1992. Prior to that time, he was a faculty member at the University of Minnesota where he received recognition for outstanding teaching in the undergraduate program and served as director of the University of Minnesota CPA Review Program. He is a Certified Public Accountant in Minnesota and holds a Ph.D. from the University of Washington. His professional memberships include the American Accounting Association, Canadian Accounting Association, American Finance Association, Public Choice Society, and the American Institute of Certified Public Accountants. Professor Daley has also been actively involved in the development and delivery of continuing professional education programs for both state CPA societies and a number of private CPA firms.

His research, on a variety of financial accounting and accounting education topics, has been published in *The Accounting Review*, the *Journal of Accounting and Economics*, and *Accounting Horizons*, among others. He has been a consultant on matters regarding financial reporting to several Fortune 1000 corporations.

Robert L. Vigeland joined the faculty of the M.J. Neeley School of Business at Texas Christian University as Professor and Chair of the Accounting Department in 1989. Prior to that time, he was faculty member at the University of Minnesota where he was honored as the outstanding teacher by the College of Business Administration in 1978 and by the Student Accounting Association in 1982 and 1983. He is a Certified Public Accountant in New York and holds a Ph.D. from Columbia University. His professional memberships include the American Accounting Association, American Finance Association, the American Institute of Certified Public Accountants, and the Texas Society of Certified Public Accountants.

His research, on a variety of financial accounting and accounting education topics, has been published in *The Accounting Review*, the *Journal of Accounting and Economics*, the *Journal of Accounting Education*, and the *Journal of Commercial Bank Lending*, among others. He has consulted with firms in the manufacturing, telecommunications, electric utility, gas utility, gas transmission, and commercial banking industries.

Contents

CONTENTS

CONTENTS

PART 1

Introduction

CHAPTER 1

The Context of Financial Reporting

¿Se habla Español?
Parlez vous Francais?
Sprechen sie Deutsch?
Do you speak accounting?

Many of you recognize that the first three questions all ask listeners about their ability to speak in a particular language: first Spanish, then French, and finally German. The fourth question may seem foolish at first, but it is really the whole point to this text. Language exists to facilitate the summarization and transmission of ideas between parties. The accounting reports, which are the focus of this text, are part of the overall system of financial reporting and are designed to summarize and transmit information.

In language, definitions and grammatical structure exist to provide a common frame of reference by which two parties can exchange ideas efficiently. This is also true about accounting. The common forms into which accounting data are organized as a report (and the definition of the elements, or pieces that make up those reports) are the language of accounting. This language emerges from the manner in which people can convey via a common system of measurement and presentation such concepts as assets, liabilities, or net worth.

A business organization exists to achieve a particular purpose. Generally, that purpose is to provide customers with some type of product or service. To provide its products or services, the organization must hire and pay employees, purchase inputs such as materials to produce its product, and acquire facilities such as office buildings, warehouses, and manufacturing plants to house all its operations. Customers pay for these goods and services by transferring something of comparable value to the business organization. This payment can be in forms such as cash, promises to pay, or the transfer of other assets such as equipment or securities that have value to the organization. We generally describe this process as the flow of economic resources. Broadly defined, **accounting** is the process of designing and maintaining an information system that focuses on these flows.

When accounting reports are used to communicate information to individuals or groups outside an organization's boundaries, we commonly refer to this form of communication as **external reporting**. There are many different types of external reports. For example, tax returns are external reports; they are submitted to the government to report the organization's economic activities. To communicate relevant information properly between the organization and the IRS, these "financial reports" must be ordered according to the "grammatical structure and definitions" (or language) of the tax code. An organization may also generate other types of special reports according to whatever rules of reporting "grammar" are arranged between the external user of the information and the company.

All these specialized reports are part of accounting's scope. However, our interest here is in only part of this process—the part that focuses on general-use reports produced by entities engaged in business for a profit. These reports are part of a financial information package commonly referred to as the **annual report to shareholders** (or **ARS**).

Before turning our attention to the common structure of the annual report, we should note that the scope of accounting as a discipline is much broader than the preparation and interpretation of annual reports. Of particular interest are the design and maintenance of internal accounting and control systems that help individuals inside of organizations monitor operations and make decisions regarding the future of the enterprise. In addition, as mentioned above, accounting also embraces issues from taxation to the design of annual reports for not-for-profit entities, such as governmental units, universities, and charities. These entities have very different communication needs than most for-profit enterprises for which the annual report was designed.

THE STRUCTURE OF FINANCIAL REPORTS

Our major focus is on the annual report to shareholders (ARS). The targeted user group for this report is typically the shareholders of the corporation. However, the information contained in this document is also commonly used by other investors such as banks, which loan money to the company, bond investors, and suppliers who use this information to assess the credit worthiness of the company.

Format of an Annual Report

The annual report of Allegheny Ludlum Corporation for 1992 is incorporated in Appendix A to this chapter as an example. While the specific format of an annual report varies considerably from company to company, Allegheny Ludlum's report is typical and can be dissected into several parts:

1. Pages 2–5 represent a letter from top management to the corporation's shareholders.
2. Pages 6–18 provide general information about the corporation's products and position in its marketplace, along with any other major issues the corporation's management desires to spotlight as important for its success.
3. Pages 19–22 provide management's discussion of the results of the corporation's operations over the past year. This section relies heavily on data that is presented later in the formal financial statements to describe, in summary form, the major features of the corporation's performance.
4. Pages 23–38 present the actual financial reports. These reports can be further broken down into the financial statements themselves on pages 23–25, the notes to those statements on pages 26–35, the auditor's report on the financial statements on page 36, and management's report on the financial statements on page 38.

From the accounting perspective of this text, only the actual financial statements and the accompanying notes (pages 23–35) are of interest to us. Ultimately, we wish to understand:

1. How the information contained in these reports and notes are compiled
2. What economic and market forces act on the form and content of these reports and generate the constant change that seems to describe the history of accounting and financial reporting

To understand and speak accounting is not simply to memorize the existing rules of accounting grammar. Rather, it is to understand the forces that give rise to these rules as well. Just as language evolves with the special needs of a culture, so does accounting and financial reporting change with the forces that are present in our economy.

Financial Reports and Aggregation

All financial reports summarize information. Large corporations enter into millions of transactions each year, but all of these are not described in detail in financial reports. Instead, a financial report seeks to:

1. Summarize data by collecting similar types of transactions and providing rules for classifying them in a meaningful manner
2. Provide the results that represent the effects of all the individual transactions

We refer to the summation as a signal of the underlying events and transactions that have been included. The process of translating events and transactions into a common format and summarizing the total effect of all similarly coded events is called **aggregation**.

To make the concept of aggregation more concrete, examine Exhibit 1.1, which is a reproduction of Allegheny Ludlum's income statement. In particular, note that the corporation reports a "Commercial and administrative" ex-

EXHIBIT 1.1
Consolidated
Statement of
Income

ALLEGHENY LUDLUM CORPORATION, AND SUBSIDIARIES
FISCAL YEAR ENDED JANUARY 3, 1993

FISCAL YEAR ENDED	JANUARY 3, 1993
Net sales	$1,036,029
Costs and expenses:	
Cost of products sold	829,494
Research, development, and technology	40,262
Commercial and administrative	39,605
Postretirement expense	22,637
Depreciation and amortization	27,578
	959,576
Income from operations	76,453
Other income (expense):	
Interest expense	(8,000)
Unrealized gain from limited partnership	8,808
Other income–net	1,538
	2,346
Income before income taxes and cumulative effect of accounting change	78,799
Income taxes	31,942
Income before cumulative effect of accounting change	46,857
Cumulative effect of accounting change (Less income tax benefit of $85,596)	(125,231)
Net (loss) income	$ (78,374)

pense in the amount of $39,605 for 1992 (dollars in thousands). This item is itself an aggregation of many types of expenses. It contains rent expense on office space, office supplies expenses, wages and salaries to sales personnel and corporate executives, and a host of other individual expense categories.

Allegheny Ludlum decided that providing a detailed list of each of these expenses did not warrant the costs involved in disclosing them. As a result, it aggregated all these expenses into a single, larger category. Note also that the corporation's management did not believe that aggregating "research, development and technology" expense with "commercial and administrative" expense was appropriate. Thus, in the same financial statement, there are examples of both aggregation and disaggregation. In this case, had management aggregated research and development expenses, the extent of the corporation's activities in new product and technology development, which may be critical to its future business opportunities, would have remained unclear. To understand why aggregation exists and why it takes the particular form we see in annual reports requires an appreciation for the economic forces that affect these decisions.

THE ECONOMIC MOTIVATION FOR FINANCIAL REPORTING

Why does financial reporting exist? Why does it take the form we observe? Detailed answers to these questions are quite complex, and even now our understanding of the answers is not complete. However, we can obtain considerable insight into the types of forces that shape financial reporting. To aid in developing this insight, we must first consider whether financial reporting would exist if regulations did not require it. After establishing that financial accounting would exist without regulation, we then turn to the issue of why there is a need for regulation. To make the economic forces that shape the answers to these questions more understandable, consider the following stylized example in which real economic forces are at play.

The example is a tale of two individuals, Mr. Gussett and Ms. Barnes. Mr. Gussett is an automotive mechanic by training. He recently inherited a considerable amount of money. He desires to purchase and manage his own company instead of working for someone else. Ms. Barnes is the sole owner of a large corporation that manufactures specialized automotive parts. The company is called AZ Automotive Parts. AZ has been in business for several years. Ms. Barnes hears of Mr. Gussett's interest in acquiring a company through a mutual friend and contacts Mr. Gussett by phone.

MS BARNES: I understand you are seeking an investment opportunity in the form of a company to buy.

MR GUSSETT: That is correct. I understand you might be interested in selling your automotive parts company. I have a good technical background in that area and am certainly interested. Can you tell me a little about the company and why you wish to sell it?

MS BARNES: Well, my business is really booming. We manufacture mostly specialized exhaust components used on high performance automobiles and supply several of the major automotive manufacturers as well as various retail outlets. The only reason I am selling is because I want to retire and spend some time traveling.

MR GUSSETT: I am very interested in your company and have used some of your products, but I know very little about the financial performance of the firm. How much are you asking for the company?

MS BARNES: I believe the company is worth $20 million. I could not consider selling it for less.

The Demand for Information

Before Mr. Gussett can decide whether to invest in AZ Automotive Parts, he must first assess the potential future profits he will generate from operating the company. He must then decide how much he is currently willing to pay to obtain the right to operate the company and receive the benefits of future operations.

If every person could observe every event that occurs in the economy and remember every detail of all these events, there would be no need for accounting. If this were the case, Mr. Gussett would already know everything that anyone could know about AZ Automotive Parts, and his conversation with Ms. Barnes would have been quite different. This is not to say that Mr. Gussett would know, with certainty, what the future profits of AZ will be. Instead, it means that Mr. Gussett would already know everything possible about the future profits that AZ might experience. He would still be uncertain about which exact outcomes will occur in future periods, and this uncertainty is the risk Mr. Gussett faces.

Since nobody, including Mr. Gussett, knows everything about AZ Automotive Parts, this situation is not realistic. Instead, demand for information regarding the company arises as a means of gathering data to estimate the future profits of the company.[1] Without some information on which to base his decision, Mr. Gussett would not be willing to negotiate for the sale of AZ Automotive Parts.

Information that may be useful in forecasting the future profits of AZ Automotive Parts can come from many sources. Trade publications that describe various products and features of the marketplace for automotive products can provide insight into the opportunities facing AZ. Forecasts of new car sales and demands for replacement parts would certainly be useful information. Government forecasts of future economic conditions will influence the entire industry. All of these sources would be available and valuable to Mr. Gussett in developing a value for AZ Automotive, but where would he get information specifically about AZ Automotive Parts?

Firm-specific information may be available by contact with retailers of AZ's products to find out how popular the products are and how many units are actually being sold. A tour of the production facility might be useful in determining how costly it is to manufacture the products. At least, it would aid in understanding how the products are actually constructed. Mr. Gussett could also ask Ms. Barnes for specific information.

The Supply of Financial Information

If Mr. Gussett requests all financial information available on AZ Automotive Parts then Ms. Barnes faces an interesting problem—financial information's unique characteristics. If Ms. Barnes provides all available information, she will convey some that is critical to the company's continued success in competing with other automotive parts suppliers. Perhaps AZ Automotive Parts has an especially efficient means of manufacturing parts or a particularly good delivery system. These might be the very secret of the company's success.

If whatever information she provides Mr. Gussett would be returned intact if he refuses to purchase the company, then Ms. Barnes would have little

---

[1] Those who have studied finance might argue that an investor should be interested in forecasting future cash flows, not "income." However, we note that even if cash flows are of ultimate interest, forecasting future income may be a more pragmatic means to forecast future cash flows. In fact, one of the major unresolved issues in financial reporting is how accounting-based measures of income may (or may not) provide users with information about future cash flows.

concern about supplying the data. However, this is not possible. Even if Ms. Barnes recovers all the reports she sends, Mr. Gussett could have easily copied or held the information in his memory. Mr. Gussett could then decide to go into business for himself and compete with Ms. Barnes, making her company less valuable, or he could supply the information to a competitor. Since it is very hard to police the transfer of information through private discussion, Ms. Barnes is naturally disinclined to give Mr. Gussett all of the data.

On the other hand, Ms. Barnes knows that without relevant data, Mr. Gussett may not bargain. To interest potential investors such as Mr. Gussett in purchasing AZ, she will need to provide some information about the firm. Just how much information she is willing to supply will be determined by her trade-off of the potential economic costs and benefits.

Some environmental considerations might influence how Ms. Barnes perceives these cost/benefit trade-offs. Ms. Barnes may be less concerned about supplying information if all firms supply similar information. Thus, she would not feel specifically disadvantaged over her competitors. This suggests that if all companies agreed to supply some minimum level of financial information, then society could be better off. However, such an arrangement may be difficult to enforce, since an individual incentive for one firm to stop participating in the agreement may exist. In these situations, regulation may prevent this violation.

Additionally, if Ms. Barnes could aggregate the data to make it difficult to determine the exact source of AZ Automotive's competitive advantage but still possible to infer something about the economic benefits of that advantage in terms of future profit potential, then Ms. Barnes would feel more comfortable about supplying this information to Mr. Gussett.

The Demand for Historical Data

The price of AZ Automotive Parts depends on how its future profits are evaluated. Different people have different expectations regarding the future business opportunities of AZ. Mr. Gussett will use many sources of information to develop his expectation of future profits, including data supplied by Ms. Barnes and the selling prices of other auto-related business investments (if available).

Information from the past is frequently used to develop forecasts. If past performance is a useful indicator of future potential, Mr. Gussett would seek historical information about the economic activities of AZ Automotive Parts. This still leaves unanswered the questions of what data will be sought and how it will be delivered.

The Demand for Financial Statements in Standardized Formats

Managers of corporations have access to a large amount of data that might be useful to some investors in determining their expectations about the company's future performance. However, it is costly to compile and transmit this information. Companies such as AZ Automotive Parts aggregate financial information to reduce these costs. We have already discovered that one cost is the possible loss of trade secrets if too much information is conveyed to outsiders. Aggregation of data conveys information about the economic performance of the company without giving sufficient detail for others to mimic.

In addition, the cost of producing a detailed report of every transaction the company entered into would be prohibitive, even if humans had the capacity to store and process all this data. The cost of production coupled with the likely "information overload," which the users may suffer due to cognitive limitations, results in a natural demand for summarized data. The forces of aggregation work to shape information systems for communication among parties within the company, as well as those between the company and external parties. In this sense, financial reports provide a means for external parties to evaluate the current and potential performance of a company, but they do not communicate all the information managers have about the firm and its opportunities. Financial reports are an economically optimal way to organize the information flows between managers and outsiders.

Investors must make trade-offs between alternative investment opportunities. Mr. Gussett can choose from many possible uses for his cash. Consequently, he needs to make a comparative analysis of how the investment in AZ Automotive Parts compares with investments in other companies. While Ms. Barnes could develop a specialized report for Mr. Gussett, she cannot spend all her time and resources producing specialized reports in response to the requests of all outsiders with an interest in AZ Automotive. Rather, Ms. Barnes avoids the cost of designing specialized reports by using a standardized format to deliver the information. Standardized reports facilitate the use of the information by users, since users will always know where to look for particular pieces of information that may be relevant to them.

Up to this point, we have used the AZ Automotive Parts example to demonstrate that financial accounting information would be demanded by investors and supplied by managers even if there were no specific regulations to require this. Costs, including the effects of information disclosures on competitive advantages and the cost of preparation and dissemination, and benefits such as the ability to interest outside investors in providing capital to the company have been traded off against one another to determine the type and amount of information distributed. Thus far, the decision regarding how much information to include and how to organize it has been left to the individual parties. Now, we turn to the potential motivation for the use of regulations in influencing the type and form of financial disclosures.

The Need for Regulation of Financial Reporting

In a capitalistic society, when a good is demanded by some parties and others are willing to produce it, the forces of supply and demand determine how much of the good will be available, as well as the price and the quality of that good. Yet financial reporting is a highly regulated process and has a large number of rules and regulations governing the way financial statement information is presented. Why is there a need for all this regulation? Why is it that the laws of supply and demand do not work here?

Part of the answers to these questions have been hinted at in the previous discussion. However, we must confess that even now the entire answer is not fully understood as new theories arise constantly and shed additional light on regulation's role in society. What we do know is that a major part of the answer lies in how information differs from other goods and services. When you buy groceries at the supermarket and consume them, you use up all the benefits present in these goods. No one else can enjoy any of the benefits of consumption after the groceries are fully consumed. Information is not like that. When Mr. Gussett uses the information supplied by Ms. Barnes, it will not be used up. Ms. Barnes can supply it to someone else at no additional cost and so can Mr. Gussett.

This feature of information can lead to a breakdown in the normal supply and demand characteristics present for other types of commodities. Better financial information can increase the efficiency with which capital markets allocate financial capital to companies in the economy. That is, investors with better information can make better decisions about where to invest their money. We all benefit by directing capital to its highest and best use in producing goods and services. When capital is employed more efficiently, the prices for goods and services provided to customers will decline to reflect this increased efficiency. Better information aids the process of identifying the highest and best use of capital.

If the amount or quality of financial information benefiting investors could be increased without imposing costs or losses on any other member of the economy, regulation would be easy. However, if improved information is costly to produce and/or it reduces the competitive advantage of firms, then costs and losses are imposed on current and future investors who buy the firm's securities. When benefits to consumers are difficult to measure accurately, it is also hard to charge them for the costs imposed on other members of the economy to compensate for the losses imposed on others. Consequently, normal forces of supply and demand for information may break down. As a result, without regulation there would be an insufficient amount of information produced to allow capital markets such as the New York Stock Exchange to function effectively.

These features give financial information a unique role as a **public good**. A public good is one that has more value to society as a whole than it does to any individual purchaser. Society as a whole can benefit greatly by the creation of financial information because of the role the information plays in facilitating economic activity. However, an individual investor may be unable to capture enough of this value personally to make the information worthwhile purchasing from a supplier. If the purchaser cannot recover the full cost of providing the information, the amount of information that is actually produced may fall short of what society as a whole desires. For this reason, society may be better off if regulation requiring the production of some minimum level of information is established.

In the United States, regulation occurs through both the public sector and the private sector. Public sector regulation generally consists of elected representatives who either serve directly as regulators or who appoint regulators to set rules of conduct for particular areas of economic activity. Public utility rates are regulated by utility commissions usually appointed by an executive branch of government. Another example is in the area of pollution control. The Environmental Protection Agency acts as a regulatory body under the President to create and enforce rules regarding acceptable levels of pollution in society.

Private sector regulation is most common in professions. Both the medical and legal professions have various regulatory boards who control admission to the profession as well as establish ethical conduct rules for members of the profession. Accounting standard setting has been undertaken primarily in the private sector, with the implicit approval of the public sector.

The task of regulators is to consider the trade-offs between the societal costs and benefits of various regulations that could be put into force and to choose those regulations in which the benefits outweigh the costs. Regulating financial reporting is complicated since the benefits to many diverse users of financial information are difficult to measure. In addition, as was discussed earlier, companies bear the cost of producing this information, while the benefits of more effectively functioning capital markets reach down to all consumers who eventually purchase products produced by these corporations.[2]

When developing financial reporting regulations, various societal groups are invited to participate. These include the companies that supply the financial information, the auditors who review the financial reports, and various representatives of user groups such as the investment banking and brokerage industries. In this way, regulators seek input from both those who supply and demand financial information in order to develop a better understanding of how the costs and benefits of new regulations might work.

Since financial reporting requires an aggregation of information regarding individual events, regulators must also decide what facets of the underlying transactions should be the focus of the aggregation process. For example, should companies be allowed to report sales on the basis of cash collections, or should firms be required to report sales on an accrual basis? If the focus of aggregation is on cash flows, then the former would be appropriate. If the focus is on the legal claims of the company, then the latter would seem to best serve the purpose. Some user groups may prefer one method; some will prefer the second; and undoubtedly others will find even more alternatives.

Given that businesses function in very complex economic environments, accountants (seeking to represent this complexity in a very aggregated form) will always find disagreement regarding what information to produce. To evaluate the strengths and weaknesses of alternative reporting methods, an accountant needs the skill to identify the important economic environment features that the financial reports need to capture for the benefit of a very diverse set of users.

---

[2] More efficient capital markets insure that scarce capital is directed toward companies who can produce the largest benefits from the use of that capital. Getting a higher level of productivity per dollar of invested capital will generally result in lower prices to consumers since more goods are made available.

The Demand for Auditing

The creation of regulations or agreements regarding the form and content of financial statements is only the beginning of a process in which information is conveyed to outsiders interested in a company. The managers of the company must then produce financial reports consistent with these agreements or regulations. At times, managers will make mistakes in the way they represent certain events or transactions in the financial statements. At other times, they may have incentives to misrepresent intentionally the consequences of certain events. In these cases, they believe that such misrepresentation is better for them than telling the truth.

This problem is a natural part of the economic setting in which companies function. Managers simply have more information than do outsiders regarding the firm. At times, managers may find it in their best interest to misrepresent certain facts. Economists call this situation a problem in **asymmetric information** because different parties have different access to information. When managers' and outsiders' incentives do not perfectly coincide and asymmetric information exists, problems arise. If no solutions were available to mitigate these problems, investors would not be willing to invest in companies they did not manage. This would severely restrict the scope of business activity. However, solutions exist and make it feasible for investors such as Mr. Gussett to negotiate an exchange of ownership even in the presence of these incentive problems.

A partial resolution to Mr. Gussett's problem may exist if he knows that Ms. Barnes needs to maintain a reputation for honesty. If Ms. Barnes intends to enter some other line of business requiring her to interact with suppliers or banks, a reputation for misrepresentation will cause her new business to suffer. This potential loss of reputation may motivate her to provide accurate data to Mr. Gussett. If Mr. Gussett is aware of Ms. Barnes' desire to maintain her reputation, he will be able to place faith in the data provided. Mr. Gussett may also be able to determine from trusted sources that Ms. Barnes has personal moral or ethical standards that allow Mr. Gussett to trust her representations.

Still other means of resolving the issue are available. Mr. Gussett and Ms. Barnes could enter into a contract in which Ms. Barnes agrees to pay penalties for every misrepresentation she makes. For example, the contract could call for Ms. Barnes to pay a monetary penalty if she overstates the amount of resources spent on research and development activities during the past year. However, it may be too costly to develop such an agreement since the list of all possible misrepresentations could be very long and hard to enforce.

While the partial solutions indicated above are at work to varying degrees, another means of reducing the effects of the incentive problem between insiders and outsiders is to have the financial information provided by insiders audited by an independent third party. An **auditor** is an independent third party who reviews the financial statements for conformity with agreed upon reporting standards. In the United States, this function is performed primarily by Certified Public Accountants (CPAs) as it relates to the information contained in an annual report.

For the benefits of the audit to be worth their cost, auditors must have some specialized skills that make them efficient at the review process. Mr.

Gussett, for example, would benefit from having AZ Automotive's financial statements reviewed by a third party instead of doing it himself. Thus, the demand for audit services arises naturally in an environment where parties with divergent economic interest have different access to information.

Summary of the AZ Automotive Parts Example

The AZ Automotive Parts example involving Ms. Barnes and Mr. Gussett is hypothetical, but it is designed to provide a very practical appreciation for the economic motives of both the suppliers and users of financial information. In the context of this example, we are able to characterize:

1. Why outsiders demand information regarding corporate performance
2. Why insiders are willing to provide some, but not all, of their information about the firm to outsiders
3. Why standardized formats and aggregated data may be useful in reducing the costs of transferring information from insiders to outsiders
4. Why regulation plays an important role in defining the minimum level of information to be contained in general financial reports
5. What the auditor's role is in resolving problems of asymmetric information between insiders and outsiders

This hypothetical case also suggests a motivation for some type of regulation of financial reporting to ensure that a minimum level of information is provided to support investors' activity in capital markets, whether those capital markets be equity markets such as the New York Stock Exchange (NYSE) or debt markets such as the banking industry. In the United States, a considerable amount of regulatory and quasi-regulatory activity has been directed at setting the form and content of financial statements. It is to these efforts that we now turn our attention.

THE REGULATION OF FINANCIAL REPORTING

The remainder of this chapter is devoted to a review of the specific process by which accounting standards are developed and implemented, both currently and historically. Throughout the remaining chapters reference will be made to various standard-setting bodies. Our purpose here is twofold.

1. To familiarize the student of accounting with the institutions that have shaped the evolution of financial reporting
2. To provide an introductory road map to the plethora of documents that currently make up existing generally accepted accounting principles (GAAP)

The institutions discussed here are only those specifically related to the process of financial reporting for businesses in the private sector. Many other accounting bodies deal with reporting for governmental organizations such as cities and towns and generating information by managerial accountants for use by decision makers inside companies. These are beyond the scope of our interest.

The Evolution of Financial Reporting Prior to 1933

Accounting practices in the United States were first imported from the British Commonwealth. In the early 1900s, the tradition was to produce for public consumption very little information regarding financial performance. In addition, no definitive standards to guide the preparation of financial statements existed. Accounting practices were left to the individual accountant to determine, and historical practice was the only guidance of any kind. Generally, firms only reported a balance sheet, which was highly summarized. It is significant that up until this time most capital for American business was contributed by the banking industry. There was little in the way of an active equity market such as the NYSE. Banks had regular contact with managers and were often represented on the board of directors. Bank representatives were more like insiders in that they had access to many sensitive types of information. As a result, general-purpose financial reports such as an annual report did little to provide the capital contributors with new information.

As the demand for capital grew with economic expansion, the concept of absentee owners who would invest financial capital in an organization but who would leave management of day-to-day activities to professional managers (or part owners) became more and more practical. Investors could purchase shares directly from a corporation, but resale of those shares necessitated finding another investor willing to buy when the initial purchaser desired to sell. Major stock exchanges were developed to facilitate this resale function. The exchanges brought buyer and seller together. Since the liquidity of these types of personal assets increased, corporations were able to issue more stocks.

The NYSE was a major force in the standardization of reporting practices during the early 1900s. It was the first American equity market to require any firm that wished to list its stock on the exchange to produce and distribute an annual financial statement to its shareholders. Again, the focus of this report was the balance sheet. It is not surprising that the NYSE sought to extend the information content of financial reports. Since the lifeblood of the NYSE was trading of equity interests and since better financial information could spur new investors to consider purchasing equity securities, the exchange had a vested interest in improving information flows between insiders and outsiders.

The only source for the development of accounting practices within the accounting profession during these years was the American Institute of Accountants (AIA), which was the predecessor organization to the American Institute of Certified Public Accountants (AICPA) that exists today. This group provided a forum for practicing accountants to discuss alternative measurement rules and presentation issues related to financial reporting, but it took no formal role in setting reporting standards.

Public Sector Regulation

In 1933, Congress passed one of the most important pieces of legislation related to accounting and financial reporting. In that year, Congress established regulations that affected the form and content of information to be made public prior to any new issue of securities to be registered with a national exchange such as the NYSE. Responsibility for defining and monitoring these disclosures was given to the newly created Federal Trade Commission (FTC). In 1934, the Securities and Exchange Commission (SEC) was created and given charge over both the information disclosures for new issues and the periodic disclosures by firms whose securities were listed on a major exchange.

Both of these actions arose as a consequence of the stock market crash of 1929, which preceded the Great Depression. The general belief is that during the period before the crash, investors speculated wildly without benefit of adequate information to evaluate the underlying performance of the companies listed on the exchanges. Whether this is true or not, the outcome was legislation empowering federal government representatives to determine minimum disclosures of information by some publicly traded firms.

The Securities and Exchange Commission   As part of its responsibility, the SEC establishes any financial reporting requirements it deems necessary. The SEC is a public sector organization specifically created by law; it cannot be disbanded except by act of Congress. The chair and commissioners of the SEC are appointed positions. As a result of the SEC acts, legal authority for determining financial reporting and disclosure standards for publicly traded firms lies in the SEC's political realm. Most of the responsibility for accounting-related matters rests with the chief accountant of the SEC. This office is responsible for ensuring that firms comply with the regulations and for developing analyses and suggestions that might lead to changes in the regulations.

The SEC's original responsibility extended only to the activities of those companies with securities registered on a major exchange such as the NYSE or American Stock Exchange (AMEX). Its authority was later expanded to all firms with securities traded in a public market, including such markets as the Over-the-Counter (OTC) market. Many corporations do not have any securities listed on any exchange, and the SEC requirements are not specifically applicable to these firms. For companies covered by SEC regulations, filing requirements extend to:

1. Annual filings (10-Ks)
2. Quarterly filings (10-Qs)
3. Registration statements
4. Proxy statements

The 10-K report, which each company with registered securities must file annually, generally includes the information contained in the company's annual report plus additional information required by the SEC. The 10-Q is a similar report prepared on a quarterly basis, and it contains quarterly financial statements along with other information. A registration statement, an extensively detailed document, is required any time a company with registered securities elects to sell a new security issue to the public. Registration statements contain the historical financial statements of the issuing entity and extensive additional information on the nature of the entity's business and the proposed use of the funds to be raised as required by SEC regulations. Finally, a proxy statement discloses information about the types of compensation of various executives along with other information not usually found in the financial reports. It also informs shareholders of any issues scheduled for a vote at an upcoming shareholders' meeting. As a result, a proxy filing is required anytime the corporation's management or its shareholders wish to have some issue brought to a vote at a shareholder's meeting.

Obviously, the SEC controls the content of the filings made under its regulations, but it also has considerable impact on the form and content of all annual reports via its influence on the private sector standard-setting process. The SEC issues various accounting and reporting requirements in its *Financial Reporting Releases* (FRRs), which establish the form and content of disclosures required in the various filings. Generally, the FRRs do not deal with issues of measurement, such as how the value of an asset should be determined, but rather deal with presentation or additional disclosures. For example, the SEC requires that companies include in their 10-K reports schedules that reconcile the changes in accounts such as accumulated depreciation and the allowance for uncollectible accounts. This detail is generally not part of the disclosures in the annual report.

The issuance of FRRs is itself significant for anyone preparing filings for the SEC or searching for information that may be contained therein, but it is not the most significant source of influence the SEC has on financial reporting. While generally accepted accounting principles have officially been developed by private sector (or quasi-private sector) groups, the SEC has had considerable impact on defining the agenda of these private sector bodies.

An accounting standard proposed by a private sector body but unsupported by the SEC would not long survive as part of generally accepted accounting principles. However, generally speaking, the SEC has followed a strategy that allows the private sector standard-setting process to function unless the SEC finds the result unacceptable. At such time, the SEC may intervene to indicate that a proposed rule will not be required for filing with the SEC or to initiate a separate process to establish different reporting standards for SEC filings.

While this does not happen often, several classic examples have shown where the SEC has simply refused to lend its support to the efforts of a private sector regulatory effort. In virtually every one of these cases, the private sector effort eventually failed. We will revisit some of these examples after introducing some of these private sector organizations and their functions.

Congress   In several situations, Congress has acted directly to affect the establishment of GAAP. Although Congress established a public sector body, the SEC, to regulate financial statement content, it retained an oversight role. In other cases, such as the use of last-in, first-out (LIFO) inventory policies, Congress influenced GAAP by encouraging the Internal Revenue Service to adopt regulations requiring any firm that used LIFO for tax purposes must also use it for financial reporting purposes. From time to time, user groups or companies who did not like standards developed by private sector groups or the SEC have encouraged congressional action. In general, the threat of legislation regarding accounting principles has been sufficient to result in changes to the standards developed by others, and actual congressional action has been rare.

Congress has acted directly (passing legislation) or indirectly (establishing regulatory bodies) to regulate financial reporting in certain industries. The banking, interstate shipping, and communication industries are examples of cases where direct governmental intervention has specified particular accounting procedures. While an extensive government regulatory structure is relatively uncommon, accountants who serve clients in these industries must have command of these specific accounting requirements.

To the extent that general financial reporting regulation in the public interest ever becomes a major economic issue in the United States, Congress has the ability—perhaps even the responsibility—to step in and set regulations. In our den.ocracy, we often turn to the system of representative government to resolve issues of social policy that cannot be resolved in the private sector. To date, the issues have been handled adequately through the cooperative effort of the SEC and the private sector. While practicing accountants generally doubt that direct congressional involvement would improve financial reporting, the choice of financial reporting standards is a social choice problem to which our government could legitimately turn its attention.

Private Sector Standard Setting—The American Institute of Certified Public Accountants (AICPA)

The AICPA is not a public sector standard-setting body. Rather, it is an industry association of accountants. However, it (and its predecessor the American Institute of Accountants) has had considerable impact on the development of accounting standards over the years. The AICPA has long set standards for the practice of public accounting among its members. These standards, referred to as *Statements on Auditing Standards* (SASs), are still the backbone of auditing practice in the United States. The AICPA has developed both ethical and procedural standards that relate to the conduct of audits by CPAs, and SASs are revised and extended continuously by the AICPA.

The AICPA is also responsible for preparing the Uniform CPA Examination, which is used by all 50 states as a requirement to qualify as a practicing CPA. While requiring prospective CPAs to take the exam is the prerogative of each individual state, the fact that all states have adopted this requirement is an indication of the importance of the AICPA in the development of the accounting profession as it relates to external financial reporting.

The AICPA has always been involved in the development of accounting standards. AICPA's predecessor, the AIA, created the Committee on Accounting Procedures (CAP), which represented the first major attempt by the public accounting community to organize an effort to develop standards for financial reporting. After demise of the CAP, the AICPA formed the Accounting Principles Board (APB) in a second attempt to establish a formal process for development of accounting standards in the private sector.

In 1972, the Financial Accounting Standards Board (FASB) was created; and for a time, this marked the end of the direct oversight by the AICPA of the formal standard-setting process. Recently, new agreements between the AICPA and the FASB have brought the AICPA back on-line as a source of definitive GAAP.

Even in the period immediately following the creation of the FASB, the AICPA had an impact on standard setting through research and discussion. In many situations where the profession desires guidance on matters that relate to a specific industry, the AICPA has developed industry audit guides, which suggest appropriate accounting and reporting treatments for events and transactions that occur only within narrowly defined industries and are not general enough for FASB deliberations.

The AICPA developed an Accounting Standards Executive Committee (AcSEC) to act as the research arm of the AICPA. AcSEC is designed to:

1. Respond to the recommendations made by other agencies charged with the responsibility of developing accounting standards
2. Address issues that the accounting profession deems appropriate regardless of other regulatory activity
3. Provide practitioners with information regarding the implementation of accounting standards

AcSEC produces documents called *Statements of Position* (SOP), which are position papers regarding a particular accounting issue. The role of SOPs as part of definitive GAAP has changed over the years. Originally, SOPs were not part of definitive GAAP, but they represented an aid to practice in specialized industries. In general, SOPs were not reviewed or in any way endorsed by the FASB. Of course, there were some exceptions. In some areas, such as accounting for long-term construction contracts, when the FASB specifically endorsed an SOP, it was elevated to the status of definitive GAAP. Recently, the FASB and AICPA have changed the status of SOPs issued by AcSEC. From now on, SOPs will be sent to the FASB for review; and if the FASB does not object to the substance of the SOP, it will become part of definitive GAAP under the new auditing standards.

The Committee on Accounting Procedures   In the late 1930s, following the establishment of the SEC, the AIA formed the CAP to aid in the development of generally accepted accounting procedures. The decision to form the CAP was probably not independent of the existence of the SEC, even though the SEC was still only in its early years of existence. From its inception, the SEC has looked to the accounting profession for assistance in the process of defining appropriate measurement and reporting standards to guide financial reporting efforts, and CAP provided a conduit for that interaction. For its part, the public accounting profession has a vested interest in actively seeking to influence this process since it is directly affected by any regulatory standards in this arena.

CAP was not designed to be a regulatory body. It did not have specific authority to dictate accounting practices even within the accounting profession. Its main purpose was to review existing practices and codify widely accepted practices that existed at that time. The CAP produced 42 *Accounting Research Bulletins* (ARBs), which formed the first major codification of accounting practice in the United States. These ARBs were then restated and reissued as ARB No. 43. Parts of this ARB still provide the basis for financial reporting methods in use today. For example, virtually all of the basic guidelines regarding the valuation of inventory and cost of sales in use today emanate from this standard. Before passing out of existence, the CAP issued additional ARBs 44 through 51. Eventually, the combination of the lack of authority and a lack of any comprehensive framework for establishing accounting practices led to the final demise of the CAP in 1959.

The Accounting Principles Board   By 1960, the AIA had become the AICPA. Following the demise of the CAP, the AICPA formed the Accounting Principles Board (APB). At this point, the accounting profession was in search of a broad set of underlying principles that could unite accounting practice and establish a framework in which all accounting and financial reporting issues could be evaluated. In addition, it sought authoritative guidance.

Since the APB had no legal authority, enforcement of its pronouncements had to come from somewhere else. One source was the SEC, but the SEC could only enforce the use of APB pronouncements on companies registered with it. To extend enforcement to all United States corporations, the AICPA created an ethics rule (Rule 203), which stipulated that the pronouncements of the APB should be considered authoritative GAAP. If accountants and auditors chose not to follow these standards, they were required to explain in the audit opinion why the alternative used was preferable to the APB standard. The failure of CPAs to abide by this requirement could result in their expulsion from the profession.

The APB was given the responsibility to develop a basic framework for accounting that would provide for the development of specific standards to guide the measurement and reporting of information in financial statements. Positions on the Board were appointed by the AICPA membership and were not paid positions. Over the years, the number of members on the Board varied from 18 to 20 professionals. Monies were set aside to support a research staff to prepare position papers on various issues, but the board members served without compensation and did not give up their affiliations with various sponsoring organizations. Board members were chosen primarily from large public accounting firms, but many were also from industry and academe. The deliberations of the Board occurred in private without input in the form of public comment. The lack of independence from the industry of public accounting would later be seen as one of the weaknesses of the APB.

To effect their responsibilities, the APB issued four statements that are devoted to the basic postulates of accounting. Not covered by ethics Rule 203, these statements were not construed as definitive GAAP. In addition, the APB issued 31 opinions regarding specific financial reporting issues as diverse as lease accounting, earnings-per-share computation, and pension reporting. These opinions were the subject of ethics Rule 203 and represented the first definitive GAAP developed in the United States. To provide continuity between CAP's and APB's efforts, the Accounting Principles Board adopted Opinion No. 6, which endorsed the findings in the ARBs and elevated this effort to the status of an APB opinion. The APB also issued Accounting

Interpretations. These documents provided specific examples of how to implement those portions of the opinions about which practitioners were unclear. The interpretations were not part of definitive GAAP under ethics Rule 203. Rather, they were developed solely as an aid to practice.

To lend support to the opinions of the APB, the SEC began to adopt APB opinions as part of the reporting requirements for publicly listed companies. This also meant that the SEC was essentially transferring its responsibilities for development of reporting requirements in the public interest to a private sector group. Several debates arose regarding the appropriateness of this behavior.

Political Conflicts and the Accounting Principles Board   Early in its existence, the APB elected to review the issue of accounting for the investment tax credit, which Congress had placed in the tax law for the first time in the early 1960s. The investment tax credit offered firms a credit against their corporate income tax bill based on a percentage of the cost of new equipment they purchased during the year. In effect, if a company spent $100,000 on new equipment, it would be given a tax credit of 7%, or $7,000. The purpose of this legislation was to spur new investment in assets covered by the credit.

Many companies wanted to recognize the entire benefit of the tax credit in their financial reports for the year in which they received it (the flow-through method). They pointed out:

1. This is the way the tax code treated it.
2. This treatment would result in higher reported net income in the year of the credit.

If they were forced to defer the credit, the companies believed investors would not fully realize the existence of this benefit and undervalue their securities in the equity market. The APB decided that any credit received should be recognized over the life of the asset (the deferral method), which provided better matching of the actual net cost of the asset against the revenues generated from its use. The APB did not appear to realize either:

1. The intensity of the opposition to this treatment
2. The political nature of the selection of accounting and reporting standards

The opponents of the deferral method lobbied the SEC. The SEC's response was to allow either method of accounting. This alone did not persuade the APB to drop the issue. Since the SEC mandate did not affect companies beyond its jurisdiction, the APB's position still affected a large number of companies. Thus, the APB appeared adamant about the use of the deferral method. The lobbying effort turned to Congress. Opponents of the APB's policy were numerous, representing considerable political clout. In addition, the opponents argued that the treatment proposed by the APB was in direct conflict with the intent of Congress in creating the tax credit. They argued that the deferral method would result in companies not investing as much as they would using the flowthrough method since the benefits would not appear in the financial statements for several years. Opponents pointed out that the intent of Congress was to spur new investment in physical assets. How could Congress allow this private sector organization to subvert its will?

It shortly became clear that Congress would act to require that firms be allowed immediate recognition of the tax credit in their financial statements, if APB did not back away from its position. In an effort to avoid the potential loss of control over the standard-setting process, the APB rescinded Opinion No. 2 and allowed firms to use either immediate recognition or deferral to account for the investment tax credit. This was the first instance in which the political process failed to support a formal private sector accounting standard-setting body designed exclusively for the purpose of developing reporting standards.

Obviously, the APB had a different view regarding which features of the investment tax credit were important to reflect in the financial statements. They saw the credit as a reduction of the initial cost of the plant and equipment. In their view of the world, the costs of plant and equipment were best reflected by spreading the initial costs as expense over several periods by use of depreciation. Therefore, it seemed natural to demand a similar treatment for any credit that reduced this cost. Companies only saw the reduction in income that would arise if the recognition of the credit was deferred. Political forces were mobilized to resolve the issue. Notice that in the end, the one group not well-represented in this process were the users of the financial statements themselves. However, this is the group that may be most affected by these types of decisions.

In summary, the fact that groups view economic events differently means that it is impossible to obtain a financial reporting system that will please everyone all the time. Political processes will be used to resolve these issues, but even they change over time. Therefore, it should be no surprise to any accountant that there is room for considerable difference of opinion regarding how transactions should be accounted for or that existing standards are not always clear-cut.

Private Sector Standard Setting—The Financial Accounting Foundation

After 14 years of operation, the APB was dissolved. Given its perception as being biased due to the exclusive presence of accountants and after several major apparent failures to recognize the political consequences of the actions it took, the APB could no longer function effectively. In 1972, the Financial Accounting Standards Board (FASB) was born.

The Financial Accounting Standards Board   To overcome the appearance that accountants were controlling the standard-setting body, a new type of governing structure was created. At the top of this structure is a nonprofit organization called the Financial Accounting Foundation (FAF). The job of the FAF is to promote improvements in financial reporting through the creation of the FASB. The FAF is basically responsible for fund-raising to support the activity of the FASB and for appointment of its members. Funding for the FAF is obtained by donations from various groups. Accounting firms, brokerage companies, and private industrial firms all contribute substantial monies to support the work of the FAF.

Membership on the seven-member board of the FASB includes not only accountants but also representatives from private industry, the financial services industry (such as investment banking and brokerage firms), and academe. Membership is a full-time, paid position, and members must give up all financial ties to former employers when appointed to the FASB in the same manner as other public servants who accept government appointments. In this way, the organization responsible for the development of accounting standards is more like a public sector organization than a group of accountants operating behind closed doors.

Even the process by which accounting standards are developed has changed. The FASB has created over 100 *Statements of Financial Accounting Standards* (SFAS). In total, these statements have revised or replaced the bulk of accounting regulations present in the opinions of the APB. Before a new standard is produced, the FASB proceeds through a long process of public commentary and debate, soliciting input from all types of financial statement users and preparers, before reaching a conclusion. A schematic diagram of this process is presented in Exhibit 1.2.

The first major step in the process of developing a new reporting standard is to have the FASB formally place the issue on its agenda. Following this step, the FASB staff undertakes background research to formulate a list of reasonable alternative accounting treatments that might be implemented. In some cases, a task force of FASB staff, practitioners, and industrial accountants is formed to support the research effort.

EXHIBIT 1.2 |

The Evolution of an Accounting and Reporting Standard

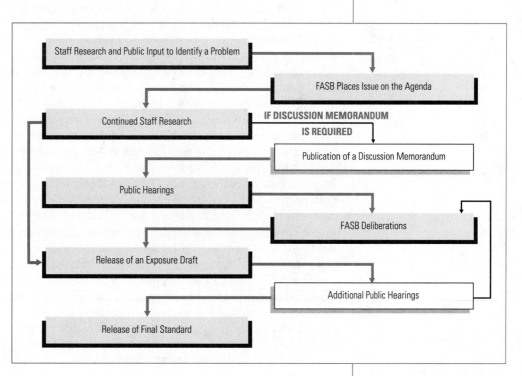

Following this, the FASB may issue a discussion memorandum. The FASB staff prepares this document, which is designed to set forth all the alternative accounting treatments identified by the staff and to stimulate discussion. The discussion memorandum is designed to stimulate discussion. Discussion memoranda are generally issued only when the FASB believes the issue is of sufficient impact to seek broad public input to their deliberations. Following the issuance of a discussion memorandum, the FASB will hold several public meetings at which anyone interested in commenting may request to speak. In addition, many position letters will be received from sources who wish to make their opinions known to the board but who do not wish to attend the public sessions.

The next document produced is the exposure draft of the *Statement of Financial Accounting Standard*. The exposure draft, a tentative version of the position taken by the FASB regarding the treatment of the accounting issue, may be issued without a discussion memorandum preceding it. The document is of sufficient detail to allow companies to evaluate the effects the change in reporting rules would have on their financial statements and to indicate to users what specific informational changes may occur. More public hearings are then scheduled to receive input on the exposure draft.

The next stage is usually the issuance of the final statement, which reflects modifications arising from comments and suggestions on the exposure draft. However, in some cases, a second exposure draft has been produced due to the substantial changes wrought in the document following the public meetings. This entire process may be completed in a few months or last for many years. Adoption of a new accounting standard originally required only a simple majority vote of the Board, but this requirement has recently been increased to a 5-2 majority.

Following the issuance of a new standard, the FASB staff may also produce a special report, commonly referred to as a "Q&A," which is short for "Questions and Answers." These reports arise as practitioners contact the FASB with questions about how certain events should be treated under the new standard. The staff then prepares responses to these questions and publishes the questions and answers to aid all preparers and users in understanding how these events will be reported. The Q&A documents have become an important part of the process that makes the new reporting standard operational.

Beyond the Q&A reports, the FASB also issues *Technical Bulletins* and *Interpretations of Statements or Opinions*. Technical bulletins usually deal only with narrow and very specialized accounting problems that arise in the application of GAAP. Interpretations are developed when the issue that has been raised applies to many companies or many circumstances. Given the broader implications, an interpretation arises due to a greater general need for clarification of a previously issued statement or opinion.

The AICPA has altered its auditing standards relating to the definition of GAAP on a couple of occasions since the FASB's existence. At present, the standards of the FASB and its interpretations are considered to be definitive GAAP, along with the portions of the APB opinions and ARBs, those that have not been overridden by more recent FASB standards. Technical bulletins are not considered definitive; rather, they are viewed as an aid to practice.

Along with the many SFASs produced, the FASB has also devoted considerable effort to developing a framework that provides basic guidance in the development of standards for financial reporting. This effort has been labeled the "Conceptual Framework," as it is intended to provide broad, general guidance on the content and use of financial reports. The output of the conceptual framework project has been six *Statements of Financial Accounting Concepts* (SFAC). These concept statements are not part of definitive GAAP. In fact, a special name was created to segregate them from the SFASs. The SFACs are designed to provide a basic conceptual structure to evaluate alternative reporting standards. The substance of these statements is discussed in more detail in Chapter 2.

Political Conflicts and the FASB   The changes to the standard-setting process evidenced by the operational changes between the APB and FASB have not eliminated the potential for significant political conflict. In the late 1970s, the FASB undertook the consideration of accounting principles for the oil and gas industry. Of particular concern was the accounting treatment for oil and gas development costs. This was shortly after a major oil crisis of the mid-1970s, and concern about oil company profitability and corporate "behavior" during the oil crisis was at its zenith in Congress.

There was a great clamor to improve financial reporting by oil and gas companies so that users, particularly those who might seek to regulate the behavior of these firms or tax them more heavily, could determine "the real economic results of operations." Congress demanded that the SEC act to develop a new set of accounting rules, and the FASB jumped into the fray in an apparent attempt to get ahead of the pack and take a leadership position. The FASB focused principally on the two alternative methods currently in use and tried to decide which of the two was more suitable.

These methods were either successful efforts or full cost. In brief, the successful efforts method allows a firm to capitalize all development costs until a well proves to be either successful or unsuccessful. If the well is unsuccessful, all development costs are written off when this determination is made. Under the full cost method, all development costs for both successful and unsuccessful wells are capitalized, and then the total cost is spread over the output of only the successful wells in a form of "depreciation" or amortization. Both methods had been in use by different companies in the oil and gas exploration business. The FASB believed that requiring a single standardized method would improve the quality of the information conveyed in financial reports for companies in this industry. Eventually, the FASB supported successful efforts when it adopted SFAS No. 19.

Following this decision, the top blew off the wellhead. Two things happened. First, the SEC refused to support this requirement because it believed the financial reporting problem was much more pervasive than the election between these two "historical cost" oriented methods of reporting exploration activity. In fact, the SEC believed that an entirely new system of financial reporting should be developed to represent the value of oil and gas resources as assets, based on their current market values. Changes in the value of this asset due to new discoveries or changes in the market price of oil and gas would be a source of income to the company (if prices went up, the company would report profits). This approach was referred to as "reserve recognition accounting."

Second, the companies that had been using the full cost method lobbied Congress to intervene in this process and prevent the FASB from forcing them to change. Most of these companies were small "wildcatters," and they argued that being forced to write off all the development cost of unsuccessful wells would severely hurt their reported profits and, thus, their ability to continue to raise capital. Given that the large oil companies predominately used the successful efforts method, the FASB's choice had, somewhat unwittingly, lined up the small producers on one side and the "big oil giants" on the other.

Given the obvious disharmony SFAS No. 19 was causing, the FASB repealed it, retreating to the position of allowing the same choice among methods that had existed prior to their activity on SFAS No. 19. It is also interesting to note that the SEC eventually gave up its attempts to develop a fully implementable version of reserve recognition accounting. Ultimately, the only impact the SEC's and FASB's multi-year efforts had was to incorporate much of the reserve recognition data into footnotes. The fact that the oil industry fell out of the spotlight of political debate during this sequence of events is greatly responsible for the fact that little was ever implemented.

The Emerging Issues Task Force   As economic transactions became more and more complicated with the advent of better and faster computer information systems, the slow process of standard setting caused problems for practitioners. They faced new and varied transactions without benefit of direction from the FASB as how to characterize the events. Complex, new arrangements such as the management buyout, a transaction by management to borrow money against the company's assets to buy out all the outside shareholders, became commonplace. Since these were new events, it was difficult to determine how old practices fit with the new circumstances. Guidance was needed.

The FASB realized it did not have the time or personnel to tackle every new problem. It had to focus on very broad and general problems and find a different way to provide specific, rapid, practical guidance to practitioners. In addition, the SEC needed specific input into this process as the decisions would certainly shape the nature of the reports it required. Subsequently, the Emerging Issues Task Force (EITF) was formed as a cooperative effort of the FASB, SEC, and practitioners of the larger CPA firms. It is basically a group of representatives from large public accounting firms, the FASB staff, and the SEC who meet on a regular basis to review specific practice issues that are put before the group.

The EITF was formed to provide a forum for discussion of those emerging issues that were not of sufficient scope to warrant the FASB's involvement but were situations for which practitioners needed specific guidance. Originally, the EITF's consensus regarding the treatment of a specific type of event would then be published for use by other practitioners. The SEC representatives are not voting members of the EITF. However, when EITF members reach a consensus, the Chief Accountant of the SEC has decided to treat that consensus as a requirement for all SEC filings as long as the SEC concurs with the decision.

Since most of the issues addressed by the EITF arise from transactions entered into by public companies, the support of the SEC implicitly gives these consensus statements the status of authoritative guidance similar to a FASB statement—at least for those companies that file financial reports with the SEC.

In reality, consensus has not been easy to reach. The EITF has provided a service in that the involvement of SEC staff allows practitioners a forum for an early opinion on the SEC's position regarding alternative accounting treatments. However, the EITF has been plagued by the difficulty of deciding when an issue is broad enough to fall within the purview of the FASB and when it is sufficiently narrow to warrant action by the EITF. Only time will determine the actual impact this working group will have. Under current auditing standards, any consensus position published by the EITF is part of definitive GAAP.

International Accounting Standards

As corporations grew internationally, problems arose in trying to satisfy the reporting requirements of many different national jurisdictions. Accounting rules in the United States were different from those of England, which differed from those of Germany, etc. As a result, several international accounting standard-setting efforts emerged. The best known of these bodies is the International Accounting Standards Committee (IASC).

These international efforts generally depend on the cooperation of national professional groups for their influence. For example, IASC can issue many accounting standards; but if the United States does not adopt them via the FASB, they carry no legal weight in this country. These international groups were designed more as a focal point for discussion of ways to overcome reporting differences between countries than as direct regulatory bodies. However, there are many accountants who believe that these organizations, particularly the IASC, will be the next stage in the evolution of financial reporting regulation as worldwide capital markets require a more global perspective on the standardization of accounting and reporting practices. Of particular concern are the problems United States-based multinationals face due to the difference in reporting practices.

For example, many managers believe the policy of requiring United States corporations to amortize goodwill, while most foreign companies are not required to do so, hurts their ability to enter into mergers. These managers argue that the periodic charge to expense from amortizing goodwill arising from such exchanges creates lower reported earnings in future years relative to foreign companies for which amortization is not required. The basis for this concern might be debatable. Most investors are aware of the differences in accounting principles, and corporations can simply disclose the amount of amortization recognized each year to allow users to make adjustments for comparative purposes. However, the issue of obtaining a level playing field in the area of accounting disclosures is a significant one in the international arena.

Another means for dealing with international differences in reporting standards is by treaty. For example, the Organization for Economic and Community Development (OECD) and the United Nations (UN) began discussions of financial reporting requirements its members would adopt as part of a treaty among the nations represented. What this means in the United States is that the executive branch of government, with oversight by the Senate, would be in the business of setting accounting standards as part of the responsibility for treaty negotiations held by the State Department. To date, these activities have not gone very far. While a discussion of the nature and impact of these international efforts is beyond the scope of this book, they do represent another facet of the public sector activity relating to the regulation of accounting standards.

A Hierarchy of GAAP

In the preceding discussions, several sources of definitive GAAP have been identified. These include:

1. *Statements of Financial Accounting Standards* issued by the FASB
2. FASB *Interpretations*
3. APB *Opinions* (to the extent they have not been superseded)
4. *Accounting Research Bulletins* (to the extent not superseded)
5. *Statements of Accounting Positions* issued by AcSEC of the AICPA
6. EITF consensus positions

Other unofficial sources include technical bulletins issued by the APB and FASB, *Statements of Financial Accounting Concepts* issued by the FASB, and international accounting standards, to name a few. Is there any means of prioritizing this extensive set of documentation?

The answer to this question is *yes*. FASB statements and interpretations, along with those parts of the APB opinions and ARBs that have not been superseded, represent the highest level of authority in GAAP. The EITF consensus statements rank second in the hierarchy, and the SOPs represent the lowest level of definitive GAAP. Exhibit 1.3 presents pictorially the evolution of definitive GAAP along with the variety of documents that are considered supplemental.

SUMMARY

The purpose of this chapter has been to provide a basic appreciation of the economic and political forces that shape the demand for and the regulation of financial reporting. The story of AZ Automotive Parts provided a backdrop for insight into why certain features of the reporting environment arise from the basic law of supply and demand for financial information. To resolve problems resulting from the nature of information, regulation of financial reporting may be beneficial to society as a whole.

The process of standard setting was reviewed, beginning with the start of the 20th century. Standard-setting bodies include the AICPA, Congress, the SEC, and the FASB (and its predecessors the CAP and APB). While the CAP and APB are no longer in existence, the FASB, EITF, and the AICPA (represented by AcSEC) are currently active in the establishment of new accounting and reporting standards that affect all for-profit entities in the United States.

EXHIBIT 1.3

Pictorial Summary of the Evolution of Private Sector Accounting Standard Setting Bodies

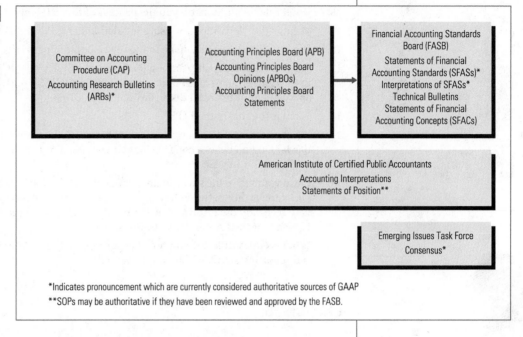

Committee on Accounting Procedure (CAP)
Accounting Research Bulletins (ARBs)*

Accounting Principles Board (APB)
Accounting Principles Board Opinions (APBOs)
Accounting Principles Board Statements

Financial Accounting Standards Board (FASB)
Statements of Financial Accounting Standards (SFASs)*
Interpretations of SFASs*
Technical Bulletins
Statements of Financial Accounting Concepts (SFACs)

American Institute of Certified Public Accountants
Accounting Interpretations
Statements of Position**

Emerging Issues Task Force Consensus*

*Indicates pronouncement which are currently considered authoritative sources of GAAP
**SOPs may be authoritative if they have been reviewed and approved by the FASB.

The chapter closed with a brief introduction to some of the international standard-setting bodies such as IASC, which may ultimately replace the FASB as the authoritative source of accounting and financial reporting standards, even in the United States.

QUESTIONS

1. What role does the concept of aggregation play in the process of financial reporting? What are the costs and benefits of aggregation?

2. Aggregation is described as grouping individual events and reporting these groups' totals in financial statements. Using the Allegheny financial reports in Appendix A, name some group totals (or accounts) in the balance sheet and income statement. Do you think the degree of aggregation used in financial statements such as those of Allegheny is too high, too low, or just right? Explain.

3. What economic forces drive the demand for accounting information?

4. What special problems does the exchange of accounting information have relative to other goods and services that are traded every day?

5. The AZ Automotive Parts example focuses on the use of accounting information for purposes of firm valuation. What other types of decision contexts might require the use of financial data?

6. List some direct and indirect beneficiaries of financial statement information.

7. Indicate several means by which the problems that arise from asymmetric information between users and suppliers of financial information may be resolved.

8. What role do auditors play in the process of financial reporting?

9. What is the motivation for using regulation in financial reporting?

10. What role does the SEC have in the regulation of financial reporting?

11. What is the relationship among the FASB, the SEC, and AICPA? What are the various sources of guidance provided by the FASB regarding the form and content of financial disclosures?

12. What is the role of the EITF?

13. What role, if any, has Congress played in setting financial reporting standards? Do you believe congressional involvement is beneficial? Why, or why not?

14. Place yourself in the shoes of an average investor. How would you feel about the choice between having financial reporting standards set in the private sector by the FASB versus having the SEC develop these requirements? How about the FASB relative to Congress?

15. What is ethics Rule 203 and how has it changed the manner in which financial reporting standards are implemented?

EXERCISES

1-1. *Institutional relationships with sources of GAAP*

Match the following sources of accounting and financial reporting guidance with the organization that produced it.

____1. APBs	A. Financial Accounting Standards Board
____2. FRRs	B. Committee on Accounting Procedures
____3. ARBs	C. AICPA
____4. SFASs	D. Securities and Exchange Commission
____5. Consensus	E. Emerging Issues Task Force
____6. Technical Bulletins	F. Accounting Principles Board
____7. SOPs	

1-2. *Financial reporting institutions*

Identify the organization associated with each of the following descriptions.

1. This organization was established by Congress to regulate the activities of organized public securities markets. It has responsibility for establishing rules regarding the form and content of information that must be made public through regular filings.

2. This organization was formed to codify accounting practices, but it had no power to enforce any of its recommendations.

3. Formed in the early 1960s, this organization was charged with the responsibility of developing specific guidance regarding the form and content of financial reports. Its members were primarily representative of the accounting profession, and they continued to hold positions in the private sector while serving in this organization.

4. This organization represents the "industry" of accounting. It implemented ethics Rule 203, which requires that all audited financial statements conform to the standards issued by the APB, unless the implementation of these standards would result in misleading financial statements due to particular circumstances.

5. This organization was formed to address current issues in accounting and financial reporting that were not of a pervasive nature but required more rapid resolution than was available through the standard-setting process of the FASB. Its members are representatives of the FASB, major public accounting firms, and an ex officio member of the SEC staff.

1-3. *Authoritative GAAP and guides to practice*

The following is a list of various sources of guidance on accounting and financial reporting matters. For a publicly traded company, indicate those sources that must be treated as authoritative guidance and those that would be considered supplementary but not necessarily authoritative.

A = Authoritative (must be followed)
S = Supplementary (may be followed)

_____ 1. *Statements of Financial Accounting Concepts*
_____ 2. FASB *Technical Bulletins*
_____ 3. EITF Consensus Statements
_____ 4. *Financial Reporting Releases*
_____ 5. AcSEC *Statements of Position*
_____ 6. *Statements of Financial Accounting Standards*
_____ 7. APB *Opinions*
_____ 8. APB *Statements*
_____ 9. FASB *Interpretations*
_____10. FASB Q&A Supplements
_____11. Internal Revenue Service Regulations

1-4. *Chronology and identity of financial reporting institutions*

The following organizations all have had some effect on the current state of financial reporting in the United States. Rank the organizations based on the time in history when each organization had its earliest effects on financial reporting with (1) being the oldest and (6) being the most recent.

_____1. Committee on Accounting Procedures
_____2. Accounting Principles Board
_____3. Securities and Exchange Commission
_____4. New York Stock Exchange
_____5. Emerging Issues Task Force
_____6. Financial Accounting Standards Board

1-5. *Evolution of net authoritative accounting standards*

The following documents are typically produced by the FASB during the process of developing a new accounting standard that has significant potential effects on the producers and users of financial statements. Order the documents in the appropriate sequence and describe what each one would typically contain.

1. Statement of Financial Accounting Standard
2. Questions and Answers
3. Discussion Memorandum
4. Exposure Draft

PROBLEMS

1-1. *Application of GAAP to research and development costs*

Cal Jones, a new staff accountant, has recently been employed by Biotechnologies Incorporated, a small, high-technology firm in your area. He is confused as to how to deal with research and development costs incurred by the company. He has identified three basic approaches to accounting for research and development costs:

1. Charge all costs to expense as incurred.
2. Add all costs to an asset and amortize the asset over some average life that reflects the average life of the benefits expected from all research and development efforts.
3. Add all costs to an asset until it can be determined whether viable products will result. If no products emerge, charge the costs to expense at the time this determination is made; otherwise amortize the costs over the expected future life of the products actually developed.

REQUIRED:

1. Explain what is meant by authoritative support for the selection of accounting principles.
2. Which approach do you think would be most favored by Biotechnologies? Why?
3. Which approach do you think would be most favored by the firm's independent auditor? Why?
4. A specific pronouncement by the FASB requires the application of Approach 1. What does this suggest to you about the relative political impact that the parties in 2 and 3 had on the determination of this social policy?

1-2.   *Standard setting and the politics of GAAP*

While attending a meeting of accountants in your area, you learn from a leading member of the profession in your state that accounting standard setting is becoming more and more political. He claims that the politicalization of the standard setting process will only serve to further erode the development of "good accounting practices."

REQUIRED:

1. Develop an argument to support the proposition that standard setting has become more political. Examine the changes in the process by which the FASB develops standards and that used by the APB.
2. What self-interest may lie behind the speaker's use of the term "good accounting practices?"
3. Develop an argument that asserts increased politicalization of standard setting results in better accounting practices than those that might exist without this process.
4. In what sense might an economist argue that there is no absolute set of "right and good" accounting practices? Does this relativist view of financial reporting imply that accountants should always be left to develop whatever reports they desire?

GAAP VERSUS RAP: THE SAVINGS AND LOAN MESS

The following article appeared in the Minneapolis *Star Tribune* on April 5, 1989. It presents an analysis of two different accounting procedures that savings and loans may have applied to determine how these institutions should recognize losses when they sell a loan they have made to another party. The savings and loan in question was one of the largest institutions in Minnesota, Midwest Federal Savings and Loan.

CASE 1.1 EXHIBIT

Accounting Method Enabled Midwest to Hide Its Problems

In January 1988, Midwest Federal Savings & Loan placed an ad in the *Star Tribune* touting "another great year."

The ad noted that the company reported net income of $8.4 million in 1987.

"And regulatory capital now stands at $142.5 million," said Harold Greenwood Jr., former Midwest chairman and chief executive.

In reality, Midwest had been broke for years.

Greenwood was deposed last month by federal regulators who took over the savings and loan institution. Now he and three of his executives are under investigation involving allegations of fraud, embezzlement, kickbacks, bribery and obstruction of justice.

For several years Midwest hasn't had any real net worth, the sum by which assets exceed liabilities. It now appears that when the final tallies come in, that might be a negative number close to two-thirds of $1 billion.

How is it that an institution in such tough shape could publicly declare only a year ago, with the backing of its regulator, the Federal Home Loan Bank Board, that it was in the pink when it actually was in the red?

The same ways a lot of other troubled S&Ls did it. They failed to write off bad loans and overstated their net worth, critics and competitors charge.

Midwest did not previously disclose to the Bank Board examiners hundreds of millions of dollars in nonperforming mobile home loans that it had bought from Green Tree Acceptance Corp., and commercial real estate investments, some of which finally were written down in the fourth quarter of 1988.

But part of the blame can be traced to Regulatory Accounting Principles (RAP), suspect accounting techniques that the Bank Board recommended to thrifts as a way

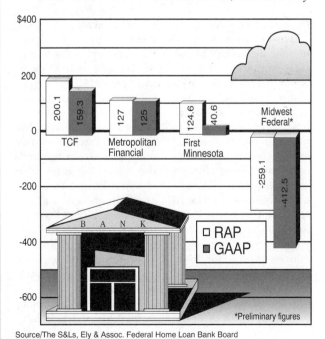

Source/The S&Ls, Ely & Assoc. Federal Home Loan Bank Board

Reprinted with permission of the Star Tribune, Minneapolis– St. Paul

to soften earnings squeezes caused by high interest rates that began a decade ago. RAP was seen as a way to ease the S&Ls into the deregulated 1980s, a temporary buffer to buoy weakened S&Ls until they could better cope in a newly competitive environment. Instead RAP only made things worse by letting some institutions and bad managers carry worthless assets on their books and essentially plug net worth with IOUs.

"RAP is crap," said Bert Ely, an accountant and S&L analyst in Washington, D.C. "Crummy regulatory accounting practices. They're absurd. Midwest was under water by December 1984."

The inherent hypocrisy of RAP accounting was underscored at a 1985 Christmas party of the Federal Savings & Loan Insurance Corp., the Bank Board's insolvent insurance fund. Staff members wore T-shirts in homage to RAP that said, "We do it with mirrors."

But the things Midwest and other thrifts did to inflate their balance sheet strength grossly were legal under regulatory accounting.

In the early 1980s, as interest rates were moving into double digits, S&Ls were caught in a bind. They were burdened with huge portfolios of low-interest long-term mortgages sold in an earlier

A difference in accounting

Here's a look at some key financial statistics of the Upper Midwest's largest S&Ls under RAP and GAAP. TCF and Metropolitan Financial both use GAAP, and their ratio of net worth to assets remains above 3 percent—considered an adequate safety cushion by the Federal Home Loan Bank Board—under both accounting practices. But Midwest Federal and First Minnesota use RAP. First Minnesota's net worth ratio drops to 1.2 percent under GAAP, while Midwest Federal goes deeper into the hole.

As of Dec. 31, 1988 (in millions of dollars):

		TCF	Metro-politan Financial	First Minnesota	Midwest Federal*
Net income		$21.5	$11.4	$11.9	−$352.4
Net worth:	RAP	$200.1	$127.0	$124.6	−$259.1
	GAAP	159.3	125.0	40.5	−412.5
Assets:	RAP	$5,296.1	$4,073.2	$3,365.1	$3,402.3
	GAAP	5,258.6	4,073.2	3,307.2	N.A.
Net worth/assets:	RAP	3.8%	3.1%	3.7%	−7.6%
	GAAP	3.0%	3.1%	1.2%	N.A.

•Midwest's results are preliminary. Audits for 1987–88 are expected to reveal a negative net worth that may top $600 million.

Source/The savings and loan associations. Ely & Associates. Federal Home Loan Bank Board. Star Tribune estimates.

regulated environment. Suddenly they were forced to offer depositors higher interest rates in the new world of competition with commercial banks and mutual funds. The Bank Board encouraged S&Ls to package and sell the old low-interest mortgages to investors, even though such sales would result in huge losses. The board reasoned that it was better for thrifts to jettison low-yielding mortgages and reinvest proceeds in higher-yielding investments.

Midwest, and others, sold hundreds of millions of dollars worth of loans.

Under Generally Accepted Accounting Principles (GAAP) such sales would be charged against earnings entirely in the year incurred. But the Bank Board allowed them to spread the loss over the life of the loans. And they were permitted to carry the remaining amount of deferred loss on their balance sheets as an asset, even though GAAP would have required the institution to take the entire loss as an immediate expense and reduced owner's equity by that amount.

Meanwhile, the capital-starved S&Ls were able to

bolster net worth by selling certain types of unsecured bonds, essentially long-term junk bonds. And since 1982 they also have been allowed to take promissory notes from the Bank Board called net worth certificates, which don't actually transfer money to the S&L.

In 1987 and 1988 Midwest sold a total of $34.6 million in subordinated debentures. About $15 million of it was to Harvey Ratner and Marv Wolfenson, Twin Cities developers and owners of the Minnesota Timberwolves basketball team. About $2.5 million was sold to businessman Stephen Adams. Midwest also has loaned money to Ratner, Wolfenson and Adams.

These were added to real equity—principally accumulated earnings for many S&Ls—and dubbed "regulatory capital." That's the item Greenwood was talking about in the ad, when he boasted that Midwest had $142.5 million.

But Midwest's December 1987 balance sheet, using RAP accounting from the Bank Board, reveals that of its $142.5 million in regulatory capital, $149 million was in deferred loan losses and $42.4 million was really debt in the form of debentures and appraised equity capital, an estimated amount by which the market value of land and office buildings exceeds the book value. That left Midwest with a negative net worth, because it was at least $49 million deficient in equity, under GAAP.

"The great variation between RAP and GAAP developed in the early 1980s, when the regulators pursued this fiction of letting thrifts sell assets but not write off the loss at once," said Ben Crabtree, financial institutions analyst at Dain Bosworth Inc. "It became a major issue when Midwest's big earnings problem started surfacing (last year). You could extract the problem they had with mobile home loans they bought from Green Tree Acceptance Corp., and questions about other issues, and they still weren't going to make it."

A key indicator of financial strength is a thrift's ratio of net worth to total assets, which measures the thickness of its equity cushion. By claiming "regulatory capital" as net worth, Midwest legally was able to say that it was as strong as Twin City Federal Savings & Loan, Metropolitan Financial Savings and First Minnesota. In fact, it was much weaker.

The stronger thrifts eschew RAP accounting. They want their strength measured by GAAP standards. The publicly held stock institutions, such as Metropolitan and TCF, must report on a GAAP basis. Midwest was a mutual association, owned by its depositors but controlled by management. It did not have to report to the Bank Board on a GAAP basis. But all S&Ls must report internally and to the IRS using GAAP principles.

"We don't even calculate RAP," said Bill Bartkowski, a vice president of Metropolitan Financial, based in Fargo, N.D.

Metropolitan and TCF to an extent were able to avoid the thrift crisis through better management of their assets and by selling stock in the mid-1980s to build capital that cushioned earlier losses. As publicly held institutions, they were allowed to claim only the funds paid in by shareholders and their accumulated profits, or retained earnings as equity capital.

First Minnesota, like Midwest, is a mutual association, but voluntarily discloses its results under GAAP. It has only a 1.2 percent equity-to-assets ratio, compared with 3 percent for Metropolitan and TCF, when its deferred loan losses from previous asset sales are subtracted from its retained earnings to arrive at a GAAP definition of equity. Midwest's net worth is -7.6 percent as of December 1988 and bound to deepen.

"The only capital requirements we have at the moment are the RAP requirements, the Federal Home Loan Bank requirements, and we have a strategic plan to meet those requirements in the future," said Jay Pfaender, vice president of marketing services at First Minnesota. "I believe it's 4.1 percent (of assets) by 1990. There are certain milestones that are being increased by the Bank Board, and we have a strategic plan in place to meet all those requirements. There has been some discussion about changing the capital requirements period, but I don't know what they're going to be.

"We support the need to increase the capital base of the S&L industry. Every dollar of net income increases our capital. We estimate by the first quarter of 1989 we will exceed 1.5 percent in GAAP net worth to equity."

Critics accuse the industry-dominated Bank Board and Congress members anxious to protect scores of local S&Ls of essentially perpetrating an accounting hoax that misled depositors—one that eventually will cost taxpayers hundreds of billions of dollars by the time the government is done reconciling insolvent institutions.

For a mutual association, accumulated profits are the only real way to increase traditional capital. In better times, healthy mutual S&Ls have converted to stock companies by raising money in the public market.

President Bush's proposed S&L restructuring legislation envisions bringing the equity-to-assets standard for S&Ls up to 6 percent, the same as is required of commercial banks.

In any case, RAP won't be around long. The Bank Board is phasing it out over the next four years. It's possible that pending legislation that would strip the Bank Board of much of its power will kill it even earlier.

"I think you'll find consistently if you ask for an honest opinion that (RAP) was the board's way of delaying the inevitable," said William Blackwell, who works with the Federal Deposit Insurance Corp. on troubled institutions for the public accounting firm of Laventhol & Horwath in Washington, D.C.

One method, referred to as RAP (for Regulatory Accounting Principles) was developed by the Federal Home Loan Bank Board, which is responsible for federal oversight of savings and loans. In this method, the savings and loan would elect to sell part of its loan portfolio to another investor at a loss. Instead of immediately recognizing the loss, the savings and loan would capitalize it as a deferred asset and amortize it over several years. For example, assume that an S&L sold a portfolio of loans it carried at $1,000,000 for cash of $850,000. The loss would be $150,000. Instead of immediately recognizing this loss, the S&L would capitalize it as an asset and amortize it over some period, say 5 years. As a result, $30,000 of the loss would be recognized in each of the next five years.

The alternative to RAP was to use standard GAAP, which requires that the loss be immediately recognized, thereby decreasing income and retained earnings (stockholder's equity) more rapidly than under RAP.

REQUIRED:

1. From what you can gather, why were the S&Ls in trouble? What role did higher interest rates have in creating this problem?
2. What did S&Ls attempt to do in terms of managing their loans to overcome the problem?
3. Why do you think it was necessary for the Federal Home Loan Bank Board to create RAP in the first place?
4. Why couldn't the FASB simply require S&Ls to use GAAP?
5. Speculate on why some S&Ls chose not to adopt RAP.
6. Congress is supposed to set regulations within which the Federal Home Loan Bank Board can operate. Obviously, Congress did not step in to stop this process. Speculate on what you think the incentives were for individual congressional representatives to interfere in the RAP versus GAAP controversy?
7. What responsibility do you think the individual auditing firms that performed the reviews on these S&Ls had in resolving the acceptability of the use of RAP or GAAP?

THE OIL AND GAS CONTROVERSY

CASE 1.2

One of the more highly debated choices of accounting and financial reporting standards over the last 20 years was that by the oil and gas producing companies to report their exploration efforts. Exploration in the oil and gas industry includes the costs of geological surveys and drilling test wells to determine the existence and quality of crude oil in an unproven area.

Until the late 1970s, companies in the oil and gas industry had used one of two basic accounting methods for the costs of exploration. These two methods were full cost and successful efforts. In both methods, the costs of drilling exploratory wells are capitalized until it is determined whether the well is viable. Once a determination as to the viability of a particular well is made, the full cost and successful efforts methods differ as to how to handle the exploratory costs.

Under the full cost method, the costs of all exploration efforts were capitalized and amortized over future years, without regard to whether the costs of drilling exploratory wells in a specific oil field actually produced a viable well. The basic support for this method was that all exploratory efforts were undertaken so that, on average, sufficient oil reserves would be identified and the firm could make a profit over all of its successful and unsuccessful efforts. In this way, matching the total exploration costs against future revenues generated from only the successful wells properly matched costs with revenues.

Under the successful efforts method, a company would only capitalize and amortize the cost of those drilling efforts that resulted in a viable well. If the exploration effort resulted in a dry well, the entire exploration cost would be expensed in the period it was determined that the well was not viable. This method focused on the matching of costs and revenues on a well-by-well basis, instead of viewing the entire exploration effort as a portfolio of opportunities.

In December 1977, the FASB released *Statement of Accounting Standard No. 19*, "Financial Accounting and Reporting by Oil and Gas Producing Companies." In general, this standard required all firms to use the successful efforts method of accounting. Within two years, the FASB found it necessary to rescind this requirement and allowed firms to use either method they wished. The evolution of this accounting standard and the surrounding political activity provide an interesting example of the process of accounting standard setting.

At the time the FASB was deliberating on this issue, several other parties became involved. In 1975, Congress passed the Energy Policy and Conservation Act of 1975, which gave the Securities and Exchange Commission the responsibility to establish uniform accounting practices in the oil and gas industry. When the FASB recommended the uniform application of successful efforts, several oil and gas companies opposed this requirement. They argued that using successful efforts would deteriorate their ability to attract capital. Expensing all unsuccessful drilling operations immediately, as required by successful efforts, would depress accounting earnings. In turn, these opponents argued that their exploration activities would be retarded, and this would harm the nation's ability to maintain energy independence.

In response to these types of concerns, the Department of Energy held a series of public meetings in February 1978. A major national consulting firm, Arthur D. Little, prepared a study that supported the opponents' claims to successful efforts. The firm's report stated that the elimination of full cost accounting would reduce domestic production by about $600 million per year, or 8% of the total annual domestic production of crude oil. In turn, this would result in larger oil imports and a further deterioration in the balance of trade with the oil exporting nations.

In a report to the SEC at about the same time, the Justice Department stated that the SEC "must determine whether the proposed mandated switch would likely affect capital market behavior in ways which would significantly disadvantage the competitive viability of any segment of the oil and gas producing industry..."

One other fact that emerged from the deliberations relating to this accounting issue was: Firms that used successful efforts tended to be the large multinational oil companies such as Exxon and Amoco. Firms that had adopted full cost were more likely to be smaller oil exploration firms.

In hearings before the Department of Energy and the SEC, several firms involved in the marketing of new security issues testified. First Boston Corporation stated that:

> In our opinion, the change to successful efforts method in financial reporting will reduce the ability of small exploration companies to attract sufficient capital to proceed with expanded exploration for domestic oil and gas.

> Weaker balance sheets, lower and increasingly volatile reported earnings as well as pressures to reduce dividends can be expected to decrease the liquidity and marketability and prices of equity securities issued by small exploration companies. Such reduction in the marketability and prices of equity securities will increase the costs and decrease the availability of this important source of capital to such companies.

In retort to this argument, Professor John Burton, former Chief Accountant of the SEC responded as follows:

> The overwhelming preponderance of results in this research [research on the stock market effects of alternative accounting approaches] has indicated that the marketplace is highly sophisticated in dealing with accounting differences and that market prices therefore adjust for these differences.

This viewpoint suggests that the choice of accounting methods has no impact on managers' underlying decisions regarding what actions they will take. In short, managers will make the same exploration decisions regardless of how the financial reports communicate the results of those decisions. If so, the security market participants are sophisticated enough to understand that the accounting differences are only superficial.

REQUIRED:

1. Do you think Congress had a legitimate basis for requiring the SEC to establish uniform reporting standards for the oil and gas industry? Why not leave this choice to each individual oil and gas producer?
2. Given that a company decided to drill a test well, would the choice of accounting method have altered the pattern of cash flows of that company?
3. In deciding whether to drill an exploratory test well, would the choice of a method to report the costs incurred in drilling influence your decision? Why or why not?
4. Speculate on why you think larger oil and gas producers all chose successful efforts, while smaller producers appeared to prefer full cost prior to the passage of the FASB standard.
5. Speculate on why the use of successful efforts might create "weaker balance sheets and increasingly volatile earnings" for firms that used full cost.
6. How much credibility do you think we should place in representations made by the members of the oil and gas industry in setting reporting standards they will have to adhere to? What about third parties such as First Boston Corporation?
7. Who do you think is right, First Boston Corporation or Professor Burton? Why?

THE INVESTMENT TAX CREDIT CONTROVERSY

CASE 1.3

In 1962, Congress first implemented the Investment Tax Credit (ITC). The ITC was designed to provide incentives for companies to invest in certain classes of assets by providing a credit against the corporation's income tax based on a percentage of the purchase price of equipment that qualified for the credit. Generally, if the equipment was held for several years before being sold or abandoned, the credit was never repaid to the government. The explicit purpose of the credit was to stimulate investment by making it cheaper for companies to purchase equipment through the immediate reduction of income taxes.

Later that same year, the Accounting Principles Board (APB) developed APB *Opinion No. 2* on accounting for the ITC. In the deliberations on this accounting standard, two basic approaches were identified. The first one, called the "flowthrough" method, simply recorded the credit as a decrease in the current period's tax expense. In that manner, the credit immediately flowed through to the net income of the company receiving it. The alternative method was called the "deferral" method. Under this approach, the credit was viewed as a reduction in the capitalized cost of the asset purchased. As such, the credit was effectively amortized over the useful life of the asset. This view of the credit argues that matching is best accomplished by taking the benefit of the credit into income over the life of the asset, not at its acquisition.

In APB *Opinion No. 2*, the APB took the position that the only "good" accounting procedure to use for the ITC was the deferral method as it provided better matching of the cost of fixed assets against the revenues generated by their use over their productive lives. Since the overwhelming majority of firms affected by this requirement had already adopted the flowthrough method, there was widespread dissatisfaction with *Opinion No. 2*.

Affected companies lobbied the SEC to rescind *Opinion No. 2* and allow them to use the flowthrough method. In response to this lobbying, the SEC announced that because of this diversity of opinion, both the deferral and the flowthrough methods would be acceptable in reports submitted to the Commission. Finding itself at odds with the SEC, the APB reversed itself with APB *Opinion No. 4*, stating that while it preferred the deferral method, the flowthrough method was also acceptable GAAP.

Congress suspended the ITC in 1966, only to reinstate it in 1967. At that time, the APB was considering the issue of accounting for income taxes. The APB included a provision in its exposure draft on deferred taxes requiring the use of the deferral method for the ITC. Firms again raised objections to this provision, and APB *Opinion No. 11* was issued without requiring the deferral method for the ITC.

Congress again abolished the ITC in 1967, only to restore it in 1971. In anticipation of the Revenue Act of 1971, the APB convinced the SEC to support its position on the deferral method. The APB issued another exposure draft proposing the mandated use of the deferral method. Facing the loss of the desired accounting treatment and unable to turn to the SEC for help, firms directly lobbied Congress. They argued that equipment purchases would increase if the benefits of the credit were reflected immediately in the earnings of firms taking advantage of the ITC. Congress accepted this argument and inserted a provision in the Revenue Act of 1971 stating that "no taxpayer shall be required, without his consent, to use for purposes of his financial reports, any particular method of accounting for the tax credit."

REQUIRED:

1. Speculate on why companies wanted to use the flowthrough method over the deferral method. Do the assertions of affected companies regarding the effects of the accounting choice on investment make sense to you?
2. Do you think that the deferral method or the flowthrough method provides better matching of revenues with the costs incurred to generate those revenues? Why?

3. Assume that the deferral method does provide better matching, is this a sufficient basis for setting financial reporting standards? Why or why not?
4. In your opinion, should the SEC have backed the APB in its original decision to require deferral? Why or why not?
5. If the SEC did not back the APB, what effect does that have on the reporting practices of firms whose securities are listed on a major exchange? What about firms whose securities are not publicly traded? Did the decision by the SEC mandate that the APB had to rescind its standard?
6. Did Congress have a legitimate basis for mandating the choice of accounting standards by law? Why was it not appropriate to leave this issue to the SEC or APB?
7. What is your opinion on the reasonableness of the APB's decision to attempt to resurrect this issue on at least two occasions following its initial failure to gain support from the SEC?

Improved Performance
with Turnaround in Domestic Economy

Financial Highlights
(In thousands of dollars, except per share data)

For the Year		Fiscal Year Ending	
	January 3, 1993	December 29, 1991	December 30, 1990
Net Sales	$ 1,036,029	$ 1,004,622	$ 1,084,908
Domestic Sales	$ 967,029	$ 892,622	$ 1,010,908
Export Sales	$ 69,000	$ 112,000	$ 74,000
Income before cumulative			
effect of accounting change (FAS 106)	$ 46,857	$ 41,110	$ 68,936
Cumulative effect of accounting change	$ (125,231)	—	—
Net (loss) income	$ (78,374)	$ 41,110	$ 68,936
Earnings per share (1):			
Income before cumulative			
effect of accounting change	$ 1.42	$ 1.25	$ 2.07
Cumulative effect of accounting change	$ (3.80)	—	—
Net (loss) income	$ (2.38)	$ 1.25	$ 2.07
Net income assuming accounting change			
had not been made	$ 1.66	$ 1.25	$ 2.07
Current Annual Dividend Rate per Share (1)	$ .88	$ .88	$ .88
Capital Expenditures	$ 25,987	$ 36,456	$ 56,975
Return on Shareholders' Equity (2) (3)	18%	11%	20%
Return on Average Capital Employed (2) (3) (4)	13%	9%	15%

At Year-End			
Working Capital	$ 299,356	$ 192,933	$ 198,187
Total Assets	$ 871,185	$ 764,482	$ 793,152
Short-Term Debt	$ —	$ 17,000	$ 15,000
Long-Term Debt Including Current Portion	$ 145,564	$ 52,800	$ 67,733
Shareholders' Equity (3)	$ 256,944	$ 364,489	$ 352,266
Per Common Share (3)	$ 7.82	$ 11.09	$ 10.72
Debt to Total Capitalization (3)	36%	16%	19%

(1) Per share data reflects the 3-for-2 stock split effective July 2, 1990.
(2) For 1992, income before cumulative effect of accounting change is used for the calculations.
(3) For 1992, equity was reduced for total cumulative effect of accounting change.
(4) Capital Employed is defined as shareholders' equity plus all long- and short-term debt and noncurrent deferred taxes.
    Income is adjusted for after-tax interest expense.

over $1 Billion in Sales

nearly $47 Million in Earnings

18% Return on Equity

13% Return on Capital

TO THE SHAREHOLDERS:

As noted in the financial highlights, we are pleased to report significant improvement in profitability for Allegheny Ludlum in 1992 — $1.66 versus $1.25 per share of common stock in the prior year — before adopting the new accounting standard for employee post-retirement benefits. Net sales increased 3 percent in 1992 to $1.04 billion as the domestic economy began to move from recession.

The restatement of 1992 income following full adoption of the new accounting standard, including an after-tax charge of $125.2 million to "catch up" as well as ongoing charges for the year, resulted in a net loss of $2.38 per share. Your Board of Directors determined that it was in our Company's best interest to make this required non-cash accounting change "early" rather than in 1993, or to amortize the one-time charge over a twenty year period. The Company's strong financial position and net worth at three times the liability made this possible. This accounting change will not affect cash flow. Further information appears in the Financial Review pages of this Annual Report.

Without the one-time charge, but recognizing ongoing charges in 1992 for postretirement benefits, Allegheny Ludlum earnings were $46.9 million, and earnings per share were $1.42. This compares to earnings of $41.1 million and earnings per share of $1.25 in 1991. With income on this basis and with equity reduced to reflect the one-time charge, return on equity for 1992 was 18 percent and return on total capital employed, one of our most important yardsticks, was 13 percent, both ratios up from the prior year.

On balance, 1992 was a good year for Allegheny Ludlum, considering the state of the economy and the performances reported by other metals companies.

The operating improvement over the prior year resulted primarily from lower raw material costs and close reins on production costs. Better customer service also contributed to the improvement in operating performance. Net income in 1992 benefited by $5.8 million after-tax from the Company's investment in a leveraged buy out firm, which has permitted a modest diversification without diverting attention

Robert P. Bozzone
President and
Chief Executive Officer

Panoramic view of the two new precision slitters and efficient coil packaging line now in operation at the Vandergrift stainless steel finishing plant.

from our core business — Specialty Materials.

A substantial reduction in inventory was achieved in 1992 through a Company-wide program to become more efficient in the use of working capital. However, these lower inventories caused a liquidation of certain LIFO layers reducing net profits by $4.3 million. This inventory reduction made $49.3 million in cash available, while improving delivery responsiveness and yields. This, coupled with the sale of $100 million in convertible subordinated debentures at an attractive interest rate earlier in 1992, as previously reported, has placed the Company in its strongest cash position in history. Cash on hand at year end was $123.6 million, an amount approaching the level of the Company's total outstanding debt. This strong cash position will permit the Company to take advantage of opportunities which may arise in 1993.

Proposed Acquisition

As announced on March 12, Allegheny Ludlum and Athlone Industries, Inc. have signed a letter of intent for Allegheny Ludlum to acquire Athlone for the equivalent of $17.50 per share. In this proposed transaction, which is valued at approximately $107 million, Allegheny Ludlum will exchange shares of its common stock for all outstanding shares of Athlone. Primarily a manufacturer of specialty steels in plate form, Athlone reported 1992 sales of $207 million.

We believe that this proposed acquisition will provide Allegheny Ludlum with an opportunity to increase operating income and earnings per share beginning in the first year by allowing us to strengthen our profitability in stainless steel plate and other high value specialty steel plate products, and providing operating and other synergies. The transaction would transform Allegheny Ludlum from a marketer to a cost-competitive producer of stainless steel plate, with a stronger focus on specialized applications. In addition, furthering our long-standing corporate goals, we will be positioned to serve more 'niches' in specialty steel markets for tool steels, heat resistant nickel alloys and other high technology materials.

Richard P. Simmons
Chairman of the Board

The merger is subject to a number of conditions, including the execution of a definitive agreement, approval by the Boards of Directors of both companies, approval by the shareholders of Athlone and clearance by governmental regulatory authorities.

Looking forward, we will continue to focus on developing strategic alliances with other companies throughout the world.

Imports-Exports

Voluntary Restraint Agreements (VRAs) which limited imports of specialty steel to a share of the U.S. market expired in March, 1992 despite our efforts to convince the government to extend the agreements until a world steel agreement was in place. We predicted imports of stainless steel sheet and strip, our major product line, would increase significantly if the voluntary agreements were permitted to expire without new and more permanent agreements with foreign nations in place to stop the subsidization of their specialty steel producers. This was exactly what happened. With world economies in recession, the domestic market became increasingly attractive to foreign producers — many of which are government owned or subsidized.

Imports of stainless steel sheet and strip increased by 22 percent to the highest level in history. "Dumped" or "subsidized" imports continue unabated. However, until we believe that we can prove "material injury" under United States trade law, a requirement necessary in order to win relief, we will continue to monitor imports and express our concerns to our government. The Specialty Steel Industry of the United States and the United Steelworkers of America have filed trade cases on stainless steel rod products where it is believed injury can be proven.

Allegheny Ludlum's exports in 1992 declined to $69 million as compared to the record of $112 million of exports in 1991. However, 1992 was still the fourth best export year in our history. Of particular note, a number of significant new export opportunities have developed relating to Allegheny Ludlum's strategy to seek niches for its specialty materials. We believe that these opportunities will continue to grow particularly with today's foreign currency relationships. However, the world economy must begin to improve before we see the full impact of these new opportunities on our plans to expand our export presence.

Serving Growing Markets

Surprisingly, in spite of the sluggish recovery in the domestic economy, the United States market demand for stainless steel sheet and strip reached record levels in 1992, up 13 percent. This follows the smallest volume decline during a recession in memory and supports our view that stainless steel markets will continue to grow. We look forward optimistically to continued market growth, starting from a higher level of demand than we had previously forecasted.

The Company's market position has never been stronger with regard to quality and delivery. You can be certain that our efforts will continue in these areas. We recognize that new competition from within and outside the United States will continue to challenge us. In support of our marketing effort, ALstrip, Allegheny Ludlum's stainless steel strip service center subsidiary, has opened its fourth processing location. Near Nashville, Tennessee, this facility will enable us to grow our business in Southern markets. ALstrip can now serve customers more quickly and efficiently in the "just in time" world in which we compete.

We believe that growth of U.S. and foreign markets for stainless steel sheet and strip will require new capacity worldwide each year of approximately 200,000 tons on average. Thus, Allegheny Ludlum must again consider expanding to continue to grow with its markets in future years. With this in mind, the first phase of the Vandergrift investment in state of the art stainless sheet and strip capacity is now complete at a cost of $85 million. As recently announced, we are making a further investment of $56 million in the Vandergrift plant.

The timetable for other future capital investments in our facilities is being examined to determine if they should be accelerated to improve costs and serve a higher level of demand than earlier anticipated. We believe that the Company is in its best position ever to compete successfully worldwide with any company which must meet a discipline of profit.

Steady Employment

We take particular pride in the fact that, as in past years, we do not have to report any major restructuring which might have resulted in plant closings or significant cutbacks in employment levels. Reductions in employment, of course, occurred at Allegheny Ludlum in the 1970s, nearly all through retirements and attrition. While productivity and efficiency continue to increase, normal retirements have made this improvement process less disruptive to the lives of our employees. This is a great source of satisfaction to everyone. During the year, 180 new production and maintenance employees were hired to replace retired employees, as well as to meet the needs for additional employees to help support the improvement in demand. The Allegheny Ludlum family today consists of over 5,400 employees and 4,300 retirees.

COILCAST™ Project

During 1992, the installation of a commercial-size prototype COILCAST™ machine at our Lockport, N.Y. plant was completed. As previously announced, with our joint venture partner Voest-Alpine Industrieanlagenbau of Linz, Austria, we aim to develop and commercialize a new lower-cost steel making process to direct cast liquid stainless and carbon steel into strip and sheet products. While recognizing that an invention of this magnitude cannot be "scheduled," we hope to commercialize this revolutionary steel making technology in the mid-nineties. We are encouraged by the progress to date.

Stock Value

Dedicated as we are to enhancing shareholder value, we are pleased to report that the total return on your investment in Allegheny Ludlum, including appreciation of the stock value and cash dividends in 1992, was 29 percent. This compares favorably to the major stock indexes used to measure performance.

Concluding Remarks

Finally, as we do each year, we close this letter with the reaffirmation that we believe firmly that we can be no better than we set out to be; that we must be willing to set ever higher standards of performance and the highest level of ethics in every area of our business; that we must be willing to deal proactively with a changing world and the new challenges and opportunities that will surely arise. We restate that our success depends on every Allegheny Ludlum employee continuing to embrace these simple concepts. For their support, we express our sincere thanks to all our employees and their families. We are pleased to report that a profit sharing pool of nearly $2 million will be distributed to all employees in recognition of their efforts.

We also take this opportunity to offer our continuing appreciation to our Board of Directors whose advice and counsel remains a key ingredient of our success.

To our shareholders we offer a humble "Thank you" for honoring us with your confidence by being shareholders of Allegheny Ludlum.

R. P. Simmons

R. P. Bozzone

March 24, 1993

Continuing Strategic Focus

Allegheny Ludlum's long-standing core strategies drive all that we do — and underlie all that is reviewed in this 1992 Annual Report. As the economic cycle turns from recession to a new period of growth and opportunity, we reaffirm these strategies to our shareholders and everyone who shares an interest in the continued success of Allegheny Ludlum.

- *To Be a Cost Competitive Producer of Special Materials*
- *To Make Major Quality Improvements to Meet Changing Customer Requirements While Remaining Cost Competitive*
- *To Find Specialty Niches Less Sensitive to Competition*
- *To Exceed Our Customers' Expectations for On-Time Deliveries and Service*
- *To Seek Opportunities to Grow in the Materials Field Horizontally and in Related Areas Vertically*
- *To Expand a Profitable Export Presence*

Specialty Materials — no other business

Allegheny Ludlum is a major producer of an extensive range of flat rolled specialty materials — stainless steels, silicon electrical steels and other high technology alloys. These highly engineered materials are produced in more than 150,000 combinations of different properties, chemistries, processing routes, finishes, forms, sizes, and other unique characteristics. Depending on specific end-use requirements, specialty materials provide exceptional resistance to corrosion, heat and abrasion, along with high strength, toughness and hardness, hygienic qualities, electrical and electronic properties, and an attractive, long-lasting appearance. Combinations of these properties as well as other advantages make specialty materials an excellent choice for countless consumer products and capital goods.

The graphic representation of Allegheny Ludlum's product lines on page 7, including their approximate selling prices, helps differentiate specialty materials from high volume carbon steels.

Turnaround Year

Pursuing our core strategies, Allegheny Ludlum posted improved 1992 sales and earnings as detailed in the Financial Highlights and Letter to Shareholders, and explained further in the Financial Review. Supplementing this information, sales revenues and operating profits since 1982 are charted to the right. During this extended period, which included two recessions, Allegheny Ludlum has reported net profits every quarter, every year, except for 1992 due to the one-time charge related to an accounting change for retiree benefits.

More Sales of Stainless Steel

In 1992 stainless steel sales revenues increased 8 percent on a year-to-year basis and represented 80 percent of total revenues. This strong growth was founded on broad market demand, the beginnings of a cyclical upward trend in the economy, and increasing recognition of the intrinsic value of stainless steel. Sales of silicon electrical steels were down reflecting lower exports of semi-finished products. Also, sales of other specialty alloys, primarily high temperature and other high technology materials, decreased with the recession in the aerospace and related industries.

The three-year sales distribution by broad product lines follows:

	1990	1991	1992
Stainless Steel	74%	77%	80%
Silicon Electrical Steel	19%	17%	16%
Other Specialty Alloys	7%	6%	4%
	100%	100%	100%

U.S. Markets Growing Again

Domestic market growth resumed and set a new record in 1992 for stainless sheet and strip steel, our major product line. As charted on page 8, demand was up 13 percent over both the previous year and the average demand for the five-year period ending in 1990. Also, domestic consumption of stainless steel sheet and strip continues to track the index of consumer durable products. Finally, the favorable position achieved by Allegheny Ludlum is highlighted on page 9 in the graphic presentation of the market growth trends of stainless sheet and strip steel compared with carbon steel.

Selling Prices Depressed

Stainless steel prices were depressed in an extremely competitive market throughout 1992, generally remaining below 1991 levels, despite a modest increase at mid-year restoring part of the past price erosion. As shown in the chart on page 8, stainless steel continues to be an excellent "buy". In the past 25 years, Type 304 stainless steel prices increased far less than other materials and the Consumer Price Index. Current selling prices lag below historic levels and do not reflect the true value of this material in our economy. Against this background, we believe that firmer stainless steel pricing would not restrain market growth. A 3 percent price increase for flat rolled stainless steel products is scheduled to become effective on May 3, as publicly announced by Allegheny Ludlum.

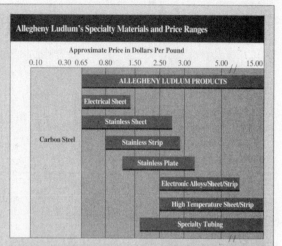

Allegheny Ludlum's Specialty Materials and Price Ranges

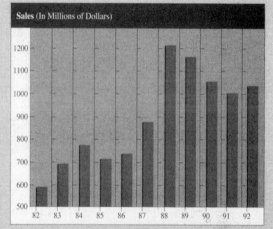

Sales (In Millions of Dollars)

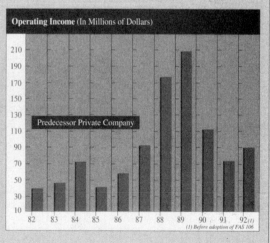

Operating Income (In Millions of Dollars)

(1) Before adoption of FAS 106

Major Markets for Allegheny Ludlum Products

Percent of Sales	1990	1991	1992
Steel service centers and distributors	40	36	40
Energy	20	17	16
Transportation - land, sea and aerospace	10	10	11
Convertors, including tubemakers	9	10	10
Commercial and domestic products	7	8	8
Exports	7	11	7
Industrial machinery and equipment	3	3	3
Construction and contractor products	2	3	3
Communications and electric equipment	1	1	1
Other markets	1	1	1
Total	100%	100%	100%

Price Trends - Stainless Steel vs. Other Materials and Indices

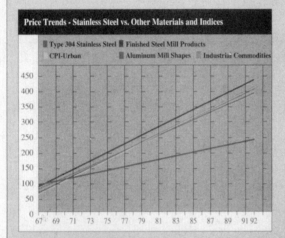

Growth of U.S. Market for Stainless Steel Sheet and Strip (In thousands of tons)

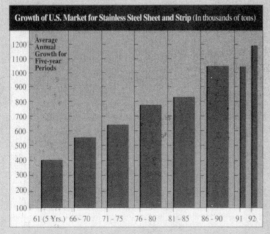

Exports Fall in World Recession

Exports decreased in 1992 to 7 percent of total sales revenue versus the 11 percent record set in the prior year. While recessions in most major world economies and lower demand for semi-finished electrical steel reduced our overall exports, we received important new business for proprietary alloys in North Sea offshore oil platforms, precision rolled stainless steel for shutter doors on computer diskettes, and other high value "niche" applications. Allegheny Ludlum plans to continue to develop global markets in the 90's, building on the widely recognized quality standards and advanced technology of its specialty materials.

Surging Imports

During 1992, imports of stainless steel sheet and strip rose to 206,400 tons, surpassing by 22 percent the record imports reported for 1991. Import penetration of these products reached 17 percent of the market in 1992. We estimate that imports in this product line alone displace over 1,000 American jobs.

Despite our best efforts, the specialty steel industry and the United Steelworkers of America (USWA) could not convince our government to extend Voluntary Restraint Agreements (VRAs) beyond March 31, 1992. Meanwhile, our government was unable to establish new agreements with steel producing nations to limit government subsidies.

As matters stand, there are no international understandings to assure fair trade in specialty steel. Foreign subsidies and dumping continue. However, the successful filing of unfair trade cases requires "material injury", which is difficult to prove under U.S. trade laws. For now, the industry and the USWA continue to carefully monitor imports and trading practices and communicate our findings and serious concerns to the new administration and the Congress.

Capital Investment Plans

In 1993 capital investments are expected to increase to about $58 million. This includes the first year of our Phase II expansion of the Vandergrift stainless steel finishing plant which will add a new anneal and pickle line and a temper rolling mill.

In addition, investments are being made to significantly increase light gauge stainless steel strip production capacity at the Company's Wallingford and Waterbury, Connecticut finishing facilities to serve projected market growth.

Stable Employment

At year end, over 5,400 men and women continued to be employed by Allegheny Ludlum. The United Steel Workers of America represents most production and maintenance employees under a labor agreement that expires March 31, 1994.

Significant improvements in safety performance continued. The OSHA Recordable Rate for 1992 improved by 30%. Serious lost workday injuries also declined by 33 percent. We share with all employees a strong commitment toward continuing to improve safety performance in all of our operations.

Allegheny Ludlum has long recognized that our future success depends on the talents of all employees. Today, more than ever before, employee education and training must be ongoing to stay ahead of the industry's rapidly changing technology.

Employees may choose from among 62 professional and personal development programs offered in our Course Catalog, or attend outside training seminars.

Whenever new equipment is installed, all affected employees attend several weeks of extensive training. Also, in-house classes are conducted for salespeople, managers, supervisors and scientists, all of whom must continuously add to their skills and talents.

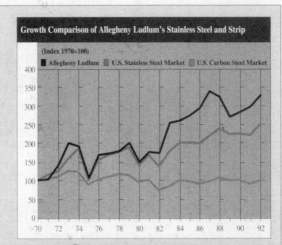

Growth Comparison of Allegheny Ludlum's Stainless Steel and Strip

(Index 1970=100)
■ Allegheny Ludlum   ■ U.S. Stainless Steel Market   ■ U.S. Carbon Steel Market

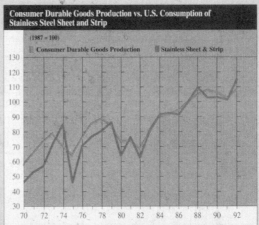

Consumer Durable Goods Production vs. U.S. Consumption of Stainless Steel Sheet and Strip

(1987 = 100)
■ Consumer Durable Goods Production   ■ Stainless Sheet & Strip

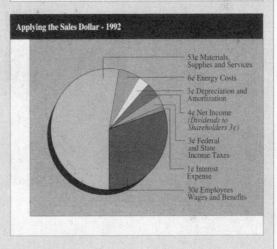

Applying the Sales Dollar - 1992

53¢ Materials, Supplies and Services
6¢ Energy Costs
3¢ Depreciation and Amortization
4¢ Net Income (Dividends to Shareholders 3¢)
3¢ Federal and State Income Taxes
1¢ Interest Expense
30¢ Employees Wages and Benefits

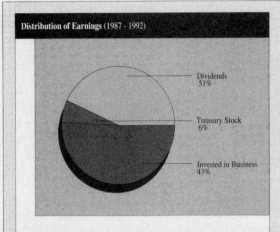

Distribution of Earnings (1987 - 1992)

Dividends
51%

Treasury Stock
6%

Invested in Business
43%

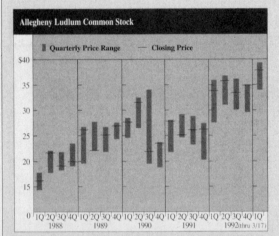

Allegheny Ludlum Common Stock

■ Quarterly Price Range   — Closing Price

Stock Price Up

Allegheny Ludlum common stock (ALS) traded between $26½ and $36⅝ per share during 1992 compared with a range of $20¼ and $29⅛ in the prior year. As noted in the chart, ALS closed at $37⅞ on March 17, 1993. Average trading volume in 1992 increased to 43,664 shares per day, versus 39,739 per day in the previous year.

The regular quarterly cash dividend rate was maintained at $.22 per share, or $.88 per share on an annual basis, during 1992. As a public company during the six year period ending December 31, 1992, the average annual total return for our common stock, assuming the reinvestment of regular quarterly cash dividends and a special cash dividend, was 18.8 percent, versus 11.0 percent for the S&P 500.

During the year, 61,600 shares were purchased under our stock repurchase program which helps provide greater liquidity for shareholders. Since inception in 1989, the Company has repurchased 1,125,300 shares at an average price of approximately $23⅞ per share. Authorization exists to repurchase an additional 1,374,700 shares.

Allegheny Ludlum offers an Automatic Dividend Reinvestment Service which also allows shareholders to make voluntary cash payments to purchase additional shares without paying brokerage commissions or service charges. A brochure describing this service is available on request.

In 1992, Allegheny Ludlum opened a new Visitor Center located within the Technical Center, in Brackenridge, PA. Pictured is a realtime display of on-line operational data from one of our facilities. Also, on view in the Center are many products made from specialty materials.

POWER OF IDEAS

Allegheny Ludlum's past and future success depends upon continuous improvement throughout all its operations. Ideas have many sources. Employee suggestions and patentable inventions improve specialty materials and customer service in addition to lowering costs. And they help make better and safer jobs.

Employee ideas under the Suggestion Awards Program generated cost savings of over $1.4 million in 1992, setting a fifth consecutive yearly record. Over 1,150 cost saving ideas were submitted, ranging from a method to prevent oxide formation on welded tubing to the elimination of paperwork on customer orders.

Eight maximum awards, each paying $7,500, were presented in 1992. Underscoring family teamwork, one award winning idea was from the father and son team of Paul and George Reesman who offered an idea that enhances both safety and productivity.

In addition, the ideas of thirteen employees resulted in twelve U.S. patents issued to Allegheny Ludlum in 1992. These employees work in many aspects of the business, from research and development at the Technical Center to plant operations in melting and finishing.

Never content with the way things are, we look for employee ideas to continue to help make major improvements in Allegheny Ludlum's operations.

Maximum award earners left to right: Paul Reesman, Jr. and son George Reesman, Bagdad; Tom Hines, Brackenridge; Mike Norvel, Claremore; Tim Klingensmith, Brackenridge. (Not shown is John Wasas of the Bagdad plant.)

Maximum award earners Bob Vance (right), Vandergrift; Glenn Sukustis (center), Brackenridge and Billy Lester, New Castle.

IMPROVING CYCLE TIME

*Time is of the essence.
Time is money.*

Old clichés, but never more true than in today's marketplace.

Allegheny Ludlum's customers expect outstanding product quality, reliable deliveries and quick responsiveness. At the same time, they want to respond to their own market opportunities, minimize their inventories, and retain the flexibility to select specific product attributes at the last possible moment.

There are two ways Allegheny Ludlum can meet these customer requirements: either carry lots of inventory as both work-in-process and finished goods, or shorten the manufacturing cycle time.

Contrary to long-held assumptions, a high inventory level is not the best answer. Carrying excessive inventories exacts a heavy price by tying up working capital dollars and valuable production space. It's also risky in a fast changing business world since predicting future customer requirements often relies too much on history.

Allegheny Ludlum's cycle time reduction process responds to our customers' needs for reliable deliveries and quick response and enables both parties to lower inventories. These seemingly conflicting tasks are accomplished by reducing the time it takes to produce our specialty materials through the complex steps of manufacturing.

A typical coil of specialty steel requires many hours of processing such as melting, annealing, rolling and slitting. When not on a piece of equipment, the coil sits in queue

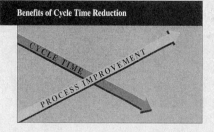

Benefits of Cycle Time Reduction

(as work-in-process inventory), and while the coil waits, no value is being added. Cycle time reduction concentrates on reducing queue time, thus lessening the total time it takes to make a coil of specialty steel from beginning to end. Improved manufacturing flexibility and responsiveness emerge from lower inventory levels and shorter production time.

Our New Castle, Indiana stainless steel sheet finishing facility provides a good example

of how reducing cycle time benefits both customers and Allegheny Ludlum. In 1992, work-in-process inventory and the number of days to move a coil through the plant were both lowered by over 60 percent, resulting in a further improvement in what we believe is an industry-leading delivery performance. The remarkable reduction in cycle time took place in a plant that had already earned an outstanding reputation for quality and service.

Cycle time reduction is a catalyst for continuous improvement. The pressure to reduce cycle time and inventory exposes and highlights problems that whose solutions lead to improved quality, cost and delivery reliability.

Through the attention and teamwork of many people in 1992, Allegheny Ludlum reduced work-in-process inventory by over $49 million throughout the Company, freeing cash resources. We're not satisfied. Lofty goals are set to further streamline processing in our plants by taking out more cycle time and inventory in order to continually improve cost, quality and customer service.

ALstrip, Inc., a subsidiary specializing exclusively in the stocking, final processing and distribution of stainless steel strip products, adds an extra dimension to the Company's efforts to reduce overall cycle time and enhance customer service.

As more manufacturing companies seek "just in time" deliveries, requiring shipments to arrive within very tight time periods, they are often best served by regional service centers. While Allegheny Ludlum relies on independent metal service centers to bring to market the preponderance of its stainless steel sheet products (more than 24 inches wide), the Company has historically sold its narrower strip products directly to end users.

ALstrip aims first, to stock finished full width coils, in order to respond to customer needs in less than normal mill lead times. Second, to provide the final processing and on-time delivery systems for customers. Third, to serve customers better by responding to both emergency shipments and small order requirements.

ALstrip provides a wide range of finishing operations including extensive slitting, oscillate winding, edging, and cut-to-length services.

The recent opening of a new service center near Nashville, Tennessee offers expanded market opportunities in the South. ALstrip is headquartered and maintains a stainless steel strip service center in Skokie, Illinois, and has established centers near Los Angeles, California and Philadelphia, Pennsylvania. Through these four regional service centers, ALstrip has become an established player in its very focused markets.

Looking forward, we expect market demand for quick response and customer service to continue as part of a growing interest in reducing cycle time.

ALstrip's slitting line for stainless steel strip at its new service center in Springfield (near Nashville), TN.

STAINLESS STEEL – THE VALUE OPTION

The Specialty Steel Industry of the United States (SSIUS), a trade association of which Allegheny Ludlum is a member, launched a new marketing program in 1992 to further expand the use of stainless steel in domestic markets. We actively support this industry-wide effort.

Consumption of stainless steel sheet and strip, Allegheny Ludlum's major products, in the United States in 1992 was approximately 1,183,000 tons. Over the past three decades, consumption has increased at an annual rate of about 4 percent and at a somewhat lower rate for other forms of stainless steel. While stainless steel usage in domestic markets has grown significantly over several decades, the per capita consumption has reached higher levels in other industrialized nations. For example, the estimated consumption of stainless steel per capita in Japan, after adjustments for imports/exports, is more than twice the U.S. rate. Japan consumes approximately 33 pounds of stainless steel per capita versus 14 pounds in the United States, as charted for several developed nations. Clearly, whether measured per capita or by gross domestic product as compared with other nations, there should be far greater consumption of stainless steel in the United States.

Recently to strengthen the public perception and understanding of the potential value of longer-lasting, low-maintenance stainless steel and stainless steel products, the SSIUS introduced a new "service mark" for stainless steel — "Stainless Steel — The Value Option". By using this mark in a wide range of promotional materials, the industry hopes to gain greater recognition and consideration of the advantages stainless steel brings to countless products and applications in the marketplace.

During the past year the SSIUS has made good progress in identifying and comparing on a country-by-country basis the relative stainless steel usage in several specific markets. The United States compares well with other developed nations in markets such as transportation and industrial/commercial machinery. However, domestic use of stainless steel in construction applications is well below that in other nations.

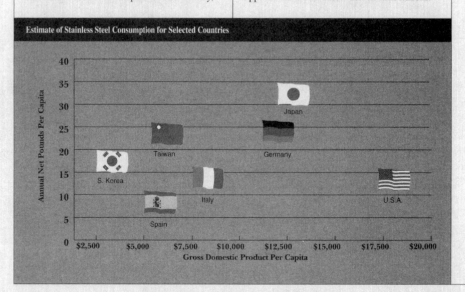

Estimate of Stainless Steel Consumption for Selected Countries

Stainless steel roofs cap the landside terminal building at the new Pittsburgh International Airport.

With this in mind, SSIUS is focusing initial efforts primarily on two marketing opportunities:

1. Applications in building and construction
2. Applications in a renewal of the nation's infrastructure

Architectural/engineering firms along with private and public owners have a high stake in lowering life cycle costs. SSIUS aims to highlight the long-term benefits of stainless steel, making it the material of choice in these and other consumer and capital goods markets. In addition to informative literature now available, several new marketing "tools" are being developed by SSIUS in cooperation with the Steel Service Center Institute and the Nickel Development Institute. A new computer software program is being prepared to assist designers and specifiers in comparing stainless steel with other materials. The program will help evaluate long-term versus short-term costs. Although stainless steel may have a higher initial cost than some other materials, it is frequently the least expensive material when total life cycle costs are calculated.

With wider recognition of its intrinsic, long-term benefits, we believe stainless steel is a material for the 21st century… available today.

STAINLESS STEEL is a strong candidate when making material selection because of its unique benefits in both consumer and capital goods applications.

STAINLESS STEEL contains 10 percent or more of chromium with or without other alloying elements and with iron as the major constituent. The chromium provides the 'stainless', corrosion resistant properties and allows the formation of a tough, adherent, invisible, corrosion-resisting chromium oxide film on the surface. If damaged, this film is self healing. The corrosion resistance and other properties of stainless steel may be enhanced by increasing the chromium content and adding nickel, molybdenum, and other elements.

There are many grades of stainless steel in thousands of combinations of sizes, finishes, and specifications to serve ever-changing needs in the marketplace.

BENEFITS OF STAINLESS STEEL
- *Corrosion resistant*
- *High strength and toughness*
- *Heat and fire resistant*
- *Hygienic qualities*
- *Hardness*
- *Impact resistant*
- *Attractive appearance*
- *Ease of fabrication*
- *Low maintenance*
- *Long-term value*

When total life cycle costs are fully evaluated, stainless steel is often the best and least expensive material option.

WORKING TOGETHER... BUILDING STRONG COMMUNITIES

More than 5,400 Allegheny Ludlum employees live and work in the communities near our plants, offices and research facility. Many represent second, third and even fourth generations of families who have been employed by the Company. Others are new employees attracted to exciting and well-paying jobs in a leading specialty materials company.

Our people are involved in almost every aspect of community life from buying local goods and services to participating in a wide range of public activities. So is Allegheny Ludlum. Together, we're strengthening the communities in which we live and work.

The Alle-Kiski Valley in Western Pennsylvania, where the families of more than 4,000 Allegheny Ludlum employees and over 3,000 retirees live, weathered the recent tough economic times better than many areas of the nation. Fortunately, the Company continued to provide good jobs and high employment levels during this difficult period. New schools and libraries were built, homes continue to be well-kept and new residents are moving in while few are leaving.

"People are attracted to this area because we're stable and they get a lot of lifestyle value here," said Highlands School District Superintendent Lou Baldasare. "We just spent $2.8 million to build the new Fairmount Elementary School in Brackenridge because our elementary enrollment is growing." This school serves children of families living near our Brackenridge and Natrona plants and Technical Center.

Fifteen miles east is the town of Leechburg where stainless and silicon steels are finished. Bruno Garelli started as a polisher in the Leechburg plant in 1928, retiring 49 years later. He's had a "shining influence" on the region. "I started making stainless steel jewelry during World War II," he said. Today Bruno Garelli's unique stainless steel awnings, mailboxes and porch railings brighten many homes in communities around Leechburg. "My own railings look as good today as when I put them up in 1960…you know how stainless steel lasts."

Near Leechburg is the community of Vandergrift. This industrial town was designed

Left, typical Victorian home in Vandergrift, PA. Right, the new Fairmount Elementary School, Brackenridge, PA.

in 1895 by Frederick Law Olmsted, whose many works include Central Park in New York City. Today, Vandergrift's well-preserved Victorian homes on beautiful tree-lined streets reflect the charm of nearly a century ago. In contrast, Allegheny Ludlum's million square foot plant showcases the very latest specialty steel finishing technology. In 1992, an office building next to the plant became the new home of our Information Technology Department.

Allegheny Ludlum recognizes its role as a neighbor in our plant communities. We support many educational, civic and charitable causes. In the 1991-93 period, as a commitment to education, area high schools were awarded almost $250,000 in math and science grants. In addition, we support and work closely with the Penn State

New Kensington Campus, the University of Pittsburgh and Carnegie Mellon University.

Also, Allegheny Ludlum provides financial support for both the Allegheny Valley and Kiski Valley YMCAs, Junior Achievement, Boy Scouts, the Salvation Army, the Pittsburgh Center for the Arts, the Pittsburgh Symphony, as well as many other educational, health and civic organizations. In addition, the Allegheny Ludlum Foundation underwrites the popular MacNeil/Lehrer NewsHour on WQED, Western Pennsylvania's public broadcasting television station.

Perhaps the public spirit and caring of Allegheny Ludlum employees is best demonstrated through employee contributions to the United Way. In 1992 the employee campaign

A basketball court in Natrona, PA. Boat dock scene along the Allegheny River, Brackenridge. Long time Vandergrift resident Thelma Orr.

Valley view of homes in Leechburg, PA.

17

New Castle is home to the Indiana Basketball Hall of Fame.

Company has made capital investments of more than $189 million in facilities to improve its competitive position.

Together, Allegheny Ludlum and the men and women who work in its plants and offices are helping to forge strong and prosperous communities — and good job opportunities in the future.

and Company match raised over $1,090,000. In addition, many employees participated in two Days of Caring, a time when volunteers learn first hand about how the United Way serves local human needs. Such activities represent the dedication of Allegheny Ludlum and our people to all our plant communities.

Also, in 1992 Allegheny Ludlum direct payroll and pension payments were more than $264 million. The states, counties, municipalities and school districts in which our employees reside benefited from more than $18 million in income, property and payroll taxes paid by the Company, including taxes withheld from employees during the year. In addition, since becoming a public company in 1987, the

Manufacturing jobs benefit more than employees and their families. They stimulate additional employment and the local economy.

The U.S. Chamber of Commerce has estimated that every 100 new manufacturing jobs create 64 additional new jobs.

Supported by Allegheny Ludlum, the Wallingford Symphony Orchestra makes its home in the Paul Mellon Art Center on the campus of Choate Rosemary Hall, Wallingford, CT.

Photo by:
Michael Melford

Management's Discussion and Analysis of Financial Condition and Results of Operations

FINANCIAL OVERVIEW

Sales and earnings (before the cumulative effect of the accounting change related to postretirement benefits) in fiscal 1992 increased reflecting higher demand for stainless steel products and improved product mix. Earnings were also impacted favorably by lower prices for raw materials and the recognition of a gain in the value of the investment in a limited partnership fund and negatively by accrued expenses related to postretirement benefits (FAS Statement No. 106) and increased charges related to inventory quantity liquidations of higher-priced material.

This financial review covers certain developments during the past three years relating to the results of operations and financial condition of the Company.

RESULTS OF OPERATIONS

Net Sales by product line were as follows:

Fiscal Year (dollars in millions)	1992	%	1991	%	1990	%
Stainless Steel	$ 831.4	80.2	$ 771.2	76.8	$ 798.4	73.6
Silicon Electrical Steel	161.1	15.6	172.2	17.1	205.8	19.0
Other Specialty Alloys	43.5	4.2	61.2	6.1	80.7	7.4
Total Net Sales	$1,036.0	100.0	$1,004.6	100.0	$1,084.9	100.0

Fiscal Year 1992 compared with Fiscal Year 1991

Net Sales

Net sales increased 3% in 1992. Shipments of 479,100 tons in 1992 were virtually the same as the 478,900 tons shipped in 1991. The increase in shipments and sales dollars occurred in the third and fourth quarters of 1992 as compared to the 1991 periods. The increase in sales in 1992 was due primarily to improved demand for stainless steel products partially offset by lower sales of semi-finished silicon steel and lower sales of specialty alloys.

Stainless steel sales increased 8% in 1992 reflecting increased domestic demand partially offset by lower selling prices and reduced export sales. Selling prices declined despite a modest price increase in June of 1992 which restored part of the price decline.

Silicon electrical steel sales decreased 6% in 1992 primarily because of decreased demand for semi-finished export products.

Other specialty alloys sales declined 29% in 1992 especially in the first and second quarters primarily due to lower demand in the aerospace and related industries and lower selling prices for most products.

Export sales decreased to $69 million compared to $112 million in 1991 reflecting a decrease in sales of semi-finished silicon export products and a general decline in the European markets.

The Company's 1993 first quarter sales and earnings are expected to exceed the 1992 first quarter (including an ongoing charge but excluding a one-time charge for postretirement benefits under FAS 106) and the most recent fourth quarter of 1992. Downward pressure on pricing appears to be continuing into the first quarter of 1993, and may continue further into the year. The Company has announced modest price increases for stainless steel products which are scheduled to become effective in May of 1993. Voluntary Restraint Agreements (VRAs) that limited certain imported products expired on March 31, 1992. While imports increased in 1992, the direct effect on the Company is unclear.

Cost and Expenses

Cost of products sold includes raw material costs, labor costs, energy costs (primarily electricity and natural gas), and other operating and support costs related to the manufacturing process. Cost of products sold as a percentage of sales decreased slightly in 1992 reflecting improved product mix and reduced raw material costs which were partially offset by lower selling prices and increased charges related to inventory quantity liquidations of higher-priced material. (See Note 2 of the Notes to Consolidated Financial Statements).

Raw material costs are the major component of cost of products sold and include expenditures for carbon and alloy scrap, nickel and nickel alloys, ferrochromium, ferrosilicon, molybdenum and molybdenum alloys, manganese and manganese alloys and other alloying materials. In 1992 raw material costs decreased 4% from 1991 on a per net ton shipped basis despite the higher costs related to inventory quantity liquidations.

Labor costs per net ton shipped increased 13% in 1992 compared to 1991. The increase primarily reflects higher labor and related premium costs as a result of producing and selling more stainless steel products, and scheduled contractual wage increases.

Energy costs per net ton shipped increased 6%. In 1992 more stainless steel products were produced and sold in a finished state resulting in a higher overall energy usage per net ton shipped. In addition, energy unit prices increased slightly in 1992.

Research, development and technology costs relate to efforts to develop new products and product applications, improved or new manufacturing methods, process improvements, quality assurance methods and cost reductions. These costs increased in 1992 reflecting higher expenses for certain projects under development, increased compensation expense reflecting salary increases, higher profit sharing and increases tied to Company financial results or common stock prices.

Commercial and administrative expenses include salaries and benefits of sales, executive and other non-manufacturing administrative personnel and related corporate support expenditures. These expenses in 1992 increased slightly over 1991 levels primarily due to higher salaries, benefits and costs for compensation plans tied to Company financial results or common stock prices. These increases were offset in part by lower legal costs.

Postretirement expense in 1992 reflects the adoption of FAS Statement No. 106 including additional non-cash accrued amounts. The 1991 and 1990 amounts reflect pay-as-you-go cash outlays.

Interest expense increased in 1992 primarily due to the issuance of $100 million of convertible subordinated debentures in the first quarter of 1992, partially offset by lower average short-term borrowings.

Unrealized gain from limited partnership was the result of recording equity income from the investment in Code, Hennessy & Simmons, a limited partnership fund.

Other income-net decreased in 1992 compared to 1991 period as a result of a cash payment the Company received in 1991 in settlement of a lawsuit for patent infringement. The 1992 period included higher investment income resulting from the investment of funds from the 1992 convertible subordinated debenture issue and funds generated from reduced inventory levels.

The **effective tax rate** of 40.5% in 1992 is lower than the 1991 rate of 43.2% primarily due to the one-time effect of the increased Pennsylvania state income tax rate in 1991 on the deferred tax liability.

The **cumulative effect of accounting change,** which resulted in an after-tax charge of $125.2 million, reflects the adoption of FAS No. 106. This accounting change did not affect cash flows.

Fiscal Year 1991 compared with Fiscal Year 1990

Net Sales

Net sales declined by 7% in 1991. Shipments of 478,900 tons in 1991 decreased 4% compared to 498,000 tons in 1990. The decline in sales was due primarily to the continued erosion of selling prices throughout 1991 in the stainless product line as well as lower shipments of silicon electrical steel.

Stainless steel sales declined 3% in 1991 despite a 2% increase in tons shipped. Selling prices continued to weaken throughout the year due to increasingly competitive pricing. This decline was partially offset by higher shipments of lower-priced export products.

Silicon electrical steel sales decreased 16%. The decrease was due to lower shipments resulting primarily from reduced demand due to a continuing slump in housing starts.

Other specialty alloys sales declined 24% in 1991 due to lower shipments and selling prices.

Export sales advanced to $112 million in 1991 compared to $74 million in 1990 reflecting increased marketing efforts as well as the favorable exchange rate of the U.S. dollar.

Cost and Expenses

Cost of products sold as a percentage of sales rose by 1.7 percentage points due primarily to selling prices declining at a rate faster than reductions in raw material costs.

In 1991 raw material costs decreased 5% from 1990 on a per net ton shipped basis, with the majority of this decrease occurring in the fourth quarter of 1991. Most raw material prices were lower compared to the 1990 year.

Labor costs per net ton shipped decreased 4% in 1991 compared to 1990. The decrease reflects improved productivity, higher shipments of less labor intensive semi-finished products and reduced employee profit sharing costs partially offset by contractual wage and benefit increases related to the four-year labor agreement that began April 1, 1990.

Energy costs per net ton shipped decreased slightly in 1991 reflecting lower unit usage per ton shipped somewhat offset by higher unit prices.

Research, development and technology costs decreased moderately in 1991 reflecting the continued emphasis on cost control as well as reduced costs for compensation plans tied to Company financial results.

Commercial and administrative expenses in 1991 increased 7% over 1990 levels primarily reflecting the recognition of higher uncollectible customer receivables and expenses related to the installation of computer software. Partially offsetting these expenses was reduced cost for compensation plans tied to Company financial results.

Interest expense decreased in 1991 due to lower average interest rates and lower long-term debt, partially offset by higher average short-term borrowings.

Other income–net declined in 1991. This was a result of reduced interest income due to less cash available for investment, partially offset by the cash payment the Company received in 1991 in settlement of a lawsuit for patent infringement.

The *effective tax rate* of 43.2% in 1991 was higher than the 1990 rate of 37.2% primarily due to increased Pennsylvania state income taxes and their one-time effect on the deferred tax liability.

Financial Condition

In 1992 cash from operations of $103.6 million, cash on hand from the prior year of $2.6 million and $100 million from the issuance of convertible subordinated debentures were used to invest $72.1 million in liquid short-term investments, purchase $26 million of capital equipment, make long-term investments of $5.2 million, repay $24.2 million of short-term and long-term debt, and pay $29 million in dividends. In addition, $51.4 million in cash remained at January 3, 1993 resulting in a combined total of $123.6 million of cash and short-term investments.

Working capital of $299.4 million at January 3, 1993 compares to $192.9 million at the end of 1991. This increase is primarily a result of increased cash generated by the issuance of debentures and inventory reductions, cash from operations and the pay-down of short-term debt and reduced accounts payable levels. The current ratios for 1992 and 1991 were 2.9 and 2.0, respectively. The debt to total capitalization ratio of 36% at the end of 1992 compares to 16% at the end of 1991. This ratio increase is primarily a result of the issuance of the $100 million convertible subordinated debentures and the reduction of equity under FAS No. 106. The ratio of total debt net of cash and investments to total capitalization was 8% at the end of 1992 and 15% at the end of 1991.

Capital expenditures of $26 million in 1992 were for equipment in all the plants and a new service center. The Company has announced plans to invest $56 million over the next two years in its Vandergrift, Pennsylvania plant. The project includes a new anneal and pickle line, a temper cold rolling mill and other auxiliary equipment. Capital expenditures in 1993 are expected to approximate $58 million, including $20 million for the Vandergrift project and $6 million for pollution abatement equipment. Many of the applicable regulations have not been issued under the Clean Air Act Amendments of 1990. When issued, such regulations may affect the Company's operations and plans for capital expenditures in the future. At this time, the Company continues to believe that it will be able to meet the new requirements while continuing its capital programs.

Internally generated funds, the availability of borrowings from existing credit arrangements and the current cash on hand should be adequate to meet foreseeable needs.

Other Matters

Although inflationary trends in recent years have been moderate, during the same period certain critical raw material costs have been volatile. The Company uses the last-in, first-out method of inventory accounting which reflects current costs in the cost of products sold. The Company considers these costs, the increasing costs of equipment and other costs in establishing its sales pricing policies and, in the past, has instituted raw material surcharges to the extent permitted by competitive factors in the marketplace. The Company continues to emphasize cost containment in all aspects of its business and, as in 1992, will continue concentrated efforts to further reduce inventories relative to sales in the current year.

In 1992, the Company, through its joint venture partner, Voest-Alpine Industrieanlagenbau GmbH, completed construction of the first COILCAST™ commercial-size prototype thin strip direct casting machine to produce stainless and carbon steel flat products directly from molten steel. Trial casts began in mid-1992 and are continuing. Although the results of this developmental work are uncertain, the COILCAST joint venture aims to commercialize the new technology in the mid 1990's.

Postretirement Benefits

In the fourth quarter of 1992, the Company adopted the Statement of Financial Accounting Standards No. 106, "Employers' Accounting for Postretirement Benefits Other Than Pensions." Previous 1992 interim period results were restated as a result of the adoption. The adoption of Statement No. 106 resulted in an initial cumulative liability of $210.8 million. The Company elected to recognize the cumulative effect of the accounting change by recording a one-time charge to net income of $125.2 million net of tax, or $3.80 per share, in the restated first quarter of 1992. In addition, the adoption resulted in an increase in postretirement benefit expense of $13.0 million and a reduction of net income before the cumulative effect of the accounting change for 1992 of $7.8 million net of tax, or $.24 per share, or $.06 per share in each quarter of 1992. The Company's cash flows were not affected by this change in accounting.

Postemployment Benefits

In November 1992, FAS Statement No. 112 was issued which relates to "Employers' Accounting for Postemployment Benefits." The statement is effective for fiscal years beginning after December 15, 1993. The Company's current accounting practices are in full compliance with provisions of the Statement.

Subsequent Event

On March 12, 1993, the Company and Athlone Industries, Inc. announced the signing of a letter of intent for the Company to acquire Athlone for the equivalent of $17.50 per share. See Note 11 of the Notes to the Consolidated Financial Statements.

ALLEGHENY LUDLUM CORPORATION AND SUBSIDIARIES
CONSOLIDATED STATEMENT OF INCOME

(In thousands of dollars except per share amounts)

Fiscal Year Ended	January 3, 1993 *(1)*	December 29, 1991 *(2)*	December 30, 1990 *(2)*
Net Sales	**$1,036,029**	$1,004,622	$1,084,908
Costs and expenses:			
Cost of products sold	**829,494**	820,668	868,661
Research, development and technology	**40,262**	35,372	36,960
Commercial and administrative	**39,605**	40,179	37,476
Postretirement expense	**22,637**	8,512	8,056
Depreciation and amortization	**27,578**	26,224	22,728
	959,576	930,955	973,881
Income from Operations	**76,453**	73,667	111,027
Other income (expense):			
Interest expense	**(8,000)**	(5,424)	(6,214)
Unrealized gain from limited partnership	**8,808**	—	—
Other income - Net	**1,538**	4,148	5,031
	2,346	(1,276)	(1,183)
Income before Income Taxes and			
Cumulative Effect of Accounting Change	**78,799**	72,391	109,844
Income taxes	**31,942**	31,281	40,908
Income before Cumulative Effect of Accounting Change	**46,857**	41,110	68,936
Cumulative Effect of Accounting Change			
(Less income tax benefit of $85,596)	**(125,231)**	—	—
Net (Loss) Income	**$ (78,374)**	$ 41,110	$ 68,936
Per Common Share:			
Income before cumulative effect of accounting change	$ **1.42**	$ 1.25	$ 2.07
Cumulative effect of accounting change	**(3.80)**	—	—
Net (loss) Income	$ **(2.38)**	$ 1.25	$ 2.07

See notes to consolidated financial statements.
(1) After adoption of FAS No. 106
(2) Before adoption of FAS No. 106

ALLEGHENY LUDLUM CORPORATION AND SUBSIDIARIES
CONSOLIDATED BALANCE SHEETS

(In thousands of dollars)

	January 3, 1993	December 29, 1991
ASSETS		
Current Assets:		
Cash and cash equivalents	$ 51,437	$ 2,645
Short-term investments	72,115	—
Trade receivables, less allowances for doubtful accounts		
of $3,235 and $3,547	95,538	92,770
Inventories	235,259	284,513
Prepaid expenses and other current assets	5,161	4,937
Total Current Assets	459,510	384,865
Properties, plants and equipment - net	362,136	364,766
Investment in limited partnership	24,409	11,665
Deferred income taxes	21,586	—
Other assets	3,544	3,186
Total Assets	$871,185	$764,482
LIABILITIES AND SHAREHOLDERS' EQUITY		
Current Liabilities:		
Short-term debt	$ —	$ 17,000
Current portion of long-term debt	7,494	4,276
Accounts payable	72,037	91,954
Accrued compensation and benefits	40,535	44,856
Deferred income taxes	13,515	19,531
Income taxes	12,353	2,734
Other accrued expenses	14,220	11,581
Total Current Liabilities	160,154	191,932
Long-term debt, less current portion	138,070	48,524
Pensions	67,054	73,039
Postretirement benefit liability	223,849	—
Deferred income taxes	—	63,250
Other	25,114	23,248
Total Liabilities	614,241	399,993
Shareholders' Equity:		
Preferred stock, par value $1: authorized—50,000,000 shares; issued—none		
Common stock, par value $.10: authorized—100,000,000 shares;		
issued—33,862,433 shares	3,386	3,386
Additional capital	164,262	164,194
Retained earnings (after adoption of FAS No. 106 in 1992)	113,169	220,544
Common stock in treasury at cost—994,294 and 1,002,661 shares	(23,873)	(23,635)
Total Shareholders' Equity	256,944	364,489
Total Liabilities and Shareholders' Equity	$871,185	$764,482

See notes to consolidated financial statements.

ALLEGHENY LUDLUM CORPORATION AND SUBSIDIARIES
CONSOLIDATED STATEMENT OF CASH FLOWS

(In thousands of dollars)

Fiscal Year Ended	January 3, 1993	December 29, 1991	December 30, 1990
Cash flows from operating activities:			
Income before cumulative effect of accounting change	$ **46,857**	$ 41,110	$ 68,936
Adjustments to reconcile income before cumulative effect of accounting change to cash flow from operating activities:			
Depreciation and amortization	**27,578**	26,224	22,728
Unrealized gain from limited partnership investment	**(8,808)**	—	—
Deferred taxes	**(5,255)**	3,921	5,994
Change in operating assets and liabilities:			
Long-term pension liability	**(5,985)**	(4,846)	(11,040)
Long-term postretirement liability	**13,022**	—	—
Deferred employee benefits	**1,312**	(433)	(3,189)
Trade receivables	**(2,768)**	9,565	(28,933)
Inventories	**49,254**	30,280	(13,690)
Trade payables	**(19,917)**	(21,201)	4,815
Income taxes payable	**9,619**	1,833	(15,262)
Net change in other current assets and current liabilities	**(1,906)**	(7,902)	3,217
Other changes	**606**	889	711
Cash Flows from Operating Activities	**103,609**	79,440	34,287
Cash flows from investing activities:			
Purchases of properties, plants and equipment	**(25,987)**	(36,456)	(56,975)
Disposals of properties, plants and equipment	**1,039**	222	435
(Purchases) sales of short-term investments	**(72,115)**	—	20,600
Increase in limited partnership investment	**(5,188)**	(4,000)	(5,375)
Limited partnership distribution	**1,252**	—	—
(Increase) decrease in notes receivable	**(414)**	(377)	24
Cash Used by Investing Activities	**(101,413)**	(40,611)	(41,291)
Cash flows from financing activities:			
(Decrease) increase in short-term debt	**(17,000)**	2,000	15,000
Issuance of convertible subordinated debentures	**100,000**	—	—
Payments on long-term debt	**(7,236)**	(14,933)	(14,773)
Dividends paid	**(28,960)**	(28,960)	(28,623)
Purchases of treasury stock	**(1,845)**	(1,264)	(17,441)
Employee stock plans	**1,637**	1,243	75
Cash From (Used by) Financing Activities	**46,596**	(41,914)	(45,762)
Increase (Decrease) in Cash and Cash Equivalents	**48,792**	(3,085)	(52,766)
Balance of cash and cash equivalents at beginning of year	**2,645**	5,730	58,496
Cash and Cash Equivalents at End of Year	$ **51,437**	$ 2,645	$ 5,730

See notes to consolidated financial statements.

ALLEGHENY LUDLUM CORPORATION AND SUBSIDIARIES
NOTES TO CONSOLIDATED FINANCIAL STATEMENTS

Note 1 — Summary of Significant Accounting Policies

Consolidation

The consolidated financial statements include the accounts of the Company and its subsidiaries. Significant intercompany accounts and transactions have been eliminated.

Business Segment

The Company operates in a single business segment, specialty steel.

Cash and Cash Equivalents

Cash includes currency on hand and demand deposits with financial institutions. Cash equivalents are short-term, highly liquid investments both readily convertible to known amounts of cash and so near maturity, three months or less, that there is insignificant risk of fluctuations in value because of changes in interest rates and thus the carrying amounts approximate market.

Short-term Investments

Short-term investments are carried at the lower of aggregate cost or market and include short-term to intermediate-term investments managed by third-party portfolio managers.

Accounts Receivable

The Company markets its products to a diverse customer base, principally throughout the United States. Trade credit is extended based upon evaluations of each customer's ability to perform its obligations, which are updated periodically. Credit losses are provided for in the financial statements and have been within management's expectations. Export sales customers generally are required to provide bank letters of credit except when considered unnecessary.

Inventories

Inventories are valued at the lower of cost or market. Cost for substantially all inventories is determined by the last-in, first-out (LIFO) method. Inventories not on LIFO (1992 — $23,373,000; 1991 — $23,606,000) are determined using the average cost method.

Properties, Plants and Equipment

Properties, plants and equipment are carried at cost. Depreciation is computed using the straight-line method at rates considered sufficient to amortize the costs over the estimated service lives. Depreciation for income tax purposes is computed principally using accelerated methods.

Investment in Limited Partnership

Investment in limited partnership is stated at the Company's pro-rata share of the limited partnership's equity. The limited partnership's net income includes unrealized gains and losses on portfolio investments. The Company has invested $16,852,500 in the limited partnership through January 3, 1993. The Chairman of Allegheny Ludlum Corporation serves on an Advisory Board of the limited partnership.

Taxes on Income

Provisions for income taxes include deferred taxes resulting from temporary differences in income for financial and tax purposes using the liability method. Such temporary differences result primarily from differences in the carrying value of assets and liabilities. The adoption in 1992 of Statement of Financial Accounting Standard No. 109, "Accounting for Income Taxes", did not affect the Company's financial statements.

Fiscal Year-End

The Company's fiscal year ends on the Sunday nearest to December 31.

Reclassifications

Certain amounts in the prior year financial statements have been reclassified to conform to 1992 presentation.

Net Income per Share of Common Stock

Net income per share is based upon the weighted average number of shares of common stock outstanding. The weighted average number of shares was 32,911,748 for this fiscal year ended January 3, 1993, 32,903,095 for the fiscal year ended December 29, 1991, and 33,300,677 for the fiscal year ended December 30, 1990. The Company's convertible subordinated debentures are not dilutive at current earnings levels.

Note 2 — Inventories

(In thousands of dollars)	January 3, 1993	December 29, 1991
Raw materials	$ 53,326	$ 63,482
Work-in-process and finished products	212,152	263,100
Supplies	11,837	11,574
Total inventories at current cost	277,315	338,156
Less allowance to reduce current cost values to LIFO basis	42,056	53,643
Total Inventories	**$235,259**	**$284,513**

Certain LIFO inventory quantities were reduced, resulting in a liquidation of items carried at costs that prevailed in prior years. The effect of the liquidations was to decrease net income in 1992 by approximately $4,252,000 and increase net income by approximately $890,000 and $36,000 in 1991 and 1990, respectively.

Note 3 — Properties, Plants and Equipment

(In thousands of dollars)	January 3, 1993	December 29, 1991
Land	$ 7,530	$ 7,472
Buildings	54,381	52,199
Machinery and equipment	435,643	413,544
	497,554	473,215
Less allowance for depreciation and amortization	135,418	108,449
Total Properties, Plants and Equipment	**$362,136**	**$364,766**

Note 4 — Credit Agreement and Long-Term Debt

Credit Agreement

The Company's Credit Agreement, dated December 28, 1990, as amended, with a group of banks, provides for borrowings of up to $100,000,000 on a revolving credit basis. Interest is payable at prime or other alternative interest rate bases, at the Company's option. Annual commitment fees range from ⅛% to ¼% on the unused portion of the credit line. The outstanding balance was paid in April 1992 from the proceeds of the debenture offering and no balance was outstanding at January 3, 1993.

The Credit Agreement has various covenants which limit the Company's ability to purchase its own stock, dispose of properties and merge with another corporation. The Company is also required to maintain certain financial ratios as defined in the agreement which also limits the amount of dividend payments. Under the most restrictive requirement, 100% of retained earnings is free of restrictions pertaining to cash dividend distributions. Borrowings outstanding under the Credit Agreement are unsecured.

Debentures

In March 1992, the Company issued $100 million of 5⅞% convertible subordinated debentures due in a single maturity on March 15, 2002. The debentures can be converted into the Company's common stock at a conversion price of $40.50 per share. The debentures can be called at a premium after three years have elapsed from date of issue.

Other

The industrial revenue bonds and capital lease obligations consist of 18 separate issues at January 3, 1993. Ten issues (aggregating $28,935,000) have an average interest rate of 5.2%, four issues ($577,000) have interest rates at the tax-free equivalent of the prime rate plus 1.0% or 1.5%, and four issues ($16,052,000) have variable interest rates, ranging from 2.4% to 6.5%. The average interest rate for all outstanding issues was 4.8% in 1992, 5.5% in 1991 and 6.1% in 1990. The variable rate obligations are subject to remarketing agreements, which provide that the bondholder may present the bonds to a remarketing agent for purchase prior to the stated maturity date. Bonds presented to the remarketing agent are then resold in the bond market.

Long-term debt consists of the following:

(In thousands of dollars)	January 3, 1993	December 29, 1991
5⅞% convertible subordinated debentures	$100,000	$ —
Industrial revenue bonds due 1993 through 2007	27,939	34,768
Capital lease obligations under industrial revenue bonds due 1993 through 2007	17,625	18,032
	145,564	52,800
Less current portion	7,494	4,276
Total long-term debt	**$138,070**	$48,524

Properties, plants and equipment include the following amounts for leases that have been capitalized:

(In thousands of dollars)	January 3, 1993	December 29, 1991
Land and buildings	$ 2,693	$ 2,693
Machinery	18,054	18,054
	20,747	20,747
Less allowance for amortization	7,075	6,022
Total leases	**$ 13,672**	$14,725

Amortization of leased assets is included in depreciation and amortization expense.

Scheduled maturities of long-term obligations for the five years succeeding January 3, 1993 are $7,494,000 in 1993, $2,976,000 in 1994, $1,992,000 in 1995, $1,940,000 in 1996, and $1,914,000 in 1997.

Interest and commitment fees paid amounted to $6,090,000 in 1992, $5,500,000 in 1991, and $5,644,000 in 1990.

Note 5 — Pension Plans and Other Postemployment Benefits

The Company and its subsidiaries have two defined benefit pension plans and several defined contribution plans, which cover substantially all of their employees. Benefits under the defined benefit pension plans are generally based on years of service and the employee's average annual compensation in the five consecutive years of the ten years prior to retirement in which such earnings were the highest. The Company funds at least the amount necessary to meet the minimum funding requirements of ERISA and the Internal Revenue Code.

The following table sets forth the funded status and amount recognized for the Company's defined benefit pension plans in the consolidated balance sheets:

(In thousands of dollars)	January 3, 1993	December 29, 1991
Actuarial present value of accumulated benefit obligations, including vested benefits of $360,880 in 1992 and $344,545 in 1991	$379,840	$371,944
Actuarial present value of projected benefit obligations for services rendered to date	$410,741	$405,488
Less plan assets at fair value, primarily listed stocks, government securities and pooled investment funds	324,999	312,721
Projected Benefit Obligations in Excess of Plan Assets	85,742	92,767
Unrecognized net gain (loss) from past experience different from assumed	(3,501)	5
Unrecognized prior service costs	(10,407)	(11,228)
Pension Liabilities	$ 71,834	$ 81,544

Pension liabilities are included in the balance sheets as follows:

(In thousands of dollars)	January 3, 1993	December 29, 1991
Accrued compensation and benefits	$ 4,780	$ 8,505
Pensions	67,054	73,039
Total Pension Liabilities	$ 71,834	$ 81,544

A summary of the net pension cost for the defined benefit pension plans is as follows:

(In thousands of dollars)	1992	1991	1990
Service cost — benefits earned during the period	$ 4,271	$ 4,508	$ 4,448
Interest cost on projected benefit obligations	32,450	32,751	32,108
Actual return on plan assets	(29,423)	(34,516)	4,698
Net amortization and deferral	3,391	10,190	(31,407)
Net Pension Cost	$ 10,689	$ 12,933	$ 9,847

The average discount rate used in determining the actuarial present value of the projected benefit obligations was 8.5% at January 3, 1993 and December 29, 1991. The rates of increase of future years' compensation levels ranged from 3% to 6% in 1992, 1991, and 1990. The expected long-term rate of return on plan assets was 9.0% in 1992, 1991 and 1990.

On November 10, 1988 the Board of Directors amended the salaried defined benefit pension plan to provide that no benefits would accrue thereunder on or after January 1, 1989. At the same time, the Board also adopted, effective January 1, 1989, a defined contribution plan. Pension costs for this plan were $4,407,000 in 1992, $4,346,000 in 1991, and $3,950,000 in 1990.

The Company has guaranteed employees who meet certain age and service criteria that at retirement their aggregate benefit from the salaried defined benefit pension plan and the defined contribution plan will not be less than the benefit which would have been payable from the salaried defined benefit pension plan if such plan had not been amended.

Other Postretirement Benefit Plans

The Company sponsors several unfunded defined benefit postretirement plans covering most salaried and hourly employees. The plans provide health care and life insurance benefits for eligible retirees. The basic health care plans are noncontributory, and the major medical options are contributory, with retiree contributions adjusted periodically. The life insurance plans are generally noncontributory.

The Company adopted the Statement of Financial Accounting Standards No. 106, "Employers' Accounting for Postretirement Benefits Other Than Pensions," in the fourth quarter of 1992. Previous 1992 interim period results were restated as a result of the adoption. The adoption of Statement No. 106 resulted in an initial cumulative pre-tax liability of $210,827,000. The Company elected to recognize the cumulative effect of the accounting change by recording a one-time charge to net income of $125,231,000, or $3.80 per share in the restated first quarter of 1992. In addition, for the year 1992, the adoption resulted in an additional pre-tax increase in postretirement benefit expense of $13,022,000 and an after-tax reduction of income before the cumulative effect of the accounting change of $7,787,000 or $.24 per share. The Company's cash flows were not affected by this change in accounting.

The following table sets forth the postretirement benefit plans' combined status reconciled with the amounts recognized in the balance sheet at January 3, 1993:

(In thousands of dollars)	Health Care	Life Insurance	Total
Accumulated postretirement benefit obligation (APBO)			
Retirees	$114,553	$10,459	$125,012
Fully eligible active participants	29,614	3,483	33,097
Other active participants	74,113	3,030	77,143
	218,280	16,972	235,252
Unrecognized net loss	(10,810)	(593)	(11,403)
Accrued postretirement benefit cost	$207,470	$16,379	$223,849

The APBO at the beginning of 1992 was $195,125,000 for the health care plans and $15,702,000 for the life insurance plans. The discount rate used in determining the APBO was 8¾ percent at January 3, 1993 and 9 percent at January 1, 1992.

Net postretirement benefit expenses for 1992 included the following components:

(In thousands of dollars)	Health Care	Life Insurance	Total
Service cost	$ 4,026	$ 189	$ 4,215
Interest cost	17,069	1,353	18,422
Net periodic postretirement benefit expense	$21,095	$1,542	22,637
Less actual cash payments	—	—	9,615
Excess expense over payments	—	—	$13,022

The annual assumed rate of increase in the per capita cost of covered benefits (the health care cost trend rate) for health care plans is 13.4 percent for 1993 and is assumed to decrease to 6 percent by 2002 and remain at that level thereafter. The health care cost trend rate assumption has a significant effect on the amounts reported. If the assumed health care cost trend rates were increased by one percentage point in each year, this would increase the APBO for health care plans as of January 3, 1993 by $29,716,000 and the aggregate of service and interest cost components of net periodic postretirement benefit expense for 1992 by $3,389,000.

The actual cash payments of retiree health care and life insurance benefits totaled approximately $9,615,000 in 1992, $8,512,000 in 1991, and $8,056,000 in 1990.

Note 6 — Shareholders' Equity

(In thousands of dollars except per share amounts)	Common Stock	Additional Capital	Retained Earnings	Treasury Shares
Balance at December 31, 1989	**$2,258**	**$165,317**	**$168,117**	**$(6,370)**
Net income			68,936	
Dividends on common stock at $.86 per share			(28,623)	
3-for-2 stock split	1,128	(1,129)	(2)	
Exercise of stock options		(22)	(14)	111
Purchase of 742,850 treasury shares at cost				(17,441)
Balance at December 30, 1990	**3,386**	**164,166**	**208,414**	**(23,700)**
Net income			41,110	
Dividends on common stock at $.88 per share			(28,960)	
Employee stock plans		28	(20)	1,329
Purchase of 57,600 treasury shares at cost				(1,264)
Balance at December 29, 1991	**3,386**	**164,194**	**220,544**	**(23,635)**
Net loss			(78,374)	
Dividends on common stock at $.88 per share			(28,960)	
Employee stock plans		68	(41)	1,607
Purchase of 61,600 treasury shares at cost				(1,845)
Balance at January 3, 1993	**$3,386**	**$164,262**	**$113,169**	**$(23,873)**

Preferred Stock

The authorized preferred stock may be issued in one or more series, with designations, powers and preferences as shall be designated by the Board of Directors. At January 3, 1993, there were no shares of preferred stock issued.

Common Stock

The Board of Directors adopted and the shareholders approved the 1987 Stock Option Incentive Plan ("Plan") in March, 1987. The Plan, which expires January 1, 1997, provides for the granting of stock options and stock appreciation rights ("Awards") of up to 1,350,000 shares of common stock to key employees.

Awards may be granted under the Plan at a price not less than the fair market value of the stock as determined by the Personnel and Compensation Committee ("Committee") on the date the Awards are granted. Awards will not be immediately exercisable and vesting of the awards will be established at the date of each grant but generally will not be more rapid than the rate of one-third of the number of shares on each of the third, fourth, and fifth anniversaries of the Award. Upon exercise of a stock appreciation right ("SAR"), the holder will receive cash, common stock or a combination thereof, as determined by the Committee, equal to the increase in fair market value over the underlying option price times the number of shares to which the right applies.

Transactions under the Plan are summarized as follows:

	Stock Options	Stock Appreciation Rights	Price Range
Balance at December 31, 1989	262,609	7,968	
Granted	299,515	—	$21.50
Exercised	(4,624)	—	16.67
Balance at December 30, 1990	557,500	7,968	
Granted	11,335	—	23.75
Exercised	(9,094)	(1,562)	16.67
Cancelled	(10,629)	(781)	16.67-21.50
Balance at December 29, 1991	549,112	5,625	
Granted	11,170	—	33.00
Exercised	(26,460)	—	16.67-22.17
Cancelled	(34,246)	—	16.67-21.50
Balance at January 3, 1993	499,576	5,625	

At January 3, 1993 there were options for 203,189 shares exercisable under the Plan.

In March, 1987, the Board of Directors adopted and the shareholders approved a Performance Share Plan for Key Employees, which provides that the Chief Executive Officer may establish certain performance objectives for a period established by the Board. The Personnel and Compensation Committee, with the advice of the Chief Executive Officer, may grant performance units payable in common stock and/or cash to key employees. Up to 450,000 shares of common stock have been reserved for the plan. Upon full or partial achievement of the performance objectives for the period, the dollar amount and/or the number of shares of common stock credited to an employee's account will be distributed to the employee in three equal annual installments.

A three-year award period under the Performance Share Plan began in 1988 and the performance objective has been achieved. Certain key employees held an aggregate of 45,500 performance units. The base value of each unit consists of $50 in cash and three shares of common stock. The final annual distribution occurred in 1993.

In addition, in March, 1991, the Board of Directors established the 1991-1993 award period under the Performance Share Plan. The performance objectives to be achieved during the 1991-1993 award period have been set, and 44 key employees hold an aggregate of 70,550 performance units. The base value of each unit consists of $50 in cash and two shares of common stock.

Note 7 — Fair Value of Financial Instruments

Fair Values of Financial Instruments
The following methods and assumptions were used to estimate the fair value of financial instruments.

Cash and cash equivalents
The carrying amount approximates fair value because of the short maturity of those instruments.

Short-term investments
The fair values are based on quoted market prices or other fair value estimates as provided by third-party portfolio managers.

Debentures
The fair value of the 5⅞% convertible subordinated debentures is based on quoted market prices.

Long-term debt
The fair values of long-term debt obligations are established from the market value of each issue if available or from market values of similar issues.

The carrying amounts and fair values of the Company's financial instruments at January 3, 1993 are as follows:

(In thousands of dollars)	Carrying Amount	Fair Value
Cash and cash equivalents	$ 46,437	$ 46,437
Short-term investments	72,115	72,115
5⅞% convertible subordinated debentures	100,000	103,000
Long-term debt	45,564	45,232

Note 8 — Taxes on Income

Income taxes (credits) consist of the following:

(In thousands of dollars)	1992	1991	1990
Current:			
Federal	$28,442	$20,928	$29,259
State	8,755	6,432	5,655
Subtotal current expense	37,197	27,360	34,914
Deferred:			
Federal	(3,393)	(388)	5,389
State	(1,862)	4,309	605
Subtotal deferred expense	(5,255)	3,921	5,994
Total income tax expense	$31,942	$31,281	$40,908
Income taxes paid	$27,379	$25,434	$50,278

The following is a reconciliation of the statutory federal income tax rate to the actual effective income tax rate:

Percent of pretax income	1992	1991	1990
Federal tax rate	34.0%	34.0%	34.0%
State and local income taxes, net of federal tax benefit	5.8	9.8	3.8
Other	0.7	(0.6)	(0.6)
Total effective income tax rate	40.5%	43.2%	37.2%

Deferred tax assets and/or liabilities result from temporary differences in the recognition of income and expense for financial and income tax reporting purposes, and differences between the fair value of assets acquired in business combinations accounted for as purchases for financial reporting purposes and their corresponding tax bases. They represent future tax benefits or costs to be recognized when those temporary differences reverse. The categories of assets and liabilities which have resulted in differences in the timing of the recognition of income and/or expense are as follows:

Deferred Tax Assets

(In thousands of dollars)	1992	1991
Postretirement benefits other than pensions	$ 89,976	$ —
Deferred compensation and other benefit plans	40,813	41,981
Other items	11,709	7,013
Total deferred tax assets	$142,498	$ 48,994

Deferred Tax Liabilities

(In thousands of dollars)	1992	1991
Basis of property, plant and equipment - net	$ 97,086	$ 96,768
Inventory valuation - net	29,788	30,085
Other items	7,553	4,922
Total deferred tax liabilities	$134,427	$131,775
Net deferred tax asset (liability)	$ 8,071	$(82,781)

Note 9 — Supplemental Operating Information

Export sales were $69,000,000 in 1992, $112,000,000 in 1991, and $74,000,000 in 1990.

Direct research and development expenditures aggregated $10,016,000 in 1992, $7,447,000 in 1991, and $8,239,000 in 1990. "Research, development and technology" in the income statement covers a broad range of activities throughout the Company.

Note 10 — Litigation

The Company is involved in various lawsuits from time to time arising in the ordinary course of business and otherwise. In July 1988, two retired former employee/shareholders filed suit against the Company and R. P. Simmons alleging damages resulting from the sale of their common stock in the Company in 1986, allegedly without being fully informed about the Company's and management's future plans. On August 6, 1991, a jury reached a verdict in the suit in favor of the Company and R. P. Simmons. On March 6, 1992, the trial court judge entered a judgment in favor of the Company and Mr. Simmons which the plaintiffs have appealed. The appeal was argued on December 9, 1992 and the parties are awaiting the appellate court's decision. The Company believes that the plaintiffs' claims are devoid of merit and is continuing to defend the case vigorously. In management's opinion, the outcome of these matters will not have a material adverse effect on the Company's financial condition.

Note 11 — Subsequent Event

On March 12, 1993, the Company and Athlone Industries, Inc. announced the signing of a letter of intent for the Company to acquire Athlone for the equivalent of $17.50 per share. The Company will exchange shares of its stock for all of the approximately 6,008,000 outstanding shares of Athlone. The exchange ratio will be determined by dividing $17.50 by the average of the closing prices of the Company's stock for the fifteen day trading period ending two days prior to closing. In any case, the Company will issue not more than 0.57302 nor less than 0.42363 of a Company share for each Athlone share. The Company will account for the transaction as a purchase, if consummated. The proposed transaction is subject to a number of conditions, including the execution of a definitive agreement, approval by the Boards of Directors of both companies, approval by the shareholders of Athlone and clearance by governmental regulatory authorities. Athlone is primarily a manufacturer of specialty steels in plate form. Its largest subsidiary, Jessop Steel, is located in Washington, Pennsylvania.

Note 12— Quarterly Data (Unaudited)

(In thousands of dollars except per share amounts)

Fiscal 1992	Restated March 29	Restated June 28	Restated September 27	January 3
			Fiscal Quarter Ended	
Net Sales	$264,397	$260,665	$254,337	$256,630
Cost of products sold as reported	214,618	210,657	209,495	201,430
Restatement for postretirement benefit expense	(2,235)	(2,234)	(2,237)	—
Cost of products sold as restated	212,383	208,423	207,258	201,430
Operating income as reported	23,655	24,128	18,613	19,636
Restatement for postretirement benefit expense	(3,148)	(3,203)	(3,228)	—
Operating income as restated	20,507	20,925	15,385	19,636
Income before cumulative effect of accounting change as reported	13,226	13,444	14,691	11,225
Restatement for postretirement benefit expense net of tax	(1,883)	(1,915)	(1,931)	—
Income before cumulative effect of accounting change as restated	11,343	11,529	12,760	11,225
Cumulative effect of accounting change net of tax	(125,231)	—	—	—
Net (loss) income	(113,888)	11,529	12,760	11,225
Per common share:				
Income before cumulative effect of accounting change as reported	.40	.41	.45	.34
Restatement for postretirement benefits expense	(.06)	(.06)	(.06)	—
Income before cumulative effect of accounting change as restated	.34	.35	.39	.34
Cumulative effect of accounting change	(3.80)	—	—	—
Net (Loss) Income	$(3.46)	$.35	$.39	$.34
Weighted average common shares outstanding	32,909,940	32,920,430	32,926,403	32,891,756

(In thousands of dollars except per share amounts)

Fiscal 1991	March 31	June 30	September 29	December 29
			Fiscal Quarter Ended	
Net Sales	$266,546	$264,774	$241,433	$231,869
Cost of products sold	217,346	223,607	199,089	180,626
Operating income	21,914	14,196	13,777	23,780
Net income	12,509	10,823	4,741	13,037
Net income per share	$.38	$.33	$.14	$.40
Weighted average common shares outstanding	32,889,017	32,911,055	32,913,939	32,898,480

REPORT OF ERNST & YOUNG, INDEPENDENT AUDITORS

Board of Directors
Allegheny Ludlum Corporation

We have audited the accompanying consolidated balance sheets of Allegheny Ludlum Corporation and subsidiaries as of January 3, 1993 and December 29, 1991, and the related consolidated statements of income and cash flows for each of the three fiscal years in the period ended January 3, 1993. These financial statements are the responsibility of Allegheny Ludlum Corporation's management. Our responsibility is to express an opinion on these financial statements based on our audits.

We conducted our audits in accordance with generally accepted auditing standards. Those standards require that we plan and perform the audit to obtain reasonable assurance about whether the financial statements are free of material misstatement. An audit includes examining, on a test basis, evidence supporting the amounts and disclosures in the financial statements. An audit also includes assessing the accounting principles used and significant estimates made by management, as well as evaluating the overall financial statement presentation. We believe that our audits provide a reasonable basis for our opinion.

In our opinion, based on our audits, the financial statements referred to above present fairly, in all material respects, the consolidated financial position of Allegheny Ludlum Corporation and subsidiaries at January 3, 1993 and December 29, 1991, and the consolidated results of their operations and their cash flows for each of the three fiscal years in the period ended January 3, 1993, in conformity with generally accepted accounting principles.

As discussed in Note 5 to the financial statements, in 1992, the Corporation changed its method of accounting for postretirement benefits other than pensions.

Ernst & Young

Pittsburgh, Pennsylvania
January 27, 1993 (except for Note 11,
as to which the date is March 12, 1993)

SELECTED FINANCIAL DATA

(In thousands of dollars except per share amounts)	1992	1991*	1990*	1989*	1988*	1987*
For Fiscal Year						
Income statement data:						
Net Sales	$1,036,029	$1,004,622	$1,084,908	$1,180,161	$1,207,512	$866,609
Operating income	76,453	73,667	111,027	208,889	175,003	90,992
Income before cumulative effect of accounting change	46,857	41,110	68,936	133,766	108,619	46,214
Cumulative effect of accounting change	(125,231)	—	—	—	—	—
Net (loss) income	$ (78,374)	$ 41,110	$ 68,936	$ 133,766	$ 108,619	$ 46,214
Per common share:						
Income before cumulative effect of accounting change	1.42	1.25	2.07	3.96	3.21	1.51
Cumulative effect of accounting change	(3.80)	—	—	—	—	—
Net (loss) income	(2.38)	1.25	2.07	3.96	3.21	1.51
Dividends declared	.88	.88	.86	.70	2.73	.13
At Year End						
Balance sheet data:						
Working capital	$ 299,356	$ 192,933	$ 198,187	$ 237,339	$ 162,956	$159,451
Total assets	871,185	764,482	793,152	784,560	703,865	648,974
Long-term debt due after one year	138,070	48,524	52,845	67,762	75,958	83,229

*Amounts related to postretirement benefits are not comparable.

COMMON STOCK DATA

	Fiscal Quarter Ended			
Fiscal 1992	March 29	June 28	September 27	January 3
Price range of common stock:				
High	$35.75	$36.625	$36.00	$34.875
Low	27.50	31.00	30.00	29.50
Dividends declared	.22	.22	.22	.22

	Fiscal Quarter Ended			
Fiscal 1991	March 31	June 30	September 29	December 29
Price range of common stock:				
High	$28.00	$29.125	$28.75	$27.625
Low	21.75	24.50	23.25	20.25
Dividends declared	.22	.22	.22	.22

The principal market on which the Company's common stock is traded is the New York Stock Exchange, using the symbol ALS. As of February 28, 1993, there were 32,917,729 shares of common stock outstanding held by 991 shareholders of record.

MANAGEMENT'S REPORT

The accompanying consolidated financial statements of Allegheny Ludlum Corporation and subsidiaries have been prepared in accordance with generally accepted accounting principles and include some amounts that are based upon Management's best estimates and judgments. Management has the primary responsibility for the information contained in the financial statements and in other sections of this Annual Report and for their integrity and objectivity.

The Company has a system of internal controls designed to provide reasonable assurance that assets are safeguarded and transactions are properly executed and recorded for the preparation of financial information. The concept of reasonable assurance is based on the recognition that there are inherent limitations in all systems of internal accounting control and that the cost of such systems should not exceed the benefits to be derived.

The Company maintains a staff of professional internal auditors, who assist in audit coverage with the independent accountants and conduct operational and special audits. The independent accountants express their opinion on the Company's financial statements based on procedures, including an evaluation of internal controls, which they consider to be sufficient to form their opinion.

The Audit and Finance Committee of the Board of Directors is composed of four non-employee members. Among its principal duties, the Committee is responsible for recommending the independent accountants to conduct the annual audit of the Company's financial statements and for reviewing the financial reporting and accounting practices.

R. P. Bozzone
President and
Chief Executive Officer

J. L. Murdy
Senior Vice President —
Finance and
Chief Financial Officer

R. R. Roeser
Controller

The Conceptual Structure of Financial Reporting

Generally accepted accounting principles (GAAP) typically set forth measurement and disclosure guidelines that apply to specific areas of financial reporting such as income taxes, pensions, and the like. The need for a new standard is often driven by a lack of consensus in accounting practice as to how certain events and transactions should be treated. In Chapter 1, we examined a number of forces that work to shape accounting standards, but this examination only provided an overview of the environmental forces. It did not attempt a more detailed study of how the Financial Accounting Standards Board (FASB) actually brings any conceptual structure to bear in the development of new standards. What framework does the FASB bring to bear on a reporting issue to create new GAAP?

From its inception in 1972, the FASB worked for over a decade to hammer out a series of documents referred to as *Statements of Financial Accounting Concepts* (SFACs). Collectively, these statements are referred to as the "conceptual framework" of financial reporting. For our purposes, only four of the SFACs are of interest: Nos. 1, 2, 5, and 6.[1] The subject matter of these four statements can be summarized as follows:

SFAC 1: Objectives of financial reporting

SFAC 2: Qualitative characteristics of accounting data

SFAC 5: Recognition and measurement in financial statements

SFAC 6: Elements of financial statements

---

[1] SFAC No. 3 has been replaced by SFAC No. 6, and SFAC No. 4 deals only with nonprofit organizations, which are beyond the scope of this text.

An SFAC differs from a *Statement of Financial Accounting Standard* (SFAS) in that it does not represent a source of definitive GAAP under Rule 203 of the ethics code. Instead, the conceptual framework attempts to set boundaries within which the FASB seeks to develop new GAAP. It also sets forth broad guidance on the definition and measurement of the elements found in financial statements.

It would be a mistake to consider the conceptual framework as something new and revolutionary. The framework is basically a distillation of existing practice. When produced, it did not challenge existing notions of financial reporting. It would also be a mistake to compare the conceptual framework with the natural laws of physics. It does not represent the discovery of some immutable natural law that must be obeyed. Instead, it represents a sort of constitution for accounting standard setting. It sets forth broad notions of what issues must be considered in the development of financial reporting standards. It provides an important lexicon over which the alternative accounting and reporting approaches debate can occur in a meaningful way. The framing of issues for debate is an important contribution of the conceptual framework and should not be understated, given the political nature of standard setting as a process for social choice. The purpose of this chapter is to provide an overview of the more important aspects of the conceptual framework.

In addition to an examination of the conceptual framework, this chapter also examines one specific accounting standard, SFAS No. 5, "Accounting for Contingencies." This standard, which is part of definitive GAAP, provides broad conceptual guidance on how uncertainty about future events should be reflected in financial statements. It has had significant impact on how a vast array of accounting and reporting issues are handled in practice. Due to its pervasive impact, this standard provides a particularly important extension to the conceptual structure of financial reporting. This standard is examined at the end of this chapter.

OBJECTIVES OF FINANCIAL REPORTING

Financial reporting is the process of communicating inside information about the past activities, current status, and future opportunities of an enterprise to interested outside parties. One of the most fundamental necessities of financial reporting is the definition of the reporting entity. Defining an accounting entity is a matter of defining the entity's boundaries so that both insiders and outsiders are identifiable. That a "bound" entity is the focus of financial reporting is sometimes referred to as the **entity concept** of financial reporting.

In developing a set of objectives for financial reporting, the FASB recognized that the economic environment where financial reporting takes place will have a significant influence on its objectives. In the United States, well-developed public equity and debt markets in which a diverse set of investors participate have long existed. The diffused nature of the capital sourcing process in the United States creates a significant number of individuals who are "outside" of the enterprise and demand information about the past performance and future potential of entities in which they invest. The demands of this group of "outsiders" are important in setting the objectives of financial reporting. In addition, the banking community is another well-established set of "outside" users, and their interests must be considered as well.

The FASB also acknowledged that financial reporting is a much broader concept than just financial statements. One of the issues that confronts accounting relates to what information should be contained within the financial statements and what should be provided outside the boundaries of these documents. Exhibit 2.1 provides an overview of how the FASB characterized the relationship among financial statements, financial reporting, and the larger domain of all information useful to users.[2]

In this structure, the basic financial statements incorporate both the statements themselves and the notes thereto. This classification embraces a concept of full disclosure. The **full disclosure principle** requires that accountants focus not only on the measurement and reporting of items in the financial statements proper but also on any explanations necessary to avoid misleading

EXHIBIT 2.1

The Context of Financial Statements Within the Broader Framework of Financial Reporting and Other Financial Information

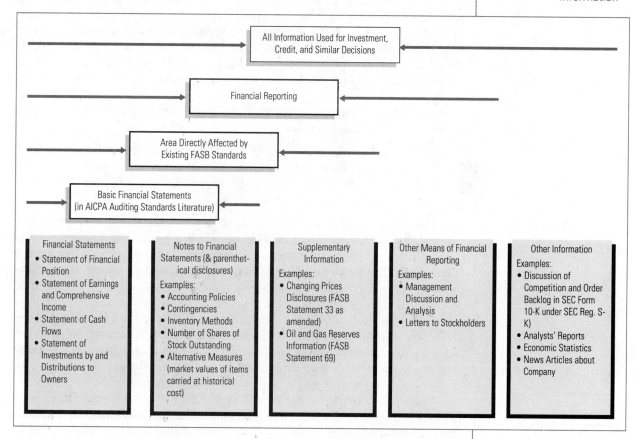

_____
[2] The diagram in Exhibit 2.1 is taken principally from that provided by the FASB in SFAC No. 5, but it was used in that statement to summarize the structure of financial reporting envisioned in SFAC No. 1.

representations in the financial statements. Notes to the financial statements help elaborate and expand information that aids users in interpreting the measurements reported in the financial statements proper.

The FASB has also incorporated all those pieces of information that normally compose the annual report to shareholders (ARS) as part of financial reporting. All information conveyed outside this format is considered other information. In general, these other sources are outside of the enterprise. Security analysts, news reporters, and government statistics bureaus are sources of information, but they do not lie in the nexus between insiders and outsiders. However, it is not clear why information disclosed by management to the SEC in a 10-K filing is not part of financial reporting in any generic sense.

The FASB also endorsed the proposition that the focus of financial reporting must be on general-purpose reporting, not the specialized needs of selected users. This represents a fundamental cost/benefit trade-off, since setting reporting standards will impose costs on some to provide information beneficial to others. If specific users have needs for information not contained in the general-purpose financial statements, they can contract directly with the enterprise to purchase the data required. Since this is likely to be stylized data for a specific use, privacy may be easier to achieve as access to the data can be controlled. In such cases, the exchange of information is similar to the exchange of any other good or service and can be handled in a similar manner. What SFAC No. 1 does not provide is any explicit means of deciding when information is of sufficiently general use to be part of the general-purpose financial statements and when it should be excluded.

In light of the above considerations, the FASB stated the objectives of financial reporting as follows:

1. To provide information useful in investment and credit decisions
2. To provide information useful in assessing cash flow prospects
3. To provide information about the enterprise resources, claims to those resources, and changes in them

Upon examination of these objectives, the first two relate to the predictive ability of financial information. This is clear in Objective 2 where assessing "prospective" cash flows is the focus, but predictive ability also lies behind Objective 1. Investment and credit decisions are based on expectations of the returns that equity or debt contributors can achieve by providing capital to an organization. Consequently, achieving these first two objectives will require a focus on the ability of financial information to *predict future cash flows.* However, the third objective is largely retrospective. It focuses on what *has* happened more than on what *will* happen. It is useful to think of this focus as one of generic performance evaluation. That is, financial reporting should provide information that is useful in *assessing the past activities* of the firm.

The FASB provided some expanded structure to communicate more fully what it intended under Objective 3. In particular, the FASB noted five important sub-components that contribute to the achievement of this objective:

3a. Providing information about an enterprise's economic resources, obligations, and owners' equity

3b. Providing information about an enterprise's financial performance during a period

3c. Providing information regarding liquidity, solvency, and funds flow

3d. Providing information about how management of an enterprise has discharged its stewardship function

3e. Incorporating management explanations and interpretations to help users understand the information provided

These sub-objectives are highly correlated with the existing reporting structure. Objective 3a is satisfied by a balance sheet; 3b, by the income statement; 3c, by the cash flow statement; and 3e, by the notes to the financial statements. This is just one example of how the conceptual framework was fit around existing reporting practices.

QUALITATIVE CHARACTERISTICS OF FINANCIAL INFORMATION

Statement of Financial Accounting Concepts No. 2 focuses on the qualitative characteristics that financial information should have. In framing SFAC No. 2, the FASB sought not only to define the key qualitative characteristics of financial information, but also to place them into the broader context of financial reporting and to order their importance. The context and hierarchy are presented in Exhibit 2.2, which is taken directly from SFAC No. 2.

The hierarchy of qualities exists within the general economic context of financial information markets. Users are varied and bring special needs and skills to the task of understanding information contained in financial reports. While some users may demand more specialized information than what is included in general-purpose financial reports, the general-purpose statements provide a baseline. This is consistent with the propositions set forth in SFAC No. 1.

In addition, the entire hierarchy is subject to a general cost/benefit analysis, which is the heart of social policy setting. However, the specific types of costs or benefits (i.e. information production, competitive disadvantage, etc.) are not identified. Furthermore, SFAC No. 2, like its predecessor SFAC No. 1, is silent as to how these costs and benefits are to be weighed in making a policy decision.

Understandability and Decision Usefulness

Users will generally prefer information that is understandable and useful within a specific decision context. **Understandability** refers to the ability of the user to determine the significance of the data to the decision at hand. The FASB indicated that financial statement disclosures should be understandable by those individuals with a reasonable comprehension of business and economic activity. Consequently, the user is presumed to have a level of "expertise."

Decision usefulness implies that different types of decisions may require different informational inputs. While user demands for specific pieces of data as inputs for decision models should be considered when making decisions about the form and content of general-purpose financial reports, consideration of all

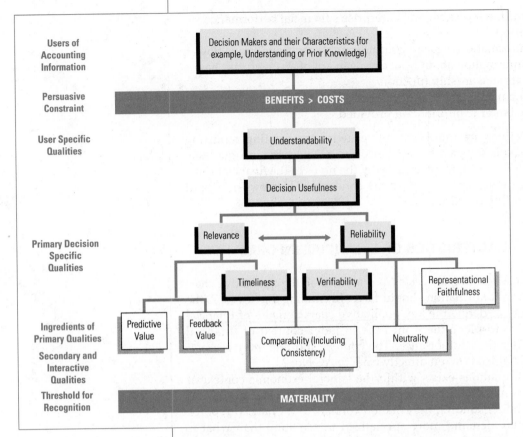

EXHIBIT 2.2

The Hierarchy of the Qualitative Characteristics of Accounting Information in Its Economic Context

possible uses is beyond the ability of any group and does not fit with the goal of providing general-purpose statements explicitly set forth in SFAC No. 1.

Qualities of the Accounting Data

The hierarchy of qualitative characteristics desired in accounting data is presented as a two-tiered system of primary and secondary qualities. Relevance and reliability are the two primary qualities. The secondary quality is comparability (including consistency). Each of the primary qualities is defined by several characteristics.

Primary Qualities   **Relevance** refers to the ability of accounting information to make a difference in a decision. To be relevant, information must possess certain qualities. These qualities are identified as predictive or feedback value and timeliness. **Predictive value** exists when the information is useful in predicting future events. This is one of the features identified in SFAC No. 1 as a central purpose of financial reporting.

Feedback value means that learning about a past outcome might alter a decision regarding a future action. This can be thought of as generic performance evaluation, which is also identified as an objective of financial reporting (Objective 3 of SFAC No. 1). Performance evaluation is a process of measuring the degree of success attained over some period of time by comparing actual outcomes with some bench mark. Comparing the total sales a salesperson obtains to a budgeted target sales figure is an example of performance evaluation. The outcome of such an evaluation may lead to a decision to retain or dismiss the salesperson. In this example, the actual sales number is provided as feedback, which in turn can alter future decisions.

Timeliness requires information that would be relevant to a decision must be delivered to the decision maker before a decision is made if it is to be valuable.

Reliability is obtained when users can depend on accounting information to represent the economic conditions or events it purports to represent. This implies that the information be error-free and unbiased and that it faithfully represents what it purports to represent. Reliability has three characteristics:

1. Verifiability
2. Representational faithfulness
3. Neutrality

Verifiability refers to those situations observed by different individuals who agree that the underlying economic event should be measured and reported in the same manner. **Representational faithfulness** exists when financial reports accurately portray similar underlying economic events similarly and different events differently. **Neutrality** is the characteristic of being free from bias or error.

The primary characteristics of relevance and reliability are more or less present in any real-life situation. Few measurements are totally free from error. Nothing short of observation of every transaction and event would be totally representationally faithful. However, these are characteristics to strive for in financial reports. In evaluating alternative reporting rules, accounting standard setters may need to trade off these characteristics due to cost factors or other political concerns. However, these characteristics provide guideposts to the development of reporting and disclosure rules.

Secondary Quality   The secondary quality is comparability (including consistency). **Comparability** refers to the development of reporting and measurement procedures that are consistent across companies (cross-sectional). **Consistency** refers to the use of the same reporting and measurement procedures by one company over time (inter-temporal). This quality is secondary because the FASB believed that there were occasions when achieving the secondary quality would be less important than achieving the primary qualities.

For example, two companies may choose different depreciation methods for financial reporting, one using straight-line and the other an accelerated method. Achieving comparability would require forcing one firm to alter its choice. However, this choice might reflect underlying differences in technology for the two companies. The firm choosing straight-line depreciation might be in an industry with little technological change. Consequently, the consumption of equipment is more uniform over time. The other firm may be in an industry where production techniques change rapidly, causing a much greater loss in productive capacity for its plant in early years of the assets' lives. The reported net book value of plant and equipment may be more relevant and reliable for the two companies when different depreciation methods are allowed, even though this results in a lack of comparability as far as the manner in which depreciation is computed.

In situations where relevance and reliability might conflict with comparability, the primary qualities are judged to be more important. Thus, the secondary quality is said to "interact" with the primary qualities to determine the selection of measurement and reporting rules.

Materiality

Materiality is a judgment regarding the significance that a choice of a particular method of presenting financial information, from a set of alternatives, might have on user decisions. Choices considered immaterial are, by definition, unimportant to users; they deserve no consideration or debate. Therefore, immaterial choices are never elevated to a debate about the degree to which they achieve the goals of relevance and/or reliability. Based on their experience, practitioners make judgments regarding which issues are material and which are not.

Conservatism

In considering the issues regarding reliability, the FASB also took a position on the use of conservatism. The FASB defined **conservatism** as:

> A prudent reaction to uncertainty to try to ensure that uncertainty and risks inherent in business situations are adequately considered.[3]

Conservatism does not imply understatement, as this would decrease the reliability of financial reports. It does imply that examination of the facts and circumstances relating to the valuation of any element in the financial statements should consider the nature of the uncertainties that are present. For example, it would not be conservative to act as if all receivables are collectible, even if none are currently past due. Some risk exists that customers will be unable to pay when the obligation comes due; and to be conservative, this should generally be reflected in an allowance for uncollectible amounts.

ELEMENTS OF FINANCIAL REPORTS

An element of a financial report is a basic category or building block around which the information contained in financial statements is organized. Initially,

---

[3] "Qualitative Characteristics of Accounting Information," *Statement of Financial Accounting Concepts No. 2* (Stamford, CT: FASB, May 1980), para. 95.

the FASB defined the elements of financial reports in SFAC No. 3, which was later amended to incorporate both for-profit, and not-for-profit entities and released as SFAC No. 6.

The FASB defined the following basic elements, and we have elected to organize them around the financial statements of which they eventually become a part.[4]

Balance Sheet (Statement of Financial Position)

The basic elements typically reported in the balance sheet are defined as follows:

Assets: Probable future economic benefits obtained or controlled by a particular entity as a result of past transactions or events.[5]

Liabilities: Probable future sacrifices of economic benefits arising from present obligations of a particular entity to transfer assets or provide services to other entities in the future as a result of past transactions or events.[6]

Equity: The residual interest in the assets of an entity that remains after deducting its liabilities.[7]

One additional feature of contemporary balance sheets is the use of accounts referred to as valuation allowances, or contra-asset (liability, equity) accounts. Examples of these accounts include the allowance for doubtful accounts and accumulated depreciation. These accounts are not to be considered independent elements. Rather, they are an integral part of the asset, liability, or equity to which they relate.

The relationships among the elements in the balance sheet is captured by the fundamental accounting identity:

$$\text{Assets} = \text{Liabilities} + \text{Owners' Equity}$$

This relationship holds by definition at all times. The identity reflects that fact since at any point in time, all value (assets) is divisible among the claimants to the corporation. The claimants may be debt holders or equity investors, but someone is entitled to all cash flows generated by the corporation. As a result, it is always true that the value of the assets is equivalent to the value of the claims against those assets.

---

[4] The FASB did identify the statement of cash flows as one of the four fundamental statements that should be produced, but it did not identify specific elements associated with this statement. Consequently, the statement of cash flows is not included in the following list of elements. SFAS No. 95 was developed later to set forth the structure of this statement.

[5] "Elements of Financial Statements," *Statement of Financial Accounting Concepts No. 6* (Stamford, CT: FASB, December 1985), para. 25.

[6] *Ibid.*, para. 35.

[7] *Ibid.*, para. 49.

Statement of Changes in Stockholders' Equity

Elements that are typically found in the statement of changes in stockholders' equity are:

Investments by owners: Increases in net assets of a particular enterprise resulting from transfers to it from other entities something of value to obtain or increase ownership in the entity.[8]

Distributions to owners: Decreases in net assets of a particular enterprise resulting from transferring assets, rendering services, or incurring liabilities by the enterprise to owners.[9]

Comprehensive income: Changes in equity which arise during a period from all transactions and events that give rise to revenues, expenses, gains, or losses during the period.

Income Statement

Elements typically included in the income statement are:

Revenues: Inflows or other enhancements of assets of an entity or settlements of its liabilities during a period from delivering or producing goods, rendering services, or other activities that constitute the entity's ongoing major or central operation.[10]

Expenses: Outflows or other using up of assets or incurrence of liabilities during a period from delivering or producing goods, rendering services, or carrying out other activities that constitute the entity's ongoing operations.[11]

Gains and losses: Increases or decreases in equity from peripheral or incidental transactions of an entity and from all other transactions or events and circumstances affecting the entity during a period except those that result from revenues, expenses, investments by owners, or distributions to owners.[12]

Income is an economic concept. Generally, income represents the increase in the value of an enterprise's net assets over a period which can be consumed by the entity and still leave the entity with the same level of financial capital at the end of the period as it had at the beginning. Another way of saying this is that, for a corporation, income is measured by the change in stockholders' equity over the period, less the effects of any transactions between the enterprise and its shareholders.

However, for financial reporting purposes, the income of a corporation is defined as:

---

[8] *Ibid.*, para. 66.

[9] *Ibid.*, para. 67.

[10] *Ibid.*, para. 78.

[11] *Ibid.*, para. 80.

[12] *Ibid.*, para. 82 and 83.

Revenues + Gains - Expenses - Losses

How successful the measure of accounting income is at providing information about the underlying economic condition of the firm and how this relationship might be improved are the central debates in much of financial reporting.

MEASUREMENT OF THE ELEMENTS CONTAINED IN THE FINANCIAL STATEMENTS

Having defined what the elements of financial reports are, how are they to be measured? When should we report a change in each element? These questions focus on the general question of how the elements are to be recognized in financial statements. **Recognition** refers to the process of formally recording or incorporating an item into the financial statements as an element therein. It includes both the initial recording of an item, as well as any subsequent changes in or removal of the item previously recorded. Recognition is separate and distinct from the concept of realization. **Realization** is the act of converting noncash resources and rights into money. While realization is a necessary condition for a cash flow, recognition may occur with or without realization.

The FASB endorsed the use of accrual accounting as the appropriate general system under which financial reports should be prepared. **Accrual basis accounting**, a system of financial reporting, attempts to record the financial effects of transactions and other events and circumstances that have cash consequences for the entity in the periods in which those transactions, events, and circumstances occur rather than only in the periods in which cash is received or paid.[13] The events, transactions, and circumstances referred to in this definition may arise because of either external or internal events. Transactions, by their definition are external exchanges. However, internal events such as placement of raw material into production or the consumption of property, plant, and equipment in the production of goods and services are also part of the set of events that accrual accounting procedures attempt to reflect.

SFAC No. 5 sets forth the basic criteria that govern recognition in the financial statements. They are:

1. The item must meet the definition of an element of the financial statements.
2. The item must have a relevant attribute that is subject to measurement with sufficient reliability.
3. The information about the item must be capable of affecting user decisions (it must be relevant).
4. The information must be representationally faithful, verifiable, and neutral (it must be reliable).

These criteria are subject to basic cost/benefit considerations. That is, even if an item meets all the criteria, it may not be included if it is too costly to pro-

---

[13] *Ibid.*, para. 139.

duce relative to the improvement the information would bring in the form of better decisions. SFAC No. 5 provides no guidance as to how to identify either the costs or benefits or how to trade them off in making this decision.

Additional Guidance on the Measurability of the Attributes Associated with an Element

Criteria 1, 3, and 4 all relate to the application of definitions that have been developed earlier in this chapter. Criterion 2 is more vague because it refers to something called an "attribute," which has not yet been defined. A measurement attribute is the trait or aspect of an element that is to be quantified. The FASB provided five examples of different traits that might be measured under current practice. They are:

2a. Historical cost
2b. Current cost
2c. Current market value
2d. Net realizable value
2e. Present (or discounted) value

Historical cost is measured by using the value of an asset, liability, or equity at the time of the original exchange, which gave rise to that element. Current cost refers to the cost to replace an asset, liability, or equity at current prices. Obviously, current cost and historical cost are equal at the point of exchange but may diverge over time. Current market value generally relates to the value that could be obtained for an asset in a sale or for settlement of a liability or equity. Net realizable value (NRV) refers to the value obtained for an asset through sale in the normal course of business less direct costs necessary to complete the sale. NRV does not consider the effect of present value on any future cash flows generated by an asset. Present value arises from discounting future cash flows.

In measuring these attributes, an assumption must be made about the measurement unit. In current practice, the general assumption is that the attributes of an element will be measured in nominal monetary units. This assumption is referred to as the **monetary unit assumption**. A nominal monetary unit is one that is not adjusted for the changes in purchasing power of money over time. However, even this practice is somewhat mixed as present value approaches will incorporate changes in the value of money if nominal, instead of real, interest rates are used in the discounting process.[14] The FASB stated that it, "expects that nominal units of money will continue to be used to measure items recognized in the financial statements. However, a change from present circumstances (for example, an increase in inflation to a level at which

---

[14] Real interest rates are determined by taking current market interest rates and removing the effects of expectations regarding future inflation rates over the period spanned by the nominal rate. For example, mortgage companies may quote a nominal rate for a 30-year, fixed rate mortgage. This rate contains both an expected real rate of return plus an inflationary premium based on the mortgage companies' beliefs about what inflation will do to the purchasing power of the money over the 30-year period. Discounting future gross cash flows by nominal interest rates can create measurements of value that adjust for inflation.

distortions become intolerable) might lead the Board to select another, more stable measurement scale.[15]

Additional Guidance on Recognition of Revenues and Gains

SFAC No. 5 also provides additional guidance regarding the recognition and measurement of elements that comprise income. Revenues and gains are to be recognized only when they are:

1. Realized or realizable
2. Earned

To satisfy the first criteria, revenues (or gains) must already be collected in cash (realized), or the enterprise must have received assets that are readily convertible into cash. Revenues are earned when the enterprise has substantially accomplished whatever performance it must complete to be entitled to the benefits represented by the revenues. This is frequently referred to as a requirement that the *earnings process be complete*. That is, the company has completed the essential steps of purchasing, manufacturing, selling, rendering service, delivering the goods, etc., which make up the core activities that the entity undertakes to generate profits. Gains frequently arise from events and transactions in which there is no "earnings process;" and, therefore, gain recognition typically depends more on meeting the realization requirement than on issues surrounding completion of the earnings process.

Note that these criteria are vague. Because there are a variety of views as to when the "earnings process is completed," a variety of alternative methods to recognize revenue are available in practice. Trying to flesh out the meaning of these guidelines is a matter of considerable professional judgment and creates a fair amount of diversity in practice. However, by setting forth these criteria and defining the terms, the debate about how revenue should be recognized in a certain situation must be framed around the concepts of realization and completion of the earnings process. It should be noted that these concepts have existed in accounting for many years and are not new to the conceptual framework. They were simply graphed into the framework because the FASB considered them useful concepts for development of future accounting standards.

Additional Guidance on Recognition of Expenses and Losses

Expenses represent the consumption of economic benefits in the generation of income. Losses represent a discovery of a decline in future benefits or incurrence of an obligation. Recognition of expenses and losses should be guided by the matching principle. The **matching principle** requires that costs, which can be directly related to the generation of revenue, should be recognized as an expense at the point when the related revenue is recognized. Costs that are indirectly related to the generation of revenue should be recognized in the period they are incurred due to the inability to draw direct linkages between

---

[15] "Recognition and Measurement in Financial Statements of Business Enterprises," *Statement of Financial Accounting Concepts No. 5* (Stamford, CT: FASB, December 1984), para. 72.

the incurrence of cost and the generation of revenues. In general, losses will be recognized when they are identified, as they represent the unanticipated decline in value of an existing asset (or incurrence of an unanticipated obligation) and should not be matched with future revenues.

BENEFITS AND LIMITATIONS OF THE CONCEPTUAL FRAMEWORK

The conceptual framework acts to focus the discussion of issues whenever choices must be made about the form and content of financial reports. Since the characteristics of relevance and reliability are the primary considerations in choosing between alternatives, the accounting profession and standard-setting process focus the discussion by all interested parties on these characteristics. Each proposed alternative can be examined in light of these characteristics. If parties can agree that one alternative provides more relevant and reliable information than another, at similar cost, then the more relevant and reliable method is preferred. If the benefits outweigh the costs, this preferred method should be implemented.

At several points throughout the preceding discussion, we pointed out that the conceptual framework does not state how the costs and benefits of alternatives will be traded off. Suppose a choice was to be made between alternative accounting procedures, one of which provided more relevant information for long-term, equity investors, while the other provided more relevant information for creditors. If it is not cost/benefit-efficient to provide both sets of information, some parties will be worse off as a result of the choice between alternatives, while some will be better off. How is this to be decided?

Decisions of this type are generally referred to as **social welfare decisions,** since the choices will impose costs on some members of society and bestow benefits on others. When organized markets that allow individuals to make their own resource allocation choices do not appear capable of solving this type of allocation problem, regulatory bodies are often formed to make these decisions. The Securities and Exchange Commission is one such regulatory body. To make these decisions, regulators must define some rule for trading off benefits to some against costs to others. This rule is called a social welfare function and is crucial to making regulatory decisions.

The FASB is not a true regulatory body in that it has no direct means of enforcing its standards. (There is no accounting police force.) However, it is setting reporting standards that affect the welfare of many participants in society. Ultimately, when the FASB makes a decision regarding what accounting policy to put forth as definitive GAAP, it is making a social welfare decision. While the conceptual framework focuses the debate over alternative financial reporting choices, it is totally silent on the social welfare function that will be adopted to resolve the disputes. Many accountants and financial statement users are disappointed that the conceptual framework does not address this missing link.

This disappointment stems partly from a lack of appreciation of the problem, not from the system's failure to fulfill its mission. Given the constantly changing environment of financial reporting, as well as the rise of competing information sources, a single, permanent social welfare function cannot be defined. Standard setters must have flexibility to alter the basis for these cost/benefit trade-offs as changes in the economic environment manifest themselves. Financial reporting exists as a response to economic forces, and it must respond when these forces change.

Another fundamental problem lies in our ability to quantify both the costs and benefits of alternative policy choices. The costs imposed by alternative financial reporting choices are often easier to assess than the benefits. Some costs are also hard to determine, such as the loss of competitive position due to increased disclosures that benefit competitors. Others, such as the cost of establishing an internal information system to collect data necessary for new disclosures, can be more readily estimated. Benefits are always stated in terms of improved effectiveness of capital markets. Assessing these benefits can be very difficult, and they are often non-quantifiable. As a result of these complexities, the social welfare function cannot be converted to simple statements contained in policy documents.

OPEB: A REAL POLICY DEBATE

The FASB has recently been involved in a policy debate that relates to the recognition of "Other Post-Employment Benefits" (OPEBs). Generally, these benefits are primarily promises made by companies to provide medical benefits to retired employees. Some of these promises are contractual, particularly when union contracts are involved. In these cases, companies cannot terminate continuation of these benefits without agreement of current and retired employees. In many cases, the promises are only enforceable at retirement. In these situations, a company may have an active plan to provide such benefits to retired employees but may also have the option to cancel the plan at any time. Cancellation may affect only employees who have not already retired, or it may affect both retired and active employees.

Unlike its provisions for pension plans, the U.S. tax code does not allow companies to make current contributions to a fund, for the ultimate payment of OPEBs, and take a tax deduction when the contribution is made. As a result, companies simply pay these benefits as they arise, called the "pay-as-you-go" method of funding. For many years, companies with these types of plans have simply charged the annual costs of these benefits to expense when paid. This was partially motivated by several factors:

1. Continuation of the plans was optional from a legal perspective.
2. Funding during the working life of the employees was impractical due to the lack of tax incentives.
3. The magnitude of the costs associated with the promise to provide future benefits was believed to be generally small.

During the late 1980s, the FASB undertook a broad project on post-employment benefits, spanning all forms of these benefits. In examining the economic reality of these OPEBs, the FASB discovered that the magnitude of these benefits far exceeded the amounts typically considered when previous decisions regarding how to account for these items were made. It was also discovered that the extent of plans that were not optional was greater than previously believed. In addition, even for those plans that were optional, the FASB argued that the companies currently maintaining such plans, without specific intent to discontinue, were indicating a long-term commitment to support these programs. As a result, current employees viewed the accruing of these benefits over their working lives as part of the compensation they received from employment. Therefore, the value of the benefit accruing in the current period should have been reflected as an expense of the period, and a liability to pay those benefits should have been accrued.

In arriving at this conclusion, the FASB was setting policy based on its assessment of the costs and benefits of imposing the requirement to accrue these costs. The FASB could have decided that while information on these plans is important, the obligation might not be incurred (therefore, it does not meet the definition of a liability) or that it could not be reliably quantified (failing the requirement of reliability). In either case, no recognition of a liability would have been appropriate in the financial statements proper. The FASB could then have decided it was sufficient to incorporate disclosure of the circumstances in the notes, or it could have decided to omit any reference to this issue.

The conceptual framework provided a focal point for the debate on this issue. There was little disagreement that information regarding these plans was relevant to financial statement users. There was little disagreement that the potential consequences of these plans could be very substantial. However, there was considerable disagreement on the reliability of the data that could be provided on the magnitude of the future costs, which is a primary characteristic of financial data set forth by the conceptual framework.

There was also considerable debate regarding the costs and benefits of accrual. Exhibit 2.3 contains the text from a *Wall Street Journal* article that reports the FASB's efforts to provide specific cost/benefit information on which to base its decision to accrue the OPEB costs during the working lives of employees. It also points out some of the political issues involved in representation of affected groups in the decision process. The FASB has not adopted a specific social welfare function; but if this practice continues, it may communicate the general decision model to other interested parties through observation of the actual trade-offs made over a large number of policy choices.

It is clear from this example of a particular policy debate that the conceptual framework and the principles of accounting that have developed through history can only serve to guide and focus the debate on the costs and benefits of various alternative policies. These concepts do facilitate useful debate by providing a common terminology for all interested parties to use in communicating their support or concerns. Since the ultimate social policy chosen will depend on the particular political and economic forces present at the time, the conceptual framework cannot of itself resolve these policy issues. While some may believe this is a failure of the framework, it can alternatively be viewed as an unrealistic expectation of such an effort.

Steps to Address Firms' Concerns

Board Issues Cost-Benefit Data to Justify a Rule, Plans Change in Voting

NEW YORK—The Financial Accounting Standards Board, the chief rule-making body for accountants, is stepping up efforts to defuse business criticism of its controversial accounting rules.

For example, the 205-page rule it just issued on post-retirement health benefits includes a section, for the first time in the FASB's 17-year history, justifying the rule on a cost-benefit basis.

The rule will reduce reported corporate profits at least $200 billion starting in 1993, and many businessmen are upset at the FASB for declining to ease the rules impact on earnings. In response to corporate criticism that some accounting rules are too costly and complex, the Securities and Exchange Commission has in recent months urged the FASB to make sure its rules are worth implementing.

In the new health-benefit rule, the FASB, based in Norwalk, Conn., says many companies haven't properly monitored or managed their health-benefit obligations for a long time. The rule boosts the credibility of financial statements by showing the real obligation of retiree health benefits and will force companies to estimate these benefits more accurately, the FASB adds. The rule forces companies to accrue or set up a reserve for such benefits rather than account for them on a "pay-as-you-go" basis each year, as is current practice.

Timothy Lucas, research director of the FASB, concedes that the new cost-benefit section was included as a response to criticism of business and government regulators. "We may very well include such cost benefit sections in future statements (rules), but we want to be sure they aren't just boilerplate and address each rule's specific benefits.

In recent months, the FASB has been the target of heavy criticism from the committee on corporate reporting of the 13,500-member Financial Executives Institute and from the accounting principles task force of the powerful Business Roundtable. Since August, both the FEI and the Roundtable have written letters to the SEC criticizing the FASB's rules for being too detailed and too expensive to implement.

The FASB usually sends only its own letter of comment to the SEC in response to business criticism. But this time the board became incensed that the FEI was criticizing FASB rules on consolidation and cash flows that the FASB thought FEI had supported. And so it sent a more stinging letter to the SEC noting these so-called inconsistencies.

The result was a private meeting called by the FEI and the FASB Dec. 14 at a New York club to discuss their differences. Says Mr. Lucas, who attended: "Not everyone kept their cool, but nobody really lost their temper. While we don't think that FEI will like everything the board does, the meeting may help clear the air." Only three FASB board members attended. If four had come, FASB rules would have required the meeting to be open to the public.

Norman Roy, FEI president, declining to discuss meeting specifics, says the get-together was part of a dialogue between businessmen and the FASB on accounting rules.

In response to its critics, the FASB next year will change its voting procedure so that a 5-to-2 vote rather than the current 4-to-3 vote is needed to issue new accounting rules. Last year, the FASB began heading its task forces, which draft new rules, with board members rather than staff, who companies have thought are tougher on business. And in 1989, the FASB also began sending a representative to attend certain key FEI meetings on accounting.

SFAS NO. 5, CONCEPTUAL STRUCTURE EMBODIED IN EXPLICIT STANDARDS

The completion of the conceptual framework has resulted in a number of new standards in areas such as accounting for income taxes, defined benefit pension plans, and OPEBs (to name a few). These new standards were a direct result of FASB's re-examination of old standards, which it believed were inconsistent with the basic tenets of the conceptual framework, or its development of standards in new areas under the conceptual framework. From 1972 through 1985, while parts of the framework were being developed, the FASB also passed a number of standards governing financial reporting.

Each new *Statement of Financial Accounting Standard* (SFAS) helps flesh out the meaning of the conceptual framework, and each new issue requires an extension of the framework in potentially significant ways. One particular standard that has had a profound effect on how uncertainty is treated in financial reporting was developed by the FASB during the period when the conceptual framework was still in development. That standard is SFAS No. 5, "Accounting for Contingencies." While the conceptual framework acknowledged the existence of the myriad of uncertainties that lie behind the representations in the financial statements, SFAS No. 5 set forth the crucial conceptual approach that has been the foundation for the treatment of these uncertainties since it was first issued in 1975. Because of its broad-based contribution to both definitive GAAP and to the development of concepts dealing with uncertainty, it is appropriate to introduce this standard at this time. Concepts such as revenue recognition, matching, conservatism, and disclosure are also fleshed out to a greater degree by this standard.

Accounting for Contingencies: Realization, Matching, and Conservatism Applied

A **contingency** is defined as *"an existing condition, situation, or set of circumstances* (emphasis added) involving uncertainty as to possible gain or loss to an enterprise that will ultimately be resolved when one or more future events occur or fail to occur."[16] In this definition, the terms gain or loss include items recorded as revenue and expense as well as those specifically treated as gain or loss. The focus on existing conditions limits the types of uncertainty to be considered to the current state of the assets, liabilities, and equities of the firm. In this manner, uncertainties as to the ability of the enterprise to (1) generate new assets in the future, (2) incur additional obligations, or (3) issue new equity claims are not within the scope of the financial accounting and, therefore, not relevant to the valuation of elements presented in the financial statements.

Contingencies that may lead to an ultimate gain (revenue) can only be recognized when realized and earned. As a result, the earnings process (if any) needs to be completed prior to gain recognition. In many cases, the earnings process is deemed completed as soon as reliable estimates of the consequences

---

[16] "Accounting for Contingencies," *Statement of Financial Accounting Concepts No. 5* (Stamford, CT: FASB, March 1975), para. 1.

of any remaining contingencies can be obtained. This is typically the case when revenue is recognized from credit sales at the point of sale, even though ultimate conversion of the resulting receivable into cash is a contingency. The decision to recognize the full amount of the receivable as revenue changes the focus of the contingency from revenue recognition to expense or loss recognition relating to the bad debts that will arise from existing credit sales. In turn, this requires an understanding of how contingent costs or losses should be recognized under the matching principle.

Product warranty is another similar example where contingencies related to future cost influence the decisions regarding revenue recognition and matching. For example, assume the revenue from the sale of a product is included in income this period, but the product warranty is likely to result in costs in future periods. Matching appears to demand that these costs be recognized in the same period that the revenue is recognized. However, the future costs are contingent on some defect appearing in the product covered by the warranty. If existence of the defect and the cost of its correction have not been identified as of the date the financial statements are prepared, this situation represents the existence of a contingency.

While the concept of matching may be best served by accruing some estimate of the future warranty costs related to current period sales, this depends critically on the nature of the contingency and the company's ability to estimate the future consequences of the warranty. If the company cannot reduce the future warranty obligation to a reliable estimate, it may be appropriate to require that no revenue from these sales be recognized.

In some cases, the issue of matching is less clear. For example, questions arise as to when possible losses from litigation should be recognized in financial statements. Should financial statements accrue the potential contingent obligations that arise from any acts entered into by the corporation or its employees in the period the acts occur? Or, alternatively, should we wait until lawsuits are actually filed? Since lawsuits take many years to progress through the courts and the outcome of a suit is often very unclear prior to a court determination, perhaps we should wait to reflect the effects of the lawsuit on income until the court decides whether any obligation exists.

After a lawsuit is decided, it is easy to go back and identify the periods when the actions that caused the suit occurred. Further, once a damage settlement has been executed, there is no problem measuring the cost of the actions that caused the injury. However, these bits of information are not available prior to the ultimate resolution of the suit. To satisfy the matching criteria, should we accrue some amount each year as a litigation contingent liability for the effects that unknown sources of future litigation might have? To aid in determining when contingencies such as litigation losses, warranty obligations, and bad debt losses should be recognized in the financial statements, the FASB created SFAS No. 5 to provide a conceptual structure to evaluate the issues.

SFAS No. 5 requires potential recognition of contingent losses but disallows recognition of any contingent gain. This treatment is partially an outgrowth of conservatism and partially related to the fact that few gain contingencies meet the requirements of the realization principle. In addressing the issue of how to report contingent losses, the FASB divided them into three categories:

1. When future events giving rise to the loss are likely to occur (also referred to as **probable events**)
2. When the chance of future events giving rise to a loss is slight (also referred to as **remote events**)
3. When the chance of future events giving rise to a loss is more than remote but less than probable

When a contingent loss falls in the first category and a reasonable estimate of the loss can be obtained, the loss must be recognized in the financial statements by accruing the loss in the period when the determination is made. If a point estimate of the loss is not possible but a range of possible losses can be determined, the lowest point in the range is accrued.[17] When a contingent loss falls in the second or third category or if it falls in the first category but has no basis for estimating its size, no accrual is required.

The categories of contingent losses are not well-specified by quantitative rules. Professional judgment is necessary to determine when a particular contingency will result in a probable loss. As such, SFAS No. 5 focuses professionals' attention on an assessment of one primary attribute of the contingency—the probability that a loss will occur. When companies sell merchandise on credit, it is likely that some portion of those credit sales will ultimately not result in cash inflows due to bad debts. Corporate managers and accountants have developed fairly accurate methods to estimate the magnitude of these bad debts. The matching principle suggests that if the revenues from credit sales are recognized at the point of sale, the cost of bad debts related to those sales should be accrued in the period the sale is recognized. SFAS No. 5 makes the criteria even more specific. Since these expenses are likely to occur and can be estimated, they meet the criteria for accrual in the period of sale. Similar arguments can be made for accruing estimates of the liabilities for future warranty costs or for future redemption of coupons when merchandise is sold under agreements of this type.

Note Disclosure and Reporting for Contingencies

The implications of SFAS No. 5 for accruing contingent gains and losses were examined above in light of their contribution to our understanding the concepts of realization, matching, and conservatism. This standard also provides an excellent example of how supplementary information provided in the notes to the financial statements can become an important part of the financial information provided by them as a whole. While the standard sets forth conceptual guidance about accruing contingent losses, it also establishes requirements for additional note disclosure related to contingencies in general.

In particular, for those contingent losses that are deemed to be reasonably possible, note disclosure, which describes the nature of the contingency, and an estimate of the magnitude (if available) of the loss are required. For contingent losses that are likely but for which no estimate of the magnitude or range

---

[17] "Reasonable Estimation of the Amount of Loss," *FASB Interpretation No. 14* (Stamford, CT: FASB, September 1976), para. 3.

of loss is possible, descriptions of the contingency are also required. Remote contingent losses need not be described, although certain contingencies that relate to guarantees of the indebtedness of other parties are encouraged even if the chance of loss is remote. The standard even allows for the description of facts surrounding contingent gains, but care must be taken to avoid unwarranted indications of realizability.

Disclosure of this type assists users in interpreting the information in the financial statements. Based on the accountants' judgment regarding the likelihood of loss, accrual of contingent losses is determined. Therefore, it is important to provide other data about existing contingencies to avoid misleading investors into believing that the accountants have attempted to capture all future losses. This is the purpose embodied by accountants accepting responsibility for disclosures that go beyond the monetary balances in the financial statements proper.

SUMMARY

This chapter reviewed the structure of the existing conceptual framework, as well as the contribution of SFAS No. 5 to the extension of this framework in the area of accounting for uncertainty. The conceptual framework represents a series of statements issued by the FASB that outlines its position regarding the goals of financial reporting, the qualitative characteristics accounting information should possess, the elements of financial statements, and the general characteristics that trigger recognition and measurement of the elements in the financial statements. This framework acts like a constitution, not an immutable law of nature, to guide the development of future reporting standards.

The conceptual framework offered little in the way of new ideas regarding the construction of accounting principles. It is basically distilled from concepts and practices that have been in place for many years, but it does bring them together into a more cohesive, integrated, and formal structure. The definitions and concepts developed in the SFACs provide an important lexicon to guide the ongoing debates regarding the construction of accounting principles. The missing link in the framework is a clear statement of what social welfare function the standard setters should adopt in executing their mission. While there are good reasons for not specifying such a rule for decision making, the absence of this guidance also makes standard setting very situation-specific and makes it appear incongruent over time and across standards. An example of a recent accounting standard debate related to other post-retirement benefits (OPEBs) was used to exemplify both the benefits and weaknesses of the conceptual framework.

Finally, SFAS No. 5, "Accounting for Contingencies," was examined. This standard represents an example of how concepts were applied to the area of accounting for future uncertainties. How uncertainty is to be treated in financial reporting is an important conceptual issue that the concepts statements do not address as richly as SFAS No. 5. This standard differentiates the treatment of contingent gains from contingent losses, deferring the recognition of contingent gains in most cases, while setting up guidelines for recognition of continent losses in general. Recognition of a contingent loss requires that it be probable of occurring and subject to reliable estimation. If these criteria are not met, note disclosure may or may not be required, depending on whether the loss is remote (no disclosure) or not.

QUESTIONS

1. In what important ways do accounting principles differ from the laws of physics?

2. What are the three major objectives of financial reporting?

3. Identify the three major financial statements and indicate the elements contained in each statement.

4. Why is the *monetary unit assumption* central to financial reporting?

5. What is meant by the concept of *recognition* in accounting?

6. What are the basic criteria for revenue recognition? How does revenue recognition relate to the concept of *matching*?

7. What does *decision usefulness* mean to you? Suppose you were deciding whether to lend money to someone, what information might you ask for? Of that information, what part is financial information and what part is not?

8. What are the two primary qualities of accounting data? What characteristic underlie each primary quality?

9. What are the secondary qualities of accounting data? Why are they considered secondary?

10. What does the concept of *conservatism* imply about the valuation of elements in the financial statements? What might it say about the valuation of plant and equipment that will be used in production instead of being offered for sale?

11. What is a contingent gain or loss? How are these accounted for?

12. What is a *remote* contingency? What is a *probable* contingency? What differences exist in how these contingencies would be reported in the financial statements?

13. How does net realizable value differ from current market value? How might the current cost of a three-year-old semitractor be determined?

14. What is a *social welfare function* and why is it important in determining financial reporting requirements?

15. Many practicing accountants argue that the conceptual framework is worthless as it provides them with no authoritative guidance to resolve reporting issues on a day-to-day basis. Comment on this view of the purpose for the conceptual framework.

EXERCISES

2-1. *Identification of the primary qualitative characteristics*

Listed below are various attributes associated with the desired qualities of accounting data. For each attribute, indicate whether it is associated with the primary qualities of relevance (RV) or reliability (RL) or with a secondary quality (S).

___ 1. Verifiability
___ 2. Timeliness
___ 3. Feedback value
___ 4. Neutrality
___ 5. Comparability
___ 6. Representational faithfulness
___ 7. Consistency
___ 8. Predictive value

2-2. *Differentiating elements, qualitative characteristics, and measurement concepts*

The following list contains references to elements (E), qualitative characteristics of accounting data (Q), or measurement concepts employed to measure and report elements in the financial statements (M). Using the appropriate letter, indicate to which category each item belongs. If the item belongs to none of these, indicate this with an (N).

___ 1. Matching
___ 2. Distributions to owners
___ 3. Reliability
___ 4. Realization
___ 5. Cash flows from operations
___ 6. Comparability
___ 7. Market value
___ 8. Gains and losses
___ 9. Net realizable value
___10. Relevance
___11. Monetary unit
___12. Consistency
___13. Assets
___14. Historical cost

2-3. *Selection of attributes for valuation*

Five years ago, Frederick Industries acquired a semitractor/trailer by paying $150,000. The truck was deemed to have a useful life of 10 years and no salvage value. Similar trucks can be purchased new from the factory today for $200,000. Frederick estimates that it might be able to sell the semi for $90,000 today, but $3,000 of preparation and transportation costs to deliver it to a purchaser would likely be incurred.

Determine each of the following values: (1) historical cost, (2) current cost, (3) current market value, and (4) net realizable value. Which value do you believe is the most reliable? Which is the most relevant to financial statement users? Defend your answer and state any assumptions you have made.

PROBLEMS

2-1. *Interplay between primary qualities*

Because you are a Certified Public Accountant and have developed a good reputation in your community, you have been invited to give a short after-dinner speech at a local chamber of commerce meeting on the relevance and reliability of financial statements. During dinner, another accountant sitting next to you comments,

"I don't understand what the fuss is about. I believe reliability should be the dominant quality in the information conveyed in financial statements, even at the expense of relevance."

REQUIRED:

1. If financial statements only contained information that auditors could fully verify and would be reliable, do you believe the value of the financial reports would be improved?
2. If only relevant information were included without consideration for reliability, what effects would this have on an auditor's position?
3. In what sense might it be reasonable to assert that the trade-off between relevance and reliability is simply a reflection of the economic forces of supply and demand for financial information?

2-2. *Conceptual framework: qualitative characteristics*

The FASB *Statements of Financial Accounting Concepts* identify the goals and purposes of financial reporting. SFAC No. 2 examines the characteristics that make accounting information useful.

REQUIRED:

1. Identify and discuss the benefits that can be expected to be derived from the FASB's conceptual framework study.
2. What are the most important qualities for accounting information as identified in SFAC No. 2? Explain why they are important.
3. SFAC No. 2 describes a number of key characteristics or qualities for accounting information. Briefly discuss the importance of any three of these qualities for financial reporting purposes.

(CMA adapted)

THE RESERVE RECOGNITION ACCOUNTING DEBATE

One of the more highly debated choices of accounting and financial reporting standards over the last 20 years was that by oil and gas producing companies to report their exploration efforts. Two basic approaches were debated: one rooted in the historical cost tradition; the other, in more of a current value system. The historical cost approach had two different options that dealt primarily with accounting for the costs of exploration such as the costs of geological surveys and the drilling of test wells to determine the existence and quality of crude oil in an unproven area. The current cost alternative was focused primarily on measuring and reporting the present value of the future cash flows that known oil reserves would generate.

Until the late 1970s, companies in the oil and gas industry had used one of two basic accounting methods for the costs of exploration. These two methods were full cost and successful efforts. In both methods, the costs of drilling exploratory wells are capitalized until it is determined whether the well is viable. Once a determination as to the viability of a particular well is made, the full cost and successful efforts methods differ as to how to handle the exploratory costs.

Under the full cost method, the costs of all exploration efforts were capitalized and amortized over future years, without regard to whether the costs of drilling exploratory wells in a specific oil field actually produced a viable well. The basic support for this approach was that all exploratory efforts were undertaken so that, on average, sufficient oil reserves would be identified and the firm could make a profit over all of its successful and unsuccessful efforts. In this way, matching the total exploration costs against future revenues generated from only the successful wells properly matched costs with revenues.

Under the successful efforts method, a company would only capitalize and amortize the cost of those drilling efforts that resulted in a viable well. If the exploration effort resulted in a dry well, the entire exploration cost would be charged to expense in the period it was determined that the well was not viable. This method focused on the matching of costs and revenues on a well by well basis, instead of viewing the entire exploration effort as a portfolio of opportunities. In December, 1977, the FASB released *Statement of Accounting Standard No. 19*, "Financial Accounting and Reporting by Oil and Gas Producing Companies." In general, this standard required all firms to use the successful efforts method of accounting.

Following the release of SFAS No. 19 by the FASB, the SEC determined it would not require firms to use successful efforts in financial reports submitted to the SEC. The SEC believed that the focus on accounting for historical development costs was misplaced and that an entirely new system of accounting, called "reserve recognition accounting," or RRA, should be instituted. RRA was required with the adoption of *Accounting Series Release (ASR) No. 253*. (ASRs were the predecessor of the FRRs that are currently promulgated by the SEC.) This release required that financial statements based on RRA should be produced as supplemental information to the historical cost based financial statements.

RRA accounting uses a very different set of assumptions to present the results of exploration activities than does the historical cost approach (under either successful efforts or full cost). In particular, under RRA, the present value of the future net revenues from proven reserves is carried as an asset on an oil and gas company's balance sheet. As more oil is discovered, the present value of the increase in proven reserves is added to the asset and reported as income for the period. As oil is transferred to production, the asset is reduced. Costs of exploration for additional oil are deducted in the period they are incurred and never capitalized.

To appreciate the implications of RRA, it is necessary to better understand some of its definitions. In particular, a proven reserve exists when wells in a potential oil field have actually begun producing oil and when geologists have estimated the size of the pool of oil using information on the rock strata and other data. An example of an unproven reserve would be fields in which no company has yet to drill a well, but geologists believe the topography is promising.

Once the geologists develop an estimate of the proven reserves, the company must then forecast the timing of its sales of these proven reserves. Of course, this is done by utilizing data on current market demand as well as competitive supply conditions. Once these volume projections are developed, current oil prices are used to convert the volume predictions into dollar of revenue. Expected extraction costs are deducted from these future revenues, based on the current cost to extract oil from the producing fields, to forecast future net revenues. The SEC then required that these future net revenues be discounted at 10 percent to obtain a present value. This amount would be reported as an asset, and increases in this amount would be reported as periodic revenues arising from exploration activities.

In support of the use of RRA, Richard Adkerson (who was the individual most responsible for developing this system) stated the following:

> Whether a company in the oil and gas producing industry is successful depends ultimately on its discoveries in relation to the costs it incurs in finding, developing, and producing oil and gas. Nonproductive costs and the lag between incurring costs and receiving revenues from productive properties consume a huge amount of capital. Determining whether the costs invested in productive properties will be recovered is complicated by the difficulty in obtaining reasonably certain and timely estimates of recoverable quantities of oil and gas. Because of these factors, measuring the economic profitability of oil and gas exploration through attempting to associate specific costs with discoveries is highly complex, involving statistical analysis typically considered beyond the scope of public financial reporting.
>
> A measurement of such economic profitability could be approached as follows:
>
> 1. Estimating recoverable volumes from the production of discoveries
> 2. Valuing the future production using a discounted cash flow technique
> 3. Associating the costs incurred directly in finding and developing discoveries with related income streams
> 4. Assigning nonproductive costs to the income streams in some manner."[18]

---

[18] Richard Adkerson, "Can Reserve Recognition Accounting Work?" *The Journal of Accountancy* (September 1979), p. 74.

Opposition to RRA also existed. Joseph Conner, a partner of a major public accounting firm and expert in the oil and gas industry, stated:

> ASR No. 253 is also a radical departure from traditional conservative methodology for developing accounting theory, in that it requires the basic testing of an entirely new notion to be conducted in full public view in the published financial statements of petroleum companies. The danger of this approach is that untried and untested, highly subjective data carrying a high risk of misinterpretation will be furnished to financial statement users who may very well believe the data to be rooted in the same sort of factual ground as historical cost data and base important economic decisions on that data.[19]

REQUIRED:

1. Briefly evaluate the reliability of the accounting data that would be produced under full cost, successful efforts, and reserve recognition accounting. Which do you believe would be most reliable?
2. Briefly evaluate the relevance of the accounting data that would be produced under full cost, successful efforts, and reserve recognition accounting. Which do you believe would be most relevant?
3. What do you think Mr. Conner meant by his statement that ASR 253 is "a radical departure from traditional conservative methodology for development of accounting theory"? What does Mr. Conner mean by the word "theory"?
4. What implications, if any, do you draw from Mr. Conner's statement that investors will misinterpret the RRA data? How does this fit into the reporting environment the FASB envisioned in its first *Statement of Financial Accounting Concepts*?

THE LEASE CONTROVERSY

CASE 2.2

All leases transfer some ownership rights in the asset from the lessor (owner of the asset) to the lessee (the party acquiring the rights under the lease). The extent of the rights transferred between the parties varies. It can lie anywhere between using the asset on a specific job for periods as short as a day to locking the lessee to many years of lease payments, after which time the lessee receives title to the asset. On both ends of this spectrum, some ownership rights are transferred in return for a periodic lease payment.

During the period the Accounting Principles Board operated, a debate arose regarding the appropriate means for the lessee to report leasing activity in the financial statements. One approach was to treat all leases as if the periodic lease payment represented the appropriate cost to recognize under the lease each year. This would avoid recording any noncurrent asset or liability that represented commitments to make lease payments in periods beyond the current year. An alternative approach was to separate leases into two different types:

---

[19] Joseph Conner, "Reserve Recognition Accounting: Fact or Fiction," *The Journal of Accountancy* (September 1979), p. 92.

1. Those that would be classified as operating leases and accounted for as described above
2. Those that were in substance a purchase of the leased asset with the lease payments providing a means to finance the acquisition

This latter group would be accounted for by recording a noncurrent asset and a liability of equal value at the inception of the lease. The asset would then be depreciated, and the lease payments would be broken down into an interest expense portion and a portion applied to reduce the recorded principal of the lease liability.

When corporations make major purchases of property, plant, and equipment, they often finance these purchases by borrowing money from banks. The banks may have a lien on the asset, which allows them a means of recovery in the event of nonpayment of the loan. In any case, the corporation generally holds the title to the asset and, within the limits imposed by the lender (if any), may use the asset in any fashion it desires or sell it if this is preferred. Payment of the loan is mandatory and cannot be avoided without foreclosure or other financial repercussions.

The financial reporting debate was eventually resolved when the FASB required the two-tiered treatment of leases. Only leases that contained non-cancellable future lease payments and those that resulted in the transfer of substantially all ownership rights between the lessor and lessee over the life of the lease, were treated as an "in-substance" sale. These leases were "capitalized" by recording an asset and liability of equal value on the lessee's books at the inception of the lease. The benefits of this policy were to make the balance sheet more reflective of the underlying economic condition of lessees involved in these types of leases.

Corporations affected by this change in policy lobbied strenuously against the new policy. They wanted information regarding the leases included in the notes to the financial statements, not reported as assets and liabilities in the financial statements proper. For many of these companies, the inclusion of the lease liability would violate various commitments they had made to lenders on other loans. These commitments related to the ratio of the book value of debt to the book value of equity, and this ratio would be significantly increased by lease capitalization. As a result, if found in violation of the terms of their loans, many of these firms would incur real costs to renegotiate these loans. These costs would include not only the time and efforts of corporate personnel, but also an increase in interest costs. (Interest rates would have increased since the original loans had been negotiated.) Severely affected companies believed that these costs incurred would not outweigh the benefits to users of information in their financial statements. They believed note disclosure could make users aware of the magnitude of these commitments without altering the content of their financial statements proper.

REQUIRED:

1. Using the concepts of relevance and reliability, build a case in support of the concept of capitalizing leases.
2. How is the concept of materiality imbedded in the two-tiered system of reporting for leases by the lessee?

3. How does the concept of full disclosure relate to the lease debate as characterized in the case?
4. How do you believe users would be affected by the decision to report information on "capital leases" in notes rather than in the financial statements proper?
5. Given the very real effects this decision had on some lessee's economic condition, do you think that the benefits outweigh the costs? Why or why not?
6. Suppose you believed the costs imposed on firms that would violate their lending agreements were too high for the benefits obtained. However, you also believed the long-term benefits of lease capitalization were significant. What policy might you implement to reduce the short-term costs for firms most severely affected and yet implement capitalization in the long term?
7. Of the alternative valuation approaches discussed in the chapter, which one seems most applicable for the capitalization of leases? Why?

THE GOLD RUSH

CASE 2.3

Companies engaged in the mining of gold follow a fairly typical pattern. They explore for new resources, then extract these resources when discovered, refine the extracted gold into saleable ingots, and finally sell the gold either to brokers or directly to customers such as large jewelry manufacturers. The selling price of gold is set in world markets where any individual trader, including the gold mining companies, is only a small part of the total volume in the marketplace.

A debate has arisen regarding the appropriate way of reporting revenues for gold mining companies. There are two basic alternatives for recognition of revenue. The first is referred to as the historical cost alternative, which requires that the gold be sold prior to recognizing any revenues. The second alternative is referred to as the market value alternative, in which revenue is recognized as soon as the gold is in marketable form.

Under the historical cost approach, companies carry gold inventory on the balance sheet at historical production costs until an exchange occurs. At that point, revenues are recognized at the selling price; and the historical production cost is charged to expense. Under this approach, companies are able to hold their gold inventories to speculate on increases in the price of gold without reporting any losses when the gold is in saleable condition. If the market price alternative were utilized, revenues would be recognized at the completion of production; and the costs of production would be matched against the revenues to determine income. In addition, any change in the market value of gold inventories would be recognized as a gain or loss during the period when prices changed.

The proponents of the historical cost alternative argue that the realization principle is violated by the market value method, which results in less relevant and reliable financial information. The information is less reliable because the revenue recognized does not represent the amount of cash generated at the time of sale. As such, it misstates the results of operations for the period since the future price of gold, at which actual sales will take place, is unpredictable.

The market value proponents argue that management's decision not to sell the gold immediately results from a decision to speculate on the future price movements in gold. As such, recognizing revenue at the completion of production, based on the selling price available at the time the gold is in saleable condition, will not only capture the results of current period operations better, but it will also limit the effects of changes in gold prices on future revenues to only the consequence of the price fluctuation. When the market value method is used, future revenue from gold already in inventory will only reflect increases or decreases in the value of that inventory.

REQUIRED:

1. Evaluate the relevance and reliability of the information produced under each of the two approaches.
2. How would the decision on when to realize revenues affect concerns regarding various contingencies such as delivery costs associated with the ultimate transfer of the gold to a customer?
3. How does the decision on the timing of revenue recognition affect the application of the matching concept?
4. Which of these two approaches would you describe as more "conservative"? Why?
5. Assuming there is no clear resolution of which proposed method is more relevant or reliable, what concept might be violated by simply allowing each company to choose its own method of reporting? Why might the violation of this concept be important enough to warrant regulation to force all companies to use one method?

CASE 2.4 ▌ INTERMEDICS CORPORATION

Intermedics Corporation, headquartered in Texas, manufactures and sells certain medical supply products. One of the company's product lines is pacemakers for individuals whose hearts do not provide sufficient electrical impulses to create a regular, strong heartbeat. The pacemaker is a small electronic device that is implanted just below the skin of the patient, typically in the chest or stomach area. The pacemaker generates a regular electronic pulse that is carried to the heart muscle via a pacing lead. The pacing lead is attached to the heart muscle in various ways, and the electronic impulse is transferred from the lead to the heart muscle through this contact. Intermedics has also produced and sold a line of pacing leads to go with their pacemakers.

Several other manufacturers of pacemakers and pacing leads are in the medical supply industry. Pacesetters, Incorporated and Medtronic Corporation are two such competitors. The industry leader is Medtronic, which has the largest share of the domestic market in the United States.

In November 1980, Medtronic sued both Pacesetters and Intermedics for infringement of a patent it held on a style of pacing lead that it claimed was being produced and sold by Intermedics and Pacesetters. (The leads were virtually identical.) Medtronic claimed damages of over $80 million at this point. Damages included all lost profits that Medtronic would have received had it sold its own pacing lead in place of the one produced by Intermedics. Arguing that it held a valid patent on the lead and that Medtronic was infringing, Intermedics responded to the suit by filing a counterclaim. At that time, Intermedics' attorneys stated they believed the case on the countersuit should prevail.

The court divided the Medtronic–Intermedics litigation into two parts:

1. A trial to determine whether Intermedics had indeed infringed on Medtronic's patent, or vice versa
2. A second set of hearings to determine settlement of damages if infringement was determined

The pre-trial hearings on the infringement suits for Pacesetters and Intermedics continued until late 1983. In September 1983, the court allowed Intermedics to proceed with discovery in preparation for actually trying the case. In June 1985, the court decided against Intermedics and for Medtronic. In addition, the jury determined there was evidence that Intermedics had willfully infringed on Medtronic's patent, thereby opening the possibility of affording Medtronic triple damages.

In August 1985, Intermedics' request for a new trial was denied; and the company was enjoined from any further production or sale of the infringing leads. Following this action, the company proceeded to appeal the court's decision. In its 1985 financial statements, Intermedics provided this description of the status of the case:

> The Company has appealed the District Court's decision and errors committed during the trial and seeks a new trial. The Company's patent counsel has advised the Company that such an appeal should be successful. However, if the appeal is unsuccessful, a damages trial will ensue.

In August 1986, Intermedics' appeal was denied; and the decision of the lower court was upheld. A special master was appointed to hear testimony regarding the damages to be awarded in the case. At this point, Medtronic was asserting damages of approximately $50 million. A hearing before the special master was scheduled for early 1988.

Intermedics is involved in several other forms of litigation, which may result in gains or losses to the firm in varying amounts. The company reported the following information regarding various accrued expenses in its 1987 and 1985 10-K reports:

In its income statement, Intermedics reports a provision for litigation losses as follows (in thousands):

	1987	1986	1985
Provision for litigation losses	$1,224	$20,821	$7,769

In its balance sheet, Intermedics reports the following data supporting its accrued liabilities (in thousands):

	November 1, 1987	November 2, 1986	November 3, 1985	October 28, 1984
Litigation provision	$28,121	$26,920	$ 8,613	$ 1,596
Payroll and other compensation	13,792	10,835	6,889	6,309
Other	9,575	10,655	11,521	10,006
	$51,488	$48,410	$27,023	$17,911

Additional information regarding the financial performance of Intermedics during the period of interest in this case is as follows (in thousands):

	1987	1986	1985	1984	1983
Reported net income or (loss)	$29,183	$6,159	$(20,046)	$3,201	$(9,455)

In Intermedics' 1985 10-K report, the following disclosure is provided as Note 1:

1. Basis of Presentation

The Company's consolidated financial statements have been presented on the basis that it is a going concern, which contemplates the realization of assets and the satisfaction of liabilities in the normal course of business.

The Company's principal loan agreement is in default, and the group of lending banks have demanded payment (deferred by agreement in principle through May 12, 1986) of the outstanding debt, $36,620,000 at November 3, 1985 (Note 11). The Company also has other significant commitments and guarantees related to ZyMOS Corporation (Note 7), to the acquisition of Infusaid Company (Notes 3 and 16), and to additional litigation liabilities (Note 16).

The Company has incurred net losses of $20,046,000 and $9,455,000 in the years ended November 3, 1985, and October 30, 1983, respectively, and net earnings of $3,201,000 in the year ended October 28, 1984.

The Company has explored various sources and methods of long-term financing to provide for the repayment of the outstanding debt to the banks and, along with funds provided from operations, to provide funding, when needed, to meet other significant unfunded obligations and possible obligations that may arise from litigation contingencies. On February 14, 1986, the Company entered into an agreement with an investment partnership under which the partnership has committed to purchase from the Company $50,000,000 of Senior Secured Increasing Rate Extendable Notes and Warrants for 3,500,000 shares (reduced under certain conditions) of Common Stock for $8.61 per share (Note 11). Upon finalization of the agreement, the proceeds from the sale of the notes will be used to repay the outstanding debt to the banks and to refinance the secured demand note of $14,747,000 relating to the Infusaid bond (Note 16). The Company will continue to explore methods of financing alternatives that may improve the Company's financial position. Management believes that working capital and cash flow from operations will be adequate to support normal, ongoing operations, research and development programs, and capital expenditure programs.

The continuation of the Company as a going concern is dependent on its ability to complete the above described or similar financing, obtain favorable resolution of litigation, and ultimately achieve profitable operations.

REQUIRED:

1. Given the criteria presented in SFAS No. 5 for recognition of contingent liabilities, what rationale would be used to determine the status of the pacing lead litigation at the following dates for purposes of financial reporting?
   (a) November 1980
   (b) November 1983
   (c) November 1985
   (d) November 1987

2. Assuming that by November 1987, the contingent liability was deemed to be probable, how much should be estimated as the potential liability to be recognized?

3. Given the information on litigation accruals provided by Intermedics, how much cash did the company actually pay out in settlement of the related litigation in 1985, 1986, and 1987, respectively? Provide the journal entries necessary to record the activity in the accrued litigation provision account.

4. How does your analysis in Requirements 1 and 2 above square with the amounts reported in the accrued litigation provision presented by Intermedics? When does it appear that Intermedics actually accrued losses from the pacing lead suit?

5. Speculate on the factors that may have influenced how Intermedics elected to present the effects of the pacing lead litigation on its financial condition.

CONTROL DATA CORPORATION

CASE 2.5

On February 14, 1986, an article appeared in *The Wall Street Journal* concerning the earnings release of Control Data Corporation for the year ended December 31, 1985. Highlights of the article are as follows:

1. Control Data reported a loss of $567.5 million for 1985, of which $297.9 was reported for the fourth quarter.
2. Control Data had reported income of $5.1 million in the previous year, 1984.
3. The information about the earnings of CDC was released on February 13, 1986, and the price of its stock fell on that day by 37 1/2 cents to $22.25 per share.

Further inspection of the financial statements for 1985 revealed that at the end of 1984, CDC reported a total stockholders' equity of $1,758.8 million and retained earnings of $1,352.8 million. This indicated that the loss reported for 1985 wiped out 32.3% of total stockholders' equity, or 42.0% of retained earnings. The financial statements also revealed that CDC had reported income of $161.7 million in 1983.

Using the information on price changes provided in the article, the announcement of this event resulted in a decline of only 1.7% in the value of a share of CDC. Another way to state this is that the daily return to holding a share of CDC's stock on the day the earnings were announced was –1.7%, while the loss appears to indicate a decline in the book value of stockholders' equity of about 32.3%

1. Does the lack of apparent association between the size of the price movement in CDC's per-share price and the magnitude of the loss reported in the financial reports suggest that accounting earnings numbers are not relevant or not reliable? Why or why not?
2. Regardless of your actual conclusion in Requirement 1, assuming there was no association between earnings announcements and price changes, would that insure that accounting earnings information was not relevant or not reliable?
3. If there was no association present between prices and accounting earnings, could we conclude that financial reporting does not matter and should be discontinued?

Financial Statement Overview

Financial accounting deals with the accounting procedures used to prepare general-purpose financial statements—those used by external decision makers such as stockholders, investors, lenders, and regulators. In this chapter, we will review the form and content of the primary financial statements: the balance sheet, income statement, statement of stockholders' equity, and cash flow statement as well as the interrelationships between the statements. The notes to the financial statements are an integral part of the statements and they will be covered throughout the text. We presume that students are already familiar with how the statements are produced—the basic methods used by accountants for recording and processing financial information and preparing financial statements. If that is not the case, the review appendix at the end of the text contains an overview of recording and processing transactions.

Accounting standard setters frequently argue that matters of economic substance are far more important than matters of form. However, the format of financial statements has attracted considerable attention from the standard setters, as we shall see.

THE INCOME STATEMENT

Income statements report the results of a firm's operations over a particular period in terms of revenues, expenses, gains, and losses. Other popular titles for these statements include the *statement of earnings* and *statement of operations*. Revenues represent increases in assets or decreases in liabilities earned by providing goods and services to customers. Revenues are most commonly earned in sales transactions but can also be earned from many other types of transactions including leases, franchises, licenses, investments, and loans. Expenses represent the costs of generating revenue—i.e., the reduction of assets or increase in liabilities required to provide goods and services to customers. Issues related to the recognition of revenues and expenses are discussed more thoroughly in Chapters 4 and 5.

The net results of transactions not directly related to the ordinary operating activities of a firm are reported separately as **gains** and **losses**. For instance, suppose a manufacturing firm sells an unneeded piece of land that had been purchased years ago as a possible expansion site. Since real estate transactions are not routine for a manufacturing firm, the revenues reported would not include the proceeds from this sale nor would the expenses include the historical cost of the land. Rather, the net results of this transaction would be reported separately as a gain if the proceeds from the sale exceed the cost of the land plus any other costs associated with the sale and as a loss if the proceeds are less than the cost of the land and any other costs.

Accountants have long debated whether such nonoperating gains or losses should even be reported on the income statement. Proponents of the *current operating performance approach* to income statements have argued that the income statement should report only the results of routine, recurring operating transactions. They advocate that nonoperating gains or losses should be handled as direct adjustments to retained earnings. Proponents of the *all-inclusive approach* (sometimes known as the *clean surplus* approach) to income statements have argued that reporting the results of nonrecurring items on the income statement reduces the probability that they will be overlooked by financial statement readers. Therefore, they advocate reporting these gains and losses on the income statement but separately from the results of routine operating transactions. As we shall see, the accounting standards have essentially adopted the all-inclusive approach.

Statement of Financial Accounting Concepts No. 6 defines the concept of "comprehensive income" as follows:

> **Comprehensive income** is the change in equity of a business enterprise during a period from transactions and other events and circumstances from nonowner sources. It includes all changes in equity during a period except those resulting from investments by owners and distributions to owners.[1]

It is interesting that while the concept of comprehensive income is advocated by SFAC No. 6, it is not followed precisely in practice. In several instances, GAAP require that certain items meeting the definition of comprehensive income be excluded from a firm's reported net income and reported separately as direct adjustments of owners' equity. We will examine one of these items when we discuss the method of accounting for certain long-term investments in marketable equity securities in Chapter 17. The only justification for excluding certain items from comprehensive income is that they are somehow different from other revenues, expenses, gains, and losses. Thus, their inclusion in net income would emphasize them inappropriately.

---

[1] "Elements of Financial Statements—A Replacement of FASB Concepts Statement No. 3 (incorporating an Amendment of FASB Concepts Statement No. 2," *Statement of Financial Accounting Concepts No. 6* (Stamford, CT: FASB, 1985), para. 70.

What Information Is Provided by the Income Statement?

The income statement is the major source of information about the firm's profitability. A firm is profitable if its net assets (assets minus liabilities) increase as a result of transactions with nonowners. Firms reporting a net income for the period (revenues and gains greater than expenses and losses) have increased their net assets as a result of transactions with nonowners. Firms reporting a net loss for a period (revenues and gains less than expenses and losses) have reduced their net assets as a result of such transactions. Most of these transactions are the results of routine operations.

Information about a firm's income (or earnings) is viewed as very important. Some financial analysts argue that the value of a firm's stock is in large part a function of the most recently reported earnings. Newspapers publishing information on daily stock prices often include ratios of firms' stock prices to their earnings on a per share basis. Analysts frequently forecast future earnings; and when the actual amounts differ significantly from these forecasted amounts, they are usually newsworthy and often are associated with an adjustment in the price of the firm's stock. While a more precise specification of the linkage between earnings and stock prices is beyond the scope of this text, the fact that such a linkage exists (or is perceived to exist by many participants in the financial markets) underlines the importance of the income statement and especially the net income amount.

The Format of the Income Statement

Accounting policy makers have long argued that matters of form are far less important than matters of economic substance. This principle of substance over form has guided policy makers in several areas to conclude that particular types of transactions should be accounted for according to their economic substance rather than their legal form. For instance, as we shall see in Chapter 18, certain lease transactions are essentially accounted for as installment sales/purchases. With all this emphasis on substance over form, it is a little surprising that accounting policy makers have devoted considerable attention to the form of the income statement.

The format of the income statement is largely dictated by *APB Opinion No. 30*, "Reporting the Results of Operations,"[2] with several other professional standards also relevant. Under GAAP, an income statement can conceivably have five distinct sections. The first four sections break down the net income of the firm into the following components:

1. Income from continuing operations
2. Income from discontinued operations
3. Extraordinary items
4. Adjustments for the cumulative effects of changes in accounting principle

---

[2] "Reporting the Results of Operations—Reporting the Effects of Disposal of a Segment of a Business, and Extraordinary, Unusual, and Infrequently Occurring Events and Transactions," *Accounting Principles Board Opinion No. 30* (New York: AICPA, 1973).

The fifth section, required of most corporations, includes the earnings amounts per share of common stock outstanding. Although it is relatively unusual for a particular firm to require all of the first four sections in a given period, for the purposes of illustration, we provide an income statement for the fictional Prairie Hardware Corp., in Exhibit 3.1, which includes all four sections.

Why are elaborate rules regarding the format of the income statement necessary? As we have already mentioned, financial analysts and the financial press pay considerable attention to the income amounts reported by firms. Given the importance of net income to financial statement users, the accounting standard setters have attempted to insure that revenues, expenses, gains, and losses are reported directly and informatively on a firm's income statement and in a consistent manner with the reporting practices of other firms. In

| **EXHIBIT 3.1** |
| Prairie Hardware Corp. Income Statement |

PRAIRIE HARDWARE CORP.
INCOME STATEMENT
For the Year Ended December 31, 1994
(000s except per share amounts)

Net sales		$290,105
Costs and expenses:		
Cost of goods sold	$146,053	
Selling and administrative expense	57,221	
Interest expense	6,157	
Other (income) expense	10,092	219,523
(1) Income from continuing operations, before taxes on income		70,582
Income tax expense		22,590
Income from continuing operations, after taxes on income		$ 47,992
(2) Loss from discontinued operations:		
Income from operations, net of income taxes of $1,256	2,669	
Loss on disposal, net of income tax benefit of $2,761	(5,867)	(3,198)
Income before extraordinary item and cumulative effect of accounting change		44,794
(3) Extraordinary loss from tornado damage, net of income tax benefit of $1,532 (see Note 1)		(3,256)
Income before cumulative effect of accounting change		41,538
(4) Cumulative effect of accounting change, net of income tax effects of $3,248		6,902
Net income		48,440
Earnings per share:		
Income from continuing operations, after taxes on income		$ 2.94
Net loss from discontinued operations		(0.19)
Income before extraordinary item and cumulative effect of accounting change		$ 2.75
Extraordinary loss, net		(0.20)
Cumulative effect of accounting change, net		0.42
Net income		$ 2.97

particular, special items, which do not reflect the results of normal, recurring events, and transactions require separate and prominent disclosure to insure that they are properly understood.

Income from Continuing Operations

The top part of the Prairie Hardware income statement, reproduced in Exhibit 3.2 below, reports the revenues, expenses, gains, and losses from the mostly routine activities of the firm. If a particular firm has no "special items," such as (1) the disposal of a segment, (2) gains or losses from unusual and infrequent events, or (3) the results of changes in accounting principles, the entire income statement will appear much like this section of the Prairie Hardware income statement with the obvious difference that the bottom line will be labeled "Net income" rather than "Income from continuing operations, after taxes on income." Under the all-inclusive approach espoused by GAAP, all revenues, expenses, gains, and losses of a firm, except those attributable to the three special items listed above, are included in this section of the income statement.

The authoritative literature does not specify a required format for the continuing operations section of an income statement. The continuing operations section of the Prairie Hardware income statement is presented in what is known as a **single-step format**. Single-step refers to the fact that income can be calculated in one step by subtracting expenses from revenues. As we can see from the Prairie Hardware statement, this is not literally true since income tax expense is not included with the other expenses and, thus, the calculation of income from continuing operations requires two steps. Nevertheless, although it is somewhat of a misnomer, the income from continuing operations section of the Prairie Hardware statement would be described as being in the single-step format. Single-step income statements offer a very simple and straightforward presentation of revenues, expenses, gains, and losses although the information presented is, of necessity, highly aggregated.

EXHIBIT 3.2
Prairie Hardware Corp. Continuing Operations Section of the Income Statement (Single-Step Format)

PRAIRIE HARDWARE CORP. Continuing Operations Section of the Income Statement (Single-Step Format) For the Year Ended December 31, 1994 (000s except per share amounts)		
Net sales		$290,105
Costs and expenses:		
Cost of goods sold	$146,053	
Selling and administrative expense	57,221	
Interest expense	6,157	
Other (income) expense	10,092	219,523
Income from continuing operations, before taxes on income		70,582
Income tax expense		22,590
Income from continuing operations, after taxes on income		$ 47,992

A **multiple-step income statement** requires several calculations to derive net income and thereby allows for a more detailed presentation of income statement information. A multiple-step presentation of the income from continuing operations section of the Prairie Hardware income statement is shown in Exhibit 3.3. Notice how the multiple-step format offers considerably more detailed information than is possible in a single-step format. It also permits reporting useful intermediate figures such as gross profit and income from operations on the statement. The additional information is particularly useful to managers who are concerned with controlling costs, and the multiple-step format is commonly used for the preparation of income statements used by managers. However, most firms believe the additional information provided

PRAIRIE HARDWARE CORP.		
Continuing Operations Section of the Income Statement		
(Multiple-Step Format)		
For the Year Ended December 31, 1994		
(000s except per share amounts)		
Sales revenue		$296,026
Less: Provision for uncollectible accounts		(5,921)
Net sales		$290,105
Cost of goods sold:		
Beginning inventory	$ 14,842	
Plus: Net purchases	142,035	
Freight-in	7,420	
Less: Ending inventory	(18,244)	146,053
Gross profit		144,052
Selling and administrative expenses:		
Commissions and salaries	32,875	
Depreciation	4,590	
Advertising	6,238	
Utilities	8,512	
Freight-out	3,894	
Miscellaneous	1,112	57,221
Income from operations		86,831
Other (income) expense:		
Interest expense	6,157	
Dividend income	(874)	
Loss on sale of building	11,438	
Other, net	(472)	16,249
Income from continuing operations, before taxes on income		70,852
Income tax expense		22,590
Income from continuing operations, after taxes on income		$ 47,992

EXHIBIT 3.3
Prairie Hardware Corp. Continuing Operations Section of the Income Statement (Multiple-Step Format)

in a multiple-step income statement is unnecessary for external reporting and use the single-step format for their published financial reports.

Income from Discontinued Operations

APB Opinion 30 requires separate reporting of the results of discontinued operations whenever a firm has disposed of a segment of its business. A *segment* is defined as:

> A component of an enterprise whose activities represent a separate major line of business or class of customer,... provided that its assets, results of operations, and activities can be clearly distinguished, physically and operationally and for financial reporting purposes, from the other assets, results of operations, and activities of the entity."[3]

For example, in December 1989, The Upjohn Company, a well-known pharmaceutical firm, decided to discontinue its industrial chemical business. Since the products and customers of the industrial chemical business were clearly separate from those of the other Upjohn operations, this transaction was treated as the disposal of a segment.

The motivation for the reporting requirements of APB Opinion No. 30 is to insure that financial statement readers are aware of the fact that the revenues, expenses, gains, and losses contributed by the discontinued operations will not be recurring. Financial statement users often base their projections of future earnings on amounts reported in the current and prior periods. Obviously, a disposed business segment cannot contribute to the earnings of future periods and the reporting requirements insure that readers can distinguish between continuing and discontinued operations.

The income from discontinued operations section of the Prairie Hardware income statement is reproduced below. Notice that two amounts are reported: (1) income from operations and (2) loss on disposal. To understand the reporting requirements for discontinued operations, let us discuss the specific nature of the segment disposal.

Income from discontinued operations:

Income from operations, net of income taxes of $1,256	$ 2,669
Loss on disposal, net of income tax benefit of $2,761	(5,867)
	$(3,198)

On October 21, 1994, the Board of Directors of Prairie Hardware Corp. approved a plan to dispose of the firm's home appliance division, a Prairie Hardware component that meets the APB Opinion No. 30 definition of a segment of the business. The plan called for a sale of the assets of the division to be completed by June 30, 1995. In this case, October 21, 1994 is known as the measurement date of the transaction, defined as "the date on which the management having authority to approve the action commits itself to a formal

---

[3] *Ibid.*, para. 13.

plan to dispose of a segment of the business, whether by sale or abandonment."[4] Assuming the sale is consummated according to plan on June 30, 1995, this date will be known as the disposal date, defined as "the date of closing the sale, if the disposal is by sale, or the date that operations cease, if the disposal is by abandonment."[5] Notice that in this case, the firm's fiscal year-end, December 31, 1994, falls between the measurement and disposal dates.

The first amount in the discontinued operations section of the Prairie Hardware income statement, income from operations of $2,669, represents the results of operating the home appliance division from the start of the year through the measurement date. The second amount, the loss on disposal of $5,867, applies to events occurring or expected to occur after the measurement date. On the measurement date, Prairie Hardware's management would be required to estimate two amounts related to the disposal:

1. The expected amount of any gain or loss from the disposal of the home appliance division's assets
2. The expected income or loss from operating the division during the phasing-out period—i.e., the period between the measurement date and the expected disposal date

If a loss on disposal of the assets of the discontinued segment is expected, it is recorded at the measurement date. If a gain is expected, it is recorded when realized at the disposal date. If operations during the phasing-out period are expected to produce losses, then these losses are included in the disposal loss. If operations during the phasing-out period are expected to produce income, this income will be recognized at the measurement date but only to the extent of expected losses on disposal of the segment's assets.

For instance, suppose that on the measurement date, management estimated the home appliance division's assets would be sold at a loss, net of taxes, of $6,742; but the division's operations from the measurement date through the disposal date would produce income, net of taxes, of $875. The reported loss on disposal is calculated as follows:

Expected loss on disposal of division assets	$(6,742)
Expected income from operations in the phasing-out period	875
Reported loss on disposal	$(5,867)

If the expected income from operations during the phasing-out period had exceeded the amount of the expected loss on disposal of division assets, then only $6,742 of income would be recognized at the measurement date, resulting in no reported loss on disposal.

Notice that both amounts in Prairie Hardware's discontinued operations section of the income statement are reported net of their related income tax effects. This implies that the tax consequences of the decision to dispose of the home appliance division are not included in the line labeled "Income taxes" in

---

[4] *Ibid.*, para. 14.
[5] *Ibid.*

the income from continuing operations section of the income statement. Rather, by reporting net of taxes in the discontinued operations section of the statement, the tax consequences are effectively reported in the same section of the income statement as the revenues, expenses, gains, and losses to which they relate. This is an example of intraperiod tax allocation. **Intraperiod tax allocation** requires that whenever an income statement has separate sections for continuing operations and any or all of the special items (discontinued operations, extraordinary items, and effects of accounting changes), the tax consequences of the items reported in each section must also be reported there. If intraperiod tax allocation were not required and just one amount for income taxes was reported in the income statement, this would effectively blur the distinctions between the items reported in the separate sections.

Since income statements typically present the revenues, expenses, gains, and losses for several (typically three) years in comparative form, restatement of prior period amounts will be necessary. For instance, in Prairie Hardware's 1992 and 1993 income statements, as originally issued, the revenues and expenses of the home appliance division were obviously reported in the continuing operations section of the income statement since the decision to dispose of the segment was not made until 1994. However, in its 1994 annual report, Prairie Hardware would be required to report the results of operating the home appliance division separately as discontinued operations. Thus, in the 1994 annual report, the income statements for 1992 and 1993 would be modified from original statements although the reported net income would be the same as originally reported.

APB Opinion No. 30 also requires the following disclosures in the notes to the financial statements accompanying the disposal of a segment.[6]

1. The identity of the segment
2. The expected disposal date, if known
3. The expected manner of disposal
4. A description of the remaining assets and liabilities of the segment at the balance sheet date
5. The income or loss from operations and any proceeds from disposal of the segment during the period from the measurement date to the date of the balance sheet

These additional disclosures are designed to provide the financial statement reader with more detailed information about the transaction without cluttering the income statement.

For an example of discontinued operations, consider the following excerpts from the 1990 annual report of Global Natural Resources, Inc.

Discontinued Operations - In March 1991, the Company agreed to sell its wholly owned subsidiary GNR Drilling Company ("Drilling") to an officer of Drilling for a nominal cash payment plus forgiveness of certain amounts owed to Drilling by the Company for contract drilling services. The loss on disposition, including estimated future costs and operating results from the segment until the date of disposition, was estimated to be $1.2 million net of

---

[6] *Ibid.*, para. 18.

income tax benefit of $.2 million. As a result there was no effect on 1991 operations from contract drilling operations. The net current assets of $2.5 million and long-term assets of $1.5 million associated with the discontinued operations are included on the balance sheet at December 31, 1990.

The loss from discontinued operations for the two years ended December 31, 1990, stated in thousands, is as follows:

	1990	1989
Net loss	$ (119)	$(570)
Estimated loss on disposition	(1,190)	--
Loss from discontinued operations	$(1,309)	$(570)

Notice that the disposal of GNR Drilling is shown as discontinued operations in the 1990 annual report even though the actual agreement was dated March 1991. Since the event is described in the 1990 annual report, the agreement was obviously entered into prior to the release of the 1990 annual report. Moreover, recall that treatment as discontinued operations only requires a commitment to dispose of a segment, not the actual disposal.

Extraordinary Items

Over the years, accounting standard setters have become increasingly selective in allowing particular gains or losses to be described on the income statement as extraordinary items. Use of the adjective "extraordinary" is clearly meant to imply that the item in question is highly unusual and is not expected to recur. The motivation for separate disclosure of the results of a truly extraordinary transaction is the same as the motivation for separate disclosure of the results of discontinued operations. An extraordinary item, while perhaps having a material effect on the current year's net income, is not likely to affect future years' income. Before there were restrictions on use of the term extraordinary item in the financial statements, losses seemed to be described in this manner more often than gains, perhaps due to managements' wish to take credit for any good news but disavow blame for any bad news.

APB Opinion No. 30 states the criteria for use of the term extraordinary item. To qualify for treatment as an **extraordinary item** on a firm's income statement, a transaction must meet both of the following criteria.[7]

1. **Unusual nature:** The underlying event or transaction possesses a high degree of abnormality and is of a type clearly unrelated to, or only incidentally related to, the ordinary and typical activities of the enterprise, taking into account the environment in which the enterprise operates.

2. **Infrequency of occurrence:** The underlying event or transaction is of a type that would not reasonably be expected to recur in the foreseeable future, taking into account the environment in which the enterprise operates.

---

[7] *Ibid.*, para. 20.

By requiring that "the environment in which the enterprise operates" be taken into account, the APB clearly intends to allow for the possibility that a particular event or transaction may qualify as an extraordinary item for one firm but not for another. For instance, a firm's geographic location might determine whether losses from flood damages were infrequent enough to qualify as extraordinary items. In addition to geography, the environmental factors that must be taken into consideration in determining whether a particular item is extraordinary include the characteristics of the firm's industry and the nature and extent of governmental regulation.

While Opinion No. 30 does not offer examples of extraordinary items, it does offer some examples of items that do not qualify.[8] These include the following:

1. Write-down or write-off of receivables, inventory, equipment leased to others, or intangible assets
2. Gains or losses from exchange or translation of foreign currencies, including those relating to major devaluations and revaluations
3. Gains or losses on disposal of a segment of a business
4. Other gains and losses from sale or abandonment of property, plant, or equipment used in the business
5. Effects of a strike, including those against competitors and major suppliers
6. Adjustment of accruals on long-term contracts

For an example of an event that does qualify, let us consider the case of Prairie Hardware Co. in more detail. On June 10, 1994, the firm's warehouse and administrative offices suffered considerable damage in a freak tornado. The firm is located in a county that has not suffered any tornado damage previously this century. The losses to buildings and grounds, equipment, and inventory totalled $4,788,000. Since these losses are deductible for income tax purposes, they also produced income tax benefits of $1,532,000. Due to the unusual nature of the loss and the infrequency of its occurrence, this loss would clearly qualify as an extraordinary item.

Once an item's status as an extraordinary item has been determined, how is it reported in the income statement? The extraordinary item section of the Prairie Hardware income statement (Exhibit 3.1) illustrates the treatment:

Extraordinary loss from tornado damage,
    net of income tax benefit of $1,532 (see Note 1)   (3,256)

Notice the location of the extraordinary item section is toward the bottom of the Prairie Hardware income statement. APB Opinion No. 30 requires that the extraordinary item section of an income statement must be located after income from continuing operations and any gain or loss from discontinued operations. Required disclosures, either in the notes or within the income statement include a description of "the nature of the extraordinary event or transaction and the principal items entering into the determination of an extra-

---

[8] *Ibid.*, para. 23.

ordinary gain or loss" and "the income taxes applicable to the extraordinary item." An acceptable note to accompany the Prairie Hardware income statement might appear as follows:

> **Note 1**: On June 10, 1994, the firm's warehouse and administrative offices were damaged by a tornado, the first such storm in the vicinity of our Midwest location this century. The losses to buildings and grounds, equipment, and inventory totalled $4,788,000 with a related tax benefit of $1,532,000.

Several other authoritative pronouncements specify that particular transactions be reported as extraordinary items even though they do not meet the "unusual nature" and "infrequency of occurrence" criteria of APB Opinion No. 30. This is done to draw the financial statement reader's attention to the item to insure that it will not be overlooked. For instance (and as discussed more fully in Chapter 14), FASB Statement No. 4 requires that material gains or losses resulting from the extinguishment of debt be treated as extraordinary items. Other pronouncements specify that certain other transactions, which are beyond the scope of this text, also be reported as extraordinary items.

A good example of an income statement containing extraordinary items can be found in the 1988 annual report of Pennzoil Co. Pennzoil's net income for 1988 includes two extraordinary items: a gain on the settlement of a lawsuit and a gain on the redemption of debentures (unsecured bonds). These two items are described more fully in Note 8 to the financial statements, excerpts of which follow:

> **(8) Extraordinary Items-**
>
> *Settlement-*
>
> Net income for 1988 reflects an extraordinary gain of $1,656 million (after expenses and estimated current and deferred taxes), or $42.62 per share, associated with the $3 billion in cash received by Pennzoil from Texaco Inc. ("Texaco") in April 1988 in settlement of all litigation between Pennzoil and Texaco arising out of Texaco's acquisition of Getty Oil Company.
>
> *Debenture Redemption-*
>
> Net income for 1988 reflects an extraordinary gain of $6.9 million (net of tax effect of $3.5 million), or $.18 per share, associated with the early redemption of $200 million of Pennzoil's 14% and 14 5/8% debentures on February 1, 1988.

The first of these items, a $1.656 million gain resulting from the settlement of a lawsuit with Texaco, Inc., seems to warrant the use of the term "extraordinary" for the amount involved, if nothing else. In a much publicized case, Pennzoil sued Texaco for interfering with its plans to acquire Getty Oil Company. After Pennzoil's claim was upheld in court and Texaco was ordered to pay more than $10 billion to Pennzoil, Texaco agreed to a cash settlement of $3 billion.[9] After legal fees and income taxes, the net gain amounted to the reported $1.656 million.

---

[9] "Texaco and Pennzoil Face New Challenges after Reaching a $3 Billion Settlement," *The Wall Street Journal* (December 21, 1987), p. 1.

When reading the description of the second item, the $6.9 million gain from the early redemption of bonds, the adjective "extraordinary" does not readily leap to mind. While redemption of long-term bonds before maturity is perhaps not the kind of transaction that occurs regularly, any faithful reader of the financial press will have observed transactions of this type often enough to make the use of the "extraordinary item" description apparently inappropriate. It seems that some rather non-extraordinary events and transactions are nonetheless treated as extraordinary items in the firm's financial statements.

It is clear that the $3 billion legal settlement from Texaco meets the APB Opinion No. 30 definition of extraordinary: It is both infrequent and unusual. While the gain on debt redemption is neither infrequent nor unusual, another authoritative pronouncement, FASB Statement No. 4, specifies that material gains or losses of this type be treated as extraordinary items. As we shall see in Chapter 13, before the FASB issued this pronouncement, some firms elected to not even report gains and losses of this type separately on their income statements, particularly if the amounts involved were gains. This practice made it difficult to distinguish between ordinary (and presumably continuing) operating income and nonrecurring debt extinguishment. With these items prominently reported as extraordinary items, such potentially misleading financial statements are no longer possible.

It will be useful to compare and contrast extraordinary items with the unusual items reported in Pennzoil's Note (9) to its financial statements.

(9) Unusual Items-

Provisions for Losses and Gains On Disposition and Write-Downs of Assets-

During the quarter ended June 30, 1988, Pennzoil's management and board of directors completed a strategic review of Pennzoil. As a result of this review, write-downs of certain assets and other charges were provided for, which Pennzoil considered appropriate to reflect permanent impairment of recorded values and other identified liabilities. The following is a summary of the write-downs and other charges provided in 1988 (in millions):

Impairments and Abandonments	$387
Write-down of Refinery Assets	115
Gain on Disposition of Oil and Gas Properties	(59)
Other Write-downs and Charges	46
	$489

The "impairments and abandonments" refer to oil and gas properties that were written down below original cost because the firm decided they "could not be economically drilled and developed given applicable lease expiration dates and anticipated future oil and gas prices." Refinery assets were written down due to "continuing operating losses and increasing difficulty in maintaining access to economical supplies of high-quality crude oil." These unusual items, then, represent the results of management decisions to dispose of and write down the values of certain productive assets. To the uninitiated, these items might seem more deserving of the extraordinary item caption than the early debt redemption described earlier.

While somewhat out of the ordinary, these unusual items do not meet the definition of extraordinary items. Given the volatile economic environment in the oil and gas business in the 1980s, write-offs of this type were relatively commonplace. Thus, under GAAP they must be presented in the continuing operations section of the income statement on a before-tax basis.

Reporting the Effects of Accounting Changes

APB Opinion No. 20 specifies how various types of accounting changes are treated in financial statements.[10] Opinion No. 20 identifies three types of accounting changes. First, as we shall see throughout this text, firms have choices available under GAAP in a number of areas. For instance, as shown in Chapter 5, firms may recognize revenue on long-term, construction-type contracts under either the completed contract or percentage of completion methods. In Chapter 8, we will show how firms may use various cost flow assumptions such as first-in, first-out (FIFO) or last-in, first-out (LIFO) in valuing their inventories. In Chapter 11, we will show that a number of depreciation methods are generally acceptable. A change in accounting principle "results from adoption of a generally accepted accounting principle different from the one used previously for reporting purposes."[11] Second, many of the amounts reported in financial statements are based on certain estimates. For instance, depreciation expense is based on an estimate of the assets' useful lives and their residual values at the end of those useful lives. As new information becomes available, some of these accounting estimates may need to be revised, resulting in a change in accounting estimate. Finally, a change in the reporting entity occurs when combined or consolidated statements are prepared for previously separate entities or vice versa.

Conceptually, accounting changes can be made on either a prospective basis or a retroactive basis. When a change is made on a prospective basis, the new principle, estimate, or reporting entity is used from the date of the change forward. No adjustments are made for amounts previously reported. When a change is made on a retroactive basis, the financial statements are made to appear as if the new principle, estimate, or reporting entity had always been in use. Retroactive changes can be effected in one of two ways:

1. By restating prior period financial statements
2. By means of a cumulative adjustment in the year of the change

Specific treatment is specified for each of the three types of accounting changes.

Changes in Accounting Principle   A change in accounting principle is difficult to reconcile with the basic accounting principle of consistency. In fact, APB Opinion No. 20 states that "in the preparation of financial statements,

[10] "Accounting Changes," *Accounting Principles Board Opinion No. 20* (New York: AICPA, 1971).

[11] *Ibid.*, para. 7.

there is a presumption that an accounting principle once adopted should not be changed in accounting for events and transactions of a similar type."[12] This presumption "may be overcome only if the enterprise justifies the use of an alternative acceptable accounting principle on the basis that it is preferable."[13] To report changes in accounting principle in a forthright manner and to avoid any misunderstanding or loss of confidence that might result from restating prior period financial statements, changes in accounting principle are generally handled on a retroactive basis by means of a cumulative adjustment on the income statement in the year of the change.

Consider a simple example to illustrate the appropriate way of reporting a change in accounting principle. Anderson Co. acquired a single piece of machinery on January 1, 1992, at a cost of $500,000. The firm has been depreciating the asset using an accelerated depreciation method (discussed more fully in Chapter 11) over an estimated useful life of five years. The asset is expected to have a value of $50,000 at the end of its five-year useful life. Effective January 1, 1994, the firm has decided to switch to straight-line depreciation. Their justification for the change is that most of the other firms in its industry use straight-line depreciation.

Since this change must be handled on a retroactive basis, we must compare the depreciation expense actually reported the past two years on an accelerated basis with the amounts that would have been reported on a straight-line basis. Without getting into the specifics of the calculations, suppose depreciation expense under the two methods would be as follows:

Year	Accelerated	Straight-line	Difference
1992	$200,000	$ 90,000	$110,000
1993	120,000	90,000	30,000
Total	$320,000	$180,000	$140,000

As you can see from this comparison, under the old accelerated depreciation method, the balance in accumulated depreciation is $140,000 greater than it would have been if the new straight-line method had been used. Thus, to make the change on a retroactive basis as required, the following journal entry would be made (ignoring tax effects):

On the date of the change in accounting principle:
Accumulated depreciation (machinery)   140,000
   Cumulative effect of accounting change   140,000
To record the cumulative effect of accounting change
  from straight-line to accelerated depreciation.

The cumulative effect of accounting change can be thought of as the effect of the change on the beginning retained earnings balance, and it must be reported on Anderson Co.'s 1994 income statement. Moreover, depreciation

---

[12] *Ibid.*, para. 15.

[13] *Ibid.*, para. 16.

expense for 1994 would be computed on the straight-line basis and would amount to $90,000 for this piece of machinery.

The change reported by Prairie Hardware Corp. is of this type. Notice how its income statement shows the cumulative effect of an accounting change. The accounting change section of its income statement is reproduced below. This presentation implies that a change in principle has occurred and has been handled on a retroactive basis.

Cumulative effect of accounting change, net of income tax effects of $3,248	6,902

If prior years' income statements had been included in comparative form, they would have to be presented as originally reported—i.e., using the old method. Moreover, the following disclosures are required:[14]

1. The effect of adopting the new accounting principle on income before extraordinary items and on net income (and on the related per share amounts) of the period must be shown.
2. Income before extraordinary items and net income computed on a pro forma basis shall be shown on the face of the income statement for all periods presented as if the newly adopted accounting principle had been applied during all periods.

The *pro forma* amounts are intended to provide the financial statement reader with income amounts computed consistently under the new method, something the income statement itself does not provide.

There are several exceptions to the general rule of reporting changes in accounting principle. In certain cases, it may not be possible to determine the cumulative effect of a change in principle. A change to the LIFO inventory method, discussed more fully in Chapter 8, is the prime example of this situation. In such cases, the change is handled prospectively with the ending balances from last period under the old method becoming the beginning balances for the current period under LIFO.

In several instances, handling a particular change in accounting principle by means of a cumulative adjustment in the year of the change might result in an adjustment of such magnitude that financial statement readers could be misled. Therefore, the following changes must be handled retroactively by means of restatements of prior period financial statements:

1. A change from the LIFO method of inventory pricing to another method
2. A change in the method of accounting for long-term, construction-type contracts
3. A change to or from the full cost method of accounting that is used in the extractive industries

As an example of such a change, consider Pennzoil's 1988 accounting change, as described below:

---

[14] *Ibid.*, para. 19.

Effective June 30, 1988, Pennzoil changed its method of accounting for oil and gas operations from the full cost method to the successful efforts method. Pennzoil's management concluded that the successful efforts method more appropriately reflects the mature nature of Pennzoil's oil and gas operations and enables investors and others to better compare Pennzoil to similar oil and gas companies, the majority of which follow the successful efforts method.

As of December 31, 1987, retained earnings were reduced by $301,584,000 as a result of the accounting change.

The cumulative effect of this change, reducing retained earnings by nearly $302 million, was so large that including this amount as an adjustment on the face of the income statement would likely mislead readers. The full cost and successful efforts methods referred to in Pennzoil's report are discussed in Chapter 11.

As we review particular areas in which there are alternatives available under GAAP and, hence, where the potential for accounting changes exists, we will discuss and illustrate accounting changes throughout the text in more detail.

Changes in Estimate   Changes in estimate are much more common than changes in principle. Estimates are prevalent in financial statements, and changes in estimates may be regularly necessary. The accounting profession was concerned about how the public's confidence in financial statements could be affected if retroactive treatment for changes in estimates were required. Frequent changes in estimate requiring either cumulative adjustment or restatement of prior period financial statements would surely cause confusion and perhaps suspicion among financial statement readers. Therefore, the APB decided to specify prospective treatment for changes in estimates. Thus, the new estimate is used from the date of change forward, and no adjustments or restatements of prior period financial statements are made.

Suppose that Anderson Co. changed the estimate of the residual value of its machinery from $50,000 to $20,000 at the same time it changed from accelerated to straight-line depreciation. Immediately after the change to straight-line depreciation, the balance in accumulated depreciation represents two years' of depreciation expense calculated on the straight-line basis based on a five-year estimated useful life and a $50,000 residual value. This leaves a net book value of $320,000.

Asset's cost	$500,000
Accumulated depreciation	180,000
Net book value	$320,000

Moreover, the asset's remaining useful life is three years. The change in the estimate of the asset's residual value to $20,000 will be handled on a prospective basis, which implies that $300,000 of the asset's cost remains to be depreciated.

Net book value	$320,000
Estimated residual value	20,000
Cost to be depreciated	$300,000

Using a straight-line depreciation calculation over a remaining useful life of three years, depreciation expense of $100,000 per year will be recorded in the usual way.

As we review particular areas that require estimates and, hence, where the potential for changes in estimates exists, we will discuss and illustrate changes in estimate in more detail.

Changes in Entity   The final type of accounting change is the change in reporting entity. Such a change will occur, for instance, as a result of certain business combinations. Whenever a change in reporting entity occurs, APB Opinion No. 20 requires that financial statements of all prior periods presented be restated "in order to show financial information for the new reporting entity for all periods."[15]

Summary of Accounting Changes   The APB's decision to handle different types of accounting changes in different ways represents its attempt to meet these conflicting objectives of:

1. Presenting comparative statements in a consistent manner
2. Avoiding the likely loss of public confidence resulting from frequent restatement of prior period financial statements

The objective of consistent presentation of comparative statements is sacrificed somewhat when changes in accounting principle are handled by means of a cumulative adjustment on the income statement in the year of the change. This is done to make sure that financial statement readers will not overlook the fact that a change has been made. Moreover, the loss of consistency is overcome somewhat by the requirement to include pro forma amounts. Consistency is also sacrificed when changes in estimate are handled prospectively. However, given the relative frequency of changes in accounting estimate, the board decided that a loss of public confidence in financial statements was likely if restatement of prior period financial statements was required for all such changes. Changes in reporting entity probably occur relatively infrequently for most firms and, therefore, restatements are less likely to undermine public confidence in the financial statements.

THE BALANCE SHEET

A **balance sheet** describes the firm's financial position at the close of business on a particular day. Balance sheets are also known as *statements of financial*

---

[15] *Ibid.*, para. 34.

position or occasionally as *statements of financial condition*. The format of the balance sheet, unlike that of the income statement, has received very little attention from accounting policy makers.

The balance sheet summarizes the amounts of a firm's various types of assets and the amounts of the various claims against those assets, namely, the firm's liabilities and owners' equity. A firm's financial position on a particular day is the result of all relevant events and transactions to date in the firm's history. Therefore, a balance sheet can be viewed as a cumulative financial record of the firm's activities.

Comparative balance sheets show balances at two or more points in time to permit comparison of the firm's financial position over time. Comparative balance sheets for Prairie Hardware Corp. as of December 31, 1993 and 1994 are provided in Exhibit 3.4.

Before providing more thorough discussions of assets, liabilities, and owners' equity, let us consider the relationship among them. The relationship between assets, liabilities, and owners' equity is known as the **fundamental accounting identity**, which holds that:

$$\text{Assets} = \text{Liabilities} + \text{Owners' Equity}$$

If a firm's balance sheet is presented with its assets on the left and its liabilities and owners' equity on the right, the two sides of the balance sheet correspond to the two sides of the fundamental accounting identity. The two sides of the equation (and the two sides of the balance sheet) are simply two ways of describing the firm's financial position.

Assets are the economic resources of the firm—things the firm has acquired in past transactions that will benefit the firm in the future. Thus, when we look at the assets listed on a firm's balance sheet, we observe the types of things in which management has invested to operate the business. As seen in Exhibit 3.4, management of Prairie Hardware Corp. has invested primarily in property, plant, and equipment with lesser amounts invested in current assets and intangibles and other assets.

How were the resources obtained to make these investments? That information is provided by the liabilities and stockholders' equity section of the balance sheet. For accounting purposes, the individuals and firms who provide financial resources to a firm are classified as either creditors or owners. **Liabilities** are a firm's obligations to its creditors and, therefore, represent the creditors' claims on the firm's assets. For the most part, these obligations are the results of contracts between the firm and its creditors or of statutory or judicial law. Creditors (and the firm's obligations to them) include employees and suppliers who have provided the firm with goods and services but who have not yet been paid in full, taxing authorities who have not yet been paid in full, and lenders who have loaned funds to a firm but who have not yet been repaid.

Owners' equity represents the owners' claims on the assets of the firm. Owners provide financial resources to a firm in two ways:

EXHIBIT 3.4
Prairie Hardware
Corp. Balance Sheet

PRAIRIE HARDWARE CORP.
BALANCE SHEET
(000s)

	DECEMBER 31	
ASSETS:	1994	1993
Cash and marketable securities	$ 6,542	$ 4,215
Accounts receivable, net of allowances	25,175	21,442
Inventories	14,777	13,626
Prepaid expenses	1,549	1,002
Other current assets	748	223
Total current assets	48,791	40,508
Property and equipment, at cost	207,373	165,423
Less: Accumulated depreciation	24,896	34,127
Net property, plant, and equipment	182,477	131,296
Intangibles and other assets	16,550	17,845
TOTAL	$247,818	$189,649

LIABILITIES AND STOCKHOLDERS' EQUITY:		
Notes payable	$ 10,005	$ 5,423
Current portion of long-term debt	12,421	10,228
Accounts payable	20,229	18,992
Taxes payable	4,591	4,320
Accrued expenses	2,674	2,548
Other current liabilities	3,216	2,981
Total current liabilities	53,136	44,492
Long-term debt, less current maturities	103,027	84,557
Common stock, 200,000 shares authorized, 37,525 and 30,025 shares issued and outstanding at December 31, 1994 and December 31, 1993, respectively	37,525	30,025
Additional paid-in capital	42,055	27,055
Retained earnings	12,075	3,520
Total stockholders' equity	91,655	60,600
TOTAL	$247,818	$189,649

1. By contributing capital—e.g., in the case of a corporation, by buying shares of stock offered by the firm
2. By not withdrawing all of the increase in the firm's net assets, which have resulted from its profitable operations—i.e., by allowing earnings of the firm to be retained and reinvested in the firm

Strictly speaking, a firm does not have a legally binding obligation to pay its owners the amount of their equity in the firm. The owners' claim is a residual one. That is, in general, distributions of a firm's assets to its owners are only permitted by law if the distributions will not impair the claims of the creditors. We can highlight the residual nature of the owners' interest in the firm by rearranging the fundamental accounting identity as follows:

$$\text{Owners' Equity} = \text{Assets} - \text{Liabilities}$$

This form of the identity shows that owners' equity is equal to the firm's net assets (assets minus liabilities). Although this relationship must hold, do not assume it implies that owners' equity is "the amount of a firm's assets that would be left over after all liabilities had been paid." There are two things wrong with such a statement. First, the book values assigned to assets and liabilities are based on the premise of a going concern and do not represent liquidation values. Second, the statement implies that the values assigned to assets and liabilities in turn determine the amount of owners' equity. This is only partially true. As we shall see more clearly in Chapters 4 and 5, in some cases the values assigned to components of owners' equity—i.e., revenues and expenses—determine the values of certain assets and liabilities, not the other way around.

Let us take a closer look at the component parts of a firm's balance sheet and, in the process, examine the balance sheet of Prairie Hardware Corp.

Assets

As we have seen, assets are, very simply, things a firm has that are expected to produce future benefits to the firm. However, not all things that have future benefits are viewed as assets. Moreover, once we identify things that meet the accounting criteria for assets, we will discuss how these assets are valued. Finally, we will discuss the typical ways assets are classified in balance sheets.

Recognition Issues   Before a firm is entitled to describe something as an asset in its financial statements, or "recognize" it, all three of the following criteria must be met:[16]

1. It must be expected to provide future benefits to the firm by being sold, used, or converted to cash.
2. It must have been acquired in a transaction that is essentially complete.
3. The firm must have the ability to control how it is used and to limit access to it.

It is not difficult to see how the items listed as assets on the Prairie Hardware Corp. balance sheet meet these criteria. A company's cash, amounts owed to it by its customers, its inventory, and productive facilities all clearly meet the accountants' definition of assets. But other items that meet Criterion 1 and are often referred to as assets in everyday conversation apparently do not. Consider the following examples.

A company's management might be tempted to recognize as an asset the extraordinary customer loyalty and goodwill they have earned through the years by paying careful attention to customers' needs. While such an item may

---

[16] *Statement of Financial Accounting Concepts No. 6, op. cit.* para. 26.

well produce some future benefits to the company, it was not acquired in a transaction and would be very difficult to value. Since such an item does not meet Criterion 2, it would not be shown as an asset on the firm's balance sheet. Goodwill purchased in an arm's-length transaction in connection with a business combination would be properly shown as an asset, however, since all criteria are met.

Employees are often described as assets of a firm but rarely appear on balance sheets. For instance, in the 1984 annual report of Eastern Airlines, the company's chairman, Frank Borman, wrote, "The Company's most important asset is the people who are Eastern." However, an examination of the assets included in Eastern's balance sheet in the same annual report did not reveal an item called "The people who are Eastern." Why not? Criterion 3 is clearly not met because firms are unable to exert sufficient control over their employees to list them as assets on their balance sheets. This was especially true in the case of Eastern Airlines, which went bankrupt in large part due to some difficult relationships with its employees' labor unions.

Valuation Issues   For the purpose of discussing how assets are valued on firms' balance sheets, we need to distinguish between monetary and nonmonetary assets. Monetary assets are those consisting of cash or the right to receive cash in the future—i.e., notes and accounts receivable. Monetary assets are typically valued at their **net realizable values**—i.e., the amount of cash they represent. Money has a time value. That is, the right to receive $1,000 in cash at a future date is worth less than $1,000 cash on hand today. The longer the firm will have to wait to receive the cash, the less it is worth today. If the cash is expected to be collected within one year or less, the reduction in time value is not significant and is usually ignored for financial reporting purposes. Therefore, notes and accounts receivable due within one year are valued at the amount expected to be collected, while those due after one year are valued at the present value of the amount expected to be collected.

Nonmonetary assets include such things as a firm's inventories, land, buildings, equipment, patents, and trademarks. The valuation of these assets is based on their historical or acquisition cost. Acquisition cost includes the full cost of acquiring an asset and making it ready for use. In some cases, GAAP require nonmonetary assets be valued at acquisition cost or market value, whichever is lower. In the case of assets with finite useful lives lasting longer than one accounting period, the acquisition cost of the asset is systematically recognized as expense using the process of depreciation or amortization. Land has an infinite life and, therefore, is not subject to depreciation or amortization.

The use of acquisition cost in the valuation of nonmonetary assets is based primarily on the principle of **objectivity**—amounts reported in the financial statements should be subject to independent verification—and the modifying convention of **conservatism**—understatement of assets and income is preferred to overstatement. Since an asset's acquisition cost has already been incurred in an arm's-length transaction, it is observable and there can be little disagreement about it. This is particularly important to auditors who independently review and report on the value of a firm's assets. Moreover, in periods of inflation such as those faced by most economies in recent history, use of acquisition cost will tend to value assets at amounts less than their current values. This increases the likelihood that asset values and income will not be overstated, consistent with the notion of conservatism in financial statements. One must question, however, whether we sacrifice the relevance of the information to decision makers in the name of objectivity.

Classification Issues   The balance sheet of Prairie Hardware Corp. shows three asset classifications:

1. Current assets
2. Property, plant, and equipment
3. Intangibles and other assets

Such a classification scheme is fairly typical. However, not all firms prepare classified balance sheets. For instance, it is standard practice in the banking industry to simply list the assets of the institution (which, of course, are predominantly monetary items) without distinguishing between current and noncurrent assets. Moreover, in some industries, the balance sheet classifications are ordered differently. Utilities, for instance, because of their very capital-intensive nature will typically list property, plant, and equipment first. We will examine the essential characteristics of the assets in the most common classifications.

> **Current assets:** The current asset classification "includes cash and other assets that are reasonably expected to be realized in cash or sold or consumed during the normal operating cycle of the business."[17] A firm's **operating cycle** can be thought of as the average period of time required for acquisition of inventory (if any), sale of goods or services to customers, collection of cash from customers, and payment of cash to suppliers. If, as is typical for most firms, the operating cycle is less than one year in length, then a one-year period is used in place of a normal operating cycle to define current assets.

A look at the Prairie Hardware Corp. balance sheet indicates the kinds of assets typically classified as current assets: cash and marketable securities, receivables, inventories, and prepaid expenses, along with the ubiquitous "other" category.

> **Property, plant, and equipment:** Property, plant, and equipment is by far the largest asset category for Prairie Hardware Corp. Assets included in this classification, also known as *fixed assets*, are typically held for use, rather than for sale, and examples include land, buildings, machinery, equipment, furniture, fixtures, trucks, and automobiles. These assets are typically used in operations over a period of years. Depreciation expense is recorded each accounting period to systematically allocate a portion of

---

[17] "Restatement and Revision of Accounting Research Bulletins," *Accounting Research Bulletin No. 43* (New York: AICPA, 1961), chap. 3A, para. 7.

the cost of these assets (except land) to each period in which they are used. The amount of depreciation recorded to date on the assets still in service is shown on the balance sheet as "accumulated depreciation." Land is deemed to have an infinite useful life and, consequently, no depreciation is recognized.

Investments: An asset classification frequently found on firms' balance sheets but missing on the Prairie Hardware Corp. balance sheet is investments. The investment classification primarily reports the investments with an expected holding period greater than one year (or one operating cycle, if longer than one year) in the securities of other firms—common and preferred stock, notes, and bonds. These should not be confused with the investments in marketable securities already noted in the firm's current assets. The current asset classification of those investments implies an expected holding period that is less than one year or one operating cycle. Some firms are also required by their debt contracts to maintain **sinking funds,** which are separate investment funds established by a debt contract to insure that the necessary funds for the repayment of debt are available as the debt instruments mature. These sinking funds are typically classified in the investments section of the balance sheet.

Intangible assets: Like property, plant, and equipment, intangible assets have useful lives exceeding one accounting period. However, unlike property, plant, and equipment, intangible assets have no tangible substance. Since the possession of tangible substance is not a criterion for asset recognition, intangible assets such as patents, copyrights, trademarks, and goodwill are included on firms' balance sheets. Like fixed assets, intangibles are systematically written off to expense over their useful lives through a process known as amortization. As we see on the Prairie Hardware Corp. balance sheet, there is no requirement, nor is it conventional practice, to report separately the accumulated amortization recorded to date.

Liabilities

As we have seen, accountants regard liabilities as obligations of a firm to its various creditors; and they can, therefore, be viewed as the creditors' claims on the firm's assets. In this section, we examine liabilities in more detail by asking:

1. Are all obligations of a firm shown as liabilities?
2. How are liabilities valued?
3. How are liabilities classified for balance sheet purposes?

Recognition Issues   Just as we observed for assets, accountants impose several criteria in determining which obligations of a firm qualify as liabilities. Obligations are recognized formally as liabilities only if all of the following criteria are met:[18]

---

[18] *Statement of Financial Accounting Concepts No. 6, op. cit.,* para. 36.

1. It must involve a future payment of cash, goods, or services at a well-specified date, upon demand, or upon the occurrence of a particular event.
2. It is unlikely that the obligation can be avoided at the firm's discretion.
3. It must be the result of events or transactions that have already occurred.

It is not difficult to see how the items listed as liabilities on the Prairie Hardware Corp. balance sheet meet these criteria. A company's obligations for notes and accounts payable, long-term debt, taxes payable, and accrued expenses all clearly meet the accountants' definition of liabilities. But other obligations, which are often referred to casually as liabilities, apparently do not. While all liabilities are obligations, not all obligations give rise to liabilities on the financial statements. The following examples illustrate these concepts.

A firm enters into a long-term lease contract to acquire office space in a particular building. The lease term is fixed at ten years and is non-cancelable. A firm enters into a purchase commitment whereby it agrees to purchase some amount of raw material over the next two years from a particular supplier. The contract (usually referred to as a "take or pay" contract) obligates the firm to take some minimum quantity of the raw material from the supplier or pay a prespecified penalty. Would such contracts give rise to liabilities on the firm's financial statements?

These are examples of executory contracts. **Executory contracts** are those that have remaining obligations to be performed by one or more of the parties. The lease contract is executory since the firm has not yet occupied the office space for the lease term. The purchase commitment is executory since the firm has neither taken the minimum quantity nor incurred the penalty. While the question of how to account for executory contracts remains controversial, the general rule that has been followed is that an obligation is only recognized to the extent of performance under the contract to date. Thus, the firm leasing office space would, in most cases, only recognize a liability to the extent that it has already occupied the premises without yet paying for it. However, since most lease contracts call for payment in advance, it is fairly unusual to observe a liability for "rent payable." The firm entering the purchase commitment would only recognize a liability when it has made purchases under the contract or has failed to make the requisite purchases and the penalty is assessed.

Valuation Issues We observed that the valuation of assets depended on whether they were monetary or nonmonetary in nature. The same can be said of liabilities. Most liabilities require that the obligation in question be settled by a cash payment or perhaps by forgoing a cash receipt. These are monetary liabilities and are valued at the present value of the amount to be paid out. Just as we saw for monetary assets, the time value of money is usually ignored when the amount is due to be paid soon. Therefore, liabilities due within one year are typically stated at the amount due to be paid rather than the present value of that amount.

Certain obligations require settlement in goods or services and are known as nonmonetary liabilities. It is conventional practice in many industries to require payment for goods or services in advance of delivery. For instance, a firm that manufactures custom machine tools collects a 25% down payment with each order. An athletic club bills its members each month for the next month's dues. In both of these cases, the firm has an obligation to its customers, which will probably not be settled by a cash payment but rather by providing the goods or services contracted for by the customer. These nonmonetary obligations are typically stated at the amount of cash received.

Classification Issues   Prairie Hardware Corp.'s balance sheet shows two classifications of liabilities: current liabilities and long-term debt. Let us examine the distinguishing characteristics of the various liability classifications.

Current liabilities are defined as that subset of all liabilities "whose liquidation is reasonably expected to require the use of existing resources properly classified as current assets, or the creation of other current liabilities."[19] Typically, any liability due (and expected to be paid) within 12 months (or one operating cycle, if longer than 12 months) is classified as a current liability. The items included in current liabilities for Prairie Hardware Corp. are fairly typical: notes payable due to lenders in the next 12 months; accounts payable, taxes payable, accrued expenses resulting from the operations of the business; that portion of the firm's debt which was originally classified as long-term debt but is now due to be repaid within 12 months; and, of course, any other types of liabilities due within 12 months.

The term **long-term debt** describes the obligations due more than 12 months (or one operating cycle, if longer) from the balance sheet date. These liabilities result from such borrowing transactions as obtaining a term loan from a bank, issuing notes and bonds payable, and borrowing under a mortgage. As discussed in Chapter 17, certain long-term lease obligations are also classified as long-term debt.

Other long-term liabilities: Although Prairie Hardware Corp. does not report any **other long-term liabilities** on its balance sheet, it is not unusual to find such a classification on firms' balance sheets. This section usually includes long-term liabilities other than those resulting from borrowing transactions. For instance, a firm might have a deferred compensation plan for various employees whereby the employees are to be paid in the future for services provided now. Such an obligation would likely be classified as other long-term liabilities.

Owners' Equity

The appearance of the owners' equity section of a firm's balance sheet depends in large part on the form of business organization: proprietorship, partnership, or corporation. For proprietorships and partnerships, it is not unusual to see a single lump sum representing owners' equity, while for a corporation, several components to owners' equity may be listed. Our focus will be on corporations, the predominant organizational form in most industries. Therefore, we will speak most often of stockholders' equity.

---

[19] *Accounting Research Bulletin No. 43, op. cit.*, chap. 3A, para. 7.

Recognition and Classification Issues Owners' equity results from two general types of activities. First, owners' equity will increase whenever one or more of the owners contributes cash or other valuable goods or services to the firm. In the case of a corporation, this type of transaction typically results from an issuance of stock by the firm, and this component of stockholders' equity is typically referred to as *paid-in* or *contributed capital*. Second, stockholders' equity will be affected by the operating performance of the firm coupled with its dividend policy. If a firm is able to increase its net assets as a result of operations—i.e., if the firm is profitable—and does not distribute assets to shareholders in an amount equal to its net income, then the firm's net assets and its stockholders' equity will increase. This component of stockholders' equity is usually referred to as *retained* or *reinvested earnings*.

Paid-in capital is appropriately recognized whenever an owner provides the firm with cash and/or other valuable goods and services. Recognition of retained earnings, of course, requires the recognition of revenues and expenses, a complicated subject covered more fully in Chapters 4 and 5.

Valuation Issues Paid-in capital is typically valued at the fair value of the cash, goods, or services contributed by the owners determined at the date of contribution. For instance, suppose two individuals start a business with one contributing $10,000 in cash and the other a printing press with a fair value of $25,000. This would create paid-in capital of $35,000. In the case of a corporation, total paid-in capital is usually broken down into two components:

1. The par or stated value of the shares issued
2. Any additional amount contributed over and above par or stated value

This latter amount is usually referred to as *additional paid-in capital* or *paid-in capital in excess of par value*. The concept of capital stock's par or stated value is discussed more fully in Chapter 14.

The amount of a firm's retained earnings is the cumulative total of net income and losses earned or incurred in each year of the firm's history less the cumulative total of dividends declared plus or minus any of the relatively few items treated as direct adjustments of retained earnings. Measurement of a firm's income is such a fundamental subject and such a major part of what accountants do that it will occupy parts of nearly every chapter in the text. Dividends can be effected through distributions of cash, stock, or other assets to shareholders and are typically valued at the fair value of whatever the firm distributes.

THE STATEMENT OF OWNERS' EQUITY

Firms are required to present reconciliations of the beginning and ending balances of their paid-in capital and retained earnings. These reconciliations are not required to be included in a single "statement of owners' equity," but that is how they are most often handled. Some acceptable alternatives include:

1. Separate statements of retained earnings and paid-in capital
2. Separate statements of paid-in capital with a statement of retained earnings combined with the income statement
3. Reconciliations included in the notes to financial statements

Prairie Hardware Corp. has taken the most popular route with a combined statement of stockholders' equity as shown in Exhibit 3.5.[20]

All that is required is an explanation of why the owners' equity account balances have changed over the year. The statement, then, is just a summary of the transactions affecting the components of owners' equity. As we can see from the Prairie Hardware Corp. statement, its paid-in capital accounts, common stock and additional paid-in capital, increased as a result of the issuance of an additional 7,500 shares of common stock for an amount that exceeded the par value of the shares. Their retained earnings increased because the firm's net income for 1993 exceeded the amount of cash dividends.

The columnar form of the Prairie Hardware Corp. statement is convenient and widely used. Its only real drawback is that if comparative statements are presented—i.e., statements for more than one year—it is typically necessary to "stack" the statements on top of each other rather than prepare them in parallel columns.

THE CASH FLOW STATEMENT

Since the FASB's issuance of Statement No. 95 in 1987, the cash flow statement is the newest required financial statement. Prior to that time, a statement of changes in financial position, which had similar purposes but was less useful than a cash flow statement, was required.

EXHIBIT 3.5
Prairie Hardware Corp. Statement of Stockholders' Equity

PRAIRIE HARDWARE CORP.
STATEMENT OF STOCKHOLDERS' EQUITY
For the Year Ended December 31, 1994
(000s)

	COMMON STOCK	ADDITIONAL PAID-IN CAPITAL	RETAINED EARNINGS
Balance, December 31, 1993	$30,025	$27,055	$ 3,520
Issuance of 7,500 shares of common stock	7,500	15,000	
Net income			48,440
Cash dividends			(39,885)
Balance, December 31, 1994	$37,525	$42,055	$12,075

[20] Of the 600 firms' financial statements surveyed in *Accounting Trends and Techniques, 1990 ed.*, 456 included a statement of stockholders' equity.

The purpose of a cash flow statement, as espoused by the FASB in a straightforward matter, is:

> The primary purpose of a statement of cash flows is to provide relevant information about the cash receipts and cash payments of an enterprise during a period.[21]

It is hoped that this information, used in conjunction with the rest of the financial statements, will help financial statement users assess a firm's ability to generate positive future net cash flows, to meet its obligations and pay dividends, and to satisfy its need for external financing, among other things.

Statement No. 95 imposes some structure on the format of the cash flow statement. The statement must explain the change in the balance of a firm's cash and its essentially equivalent to cash assets during the period. These **cash equivalents** are very liquid, short-term investments, which are typically made to earn a return on otherwise idle cash balances.

Classification of Cash Flows

A **cash flow statement**, then, is essentially nothing more than a summary of cash receipts and cash expenditures formatted in a particular way. Statement No. 95 requires these receipts and expenditures to be classified as the result of one of three mutually exclusive types of transactions: investing activities, financing activities, and operating activities. To illustrate what is included in these three categories, let us take a look at a cash flow statement prepared by Prairie Hardware Corp. shown in Exhibit 3.6, which is presented in accordance with the provisions of Statement No. 95. As you can see, the cash flow statement for Prairie Hardware Corp. classifies cash receipts and expenditures into three categories: cash flows from operating activities, cash flows from investing activities, and cash flows from financing activities. The essential characteristics of each type of activity are examined below.

Operating Activities   Firms' operating activities can be viewed as those directly involved in providing goods and services to customers. The FASB takes the approach that if activities are neither investing nor financing in nature, then they are, by default, operating activities. As a general rule, "cash flows from operating activities are generally the cash effects of transactions and other events which enter into the determination of net income."[22] The operating cash flows of Prairie Hardware Corp. represent amounts received from customers and amounts paid for various expense items.

Investing Activities   Firms invest in a wide variety of assets, including productive assets such as machinery and equipment, real estate, debt or equity securities, and loans to individuals or other firms. Any cash paid or received

---

[21] "Statement of Cash Flows," *Statement of Financial Accounting Standards No. 95* (Stamford, CT: FASB, 1987), para 4.

[22] *Ibid.,* para. 21.

EXHIBIT 3.6
Prairie Hardware
Corp. Cash Flow
Statement

PRAIRIE HARDWARE CORP.
CASH FLOW STATEMENT
For the Year Ended December 31, 1994
(000s)

CASH FLOWS FROM OPERATING ACTIVITIES:	
Collections from customers	$302,517
Payments for operating expenses	(247,328)
Net cash flows from operating activities	55,189
CASH FLOWS FROM INVESTING ACTIVITIES:	
Proceeds from disposal of plant and equipment	13,938
Purchase property , plant, and equipment	(74,660)
Net cash flows from investing activities	(60,722)
CASH FLOWS FROM FINANCING ACTIVITIES:	
Cash dividends	(39,885)
Issuance of stock	22,500
Increase notes payable	4,582
Increase long-term debt	20,663
Net cash flows from financing activities	7,860
Increase in cash and marketable securities	$ 2,327
Beginning cash and marketable securities	4,215
Ending cash and marketable securities	$ 6,542

in connection with the acquisition or disposal of these investment assets is classified on the cash flow statement as a cash flow from investing activities. Prairie Hardware's investing activities included the following: the purchase of new property, plant, and equipment and the disposal of some old plant and equipment.

Financing Activities   Firms obtain financing from owners and lenders. Any cash paid to or received from owners (including dividends) or paid to or received from lenders in connection with borrowing activity (except interest) is viewed as a financing cash flow. Prairie Hardware's financing activities include the following: cash dividends, issuance of stock, borrowing with notes payable and long-term debt.

Formats of the Cash Flow Statement

FASB Statement No. 95 allows some flexibility in the format of the cash flow statement. Firms may present cash flows from operating activities under either the direct or indirect format. Prairie Hardware Corp. has chosen the direct format. It simply lists the firm's operating cash flows directly. The alternative indirect approach derives net cash flows from operating activities by a series of adjustments to net income. Although firms are "encouraged" to present the net cash flows from operating activities by the direct method, the indirect method is also permitted. Moreover, firms using the direct method are also required to present the indirect derivation in a supporting reconciliation schedule. Therefore, for all intents and purposes, the indirect method is required and the direct method is optional. We present this reconciliation schedule for Prairie Hardware Corp. in Exhibit 3.7.

Perhaps the most controversial part of Statement No. 95's requirements are those provisions dealing with how cash flows from operating activities are to be presented. In fact, based in large part on the rules for presenting operating cash flows, three of the seven FASB members voted against Statement No. 95, leaving only the barest of majorities in favor of the standard.

Under the now superseded APB Opinion No. 19, firms were required to present funds provided or used by operations on their statements of changes in financial position (SCFP) and were permitted to present this in either the direct and indirect formats. While both approaches yield the same total, they do not provide the same level of detail. The direct approach provides information about which transactions generated cash inflows from operating activities ("collections from customers") and which transactions generated cash outflows from operating transactions ("paid for interest," etc.). The reconciliation approach of the indirect method only provides the net inflow or outflow of cash from operating activities. On the other hand, the indirect calculation permits a reconciliation of net operating cash flow with net income, whereas the

EXHIBIT 3.7

Prairie Hardware Corp. Reconciliation of Net Income and Net Operating Cash Flows

PRAIRIE HARDWARE CORP. RECONCILIATION OF NET INCOME AND NET OPERATING CASH FLOWS For the Year Ended December 31, 1994 (000s)		
Net income		$48,440
Adjustments to reconcile net income to net operating cash flows:		
Depreciation	6,275	
Amortization	1,295	
Loss on disposal, before taxes	8,628	
Extraordinary loss, before taxes	4,788	
Cumulative effect of accounting change, before taxes	(10,150)	
Increase in accounts receivable	(3,733)	
Increase in inventories	(1,151)	
Increase in prepaid expenses	(547)	
Increase in other current assets	(525)	
Increase in accounts payable	1,237	
Increase in taxes payable	271	
Increase in accrued expenses	126	
Increase in other current liabilities	235	6,749
Net operating cash flows		$55,189

direct method does not. The indirect approach has traditionally been (and still is) more widely followed and led to SCFPs that were less informative than they might have been since they lacked the detailed information about operating cash inflows and outflows.

The prevalence of the indirect method in connection with the old statements of changes in financial position has led to much confusion. For instance, notice how depreciation is added to net income on Prairie Hardware's reconciliation schedule (Exhibit 3.7). The indirect presentation leads many users of financial statements to conclude that depreciation is a "source of funds" since it is a positive quantity on the statement. For instance, consider the following quote from the business press:

> Cash flow will fatten whenever capital spending—a main user of cash—decreases and depreciation—a big cash booster—increases.[23]

Of course, depreciation is not a source of funds at all. When depreciation is recorded as an expense, no cash is received. Rather, depreciation is readded on the reconciliation because it is an expense that was subtracted to derive net income but one that required no funds in the same period. Because this confusion existed over the indirect method, many (including three members of the Board) hoped the FASB would require the direct method.

Instead, the FASB opted for its compromise position: The direct method is preferable but, if used in the cash flow statement, the indirect method must also be included in the form of the reconciliation of net income to net cash flow provided by operating activities, as shown in Exhibit 3.7. The fact that firms can (and most do) present their operating cash flows by the indirect method means that some financial statement readers are probably still confused by what the calculation shows.

What does Prairie Hardware's cash flow statement (Exhibit 3.6) tell us? From the comparative balance sheets in Exhibit 3.4, we observe that Prairie Hardware's cash balance increased by $2,327,000. Why? The statement of cash flow tells us the following: The firm was able to increase its cash balance by $55,189,000 as the result of operating events and transactions. An additional $7,860,000 was obtained from the various financing activities such as the increase in common stock and several borrowing transactions, net of dividend payments. This was sufficient to allow for net cash outflows for investment purposes of $60,722,000 with $2,327,000 "left over" to increase the cash balance. Thus, the statement reveals the nature of the transactions contributing to the change in Prairie Hardware Corp.'s cash balance.

FINANCIAL STATEMENT INTERRELATIONSHIPS

Before concluding our overview of the financial statements, it is important to note the interrelationships among them. Too often students regard them as largely independent. This is certainly not the case. As shown in Exhibit 3.8, the

---

[23] Leah J. Nathans, "Why 'Cash Flow' Might Still Be Magic Word," *Business Week* (December 25, 1989), p. 114.

EXHIBIT 3.8
Financial Statement
Interrelationships for
Prairie Hardware
Corp.—1994

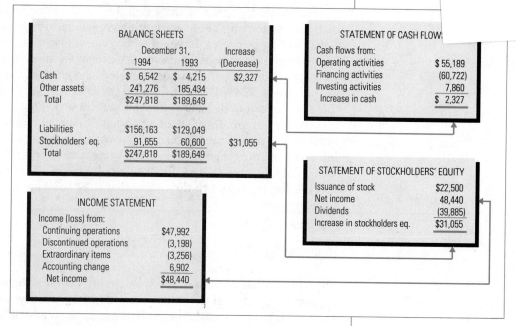

cash flow statement, the statement of stockholders' equity, and the income statement all provide detailed explanations for the changes in particular amounts reported on the balance sheets. Using the terminology of economists, the amounts reported on a balance sheet are stock variables, while the amounts reported on the cash flow statements, stockholders' equity, and income are all flow variables. A **stock variable** (e.g., the amount of inventory on hand at the balance sheet date) describes some quantity at a point in time. A **flow variable** (e.g., the cost of goods sold during a period) describes changes in some quantity over a period of time. The stock variables on a firm's balance sheet are measured in terms of dollars at a point in time, while the flow variables on the other statements are measured in terms of dollars per period.

Obviously, if the statements of income, stockholders' equity, and cash flows are to explain changes in the balance sheet, then the statements cannot be independent. For instance, any decision that affects amounts reported on the income statement will clearly affect the statement of stockholders' equity and the balance sheet. If a firm is trying to choose between straight-line depreciation and some other method, it must understand that (ignoring tax effects) the choice will affect the amount of depreciation expense reported on the firm's income statement, the net income reported on the income statement and statement of stockholders' equity, and the stockholders' equity and net property, plant, and equipment reported on the firm's balance sheet. Likewise, if a firm is trying to choose between valuing its inventory at average cost or FIFO cost, it must understand that (again, ignoring tax effects) the choice will affect the inventory and stockholders' equity balances reported on the balance sheet, the cost of goods sold and net income reported on the income statement, and the net income reported on the statement of stockholders' equity.

Notice that neither of the examples cited above had any impact on the cash flow statement. These accounting choices, which are made only for financial reporting purposes, have no cash consequences. However, some accounting choices may also be made for tax purposes. In such cases, some indirect cash consequences will occur as a result of the effect of the choice on the firm's tax payments. We will be considering the effects of accounting choices such as these in considerable detail throughout the text. Please note, however, that intermediate accounting is concerned with financial reporting issues governed by GAAP. The tax law specifies its own accounting rules; and, in general, firms are not obligated to follow the same accounting rules on their financial statements that are followed on their tax returns. Therefore, we will only be considering tax issues to the extent that they have an impact on firms' financial statements.

SUMMARY

This chapter has examined the principal financial statements—balance sheet, income statement, statement of stockholders' equity, and cash flow statement—the information conveyed by each, their format, and interrelationships.

The income statement reports the results of a firm's operations over a particular period in terms of revenues, expenses, gains, and losses. Net income and the income statement may be broken down into as many as four parts: income (or loss) from continuing operations, income (or loss) from discontinued operations, extraordinary items, and the cumulative effects of changes in accounting principles.

The rules for reporting special items on firms' income statements are designed to make the income statements more useful by highlighting unusual and nonrecurring items. If financial statement readers use reported income amounts to forecast future amounts, then the special item reporting rules make it less likely that nonrecurring items will be used in making such projections. These very detailed rules governing the format of the income statement underscore the perceived importance of the amount of net income firms report.

On the disposal of a segment of their business, firms will separately report the results of discontinued operations. Two amounts are typically reported for discontinued operations: the income (or loss) from operations of the discontinued segment and the gain (or loss) on disposal. Both amounts are reported net of tax effects.

Gains and/or losses resulting from transactions that are both infrequent and unusual will be reported as extraordinary items, net of taxes. Accounting changes are of three types: changes in principle, changes in estimate, and changes in entity. Only the cumulative effects of certain changes in accounting principle are reported on the firms' income statements on a net of tax basis.

The balance sheet describes the firm's financial position at the close of business on a particular day in terms of its assets and the claims against those assets, namely liabilities and stockholders' equity. Assets and liabilities are commonly classified as current and noncurrent. Stockholders' equity is commonly broken down into amounts paid-in or contributed by owners and retained earnings.

The statement of stockholders' equity explains why the balances in the stockholders' equity accounts changed over the course of the period. Either a single statement or multiple statements to accomplish this purpose are acceptable.

The cash flow statement reports the cash transactions of the firm in three mutually exclusive classifications: cash flows from operating activities, cash flows from investing activities, and cash flows from financing activities. In addition, any noncash financing and investing activities must be reported.

Financial statements are interrelated. The balance sheet describes the firm at a point in time, while the statements of income, stockholders' equity, and cash flows describe changes over time. Therefore, the statements of income, stockholders' equity, and cash flows explain, in part, why various balances shown on the balance sheet have changed over time.

QUESTIONS

1. Explain the difference between the *all-inclusive* and the *current operating performance* approaches to income statements.

2. Briefly explain the purpose of an income statement.

3. Explain the difference between *single-step* and *multiple-step* income statements.

4. The following terms are related to accounting for discontinued operations. Define them.

   (a) Measurement date

   (b) Disposal date

   (c) Segment

   (AICPA adapted)

5. A discontinued operations section of an income statement typically reports two amounts. What are they? Briefly describe what is included in each.

6. A financial statement reader is confused. During 1994, Discontinuous Technologies, Inc. (DTI) disposed of its desktop nuclear reactor business. When comparing the 1993 amounts reported in the income statement included in the 1994 annual report with the 1993 amounts reported in the 1993 annual report, he notices numerous differences in the reported revenues and expenses although the net income amounts agree. Explain how these discrepancies occurred.

7. Explain how *intraperiod tax allocation* applies to the reporting of special items.

8. Why is a separate section reporting the results of discontinued operations required?

9. APB Opinion No. 20 identifies three types of accounting changes. Identify them and briefly explain the required method of reporting them.

10. Explain how (1) an accounting change from the LIFO inventory method to the FIFO method, (2) an accounting change from the FIFO inventory method to the LIFO method, and (3) an accounting change from the FIFO inventory method to the average cost method would be handled. Why are these handled differently?

11. Why are changes in accounting estimates not handled in the same manner as changes in accounting principle?

12. How are changes in accounting principle required by the issuance of new FASB pronouncements handled?

13. What are the two criteria for classifying a gain (or loss) as an *extraordinary item*? Why are some items that do not meet these criteria—e.g., gains (or losses) from the early extinguishment of debt—still classified as extraordinary items?

14. Which of the following items would be classified as extraordinary items?

    (a) Write-down or write-off receivables, inventory, equipment leased to others, or intangible assets

    (b) Gains or losses from exchange or translation of foreign currencies, including those relating to major devaluations and revaluations

    (c) Gains or losses on disposal of a segment of a business

    (d) Other gains and losses from sale or abandonment of property, plant, or equipment used in the business

    (e) Effects of a strike, including those against competitors and major suppliers

    (f) Adjustment of accruals on long-term contracts.

15. What is the *fundamental accounting identity*? Explain why it must always hold.

16. Define the following terms:

    (a) *Asset*

    (b) *Liability*

    (c) *Owners' equity*

17. What conditions are necessary before assets are recognized in a firm's financial statements?

18. Distinguish between monetary and nonmonetary assets and explain how assets of each type are valued in a firm's financial statements.

19. Define the term *operating cycle* and explain how it is used in determining how to classify a firm's assets.

20. What conditions are necessary before liabilities are recognized in a firm's financial statements?

21. Explain what an *executory contract* is and how, in general, it is recognized in a firm's financial statements.

22. Distinguish between monetary and nonmonetary liabilities and explain how liabilities of each type are valued in a firm's financial statements.

23. Distinguish between paid-in capital and retained earnings.

24. Determine how each of the following items would be classified on a firm's cash flow statement. Use these identifiers: (i) an operating activity, (ii) an investing activity, or (iii) a financing activity.

    _____ (a) Cash paid for dividends

    _____ (b) Cash borrowed from the bank

    _____ (c) Cash collected from customers

    _____ (d) Cash paid to sales employees

____ (e) Cash paid to acquire new equipment

____ (f) Cash paid to suppliers of inventory

____ (g) Cash received from sale of common stock

25. Explain how, if at all, the choice of a method of calculating depreciation will affect amounts reported on a firm's

(a) Balance sheet

(b) Income statement

(c) Statement of owners' equity

(d) Cash flow statement

EXERCISES

3-1. *Discontinued operations*

The board of directors of River Research Corp. met on October 1, 1994, and approved the sale of the firm's computer software division to Carp Computing Corp., effective immediately. No previous plan of disposal had ever been discussed or approved. The sales price agreed to was $2,300,000, and the net assets of the computer software division had a net book value of $2,000,000. The division reported year-to-date revenues of $550,000 and expenses (other than income taxes) of $650,000 in 1994. Assume an income tax rate of 40% applies in all cases.

REQUIRED:

Prepare the discontinued operations section of River Research Corp.'s income statement for the year ended December 31, 1994, in good form.

3-2. *Change in estimate*

Effective January 1, 1994, Mountain Mfg. Corp. revised the estimate of the useful life and residual value of a piece of machinery used in its operations. The machine, acquired on January 1, 1992, at a cost of $400,000, has been depreciated on the straight-line basis. The estimates of the asset's useful life and residual value are as follows:

	Original Estimate	Revised Estimate
Useful life	10 years	12 years
Residual value	$20,000	$34,000

REQUIRED:

Prepare an original and revised depreciation schedule showing depreciation expense and ending net book value for each year of the asset's useful life. Ignoring income tax effects, how will this change affect income for 1994?

3-3. *Change in principle*

Old Fashioned, Inc. has been recognizing bad debt expense by the direct write-off method. That is, bad debt expense has been recognized whenever an account is written off as uncollectible. Effective January 1, 1994, the firm has decided to change to the allowance method and recognize bad debt expense on an estimated basis in the amount of 2% of net sales. Of the accounts receivable balance of $345,000 outstanding at January 1, 1994, management estimates that $8,400 will prove to be uncollectible. The following activity occurred in 1994:

Sales on account	$3,642,000
Collections on account	3,583,000
Accounts written off	68,000

REQUIRED:

1. Calculate the amount of bad debt expense to be reported for the year ended December 31, 1994.
2. Calculate the amount of the cumulative effect of the accounting change to be reported on the 1994 income statement, assuming a 40% income tax rate applies. Be sure to indicate whether the cumulative effect of the accounting change would increase or decrease net income.
3. Calculate the total effect of this accounting change on reported net income for 1994.

3-4. *Extraordinary items*

For each of the following items, indicate whether it should properly be reported as an extraordinary item and briefly explain why.

1. On September 23, 1994, American Realty Co. suffered a $1,500,000 casualty loss when one of its buildings was badly damaged in a flood. The building is located in an area that has seen severe flooding three times in the past 20 years.
2. On January 17, 1994, Marigold Marketing Co. experienced a $1,250,000 gain on the early redemption of its outstanding bonds.
3. On July 14, 1994, Robertson Robotics Corp. wrote down its inventory by $605,000 because its market value had fallen below cost by that amount.
4. On December 3, 1994, Carolina Canning Co. was assessed an additional $1.3 million in income taxes by the Internal Revenue Service after an audit of the firm's income tax returns for the years 1989-1992.
5. On March 8, 1994, Elite Electronics Co., a manufacturer of stereo headphones, was ordered by the Superior Court of California to pay $1,500,000 to the estate of a customer who had been electrocuted while using one of the firm's products. This is the only product liability judgment against the company in its 28-year history.

3-5. *Discontinued operations*

In the years ended December 31, 1994 and 1993, Florida Fresh Fruit Co. reported the following amounts:

	1994	1993
Revenues	$120,000	$105,000
Operating expenses	95,000	85,000
Income before taxes	25,000	20,000
Income tax expense	10,000	8,000
Net income	$ 15,000	$ 12,000

These amounts include the results of operation of the firm's Freshly Squeezed Juice (FSJ) division, which was sold on November 15, 1994. The sale of the division produced a loss (before tax) of $1,250, which is not included above. The decision to sell the division had been made at the June 30, 1994 meeting of the board of directors. The results of operation for the FSJ division were as follows:

	7/1 – 11/15/94	1/1 – 6/30/94	1/1 – 12/31/93
Revenues	$ 6,500	$14,000	$23,000
Operating expenses	8,900	16,800	24,200
Loss before taxes	(2,400)	(2,800)	(1,200)
Income tax benefit	960	1,120	480
Net loss	$ (1,440)	$ (1,680)	$ (720)

REQUIRED:

Prepare a comparative 1994/1993 income statement, suitable for inclusion in the firm's 1994 annual report, in accordance with APB Opinion No. 30.

3-6. *Extraordinary item*

Fort Worth Foundry, Inc. has prepared the following income statement for the year ended December 31, 1994:

Sales	$1,400,500
Cost of goods sold	1,050,200
Selling, general, administrative expense	250,100
Income before taxes	100,200
Income taxes	40,080
Net income	$ 60,120

The firm's independent public accountant has advised that a $28,000 litigation loss, included in "Selling, general, and administrative expense," meets the criteria for an extraordinary item. Assume that an income tax rate of 40% applies to all items on the income statement.

REQUIRED:

Prepare an income statement, in good form, with the litigation loss classified as an extraordinary item.

3-7. *Change in estimate*

Twin Cities Temporaries, Inc. has been recognizing bad debt expense by the allowance method in an amount equal to 2% of sales. In connection with the audit of the firm's 1993 financial statements, the firm's independent public accountant has analyzed the firm's allowance for bad debts and has determined that the balance is $14,000 less than necessary and that the firm's collection experience in recent years has been that approximately 3% of net sales ultimately prove to be uncollectible.

REQUIRED:

Explain how this situation should be dealt with in the firm's 1993 and 1994 income statements.

3-8. *Change in principle*

After using the straight-line depreciation method since its inception on January 1, 1991, Trendy Computer Corp. has decided, effective January 1, 1994, to adopt an accelerated depreciation method. This method will more closely approximate the actual decline in value of its productive equipment. The firm has calculated depreciation using both methods each year, with the following results:

	Straight-line	Accelerated
1991	$125,000	$175,000
1992	245,000	315,000
1993	320,000	445,000

REQUIRED:

Explain how this change will be handled in the firm's 1994 income statement. Assume a 40% income tax rate applies to Trendy Computer Corp.

3-9. *Discontinued operations*

The four firms discussed below have all decided to dispose of a segment of their businesses in 1994, but none has completed the disposal by year-end.

REQUIRED:

For each firm, determine the amounts that would be reported in the discontinued operations section of the firm's income statement for (1) operating income or loss and (2) disposal gain or loss. All amounts shown are net of income taxes.

	Firm A	Firm B	Firm C	Firm D
Operating income (loss) from start of year to the measurement date	$ 20,000	$(45,000)	$100,000	$75,000
Operating income (loss) from measurement date to year-end	(12,500)	(26,000)	14,300	6,500
Gains (losses) realized from sale of assets prior to year-end	15,000	(14,000)	(27,500)	7,500
Estimated operating income (loss) after year-end	(16,000)	(13,200)	(11,500)	(3,200)
Estimated gains (losses) from sale of assets after year-end	48,000	(64,000)	35,000	(25,300)

3-10. *Asset recognition*

Determine whether each of the following items would be recognized as an asset and, if so, at what amount it would be reported on the firm's balance sheet.
1. A building, with a book value of $250,000, is appraised at a market value of $350,000.
2. The firm's investment bankers estimate that the firm, as a going concern, is worth $1,000,000 more than the book value of the firm's net assets.
3. The firm has received an offer to purchase a parcel of undeveloped real estate that it owns for a price of $2,500,000. The land was acquired ten years ago at a cost of $750,000. The firm has no plans to sell the land at this time.
4. The firm acquires a patent at a cost of $250,000 on a product it has developed. The firm estimates that the market value of this patent is $5,000,000.

3-11. *Balance sheets*

The following assets, liabilities, and owners' equity items are listed in alphabetical order:

Accounts payable	$ 37,850
Accounts receivable	24,500
Accrued expenses	1,450
Accumulated depreciation	116,250
Buildings	270,450
Cash	10,000

Common stock	157,500
Equipment	221,100
Intangibles	15,500
Inventories	52,500
Investments, noncurrent	105,200
Land	125,000
Long-term debt	275,000
Notes payable, current	115,000
Prepaid expenses	750
Retained earnings	121,950

REQUIRED:

Prepare a classified balance sheet in good form.

3-12. *Liability recognition*

Determine whether each of the following items would be recognized as a liability and, if so, at what amount it would be reported on the firm's balance sheet.

1. The firm has been sued by a customer for damages of $1,500,000 incurred while using the firm's products. The suit has just been filed, and the firm's legal counsel is unable to assess the likelihood of any obligation.
2. The firm has received $25,000 from a customer as an advance payment for services that have yet to be delivered.
3. The firm has purchased merchandise on account from a supplier in the amount of $27,400 due in 30 days.
4. The firm has borrowed $10,000 at 10% interest, agreeing to pay $11,000 in one year.

3-13. *Income statements*

The following revenues, expenses, gains, and losses are listed in alphabetical order:

Cost of goods sold	$ 72,490
Extraordinary casualty loss, net	6,402
Gain on sale of investments	5,180
General and administrative expenses	16,550
Income taxes	2,575
Sales	145,250
Sales commissions	16,805
Wage expense	31,292

REQUIRED:

Prepare an income statement in good form.

3-14. *Cash flow statements*

The following cash flows are listed in alphabetical order:

Cash dividends paid	$ 20,400
Collections from customers	275,409
Income taxes paid	13,921
Interest paid	6,420

Long-term debt retired	35,900
Paid to employees and suppliers	161,255
Purchase of equipment	74,260
Purchase of investments	16,950
Proceeds from sale of land	25,500

REQUIRED:

Identify each of these cash flows as an operating, investing, or financing activity and prepare a cash flow statement in good form.

3-15. *Statement of stockholders' equity*

Tucker Technology Co. reported the following balances in stockholders' equity at December 31, 1993:

Common stock, $5 par value	$125,000
Additional paid-in capital	375,000
Retained earnings	450,000
Total stockholders' equity	$950,000

During 1994, the following events and transactions affecting these balances occurred:
(a) The firm sold 5,000 shares of common stock for $25 per share.
(b) Net income of $139,000 was earned for the year.
(c) Cash dividends of $114,000 were declared and paid.

REQUIRED:

Prepare a statement of stockholders' equity in good form for the year ended December 31, 1994.

PROBLEMS

3-1. *Discontinued operations*

Boston Boat Works Co. decided on December 31, 1994 to dispose of its recreational boat division and concentrate on the manufacture of commercial vessels. This decision qualifies as the disposal of a segment under APB Opinion No. 30. Revenues and expenses for 1994 and 1993 are as follows:

	(000s)	
	1994	1993
Sales	$250,000	$220,000
Expenses:		
Cost of goods sold	150,000	130,000
Other operating expenses	45,000	38,000
Income taxes	18,000	17,000

Management expects to sell the recreational boat division within six months at an estimated loss of $6,500,000, net of taxes. Operations during the phasing-out period are expected to produce a loss of $1,500,000, net of taxes. These expected losses have not yet been recorded. Revenues and expenses of the recreational boat division included in the above amounts are as follows:

	(000s)	
	1994	1993
Sales	$80,000	$75,000
Expenses:		
Cost of goods sold	56,000	53,000
Other operating expenses	12,000	11,000
Income taxes	4,000	3,500

REQUIRED:

Prepare comparative income statements for 1994 and 1993 in good form according to APB Opinion No. 30.

3-2. *Discontinued operations*

On September 20, 1994, the board of directors of General Technology Co. voted to adopt a plan for disposing of the firm's Genetic Engineering Laboratory Division (GELD) through a sale of the division as an operating unit no later than June 1, 1995. The fiscal year-end for General Technology Co. is December 31. The revenues and expenses of General Technology Co. (including GELD) for the years ended December 31, 1994 and 1993 are as follows:

	(000s)	
	1994	1993
Sales	$295,452	$272,895
Expenses:		
Cost of goods sold	189,089	169,176
Selling and administrative	46,291	45,911
Interest	4,588	4,329
Other	12,891	241
Income taxes	13,630	17,036
Total expenses	$266,489	$236,693

The revenues and expenses of GELD alone for the years ended December 31, 1994 and 1993 are as follows:

	(000s)	
	1994	1993
Sales	$59,090	$57,308
Expenses:		
Cost of goods sold	39,709	38,910
Selling and administrative	10,184	11,478
Interest	1,055	1,082
Other	7,256	111
Income taxes	284	1,833
Total expenses	$58,488	$53,414

The 1994 revenues and expenses for GELD include the results of operations from September 20 through December 31, the estimated results of operations for the rest of the phasing-out period, and the estimate loss from ultimate sale of the division. Here is a break-down of the 1994 revenues and expenses for GELD:

	(000s)		
	1/1 - 9/19	9/20 - 12/31	Disposal*
Sales	$ 44,318	$ 14,772	
Expenses:			
Cost of goods sold	29,385	10,324	
Selling and administrative	7,740	2,444	
Interest	781	274	
Other	100	33	$ 7,123
Income taxes	2,020	543	(2,279)
Total expenses	$ 40,026	$ 13,618	$ 4,844

*Includes the estimated results of operations for the remainder of the phasing-out period

REQUIRED:

Prepare comparative income statements for General Technology Co. for 1994 and 1993 showing the results of discontinued operations in good form.

3-3.   *Extraordinary items*

QRC, Inc. experienced the following events and transactions during 1994. For each one, discuss whether treatment as an extraordinary item is appropriate.

1. QRC restructured its operations during 1994 at a pre-tax cost of $2,500,000. These costs consist of employee severance costs and write-offs of obsolete inventory and plant and equipment. This is the first restructuring in the firm's history.
2. The firm sold its long-term investment in Alphatronics, Inc. at a pre-tax gain of $500,000. This is the only long-term investment the firm has ever held, and it is unlikely that any other long-term investments will be made in the next five years.
3. A strike at a major supplier required QRC to shut down one of its assembly lines for six weeks during the year at a pre-tax cost of $2,250,000.
4. The firm refinanced some of its long-term bonds and experienced a pre-tax gain of $700,000.

3-4.   *Extraordinary item; accounting change*

Houston Oil Works, Inc. prepared the following income statement for the year ended December 31, 1994 (amounts in $000s).

Sales	$2,450,000
Cost of goods sold	1,875,000
Gross profit	$ 575,000
Selling and administrative expense	245,000
Other expenses	295,000
Income before taxes	35,000
Income taxes	14,000
Net income	$ 21,000

Additional information:

1. Depreciation expense of $725,000,000, calculated on a straight-line basis, is included in "Cost of goods sold." In prior years, depreciation was calculated on an accelerated basis. At December 31, 1993, the balance in accumulated depreciation reported by the firm was $4,575,000,000. If the firm had been using straight-line depreciation all along, the balance in accumulated depreciation would have been $3,880,000,000.
2. An extraordinary loss of $210,000,000 is included in "Other expenses." This loss resulted from damage caused by a tidal wave to one of the firm's offshore drilling platforms in the Gulf of Mexico.
3. Income taxes at 40% apply to all items.

REQUIRED:

Prepare a revised income statement for the firm in accordance with generally accepted accounting principles.

3-5. *Accounting changes*

Effective January 1, 1994, Union Carbon Corp. changed from an accelerated depreciation method to the straight-line method and revised its estimate of the useful life of its manufacturing plant. The plant was acquired on January 1, 1989, at a cost of $4,750,000, and the original estimate of its useful life was 25 years. It was estimated to have a salvage value of $250,000. Effective January 1, 1994, the plant's total useful life is estimated to be 30 years.

The following amounts have been recognized to date as depreciation expense under the accelerated depreciation method formerly in use:

1989	$380,000
1990	349,600
1991	321,632
1992	295,901
1993	272,229

REQUIRED:

Assume a 40% income tax rate. Calculate the following amounts that would be reported in the firm's income statement for the year ended December 31, 1994.

1. The cumulative effect of the accounting change
2. Depreciation expense for 1994

3-6. *Financial statement interrelationships: cash basis vs. accrual basis*

The following information is available for B&C Industries, Inc.

Balance Sheet
December 31, 1994

Cash	$ 10,000	Payables	$ 40,000
Receivables	40,000	Stockholders' equity	120,000
Inventory	60,000		
Plant & equipment	50,000	Total liabilities &	
Total assets	$160,000	stockholders' equity	$160,000

Income Statement
For the Year Ended December 31, 1994

Sales		$400,000
Cost of goods sold:		
Inventory, January 1	$ 65,000	
Purchases	235,000	
Goods available for sale	300,000	
Inventory, December 31	60,000	240,000
Gross profit		160,000
Depreciation expense		5,000
Other operating expenses		135,000
Net income		$ 20,000

Cash Flow Statement
For the Year Ended December 31, 1994

Cash flows from operating activities:	
Collections from customers	$ 380,000
Payments on accounts payable	(375,000)
Net cash flows from operations	5,000
Cash flows from investing activities:	
Purchase of plant and equipment	(11,000)
Cash flows from financing activities:	
Dividends	(18,000)
Change in cash balance	$ (24,000)

REQUIRED:

Prepare a balance sheet as of December 31, 1993.

3-7. *Financial statement interrelationships: cash basis vs. accrual basis*

The following information for Morgan Corp. is available:

MORGAN CORP.
Balance Sheet

	December 31, 1994	December 31, 1993
Cash	$ 100	$ 150
Accounts receivable	650	540
Merchandise inventory	800	720
Prepaid rent	145	155
Property, plant, and equipment	1,500	1,800
Total assets	$3,195	$3,365
Accounts payable	$ 225	$ 255
Wages payable	110	145
Interest payable	60	65
Notes payable	500	400
Paid-in capital	1,000	800
Retained earnings	1,300	1,700
Total liabilities & equity	$3,195	$3,365

MORGAN CORP.
Cash Flow Statement
For the Year Ended December 31, 1994

Cash flows from operating activities:	
Collections from customers	$ 4,200
Payments to suppliers	(2,400)
Payments to employees	(1,200)
Payments for rent	(500)
Payments for interest	(75)
Net cash flows from operations	$ 25
Cash flows from financing activities:	
Bank borrowings	$ 250
Paid in by owners	200
Bank borrowings repaid	(150)
Cash dividends paid	(375)
Net cash flows from financing activities	(75)
Net change in cash balance	$ (50)

REQUIRED:

Prepare an income statement for the year ended December 31, 1994.

3-8.   *Balance sheet and income statement*

The following alphabetical listing of accounts and balances is taken from the adjusted trial balance of Ryan Motors, Inc. as of December 31, 1994:

Accounts payable	$ 8,403
Accounts receivable	14,872
Accrued expenses	255
Accrued interest receivable	80
Accumulated depreciation	4,542
Additional paid-in capital	8,795
Advertising expense	1,743
Allowance for doubtful accounts	726
Bad debt expense	431
Cash	1,245
Common stock	5,600
Cost of goods sold	154,245
Customer deposits	500
Depreciation expense	1,275
Furniture and fixtures	14,838
Income tax expense	55
Income taxes payable	55
Insurance expense	480
Interest expense	2,395
Interest revenue	80
Inventories	23,144
Notes payable—banks	5,200
Notes payable—long-term	12,240
Notes receivable	2,400
Other expenses	436
Prepaid expenses	300
Rent expense	12,480
Retained earnings	10,471
Salary expense—administration	16,203
Salary expense—sales	23,197
Sales revenue	213,824
Travel and entertainment expense	872

REQUIRED:

Prepare a balance sheet as of December 31, 1994 and an income statement for the year then ended in good form.

3-9. *Cash flow statement*

The following summary of cash receipts and expenditures is provided by Ajax Corp.:

AJAX CORP.
Summary of Cash Receipts and Expenditures
For the Year Ended December 31, 1994
(000s omitted)

Cash receipts:	
Collections from customers	$23,370
Proceeds from short-term borrowing	250
Proceeds from sale of fixed assets	875
Total cash receipts	$24,495
Cash expenditures:	
Paid to purchase fixed assets	2,000
Paid for interest	90
Paid to retire short-term notes payable	100
Paid for cash dividends	600
Paid to suppliers	15,090
Paid to employees	5,390
Paid for taxes	1,000
Paid to retire long-term debt	75
Total cash expenditures	24,345
Increase in cash balance	$ 150

REQUIRED:

Prepare a cash flow statement in good form for Ajax Corp. for the year ended December 31, 1994.

3-10. *Statement of stockholders' equity*

Thompson Enterprises, Inc. reports the following information:

From the firm's cash flow statement:

Cash flows from financing activities:	
Proceeds from sale of stock	$ 34,500,000
Cash dividends paid	(4,250,000)
Funds used to retire long-term debt	(24,700,000)
Net cash flows from financing activities	$ 5,550,000

From the firm's balance sheet:

	12/31/94	12/31/93
Stockholders' equity:		
Common stock, $1 par	$ 19,000,000	$ 17,850,000
Additional paid-in capital	395,000,000	361,650,000
Retained earnings	276,500,000	245,900,000
Total	$690,500,000	$625,400,000

REQUIRED:

Prepare a statement of stockholders' equity in good form for the year ended December 31, 1994.

3-11. *Cash flow statement*

Superior Products Corp. reports the following cash receipts and disbursements for the year ended December 31, 1994:

Acquire patents	$ (1,394)
Acquire property, plant, and equipment	(8,094)
Cash dividends	(5,899)
Collections from customers	111,973
Investments	(1,219)
Payments to suppliers and employees	(100,471)
Payments for interest	(2,950)
Payments for taxes	(293)
Purchase treasury stock	(119)
Repay long-term debt	(2,463)
Repay notes payable	(505)
Sale of Davenport facility	11,868
Increase in cash balance	$ 434

REQUIRED:

Identify each of these cash flows as an operating, investing, or financing activity and prepare a cash flow statement in good form.

3-12. *Balance sheet and income statement*

The following is an alphabetical listing of the accounts of Marvin Hardware Co. and their balances as of December 31, 1994:

Accounts payable	$ 17,621
Accounts receivable	34,092
Accrued expenses	1,005
Accrued interest receivable	133
Accumulated depreciation	12,376
Additional paid-in capital	16,451
Advertising expense	4,095
Allowance for doubtful accounts	1,065
Bad debt expense	1,282
Cash	458

Common stock	$ 17,773
Cost of goods sold	63,692
Depreciation expense	4,810
Furniture and fixtures	37,451
Income tax expense	1,245
Income taxes payable	136
Insurance expense	3,562
Interest expense	2,710
Interest revenue	133
Inventories	29,463
Notes payable—banks	5,000
Notes payable—long-term	17,250
Notes receivable	1,475
Other expenses	245
Prepaid expenses	713
Rent expense	12,671
Retained earnings	11,510
Salary expense	23,791
Sales revenue	128,158
Travel and entertainment expense	6,590

REQUIRED:

Prepare a balance sheet as of December 31, 1994 and an income statement for the year then ended for Marvin Hardware Co.

3-13. *Financial statement interrelationships*

Arnold Aviation, Inc. reports the following amounts:

ARNOLD AVIATION, INC.
Balance Sheet
December 31, 1993
($000s)

Cash	$ 4,525	Notes payable	$ 5,500
Accounts receivable	26,083	Accounts payable	15,672
Inventories	38,711	Accrued expenses	2,609
Total current assets	69,319	Total current liab.	23,781
Plant and equipment	24,056	Long-term debt	30,023
Less: Accum. depr.	(7,307)		
Net plant and equip.	16,749	Common stock	40,512
		Retained earnings	3,833
Investments	12,081	Total stockholders' eq.	44,345
		TOTAL LIABILITIES	
TOTAL ASSETS	$98,149	AND EQUITY	$98,149

ARNOLD AVIATION, INC.
Income Statement
Year Ended December 31, 1994
($000s)

Sales revenue		$ 125,903
Cost of goods sold*	$(87,894)	
General and administrative expense	(32,012)	
Depreciation expense	(1,357)	
Interest expense	(3,011)	
Loss on plant abandonment	(1,459)	(125,733)
Income before nonrecurring gain		170
Gain on sale of investments		2,840
Net income		$ 3,010

*Cost of goods sold is calculated as follows:

Beginning inventory	$ 38,711
Purchases	90,106
Ending inventory	(40,923)
Cost of goods sold	$ 87,894

ARNOLD AVIATION, INC.
Statement of Stockholders' Equity
Year Ended December 31, 1994
($000s)

	Common Stock	Retained Earnings
Balance, December 31, 1993	$40,512	$ 3,833
Net income		3,010
Cash dividends		(2,867)
Balance, December 31, 1994	$40,512	$ 3,976

ARNOLD AVIATION, INC.
Cash Flow Statement
Year Ended December 31, 1994
($000s)

Cash flows from operating activities:	
Collections from customers	$121,873
Payments to supplies of inventory	(90,593)
Payments for general and administrative expense	(31,805)
Payments for interest	(3,011)
Net cash flows from operating activities	(3,536)
Cash flows from investing activities:	
Proceeds from sale of investment	14,921
Purchase plant and equipment	(3,140)
Net cash flows from investing activities	11,781
Cash flows from financing activities:	
Cash dividends	(2,867)
Retire notes payable	(1,000)
Retire long-term debt	(5,000)
Net cash flows from financing activities	(8,867)
Net decrease in cash balance	$ (622)

REQUIRED:

Prepare a balance sheet for Arnold Aviation, Inc. as of December 31, 1994.

3-14. *Financial statement interrelationships*

Gordon Manufacturing Co. has provided the following financial statements: a balance sheet as of December 31, 1993; and statements of income, stockholders' equity, and cash flows for the year ended December 31, 1994.

GORDON MANUFACTURING CO.
Balance Sheet
December 31, 1993
($000s)

Cash	$ 6,084		Notes payable	$ 15,200
Accounts receivable	49,026		Accounts payable	28,749
Inventories	55,922		Accrued wages	2,744
Prepaid insurance	2,032		Taxes payable	4,979
Total current assets	113,064		Total current liab.	51,672
Plant and equipment	69,200		Long-term debt	47,592
Accum. depr.	(20,436)			
Net plant and equip.	48,764		Common stock	20,455
			Add. paid-in capital	40,105
Investments	12,944		Retained earnings	29,611
Intang. assets, net	14,663		Total stock. equity	90,171
			Total Liabilities	
Total Assets	$189,435		and Equity	$189,435

GORDON MANUFACTURING CO.
Statement of Stockholders' Equity
Year Ended December 31, 1994
($000s)

	Common Stock	Additional Paid-In Capital	Retained Earnings
Balance, December 31, 1993	$20,455	$40,105	$29,611
Net income			16,963
Dividends			(10,197)
Sale of stock	5,495	10,139	
Balance, December 31, 1994	$25,950	$50,244	$36,377

GORDON MANUFACTURING CO.
Statement of Income
Year Ended December 31, 1994
($000s)

Sales revenue		$ 307,985
Cost of goods sold		(184,209)
Gross profit		123,776
Wage expense	$(74,509)	
Depreciation expense	(6,549)	
Insurance expense	(6,055)	
Amortization of intangibles	(1,718)	
Income tax expense	(10,402)	
Loss on sale of investment	(1,490)	
Interest expense	(7,655)	
Gain on sale of plant	815	$(107,563)
Income before extraordinary item		16,213
Extraordinary item:		
Gain on early debt retirement		750
Net income		$ 16,963

GORDON MANUFACTURING CO.
Cash Flow Statement
Year Ended December 31, 1994
($000s)

Cash flows from operating activities:	
Collections from customers	$ 303,928
Payments for inventory purchases	(183,791)
Payments for insurance	(6,998)
Payments for wages	(74,598)
Payments for taxes	(10,280)
Payments for interest	(7,655)
Net cash flows from operating activities	20,606
Cash flows from investing activities:	
Sale of investments	6,250
Sale of plant	2,535
Acquisition of plant and equipment	(11,661)
Net cash flows from investing activities	(2,876)
Cash flows from financing activities:	
Long-term debt retired	(6,750)
Dividends paid	(10,197)
Repay notes payable	(15,200)
Issuance of stock	15,634
Net cash flows from financing activities	(16,513)
Change in cash balance	$ 1,217

Note 1: Cost of goods sold is determined as follows:

Beginning inventory	$ 55,922
Purchases	185,744
Ending inventory	(57,457)
Cost of goods sold	$ 184,209

Note 2: The gain on the sale of plant is computed as follows:

Proceeds on sale		$2,535
Cost	6,299	
Less: Accumulated depreciation	(4,579)	1,720
Gain		$ 815

REQUIRED:

Prepare a balance sheet for Gordon Manufacturing Co. as of December 31, 1994.

CASE 3.1

SUPER RITE FOODS, INC.

Note: This case is based on the 1988 annual report of Super Rite Foods, Inc. Certain amounts have been reclassified in the restated financial statements provided below. In particular, the restated cash flow statement presents cash flows from operating activities in the direct format, whereas the original statement presented it in the more common indirect format. These restatements involve the authors' assumptions, which may or may not correspond to actual events and transactions of the company. They have been made only for computational convenience and to permit the use of these financial statements in a case study.

SUPER RITE FOODS, INC.
Balance Sheet
February 27, 1988
($000s)

Cash	$ 3,329
Receivables	10,035
Inventories	45,439
Total current assets	58,803
Property, plant, equipment	60,957
Accumulated depreciation	(17,362)
Property, plant, equipment, net	43,595
Other assets (principally intangibles)	12,195
Total Assets	$114,593
Notes payable	$ 9,000
Accounts payable	28,598
Current portion of long-term debt	7,895
Accrued expenses	3,995
Income taxes payable	445
Total current liabilities	49,933
Deferred income taxes	4,414
Long-term debt	22,876
Common stock	252
Capital surplus	9,443
Retained earnings	27,675
Shareholders' equity	37,370
Total Liabilities and Equity	$114,593

SUPER RITE FOODS, INC.
Income Statement
For the Year Ended March 4, 1989
($000s)

Net sales	$756,576
Cost of goods sold	641,683
Selling, general, administrative expense	99,456
Interest expense	2,985
Income before tax	12,452
Provision for income taxes	5,042
Net income	$ 7,410

SUPER RITE FOODS, INC.
Statement of Cash Flows
For the Year Ended March 4, 1989
($000s)

Cash flow provided by operating activities:	
Collections from customers	$ 751,846
Payments for inventory purchases	(637,227)
Payments for selling, general, admin. expense	(88,320)
Payments for interest	(2,985)
Payments for income taxes	(4,015)
Net cash provided by operations	19,299
Cash flow provided by investing activities:	
Purchase property, plant, equipment	(8,017)
Sell property, plant, equipment	765
Net cash used by investing activities	(7,252)
Cash flow provided by financing activities:	
Equity financing	87
Decrease in borrowing	(10,388)
Dividends	(1,210)
Net cash used by financing activities	(11,511)
Net change in cash	536
Cash at year start	3,329
Cash at year-end	$ 3,865

Additional information:

a. "Selling, general, and administrative expense" includes depreciation expense of $5,594 and amortization of intangibles of $2,049.

b. The provision for income taxes includes the following amounts:

Taxes currently due	$4,712
Deferred taxes	330
Total	$5,042

REQUIRED:

Prepare a balance sheet as of March 4, 1989. **Note:** Given the limited information provided, it will *not* be possible to prepare a balance sheet with as much detail as the February 27, 1988 balance sheet provided.

CASE 3.2

NATIONAL GYPSUM COMPANY

The following is an excerpt from the notes to financial statements included in the 1988 annual report of National Gypsum Co.

Discontinued Operation

On August 16, 1988, the Company entered into a definitive agreement under which Armstrong World Industries, Inc. ("Armstrong") would purchase all the outstanding shares of capital stock of American Olean, a wholly-owned subsidiary of the Company.

On October 3, 1988, the Company completed the sale of American Olean to Armstrong for approximately $328 million, net of related sale expenses. Taking 1989 expenses into consideration, after-tax proceeds are expected to be approximately $240.3 million.

The following is a summary of the amounts shown on the Consolidated Statements of Operations as earnings and loss from the discontinued operation (000s):

	Year Ended December 31, 1988	Year Ended December 31, 1987
Net sales	$163,111	$ 207,329
Earnings before taxes	$ 6,178	$ 10,522
Income tax (expense) benefit	(3,198)	(5,018)
Loss on disposal, including applicable income tax expense of $6,031	(63,990)	—
Post-measurement loss from operations, less applicable income tax benefit of $1,267	(1,935)	—
Earnings (loss) from discontinued operation	$ (62,945)	$ 5,504

During the fourth quarter of 1988, the Company decreased the original September 30, 1988 estimated loss on disposal by $12.9 million, net of related tax effect, primarily due to final settlements with the purchaser and an in-depth review and quantification of remaining liabilities.

The post-measurement loss from operations increased by $2.6 million during the fourth quarter of 1988 primarily due to final closing adjustments.

REQUIRED:

Prepare a suitable discontinued operations section for inclusion in the firm's 1988 income statement, showing the income or loss from operations and the gain or loss on disposal of the segment, in accordance with APB Opinion No. 30.

CROWLEY MILNER & CO.

CASE 3.3

The following excerpts have been taken from the 1988 annual report of Crowley Milner & Co.

Industry Description

The Company is engaged in the operation of retail department stores in the Detroit-metropolitan and suburban Flint, Michigan areas. In addition to its own merchandise, it offers certain goods and services through leased departments. The Company began reporting on a 52/53 week fiscal year commencing with the year ended January 30, 1988.

Restructuring

During the fiscal year ended January 30, 1988, the Company recorded a restructuring charge of $2,298,000, which increased the net loss by $1,241,000 or $2.44 per share. The charge consists of costs related to closing the Grand River store, sale of the Fashion Distribution Center, the write off of obsolete point of sale equipment, and a reduction in the remaining estimated useful lives of store fixtures.

REQUIRED:

Based on the limited information provided here, discuss the following questions:
1. Does the restructuring described above qualify as the disposal of a segment?
2. Does the restructuring described above qualify as an extraordinary item?
3. Does the reduction in the remaining estimated useful lives of store fixtures qualify as a change in accounting estimate? How would this affect the restructuring charge?
4. How would you present the restructuring charge on the firm's income statement? Justify your answer.

PENNZOIL COMPANY

PENNZOIL COMPANY
Consolidated Statement of Income
(Dollar amounts expressed in thousands except per share amounts)

	Year Ended December 31,		
	1988	1987	1986
Revenues			
Net sales	$2,088,412	$1,786,498	$1,782,177
Other income, net	185,488	49,804	139,046
	2,273,900	1,836,302	1,921,223
Costs and Expenses			
Cost of sales	1,341,896	1,109,570	1,001,658
Selling, gen. and admin. exp.	295,311	219,551	228,762
Depr., depletion and amort.	203,046	201,897	227,375
Exploration expenses	76,415	64,671	144,858
Taxes, other than income	38,703	36,396	52,166
Provisions for losses and gains on disposition and write-downs of assets (Note 9)	489,300	—	—
Interest charges	150,508	157,759	165,303
Interest capitalized	(23,619)	(38,957)	(37,274)
Income (Loss) Before Income Tax, Equity in Proven Properties Inc. and Extraordinary Items	(297,660)	85,415	138,375
Income tax (benefit)	(123,999)	24,812	39,393
Equity (loss) in net income of Proven Properties Inc.	(13,299)	(15,089)	(76,312)
Income (Loss) Before Extraordinary Items	(186,960)	45,514	22,670
Extraordinary Items (Note 8)	1,662,402	—	(23,098)
Net Income (Loss)	$1,475,442	$ 45,514	$ (428)
Preference common stock dividends	$ 15,690	$ 15,690	$ 15,690
Earnings (Loss) Available for Common Stock	$1,459,752	$ 29,824	$ (16,118)
Earnings (Loss) per Share			
Before extraordinary items	$ (5.22)	$ .72	$ .17
Extraordinary items	42.80	—	(.56)
Total	$37.58	$ .72	$ (.39)
Dividends per Common Share	$ 2.60	$2.20	$2.20

Information from the notes to the 1988 Pennzoil annual report:

1. Effective June 30, 1988, Pennzoil changed its method of accounting for oil and gas operations from the full cost method to the successful efforts method. Pennzoil's management concluded that the successful efforts method more appropriately reflects the mature nature of Pennzoil's oil and gas operations and enables investors and others to better compare Pennzoil to similar oil and gas companies, the majority of which follow the successful efforts method.

As of December 31, 1987, retained earnings were reduced by $301,584,000 as a result of the accounting change.

(8) Extraordinary Items-

Settlement-

Net income for 1988 reflects an extraordinary gain of $1,656 million (after expenses and estimated current and deferred taxes), or $42.62 per share, associated with the $3 billion in cash received by Pennzoil from Texaco Inc. ("Texaco") in April 1988 in settlement of all litigation between Pennzoil and Texaco arising out of Texaco's acquisition of Getty Oil Company.

Debenture Redemption-

Net income for 1988 reflects an extraordinary gain of $6.9 million (net of tax effect of $3.5 million), or $.18 per share, associated with the early redemption of $200 million of Pennzoil's 14% and 14 5/8% debentures on February 1, 1988.

(9) Unusual Items-

Provisions for Losses and Gains on Disposition and Write-Downs of Assets

During the quarter ended June 30, 1988, Pennzoil's management and board of directors completed a strategic review of Pennzoil. As a result of this review, write-downs of certain assets and other charges were provided for, which Pennzoil considered appropriate to reflect permanent impairment of recorded values and other identified liabilities. The following is a summary of the write-downs and other charges provided in 1988 (in millions):

Impairments and Abandonments	$ 387
Write-down of Refinery Assets	115
Gain on Disposition of Oil and Gas Properties	(59)
Other Write-downs and Charges	46
	$ 489

REQUIRED:

Financial analysts and other users of financial statements frequently calculate the amount of a firm's income that is based on normal, recurring events and transactions. From the information above taken from the 1988 annual report of Pennzoil Company, calculate the amount of the firm's 1988 net income based on normal, recurring events and transactions.

PART 2

Revenue and Expense Recognition

CHAPTER 4

Revenue and Expense Recognition Related to Delivery of Goods and Services

The accounting profession frequently faces some of the most controversial issues in matters of revenue and expense recognition. For example, the Financial Accounting Standards Board (FASB) recently dealt with such issues as how to recognize revenue on the sale of extended product warranties, how and when to recognize income tax expense, and when to recognize the cost of employee retirement benefits as an expense. Many, if not most, of the accounting issues requiring SEC enforcement activity involve questions of revenue and expense recognition.[1]

As we have seen, revenues represent amounts received and/or receivable for goods and services provided to customers. Expenses represent the costs of providing those goods and services. One reason why revenue and expense recognition is such a complicated issue is the diversity of types and forms of business operations. Firms earn revenue by providing a wide variety of goods and services to their customers under the terms of many types of contracts. A retailer such as J.C. Penney generates revenue by making cash and credit sales to consumers. A defense contractor such as General Dynamics generates revenue by making sales to the U.S. military and other customers under long-term contracts. A bank such as Chase Manhattan Bank generates revenues by providing a wide variety of loans and services to business and individual customers. Many companies such as McDonald's generate at least some of their revenues in franchising contracts by allowing individuals and other companies to use the McDonald's trademarks and providing them with goods and such services as advertising, training, management consulting, and new product development.

---

[1] E.K. Park Feroz and V. Pastena, "The Financial and Market Effects of the SEC's Accounting and Auditing Enforcement Releases," *Journal of Accounting Research* (Supplement 1991), p. 112.

Not surprisingly, the differences in the way firms provide goods and services to customers lead to differences in the way revenues are recognized. We will show how the variations in revenue recognition methods used in practice are related to fundamental economic differences in the way firms generate revenue.

The general answer to the question of when revenue and expense should be recognized has two parts. The first part, referred to as the *realization principle*, states that revenue should be recognized as soon as:

1. It has been earned
2. The fair value of the consideration received is determinable

The second part, known as the *matching principle*, states that expenses should be recognized in the same period as the revenues to which they relate. Taken together, the realization and matching principles imply that, in general, when a firm recognizes revenue also determines when it recognizes the related expenses.

To earn revenue, a firm must demonstrate **substantial performance** under the contract with the customer, and a **genuine exchange** transaction must occur. The most obvious way to demonstrate substantial performance is by delivery of the goods and services to the customer. The situations described later in this chapter will all be based on delivery of goods and services as the criterion for substantial performance. In the next chapter, we will consider some other situations in which delivery is not required to demonstrate substantial performance. Questions about whether a genuine exchange transaction has occurred arise in a number of situations, notably sales with a right of return, transactions in which the seller has continuing involvement with the item "sold," and sales to related parties. In all of these situations, there are good reasons to question whether a genuine exchange transaction has occurred—i.e., whether or not the risks and rewards of ownership have been transferred from the seller to the buyer.

The second condition of the realization principle states that revenue cannot be recognized until the fair value of the consideration received is determinable. The consideration received by firms in exchange for the goods and services they provide to their customers takes many forms. They receive assets (most often cash), a promise to receive cash or other assets in the future (notes and accounts receivable), or sometimes the firm's liabilities to its customer are forgiven. Whenever the consideration received from the customer is not in the form of cash, some questions as to its fair value may exist. Will notes and accounts receivable be collected? When? What is the fair value of noncash assets received or liabilities forgiven? According to the realization principle, a firm may not recognize revenue until such questions are resolved.

Firms frequently encounter problems in applying the matching principle because the firm's performance under the contract, while substantial enough to warrant revenue recognition, is not complete. For example, manufactured products are frequently sold with limited product warranties and maintenance contracts bundled into the sales price. If revenue is recognized when the product is sold to the customer, applying the matching principle would require that the costs associated with warranties and maintenance agreements be accrued on an estimated basis. If the amount of remaining costs yet to be incurred is potentially large and difficult to estimate, this raises questions about whether the firm's performance has been substantial enough to justify revenue recognition.

Two chapters will be required to examine the full implications of revenue recognition methods. We begin this chapter by examining the financial statement implications of various revenue recognition principles in rather general terms. This will demonstrate the relationship between revenue and expense recognition methods and asset and liability valuation. Next, we will look at some of the specific problems encountered and issues considered in recognizing revenue upon the delivery of goods or services to customers and matching the related expenses. In Chapter 5, we examine some situations that require recognition of revenue upon production of a firm's products or collection of cash from customers.

THE IMPLICATIONS OF REVENUE RECOGNITION

We begin the discussion of revenue and expense recognition with definitions of the terms.

Revenues are inflows or other enhancements of assets of an entity or settlements of its liabilities (or a combination of both) from delivering or producing goods, rendering services, or other activities that constitute the entity's ongoing major or central operations.[2]

Expenses are outflows or other using up of assets or incurrences of liabilities (or a combination of both) from delivering or producing goods, rendering services, or carrying out other activities that constitute the entity's major or central operations.[3]

Paraphrasing the FASB's definitions, revenues represent the value of goods or services a firm provides to its customers, while expenses represent the costs of those activities undertaken to generate revenues. When revenues exceed expenses, a firm reports income. Thus, income can be viewed as the net value added by a firm in providing goods and services to customers. The basic accounting question involving revenues and expenses is when accounts should formally recognize this added value.

Before examining the timing of revenue and expense recognition as specified by GAAP, let us begin by considering a simple example. We use this example to illustrate the financial statement implications of revenue and expense recognition principles and to motivate the discussion that follows. During our discussion of this example, we will not concern ourselves with what GAAP require in regard to revenue and expense recognition. Rather, we will simply consider the use of some alternative methods of revenue recogni-

---

[2] "Elements of Financial Statements," *Statement of Financial Accounting Concepts, No. 6* (Stamford, CT: FASB, 1985), para. 78.

[3] *Ibid.,* para. 80.

tion and how the selection of these methods would affect the firm's resulting financial statements.

An Example

Northwestern Mining Co. started operations on January 1, 1994, with $300,000 in cash contributed by its sole shareholder. On the same date, the firm spent $200,000 in cash to acquire the mining rights to a property in North Dakota. According to geological estimates, the mine contains 10,000 tons of a mineral ore that is widely used in the manufacture of certain metal alloys. The current market value of this mineral ore is $100 per ton. Depletion of the mine will be recognized by using a method known as unit-of-production and, therefore, depletion cost per unit is computed at $200,000/10,000 tons or $20 per ton. The cost of extracting the ore is $50 per ton, and the cost of shipping it is $5 per ton. All extraction and shipping costs are paid in cash. During the year ended December 31, 1994, the company extracted 1,000 tons of ore, sold 800 tons on account at $100 per ton, and collected the selling price on 750 tons. In addition, $6,000 of general and administrative costs were incurred and paid.

When does Northwestern Mining Co. add value? Conceivably, we could say that the firm begins adding value at the acquisition of the mine and continues adding value throughout its operating cycle as the mineral ore is first extracted from the ground and then delivered to its customers. Alternatively, we could say that since the sales are made on account and, therefore, there is some risk of not collecting the receivables, we should wait until the cash is collected to be certain that value has indeed been added.

Accountants usually wait for a particular event or transaction to occur before amounts are recorded in the accounts. Therefore, accountants typically select a **critical event** in a firm's operations for the purposes of recognizing revenue. For Northwestern Mining Co., only four discrete events are probably possible choices as a critical event for revenue recognition: the acquisition of the mine, the extraction of mineral ore, the delivery of mineral ore to customers, and the collection of the proceeds. Let us consider the implications of using each of these events as the critical event that triggers the recognition of revenues and expenses.

Whatever critical event we choose for recognizing revenues for Northwestern Mining Co., the matching principle dictates that we must use the same event to recognize expenses. In this example, three costs are directly related to revenues (variable costs). First, for each $100 of revenue from the sale of a ton of mineral ore, the firm must extract a ton of ore, using up mineral rights costing $20. This cost is referred to throughout the example as *depletion cost*. In addition, the company must pay $50 to extract each ton of ore and another $5 to ship the ore to customers. Costs such as these, which are directly related to revenues on a cause-and-effect basis, are easy to match with revenues. But what about the general and administrative costs of running the business? There is no direct relationship between a dollar spent on general and administrative activities and revenue. Therefore, we typically treat such costs as **period expenses**—i.e., expenses that cannot be directly matched with revenues and, therefore, are recognized in the period the costs were incurred.

Some costs, such as advertising and research and development costs, are routinely treated as period costs because their relationships with revenues are difficult to gauge.

We can summarize the selling price and variable costs in this example on a per unit basis as follows:

		Per Unit
Selling price		$100
Depletion cost	$20	
Extraction cost	50	
Shipping cost	5	75
Contribution to fixed costs		$ 25

Thus, every ton sold will contribute $25 toward the fixed cost ($6,000) of general and administrative costs this period. This amount is often referred to as the **contribution margin** of the firm.

It will probably come as no surprise that a firm's choice of critical event affects the amounts of revenues and expenses reported on its income statement. As we shall see, the decision of when to recognize revenue will also affect the balance sheet. The values assigned to some of the firm's assets and liabilities depend on the timing of revenue recognition. We show the relationships between asset and liability valuation and revenue recognition by examining how the financial statements will vary as the critical event for revenue recognition purposes varies from the time of mineral extraction to the time of sale to the time of collection. We begin by examining the cash consequences of the transactions described.

Cash Basis Accounting

Under strict cash basis accounting, revenues and expenses merely represent the amounts of cash receipts and disbursements. This, of course, is inconsistent with the realization and matching principles; but it provides a useful baseline comparison with the several variations of accrual accounting presented next.

A statement of cash receipts, disbursements, and changes in cash balance for Northwestern Mining Co. is presented in Exhibit 4.1. Notice that the cash balance has decreased by $185,000 over the course of the year, largely due to the purchase of the mine. Under accrual accounting, this transaction would be treated as a capital expenditure—i.e., the mine would be recorded as an asset and expensed over its useful life. However, under strict cash basis accounting, all cash disbursements are treated alike with the end result that Northwestern Mining Co. would report a decrease in cash (a "loss") of $185,000 for 1994. Subsequent years would benefit by not having to bear any of the cost of the mine since it has been fully recognized upon acquisition.

One obvious problem with cash basis accounting is that expenditures that benefit multiple periods, such as the purchase of the mine by Northwestern Mining, are fully recognized in a single period. More generally, the timing of

NORTHWESTERN MINING CO.
Statement of Cash Receipts, Disbursements,
and Changes in Cash Balance
For the Year Ended December 31, 1994

Cash receipts	
Collections from customers	$ 75,000
Cash disbursements:	
Purchase of mine	200,000
Extraction costs paid	50,000
Shipping costs paid	4,000
General and administrative expenses paid	6,000
Total disbursements	260,000
Decrease in cash	185,000
Beginning cash balance	300,000
Ending cash balance	$115,000

cash receipts need not coincide with the timing of providing goods and services to customers. Moreover, the timing of cash disbursements need not coincide with the consumption of resources to provide goods and services. The accrual basis, with its realization and matching principles, is not primarily concerned with when cash is received. Rather, it is concerned with when the right to receive cash or other consideration has been earned by providing goods and services to customers. We begin consideration of accrual accounting by considering revenue recognition upon collection of cash.

Revenue Recognition at the Time of Collection

A time line showing the sequence of transactions and the resulting valuation of assets for revenue recognition at the time of collection is shown in Figure 4.1. If revenue is not recognized until the firm collects cash from its customers, then no net increase in value will be recognized in the accounts until units of the mineral have been sold and the sales price has been collected. This implies that inventory and receivables will effectively be stated at their cost. In this case, since revenue will not be recognized when the ore is sold but rather as the cash is collected from customers, the sales are recorded without any revenue or expense being recognized. The sales transactions in the aggregate involve a transfer of costs from inventory ($56,000), the payment of shipping costs ($4,000), in exchange for accounts receivable ($80,000). However, the receivables include $20,000 of additional value (income) that cannot be recognized until the critical event, collection, has occurred. Thus, the $20,000 of income is initially deferred pending the collection of the receivables. The following summary journal entry shows how sales are recorded if revenue is to be recognized upon collection rather than sales:

FIGURE 4.1
Revenue
Recognition at
Collection

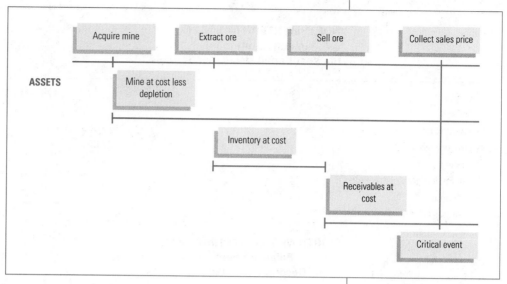

Accounts receivable	80,000	
Inventory (800 tons × $70)		56,000
Cash (for shipping costs)		4,000
Deferred profit on sales		20,000

The deferred profit on sales account is usually shown as a contra-asset to accounts receivable, leaving a net amount of $60,000 shown for receivables. This represents their cost ($56,000 cost of the mineral plus $4,000 to ship).

When the accounts receivable are collected from customers, the amount collected ($75,000) is recognized as revenue. The costs to be matched as expenses with that revenue include the depletion cost of $15,000 (750 tons × $20), extraction cost of $37,500 (750 tons × $50), and shipping cost of $3,750 (750 tons × $5). Therefore, as collections occur, the accounts receivable balance is reduced by the amount collected, $75,000; and the deferred profit on sales account is reduced by the profit that has now been earned, $18,750 (750 tons × $25). The general and administrative cost ($6,000) is treated as an expense of the period.

The financial statements that result when revenue is recognized at the time of collection are included in Exhibit 4.2. The revenues, depletion cost, extraction cost, and shipping cost are all just the per unit amounts multiplied by the 750 tons for which collections were made by year-end. The inventory balance shown at year-end relates to 200 tons of ore. Recall that 1,000 tons were extracted and 800 were sold, leaving 200 tons in inventory at year-end. Notice on the balance sheet that inventory is carried at $14,000, which represents cost (200 tons × $70). The balance shown at year-end for accounts receivable relates to 50 tons of ore. Recall that 800 tons were sold and the proceeds were collected for 750 tons, leaving accounts receivable at year-end for 50 tons of ore. Accounts receivable are carried at a net amount of $3,750 for 50 tons at $75 per ton. This represents the cost, rather than the net realizable value, of the receivables. Thus, when revenue is recognized at the time of collection, both

| **EXHIBIT 4.2**

Financial
Statements—
Revenue
Recognition at the
Time of Collection

NORTHWESTERN MINING CO.
Income Statement
For the Year Ended December 31, 1994

Revenue		$75,000
Expenses:		
Depletion cost	$15,000	
Extraction cost	37,500	
Shipping cost	3,750	
General and administrative cost	6,000	62,250
Net income		$12,750

NORTHWESTERN MINING CO.
Balance Sheet
December 31, 1994

Cash		$115,000
Accounts receivable	$ 5,000	
Less: Deferred profit	(1,250)	3,750
Inventory		14,000
Total current assets		132,750
Mine, net of accumulated depletion		180,000
Total assets		$312,750
Capital stock		$300,000
Retained earnings		12,750
Total liabilities and equity		$312,750

receivables and inventory are carried at their cost. This is a direct consequence of the decision to recognize revenue and expenses at the time of collection.

Please note that recognizing revenue at the time of collection is not the same as cash basis accounting. When recognizing revenue at the time of collection, we have applied the matching principle and only recognized as expenses the costs that pertain to the $75,000 of revenues recognized. Under cash basis accounting, all amounts paid are recognized as expenses.

Revenue Recognition at the Time of Sale

A time line showing the sequence of transactions and the resulting valuation of assets for revenue recognition at the time of sale is shown in Figure 4.2. A sale or, more precisely, delivery of goods to customers is the event used most frequently for revenue recognition. Upon delivery of goods to customers in connection with a sale on account, the company effectively converts inventory

FIGURE 4.2

Revenue
Recognition at Sales

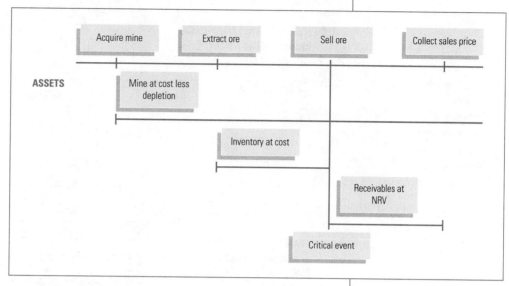

into accounts receivable. If revenue is recognized upon delivery, an increase in value is recognized as inventory (carried at cost) and is converted to accounts receivable (carried at *net realizable value*, NRV, or the amount of future cash they represent).

The income statement and balance sheet for the firm, assuming revenue is recognized at the point of sale, are shown in Exhibit 4.3. The sales revenue and the expenses for depletion, extraction, and shipping are simply the per unit amounts times the 800 tons of mineral ore sold during the year. Inventory is stated at $14,000 (its cost) on the balance sheet. Since accounts receivable are stated at $5,000 on the balance sheet for 50 tons, we can also see that accounts receivable are carried at their net realizable value of $100 per ton. The difference between the valuation of these two assets is due to revenue recognition at the time of sale. By recognizing revenue upon sales, the firm added value (the expected profit contribution of $25 per ton) to the cost of inventory ($70) and the cost of shipping ($5) to obtain the accounts receivable balance ($100). Thus, inventory at $70 per ton became accounts receivable at $100 per ton. These valuations for inventory and accounts receivable are a direct result of revenue recognition at the time of sale.

Revenue Recognition at the Time of Mineral Extraction

A time line showing the sequence of transactions and the resulting valuation of assets for revenue recognition at the time of mineral extraction is shown in Figure 4.3. Suppose the firm recognizes revenue as soon as the mineral ore is extracted. If revenue is recognized at this point in the firm's operating cycle, then value will be added in the accounts as the firm produces its inventory. This implies that inventory will not be carried at cost but rather at market value and liabilities will have to be accrued to match expenses not yet incurred with revenue properly. Since the extraction of ore is the critical event

EXHIBIT 4.3

Financial
Statements—
Revenue
Recognition at the
Time of Sale

NORTHWESTERN MINING CO.
Income Statement
For the Year Ended December 31, 1994

Revenue		$80,000
Expenses:		
Depletion cost	$16,000	
Extraction cost	40,000	
Shipping cost	4,000	
General and administrative cost	6,000	66,000
Net income		$14,000

NORTHWESTERN MINING CO.
Balance Sheet
December 31, 1994

Cash	$115,000
Accounts receivable	5,000
Inventory	14,000
Total current assets	134,000
Mine, net of accumulated depletion	180,000
Total assets	$314,000
Capital stock	$300,000
Retained earnings	14,000
Total liabilities and equity	$314,000

for revenue recognition, the extraction of 1,000 tons of ore results in the recognition of $100,000 (1,000 × $100) of revenue. Inventory is recorded at its market value. Since 1,000 units worth of revenues have been recognized, 1,000 units worth of expenses must be matched with them. The depletion cost of $20,000 (1,000 tons × $20) and the extraction cost of $50,000 (1,000 tons × $50) have already been incurred, but the shipping cost of $5,000 (1,000 × $5) will not be paid until the ore is shipped to the customers. Since that will occur some time after the extraction of the ore, it is necessary to record a liability for accrued expenses in the initial amount of $5,000.

When 800 tons of ore are sold, no revenue is recognized. That has already occurred when the mineral ore was extracted. Therefore, all we need to recognize is that inventory has been converted into accounts receivable. Thus, 800 units of inventory valued at $100 become 800 units of accounts receivable valued at the same amount. With the shipping cost of $4,000 incurred and paid at the time of sale, the liability for accrued expenses recognized earlier is reduced by this amount, leaving an accrued liability of $1,000 for the estimated cost of shipping the 200 tons of ore remaining in inventory. It is not necessary to

FIGURE 4.3

Revenue
Recognition at Ore
Extraction

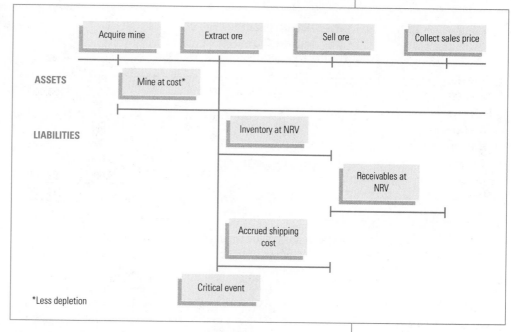

accrue this liability under revenue recognition at the time of sale or collection since no revenue (and, hence, no expenses) was recognized for amounts produced but not yet sold.

Financial statements that reflect the recognition of revenue at the time of mineral extraction are included in Exhibit 4.4. Revenues and expenses are simply the per unit amounts times the 1,000 tons of ore extracted. The balance sheet shows inventory stated at $20,000, or $100 per ton, and accounts receivable stated at $5,000, or $100 per ton. Notice that both assets, which exist after the critical event of mineral extraction has occurred, are carried at the market value of the ore. Once again, the point at which revenues are recognized determines the valuation of assets and liabilities on the balance sheet.

Revenue Recognition at the Time of Mine Acquisition

One last iteration of this exercise is necessary to consider the implications of revenue recognition at the time Northwestern Mining Co. acquired the mineral rights to the property in North Dakota.

A time line showing the sequence of transactions and the resulting valuation of assets for revenue recognition at the time of mine acquisition is shown in Figure 4.4. If revenue is recognized at the time the mine is acquired, then revenue equal to the total quantity of ore contained in the mine (10,000 tons) times the market value of the ore ($100 per ton), or $1,000,000, is recognized. The costs to be matched with this revenue include the total cost of the mine ($200,000), the expected cost of extracting the ore (10,000 tons × $50, or $500,000), and the expected cost of shipping the ore to customers (10,000 tons × $5). These latter two costs have not yet been incurred and are, therefore,

EXHIBIT 4.4
Financial
Statements—
Revenue
Recognition at the
Time of Mineral
Extraction

NORTHWESTERN MINING CO.
Income Statement
For the Year Ended December 31, 1994

Revenue		$100,000
Expenses:		
Depletion cost	$20,000	
Extraction cost	50,000	
Shipping cost	5,000	
General and administrative cost	6,000	81,000
Net income		$19,000

NORTHWESTERN MINING CO.
Balance Sheet
December 31, 1994

Cash	$115,000
Accounts receivable	5,000
Inventory	20,000
Total current assets	140,000
Mine, net of accumulated depletion	180,000
Total assets	$320,000
Accrued shipping costs	$ 1,000
Capital stock	300,000
Retained earnings	19,000
Total stockholders' equity	319,000
Total liabilities and equity	$320,000

shown as a liability for accrued expenses. As the ore is extracted and sold, it moves through the accounts at market value of $100 per ton; and as extraction and shipping costs are incurred, the previously recognized liability for accrued expenses is paid off.

The financial statements that reflect revenue recognition at the acquisition of the mining rights to the property are shown in Exhibit 4.5. On the income statement, the amounts for revenue and expenses for depletion, extraction, and shipping are the per unit costs times the 10,000 tons of ore acquired with the mine. On the balance sheet, notice that the mine is carried at $900,000, which represents the market value ($100 per ton) of the 9,000 remaining tons of ore in the mine. Thus, value has been added as soon as the mine was acquired.

FIGURE 4.4

Revenue
Recognition at Mine
Acquisition

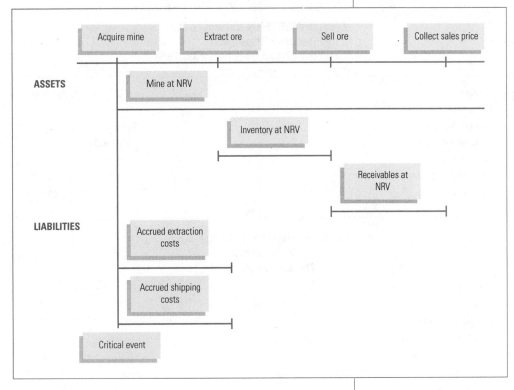

Summary

To summarize this section, we have observed that a firm's choice of a critical event for revenue recognition affects not only the amounts reported as revenues and expenses on its income statement but also the amounts reported as assets and liabilities. In the Northwestern Mining Co. example just completed, the valuation of the firm's mining property, inventory, accounts receivable, and accrued expenses were all affected by the choice of critical event for revenue recognition. The sooner revenue is recognized, the sooner the firm's balance sheet must reflect this value added. The most aggressive revenue recognition method we examined involved recognizing revenue at the time the mine was acquired. Under this approach, the mining property, inventory, and accounts receivable all were carried at the market value of the ore they represented. Under the matching principle, it was necessary to recognize a substantial liability for costs recognized as expenses but not yet incurred. The most conservative revenue recognition method we examined involved recognizing revenue when the cash was collected from customers. Under this approach, all the assets were stated at cost; and it was not necessary to recognize any liability for accrued expenses.

EXHIBIT 4.5

Financial
Statements—
Revenue
Recognition at the
Time of Mine
Acquisition

NORTHWESTERN MINING CO.
Income Statement
For the Year Ended December 31, 1994

Revenue		$1,000,000
Expenses:		
Depletion cost	$200,000	
Extraction cost	500,000	
Shipping cost	50,000	
General and administrative cost	6,000	756,000
Net income		$ 244,000

NORTHWESTERN MINING CO.
Balance Sheet
December 31, 1994

Cash	$115,000
Accounts receivable	5,000
Inventory	20,000
Total current assets	140,000
Mine, net of accumulated depletion	900,000
Total assets	$1,040,000
Accrued expenses	$ 496,000
Capital stock	300,000
Retained earnings	244,000
Total stockholders' equity	544,000
Total liabilities and equity	$1,040,000

WHEN SHOULD REVENUE BE RECOGNIZED?

We have just observed the financial statement implications of recognizing revenues at different points in a firm's operating cycle. How do firms decide what is the appropriate time for revenue recognition? If managers are interested in making their firms look as good as possible, it would appear that they would prefer recognizing revenue as early in the firm's operating cycle as possible.[4] However, earlier recognition of revenue introduces more uncertainty into the financial statements.

---

[4] Please note that managers will have exactly the opposite incentives for tax reporting purposes. As we shall see, firms are free in most cases to select different accounting principles for tax and financial reporting purposes.

For instance, in the Northwestern Mining Co. example just considered, recognizing revenue at the time mining rights were acquired introduced considerable uncertainty into the financial statements even in such a simple case. How could the firm be sure that the geological estimates of the mine's capacity were accurate? Moreover, how could it be sure that all 10,000 tons of ore would eventually be sold? And how could it be sure about the ultimate selling price and extraction cost? Once the ore was sold, how could Northwestern be sure customers would not return it? And how could it be sure that no customers would default on their obligation to pay for the ore? By waiting until the ultimate collection of cash from the customers, Northwestern could avoid most of this uncertainty. At collection, the firm will know exactly how many units have been sold, the selling price of all units sold, as well as the amount of uncollectible accounts. The only residual uncertainty will involve sales returns if allowed by the contract.

Thus, the issue of when to recognize revenue seems to come down to just how much uncertainty accountants are willing to accept in the financial statements. In general, as revenue is recognized earlier in a firm's operating cycle, the amount of uncertainty in the reported revenues and expenses increases.

Statement of Financial Accounting Concepts No. 5 states that revenues and gains must be (1) realized or realizable and (2) earned before they can be recognized.

1. Revenues and gains generally are not recognized until realized or realizable. Revenues and gains are realized when products (goods or services), merchandise, or other assets are exchanged for cash or claims to cash. Revenues and gains are realizable when related assets received or held are readily convertible to known amounts of cash or claims to cash.
2. Revenues are not recognized until earned. An entity's revenue-earning activities involve delivering or producing goods, rendering services, or other activities that constitute its ongoing major or central operations, and revenues are considered to have been earned when the entity has substantially accomplished what it must do to be entitled to the benefits represented by the revenues.[5]

When a firm meets these criteria will depend on the nature of its operations. Assuming a genuine exchange is involved, these criteria are met by most firms when products or services are delivered to customers. Notice, however, that all uncertainty has typically not been removed at this point in a firm's operating cycle. Costs such as bad debts and warranty costs will not have been incurred by this point, but the accounting profession generally believes these items can be recognized and matched with revenues adequately on an estimated basis. The genuineness of the exchange will be questionable whenever the transaction was not entered into at arm's-length, the seller has continuing involvement with the assets sold (e.g., the buyer has the right to return the goods or the transaction is a consignment), or the buyer is a related party.

---

[5] "Recognition and Measurement in Financial Statements of Business Enterprises," *Statement of Financial Accounting Concepts No. 5* (Stamford, CT: FASB, December, 1984), para. 83.

A firm will sometimes enter into a contract to provide a particular product to a customer before that product has been produced. In such cases, the firm earns revenues as production proceeds. As long as reliable estimates are available regarding how much of the total production has been completed in a particular period, the firm is allowed to recognize revenues during the production process by means of the percentage of completion method. If reliable estimates are not available, then recognizing revenue on a percentage of completion basis would entail too much uncertainty. The firm must then wait until production is complete and recognize revenue by the completed contract method.

In other instances, a firm may lend money or lease assets to its customers; and it earns revenues continuously while providing customers the right to use the borrowed funds or the leased assets. Accordingly, revenues are recognized as time passes. Another firm may produce agricultural products, precious metals, or marketable securities that can be sold without any significant sales effort and at prices that may be readily determined in advance. These assets must be "readily convertible into known amounts of cash or claims to cash." That is, they must have " interchangeable (fungible) units and quoted prices available in an active market that can rapidly absorb the quantity held by the entity without significantly affecting the price."[6] Such firms will recognize revenue upon "completion of production or when prices of the assets change."[7]

In some instances, collectibility of a firm's revenues for goods or services provided is doubtful. Even if they have been earned, such revenues do not pass the test of being realizable; and recognizing revenues prior to their collection would introduce too much uncertainty into the financial statements. Accordingly, the firm would probably recognize revenue at the time of cash collection.

With regard to the Northwestern Mining Co. example, introduced in the last section, which of the four critical events would appear to be the most appropriate choice for revenue recognition under GAAP? Recognizing revenue at the time the mine is acquired appears to be too early. The firm has not earned the revenue by providing goods to its customers, and the revenue is far from realizable. The resulting uncertainty in the financial statements would be substantial. Despite all the uncertainty in such a revenue recognition approach, it is interesting to note that a very similar approach, called reserve recognition accounting, was proposed for the oil and gas industry in the 1970s but never implemented. Reserve recognition accounting is discussed in Chapter 5.

It is also hard to argue that Northwestern should wait until collection of cash to recognize revenue. In this simple example, no problems with bad debts or sales returns appears to exist; however, there is simply not enough uncertainty to warrant waiting until collection to recognize revenue. Revenue has clearly been earned and is realizable earlier in the firm's operating cycle.

Revenue recognition at the time of sale is probably the most comfortable choice in that it is familiar and well understood. At the point of sale, revenue

---

6 *Ibid.*

7 *Ibid.*, para. 84(e).

has obviously been earned; and Northwestern's lack of any significant problems with bad debts and returns makes the realization of revenue beyond question. However, suppose the company has a contract with a metal alloy manufacturer to provide all mineral ore extracted from the mine at the prevailing market price. In such a situation, a case could be made for recognizing revenue at the time it is extracted from the mine. At that point, the only activity still required is shipping the ore to the customer; the only significant uncertainty, the selling price. If the selling price differs from the market price prevailing when the ore is mined, Northwestern can make a simple adjustment to reflect the difference. This is precisely how many mining companies recognize revenue.

In summary, accountants recognize revenue when it (1) has been earned and (2) has been realized or is realizable. Judgment is involved in deciding when both of these criteria have been met. Recall that information in financial statements must be both reliable and relevant to be useful. If revenue is recognized too early in the operating cycle, the result may well be an unacceptably high level of uncertainty in the firm's financial statements. The resulting information may not be reliable enough to be useful. If, on the other hand, revenue is recognized too late in the operating cycle, then it will not be a good indicator of the firm's productive effort during the period. Thus, the resulting information may not be relevant enough to be useful. This trade-off between reliability and relevance is the main issue that must be dealt with in deciding when a firm should recognize revenue.

We will now illustrate some of the problems in recognizing revenue upon delivery of goods and services to customers. Most companies provide goods and services to customers in sales contracts, and we consider this situation first.

REVENUE RECOGNITION RELATED TO SALES

The majority of firms providing goods and/or services to their customers recognize revenue at the point of sale. With a look at some revenue recognition problems encountered by Datapoint Corporation, we begin the discussion of revenue recognition related to sales.

Datapoint Corporation

Datapoint Corp. is a manufacturer of computer and telecommunications products. Datapoint sold its first shares of stock to the public in 1970, and the firm reported its first profitable year in 1973. For a remarkable 39 consecutive quarters, the firm reported increasing net income. Annual sales and net income reached their peaks in the fiscal year ended June 31, 1981, at $396.2 million and $48.8 million, respectively. Then, in the third quarter of fiscal 1982, the firm reported a loss of $23 million on revenues of $99.4 million. Included in this net loss was $4.4 million attributable to the reversal of an estimated $15 million in revenues recorded in previous periods.[8]

---

[8] "Datapoint Posts $23 Million Loss for Its 3rd Period," *The Wall Street Journal* (June 17, 1982), p. 2.

At issue were sales returns. Datapoint, like most firms, recognized revenue on sales when its goods were shipped to customers. In its zeal to continue the remarkable trend of increasing earnings, Datapoint had apparently been overly aggressive in shipping unordered merchandise to its distributors. In one particularly troublesome instance, at the end of one quarter, the company sent a shipment of computers to a fictitious party, one "Joe Blow," at a resort hotel in Texas because the real customer was not yet ready to take delivery. The end result was that the correct customer ultimately received the computers when he was ready for them, but the early shipment via a circuitous route enabled Datapoint to record revenue before the end of an accounting period.[9] Datapoint apparently pushed too hard in some cases, causing unexpectedly large sales returns in subsequent periods. Thus, some $15 million of revenue recorded by Datapoint at the time of sale was never collected because the merchandise was returned.

For most firms, the sales event or, more precisely, the delivery of goods or services to customers is deemed most appropriate time for recognizing revenue. Since the product or services have been delivered to the customer, there is usually little question that revenues have been earned. Since the price has been set, the amount of revenue seems readily determinable. However, several issues complicate measurement of the amount of revenue to be recognized. Most firms have to deal with the problems of bad debts and sales returns and allowances. Both of these problems imply that firms may never receive the full sales price of the products or services delivered to their customers. Moreover, not all costs have necessarily been incurred by the time of delivery. For instance, costs are incurred to collect revenues, including those preparing and sending invoices and periodic statements of account, and to employ collection agents to help with difficult cases. In addition, many goods or services sold to customers are covered by warranties, which can obligate the seller to repair or replace the products for a number of years after the date of sale. An application of the matching principle is more difficult when the expenses to be matched with revenues include some costs that have not yet been incurred.

Problems in Recognizing Revenues for Sales Transactions

In a number of situations, recognizing revenue for sales transactions presents difficulties. If revenue is recognized before it has been collected, the amount of revenue to be recognized is uncertain. Uncollectible accounts, discounts, and sales returns may all contribute to a firm collecting less than the full invoice amounts. In some cases, despite the fact that a sale has occurred, we conclude that revenue has not been earned because the selling firm still has outstanding obligations.

Uncollectible Accounts   A firm may not collect the entire sales amount for a variety of reasons. First, some customers will simply default on their obligations and the selling firm may, as a practical matter, have no real recourse to

---

9 "Fall from Glory," *The Wall Street Journal* (May 27, 1982), p. 1.

the buyer. If a customer files bankruptcy, the selling firm will have to join all the customer's other creditors and may collect little or nothing of the amounts owed to it. Alternatively, the firm may decide that the legal cost of pursuing a customer who has defaulted is in excess of the amount it can reasonably expect to collect. Regardless of the reason, the selling firm will collect less revenue than it has earned. When a firm recognizes revenue at the time of sale, it generally will recognize expected bad debts on an estimated basis by the allowance method, described fully in Chapter 7. If bad debts are a serious problem, the realization principle may not be met; and the firm would be forced to recognize revenue upon collection of cash, using one of the methods illustrated in Chapter 5.

Discounts   A firm may offer its customers discounts for prompt payment for sales made on account. For instance, if the terms of the sale are 2/10, net 30, customers are only required to remit 98% of the sales amount if they do so within 10 days. Not all customers take advantage of these discounts. To avoid overstating the amount of revenue at the date of sale, the firm may need to deal with discounts and bad debts on an estimated basis. However, given the relatively short discount periods typically offered, there is usually little concern that sales discounts will significantly affect the amount of revenues reported in an accounting period. We examine the techniques for dealing with these problems in detail in Chapter 7.

Sales with the Right of Return   Another reason why a firm may not collect the entire sales amount is due to the customers' right of return. Retail establishments are typically fairly liberal in allowing their customers to return merchandise that is defective or the wrong size or color, or whatever. Book publishers typically allow bookstores to return unsold copies for full refund. In addressing the issue of revenue recognition when customers have the right to return merchandise, the FASB has concluded that revenue shall be recognized at the time of sale only when all of the following six criteria are met:

1. The seller's price to the buyer is substantially fixed or determinable at the date of sale.
2. The buyer has paid the seller, or the buyer is obligated to pay the seller, and the obligation is not contingent on the resale of the product.
3. The buyer's obligation to the seller would not be changed in the event of theft or physical destruction or damage of the product.
4. The buyer acquiring the product for resale has economic substance apart from that provided by the seller.
5. The seller does not have significant obligations for future performance to directly bring about resale of the product by the buyer.
6. The amount of future returns can be reasonably estimated.[10]

----

10 "Revenue Recognition When Right of Return Exists," *Statement of Financial Accounting Standards No. 48* (Stamford, CT: FASB, June, 1981), para. 6.

With the exception of Item (4), these six criteria are probably self-explanatory. Criterion (4) prevents a firm from creating an entity "on paper"—that is, with no employees or facilities—for the express purpose of recording revenues. This would prevent a similar Datapoint shipment to a fictitious "Joe Blow" from counting as revenue.

When all six criteria are met, "sales revenue and cost of sales must be reduced to reflect estimated returns."[11] This is usually handled with a reserve for sales returns. For instance, suppose Carper Hollins Publishing Co. sells to bookstores with a full right of return for six months. That is, these bookstores may return any unsold books for full refund up to six months after the date of sale. Carper Hollins' experience has been that 20% of the books sold to bookstores are returned. During 1994, Carper Hollins reported sales of $120,000. The cost of books sold was $75,000. Thus, revenue should be reduced by $24,000 (20% of 120,000), and cost of goods sold should be reduced by $15,000 (20% of $75,000) for the estimated sales returns. This is usually handled by recognizing a provision for (estimated cost of) sales returns of $9,000 (the revenue reduction of $24,000 less the cost of goods sold reduction of $15,000). To record the sales, cost of goods sold, and estimated returns, Carper Hollins would make the following entries:

Accounts receivable	120,000	
Sales revenue		120,000
To record 1994 sales on account.		

Cost of goods sold	75,000	
Inventory		75,000
To record cost of books sold in 1994.		

Provision for sales returns	9,000	
Allowance for sales returns		9,000
To record estimated sales returns for 1994.		

The provision for sales returns account is typically reported on the income statement as either a reduction of revenue or as a selling expense. The allowance for sales returns account is typically shown as a contra-asset to receivables.

Suppose a bookstore returns all copies of a slow-selling romance novel to Carper Hollins. These books had originally been sold to the bookstore for $3,200 and had a cost of $2,000. The return would be recorded as follows:

Inventory	2,000	
Allowance for sales returns	1,200	
Accounts receivable		3,200
To record actual returns.		

Since it is based on estimates of sales returns, the allowance for sales returns must be reviewed periodically to see whether experience has confirmed the estimates of returns. If the balance is inappropriate, an adjustment in the current and future periods would be necessary for the change in estimate.

---

[11] *Ibid.*, para. 7.

Suppose a sale with the right of return does not meet all the criteria that allow revenue recognition. How is this transaction recorded without recognizing revenue? The usual treatment is to defer gross profit on the sale until the return period has expired. Thus, if the transaction does not meet all the criteria for revenue recognition, we conclude that it is not appropriate to recognize any value added until the customer's right to return the goods has lapsed as follows:

Accounts receivable	120,000	
Inventory		75,000
Deferred gross profit on sales with right of return		45,000
To record sales with right of return that do not meet the		
criteria for revenue recognition.		

Suppose by the end of the period, books that originally sold for $15,000 and cost $9,375 were actually returned and that the return period has expired (and revenue has been earned) on books that sold for $60,000 and cost $37,500. If revenue was *not* recognized at the time of the sale, these transactions would be recorded as follows:

Inventory	9,375	
Deferred gross profit on sales with right of return	5,625	
Accounts receivable		15,000
To record sales returns.		
Cost of goods sold	37,500	
Deferred gross profit on sales with right of return	22,500	
Sales revenue		60,000

The deferred gross profit on sales with right of return account is usually shown as a liability, similar to the liabilities for unearned revenue shown by airlines, insurance companies, and magazine publishers.

Consignment Sales In a **consignment** (also known as a *consignment sale*), the parties involved are known as the consignor and the consignee. The consignor delivers goods to the consignee, who agrees to sell the consignor's goods for a commission or fee and to exercise a reasonable standard of care in protecting these goods from damage or loss. When the goods are sold, the consignee will typically remit the sales proceeds (less the agreed upon commission or fee) to the consignor. Similar to consignment sales, **sales on approval** involve goods that are shipped to a potential buyer who has the right to return them if they are not satisfactory. The nature of the contract involving consignments and sales on approval requires that revenue not be recognized upon shipment. Rather, the consignor would recognize revenue when the consignee sells the goods. The seller on approval would not recognize revenue until the customer has decided to accept, rather than return, the goods.

When Revenue Is Not Earned at the Time of Sale A number of instances occur when revenue has not been earned despite the existence of a sale transaction. For example, consider the sale of an airline ticket to a passenger for a flight to be taken next month. Airlines frequently offer special "super saver" fares to encourage customers to buy tickets early, often more than a month prior to the date of the flight. Has revenue been earned upon the sale of such a ticket? What the customer is really buying is transportation services, which will not be delivered until the date of travel. Therefore, even though a sale has taken place, revenue would not be recognized until the ticket is used. Between the date the ticket is sold and the date of travel, the airline would report a liability for unearned revenue, often called an "air traffic liability" by the airlines. If the ticket price was $500, the airline would make the following entries:

1. At the date the ticket is sold:

Cash	500	
Air traffic liability		500
To record the sale of airline ticket.		

2. At the date the ticket is used:

Air traffic liability	500	
Revenue		500
To record revenue earned upon usage of ticket.		

Sale of Extended Warranties   Similar situations exist in other industries. For instance, in a recent pronouncement, the FASB dealt with the issue of how to recognize revenue on the sale of extended warranties frequently offered by retailers and manufacturers.[12] When consumers purchase automobiles or appliances, they are usually offered the opportunity to purchase an extended warranty, which covers a period after the manufacturer's warranty expires. Has revenue been earned upon the sale of an extended product warranty? The FASB decided that it has not. Instead, the seller must initially recognize a liability for unearned revenue. Revenue is to be recognized on a straight-line basis over the period covered by the extended warranty.

For instance, suppose Crazy Louie's Electronics Co. sells a 27-inch color television together with a 36-month extended warranty. The television sells for $800, and the extended warranty sells for $72. The extended warranty coverage begins upon expiration of the manufacturer's 3-month factory warranty. Crazy Louie's would account for the extended warranty this way:

1. At the date of sale:

Cash	872	
Sales revenue		800
Unearned warranty revenue		72
To record sale of merchandise and extended warranty.		

2. Each month starting four months after the sale:

Unearned warranty revenue	2	
Warranty revenue		2
To record warranty revenue earned each month ($72 ÷ 36 months = $2 per month).		

---

[12] "Accounting for Separately Priced Extended Warranty and Product Maintenance Contracts," *Technical Bulletin 90-1* (Stamford, CT: FASB, 1990).

Similar accounting treatment is applied in other situations where revenue has not been earned at the date of sale. A magazine publisher will not recognize but will treat revenue as initially unearned upon the sale of subscriptions. With the mailing of each issue, a *pro rata* amount is recognized as revenue. Similarly, an insurance company will not recognize revenue upon the sale of a policy. Rather, the revenue will be treated initially as unearned and recognized with the passage of time.

Installment Sales   Many retail establishments sell merchandise to customers on the installment plan or flexible revolving credit arrangements. In most cases, revenue is deemed to be earned at the time of sale even though collection of the revenues may require many months. While the extended collection period adds uncertainty to the process, in most cases the amount of uncertainty is not sufficient to require a delay in revenue recognition beyond the point of sale. When a delay in revenue recognition is appropriate, the firm will be required to use one of the methods of revenue recognition, illustrated in Chapter 5, at the time of collection.

For example, suppose California Appliance Co. sells a refrigerator on the easy payment plan. The customer agrees to a monthly payment of $29 for 36 months. The refrigerator sells for a cash price of $800. With 36 payments of $29 or $1,044 in total, the customer is paying $244 ($1,044 – $800) for the right to pay for the refrigerator in installments. When revenue is recognized at the time of sale, we recognize the cash selling price as sales revenue. The rest of the amount to be collected represents interest revenue, which will be recognized over the period the installment receivable is outstanding. At the date of sale, California Appliance would record the transaction this way:

1. To record the installment sale:

Installment receivables	1,044	
Sales revenue		800
Unearned interest revenue		244

Unearned interest revenue would be shown on the firm's balance sheet as a contra-asset account—i.e., as a reduction of the installment receivables. The cost of the refrigerator to California Appliance Co. would be recognized as cost of goods sold at this point also.

Interest revenue is recognized by the **effective interest method**. To apply this method, we must first determine the **effective interest rate**, which, when used to determine the present value of the installment payments, will yield a present value equal to the cash selling price of the asset sold. Thus, we need to find the rate of interest that will give the annuity of 36 monthly payments of $29 a present value of $800. This implies a present value factor of $800 ÷ $29 or 27.586, which, from Table 2 at the end of the text, implies an interest rate of 1.5% per month. Thus, interest for the first month is $800 × 1.5% or $12. Of the monthly payment of $29, $12 applies to interest; and the rest, $17, represents a reduction of the amount due from the customer. The entry to record the first month's interest revenue and collection of the installment would be:

2. To record first month's interest and installment collection:

Cash	27	
Unearned interest revenue	12	
Installment receivables		27
Interest revenue		12

After collection of the first installment, California Appliance Co. would report the following balances:

Installment receivables (35 × $29)	$1,015
Unearned interest revenue ($244 – $12)	232
Net installment receivables	$ 783

Interest for subsequent months would be computed on the net installment receivable balance. Each monthly payment would be split between interest and principal in this fashion. As the principal is repaid, less of each monthly payment will apply to interest and more will apply to reduction of the principal amount. The 36th and final installment payment will leave the net installment receivable balance at zero.

Thus, installment sales are treated as a part sale and part loan. Sales on revolving credit accounts are accounted for in a similar fashion. Revolving credit terms are somewhat more flexible in that a fixed monthly payment is not required although there will usually be a minimum payment provision. With installment sales or sales on revolving credit terms, revenue on the sale is usually recognized upon delivery of the merchandise to the customer. However, interest revenue on the loan has not yet been earned at this point; and its recognition is delayed until time passes. In some cases, the collectibility of installments is uncertain, and revenue is not recognized at the time of sale. We consider these situations in the next chapter.

Problems in Measuring Expenses at the Time of Sale

Once revenue is recognized at the point of sale, the matching principle dictates that all costs to generate that revenue must be recognized as expenses. We will be considering some of the problems of expense recognition throughout the text. For instance, the amount of expense recognized for the cost of goods sold will depend on the inventory cost flow assumption used, as we shall see in Chapter 8. The amount of depreciation expense recognized will depend on the depreciation method used as well as the estimated useful lives of the firm's productive assets, as we shall see in Chapter 11. The treatment of costs that are contingent upon the occurrence of some event were introduced in Chapter 2 and are discussed further below.

Frequently, the matching principle requires expenses be recognized for costs that have not yet been incurred. For instance, it is very common for manufacturers and retailers to offer a product warranty with the products they sell. The matching principle dictates that warranty costs be matched with the revenue from the sale of the product. Since these warranty costs have not yet been incurred at the date of sale, they must be recognized on an estimated basis. For example, suppose Home Electronics, Inc. sells audio equipment covered by a 5-year limited warranty. Based upon the company's experience, warranty claims amount to 2% of sales in the first year of warranty coverage and .5% in years two through five. Thus, total warranty claims during the 5-year warranty period are expected to amount to 4% of sales. Suppose the company's sales in 1994 amount to $4,500,000 and warranty claims on these sales paid prior to the end of 1994 amounted to $58,000. These transactions would be accounted for this way:

1. As the sales occur:

Warranty expense	180,000	
Estimated liability for warranty claims		180,000
To accrue estimated warranty expense for 1994 sales		
($4,500,000 × 4%).		

2. As the claims are paid:

Estimated liability for warranty claims	58,000	
Cash		58,000
To record warranty claims paid.		

Subsequent payments of warranty claims for merchandise sold in 1994 would be handled in the same manner as Entry 2. If the actual payments for warranty claims differ from the estimates by an amount large enough to suggest the firm's estimate is not accurate, the firm will be required to make a change in estimate. Changes in estimates were discussed in Chapter 3. In brief, the firm would not restate amounts previously reported for changes in estimates but rather would adjust amounts reported as warranty expense in subsequent periods.

The estimated liability for warranty claims account is an example of a contingent liability, introduced in Chapter 2. The firm is only liable if customers return their merchandise purchases for warranty service. Under the terms of FASB Statement No. 5, contingent liabilities are only accrued when it is probable that an obligation has been incurred and the amount of the obligation can be estimated.[13] In general, the obligation for warranty claims meets this definition because it is likely that customers will make warranty claims and a firm can use its experience or that of other firms in its industry to make a reasonable estimate of the amount of warranty claims. If the firm is unable to make a reasonable estimate of warranty claims and the range of potential warranty claims is wide, it "may raise a question about whether a sale should be recorded prior to the expiration of the warranty period or until sufficient experience has been gained to permit a reasonable estimate of the obligation."[14] This suggests that if a firm is unable to accrue expenses on an estimated basis, then the revenue to which those expenses relate should not be recognized.

As the example of warranty costs demonstrates, the matching principle requires firms to recognize, as expenses, costs that have not yet been incurred.

---

[13] "Accounting for Contingencies," *Statement of Financial Accounting Standards No. 5* (Stamford, CT: FASB, 1975), para. 8.

[14] *Ibid.*, para. 25.

If considerable uncertainty exists about costs yet to be incurred, then it is questionable whether the firm has truly earned the revenue. When a firm sells a product covered by a warranty and cannot make a reasonable estimate of the costs of future warranty claims, then the amount of the warranty claims will probably be large. This implies that the firm will have to make considerable effort after the date of sale to earn the revenue from the transaction. Therefore, revenue has not truly been earned by mere delivery of the product to the customer and should not be recognized at that point. We will see similar arguments in Chapter 17 applied to the issue of when and how firms should recognize revenue from certain lease transactions.

REVENUE RECOGNITION FOR LENDING TRANSACTIONS

In lending transactions, the lender allows the borrower to use funds for some prespecified period of time. The borrower agrees to repay the amount loaned plus interest. The FASB has taken the position that the difference between the net amount loaned and the amount to be repaid represents interest and should be accounted for as such. Lenders frequently charge their customers certain fees, known as **loan origination fees** or **points**, at the beginning of the loan. Although these fees have been received when the loan agreement was signed, they have not yet been earned; and FASB Statement No. 91 requires that they be "deferred and recognized over the life of the loan as an adjustment of yield."[15] Since the loan contract allows the borrower to use the funds until payments are due, interest revenue is not recognized until time passes. The loan origination fees are viewed as part of the revenue earned on the loan contract and are treated in the same fashion.

As we saw with installment sales, interest revenue is recognized by the effective interest method. Initially, the loan is recorded at the amount loaned adjusted by any loan origination fees collected. As time passes, interest on the net loan amount is recognized at the effective rate. For instance, suppose First Bank & Trust Co. of Toledo makes a $15,000, 5-year second mortgage loan at a stated annual rate of 8.5%. For simplicity, assume the mortgage payments are due annually at the end of each year. This second mortgage would require an annual payment of $3,806.49. Now suppose the bank charges the customer a loan origination fee of $194.10 payable at closing. Since the bank is lending $15,000 but receiving $194.10 from the customer, the transaction will be accounted for as a loan of the net amount of $15,000 − $194.10, or $14,805.90. Effectively, the bank has loaned the customer $14,805.90 in exchange for the promise of five annual payments of $3,806.49. What is the effective interest rate in this transaction? Solving for the factor ($14,805.90 ÷ $3,806.49, or 3.8896) and using Table 2 at the end of the text results in an effective interest rate of 9%.

---

[15] "Accounting for Nonrefundable Fees and Costs Associated with Originating or Acquiring Loans and Initial Direct Costs of Leases," *Statement of Financial Accounting Standards No. 91* (Stamford, CT: FASB, 1986), para. 5.

A loan amortization table for this second mortgage loan is contained in Exhibit 4.6. It shows how the annual payments of $3,806.49 repay the net loan amount of $14,805.90 plus interest of 9 percent on the outstanding balance. Using this table, we can illustrate how First Bank & Trust Co. of Toledo should account for this mortgage loan.

1. At the closing date:

Cash	194.10	
Mortgage loan receivable	14,805.90	
Cash		15,000.00
To record mortgage loan.		

The debit and credit to cash are necessary because the bank is both paying out and receiving cash at the closing. After one year has passed, the bank would recognize one year's interest revenue at the effective rate of 9% on the net loan amount, or $1,332.53. The entry to record interest revenue and the receipt of the first payment would appear this way:

2. At the end of the first year outstanding:

Cash	3,806.49	
Interest revenue		1,332.53
Mortgage loan receivable		2,473.96
To record first year's interest and payment received.		

This would leave a balance in the mortgage loan receivable account of $9,635.33. Interest for subsequent years is shown in the amortization table and would be recorded by similar entries. Thus, whether the lending contract calls it interest or loan origination fees, revenue is recognized in the same way — as it is earned over the period the loan is outstanding.

REVENUE RECOGNITION FOR LEASING TRANSACTIONS

Many firms provide goods to their customers in lease transactions rather than sales. Lease transactions are covered in much more detail in Chapter 17. We only touch on some revenue and expense recognition issues here. In a lease

EXHIBIT 4.6
Loan Amortization Table

	Loan Amortization Table — First Bank & Trust Company of Toledo			
PAYMENT NO.	9% INTEREST	PAYMENT	AMORTIZATION	LOAN BALANCE
1	1,332.53	3,806.49	(2,473.96)	12,331.94
2	1,109.87	3,806.49	(2,696.62)	9,635.33
3	867.18	3,806.49	(2,939.31)	6,696.02
4	602.64	3,806.49	(3,203.85)	3,492.17
5	314.32	3,806.49	(3,492.17)	0.00

transaction, the **lessor** provides the use of an asset or assets for a period of time specified by the contract (the **lease term**). In return, the **lessee** agrees to make a series of payments as consideration for the use of the asset. At what point is it appropriate for the lessor to recognize revenue in leasing transactions? The FASB has taken the approach that the legal form of the transaction is much less significant than its economic substance. Therefore, the lease contract must be examined to determine when revenue has been earned.

Some long-term lease contracts transfer virtually all the risks and rewards of ownership from the lessor to the lessee. In these transactions, known as **sales-type leases**, the lessor is essentially selling the asset to the lessee. Sales revenue is recognized at the inception of the lease, and the cost of the asset is matched with the revenue as an expense. The lessor also provides financing in these transactions, requiring the recognition of interest revenue over the lease term. Essentially, the transaction would be accounted for similarly to the installment sale discussed previously.

In many long-term lease transactions, the lessor is a financial institution rather than a dealer or manufacturer. These lessors exchange physical assets (e.g., aircraft) for financial assets (e.g., loans). These transactions are accounted for as **direct financing leases**, essentially an installment loan in disguise.

When leases do not transfer the risks and rewards of ownership to the lessee, they are accounted for as **operating leases**. That is, the lease payments will be recognized as rent revenue as they are earned. For many operating leases, the terms of the contract require payments in advance. Thus, they are initially recorded by the lessor as unearned rent revenue until earned—i.e., until time has passed and the lessee has had the use of the leased asset. Only then can the lessor recognize rent revenue. For instance, suppose on July 1, 1994, San Diego Realty (the lessor) leases a boat yard to Harbor Yachts (the lessee). Harbor Yachts agrees to a 12-month lease calling for monthly payments of $20,000 and agrees to pay the first and last months' rent at the signing of the contract. San Diego Realty would account for this transaction as an operating lease this way:

1. At inception of the lease at July 1, 1994:

Cash	40,000	
Unearned rent revenue		40,000

To record the signing of the lease and receipt of first and last months' rent.

After one month had elapsed, the rent for July could be recognized as revenue earned.

2. At July 31, 1994:

Unearned rent revenue	20,000	
Rent revenue		20,000

To record rent earned in July.

Thus, revenue may be recognized by lessors in three ways: as sales revenue, interest revenue, or rent revenue. Which method is applied depends on the particular terms of the lease contract and when revenue is deemed to have been earned by the lessor.

REVENUE RECOGNITION FOR FRANCHISING TRANSACTIONS

Franchising has become a popular way of doing business for firms in many diverse industries. Restaurants, law firms, real estate firms, automobile maintenance establishments, and many others are run as franchise operations. A **franchise** is a contract between two parties, known as the **franchiser** and the **franchisee**. The franchiser allows the franchisee to operate a business in exchange for the franchisee's promise to pay fees to the franchiser. Both the franchisee and the franchiser provide economic resources to the business. The franchiser typically provides trademarks, advertising, a reputation for quality goods or services, consulting services, and in some cases, products and equipment. To operate the business, the franchisee typically provides capital, labor, and management. The primary advantage to doing business as a franchiser is that a firm can typically grow more rapidly since much of the growth is financed by the franchisees. The primary disadvantage is the franchiser will typically have less control over the operations of a franchised business than a business that is owned outright.

Franchisees typically pay two types of fees to franchisers. The **initial franchise fee** represents consideration paid for "establishing the franchise relationship and providing some initial services."[16] In general, these initial services include various kinds of assistance to help the franchisee successfully start the business. The continuing franchise fee represents "consideration for the continuing rights granted by the franchise agreement and for general or specific services during its life."[17]

Both types of fees paid to the franchiser represent payments for services provided to the franchisee. Consistent with the basic principles of revenue recognition discussed in this chapter, these fees may not be recognized as revenues until they have been earned—i.e., until the services have been substantially performed. Under the provisions of SFAS No. 45, "the commencement of operations by the franchisee shall be presumed to be the earliest point at which substantial performance has occurred, unless it can be demonstrated that substantial performance of all obligations... has occurred before that time."[18] Therefore, most franchisers will recognize initial franchise fees as revenues upon the franchisee's start of operations.

Franchise fees received by the franchiser but not yet earned are accounted for as a liability for unearned revenue. For instance, suppose Diversified Restaurants Co. (the franchisee) enters into a franchise agreement with the Burger Czar Corp. (the franchiser) on April 1, 1993 to operate a fast-food Burger Czar restaurant and pays an initial franchise fee of $50,000 at the signing of the contract. The franchise agreement lists the initial services to be provided by Burger Czar Corp., and these initial services are substantially complete on June 1, 1994, at which time the restaurant opens. Burger Czar would account for these initial fees as follows:

---

[16] "Accounting for Franchise Fee Revenue," *Statement of Financial Accounting Standards No. 45* (Stamford, CT: FASB, 1981), para. 26.

[17] *Ibid.*

[18] *Ibid.*, para. 5.

1. On April 1, 1993:

Cash	50,000	
Unearned franchise fees		50,000

To record receipt of initial franchise fee.

2. On June 1, 1994:

Unearned franchise fees	50,000	
Franchise fee revenue		50,000

To recognize initial franchise fees earned as revenue.

In unusual cases, the franchise fees may be collectible over an extended period of time; and there may be significant uncertainty as to whether they are collectible. In such cases, SFAS No. 45 prescribes use of the installment or cost recovery methods, as illustrated in Chapter 5.

SUMMARY

Revenues are recognized according to the realization principle, which states they should be recognized when earned and when the fair value of the consideration received is determinable. Costs are recognized as expenses by matching them with the revenues to which they relate. When this relationship is difficult or impossible to establish, costs are expensed as incurred—i.e., treated as period expenses.

The timing of revenue recognition will affect not only the amounts reported on the income statement, but also those reported for various assets and liabilities. Selecting the appropriate time for revenue recognition involves a trade-off between relevance and reliability. Unless a firm waits until all revenues have been collected and all related costs have been incurred, uncertainty about the amount of revenues and expenses will be introduced into the financial statements. However, waiting until all uncertainty has been eliminated may render the financial statements irrelevant to the current period's operations.

Many firms recognize revenue at the time of sale. This entails numerous uncertainties about the amount of revenues, due to sales returns and uncollectible accounts and related expenses that have not yet been incurred, such as warranty costs. Revenue recognition for lending, leasing, and franchising transactions all involve the basic principles of revenue recognition as goods or services are provided to customers.

QUESTIONS

1. What are *revenues*? What are *expenses*? How does the answer to the question of when to recognize revenue also determine when a firm recognizes expenses?

2. Give some examples of costs that are not typically matched with revenues but, rather, are matched with the period in which they are incurred. Why are these costs not matched with revenues?

3. How does a firm's choice of a revenue recognition principle affect the balances of assets and liabilities reported on its balance sheet?

4. If a firm recognizes revenue at the time of production rather than at the time of sale, would it report higher or lower total assets ? Why?

5. Describe how earlier revenue recognition affects the uncertainty in financial statements.

6. Describe how selecting a revenue recognition principle involves a trade-off between relevance and reliability.

7. What are the criteria for revenue recognition?

8. Why do most firms recognize revenue at the time of sale?

9. What problems exist in recognizing revenue at the time of sale? What problems exist in matching expenses with revenue recognized at the time of sale?

10. If a firm's customers have the right to return merchandise, under what conditions can the firm recognize revenue at the time the merchandise is sold?

11. How is revenue recognized on consignment sales and sales on approval?

12. How does an airline recognize revenue from the sale of advance tickets?

13. How does an appliance retailer recognize revenue from the sale of extended product warranties?

14. When are franchisers permitted to recognize revenue from initial franchise fees?

15. A growing, profitable firm is trying to choose between recognizing revenue at the time of sale and recognizing revenue at the time of collection. What are the implications of this choice for the firm's reported net income and total assets? What do GAAP have to say with regard to this choice?

EXERCISES

4-1. *Balance sheet implications of alternative revenue recognition criteria*

Mountain Mining Corp. produces a precious metal whose price is fixed by law at $35 per ounce. It started operations on January 1, 1993 with only two assets: $50,000 in cash and a mine acquired for $1,500,000. The mine contains an estimated 150,000 ounces of the precious metal. During 1993, the following activities took place:

1. Ore was extracted from the mine and refined into 10,000 ounces of the precious metal. Refining costs of $150,000 were paid in cash.
2. 9,500 ounces of the precious metal were sold on account, and delivery costs of $4,750 ($.50 per ounce) were paid in cash.
3. $315,000 was collected from customers. There are no bad debts.

REQUIRED:

Calculate the ending balances in inventory, accounts receivable, and accrued expenses for Mountain Mining Corp. under the three alternative revenue recognition criteria:

1. Revenue recognized at production of precious metal
2. Revenue recognized at sale of precious metal
3. Revenue recognized at collection of cash

4-2. *Income statement implications of alternative revenue recognition criteria*

Refer to the data in the previous exercise.

REQUIRED:

Prepare income statements under the three alternative revenue recognition criteria:

1. Revenue recognized at production of precious metal
2. Revenue recognized at sale of precious metal
3. Revenue recognized at collection of cash.

4-3. *Warranty costs*

Treated, Inc. sells a line of cellular telephones covered by a 3-year warranty. The costs of warranty claims over the warranty period as a percentage of sales are estimated to occur as follows:

First 12 months	2%
Second 12 months	1%
Third 12 months	1%

During the first three years of the company's operations, the following sales and warranty expenditures took place:

Year	Sales	Warranty Expenditures
1993	$ 50,000	$ 450
1994	90,000	1,150
1995	150,000	3,250

REQUIRED:

1. Compute warranty expense for each year.
2. Compute the balance in warranty-related liabilities at December 31, 1995.
3. Does the firm's estimate of the cost of warranty claims appear reasonable? Why or why not?

4-4. *Unearned revenue: airlines*

South Central Airlines (SCA) reports the following amounts:

	December 31,	
	1994	1993
Unearned passenger revenue	68,200	71,600

During 1994, SCA sold passenger tickets for $839,800. No tickets were submitted for refunds.

REQUIRED:

1. Calculate passenger revenue earned in 1994.
2. Prepare summary journal entries to record ticket sales and passenger revenue earned in 1994.

4-5. *Warranty costs: sale of extended warranties*

Appliance King became an authorized dealer for American Electric (AE) refrigerators effective January 1, 1994, the day AE introduced its line of refrigerators. Appliance King is one of more than 1,000 dealers nationwide carrying AE appliances. AE appliances are covered by a 1-year factory warranty. Appliance King also offers consumers the opportunity to extend the warranty coverage for an additional year at a cost of $50. The extended warranty period starts upon expiration of the factory warranty. AE estimates that the average regular factory war-

ranty cost per refrigerator will amount to $20. Appliance King estimates that the average extended warranty cost per refrigerator will amount to $10. The following activities took place in 1994:

	American Electric	Appliance King
Refrigerators sold (units)	20,000	100
Extended warranties sold (units)	N/A	40
Warranty claims paid	$165,000	$ 0

REQUIRED:

1. Calculate the balance in any warranty-related liability on American Electric's books at December 31, 1994.
2. Calculate the balance in any warranty-related liability on Appliance King's books at December 31, 1994.

4-6.   *Unearned revenue: season ticket sales*

The Toledo Mud Hens sell a season ticket for $100 on April 1, 1994. The season ticket entitles the ticket holder to attend all 25 home games. The first home game of the season occurs on April 30.

REQUIRED:

Prepare all journal entries necessary in April relating to the season ticket sold on April 1, 1994.

4-7.   *Sales with right of return*

Great Western Music (GWM) produces compact discs and cassettes of country and western music and sells its recordings to record stores with a full right of return for 12 months. During 1994, the firm's first year of operations, GWM reported sales on account of $125,000 and costs of recordings sold of $75,000. Management estimates that 10% of the recordings sold will be returned. By December 31, 1994, recordings that had been sold for a total of $6,500 and cost $3,900 to produce are returned by customers.

REQUIRED:

Assume GWM meets all criteria for revenue recognition at the time of sale. Prepare all journal entries dealing with sales and sales returns for 1994.

4-8.   *Sales with right of return*

Refer to the information given in the previous exercise.

REQUIRED:

Assume GWM does not meet all criteria for revenue recognition at the time of sale. Prepare all journal entries dealing with sales and sales returns for 1994.

4-9.   *Unearned revenue: magazine subscriptions*

New York Illustrated reports the following balances:

	December 31,	
	1994	1993
Unearned subscription revenue	14,500	15,850

Subscription revenue for 1994 was $187,600.

REQUIRED:

1. Calculate subscriptions sold during 1994.
2. Prepare summary journal entries to record subscriptions sold and subscription revenues earned in 1994.

4-10. *Lending transactions*

On July 1, 1993, Last National Bank and Trust makes a 15-year mortgage loan in the amount of $150,000. The loan carries a 7.75% interest rate and requires annual payments of $17,258, starting June 30, 1994. The borrower is required to pay one point (1% of the loan amount, or $1,500) plus a loan origination fee of $781, giving the loan an effective rate of 8%.

REQUIRED:

Prepare journal entries to record:
1. The issuance of the loan
2. The first payment received on June 30, 1994

4-11. *Installment sales*

On December 1, 1994, Great Falls Electronics sells a large screen television set for 36 monthly installments of $86.77. The cash selling price for this TV is $2,400.

REQUIRED:

1. Calculate the effective monthly interest rate in the installment sale.
2. Prepare journal entries to record the sale on December 1 and the collection of the first installment on December 31.
3. Show how the installment receivable would be reported on the firm's balance sheet at December 31, 1994.

PROBLEMS

4-1. *Implications of alternative revenue recognition methods*

Custom Windows, Inc. manufactures and installs aluminum storm windows. Sales representatives take orders from customers and a $25 down payment is collected at that time. Upon installation, the customer is billed for the balance of $75 per window. The sales representative is paid a commission of $15 per window at the date the order is taken. The firm maintains only one inventory: windows that have been ordered and manufactured but not yet installed. The firm recognizes revenue upon installation of the windows.

Selling price and costs per unit are summarized below:

Selling price	$100.00
Manufacturing cost	40.00
Installation cost	20.00
Sales commission	15.00
Profit per unit	$ 25.00

The firm's income statement and balance sheets appear as follows:

CUSTOM WINDOWS, INC.
Income Statement
For the Year Ended December 31, 1994

Revenues	$60,000
Manufacturing expense	24,000
Installation expense	12,000
Commission expense	9,000
Net income	$15,000

CUSTOM WINDOWS, INC.
Balance Sheets

	1994	1993
Cash	$ 8,500	$5,000
Accounts receivable	7,500	-
Inventory	8,000	-
Deferred commissions	6,000	-
Total assets	$30,000	$5,000
Liability for customer advances	$10,000	$ -
Owners' equity	20,000	5,000
Total equities	$30,000	$5,000

REQUIRED:

1. Calculate the number of windows:
   (a) Ordered in 1994
   (b) Manufactured in 1994
   (c) Installed in 1994
   (d) Paid for in full in 1994.
2. Prepare a balance sheet at December 31, 1994, and an income statement for the year then ended that reflects revenue recognition at the time the windows are ordered. *Note:* You may find it appropriate to add or delete certain accounts.

4-2. *Franchising transactions*

Nuclear Lawns, Inc. (NLI) is a franchiser in the lawn care industry. On January 1, 1993, NLI entered into a franchise agreement with John Appleby, the franchisee, calling for an initial franchise fee of $35,000, payable immediately. The initial franchise fee covers the following services to be provided by NLI by the dates indicated:

Training	$ 8,000	December 31, 1993
Management consulting	12,000	December 31, 1994
Advertising	15,000	December 31, 1994
Total	$35,000	

The percentages of the agreed upon services completed by NLI as of December 31, 1993 and 1994 were as follows:

	12/31/93	12/31/94
Training	100%	
Management consulting	40%	100%
Advertising	75%	100%

REQUIRED:

1. Calculate the amount of initial franchise fee revenue to be recognized by NLI in 1993 and 1994.
2. Prepare journal entries to record the receipt of the initial franchise fee on January 1, 1993, and the revenue earned in 1993 and 1994.

4-3. *Sale of extended warranties, liability for product warranties*

Joe's Appliances, Inc. has been an authorized dealer for Kool King refrigerators since January 1, 1993. Kool King appliances are covered by a 1-year factory warranty. At the date a refrigerator is sold, retail buyers can purchase extended warranty coverage from Joe's for $25 per year for up to 4 years. The estimated average cost of warranty repairs is $15 per year for the first 5 years of the asset's life. Kool King will reimburse Joe's for the cost of any factory warranty service it performs but not for the cost of extended warranty service.
The following activities took place in 1993 and 1994:

	1993	1994
Kool King sales to Joe's (units)	200	400
Warranty claims paid by Kool King		
Units sold in 1993	$1,400	$1,550
Units sold in 1994	0	2,950
Joe's retail sales (units)	190	405
Extended warranty coverage sold (units):		
No extended coverage	100	200
1-yr. extended coverage	50	105
2-yr. extended coverage	20	50
3-yr. extended coverage	10	30
4-yr. extended coverage	10	20
	190	405
Extended warranty claims paid	0	$710

Sales take place evenly throughout the year. Based on their experience in 1993 and 1994, neither Kool King nor Joe's will revise the estimate of the annual cost of warranty repairs.

REQUIRED:

1. Prepare any journal entries necessary to record factory warranty expense and warranty payments by Kool King from the sales to Joe's in 1993 and 1994.
2. Prepare any journal entries necessary to record the sale of extended warranty coverage and payment of extended warranty claims by Joe's in 1993 and 1994.
3. Calculate the balances in any warranty-related liabilities on Kool King's and Joe's books on December 31, 1994.

4-4. Franchises

Pay Less Tax, Inc. (PLTI) is a franchiser in the tax return preparation business. On August 1, 1994, PLTI entered into a franchise agreement with George Geek, calling for an initial franchise fee of $36,000, payable immediately. The initial franchise fee covers the following services to be provided by PLTI:

	Revenue	Cost
Training	$20,000	$12,000
Site selection assistance	4,000	2,000
Management consulting	8,000	7,000
Advertising	4,000	3,000
Total	$36,000	$24,000

Total costs incurred by PLTI by December 31, 1994 and 1995, to fulfill its obligations under the contract were as follows:

	12/31/94	12/31/95
Training	$4,000	$12,000
Site selection assistance	2,000	2,000
Management consulting	2,000	7,000
Advertising	1,000	3,000
Total costs incurred	$9,000	$24,000

REQUIRED:

1. If there are no uncertainties about Mr. Geek's ability to pay and if the initial franchise fee revenue is recognized according to SFAS No. 45, determine the amounts of revenue and expense PLTI will recognize in the years ended December 31, 1994 and December 31, 1995.
2. Prepare journal entries for 1994 and 1995.

4-5. Sales with right of return

American Test Instruments, Inc. (ATI) sells its products with a 90-day unconditional right of return. The following information is taken from the firm's 1994 annual report:

Balance sheet data:

	December 31, 1994	1993
Accounts receivable	$17,500	$15,000
Less: Allowance for sales returns	(4,100)	(3,200)
Net receivables	$13,400	$11,800

Income statement data:

Sales revenue	$ 205,000
Cost of goods sold	(123,000)
Provision for sales returns	(8,200)

REQUIRED:

1. What do the "allowance for sales returns" amounts shown on the balance sheet represent?

2. What does the "provision for sales returns" amount shown on the income statement represent?

3. Does ATI apparently meet the conditions for revenue recognition at the time of sale? How do you know?

4. Prepare summary journal entries to record sales, cost of goods sold, estimated returns, actual returns, and collections on account for 1994. Assume cost of goods sold is 60% of sales in all cases.

4-6.   *Sales with right of return*

Columbus Record Club (CRC) operates as follows: On the first of each month, members are sent a brochure describing that month's selection. If the member does not return the postcard provided by the end of the month, CRC automatically ships the selection to the member, who is billed for $16. CRC's cost is $8 per selection. The member has the right to return the selection for a full refund until the end of the following month. During 1994, the first year of operations for the club, the following activities took place:

Selections shipped	1,200
Selections returned	250
Cash collected from members	$12,800

At December 31, 1994, a total of 100 selections had been shipped to members and were still eligible for return. Management estimates that 20 of these will actually be returned.

REQUIRED:

1. Assume that CRC meets all criteria for revenue recognition at the time of sale. Prepare all journal entries to record sales, cost of goods sold, collections, and actual and estimated returns for 1994.

2. Assume that CRC does *not* meet all criteria for revenue recognition at the time of sale. Prepare all journal entries to record sales, cost of goods sold, collections, and actual and estimated returns for 1994.

4-7.   *Deferred income: sales with right of return*

Advanced Computer Devices, Inc. (ACD) manufactures semiconductor products for use in the computer industry and distributes its products, in part, through a network of independent distributors. The company's 1994 annual report contains the following note to the consolidated financial statements.

Accounting policies (in part):

Deferred income on shipments to distributors. Sales are made to distributors under agreements allowing the right of return on unsold merchandise held by the distributors. These agreements can be canceled by either party upon written notice, at which time the company is generally obligated to repurchase unsold inventory. Accordingly, recognition of sales to distributors and related gross profit are deferred until the merchandise is resold by the distributors.

Included in the current liabilities on the company's balance sheets are the following amounts:

	December 31,	
	1994	1993
Deferred income on shipments to distributors	$3,900	$3,550

The 1994 income statement reports the following amounts:

Sales	$115,500
Cost of goods sold	69,300
Gross profit	$ 46,200

All of ACD's products are priced to yield a gross profit equal to 40% of selling price.

REQUIRED:

1. Explain why ACD defers gross profit on sales to distributors until the merchandise is resold by the distributors.
2. Calculate the sales price of merchandise shipped to distributors in 1994, assuming no merchandise was actually returned.
3. Prepare summary journal entries to record:
   (a) Shipments of merchandise to distributors
   (b) Shipments of goods by distributors in 1994

4-8. *Lending transactions*

On January 1, 1994, Jumbo Real Estate Co. obtains a $250,000 mortgage from the Last Bank in Texas. The loan carries an 8.5% rate with annual payments of $63,441 for 5 years. Jumbo Real Estate was required to pay the following fees in connection with the mortgage:

Appraisal fee	$ 500
Loan origination fee	235
One point	2,500

REQUIRED:

1. Calculate the effective yield on this mortgage.
2. Prepare a mortgage amortization table.
3. Prepare journal entries to record the issuance of the mortgage loan and the receipt of the first payment.

4-9. *Sales on revolving credit terms*

Electronics World, Inc. offers revolving credit terms to its customers who qualify. The accounts carry an interest rate of 1.5% per month; and the customer must pay, at a minimum, an amount equal to 4% of the balance at the beginning of each month or $50, whichever is greater. On July 1, 1994, the company sells a home computer system for $1,350. The customer puts the purchase on her revolving credit account and makes the minimum payments at the end of each month.

REQUIRED:

1. Calculate the total amount of revenue recognized by Electronics World in the year ended December 31, 1994.
2. Prepare journal entries to record the sale on July 1, 1994 and receipt of the first payment on July 31.

4-10. *Revenue and cash flow*

Brick Publishing Co. publishes several monthly magazines and various paper-backs of the "how to do it" variety. Most magazine sales are by subscription, and revenue is recognized as the magazines are sent to the subscribers. Books are sold with a 12-month right of return; and revenue, less a provision for returns, is recognized at the time of sale. All books are sold with a 100% markup on cost—i.e., a book costing $5 to produce would sell for $10. Brick Publishing Co. reports the following amounts:

Balance sheet data:

	December 31,	
	1994	1993
ASSETS:		
Accounts receivable	$154,200	$ 148,750
Less: Allowance for sales returns	(4,850)	(4,510)
Net accounts receivable	149,350	144,240
LIABILITIES:		
Unearned portion of paid subscriptions	42,875	39,900

Income statement data:

Sales	$1,945,020
Less: Provision for sales returns	(67,240)
Net sales	$1,877,780

REQUIRED:

Calculate the amount of cash collected from customers during 1994.

PACIFIC GAS AND ELECTRIC COMPANY

The following is an excerpt from the 1987 annual report of Pacific Gas and Electric Company (all amounts in $ thousands):

Income statement excerpts:

	1987	1986	1985
Total operating revenues	$7,185,701	$7,816,661	$8,430,981
Income before change in recording unbilled revenues	597,194	1,081,223	1,030,805
Cumulative effect as of January 1, 1987 of accruing unbilled revenues, net of income taxes of $77,045	91,323	-	-
Net income	$ 688,517	$1,081,223	$1,030,805

Balance sheet excerpts:

	December 31, 1987	1986
Accounts receivable from customers (including unbilled amounts of $311,604 in 1987)	$962,922	$556,648

Excerpts from the notes to the financial statements:

Before January 1, 1987, revenues were recognized when customers were billed on a cycle basis. Beginning in 1987, the Company began accruing revenues for service provided but unbilled at the end of each month to match revenues and expenses more closely. If this accounting method had been used in prior years, consolidated net income for the periods prior to January 1, 1987, would not have been materially different.

REQUIRED:

1. Calculate the unbilled amount added to accounts receivable on January 1, 1987, as a result of the cumulative adjustment for the accounting change.
2. Calculate the amount of revenues billed in 1987.
3. Despite the fact that the cumulative effect of the change amounted to $91,323,000, the note states that "if this accounting method had been used in prior years, consolidated net income for the periods prior to January 1, 1987, would not have been materially different." Explain this apparent contradiction.
4. Explain how the new method of revenue recognition will "match revenues and expenses more closely."
5. The firm's ability to manage its accounts receivable balance efficiently is often assessed by measuring the accounts receivable turnover ratio. In general, the higher the turnover ratio, the more efficient the firm is in managing receivables. Calculate the receivables turnover ratio (revenues ÷ ending accounts receivable) for 1987 under both the old and new methods of revenue recognition. If a financial analyst was unaware of the change in revenue recognition, what would she conclude about management's efficiency in managing receivables?

REPUBLIC AIRLINES

The following note is taken from the 1985 annual report of Republic Airlines:

Passenger Revenue: Passenger revenue is recognized when the transportation service is provided. Tickets sold but unused are classified as a current liability.

The current liability referred to in the note is known as an air traffic liability, and Republic Airlines reported the following balances in this account in its 1985 annual report:

	12/31/85	12/31/84
Air traffic liability	$128,647,000	$84,661,000

When Republic Airlines sells tickets directly to customers, the firm typically receives cash (either currency or a negotiable instrument) at the time of sale. When a travel agent sells a Republic Airlines' ticket, the airline still records an air traffic liability for the amount of the ticket. However, since it has not yet received cash, it will record accounts receivable (from the travel agent) instead of cash. Republic Airlines reported the following balances in accounts receivable in its 1985 annual report:

	12/31/85	12/31/84
Accounts receivable	$158,108,000	$109,193,000

For the year ended December 31, 1985, Republic Airlines reported passenger revenues of $1,598,237,000.

REQUIRED:

Suppose Republic Airlines recognized revenue upon collection of cash from its customers and travel agents. Calculate the amount of passenger revenue that would have been reported for the year ended December 31, 1985.

CONSUMER REPORTS

The following excerpts are taken from an article entitled "Who Needs an Extended Warranty?" in the January, 1991 issue of *Consumer Reports*.

Retailers have been tight-lipped about their profits on warranty sales. But recently they've divulged this once-secret information, as part of an industry-wide examination of accounting procedures. It sheds new—and quite unflattering—light on the extended warranty business.

We obtained an "issues paper" prepared by several large consumer- electronics chains for the Financial Accounting Standards Board (FASB), a group that establishes generally accepted accounting procedures. That document and material we received from other sources show that warranty sales are far more lucrative for many retailers than anything else in the store.

According to the retailers themselves, only 12 to 20 percent of people who buy a warranty will ever use it. And many warranty-holders who do call for service don't need repair work, but simply help of an "educational" nature. In other words, they didn't understand the instructions.

Since warranties usually don't require the seller to provide any regular service or maintenance, and since actual repairs are so infrequent, the profit margin is enormous. Retailers estimate that for every dollar they take in from selling extended warranties, they will have to spend between 4 and 15 cents on service.

REQUIRED:

1. What did the consumer-electronics industry hope to accomplish by providing the FASB with the "issues paper" described in the *Consumer Reports* article?
2. Was the consumer-electronics industry successful in their lobbying efforts before the FASB?
3. How is the release of this information by *Consumer Reports* likely to affect the sales of extended warranties?

CASH AMERICA INVESTMENTS, INC.

CASE 4.4

The following information is taken from the 1991 annual report of Cash America Investments, Inc.:

The Business of Cash America

Cash America Investments, Inc. is engaged in acquiring, establishing and operating pawnshops that lend money on the security of pledged tangible personal property. Pawnshops function as convenient sources of consumer loans and as retailers of previously owned merchandise acquired in forfeited pawn transactions.

The pledged property is held through the term of the loan, which generally is one month with an automatic 60-day extension period. In the event the borrower does not pay or renew his loan, the unredeemed collateral is forfeited to the Company and then becomes inventory available for sale in the retail operations of the pawnshop.

Summary of Significant Accounting Policies (in part)

Loans and Income Recognition

Pawn loans ("loans") are generally made on the pledge of tangible personal property for one month with an automatic 60-day extension period ("the loan term"). Pawn service charges on loans are recorded on a constant yield basis over the loan term.

If the loan is not repaid, the principal amount loaned plus accrued pawn service charges become the carrying value of the forfeited collateral ("inventory") which is recovered through sale.

Inventory

Inventory represents merchandise acquired from forfeited loans, merchandise purchased directly from the public and new merchandise purchased from vendors.

Inventory is stated at the lower of cost or market.

The Company provides an allowance for shrinkage and valuation based on management's evaluation of the merchandise. The allowance deducted from the carrying value of inventory amounted to $1,490,000 and $1,265,000 at December 31, 1991 and 1990, respectively.

Note 2—Acquisitions (in part)

During 1991, the Company acquired 17 pawnshops in individual purchase transactions occurring throughout the year for an aggregate cash consideration of $10,790,000.

Consolidated Balance Sheets—December 31 (in part)

Dollars in thousands	1991	1990
Loans	$28,990	$23,305
Inventory, net	35,610	30,335
Service charges receivable	7,786	6,477

Consolidated Income Statement—Year Ended December 31, 1991 (in part)

Dollars in thousands	
Revenues	
Sales	$86,540
Pawn service charges	51,141
Cost of sales	68,716

Consolidated Statement of Cash Flows—Year Ended December 31, 1991 (in part)

Dollars in thousands	
Cash flows from operating activities	
Sales	$ 86,540
Pawn service charges	28,757
Cash flows from investing activities	
Loans forfeited and transferred to inventory	40,622
Loans repaid or renewed	93,920
Loans made, including loans renewed	(138,210)

REQUIRED:

1. Prepare summary journal entries to reflect the following activities for 1991:
   (a) Loans made, including loans renewed (Treat loans renewed as new loans.)
   (b) Pawn service charges earned
   (c) Loans repaid or renewed (Treat loans renewed the same as loans repaid.)
   (d) Pawn service charges collected
   (e) Loans forfeited and transferred to inventory
   (f) Merchandise sold

2. Does the amount shown as inventory on the Cash America balance sheet reflect the value of all the merchandise on hand at the balance sheet date? Explain.

3. From the description of the firm's accounting policies, it seems to be recognizing pawn service charge revenue on pawn loans that have been forfeited. Does this not violate the realization principle? Explain.

4. Suppose Cash America changed its accounting policies so that it only recognizes revenue on pawn loans actually repaid and merchandise sold. Describe how the financial statements would differ.

5. Calculate the average annual yield on pawn loans in 1991.

Revenue and Expense Recognition Related to Production and Collection

In Chapter 4, we observed that many firms recognize revenue upon delivery of goods and services to their customers. Recall that the decision of when to recognize revenues usually involves a trade-off between relevance and reliability. Relevance dictates recognizing revenue and expense as soon as it has been earned. Reliability dictates that revenue should not be recognized until most of the uncertainty regarding the amounts of revenue and expense to recognize have been eliminated. For many firms, relevant and reliable measures of revenue and expense can be obtained at the point of delivery of products or services to customers. This, then, is a very suitable point for revenue and expense recognition.

In this chapter, we consider some situations in which revenues and expenses are recognized at points in the firms' operating cycles other than the delivery of goods and services. In some cases, we will observe revenue recognized at or during production of firms' products. This is the point where recognition is deemed to be more relevant, and the uncertainty involved is not so great as to impair the reliability of the financial statements. In other cases, we will observe revenue recognized at the point of collection of cash from the customers. In some cases, it is not until this point that the inherent uncertainty can be limited enough to produce reliable financial statements. Before moving into a discussion of these methods of revenue and expense recognition, consider the following Wedtech Corp. example, which illustrates some of the difficulties in revenue recognition relevant to our discussion in this chapter.

WEDTECH CORPORATION

In December of 1986, Wedtech Corp. filed for protection from its creditors under Chapter 11 of the federal bankruptcy law. Wedtech was a defense contractor based in New York City; and in the three years prior to the bankruptcy filing, the firm had reported the following amounts of revenues and net income (in $ millions):

	Revenues	Net Income
1985	$117.5	$9.7
1984	72.4	4.7
1983	27.4	4.9

The amounts and rapid growth of revenues and net income reported by Wedtech over this period hardly give the impression of imminent financial distress.

Wedtech's initial public offering of common stock was in August of 1983. By the time it filed for bankruptcy, the corporation had raised a total of $155 million by selling stocks and bonds to investors.[1] The last security offering by Wedtech was a $75 million bond issue in August, 1986, just four months prior to the bankruptcy filing.[2] This, too, suggests that investors were unaware of the firm's financial difficulties just prior to the bankruptcy filing.

An article in *The Wall Street Journal* reported that the investment community was quite surprised at the bankruptcy filing.

> Wall Street analysts and thousands of investors in more than $160 million of Wedtech's stocks and bonds are puzzled and upset about Wedtech. A major question being asked is how did Wedtech fool so many people for four years about its earnings?[3]

According to the article, there were many alleged answers to the last question, including the possibility of fraud by management. However, Wedtech's use of the percentage of completion method for recognizing revenues on government contracts appeared to have been directly related to the alleged overstatement of revenues and income.

Many of Wedtech's contracts were long-term and supplied the U.S. military services with various items. As we shall see, under the percentage of completion method, revenues are recognized based on management's estimate of the proportion of the total contracted work performed in a particular year. Thus, suppose Wedtech had a $10 million contract to supply equipment to the U.S. Army over a three year period at an estimated total cost of $9 million. The total expected income from this contract is $10 million in revenue minus $9 million in expenses, or $1 million. If Wedtech's management estimated that

---

[1] "Wedtech's Data Called False," *New York Times* (February 10, 1987).

[2] *Ibid.*

[3] "Wedtech Used Gimmickry, False Invoices to Thrive," *The Wall Street Journal* (February 23, 1987), p. 6.

50% of the contracted work had been performed in 1985, it would recognize 50% or $5 million in revenue and 50% or $500,000 in income.

But how did Wedtech's use of the percentage of completion method lead to an apparent overstatement of revenues and income? Suppose Wedtech's management erred in its estimates of the amount of work performed in a particular year. For instance, suppose the estimate of the proportion of the work done in 1985 was based on the proportion of the total expected cost incurred that year. That is, if Wedtech had incurred $4.5 million of costs under this contract and the total expected cost was $9 million, management might have estimated the contract to be 50% complete. But what if the firm had not been able to control costs adequately and the contract turned out to cost a total of $10 million to complete? Thus, based on the costs incurred in 1985, the contract was really only 45% complete. Moreover, the total income on this contract would be exactly zero. But as we just saw, the firm would have recognized $500,000 of income on a contract that would eventually just break even. Part of the overstatement of Wedtech's revenues and income is alleged to have occurred in this way.[4]

The Wedtech experience illustrates the inherent trade-offs between relevance and reliability in the choice of revenue recognition method. Firms that engage in long-term contracts earn revenue by producing products or services according to the contracts' terms. Since these contracts often span several years and if revenue is not recognized until a particular contract has been completed, then at least some (and perhaps most) of the revenue from that contract will have been recognized in a period other than the one in which it was earned. If revenue is recognized when the contract is signed, then revenue will have been recognized before any has been earned. The preferred approach is to recognize revenue based on the amount of work performed each period, thereby recognizing revenue as it has been earned. The problem with this approach is that determining the relative amount of work performed in a period requires reliable estimates of the amount and cost of work yet to be performed. As we saw in the case of Wedtech, reliable estimates are not always available, resulting in potentially unreliable measures of income.

REVENUE RECOGNITION RELATED TO PRODUCTION

There are basically two types of firms that employ revenue recognition methods related to production. First, firms like Wedtech, which are engaged in long-term construction or production contracts, either recognize revenue as production proceeds or at the conclusion of production. Second, firms that produce certain commodities, which can be sold at well-defined market prices with little sales effort, recognize revenue at the point of production. We will examine both types of firms, starting with firms engaged in long-term, construction-type contracts.

---

[4] *Ibid.*

Long-Term Contracts

Firms engaged in long-term contracts include building contractors, interior decorators, shipyards, and government contractors such as Wedtech, our earlier example. For such firms, completion of the construction or production called for under a particular sales contract may require several years. The firm will not earn all its revenue until the long-term project required under the contract has been completed. If revenue were only recognized upon completion of the project, then a firm would report no revenue at all while the project is underway but would then report the entire revenue amount upon completion of the project. In such a case, the income statements produced would offer little relevant information about the profitability (or even the level) of the firm's activities while the project is underway.

Thus, many firms will recognize revenues from long-term contracts by the **percentage of completion method**. Under this method, revenue is recognized as work on the project progresses. As we have seen in Chapter 3, recognizing revenue prior to a project's completion unavoidably introduces uncertainty into the financial statements because estimates of the cost of work required to complete the project are necessary. When firms are unable to make reliable estimates, they will recognize revenue upon completion of the project by the **completed contract method**. In hindsight, it appears that Wedtech management was not capable of making the reliable estimates required by percentage of completion accounting; thus, the firm should have used completed contract accounting. Let us examine the differences between these two approaches in general terms before turning to a specific example.

Completed Contract Method   Under the completed contract method, a firm recognizes no revenue under a particular contract until the contract has been completed. As costs of completing the contract are incurred, they are recorded as an asset usually called Costs of Uncompleted Contracts (CUC). Upon completion of a contract, the contract price is recognized as revenue; and all of the costs recorded as CUC are recognized as expenses, thus matching them with the revenue earned under the contract. Since no revenue is recognized until the contract has been completed, the balance in CUC includes no value added by the construction or production process. Rather, it is stated at cost.

If revenue is recognized at the completion of the contract, then a firm could conceivably report no revenue for a period of years followed by a very large amount of revenue in the period the project is completed. Such income statements are potentially misleading in that the amount of revenue recognized in a period may not be related to the amount of productive effort the firm expended during the same period. However, financial statements prepared under the completed contract method are reliable in the sense that they are not based on estimates of the amount of work completed to date on contracts still in progress. Moreover, the completed contract method tends to produce more conservative financial statements, those that tend to understate a firm's assets and income. Of course, saying that a particular accounting method is conservative is just another way of saying that relevance has been sacrificed in the name of reliability.

Percentage of Completion Method   Firms employing the percentage of completion method recognize revenue each period based on management's estimates of the percentage of the total contracted work performed during the period. As the firm incurs costs of working on the contract, it records them as CUC. At the end of each accounting period, management will estimate the percentage of work done that period and accrue income, adding it to the balance in CUC. For instance, if management estimates that during a particular period the firm has completed 25% of a contract that is expected to produce income of $1,000,000, then $250,000 (25% of $1,000,000) will be accrued and added to the balance in CUC. However, if a contract is expected to produce a loss, then the firm will accrue the entire loss.[5] Thus, at any point in time, the balance in CUC under the percentage of completion method will include a *pro rata* share of any income expected from projects under construction and the entire expected loss on projects expected to produce losses.

Choosing Between Completed Contract and Percentage of Completion   Under FASB Statement No. 56, "the percentage of completion and completed contract methods are not intended to be free choice alternatives for the same circumstances."[6] How then do firms make the choice? The choice between completed contract accounting and percentage of completion accounting depends on the reliability of the estimates required. Applying the percentage of completion method requires estimates of the percentage of work done in a particular period and an estimate of the total profit or loss to be realized on the project. When such estimates are "reasonably dependable, the percentage of completion method is preferable."[7] Otherwise, the completed contract approach is preferable.

Accounting for Interim Billings and Collections on Long-Term Contracts   Under both completed contract and percentage of completion accounting, revenue is recognized independently of the timing of billings and collections. Most long-term contracts will provide for one or more interim payments (progress payments) to the contractor prior to the completion of the project. Since these progress payments are not events that trigger the recognition of revenue, how do contractors record interim billings and collections? When a customer is billed for an interim payment, the contractor records the amount due as a debit to an account receivable. The credit is then recorded to a Billings account. Billings are not reported separately on the firm's balance sheet but, rather, are deducted from the balance in CUC. Thus, the difference between the amount of CUC and Billings is reported. If, for a particular con-

5 "Long-Term Construction-Type Contracts," *Accounting Research Bulletin No. 45* (New York: AICPA, 1955), para. 6.

6 "Designation of AICPA Guide and Statement of Position (SOP) 81-1 on Contractor Accounting and SOP 81-2 Concerning Hospital-Related Organizations as Preferable for Purposes of Applying APB Opinion 20," *Statement of Financial Accounting Standards No. 55* (Stamford, CT: FASB, 1982), para. 6.

7 *Accounting Research Bulletin No. 45, op. cit.*, para. 15.

tract, the firm's balance in CUC exceeds the total amount billed, the firm will report the difference as an asset. This accounting indicates that the firm has not yet recovered all of costs of the uncompleted contract through billings and, thus, will be able to bill and collect additional amounts. If the amount billed exceeds the total CUC balance, the firm reports the difference as a liability, which indicates the firm has billed its customers for amounts exceeding the costs of the uncompleted contracts and, therefore, has an obligation to them to provide additional construction services for the amounts already billed. The accounting for interim billings will become more clear in the following example.

Applying the Methods

Suburban Construction Corp. worked on two contracts, A and B, during its first two years of operations. Information on the two contracts is as follows:

	Contract A	Contract B
Contract price	$10,000,000	$7,500,000
Year 1:		
Costs incurred this period	$ 4,000,000	$1,500,000
Estimated costs to complete	4,000,000	4,500,000
Amounts billed this period	2,500,000	3,500,000
Amounts collected this period	2,000,000	2,400,000
Year 2:		
Costs incurred this period	$ 4,000,000	$5,000,000
Estimated costs to complete	0	0
Amounts billed this period	7,500,000	4,000,000
Amounts collected this period	7,000,000	5,100,000

Completed Contract Accounting Let us begin by examining the journal entries to record the various transactions involved with the two contracts under the completed contract method.

Year 1

1. To record the construction costs incurred this period:

Costs of uncompleted contract A	4,000,000	
Costs of uncompleted contract B	1,500,000	
Various accounts		6,500,000

Without additional information, it is impossible to specify which accounts would be credited; but it is likely that cash, accounts payable, accumulated depreciation, and various prepaid and accrued expenses would all be involved.

2. To record interim billings made during the period:

Account receivable—contract A	2,500,000	
Account receivable—contract B	3,500,000	
Billings—contract A		2,500,000
Billings—contract B		3,500,000

3. To record collections on account during the period:

Cash	4,400,000	
Account receivable—contract A		2,000,000
Account receivable—contract B		2,400,000

Notice that since neither contract was completed during Year 1, no revenue has been recognized and the balances in CUC are merely the costs incurred to date on the two contracts.

At the end of Year 1, the total billings on Contract A under construction of $2,500,000 is less than the balance in costs of uncompleted contract of $4,000,000. Suburban would report the difference of $1,500,000 as an asset (costs of uncompleted contracts in excess of billings) on the December 31, Year 1 balance sheet. However, on Contract B, the total billings of $3,500,000 exceed the balance in cost of uncompleted contract of $1,500,000. Thus, Suburban would report the difference of $2,000,000 on the balance sheet as a liability (billings in excess of costs of uncompleted contracts).

Year 2

4. To record the construction costs incurred this period:

Costs of uncompleted contract A	4,000,000	
Costs of uncompleted contract B	5,000,000	
Various accounts		9,000,000

5. To record interim billings made during the period:

Account receivable—contract A	7,500,000	
Account receivable—contract B	4,000,000	
Billings—contract A		7,500,000
Billings—contract B		4,000,000

6. To record collections on account during the period:

Cash	12,100,000	
Account receivable—contract A		7,000,000
Account receivable—contract B		5,100,000

7. To record completion of Contracts A and B, closing out Billings and CUC:

Billings—contract A	10,000,000	
Billings—contract B	7,500,000	
Sales revenue—contract A		10,000,000
Sales revenue—contract B		7,500,000
Cost of goods sold—contract A	8,000,000	
Cost of goods sold—contract B	6,500,000	
Costs of uncompleted contract A		8,000,000
Costs of uncompleted contract B		6,500,000

Under the completed contract method, Suburban would record all revenue and the related cost of goods sold in the year the contracts are completed. Thus, Suburban Contractors would report $0 and $17,500,000 of sales revenue and $0 and $14,500,000 of cost of goods sold in Years 1 and 2, respectively. You may have noticed that management erred in its estimate of the costs necessary to complete Contract B at the end of Year 1. Costs of $4,500,000 were estimated but actual costs to complete the contract amounted to $5,000,000. This estimation error had no effect on the results under the completed contract method since revenue is not recognized on the basis of estimates. As we shall see next, this will not be the case under the percentage of completion method.

Percentage of Completion Accounting   Suburban would essentially make the same entries under the percentage of completion method in Year 1. The costs of working on the two contracts would be recorded as assets, but the title of the asset account would differ. Since the percentage of completion method adds value to the accounts during the performance of the contract, Suburban would record the costs plus estimated earnings on uncompleted contracts as an asset. Thus, the title of the account is changed to Costs and Estimated Earnings on Uncompleted Contracts.

In addition to the entries necessary under the completed contract approach, Suburban would need to make the following entry to accrue income based on management's estimates of the expected income and amount of work performed on each contract this period. In this example, the percentage of completion is determined using the **cost-to-cost method**, so named because it involves a ratio of the cost incurred to date to the total expected contract costs.

Year 1

8. To recognize revenue and expense based on current estimates:

Costs and estimated earnings of uncompleted contract A	*1,000,000	
Costs and estimated earnings of uncompleted contract B	**375,000	
Cost of goods sold—contract A	4,000,000	
Cost of goods sold—contract B	1,500,000	
Sales revenue—contract A		5,000,000
Sales revenue—contract B		1,875,000

These amounts are calculated as follows:

	Contract A	Contract B
1. Contract price	$10,000,000	$7,500,000
2. Costs incurred to date	4,000,000	1,500,000
3. Estimated costs to complete	4,000,000	4,500,000
4. Total estimated costs (line 2 + 3)	8,000,000	6,000,000
5. Estimated contract income (line 1 – 4)	2,000,000	1,500,000
6. Estimated percentage complete (line 2 ÷ 4)	50%	25%
7. Estimated contract income earned to date (line 6 × 5)	1,000,000	375,000
8. Amounts already recognized	0	0
9. Amount recognized this period	*1,000,000	**375,000

After Entry 8 is made, the balances in the costs and estimated earnings of uncompleted contracts accounts will reflect the amount of revenue Suburban would recognize to date.

At the end of Year 1, the total billings on uncompleted Contract A of $2,500,000 are less than the total costs and estimated earnings of uncompleted contract balance of $5,000,000 ($4,000,000 of construction costs + $1,000,000 of accrued earnings). Suburban would report the difference of $2,500,000 as an asset called "costs and estimated earnings on uncompleted contracts in excess of billings" on the December 31, Year 1 balance sheet. On Contract B, the total billings of $3,500,000 exceed the costs and estimated earnings of uncompleted contract balance of $1,875,000 ($1,500,000 of construction costs + $375,000 of accrued earnings). Suburban would report the difference of $1,625,000 as a liability called "billings in excess of costs and estimated earnings on uncompleted contracts" on the December 31, Year 1 balance sheet. Thus, we see how recognizing revenue on the percentage of completion method resulted in adding value to the accounts sooner, resulting in a larger asset balance for Contract A ($2,500,000 under the percentage of completion method compared with $1,500,000 under the completed contract method) and a smaller liability balance for Contract B ($1,625,000 under the percentage of completion method compared with $2,000,000 under the completed contract method).

Notice that the amount of revenue recognized has nothing to do with the amount that Suburban has been able to bill the customer under the terms of the contracts. On Contract A, Suburban recognized revenue of $5,000,000 in Year 1 under the percentage of completion method, while it billed only $2,500,000 under the terms of the contract. On Contract B, Suburban recognized revenue of $1,875,000 in Year 1 under the percentage of completion method, while its contract allowed $3,500,000 in billings.

The amount a contractor can bill a customer during the contract is specified by the contract and will reflect the contractor's financial needs and the customer's willingness to provide interim financing. It may or may not be related to the contractor's performance under the contract. Therefore, under accrual accounting, it has no bearing on the decision of when to recognize revenue. Companies recognizing unbilled revenue under the percentage of completion method will typically disclose the cumulative amount of unbilled revenue recognized in the notes to the financial statements.

Year 2

9. To record revenue and expense for year 2:

Construction in progress—contract A	*1,000,000	
Construction in progress—contract B	**625,000	
Cost of goods sold—contract A	4,000,000	
Cost of goods sold—contract B	5,000,000	
Sales revenue—contract A		5,000,000
Sales revenue—contract B		5,625,000

These amounts are calculated as follows:

	Contract A	Contract B
1. Contract price	$10,000,000	$7,500,000
2. Costs incurred to date	8,000,000	6,500,000
3. Estimated costs to complete	0	0
4. Total costs (line 2 + 3)	8,000,000	6,500,000
5. Estimated contract income (line 1 – 4)	2,000,000	1,000,000
6. Estimated percentage complete (line 2 ÷ 4)	100%	100%
7. Contract income earned to date (line 6 × 5)	2,000,000	1,000,000
8. Amounts already recognized	1,000,000	375,000
9. Amount recognized this period	*1,000,000	**625,000

The amount of earnings Suburban recognized in Year 2 on Contract B includes a change in estimate. At the end of Year 1, management thought it was 25% complete on a project that would yield a total of $1,500,000 in earnings. However, the total earnings on the contract only amounted to $1,000,000. Therefore, the firm was only about 23% complete ($1,500,000 ÷ $6,500,000) on a project that would yield only $1,000,000 in earnings. While it is clear that too much has been accrued for estimated earnings in Year 1, the firm would not make any retroactive adjustments. Instead, as described in Chapter 3 on changes in estimate, the amount Suburban would record as revenue and expense in Year 2 reflects the totals that should be recognized under the revised estimate.

10. To record completion of Contracts A and B, closing out Billings and CUC:

Billings—contract A	10,000,000	
Billings—contract B	7,500,000	
Costs and estimated earnings of uncompleted contract A		10,000,000
Costs and estimated earnings of uncompleted contract B		7,500,000

Notice, once again, that the balances in the costs and estimated earnings on uncompleted contracts accounts reflect the total revenues Suburban would recognize to date. Since both of these contracts are now completed, balances equal to the total contract prices are found in the costs and estimated earnings accounts just prior to their being closed out.

Other Issues in Accounting for Long-Term Contracts

In addition to the question of how to recognize revenue for long-term contracts, these contracts also frequently raise some other accounting questions. These include how to account for amounts retained by the customer, what costs to include as product costs, and how these contracts are treated for tax purposes.

Retainages Some long-term contracts allow the buyer to retain a portion of the contract price pending the occurrence of some event, usually final inspection and testing of the goods provided under the long-term contract. These amounts, known as **retainages** or **retentions**, are usually classified as receivables although, under the terms of the contract, they are not yet receivable. For instance, the notes to the 1991 financial statements of Offshore Pipelines, Inc., reveal the following:

> Included in contract receivables are amounts representing retainages on contracts of $2,290,077 at July 31, 1991, of which $904,000 is expected to be collected in fiscal year 1993 and the balance of the receivables is expected to be collected within one year. Retainage balances at July 31, 1990 were not material.

What Costs are Treated as Product Costs?   As we have seen, some costs are treated as product costs and carried on the balance sheet as an asset until revenue from the sale of that asset has been recognized. At that point, these product costs are matched with that revenue as an expense. Other costs are treated as period costs and simply recognized as an expense as incurred. Some companies, especially government contractors, enter into contracts in which the contract price is based on the contractor's costs. Under cost accounting standards agreed to by both parties, selling, general, and administrative costs are treated as product costs. Most other companies treat these as period costs.

For example, F. A. Tucker Group, Inc., involved in maintaining, upgrading, and constructing transmission lines, distribution systems, and substations for public power authorities and electrical utilities, treats selling, general, and administrative costs as period costs, as evidenced by this excerpt from their 1991 annual report.

> **Revenue Recognition** - The Companies recognize revenue on construction contracts using the percentage-of-completion method, measured by the ratio of cost incurred to date on the contract to management's estimate of the contract's total cost. Contract cost includes all direct material and labor costs and those indirect costs related to contract performance, such as supplies, tools, repairs and equipment cost. *Selling, general and administrative expenses are charged to expense when incurred* (emphasis added).

On the other hand, LTV Aerospace and Defense Company, a large government contractor, treats general and administrative costs as product costs.

> Fixed price contracts in progress are stated at accumulated costs, less amounts allocated to products delivered (in accordance with defined contract terms), based upon the estimated total cost of the products *(including general and administrative costs)...* (emphasis added).

Only those companies that work on cost-based contracts treat selling, general, and administrative costs as product costs.

Tax Considerations   For tax reporting purposes, companies that work under long-term contracts often have an incentive to prefer the completed contract method of reporting revenues and expenses. Under the completed contract method, revenues and expenses are recognized upon completion of a contract, not before. Thus, the payment of taxes on income can also be deferred until completion of the contract if taxable income is computed according to the completed contract method. Until recently, many companies engaging in long-term contracts used completed contract accounting for tax purposes, while using percentage of completion for financial reporting purposes. However, the tax law has been revised and requires percentage of completion for tax purposes in most cases where it is used for financial reporting.

Summary of Accounting for Long-Term Contracts

We have seen that long-term contracts are accounted for by either the completed contract or the percentage of completion methods. The choice between the two methods depends on whether reliable estimates can be made of:

1. The percentage of total work performed in a particular period
2. The costs necessary to complete the contract

If reliable estimates can be made, then the percentage of completion is the required method. Otherwise, firms use the completed contract method. This reflects the trade-off between relevance and reliability introduced in the last chapter. Revenue recognition by the percentage of completion method is deemed to be more relevant but is inherently less reliable because it is based on management's estimates.

Firms using the percentage of completion method recognize revenue earlier and, assuming the firm's contracts are profitable, report higher net assets than they would under the completed contract method. As we have seen, the higher total assets under percentage of completion accounting result from the value added to the firm's assets through the recognition of revenues and expenses.

Revenue Recognition at Production for Certain Commodity Producers

As we noted earlier in the chapter, some firms produce or sell products such as agricultural commodities, precious metals, or marketable securities that can be sold without any significant sales effort at prices that may be readily determined in advance because an efficient and active market exists. If these assets are "readily convertible into known amounts of cash or claims to cash"—i.e., if they have "interchangeable (fungible) units and quoted prices available in an active market that can rapidly absorb the quantity held by the entity without significantly affecting the price"—then such firms will recognize revenue upon "completion of production or when prices of the assets change."[8]

As we have seen in Chapter 4, revenue recognition at production implies that inventories are stated at market value. Since little effort is required to sell these products, costs to sell are relatively insignificant and the accrual of such costs as expenses before the costs have been incurred is typically not necessary. When these market values change, inventories are "marked to market," and the adjustment of the assets' market values are also recorded as an adjustment to revenues for the period.

Among commodity merchandising firms, it is industry practice to recognize as revenue the difference between the sales price and the cost of products. Thus, what these firms call "revenue" is analogous to what most firms call "gross profit," the difference between revenues and cost of goods sold. For example, the following note was taken from the 1988 annual report of The Pillsbury Company.

Net sales

Net sales include trading margins rather than total sales, from merchandising grain, feed ingredients, and export flour.

Reserve Recognition Accounting

In the 1970s, a period of considerable economic and political turmoil for the oil and gas industry, the SEC proposed that oil and gas producing companies adopt a procedure known as reserve recognition accounting (RRA). Essentially, RRA called for the recognition of oil and gas revenues at the time the reserves are discovered underground. Thus, the SEC proposed that revenues be recognized even earlier in these firms' operating cycles: before actual production (extraction) of the oil and gas. This would have resulted in the oil and gas reserves, arguably the most important assets of oil and gas producing companies, being valued at their current market value less the costs of extraction. RRA, ultimately deemed to be infeasible, was never implemented; but it is interesting to note how earlier recognition of revenues would have resulted in value being added to the balance sheets of affected firms earlier than under more conventional revenue recognition alternatives. More details on RRA are contained in Appendix 5.1.

REVENUE RECOGNITION RELATED TO COLLECTION

In general, recognition of revenue as cash collections from customers are made is only appropriate for financial reporting purposes when substantial uncertainties exist as to the amount that will ultimately be collected.[9] In such cases, the revenues, while earned, do not meet the definition of being "realizable" because there is some question as to the amount of cash they represent. Therefore, firms will wait until the revenues are collected before recognizing them. In this section, we illustrate two methods that accomplish this—**the cost recovery method** and the **installment sales method**. We demonstrate that what really distinguishes these methods is how they recognize expense rather than revenue.

The installment sales method has its widest application in the real estate industry, as briefly introduced in Appendix 5.2. It is also used by some firms for tax reporting purposes. The earlier firms recognize revenues for tax purposes, the earlier they will have to include those revenues in their taxable income and pay income taxes. Moreover, if firms make installment sales to their customers and recognize revenue for tax purposes before they collect the

---

8 "Recognition and Measurement in Financial Statements of Business Enterprises," *Statement of Financial Accounting Concepts No. 5* (Stamford, CT: FASB, December 1984), para. 83, 84).

9 *Accounting Principles Board Opinion 10: Omnibus Opinion* (New York: AICPA, 1966), para. 12.

installments, then they may end up paying taxes on revenues they have yet to collect. Fortunately, the tax law recognizes this problem and allows firms to recognize revenue under the installment sales method in some cases.

Cost Recovery Method

A firm uses the cost recovery method when enough uncertainty exists about the collectibility of revenues that it doubts whether the costs of its goods or services sold will be recovered. Under the cost recovery method, a firm will not recognize income from a sale until it has fully recovered the cost of the goods or services sold. At the date of sale, the firm makes a journal entry to recognize revenue and cost of goods or services sold but to defer the gross profit on the sale. This gross profit remains deferred until revenues equal to the cost of goods or services sold have been collected. Once costs have been recovered, the firm recognizes additional collections as gross profit.

For example, suppose Flagship Enterprises, Inc. makes a sale to Shady Oak, Inc. on April 1, 1993. Because of considerable concern about the collectibility of the receivable from Shady Oak, Inc., Flagship's management would account for this transaction under the cost recovery method. The goods sold cost Flagship $42,000, and the sales contract calls for monthly payments of $2,000 (due on the last day of each month) for 36 months. Thus, if collections are made according to the contract schedule, Flagship would recover its costs after it has collected the 21st monthly installment of $2,000 on December 31, 1994. Once the costs have been recovered, Flagship would recognize the remaining installments as gross profit. Assuming all installments are collected on a timely basis, Flagship would recognize gross profit as follows:

	1993	1994	1995	1996
Gross profit recognized	$0	$0	$24,000	$6,000

The journal entries necessary to account for this transaction under the cost recovery method would be as follows:

1. To record sale on April 1, 1993:

Installment accounts receivable	72,000	
Inventory		42,000
Deferred gross profit		30,000

2. To record collection of the first 21 installments:

Cash	2,000	
Cost of goods sold	2,000	
Installment accounts receivable		2,000
Sales revenue		2,000

Until the cost of the goods sold has been fully recovered, expenses would be recognized in amounts equal to the amounts collected from customers, yielding no gross profit. Once the cost has been fully recovered, revenue is recognized for each subsequent collection. However, no expense is recognized because the cost of the goods sold will have been fully recognized as an expense by that point.

3. To record collection of the final 15 installments and recognize gross profit:

Cash	2,000	
Deferred gross profit	2,000	
Installment accounts receivable		2,000
Sales revenue		2,000

Under the cost recovery method, the income statements will report the sales and cost of goods sold. The balance in deferred gross profit is typically offset against the receivable from the sale on the firm' balance sheets. Thus, this transaction would affect Flagship's income statements and balance sheets for the four years as shown in Exhibit 5.1.

Notice how the balance in deferred gross profit on the balance sheet does not change until the firm has recovered its $42,000 cost by collecting that amount of installments from customers. Once the costs have been recovered, each additional installment collection results in recognition of gross profit of an equal amount.

One could argue that the cost recovery method does not adhere to the matching principle very well. In the example just considered, all of the costs were effectively matched with the first 21 installment collections (resulting in no gross profit being recognized with these collections), and no costs were matched with the last 15 installment collections (resulting in gross profit equal to the amount collected being recognized with each of these collections). Of course, since considerable concern existed about whether all of these collections would be made, Flagship's matching costs on a *pro rata* basis with collections

EXHIBIT 5.1

Income Statement Effects and Balance Sheet Effects—Cost Recovery Method

FLAGSHIP ENTERPRISES, INC.
Income Statement Effects
Cost Recovery Method

	YEAR ENDED DECEMBER 31,			
	1993	1994	1995	1996
Sales revenue	$18,000	$24,000	$24,000	$6,000
Cost of goods sold	18,000	24,000	0	0
Gross profit	$ 0	$ 0	$24,000	$6,000

FLAGSHIP ENTERPRISES, INC.
Balance Sheet Effects
Cost Recovery Method

	DECEMBER 31,			
	1993	1994	1995	1996
Installment receivable	$54,000	$30,000	$ 6,000	$ 0
Less: Deferred gross profit	30,000	30,000	6,000	0
Net receivable	$24,000	$ 0	$ 0	$ 0

might have resulted in the recognition of income, which would never be realized. Hence, the matching principle gets sacrificed in the name of conservatism.

Installment Sales Method

The installment sales method, used in some cases for tax reporting purposes but relatively rarely for financial reporting purposes, is similar to the cost recovery method just illustrated. Under both methods, the gross profit from an installment sale is initially deferred. The primary difference between the two methods is: Under the installment sales method, the deferred gross profit is recognized on a *pro rata* basis with each installment collection; while under the cost recovery basis, gross profit is not recognized until all costs have been recovered. Thus, the installment sales method will recognize gross profit somewhat earlier than the cost recovery method.

Let us examine the installment sales method by using the Flagship example we just considered under the cost recovery method. If Flagship had accounted for the sale to Shady Oak, Inc. under the installment sales method, the results would have been as follows:

First, we calculate a gross profit percentage as the expected gross profit on the sale divided by the sales amount:

1. Sales revenue	$72,000
2. Cost of goods sold	42,000
3. Gross profit	$30,000
4. Gross profit percentage (100 × line 3 ÷ line 1)	41.67%

Applied to each installment collection, this percentage determines the amount of gross profit to be recognized with each collection. Thus, given the timing of the installment collections, Flagship would recognize gross profit as follows under the installment sales method:

	1993	1994	1995	1996
No. of installments collected	9	12	12	3
Gross profit per installment*	$ 833	$ 833	$ 833	$ 833
Gross profit recognized	$7,500	$10,000	$10,000	$2,500

* $30,000 ÷ $72,000 × $2,000 = $833

To account for this transaction under the installment sales method, Flagship would need to make the following journal entries:

1. To record sale on April 1, 1993:

Installment accounts receivable	72,000	
Inventory		42,000
Deferred gross profit		30,000

This first entry is identical to that made earlier under the cost recovery method. However, under the installment sales method, a portion of the deferred gross profit is recognized with each installment collected.

2. To record collection of installments:

Cash	2,000	
Deferred gross profit	833	
Cost of goods sold	1,167	
Installment accounts receivable		2,000
Sales revenue		2,000

The effect on Flagship's income statements and balance sheets for the four years under the installment sales method would be as shown in Exhibit 5.2.

If you compare these amounts with those reported under the cost recovery method, you will notice that the installment sales method reports gross profit earlier than the cost recovery method. As a result, the installment sales method reports higher asset values.

SUMMARY

Two types of firms recognize revenue related to their production. First, firms engaged in long-term construction or production contracts either recognize revenue as production proceeds or at the conclusion of production. Second, firms that produce certain commodities, which can be sold at well-defined market prices with little sales effort, recognize revenue at the point of production. Long-term contracts are accounted for by either the completed contract or the percentage of completion methods. The choice between the two methods depends on whether reliable estimates can be made of:

EXHIBIT 5.2
Income Statement Effects and Balance Sheet Effects—Installment Sales Method

FLAGSHIP ENTERPRISES, INC.
Income Statement Effects
Installment Sales Method

	YEAR ENDED DECEMBER 31,			
	1993	1994	1995	1996
Sales revenue	$18,000	$24,000	$24,000	$6,000
Cost of goods sold	7,500	10,000	10,000	2,500
Gross profit	$10,500	$14,000	$14,000	$3,500

FLAGSHIP ENTERPRISES, INC.
Balance Sheet Effects
Installment Sales Method

	DECEMBER 31,			
	1993	1994	1995	1996
Installment receivable	$54,000	$30,000	$6,000	$ 0
Less: Deferred gross profit	22,500	12,500	2,500	0
Net receivable	$31,500	$17,500	$3,500	$ 0

1. The percentage of total work performed in a particular period
2. The costs necessary to complete the contract

If reliable estimates can be made, then the percentage of completion is the preferable method. Otherwise, firms should use the completed contract method.

There are two methods of revenue recognition related to the collection of revenues: cost recovery and installment sales. These methods are inconsistent with accrual accounting and, therefore, are only appropriate for financial reporting purposes when substantial uncertainties exist as to the amount that will ultimately be collected.

Appendix 5.1—Reserve Recognition Accounting

The SEC proposed **reserve recognition accounting (RRA)** in the mid-1970s for use in the oil and gas industry as a replacement for revenue recognition at the time of sale. The SEC's intent was to report the most important assets of oil and gas firms, namely their **proven reserves** of oil and gas, at market value on the firms' balance sheets. Proven reserves are the quantities of oil and gas that can be extracted at commercially feasible costs. If revenue were recognized upon discovery of proven reserves, then the firms would carry the reserves at their market value less the cost of extraction. The problem: Proven reserves are underground and not directly observable. Engineers and geologists estimate the amount of proven reserves from information on rock strata and other data. As more data become available, these estimates are revised. The problem with RRA should be immediately apparent. Recognizing revenue based on geological estimates of proven reserves would introduce considerable uncertainty into the financial statements.

Consider the following simple example. Blackfoot Oil Company purchased an oil field for $1,740,760 on the first day of 1993. The field had proven reserves of oil estimated at 300,000 barrels. On the first day of the year, oil was selling at $15/barrel, and Blackfoot estimated it would cost $8/barrel to extract the reserves. Blackfoot also estimates it could produce 100,000 barrels a year for 3 years. For simplicity, assume Blackfoot is financed totally with equity and that all cash flows occur on the last day of the year. Exhibit 5.3 demonstrates the valuation of Blackfoot's proved reserves using a discount rate of 10%, along with a summarized balance sheet for the company as of January 1, 1993.

If during 1993, Blackfoot produced and sold the 100,000 barrels expected for cash, at the $15/barrel price, with cash production costs of $8/barrel, the company would have only 200,000 barrels of proved reserves at the end of 1993. Assuming that the prices have not changed by year-end, Exhibit 5.4 demonstrates how these reserves would be valued and provides summarized financial statements for the period based on RRA. The value of the proved reserves has fallen, and this decrease represents an expense for Blackfoot. In addition, the out-of-pocket production costs also represent an expense of the period. In the end, income for 1993 is $174,160, which is equal to a 10% return on the beginning value of the proved reserves ($1,740,760 × 10%), subject to rounding error.

Other factors also influence the way income is recognized under RRA. Suppose that in addition to the production activity described above for 1993, the company entered into exploration and development efforts, which cost $50,000 and $600,000, respectively. The result of these efforts was the discovery of an additional 180,000 barrels of proved reserves, which the company

BLACKFOOT OIL COMPANY
Valuation of Crude Oil Reserves Under RRA
as of January 1, 1993

	1993	1994	1995
Cash inflow from crude oil sales	$1,500,000	$1,500,000	$1,500,000
Cash outflow for production costs	800,000	800,000	800,000
Net cash inflow	$ 700,000	$ 700,000	$ 700,000
Discount factor	× .9091	× .8264	× .7513
Present values	$ 636,370	$ 578,480	$ 525,910
Total present value = $1,740,760			

BLACKFOOT OIL COMPANY
Balance Sheet
January 1, 1993

ASSETS:		EQUITY:	
Oil reserves	$1,740,760	Contributed capital	$1,740,760

BLACKFOOT OIL COMPANY
Valuation of Crude Oil Reserves Under RRA
December 31, 1993

	1994	1995
Cash inflow from crude oil sales	$1,500,000	$1,500,000
Cash outflow for production costs	800,000	800,000
Net cash inflow	$ 700,000	$ 700,000
Discount factor	× .9091	× .8265
Present values	$ 636,370	$ 578,550

Total present value = $1,214,920

BLACKFOOT OIL COMPANY
Statement of Income
For the Period Ended December 31, 1993

Revenues	$1,500,000
Cost of production	800,000
Gross margin	$ 700,000
Amortization of proved reserves	525,840[a]
Income	$ 174,160

BLACKFOOT OIL COMPANY
Balance Sheet
December 31, 1993

ASSETS:		EQUITY:	
Cash	$ 700,000	Contributed capital	$1,740,760
Oil reserves	1,214,920	Retained earnings	174,160
	$1,914,920		$1,914,920

Supporting calculation:	
Oil reserves, January 1	$1,740,760
Oil reserves, December 31	1,214,920
Amortization	$ 525,840[a]

expects to extract uniformly over the two-year period 1994–1995. The discovery of new reserves would also generate income for the period under RRA. Exhibit 5.5 demonstrates the effect of this new discovery on Blackfoot's financial statements. Income in this example would have risen relative to the example in Exhibit 5.4 due to the effects of oil and gas exploration and development. The additional revenues from new discoveries would have been

$1,093,428, and the costs of $650,000 for exploration and development would have been matched against these revenues. The net result is an increase in income of $443,428.

An alternative way of thinking about RRA is to note that the income for any period is simply the sum of the results of actual production plus (or minus) the change in the present value of the proven reserves. In Exhibit 5.4 where no new oil reserves are discovered, the present value of proved reserves falls as they are actually converted into cash flows via production and sale. This decline reduces income from production. In Exhibit 5.5, the net effect of increases from new discoveries and declines from production is a net increase of $567,588, which is exactly equal to the increase in the present value of the proven reserves during the year.

There are many other factors that influence how the present value of proven reserves changes throughout the year under RRA. Selling prices and production costs will change, resulting in revision of estimates of future cash flows. When profit margins increase or decrease, unexpected gains or losses, respectively, will be recognized. In addition, estimates of proved reserves will be revised as new information becomes available. Production schedules may also be revised to change the rate of production in response to price changes. Finally, Blackfoot may elect to sell some of its proved reserves prior to extraction or purchase more reserves from other companies. These changes will also be reflected in the present value of proved reserves at the end of the period and, thus, affect income for the period. Note that the determination of gain or loss on sale of oil and gas properties would be determined by matching the decline in the value of the proven reserves against the selling price of the properties.

EXHIBIT 5.5

Blackfoot Oil
Company Valuation
of Crude Oil
Reserves Under
RRA

BLACKFOOT OIL COMPANY
Valuation of Crude Oil Reserves Under RRA
December 31, 1993

	1994	1995
Cash inflow from crude oil sales	$2,850,000	$2,850,000
Cash outflow for production costs	1,520,000	1,520,000
Net cash inflow	$1,330,000	$1,330,000
Discount factor	× .9091	× .8265
Present values	$1,209,103	$1,099,245
Total present value	$2,308,348	
Present value without new reserves (from Exhibit 5.2)	1,214,920	
Value of new reserves	$1,093,428	

BLACKFOOT OIL COMPANY
Statement of Income
For the Period Ended December 31, 1993

Revenues from production	$1,500,000
Costs of production	800,000
Income from production	$ 700,000
Revenues from discoveries	1,093,428
Amortization of proved reserves	525,840
Income from changes in proved reserves	567,588
Income before exploration and development costs	1,267,588
Cost of exploration and development	650,000
Income	$ 617,588

BLACKFOOT OIL COMPANY
Balance Sheet
December 31, 1993

ASSETS:		EQUITY:	
Cash	$ 50,000	Contributed capital	$1,740,760
Oil reserves	2,308,348	Retained earnings	617,588
	$2,358,348		$2,358,348

Appendix 5.2—Reserve Recognition Accounting in the Real Estate Industry

In this Appendix, we briefly examine some of the specialized revenue recognition procedures used by firms selling real estate. These specialized accounting principles are necessary because the complexity of these transactions makes it difficult to determine when the general criteria for revenue and expense recognition have been met. Our objective is not to explore the relevant accounting issues in depth but, rather, to provide a general overview. The accounting procedures required by real estate firms are technically complex, and a thorough examination of them is beyond the scope of this text.

Real estate transactions are contractually complex, and it may be difficult to determine the appropriate point for revenue recognition under the general guidelines outlined in the chapter. Therefore, the FASB issued SFAS No. 66 in 1982 to provide more specific guidance in accounting for real estate sales transactions.[10] SFAS No. 66 recognizes two broad classes of real estate sales transactions: retail land sales and all other sales of real estate. This distinction is drawn because the procedures and terms of the two types of sales typically differ.

The general conditions applying to sales other than retail land sales are that revenue shall be recognized at the time of sale (called the *full accrual method*) only when the amount of revenue to be collected can be reasonably determined and the seller's obligations under the contract are substantially complete. For these general conditions to be considered met, SFAS No. 66 imposes a number of precise tests, which look at whether:

1. The sale has actually been consummated
2. The amounts paid by the buyer demonstrate ability to pay
3. The receivable can be subordinated (i.e., whether the seller can be reduced to a lower creditor status by future property loans)
4. The usual risks and rewards of ownership have been transferred from the seller to the buyer.

---

[10] "Accounting for Sales of Real Estate," *Statement of Financial Accounting Standards No. 66* (Stamford, CT: FASB, 1982), para. 5.

If any of these tests are not met, then the seller will account for the transaction under the percentage of completion method, the installment method, or, if the sale has not yet been consummated, the deposit method.

In retail land projects, a developer acquires a parcel of land, develops and subdivides it, and sells individual lots to retail customers. Several features distinguish retail land sales contracts. In many contacts, a refund period exists during which time the buyer may back out of the contract and receive a full refund of payments made to date. The purchase price is usually paid over an extended period of time. The collection experience with retail customers typically differs from that with other customers. It is not unusual for sales to be made before development has been completed.

As we have seen, in sales transactions, revenue is typically recognized at the point of sale when title passes from the seller to the buyer. However, in retail land sales, the **full accrual method** of revenue recognition—i.e., revenue recognition at the point of sale—is only applied when the following conditions imposed by SFAS No. 66 are met:

1. The refund period has expired, and the buyer has made all required payments to date.
2. The cumulative payments amount to at least 10% of the sales price.
3. Collectibility is reasonably assured.
4. The receivable on the loan cannot be made subordinate (i.e., a lesser claim) to new loans on the property.
5. The developer's obligations are complete.[11]

These precisely specified criteria for revenue recognition are designed to insure that revenue has been earned and is realizable.

If all of these criteria are not met, then the transaction will be accounted for under the percentage of completion method, the installment method, or the deposit method depending on the particular circumstances of the contract.

QUESTIONS

1. How do firms engaged in long-term, construction-type contracts choose between the percentage of completion and completed contract methods?

2. In accounting for a long-term construction contract using the percentage of completion method, how is the interim billings on contracts account classified on the balance sheet?

   (AICPA adapted)

3. A company used the percentage of completion method to account for a 4-year construction contract. How, if at all, would income previously recognized and interim billings to date be used in the calculation of the income recognized in the second year?

   (AICPA adapted)

---

[11] *Ibid.*, para. 45.

4. On what is the calculation of the income recognized in the second year of a 4-year construction contract, which is accounted for using the percentage of completion method, based?
(AICPA adapted)

5. In accounting for a long-term construction contract for which there is a projected profit, would the balance in the appropriate asset accounts at the end of the first year of work using the completed contract method be higher or lower than the amounts reported under the percentage of completion method? Explain your answer.
(AICPA adapted)

6. When should an indicated loss on a long-term contract be recognized under the completed contract method? Under the percentage of completion method?
(AICPA adapted)

7. Why is the installment sales method generally not acceptable for financial reporting purposes?

8. In what sense does the cost recovery method violate the matching principle? Why does the accounting profession tolerate this violation?

9. Give two examples of sales transactions for which it would *not* be appropriate to recognize revenue at the time of the sale.

10. Why are different revenue recognition principles necessary for retail land sales and for other real estate sales?

EXERCISES

5-1. *Percentage of completion method*

Hansen Construction, Inc., uses the percentage of completion method of recognizing revenue. During 1993, Hansen started work on a $3,000,000 fixed-price construction contract. The accounting records disclosed the following data for the year ended December 31, 1993:

Costs incurred	$ 930,000
Estimated cost to complete	2,170,000
Interim billings	1,100,000
Collections	700,000

REQUIRED:

1. Prepare summary journal entries to record the following 1993 activities related to this contract:
   (a) Construction costs incurred
   (b) Progress billings
   (c) Collections
2. Calculate the amount of income or loss (if any) Hansen should recognize for 1993 and prepare a journal entry to record it.
3. Assume this is the only contract in progress at December 31, 1993. Show how the balances in construction in progress and billings would be reported on the firm's balance sheet as of that date.
(AICPA adapted)

5-2.   *Completed contract method*

Refer to Exercise 5-1. Suppose Hansen Construction, Inc. has consistently used the completed contract method and that all facts pertaining to this fixed-price contract are as described above.

REQUIRED:

1. Prepare summary journal entries to record the following 1993 activities related to this contract:
   (a)   Construction costs incurred
   (b)   Progress billings
   (c)   Collections
2. Calculate the amount of income or loss (if any) Hansen should recognize for 1993 and prepare a journal entry to record it.
3. Assume this is the only contract in progress at December 31, 1993. Show how the balances in construction in progress and billings would be reported on the firm's balance sheet as of that date.
   (AICPA adapted)

5-3.   *Percentage of completion method vs. completed contract method*

During 1991, Landy Construction Company started work on a $7,500,000 fixed-price construction contract, which was completed in 1994. The accounting records disclosed the following data:

	Cumulative Contract Costs Incurred	Estimated Costs at Completion
At 12/31/91	$ 500,000	$5,000,000
At 12/31/92	2,750,000	5,500,000
At 12/31/93	5,000,000	6,000,000

REQUIRED:

1. Calculate the amount of income or loss Landy would recognize on this contract for the years ended December 31, 1991, 1992, and 1993 under the percentage of completion method.
2. Calculate the amount of income or loss Landy would recognize on this contract for the years ended December 31, 1991, 1992, and 1993 under the completed contract method.
   (AICPA adapted)

5-4.   *Percentage of completion method*

On April 1, 1993, Pine Construction Company entered into a fixed-price contract to construct an apartment building for $6,000,000. Pine appropriately accounts for this contract under the percentage of completion (cost-to-cost) method. Information relating to the contract is as follows:

	December 31,	
	1993	1994
Percentage of completion	20%	60%
Estimated costs at completion	$4,500,000	$4,800,000
Income recognized (cumulative)	300,000	720,000

REQUIRED:

What is the amount of contract costs incurred during the year ended December 31, 1994?

5-5. *Percentage of completion method vs. completed contract method*

In 1994, Long Corporation began construction work under a 3-year contract. The contract price is $800,000. Long uses the percentage of completion method for financial accounting purposes. The income to be recognized each year is based on the proportion of cost incurred to total estimated costs for completing the contract. The financial statement presentations relating to this contract at December 31, 1994, follow:

Balance Sheet:

Accounts receivable—construction contract billings	$15,000
Construction in progress	50,000
Less: Contract billings	47,000
Costs of uncompleted contract in excess of billings	3,000

Income Statement:

Income (before tax) on the contract recognized in 1994	$10,000

REQUIRED:

1. How much cash was collected in 1994 on this contract?
2. What was the initial estimated total income before tax on this contract?
3. What amounts would have been reported on the firm's balance sheet and income statement if the contract had been accounted for under the completed contract method?

(AICPA adapted)

5-6. *Percentage of completion method vs. completed contract method*

On January 10, 1993, Marr Construction Co. began work on a $6,000,000 construction contract. At the inception date, the estimated cost of construction was $4,500,000. The following data relate to the progress of the contract:

Income recognized at 12/31/93	$ 600,000
Costs incurred 1/10/93 through 12/31/94	3,600,000
Estimated cost to complete at 12/31/94	1,200,000

REQUIRED:

1. How much income should Marr recognize for the year ended December 31, 1994, under the percentage of completion method? Under the completed contract method?
2. If the estimates of the costs to complete the contract are accurate and the job is completed by December 31, 1995, how much income will Marr recognize for the year ended December 31, 1995 under the percentage of completion method? Under the completed contract method?
3. If the contract is completed by December 31, 1995, at a total cost of $5,200,000, how much income will Marr recognize for the year ended December 31, 1995, under the percentage of completion method? Under the completed contract method?

5-7. *Installment sales method*

June Department Store started making installment sales to customers during 1994 and uses the installment sales method to recognize revenue on these transactions. At December 31, 1994, the balance in deferred gross profit was $27,000, and $18,000 of gross profit was recognized during 1994. The gross profit percentage applicable to 1994 is 30%.

REQUIRED:

1. What was the amount of installment sales made in 1994?
2. What was the amount of collections on installment sales made in 1994?

5-8. *Cost recovery method*

On October 31, 1993, Malone Machinery Co. sold some assets to Culhane Corp. for $24,000, payable in 12 monthly installments of $2,000. Prior to the sale, the assets were carried on Malone's balance sheet at their cost of $20,000. The sale was accounted for by the cost recovery method.

REQUIRED:

1. Prepare journal entries to record the sale.
2. Determine the amount of income to be reported on this sale for the years ended December 31, 1993 and 1994.

5-9. *Installment sales method*

Thompson Motors, Inc. made installment sales in 1994 for the first time. The following data summarize the activities for 1994:

Installment sales	$400,000
Costs of installment sales	260,000
Collections on installment sales	160,000

REQUIRED:

1. Calculate the gross profit percentage for 1994.
2. Prepare journal entries to record the installment sales, the deferral of gross profit, the collection of installment receivables, and the recognition of gross profit.

5-10. *Cost recovery method*

Dairy Princess Corp. (DPC) is a franchisor in the soft ice cream business. On June 1, 1993, DPC entered into a franchise agreement with Don Corleone, the franchisee, and called for an initial franchise fee of $50,000 payable in 5 equal annual installments of $10,000 from June 1, 1993 - June 1, 1997. DPC's cost of providing the services covered by the initial franchise fee is $42,000, and these costs are incurred immediately. Because the initial franchise fee is collectible over an extended period of time and because considerable uncertainty exists regarding Don Corleone's ability to pay, DPC will account for these costs under the cost recovery method.

REQUIRED:

1. Prepare journal entries relevant to the initial franchise fee on June 1, 1993.
2. Calculate the amount of income to be recognized from the initial franchise fee each year over calendar years 1993–1997.

5-11. *Revenue recognition at production*

Mountain Mining Corp. produces a precious metal whose price is fixed by law at $35 per ounce. It started operations on January 1, 1993 with only two assets— $50,000 in cash and a mine acquired for $1,500,000—and no liabilities. The mine contains an estimated 150,000 ounces of the precious metal. The firm recognizes revenue at the time of production. During 1993, the following activities took place:

(a) Ore was extracted from the mine and refined into 10,000 ounces of the precious metal. Refining and extraction costs of $150,000 were paid in cash.

(b) 9,500 ounces of the precious metal were sold on account and delivery costs of $4,750 ($.50 per ounce) were paid in cash.

(c) $315,000 was collected from customers. There are no bad debts.

REQUIRED:

Prepare an income statement for 1993 and a balance sheet as of December 31, 1993.

PROBLEMS

5-1. *Percentage of completion method vs. completed contract*

Northwestern Remodelers, Inc. is a building contractor specializing in residential remodeling work. During its first year of operations, the following activities took place:

(a) On January 2, the firm's owners contributed $20,000 in cash.

(b) On January 2, the firm borrowed $80,000 from First Bank and Trust Co. The loan is in 5 years, and annual interest at 15% is due each December 31.

(c) Construction machinery and equipment costing $50,000 was acquired on January 3 and was paid for in cash.

(d) During the year, the firm entered into four contracts to provide remodeling services to homeowners. The status of the four contracts at year-end is as follows:

	A	B	C	D
Contract price	$25,000	$40,000	$30,000	$50,000
Costs incurred to date:				
Depreciation	1,500	2,500	0	3,000
Other	18,500	12,500	0	22,000
Total	$20,000	$15,000	$ 0	$25,000
Total estimated costs	$20,000	$30,000	$24,000	$40,000
Amount billed	25,000	25,000	5,000	35,000
Amount collected	20,000	22,500	5,000	25,000

All costs other than depreciation incurred to date have been paid in cash.

(e) General and administrative costs of $2,500 were incurred and paid in cash.

(f) Interest on the bank loan was paid on December 31.

(g) On December 31, the owners withdrew $5,000 in cash from the firm.

REQUIRED:

1. Prepare an income statement for the year and balance sheet as of December 31 assuming the firm recognizes revenue on the completed contract basis.
2. Prepare an income statement for the year and balance sheet as of December 31 assuming the firm recognizes revenue on the percentage of completion basis.
3. Briefly discuss how the choice between the completed contract method and percentage of completion would be made.

5-2. *Percentage of completion method*

Curtiss Construction Company, Inc., entered into a firm, fixed-price contract with Axelrod Associates on July 1, 1992, to construct a four-story office building. At that time, Curtiss estimated that it would take between two and three years to complete the project. The total contract price for construction of the building is $4,000,000. Curtiss appropriately accounts for this contract under the completed contract method in its financial statements and for income tax reporting. The building was deemed substantially completed on December 31, 1994. Estimated percentage of completion, accumulated contract costs incurred, estimated costs to complete the contract, and accumulated billings to Axelrod under the contract were as follows:

| | At December 31, | | |
	1992	1993	1994
Percentage of completion	10%	60%	100%
Contract costs incurred	$ 350,000	$2,500,000	$4,250,000
Estimated costs to complete the contract	3,150,000	1,700,000	—
Billings to Axelrod	720,000	2,160,000	3,600,000

REQUIRED:

1. Prepare schedules to compute the amount to be shown as "Costs of uncompleted contract in excess of related billings" or "Billings on uncompleted contract in excess of related costs" at December 31, 1992, 1993, and 1994. Ignore income taxes. Show supporting computations in good form.
2. Prepare schedules to compute the profit or loss to be recognized as a result of this contract for the years ended December 31, 1992, 1993, and 1994. Ignore income taxes. Show supporting computations in good form.

(AICPA adapted)

5-3. *Percentage of completion method*

On April 1, 1993, Butler, Inc., entered into a cost plus fixed-fee contract to construct an electric generator for Dalton Corporation. At the contract date, Butler estimated that it would take two years to complete the project at a cost of $2,000,000. The fixed fee stipulated in the contract is $300,000. Butler appropriately accounts for this contract under the percentage of completion method. During 1993, Butler incurred costs of $700,000 related to the project, and the estimated cost at December 31, 1993, to complete the contract is $1,400,000. Dalton was billed $500,000 under the contract.

REQUIRED:

Prepare a schedule to compute the amount of gross profit Butler will recognize under the contract for the year ended December 31, 1993.

(AICPA adapted)

5-4.   *Real estate transactions*

Breezey Mountain Estates, Inc. sells vacation homes in Montana. The following terms are typical of those offered by the firm:

(a) A $75,000 home can be purchased for no down payment with monthly payments of $900 for 15 years.

(b) The buyer has the right to cancel the contract during the first 6 months and have all payments returned.

REQUIRED:

Assuming that collectibility is reasonably assured, no subordination of the receivable is possible, and Breezy Mountain Estates has fulfilled all of its obligations, can Breezy Mountain Estates apply the full accrual method of revenue recognition at the:

1. Date of sale?
2. Expiration of the refund period?

5-5.   *Revenue recognition at production*

Green River Gold Mining, Inc. recognizes revenue at the time it produces gold bullion. Assume that the price of gold has been constant at $250 per ounce over 1994 and that the firm started the year with 5,000 ounces of gold in inventory. During the year, the following activities took place:

(a) 10,000 tons of ore were extracted from the mine at a total extraction cost of $500,000.

(b) All of the ore was refined into 40,000 ounces of gold bullion at a total refining cost of $2,900,000.

(c) 38,000 ounces of gold were sold for a total of $9,500,000.

(d) General and administrative expenses amounted to $425,000.

REQUIRED:

1. Calculate the income for 1994.
2. Calculate the balance in the gold inventory account at December 31, 1994.

5-6.   *Installment sales method*

Royal Stores sells merchandise on the installment plan. The following data cover the first three years of the firm's operations:

	1991	1992	1993
Installment sales	$360,000	$480,000	$570,000
Costs of installment sales	226,800	288,000	336,300
Collections on installment sales			
- made in 1991	120,000	180,000	60,000
- made in 1992		165,000	240,000
- made in 1993			188,000

REQUIRED:

Calculate the gross profit recognized each year under the installment sales method of revenue recognition.

5-7.   *Installment sales method*

Roger's Retail uses the installment sales method and reports the following balances in deferred gross profit:

	12/31/94	12/31/93
Deferred gross profit	$285,600	$216,000

All of Roger's installment sales are due in 12 monthly installments, and the firm collected installments totalling $960,000 during 1994. There were no bad debts during 1994. The gross profit percentages applying to 1994 and 1993 were 34% and 36%, respectively.

REQUIRED:

1. Calculate the amount of the gross profit recognized in 1994.
2. Prepare summary journal entries to record the following activities:
   (a) 1994 installment sales and costs of installment sales
   (b) 1994 collections on installment sales

5-8. *Cost recovery method*

Pay Less Tax, Inc. (PLTI) is a franchisor in the tax return preparation business. On August 1, 1994, PLTI entered into a franchise agreement with George Geek, which called for an initial franchise fee of $36,000, payable in 24 monthly installments of $1,500 beginning immediately. The initial franchise fee covers the following services to be provided by PLTI:

	Revenue	Cost
Training	$20,000	$12,000
Site selection assistance	4,000	2,000
Management consulting	8,000	7,000
Advertising	4,000	3,000
Total	$36,000	$24,000

All costs were incurred by PLTI by December 31, 1994.

REQUIRED:

Suppose that the initial franchise fee is accounted for by the cost recovery method because of concern over Mr. Geek's ability to pay. Determine the amount of revenue and expense to be recognized by PLTI in the years ended December 31, 1994, 1995, and 1996.

5-9. *Installment sales method vs. cost recovery method*

Speedy Lube, Inc. is a franchisor in the automobile maintenance business. On September 1, 1993, Speedy Lube entered into a franchise agreement with Jack Harris, which called for the payment of an initial franchise fee of $36,000 payable in 24 monthly installments of $1,500 starting September 1, 1993. The cost of the services that Speedy Lube will provide in return for the initial franchise fee were $10,000 incurred on September 1, 1993, and $14,000 incurred on December 1, 1993. Because the collectibility of the initial franchise fee is questionable, Speedy Lube must account for these fees under either the installment sales method or the cost recovery method.

REQUIRED:

1. Prepare journal entries relevant to the recording of initial franchise fees by Speedy Lube for the year ended December 31, 1993 under the:
   (a) Installment sales method
   (b) Cost recovery method

2. Calculate the amount of income Speedy Lube will recognize for each year ended December 31, 1993–1995 under both revenue recognition methods.
3. Which method would Speedy Lube probably prefer? Why? Ignore tax considerations.

5-10. *Balance sheet implications of alternative revenue recognition methods*

Happy Valley Contractors, Inc. worked on four contracts during its first year of operations. Information on the status of these contracts is as follows:

	A	B	C	D
Contract price	$50,000	$120,000	$45,000	$25,000
Costs incurred to date:				
Depreciation	3,000	7,500	0	1,500
Other	37,000	37,500	0	11,000
Total	$40,000	$45,000	$ 0	$12,500
Total estimated costs	$40,000	$90,000	$36,000	$20,000
Amount billed	50,000	75,000	7,500	17,500

REQUIRED:

1. Show how the balances in Construction in Progress and Billings would be reported on the firm's year-end balance sheet under the
   (a) Completed contract method
   (b) Percentage of completion method
2. Explain why the revenue recognition principle affects these balance sheet amounts.

5-11. *Real estate sales/installment method*

Great Minnesota Real Estate Co. sells a property with a cost of $600,000 on June 1, 1994, under the following terms:

Total selling price	$1,000,000
Cash down payment	150,000
First mortgage payable to seller	850,000

By December 31, 1994, the seller has received $35,000 of principal on the first mortgage. The down payment is deemed to be inadequate for full profit recognition, and the firm will recognize revenue under the installment method.

REQUIRED:

Calculate the amount of profit to be recognized on this transaction for the year ended December 31, 1994.

PEABODY CORP.

Peabody Corp. builds pollution control devices for electric utilities and heavy industry. It recognizes revenue on the percentage of completion basis. In 1980, it completed a project for a Colorado utility and disclosed that the project had cost $9 million more than had originally been estimated. Although the project had been under construction for several years, this was the first disclosure of any cost overruns. Information on this project is as follows:

Total contract price (fixed)	$61,500,000
Original estimate of total contract cost	52,000,000
Costs incurred prior to 1980	46,800,000

While the project was under construction, Peabody estimated percentage of completion by the cost-to-cost method by calculating the costs incurred to date as a percentage of the original estimate of the total contract cost. This percentage was then applied to the expected income from the project to yield the total income recognized on the project to date.

REQUIRED:

1. Calculate the income from this project that had been recognized by Peabody prior to 1980.
2. Calculate the total income from the project.
3. Calculate the income or loss from this project reported by Peabody in 1980.
4. Given the magnitude of the cost overrun, does it appear reasonable that the entire overrun occurred in 1980?
5. Assume that the cost overrun actually occurred prior to 1980. By how much, in total, had Peabody's income (before taxes) prior to 1980 been overstated by the failure to include the cost overruns in the calculation of the percentage of completion?
6. How could Peabody have estimated the percentage of completion more accurately and avoided the problems reported here?

LTV AEROSPACE AND DEFENSE COMPANY

LTV Aerospace and Defense Company (LTVAD) manufactures aircraft, missiles, and various electronic components used for military and commercial applications. Most of its contracts are with the federal government and are of two types:

1. Cost-reimbursement contracts permit the company to recover its costs plus a fee, which may be fixed or determined according to any one of a variety of different formulas. Cost-reimbursement contracts are generally applied to products and processes in the development stage—i.e., not yet ready for production.

2. Fixed-price contracts permit the company to recover a fixed price per unit delivered. Fixed-price contracts are generally applied to products and processes in production.

LTVAD's Summary of Significant Accounting Policies contained in its 1993 annual report described the firm's accounting methods as follows:

Inventories

Fixed-price contracts in progress are stated at accumulated costs, less amounts allocated to products delivered (in accordance with defined contract terms), based on the estimated total cost of the contracts determined under the learning curve concept, which is based on a predictable decrease in unit cost as production techniques become more efficient through repetition.

In accordance with industry practice, inventories include amounts relating to contracts and programs having production cycles longer than one year and, therefore, a portion thereof will not be realized within one year.

Revenue and profit recognition

Sales and profits under fixed-price contracts are based on contract terms and estimated final costs and generally are recorded as items are delivered in accordance with contract terms. Sales and profits under certain fixed-price contracts, primarily full-scale engineering and development contracts, requiring substantial performance over several periods prior to commencement of deliveries, are recognized under the percentage of completion (cost-to-cost) method of accounting. Sales and fees from cost-reimbursement contracts are recognized using the percentage of completion (cost-to-cost) method of accounting and are recorded as costs are incurred in the proportion that costs incurred bear to total estimated costs at completion. Incentive fees are recognized using the percentage of completion method when sufficient information is available to relate actual performance to target performance. Losses on contracts are recognized in full when identified.

Consider two hypothetical contracts of the type regularly entered into by LTVAD.

Contract A

LTVAD agrees to deliver 100 surface-to-surface missiles (SSMs) at a fixed price of $24,800 each. Management expects that production will take two years to complete and the average final cost per unit will be $21,080, computed as follows:

Units	Cost
1–10	$ 235,000
11–60	1,050,000
61–100	823,000
	2,108,000

Contract B

LTVAD agrees to deliver a prototype electronic device to military specifications. The contract calls for payment to LTVAD equal to its costs incurred plus a fee of $100,000 if the total contract costs do not exceed $1,000,000. Management estimates the contract will take 18 months to complete at a cost of $920,000.

During 1994, the following activities take place:

	Contract A	Contract B
Units delivered	8	N/A
Costs incurred	$ 237,500	$620,000
Estimated costs to complete	1,944,900	315,000
Amounts billed	190,000	620,000
Amounts collected	148,000	465,000

REQUIRED:

Using LTVAD's description of its accounting methods and the facts given about these hypothetical contracts, determine the amounts that Contracts A and B would contribute to the amounts reported by LTVAD for:
1. Revenue for 1994
2. Expense (ignore income taxes) for 1994
3. Inventory at December 31, 1994
4. Receivables at December 31, 1994

F. A. TUCKER GROUP, INC.

F. A. Tucker Group, Inc. is an electrical contractor to public power authorities and electrical utilities, supplying personnel and equipment to maintain, upgrade, and construct distribution systems, transmission lines, and substations. The group also provides installation services, engineering, and project managerial services. The group reported sales of $32,337,000 and cost of goods sold of $26,519,000 in the year ended December 31, 1991.

The following excerpts from the notes to the financial statements are taken from the 1991 annual report:

Revenue Recognition—The Companies recognize revenue on construction contracts using the percentage-of-completion method, measured by the ratio of cost incurred to date on the contract to management's estimate of the contract's total cost. Contract cost includes all direct material and labor costs and those indirect costs related to contract performance, such as supplies, tools, repairs and equipment cost. Selling, general and administrative expenses are charged to expense when incurred.

Provision for estimated losses on uncompleted contracts are recorded in the period in which such losses are determined. Changes in job performance, job conditions and estimated profitability including those arising from contract penalty provisions, and final contract settlements may result in revisions to costs and income and are recognized in the period in which the revisions are determined.

The asset, "Costs and estimated earnings in excess of billings on uncompleted contracts," represents revenues recognized in excess of amounts billed. The liability, "Billings in excess of costs and estimated earnings on uncompleted contracts," represents billings in excess of revenues recognized.

Accounts Receivable—Accounts receivable consist of the following at December 31:

	1991	1990
Contract receivables	$3,571,286	$5,209,916
Contract retainages	485,258	1,113,881
	$4,056,544	$6,323,797

Contracts in Progress—Details of contracts in progress are as follows at December 31:

	1991	1990
Costs incurred on uncompleted contracts	$17,619,173	$10,759,792
Estimated earnings	3,369,567	1,627,127
	$20,988,740	$12,386,919
Less billings to date	20,980,512	12,278,077
	$ 8,228	$ 108,842

Included in the accompanying balance sheets under the following captions:

	1991	1990
Costs and estimated earnings in excess of billings on uncompleted contracts	$ 173,999	$ 529,555
Billings in excess of costs and estimated earnings on uncompleted contracts	(165,771)	(420,713)
	$ 8,228	$ 108,842

REQUIRED:

Assume that all contracts in progress at December 31, 1990 were completed by December 31, 1991. Calculate the following amounts F.A. Tucker Group would have reported if it had used completed contract accounting:

1. Revenues, 1991
2. Cost of goods sold, 1991
3. Accounts receivable, December 31, 1991
4. Billings to date, December 31, 1991
5. Ignoring income taxes, what effect would completed contract accounting have on the net assets at December 31, 1991?

PART 3

Valuation and Representation of Assets

CHAPTERS

CHAPTER 6

Cash and Short-Term Investments in Marketable Securities

Cash flow is the lifeblood of any business organization. **Liquidity** is the term used to describe an enterprise's ability to generate sufficient cash to meet creditors' demands when obligations come due. Higher liquidity implies a greater amount of available resources to pay bills when due. The major source of cash for any company arises from the sale of its goods and services. Often these sales are initially on credit, requiring that the entity forego the use of the cash generated from the sale until it is collected. Other sources of cash include new debt issues, issues of stock, or sales of property, plant, and equipment.

When companies expect future expansion of operations by acquiring new property, plant, and equipment, expanding inventory, or acquiring an entire business unit, they may need to amass cash over time to fund planned growth. Rather than holding excess cash in non-interest bearing demand deposits, corporations often have cash management programs, which place excess cash balances in some form of temporary investment that earns a return. These investments range from government treasury bills, which mature in a few days, to other corporations' equity securities, which have no maturity at all.

Due to the close operational linkage between excess cash balances and short-term investments, some companies view the sum of their cash balances and the value of short-term investments as interchangeable assets that together represent the corporations' available liquid assets. As a result, corporations commonly report these two assets as a single asset in their balance sheets. Depending on the types of securities purchased as short-term investments and the relative value of all these investments, other companies elect to disclose separately the balances of cash and short-term investments in the balance sheet. Regardless of the disclosure choice, the management of cash balances is the driving force behind most short-term investments. For this reason, we consider accounting and reporting issues for both asset categories simultaneously in this chapter.

CASH

Cash, an asset, includes all of the following types of individual assets:

1. Petty cash
2. Demand deposits
3. Time deposits
4. Undeposited checks
5. Foreign currencies
6. Bank drafts
7. Money orders

Petty cash refers to cash balances kept on hand at various locations to pay for minor expenditures such as postage and other small out-of-pocket expenditures. Petty cash funds are referred to as "imprest funds" because the petty cash always contains cash and receipts for expenditures and totals a constant amount. For example, if a petty cash fund were established on January 1, 1994, in the amount of $50, the company would record the following journal entry:

January 1, 1994:
Petty cash   50
   Cash   50
To establish the petty cash fund.

If postage of $12 was paid out of petty cash, then a receipt for the postage charges would replace the cash removed. At some point, the cash balance of petty cash would be restored by transferring an amount equal to the value of the disbursement receipts. Suppose that another postage charge of $15 was also paid out of petty cash prior to replenishing the balance on February 17, 1994. In this case, the company would restore the $50 petty cash balance, transferring $27 from its bank balance into petty cash. The following entry would record this event:

February 17, 1994:
Postage expense   27
   Cash   27
To replenish petty cash and record expenses to date paid from
 petty cash.

While cash in the fund and receipts should always equal the fund's balance, several events could cause the fund not to balance:

1. Receipts may be lost or not completed.
2. Errors may occur in disbursing cash (either too little or too much cash is disbursed).
3. Receipts may be written for an incorrect amount.
4. Money from the fund may be lost or stolen.

As a result, it may not be possible to identify every expenditure out of the petty cash fund when it is time to replenish the cash balance.

When the cash in the fund and the total receipts do not equal the fund's balance, the cash (over) and short account is typically charged for any discrepancy between the verifiable expenditures and the current balance of petty cash. If there is more cash than can be accounted for, cash (over) and short is credited for the excess. If there is less cash, cash (over) and short is debited. Ultimately, this account is an income statement account, which will be closed to retained earnings after the financial statements are prepared.

Since the petty cash fund should always account for a fixed amount of funds, and this is a relatively immaterial balance for most companies, the total value of the petty cash fund ($50 in the example above) is included in the balance of cash reported in the balance sheet.

Demand deposits and **time deposits** represent amounts on deposit in checking and savings accounts, respectively. When a company holds checks that have not yet been deposited or foreign currencies that are not yet converted into U.S. dollars, the dollar value of these items is also included in the definition of cash. Checks written by a company but not yet been presented to the bank for payment are also included in the definition of cash (by reducing the cash balances reported as being on deposit with the bank). **Bank drafts** are commitments by banking institutions to advance funds on demand by the party to whom the draft was directed. **Money orders** are similar financial instruments to bank drafts, but they need not be drawn on a bank. Both of these instruments represent claims to cash balances and are included in the definition of cash.

Balance Sheet Classification of Cash

Generally, cash will be reported as a current asset. However, if the checks written exceed the available cash balance, an **overdraft** has occurred, resulting in a negative balance for cash. When this occurs, the negative balance should be reported as a current liability, not as a negative asset. Overdrafts are accounted for as a temporary loan.

Compensating Balances

A **compensating balance** is the minimum balance that must be kept on deposit with the bank (usually in a checking account) as part of a lending agreement. Banks often require compensating balances in line-of-credit agreements to provide collateral and to lock in a minimum amount of funds, which can be invested without fear of having it withdrawn by the depositor. A **line-of-credit** is a commitment from a bank to make loans to the company on demand up to a prespecific maximum limit. No loan actually exists until the company activates part, or all, of the line-of-credit. Line-of-credit agreements contain a variety of terms, including provisions for how interest rates will be determined for any outstanding balance.

Since compensating balances do not represent amounts the company must pay to the bank, they do not reduce the cash balance reported in the balance sheet. In effect, they restrict the use of those funds. Before the company can draw down the account balance below the minimum, it must obtain approval or pay special fees. A compensating balance requirement effectively increases the cost of the loan by the opportunity cost of losing the use of these funds during the period covered by the minimum balance requirement. Since they do not represent resources actually consumed, economic opportunity costs of this type are not directly reflected as expenses in the company's financial statements.

If the restriction imposed by the compensating balance requirement on the use of the cash asset is deemed material to the company's financial position, additional note disclosures of such restriction may be necessary. Exhibit 6.1 provides an example, taken from the financial reports of Pioneer Hi-Bred International Corporation, of a note disclosure relating to compensating balances that might be incorporated into the financial statements.

SHORT-TERM INVESTMENTS AND CASH EQUIVALENTS

Short-term investments in marketable securities is an asset category that represents investments in debt or equity securities of other entities, where management's intent is to liquidate the investment within one year or the next operating cycle, whichever is longer. Liquidation may occur by the sale of the security for cash in the open market or the maturity of a debt security. Examples of debt securities include bonds, notes, and commercial paper. Examples of equity securities include common stock, preferred stock, and stock options.

Short-term investments in marketable securities are further divided into two groups, depending on whether the securities are cash equivalents. *Cash equivalents* include only those short-term investments that will mature within 90 days of the date they were acquired by the investor. Securities that often meet the definition of a cash equivalent include government treasury bills, commercial paper (short-term notes issued by corporations), and certificates of deposit. On occasion, high-grade bonds issued by other corporations may be cash equivalents if the maturity date of these bonds is less than or equal to 90 days at the time of acquisition.

The distinction between short-term investments that qualify as cash equivalents and those that do not is particularly important in the construction of the statement of cash flows. Corporations may elect to define cash for purposes of the construction of the statement of cash flows, as either:

1. Cash, or
2. Cash and cash equivalents.

Once they make this election, corporations are expected to continue to apply the same definition consistently from period to period. If corporations

---

DISCLOSURE OF COMPENSATING BALANCES **PIONEER HI-BRED INTERNATIONAL CORPORATION**	**❘ EXHIBIT 6.1** Pioneer Hi-Bred International
During the year, additional lines of credit were available to meet peak borrowing periods. Two of these lines of credit require compensating balances totaling $230,620. Others call for a fee payment based on a rate of 3/8% of the respective lines.	Corporation Disclosure of Compensating Balances

elect to change the definition of cash for the construction of their statements of cash flows, it is deemed a change in accounting principle, which requires restatement of prior years' statements of cash flows to be consistent with the current year's definition. Short-term investments that are not cash equivalents can never be included in the definition of cash for purposes of constructing the statement of cash flows.

The treatment of cash equivalents can, at times, make the articulation between the statement of financial position and the statement of cash flows difficult to understand. In its cash flow statement for a recent year, Honeywell, Inc. reported the following (amounts in millions):

Increase (decrease) in cash and cash equivalents	$(222.8)
Cash and cash equivalents at beginning of year	366.5
Cash and cash equivalents at end of year	$ 143.7

However, in its balance sheet, Honeywell reported a balance of $180.4 million for an asset category described as cash and temporary cash equivalents. How can we reconcile these two amounts ($143.7 million in the statement of cash flows and $180.4 million in the balance sheet) for what appears to be the same category of asset? The answer to this question lies in understanding the difference between temporary cash investments as a whole and the subcategory of cash equivalents.

Honeywell must have included certain short-term investments that were not cash equivalents in the amount reported in its balance sheet ($180.4 million). Since the statement of cash flows must employ a more limited definition of cash and cash equivalents, the amount reported there ($143.7 million) would exclude certain short-term investments. By implication, Honeywell must have held short-term investments ($36.7 million) that did not mature within 90 days of the date on which these securities were acquired.

Liquidity and the Selection of Short-Term Investments

Companies attempt to maximize their use of cash balances by placing excess cash into some type of investment that might earn a return. Central to this decision is maintaining liquidity while still obtaining a return on the cash not used. Maintaining liquidity requires that investments must be readily marketable (easily convertible into cash). Well-organized markets exist to trade commercial paper (short-term corporate debt), government treasury bills, corporate bonds, corporate stocks, options, and other securities. These types of financial instruments represent possible short-term investments that allow companies to earn returns on excess funds while maintaining an ability to convert the instrument to cash, virtually on demand, by sale to other investors.

Debt Versus Equity Securities: A Brief Comparison of Alternative Short-Term Investments

Debt securities differ from equity securities in a variety of ways that are too numerous to exhaust in the discussion here. However, there are some important comparative features we need to review to understand the issues relating to accounting for short-term investments as they relate to each type of security.

Debt securities typically have two important features:

1. In the event that a corporation becomes insolvent, debt holders generally must be paid in full before equity holders receive any distributions of assets.
2. Debt securities promise fixed cash payments to investors at specific points in time.

The commitment to make fixed payments at specific points in time allows investors who purchase the debt securities to take actions in the event of non-payment. Such actions include foreclosure and renegotiation of the terms of the debt. These actions are typically not available to equity investors in the event that a dividend is not paid when expected.

The market value of a debt security is affected principally by two forces:

1. The term structure of interest rates in the economy
2. The default risk of the debt

The **term structure of interest rates** refers to the interest rates required in the financial markets for securities with a duration (length of life) equivalent to the debt security under examination. Different interest rates exist for different maturities, with short maturities generally having the lowest equivalent annual rate of interest and long-term (20–30 year bonds) having the highest equivalent annual rate of interest. Term structure is affected by the general expectations of investors regarding the future levels of economic activity on the whole. When the economic outlook is good, interest rates will decline. When the outlook is poor, interest rates will rise.

Default risk refers to the likelihood that the issuing corporation will not be able to make all the promised cash payments at the scheduled dates. It is a risk related to the individual corporation's future performance. If default risk is high, investors will require a very high interest rate when discounting the future cash flows under the debt to compensate for the high level of risk that payment will not be forthcoming. When default risk becomes a major issue in valuing debt securities, the security may become unmarketable.

The market value of a debt security may be more or less susceptible to changes in the term structure. Debt securities with short maturities (such as two or three months) will not vary greatly in value even if the term structure changes dramatically. This situation arises because of the very short period over which the remaining cash flows under the debt security will be received. With longer duration debt (debt with several years of cash flows remaining), changes in the term structure can dramatically affect the market value of the security.

Recalling the definition of a cash equivalent, it is clear that one attribute of a cash equivalent is that its market value will not be very sensitive to changes in the term structure of interest rates. Remember, it must mature within 90 days of the date the investor corporation acquires the security to qualify as a cash equivalent. In addition, for debt securities within 90 days of maturity, any significant default risk will be more apparent and less likely to change dramatically in the period leading up to maturity. The insensitivity of the market value of such securities to fluctuation is a major reason why cash equivalents were defined in this fashion.

Since maintenance of liquidity is a company's primary consideration in the selection of short-term investments, debt securities with significant default risk are simply not considered acceptable. Consequently, it is rare that investments in debt securities for short-term purposes are materially affected by changes in default risk.

In the absence of default, an investor who purchases a debt security and holds it to maturity will receive a rate of return equivalent to the market rate of interest used to determine the purchase price when the debt security was acquired. This rate of interest is referred to as the yield-to-maturity. **Yield-to-maturity** is the equivalent annual interest rate that, when compounded over the life of the debt, would make the present value of the future cash flows equivalent to the price paid by the purchaser. It represents the actual yield that an investor will receive if the security is held to maturity and no default occurs.

The fact that yield-to-maturity can be determined at the date of purchase does not imply that the investor does not face the risk of changes in term structure and of default. While the investor's intention at the time of purchase may be to hold the debt to maturity, should it be necessary to sell the security to raise cash during the life of the debt, the holder still faces the risk that the term structure will have changed and caused the market value of the debt to rise or fall since acquisition. We will return to these observations later when we examine the debate over the use of historical cost or market value as a valuation basis for financial reporting relating to these investments.

Equity securities generally do not have promised cash flows, which must occur at fixed points in time. By definition, equity securities are claims on the corporation's residual cash flows. Residual in this context means any cash flows that remain after all debt claimants have been satisfied. Equity securities are also affected by changes in interest rates, as well as a large number of other events. For example, if a corporation develops a valuable new product without increasing the amount of outstanding debt, two things are likely to happen:

> The existing debt's default risk is likely to decrease somewhat due to the addition of the new product's future cash flows, which will cover the company's fixed future cash payments on the debt.
> The equity value of the corporation may increase since the equity holders benefit from the increases in future profitability as a result of the new product.

Compared to debt securities, the value of an equity security is much more sensitive to a variety of factors. Many corporate money managers refuse to purchase equity securities as short-term investments because of their volatility. However, high-quality equity securities issued by very large, stable corporations can provide an opportunity for increased return without taking undue risk of loss in value.

Finally, in addition to the risk differences that exist between debt and equity securities, there are also differences in how income from these investments are taxed. Generally, interest income is taxed in full when earned. Dividend income earned by one corporation through investments in another corporation are partially excluded from taxable income. This makes equity securities a more attractive investment from a tax perspective. The interplay between the tax benefits of equity and the higher risks inherent in such investments will ultimately determine the extent to which a corporation considers equities a viable short-term investment.

ACCOUNTING FOR SHORT-TERM INVESTMENTS

Securities held for the short-term are referred to as **trading securities**. Current accounting rules for trading securities require that the portfolio be represented in the balance sheet, with all unrealized gains or losses reported in the income statement. An unrealized gain or loss arises whenever the market value of the security at the end of an accounting period differs from its existing carrying value. Under this approach, this difference must be recognized in the financial statements as income or loss, regardless of the fact that it has not been realized by exchange. The accounting literature sometimes refers to this process as a **mark-to-market approach**, since all securities are adjusted to current market value at the end of the period.

The accounting treatment for investments, both short- and long-term, has changed considerably over the past 25 years. In the 1960s and early '70s, the cost method was used for all these investments. Under the cost method, income is represented by dividend, interest, and realized gains or losses on sales of securities. In the mid-1970s, a hybrid method, referred to as the *lower-of-cost-or-market (LCM)* approach, was adopted in which the treatment of short-term and long-term investments differed. Under LCM, the short-term portfolio was marked to market whenever the portfolio's market value was below cost. However, if the market value of the portfolio was above cost, no appreciate was recognized until sale. The full mark-to-market approach was only adopted in 1993 and is applicable to all fiscal years after December 31, 1993. When accounting for noncurrent investments is examined in Chapter 16, we will take a closer look at the evolution of the reporting requirements for investments in general.

Application of the market value approach requires an understanding of three elements:

1. Recognition of interest and dividend income
2. Measurement and recognition of realized gains and losses
3. Measurement and recognition of unrealized gains and losses for each period

Each of these is addressed below.

Recognition of Interest Income and the Effect of Gains and Losses on Debt Securities Purchased and Disposed of Within a Period

Under the mark-to-market approach, interest income is accrued only for the contractual interest earned during a period. In general, there are two different types of debt securities that companies purchase for their trading portfolios:

1. Interest bearing debt
2. Non-interest bearing debt

When the debt contract explicitly calls for both periodic payments of interest (called the *face* or *stated interest*) and repayment of principal, it is referred to as an **interest bearing** debt. Most corporate bonds and notes are of this type. If a debt contract contains only a promise to pay a lump sum at the maturity of the debt, it is referred to as a **non-interest bearing** debt. Short-term government securities such as treasury bills (T-bills) are non-interest bearing in that they promise to pay a lump sum of $10,000 at the end of a specified time period such as 90 days.

In general, the purchase price of an interest bearing debt security is often close to its maturity value (referred to as the *face value*) of the debt. If bonds do trade at a price below maturity value, the difference between the maturity value and the existing market price is referred to as a **discount**. When bonds trade at prices above maturity value, the difference is referred to as a **premium**. A discount or premium arises because the face interest rate on the debt differs from the rate of interest currently demanded by investors. When the market rate is above the face rate, the bond trades at a discount. When market rates are below the face rate, the bonds trades at a premium. Since government treasury bills never have a face interest rate, they always trade at a discount. The investor in a government T-bill obtains a return from the appreciation of the debt from the date of purchase to maturity.

Interest Bearing Debt   Measurement and recognition of income from interest bearing debt securities require that income be recognized based on the accrual of interest for the period of time the security was held. For example, Barren's Corporation purchased a bond issued by Mathes, Inc. on July 1, 1994. The bond has a maturity value of $100,000, a 9% face rate, and will mature on July 31, 1994. Interest on the bond is paid semi-annually on January 31 and July 31. Assuming the probability of default is small, this bond will trade very close to its maturity value due to the short period of time between the purchase date and maturity date. Assume that the purchase price of the bond was 100.4 plus accrued interest.

The price 100.4 refers to the percentage of maturity value that must be paid for the bond. In this case, it implies a purchase price of $100,400. The term "plus accrued interest" refers to the fact that the purchaser of the bond must pay the previous owner for all interest accrued, at the face rate, from the last interest payment date to the date of purchase. The holder of the bond at the next interest payment date will receive the entire six-month interest payment. Consequently, when the bond is purchased between interest payment dates, the purchaser pays the accrued interest to date, then collects the entire six-month interest payment from the issuing company, which reimburses the purchaser for the accrued interest paid out at purchase plus any interest actually earned by the purchaser from the date of purchase. In this case, the computation of the total cost of the bond appears as follows:

Bond: $100,000 × 1.004	$ 100,400
Interest: $100,000 × 9% × 5 months ÷ 12 months	3,750
	$ 104,150

At the date of purchase, Barren's would record the acquisition as follows:[1]

July 1, 1994:

Short-term investments	100,400	
Interest receivable	3,750	
Cash		104,150

To record the acquisition of the bond as a short-term investment.

If this bond is held to maturity, Barren's will receive the maturity value of the bond, $100,000, plus interest at the face rate for six months, $4,500 ($100,000 × 9% × 6 months ÷ 12 months), a total of $104,500. Barren's would record this transaction as follows:[2]

July 31, 1994:

Cash	104,500	
Interest receivable		3,750
Short-term investments		100,400
Income from investments		350

To record interest income at maturity of the bond.

The interest income of $350 represents interest accruing at the face rate for one month, $750 ($100,000 × 9% × 1 month ÷ 12 months), less the decline in the value of the bond from $100,400 at purchase to only $100,000 at maturity, a loss of $400. This income is realized during the accounting period as the maturity of the bond results in the realization of the $400 loss and collection of interest in the realization of the $750 of income. In effect, the loss arises from a decline in the purchase premium. When a bond of this type is classified as a long-term investment, amortization of the premium or discount is required on a periodic basis. However, with the use of the mark-to-market approach for trading portfolios, amortization is not necessary for bonds in the short-term portfolio.

Suppose that instead of holding the bond to maturity, Barren's sells the bond for 100.2 plus accrued interest after holding it only 15 days (one-half of a month). The selling price of the bond would be computed as follows:

Selling price:	
Bond: $100,000 × 100.2%	$ 100,200
Interest: $ 100,000 × 9% × 5.5 months ÷ 12 months	4,125
	$ 104,325

---

[1] The debit to interest receivable may be replaced with a debit to interest income. This would remove the necessity of adjusting the interest receivable in 30 days when the next interest payment is actually received.

[2] If interest income had been debited for $3,750 in the entry to record the acquisition of the bonds, there would be no credit to interest receivable in the entry below. Instead, interest income would have a credit of $4,100, resulting in a net balance in interest income of $350.

Since the total cost of the bond at purchase was $104,150, this selling price implies that Barren's generated income of $175 from this investment over the 15-day holding period. This amount includes interest accruing at the 9% face rate of $375 ($100,000 × 9% × .5 months ÷ 12 months) less the decline in the value of the bond from 100.4 at purchase to 100.2 at sale, of $200. Barren's entry to record this transaction would appear as follows:[3]

July 16, 1994:

Cash	104,325	
Interest receivable		3,750
Short-term investments		100,400
Income from investments		175
To record interest income and sale of the bond.		

In the preceding example, the bond was purchased and sold (or it matured) within the same accounting period. This is a common occurrence for securities held in the short-term portfolio. Note that upon the sale of a debt security, the "gain or loss" that arises because the selling price is different from the carrying value of the debt is reported as part of interest income. When debt securities are purchased and disposed of in the same accounting period, there is no need to:

1. Accrue face interest earned by the end of the accounting period, or
2. Worry about any revaluation due to the need to mark the security to market at the end of the accounting period

However, some debt securities may be purchased in one period only to mature or be sold in a later period. For example, Deakon Corporation purchased $100,000 of bonds issued by Lake Company on July 1, 1994, by paying 99.8 plus accrued interest. The bonds pay interest of 10% annually on June 30 and mature on June 30, 1995. Deakon has a fiscal year-end of December 31. In this acquisition, there is no accrued interest because the bonds were purchased immediately after an interest payment date. As a result, Deakon would record the acquisition with the following entry:

July 1, 1994:

Short-term investments	99,800	
Cash		99,800
To record the purchase of the Lake Company bonds.		

Under mark-to-market, no amortization of the purchase discount is necessary. The accrued interest on the bonds to December 31, 1994, must be recognized as follows:

December 31, 1994:

Interest receivable	5,000	
Income from investments		5,000
To accrue interest on the bonds to the end of the fiscal year.		

---

[3] If interest income had been debited for $3,750 in the entry to record the acquisition of the bonds instead of debiting interest receivable, the credit to interest receivable in the following entry would not exist. Instead, interest income would be credited for $3,925, leaving a net balance in interest income of $175.

The adjustments necessary to deal with the mark-to-market requirements will be discussed shortly.

Non-Interest Bearing Debt   Non-interest bearing debt securities are handled in a fashion similar to interest bearing debt except that there is no accrual of interest at the end of an accounting period and the total purchase price never has any accrued interest component. For example, assume that Franklin Enterprises purchases a $10,000 T-bill on April 1, 1994. The T-bill matures in 90 days and was purchased at 97. Franklin's journal entry to record the acquisition is as follows:

April 1, 1994:
Short-term investments	9,700	
Cash		9,700

To record the purchase of the T-bill.

If the T-bill is held to maturity, Franklin would make the following entry:

June 30, 1994:
Cash	10,000	
Short-term investments		9,700
Income from investments		300

To record interest income at maturity of the T-bill.

If Franklin had elected to sell the T-bill prior to maturity for 98.5 on June 1, 1994, the entry would appear as follows:

June 1, 1994:
Cash	9,850	
Short-term investments		9,700
Income from investments		150

To record interest from the sale of the T-bill.

If we assume Franklin had a fiscal year-end of May 31, 1994, then the company would make no entry to accrue interest at that time since no face interest is being accrued under the terms of the debt agreement.

Dividend Income and the Effect of Equity Securities Purchased and Sold Within a Period

Accounting for the acquisition and dividend income of equity securities is somewhat less complex than accounting for interest on debt securities. When equity securities are acquired, the total cost of the securities is recorded as the carrying value of the asset. For example, assume that on October 1, 1994, Able Corporation acquires 10,000 shares of Baker Company for $6 per share, paying a brokerage fee of 5% on the purchase. The total cost of the shares is $63,000 ($60,000 for the shares + $3,000 for commissions). Able records this acquisition as follows:[4]

---

[4] The brokerage fees may also be treated as an expense of the period, but these costs must be handled uniformly across investments and across periods.

October 1, 1994:

Short-term investments	63,000	
Cash		63,000

To record purchase of the Baker Company stock.

Dividend income from shares arises whenever the issuing company declares a dividend. The declaration of a dividend by the issuing company's board of directors commits the company to distribute the dividend at a future point in time. The date the directors declare the dividend is referred to as the **date of declaration**. The date the dividend is actually distributed is referred to as the **date of distribution**.

When a dividend is declared, and **ex dividend date** is also set. The ex dividend date is the date on which the rights to the dividend attach to a particular investor. The investor who owns the shares at the close of business on the ex dividend date will have the right to receive the dividend when it is distributed. Investors who sell the shares between the date of declaration and the ex dividend date transfer the right to receive the dividend to the purchaser of the shares. Investors who sell the shares after the ex dividend date, but before the date of distribution, retain the right to the dividend.

From the investor's point of view, the ex dividend date represents the date on which the investor has earned the dividend and, therefore, represents the date on which the accounting records should reflect that income by creating a receivable to reflect the future cash to be collected when the dividend is paid. For example, assume that Baker Company declared dividends of $1 per share on November 1, 1994, with an ex dividend date of November 15, payable on December 1. Able Corporation would make the following entries to record the income and receipt of the dividend:[5]

November 15, 1994:

Dividend receivable	10,000	
Income from investments		10,000

To accrue the dividend on Baker shares at the ex dividend date.

December 1, 1994:

Cash	10,000	
Dividend receivable		10,000

To record collection of the dividend on the date of distribution.

If the stock is sold during the same accounting period in which it was acquired, gain or loss on the sale is determined by comparing the selling price (net of any transactions costs such as commissions) to the carrying value of the security. Since the gain or loss arises from an exchange, it is a realized gain or loss and must be recognized in income for the period. Suppose that Able sold 3,000 shares of Baker stock for $7.50 per share on December 15, 1994. Able's entry to record the transaction would appear as follows:

---

[5] In general, if the dividend is declared and paid within the same accounting period, the investor will often record income when the dividend is received. However, if a dividend receivable exists at year-end because the issuer declared, but has not yet paid, the dividend, the receivable should be accrued.

December 15, 1994:
Cash   22,500
   Short-term investments   18,900
   Income from investments   3,600
To record the sale of 3,000 Baker Company shares at a gain.

Mark-To-Market Requirements

Based on the guidelines in SFAS No. 115, "Accounting for Certain Investments in Debt and Equity Securities," which the FASB released in May 1993, securities held in the short-term portfolio at the end of any fiscal period must be revalued to current market value. This revaluation permanently changes the carrying value of the individual securities. The carrying value of the securities before the mark-to-market adjustment may arise from:

1. An historical purchase price if the security was purchased in the current fiscal period, or
2. The market value of the security at the end of the last fiscal period the security has been held over the entire current period

In any case, the process of resetting this carrying value from the old level to the current market price gives rise to unrealized gains and losses. Unrealized gains arise when the current market price at the end of the period is above the old carrying value. Unrealized losses arise when the market price is below the carrying value. These gains and losses are unrealized because no exchange has taken place by the end of the period. Nonetheless, these gains and losses must be recognized in income for the period.

Returning to the Deakon Corporation investment in Lake Company bonds, recall that Deakon had a fiscal year-end of December 31. It had purchased the bonds at 99.8 and accrued all interest to December 31, 1994, in the previous analysis. Under mark-to-market, Deakon will also be required to revalue the debt to current market value at December 31. Assume that the bond is trading at 100.1 plus accrued interest on December 31, 1994. Since the accrued interest on the bond has already been recognized as income, Deakon's only concern is recording the change in value of the bond from 99.8 up to 100.1. The company would accomplish this with the following journal entry:

December 31, 1994:
Short-term investments   300
   Income from investments   300
To accrue the unrealized gain on Lake Company bonds.

Once this entry is made, the carrying value of the bonds now becomes $100,100 plus the accrued interest receivable of $5,000. This affects the determination of investment income in the next period. Consider the following three examples:

1. The bonds are sold on January 1, 1995, at 100.1 plus accrued interest
2. The bonds are sold on April 1, 1995, at 100 plus accrued interest
3. The bonds are held to maturity on June 30, 1995

If the bonds are sold on January 1, Deakon would make the following entry to record the sale:

January 1, 1995:
Cash	105,100	
Interest receivable		5,000
Short-term investments		100,100

To record the sale of the bonds on January 1, 1995.

No income is generated from the sale of these securities since the selling price is equivalent to the market value at December 31, 1995, and no interest has accrued since that date. Had the bonds not been revalued to market, the $300 of income recorded on December 31, 1994, would have been recognized on January 1, 1995, when the bonds were sold.

If the bonds are sold on April 1, 1995, for 100.0 plus accrued interest, the total cash proceeds from the sale would be $107,500 ($100,000 × 100.0% + $100,000 × 10% × 9 months ÷ 12 months). Deakon's entry to record this event would appear as follows:

April 1, 1995:
Cash	107,500	
Interest receivable		5,000
Short-term investments		100,100
Income from investments		2,400

To record the sale of the bonds on April 1, 1995.

The income of $2,400 represents the sum of the interest accruing at face from January 1, 1995, to April 1, 1995, or $2,500, less the decline in the market value of the bond from 100.1 at January 1, 1995, to 100.0 at April 1, 1995, or a $100 loss. Had there been no revaluation of the bonds at December 31, 1994, the income from the sale on April 1 would have been $300 higher.

Finally, if the bonds are held to maturity, the following entry would be appropriate:

June 30, 1995:
Cash	110,000	
Interest receivable		5,000
Short-term investments		100,100
Income from investments		4,900

To record the maturity of the bonds.

In this case, the income of $4,900 represents the recognition of an additional $5,000 of income from accrual of face interest less the $100 decline in value of the bond from January 1, 1995, to maturity.

The same valuation procedures would be applicable to a non-interest bearing bond as well. Any unrealized gain or loss would be recognized at the end of the fiscal period, and investment income in future periods would be altered by this revaluation. Revaluation of equity securities is also handled in the same fashion. For example, returning to the Able Corporation investment in 10,000 shares of Baker stock, recall that Baker paid $6 per share for the stock on October 1, 1994, and sold 3,000 shares on December 15, 1994. Assume further that Able has a fiscal year-end of December 31, 1994, and the Baker stock was trading at $5.75 per share on that date. The mark-to-market adjustment for these shares requires that Able recognize a loss from the decline in market value of the shares. Able had a carrying value for these shares of $44,100 (70% of the $63,000 cost recorded at acquisition). The market value of the shares is currently $40,250 (7,000 shares × $5.75). Mark-to-market requires a reduction of $3,850, recorded as follows:

December 31, 1994:
Income from investments   3,850
   Short-term investments   3,850
To record the unrealized loss on Baker stock.

After the December 31, 1994, adjustment, the carrying value of the Baker shares is now permanently lowered to $40,250, or $5.75 per share. Any sales of these shares in the next fiscal period will result in a gain if the selling price is above $5.75 per share, or a loss if below this amount. Suppose that 2,000 shares were sold at $6.25 on February 1, 1995. Able's entry to record this event would appear as follows:

February 1, 1995:
Cash   12,500
   Short-term investments   11,500
   Income from investments   1,000
To record the sale of 2,000 shares of Baker stock and to realize
  gain of $1,000.

SUMMARY OF THE MARK-TO-MARKET METHOD

Conceptually, the mark-to-market approach recognizes income based on accrued interest earned, dividends earned, realized gains and losses in the period, and any unrealized gain or loss arising from the process of revaluation at the end of the period for securities still held in the trading portfolio at that time. All securities are revalued to market at the end of each accounting period, and this is a permanent change in the carrying value of the security. Since this process is applied to all debt and equity securities in the trading portfolio, both unrealized gains and losses are likely to exist within the portfolio; and the net effect of these adjustments will ultimately be reflected in income for the period.

Accounting for the short-term portfolio of trading securities represents a market value that is a reliable basis for reporting the value of an asset and for measuring income. As with the recognition of income at the completion of production in the precious metals extraction industry, the view taken for valuation of these securities is that a readily available market price quotation will provide a reliable basis for measuring the value without the investor's execution of an exchange. The presumption that the market price is reliable depends on the existence of sufficient depth in the market to absorb any quantity of shares or bonds the investor might elect to deliver. Given the investors' liquidity demands relating to the selection of short-term investment securities, the vast majority of securities that qualify for consideration under the mark-to-market approach will be traded in deep, well-organized markets with reliable price quotations.

SHORT-TERM INVESTMENTS AND THE CASH FLOW STATEMENT

Activity relating to short-term investments that are not cash equivalents but do affect the entity's cash flows are reported in the cash flow statement as investing cash flows. When cash is paid to acquire short-term investments that are not cash equivalents, this represents an investing cash outflow. When such securities are sold for cash, this represents an investing cash inflow.

The only operating cash flows that arise from short-term investments are cash inflows from the receipt of interest payments and from the receipt of dividend payments on investments. All other elements of income from investments that arise from gain or loss on sale or unrealized gains and losses from the mark-to-market process are not operating cash flows. If the indirect method is used to prepare the statement of cash flows, these items will be removed from income to convert net income from operations to cash flows from operations.

For securities that qualify as cash equivalents, the treatment of cash inflows and outflows, as well as unrealized gains and losses, will depend on whether management elects to define cash to include or exclude these securities for purposes of constructing the cash flow statement. If cash equivalents are included in the definition of cash for this purpose, the cash flow statement will reconcile the changes in the cash plus cash equivalents, and no specific identification of cash flows related to cash equivalents is required. In addition, any unrealized gain or loss for the period will not be deducted from income to obtain cash flows from operations since these gains and losses are part of the valuation of the cash and cash equivalents. If cash equivalents are excluded from the definition of cash for purposes of the cash flow statement, the financial statement effects of the cash equivalents are treated just like any other short-term investment.

ACCOUNTING FOR OTHER TYPES OF EQUITY SECURITIES

Special problems arise in the valuation of investments when convertible securities such as stock rights are distributed by a corporation. Additional adjustments also need to be made when securities such as stock warrants or options are acquired as part of the investment portfolio.

Stock Rights

A **stock right** is a security issued by a corporation to its shareholders and grants an opportunity to the right holder to purchase shares of the issuing corporation at a fixed price for a limited period of time. Rights are usually outstanding for only a matter of weeks. In addition, rights are awarded without compensation. Consequently, the investor pays nothing in the form of consideration to acquire the rights.

When stock rights are issued to current stockholders as a means of obtaining new capital, the investors receive rights to purchase new shares in proportion to their previous holdings. For instance, if an investor held 10% of a company's stock, and the company issued rights to purchase another 500,000 shares of stock to its shareholders, the investor would receive rights for 50,000 shares.

Rights can be sold to other investors, exercised, or allowed to lapse without any action at all. When rights are received, the investor pays nothing for them directly. However, the issuance of the rights has diluted the value of the stock the investor holds since there is now a potential for many more outstanding shares.

When rights are received from the issuing corporation, both the existing share investment and the rights received should be valued at existing market value if the investment is short-term. This may involve the recording of an unrealized gain or loss when the rights are received. For example, assume FML Corporation holds 10,000 shares of Livermore Company, which it just purchased at $470,000. On May 25, 1994, Livermore issued stock rights to acquire 20% of the outstanding shares at $51 per share. The rights expire on July 25, 1994. Following the rights issue, the price of the stock without rights was $52; and the rights were trading at $1.50 each. Recording the effects of the rights distribution would be accomplished as follows:

May 25, 1994:
Short-term investments   53,000
   Income from investments   53,000
To record the revaluation of shares and receipt of rights.

The effect of this journal entry is to increase the carrying value of the investment in Livermore from $470,000 up to $523,000. The new carrying value can be broken down as follows:

Shares:	10,000 shares × $52/share	$520,000
Rights:	2,000 rights × $1.50/share	3,000
		$523,000

Clearly, only $3,000 of the increase reflects the value of the rights themselves. The remaining $50,000 is appreciation on the shares from the date of purchase to the date the rights were issued.

Following their receipt, rights are accounted for like any other equity security. Sale to a third party prior to the end of the accounting period will result in recognition of gain or loss based on a comparison of the selling price to the carrying value of $1.50 per right. For example, if FML sold 1,000 rights at $1.55 on June 20, 1994, the following entry would record the gain:

June 20, 1994:
Cash   1,550
   Short-term investments   1,500
   Income from investments   50
To record income from sale of rights.

If the rights are allowed to lapse, a loss of $3,000 would be recorded when they expire. If the rights are exercised before the end of the fiscal period, then additional shares will be acquired. These shares should be placed in the short-term portfolio at the existing market price on the date the rights are exercised. The cash payment of $51 per share ($102,000 ÷ 2,000 shares) and the removal of the rights from the short-term portfolio at $1.50 each ($3,000 ÷ 2,000 shares) may result in a gain or loss at exercise if the market price of the shares is not $52.50. For example, assume that the share price at exercise on July 1, 1994, was $53/share. A gain of $1,000 [2,000 shares × ($53.00 – $52.50)] would occur at exercise. FML would make the following entry to record the exercise:

July 1, 1994:

Short-term investments	103,000	
Cash		102,000
Income from investments		1,000
To record the exercise of the rights and the receipt of shares		
at fair value.		

The increase in the short-term investments account is actually a net effect. The shares acquired are entered at $53.00 per share, or $106,000, but the rights are removed, reducing this value by $3,000.

If the rights are still part of the investment portfolio at the end of a fiscal period, the same rules for revaluation to market are applied to the rights to establish a new carrying value equal to the market value at the end of the period.

Stock Warrants and Options

Stock warrants are similar to rights in that they are issued by corporations and represent a right to acquire shares at a fixed price over a certain period of time. They differ in that when a company issues warrants, it generally receives compensation. In addition, the life of a warrant is generally much longer, sometimes spanning several years. Both warrants and options may be purchased from other investors as well as obtained directly from the issuing corporation.

Stock options are securities with characteristics similar to rights and warrants except they are created by one investor and sold to another. A stock option provides the right to purchase (a *buy* option) or sell (a *put* option) shares of stock in a specific corporation for a fixed price over a certain period of time. Since option contracts are written between investors, when the options are exercised, the exchange of shares does not directly affect the corporation that originally issued the shares. Options are outstanding only a few months.

When stock rights, warrants, or options are acquired from a third party, the price paid is established as the carrying value of the investment. Exercising, selling, holding the security over multiple fiscal periods, and allowing the security to lapse after purchase will result in the same types of entries presented above for rights received directly from a corporation.

Stock Dividends and Splits

Stock dividends *and* **stock splits** *both* represent situations in which the issuing corporation elects to distribute additional shares to each of its current shareholders. When this occurs, additional shares are distributed to the investor based on the requirements of the dividend or split. Accounting for these events simply requires that the post-dividend or post-split market value per share be assigned to all shares following the dividend or split. If this valuation changes the carrying value of the investment in total, income or loss is recognized. The new carrying value of each post-dividend or post-split share will equal the market value of a share on the date the dividend or split is distributed. If some or all of the shares are sold subsequent to the dividend or split, income or loss will be determined by comparing the selling price of the shares to the new carrying value.

SUMMARY

The asset cash represents many forms of currency and near cash assets such as demand deposits, foreign currency, and others. To manage cash balances effectively, corporations often place excess cash into short-term investments referred to as trading securities. These types of investments have the common characteristic of being highly liquid. When these investments mature within 90 days of acquisition, they are defined as cash equivalents. If maturity is beyond 90 days, they are referred to as short-term investments, temporary investments, trading securities, or any other of several titles designed to convey the fact that they are expected to be converted to cash within the next year or operating cycle.

Reporting the effects of these investments requires the application of the mark-to-market process. Interest accrued during the period, dividends earned in the period, and any gains or losses realized during the period are recognized as appropriate. In addition, each security in the portfolio at the end of any fiscal period must be revalued to market value at that date. This revaluation requires the recognition of unrealized gains and losses to the extent that the previous carrying value of the security differs from its end-of-period market value.

Use of market value for both balance sheet representation and income measurement is motivated by both the strategic nature of these investments and the fact that reliable market values can be obtained for investments of this type. Fluctuations in market value directly affect the liquidity of the companies that elect these investments; and the application of market value concepts results in improved measures of liquidity when markets are deep and prices are reliable.

QUESTIONS

1. Identify five subcomponents that are typically included in the classification of *cash* in the balance sheet.

2. What is the most important characteristic of all securities that are purchased as short-term investments?

3. How do securities that can be classified as cash equivalents differ from those classified as short-term investments in general?

4. What types of restrictions may exist on cash balances and how should these affect the presentation of cash in the balance sheet?

5. The use of historical cost to value short-term investments would not recognize any unrealized gain or loss from differences between current market value and historical cost at the end of an accounting period. Explain why it may be said that the choice of historical cost or market value to measure income and represent the value of *cash equivalents* in the balance sheet is likely to be unimportant (i.e., result in immaterial differences).

6. The use of historical cost to value short-term investments would not recognize any unrealized gain or loss from differences between current market value and historical cost at the end of an accounting period. Why would it be likely that the application of the *mark-to-market approach*, rather than historical cost, would have more effect on firms with short-term investments in equity securities than on firms that make these investments in debt securities?

7. What is realized gain or loss as it relates to marketable equity securities?

8. What is a recognized gain or loss on marketable equity securities? How does it differ, if at all, from a realized gain or loss?

9. What is a *stock right*? *Stock warrant*? *Stock option*?

10. How might the acquisition of stock rights differ from the acquisition of warrants or options? How might it be similar?

11. How is the receipt of stock rights from the issuing corporation similar to the receipt of stock dividends or stock splits?

12. When stock rights or warrants are exercised, how does the investor determine the carrying value of the shares acquired?

EXERCISES

6-1. *Petty cash*

In September, 1994, Matchup Corporation began a petty cash fund by drawing a check for $1,000 and placing the cash in a safe in the office. Petty cash is used for reimbursement of various small expenditures, postage, and freight. Office employees may also cash personal checks of $25 or under against petty cash. At the end of September, the following receipts and cash balance were present in petty cash:

Postage costs	$126
Advance to Arthur Brown, sales representative	200
Freight-in on supplies	74
Personal checks	125
Supplies	467
Cash balance	8

REQUIRED:

Prepare the journal entry to record the creation of the petty cash fund and the replenishment of the fund at the end of September.

6-2.   *Petty cash—cash over/short*

Baker Enterprises maintains a petty cash fund in the amount of $5,000 for emergency needs and the payment of small out-of-pocket expenditures. The fund is replenished at the end of each month. During the month of March, 1994, the following items were paid for out of petty cash:

Office equipment	$2,300
Office supplies	1,228
Mileage allowance for sales personnel	336
Postage	647

At the end of the month, a count of the cash remaining indicated a balance of $526.

REQUIRED:

Prepare the journal entry to record the replenishment of petty cash at the end of March.

6-3.   *Cash equivalents—definition and disclosure*

Tallent Corporation had the following account balances at December 31, 1994:

Cash on hand and in banks	$975,000
90-Day T-bills	500,000
6-month certificates of deposit	600,000
Cash legally restricted for additions to plant	250,000

REQUIRED:

How much should Tallent report as cash and cash equivalents in the current assets portion of its balance sheet?

6-4.   *Overdrafts—classification and disclosure*

At the end of the fiscal year, Blake Corporation had a balance in its checking account of $50,000 according to the bank. However, Blake had outstanding checks in the amount of $55,000 issued at that time. There were no other differences between the balance reported by the bank and the balance in cash recorded on Blake's books.

REQUIRED:

How would Blake represent the balance of cash in its balance sheet at year-end?

6-5.   *Bond investments—purchase and sale within the year*

On February 14, 1993, Signet Corporation acquired bonds of Giant Enterprises as a short-term investment. The bonds had a face value of $200,000 and a face interest rate of 10%. Interest was paid on June 30 and December 31 each year. The bonds mature on December 31, 1993. Signet paid 100.4 plus accrued interest for the bonds. Signet sold the bonds on November 1, 1993 for 99.9 accrued interest.

REQUIRED:

Prepare all journal entries necessary to record the activities relating to the Giant bonds. (Round all computations to whole dollars.)

6-6.   *Bond investments—interest income and mark-to-market at year-end*

On March 10, 1994, Frank Corporation purchased bonds issued by Renner, Inc. as a short-term investment. The bonds had a face value of $650,000 and a face interest rate of 8%. Interest is paid on March 1 and September 1 each year. The bonds mature on September 1, 1998. Frank paid 97.0 plus accrued interest to acquire the bonds. On January 15, 1995, Frank sold these bonds for 99.2 plus accrued interest. Frank has a December 31 fiscal year-end. At December 31, 1994, the bonds were trading at 99.4 plus accrued interest.

REQUIRED:

Prepare all journal entries required in 1994 and 1995 to record the activity relating to the bonds under the mark-to-market approach. (Round all computations to whole dollars.)

6-7.   *T-bills—income and mark-to-market at year-end*

Baker Corporation has a policy of investing its excess cash balances in short-term government treasury bills, which mature in 90 days or less. On March 15, 1994, Baker purchased $500,000 of these treasury bills at 98.0. These matured on June 15, 1994. On December 15, 1994, the company acquired $300,000 of treasury bills maturing on February 15, 1995, for 97.0. All treasury bills were held to maturity. Baker has a December 31 fiscal year-end, and the treasury bills were trading at 97.4 on December 31, 1994.

REQUIRED:

Prepare journal entries to record the activities relating to the investments in treasury bills for 1994 and 1995 using the mark-to-market approach.

6-8.   *T-bills—income and mark-to-market at year-end*

Lee Enterprises acquired $100,000 of treasury bills on December 1, 1994 at a price of 98.2. The bills mature on February 15, 1995. The bills had a quoted price of 98.7 on December 31, 1994. Lee sold the bonds at 99.3 on January 15, 1995. Lee has a December 31 fiscal year-end.

REQUIRED:

Prepare entries to record the activities relating to the treasury bills for both 1994 and 1995 under the mark-to-market approach.

6-9.   *Share investments—purchase and sale within year with dividends*

Bracken Industries acquired 1,000 shares of Microdyne Corporation at $12 per share on January 27, 1994, as a short-term investment. On July 1, 1994, Microdyne declared a $2 per share cash dividend, payable to the holders of record on July 15, distributable on August 1. Bracken sold the shares on October 10, 1994, for $11.50 per share.

REQUIRED:

Prepare the journal entries to record the activities relating to Bracken's investment in Microdyne during 1994.

6-10.   *Share investments—income and mark-to-market at year-end*

As part of its cash management strategy, King Corporation acquired 2,000 shares of Denmore Corporation at a price of $8 per share on July 23, 1993. Commissions on the purchase were 10% and were included in the $8 price. On December 12, 1993, Denmore declared a cash dividend of $3 per share, payable to the holders of record on December 31, and distributable on January 15, 1994. At year-end, the market price of the stock was at $6.75 per share. King has a December 31 fiscal year-end.

REQUIRED:

Prepare all journal entries necessary to record the activities relating to the investment in Denmore common stock. How will the dividends receivable at year-end be presented in King's balance sheet?

6-11. *Share investments—mark-to-market investments*

During 1994, Garr Company purchased marketable securities as a short-term investment. None of the securities were sold during 1994. At December 31, 1994, the following information was available:

Security	Carrying Value	Market
A	$245,000	$230,000
B	180,000	182,000

REQUIRED:

What adjustments, if any, would be required at December 31, 1994?

6-12. *Share investments—sale in subsequent periods, mark-to-market*

Referring to the information in Exercise 11, assume that Garr Company sold Security A during 1995 for $233,000 but held on to Security B. At the end of 1995, the market value of Security B was $188,000.

REQUIRED:

Prepare the journal entry to record the sale of Security A. What adjustments, if any, would be required at December 31, 1995?

6-13. *Share investments—mark-to-market, measurement of gain from sale*

During 1994, Rex Company purchased marketable securities as a short-term investment. The purchase price and market values at December 31, 1994 were as follows:

Security	Purchase Price	Market
A—100 shares	$ 2,800	$ 3,400
B—1,000 shares	17,000	15,300
C—2,000 shares	31,500	29,500

Rex sold 1,000 shares of Security B stock on January 31, 1995, for $15 per share, incurring brokerage fees of $1,500.

REQUIRED:

1. What is the unrealized gain or loss at December 31, 1993?
2. What adjustments, if any, will Rex make regarding the valuation of marketable securities on December 31, 1994?
3. Prepare the journal entry to record the sale of Security B's stock. How would this entry appear if Rex had used the historical cost method of accounting for short-term investments, which does not recognize any of the unrealized gains or losses?

6-14. *Share investments—mark-to-market portfolio analysis*

Burr Corporation began operations on July 1, 1994. At December 31, 1994, Burr had the following portfolio of short-term investments in marketable securities:

Aggregate Cost	$185,000
Aggregate Market Value	150,000

REQUIRED:

Prepare all adjusting entries required at December 31, 1994, to reflect properly the investments in marketable securities in Burr's balance sheet. If the market value of the current portfolio rises to $200,000 by the end of 1995, what entry will be required (assuming none of the securities are sold and no new securities are purchased)?

6-15. *Share investments—mark-to-market, measurement of gain from sale*

On December 31, 1994, Ball Company purchased marketable securities as a temporary investment. At the end of 1995, the following data was available regarding these investments:

Security	Original Cost	Carrying Value At January 1, 1995	Market
A	$37,000	$39,000	$36,000
B	52,000	50,000	55,000
C	95,000	96,000	85,000

REQUIRED:

What is the amount of the unrealized gain or loss to be recognized as of December 31, 1994? Suppose Security A was sold on January 1, 1995, for the indicated market value at December 31, 1994. How much of a realized gain or loss would be recognized on that sale under the mark-to-market approach?

6-16. *Share investments—stock dividends under mark-to-market*

Huff Company acquired 2,000 shares of Post, Inc. common stock on October 5, 1994, at a cost of $44,000. On December 31, 1994, the market price of the stock was at $25 per share. On April 10, 1995, Post distributed a 10% common stock dividend when the market price of the stock was $30 per share. On December 20, 1995, Huff sold 200 shares of its Post stock for $6,400.

REQUIRED:

Prepare all journal entries necessary to record the activities relating to the stock in 1995.

6-17. *Share investments—warrants under mark-to-market*

On February 24, 1994, Black Company purchased 2,000 warrants to purchase shares of Winn Corporation's common stock for $4,000. Each warrant allows the holder to acquire one share of common stock at a price of $32 per share. On March 1, 1994, Black sold 500 warrants at a price of $2.50 per warrant. The remainder of the warrants were exercised on April 15, 1994. The market value of Winn shares on April 15, 1994, was $37 per share.

REQUIRED:

Prepare the journal entries necessary to record the investment in the warrants and their eventual disposition.

6-18. *Share investments—rights offerings under mark-to-market*

Rice Company owns 300 shares of Wood Corporation common stock acquired on July 24, 1994, at a total cost of $11,000. On December 2, 1994, Rice received 300 stock rights from Wood. Each right entitles the holder to acquire one share of Wood's common stock at $45. The market price of Wood's stock on this date, ex rights, was $50, and the market price of each right was $5. Rice sold the rights on the same day for $5 a right, less commission fees of $90.

REQUIRED:

Prepare a schedule to determine the amount of gain or loss to be recorded as a result of the activity relating to the rights.

PROBLEMS

6-1. *Investments in various securities, recording acquisition and classification as a cash equivalent*

Barnwell Enterprises acquired the following short-term investments during 1994:
   (a) Government treasury bills with a maturity value of $100,000 and a 90-day maturity, purchased at 98.
   (b) 40 of Newmo Corporation's $1,000 face value bonds at 101. The interest rate on the bonds was 7% paid semiannually. The bonds matured 60 days after purchase.
   (c) 10,000 shares of Berkley Company common stock at $43 per share.
   (d) 30 bonds of Baker Company. Each bond has a face value of $1,000 and pays interest at 10%. These bonds were purchased at face value and have a maturity date 5 years from the date of purchase.
   (e) 2,000 shares of Donnelly Company preferred stock at a price of $102 per share.

REQUIRED:

1. Prepare the journal entries to record the purchase of each of these investments.
2. Which of these investments could be classified as cash equivalents?

6-2. *Investments in shares, various transactions, comparison of income under historical cost and mark-to-market*

On January 1, 1994, Franklin Corporation acquired the following short-term investments in equity securities:

Company	Stock	No. of Shares	Cost per Share
Ivory	Common	1,500	$32
Pearl	Common	800	7
Flint	Preferred (nonconvertible)	200	23

Per share data subsequent to the acquisition are as follows:

December 31, 1994 (Market value per share):

Ivory	$26
Pearl	$ 8
Flint	$22

July 15, 1995 (Ex dividend date for cash dividends per share):

Ivory	$1
Flint	$3

July 30, 1995 (Cash dividends received per share):

Ivory	$1
Flint	$3

December 15, 1995 (Sold all Flint stock at $27 per share.)

Dec. 31, 1995 (Market value per share):

Ivory	$22
Pearl	$19
Flint	$33

REQUIRED:

1. Give all entries indicated for Franklin Corporation for 1994 and 1995, assuming no investment in marketable securities existed prior to January 1, 1994. Use the requirements of GAAP to formulate your response.
2. Show how Franklin Corporation's income statement and balance sheet would reflect the effects of short-term investments in 1994 and 1995, under GAAP.
3. How much would Franklin's reported income change if the strict historical cost (nonrecognition of unrealized gains and losses) approach had been used to account for the investments in marketable equity securities?

6-3. *Equity securities, short-term investment strategy, mark-to-market*

On December 31, 1994, Blackburn Corporation's portfolio of short-term investments in marketable equity securities was as follows:

Security	Shares	Cost per Share	Market Share
IBM	50	$104	$123
Control Data Corporation	100	36	40
Cray Computers	200	12	15

All securities were purchased on March 29, 1994. Blackburn has a December 31 fiscal year-end.

Transactions relating to this portfolio during 1995 were as follows:

(a) On March 15, IBM declared and distributed a 20% stock dividend. The market value of a share of IBM after the dividend was $120.
(b) On June 12, 20 shares of Cray Computers were sold at $13 per share.
(c) On August 15, 300 shares of DEC Computers were purchased at $75 per share.
(d) On November 30, Control Data Corporation shares split 2-for-1. The market price of Control Data stock following the split was $23.50 per share.

Market value per share, as of December 31, 1995 were as follows:

IBM	$102
Control Data	24
Cray	10
DEC	70

REQUIRED:

1. Give the entries that Blackburn should make to record the activities relating to the short-term investments from March 29, 1994 through December 31, 1995, using the mark-to-market approach.

2. Assuming that Blackburn's decision to purchase these short-term investment securities was motivated by a desire to obtain a return from excess cash balances while maintaining liquidity and reasonable risk, identify the pros and cons of Blackburn's investment strategy.

3. What amounts will be reported in Blackburn's income statement and balance sheet for fiscal 1995?

6-4. *Investments in bonds, income recognition, valuation under mark-to-market, classification as cash equivalents*

On April 1, 1994, Mattress Corporation purchased bonds of Spread Corporation for 101 plus accrued interest. The bonds had a maturity value of $10,000 and a contractual interest rate of 9%. Interest is paid semiannually on January 31 and July 31, respectively. Mattress has a December 31 fiscal year-end. The bonds mature on January 31, 1995.

On November 15, 1994, half of these bonds were sold at 100 1/2 plus accrued interest. At December 31, 1994, the Spread Corporation bonds had a quoted price of 99 7/8 plus accrued interest.

REQUIRED:

1. Would the Spread Corporation bonds qualify as cash equivalents at April 1, 1994? Would your answer change at December 31, 1994?

2. Using the mark-to-market approach, prepare all journal entries necessary to record the activities relating to this investment during 1994.

6-5. *Bond investments, comparison of historical cost and mark-to-market*

At December 31, 1993, Maynerd Corporation held the following portfolio of short-term investments in debt securities:

Security	Maturity Value	Interest Rate	Payable	Cost	Cash Date Purchased
A Corp. bonds	$ 20,000	6%	Nov. 1	$19,900	December 1, 1993
B Corp. bonds	50,000	9%	Dec. 31	51,500	December 31, 1993
T-bills	100,000	-	-	97,000	November 15,1993

Interest on the A and B Corporation bonds is paid annually, and the cash cost indicated in the above schedule includes accrued interest to the date of purchase where applicable. Maynerd had not held any short-term investments prior to the purchase of the T-bills on November 15, 1993.

Maturities of the debt securities held as short-term investments as of December 31, 1993 were as follows:

Security	Maturity Date
A Corp. bonds	November 1, 1995
B Corp. bonds	December 31, 1995
T-bills	February 13, 1994

Market values of these debt securities at December 31, 1993 were as follows:

A Corp. bonds	95 plus accrued interest
B Corp. bonds	103 plus accrued interest
T-bills	98 1/4

Transactions relating to the portfolio of short-term investments in debt securities during 1994 were as follows:

(a) February 13, T-bills matured and were converted to cash.
(b) July 15, sold the B Corp. bonds at 99 plus accrued interest.
(c) November 1, interest was paid on the A Corp. bonds.
(d) At December 31, 1994, the A Corp. bonds had a market value of 97 plus accrued interest.

REQUIRED:

1. Prepare a schedule to determine investment income from the short-term investments in debt securities for both 1993 and 1994, applying the mark-to-market approach.
2. Prepare a schedule to determine investment income from the short-term investments in debt securities for both 1993 and 1994, assuming that no unrealized gain or loss will be recognized (basically the historical cost approach). How much difference does the nonrecognition of unrealized gains and losses have on reported income for 1993 and 1994?
3. Prepare all journal entries necessary to record the activities relating to the short-term investments in debt securities during 1993 and 1994, using the mark-to-market approach.

6-6. *Equity investments, various events under mark-to-market*

Blanket Corporation had the following marketable equity securities on hand at the end of 1994 (all were purchased during 1994):

Securities	Cost	Market
2,000 shares of A Co. Common	$ 20,000	$ 24,000
5,000 shares of B Co. Common	25,000	30,000
7,000 shares of C Co. Common	210,000	175,000
1,000 shares of D Co. Common	50,000	76,000
8,000 shares of E Co. Common	48,000	45,000

All of these securities are included in Blanket's current marketable equity security portfolio.

During 1995, none of the shares held by Blanket paid dividends. Blanket entered into the following transactions during the year:

(a) Sold 500 shares of D Co. stock at $80 per share.
(b) Sold 3,000 shares of E Co. stock at $5 per share.
(c) Purchased 3,000 shares of F Co. stock at $12 per share.
(d) Purchased an additional 5,000 shares of A Co. stock at $13 per share

At the end of 1995, market values for each company's stock appeared as follows:

A Co.	$13.00 per share
B Co.	6.50 per share
C Co.	27.00 per share
D Co.	65.50 per share
E Co.	1.50 per share
F Co.	11.00 per share

REQUIRED:

1. Prepare the journal entries necessary to record the purchases and sales of securities for the current marketable equity security portfolio during 1995.

2. Determine the amount of the unrealized gains or loss to be recognized at the end of 1994 and 1995.

3. Prepare any journal entries necessary to record the mark-to-market adjustments at the end of 1994 and 1995.

6-7. *Bond investments, accrued interest, income measurement under mark-to-market*

Winslow Corporation manages its cash resources by acquiring short-term investments in T-bills and high-grade commercial paper that matures in less than 90 days. A summary of the activities related to these investments for 1995 is as follows:

	Carrying Value January 1, 1995	Maturity Value	Maturity Date
T-Bills	$47,950	$50,000	February 14, 1995
X Corporation 15% Commercial Paper	24,100	24,000	January 31, 1995
Z Company 18% Commercial Paper	14,950	15,000	January 15, 1995
Total	$87,000		

Accrued Interest Receivable at January 1, 1995:

X Corporation 15% Commercial Paper	$300
Z Company 18% Commercial Paper	225
Total	$525

The carrying value of the securities is equivalent to their market value on December 31, 1994.

During 1995, the above investments all matured and the maturity values were paid in full. In addition, Winslow entered into the following additional investments:

(a) March 15, 1995: Purchased $30,000 of 90-day T-bills at 97.6 with a maturity of May 30, 1995.

(b) May 20, 1995: Purchased $65,000 of S Company's newly issued 17% commercial paper at face value. The debt will mature on July 20, 1995.

(c) November 30, 1995: Purchased $70,000 of new T-bills at 97; these mature on February 28, 1996.

(d) December 15, 1995: Purchased $55,000 of K Corporation's newly issued 12% commercial paper at 99.5. This debt will mature on January 15, 1996.

Market values for the securities still held on December 31, 1995, were as follows:

T-bills	98.4
K Corporation Commercial Paper	100.0 plus accrued interest

REQUIRED:

1. Prepare the journal entries to record all activities in the short-term investments of Winslow implied by the above information.

2. Prepare a schedule that summarizes the investment income of Winslow, by source, within the short-term investment portfolio and a schedule reconciling the ending balances of the short-term investment and accrued interest receivable accounts.

6-8. *Equity investments, various transactions under mark-to-market, preparation of schedules instead of journal entries*

Majestic Enterprises began fiscal 1994 with the following portfolio of short-term investments:

(a) Common stock of North Company: 2,000 shares, purchased at $53 per share. Current market value was $67 per share.

(b) Common stock of South Company: 10,000 shares, purchased at $20 per share. Current market value was $15 per share.

(c) Common stock of Current Corporation: 8,000 shares purchased at $12 per share. This stock is not traded on an organized market, but Majestic classified it as current due to a pending sale of the security. Majestic expects to sell the shares for approximately $15 each.

(d) Options to purchase common stock of East Company: 12,000 options purchased at $3 per share. Options allow the holder to acquire one share of Each Company common stock for $25. Current market price of Each Company common stock was $29 per share, and the current market price of the options was $7.

(e) Preferred stock of West, Incorporated: 5,000 shares of 8%, $100 par, cumulative preferred stock, purchased at a price of $98. Current market price is $102.

During 1994, Majestic sold the Current Corporation stock for $16 per share. The options on East Company stock were also sold for $10 per option. Majestic also purchased 10,000 shares of stock in Kadavor Corporation for $18 per share as a short-term investment. Dividends from the investments in stock were as follows:

North	$2.00 per share
South	5.00 per share
West	8.00 per share

At the end of 1994, the following information was available regarding market values for the investments:

North	$ 69 per share
South	17 per share
West	101 per share
Kadavor	18 per share

REQUIRED:

1. Prepare the balance sheet presentation of the short-term investment account as of December 31, 1994.
2. Prepare a schedule to determine the income from investments, not including the gains and losses from disposition.
3. Prepare a schedule to determine the gains and losses from sale of investments during 1994.

6-9. *Equity and debt securities in the same portfolio, application of mark-to-market*

Brat Industries reported the following information relating to its portfolio of short-term investments for 1995:

Held as of January 1, 1995:

(a) 2,000 shares of Beta Company stock originally purchased in 1994 at a cost of $35,000. Market value at January 1, 1995, was $39,000.

(b) 5,000 warrants to purchase 5,000 shares of Gamma Corporation. The warrants were purchased for $10,000 on December 1, 1994. Each warrant entitles the holder to purchase one share of stock at $12 per share. The value of each warrant at December 31, 1994, was $1.50.

(c) $100,000 of face value bonds issued by Delta Company. The bonds were purchased at December 1, 1994, at 102. The face rate on the bonds is 12%, and they pay interest on May 31 and November 30 each year. The bonds mature on December 1, 1999. They had a market value of 101.8 plus accrued interest as of December 31, 1994.

(d) 8,000 shares of Lambda Company that were purchased in 1994 at a price of $32,000. At December 31, 1994, the market value of the shares was $30,000, ex dividend, and there was a dividend declared but unpaid of $1 per share. The dividend was to be distributed on January 15, 1995.

During 1995, Brat completed the following transactions:

(a) On February 1, Brat received a distribution of stock rights from Beta Company. The rights allowed the holder to obtain 200 shares of common stock at $16 per share. The market price of the stock at the date of the rights issue was $18 per share, and the rights were trading at $3 per right following the issuance. On February 26, Brat sold 150 of the rights immediately before expiration at $2.50 per right and exercised the remainder.

(b) The warrants for Gamma Corporation were exercised on May 12, 1995. Gamma Corporation declared a dividend of $1.50 per share on June 1, payable on July 1. Brat sold 2,000 shares of Gamma on August 15 for $15 per share.

(c) On June 1, the bonds of Delta were sold for 101.5.

(d) On December 1, Brat purchased $100,000 worth of 90-day T-bills at 96.5.

At the end of 1995, market values of the securities held in the portfolio were as follows:

Beta Company	$22.00 per share
Gamma Corporation	17.00 per share
Lambda Company	3.00 per share
T-bills	97.75 plus accrued interest

REQUIRED:

1. Determine the amount of investment income to be recognized by Brat on its short-term investments.
2. Prepare journal entries to record the transactions for the period.
3. Prepare an adjusting entry to reflect properly the application of the mark-to-market rule.

6-10. *Equity securities, multi-period application of historical cost and mark-to-market*

Black Corporation held the following portfolio of marketable equity securities at the beginning of 1994 (all securities purchased in 1993):

Securities	No. of Shares	Cost	Market
Bea Company	12,000	$ 60,000	$ 63,000
Dee Corporation	20,000	100,000	105,000
Kay Company	15,000	225,000	223,125
		$385,000	$391,125

During 1994, the Bea Company stock was sold for $65,000, and 5,000 shares of Ell Company stock were purchased at $18 per share. At the end of 1994, market values were as follows:

Dee Corporation	$ 4.00 per share
Kay Company	14.00 per share
Ell Company	18.50 per share

During 1995, the Kay Company stock was sold for $202,500. At the end of 1995, the market values of the remaining securities were as follows:

| Dee Corporation | $ 3.50 per share |
| Ell Company | 19.00 per share |

During 1996, the remaining investments were liquidated for a total of $180,000.

REQUIRED:

1. Prepare an analysis of the gains and losses from the equity investments that Black Corporation would have reported under a strict application of the historical cost valuation approach (implying that no unrealized gains or losses would be recorded).
2. Prepare an analysis of the gains and losses from the equity investments that Black would report using the mark-to-market approach.
3. Assuming all of these equity securities are traded on the New York Stock Exchange, present an argument for and against the use of each of these methods.

CASE 6.1

CLAROSTAT MANUFACTURING/COORS COMPANY

Clarostat Manufacturing Company, Inc. reported the following information as part of the current asset section of its balance sheet at December 31, 1986:

	1986	1985
Current Assets:		
Cash	$ 706,698	$ 562,763
Certificates of deposit	705,223	1,331,915
Trade receivables, less allowance for doubtful accounts of $33,000 in 1982 and $25,000 in 1981	2,339,917	2,701,393
Inventories	3,545,648	3,820,157
Prepaid expenses	450,437	391,548
Total Current Assets	$7,747,923	$8,807,776

Adolph Coors Company reported the following information as part of its balance sheet at December 31, 1986:

	1986	1985
Current Assets:		
Cash, including short-term interest bearing investments of $127,724 in 1986 and $125,927 in 1985	$150,464	$166,131
Accounts and notes receivable	99,560	90,698
Inventories:		
Finished	18,464	14,927
In process	31,037	26,738
Raw materials	68,409	70,296
Packaging materials	38,632	30,989
Total inventory	156,542	142,950
Accumulated income tax prepayments	5,216	3,238
Prepaid expenses and other assets	61,255	51,567
Total Current Assets	$473,037	$454,584

REQUIRED:

1. Compare and contrast the presentation of cash for these two companies. What can you deduce from these disclosures regarding the likelihood that each company's short-term investments qualify as cash equivalents?
2. When would it be appropriate, if ever, to report the value of time deposits or certificates of deposit as cash for balance sheet purposes?
3. How much cash does Coors actually have immediately available? What does the relationship between available cash and short-term investments in these two years imply about what Coors might be doing with its cash management policies?

SCOPE INDUSTRIES

Prior to December 31, 1993, accounting for marketable equity and debt securities was done on a different basis than it is now. Equity securities were marked-to-market only if the total market value of the portfolio of equity securities was below cost (an aggregate unrealized loss existed). If aggregate market value was above cost, the securities were carried under the historical cost method (no aggregate unrealized gains were recognized). In general, debt securities were carried at historical cost (no unrealized gains or losses were recognized). The case that follows arose under the old rules for valuation of these investments, and the data provided should be interpreted in that light. The case questions focus on how the financial statements would appear had the recently adopted approach been in use when the reported statements were produced.

Scope Industries has a June 30 fiscal year-end. On June 30, 1982, Scope included the following as part of its financial statements:

	1982	1981
Current Assets:		
Cash	$ 219,088	$ 223,265
Short-term investments, at cost which approximates market	150,000	200,000
Marketable securities, at cost (Market $3,240,632 in 1982 and $4,046,200 in 1981 – Note 2)	3,250,412	1,498,865
Accounts and notes receivable, less allowance for doubtful accounts of $151,509 in 1982 and $213,954 in 1981	3,235,984	2,293,495
Inventories	644,888	595,474
Prepaid expenses	363,390	260,149
Total Current Assets	$7,863,762	$5,071,248

Note 1: Summary of Significant Accounting Policies

Marketable Securities

Marketable securities are stated at the lower of aggregate cost or market at the balance sheet date and consist of common and preferred stocks. Dividend and interest income are accrued as earned. The cost of marketable securities sold is determined by the specific identification method, and realized gains or losses are reflected in income.

Note 2: Marketable Securities

At June 30, 1982, gross unrealized gains and losses were as follows:

	Current Marketable Securities
Gross Unrealized Gains	$ 455,878
Gross Unrealized Losses	(465,658)

Included in revenues is a net gain of $131,269 (1982), $64,510 (1981), and $282,732 (1980) realized on the sale of marketable securities. On July 1, 1981, the company realized an additional gain before income taxes of $2,466,336 on the sale of marketable securities with a cost basis of $728,664.

REQUIRED:

1. What percentage of total current assets are represented by investments in marketable equity securities at cost in 1981 and 1982? Would you consider this to be a material amount?
2. In the note on marketable securities, Scope indicates that dividends and interest income are accrued as earned. When is interest earned? When are dividends earned?
3. What does the reference to specific identification in the description of accounting policies relating to marketable securities mean? How else might cost be assigned to securities sold during the period? Would this be an issue if the mark-to-market method had been employed?
4. What was the net unrealized gain or loss at the end of 1981? At the end of 1982? What should Scope have done to apply the mark-to-market method?
5. Prepare the journal entry Scope would have used to record the sale of securities on July 1, 1981, referred to specifically in the note disclosure.
6. Assume that Scope sold other securities from the portfolio for $365,388 during 1982. Prepare the journal entry to record these sales.
7. Given the sales of securities in (5) and (6), how much cash did Scope expend to purchase new marketable equity securities during 1982?
8. How much of a realized gain or loss on sales of marketable securities would Scope have recorded in 1982 if it had employed the mark-to-market approach at the end of 1981? In responding to the question, assume that any unrealized gain or loss as of the end of 1981 related to securities sold in 1982.
9. How would the cash outflows for the purchase of marketable securities and the cash inflows from the sales of securities appear in Scope's cash flow statement?

CASE 6.3   MOTT'S SUPERMARKETS, INC.

Prior to December 31, 1993, accounting for marketable equity and debt securities was done on a different basis than it is now. Equity securities were marked-to-market only if the total market value of the portfolio of equity securities was below cost (an aggregate unrealized loss existed). If aggregate market value was above cost, the securities were carried under the historical cost method (no aggregate unrealized gains were recognized). In general, debt securities were carried at historical cost (no unrealized gains or losses were recognized). The case that follows arose under the old rules for valuation of these investments, and the data provided should be interpreted in that light. The case questions focus on how the financial statements would appear had the recently adopted approach been in use when the reported statements were produced.

Mott's Supermarkets, Inc. reported the following information in its December 31, 1982 annual report to shareholders:

Note 4: Investments

In accordance with FASB Statement No. 12 issued December 1975 (*this is the old standard that is no longer applicable*), marketable equity securities are stated at the lower of aggregate cost or market value. Specific cost was used in computing realized gain or loss. A summary of cost, market value, and gains and losses follows:

	January 1, 1983	January 2, 1982	January 3, 1981
Aggregate Cost	$10,350	$ 10,212	$ 26,695
Aggregate Market	6,538	5,725	166,364
Gross Unrealized Gains	-	-	144,131
Gross Unrealized Losses	3,812	4,487	4,462
Net Realized Gain or Loss			
Included in Net Income	-	143,208	515,919

In responding to the following questions you may assume that no short-term investments existed in financial statements prior to January 3, 1980. Also assume that the entire gross unrealized gain reported as of January 3, 1981 was related to securities sold in the period covered by the January 2, 1982 financial statements. In addition, assume that no new securities were purchased during 1981, and any change in the historical aggregate cost of securities from January 2, 1982 to January 1, 1983 are the result of new purchases.

REQUIRED:

1. What was the net unrealized gain or loss on January 1, 1983? At January 3, 1981? What should Mott's have done in each of the three years presented if it had employed the mark-to-market approach?
2. Prepare all necessary journal entries to make any year-end adjustments implied by the mark-to-market approach at the end of each fiscal year presented by Mott's.
3. What do you think Mott's means when it says, "Specific costs was used in computing realized gains and losses"? Is this process necessary under the mark-to-market approach?
4. Prepare the journal entry Mott's used to record the sale of securities in 1982 under the historical cost approach. Reconstruct this entry as if Mott's had always used the mark-to-market approach.
5. How much cash did Mott's expend in purchasing additional equity securities during 1982–1983? Prepare the journal entry to record this activity.

CHAPTER 7

Receivables

Allegheny Ludlum Corporation reported an item labeled "Trade receivables" in the current asset section of its balance sheet as of January 3, 1993. Exhibit 7.1 displays the current asset section of that financial statement. The disclosure indicates that the amounts reported for the value of the asset are net of allowances for doubtful accounts. Based on the amounts reported, the net trade receivables appear to be approximately 20% of total current assets at January 3, 1993. This represents a significant source of future cash flow to maintain the liquidity of the corporation.

However, the disclosure does not provide answers to many questions relating to receivables. What is a trade receivable? How does a trade receivable differ from any other receivable, if at all? What is the purpose of an allowance for doubtful accounts? How is the allowance determined? Why does it change? How was the value of trade receivables itself determined? The answers to these questions, as well as others relating to accounting and reporting events and transactions relating to receivables, are the subject of this chapter.

RECEIVABLES—DEFINITIONS AND BASIC VALUATION

A **receivable** is a contractual right to collect cash at some point in the future. Receivables arise through exchanges in which one entity extends credit to another and accepts a promise to pay in return for whatever consideration is involved. The company accepting the receivable may deliver services, goods, money, or other assets as exchange. **Accounts receivable** represent rights to collect cash obtained in the exchange for the goods and services based on the terms of trade. **Notes receivable** are rights, formalized into a specific financial instrument called a promissory note, to collect cash. A **promissory note** is a

EXHIBIT 7.1		
Allegheny Ludlum Corporation—Trade Receivables and Current Assets	**ALLEGHENY LUDLUM CORPORATION** **Trade Receivables and Current Assets** **Consolidated Balance Sheet** **As of January 3, 1993**	

	JANUARY 3, 1993	DECEMBER 29, 1991
Assets		
Current Assets:		
Cash and cash equivalents	$ 51,437	$ 2,645
Short-term investments	72,115	-
Trade receivables, less allowances for doubtful accounts of $3,235 and $3,547	95,538	92,770
Inventories	235,259	284,513
Prepaid expenses and other current assets	5,161	4,937
	$459,510	$384,865

legal document executed by a borrower and a lender setting forth the rights and responsibilities of both parties, along with the timing of any cash flows for payment of interest and principal. A promissory note may be accepted by a seller of goods and services as consideration for delivery, or it may arise because one party loans money to another.

A **trade account receivable** arises from the sale of a company's usual goods and services, in the normal course of business, because the seller elects to extend credit to its customers. As discussed in Chapters 4 and 5, a trade receivable is usually recognized at the point-of-sale, assuming that collection is not in serious doubt. However, revenue need not be recognized when a receivable is created, as in the case of receivables for interim billings on long-term construction contracts. All trade accounts receivable have two features in common:

1. They are generated in the normal course of providing the goods or services, which represent the primary source of revenues for the company
2. Terms of payment are covered by the billing invoice, or the terms of trade common to the industry

While receivables may be created through a variety of transactions, their valuation for purposes of financial reporting is governed by the concept of *net realizable value* (NRV). In the case of receivables, NRV generally means the present value of the expected cash flows to be collected under the terms of the receivable. Determining the present value always requires some assumptions regarding the effect of interest rates on the future gross cash flows. Determining expected cash collections requires additional assumptions regarding the effects of the terms of trade, potential nonpayment by the debtor, and others. The principal theme of this chapter is to provide a reasonably comprehensive examination of how the concept of net realizable value is made operational in the preparation of financial statements. The principal focus will be on trade receivables, but the principles developed are applicable to any account or note receivable.

301

MOTIVATIONS FOR THE USE OF CREDIT

As with all business decisions, the decision to grant credit to customers is the result of a cost/benefit trade-off. The costs of extending credit include:

1. Evaluating the creditworthiness of the customer, which may include support of a credit department
2. Monitoring and recording collections
3. Incurring actual bad debts, which ultimately go uncollected
4. Foregoing interest on the cash that otherwise would have been collected at the time of sale

The benefits of extending credit are less easily identified.

Credit markets, like other capital markets, function on partial information regarding the ability of a borrower to repay any loans. If sellers did not provide credit, purchasers would have to look to other sources to obtain the necessary capital to finance the acquisition of goods and services—or go without purchasing them.

The purchaser's need for credit to finance the acquisition of goods or services varies considerably over both the short and long run, just as the level of a company's operations varies with economic conditions. Raising capital results in two types of cost:

1. The return that must be provided to investors to attract capital (interest)
2. Transaction costs of raising capital

Transaction costs include items such as the time to prepare documents to apply for a bank loan or the cost to register securities if the capital is to be raised in a public capital market. Transaction costs can be reduced or avoided if capital can be supplied by sources that have a cost advantage in assessing the creditworthiness of the borrower.

This is where *trade credit* (extension of credit by suppliers to customers for purchases of inventory or services) plays an important role, particularly in the manufacturing sector. Suppliers often have two advantages over other providers of capital. Because they typically supply a large number of customers in similar industries, they are likely to have better information regarding the nature of the current economic conditions in the industry and firm-specific information on which firms are better credit risks. In addition, as sellers of the merchandise, suppliers can more easily foreclose on the goods in the event of nonpayment. This can reduce the costs of collection. These forces work to create a capital market between sellers and purchasers, but it is a market limited to financing only the purchases of goods from the seller. If sellers can take advantage of their position in this capital market, the additional profits they can generate may more than offset the costs necessary to support the credit extension and collection process.

There are other reasons for providing customer credit, particularly in the retail industry. One of the key competitive features of the retail industry is customer service. One means of making it easier for customers to purchase goods from a retailer is to provide "in-house" financing. With the rise of bank credit cards, many retailers determined that the costs of maintaining their own credit operations were far in excess of the fees charged by credit card companies. As a result, some retailers stopped offering in-house credit and began accepting only bank cards. This is an example of a capital market where the information available to banks regarding an individual consumer's creditworthiness is likely to be just as extensive as that available to the retailer. Given the economies of scale in managing a large credit operation, bank cards displaced many store-specific credit cards. Even in this environment, however, many large retailers still provide in-house credit, usually with many different payment options to give the consumer a higher level of service than can be obtained through standard bank cards.

SALES DISCOUNTS AND THE VALUATION OF RECEIVABLES

Sales discounts are incentives offered to encourage early payment of invoice amounts. Sales discounts are used by sellers to expedite collection of cash to reduce the opportunity cost of funds tied up in receivables. For instance, the two-price system Amoco Oil Company used to allow cash purchasers to pay less than credit purchasers is an example of a sales discount offered to retail customers.

More often, discounts are offered at the wholesale, rather than the retail, level. These incentives allow the purchaser a discount from the full sales price for prompt payment of the balance due, but they generally do not require a cash purchase. For example, a 2% discount for payment within 10 days might be included to encourage payment of a balance that may not be due for 30 days. Sales discounts are usually stated as a percentage of the total invoice price that can be deducted for payment within a given period. For instance, a wholesaler might adopt a credit policy of payment in 30 days, but he or she may also adopt a discount of 2% of the invoice price if payment is made within 10 days. Such a policy is often referred to as "two-ten, net 30" or written 2/10, n/30. This refers to the 2% discount for payment in 10 days or the net invoice in 30 days.

These credit terms give accountants problems in matching as well as in valuation. To the extent that the purchaser eventually takes these incentives, the ultimate cash flow generated by the sale will be below the gross invoice price of the goods or services sold. If these differences are material, a question arises as to whether they should be treated as an expense in the period the original sale is recognized or be deducted from income in the period the discount is actually taken. Matching demands that all costs incurred to generate revenue be charged to expense when the revenue is recognized. In addition, valuation of the receivable based on net realizable value would require that any expected discounts reduce the value of the receivable since they represent amounts the seller does not expect to collect.

To satisfy both the matching concept and the use of net realizable value to represent receivables in the balance sheet, it is preferable to accrue the future costs of discounts associated with existing receivables in the period the revenue is recognized, rather than record expense at the point the discount is actually taken. This accrual will increase the expense of the period and decrease the recorded value of the receivable. Accrual of the effect of discounts on future cash collections is preferable only when reliable estimates of the future discount experience can be obtained.

In general, incorporating sales discounts into the determination of the NRV can be done by creating a contra-asset, or an allowance, account. The balance in this account reflects the difference between the gross receivable and the amount that is expected to be collected after including the effects of discounts. The allowance account is decreased whenever customers take the discounts. It increases when accruals are made to reflect the expense for the period.

Generally, the accrual of the expense for the period can be done once, at the end of the accounting period. At that time, an analysis can be performed to determine the amount of future discounts expected to be taken on currently outstanding receivables; and an adjustment to the allowance account can be made. This adjustment would be charged to an expense for the period.

For example, assume the Karrol Industries offered discounts to its customers. At the beginning of 1994, Karrol reported the following amounts in its balance sheet:

Accounts receivable	$100,000
Allowance for sales discounts	(5,000)
Net accounts receivable	$ 95,000

During 1994, the customers actually took discounts of $40,000. At year-end, Karrol estimated that discounts relating to the outstanding receivables would be $7,000. Based on this estimate, Karrol performed an analysis to determine the adjustment required to the allowance account to reflect properly the effect of discounts on income and receivables for the period. This analysis appears in Exhibit 7.2. The analysis indicates a need for an adjustment in the amount of a $42,000 increase in the allowance account. The journal entries Karrol would use to record this activity throughout 1994 would appear as follows:

Various dates as collections occur:		
Allowance for sales discounts	40,000	
Accounts receivable		40,000
To record discounts taken at the time of payment.		
December 31, 1994:		
Sales discount expense	42,000	
Allowance for sales discounts		42,000
To record the year-end adjustment to the allowance account in order to have the balance reflect expected future discounts on outstanding receivables.		

If no discounts were ever taken, there would be no need for the accrual of an allowance for sales discounts. On the other hand, if all discounts were always taken, it would be simpler to record the receivable at the net collectible amount when the sale occurred. This would eliminate any need for adjustment when the discounts were actually taken since revenues would already have been reduced by the effect of the discount. While these two extreme situations never actually occur, they do suggest alternatives to the use of an allowance account where experience indicates that discounts are either pre-

EXHIBIT 7.2

Karrol Industries—
T-Account Analysis
of Allowance for
Sales Discounts

KARROL INDUSTRIES
T-Account Analysis of Allowance for Sales Discounts

ALLOWANCE FOR SALES DISCOUNTS

		Beginning balance	$5,000
Discounts taken	$40,000		
Subtotal	$35,000		
		Sales discount expense accrual	?
		Ending balance	$7,000

Solving for the sales discount expense accrual:

Ending balance − subtotal = $35,000 − $(7,000) = $42,000

dominantly ignored, or predominantly taken, by customers. These methods are referred to as the gross method and the net method of handling discounts, respectively.

Under the **gross method** of accounting for sales discounts, the sale and related receivable are recorded for the entire invoice price. This is identical to the allowance method discussed earlier. If the customer takes advantage of the discount, the discount is recorded as an expense in the period it is taken. The gross method is typically chosen when discounts are not material.

Under the **net method**, the initial sale and receivable are recorded net of the discount. If the discount is taken, nothing is recorded. If the customer fails to pay within the discount period, an entry is made to record the foregone discount as additional revenue. This revenue is commonly classified as interest revenue. The net method is typically selected when discounts are material and commonly taken. For example, assume that Wenner Corporation sold merchandise to Blackburn, Inc. at a price of $1,000 and terms 1/10, n/60. Exhibit 7.3 displays the basic entries associated with the gross and net methods of accounting for sales discounts, assuming that all events described occur within a single year.

In summary, the determination of net realizable value in the presence of sales discounts requires some method of incorporating the effects of the discounts on the gross receivable. When this effect is not material, the gross method provides a reasonable means of tracking the company's experience with sales discounts, even though it technically does not achieve optimal matching or valuation of the receivables. The net method is often employed when discounts are material and commonly taken by customers. The net method may also not achieve optimal matching if it is possible to predict, with reasonable accuracy, that the amount of the discounts associated with receivables on the balance sheet date will not be taken. However, if these amounts are themselves not material, the net method will yield acceptable results. If either method results in receivable values that differ materially from the expected future cash collections due to the treatment of discounts, the allowance method should be employed to value correctly the receivables at net realizable value.

EXHIBIT 7.3

Wenner
Corporation—
Journal Entries for
Sales Discounts—
Gross Versus Net
Method

WENNER CORPORATION
Journal Entries for Sales Discounts
Gross Versus Net Method

THE GROSS METHOD			THE NET METHOD		
At sale:			At sale:		
Accounts receivable	1,000		Accounts receivable	990	
Revenue		1,000	Revenue		990
At payment: if discount is taken:			At payment: if discount is taken:		
Cash	990		Cash	990	
Sales discount expense	10		Accounts receivable		990
Accounts receivable		1,000			
At payment: if discount is not taken:			At payment: if discount is not taken:		
Cash	1,000		Cash	1,000	
Accounts receivable		1,000	Interest revenue		10
			Accounts receivable		990

USE OF BANK CREDIT CARDS FOR RETAIL OPERATIONS

When bank credit cards such as Visa and MasterCard became widespread, many retail companies decided to disband their own credit operation and began accepting charges from these national consumer credit operations. Credit card companies will agree to accept any authorized charge to a card they have issued and not hold the merchant liable for any uncollected balances as long as the merchant has followed the rules set forth by the credit card operation. Generally, these rules relate to verification of acceptance of the charge at the time of sale through contact with the credit card company for amounts above a certain limit and an agreement for handling merchandise returns.

Credit card companies generate revenues in two ways:

1. Interest on unpaid balances from customers who choose to extend their payment program
2. Fees charged to retailers and card holders

The fees charged to retailers depend on the volume of activity, both in terms of numbers of charges and dollar amounts. Generally, the merchant receives 90–98% of the selling price for merchandise charged on these types of cards. The larger the dollar volume, the higher the percentage retained by the merchant, since large volume is more cost-efficient for the credit card processing operation.

These discounts can be accounted for using either a gross or net method, depending on how the merchant wishes to track the costs of credit card sales. Since all credit card sales will have a discount imposed, the question is one of how much cost will ultimately be incurred. Most large retail operations use the net method, recording the revenue at the selling price of the goods less the discount charged by the credit card issuer. For example, assume Dunston's

Department Stores had $3,000,000 of credit card sales for the month of September 1993. The credit card issuer charged a discount of 3% for this level of volume. Dunston's would record the following entry:

September 30, 1993:
Accounts receivable   2,910,000
　　Revenues   2,910,000
To record revenues and the amounts receivable from the
　credit card operation.

Since one advantage of allowing customers to use credit cards is to expedite the cash collection, this receivable is outstanding only long enough for the credit card company to receive the documents supporting the charges and to transfer cash to the merchant. This would not extend beyond a few days.

UNCOLLECTIBLE ACCOUNTS AND THE VALUATION OF RECEIVABLES

Companies that sell on credit also incur losses from accounts that are never collected. The magnitude of these losses is a direct result of the nature of the policies regarding credit extension. Companies that place more effort in screening customer credit are likely to have fewer bad debts. If these losses are not material, a company may elect to treat the costs associated with uncollectible accounts as an expense at the time it proves uncollectible. This approach is referred to as the **direct write-off method** of accounting for bad debts and is conceptually similar to the gross method of accounting for sales discounts.

If the anticipated level of uncollectible accounts is material to either the measurement of the net realizable value of receivables, or income for the period, an **allowance method** of accounting for uncollectible amounts must be employed. The allowance method accrues expected bad debt losses based on expectations regarding future collections. Conceptually, the use of an allowance for uncollectible accounts is similar to the use of the allowance for sales discounts. In the discussion that follows, the direct method is examined first, followed by the allowance method.

The Direct Write-off Method

Assume Davidson Manufacturing sold $25,000 of merchandise on credit on July 14, 1994, and this amount eventually proved to be uncollectible on February 14, 1995. Davidson has a fiscal year-end of December 31. If the direct method of accounting for bad debts were utilized, Davidson would make the following entries relating to this sale and failure to collect:

July 14, 1994:
Accounts receivable   25,000
　　Revenue   25,000
To record the sales of merchandise in 1992.

February 14, 1995:

Bad debt expense	25,000	
Accounts receivable		25,000

To record the write-off of the receivable as uncollectible in 1993.

If at some point after February 14, 1995, a portion of this receivable was actually recovered unexpectedly, Davidson would reverse the entry that recorded the bad debt, reinstate the receivable to the extent it was collected, then record the cash collection. For example, assume that on October 1, 1995, Davidson collected $3,000 of the unpaid receivable through the liquidation of the debtor in bankruptcy. At that point, Davidson would record the following entry:[1]

October 14, 1995:

Cash	3,000	
Bad debt expense		3,000

To record the collection of a previously written-off balance.

The decision to classify a receivable as ultimately uncollectible and, therefore, to write off the remaining balance is typically one of managerial judgment as to when the receivable has become worthless. Some companies write off accounts only when they discontinue any attempts at collection. Others may use more conservative criteria and write off accounts as soon as they become past due for some period of time.

The decision to write off an account may be made by applying various criteria that have been developed from past experience with poor paying accounts. For example, in a recent annual report, Dayton Hudson Corporation (a major retailer in the Midwest) reported that: "Our policy is to write off accounts receivable when any portion of the balance is 12 months past due, or when the required payments have not been made for six consecutive months." While this appears to be an objective standard—and it may be determined based on the past experience of the company with regard to recoveries after accounts are as far delinquent as indicated in its policy—the policy is still based on judgment. This policy is subject to change whenever management believes it might be appropriate. This leaves room for changes that are manifestations of changing economic environments, but it also creates opportunities for management to manipulate reported balances through decisions of this type.

The Allowance Method

If a company's bad debt experience suggests that future losses associated with uncollectible accounts will be material, it is desirable to quantify and measure the size of the potential bad debt losses and to record them in the period that

---

[1] The entry could be separated into two steps as follows:

Accounts receivable	3,000	
Bad debt expense		3,000
Cash	3,000	
Accounts receivable		3,000

However, the net effect of these entries is captured by the entry in the text.

the revenue from the original sale occurred. This approach obtains a better matching of expenses to revenue. The use of a valuation allowance to reflect the expected amount of gross uncollectible receivables due to bad debts also achieves a better measure of net realizable value for purposes of measurement and reporting.

Accrual of bad debt losses as expense prior to the actual write-off of an account is also appropriate under the guidelines established for the recognition of contingent losses in SFAS No. 5. The existence of future losses from nonpayment of some receivable balances is probable. This implies that if a reliable estimate of those losses is possible, their accrual is mandated under SFAS No. 5. When these costs are accrued, they are reported as an expense of the period and reduce the value of the receivables through the creation of a valuation allowance.

Determining the Magnitude of the Allowance for Uncollectible Accounts   The two basic approaches for estimating the losses from accounts that will prove uncollectible are the **percentage of sales** and the **percentage of receivables**. Most companies use both these methods as a means of cross-checking the reasonableness of the results obtained from either one individually. The two methods are differentiated by their focus in obtaining an estimate of the remaining anticipated future losses at the balance sheet date. The percentage of sales method attempts to link losses to the magnitude of credit sales for the period without reference to the actual balance remaining in gross receivables at the balance sheet date. The percentage of receivables method directly estimates the amount of future losses as a percentage of the ending balance of the gross receivables. The application of either method will determine both of the following:

1. The expense to be recognized in the period, which measures the amount of bad debts estimated to relate to current period sales
2. The ending balance in the allowance account, which represents an estimate of the magnitude of uncollectible balances included in the gross receivable at the balance sheet date

During each period, the allowance account is increased by the current period's bad debts expense and reduced by the amounts of any accounts actually written off.

Application of the Percentage of Sales Method   Assume that Daco Enterprises begins 1994 with the following balances on January 1:

Accounts receivable	$1,200,000
Allowance for uncollectible accounts	(50,000)
Net receivables	$1,150,000

Daco sells all of its merchandise on credit and has historically experienced about 4% of its sales to be uncollectible. Sales for the current year were

$3,000,000. Collections on trade receivables were $2,800,000 for the year. Daco had net write-offs (accounts written off less accounts collected that had previously been written off) of $122,000. Using the percentage of sales method, the company would make the following journal entries to record the activities relating to receivables and the allowance account:

Various dates throughout the year:

Accounts receivable	3,000,000	
Revenues		3,000,000

To accrue revenues from credit sales throughout the year.

Various dates throughout the year:

Cash	2,800,000	
Accounts receivable		2,800,000

To record collections on receivables throughout the year.

When the allowance method is used, accounts that prove to be uncollectible in the period are not charged to expense. Rather, they reduce the magnitude of the allowance that has been established to absorb such losses when realized.

Various dates throughout the year:

Allowance for uncollectible accounts	122,000	
Accounts receivable		122,000

To record accounts written off during the year.

Under the percentage of sales approach, the current period expense is estimated as a percentage of credit sales. Using an estimate of 4% of credit sales yields an expense estimate of $120,000 (4% × $3,000,000 = $120,000).

To record the accrual of bad debt expense
December 31, 1994:

Bad debt expense	120,000	
Allowance for uncollectible accounts		120,000

To accrue the estimated bad debt expense for the year.

The ending balance of the allowance for uncollectible accounts results from the consequences of the entries indicated above. In this example, the balances in receivables and the allowance account would appear as follows at the end of the year:

Accounts receivable	$1,400,000
Allowance for uncollectible accounts	(48,000)
Net receivables	$1,352,000

Application of the Percentage of Receivables Method Assume the same information regarding the operations of Daco, except that the company estimates 4% of the ending balance of accounts receivable typically prove uncollectible and uses the percentage of accounts receivable method, instead of the percentage of sales method, to estimate bad debt expense. Daco would record revenues, collections, and the write-offs of uncollectible accounts in exactly the same fashion as before, but it would determine the current period expense differently. In particular, Daco would estimate the desired ending balance in the allowance for bad debts. In this case, this desired balance is $1,400,000 × 4%, or $56,000. Given this information, Daco would perform an analysis similar to that presented in Exhibit 7.4.

The purpose of this analysis is to determine the amount of the current period expense that must be recognized to support the desired ending balance of $56,000. The analysis indicates that amount must be $128,000, which is recorded via the following journal entry:

December 31, 1994:
Bad debt expense   128,000
    Allowance for uncollectible accounts   128,000
To accrue the estimated bad debt expense for the year.

In the Daco example, the percentage of sales method does not provide precisely the same estimate of the bad debt expense for 1994 as does the percentage of receivables method. The difference in this case is $8,000, which might be immaterial to the financial statements. If so, either method may be used. However, if the difference is deemed material, additional information may be necessary to resolve which of the two methods provides a more reliable estimate. Perhaps collections are slowing down such that the relationship between sales and collections has changed. Slower collections mean higher receivables for the same level of sales. This might explain the higher expense estimate arising from the percentage of receivables method. If the slower collections also imply higher uncollectible amounts, the percentage of receivables estimate may be more appropriate.

Aging and the Interplay Between the Percentage of Sales and Receivables Approaches   When the percentage of receivables method is employed to estimate the ending balance of the allowance for doubtful accounts, it is typical to stratify the receivable balances into groups based on their age. The likelihood of an account going unpaid increases with the length

EXHIBIT 7.4
T-Account Analysis of Allowance for Uncollectible Accounts— Application of the Percentage of Receivables Method

**T-Account Analysis of Allowance for Uncollectible Accounts
Application of the Percentage of Receivables Method**

ALLOWANCE FOR UNCOLLECTIBLE ACCOUNTS			
		Beginning balance	$50,000
Accounts written off	$122,000		
Subtotal	$ 72,000		
		Bad debt expense accrual	?
		Ending balance	$56,000

Solving for the bad debt expense accrual:
Ending balance − subtotal = $56,000 − $(72,000) = $128,000

of time it has been outstanding. A better estimate of the total amount of uncollectible accounts expected from a population of receivables can be determined by breaking the population down into strata and applying a likelihood of non-payment to each strata separately. Such a process is demonstrated in Exhibit 7.5 for Partial, Inc. Since this process generally requires more information than a simple percentage of sales, estimates of the allowance balance from the aging approach are generally considered to be more reliable.

CHANGES IN ACCOUNTING METHODS AND ACCOUNTING ESTIMATES IN THE VALUATION OF RECEIVABLES

When a company changes from the direct write-off method to the allowance method of accounting for uncollectible accounts, it makes a change in accounting principle. There are two possible situations in which this might arise. If bad debt losses were immaterial in the past, but have become material, then the change will likely be treated prospectively. This application arises because the beginning balance of the allowance account is immaterially different from zero but during the period the situation has changed, resulting in a material ending balance. If bad debt losses have always been material, the use of the direct write-off method was a violation of GAAP. The change is treated as an error correction, which requires restatement of all prior period financial statements.

Since the percentage of sales and percentage of receivables methods are simply different approaches to developing an estimate of the bad debt expense and ending allowance account, the firm's decision to switch from one method to the other is not a change in accounting principle. Rather, it is simply a change in estimate, which requires disclosure only if the effect is highly material.

DISCLOSURES RELATING TO RECEIVABLES

Trade receivables are generally reported as part of current assets, net of any valuation allowances that reduce the gross value of the receivable to expected

PARTIAL, INC. Aging of Accounts Receivable			
	RECEIVABLE BALANCE	PERCENTAGE UNCOLLECTIBLE	ESTIMATED ALLOWANCE
Current	$100,000	0.2%	$ 200
31 to 60 days	20,000	1.0%	200
61 to 90 days	5,000	7.0%	350
91 to 120 days	3,000	10.0%	300
Over 120 days	1,000	45.0%	450
Total	$129,000		$1,500

EXHIBIT 7.5

Partial, Inc.—Aging of Accounts Receivable

net realizable value. This format was demonstrated in the excerpt from the financial statements of Allegheny Ludlum Corporation in Exhibit 7.1. Typically, trade receivables are included in the current asset category of receivables. Current receivables may also include rights to collect cash from the sale of assets other than inventory, if the cash collections are expected to occur within the next operating cycle or one year. In addition, other miscellaneous receivables may also be included in the current receivables balance.

Expenses related to credit sales such as the costs of discounts and allowances and bad debts may be reported in several different ways. Some companies elect to reduce the amounts reported as revenue for the costs of credit sales, especially the costs associated with sales discounts and credit card sales. This treatment makes net revenue comparable for firms that use either the gross or net method of accounting for discounts and allowances. Bad debt expense is more commonly included in the category of selling, general, and administrative expense.

The treatment of receivables, and related accounts, in the statement of cash flows depends on the event that gave rise to the receivable. Any cash flows related to collection of a receivable that arose from the sale of inventory or services in the normal course of business is considered an operating cash flow. Under the direct method of reporting cash flows from operations, the cash collections from customers must be reported as a line item. Under the indirect method, bad debt expense must be added back to net income to convert net income to cash flow from operations. In addition, the change in net accounts receivable will appear as another reconciling item. Increases in net accounts receivable are deducted from net income to obtain cash flows from operations, while decreases are added.

Collections of receivables that arise from the sale of other assets or loans made by the entity are investing cash flows, not operating cash flows. These cash inflows would then be reported as investing cash inflows in the statement of cash flows.

IMPUTED INTEREST

When a company sells on credit, the costs of this process must be recovered if the company is to stay in business. One means of doing this is to charge interest from the date of the sale. Interest charges can be structured such that they provide a competitive return to the seller from entering into credit operations. Usually, trade receivables have a 30-to-90-day non-interest bearing period before interest charges begin to accrue. Although this practice appears to provide "interest free" financing, this is not the case.

In the absence of an explicit interest charge, the selling price is established to cover the cost of credit sales and must include an implicit interest charge. The price of a unit must reflect both the cost of providing the good or service and the cost of providing credit to credit purchasers. A common example of this occurs in the retail gasoline business. Some companies, such as Amoco Oil Company, provide a two-price system, one for credit purchases and a second, lower price for cash purchases. This system specifically charges all credit sales customers for the costs of maintaining the credit sale option. Purchasers who use cash need not pay for this service since they do not use it. In any case, the effect of having price reflect both product and financing costs is that revenues (which are recognized on price) contain elements of both.

The payment period on most trade receivables is short. Consequently, the difference between the invoice value and the discounted value of the future payment is typically not material enough to warrant concern. If the payment period is longer, the effect of imputed interest on both revenue recognition and valuation of the receivable is more pronounced. As a result, the need to consider discounting of receivables arises as a natural response to differing credit policies.

Valuation of Trade Receivables

To appreciate the implications of imputed interest on the revenue from sales on credit and why this is generally not a material issue for trade receivables, consider the following example. Major Company sold merchandise on credit to Minor Company for $10,000 payable in 30 days. The present value of this receivable would not be $10,000. Assuming that Major could borrow funds at a rate of 12% annually, the present value to Major of the receivable would be computed as:

$$\$10,000 \times (\text{Present Value of } \$1, \text{ at } 1\%, \text{ for 1 period}) =$$
$$\$10,000 \times .9901 = \$9,901$$

In this case, the difference between the present value of $9,901 and the face value of $10,000 is the implicit interest of $99. How should the implicit interest be accounted for?

In most cases, receivables that carry no interest rate (or a rate that is less than the prevailing market rate at the time the receivable arises) are required to be discounted. The original value of the receivable is then recorded at the discounted value. The difference between the face amount and discounted value is accrued as interest income over the life of the receivable.[2] Short-term trade receivables are exempt from this requirement, as long as they mature within one year. This exemption is motivated primarily by a lack of materiality.[3]

Discounting receivables does not change the total amount of cash to be collected. It does change the value of the revenue recognized at sale and the interest revenue recognized over time following the sale. If the sale and collection of the receivable occur in the same accounting period, discounting has no effect on total revenue; but it does change the classification of some of the revenue from sales to interest revenue. In the case of Major Company, discounting would result in sales revenue of $9,901 and interest revenue of $99. Total revenues would be $10,000, regardless of whether discounting is employed. Even if collection occurs in a later period, the small size of any imputed inter-

---

[2] "Interest on Receivables and Payables," *Accounting Principles Board Opinion No. 21*, August, 1971.

[3] *Ibid.*, para. 3.

est would suggest that any misstatement of the net realizable value of receivables (and the related effect on total revenue) that arises from not discounting future cash flows would be immaterial.

Valuation of Installment Receivables

Not all trade receivables are short-term. Some companies sell merchandise on the installment basis, which spreads payments out over a number of months. This is particularly common in the sale of consumer durable goods such as television sets, automobiles, washers, dryers, and the like. When such a sale occurs, two possible situations may arise. First, the installment sales contract may call for interest payments at a rate that is reasonable given the market conditions at the time of the sale. Alternatively, the interest rate may differ from the market rate of interest. Providing below market rate financing is a common practice in the automobile industry to increase sales.

When the interest rate in the installment sale contract (referred to as the **contractual rate**) differs materially from the market rate of interest on similar exchanges, the economic reality of the situation suggests that representation of the installment receivable, and revenue therefrom, based on the reported selling price may materially misrepresent the economic substance of the exchange. Since the installment receivable agreement sets forth the pattern of future cash flows for both interest (at the contractual rate) and the principal payments, determining the net realizable value of this receivable requires that the future cash payments under the contract be discounted using the prevailing market rate of interest at the time of the original exchange instead of the contractual rate of interest. The resulting discounted value is recorded as the value of the receivable and the revenue from the sale. As time passes, interest is accrued on the receivable using the market interest rate at the date the exchange originated.

Assume Fastdrive Automotive sold an auto to a customer on January 1, 1994. The contract price was $8,000. The installment contact calls for no money down and payments over 18 months at a contractual interest rate of 6%. Using the tables for the present value of an annuity at 1/2% for 18 periods, the annuity payment required under the installment contract is $465.85 per month ($8,000 ÷ 17.1728). Assume that at the time of the sale, banks were lending money for car loans of this type at 15%. How should Fastdrive record the sale?

Exhibit 7.6 presents the computation of the present value of the installment contract at 15%, as well as the breakdown of interest (at the market rate) and principal for each payment. As a result of these computations, Fastdrive would prepare the following journal entry to record the sale of the automobile:

January 1, 1994:

Accounts receivable	7,467.34	
Sales		7,467.34

To record the receivable at its present value when discounted at the market rate of interest.

When the first payment is received, the following entry will be recorded:

FASTDRIVE AUTOMOTIVE
Imputing Interest on Installment Contracts

Computation of present value:

$465.85 × (present value of an annuity of $1, at 1.25%, for 18 periods)

$465.85 × 16.0295 = $7,467.34

Amortization table for the installment contract:

Payment	(1) Principal Prior to Payment	(2) Interest Portion [1.25% × (1)]	(3) Principal Portion [Payment − (2)]	(4) Balance [(1) − (3)]
1	$7,467.34	$ 93.34	$ 372.51	$7,094.83
2	7,094.83	88.69	377.16	6,717.67
3	6,717.67	83.97	381.88	6,335.79
4	6,335.79	79.19	386.66	5,949.13
5	5,949.13	74.36	391.49	5,557.64
6	5,557.64	69.47	396.38	5,161.26
7	5,161.26	64.51	401.34	4,759.92
8	4,759.92	59.49	406.36	4,353.56
9	4,353.56	54.41	411.44	3,942.12
10	3,942.12	49.27	416.58	3,525.54
11	3,525.54	44.06	421.79	3,103.75
12	3,103.75	38.79	427.06	2,676.69
13	2,676.69	33.45	432.40	2,244.29
14	2,244.29	28.05	437.80	1,806.49
15	1,806.49	22.58	443.27	1,363.22
16	1,363.22	17.04	448.81	914.41
17	914.41	11.43	454.42	459.99
18	459.99	$ 5.86	$ 459.99	0
	Totals	$917.96	$7,467.34	

EXHIBIT 7.6

Fastdrive
Automotive—
Imputing Interest
on Installment
Contracts

January 31, 1994:

Cash	465.85	
Accounts receivable		372.51
Interest revenue		93.34

To record the receipt of the first payment.

Future entries to record payments would appear similar to the one above, but with the appropriate amounts entered as interest revenue and principal reduction.

Valuation of Notes Receivable

Notes receivable generally differ from accounts receivable in two important ways:

1. Their maturity
2. The exchange that gives rise to them is often not part of the operating cycle

When assigning a value to a note, these two features become very important. Where short-term, trade receivables were exempt from imputing of interest due to their nature and maturity structure, notes are not exempt unless they are taken in exchange for the sale of inventory (trade notes). Trade notes are treated just like trade receivables. (Interest is imputed only when collection extends beyond one year and the contractual interest rate is not equal to the market rate of interest when the sale occurred.) All other notes are subject to the requirement that they be presented in the balance sheet at the present value of the future cash flows required by each note. The process of imputing interest on a note is identical to imputing interest on an installment receivable, which was discussed earlier. An example of how the present value of a note interacts with the net carrying value of the note to determine the gain or loss recognized from the sale of property, plant, and equipment is captured in Exhibit 7.7.

In this example, Deca Corporation sold a piece of land it owned to Lowenstein, Incorporated on January 1, 1994. Deca accepted a non-interest bearing note due on December 31, 1996, in the amount of $12,000 in exchange for the land, which had a book value of $10,000. The market rate of interest for similar types of transactions was 13% at the time of the sale. Discounting the promised cash flows under the note at the market rate of interest results in a present value of $8,317, which represents the selling price of the land. Since the face value of the note is $12,000, the difference between the present value and the face value is recorded as a discount (valuation allowance) associated with the note receivable.

If Deca were to produce a balance sheet at the date of the sale, the entire value of the note would not be classified as a current asset. In particular, the current portion of the note receivable would be represented by the present value of the cash to be collected at the end of the first year, which is zero. As a result, the entire balance of the note receivable would be classified as noncurrent, until the end of 1991 when the collection of the one and only cash payment comes within the next year. Over time, interest income is recognized based on the amortization of the discount and uses the concepts of present value. However, the interest rate used is always the market rate when the transaction that originated the note occurred.

GENERATING CASH FROM RECEIVABLES PRIOR TO MATURITY

Accounts and notes receivable represent rights to collect cash. When a firm determines that the cost of waiting to collect the cash represented by the receivables is too high, it may elect to convert these receivables immediately into cash. There are several means of accomplishing this. The alternatives differ primarily in the types of risks that are exchanged. Typical examples of these transactions involving receivables include pledging, assigning, and factoring. When notes are transferred the process is typically referred to as *dis-*

counting. From a financial reporting perspective, the form of the transaction is not important. The crucial issue for financial reporting is whether the transfer represents a sale of receivables or borrowing using the receivables as security.

If a transfer of receivables is treated as a sale, the asset will be removed from the books of account; and any gain or loss on the transfer will be recognized immediately. If the transfer is classified as a borrowing, the asset is not deemed to be disposed of and remains on the transferee's books. In addition, a liability for the amount of the loan that arises in the transfer must be recognized on the transferee's books. Clearly, the distinction between a sale and a borrowing has substantial effects on both the income statement and the balance sheet. As each form of transfer is examined, keep in mind that the accounting treatment is dependent on our assessment of the transfer as a sale or borrowing.

Determining the Present Value of a Note
Exchange of Land for a Note

EXHIBIT 7.7
Determining the
Present Value of a
Note—Exchange of
Land for a Note

Computation of present value:

$12,000 × (present value of $1, at 13%, in 3 periods)
$12,000 × .6931 = $8,317

Amortization schedule for the note:

Principal	Accrued Interest at 13%	Principal + Interest
$8,317	$ 8,317 × .13 = $1,081	$8,317 + $1,081 = $ 9,398
	9,398 × .13 = 1,222	8,317 + 2,303 = 10,620
	10,620 × .13 = 1,380	8,317 + 3,683 = 12,000

Journal entries:

January 1, 1994:

Notes receivable	12,000	
Loss on sale of land	1,683	
Discount on notes receivable		3,683
Land		10,000

To record the exchange of land for a non-interest bearing note.

December 31, 1994:

Discount on notes receivable	1,081	
Interest revenue		1,081

To record interest revenue imputed on the note for 1994.

December 31, 1995:

Discount on notes receivable	1,222	
Interest revenue		1,222

To record interest revenue imputed on the note for 1995.

December 31, 1996:

Cash	12,000	
Discount on notes receivable	1,380	
Interest revenue		1,380
Notes receivable		12,000

To record interest revenue imputed on the note and repayment of the note in 1996.

Pledging of Receivables

Pledging of receivables is a means of providing a security interest in the receivables (referred to as *collateral*) to a third party in exchange for a loan. A pledging of receivables does not transfer either title to the receivables or risks of ownership from the firm to the lender. Pledging does guarantee that if the loan is not repaid, the lender has the right to obtain title to the receivables and collect any proceeds under those agreements. However, if the proceeds of those collections are still insufficient to pay the principal and interest on the loan, the company is still liable for any shortfall. In short, pledging never transfers the risk of loss from the firm to the lender. As a result, a sale has not occurred since ownership of the asset is never expected to be transferred and risk of loss is never transferred between the parties.

Corporations commonly maintain lines-of-credit with their banks. Such lines-of-credit are often secured by having the companies pledge their inventories and receivables as collateral against any outstanding balance. No special accounting procedures are required when assets are pledged. If the restrictions on receivables from such collateral agreements are material, they should be disclosed in the notes to the financial statements. An example of such disclosure for Pioneer Hi-Bred International, Inc. is presented in Exhibit 7.8.

Assignment of Receivables

An **assignment of receivables** is a transfer of right to the cash collections from the receivables to a third party. An assignment differs from a pledging in that the right to collect cash is transferred when the assignment is executed. This does not occur when assets are pledged. The company assigning the receivables is called the **assignor**, and the third party receiving the right to collections is the **assignee**. The assignee advances money to the assignor based on the value of the receivables being assigned. Generally, the assignor collects the receivables and remits the collections to the assignee until the loan is repaid. In this way, customers are never aware that their receivable has been assigned to another party. In extreme cases, the assignee may require customers to make payment directly to itself.

The essence of an assignment does not differ materially from that of a pledging, except to the extent that the transferee receives a security interest in the receivables. For example, if the assignee elects to have customers make

EXHIBIT 7.8	PIONEER HI-BRED INTERNATIONAL, INC.
Pioneer Hi-Bred International, Inc.— Disclosure of Receivables Pledged as Collateral for a Loan	**Disclosure of Receivables Pledged as Collateral for a Loan**

Note 5: Pledged Assets, Notes Payable, Lines of Credit, and Long-Term Debt

The long-term debt with an August 31, 1982 balance of $17,621,680 bears interest at 4-14 3/4% and requires varying annual principal payments through 2008. $10,726,290 of this long-term debt is collateralized by receivables of $10,030,965, inventories of $11,715,745, and property and equipment with a depreciated cost of $15,789,319.

payment directly to itself, then a higher level of security is provided than if payments are directed to the assignor. Payments going to the assignor may be redirected and not used to repay the assignee for the advances. Similarly in a pledge situation, the firm pledging the receivables may redirect proceeds from its collection to activities other than repayment of the loan. Since an assignment actually empowers the assignee to take possession of the receivables at any time, the assignee can obtain greater control over the cash flows from collection of the receivables. An assignment does transfer control of the receivable, but it does not transfer risks of ownership. Since risk of ownership is not materially altered, an assignment is not a sale of receivables.

In general, the terms of an assignment include a fee charged by the assignor for providing the cash advance. It is also possible that the assignor will charge interest on any unpaid portion of the advance at periodic intervals over the life of the assignment. In addition, the assignor will typically assign receivables with a value in excess of the amount of the advance. Such assignment provides the assignee a cushion to absorb bad debts, sales discounts, and sales returns that might reduce the ultimate collections on the receivables assigned. The costs of the assignment are basically interest costs and should be recognized as expense over the life of the assignment. The advance should create a liability of equal value.

For example, assume that Jake Industries assigned $100,000 in trade receivables to Midtown Finance on January 1, 1994, in exchange for an advance of $80,000. Midtown charged a finance fee of $3,900, which is deducted from the loan proceeds; no other interest charges are to be paid. These fees represent the interest costs of the loan and are prepaid in this example. The interest costs must be recognized as an expense over the life of the loan. Collections were anticipated to pay off the loan within 45 days. Actual collections on the receivables were $60,000 on January 31 and $37,000 on February 15. Jake would have used the following journal entries to record the effect of the assignment:

January 1, 1994:

Cash	76,100	
Prepaid expense (interest)	3,900	
Loan payable		80,000
To record the receipt of the loan proceeds and the prepaid financing costs.		
Accounts receivable assigned	100,000	
Accounts receivable		100,000
To reclassify the accounts receivable that were assigned under the terms of the loan.		

The reclassification of receivables as accounts receivable assigned in the second entry above is designed to segregate those receivables for which collections are directed to repayment of an advance from those whose collections are unencumbered.

January 31, 1994:

Cash	60,000	
Accounts receivable assigned		60,000
To record collection of assigned receivables.		

Loan payable	60,000	
Cash		60,000
To repay part of the loan balance with collections.		

Interest expense	2,600	
Prepaid expenses (Interest)		2,600
To amortize the prepaid interest on the loan:		
$3,900 ÷ 45 days × 30 days.		

February 15, 1994:

Cash	37,000	
Accounts receivable assigned		37,000
To record collections of assigned receivables.		

Loan payable	20,000	
Accounts receivable	3,000	
Cash		20,000
Accounts receivable assigned		3,000
To record final payment on the loan and reclassify the remaining receivables.		

Interest expense	1,300	
Prepaid expenses (interest)		1,300
To amortize the remaining prepaid interest on the loan:		
$3,900 – $2,600.		

When assigned receivables exist at the balance sheet date, special disclosure requirements exist. Since the loan that arose as part of the assignment process has a direct claim against a particular asset, the assigned receivables, the loan may not be classified as part of the liability section of the balance sheet. At the discretion of management, the loan may be used to offset directly the assigned accounts receivable asset; and the net amount is reported in the asset section of the balance sheet.

In the example presented above, if Jake has a fiscal year-end of January 31, it would report the following in the current asset section of its balance sheet as it relates to the assigned receivables:

Accounts receivable assigned	$ 40,000
Loan payable to assignee	(20,000)
Equity in assigned receivables	$ 20,000

Factoring or Sale of Receivables

A **factor** is an entity in the business of acquiring receivables from companies in exchange for cash. A factor usually takes possession of the receivables and directly collects the balances from customers. A factoring can occur *with* or *without recourse*. **Recourse** refers to the factor's requirement that the company transferring the receivables make payments for any uncollectible accounts or otherwise compensate the factor in the event of noncollection. Recourse creates a contingent liability for the company-transferor since additional monies may have to be paid to the factor if certain events occur. When receivables are factored **without recourse**, all ownership rights and risks of ownership are transferred from the firm to the factor. As a result, a nonrecourse factoring is always accounted for as a sale of receivables. What is less clear is whether there are any circumstances when a recourse factoring constitutes a sale since the recourse provision always leaves some risk of loss with the firm transferring the receivables.

SFAS No. 77, "Reporting by Transferors for Transfers of Receivables with Recourse," sets forth the criteria for determining when a sale of receivables has occurred. Prior to the adoption of this standard, the assessment of the substance of a factoring, to determine whether it qualified for treatment as a sale, would have been done using the general guidelines for income recognition:

1. Income must be earned
2. Income must be realizable

Income is earned when the seller's performance is substantially completed and when substantially all of the risks of ownership are transferred. When some risk of ownership remains or some small portion of the seller's performance is yet to be completed at the point-of-sale, income is generally recognized at the time of the transfer as long as reliable estimates of the future costs to be incurred due to the retention of risk or requirement for future performance can be obtained. If the risk of ownership retained by the seller is extensive or if the future costs cannot be reliably estimated, no income should be recognized at the point-of-sale.

The problem with factoring was that accountants and auditors were having difficulty deciding what criteria to use to make the judgment that "substantially all" of the risks of ownership had been transferred. Some accountants believed that retention of any risk was sufficient to prevent treatment of the transaction as a sale. Others believed that as long as quantifiable estimates of future expected losses (costs) could be obtained, the presence of recourse should not prevent treatment as a sale. This conflict within the profession led the FASB to develop a specific standard.

SFAS No. 77 sets forth conditions that must be satisfied to treat a recourse factoring as a sale:

1. The transferor surrenders control of the future benefits embodied in the receivables.
2. The transferor's obligation under the recourse provision can be reasonably estimated.
3. The transferee cannot require the transferor to repurchase a material amount of the receivables.

The above criteria do not require that the transfer occur without recourse in order for it to be treated as a sale. Surrendering control of the receivables is accomplished when the collection of the receivable is unconditionally transferred to the factor. If the transferor holds an option to repurchase the receivables at the transferor's discretion, control has not been transferred.

The requirement that a reasonable estimate of any future obligation be obtainable is meant to limit the treatment of a transfer as a sale to only those situations in which the likelihood of any contingent liability can be determined. If the transferor has no experience with factoring and is unable to develop a means to obtain a reasonable estimate of the future costs arising from the factoring of the receivables, no sale will be recorded due to the high level of uncertainty involved.

The last requirement limits the definition of a sale to only those transfers where the factor takes the receivables without recourse, or where the amount of such recourse is not deemed to be material. This provision allows recourse transfers to be accounted for as a sale provided that the expectations of the parties regarding any subsequent return of receivables is immaterial to the entire transaction.

The Structure of a Factoring Agreement   Many terms of a factoring agreement are similar to those of an assignment. The factor typically charges a finance fee, which is deducted from the gross proceeds received by the firm transferring the receivables. Periodic interest charges on uncollected amounts may also be charged, but this is less common in a factoring agreement than in an assignment. The factor also typically imposes a "holdback" provision.

A **holdback** is a percentage of the total factored receivables that is set aside to absorb the effects of bad debt losses, sales discounts, sales returns, and other types of costs that will ultimately decrease the cash collections associated with the factored receivables. As these losses are incurred, the amount of the holdback is drawn down to compensate for these losses. A holdback provision can exist regardless of whether the transfer is with or without recourse.

If the actual losses are less than the holdback, the excess holdback is repaid to the firm originally transferring the receivables. In this sense, the amount of the holdback actually belongs to the company transferring the receivables until actual losses are incurred to offset this balance. If the holdback is too small, the factor will incur losses. When a factoring is without recourse, any losses suffered by the factor must be borne by the factor. In a recourse factoring, these losses can be collected from the firm originally transferring the receivables.

Transfers Without Recourse   If the receivables are transferred to the factor without recourse, the transfer is a sale. For example, assume that on March 3, 1994, Getta Company sold, without recourse, receivables with a face value of $25,000 to Magna, Inc. Getta had previously established an allowance for doubtful accounts relating to these receivables in the amount of $5,000. Magna required a holdback of $7,000 and imposed a finance charge of 4% of the gross receivables. As a result, Getta actually received cash of $17,000 [$25,000 — (4% × $25,000) – $7,000] on the date of the factoring. Getta would make the following journal entry to record the sale:

March 3, 1994:

Cash	17,000	
Loss on sale of receivables[4]	1,000	
Due from factor	7,000	
Accounts receivable		25,000

To record the sale of receivables without recourse.

---

[4] This amount is often charged to interest expense since it represents a cost of financing related to the early conversion of receivables to cash.

In the journal entry above, the due from factor account represents the remaining interest held by Getta in the factored receivables. The existing allowance for doubtful accounts has a balance of $5,000, reflecting the expected losses that the holdback of $7,000 is designed to absorb. On net, Getta expects to get $2,000 cash back when the receivables are finally collected, and this is represented by the net asset (due from factor – allowance for uncollectible accounts). Alternatively, Getta could have closed out the allowance for uncollectible accounts against the due from factor and reported the due from factor balance as $2,000. If Magna had not required a holdback as part of the agreement, the due from factor account would not be necessary, and the allowance for uncollectible accounts would be closed out in determining the loss on sale.

Suppose that the actual bad debt losses from the factored receivables was $4,000. This would imply that the factor must return the difference between the holdback of $7,000 and the actual losses of $4,000 to Getta. Assuming this settlement was achieved on April 30, 1994, Getta would journalize this event as follows:

April 30, 1994:

Cash	2,000	
Allowance for uncollectible accounts	5,000	
Due from factor		7,000
To record settlement of the holdback.		

Had the actual losses exceeded the holdback, Getta would receive no cash from Magna; but due to the no recourse provision, Getta would not be required to make up the difference. As a result, the receivable from the factor would simply be written off against the allowance for uncollectible accounts as follows:

April 30, 1994:

Allowance for uncollectible accounts	7,000	
Due from factor		7,000
To write off the receivable from the factor due to higher than anticipated bad debt losses on factored receivables.		

When a transfer of receivables is reported as a sale, the proceeds from the transfer should be reported in the notes to the financial statements for each period for which an income statement is presented. In addition, the balance of the uncollected receivables at the balance sheet date should be reported in the notes, if available. An example of the disclosure for a nonrecourse sale of receivables for Firestone Tire and Rubber Company is presented in Exhibit 7.9.

Transfers With Recourse If accomplished with recourse, the exchange may be accounted for as a sale if it meets the conditions identified above. When a recourse transfer is accounted for as a sale, any contingent liability related to the recourse provision should also be recorded at the time of the sale and entered into the determination of gain or loss on the sale.

When the transfer does not qualify as a sale, the amount of the proceeds from the transfer will be recorded as a liability. The receivables and any allowance accounts associated with them are not altered. For example, if in the Getta example above, the receivables had been factored with recourse and the

EXHIBIT 7.9

Firestone Tire and
Rubber Company—
Disclosure of
Nonrecourse Sales
of Receivables

FIRESTONE TIRE AND RUBBER COMPANY
Disclosure of Nonrecourse Sales of Receivables

Notes to the Financial Statements

… the Company sold certain retail accounts receivable and related finance income to a bank in a gross amount sufficient to provide net proceeds of $100,000,000. The company will act as agent for the buyer in collection and administration of receivables sold.

conditions for treatment as a sale were not met, the company would have made the following entry:

March 3, 1994:
Cash	17,000	
Prepaid interest	1,000	
Liability for factored receivables		18,000

To record the transfer of receivables with recourse.

As the receivables are collected, the accounts receivable balance is reduced along with the liability for factored receivables. In addition, the prepaid interest should be amortized over the life of the factoring arrangement.

If we assume that actual losses were $4,000, the final settlement of this factoring arrangement on April 1, 1994, would be recorded as follows:

April 30, 1994:
Cash	3,000	
Liability for factored receivables	18,000	
Allowance for uncollectible accounts	4,000	
Accounts receivable		25,000

To record settlement of the holdback.

In the event that the actual losses exceeded the holdback, Getta would be required to make a payment to Magna for the difference. This would be recorded as a credit to cash and the debit to the allowance for uncollectible accounts. The effect of the higher than expected bad debt experience will then be felt through the current period's accrual of bad debt expense, which is reflective of the source of the additional costs incurred due to the recourse provision.

If the magnitude of the receivables factored under an arrangement accounted for as a borrowing are significant, note disclosure of this information is appropriate. In addition, the company's accounting policies should indicate how recourse transfers are accounted for, as a sale or borrowing, and if these transactions are material. An example of disclosures used by The Singer Company relating to receivables transferred with recourse are presented in Exhibit 7.10.

Discounting of Notes Receivable

Discounting of notes receivable is a practice very similar to that of factoring accounts receivable. Discounting of notes can occur either with or without recourse. Notes are usually discounted with financial institutions such as banks. To determine the proceeds received by the holder of the note when it is

EXHIBIT 7.10

The Singer
Company—
Disclosures
Regarding Transfers
of Receivables with
Recourse

THE SINGER COMPANY
Disclosures Regarding Transfers of Receivables with Recourse

Notes to the Financial Statements

1. Significant Accounting Policies

... Receivables discounted with recourse are considered a financing arrangement and, accordingly, the liability for such receivables is included in notes and loans payable. Earned carrying charges and discounts and related financing expenses are recognized as the receivables are collected.

7. Accounts Receivable

... Included in accounts receivable at December 31, 1982 and 1981, respectively, are $9.7 million and $10.5 million of trade receivables with varying maturities discounted on a recourse basis principally with foreign unaffiliated financial institutions.

---

tendered, the bank will compute a discount that will be subtracted from the collections on the note due at maturity. This discount is stated as an interest rate and works as follows.

Assume Borrowmore Company accepted a 60-day note on September 1, 1994, in the amount of $10,000, with interest accruing at 12% in exchange for merchandise sold. On October 1, Borrowmore discounted the note, without recourse, at its bank at a rate of 16%. Assuming the original 12% rate was a reasonable market rate of interest at the time of the original sale, Borrowmore would record the following series of entries relating to this note:

September 1, 1994:		
Notes receivable	10,000	
Sales		10,000
To record the initial sale of merchandise.		
October 1, 1994:		
Accrued interest receivable	100	
Interest revenue		100
To accrue interest on the note up to the date of discounting.		
Cash	10,064	
Interest expense	36	
Notes receivable		10,000
Accrued interest receivable		100
To record the discounting of the note as a transfer without recourse.		

To calculate the amount of cash collected when the note is discounted:

1. Take the total proceeds at maturity under the note and multiply by the discount rate to determine the size of the discount.
2. Then, subtract the discount from the total proceeds.

In this case, these computations are as follows:

$$\text{Total Proceeds} = \$10,000 + (\$10,000 \times 12\% \div 12 \text{ months} \times 2 \text{ months}) = \$10,200$$

$$\text{Discount} = \$10,200 \times 16\% \div 12 \text{ months} \times 1 \text{ month} = \$136$$

$$\text{Cash Proceeds} = \$10,200 - \$136 = \$10,064$$

If the note discounted by Borrowmore was with recourse and did not qualify for treatment as a sale, the transaction would be treated as a loan collateralized by the note; and the following entry would be made at the discount date:

October 1, 1994:
Cash	10,064	
Interest expense	36	
Notes receivable—discounted		10,000
Accrued interest receivable		100

To record the discounting of the note as a collateralized
borrowing.

As a collateralized borrowing, the note may be paid when it comes due, or the maker may default. If the note is paid by the maker, Borrowmore would simply remove both the notes receivable and the notes receivable—discounted accounts from its books. If the note is dishonored, the bank may return it to Borrowmore, and the company must make good on the note plus the interest. Of course, Borrowmore may then attempt to collect from the maker of the note directly. The entry Borrowmore would use to record a default situation would appear as follows:

October 31, 1994:
Notes receivable—discounted	10,000	
Accrued interest receivable	200	
Cash		10,200

To remove the contingent liability for the discounted note, record
the right to collect interest on the note, and the payment to the
bank of the principal and interest due to default of the maker.

Reporting Pledges, Assignments, Transfers to Factors, and Discounts in the Statement of Cash Flows

When any of these activities are engaged in during the period, a determination must be made as to whether the cash generated is from operating, investing, or financing activities for purposes of classification in the statement of cash flows. The classification issue does not relate to the collection of cash from the original receivable. Those cash flows are classified according to the source of the receivable. The cash flows of interest here relate to the inflow from the loan or sale arising from the pledge, assignment, factoring, or discounting, and the related cash outflow for repayment of any amounts borrowed.

In general, whenever the transaction gives rise to a financing arrangement, cash inflows from the financing transaction and cash outflows to repay the obligation will be classified as a financing cash flow. This applies to the use of pledging, assignments, factoring (if the transaction is not deemed to be a sale), and discounting with recourse. When a factoring of receivables or discounting of a note is accounted for as a sale, the cash inflow will be classified in the same fashion as the cash collections from the receivable or note would have been classified.

For example, if a receivable arose from the sale of goods and was factored without recourse, resulting in a sale for accounting purposes, the cash inflow from the sale would be classified as an operating cash flow since the collection of the receivable would have been classified as an operating cash flow had it been collected in the normal course of business. A receivable that arose from the sale of plant and equipment would give rise to an investing cash flow if factored in an exchange accounted for as a sale because the cash collections on the receivable would have been classified as investing had it been collected in the normal course of business.

SUMMARY

A company's cash management policies are influenced by its decision to sell products or services on credit. Cash only sales are common in industries such as the retail grocery business. Generally, the decision to extend credit carries a whole host of other issues that must be dealt with, including offering of sales discounts, determining payment periods, setting interest rates for receivables, and estimating the cost of bad debts that will arise.

To achieve better matching of expenses and revenues, as well as reflect the value of receivables in the balance sheet at net realizable value, the costs associated with credit sales are accrued, when material, and generally reported as part of an allowance account, which serves to reduce the gross receivable to its net realizable value.

When sales discounts are employed, an allowance may be necessary to reflect the discounts management expects customers to take when payments on currently open receivable balances are made in future periods. Many companies adopt either a *net* or *gross method* of accounting for sales discounts as a reasonable approximation for the allowance method under certain circumstances. When discounts are normally taken, the net method may provide a reasonable estimate of the effects of discounts on future cash collections. When discounts are rarely taken, the gross method accomplishes a similar goal.

Generally, the valuation of receivables will require imputing interest unless the receivable:

1. Already accrues interest at the market rate as of the date the receivable was created, or
2. Represents an account receivable that is due within one year

When interest is imputed, interest revenue will be recognized over the life of the receivable and based on the market rate of interest existing at the time of the original exchange which gave rise to the receivable.

Losses that arise from unpaid accounts also create a problem in matching and valuation of receivables. Generally, an allowance for uncollectible accounts is necessary to reduce the receivable to its net realizable value. When the allowance method is used, bad debt expense is accrued based on estimates of future nonpayment. Two techniques for estimating the periodic bad debt expense were examined:

1. Percentage of sales method
2. Percentage of receivables method (of which aging is a special case)

The accrual of bad debt expense increases the balance of the allowance account. Accounts that are deemed uncollectible are written off against the allowance account, not directly charged to expense. Companies whose credit policies result in only small bad debt losses may use the direct write-off method to account for such losses. However, this is based on a lack of materiality. If bad debt losses are material, the allowance method must be employed.

In some situations, companies find it advantageous to convert notes or receivables into cash prior to the normal collection point. This can be done by borrowing against the receivables either by pledging or assigning them to a third party or by physical transfer of the receivables to a factor. Transfer of the receivables to a factor may be done with or without recourse against the transferor and may or may not result in a sale of the receivables for financial reporting purposes.

QUESTIONS

1. What is a *trade receivable* and why is it different from other types of receivables?

2. What factors need to be considered in making the decision to sell on credit?

3. Why is interest not imputed on most trade receivables?

4. What is a *sales discount*, and what alternative accounting procedures are available for recording sales discounts?

5. Describe how a 3-year note with a below market interest rate would be valued for presentation in the note holder's balance sheet.

6. What is an *allowance for uncollectible accounts*? What alternatives are available for determining the value of this account?

7. How should the allowance for doubtful accounts be classified in the balance sheet?

8. Compare and contrast the use of an aging of accounts receivable with the use of the percentage of sales method for determining the provision for bad debts. What are the strengths and weaknesses of each?

9. Name three ways to convert receivables into cash prior to collection and describe how they work.

10. What role does *recourse* play in recording the factoring of receivables or discounting of a note?

11. How should *pledged* assets be disclosed in the balance sheet of the firm pledging the assets?

12. Is it appropriate to offset liabilities under *assignments of receivables* directly against the receivable balance? Why or why not?

EXERCISES

7-1. *Sale exchanges with below market rate financing—single future payment*

Creditsales, Inc. sells a number of items through the use of low-interest note financing as an inducement to the buyer. On March 31, 1994, the company sold a major appliance and received a non-interest bearing note in exchange. The note promises to pay $15,000 at the end of 2 years. The market rate of interest for notes of this type is 12%.

REQUIRED:

Prepare the journal entries Creditsales will use to record the sale, interest accruals, and final collection of the note, assuming Creditsales has a September 31 fiscal year-end.

7-2.   *Sale exchanges with below market rate financing—monthly payments*

Wrecker's Automotive sold a car to Mary McCarthy on January 1, 1994. The sale required that Mary put down $1,000 and make installment payments at the end of each of the next 5 years in the amount of $2,000 per year. The note requires interest on the unpaid balance at a rate of 6% per year. The market rate for notes of this type is 15%. Wrecker's has a calendar-year fiscal period.

REQUIRED:

Prepare an amortization schedule for this note indicating how much interest revenue should be reported for each year during the life of the note. Prepare the journal entry to record the sale. Prepare the journal entry to record the activities relating to the note in 1997.

7-3.   *Fixed asset sales with below market rate financing—multiple payments*

On June 30, 1993, ABC sold a piece of land to XYZ in exchange for a 3-year, non-interest bearing note requiring payments of $10,000 per year. The market rate of interest on such notes is 12%. An initial down payment of $50,000 was also paid. The present value of an annuity of $1 for 3 years at 12% is 2.40. ABC had a book value for the land of $30,000. The collection of the note is reasonably assured.

REQUIRED:

1. Prepare an amortization schedule for the note.
2. Prepare all journal entries necessary to record the activities relating to the note assuming ABC has a fiscal year-end of December 31.

7-4.   *Sales discounts—gross and net method*

Martin Company sells merchandise on credit terms that are 2/10, n/30. Credit sales for the months of January through March, 1994, were as follows:

January	$540,000
February	620,000
March	480,000

Martin's experience with collections from these sales was that 60% of each month's sales are collected during the discount period, with the remainder collected within 30 days.

REQUIRED:

Prepare the journal entries to record Martin's sales and collections under both the net and gross method of recording sales discounts. Assume that no allowance account is established under the gross method.

7-5.   *Sales discounts—application of the allowance concept*

Lynch Corporation sells merchandise on credit terms of 5/10, n/60. Lynch uses the gross method of accounting for sales discounts but establishes an allowance for future discounts due to the material size of the discount. On January 1, 1994, Lynch reported the following information:

Accounts receivable (gross)	$3,400,000
Allowance for sales discounts	(150,000)
Net accounts receivable	$3,250,000

During 1994, credit sales were $17,000,000. Cash collections amounted to $16,200,000, and discounts taken during the year were $690,000. At year-end, an assessment of the open balances indicated that discounts of $162,000 were expected to be taken as the receivable balances were collected in 1995.

REQUIRED:

Prepare all journal entries necessary to record the activities relating to the sales discounts during 1994.

7-6. *Trade receivables and bad debts—expense recognition and balance sheet presentation*

Rex Company had the following information relating to its accounts receivable at December 31, 1993, and December 31, 1994:

Accounts receivable at 12/31/93	$1,200,000
Allowance for uncollectible accounts at 12/31/93	(60,000)
Credit sales for 1994	5,300,000
Collections from customers for 1994	4,650,000
Accounts written off during 1994	75,000

Rex Company uses the percentage of sales method of estimating uncollectible accounts and has established a rate of 3% of credit sales for this purpose.

REQUIRED:

1. Prepare the journal entry to record the provision for bad debts for 1994.
2. Prepare the presentation of the information on accounts receivable that should be included in the current asset section of Rex Company's balance sheet as of 12/31/94.

7-7. *Aging and bad debts*

Bryan Corporation has prepared the following aging schedule for its accounts receivable:

Current	$400,000
30–60 days	120,000
61–90 days	50,000
Over 90 days	20,000

Bryan has estimated that 1% of its current accounts, 5% of its 30–60 day-old accounts, 8% of its 61–90 day-old accounts, and 10% of the past-90 days accounts will be uncollectible.

In addition, Bryan has prepared the following analysis of the activity in the allowance for uncollectible accounts for the period:

Beginning balance	$ 15,000
Write-offs during the year	(6,000)

REQUIRED:

1. Prepare an aging schedule for Bryan Corporation.
2. Prepare the journal entry to record the provision for bad debts for the current year.

7-8.   *Bad debts—comparison of allowance and direct write-off*

All of Jade Company's sales are on credit. The following information is available for 1994:

Allowance for uncollectible accounts at 1/1/94	$ 9,000
Sales	475,000
Accounts written off as uncollectible	10,000

Jade's provision for bad debts is at the rate of 5% of sales.

REQUIRED:

1. What is the ending balance of the allowance for uncollectible accounts as of 12/31/94?
2. What journal entry would Jade make to record the provision for bad debts using the allowance method?
3. What journal entry would Jade use if it elected to use the direct write-off method?
4. What factors would influence your opinion regarding which of the two methods of accounting for bad debts should be used?

7-9.   *Provision for bad debts—alternative methods of estimation and change in method*

Yentl Industries reported the following information related to credit operations during 1993:

Credit sales	$5,600,000
Accounts written off	140,000
Beginning accounts receivable (gross)	900,000
Ending accounts receivable (gross)	1,200,000

REQUIRED:

1. Compute bad debt expense assuming that Yentl uses the direct write-off method.
2. Compute bad debt expense assuming that Yentl uses the percentage of sales method and a 3% bad debt percentage.
3. Compute bad debt expense using the percentage of receivables method and a 4% rate of bad debts.
4. If Yentl had been using the direct write-off method and elected to switch to the percentage of receivables method, how would the change be accounted for?
5. If Yentl had been using the percentage of sales method and had a beginning balance for the allowance for uncollectible accounts of $30,000, and switched to the percentage of receivables method in 1993, how would this change be accounted for?

7-10.   *Bad debts—recreation of journal entries from financial statement data*

Black, Inc. included the following disclosures in its financial statements for 1994 (dollars in thousands):

	1994	1993
Receivables	$1,310.2	$1,286.4

Note 9: Receivables

Receivables have been reduced by an allowance for doubtful accounts as follows:

Receivables—current	$	26.7	$	20.3

Bad debt expense for 1994 amounted to
$145.67.

REQUIRED:

1. Determine the amount of receivables that were written off during 1994.
2. Prepare journal entries to record the activities in the allowance for doubtful accounts.
3. How much would 1994 reported income have been affected if Black had used the direct write-off method compared to the allowance method actually employed?

7-11. *Credit card sales*

Avco Merchandising sells most of its merchandise to customers who use credit cards. Avco processes all credit card receipts once a month at the end of each month. Avco is charged a fee of 4% of all credit card purchases. Credits issued for return merchandise are deducted from total charges to determine the amount subject to collection from credit card companies. Activities for the month of April, 1993, appeared as follows:

Accounts receivable from credit card companies at April 1	$360,000
Credit card sales for April	290,000
Merchandise returns resulting in credits to charge cards	5,000
Cash collected from credit card companies	360,000
Cash sales for April	45,000

REQUIRED:

Prepare journal entries to record the activities in the accounts receivable from credit card companies for April, 1993.

7-12. *Receivables—assignments*

Quickturn Corporation has adopted a policy of assigning accounts receivable to its bank in return for cash whenever a receivable is not collected within 10 days of a sale. During the month of October, 1994, the company assigned receivables with a face value of $250,000 to the bank in return for cash of $200,000. The bank charges interest on assignments of this type at a rate of 2% of the gross loan, which is deducted from the cash advanced on the receivables.

During November, cash in the amount of $220,000 was collected on these receiv-ables by Quickturn, and the loan was paid off. The balance of the receivables reverted to Quickturn when the loan was paid.

REQUIRED:

1. Prepare the journal entries Quickturn would use to record the assignment and collection of the receivables.
2. How would the assigned receivables and related loan be disclosed in the balance sheet at the end of October?

7-13. *Transfer of receivables—with and without recourse*

Lasker, Incorporated is considering the transfer of $750,000 of its receivables to a factor. If Lasker transfers the receivables with recourse, the factor will pay Lasker

$675,000. If the company transfers the receivables without recourse, the factor will only pay $625,000. Lasker has established an allowance for uncollectible accounts based on 5% of credit sales.

REQUIRED:

1. Prepare the entry used by Lasker to record the transfer of receivables without recourse.
2. Prepare the entry used by Lasker to record the transfer with recourse, assuming the transfer does not qualify for treatment as a sale.

7-14. *Discounting of notes receivable—with and without recourse*

Grow, Inc. received a 90-day, 10% note with a face value of $2,000 in exchange for a loan of $2,000 cash made to Debtor Corporation. Grow held the note for 45 days and then discounted it with its bank. The bank discounted the note at 12%.

REQUIRED:

1. Prepare the entry Grow would use to record the activities relating to the note, assuming the note was discounted without recourse.
2. Prepare the entries Grow would use to record the activity relating to the note, assuming the note was discounted with recourse and paid by Debtor at maturity.
3. How would your response above change if the note had been dishonored by Debtor?

7-15. *Discounting of notes receivable*

XYZ Co. took a 90-day, $50,000, 12% note in exchange for some merchandise. Then after 30 days, XYZ discounted the note with its bank at 15%.

REQUIRED:

How should XYZ record this activity, assuming the transfer does not meet the conditions for a sale?

PROBLEMS

7-1.   *Accounting for bad debts—allowance and provision under a variety of alternative estimation techniques*

Farina Corporation operates in an industry that has a high rate of bad debts. On January 1, 1993, Farina reported an accounts receivable balance of $450,000, with a related allowance for uncollectible accounts of $40,000. During 1991, Farina wrote off accounts with a value of $24,000 and recovered $6,000 of previously written off accounts. On December 31, 1993, before any year-end adjustments, the balance in Farina's accounts receivable was $505,000. No entry has been made for the current period's provision for bad debts expense. Sales for the year are summarized as follows:

Credit sales	$2,230,000
Cash sales	860,000
Total sales	$3,090,000

Farina wishes to compute its current period expense. Historically, about 2% of credit sales result in bad debts, and Farina has used this estimate to compute its annual bad debt expense. An aging of the accounts receivable revealed the following:

Days Outstanding	Amount	Probability of Collection
Less than 15 days	$300,000	.98
16–30 days	100,000	.90
31–45 days	50,000	.80
46–60 days	30,000	.70
61–75 days	10,000	.60
Past 75 days	15,000	.00

REQUIRED:

1. Prepare the computation of Farina's provision for bad debts using the percentage of sales method.
2. Prepare the computation of Farina's provision for bad debts using an aging of Farina's accounts receivable.
3. Prepare the journal entry Farina would use to record the provision for bad debts using the aging method.
4. Prepare the journal entries necessary to record the write-off of uncollectible accounts and the recovery of previously written-off accounts for Farina.

7-2. *Essay on accounting for bad debts—general concepts*

Baker Company has significant amounts of trade accounts receivable. Baker uses the allowance method to estimate bad debts instead of the direct write-off method. During the year, some specific accounts were written off uncollectible, and some that were previously written off as uncollectible were collected.

REQUIRED:

1. What are the deficiencies of the direct write-off method?
2. What are the two basic allowance methods used to estimate bad debts, and what is the justification for each?
3. How should Baker account for the collection of the specific accounts receivable previously written off?
   (AICPA adapted)

7-3. *Accounting for bad debts—allowance and provision under aging and changes in method of estimation*

From inception of operations to December 31, 1994, Haymarket Corporation provided for uncollectible accounts receivable under the allowance method. Provisions for bad debts were made monthly at 2% of credit sales, bad debt write-offs were charged to the allowance account, recoveries of previously written off accounts were credited to the allowance account, and no year-end adjustments were made. Haymarket's usual credit terms require payment in full within 30 days. The balance in the allowance for uncollectible accounts was $130,000 at January 1, 1994. During 1994, credit sales totalled $9,000,000. Interim provisions for bad debts were made at 2% of credit sales, and $90,000 of specific accounts were written off during the year. Recoveries of previously written off accounts amounted to $15,000 during 1994.

An aging of the accounts of Haymarket was performed for the first time as of December 31, 1994. A summary of this aging follows:

Classification by Month of Sale	Balance	Percent Uncollectible
Nov-Dec, 1994	$1,140,000	2%
Jul-Oct, 1994	600,000	10%
Jan-June, 1994	400,000	25%
Pre-1/1/94	130,000	75%
	$2,270,000	

Based on a review of those accounts in the "pre-1/1/94" classification, additional receivables totalling $60,000 were written off at year-end.

REQUIRED:

1. Prepare a schedule to estimate the ending balance of the allowance account using the aging method.
2. Prepare the journal entries relating to the activities in the allowance for uncollectible accounts during 1994.
3. How should the adjustment from the percentage of sales method to the aging method be treated in Haymarket's income statement for 1994?
   (AICPA adapted)

7-4.   *Receivables—sales discounts, factoring, financial statement presentation*

On January 1, 1994, Kary Corporation reported the following data in its balance sheet:

Accounts receivable	$1,800,000
Allowance for uncollectible accounts	(400,000)

On July 1, 1994, Kary Corporation sold special-order merchandise on credit for $1,200,000. Kary received a note bearing interest at the market rate of 12%. The note is payable in 3 years with interest payments required on July 1 of each year. On September 1, 1994, Kary sold special-order merchandise for $900,000 and received a non-interest bearing note due in 2 years. The market rate of interest on such notes was still 12%.

During 1990, Kary also sold merchandise under its normal credit plan, which requires payment in 30 days but offers a discount of 1% for customers paying within 10 days. These sales amounted to $13,650,000 for the year. Of these amounts, 40% were collected within the 10-day discount period. None of the receivables in the beginning balance of accounts receivable were entitled to take a discount. Kary uses the percentage of sales method to determine its provision for bad debts at a rate of 4% of credit sales. Kary wrote off $430,000 of uncollectible accounts during the year. Cash acquired through normal collections of accounts receivable during 1990 amounted to $11,660,000.

On November 1, 1994, the company assigned $1,000,000 of its accounts receivable to Deadhead Finance Company on a recourse basis. Deadhead advanced 75% of the face value and charged interest of 15% on the outstanding balance of the receivables at the end of each month. During November, $800,000 of these receivables were collected, with the remainder being collected in full during December. On December 31, 1994, the company factored $1,500,000 of receivables without recourse. The factor withheld 4% of the balance as uncollectible and charged a 5% finance charge.

REQUIRED:

1. Prepare entries to record the sale of special-order merchandise in exchange for each note. Supporting computations should be presented when appropriate.
2. How much interest revenue should Kary report at December 31, 1994, assuming Kary uses the gross method to report sales discounts?
3. Prepare entries to record collections of those receivables where the discount for early payment was taken using both the gross and net methods.
4. Prepare the entries necessary to record the assignment of receivables and the factoring of receivables. How should these be reported in Kary's financial statements at December 31, 1994?
5. Prepare the presentation of the information on accounts receivable to be included in the current asset section of Kary's balance sheet as of December 31, 1994.

7-5. *Essay—note received in exchange for fixed assets, valuation, and presentation*

Business transactions often involve the exchange of property, goods, or services for notes or similar instruments that may stipulate no interest rate or an interest rate that varies from prevailing rates.

REQUIRED:

1. When a note is exchanged for property, goods, or services, what value should be placed upon the note:
   (a) If it bears interest at a reasonable rate and is issued in a bargained transaction entered into at arm's length? Explain.
   (b) If it bears no interest and/or is not issued in a bargained transaction entered into at arm's length? Explain.
2. If the recorded value of a note differs from the face value:
   (a) How should the difference be accounted for? Explain.
   (b) How should this difference be presented in the financial statements? Explain.
   (AICPA adapted)

7-6. *Long-term receivables—valuation, income determination, and presentation*

Linden, Inc., had the following long-term receivable account balances at December 31, 1994:

> Note receivable from sale of division $1,500,000

Transactions during 1995 and other information relating to Linden's long-term receivables were as follows:

(a) The $1,500,000 note receivable is dated May 1, 1994, bears interest at 9%, and represents the balance of the consideration received from the sale of Linden's electronics division to Pitt Company. Principal payments of $500,000 plus appropriate interest are due on May 1, 1995, 1996, and 1997. The first principal and interest payment was made on May 1, 1995. Collection of the note installments is reasonably assured, and the interest rate of 9% approximated the market rate of interest on notes of this type as of May 1, 1994.

(b) On April 1, 1995, Linden sold a patent to Bell Company in exchange for a $100,000 non-interest bearing note due on April 1, 1998. There was no established exchange price for the patent, and the note had no ready market. The prevailing rate of interest for a note of this type at April 1, 1995, was 15%. The patent had a carrying value of $40,000 at January 1, 1995, and the amortization for the year ended December 31, 1995, would have been $8,000. The collection of the note receivable from Bell is reasonably assured.

(c) On July 1, 1995, Linden sold a parcel of land to Carr Company for $200,000 under an installment sale contract. Carr made a $60,000 cash down payment on July 1, 1995, and signed a 4-year, 16% note for the $140,000 balance. The equal annual payments of principal and interest on the note will be $50,000 payable on July 1, 1994, through July 1, 1999. The land could have been sold at an established cash price of $200,000. The cost of the land to Linden was $150,000. Circumstances are such that the collection of the installments on the note is reasonably assured.

REQUIRED:

1. Prepare the long-term receivables section of Linden's balance sheet at December 31, 1995.
2. Prepare a schedule showing the current portion of the long-term receivables and accrued interest receivable that would appear in Linden's balance sheet at December 31, 1995.
3. Prepare a schedule showing interest income from the long-term receivables and gains recognized on sale of assets that would appear on Linden's income statement for the year ended December 31, 1993.
   (AICPA adapted)

7-7. *Notes receivable—receipt, income determination, discounting*

Easy Touch Corporation often accepts notes in exchange for its merchandise. As a result, the balance in its notes receivable account at the beginning of 1994 was as follows:

Note	Date of Note	Initial Term	Face Interest Rate	Face Amount
A	3/31/93	12 months	15%	$10,000
B	9/30/93	8 months	12%	5,000
C	12/31/92	24 months	10%	7,000
D	12/31/93	6 months	8%	9,000
E	12/31/93	2 months	6%	12,000

The interest payment terms of each note differ. For any note with a maturity of one year or less from the date of origin, interest is to be paid at maturity. For notes whose term exceeds one year, interest is paid on the anniversary date of the note. Interest rates on the notes are determined based on the existing market rate of interest for similar term notes at the date of origin.

During 1994, Easy Touch discounted notes A, C, and D as follows:

Date Discounted	Bank Discount Rate
2/28/94	9%
10/31/94	12%
5/31/94	8%

Notes A and D were discounted without recourse. Note C was discounted with recourse. At the date note C was discounted, Easy Touch was not able to develop a reliable estimate of any future losses that might arise from the recourse provision. Notes B and E were collected during the year.

After discounting note C, it was dishonored at maturity and returned to Easy Touch. The bank charged Easy Touch a fee of 10% of the interest and principal of the note as a penalty for dishonor. Easy Touch is attempting to recover the amounts due on this note, but believes recovery will not exceed 40% of the amounts due (including the penalty that it is trying to recover).

REQUIRED:

1. Prepare journal entries to record the activities relating to these notes during 1994. Provide supporting computations.
2. How does the existence of recourse alter the underlying economic features of discounting? How does this influence the manner in which the effect of discounting is presented in the financial statements, if at all?

7-8. *Factoring of receivables*

Clover Corp. reported the following information in the notes to its December 31, 1994, financial statements regarding transfers of receivables without recourse: In December, 1994, the Company entered into an agreement with a financial institution whereby the Company has the right to sell undivided fractional interests in designated receivables on an ongoing basis, without recourse, as evidenced by receivable certificates (not to exceed $100,000,000 at any time). During the period December 8 through December 31, 1994, proceeds totaling $195,508,000 were received. Losses totaling $1,741,000 were recognized on these sales.

REQUIRED:

1. Assuming that an allowance for 1% of the receivables transferred from Clover to the financial institutions existed at the point-of-sale, and that there was no holdback provision related to the sale, prepare the journal entry to record the sales of receivables made by Clover.
2. What conditions must be met regarding the transfer of receivables for it to be treated as a sale? How do these conditions relate to the general guidelines for revenue or income recognition?
3. How would Clover's financial statements have been affected if the above transactions had been accounted for as a borrowing instead of a sale?

7-9. *Reconstruction of information, valuation of receivables, basis for a loan*

Daycor Corporation has approached your bank regarding the possibility of a loan to support its expansion. Since Daycor is a relatively new company, and a customer with whom your bank has not done business before, you suggested the possibility of providing a loan secured against current receivables. Daycor has provided you with a listing of its outstanding receivables totaling $23,000,000. Your bank has a policy of never loaning more than 80% of the net realizable value of receivables in cases like Daycor's.

Upon further investigation you discover the following facts:

(a) Daycor uses the direct write-off method of accounting for bad debts. Over the past 3 years, the following information regarding bad debts is available:

| | Year of Write-off | | | |
Write-offs Year of Sale	1992	1993	1994	Total Credit Sales
1992	1.7	1.0	-	$45.6
1993	-	2.2	1.9	56.0
1994	-	-	3.2	68.4

| | Year of Recovery | | | |
Recoveries Year of Sale	1992	1993	1994	Total Credit Sales
1992	–	0.2	0.1	$45.6
1993	–	–	0.4	56.0
1994	–	–	0.3	68.4

(b) The company uses the gross method of accounting for sales discounts. Generally, sales discounts of 1% are offered for payment within 30 days of invoicing. You discover that approximately 70% of the available discounts are taken. A review of the receivables that constitute Daycor's current balance indicates that 60% of these receivables are still entitled to the discount.

(c) Daycor accounts for sales returns when they occur. Historically, returns have amounted to approximately 3% of gross sales.

(d) All Daycor's sales are on credit.

REQUIRED:

What, in your opinion, is the maximum amount of the loan your bank would make to Daycor under current policies? Justify your response as if you were explaining the basis for your opinion to your supervisor at the bank.

7-10. *Factoring—an analysis of alternative proposals*

Barron Corporation is considering the possibility of factoring some of its accounts receivable to raise cash. Barron has identified receivables whose gross value is $500,000 for this purpose. These receivables are all from repeat customers with the highest credit ratings. As a result, Barron estimates that uncollectible accounts within this pool will be only 0.3% of the gross receivables. Sales returns from these customers typically average about 1% of the sales price and all sales are on credit.

Barron has discussed factoring with two different factors, Bestline Factors and Only-If-Necessary Credit Corporation (OIN). Bestline is willing to purchase these receivables under the following terms:

(a) A holdback of 5% of the gross receivables is to be maintained to cover any uncollectible amounts and the effects of sales returns. Any costs in excess of this amount are borne by Bestline. Should the actual experience be under 5%, any excess holdback will be returned to Barron.

(b) A discount of 3% of gross receivables will be charged as a factoring fee.

OIN is willing to purchase the receivables on the following terms:

(a) A holdback of 2% is required, but any costs in excess of this amount are borne by Barron and will require that Barron pay an additional 10% service fee for all costs in excess of the holdback.

(b) A discount of 2% of gross receivables will be charged as a factoring fee.

Assume that after the factoring decision is made, the actual collections resulted in uncollectible accounts of $12,000 and sales returns of $7,000.

REQUIRED:

1. Prepare the journal entries assuming that Barron accepted the Bestline offer.
2. Prepare the journal entries assuming that Barron accepted the OIN offer and that Barron believed that its estimates of future costs associated with the remaining contingencies were reliable.
3. Given the facts at the time of the factoring decision, which alternative would you suggest Barron take and why?
4. What role does Barron's ability to forecast future bad debts and sales returns have on the treatment of the factoring with either Bestline or OIN at the time the factoring agreement is executed and the receivables transferred?

DAYTON HUDSON CORPORATION

The following discussion appeared in the annual report to shareholders of the Dayton Hudson Corporation as of February 1, 1986 (all dollar figures are in thousands):

> Our percentage of credit sales to total sales was 41% in 1985 and 1984, compared with 39% in 1983. Continued growth of third-party credit card sales throughout our companies in 1985 led to a slight increase in the portion of sales produced by these cards and an equivalent decrease in the portion of sales produced by internal credit cards. We recorded financing charge revenues of $144,065 on internal credit sales of $2,278,723 in 1985; $136,256 on sales of $2,186,890 in 1984; and $124,341 on sales of $1,902,572 in 1983. The provision for bad debts as a percentage of internal credit sales increased to 2.8% in 1985, compared with a favorable 1.8% in 1984 and 2.0% in 1983. The increase is due to higher losses resulting from initial market entries and caution outlook for potential losses on year-end receivables.

The following disclosures were contained in the financial statements presented in the annual report:

	1985–86	1984–85	1983–84
Revenues	$8,793,372	$8,009,030	$6,963,255
Earnings before taxes	524,574	479,342	450,670
Current Assets:			
Accounts receivable (net of allowance for doubtful accounts of $34,672 and $26,520)	$1,060,129	$1,103,922	

Dayton Hudson defined revenues as gross sales plus financing revenues, less the provision for bad debts.

REQUIRED:

1. Based on the percentages provided by Dayton Hudson, prepare the entries to record the provision for bad debts in each of the three years discussed.
2. Assuming that Dayton Hudson did not recover any collections on previously written-off accounts in 1985–86, what amount of accounts receivable were written off to the allowance account during 1985–86?
3. Prepare the journal entries to record Dayton Hudson's sales on internal credit accounts for each of the three years discussed.
4. How much were the gross revenues from sales in 1986?
5. How much cash was collected, in total, from customers from sales of merchandise during 1985–86?
6. How much was collected on Dayton Hudson internal credit accounts (assuming all accounts receivable relate to these credit accounts)? Prepare the journal entry to record these collections.
7. What were the total credit sales, in dollars, for 1986?
8. What percentage of total credit sales represents sales on internal credit accounts of Dayton Hudson?

CASE 7.2

BORG WARNER

In its annual report to shareholders dated December 31, 1982, Borg Warner Corporation included the following information regarding receivables in its notes to the financial statements:

Receivables are as follows at December 31 (dollars in millions):

	1982	1981
Customers	$311.7	$311.8
Other	139.4	76.1
Gross receivables	$451.1	387.9
Less allowance for losses	21.5	23.1
Net receivables	$429.6	$364.8

Selling, general, and administrative expenses include provisions for losses on receivables of $3.6 million in 1982, $7.9 million in 1981, and $4.7 million in 1980. Included in other receivables at December 31, 1982, is $70.5 million related to the sale of Morse Industrial operations. This amount was subsequently collected in January, 1983.

REQUIRED:

1. Prepare the journal entries to record the provision for losses on receivables during 1981 and 1982.
2. Assuming Borg Warner reinstated $1.2 million dollars of previously written-off accounts in 1982, what was the dollar amount of the accounts written-off in 1982?
3. Prepare the journal entries for the reinstatement and the write-offs from (2) above.
4. Prepare the journal entry Borg Warner would use to record the collection of the other receivable relating to the sale of Morse Industrial in 1983.
5. What percentage of the ending balance of receivables from customers is represented by the balance in the allowance for losses account for 1981 and 1982? Is it increasing or decreasing? What if anything can this tell you about the credit policies of Borg Warner?

LONE STAR INDUSTRIES

In its December 31, 1982, financial statements, Lone Star Industries, Inc., reported the following:

Receivables consist of the following (in thousands):

	1982	1983
Trade	$101,479	$ 96,482
Other	16,965	7,706
Total receivables	$118,444	$104,188
Less:		
Allowance for doubtful accounts	9,476	6,788
Receivables sold	65,805	-
Net receivables	$ 43,163	$ 97,400

In July 1982, the company entered into an agreement under which it has a right to sell certain receivables on an ongoing basis to financial institutions through May 1984. At December 31, 1982, receivables sold to the financial institutions were net of receivables due from the financial institutions of $4,771,000. This amount has been held back by the financial institutions under a partial recourse provision of the agreement.

REQUIRED:

1. What conditions must be met regarding the transfer of receivables for it to be treated as a sale?
2. Was this a sale of receivables or a financing transaction? Why or why not?
3. Assuming that $60,000,000 in cash was paid when the receivables classified as receivables sold were transferred and that these receivables had an allowance for doubtful accounts in the amount of 2% of the gross outstanding balance, prepare a journal entry to record the transfer of the receivables as described in the financial statements as of December 31, 1982.

Inventories and Cost of Goods Sold: Basic Issues

The intricacies of accounting for inventories and cost of goods sold require two chapters for reasonably complete coverage. In this chapter, we address the basic issues of accounting for inventories and determining the cost of goods sold: the reasons firms hold inventory, the items included in inventory, the components of inventory cost, inventory cost flow assumptions, and inventory valuation in the financial statements. In Chapter 9, we examine some inventory estimation techniques and alternative valuation methods.

This material requires such a substantial amount of coverage for several reasons. First, the amounts involved for many firms are large. For any firm that provides products to customers, inventory will be a very significant item on its balance sheet, and cost of goods sold will be one of the largest expense items on its income statement. For example, of the 24 retail department stores included in Exhibit 8.1,[1] inventories amounted to 22.7%, on average, of total assets, and cost of goods sold averaged 74.7% of net sales. Second, accounting procedures for inventory are complex. There are different ways of keeping track of inventory quantities, and several assumptions are available regarding the flow of inventory costs. Even some of the inventory cost components can be accounted for in a number of ways. The choices available to firms will affect both the inventory amounts and the cost of goods sold. The material amounts involved and the complex and numerous accounting procedures available make accounting for inventories a subject worthy of considerable study.

ARB No. 43 defines **inventories** as follows:

> The term inventory is used to designate the aggregate of those items of tangible personal property that (a) are held for sale in the ordinary course of busi-

---

[1] Data provided by Standard & Poor's Compustat Services, Inc., using COMPUSTAT PC Plus.

The Significance of Inventories and Cost of Goods Sold for Retail Department Stores
($ millions except for percentages)
1991 Compustat Annual Industrial File

COMPANY NAME	INVENTORY	TOTAL ASSETS	PERCENTAGE	COST OF GOODS SOLD	SALES	PERCENTAGE
Alexander's Inc	$ 47.3	$ 188.1	25.2%	$ 321.6	$ 430.3	74.7%
Allied Stores	440.2	3,024.4	14.6%	1,775.9	2,653.6	66.9%
Anthony (C.R.) Co	82.6	161.9	51.0%	270.9	397.3	68.2%
Bon-Ton Stores Inc	44.1	153.1	28.8%	164.8	284.0	58.0%
Carter Hawley Hale Stores	550.4	2,045.2	26.9%	2,044.3	2,982.8	68.5%
Crowley Milner & Co	11.8	40.3	29.4%	69.3	112.3	61.7%
Dillard Dept Stores	889.3	3,008.0	29.6%	2,342.1	3,734.0	62.7%
Federated Dept Stores	851.4	6,125.7	13.9%	3,194.3	4,701.8	67.9%
Gottschalks Inc	52.3	207.9	25.1%	191.2	295.4	64.7%
Jacobson Stores	73.6	240.8	30.6%	253.3	400.5	63.3%
Macy (R.H.) & Co.	1,452.7	4,811.6	30.2%	4,443.1	6,960.7	63.8%
May Department Stores Co	1,628.0	8,295.0	19.6%	6,702.0	10,066.0	66.6%
Mercantile Stores Co Inc	393.3	1,596.6	24.6%	1,607.4	2,393.8	67.1%
Meyer (Fred) Inc	378.3	905.8	41.8%	2,364.9	2,476.1	95.5%
Montgomery Ward Hldg	927.0	3,802.0	24.4%	4,029.0	5,464.0	73.7%
Neiman-Marcus Group Inc	288.5	1,072.2	26.9%	1,199.9	1,772.5	67.7%
PBL Acquisition Corp	38.2	163.5	23.4%	82.4	144.0	57.2%
Peebles Inc	38.2	163.6	23.3%	82.4	144.0	57.2%
Penney (J.C.) Co	2,657.0	12,325.0	21.6%	15,978.0	17,410.0	91.8%
Proffitts Inc	22.9	88.7	25.9%	65.2	102.8	63.5%
Pubco Corp	34.3	85.9	39.9%	93.3	135.7	68.8%
Schottenstein Stores CP	251.6	611.0	41.2%	694.5	1,133.1	61.3%
Strawbridge & Clothier	138.8	645.6	21.5%	731.4	981.7	74.5%
Zions Co-Operative Mercantil	35.8	124.0	28.9%	131.8	205.1	64.3%
Average			22.7%			74.7%

ness, (b) are in process of production for such sale, or (c) are to be currently consumed either directly or indirectly in the production of goods or services to be available for sale.[2]

The three parts of this definition correspond to the three usual classifications of inventory:

- Finished goods
- Work in process
- Raw materials

EXHIBIT 8.1

The Significance of Inventories and Cost of Goods Sold for Retail Department Stores

[2] "Restatement and Revision of Accounting Research Bulletins," *Accounting Research Bulletin No. 43*, (New York: AICPA, 1953), ch. 4, para. 3.

Only a firm that manufactures its products will have inventory in all three classifications. Retail and wholesale firms will typically only have inventory of the type described in part (a) of the definition above, while companies that deal primarily in a service (airlines, for instance) will typically only have inventory of the type described in part (c) of the definition.

The basic rule applied to inventories is that they be stated at cost except "when the utility of the goods is no longer as great as its cost."[3] In such cases, the inventory is stated at cost or market value, whichever is lower. Hereafter, we will refer to this valuation principle as the **lower-of-cost-or-market** or **LCM** rule. Before examining how and why that valuation rule is applied, we need to understand first what is meant by the cost of inventories. This necessitates answering the following questions:

1. Why do firms hold inventory?
2. What items are included in the inventory classifications?
3. How do firms keep track of inventory quantities?
4. What are the components of inventory cost?
5. What inventory cost flow assumptions can be made and why?
6. What special problems are presented by the LIFO cost flow assumption?

After considering inventory cost in this complete manner, we will be in a better position to examine how the LCM rule is applied in valuing inventories.

WHY FIRMS HOLD INVENTORY

As ARB No. 43's definition of inventory indicates, firms hold inventory because they provide one or more products to customers. Whether firms manufacture their own products or resell those manufactured by other firms, they need to hold some inventory to meet the demand for their products. In addition to keeping inventories of finished goods ready to sell, manufacturing firms must also keep inventories of those goods in various stages of completion, which will become finished goods to satisfy future demand.

The Costs and Benefits of Holding Inventory

How much inventory a firm holds depends on a variety of factors. In general, firms need to balance the cost of holding inventories with the cost of not holding them. The costs of holding inventories (frequently known as *inventory carrying costs*) are directly related to the firm's amount of investment in inventory and the length of time the inventory is held. These costs include capital tied up in inventory, taxes levied on inventory, insurance, storage, and record keeping. As we shall see, most of these costs are accounted for separately from the cost of the items in inventory. Nevertheless, since these carrying costs vary directly with the amount of inventory held by the firm, firms have a real economic incentive to minimize their inventory holdings.

---

[3] *Ibid.*, para. 8.

Firms will also incur costs when they do not hold enough inventory. Firms with insufficient inventory are likely to lose business and revenues as customers seek alternative suppliers that can satisfy their demands. This lost revenue is frequently referred to as the costs of *stock-outs*.

Determining Optimal Inventory Quantities

The problem of determining an optimal amount of inventory to hold is compounded by the fact that unit costs typically vary with order size (for a wholesale or retail firm) or with the size of a production run (for a manufacturing firm). That is, **economies of scale** usually imply that the larger the order or the lot size, the lower the unit cost. There are certain costs (often referred to as *order costs*) that are essentially constant, regardless of order size or the size of a production run. These order costs might include those of preparing and following up on material requisitions, setting up productive facilities to manufacture the inventory, and handling materials. If these order costs are spread over a larger number of units, the resulting cost per unit will be lower. Thus, while firms have some incentives to minimize their inventory holdings, economies of scale might encourage larger inventory holdings.

Researchers in operations management and production have developed a variety of inventory models, which are generically known as **economic order quantity (EOQ)** models, to help firms manage their inventory holdings. These models use estimates of order costs, carrying costs, stock-out costs, time required for production or order procurement, and demand for inventory to determine an optimal inventory size for the firm. A simple EOQ model is illustrated in Exhibit 8.2. One outcome of these inventory management models has been an increasing use of the so-called **just-in-time (JIT)** inventory management technique. Firms using JIT methods work with their suppliers and arrange for delivery of inventory exactly when it is needed for production, thereby minimizing carrying costs.

There are many variations of EOQ models, and they all require forecasts of demand for firms' products. Given the difficulty of predicting consumer preferences and the uncertainties of the economy, these forecasts are subject to considerable error. As a consequence, even firms employing state-of-the-art inventory management techniques still find themselves with inadequate or excessive inventory levels from time to time.

ITEMS INCLUDED IN THE INVENTORY CLASSIFICATION

In general, firms include those items in their inventory that they own. In the simplest kinds of purchase and sales transactions, legal title to goods passes as the goods themselves change hands. In such cases, a firm's inventory will consist of those items in its possession that it owns. But in certain types of transactions, title to goods may pass either before or after the goods change hands. As a result, a firm may have goods in its possession that it does not own or may have title to goods it does not physically possess. Thus, questions may arise as to which firm should include particular goods in its inventory.

EXHIBIT 8.2
The Classical
EOQ Model

The Classical EOQ Model

Let C = The purchase cost of a unit
U = Estimated annual usage (in units)
O = Cost of processing one order
K = Cost of carrying inventory, expressed as a percentage of the purchase cost of units on hand
Q = Quantity ordered
TC = Total annual cost of carrying the inventory and ordering

The model assumes that inventory usage is constant so that the average inventory quantity on hand is $Q/2$ units. We can express the total annual cost of carrying inventory and placing orders as follows:

$$TC = KC\frac{Q}{2} + O\frac{U}{Q}$$

The quantity $KCQ/2$ represents the total carrying costs: the carrying cost percentage (K) times the average dollar investment in inventory ($CQ/2$). The quantity OU/Q represents the total ordering costs: the number of orders (U/Q) times the cost per order (O). We want to find the value of order quantity (Q), which results in minimum total annual cost of carrying inventory and placing orders. This requires we differentiate the expression with respect to Q, set the derivative equal to zero, and solve for Q. Without going through the mathematics, this yields:

$$Q = \sqrt{2\frac{UO}{CK}}$$

Let us apply this model to an inventory item costing $100 ($C$ = 100), with an estimated annual usage of 2,000 units (U = 2,000), an order cost of $50 per order ($O$ = 50), and carrying costs of 20% per annum. Thus,

$$
\begin{aligned}
C &= \quad \$100 \\
U &= \quad 2,000 \\
O &= \quad \$\ 50 \\
K &= \quad .20
\end{aligned}
$$

Solving for Q yields an economic order quantity of:

$$Q = \quad 100$$

This implies an average (inventory quantity of 100/2 or 50 units and an average inventory balance of 50 × $100 or $5,000. Experiment with other values for C, U, O, and K and see how the optimal order quantity changes.

Questions of this sort are usually resolved in favor of the firm with title to the goods. That is, the firm with title to particular goods will generally include them in its inventory accounts. However, in some transactions, title is not enough to insure that goods are included in a firm's inventory accounts. The accountant needs to exercise judgment as to the intent of the parties in particular contracts to decide which firm includes the goods in its inventory.

Goods in Transit

When goods are in transit at the date of the firm's balance sheet, it is necessary to review the contract's terms to determine who has title to the goods and whether they should be included in the buyer's or seller's inventory. The contract will specify the shipping terms. Usually, goods are shipped F.O.B. (free on board) shipping point or F.O.B. destination. This determines when title passes from seller to buyer. When the sales contract specifies that the goods are shipped F.O.B. shipping point, then legal title to goods changes when they are delivered to a common carrier. The buyer will have title to (and be responsible for) the goods while they are in transit to the buyer's location. If the buyer's normal practice is to record purchases of inventory upon receipt of the goods, then an adjustment will be necessary to record inventory purchases shipped F.O.B. shipping point and in transit at the end of an accounting period. This adjustment will simply involve recording additional purchases in the usual form.

When the sales contract specifies that the goods are shipped **F.O.B. destination**, then title to the goods changes when the common carrier delivers them to the buyer. The seller will continue to have title (and be responsible for) the goods while they are in transit to the buyer's location. If the seller's normal practice is to record sales upon shipment of the goods, then an adjustment will be necessary for inventory sales shipped F.O.B. destination and in transit at the end of an accounting period. This adjustment will reverse the sales and cost of goods sold entries already recorded for those sales still in transit at the end of the period.

Consignments and Sales on Approval

Consignments and sales on approval also may lead to situations when ownership and possession do not coincide. In a *consignment* (also known as a *consignment sale*), the parties involved are known as the consignor and the consignee. The **consignor** delivers goods to the consignee. The **consignee** agrees to attempt to sell the goods for the consignor for a commission or fee and to exercise a reasonable standard of care in protecting the goods from damage or loss. When the goods are sold, the consignee will typically remit the sales proceeds (less the agreed upon commission or fee) to the consignor. In **sales on approval**, the goods are shipped to a potential buyer who has the right to return them if they are not satisfactory.

The general rule that the title holder to goods includes them in inventory also applies to consignments and sales on approval. Thus, goods out on consignment (or out on approval) remain in the inventory of the consignor (seller) until a sale occurs.

Sales With the Right of Return

It is common practice in certain industries (publishing, for instance) for sellers to grant buyers liberal privileges to return goods for a full refund or adjustment of the amount owed. Bookstores will ordinarily have the right to return unsold copies of books and magazines to the publisher after some agreed upon interval of time. Such sales with the right of return have been the subject of a FASB pronouncement. The FASB has ruled that if the amount of returns expected can be "reasonably estimated," then revenue should be recognized on sales with the right of return and the goods should not be included in the inventory of the seller.[4] If there is enough uncertainty in a particular case to preclude reasonable estimation of the amount of returns, no sales revenue is recorded; and the seller will continue to carry the items in inventory.

Installment Sales

A somewhat similar situation exists with installment sales. In installment sales, the buyer pays for the goods purchased over an extended period of time. Thus, the seller is not only selling the goods, but is also providing some of the financing for the transaction. Since the collection period is significantly longer with installment sales than for ordinary sales on account that require payment in 30 to 60 days, the risk of bad debts is correspondingly higher. As a protection against this added risk, the seller often retains legal title to the goods (or a lien on the title) until all installments are collected. Should the buyer default on the contract, the seller has the right to repossess the goods. If the seller retains title, should the goods be included in its inventory until all installments are collected? As we saw in Chapter 5, unless the risk of default is unacceptably high, the seller will recognize revenue from installment sales at the date of sale and will, therefore, not include the goods in its inventory.

Product Financing Arrangements

Consider the following contract, which may appear a bit strange at first glance. Roberts Corp. sells some of its inventory to Brown, Inc. and, in the same contract, agrees to repurchase it in the future at a prespecified price. Why would the parties agree to such a contract? The transaction, which is known as a "parking transaction," seems to accomplish little other than the obvious result that Roberts "parks" some of its inventory for awhile at Brown, Inc.

However, Roberts (the "seller") has accomplished several things here. First, it has secured a sure supply of inventory it will require in the future, perhaps at a favorable price. Moreover, it has effectively financed the transaction through the sale and repurchase agreement with Brown. That is, the proceeds from the sale will probably cover the cost of the original purchase. Another possible advantage of structuring the transaction in this way is that some states impose a personal property tax on firms' inventories. Roberts may be able to avoid this tax by transferring title temporarily to the out-of-state Brown, Inc.

Brown (the "buyer") can probably use the inventory to secure a loan to pay for the purchase, thus not adversely affecting its working capital, and can structure the transaction so that it will earn a positive return. Moreover, if Brown uses the LIFO inventory method, such transactions may prevent liquidations of older LIFO inventory layers, which, as we shall see shortly, can have some unfavorable consequences.

If this transaction is, in substance, a financing arrangement, it will be accounted for as such, despite the fact that the contract is technically a sale. This reflects the accounting profession's desire to have the accounting treat-

---

[4] "Revenue Recognition When Right of Return Exists," *Statement of Financial Accounting Standards No. 48* (Stamford, CT: FASB, 1981).

ment follow the economic substance of a transaction rather than its legal form. Brown would be required to report a liability for the repurchase of the goods and would continue to carry the goods in its inventory. The FASB has specified the following conditions which, if both are met, would cause the transaction to be regarded as a financing arrangement rather than a sale:[5]

1. The seller is required to repurchase the product, a substantially identical product, or processed goods of which the product is a component, at specified prices.
2. The payments the buyer will receive are established by the contract, and the amounts will be adjusted, as necessary, to cover substantially all fluctuations in costs incurred by the buyer in purchasing and holding the product (including interest).

KEEPING TRACK OF INVENTORY QUANTITIES

Firms use two general types of inventory record keeping systems to keep track of their inventory quantities: the **periodic inventory system** and the **perpetual inventory system**. The names given to these systems are quite descriptive. Under the periodic system, inventory quantities are determined periodically by means of a physical count; while under the perpetual system, detailed records are maintained perpetually so that, ideally, inventory quantities are determinable at any time. These two systems for keeping track of inventory quantities are not mutually exclusive. Many firms will use one system as a check on the other. For instance, even firms with very sophisticated perpetual inventory systems will periodically take a physical inventory count and compare the quantities in the perpetual records with those observed in the count.[6]

As we shall see, firms' choices of inventory record keeping systems can interact with their choices of cost flow assumptions to affect the value assigned to inventory and cost of goods sold. That is, under some cost flow assumptions, the amount reported for inventory and cost of goods sold will depend, in part, on whether the periodic or perpetual system is used. However, just because firms have perpetual records does not mean they must use them for financial reporting purposes. For financial reporting purposes, many firms will use a periodic calculation for inventory and cost of goods sold even though they may be keeping track of inventory quantities with perpetual records. Before exploring the interaction of the cost flow assumption and the record keeping system, we need to understand more fully how these two systems operate.

---

[5] "Accounting for Product Financing Arrangements," *Statement of Financial Accounting Standards No. 49* (Stamford, CT: FASB, 1981).

[6] Generally accepted auditing standards require the independent public accountant to observe the taking of the physical inventory count in connection with an audit of the firm's financial statements.

Periodic Inventory System

Under the periodic system (strictly applied), firms will take a physical count of their inventory once each period and use the quantities so determined to compute both their ending inventory and cost of goods sold. To convert quantities to costs, the quantities will be priced at amounts appropriate to the cost flow assumption in use. During the period, inventory purchases are recorded in a temporary account usually called purchases, which is closed out at the end of the accounting period. The sum of inventory at the start of the period, plus the cost of goods purchased during the period, yields an amount known as the cost of goods available for sale. Cost of goods sold is a residual amount under the periodic system—it is determined by subtracting the ending inventory from the cost of goods available for sale, as follows:

Inventory at December 31, 1993	$ 55,000
Inventory purchases during 1994	225,000
Cost of goods available for sale	$280,000
Inventory at December 31, 1994	(45,000)
Cost of goods sold in 1994	$235,000

In essence, whatever is not on hand at the end of the period is assumed to have been sold under the periodic system.

If we assume that all inventory purchases in this example were made on account, the journal entries to record the purchases of inventory and cost of goods sold would appear as follows:

1. To record inventory purchases on account:

Purchases	225,000	
Accounts payable		225,000

2. To adjust inventory to the amount determined by the year-end physical inventory and to close the purchases account:

Cost of goods sold	235,000	
Purchases		225,000
Inventory		10,000

The $10,000 credit in the second journal entry reduces the balance in inventory from the $55,000 balance reported at December 31, 1993, to the $45,000 balance determined to be on hand at December 31, 1994.

The periodic system has the advantage of being fairly inexpensive to implement. No costly detailed records are required. But several very real disadvantages must be weighed against the apparent cost savings.

First, without detailed records, inventory management and control are difficult. Deciding when to reorder particular items and identifying slow-moving inventory require observation of the actual stocks of goods on hand. It is not possible to identify cases of pilferage or spoilage since goods not on hand when the inventory is taken are assumed to have been sold.

Second, interim financial reporting is more difficult when the periodic system is used. Since cost of goods sold and inventory values cannot be determined under the periodic system without a physical count of the inventory, firms must either take a physical count for each interim period or use an estimation technique (illustrated in Chapter 9) for the preparation of interim financial statements. Due to the nuisance and expense of a physical count, most firms opt for estimation of interim inventory amounts.

For these reasons, the periodic system is probably more suitable for inventories that have relatively few different items with low unit values. When unit values are low, the higher cost of a perpetual record system is more likely to exceed the benefits of better inventory control. For instance, a grain elevator operator may find that a periodic inventory system is perfectly adequate. Cases with more complexity and/or more costly inventory items are better served by perpetual inventory records.

Perpetual Inventory System

Firms using a perpetual inventory system will update their inventory and cost of goods sold account balances with each purchase and sale transaction. Thus, the balance in the inventory account at any particular point in time should correspond to the cost of the goods actually on hand. No temporary purchases account is necessary—purchases are debited directly to the inventory account. The same transactions discussed above for a firm using the periodic system would be handled as follows under the perpetual system:

1. To record inventory purchases on account:

Inventory	225,000	
Accounts payable		225,000

2. To record cost of goods sold:

Cost of goods sold	235,000	
Inventory		235,000

When firms use the perpetual system in conjunction with a periodic physical count of the goods on hand, they can discover errors in the records. The cause for these errors can then be investigated and necessary adjusting entries made. If we assume a $5,000 discrepancy is uncovered, the adjustments would be made as follows:

1. To record a $5,000 inventory shortage:

Inventory shortage	5,000	
Inventory		5,000

2. To record a $5,000 inventory overage:

Inventory	5,000	
Inventory overage		5,000

The inventory shortage/overage accounts are typically closed out at the end of the period to cost of goods sold.

A perpetual inventory system is more costly to maintain than a periodic system. The detailed records of a perpetual system will require more human and data processing resources. However, the availability of affordable computers, optical character recognition devices, and universal product bar codes, which can be found on most consumer products, has made perpetual inventory systems both feasible and cost-effective in a wide variety of settings where the cost was formerly prohibitive. Many retail establishments (including supermarkets with tens of thousands of items in inventory with relatively low unit costs) employ these technological advances to maintain perpetual inventory systems. As the consumer purchases the goods, the firms' point-of-sale systems record the sale and update the inventory records simultaneously.

The ability to manage and control inventory is greatly enhanced with perpetual records; and as the costs of such systems continue to decrease, more and more firms will find the benefits outweigh the costs.

COMPONENTS OF INVENTORY COST

Thus far, we have been discussing inventories in terms of physical quantities. These quantities must obviously be priced at appropriate unit costs for financial reporting purposes. But what are the appropriate costs? Firms include in inventory all the costs of acquiring or producing goods and making them available for sale. Exactly what cost components a particular firm includes in inventory depends on the nature of its operations. Merchandising firms (retailers and wholesalers), such as those listed in Exhibit 8.1, buy and resell goods. The cost of inventory for these firms will consist of the costs incurred to acquire the goods in purchase transactions plus any related shipping and handling costs. Manufacturing firms acquire raw material and add value through the manufacturing process. The cost of inventory for these firms will include the costs of acquiring raw materials plus manufacturing costs such as labor, depreciation of manufacturing machinery and equipment, electricity, maintenance, and supervision. Depending on their stage in the production process, inventories are classified as raw materials, work in process, or finished goods.

Costs assigned to inventory are known as **product costs**. Costs not directly related to inventory are not assigned to inventory but, rather, are treated as expenses of the period in which they are incurred, or *period expenses*. The definitions of product costs and period expenses are vague, and what is treated as a product cost by one firm may be treated as a period cost by another firm.

Manufactured Inventories

A case can be made for treating all costs related to the manufacturing process as product costs since these costs were incurred for the purpose, directly or indirectly, of producing inventory. However, when the costs in question are only indirectly related to the product (i.e., "overhead"), it becomes difficult to make the allocations necessary to treat these costs as product costs. Therefore, they may be treated as period costs as a practical matter.[7] However, please

---

[7] One of the less popular provisions of the Tax Reform Act of 1986 was a change in the definition of the cost of inventory for tax reporting purposes. Under the 1986 law, firms are required to treat certain costs as product costs that had previously been treated as period costs. This may result in costs being treated as product costs for tax purposes and period costs for financial reporting purposes. These "temporary differences" will affect the calculation of deferred taxes as illustrated in Chapter 20.

note that ARB No. 43 states very explicitly that "exclusion of all overhead costs from inventory costs does not constitute an accepted accounting procedure."[8]

Students of managerial accounting will recall that fixed manufacturing costs (i.e., those that do not vary with output) are handled in one of two ways. Under a **variable** or **direct costing approach**, only the variable manufacturing costs are treated as product costs. All fixed manufacturing costs are treated as expenses of the period. Under the **full** or **absorption costing approach**, all costs, both fixed and variable, are treated as product costs. The rationale behind the variable costing approach is that since managers only have direct control over variable costs, only these costs should be included in reports to evaluate managers' performance. Moreover, the segregation of fixed and variable costs is very useful in analyzing the marginal effects of managerial decisions. Despite its admitted benefits as a management accounting technique, variable costing remains unacceptable as a financial reporting technique since it understates the cost of inventories. However, firms may use a variable costing system for managerial purposes and make end-of-period adjustments to include fixed manufacturing costs in product costs for financial reporting purposes.

Purchased Inventories

We now turn to a discussion of the accounting treatment for certain specific cost components for purchased inventories. When firms purchase goods for their inventories, the purchases are recorded with debits to purchases (under the periodic system) or inventory (under the perpetual system) for the invoice amounts of the purchases. We will examine briefly how these invoice amounts are adjusted for purchase discounts, returns and allowances, shipping, and handling charges. We will also consider how a lump-sum purchase price is allocated to the various items acquired.

Purchase Discounts   Suppliers commonly offer discounts to customers to encourage prompt payment. Suppose a particular supplier offers a 5% discount off the invoice price of $5,000 if payment is received within 10 days of delivery of the goods rather than in the maximum 30-day period allowed. These terms would be abbreviated 5/10, net 30. The firm making this purchase can record the discount in one of two ways. If the firm does not routinely take advantage of purchase discounts, it will use the *gross method*—it will record the purchase at gross price, and an adjustment for purchase discounts will be necessary only in those unusual situations in which the discount is taken. To record the purchase and payment, net of discount, the following entries are appropriate for a periodic inventory system under the gross method:

1. To record the purchase on account:

Purchases	5,000	
Accounts payable		5,000

---

[8] *Accounting Research Bulletin No. 43, op. cit.*, ch. 4, para. 5.

2. To record payment, net of discount:

Accounts payable	5,000	
Cash		4,750
Discounts taken		250

The discounts taken account, like purchases, is a temporary account that will be closed out at the end of the period in the calculation of cost of goods sold. The net result of these two entries is to record the purchase at the net-of-discount amount. If, as expected, the company does not take advantage of the discount offered, the resulting journal entry is straightforward, involving only cash and accounts payable.

3. To record payment at gross price:

Accounts payable	5,000	
Cash		5,000

If company policy is to take all or most discounts offered by suppliers, it will be simpler to use the *net method*—record purchases at the net-of-discount amount in the first place. Then, adjustments will only be necessary for discounts not taken. Under the net method, the purchase and payment, net of discount, would be recorded as follows:

1. To record a purchase on account, net of available discount:

Purchases	4,750	
Accounts payable		4,750

2. To record the payment on account within the discount period:

Accounts payable	4,750	
Cash		4,750

Suppose the accounts payable clerk is on vacation and the invoice is not processed for payment in time to take advantage of the discount. The following entry would be necessary to record the payment and discount lost:

3. To record payment on account after the discount period has lapsed:

Accounts payable	4,750	
Discounts not taken	250	
Cash		5,000

Discounts not taken can be thought of as the firm's cost of not paying for the purchase within 10 days or its cost of financing the purchase over a longer period. Under this interpretation, the firm would include the amount of discounts not taken with interest expense on its income statement, since the expense represents a financing cost. Also note that the firm may need to make an end-of-period adjustment under the net method to record discounts lost on outstanding payable balances past the discount period.

Whether firms use the gross method or the net method of recording purchase discounts is, like all accounting choices, a matter of managements' discretion. The differences between the two methods are likely to be slight. Under the gross method, a slight mismatching of discounts with purchases may occur since discounts could be taken in the accounting period following the purchase. However, the discount periods are typically brief and the potential for mismatching will not likely result in material differences. Although it would probably be more convenient for firms that routinely take advantage of purchase discounts to use the net method, the gross method seems to be more popular. Perhaps managers would rather point proudly to the amount of "purchase discounts taken" than be required to admit the amount of "purchase discounts lost."

Regardless of the method used to record purchase discounts, firms are not wise to forego them. In the example above, when the firm did not take advantage of 5/10, net 30 terms offered on the $5,000 invoice amount, it effectively paid $250 to use $4,750 for an extra 20 days. This works out to a whopping 95% annual interest rate:

$$\$250 \div \$4{,}750 \times 360 \text{ days} \div 20 \text{ days} = 95\%$$

The firm should obtain bank financing to permit it to take advantage of such generous terms from its supplier.

Returns and Allowances   If goods purchased are found to be unsatisfactory, they will either be returned to the supplier or the supplier will grant an allowance (reduction of the purchase price). In either case, it is necessary to record the transaction as a **purchase return** or **purchase allowance** since the amount of purchases has effectively been reduced. Suppose some of the goods purchased in the above transaction are found to be below the firm's standards and are returned to the supplier for a full adjustment of $800. The usual way to record this transaction under the periodic system is as follows:

Accounts payable	800	
Purchase returns and allowances		800

Using a separate purchase returns and allowances account will help management keep track of the extent of problems with returns and allowances. Management needs to monitor returns and allowances for a number of reasons. Purchase returns are costly to process. Increases in returns may indicate particular suppliers are having trouble providing goods that meet the company's requirements. As companies adopt highly efficient and automated inventory management techniques such as just-in-time inventory management, purchase returns have the potential to disrupt a firm's operations.

Shipping and Handling Costs

If shipping and handling charges are included on the supplier's invoice, they can simply be recorded as part of the cost of the purchase and included in the debit to purchases (or inventory in a perpetual system). Sometimes, a separate invoice will be received from the carrier for the freight charges, and in periodic systems, these charges are usually recorded separately with a debit to an account titled freight-in or transportation-in. This account is closed at the end of period to cost of goods sold. When a perpetual system is used, the freight charges are either recorded with a direct debit to inventory or separately in a freight-in account. If the latter approach is taken, the freight charges are typically treated as a period cost and included, in full, in the cost of goods sold for the period. It should be recognized that this violates the matching principle somewhat since these freight charges cover some goods that have not yet been sold and some goods sold this period but expensed last period. The amount of the mismatching is unlikely to be troublesome, however, unless there are dramatic changes in inventory levels from period to period.

INVENTORY COST FLOW ASSUMPTIONS

We have seen what items and what costs are included in inventories, as well as the periodic and perpetual inventory systems for keeping track of inventory quantities. Our discussion of the cost of inventory can now be completed by considering the different **cost flow assumptions** that firms can make about their inventories.

Inventory cost flow assumptions are not always necessary. In many cases, it is possible and practical to identify the specific cost of each item in inventory. For instance, an automobile dealer can keep track of each vehicle by its serial number. Unless the dealer's volume is exceptionally high, it would not require an inordinate amount of bookkeeping effort to apply the **specific identification method**. That is, it would value inventory and cost of goods sold at the actual costs of the items either in inventory or sold during the period.

In other cases, specific identification may literally be impossible to apply and assumptions about inventory cost flows must be made. Consider, for instance, a home heating oil distributor. Once the oil is stored in the company's storage tanks, it loses its identity. When oil is taken from a tank, it is impossible to determine what price was paid to acquire it. Therefore, determination of values for inventory and cost of goods sold will require an assumption as to how the costs flow through inventory.

Firms commonly use inventory cost flow assumptions, whether necessary or not, to either simplify the bookkeeping process or to achieve other particular results, which are discussed below. While it may be intuitively appealing to think of cost flow assumptions in terms of the physical flow of goods, it is not necessary for the physical flow of goods to match the assumed flow of costs. All of the cost flow assumptions discussed below are available to firms, regardless of the nature of their business and the physical flow of units in and out of inventory. We will examine the available cost flow assumptions briefly and then turn to an example that permits a comparison of their effects.

First-in, First-out (FIFO)

The **first-in, first-out (FIFO) method** assumes that costs flow through inventory in chronological order. That is, costs are assumed to flow as if the units are sold in the same order they were purchased. If oldest units are sold first, then the first costs into inventory will always be the first ones out. This also implies that the costs that remain in inventory will be the last ones in or the costs of the most recently acquired units. Thus, an alternative description of the FIFO cost flow assumption that focuses on the costs that remain in inventory is *last-*

in, still-here or *LISH*. FIFO results in inventory being stated at the costs of the most recently acquired units and cost of goods sold being stated at somewhat older costs.

The "age" of the costs assigned to the cost of goods sold figure depends on the average length of time inventory is held by the firm or, conversely, on how quickly inventory is sold (or "turns over"). Average holding period and inventory turnover are two ways of capturing the same idea. An average holding period of a month implies inventory turns over 12 times a year and vice versa. Under FIFO, the slower the inventory turnover, the older the reported costs of the inventory.

FIFO has a nice intuitive feature in that the flow of costs often corresponds to the physical flow of goods. In many industries, the physical goods flow in a FIFO fashion. Where obsolescence or spoilage is a potential problem, firms will naturally try to sell their older units first. Despite this intuitive appeal and the resulting ease of application, over the past decade, FIFO has not been the clear favorite among cost flow assumptions.[9] We will pursue the reasons for this later in the chapter.

Last-in, First-out (LIFO)

The **last-in, first-out (LIFO) method** assumes that costs flow in reverse chronological order. That is, costs flow as if the most recently acquired units are sold first. If the most recent units are sold first, then the last costs into inventory will always be the first ones out. This also implies that the costs that remain in inventory will be the first ones in or the costs of the first units acquired. Thus, an equivalent description of the LIFO method that focuses on the costs that remain in inventory is *first-in, still here* or *FISH*. If a firm has been using LIFO for 30 years, then it is likely that there will be some 30-year-old costs accumulated in the inventory figure on its balance sheet. Thus, LIFO results in inventory being stated at old (and perhaps very old) costs, while cost of goods sold will usually be stated at the costs of the most recent purchases.

LIFO has a number of problems. First, it is not very intuitively appealing. While some commodity inventories, such as coal, are stored in a pile so the first units put into the pile will be the last to be sold or used, there are not many situations in which the physical goods flow in a LIFO fashion. Second, stating inventory at old costs severely impairs the usefulness of the balance sheet, as we shall see later in the chapter. Despite these shortcomings, LIFO has become an increasingly popular method. There are sound economic reasons for this trend, which will be discussed later in the chapter.

Average Cost

The **average cost method** produces results that typically fall somewhere between the LIFO and FIFO extremes. As the name implies, both inventory and cost of goods sold are stated at an average cost figure. Neither inventory nor cost of goods sold will be stated at a particularly current figure.

---

[9] According to *Accounting Trends & Techniques*, 1990 edition, FIFO was used by 401 firms; LIFO, by 366 firms; and average cost, by 200 firms.

The Cost Flow Assumptions Illustrated

To illustrate these three cost flow assumptions and gain some insight into their effects, consider the following simple example:

INVENTORY EXAMPLE

Date	Units	Cost/Unit	Sales(Units)	Balance (Units)
		Purchases		
February 12	11,000	$6.00		11,000
April 15	14,000	6.50		25,000
September 10			20,000	5,000
November 28	10,000	6.40		15,000

Ending inventory and cost of goods sold for the month can be calculated under each of the three inventory cost flow assumptions discussed above. Calculations will be illustrated under both the periodic and perpetual inventory systems because for both LIFO and average cost, the results will be affected by the inventory system in use.

FIFO Flow, Periodic System   Applying the FIFO method to these data would result in the following ending inventory and cost of goods sold:

FIFO ending inventory:			
10,000 units	×	$6.40	$64,000
5,000 units	×	$6.50	32,500
Total			$96,500

To calculate FIFO ending inventory, start with the most recent purchases and work backward. The cost of the 15,000 units in ending inventory is assumed to consist of the cost of the 10,000 units purchased on February 12 and the cost of 5,000 of the units purchased on April 15.

FIFO cost of goods sold:			
Beginning inventory			$ –
Purchases:			
11,000 units	×	$6.00	$ 66,000
14,000 units	×	$6.50	91,000
10,000 units	×	$6.40	64,000
Total purchases			$221,000
Cost of goods available			$221,000
Less: Ending inventory			96,500
Cost of goods sold			$124,500

The cost of goods sold calculation is similar in approach for all three cost flow assumptions under the periodic system. The cost of the purchases is added to the cost of the beginning inventory to yield the cost of the goods available for sale during the period. From this amount, subtract the cost of the ending inventory to yield the cost of goods sold. What will differ across the three cost flow assumptions is the cost of the ending inventory. Had there been any beginning inventory in this example, that too might have differed.

FIFO Flow, Perpetual System   Under a perpetual inventory system, the calculation will look a bit different but the results will be identical to those under FIFO, periodic system.

Date	Transaction	Units	Cost/Unit	Total Cost
2/12	Purchase	11,000	$6.00	$ 66,000
4/15	Purchase	14,000	6.50	91,000
		25,000		157,000
9/10	Sale	(11,000)	6.00	(66,000)
		(9,000)	6.50	(58,500)
		5,000		32,500
11/28	Purchase	10,000	6.40	64,000
12/31	Balance forward	15,000		$ 96,500

Notice how both the inventory cost ($96,500) and the cost of goods sold ($66,000 + $58,500 = $124,500) are exactly the same as those calculated above on the FIFO periodic basis. This is no coincidence. FIFO, alone among the three cost flow assumptions considered here, will always yield the same results under perpetual and periodic calculations.

LIFO Flow, Periodic System   Applying the LIFO method to these data would result in the following ending inventory and cost of goods sold for a periodic inventory system:

LIFO ending inventory:			
11,000 units	×	$6.00	$66,000
4,000 units	×	$6.50	26,000
Total			$92,000

In the calculation of LIFO ending inventory, begin with the oldest units and work forward. The cost of the 15,000 units in ending inventory is assumed to consist of the cost of the 11,000 units purchased on February 12 plus the cost of the 4,000 of the units purchased on April 15.

LIFO cost of goods sold:

Beginning inventory	$ —
Purchases	221,000
Cost of goods available	$221,000
Less: Ending inventory	92,000
Cost of goods sold	$129,000

Notice that the only difference between LIFO and FIFO in the cost of goods sold periodic calculations in this example is the amount of ending inventory. In a calculation with beginning inventory, it is likely that both beginning and ending inventories will differ. Due to the increasing cost of the items in inventory, the ending inventory is lower in this example under LIFO than under FIFO. Therefore, LIFO cost of goods sold is higher than that under FIFO.

LIFO Flow, Perpetual System   Under a perpetual inventory system, the LIFO method will typically yield different results than those obtained when LIFO is used in a periodic system.

Date	Transaction	Units	Cost/Unit	Total Cost
2/12	Purchase	11,000	$6.00	$ 66,000
4/15	Purchase	14,000	6.50	91,000
		25,000		157,000
9/10	Sale	(14,000)	6.50	(91,000)
		(6,000)	6.00	(36,000)
		5,000		30,000
11/28	Purchase	10,000	6.40	64,000
12/31	Balance forward	15,000		$ 94,000

Notice how the amounts for ending inventory ($94,000) and cost of goods sold ($91,000 + 36,000 = $127,000) differ from the comparable amounts calculated on a LIFO periodic basis above. The reason for this discrepancy is that when LIFO is applied on a periodic basis, the costs of units purchased after the last sale has taken place still enter into the cost of goods sold calculation. The LIFO periodic cost of goods sold consists of the following:

10,000 units	×	$6.40	$ 64,000
10,000 units	×	6.50	65,000
Total			$129,000

Notice that the units purchased at a unit cost of $6.40 were purchased after the date of the sale of 20,000 units. Nevertheless, the LIFO periodic cost of goods sold calculation includes these costs. When applied perpetually, the cost of units purchased after a particular sale obviously cannot be included in the cost of goods sold calculation. Because of the difficulties in applying LIFO on a perpetual basis, it is rarely done. Instead, perpetual records will probably be kept on a FIFO basis, and an end-of-period adjustment is made to put the firm on a LIFO basis. This is often done using the dollar value LIFO method, illustrated in Chapter 9.

Average Cost Flow, Periodic System   Applying the average cost method to these data would result in the following ending inventory and cost of goods sold under a periodic system:

Average cost ending inventory:	
Cost of goods available for sale	$221,000
Units available	35,000
Average cost per unit	$ 6.314
Units in ending inventory	× 15,000
Cost of ending inventory	$ 94,710

The average cost calculation divides the cost of the goods available for sale by the number of units available to yield an average unit cost. This average cost is then applied to the number of units in ending inventory to yield the cost of ending inventory.

Average cost of goods sold:	
Beginning inventory	$ –
Purchases	221,000
Cost of goods available	$221,000
Less: Ending inventory	94,710
Cost of goods sold	$126,290

Average Cost Flow, Perpetual System   Under a perpetual inventory system, the average cost calculations will differ. In the periodic calculation, the average cost was computed for the entire period. If perpetual records are to be maintained, it is not possible to wait until the end of period to calculate an average cost. Instead, a moving average cost must be calculated before each sales transaction.

Date	Transaction	Units	Cost/Unit	Total Cost
2/12	Purchase	11,000	$6.00	$ 66,000
4/15	Purchase	14,000	6.50	91,000
		25,000		157,000
9/10	Sale	(20,000)	$6.28*	$(125,600)
		5,000		31,400
11/28	Purchase	10,000	6.40	64,000
12/31	Balance forward	15,000		$ 95,400

* $157,000 ÷ 25,000 units = $6.28/unit

Recap

It may be useful to recap the results of the three methods:

| | Periodic Inventory System | | | Perpetual Inventory System | | |
	FIFO	LIFO	Average	FIFO	LIFO	Average
Inventory	$ 96,500	$ 92,000	$ 94,710	$ 96,500	$ 94,000	$ 95,400
Cost of goods sold	124,500	129,000	126,920	124,500	127,000	125,600

In this period of generally (but not steadily) rising prices for the item in inventory, FIFO ending inventory is greater than LIFO; and FIFO cost of goods sold is lower than LIFO. This should come as no surprise. Since FIFO ending inventory is based on the costs of the most recent purchases and LIFO is based on the costs of the oldest purchases, in periods of rising prices, FIFO inventory will be higher in amount than LIFO. LIFO cost of goods sold, on the other hand, is based on the most recent costs, while FIFO cost of goods sold is based upon somewhat older costs. Thus, in a period of rising prices, LIFO cost of goods sold will typically be higher in amount than FIFO. The results of the average cost method are, as expected, between those of LIFO and FIFO.

Regardless of which cost flow assumption firms select (or which combination of cost flow assumptions for different parts of a firm's inventories), they must disclose their choices in the summary of significant accounting policies as required by APB Opinion No. 22. When firms change their cost flow assumptions, the resulting changes in accounting principle must be presented in accordance with the provisions of APB Opinion No. 20.

LIFO ISSUES

Why has the LIFO method become more popular in American businesses? To understand the motivations, let us examine the disclosures made by The Coleman Company, Inc., when it adopted the LIFO inventory method in 1974. For reasons we explain later, 1974 was a big year in terms of the number of firms adopting LIFO. By looking at an example drawn from that era, we can begin to appreciate the political and economic forces that encourage firms to adopt LIFO.

Example: The Coleman Company, Inc.

In 1974, The Coleman Company, Inc., along with many other firms, adopted the LIFO inventory method. In its annual report for that year, the change to the LIFO method was explained and described as follows:

> Effective January 1, 1974, the Company changed its method of determining cost for substantially all inventories from the first-in, first-out (FIFO) method to the last-in, first-out (LIFO) method. The LIFO method was adopted to provide a better matching of current costs and revenues in determining the results of operations by excluding from inventories the effect of inflationary cost increases.

Since the December 31, 1973 inventory valued at FIFO is considered to be the opening LIFO inventory, there is no cumulative effect of the change on prior years. The change to LIFO decreased inventory values at December 31, 1974 by $8,845,000 and reduced 1974 net income by $4,405,000 ($.60 a share).

To put the effects of this change into perspective, the $8,845,000 reduction of inventory values accompanying the change to LIFO represented a 16% reduction of the FIFO value of the same inventory. Moreover, the $4,405,000 reduction of earnings amounted to a reduction of nearly 56% of earnings computed under FIFO.

Now exactly why would a company voluntarily choose to adopt an accounting method for inventory that results in a 16% reduction of inventory and a staggering 56% reduction of earnings? According to the company, the reason was to provide a "better matching of current costs and revenues." That sounds noble enough, but one wonders if that was Coleman's purpose, why did it wait until 1974 to make the change? LIFO, after all, had been around for years.[10] Moreover, is adherence to the matching principle really important enough to management to warrant the severe financial statement consequences observed here? We will address these issues in due course and try to provide a more satisfying answer to the question of why firms use LIFO.

The Incentive to Adopt LIFO

As we have already seen, in periods of rising prices, the LIFO method generally yields a higher cost of goods sold figure and, hence, a lower net income than either FIFO or average cost. Once this relationship became well known, firms began to urge the Internal Revenue Service (IRS) to allow them to use LIFO for tax reporting purposes. Their motivation for doing so was apparent. By reporting higher cost of goods sold, they would report lower taxable incomes and, therefore, pay less in income taxes. The IRS, perhaps recognizing that widespread adoption of LIFO had the potential to reduce income tax payments, initially denied the requests for allowing the use of the LIFO method.[11]

As we shall see in Chapter 20, firms are, by and large, free to choose one set of accounting principles for financial reporting purposes and another set for tax reporting purposes. These "two sets of books" essentially allow firms to eat their cake and have it too—they can report relatively low income to the taxing authorities and relatively high income to their stockholders, bankers, etc. In the case of LIFO, however, that is not the case. After a number of years of pressure to allow the LIFO method, the IRS finally relented to a very limited extent in

---

[10] The LIFO method first gained widespread use in the petroleum industry in the mid-1930s. It has been widely available for tax purposes since 1939. See H. Davis, "History of LIFO," *Journal of Accountancy* (May, 1983), pp. 96–114, for more details.

[11] There is some question about whether the tax saving feature of LIFO was widely anticipated in LIFO's early years. In a report of the American Institute of Accountants Committee on Federal Taxation issued in 1938, which recommended LIFO be allowed for tax purposes, it was argued that use of LIFO would not result in lower tax payments than those under FIFO. It may be difficult for us to understand now, but in 1938 the expectation was that prices would probably change cyclically but without any upward general trend. This point is discussed further in H. Davis, "History of LIFO," *op cit.*, p. 104.

1938 and much more generally in 1939. However, it imposed the "conformity rule"—a requirement that firms must also use the LIFO method for financial reporting purposes if they wished to use it for tax purposes. Essentially, it appears that the IRS was saying to management, "We believe LIFO is only appropriate if the firm genuinely believes it produces the best measure of income and is willing to use it for financial reporting purposes." This was its way of seeing whether all the arguments it had been hearing about the theoretical merits of the LIFO method were sincere or merely self-serving.

For years, many firms decided to forego the tax advantages of using LIFO in periods of rising prices because they were afraid of the consequences of reporting lower income and total assets in their published financial statements. They were concerned that this would make it harder for them to raise capital and would increase stockholder dissatisfaction. The paradox is that the firms would have been better off in a real economic sense if they had adopted LIFO—their tax payments would have been lower, but their financial statements would have appeared worse, and in many cases, much worse. Numerous research studies on this issue have failed to document that the market values of the common stock of companies adopting LIFO were adversely affected by the change, despite the adverse financial statement effects.[12]

In the early 1970s, when inflation hit double-digit levels, more and more firms found the tax advantages of using LIFO just too attractive to pass up any longer and adopted LIFO. Moreover, the IRS relaxed the LIFO requirements somewhat and began to allow firms using LIFO to make footnote disclosure of the current costs of beginning and ending inventories and the amount of income or loss that the firms would have reported under an alternative method.[13] Thus, the combination of extraordinarily high rates of price increases and a relaxation of the conformity rule accounted for the unusually large number of firms adopting LIFO in 1974. Since that time, we continue to observe that interest in the LIFO method is directly related to the rate of inflation in inventory prices. For instance, *The Wall Street Journal* reported in its regular "Business Bulletin" feature on April 27, 1989, that concern over inflation has prompted many small companies to consider switching to LIFO.

In the year firms adopt LIFO, most do not admit in their financial statements that in adopting LIFO they avoid the payment of income taxes. Rather, as we saw with The Coleman Company, Inc., they are more politically astute, simply stating that LIFO was adopted "to provide a better matching of current costs and revenues in determining the results of operations by excluding from inventories the effect of inflationary cost increases." This explanation requires some clarification.

In a period of rising prices, companies using FIFO or the average cost method will report an amount for cost of goods sold that is lower than that

[12] See, for instance, G. Biddle and F. Lindahl, "Stock Price Reactions to LIFO Adoptions: The Association Between Excess Returns and LIFO Tax Savings," *Journal of Accounting Research* (Autumn 1982), pp. 551–588, and references cited therein.

[13] This was formalized in *U.S. Treasury Regulation 1.472-2(e)*, issued in 1981, but revenue rulings and revenue procedures issued from 1973 through 1979 allowed exemptions to the conformity rule in an increasing number of cases.

reported under LIFO (as long as inventory quantities are not decreasing) because older and, therefore, lower costs are matched with revenues. But these units sold will have to be replaced at the new higher costs if the companies are to continue their operations. Therefore, the higher profits under FIFO or average cost do not represent amounts that companies could distribute to shareholders as a dividend without effectively impairing their ability to continue operations at the current level. Under LIFO, these illusory "inventory profits" or "realized holding gains" are typically avoided because more current (and higher) costs of inventory are matched with revenues.

Changing To and From the LIFO Method

We observed in Chapter 3 that firms may only make changes in accounting principle when the new method is preferable to the old one. Moreover, when firms make a change in accounting principle, the cumulative effect of the accounting change is generally reported on the income statement in the year of the change. A review of The Coleman Company, Inc., annual report for 1974 revealed no such item on the firm's income statement. Why not? Changes to or from the LIFO method are an exception to the general rule of reporting the cumulative effect of accounting changes on the income statement. Calculating the cumulative effect on retained earnings at the beginning of the period of a change to LIFO would be difficult, if not impossible. It would require a detailed examination of all of the inventory records since the inception of the firm to calculate the LIFO cost of inventory as if LIFO had been in use all along. Even if such data were available, the calculation would be quite difficult. Therefore, when firms adopt the LIFO method, they simply use the ending inventory cost under their old method as their beginning LIFO cost and proceed from there to apply the LIFO method. Moreover, firms are required to report the effect of the change on income for the period as The Coleman Company, Inc., did when it stated, "The change to LIFO decreased inventory values at December 31, 1974 by $8,845,000 and reduced 1974 net income by $4,405,000 ($.60 a share)."

APB Opinion No. 20 earmarked several accounting changes for special consideration. These changes "are such that the advantages of retroactive treatment in prior period reports outweigh the disadvantages"; and, therefore, they are handled by restatement of prior period amounts, rather than by means of a cumulative adjustment, on the income statement.[14] The end result of restatement or a cumulative adjustment is the same—the balance in retained earnings will appear as if the new accounting method had always been used. However, the difference between the two approaches is that restatement avoids a cumulative adjustment on the income statement. One change to receive this special treatment is any change from the LIFO method to any other cost flow assumption. Other changes include those in accounting for long-term contracts (see Chapter 5) and those to or from the full cost method used in the extractive industries (see Chapter 10).

---

[14] "Accounting Changes," *Accounting Principles Board Opinion No. 20* (New York: AICPA, 1971), para. 27.

While APB Opinion No. 20 did not specify what is special about these changes, it is apparent that in each case, the cumulative adjustment required for such a change would be very large, perhaps large enough to dominate the income statement. While the APB clearly preferred the cumulative adjustment approach to make the existence of the accounting change as obvious as possible, it was concerned that this approach might be potentially misleading when the cumulative adjustments are relatively large. Therefore, when firms switch from the LIFO method, they do so by restating prior period amounts rather than reporting a cumulative adjustment. Changes of cost flow assumptions not involving the LIFO method are handled in the usual way—by means of a cumulative adjustment in the year of the change.

Advantages of LIFO

LIFO has become popular because it clearly offers firms some very real advantages.

Tax Savings   The primary reason why firms adopt LIFO is the tax savings available. However, firms must comply with the conformity rule and use LIFO for both tax reporting and financial reporting purposes. Effectively, LIFO shelters income from taxation by charging price increases to cost of goods sold rather than to inventory. The difference between the LIFO cost of inventory and its cost under a different cost flow assumption is the total amount of income that has been sheltered from taxation. The potential savings are very substantial. For instance, as shown in the Case 8.1 (at the end of this chapter), Deere & Company has sheltered more than $1 billion of income from taxation by using LIFO.

Matching   LIFO is often said to match current costs with revenues better than the other cost flow assumptions. It does this by always charging the costs of the most recently acquired units to cost of goods sold. Thus, the income reported under LIFO is said to be more relevant in that it does not include any of the so-called "inventory profits." However, as we show in the next section, this is not always the case. When LIFO inventories are liquidated, old LIFO costs are matched with revenues and income will include "inventory profits," perhaps in substantial amounts. While firms usually invoke the matching principle to justify a switch to LIFO, one must wonder whether as many firms would use LIFO if it were not available for tax purposes.

Problems with LIFO

While LIFO does avoid the payment of income taxes and the "problem" of inventory profits, it creates serious problems for the financial statement user.

Comparability   One major problem LIFO creates is a lack of comparability. It probably seems reasonable that the financial statements of a firm using LIFO cannot be compared with those of a firm using FIFO. The differences between the firms would be difficult to characterize. Are the differences due to real differences between the firms or merely to the fact that one uses LIFO and the other uses FIFO? What is perhaps less obvious is that the financial statements of two firms using LIFO cannot be easily compared either. This is because the amount of the difference between LIFO cost of inventory and current cost depends on how long the firm has been using LIFO. If the firm has been using LIFO for only a short while, then the LIFO cost of its inventory will not be too different from FIFO cost. However, if the firm has been using LIFO for 20 years, then inventory will include some 20-year-old costs, and LIFO inventory will differ significantly from FIFO.

Inventory Liquidations   Another problem with LIFO is that the cost of goods sold figure and, hence, the firm's income, can be significantly affected by changes in the level of purchasing or production. This can be easily demonstrated with a simple example. Consider the following data used to calculate a firm's cost of goods sold:

Beginning inventory	1,000	×	$5.00	=	$ 5,000
Purchases:						
Jan. 1 – June 30	5,000	×	$7.00	=	35,000
July 1 – Dec. 31	6,000	×	$7.50	=	45,000
	11,000				80,000
Available for sale	12,000				85,000
Ending inventory	1,000	×	$5.00	=	5,000
Cost of goods sold	11,000				$80,000

Now suppose that for some reason, purchases in the second half of the year only amounted to 5,500 units instead of the 6,000 reported above. The revised cost of goods sold calculation would appear as follows:

Beginning inventory	1,000	×	$5.00	=	$ 5,000
Purchases:						
Jan. 1 – June 30	5,000	×	$7.00	=	35,000
July 1 – Dec. 31	5,500	×	$7.50	=	41,250
	10,500				76,250
Available for sale	11,500				81,250
Ending inventory	500	×	$5.00	=	2,500
Cost of goods sold	11,000				$78,750

Notice that for the same number of units sold (11,000), the cost assigned to those units sold is now $78,750, instead of the $80,000 calculated above.

How can changing the level of purchasing (or production for a manufacturing firm) affect the cost of goods sold calculation? Under LIFO, old costs remain on the balance sheet. If the firm, intentionally or otherwise, allows its inventory levels to fall, it will liquidate or "dip" into those old costs (called LIFO layers), allowing them to flow out to the cost of goods sold calculation. Thus, in a period where the current cost of the item is $7.50, LIFO matches an old $5.00 unit cost with revenues. This is what accounts for the decrease in cost of goods sold.

As we have already seen in The Coleman Company, Inc., case above, it is frequently said of LIFO that it matches current costs with current revenues. We have just seen that this is not strictly true. If inventory levels are allowed to fall, LIFO will match older costs with current revenues.

Interim Reporting   Related to the problem of inventory liquidations is the problem LIFO presents for interim financial reporting. In 1973, the Accounting Principles Board decided that interim periods, typically quarters, must be viewed as an integral part of the fiscal year.[15] This implies that the results of operations for a year should equal the sum of the results of operations for the four quarters. This seems reasonable enough; but under LIFO, this result will often not be obtained routinely.

As we observed in the examples above, LIFO can produce different results, depending on whether it is applied under a periodic system or a perpetual system. What causes the differences is the effect of temporary liquidations of LIFO inventory layers that will be replenished by year-end. This is the same cause of the interim reporting problems presented by LIFO.

Suppose a ski shop using the LIFO method routinely allows its inventory level to fall in the off-season but replenishes it later in the year. Thus, although in a particular quarter inventory quantities may decrease, on an annual basis no decrease is expected. If a quarter is viewed as a separate reporting period, then the decrease in inventory quantities in the off-season will produce a partial liquidation of LIFO layers as discussed above. However, as APB Opinion No. 28 requires, the quarters must be viewed as integral parts of the year; and partial liquidations that are expected to be replenished by year-end must be ignored. The following example illustrates the problem.

Seasonal Ski Shop uses the LIFO method and reports the following amounts:

Beginning inventory:	500 pairs	×	$100.00	=	$ 50,000
Purchases, 1st quarter	600 pairs	×	$125.00	=	75,000
Purchases, 2nd quarter	800 pairs	×	$137.50	=	110,000
Total purchases	1,400				$185,000
Sales, 1st quarter	800 pairs				
Sales, 2nd quarter	600 pairs				
Total sales	1,400 pairs				

If LIFO is applied to the two quarters independently, cost of goods sold would be calculated as follows:

15 "Interim Financial Reporting," *Accounting Principles Board Opinion No. 28*, (New York: AICPA, 1973).

	1st Qtr.	2nd Qtr.
Beginning inventory	$ 50,000	$ 30,000
Purchases	75,000	110,000
Cost of goods available for sale	$125,000	$140,000
Less: Ending inventory	(30,000)*	(57,500)**
Cost of goods sold	$ 95,000	$ 82,500

* 500 pr. + 600 pr. − 800 pr. = 300 pr. × $100 = $30,000

** 300 pr. + 800 pr. − 600 pr. = 500 pr.

Under LIFO, these units would be valued as follows:

300 pr.	×	$100.00	=	$30,000
200 pr.	×	$137.50	=	27,500
500 pr.				$57,500

Under this approach, the total cost of goods sold for the first half-year would be:

Cost of goods sold:

1st quarter	$ 95,000
2nd quarter	82,500
Total, first half	$177,500

Alternatively, consider the half-year as a single period. Under this approach, cost of goods sold can be calculated as follows:

Beginning inventory:	500 pairs	×	$100.00	=	$ 50,000
Purchases, 1st quarter	600 pairs	×	$125.00	=	$ 75,000
Purchases, 2nd quarter	800 pairs	×	$137.50	=	110,000
Total purchases	1,400 pairs				$185,000
Available for sale	1,900 pairs				$235,000
Ending inventory	500 pairs				50,000*
Cost of goods sold					$185,000

*500 pairs × $100 = $50,000

Notice that the cost of goods sold for the half-year in the second calculation ($185,000) does not equal the sum of the two quarterly cost of goods sold amounts from the first calculation ($177,500). Because sales of 800 pairs of skis exceeded the quantity purchased in the first quarter (600 pairs), a partial liquidation of LIFO inventory has taken place in the first quarter. However, that partial liquidation of inventory quantities has been replenished by the end of the second quarter. Under generally accepted accounting principles, if the liquidation is temporary, it is assumed not to have taken place; and cost of goods sold "shall include the expected replacement cost of the liquidated LIFO base."[16]

Thus, the first quarter cost of goods sold in this example should include the expected cost of replacing the 200 pairs of skis that came out of beginning inventory. If we assume Seasonal Ski Shop anticipated the price increase to $137.50 per pair of skis in the second quarter, its entry to record cost of goods sold for the first quarter would be as follows:

1. To record cost of goods sold for the first quarter:

Cost of goods sold (600 pr. × $125.00)	75,000	
Cost of goods sold (200 pr. × $137.50)	27,500	
Inventory (600 pr. × $125.00)		75,000
Inventory (200 pr. × $100.00)		20,000
Excess of replacement cost over LIFO cost of layer temporarily liquidated		7,500

The account excess of replacement cost over LIFO cost of layer temporarily liquidated would be included on the interim balance sheet at the end of the first quarter as a current liability.

Seasonal Ski Shop would record purchases and cost of goods sold for the second quarter as follows:

2. To record purchase of 800 pairs of skis × $137.50:

Inventory (200 × $100.00)	20,000	
Inventory (600 × $137.50)	82,500	
Excess of replacement cost over LIFO cost of layer temporarily liquidated	7,500	
Accounts payable		110,000

3. To record cost of goods sold in the second quarter:

Cost of goods sold (600 × $137.50)	82,500	
Inventory		82,500

Notice how under this approach, the sum of the cost of goods sold for the first quarter ($102,500) plus cost of goods sold for the second quarter ($82,500) is $185,000, or the same amount we calculated above for the half-year as a whole.

Restating LIFO Financial Statements

Because of these problems, it is essential that users of financial statements have the ability to convert from the LIFO method to a method such as FIFO or average cost, which does not have the same problems.

To illustrate how this is accomplished, consider the following information taken from the 1989 annual report of Clark Equipment Co.

The "Summary of Significant Accounting Policies" section of Clark's annual report contains the following explanation of how the company accounts for inventories:

---

[16] "Interim Financial Reporting," *Accounting Principles Board Opinion No. 8*, (New York: AICPA, 1973), para. 14b.

Inventories are valued at the lower of cost or market by the last-in, first-out (LIFO) method for domestic inventories and by the first-in, first-out (FIFO) method for foreign subsidiaries. If the FIFO method of inventory accounting had been used worldwide, inventories would have increased by $62.8 million at December 31, 1989 and $59.7 million at December 31, 1988.

The balance sheet showed that inventories at December 31, 1989, and December 31, 1988, were $180.0 million and $152.1 million, respectively. The 1989 cost of goods sold was $1,133.7 million. The effective income tax rate was 42.3%.

If Clark had used FIFO instead of LIFO as an inventory flow assumption, what would its 1989 cost of goods sold have been? The following calculation shows the answer to this question (in $ millions):

	LIFO	Adjustment	FIFO
Beginning inventory	$ 152.1	$59.7	$ 211.8
+ Cost of goods acquired	1,161.6	–	1,161.6
– Ending inventory	180.0	62.8	242.8
= Cost of goods sold	$1,133.7	$ (3.1)	$1,130.6

We have recreated the LIFO cost of goods sold calculation and adjusted the beginning and ending inventory amounts to FIFO. While the cost of goods acquired amount was not given, it was easily calculated. We observe that inventory, under LIFO, increased from $152.1 million to $180.0 million, an increase of $27.9 million. This implies that cost of goods acquired must have exceeded cost of goods sold by this amount. Since cost of goods sold is given at $1,133.7 million, cost of goods acquired must have been $1,161.6 million.

The difference between the LIFO value of inventory and its FIFO value, sometimes called the **LIFO reserve**, was $59.7 million on December 31, 1988, and $62.8 million on December 31, 1989. This increase in the LIFO reserve of $3.1 million indicates that the cost of Clark's inventory has increased during the year ended December 31, 1989, resulting in a wider disparity between LIFO and FIFO costs. The net effect of the two adjustments to the cost of goods sold calculation is to decrease it by the change in the LIFO reserve. Thus, FIFO cost of goods sold would be lower and income before taxes would be higher by $3.1 million than the comparable amounts reported under LIFO.

Why would Clark want to report income before taxes lower by $3.1 million than the amounts it could report under FIFO? The use of LIFO enables Clark to obtain the tax benefits it can produce. At the firm's reported effective tax rate of 42.3%, Clark's tax savings for this year alone are:

$$\$3.1 \text{ million} \times 42.3\% = \$1.3 \text{ million}$$

How much has Clark saved in total since adopting the LIFO method? If we assume that the tax rate has been steady at roughly 40%, then its cumulative savings amount to:

$$\$62.8 \text{ million} \times 40\% = \$25.1 \text{ million}$$

The reason for the attractiveness of the LIFO method in periods of rising prices is apparent in this example.

What price has Clark had to pay for the tax benefits of LIFO? It is reporting an inventory amount that is $62.8 million lower than the amount it would report under FIFO. Moreover, Clark's owners' equity is lower by roughly the following amount:

$$\$62.8 \text{ million} \times (1 - .40) = \$37.7 \text{ million}$$

Clark's reported net income has been lower each year as well, assuming there has been a steady increase in the LIFO reserve each year. Thus, while Clark's financial statements have appeared much worse under LIFO, the firm is clearly better off with a cumulative tax savings of $25.1 million. Such are the mysteries of LIFO.

This example can be used to consider the effect of LIFO on certain key ratios derived from the financial statements. This can be illustrated best by looking at the **inventory turnover ratio**, a measure of how quickly inventory moves through the firm. This ratio is usually defined as:

$$\text{Inventory turnover} = \text{Cost of goods sold} \div \text{Inventory}$$

Using the figures for Clark, the inventory turnover ratio can be calculated under both LIFO and FIFO.

$$\text{LIFO:}\quad \$1{,}133.7 \div \$180.0 = 6.30$$

$$\text{FIFO:}\quad \$1{,}130.6 \div \$242.8 = 4.66$$

Under LIFO, inventory appears to be turning over much more rapidly than it actually is. The reason for this anomaly is that, under LIFO, the cost of goods sold figure is stated at very current costs, while the inventory, at least in part, is stated at very old costs. Since costs have been rising, the result is a much inflated inventory turnover. The point of this example is that any ratios derived from LIFO financial statements should be treated very cautiously, especially those involving the inventory figure, which is likely to involve costs old enough to render it useless.

What can we conclude about the LIFO inventory method? While it is a marvelous way of minimizing income tax payments in periods of rising prices, it leaves much to be desired as a financial reporting technique.

THE LOWER-OF-COST-OR-MARKET RULE

We have now seen how inventory cost is determined. Inventory cost is a function of the cost flow assumption employed and the method used to determine inventory quantities. Our treatment of the basic issues in accounting for inventory and cost of goods sold will be complete once we consider the valuation rule applied to inventories—the lower-of-cost-or-market value.

While inventories are generally valued at their historical cost, the accounting profession decided that "a departure from the cost basis of inventory pricing is required when the utility of the goods is no longer as great as its cost."[17] "Utility of the goods" is a difficult concept to measure directly, and the profession wisely decided to measure this through market values. Thus, when market value of inventory falls below cost, it is necessary to write the inventory down to the lower market value.

This *lower-of-cost-or-market (LCM) rule* is a direct application of conservatism in accounting. Notice that under this rule, inventories can be written down below original cost but are never written up above cost. Apparently, overstatement of asset values is deemed to be a far more serious problem than understatement.

Application of the LCM Rule

We have spent the bulk of this chapter discussing how inventory costs are determined. But what is meant by market value of inventories? In general, **market value** means the replacement cost of the inventory whether replacement is effected by purchasing or producing the inventory. However, GAAP places some limits on the definition of market value for the purposes of applying the LCM rule. The maximum amount for market value is the *net realizable value (NRV)* of the inventory ("estimated selling price in the ordinary course of business less reasonably predictable costs of completion and disposal"), while the minimum amount for market value is "net realizable value reduced by an allowance for an approximately normal profit margin."[18]

For example, consider a finished item in inventory that sells for $18. The firm's prices are set at an average markup of 80% over cost. Thus, selling price is 180% of average cost, or cost is 55.6% (100 ÷ 180) of selling price. Thus, a normal profit margin is 44.4% of selling price, or $8 for the item under consideration. In this situation, the maximum amount for market value under the LCM rule is $18, and the minimum is $10 ($18 − 8). As long as the replacement cost of the unit is greater than $10 but less than $18, it will be used as market value in applying the LCM rule.

If these definitions of the maximum and minimum amounts for market value in the LCM rule are to be anything more than a set of arbitrary rules, then there must be some reason for them. The rule clearly seems to indicate that under normal circumstances, the replacement cost of an item is the best measure of its market value. The maximum and minimum amounts are designed to deal with those unusual situations when the use of replacement cost does not make sense. For instance, if the cost of replacing a unit in inventory (say, $20) has risen above the net realizable value of the unit ($18), it is unlikely that the item will be replaced, and the item's market value is clearly not as high as replacement cost would seem to indicate. Alternatively, the firm may

---

[17] *Accounting Research Bulletin No. 43, op. cit.,* ch. 4, para. 8.

[18] *Ibid.,* para. 9.

have a long-term contract to supply an item to a customer at a fixed price. In such cases, even if the replacement cost of the item falls sharply, the nature of the contract will prevent the value of the item from falling as much as the decline in replacement cost would seem to indicate.

Taken together, the maximum and minimum amounts for market value can be said to define the "ceiling and the floor of a market range." If replacement cost falls within the "market range," then it is used in applying the LCM rule. If replacement cost is greater than NRV, use NRV (the "ceiling") as market value in applying the LCM rule. If replacement cost is less than NRV – normal profit margin or NPM, use NRV – NPM (the "floor") as market value in applying the LCM rule. See Figure 8.1.

To illustrate the application of the LCM rule, consider the following example of four items taken from the inventory of Basic Business Products, Inc.:

	Item A	Item B	Item C	Item D
Cost	$40	$16	$55	$27
Net realizable value	52	27	60	25
Replacement cost	46	17	54	26
NRV – NPM	45	19	52	23
LCM	40	16	54	25

To apply the LCM rule to these four items, first determine the market value, then compare it with cost, and finally select the lower amount of the two.

Item A: Replacement cost of $46 is in the "market range" and, therefore, is used as market value. Since market value is greater than cost of $40, Item A would be carried at $40 per unit under the LCM rule.

Item B: Replacement cost of $17 is less than (NRV – NPM) of $19 and, therefore, below the "market range." $19 is then used as market value; and since it is greater than the cost of $16, Item A would be carried at $16 per unit under the LCM rule.

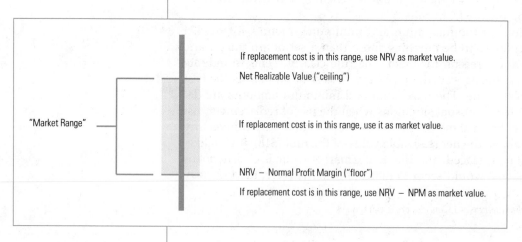

If replacement cost is in this range, use NRV as market value.

Net Realizable Value ("ceiling")

"Market Range"

If replacement cost is in this range, use it as market value.

NRV – Normal Profit Margin ("floor")

If replacement cost is in this range, use NRV – NPM as market value.

| FIGURE 8.1
The Lower-of-Cost-or-Market Value Rule

Item C: Replacement cost of $54 is in the market range and below the cost of $55. Therefore, Item C would be carried at $54 per unit under the LCM rule.

Item D: Replacement cost of $26 is above NRV of $25 and, therefore, above the "market range." $25 is then used as market value; and since this is less than the cost of $27, Item D would be carried at $25 under the LCM rule.

For Items C and D, which are effectively written down below their cost, the new lower carrying value will be treated as cost in subsequent periods.

The examples above have demonstrated application of the LCM rule on an item-by-item basis. It may also be applied to categories of inventory or to inventory as a whole. In general, more write-downs will be necessary when the LCM rule is applied to individual items than when it is applied to categories of inventory or inventory as a whole. The reason for this is that when looking at groups of inventory items, declines in market values of particular items may be offset by increases in the market values of other items. This "offsetting" is not possible when the unit of analysis is a single item.

To record the write-down of inventory amounts to a market value below cost, two approaches are possible. Perhaps the simplest approach is to reduce inventory and increase cost of goods sold by the amount of the adjustment. A somewhat more elaborate, but perhaps more useful, alternative is to use a separate allowance account to record the decrease in the carrying value of the inventory and a separate loss account to record the adjustment.

To illustrate these two approaches, assume there are 1,000 units of Item C (above) in inventory, each of which has a cost of $27 and a market value of $25. To write down the inventory in this situation, either of the following entries would be appropriate for a perpetual inventory system:

1. To write down inventory to LCM:

Cost of goods sold	2,000	
Inventory		2,000

2. To write down inventory to LCM:

Inventory loss from decline of market value below cost	2,000	
Allowance to record inventory at LCM		2,000

The advantage of the second adjusting entry is that losses from declines in market value of inventory are accounted for separately rather than buried in with cost of goods sold. This separate accounting is preferable since the loss really had nothing to do with the sale of goods and, therefore, its inclusion with cost of goods sold is inappropriate.

Purchase Commitments

Closely related to the LCM rule is the treatment of losses on purchase commitments. Some companies enter into long-term contracts with their suppliers to insure an uninterrupted supply of some crucial item of inventory. For instance, suppose a steel mill enters into a long-term contract with a coal mining company to purchase the coal required to operate its blast furnaces. Under this contract, the steel mill is required to purchase a minimum quantity of coal in the upcoming year at some prespecified price. When such contracts (sometimes known as "take or pay" contracts) exist and result in commitments of a material amount, disclosure of the nature and amount of the commitments is necessary. This is handled by a footnote to the financial statements. No formal entry is required to record the purchase contract until goods are actually shipped by the seller.

Suppose the contract between the steel mill and the coal mine calls for purchase of a minimum of 5 million tons of coal at a price of $52.00 per ton in the upcoming year. Suppose further that since this contract was executed, the market price of coal has fallen to $50.00 per ton at the end of the current fiscal year. Under generally accepted accounting principles, the steel mill would be required to accrue a loss from the contract in the period in which the prices decline rather than when the purchases are actually made.[19] Thus, at the end of the current period, the steel mill would be required to record a loss of $2.00 per ton on the minimum required purchase of 5 million tons, or $10 million, as follows:

1. To accrue loss of $2 per ton on the commitment to purchase 5 million tons of coal:

Purchase commitment loss	10,000,000	
Accrued purchase commitment loss		10,000,000

On the date the coal is actually purchased, it will be recorded at its market value, which is lower than the cost incurred under the long-term contract.

2. To record purchase of 5 million tons of coal at contract price of $52 when market price is $50:

Coal inventory	250,000,000	
Accrued purchase commitment loss	10,000,000	
Cash		260,000,000

Thus, the inventory is effectively recorded at the lower-of-cost-or-market value. The motivation for this accounting treatment is exactly the same as that for the LCM rule illustrated above—conservatism.

As you would probably expect, if the market price of coal recovers to $52 or above per ton before any purchases are made, the accrued loss would be eliminated. The entry is as follows:

3. To record recovery of accrued loss on long-term purchase commitments for coal:

Accrued purchase commitment loss	10,000,000	
Recovery of commitment loss		10,000,000

This, too, is consistent with the LCM valuation approach. By eliminating the accrued loss, the subsequent purchase will be recorded at cost. Notice that no accrued gain is recognized if the market price of coal goes above $52 per ton. That would lead to recording the subsequent purchase at a market value above cost, which is inconsistent with the LCM rule.

---

[19] *Accounting Research Bulletin No. 43, op. cit.,* ch. 4, para. 16.

SUMMARY

This chapter has covered the basic issues of accounting for inventories and cost of goods sold. Inventories are valued at LCM—the lower-of-cost-or-market value. Cost is determined both by the firm's cost flow assumption and record keeping system. Cost flow assumptions include first-in, first-out (FIFO); last-in, first-out (LIFO); and average cost. Record keeping systems used include the perpetual inventory system and the periodic inventory system. Perpetual inventory systems and periodic inventory systems are not mutually exclusive. Firms often use a perpetual inventory system for control purposes but calculate and report their cost of goods sold on a periodic basis.

LIFO has become increasingly popular due in large part to the tax savings it affords in periods of rising prices, which have been characteristic of the U.S. economy in recent decades, and the "conformity rule" that requires its use for financial reporting purposes if it is used for tax purposes. Despite its popularity, LIFO presents a number of problems to the user and preparer of financial statements, including the problems of LIFO liquidations, interim reporting, profit manipulation, and the distortion of the relationship between the balance sheet and income statements.

Market value, for the purposes of applying the LCM rule, is defined as replacement cost subject to maximum and minimum limitations. The maximum or "ceiling" amount for market value is the net realizable value of the item in inventory. The minimum or "floor" amount for market value is the net realizable value minus a normal profit margin.

QUESTIONS

1. If goods shipped *F.O.B. destination* are in transit at the end of an accounting period, are they included in the buyer's or seller's inventory? Why?

2. Who has title to goods out on consignment? Who includes them in inventory?

3. Penny Publishing Co. sells the books it publishes to bookstores and allows its customers to return any copies unsold after six months. On average, Penny has experienced a 10% return rate. Should Penny include 10% of the books sold over the past six months in its inventory on the grounds that it is likely to get them back? Why or why not?

4. How should the following items affect the costs to be included in a manufacturer's inventory?
   (a) Insurance on raw materials while in transit
   (b) Cash discounts taken on purchased raw materials
   (AICPA adapted)

5. What are the advantages and disadvantages of the *periodic inventory system*?

6. What are the advantages and disadvantages of the *perpetual inventory system*?

7. Explain why it is not always possible or practicable to account for inventories with the *specific identification method*.

8. Which method of inventory pricing best approximates specific identification of the actual flow of costs and units in most manufacturing situations?
(AICPA adapted)

9. In a period of rising prices, the use of which inventory cost flow methods would typically result in the highest cost of goods sold?
(AICPA adapted)

10. Explain why the following statement is true or false:
The use of LIFO permits some control by management over the amount of net income for a period through controlled purchases, which is not true with FIFO.
(AICPA adapted)

11. When a firm using the LIFO method liquidates some of its inventory, how will net income typically be affected? Why?

12. How are seasonal LIFO inventory liquidations accounted for on interim financial statements?

13. How should freight costs incurred in the transfer of consigned goods from the consignor to the consignee be accounted for?
(AICPA adapted)

14. What accounting treatments are available for cash discounts permitted on purchased raw materials? Which of these methods do you recommend? Why?
(AICPA adapted)

15. Why do firms such as IBM and Apple Computer choose not to use the LIFO inventory method?

EXERCISES

8-1. *Items included in inventory*

The inventory of Roberts & Co. at December 31, 1993, was $2,500,000 based on a physical count of goods on hand. The following transactions may require adjustments:

(a) Goods shipped F.O.B. shipping point from a vendor on December 28, 1993, to Roberts & Co. were received on January 3, 1994. Their cost was $75,000.

(b) Goods shipped F.O.B. destination to a customer on December 30, 1993, arrived on January 2, 1994. Their cost was $116,000.

(c) Included in the physical count were goods that were prepared for shipment on December 31, 1993. These goods, costing $71,000, were to be shipped F.O.B. shipping point. The invoice was sent to the customer on December 31, but the goods were not picked up by the carrier until January 2, 1994.

(d) Included in the physical count were goods costing $30,000 that had been received on consignment from Thomas Brothers Co.

REQUIRED:

What amount should Roberts & Co. report as inventory on its December 31, 1993, balance sheet?

8-2. *Costs included in inventory*

Dean Sportswear, Inc., regularly buys sweaters from Mill Company and is allowed a trade discount of 30% from the list price. Dean made a purchase on

March 20, 1993, and received an invoice with a list price of $6,000, a freight charge of $150, and payment terms of net 30 days.

REQUIRED:

At what amount should Dean record the purchase?
(AICPA adapted)

8-3.   *Purchase discounts*

Dixon Menswear Shop regularly buys shirts from Colt Company and is allowed trade discounts of 20% from the list price. Dixon purchased shirts from Colt on May 27, 1993, and received an invoice with a list price amount of $5,000 and payment terms of 2/10, n/30. Dixon uses the net method to record purchases.

REQUIRED:

At what amount should Dixon record the purchase?
(AICPA adapted)

8-4.   *Costs included in inventory*

The following costs were among those incurred by Woodcroft Corporation during 1993:

Merchandise purchased for resale	$500,000
Sales commissions	40,000
Interest on notes payable to vendors	5,000

REQUIRED:

How much should be charged to the cost of the merchandise purchases?
(AICPA adapted)

8-5.   *Manufactured inventories*

Danforth Manufacturing Co. reports the following amounts:

Gross profit for 1993	$ 61,000
Cost of goods manufactured in 1993	437,000

	Raw Materials	Work in Process	Finished Goods
Balance, December 31, 1992	$16,000	$7,000	$41,000
Balance, December 31, 1993	24,000	9,000	38,000

REQUIRED:

Calculate sales for 1993.

8-6.   *Costs included in inventory*

Glen Company has the following data pertaining to the year ended December 31, 1993:

Purchases	$450,000
Beginning inventory	170,000
Ending inventory	210,000
Freight-in	50,000
Freight-out	75,000

REQUIRED:

Determine the cost of goods sold for 1993.

(AICPA adapted)

8-7. *Purchase commitments*

During 1993, R Corp., a manufacturer of chocolate candies, contracted to purchase 100,000 pounds of cocoa beans at $1.00 per pound, delivery to be made in the spring of 1994. Because a record harvest is predicted for 1994, the price per pound for cocoa beans had fallen to $.80 by December 31, 1993.

REQUIRED:

What journal entry (if any) is necessary to reflect in 1993 the effect of the commitment of R Corp. to purchase the 100,000 pounds of cocoa?

(AICPA adapted)

Exercises 8-8 through 8-13 are based on the following information:

The following information was available from the inventory records of the Alexander Company for January 1993:

	Units	Unit Cost	Total Cost
Balance at January 1, 1993	5,000	$13.685	$ 68,425
Purchases:			
January 6, 1993	3,750	14.420	54,075
January 26, 1993	8,500	15.050	127,925
Sales:			
January 7, 1993	4,500		
January 31, 1993	8,000		
Balance at January 31, 1993	4,750		

8-8. *Average cost method: perpetual system*

REQUIRED:

Calculate inventory at January 31, 1993, and cost of goods sold for the month then ended, assuming Alexander uses the perpetual inventory system and the average cost inventory method.

8-9. *Average cost method: periodic system*

REQUIRED:

Calculate inventory at January 31, 1993, and cost of goods sold for the month then ended, assuming Alexander uses the periodic inventory system and the weighted average cost inventory method.

8-10. *LIFO method: perpetual system*

REQUIRED:

Calculate inventory at January 31, 1993, and cost of goods sold for the month then ended, assuming Alexander uses the perpetual inventory system and the LIFO cost inventory method.

8-11. *LIFO method: periodic system*

REQUIRED:

Calculate inventory at January 31, 1993, and cost of goods sold for the month then ended, assuming Alexander uses the periodic inventory system and the LIFO cost inventory method.

8-12. *FIFO method: perpetual system*

REQUIRED:

Calculate inventory at January 31, 1993, and cost of goods sold for the month then ended, assuming Alexander uses the perpetual inventory system and the FIFO cost inventory method.

8-13. *FIFO method: periodic system*

REQUIRED:

Calculate inventory at January 31, 1993, and cost of goods sold for the month then ended, assuming Alexander uses the periodic inventory system and the FIFO cost inventory method.

Exercises 8-14 through 8-16 are based on the following information:

Marsh Company had 750 units of Product A on hand at January 1, 1993, costing $25.20 each. Purchases of Product A during the month of January were as follows:

	Units	Unit Cost
Jan. 10	1,000	$26.40
Jan. 18	1,250	27.60
Jan. 28	500	28.80

A physical count on January 31, 1993, shows 1,250 units of Product A on hand.

8-14. *LIFO method: periodic system*

REQUIRED:

What is the cost of the inventory at January 31, 1993, and the cost of goods sold for the month then ended under the LIFO method?

8-15. *FIFO method: periodic system*

REQUIRED:

What is the cost of the inventory at January 31, 1993, and the cost of goods sold for the month then ended under the FIFO method?

8-16. *Average cost method: periodic system*

REQUIRED:

What is the cost of the inventory at January 31, 1993, and the cost of goods sold for the month then ended under the average cost method?

8-17. *Moving average unit cost*

REQUIRED:

Frey Company recorded the following data pertaining to Raw Material Y during January 1993:

Date	Units Received	Unit Cost	Units Issued	Units on Hand
1/1/93		$250		2,400
1/8/93			1,200	1,200
1/20/93	3,600	$300		4,800

REQUIRED:

Calculate the moving average unit cost of Y inventory at January 31, 1993.

8-18. *Restatement from LIFO to FIFO*

The Southwestern Company reported the following amounts (000s omitted):

	12/31/93	12/31/92	12/31/91
Inventory at LIFO cost	$55,773	$ 44,846	$42,115
LIFO reserve	49,788	105,467	18,723

Its cost of goods sold was $159,652 for the year ended December 31, 1993 and $209,331 for the year ended December 31, 1992.

REQUIRED:

What would Southwestern Company's cost of goods sold have been for both years under the FIFO method? How can you explain the large decrease in the LIFO reserve for the year ended December 31, 1993?

8-19. *Lower-of-cost-or-market value rule*

At December 31, 1993, the following data pertain to an inventory item held by American Novelty Company:

Estimated selling price	$83
Normal profit margin	17
Estimated cost of disposal	1
Cost	70
Replacement cost	62

REQUIRED:

Under the lower-of-cost-or-market rule, at what amount should this inventory item be valued?

8-20. *Lower-of-cost-or-market value rule*

Horsepower Corporation has two products in its ending inventory, each accounted for at the lower-of-cost-or-market. A profit margin of 25% on the selling price is considered normal for each product. Specific data with respect to each product follows:

	Product A	Product B
Historical cost	$42.50	$ 67.50
Replacement cost	37.50	69.00
Estimated cost to dispose	12.50	39.00
Estimated selling price	75.00	150.00

REQUIRED:

In applying the lower-of-cost-or-market rule, what unit values should Horsepower use for Products A and B?

PROBLEMS

8-1. *Cost flow assumptions: periodic vs. perpetual systems*

The inventory records of Herbert Corp. include the following information:

	Units	Cost/Unit	Total Cost
Balance, 1/1/93	400	$20	$8,000
Purchases:			
2/24/93	200	21	4,200
9/23/93	100	22	2,200
12/28/93	100	23	2,300
Sales:			
6/16/93	300		
11/15/93	300		

REQUIRED:

Calculate the 1993 cost of goods sold and the December 31, 1993, ending inventory for *both* periodic and perpetual inventory systems assuming the following cost flow assumptions:

1. First-in, first-out
2. Last-in, first-out
3. Average cost

8-2. *Alternative cost flow assumptions*

Boston Beanies, Inc. is a hat retailer. Information for the quarter ended June 30, 1993, is as follows:

	Units	Cost/Unit	Total Cost
Inventory, April 1	16,000	$5.00	$ 80,000
Purchase, April 20	12,800	5.20	66,560
Purchase, May 12	8,000	5.18	41,440
Purchase, May 31	11,200	5.40	60,480
Purchase, June 20	19,200	5.30	101,760

During the quarter, Boston Beanies sold 43,200 hats at $12 each.

REQUIRED:

Calculate gross profit for the quarter under the FIFO, LIFO, and average cost methods.

8-3. *Manufactured inventories*

Baltimore Ballistics is a manufacturing company. It reports the activities for 1994:

Activities in 1994:	
Raw materials purchased	1,025,450
Direct factory labor costs	2,230,500
Factory overhead costs	3,521,050

Inventory balances at the end of 1993 and 1994 are as follows:

	December 31, 1994	1993
Inventory balances:		
Raw materials	$112,650	$103,200
Work in process	48,490	42,925
Finished goods	123,820	125,665

REQUIRED:

Calculate the cost of goods sold for 1994.

8-4.   *Manufactured inventories*

Camden Can Company manufactures aluminum beer kegs. Information for 1993 is as follows:

Beginning inventory	5,000 kegs × $10.00 per keg
Fixed manufacturing cost for 1993	$50,000
Variable manufacturing cost for 1993	$8.00 per keg

Camden expects to sell 20,000 kegs during 1993 but has the capacity to produce 25,000 kegs.

REQUIRED:

1. If the company sells 20,000 kegs, calculate FIFO cost of goods sold assuming that 20,000 kegs are produced.
2. If the company sells 20,000 kegs, calculate FIFO cost of goods sold assuming that 25,000 kegs are produced.
3. Explain why the cost of goods sold depends on the volume of production.

8-5.   *Items included in inventory, cost of goods sold, accounts payable*

Layne Corporation, a manufacturer of small tools, provided the following information from its accounting records for the year ended December 31, 1993:

Inventory at December 31, 1993 (based on physical count of goods in Layne's plant at cost on December 31, 1993)	$1,750,000
Accounts payable at December 31, 1993	1,200,000
Net sales (sales less sales returns)	8,500,000

Additional information is as follows:
(a) Included in the physical count were tools billed to a customer F.O.B. shipping point on December 31, 1993. These tools had a cost of $28,000 and were billed at $35,000. The shipment was on Layne's loading dock waiting to be picked up by the common carrier.
(b) Goods were in transit from a vendor to Layne on December 31, 1993. The invoice cost was $50,000, and the goods were shipped F.O.B. shipping point on December 29, 1993.
(c) Work-in-process inventory costing $20,000 was sent to an outside processor for plating on December 30, 1993.
(d) Tools returned by customers and held pending inspection in the returned goods area on December 31, 1993, were not included in the physical count. On January 8, 1994, the tools costing $26,000 were inspected and returned to inventory. Credit memos totaling $40,000 were issued to the customers on the same date.

(e) Tools shipped to a customer F.O.B. destination on December 26, 1993, were in transit at December 31, 1993, and had a cost of $25,000. Upon notification of receipt by the customer on January 2, 1994, Layne issued a sales invoice for $42,000.

(f) Goods, with an invoice cost of $30,000, received from a vendor at 5:00 p.m. on December 31, 1993, were recorded on a receiving report dated January 2, 1994. The goods were not included in the physical count, but the invoice was included in accounts payable at December 31, 1993.

(g) Goods received from a vendor on December 26, 1993, were included in the physical count. However, the related $60,000 vendor invoice was not included in accounts payable at December 31, 1993, because the accounts payable copy of the receiving report was lost.

(h) On January 3, 1994, a monthly freight bill in the amount of $4,000 was received. The bill specifically related to merchandise purchased in December 1993, one-half of which was still in inventory at December 31, 1993. The freight charges were not included in either the inventory or in accounts payable at December 31, 1993.

REQUIRED:

Using the format shown below, prepare a schedule of adjustments as of December 31, 1993, to the initial amounts per Layne's accounting records. If the transactions would have no effect on the initial amount shown, state NONE. (AICPA adapted)

	Inventory	Accounts Payable	Net Sales
Initial amounts	$1,750,000	$1,200,000	$8,500,000
Adjustments—			
increase			
(decrease)			
a.			
b.			
.			
.			
.			
Total adjustment	_____	_____	_____
Adjustment amounts	$_____	$_____	$_____

8-6.   *Change from FIFO to LIFO*

The Odessa Manufacturing Company manufactures two products: belts and pulleys. At December 31, 1993, Odessa used the first-in, first-out (FIFO) inventory method. Management is considering a change, effective January 1, 1994, to the last-in, last-out (LIFO) inventory method. If the change were made, the ending FIFO inventory of 1993 would be used as the beginning inventory for 1994 for the LIFO method. Any layers added during 1994 should be costed by reference to the first acquisitions of 1994, and any layers liquidated during 1994 should be considered a permanent liquidation.

The following information was available from Odessa's inventory records for the two most recent years:

	Belts		Pulleys	
	Units	Unit Cost	Units	Unit Cost
1993 production:				
January 7	5,000	$4.00	22,000	$2.00
April 16	12,000	4.50		
November 8	17,000	5.00	18,500	2.50
December 13	10,000	6.00		
1994 production:				
February 11	3,000	7.00	23,000	3.00
May 20	8,000	7.50		
October 15	20,000	8.00		
December 23			15,500	3.50
Units on hand:				
December 31, 1993	15,000		14,500	
December 31, 1994	16,000		13,000	

REQUIRED:

Compute the effect on income before income taxes for the year ended December 31, 1994, if the Odessa Manufacturing Company changes from the FIFO to the LIFO method.

(AICPA adapted)

8-7.   *Restatement from LIFO to LIFO: effects of inventory liquidation*

Portable Technology Inc. reported the following inventory balances ($000s):

	12/31/93	12/31/92
Inventory at LIFO cost	$26,195	$31,920
LIFO reserve	20,858	21,531
Inventory at FIFO cost	$47,053	$53,451

The LIFO cost of goods sold reported on the firm's income statement for the year ended December 31, 1993 was $801,765,000. The notes to the financial statements reveal that if there had been no decrease in inventory quantities during the year, then LIFO cost of goods sold would have been higher by $1,480,000.

REQUIRED:

1. Calculate the cost of goods sold under the FIFO cost flow assumption.
2. How did the decrease in inventory quantities affect the FIFO cost of goods sold and ending inventory balance?
3. Calculate the amount of the LIFO reserve that would have been reported if there had been no decrease in inventory quantities during the year.

8-8.   *LIFO vs. FIFO: effects of inventory liquidation*

Amalgamated Oil Company is a home heating oil distributor. It uses the last-in, first-out (LIFO) method of valuing its inventory but also discloses information about the first-in, first-out (FIFO) cost of its inventory in the notes to its financial statements. Its beginning inventory consists of the following:

Units	LIFO Unit Cost	FIFO Unit Cost
100,000 gal.	$.80	$1.10

Amalgamated expects to sell 1,000,000 gallons of oil during the year. The firm has a contract with its supplier, which calls for a constant purchase price of $1.20 during the year. However, due to shortages of oil, Amalgamated might not be able to purchase as much as it would like.

REQUIRED:

1. If Amalgamated sells 1,000,000 gallons of oil during the year, calculate the ending inventory cost and cost of goods sold for the year under both LIFO and FIFO if it purchases the following two alternative quantities:
   (a) 1,050,000 gallons
   (b) 950,000 gallons
2. In a period of rising prices, will the LIFO method always produce a higher cost of goods sold than FIFO? Explain by reference to your calculations in Requirements 1a and 1b.

8-9. *Interim reporting under LIFO*

MBI Corp. is an importer of cocoa and uses the LIFO inventory method. Information for 1993 is as follows (units are metric tons):

	Qty.	Purchases Price	Total	Sales Qty.
Beginning inventory	10,000	$1,000	$10,000,000	
First quarter	5,000	1,100	5,500,000	6,000
Second quarter	8,000	1,200	9,600,000	10,000
Third quarter	12,000	1,250	15,000,000	10,000
Fourth quarter	13,000	1,250	16,250,000	12,000
Total	38,000		$46,350,000	38,000
Ending inventory	10,000			

REQUIRED:

1. Calculate the amount MBI would report as cost of goods sold for the year.
2. Calculate the amount that MBI would report as cost of goods sold for each quarter on the quarterly financial statements, assuming that any liquidations of inventory that occurred were expected to be replenished by year-end at the price actually paid during the fourth quarter.
3. Calculate the amount of the LIFO reserve at year-end.
4. Suppose that because of a transportation workers' strike, MBI had only been able to purchase 10,000 metric tons during the fourth quarter. Assuming a tax rate of 40%, calculate the effect of the strike on the firm's tax liability for 1993 compared with the planned fourth quarter purchases of 13,000 metric tons.

8-10. *Effect of the LIFO method on management decisions*

Carter Commodity Corp. is a peanut processor, and it uses the LIFO inventory method. At the start of 1993, its inventory consisted of the following layers:

1990	5,000 bushels at $2.70	$13,500
1991	18,000 bushels at $3.00	54,000
1992	2,000 bushels at $3.75	7,500
	25,000	$75,000

Carter tries to maintain an inventory of 25,000 bushels, but, due to unfavorable weather, there has been a shortage of peanuts in 1993; and the price has risen dramatically, as shown below:

Date	Price
12/31/92	$4.00
3/31/93	5.25
6/30/93	6.10
9/30/93	6.00

As of September 30, 1993, Carter has purchased 100,000 bushels at an average cost of $5.50 per bushel. However, it has processed and sold 115,000 bushels, leaving only 10,000 bushels in inventory on that date.

By year-end, the price per bushel is expected to fall to $4.50 and stay at that level. Management is trying to decide whether it should (1) replenish inventories during the fourth quarter by purchasing 15,000 more bushels than it will process or (2) replenish inventories after year-end.

REQUIRED:

1. Calculate cost of goods sold for 1993 under the assumption that Carter purchases 45,000 bushels during the fourth quarter at an average price of $5.10 and processes and sells 30,000 bushels.
2. Calculate cost of goods sold for 1993 under the assumption that Carter purchases 30,000 bushels during the fourth quarter at an average price of $5.10 and processes and sells the same quantity.
3. Carter pays income taxes at a 40% rate. Calculate the difference in Carter's tax liability between Alternatives 1 and 2.
4. What advice would you offer to management about whether it should replenish the inventory during the fourth quarter or after year-end? Would your advice differ if the firm used the FIFO inventory method? Be specific and show any calculations in good form.

8-11. *Liquidation of LIFO inventories*

Harbor Commodity Co. uses the LIFO inventory method. In 1993, the cost of its inventory has risen rapidly as indicated below:

	Units	Cost/Unit
Beginning inv.	10,000	$ 6.43
Purchases:		
1st quarter	30,000	8.48
2nd quarter	40,000	10.51
3rd quarter	25,000	12.67
4th quarter	32,000	13.89
Total	127,000	
Ending inventory	8,000	

At the beginning of the year, the FIFO cost of the inventory was $7.88 per unit.

REQUIRED:

1. Calculate the cost of goods sold for 1993.
2. Suppose the company had purchased enough during the fourth quarter at the prevailing price of $13.89 per unit to avoid any liquidation of inventory quantities. What would the cost of goods sold have been?
3. Calculate the cost of goods sold for 1993 on a FIFO basis.
4. Will liquidations of LIFO inventories always result in lower cost of goods sold than would have been reported under FIFO? Explain your answer.

8-12. *LIFO reserve*

LMI reports the following amounts in its annual report (000s):

	1993	1992
Raw materials	$2,146	$2,525
Work in process	454	760
Finished goods	1,626	2,077
	$4,226	$5,362
Less reduction to LIFO cost	1,458	1,345
Ending inventories, at LIFO cost	$2,768	$4,017

REQUIRED:

How much higher or lower would LMI's income before taxes have been in 1993 if the firm had *not* used the LIFO method? Notice that a liquidation of LIFO inventories has occurred here. Explain your answer.

CASE 8.1

DEERE & COMPANY

The following balance sheets and income statements are excerpted from the 1983 annual report of Deere & Company.

CONSOLIDATED BALANCE SHEET, DEERE & COMPANY
(In thousands of dollars except per share amounts)

	OCTOBER 31, 1983	1982
ASSETS:		
Current assets:		
Cash	$ 56,574	$ 48,101
Short-term investments—at cost, which approximates market value	158,310	4,268
Refundable income taxes	62,736	75,204
Receivables from affiliates	167,883	215,934
Trade receivables, net	2,723,633	2,660,897
Inventories	632,497	760,945
Total current assets	3,801,633	3,765,349
Property and equipment—at cost	2,482,833	2,525,951
Less accumulated depreciation	1,328,018	1,197,891
Property and equipment, net	1,154,815	1,328,060
Investments and advances	826,528	781,233
Other assets	60,034	16,812
Deferred charges	37,002	44,225
Total	$5,880,012	$5,935,679

LIABILITIES AND STOCKHOLDERS' EQUITY:		
Total current liabilities	$2,151,458	$2,395,570
Long-term debt	1,180,295	897,682
Other noncurrent liabilities	272,292	254,231
Stockholders' equity:		
Common stock	487,879	485,953
Retained earnings	1,877,448	1,904,968
Cumulative translation adjustment	(86,635)	
Treasury stock	(2,725)	(2,725)
Total stockholders' equity	2,275,967	2,388,196
Total	$5,880,012	$5,935,679

STATEMENT OF CONSOLIDATED INCOME, DEERE & COMPANY
(In thousands of dollars except per share amounts)

ASSETS:	YEAR ENDED OCTOBER 31,	
	1983	1982
Sales and other income	$4,116,790	$4,770,542
Less:		
Cost of goods sold	3,288,087	3,821,761
Research and development expense	212,224	242,459
Selling, administrative, and general expense	474,179	511,512
Interest expense	229,868	266,581
Other charges	10,496	8,501
Total	$4,214,854	$4,850,814
Income (loss) of consolidated group before taxes	(98,064)	(80,272)
Provision (credit) for income taxes	(46,431)	(40,821)
Income (loss) of consolidated group	(51,633)	(39,451)
Equity in income of unconsolidated subsidiaries and affiliates	74,918	92,349
Net income	$ 23,285	$ 52,898
Net income per share:	$ .34	$ .78

The Deere & Company 1983 annual report also includes the following note regarding the firm's inventories:

Substantially all inventories owned by Deere & Company and its United States subsidiaries are valued at cost on the "last-in, first-out" (LIFO) method. Where local tax and accounting regulations permit, inventories of subsidiaries outside the United States are also generally valued using LIFO methods. Remaining inventories outside the United States are generally valued at the lower of cost, on the "first-in, first-out" (FIFO) basis, or market. The current cost value of gross inventories on the LIFO basis represented 91 percent of total worldwide gross consolidated inventories at current cost value on both October 31, 1983 and 1982.

Company-owned raw material, work-in-process, and finished goods inventories at October 31, 1983 were $632 million compared with $761 million one year ago. During 1983 and 1982, the company's inventories declined due to the lower levels of production. As a result, lower costs were matched against current year revenues, the effect of which was to increase 1983 and 1982 net income by $41.7 million, or 62 cents per share, and $20.8 million, or 31 cents per share, respectively.

During the fourth quarter of 1982, in conjunction with an examination completed by the Internal Revenue Service of certain prior years' United States federal income tax returns, the company increased the valuation of its slow-moving service parts inventories. As a result, 1982 net income was increased by $13.2 million, or 20 cents per share.

If all the company's inventories had been valued on a current cost basis, which approximates FIFO, estimated inventories at October 31, 1983 would have been approximately $1,695 million compared with approximately $1,885 million at October 31, 1982.

The dollar-value method used to price the inventories on a LIFO basis makes it impracticable to classify the inventories according to raw materials, work-in-process, finished goods and supplies.

Note: Assume a 50% income tax rate in answering the following questions.

REQUIRED:

1. What was the amount of Deere & Company's "LIFO reserve" on October 31, 1983 and 1982?
2. Calculate the following amounts that Deere & Company would have reported for 1983 if inventories were valued at FIFO cost:
   (a) Cost of goods sold
   (b) Net income
3. Calculate the following amounts that Deere & Company would have reported at October 31, 1983 and 1982 if inventories were valued at FIFO cost:
   (a) Total current assets
   (b) Total assets
4. Calculate the following financial ratios for Deere & Company for 1983 under both the LIFO and FIFO cost flow assumptions:
   (a) Current ratio
   (b) Inventory turnover ratio
   (c) Total asset turnover
   (d) Return on equity
   (e) Return on assets
5. Estimate the total cumulative tax savings of Deere & Company that have resulted from the use of the LIFO method. Did the company reduce its tax expense in 1983 as a consequence of the LIFO method? Why or why not?
6. It is often stated that LIFO matches current costs with revenues. Is this statement true for Deere & Company in 1983? Why or why not?
7. Summarize the effects of the LIFO method on the 1983 financial statements of Deere & Company.

CASE 8.2

FARMER BROTHERS COMPANY

Farmer Brothers Company is in the coffee business, and the firm uses the LIFO inventory method for its coffee inventories. During July 1975, bad weather destroyed much of the Brazilian coffee crop, resulting in rapidly increasing world coffee prices in 1976 and early 1977. The effect of this on Farmer Brothers was described by the chairman of the board in his 1977 letter to stockholders, as follows:

> The much publicized Brazilian frost of July [1975] and the shortage of coffee which it allegedly created, was used by producing countries to drive the cost of green coffee to record highs. This situation, combined with our use of the Last-In-First-Out method of costing, which channels the latest and most expensive purchases into costs of goods sold and applies those costs against sales made at prices based on earlier and lower costs, resulted in a pre-tax loss of $11,745,859 for fiscal 1977. This loss will enable the company to recover approximately $5,600,000 as a refund of income taxes paid in prior years.

Farmer Brothers' consolidated balance sheets and income statement that were included in the fiscal 1977 annual report are reproduced at the end of the case. Also included in the fiscal 1977 annual report was the following discussion and analysis by management:

> The continuing escalation of green coffee costs through most of fiscal 1977 was directly responsible for the large losses incurred by the company. During the period between January 1, 1977, and March 15, 1977, green coffee costs rose from $2.00 to $3.40 per pound. Farmer Bros. Co., in order to remain competitive, was forced to absorb a portion of additional cost; consequently, our selling prices did not reach a level which would produce reasonable gross profit margins until May 1977. Because the company utilizes the Last-In-First-Out method of accounting for coffee costs, its latest purchases are channeled directly into costs of goods sold and are applied against sales which were made at prices based on earlier and lower priced green coffee purchases. The combination of the LIFO method of accounting and the delay in increasing selling prices produced heavy losses during the third quarter. Fourth quarter operations resulted in the recovery of eight million of the 19 million dollar pre-tax loss incurred in the first nine months. The recovery can be attributed to two factors. First, at March 31, 1977, in anticipating the replacement of (liquidated) LIFO inventory, the company used $3.00 per pound as an estimated cost. Management, however, did not replenish the inventory at the time green coffee was priced at $3.00 but waited and made its purchases at an average price of $2.32 per pound. The difference between the $3.00 estimate and the $2.32 actual cost accounted for approximately $4,750,000 of the fourth quarter profit [before taxes]. Second, the increase in selling prices raised our gross margins to a more reasonable level and this accounted for $3,940,000 in fourth quarter profits, while the addition of 1.9 million pounds of coffee to our LIFO base served to reduce the fourth quarter profit and increase the loss for fiscal 1977.

During fiscal 1977, Farmer Brothers sold 39,545,000 pounds of coffee at a LIFO cost of $93,900,000. Its ending inventory at June 30, 1977, included 19,700,000 pounds of coffee, up from 17,800,000 pounds at June 30, 1976, and 12,800,000 pounds at June 30, 1975. The notes to the financial statements included the following information about inventory costs:

Inventories consist of the following:

	1977	1976	1975
Coffee	$ 9,920,842	$ 7,706,245	$ 5,317,537
Allied products	5,400,394	5,594,160	5,887,303
Brewmatic equipment	2,505,611	2,134,388	2,362,052
Total	$17,826,847	$15,434,793	$13,566,892

Coffee and allied products inventories are stated at LIFO cost while all other inventories are stated at FIFO cost. Current cost of coffee and allied products inventories exceeded the LIFO cost by $40,800,000, $12,700,000, and $2,600,000 at June 30, 1977, 1976, and 1975, respectively.

For the purpose of this case analysis, assume the following information. The firm's effective income tax rate in all years is 50 percent. The cost of carrying inventory consists primarily of the cost of capital, which was approximately one-half percent per month at June 30, 1977.

FARMER BROTHERS COMPANY
CONSOLIDATED STATEMENT OF INCOME AND (LOSS)

	YEARS ENDED JUNE 30,	
	1977	1976
Sales	$135,271,053	$87,156,483
Cost of goods sold	124,267,341	64,799,214
Gross profit	11,003,712	22,357,269
Selling expense	19,615,507	17,752,185
General and administrative expense	3,485,365	2,962,941
	23,100,872	20,715,126
Income (loss) from operations	(12,097,160)	1,642,143
Other income, net	351,301	444,268
Income (loss) before provision (credit) for taxes	(11,745,859)	2,086,411
Provision (credit) for taxes on income	(5,759,600)	1,098,039
Net income (loss)	$ (5,986,259)	$ 988,372
Net income (loss) per average common share outstanding	$ (3.04)	$ .50

FARMER BROTHERS COMPANY CONSOLIDATED BALANCE SHEET

	JUNE 30,	
ASSETS:	1977	1976
Current:		
Cash	$ 2,228,019	$ 587,965
Marketable securities, at cost (approximates market)	3,599,154	3,101,902
Accounts receivable, less allowance for doubtful accounts of		
$480,000 in 1977 and $375,000 in 1976	13,434,729	7,976,904
Federal and state income taxes receivable	5,973,213	1,422,582
Inventories	17,826,847	15,434,893
Prepaid expenses	679,860	460,541
Total current assets	$43,741,822	$28,984,787
Properties and equipment, at cost, less accumulated		
depreciation	10,009,444	8,731,176
Cash surrender value of life insurance	787,868	753,783
Other assets	1,023	6,952
	$54,540,157	$38,476,698

LIABILITIES:		
Current:		
Accounts payable, including accruals	$21,219,262	$11,144,547
Short-term borrowings	12,887,518	—
Deferred taxes	115,267	105,422
Total current liabilities	$34,222,047	$11,249,969
Long term:		
Notes payable	626,156	626,156
Deferred taxes	31,024	166,169
	$34,879,227	$12,042,294

SHAREHOLDERS' EQUITY:		
Capital shares:		
Common	$ 1,968,037	$ 1,968,037
Additional paid-in capital	1,290,687	1,290,687
Retained earnings	16,402,206	23,175,680
	19,660,930	26,434,404
	$54,540,157	$38,476,698

REQUIRED:

1. Management's discussion and analysis reveal that as of March 31, 1977 (the end of the firm's third quarter), the firm had temporarily liquidated some of its inventory, which it expected (and did) replenish prior to year-end. Explain how the fact that it replenished the inventory at $2.32 per pound as opposed to the $3.00 per pound expected at March 31, 1977, contributed $4,750,000 [pre-tax] to fourth quarter profit and calculate the approximate quantity of coffee inventory that was temporarily liquidated.

2. Coffee prices were declining at June 30, 1977, yet management of Farmer Brothers decided to increase the firm's coffee inventory by 1.9 million pounds to 19.7 million pounds. Assume that purchases of the last 1.9 million pounds of coffee in fiscal 1977 were made at the year-end price of $2.25 per pound and that the firm could have delayed these purchases by 4 months without any operating problems. At that time, the price was expected to be $2.00 per pound. Moreover, assume that year-end coffee inventory quantities are not expected to decrease in the foreseeable future. Given these assumptions, was management's decision to increase inventory quantities by 1.9 million pounds in 1977 at the higher prevailing price a rational economic decision? Explain your answer fully.

3. Calculate the cost of goods sold for the year ended June 30, 1977, under the FIFO method.

4. How would the FIFO cost of goods sold computed in Requirement 3 have been affected if coffee inventory quantities had not increased by 1.9 million pounds but rather remained constant at 17.8 million pounds? Answer as specifically as you can.

Inventories and Cost of Goods Sold: Estimation Techniques and Alternative Valuation Methods

In the last chapter, we described the basic inventory accounting principles that exist under generally accepted accounting principles (GAAP). To recap, inventories are accounted for at the *lower-of-cost-or-market value*, and cost may be determined by *specific identification* or a cost flow assumption such as *first-in, first-out (FIFO)*; *last-in, first-out (LIFO)*, or *average cost*. In this chapter, we introduce some computational techniques used to value inventories for financial reporting and other purposes as well as some alternatives to the LCM valuation rule specified by GAAP.

First, we introduce some techniques that yield estimates of the inventory balance and cost of goods sold. These estimates are necessary or useful in a number of situations. Firms using a *periodic inventory system* must take a physical count of their inventories to determine inventory quantities and then apply unit costs to determine inventory costs. Since this is typically a costly and time-consuming process, most firms will take a physical inventory only once a year. These firms may need to prepare interim financial statements, and, thus, they require estimates of the inventory balances at the end of interim periods. The *gross profit method* is one convenient way of obtaining inventory balance estimates. Firms in retail industries often have many different items in inventory with relatively low unit costs. Moreover, managers of these retail establishments are more concerned about the retail value of inventories rather than their costs. One way of simplifying the task of keeping track of the cost and retail values of so many items in inventory is to use *retail inventory methods*. These methods allow retail establishments to estimate the cost of their inventories under particular cost flow assumptions, while internal records are maintained based on the retail value of the merchandise. Many firms want the tax savings available under the LIFO inventory method without having to maintain their inventory accounts on that basis. The *dollar value LIFO method* permits firms to do just that by a technique that estimates the LIFO cost of inventory.

Bear in mind that the chief virtues of these techniques are their convenience and substantially reduced bookkeeping costs. While they are somewhat imprecise, the accounting profession has found their benefits outweigh the costs of such imprecision. The approximations have been shown to be accurate enough that, over the years, these techniques have become part of the set of GAAP.

Later in this chapter, we consider some alternatives to the lower-of-cost-or-market (LCM) valuation principle. While GAAP require valuation at LCM in most cases for financial reporting purposes, other valuation principles are used occasionally for financial reporting purposes and are more widely used for managerial accounting and decision-making purposes. The alternative valuation principles introduced in this chapter are *direct costing, full absorption costing, standard costing,* and current cost valuation principles including both *net realizable value (NRV)* and *replacement cost.*

ESTIMATION TECHNIQUES

The use of estimates in financial accounting is widespread. For instance, depreciation is based upon the estimated useful lives of the assets and bad debt expense is based upon estimates of uncollectible accounts. Estimation techniques are applied to inventories in a number of situations as we illustrate in this section.

Dollar Value LIFO

The vast majority of firms using the LIFO method implement it with the **dollar value LIFO** technique. By preparing financial statements using LIFO, firms can realize the tax savings it offers. By using the dollar value technique, firms can report on a LIFO basis without having to maintain their inventory records on that basis. As we saw in Chapter 8, maintaining inventory records is complex. Moreover, inventory records maintained at LIFO cost are not particularly useful for management decision making. The old and layered costs at which LIFO inventories are stated are simply not relevant for most managerial decisions regarding inventory prices and quantities. When using the dollar value LIFO technique, firms can maintain their inventory records by whatever cost flow assumption they prefer. At the end of each accounting period, an entry is made to adjust the inventory value to approximate LIFO cost as determined by the dollar value LIFO calculation. In a period of rising inventory prices, the entry to restate inventory from FIFO cost, say, to LIFO cost would typically involve an increase in cost of goods sold and a reduction of inventory value (an increase in the *LIFO reserve*).

All LIFO calculations illustrated in Chapter 8 involved LIFO applied to individual items in inventory. Even in such simple settings, the complexity of the LIFO method was apparent. When a more realistic situation is considered—a firm with numerous items in inventory—the complexity of applying LIFO increases substantially. Techniques have evolved over time to simplify the application of LIFO in such complex cases with the result that today no firm needs to avoid the use of LIFO simply because of its complexity.

The first simplification technique employed was the use of **inventory pools** for the application of LIFO. Inventory pools are groupings of specific goods; and these groupings, instead of individual items in inventory, are the units of analysis in LIFO calculations. Originally, inventory pools were viewed as "natural" groupings of items—those with similar characteristics and price movements. A computer manufacturer, for instance, might form pools of parts such as circuit boards, disk drives, and power supplies. Within each pool, however, there would be parts of different specifications (e.g., 100, 200, and 500 megabyte disk drives). Instead of applying LIFO to the numerous, different items in each pool, the manufacturer would apply LIFO to each pool based on some appropriate unit of measure. The savings in terms of clerical effort alone from such an approach can be substantial. In carefully selected pools of homogeneous items, the difference between a pooled LIFO calculation and a LIFO calculation based on individual items will be minimal.

One problem with this approach: As their businesses change, the companies will probably need to redefine their inventory pools. Companies frequently get out of certain lines of business and move into entirely new ones. Technological changes will render some inventory items obsolete and will result in the introduction of new items. As their businesses change, so will the composition of the firms' inventories, thus necessitating the determination of new pools.

Related to this problem is the fact that particular pools of similar items, just as individual items, can occasionally be liquidated entirely or in part, leading to the problem of LIFO liquidations discussed in Chapter 8. While the likelihood of liquidation decreases as the number of items in a pool increases, liquidations may still take place under the pooled LIFO approach. For instance, suppose the computer manufacturer discussed above faces a declining demand for computers based upon a particular microprocessor. The manufacturer's appropriate business response to such a decrease in demand would be to cut back the inventory of components to build these machines. If all of these component parts are in a single pool, some liquidation of older LIFO inventory layers is inevitable. If, on the other hand, component parts for various computers were in a single pool, the manufacturer might avoid or decrease the likelihood of LIFO liquidation if the declining demand for certain products is offset by an increase in the demand for other products.

An alternative approach to inventory pools that substantially avoids these problems is to measure pools not in terms of their physical quantities of goods but, rather, in terms of their total dollar value. This is the idea behind dollar value LIFO. If pools are measured in terms of dollar value, rather than, say, megabytes, there is no reason why the computer manufacturer could not put all of the inventory of memory storage devices into a single pool. If disk drives are ever replaced by flash memory cards, there is no problem. Under the dollar value LIFO technique, the replacement of one item by another is permissible, providing the new item "fits" into the pool.[1]

---

[1] The rules governing the use of the dollar value LIFO technique are contained in the U.S. Treasury Regulations, sec. 1.472-8. Although these rules were written to govern the use of dollar value LIFO for tax purposes, they have become part of GAAP and, thus, apply for financial reporting purposes.

Firms using the dollar value LIFO technique must create at least one inventory pool for each "natural business unit," although a multiple-pools approach is also permitted. As we have seen, more goods in a pool reduces the likelihood of dipping into old LIFO cost layers.

The dollar value LIFO technique works as follows. The year LIFO is adopted is referred to as the **base year**. For each of the inventory pools, the following steps are performed:

1. Determine the current cost of ending inventory
2. Apply appropriate price indexes to determine the base period cost of the ending inventory
3. Identify the LIFO layers in the inventory
4. Convert each layer from base period cost to the cost that applied in the year the layer was added

The price indexes used in the calculation are either drawn from relevant indexes published by the federal government or are calculated by the firm. We will examine the issue of how such indexes are calculated later in the chapter.

In the following example, the procedures may at first appear complex. Remember: The objective of the method is to approximate the results of applying LIFO by means of an end-of-period adjustment. Under LIFO, inventory is carried in layers. The dollar value LIFO technique estimates the layers in inventories added each year. Each layer is priced appropriately by employing an index of prices relative to those of the base period.

An Example   Madison Manufacturing Corp. adopted LIFO in 1992. The following information pertains to the firm's Inventory Pool No. 3:

Madison Manufacturing Corp.
Inventory Pool No. 3
Data for Dollar Value LIFO Calculations

	1992	1993	1994
Ending inventory at current prices	$300,000	$600,000	$875,000
Price index (1992 = 100)	100	120	140

The first step in the process is to convert the inventory values at current prices to inventory values at base period prices. Notice that the price index increases each year. Since this index is constructed to capture the prices of items in Inventory Pool No. 3, these index increases indicate the costs of goods in the pool are increasing. Thus, when observing the increasing values of inventory at current prices, it is impossible to tell if the firm has more inventory quantity or just higher-priced inventory. By converting to base period prices, we are effectively stating inventory values in terms of a common denominator. With each of the three years' inventories stated at base period prices, we can determine whether inventory quantities have increased.

To determine inventory at base period prices, first calculate a ratio of price indexes to capture the prices in 1993 and 1994 relative to the base period of

1992. For instance, the price index for this pool was 120 at the end of 1993 compared with 100 a year earlier. Putting these indexes in ratio form tells us that 1993 prices are 1.2 times the 1992 prices. Then, dividing the ending inventories at current prices by the ratio of price indexes will "deflate" the ending inventory values from current prices back to base period prices. Thus, the $600,000 of inventory at current prices in 1993 is equivalent to $500,000 $600,000 ÷ 1.2) of inventory at base period prices.

Madison Manufacturing Corp.
Inventory Pool No. 3
Calculations of Ending Inventory at Base Period Prices

	1992	1993	1994
Ending inventory at current prices	$300,000	$600,000	$875,000
Relative price index	1.00	1.20	1.40
Ending inventory at base prices	$300,000	$500,000	$625,000
Layer added		$200,000	$125,000

With ending inventories now stated in terms of base period prices, it is apparent that inventory quantities have, in fact, increased each year; and it is possible to identify the LIFO layers at base period prices. At base period prices, a layer of $200,000 was added to the base (1992) layer of $300,000 in 1993, and another layer of $125,000 was added in 1994. But, since each of the layers was not added in the base period, it is necessary to multiply the base period cost of each layer by the relative price index for that period to price the layers correctly. The dollar value LIFO calculations for 1993 and 1994 follow:

December 31, 1993	Base	Index	LIFO
1992 (Base year) layer	$300,000	1.00	$300,000
1993 layer	200,000	1.20	240,000
Total	$500,000		$540,000

December 31, 1994	Base	Index	LIFO
1992 (Base year) layer	$300,000	1.00	$300,000
1993 layer	200,000	1.20	240,000
1994 layer	125,000	1.40	175,000
Total	$625,000		$715,000

The dollar value LIFO technique also works when inventory layers are liquidated rather than added. To consider a calculation involving a partial liquidation of LIFO inventory layers, suppose that inventory at December 31, 1994, amounted to $525,000 at current prices. Deflating this to base period prices would yield $525,000 ÷ 1.40 = $375,000. Comparing this with the balance of $500,000 in base period prices at the end of 1993 reveals that not only has no layer been added in 1994, but also a substantial portion of the 1993 layer has been liquidated. The rest of the dollar value LIFO calculation for this situation is as follows:

December 31, 1994	Base	Index	LIFO
1992 (Base year) layer	$300,000	1.00	$300,000
1993 layer	75,000	1.20	90,000
Total	$375,000		$390,000

The dollar value technique is widely used because of its convenience. When inventory pools are constructed carefully and appropriate price indexes are used, the technique will yield a close approximation of the results of applying LIFO as illustrated in the previous chapter at a fraction of the cost. Dollar value LIFO is an acceptable procedure for tax reporting and financial reporting.

Price Indexes   The origin of price indexes is all that remains to be considered in the discussion of the dollar value LIFO technique. Many firms construct their own indexes because no published indexes that accurately capture the price changes of the particular mix of items they carry in inventory are available. Two methods are used to construct these indexes: double extension and link-chain. In both methods, firms may use their entire inventories or, if the number of items in inventory is very large, they may apply the calculations to a representative sample of inventory items. Let us briefly examine each method.

Double Extension Method   Under the **double extension method**, the ending inventory is priced twice ("double extended") at current prices and again at base period prices. The index for the period, then, is just the following ratio:

$$\frac{\text{Ending Inventory at Current Prices}}{\text{Ending Inventory at Base Period Prices}} = \text{Price Index}$$

While conceptually simple, the mechanics of the double extension method can be quite cumbersome for firms with large and complex inventories. For firms that have been using LIFO for a long period of time, some of the items in their current inventories may not have even existed in the base period. Obviously, it is not possible to determine the base period prices of items introduced after the base period. The link-chain method offers a way of dealing with this problem of changing inventory pools.

Link-Chain Method   Under the **link-chain method**, an annual index is constructed each year by the double extension approach, as follows:

$$\frac{\text{Ending Inventory at Current Prices}}{\text{Ending Inventory at Beginning-of-Year Prices}} = \text{Annual Price Index}$$

These annual indexes are then linked or multiplied to obtain an index that captures the cumulative changes in inventory prices.

An Example of Index Calculation   To illustrate the calculation of indexes under the double extension and link-chain methods, consider the following data about the value of inventory at Howard's Hardware, a small retail establishment that adopted the LIFO method using the dollar value LIFO technique effective January 1, Year 1. Our task is to calculate the price index to use in the dollar value LIFO calculation for the year ended December 31, Year 3, under both calculations.

	Total Inventory Valued at		
Date	Current Prices	Start-of-Period Prices	Base Period Prices
January 1, Year 1	$250,000	$250,000	$250,000
December 31, Year 1	302,400	280,000	280,000
December 31, Year 2	372,600	324,000	300,000
December 31, Year 3	375,705	341,550	275,000

Under the double extension calculation, the inventory at December 31, Year 3 is priced twice—first at current prices and then at base period prices. The index is just the ratio of these two amounts:

	Total Inventory Valued at		
Date	Current Prices	Base Period Prices	Index
December 31, Year 3	$375,705	$275,000	1.366

Under the link-chain method, an index is calculated to capture the yearly price changes that are then multiplied to obtain an index that captures the total price change since the base period. The yearly indexes are calculated by pricing each year-end inventory twice—first at current prices and then at start-of-period prices. The yearly index is just the ratio of these two amounts:

	Total Inventory Valued at		
Date	Current Prices	Start-of-Period Prices	Ratio
December 31, Year 1	$302,400	$280,000	1.080
December 31, Year 2	372,600	324,000	1.150
December 31, Year 3	375,705	341,550	1.100
Index			1.366

The resulting index at December 31, Year 3, is the result of multiplying the three annual indexes for Years 1 through 3.

Notice that in this simple example, the results of the two calculations produce the same index for the year ended December 31, Year 3. This will usually not be the case for several reasons. First, in our example, there were no items in the inventory at the end of Year 3 that did not exist at January 1, Year 1. Therefore, we were able to obtain base period prices for all items in inventory at the end of Year 3. In industries with high rates of technological change, it will not be possible to obtain base period prices for some items in inventory, and the link-chain method, which only requires prices at the start of each year, is the only way these firms can calculate their own indexes. Second, our example used the entire inventory in the calculation, but firms will frequently construct their indexes based on a representative sample of inventory items. If the composition of the samples changes over time, the two calculations need not yield the same index values.

Published Indexes   Whenever it is impractical to calculate an index, the IRS will permit firms to use an index derived from published price level statistics.[2] Needless to say, the use of published price level statistics will greatly simplify the dollar value LIFO procedure. However, because of the difficulty many firms face in finding a published index that accurately captures the price changes of the items in their inventories, the use of published indexes is probably not as widespread as you might expect given their convenience.

Retail Inventory Method

The **retail inventory method** allows firms to keep track of their inventories at retail values and still provides a reliable estimate of the goods' costs for financial reporting purposes. Imagine the clerical burden involved in running a retail establishment that has thousands of different items, often in different sizes and colors, in inventory. As indicated in Chapter 8, technological innovations are making it increasingly possible for retail firms to install fairly sophisticated perpetual inventory systems. However, even in such cases, any procedures that permit simplification of the record keeping function are undoubtedly welcome.

As the retail inventory method is typically applied, each department will keep track of the following amounts:

- The cost (including freight-in) and retail value of goods purchased
- Any and all adjustments to retail values such as markups, markdowns, employee discounts, or allowances for soiled or damaged merchandise
- Sales[3]

All this information is necessary to apply the retail method. Each department will typically apply the retail method because margins (differences between selling prices and costs) frequently vary across departments. As a result, the relationship between cost and retail value of merchandise, which is at the heart of the retail method, may not be the same for different types of goods.

Advantages of the retail method include the following:

1. Records are maintained and physical inventories are taken on the basis of retail prices. Since these amounts are typically marked on tags or labels affixed to the merchandise or shelves, this is considerably easier than trying to determine costs.

---

[2] Treasury Regulations, sec. 1.472-8(e).

[3] C.P. Jannis, C.H. Poedtke, Jr., and D.R. Ziegler, *Managing and Accounting for Inventories: Control, Income Recognition, and Tax Strategy*, 3rd ed., (New York: John Wiley & Sons, 1980), p. 295.

2. An estimate of the inventory balance can be obtained at any point in time without performing a physical inventory count.
3. Then once a count is taken, a comparison of the actual inventory balance with the estimate from the retail method serves as a reasonably effective control device. Such a comparison may reveal shortages or overages.

The efficacy of the retail method has been recognized by the accounting profession and the IRS and is permitted for both financial reporting and tax purposes.

The retail method operates in the following way. Each department will calculate the relationship between the costs and retail values of its merchandise. This cost percentage is applied to the retail value of the ending inventory to reduce it to cost. Consider the following example:

	Cost	Retail
Beginning inventory	$ 2,800	$ 4,200
Purchases	10,400	17,800
Goods available for sale	$13,200	$22,000
Cost percentage	60%	

The *cost percentage* is calculated as the cost of the goods available for sale divided by their retail value—in this case, $13,200 + $22,000 = .60. Suppose the sales for the period were $17,500. The ending inventory at cost can be approximated as follows:

	Cost	Retail
Goods available for sale	$13,200	$22,000
Sales		17,500
Ending inventory at retail		$ 4,500
Ending inventory at cost (60% of retail value)	$ 2,700	
Cost of goods sold	$10,500	

In this example, there are no adjustments to the retail values of the inventories. A more involved example will include these adjustments and illustrate how to deal with them. Before turning to such an example, we need to consider the nature of these adjustments.

Adjustments to Retail Value   As any dedicated shopper knows, retail prices are not constant. Much merchandise is seasonal. If you are shopping for a winter coat, prices are usually highest (and selection greatest) when new merchandise is introduced. Later in the season, the prices will typically be lower but the selection will not be as great.

Let us consider these price adjustments from the retailer's perspective. If the price of an item is raised above its original retail price, this is referred to as a **markup**. Markups may be necessary for several reasons. The original price may have been incorrectly set, and the markup is made to correct the error. Alternatively, a markup may be made because demand for the item exceeds expectations or the quantity provided by the supplier is less than expected. **Markdowns** involve reducing the prices of items below their original retail prices. Markdowns are common on seasonal goods or may be necessary if the buyer has not judged consumers' tastes correctly. On occasion, markups and markdowns will be canceled in part or in total, and prices will be written down (in the case of a **markup cancellation**) or written up (in the case of a **markdown cancellation**). These markup and markdown cancellations are similar in their effect to markdowns and markups, respectively. However, a markup cancellation can only occur after a markup has already been taken, and the amount of a markup cancellation cannot exceed the amount of the markup already taken. The same relationship exists between markdown cancellations and markdowns.

Suppose an item is originally priced to sell for $10.00. A while later, it is marked up to $13.00, followed shortly by a return to the original price. Toward the end of the season, the retailer marks the remaining units of the item down to $8.00 for a short while and finally settles on a price of $9.00. Figure 9.1 classifies these price changes. The bold line maps the path of the item's price over time.

Other adjustments to the retail price may be recorded separately. For instance, stores will commonly offer their employees a discount. Items used as "demos" in a showroom may also be sold at reduced prices. Why not just call these adjustments markdowns and record them accordingly? The amounts of markdowns taken in a particular period by a store or department are often used to evaluate the performance of the merchandise buyer. Since employee discounts or reduced prices on "demos" are not attributable to the buyer's performance, they are often recorded in separate accounts.

FIGURE 9.1
Changes in Retail
Prices over Time

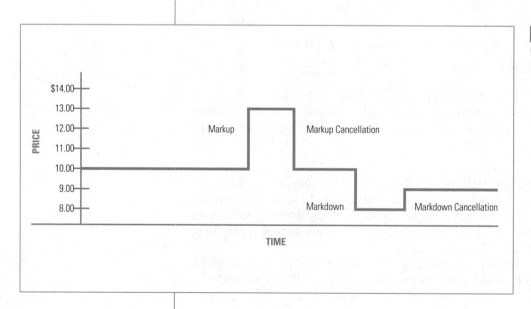

To illustrate how these adjustments to retail prices are handled under the retail method, let us expand the previous example somewhat.

	Cost	Retail
Beginning inventory	$ 2,800	$ 4,200
Purchases	10,400	17,800
Markups		1,200
Markup cancellations		(400)
Net markups		800
Markdowns		(700)
Markdown cancellations		225
Net markdowns		(475)
Employee discounts		(200)
Goods available for sale	$13,200	$22,125
Sales (net of employee discounts)		(17,300)
Ending inventory (retail)		$ 4,825

If a cost percentage is calculated after all adjustments to retail prices, it will have a value in this case of $13,200 ÷ $22,125 or 59.7%. However, remember that the purpose of this cost percentage is to determine the approximate cost of the ending inventory. The question, then, is to what extent do these adjustments pertain to items that are still in inventory? The employee discounts arose when employees purchased merchandise at less than full retail price. Obviously, these goods are no longer in inventory, and the $200 employee discounts should not enter into the calculation of the cost percentage.

But what about the net markups and net markdowns? It is probably not possible to determine the extent to which these amounts apply to goods that are still in inventory and the extent to which they apply to goods already sold. The way this problem is typically handled in the conventional retail method is to include net markups in the calculation of the cost percentage but to exclude the net markdowns. Thus, the cost/retail percentage in this case would be $13,200 ÷ $22,800 or 57.89%, calculated as follows:

	Cost	Retail
Beginning inventory	$ 2,800	$ 4,200
Purchases	10,400	17,800
Markups		1,200
Markup cancellations		(400)
Net markups		800
Subtotal	$13,200	$22,800
Cost percentage		57.89%

Applying this percentage to complete the calculations of ending inventory and cost of goods sold will yield the following results:

	Cost	Retail
Subtotal	$13,200	$22,800
Markdowns		(700)
Markdown cancellations		225
Net markdowns		(475)
Employee discounts		(200)
Goods available for sale	$13,200	$22,125
Sales (net of employee discounts)		(17,300)
Ending inventory at retail		4,825
Ending inventory at cost (57.89% of retail)	$ 2,793	
Cost of goods sold	$10,407	

The approach illustrated above is often said to approximate the results under the lower-of-cost-or-market (LCM) approach. By excluding markdowns from the calculation, the retail value used in the calculation of the cost percentage is higher than it would otherwise be, and the cost percentage is correspondingly lower. Thus, figuring the cost percentage in this way will clearly yield a lower amount for ending inventory at cost, but in what sense does it approximate the LCM approach?

When an item is marked down, its market value (net realizable value) has fallen. By excluding these markdowns from the calculation of the cost percentage and applying the cost percentage to the retail value of the ending inventory after markdowns, the ending inventory will be stated at an amount less than its cost.[4] Since the cause of inventory being stated below cost is the decline in its market value, it is said that this procedure approximates the LCM rule. The approximation may not be particularly good. Recall from Chapter 8 that the usual definition of market value is replacement cost, which is ignored fully here. Thus, the procedure illustrated here may well result in inventory being stated at an amount below cost when market value (replacement cost) is above cost.

The real advantage of the retail inventory method is the ability to maintain inventory records on the basis of retail values, which retail establishment managers find most useful, yet still report them on the basis of cost. Whether or not the retail method approximates the LCM approach is, frankly, a less important issue. Let us just conclude that as the conventional retail inventory method is usually applied, the retail method will yield an amount for ending inventory that is probably less than its cost whenever markdowns have taken place.

---

[4] If both markups and markdowns are included in the calculation of the cost percentage, the retail method will yield an amount for ending inventory that approximates *average cost*.

One more variation of the retail method, which is designed to approximate the LIFO cost of the ending inventory, needs to be examined. This variation is best viewed as a combination of the retail method, just illustrated, with the dollar value LIFO method, illustrated earlier.

LIFO Retail **LIFO retail** allows retail firms to keep their records based on retail prices but permits them to use LIFO for financial reporting and tax purposes. Therefore, it combines the retail method and the dollar value LIFO method into what is sometimes called the *dollar value LIFO retail method*.

Accounting theorists and the IRS initially were reluctant to allow application of the LIFO method to retail inventories. Since retailers often completely liquidate their stocks of particular items and do not replace them with identical items but, rather, substitute the newest styles, colors, and models, LIFO was considered inappropriate. The Commissioner of Internal Revenue denied the initial adoption of LIFO by retailers in 1941. In the resulting court case, *Hutzler Bros. vs. U.S.*, the Tax Court upheld the retailers' right to use LIFO, arguing that both the retail method and LIFO were already acceptable and, therefore, a method combining two acceptable approaches was acceptable.[5] All the early LIFO retail adopters had used in their calculations indexes that were compiled by an industry association. The Tax Court ruling required the use of indexes compiled by the Bureau of Labor Statistics.[6]

LIFO retail is a combination of the conventional retail method and dollar value LIFO. It differs from the conventional retail method (already illustrated) because of the necessity to identify inventory layers and their associated costs, which requires restatement of current retail prices to their base period prices. Moreover, separate cost percentages are computed and kept track of each year. Also, the calculation of the cost percentages differs slightly from that used in the conventional retail method since the objective is to approximate the actual cost of each layer rather than lower-of-cost-or-market as in the conventional retail method.

However, LIFO retail is similar to the conventional retail method in its basic approach. The inventory pools typically used correspond to departments or lines of merchandise with comparable markup percentages. Inventory records are kept based on the retail values of the inventories; and for each pool, records must be kept of purchases, sales, and adjustments to retail prices such as markups and markdowns.

To illustrate the procedures involved in LIFO retail, let us return to the example used earlier in the chapter to illustrate the conventional retail method and expand it somewhat. The facts are as follows:

---

[5] *Hutzler Bros. vs. U.S.*, 8 T.C. 14 (1947).

[6] H.Z. Davis, "History of LIFO," *Journal of Accountancy* (May, 1983), p. 108.

	Cost	Retail
Inventory at 12/31/92	$ 2,800	$ 4,200
1993 activity:		
Purchases	10,400	17,800
Markups		1,200
Markup cancellations		(400)
Net markups		800
Markdowns		(700)
Markdown cancellations		225
Net markdowns		(475)
Employee discounts		(200)
Sales (net of employee discounts)		(17,300)
Inventory at 12/31/93 (retail)		$ 4,825
1994 activity:		
Purchases	$12,300	$ 20,100
Markups		1,200
Markup cancellations		(800)
Net markups		400
Markdowns		(1,300)
Markdown cancellations		600
Net markdowns		(700)
Employee discounts		(100)
Sales (net of employee discounts)		(19,725)
Inventory at 12/31/94 (retail)		$ 4,800

With this information, it is possible to calculate cost percentages for the base period (1992) and for 1993 and 1994. Separate cost percentages for each period are needed to price each layer in the inventory properly. The cost percentages are calculated, including the effects of both markups and markdowns. The implicit assumption in this calculation is that the markups and markdowns occurring in a particular period (net of any cancellations) apply only to goods purchased that period, not to goods included in the beginning inventory. How literally true this assumption is depends on the particular facts in each case. If the assumption is not literally true, then the implication is that the approximation provided by the LIFO retail method probably contains some error. Calculating cost percentages for the base period, 1993, and 1994 yields the results shown on the top of the next page.

Notice that if the assumption about markups and markdowns applying only to goods purchased that year holds, then each year's cost percentage pertains only to that year's activity.

	Cost	Retail
Inventory at 12/31/92	$ 2,800	$ 4,200
1992 cost percentage	66.67%	
1993 activity:		
Purchases	$10,400	$17,800
Markups		1,200
Markup cancellations		(400)
Net markups		800
Markdowns		(700)
Markdown cancellations		225
Net markdowns		(475)
1993 layer	$10,400	$18,125
1993 cost percentage	57.38%	
1994 activity:		
Purchases	$12,300	$20,100
Markups		1,200
Markup cancellations		(800)
Net markups		400
Markdowns		(1,300)
Markdown cancellations		600
Net markdowns		(700)
1994 layer	$12,300	$19,800
1994 cost percentage	62.12%	

Suppose further that the Bureau of Labor Statistics has provided the following indexes of price levels applicable to this firm:

Date	Price Index
12/31/92	100
12/31/93	102
12/31/94	105

Thus, prices are 2% higher at December 31, 1993, and 5% higher at December 31, 1994, than they were at December 31, 1992. With these indexes, it is possible to restate from current prices to base period prices. The LIFO retail calculations for December 31, 1993 and 1994 would appear as follows, assuming that the year ended December 31, 1992 is the base period—i.e., the period in which LIFO was adopted. (Note: All calculations are rounded to the nearest dollar.) It is first necessary to calculate ending inventories at base period retail prices:

December 31, 1993:

Ending inventory at current retail prices	$4,825
Relative price index 102 ÷ 100	÷ 1.02
Ending inventory at base period retail prices	$4,730

Comparing this with the retail value of the December 31, 1992, inventory of $4,200 makes it clear that more inventory is on hand, not just higher priced inventory. Next, the value of each of the layers must be converted from retail values to costs using the cost percentages computed above. The final step in the process is to convert from base period costs to costs of the appropriate period using the price level indexes provided by the Bureau of Labor Statistics. The rest of the December 31, 1993, calculation is as follows:

	Base Retail	Cost Percentage	Base Cost	Price Index	LIFO
Base layer	$4,200	66.67%	$2,800	1.00	$2,800
1993 layer	530	57.38%	304	1.02	310
Total	$4,730		$3,104		$3,110

Notice how this calculation resembles the dollar value LIFO method with the added step of the conversion from base period retail prices to base period costs. This extra step is necessary because inventories are carried on the books at their retail prices rather than at cost.

December 31, 1994:

Ending inventory at current retail prices	$4,800
Relative price index 105 ÷ 100	÷ 1.05
Ending inventory at base period retail prices	$4,571

Comparing this amount with the previous year's ending inventory at base period prices ($4,730) shows that no new layer was added in 1994 and, in fact, a partial liquidation has occurred. The rest of the calculation for 1994 is as follows:

	Base Retail	Cost Percentage	Base Cost	Price Index	LIFO
Base layer	$4,200	66.67%	$2,800	1.00	$2,800
1993 layer	371	57.38%	213	1.02	217
1994 layer	0	62.12%	0	1.05	0
Total	$4,571		$3,013		$3,017

Strictly speaking, the line labeled "1994 layer" is unnecessary and is included just for the sake of completeness. There is no 1994 layer since inventory quantities decreased in 1994.

The LIFO retail method may seem enormously complex upon first examination. However, it is important to remember that this approximation technique is valuable because it is actually simpler and less costly than the alternatives of keeping records on both the costs and retail values of the inventory. LIFO retail offers the same advantages listed above for the conventional retail method with the added advantage of permitting firms to achieve the tax savings LIFO offers in a period of rising prices.

Gross Profit Method   The purpose of the **gross profit method** is to allow firms to estimate the cost of their ending inventories. Related to the retail inventory method, the gross profit method exploits the relationship that typically exists between the selling price of goods and their costs. In many firms, this relationship is quite stable. For instance, a retailer or wholesaler may set selling prices (or "mark up" the goods) uniformly at 50% over cost. In such a situation, the gross profit method will work quite well. If different categories of goods are marked up differently, the gross profit method will still work reasonably well, unless the mix of items (and markups) in inventory changes over time. This point will be discussed further below.

Before demonstrating the use of the gross profit method, let us consider some of the situations calling for its application. Suppose a company uses a periodic inventory system and has no perpetual records whatsoever. Such a firm is a likely candidate to use the gross profit method in those situations where it is either impossible or very costly to determine inventory balances by taking physical inventory. For instance, suppose some inventory is either stolen or destroyed. Obviously, even if the firm was willing to take a physical inventory, that would be impossible since no inventory is on hand to count. Applying the gross profit method will allow the firm to estimate the cost of the inventory destroyed or stolen. Also, the firm may use the gross profit method for the purposes of preparing its quarterly financial statements. This will allow the firm to issue financial statements without having to take a physical inventory four times in a year. The firm's auditors may also employ the gross profit method as a check on the reasonableness of the reported balance. While generally accepted auditing standards require auditors to observe the taking of the physical inventory, physical inventories are frequently taken at sometime other than year-end. In such a case, using the gross profit method will help the auditor "roll the balance forward" from the date of the physical inventory to the year-end.

To illustrate the gross profit method, consider the following simple example. A fire at Accident Prone, Inc.'s warehouse destroyed the building and its contents. The firm uses a periodic inventory system and maintains no perpetual records at all. At the end of the last fiscal year, the reported inventory balance was $120,000. On the date of the fire, the ledger shows a balance in the purchases account of $600,000 and a balance in the sales account of $1,170,000. Both balances reflect year-to-date activity. Company policy is to set the selling price of its goods at a markup of 80% over cost—i.e., an item costing $10 would be priced to sell for $18. What was the approximate cost of the inventory destroyed in the warehouse fire?

Before proceeding, let's clarify the firm's pricing policy. In the most general terms, a firm's selling price is equal to the cost of the goods plus a markup. This markup can be expressed either as a percentage of the cost of the goods or as a percentage of the goods' selling price. In this case, the markup was expressed as a percentage of cost. Thus,

Selling Price	=	Cost + Markup
	=	Cost + 80% of Cost
	=	180% of Cost

What we need to extract from this is the relationship between cost and selling price. This is easily done. Since selling price is 180% of cost, it follows that:

Cost	=	Selling Price ÷ 180%
	=	55.56% of Selling Price

The markup relationship could also be expressed as a percentage of selling price. In this example, the selling price is 180% of cost, or cost is selling price divided by 180%. Thus,

Markup	=	80% of Cost
	=	80% of Selling Price ÷ 180%
	=	44.44% of Selling Price

This, of course, yields the same relationship between cost and selling price as before:

Cost	=	Selling Price − Markup
	=	Selling Price − 44.44% of Selling Price
	=	55.56% of Selling Price

In general, a markup of X percent of cost is equal to a markup of $X ÷ (100 + X)$ percent of selling price.

If such a relationship between the selling price and cost of goods exists, it can be used to approximate the cost of goods sold and the cost of goods in inventory at any time. If the cost of Accident Prone, Inc.'s goods is equal to 55.56% of selling price, the cost of goods destroyed in the warehouse fire can be estimated as follows:

Beginning inventory		$120,000
Plus: Purchases		600,000
Cost of goods available for sale		$720,000
Approximate cost of goods sold to date:		
Sales	$1,170,000	
Percentage	55.56%	
Cost of goods sold	$ 650,000	650,000
Cost of inventory destroyed by fire		$ 70,000

It is not unusual for a firm to apply different markup percentages to different items in inventory. In such a case, the relationship between selling price and cost will only hold on average. Suppose, for example, Slightly Diversified Corp. (SDC) carries two items in inventory. Item A costs $65 and sells for $100. Item B costs $18.75 and sells for $37.50. In 1994, the sales and cost of sales by item were as follows:

	Units	Sales	Cost of Sales	Cost Percentage
Item A	1,000	$100,000	$ 65,000	65%
Item B	4,000	150,000	75,000	50%
Overall		$250,000	$140,000	56%

If this overall cost percentage of 56% is used in a gross profit method calculation, the accuracy of the results will depend on the product mix at the time. To illustrate, consider the following information from the first quarter of 1995:

	Units	Cost/Unit	Total Cost
Beginning inventory:			
Item A	100	$ 65.00	$ 6,500
Item B	400	18.75	7,500
Total			$14,000

	Units	Cost/Unit	Total Cost
Purchases:			
Item A	500	$ 65.00	$32,500
Item B	1,000	18.75	18,750
Total			$51,250

	Units	Price/Unit	Total Sales
Sales:			
Item A	400	$100.00	$40,000
Item B	900	37.50	33,750
Total			$73,750

Now with all this information, there is no reason to apply the gross profit method. We can easily calculate the actual ending inventory:

	Units	Cost/Unit	Total Cost
Ending inventory:			
Item A	200*	$65.00	$13,000
Item B	500**	18.75	9,375
Total			$22,375

* 100 + 500 - 400 = 200 units
** 400 + 1,000 - 900 = 500 units

To determine how well (or how poorly) the gross profit method will perform in such a case, let us apply it and compare the results with the actual ending inventory amount above.

Beginning inventory		$14,000
Plus: Purchases		51,250
Cost of goods available for sale		$65,250
Approximate cost of goods sold to date:		
Sales	$73,750	
Percentage	56%	
Cost of goods sold		41,300
Cost of ending inventory		$23,950

The approximation provided by the gross profit method differs from the actual ending inventory by $1,575 or about 7% of the actual amount:

Estimated ending inventory	$23,950
Actual ending inventory	22,375
Difference	$ 1,575

The reason for this difference is the change in the mix of the inventory. At the start of the year, Item A comprised approximately 46% ($6,500 ÷ $14,000) of the inventory cost, while at the end of the first quarter, it comprised approximately 58% ($13,000 ÷ $22,375) of the cost of the inventory. This change in mix implies that the historical cost percentage of 56% does not apply strictly to the goods actually sold during the first quarter.

Thus, the gross profit method is clearly an estimation technique and, like all estimation techniques, is prone to some errors. The amount of error depends on the difference between the historical cost percentage used and the actual cost percentage during the period. Some accounting systems may provide enough information to adjust the cost percentages. Those that need the gross profit method probably will not.

ALTERNATIVE VALUATION APPROACHES

In this section, some alternatives to the LCM valuation rule are considered. Some of these alternatives are used for financial reporting purposes in selected situations, but all may be used for managerial purposes. We discuss these alternatives to underscore an important point. Just because GAAP do not specify a particular valuation principle does not mean it is useless. Firms may find they can make better decisions if alternatives to GAAP are used. For internal purposes, firms are free to use whatever accounting methods they deem appropriate to their particular circumstances. However, the use of an alternative to the LCM rule for managerial purposes but LCM for financial reporting purposes imposes an additional cost on firms because they will either have to keep a separate set of records in conformity with the LCM rule or make end-of-period-adjustments to the records to insure that they conform with GAAP.

Variable Costing vs. Full Absorption Costing

The proper treatment of fixed manufacturing costs (i.e., those that do not vary with output) has been an issue of concern in managerial accounting circles for some time. These fixed manufacturing costs tend to be handled in one of two ways. In a **variable** or **direct costing system**, only those costs that vary with output are treated as product costs. Fixed manufacturing costs are treated as period expenses. In a **full absorption costing system,** all manufacturing costs, whether variable or fixed, are included in product costs. What is the motivation for excluding fixed manufacturing costs from product costs in the variable costing approach? Managers have no short-term control over fixed costs. Therefore, it is unfair to saddle particular managers with costs they cannot control and to evaluate their performance in the short-term based on these fixed costs. It is also very useful for decision-making purposes to keep fixed and variable costs segregated. This segregation of fixed and variable costs will permit managers to analyze the effects of their decisions at the margin. While managers may be interested in variable costing for internal purposes, the exclusion of fixed manufacturing costs from the cost of inventories is expressly prohibited by GAAP.

While the accounting profession has required absorption costing for financial reporting purposes to avoid the problem of understating the cost of inventories, it is interesting to note that in so doing, they have made firms' cost of goods sold dependent on the number of units produced in a period. By varying the amount of production in a particular period, managers can affect the amount of fixed manufacturing costs "absorbed" by units produced and, thereby, affect the cost of units sold. The following example will illustrate this issue.

Small Business, Inc. is considering whether to increase its annual production from the originally planned 1,000 units to a proposed 1,250 units. The fixed manufacturing costs for the year amount to $100,000, and the variable manufacturing costs amount to $500 per unit produced. It is possible to compute the unit cost under the two production levels.

	1,000-Unit Production	1,250-Unit Production
Manufacturing costs:		
Fixed	$100,000	$100,000
Variable	500,000	625,000
Total	$600,000	$725,000
Per unit	$ 600	$ 580

Thus, just by increasing the quantity of units produced, unit cost decreases by $20 per unit. If the sales for the period amount to 1,000 units, the reduction of cost of goods sold and the increase in gross profit for the period will amount to $20,000. There are, of course, limits on the extent to which management can use this technique to increase income, including production capacity constraints and the necessity of increasing the investment in working capital. However, it has been observed that production activity often increases toward the end of the period as managers find their results of operations to be somewhat below expectations.

Standard Costs

Many manufacturing firms (and some service companies as well) employ a standard costing system to control their productive operations. Periodically, **standard costs** are set as to what a unit of output should cost under the conditions that managers can reasonably be expected to achieve. These standards are typically broken down into component parts—such as raw material standard cost, direct labor standard cost, indirect labor standard cost, etc.—to allow managers to pinpoint the source of any problems. Actual costs are compared to standard costs, and any differences (referred to as *variances*) are investigated and managers are held accountable for them.

Standard costs are an acceptable alternative to specific identification, FIFO, LIFO, or average cost for financial reporting purposes provided that "at the balance sheet date standard costs reasonably approximate costs computed under one of the recognized bases."[7] Many firms that use a standard cost system for managerial accounting purposes will also use it for financial reporting purposes. Take, for example, the following excerpt from the summary of significant accounting policies of Advanced Micro Devices, Inc., contained in the firm's 1991 annual report:

> Inventories are stated principally at standard costs adjusted to approximate the lower of cost (first-in, first-out) or market (net realizable value).

Net Realizable Value

GAAP states that "only in exceptional cases may inventories be stated above cost" and that these "exceptions must be justifiable by inability to determine appropriate approximate costs, immediate marketability at quoted market price, and the characteristic of unit interchangeability."[8] One well-known example of a situation where inventories are carried at *net realizable value (NRV)* or "estimated selling price in the normal course of business less reasonably predictable costs of completion and disposal" because of the "inability to determine appropriate approximate costs" is the meat packing business. In this business, a single input (e.g., a hog or head of cattle) yields numerous outputs (steaks, roasts, chops, and various by-products). It is impossible to allocate the cost of the input to the many outputs in anything other than an arbitrary way. Therefore, meat packers will often value their inventories at net realizable value. Instances of pricing inventories at net realizable value

---

7 "Restatement and Revision of Accounting Research Bulletins," *Accounting Research Bulletin No. 43*, (New York: AICPA, June 1953), ch. 4, para. 6.

8 *Ibid.*, ch. 4, para. 16.

because of their "immediate marketability at quoted market price" can be found in the case of precious metals and agricultural products. In all such cases, full footnote disclosure of the fact is required.

Replacement Cost

Accounting theorists have long argued for valuation of inventories at their current replacement cost; and, for a while, supplementary disclosure of the current costs of inventories were required by both the Securities and Exchange Commission and the Financial Accounting Standards Board for large corporations. Despite some very attractive features of this approach, discussed below, it was never popular with either preparers of financial statements or most users. Preparers found information on the replacement costs of inventories difficult and costly to obtain. Financial statement users never seemed to have much interest in the information despite the accounting profession's claims that this information was essential to understand a company's financial situation during periods of changing prices. As a consequence, these supplementary disclosures of replacement cost information are no longer required, and few firms offer them voluntarily.

Perhaps the most desirable feature of accounting for inventories at their **replacement cost** is that it allows the firm's income to be separated into two components—**operating profit** and **holding gains**. A firm has an operating profit every time it sells a unit of inventory for more than its cost to replace that unit. Holding gains (losses) occur when a firm has (or is "holding") one or more units of an item in inventory at a time when the replacement cost increases (decreases).

The advantage to separating income into these two components is that holding gains, while they certainly reflect an increase in the firm's wealth, do not represent income that could be distributed to the firm's owners without effectively impairing the firm's ability to continue in business. The point is simply that in order to continue in business, a firm will have to replace units in inventory as they are sold. If the replacement cost has increased, part of the total gross profit from the just completed sale will have to go toward replacing the unit sold at its new higher cost.

To illustrate this point, consider the following very simple example. Barkley Corp. deals in widgets. On January 1 of the current period, its supplier announced a price increase from $10 to $12 per widget. The following activity occurred:

Beginning inventory	100 units at $10	=	$ 1,000
Purchases	900 units at $12	=	10,800
Available for sale	1,000 units		$11,800

Suppose that all 1,000 units available for sale are sold for $20 and there are no other operating expenses. Under the traditional historical cost approach, the firm's income would be calculated as follows:

Historical cost approach:

Sales (1,000 × $20)	$20,000
Beginning inventory	$ 1,000
Plus: Purchases	10,800
Available for sale	$11,800
Minus: Ending inventory	0
Cost of goods sold	$11,800
Income (historical cost)	$ 8,200

Notice that since all inventory has been sold, there is no reason to specify a *cost flow assumption*.

Under the replacement cost approach, this gross profit would be broken down into operating profit and holding gains as follows:

Replacement cost approach:

Sales	$20,000
Replacement cost of goods sold (1,000 × $12)	12,000
Operating profit	$ 8,000
Holding gains [100 × ($12 − $10)]	200
Gross operating profit plus holding gains	$ 8,200

The cost of replacing the 1,000 units sold during the period was $12; and under replacement cost accounting, this amount is matched with revenues for all 1,000 units, regardless of when they were acquired and at what price. The holding gain arises from the fact that there were 100 units in beginning inventory at a cost of $10 when the replacement cost increased to $12.

A basic principle of replacement cost accounting is that holding gains (also known as "inventory profits") do not represent "spendable income." To demonstrate this, suppose that the management of Barkley Corp. decided to declare and distribute a cash dividend of $8,200, an amount equal to its historical cost income for the period. If for the sake of simplicity, it is assumed that all sales and purchases are for cash, the amount of cash generated by operations would be $9,200 (sales of $20,000 − purchases of $10,800). If $8,200 of this is distributed to the owners, only $1,000 will be left. At the current replacement cost of $12 per widget, Barkley will only have enough cash to purchase about 83 widgets ($1,000 ÷ $12), fewer than the 100 units with which it started the period.

If, on the other hand, only $8,000 (an amount equal to the operating profit) is distributed to the owners of the firm, $1,200 will be left, which is exactly the amount needed to replace the 100 widgets that were in beginning inventory. Thus, operating profits represent amounts that the firm could spend without impairing its ability to continue in business.

LIFO and FIFO in a Replacement Cost Context

One way of characterizing the differences between the cost flow assumptions illustrated in Chapter 8 is by the extent to which they include holding gains (or losses) in income. Holding gains that are included in income are known as *realized* holding gains. It was observed in Chapter 8 that, in general, LIFO matches current costs with revenue. As seen in the above example, when current replacement costs are matched with revenues, the result is pure gross operating profit. Thus, the statement that LIFO matches current costs with revenues is another way of stating that LIFO gross profit includes no realized holding gains. What happens to the holding gains under LIFO? They remain unrealized, in a sense, just sitting on the balance sheet as the difference between current cost and LIFO cost (the *LIFO reserve*) gets larger and larger over time as prices rise. These unrealized holding gains are only realized under LIFO when a LIFO liquidation occurs and some of the old historical costs that have accumulated on the balance sheet are matched with revenues.

FIFO tends to include more realized holding gains in income than LIFO, except when LIFO liquidations take place. It was observed in Chapter 8 that FIFO can be thought of as the *last-in, still-here* method. Thus, the costs of FIFO inventories tend to be much closer to current costs than the costs of LIFO inventories because FIFO inventories are carried at the costs of the most recent purchases. As a consequence, the inventory costs assigned to cost of goods sold under FIFO tend to be somewhat older; and, hence, there is a greater chance that some noncurrent costs are matched with revenues under FIFO.

To illustrate this difference between LIFO and FIFO, consider the following example. Morris Merchandise Co. sells a single product. Data from its most recent year's operations follows.

	Units		Cost/Unit		Total Cost
Inventory at 1/1	5,000 units	at	$250	=	$ 1,250,000
Purchases:					
1/1 – 6/30	20,000 units	at	$275	=	$ 5,500,000
7/1 – 12/31	36,000 units	at	$280	=	10,080,000
Total	56,000				$15,580,000
Sales:					
1/1 – 6/30	23,000 units	at	$375	=	$ 8,625,000
7/1 – 12/31	30,000 units	at	$380	=	11,400,000
Total	53,000				$20,025,000
Inventory at 12/31	8,000 units				

Notice that in both parts of the year, the firm's pricing policy is to sell the product for $100 more than its current replacement cost. Thus, the firm enjoys a gross operating profit of $100 on each of the 53,000 units sold for total gross operating profit of $5,300,000. Let us compare the gross profits computed under FIFO and LIFO with this bench mark:

FIFO:

Sales		$20,025,000
Cost of goods sold:		
1/1 inventory	1,250,000	
Purchases	15,580,000	
12/31 inventory	(2,240,000)*	14,590,000
FIFO gross profit		$ 5,435,000

* 8,000 units × $280 = $2,240,000

LIFO:

Sales		$20,025,000
Cost of goods sold:		
1/1 inventory	1,250,000	
Purchases	15,580,000	
12/31 inventory	(2,075,000)**	14,755,000
LIFO gross profit		$ 5,270,000

** 5,000 units	×	$250	=	$1,250,000
3,000 units	×	$275	=	825,000
8,000 units				$2,075,000

FIFO gross profit apparently includes $135,000 of realized holding gains since it exceeds gross operating profit by that amount ($5,435,000 − $5,300,000). This will occur whenever current costs are not matched with current revenues. In the case of FIFO, the first 5,000 units sold in the first six months of the year had a current cost of $275 but were assigned a FIFO cost of $250 for a realized holding gain of $25 per unit on 5,000 units or $125,000. In the second half of the year, the first 2,000 units sold were assigned a FIFO cost of $275 when their replacement cost was $280 for an additional holding gain of $5 per unit on 2,000 units, or $10,000. This yields a total for the year of $125,000 plus $10,000 or $135,000 under FIFO.

LIFO gross profit apparently includes $30,000 of holding *losses* ($5,270,000 − $5,300,000). How can LIFO produce realized holding losses in a period of rising prices? The LIFO cost assigned to 6,000 units in the first half of the year was $280, while the actual replacement cost in the period was $275. This yields a holding loss of $5 per unit on 6,000 units or $30,000.

Thus, even in a period with no LIFO liquidation, it is not always strictly true that "LIFO matches current costs with revenues." It is safe to conclude, however, that in the absence of liquidations of old LIFO layers, LIFO gross profit will, in general, include less realized holding gains and/or losses than FIFO gross profit.

SUMMARY

This chapter has looked at two extensions of the basic inventory accounting principles introduced in Chapter 8. First, some very useful approximation techniques were examined. These allow firms to arrive at good working approximations of the results of more complicated inventory accounting procedures. These approximation techniques have a wide range of uses in reporting for managerial, financial, and tax purposes.

The dollar value LIFO method allows firms to prepare their financial statements on a LIFO basis while maintaining their internal inventory records on the basis of some other cost flow assumption. The technique involves a year-end adjustment using published or internally constructed indexes of the change in inventory prices.

The retail inventory method allows firms to prepare their financial statements with inventories stated at cost, while maintaining their internal inventory records on the basis of retail value. The variations of this technique all involve the application of a cost percentage to the year-end retail value of the firms' inventories.

The LIFO retail method combines the dollar value LIFO method with the retail method to allow firms to prepare their financial statements on a LIFO cost basis, while maintaining their internal inventory records on the basis of retail value.

The gross profit method is related to the retail method in that it relies on the relationship between the cost of firms' inventories and their retail value to produce estimates of inventory values when it is inconvenient or impossible to determine their costs using traditional methods.

Second, some alternatives to the LCM valuation rule were considered. Some of these alternatives are used for financial reporting purposes in special cases, while others are useful primarily for managerial and analytical purposes.

Under a variable costing approach, only those costs that vary with output are included in inventory cost, while under a full absorption costing approach, all costs, whether fixed or variable, are included in inventory cost. While GAAP require full absorption costing, this makes cost of goods sold depend on the quantity manufactured as well as the quantity sold.

Standard costs are set by managers as realistic goals that manufacturing employees should be able to meet. They are used for financial reporting purposes if they reasonably approximate cost under a FIFO, LIFO, or average cost flow assumption.

Some industries value their inventories at net realizable value, or "estimated selling price in the normal course of business less reasonably predictable costs of completion and disposal."

Accounting for inventories at their replacement costs allows firms' income to be separated into operating profit (sales price minus the cost to replace) and holding gains (increase in the cost of replacing inventory). Holding gains do not represent income that firms could spend without effectively impairing their ability to continue operating at the same level.

Finally, FIFO and LIFO were compared in terms of the extent to which they include realized holding gains in income. In general, LIFO was found to include fewer realized holding gains in income than FIFO except when liquidations of old LIFO cost layers occur.

QUESTIONS

1. What are the advantages to a retail firm of using the conventional *retail method*? The *LIFO retail method*?
2. What uses are there for the *gross profit method*?
3. Why is it necessary to pay attention to the mix of items in inventory in applying the gross profit method?
4. Is the mix of items in inventory also a concern in the retail inventory methods? Why?
5. Why is it probably more appropriate for a retail department store to apply the retail inventory method by department rather than for the entire store?
6. Under the retail inventory method, how is freight-in on inventory purchases included in the calculation?
7. If a retail firm records its purchase returns separately, how should this item be handled in the conventional retail method?
8. What are the advantages of using the *dollar value LIFO* inventory method as opposed to the conventional LIFO method?
9. What is an *inventory pool*?
10. How does the use of inventory pools simplify accounting for inventories?
11. In what inventory methods are inventory pools typically employed?
12. How does the use of published *price level indexes* simplify the application of the dollar value inventory technique?
13. What are *inventory profits*?
14. Which cost flow assumption, LIFO or FIFO, will typically produce more inventory profits? Why?
15. Under what circumstances will LIFO include more holding gains in income than FIFO?

EXERCISES

9-1.   *Gross profit method*

The following information appears in Dix Company records for the year ended December 31, 1994:

Merchandise inventory, 1/1/94	$ 275,000
Purchases	1,125,000
Sales	1,500,000

On December 31, 1994, a physical inventory revealed that the ending inventory was only $300,000. Dix's gross profit on sales has remained constant at 30% in recent years. Dix suspects that some inventory may have been pilfered by one of the new employees.

REQUIRED:

At December 31, 1994, what is the estimated cost of missing inventory?
(AICPA adapted)

9-2.   Gross profit method

On September 30, 1995, a fire at Brock Company's only warehouse caused severe damage to its entire inventory. Based on recent history, Brock has a gross profit of 30% of net sales. The following information is available from Brock's records for the nine months ended September 30, 1995:

Inventory at 1/1/95	$ 550,000
Purchases	3,000,000
Net sales	4,000,000

A physical inventory disclosed usable damaged goods which Brock estimates can be sold for $50,000.

REQUIRED:

Using the gross profit method, calculate the estimated loss from the fire at September 30, 1995.
(AICPA adapted)

9-3.   Gross profit method

Nada Co.'s pricing structure has been established to yield a gross margin of 40%. The following data pertain to the year ended December 31, 1993:

Sales	$1,000,000
Inventory, January 1, 1993	500,000
Purchases	400,000
Inventory, per actual count at December 31, 1993	80,000

Nada is satisfied that all sales and purchases have been fully and properly recorded but is concerned about the possibility of inventory shortages.

REQUIRED:

How much might Nada reasonably estimate as a shortage in inventory at December 31, 1993?
(AICPA adapted)

9-4.   Retail method

At December 31, 1994, the following information was available from Moore Company's accounting records:

	Cost	Retail
Inventory, 1/1/94	$ 29,400	$ 40,600
Purchases	166,600	231,000
Additional markups	–	8,400
Available for sale	$196,000	$280,000

Sales for the year totaled $221,200, and markdowns amounted to $2,800.

REQUIRED:

Calculate the cost of inventory at December 31, 1994, under the conventional retail method, which approximates the lower of cost or market value.

(AICPA adapted)

9-5. *Retail method*

Shannon Retail Co. uses the conventional retail method and reports the following amounts for 1995:

	Cost	Retail
Inventory, 1/1/95	$ 36,000	$ 60,000
Purchases	220,000	420,000
Sales		400,000
Net markups		3,000
Net markdowns		7,500

REQUIRED:

Calculate ending inventory and cost of goods sold for the year under the conventional retail method.

9-6. *Retail method*

Hutch Co. uses the conventional retail method and reports the following amounts:

	Cost	Retail
Inventory, 1/1/94	?	$ 175,000
Purchases	$1,054,100	1,925,000
Sales		1,940,000
Markups		40,000
Markdowns		65,000
Inventory, 12/31/94	$ 72,900	$ 135,000

REQUIRED:

Calculate the cost ratio used at year-end and the cost of the inventory at January 1, 1994.

9-7. *Retail method*

The Good Trader Company values its inventory by using the conventional retail method. The following information is available for the year 1993.

	Cost	Retail
Beginning inventory	$ 80,000	$140,000
Purchases	297,000	420,000
Freight-in	4,000	
Shortages	—	8,000
Markups (net)	—	10,000
Markdowns (net)	—	2,000
Sales	—	400,000

REQUIRED:

At what amount would the Good Trader Company report its ending inventory?

(AICPA adapted)

9-8. *Dollar value LIFO*

Dalton Company adopted the dollar value LIFO inventory method on January 1, 1993. In applying the LIFO method, Dalton uses internal price indexes and the multiple-pools approach. The following data were available for Inventory Pool No. 1 for the two years following the adoption of LIFO:

	Current Inventory		
	At Current Year Cost	At Base Year Cost	Internal Price Index
1/1/93	$100,000	$100,000	1.00
12/31/93	126,000	120,000	1.05
12/31/94	140,800	128,000	1.10

REQUIRED:

Use the dollar value LIFO method to calculate inventory at December 31, 1993.

(AICPA adapted)

9-9. *Dollar value LIFO*

Since January 1, 1993, Boyd Manufacturing Co. has used the dollar value LIFO method applied to a single inventory pool. The current costs of its inventory and the values of the price index used in the calculation at the end of the last three fiscal years are as follows:

	12/31/94	12/31/93	1/1/93
Inventory at current cost	$19,030	$17,472	$16,600
Price index (1992=100)	110	104	100

Inventory purchases in 1994 and 1993 were $196,310 and $173,400, respectively.

REQUIRED:

Calculate ending inventory at December 31, 1993, and 1994 and the cost of goods sold for 1993 and 1994 under the dollar value LIFO method.

9-10. *Dollar value LIFO*

Since January 1, 1992, Carlisle Corp. has used the dollar value LIFO method applied to a single inventory pool. The current costs of its inventory and the values of the price index used in the calculation at the end of the last three fiscal years are as follows:

	12/31/93	12/31/92	1/1/92
Inventory at current cost	$51,600	$41,040	$40,000
Price index (1991=100)	120	108	100

Inventory purchases in 1993 and 1992 were $642,000 and $476,000, respectively.

REQUIRED:

Calculate ending inventory at December 31, 1992, and 1993 and the cost of goods sold for 1992 and 1993 under the dollar value LIFO method.

9-11. *Dollar value LIFO retail method*

Dorothy's Draperies, Inc. has used the dollar value LIFO retail method since January 1, 1993. Information for the three most recent years is as follows.

	12/31/94	12/31/93	1/ 1/93
Inventory at current retail	$82,880	$82,080	$74,000
Cost percentage for the year	58%	62%	60%
Price level index (1992=100)	112	108	100

REQUIRED:

Calculate LIFO retail ending inventory at December 31, 1993 and 1994.

9-12. *Dollar value LIFO retail method*

On December 31, 1992, Jason Company adopted the dollar value LIFO retail inventory method. Inventory data for 1993 are as follows:

	LIFO Cost	Retail
Inventory, 12/31/92	$360,000	$500,000
Inventory, 12/31/93	?	660,000
Increase in price level for 1993		10%
Cost to retail ratio for 1993		70%

REQUIRED:

Use the LIFO retail method to calculate Jason's inventory at December 31, 1993.
(AICPA adapted)

PROBLEMS

9-1. *Dollar value LIFO method*

The Barometer Company manufactures one product. On December 31, 1992, Barometer adopted the dollar value LIFO inventory method. The inventory on that date using the dollar value LIFO method was $200,000.
Inventory data are as follows:

Year	Inventory at Respective Year-end Prices	Price Index (Base Year 1992)
1993	$231,000	1.05
1994	299,000	1.15
1995	300,000	1.20

REQUIRED:

Compute the inventory at December 31, 1993, 1994, and 1995, using the dollar value LIFO method for each year.
(AICPA adapted)

9-2. *LIFO retail inventory method*

The Jericho Variety Store uses the LIFO retail inventory method. Information relating to the computation of the inventory at December 31, 1993, follows:

	Cost	Retail
Inventory, January 1, 1993	$ 29,000	$ 45,000
Purchases	120,000	172,000
Freight-in	20,000	
Sales		190,000
Net markups		40,000
Net markdowns		12,000

REQUIRED:

Assuming that there was no change in the price index during the year, compute the inventory at December 31, 1993, using the LIFO retail inventory method.
(AICPA adapted)

9-3. *Dollar value LIFO retail method*

Farsighted, Inc. has been using the conventional retail method for some time and is considering adoption of the dollar value LIFO retail method using a published price index. Farsighted's records reveal the following:

	Cost	Retail
Inventory, 12/31/92	$ 247,819	$ 450,580
Purchases	2,262,712	3,800,920
Sales		3,706,600
Markups		14,300
Markdowns		44,000
Inventory, 12/31/93		515,200

The price index Farsighted, Inc. would use if LIFO retail is adopted for 1993 has the following values.

	Index
12/31/92	100
12/31/93	112

REQUIRED:

Calculate 12/31/93 inventory and cost of goods sold for 1993 under the following methods:
1. Conventional retail
2. Dollar value LIFO retail (adopted effective 1/1/93)

9-4. *Dollar value LIFO*

On January 1, 1991, Grover Company changed its inventory cost flow assumption to the dollar value LIFO cost method from the FIFO cost method for its raw materials inventory. The change was made for both financial statement and income tax reporting purposes. Grover uses the multiple-pools approach under which substantially identical raw materials are grouped into LIFO inventory pools. Published price level indexes are used in valuing annual incremental layers. The composition of the December 31, 1993, inventory for the Class F inventory pool is as follows:

	Base Cost	Index	LIFO Cost
Base year inventory, 1991	$ 90,000	1.00	$ 90,000
Incremental layer, 1992	30,000	1.10	33,000
Incremental layer, 1993	20,000	1.25	25,000
Inventory, December 31, 1993	$140,000		$148,000

Data for 1994–1995:

	Purchases	FIFO Cost of Ending Inventory	Index
Year ended December 31, 1994	$165,600	$154,000	1.40
Year ended December 31, 1995	306,000	240,000	1.60

REQUIRED:

1. Prepare a schedule to compute the dollar value LIFO amount of the Class F inventory pool at December 31, 1994.
2. Prepare a schedule to compute the cost of Class F raw materials used in production for the year ended December 31, 1994.
3. Prepare a schedule to compute the dollar value LIFO amount of the Class F inventory pool at December 31, 1995.
   (AICPA adapted)

9-5. *Dollar value LIFO method*

On January 1, 1992, Lucas Distributors, Inc., adopted the dollar value LIFO inventory method for income tax and external financial statement reporting purposes. However, Lucas continued to use the FIFO inventory method for internal accounting and management purposes. In applying the LIFO method, Lucas uses internal conversion price indexes and the multiple-pools approach under which substantially identical inventory items are grouped into LIFO inventory pools. The following data were available for Inventory Pool No. 1, comprises Products A and B, for the two years following the adoption of LIFO:

	FIFO Basis per Records		
	Units	Unit Cost	Total Cost
Inventory, 1/1/92			
Product A	12,000	$30	$360,000
Product B	8,000	25	200,000
			$560,000
Inventory, 12/31/92			
Product A	17,000	35	$595,000
Product B	9,000	28	252,000
			$847,000
Inventory, 12/31/93			
Product A	13,000	40	$520,000
Product B	10,000	32	320,000
			$840,000

REQUIRED:

1. Prepare a schedule to compute the internal conversion price indexes for 1992 and 1993. These are calculated as the ratio of the ending inventory priced at current FIFO cost to the ending inventory priced at base period FIFO costs. Round indexes to two decimal places.
2. Prepare a schedule to compute the inventory amounts at December 31, 1992 and 1993, using the dollar value LIFO inventory method.
   (AICPA adapted)

9-6.   *Dollar value LIFO retail*

Spirit Enterprises maintains its inventory records on the basis of retail prices but has used the dollar value LIFO retail method for financial reporting purposes since 1984. Information from the firm's 1993 records reveals the following:

	Retail Price
Inventory, 12/31/92	$ 250,125
Purchases	2,525,000
Sales	(2,410,097)
Markups	11,500
Markdowns	(62,500)
Inventory, 12/31/93	$ 314,028

Values of the price index used in the LIFO retail calculations at relevant dates are as follows:

	Index (1960 = 100)
12/31/84 (Base year)	160.0
12/31/92	184.0
12/31/93	195.2

Cost of goods purchased in 1993 was $1,533,880. The cost of the inventory at 12/31/92 under the LIFO retail method was $120,060.

REQUIRED:

Calculate the cost of the inventory at 12/31/93 under the dollar value LIFO retail method.

9-7.   *Operating income vs. holding gains*

Nolead, Inc. is a gasoline retailer offering only unleaded regular gasoline. During June, 1993, Nolead had the following inventory transactions.

	Gallons	Cost/Gallon	Total
Inventory, 5/31/93	12,500	$.80	$ 10,000
Purchases:			
June 1–10	75,000	.82	61,500
June 11–20	85,000	.84	71,400
June 21–30	68,000	.88	59,840
Total	228,000		$192,740

Sales activity for the month was as follows:

	Gallons	Price/Gallon	Total
June 1–10	80,500	$.90	$ 72,450
June 11–20	78,000	.94	73,320
June 21–30	72,000	.98	70,560
Total	230,500		$216,330

REQUIRED:

Calculate gross operating income and holding gains for the month of June.

9-8.   *FIFO and holding gains*

Refer to the data for Nolead, Inc. in Problem 9-7.

REQUIRED:

Calculate gross profit for the month on a FIFO basis. Are any holding gains included in FIFO gross profit? Why?

9-9.   *LIFO and holding gains*

Refer to the data for Nolead, Inc. in Problem 9-7.

REQUIRED:

Calculate gross profit for the month on a LIFO basis. Are any holding gains included in LIFO gross profit? Why?

ADVANCED MICRO DEVICES, INC.

Advanced Micro Devices, Inc. is a semiconductor manufacturer. The following information is taken from the firm's 1991 annual report.

Information from the Consolidated Balance Sheets:
December 29, 1991; December 30, 1990; and December 31, 1989
(In Thousands)

	1991	1990	1989
Inventories:			
Raw materials	$ 19,556	$ 21,049	$ 22,518
Work-in-process	39,100	34,892	31,246
Finished goods	32,835	34,101	36,727
Total inventories	$ 91,491	$ 90,042	$ 90,491

Information from the Consolidated Statements of Operations:
Three Years Ended December 29, 1991
(In Thousands)

	1991	1990	1989
Net sales	$ 1,226,649	$ 1,059,242	$ 1,104,606
Expenses:			
Cost of sales	658,824	678,507	643,427
Research and development	213,765	203,651	201,764
Marketing, general and administrative	244,900	228,204	220,983
	$ 1,117,489	$ 1,110,362	$ 1,066,174
Operating income (loss)	$ 109,160	$ (51,120)	$ 38,432
Litigation judgment		(27,738)	
Interest and other income	57,007	33,588	27,213
Interest expense	(20,880)	(8,282)	(15,790)
Income (loss) before taxes on income	$ 145,287	$ (53,552)	$ 49,855
Provision for taxes on income			3,803
Net income (loss)	$ 145,287	$ (53,552)	$ 46,052

Information from the Notes to
Consolidated Financial Statements:
December 29, 1991, December 30, 1990, and December 31, 1989

1. Accounting Policies

Inventories. Inventories are stated principally at standard costs adjusted to approximate the lower of cost (first-in, first-out) or market (net realizable value).

The following additional information is also available:
(a) The Bureau of Labor Statistics of the U.S. Department of Labor publishes producer price indexes (PPI). Values of the PPI for semiconductors (base period = 6/81) were as follows:

December 1991	100.8
December 1990	104.0
December 1989	106.2
December 1988	109.0

(b) AMD's total inventory at December 31, 1988, was $90,487,000.

Assume the following:

(a) AMD's reported inventory amounts are approximately equal to the current costs of the inventories at the balance sheet dates.

(b) The PPI for the semiconductor industry accurately captures the prices of items in AMD's inventory.

REQUIRED:

1. Apply the dollar value LIFO method (adopted effective December 31, 1988) to calculate the LIFO value of AMD's inventory at December 31, 1988, 1989, 1990, and 1991.
2. Calculate the cost of goods sold amounts that AMD would have reported on a LIFO basis for the years ended December 31, 1989, 1990, and 1991.
3. Calculate the income (loss) before taxes on income that AMD would have reported on a LIFO basis for the years ended December 31, 1989, 1990, and 1991.
4. Speculate on why AMD does not use the LIFO method.

CASE 9.2

E. I. DU PONT DE NEMOURS AND COMPANY

The 1984 Consolidated Income Statement for E. I. du Pont de Nemours and Company appeared as follows (amounts in millions):

Sales	$35,915
Other income	303
Total	36,218
Cost of goods sold	23,983
Selling, general, and administrative expenses	2,024
Depreciation, depletion, and amortization	1,736
Exploration expenses	524
Research and development expenses	1,097
Interest and debt expense	565
Taxes other than on income	2,345
Total	$32,274
Earnings before income taxes	3,944
Provision for income taxes	2,513
Net income	$ 1,431

The summary of significant accounting policies reveals the following:

Inventories

Substantially all inventories are carried at cost as determined by the last-in, first-out (LIFO) method; in the aggregate, such valuations are not in excess of market. Elements of cost in inventories include raw materials, direct labor and manufacturing overhead. Stores and supplies are valued at cost or market, whichever is lower; cost is generally determined by the average cost method.

Note 8, Inventories, contains the following information:

The liquidation of LIFO inventory quantities carried in the aggregate at lower costs prevailing in prior years increased 1982 net income by approximately $51.

The Supplemental Inflation Disclosure reveals the following:

Conventional financial statements measure results in historical dollars and therefore do not reflect fully the effects of changing prices. Additional perspective is provided using the current cost accounting method, under which depreciation, depletion and amortization (DD&A) expense and costs of goods sold are adjusted using indices representative of costs incurred by the company. The effect of these adjustments in 1984 was as follows:

Income from continuing operations	$1,431
DD&A adjustment	(231)
Cost of goods sold adjustment	(33)
Current cost income from continuing operations	$1,167

The DD&A adjustment reflects the cumulative effect of higher replacement costs for property, plant and equipment (PP&E), which costs are not necessarily indicative of fair values or actual costs that would be incurred in replacing the company's productive capacity, and in particular, its natural resource assets. The adjustments to costs of goods sold reflects the effect of LIFO inventory liquidations.

REQUIRED:

1. Explain how the liquidation of LIFO inventory quantities increased 1982 net income.
2. Explain how the current cost adjustments to costs of goods sold reflects the effect of LIFO inventory liquidations.
3. Explain why the cost of goods sold adjustment in the Supplemental Inflation Disclosure is not the same amount as the effect of the LIFO liquidation on net income.

Acquisition of Property, Plant, and Equipment

Property, plant, and equipment often represents the largest asset category in firms' balance sheets. These assets, also known as **productive assets** or **fixed assets**, are those with useful lives greater than one year that firms hold for use rather than for sale. Firms invest in this type of asset to house their operations and produce their products and/or services. The magnitude of firms' investments in plant and equipment will depend on how they choose to produce their products and services. Firms that require a significant investment in plant and equipment are said to be **capital intensive**. For example, an electric utility requires a very large investment in facilities for the generation and transmission of electricity. Detroit Edison, in its 1990 annual report shows $9.053 billion of property, plant, and equipment, which is 86% of its total assets. Other capital intensive industries include heavy manufacturing and airlines.

Because the amounts involved are so large for many firms, the accounting methods applied to property, plant, and equipment can have a significant impact on firms' financial statements. Interestingly enough, as we shall see in this chapter and especially the next, quite a number of alternative accounting methods are available for these assets. The combination of the large dollar amounts involved and the flexibility in available accounting methods make this area particularly interesting.

Exhibit 10.1 presents some information from The Dow Chemical Company's notes to its financial statements for 1990. Approximately 34% of Dow Chemical's total assets was in the category of Plant Properties. Examination of the schedule of plant properties reveals that Dow Chemical breaks its Plant Property down into 11 categories. These categories give a good idea of the kinds of assets typically included under the heading of property, plant, and equipment for a large industrial corporation.

How are the values in Exhibit 10.1 determined? Why do accountants have different rules for the valuation of property, plant, and equipment than those existing for inventory or other assets? These questions are the subject of this chapter. Chapter 11 deals with methods of recognizing the cost of property, plant, and equipment as expense (depreciation and depletion), as well as accounting for the disposal of these assets.

CHARACTERISTICS OF PROPERTY, PLANT, AND EQUIPMENT

In this section, we show how the accounting methods used for productive assets relate to the assets' characteristics. In very general terms, productive assets are initially recorded at their cost. The costs are recognized as expenses over their useful lives through the process known as *depreciation*. In this chapter, we consider issues related to determining the cost of property, plant, and equipment.

The accounting methods applied to productive assets differ significantly from those for other assets, namely short-term investments and inventory, because productive assets have different characteristics and different markets. By comparing and contrasting productive assets with other assets we have already considered, we can appreciate the need for their different accounting treatment.

Unlike inventory and short-term investments, productive assets are held for use rather than for sale. If an asset will be used rather than sold, then that asset's current market value is not particularly relevant. Far more important is the asset's ability to generate positive future cash flows through its use. Therefore, the market values used for short-term investments and the lower-of-cost-or-market value rules for inventories are not extended to productive assets.

EXHIBIT 10.1

The Dow Chemical Company—Plant Properties

THE DOW CHEMICAL COMPANY Plant Properties		
	1990	1989
Land	$ 310	$ 281
Land and waterway improvements	551	492
Buildings	1,892	1,623
Transportation and construction equipment	163	159
Machinery and equipment	12,238	11,002
Utility and supply lines	1,220	1,066
Wells	144	137
Office furniture and equipment	624	468
Mineral reserves	35	31
Other	232	185
Construction in progress	1,740	1,256
Total	$19,149	$16,700

The markets for productive assets also differ from those for short-term investments and, to a lesser extent, from those for inventory items. Monetary assets such as receivables and investment securities are claims to cash flows that can be bought and sold with very small transactions costs. Transferring bonds from one owner to another is less costly than shipping equipment from a manufacturer to a purchaser. Given the ease of transactions, markets for trading monetary assets are well-developed and generally centralized. Since markets for inventory items are not as well-formed, market values for these items are more difficult to evaluate.[1] However, inventories are held for sale to generate revenues. Thus, it is appropriate to attempt to measure the realizable value of items in inventory and then recognize losses when declines in selling prices of inventory items can be identified.

Markets for assets classified as property, plant, and equipment typically are not centralized and not as well-developed. Consequently, these assets cannot be readily bought and sold in centralized markets. This does not mean they have no value. Rather, these assets tend to be more specialized, and markets for used assets where many buyers and sellers come to trade assets are not typical. For example, compare a truck to the commodity, gold. The number of differing types of trucks is large, ranging from a Chevrolet 1/2-ton pickup to a Ford diesel cab and trailer. Each vehicle differs slightly in its character, the options it has, and the value of the vehicle in service, even though both are trucks. On the other hand, all gold is basically the same, differing only in level of purity. Since gold can easily be classified as to its purity and the number of traders demanding and providing it is relatively large, a well-organized market has developed for trading. Such a market is not as likely for trucks due to the number of dimensions on which they can vary.

These differences in the organization and structure of markets imply that it is difficult to determine market values of assets traded in most product markets. Without well-organized markets from which to observe transactions prices for similar assets, valuation of assets not held for sale becomes a subjective process of attempting to assign value to the assets' unique attributes. Using these subjective values for financial reporting purposes would result in unreliable financial statements. Thus, the valuation of property, plant, and equipment for financial statement purposes relies heavily on the use of historical acquisition prices, not current market values.

VALUATION OF PROPERTY, PLANT, AND EQUIPMENT

Valuation of property, plant, and equipment is similar to inventory valuation, with the exception that the lower-of-cost-or-market rule is generally not applied. The general guideline is that all costs incurred to bring the asset to productive use are capitalized as part of the asset's acquisition costs. The lower-of-cost-or-market rule is not applied because productive assets, unlike inventories, are not held for sale. As we shall see, when there is a basis for

---

[1] The well-developed markets for various commodity items such as precious metals and agricultural products are an obvious exception.

determining that a plant asset has lost value due to its inability to produce products or services profitably, then a write-down or write-off of the asset is considered.

Real Property

Real property, or land, may be acquired for an office or manufacturing site or held partly as an investment and partly for potential future expansion. When land is held as an investment, the property is generally classified as a noncurrent investment, not part of property, plant, and equipment. The classification as property, plant, and equipment is reserved for assets placed in service or under construction. Regardless of the manner in which the property will be used, valuation of the property in the balance sheet will depend on the acquisition price plus any cost related to bring the land to productive use. These costs include various transactions costs incurred to acquire the property as well as the costs of improvements.

Transactions costs associated with the acquisition of land include legal fees, title transfer fees, commissions paid to brokers, and other closing costs. Property taxes the purchaser pays would generally not be considered part of the capitalized value of the property, but rather as a period expense. The only exception to this may be when land is purchased for speculation. Here, the capitalization of property taxes acts as a deferral of the cost to be matched against the future selling price of the land. In this case, it would be appropriate to evaluate the relationship between the land's carrying value and its appraised market value since capitalization of costs in excess of an expected selling price is inappropriate. Another transaction cost capitalized as part of the cost of land is that of any option acquired on the parcel prior to actual purchase. Purchase of an option allows the buyer the right to purchase the property at a fixed price over some period of time. If the option is allowed to go unexercised, the cost of the option is charged to expense. If the option is exercised, the purchase price of the option is included in the capitalized value of the land acquired.

Improvements to land are generally capitalized. Some of these types of costs are capitalized as part of the land's value, while others are treated as a separate category of land improvements. The difference between these two approaches lies in the nature of the expenditure. If incurred for improvements that permanently alter the property and thus have an indefinite future life, the expenditures should be capitalized as part of the property's value. Examples of these expenditures would include landscaping, demolition of buildings on the site to prepare it for the intended use, and special assessments for installation of such public services as sewers, curb and gutter, or sidewalks on the property. Land improvements that have limited lives would include parking lots, fencing, and other amenities that will require replacement over the life of the land. These expenditures should be capitalized and charged to expense over their expected useful lives.

Buildings, Machinery, and Equipment

The major component of the capitalized cost of buildings, machinery, and equipment is typically their purchase price. However, in addition to purchase price, other costs may be capitalized if they relate directly to bringing the asset into productive use. Also, the purchase price of assets is not always the invoice price. If the seller allows purchase discounts, the actual cost of the equipment is the invoice price less the discount, similar to the net method of recording purchase discounts for inventory as discussed in Chapter 8. Other costs that are typically included in the capitalized value of these assets include freight charges for delivery of equipment, sales taxes (if applicable), in-transit insurance costs, and installation costs. In those cases where a production facility needs to be rearranged due to the acquisition of some new equipment, the cost of the rearrangement should be capitalized as part of the cost of bringing the new asset into productive use.

Leasehold Improvements

Many companies prefer to lease, rather than own, their places of business. For instance, the 1992 annual report of Albertson's, Inc., a large retail food and drug chain, contains the following description of its activities:

> The Company leases a portion of its real estate. The typical lease period is 25 to 30 years and most leases contain renewal options. Exercise of such options is dependent on the level of business conducted at the location. In addition, the Company leases certain equipment. Some leases contain contingent rental provisions based on sales volume at retail stores or miles traveled for trucks.

In most cases, these leased assets are not included in the company's property, plant, and equipment, but any improvements the company makes to the assets are included. For instance, Albertson's 1992 Summary of Significant Accounting Policies states that "the costs of major remodeling and improvements on leased stores are capitalized as leasehold improvements." Much of the U.S. retail trade is conducted in leased facilities, and leasehold improvements can be a large component of property, plant, and equipment for such firms. Leasehold improvements are not accounted for any differently than other productive assets. They are initially recorded at cost as described above.

PROBLEMS IN DETERMINING THE COST OF PROPERTY, PLANT, AND EQUIPMENT

In certain situations, it may be difficult to determine the cost of property, plant, and equipment. When a package of assets is acquired in a lump-sum purchase, the package's purchase price must then be allocated to the individual assets in the group to determine each asset's cost. Some companies construct their own assets, and the question arises as to which costs should be capitalized as the cost of the asset. Similarly, the issue arises as to whether interest cost should be capitalized as part of the cost of self-constructed assets. Finally, how is the cost of an asset determined when the asset is acquired in a nonmonetary exchange—i.e., when the price is not paid in cash or some other monetary consideration? We consider each of these issues in turn.

Lump-Sum Purchases

When multiple assets are acquired for a single purchase price, the documents of transfer do not indicate a valuation of each individual asset acquired. These transactions are referred to as **lump-sum purchases**. For example, when land and a building are acquired, the documents of sale do not generally indicate the value of the land and building separately. For accounting purposes, some allocation of the purchase price across the various assets is required. This is particularly true for the joint acquisition of land and buildings where one asset is subject to depreciation and the other is not. Generally, the procedure is to obtain separate estimates of each asset's fair market value and then allocate the purchase price to each asset based on the pro-rata contribution each makes to the sum of the individual fair market values. Exhibit 10.2 demonstrates this process.

Self-Constructed Assets

In many cases, the acquisition of certain assets carries with it a need for some type of self-construction on either a limited or extended scale. **Self-constructed assets** are those in which a company has used some of its own labor or capital resources to construct or install. Buildings and equipment are frequently

EXHIBIT 10.2
Allocation of
Purchase Price in
Lump-Sum
Acquisitions

Allocation of Purchase Price in Lump-Sum Acquisitions

On May 15, 1993, Delta Company acquired a parcel of land on which a building had been constructed for a total purchase price of $300,000, which it paid in cash. Independent appraisals of the land and building indicate the land is valued at $80,000 and the building is valued at $240,000, for a total value of $320,000.

To allocate the purchase price over the land and building, Delta would use the following allocation procedure:

Asset	Estimated Fair Value	Percent of Total Fair Value	Recorded Acquisition Cost
Land	$ 80,000	25.0%	$ 75,000
Building	240,000	75.0%	225,000
Totals	$320,000	100.0%	$300,000

Journal Entry to Record Acquisition of Land and Building:

May 15, 1993:

Land	75,000	
Building	225,000	
Cash		300,000

To record the acquisition of land and building in a single purchase on May 15.

self-constructed. An important accounting issue for self-constructed assets is how to determine the magnitude of the costs that will be capitalized as part of the plant asset. While some argue that only the marginal costs incurred, such as direct labor and materials, should be allocated to the installation, generally accepted accounting principles rely on the same full cost approach that is used in representing inventory costs. In the case of self-constructed assets, the direct costs, as well as a portion of the overhead of the manufacturing operation, should be allocated to the asset's cost and capitalized. The full cost approach results in allocation problems similar to those for inventory. One issue not resolved by this method is the capitalization of interest costs on capital used to finance major construction projects.

Interest Capitalization

Interest costs represent the cost of using borrowed funds and generally are expensed as incurred. Accountants view the decision to acquire an asset as separate from and independent of the means of financing the purchase. Thus, when assets are acquired with borrowed funds, the asset's cost typically does not include any interest cost. Instead, interest costs are viewed as period costs and expensed.

A major exception to this general rule is contained in *FASB Statement of Financial Accounting Standards No. 34*, "Capitalization of Interest Costs," which requires interest capitalization on all assets constructed for a firm's own use or for sale or lease as discrete projects.[2] That is, the cost of assets constructed for a firm's own use or for sale or lease as discrete projects may include interest costs.

There is frankly little theoretical support for the treatment specified in SFAS No. 34. In recent theories of finance, the decision to purchase an asset is dependent on capital structure—i.e., how the firm finances the acquisition of its assets. These theories allow for the possibility that the cost of acquiring an asset depends on the method of financing its acquisition. In turn, this offers some justification for capitalization of financing costs such as interest. However, these theories would seem to apply equally to self-construction or outright purchase of assets. At present, interest capitalization only applies to the interest incurred on self-constructed assets. Some historical perspective may help explain this pronouncement.

Historically, interest capitalization began in the public utility industry. Since utility firms typically enjoy some degree of monopoly, they are regulated by state and federal authorities. In general, these electric, gas, and telecommunications firms are allowed to recover, through the rates they charge their customers, the cost of providing their services. This includes the cost of the capital they have invested in utility plant and equipment. Many regulators have been unwilling to pass on the costs of capital incurred during a period of construction to current rate payers. They believe it is unfair to make consumers pay for any costs associated with a plant that is not yet providing any service. Therefore, as a means of deferring these costs to be paid by rate payers

---

[2] "Capitalization of Interest Costs," *Statement of Financial Accounting Standards No. 34* (Stamford, CT: FASB, 1979), para. 9.

who will benefit from the plant when it is completed, the firms capitalize the cost of the capital during the period of construction. Thus, when the plant is completed and goes into service, the cost to be recovered in rates will include the cost of capital incurred (but not recovered in rates) during the period of construction. Note that utilities capitalize not only interest costs (the cost of debt capital), but also the cost of equity capital.

While this practice makes sense for rate regulated firms, it is unclear whether it is appropriate for unregulated firms. Since rates (prices) are determined by competitive market forces, not set by regulation, it is unclear what role capitalization plays for unregulated firms. Nevertheless, many private sector corporations began capitalizing interest on construction in progress during the early 1970s. The justification was often the notion that all costs incurred prior to placing an asset into productive use should be capitalized and matched against the revenues generated from its use in future years. Historical records indicate that during the early 1970s corporate profits were falling, and one effect that capitalization of interest had was to buoy reported profits by delaying the recognition of interest costs as expense. How much of an effect this had on managerial decisions to utilize this accounting treatment is not clear.

In 1974, the SEC became concerned about the practice of interest capitalization and placed a moratorium on the use of interest capitalization until the issue could be examined more closely. The moratorium prevented firms from adopting this accounting policy if they had not done so previously. However, it did not prevent firms that had already capitalized interest in previous periods from continuing to do so. With the SEC's encouragement, the FASB examined the issue of interest capitalization and issued SFAS No. 34. Thus, SFAS No. 34 can be seen as a politically acceptable way of controlling the spread of an accounting practice from the regulated arena where it had appropriate justification to the unregulated arena where it did not.

Under SFAS No. 34, assets qualifying for interest capitalization include those constructed or otherwise produced for an enterprise's own use (including those produced by other parties where deposits or progress payments are required during construction) and those intended for sale or lease that are constructed or otherwise produced as discrete projects. The latter group consists of items of inventory in industries with long production cycles. Some assets are explicitly excluded:

1. Those already in place or in use in production
2. Those that are not being used in production and for which no activities are underway to place them in productive use

Land held for speculation would fall under the second exception.

The computation of the interest to be capitalized is based on a notion of "avoidable cost." That is, the calculation attempts to identify the interest cost that could have been avoided if the funds invested in the construction project had been used instead to reduce (or avoid) indebtedness. Two elements are necessary to make this computation:

1. The amount of average investment in the construction project over the period
2. An interest rate that captures the cost of debt capital used to support the construction project

The average investment in the construction project is determined by accumulating the construction expenditures over time, and then computing a weighted average cost on an annual basis. Accumulation of the expenditures begins and continues as long as three conditions are satisfied:

1. Expenditures for the asset have been made.
2. Activities necessary to prepare the asset for use are in progress.
3. Interest cost has been incurred.[3]

Accumulation of expenditures ceases when the asset is substantially ready for use.

Exhibits 10.3 and 10.4 are examples of the process Acorn International uses to determine the amount of interest to be capitalized on construction in progress. The first step in the process is to compute the average annual accumulated expenditures on the construction projects. This process is described in Exhibit 10.3. This computation is used to determine the average level of expenditures on the construction project over the entire year. As these expenditures are made, they are recorded as Construction in Process (CIP). To determine a weighted average balance for the year in CIP, the beginning balances each month are summed; and the total is divided by 12 to obtain the average. In this particular example, there was a zero balance in CIP for Acorn over the first nine months, and these are deleted from the computation.

The amount of interest cost capitalized is determined by applying an interest rate or rates (known as the *capitalization rate*) to the average accumulated expenditure balance. Exhibit 10.4 demonstrates how the capitalization rate is determined. When loans are taken out specifically to support the construction project, the interest rates on these loans would be applied first to determine the capitalized interest. In Acorn's case, it acquired a loan of $100,000 on October 1, 1995, to help support the first progress payment. Care must be taken to use the annual average balance of these loans, not the total amount borrowed, in order to base the interest computation on the same annual average as the expenditures. In this case, the $100,000 loan was outstanding for three months, so the average annual balance was $25,000. Since the average annual accumulated expenditures were $109,000, the balance of $84,000 is assumed to be financed with other interest bearing debt, which could have been paid off had the cash not been used to pay construction costs.

The next step is to compute a weighted average annual interest rate on the other outstanding debt. This is accomplished by weighting the interest rates on this debt by the portion of the total interest bearing debt outstanding. In this example, the weighted average interest rate on other debt was 11.6%. To compute the capitalized interest for the period, the interest rates are applied to the balances that the respective debt supports to obtain a total capitalized

---

[3] *Ibid.*, para 17.

EXHIBIT 10.3

Example of Interest
Capitalization
Determination of
Average
Accumulated
Expenditures

Example of Interest Capitalization Determination of Average Accumulated Expenditures

Acorn International entered into a fixed-price contract with Elm, Inc. on October 1, 1995, to construct a building at a total cost of $1,000,000. Construction was expected to take eight months. Progress payments of $300,000, $150,000, and $108,000 were made on the first of the month for the last three months of Acorn's fiscal year, which ends on December 31, 1995. Acorn had debt outstanding during this period as follows:

Debt	Book Value	Yield
Short-term line-of-credit	$3,000,000	12%
First mortgage bond	5,000,000	10%
Debenture bond	2,000,000	15%
Construction loan on the project	100,000	11%

The construction loan was taken out at the time of the first progress payment.

Determination of the Average Accumulated Expenditures:
  Balance of Construction in Process as of

October 1, 1995	$ 300,000
November 1, 1995	450,000
December 1, 1995	558,000
Total	$1,308,000
Weighted Average Balance = $1,308,000 ÷ 12 =	$ 109,000

interest of $12,494. The last step in determining the amount of capitalized interest is to ensure that the total interest capitalized does not exceed the total interest costs incurred. Given the large amount of debt that Acorn has outstanding, this is not a limitation in this example. The journal entry below assumes that all interest costs were charged to expense prior to determining the amount to be capitalized.

December 31, 1995:

Construction in progress	12,494	
Interest expense		12,494

To capitalize interest cost already recognized as expense at
  December 31, 1995.

    Disclosures related to interest costs require that in periods when no interest is capitalized, the total interest cost charged to expense be disclosed. This is usually accomplished by listing interest expense on the face of the income statement as an expense category or by including the disclosure in the note on long-term debt. When interest is capitalized in the period, the total interest costs and the amount capitalized must be disclosed, typically in a note.

Nonmonetary Exchanges

In general, when an asset is purchased, it is recorded at its cost—i.e., the value of the consideration the purchaser gives up. **Monetary exchanges** are those in which the consideration given up to acquire an asset is cash, a near cash asset,

Example of Interest Capitalization
Determination of Average Annual Interest Rates and Amount of
Capitalized Interest for Acorn International

| EXHIBIT 10.4

Acorn
International—
Example of Interest
Capitalization—
Determination of
Average Annual
Interest Rates and
Amount of
Capitalized Interest

Determination of the Annualized Interest Rate:

Debt specifically used to finance construction = $100,000 at 11%

Debt was outstanding from 10/1 to 12/31 (3 months):

Annualized Outstanding Debt = $100,000 × 3/12 = $25,000

Weighted Average Accumulated Expenditures	$109,000
Amount Financed Directly by Construction Debt	(25,000)
Amount Financed by Other Debt	$ 84,000

Weighted Average Annual Interest Rate on Nonconstruction Debt:

Debt Instrument	Interest Rate	Amount	Percent of Total Amount	Weighted Average Rate
Short-term line-of-credit	12%	$ 3,000,000	30%	3.6%
First mortgage bond	10%	5,000,000	50%	5.0%
Debenture bond	15%	2,000,000	20%	3.0%
Totals		$10,000,000	100%	11.6%

Determination of Interest to be Capitalized:

Interest on Construction Debt	=	$ 25,000	×	11.0%	=	$ 2,750
Interest on Other Debt	=	84,000	×	11.6%	=	9,744
Total		$109,000				$12,494

or a promise to make future cash payments. In these cases, the asset's purchase price is determined by the fair market value of the monetary asset surrendered or liability assumed in the exchange. Monetary items have readily determinable fair values since they represent cash or claims to cash that can be readily traded. When the purchaser uses nonmonetary assets or equity claims as consideration, the determination of the asset's acquisition price is less clear. These exchanges are referred to as **nonmonetary exchanges** and are the subject of APB Opinion No. 29 and recent deliberations by the Emerging Issues Task Force.

In general, APB Opinion No. 29 specifies that fair values should be used to record these transactions. That is, "the cost of a nonmonetary asset acquired in exchange for another nonmonetary asset is the fair value of the asset surrendered to obtain it, and a gain or loss should be recognized on the exchange."[4] If the market value of the asset acquired is more readily determinable than that of the consideration given up, then the asset's market value will be used to record the exchange.

---

[4] "Accounting for Nonmonetary Transactions," *Accounting Principles Board Opinion No. 29* (New York: AICPA, 1973), para. 18.

There are two exceptions to this general rule of using fair values to record nonmonetary exchanges. First, when fair values of the consideration given up and the asset acquired are not determinable, then the asset acquired will be recorded at the book value of the consideration given. Second, when similar productive assets are exchanged, the transaction is deemed to be "not essentially the culmination of an earning process," and the asset acquired is recorded at the book value of the asset given up.[5]

Asset Acquired by Issuing Stock   Assume that Peterson Corporation exchanged 10,000 shares of its $1 par common stock for a piece of land on April 30, 1995. Peterson's common stock is traded on a major exchange at $15 per share. A recent appraisal of the real estate indicated a value of $120,000. This is a nonmonetary exchange in which both the asset acquired and the shares given as consideration have reasonably determinable fair values, but these values differ. Based on the share price, the land must be worth $150,000, while the appraisal indicates a value of only $120,000. Which of these fair values is more reliable is a judgment issue. However, the stock price is generally considered more reliable unless there are indications of major fluctuations in this price over a short period. Assuming this is the judgment of the individuals involved, Peterson's journal entry to record the land purchase would appear as follows:

April 30, 1995:

Land	150,000	
Common stock at par		10,000
Additional paid-in capital		140,000

To record acquisition of land in exchange for 10,000 shares of stock.

Asset Acquired in Exchange for Stock Held as an Investment   Suppose Peterson gives 10,000 shares of Brown Corporation stock, which it held as an investment carried at $110,000, in exchange for the land, recently appraised at $120,000 on May 15, 1993. Peterson will recognize a gain or loss for the difference between the carrying value of the Brown Corporation stock and its fair value. However, if Brown Corporation is a privately held company with no traded shares, it is likely that the fair value of its stock is less reliable than the appraisal value of the real estate. Thus, the $120,000 value placed on the land will be used to determine the gain or loss on the sale of the Brown Corporation stock. Peterson's journal entry to record the land purchase would appear as follows:

May 15, 1995:

Land	120,000	
Investment in Brown Corp. stock		110,000
Gain on exchange		10,000

To record acquisition of land in exchange for shares of Brown Corp. stock.

---

[5] *Ibid.*, para. 21.

Exchanges of Similar Productive Assets   When similar productive assets are exchanged, the asset structures of both the seller and purchaser are virtually unchanged. For example, assume two companies that manufacture wood products exchange lathes, which are essentially the same except one can accommodate larger pieces of lumber than the other. Following the exchange, both firms have virtually the same future revenue opportunities as before. In both cases, any value in the lathes is expected to be realized by production of future goods for sale, not by sale of the lathes themselves. If these firms are allowed to value the acquired lathes at their fair values, gains or losses will arise without any fundamental change in the companies' underlying ability to generate future profits. Carried to an extreme, managers of companies could generate gains from swapping similar assets whose value has increased without any substantive changes in the companies' real profitability.

It is this characteristic of exchanges of similar productive assets that lead accountants to assert that these types of exchanges are "not essentially the culmination of an earning process" and gains should not be recognized. However, conservatism dictates that if the book value of the asset given up in the exchange exceeds the fair value of the asset acquired, a loss must be recognized to prevent the acquired asset from being recorded at more than its fair value. When dissimilar assets are exchanged, there is a cost to the company in that the realization of the benefits contained in the new asset will require a substantially different series of events than would realization of the benefits in the asset given as consideration. Here, the earnings process is deemed to be complete since the realization of future benefits depends on an entirely different process.

Assume that on July 17, 1995, Kline Company gives a parcel of land it purchased several years ago for $40,000 in exchange for a different parcel of land owned by Field Company. Field had paid $65,000 for the land some years ago. Both firms are in the business of manufacturing chemicals. Appraisals of both parcels indicated a market value of $60,000 for each. This is an exchange of similar productive assets. Kline would carry the old book value of its land over to the new land as follows:

```
July 17, 1995:
Land (new)                                                     40,000
   Land (old)                                                            40,000
To record the exchange of land for land on the books of Kline.
```

Field has realized a loss of $5,000 ($60,000 − $65,000) on the exchange. Under APB No. 29, losses are recognized immediately. Field would prepare the following entry:

```
July 17, 1995:
Land (new)                                                     60,000
Loss on exchange of land                                        5,000
   Land (old)                                                            65,000
To record the exchange of land for land on the books of Field.
```

Exchanges of Similar Productive Assets with Significant Boot   In many cases, the consideration given is partly in the form of a similar asset and partly in the form of a dissimilar asset, debt, or equity. This occurs quite frequently with trade-ins. For example, an old truck might be traded in on a new truck, with the difference in values equaled by an additional cash payment. In these cases, the dissimilar asset, debt, or equity is called **boot**. When an exchange involves boot, several possible treatments may be applicable. When the major portion of consideration is in the form of boot, full gain or loss recognition is considered appropriate if a fair value for the similar assets can be determined. Specific determination of when the magnitude of the boot is sufficient to warrant use of full fair value is not available. Professional judgment must be applied.

Assume that on August 31, 1995, Nate's Trucking Company swaps an old truck with a net book value of $10,000 (original purchase price of $70,000 and accumulated depreciation of $60,000) for a newer truck owned by Lee Trucking. Lee Trucking purchased its truck for $80,000 and has recorded accumulated depreciation of $20,000 as of the date of the exchange. Nate will pay cash of $78,000 plus the old truck to acquire the newer truck. Recent sales of trucks similar to the one Nate's is trading in indicate a market value of $12,000. Since the boot represents the major portion of the consideration in this case, and data sufficient to estimate a fair value for the truck traded-in are available, full fair value ($90,000) should be used to record the purchase price of the new truck. Nate's would make the following entry:

August 31, 1995:

Trucks (newly acquired)	90,000	
Accumulated depreciation	60,000	
Gain on disposal of old truck		2,000
Trucks (previously owned)		70,000
Cash		78,000

To record exchange of trucks plus cash by Nate's
Trucking Company, the payor of boot.

Lee Trucking would also use full fair value and record the following entry:

August 31, 1995:

Trucks (newly acquired)	12,000	
Cash	78,000	
Accumulated depreciation	20,000	
Gain on disposal of old truck		30,000
Trucks (previously owned)		80,000

To record exchange of trucks plus cash by Lee Trucking, the
recipient of boot.

Exchanges of Similar Productive Assets with Minor Boot   If the boot is a minor portion of the total consideration in the exchange, the accounting treatment will depend on whether the firm is receiving or paying the boot. For the entity paying the boot, the transaction is essentially handled as a straight exchange, with no gains recognized but any loss recognized immediately. For the entity receiving the boot, the accounting treatment effectively breaks the transaction down into two parts:

1. An exchange of similar assets with the old asset's book value carried over to the new asset
2. An exchange of dissimilar assets essentially handled as an ordinary sale with full gain or loss recognition

The amount of the old asset's book value allocated to each part is based on the relative size of the boot to the fair value of the total consideration.

Assume that on October 27, 1994, Bill's Car Rental swapped a two-year old automobile for a newer version of the same model owned by Worldwide Car Rentals. The net book value of the old auto on Bill's books was $12,000 (original cost was $18,000). Worldwide carried its vehicle at $18,000 (original cost was $21,000). Bill's pays cash of $4,000 along with the two-year old vehicle to obtain the newer model. Information obtained on the resale value of vehicles similar to Bill's indicates it was worth $16,000 compared to a $20,000 value for Worldwide's vehicle at the time of the swap.

In this case, since boot is not a major portion of the consideration, full fair value would not be appropriate. Since Bill's provided the boot as additional consideration, no gain recognition is allowed, even though Bill's has received an asset worth $20,000 at fair value in exchange for assets with a book value of $16,000 ($4,000 cash and $12,000 of net book value for the auto). Bill's would make following journal entry:

```
October 27, 1994:
Automobiles (new)                                    16,000
Accumulated depreciation                              6,000
   Automobiles (old)                                            18,000
   Cash                                                          4,000
To record exchange of similar productive assets with boot by
 Bill's Car Rental, the payor of the boot.
```

Since Bill's records the new auto at only $16,000, the future depreciation charges will be lower, increasing future earnings relative to the use of full fair value.

Worldwide is receiving boot. As a result, the transaction is broken down into two parts based on the relative size of the boot to the total fair value of the consideration received. All gains or losses arising from the portion of the exchange related to the boot are recognized, while only losses from the portion of the exchange related to the similar assets are recognized. Computation of gain/loss on each part of the transaction would occur as follows:

Cash received	$ 4,000
Fair value of automobile received	16,000
Fair value of all consideration	$20,000
Cash ÷ fair value of all consideration =	.20

This proportion is applied to the net book value of the old asset to determine the amount treated as a sale with the rest treated as an exchange of similar productive assets.

Net book value of old automobile	$18,000
Amount sold for cash (.20 × $18,000)	3,600
Amount exchanged for similar productive asset	$14,400

The sale part of the transaction produces a gain of $400, which must be recognized.

Sales proceeds	$4,000
Book value sold for cash	3,600
Gain on sale	$ 400

The exchange part of the transaction produces a gain, which is not recognized.

Fair value of automobile received	$16,000
Book value exchanged for similar productive asset	14,400
Gain on exchange	$ 1,600

The journal entry Worldwide would make to record this exchange appears as follows:

```
October 27, 1994:
Cash                                            4,000
Automobiles (new)                              14,400
Accumulated depreciation                        3,000
    Automobiles (old)                                      21,000
    Gain on disposal                                          400
To record exchange of automobiles plus the receipt of cash.
```

ACCOUNTING FOR POST-ACQUISITION EXPENDITURES ON PLANT AND EQUIPMENT

Following the acquisition of plant assets, companies incur various costs to maintain, improve, and replace part or all of these assets. The accounting issue is whether to treat these post-acquisition costs as period costs and charge them to expense as incurred or to capitalize them as part of the plant assets' costs. By capitalizing these costs, companies would match them with future revenues generated by the use of the assets.

The general rule is that post-acquisition expenditures are capitalized if they significantly increase the asset's life, the quality or quantity of the output generated by the asset, or otherwise increase the asset's value. If expenditures are for normal maintenance activities and merely maintain the status quo, they should be charged to expense. Accountants usually classify these expenditures into five categories:

1. Normal maintenance
2. Extraordinary repairs
3. Replacements
4. Additions
5. Improvements

Normal maintenance is represented by any recurring costs that are necessary to maintain the asset's normal working condition. Examples would be machine lubrication, periodic inspections, and replacement of minor components such as belts and filters. While these types of expenditures are necessary to maintain the asset's value and avoid breakdown, their regularity and expected nature are assumed not to add value to the asset other than assuring its salvage value. Normal maintenance costs are charged to expense as incurred.

Extraordinary repairs are infrequent and typically involve an attempt to restore productive capacity by rebuilding part or all of the asset. For example, rebuilding an electric generator would likely qualify as an extraordinary repair. These types of repairs typically extend the useful life of the asset and, therefore, can be capitalized as part of the plant asset's value. **Replacements** are similar to extraordinary repairs; they extend the asset's life by replacement of components within the asset. For example, replacing a furnace in a building would constitute a replacement that would extend the building's useful life. If the accounting records do not identify the original costs of components replaced in the repair, the transaction is accounted for as an extraordinary repair. However, when the book value of the component being replaced can be separately identified in the accounting records, it is accounted for as a replacement. When the cost of replaced components can be individually identified, the acquisition cost and accumulated depreciation on the component replaced should be removed from the accounting records and replaced with the acquisition cost of the new component. For example, trucking companies, recognizing that different components of their trucks wear out at different intervals, often capitalize the costs of tires, engines, and transmissions separately from the truck chassis to facilitate accounting for replacements. Thus, the difference between extraordinary repairs and replacements is not in the nature of the transaction but, rather, in the method used to account for the original acquisition.

Extraordinary Repairs

In 1980, Bradley Corporation acquired a building for use as office space. On October 23, 1995, Bradley needed to replace the heating plant in the building and paid $15,000 for this service. First, assume Bradley is unable to separate the heating plant's cost from the remainder of the building's cost. In this case, the replacement would qualify as an extraordinary repair. Two methods have been adopted for recording extraordinary repairs. The first approach is to capitalize the cost of the repair into the asset's gross value. The journal entry under this approach is presented below:

October 23, 1995:
Buildings   15,000
   Cash   15,000
To record the extraordinary repair on the heating plant on
  October 23.

The second approach reduces the asset's accumulated depreciation by the amount of the repair. Under this approach, the entry would appear this way:

October 23, 1995:
Accumulated depreciation—buildings   15,000
   Cash   15,000
To record the extraordinary repair on the heating plant on
  October 23.

In both of these alternatives, the building's net book value is increased by the cost of the extraordinary repair. Increasing the asset's gross value is the preferable treatment.

If Bradley had originally allocated a portion of the building's cost to the heating plant, then the replacement of the system could be recorded as a replacement, not an extraordinary repair.

Replacement

Assume that the original cost of the heating plant was $10,000, and it had accumulated depreciation of $9,500 at the date of removal. Bradley's journal entries to record the replacement would appear as follows:

October 23, 1995:
Accumulated depreciation—buildings   9,500
Loss on disposal of heating plant   500
   Buildings   10,000
To record the removal of the cost for the old heating system
  on October 23.

October 23, 1995:
Buildings   15,000
   Cash   15,000
To record the acquisition costs of the new heating plant.

Periodic Rebuilding

Sometimes a productive asset will require **periodic rebuilding** or **refurbishment**. That is, built into a firm's estimate of an asset's useful life is the expectation that a component will require periodic rebuilding or refurbishment several times over the asset's useful life. For example, firms in the glass industry must periodically reline their furnaces. These costs are much more substantial than routine maintenance costs but are just as predictable. Firms typically account for these costs in one of two ways. The accrual method recognizes these costs as expenses before the rebuilding occurs. Every year, a pro-rata portion of the expected cost is charged to expense and credited to an accrued liability for rebuilding. When the actual rebuilding expenditure occurs, it is simply charged against the accrued liability. The other alternative is to simply capitalize these costs as incurred and recognize them as expense over the time period until the next rebuilding is expected.

Assume Crystal Clear Glass Co. must reline its glass furnace every five years at a cost of $5,000,000. If these expenditures were accounted for under the accrual method, each year before a rebuilding expenditure is made, the firm would recognize one-fifth of the expected total cost as an expense as follows:

Years 1–5:
Relining expense   1,000,000
   Accrued liability for furnace relining   1,000,000
To accrue one year's cost of furnace relining.

When the expenditure is actually made, it would be recorded as follows:

Year 5:
Accrued liability for furnace relining   5,000,000
   Cash   5,000,000
To record expenditure for furnace relining.

Under the capitalization method, the expense is recognized after the relining has been completed. First, the expenditure will be capitalized as part of the cost of the furnace.

Year 5:
Furnace relining   5,000,000
   Cash   5,000,000
To record expenditure for furnace relining.

Then, this expenditure will be systematically recognized as an expense through the depreciation calculation. Assuming a straight-line method is used, the following entry will be made each year:

Years 6–10:
Depreciation expense   1,000,000
   Accumulated depreciation   1,000,000
To recognize cost of furnace relining as an expense.

As this example illustrates, the capitalization approach delays the recognition of relining expense relative to the accrual method. Under the accrual method, the relining cost is viewed as a cost of current use of the furnace; while under the capitalization approach, the relining cost is viewed as a cost of future use of the furnace.

Additions represent expenditures to add components to existing assets. Building additions, where additional floor space is created by adding a wing or additional floor to an existing building, are one of the most common forms of additions. Costs of additions are capitalized as new assets.

Improvements, also known as **betterments**, are expenditures related to changes in existing assets that increase the efficiency or quality of the output the asset produces. Improvements often occur simultaneously with extraordinary repairs as new technology is built into old equipment when it undergoes substantial repairs. When this happens, the cost of the improvement is typically treated as part of extraordinary repair costs. Sometimes an improvement can be made by simply adding components to existing assets. In these cases, the cost of the improvements are capitalized in a fashion similar to those for additions. Finally, a redesign of the production facilities' layout, which does not actually change the nature of any individual asset, is an improvement. When costs are incurred to rearrange plant assets to take advantage of the new layout, the firm should capitalize these costs as part of its plant.

ACCOUNTING FOR EXPLORATION AND DEVELOPMENT COSTS IN THE EXTRACTIVE INDUSTRIES

Firms in the extractive industries account for their productive properties (e.g., coal mines and oil wells) in a manner consistent with the way manufacturing firms account for their plant and equipment. At acquisition, the costs of these properties are capitalized and systematically charged off to expense over their estimated useful lives. This expense recognition process is known as *depletion* and is discussed in Chapter 11. In this chapter, we need to consider some issues in determining the cost of properties in the extractive industries. We will discuss these issues in the context of the oil and gas industry although they apply to all extractive industries.

There are three basic steps in the process of obtaining oil and gas to sell:

1. Exploration for oil and gas reserves
2. Development of fields to obtain access to reserves for which production is expected to be feasible
3. Actual production or extraction of crude oil and gas from the wells

Expenditures for geological surveys of potential fields and drilling exploratory or test wells are **exploration costs**. **Development costs** include expenditures to prepare sites for drilling and the actual costs of drilling and equipping the wells to be used for production. **Production costs** are those costs incurred for operating and maintaining wells and related equipment, including labor, materials, supplies, and taxes.

While production costs are relatively easily matched with the revenues generated from the sale of oil and gas, exploration and development costs are incurred well in advance of the generation of revenues and, therefore, are more difficult to match with revenues. Moreover, not all test wells prove successful. Those that prove unsuccessful, known as *dry holes*, are abandoned without ever producing any revenues. Therefore, the issue arises as to how to account for the costs of dry holes.

Generally, exploration costs, other than those for drilling test wells, are charged to expense as period costs. Several reasons for this exist. First, these costs are generally small in relation to other pre-production costs. Second, these costs are often incurred prior to the acquisition of any drilling rights. The results of early exploration efforts indicate where the firm should seek drilling rights. Even when drilling rights are acquired, it is difficult to identify particular exploration costs with particular drilling rights purchased. All these factors lead to the treatment of charging these costs to expense as incurred.

Other pre-production costs (mainly costs of drilling and equipping wells) are substantial, and all firms capitalize these costs until the commercial viability of a given well or field can be determined. When a well proves successful, there is little debate that the development costs of the successful wells should be capitalized and charged to expense over the field's estimated useful life. When a well is abandoned, there are two alternative accounting methods for these pre-production costs. In **successful efforts accounting**, the development costs of dry holes are charged to expense when the well is abandoned. Under **full cost accounting**, the costs of dry holes are capitalized and written off to expense along with the successful wells.

The choice between these methods depends on whether one views oil and gas exploration on a case by case basis or as a portfolio of efforts. The proponents of successful efforts accounting view each well or field as a separate development project. In contrast, the proponents of full cost accounting view all the company's exploration and development activities as a portfolio. Dry holes are simply viewed as one of the costs necessary to produce oil and gas, and their costs should be matched with the revenues generated by successful development. Exhibit 10.5 provides a brief example of how these two methods differ for a firm that is just entering the oil and gas exploration business. If exploration and development costs are growing, then the full cost method will tend to defer a larger portion of the costs to future periods relative to successful efforts. This makes the profitability of firms using full cost appear larger in the early years as they grow. Also, firms using full cost will report higher assets than those using successful efforts since more costs are capitalized. While the reported income in any individual year may be higher or lower, the

---

Successful Efforts Versus Full Cost Accounting

| **EXHIBIT 10.5**
Successful Efforts
Versus Full Cost
Accounting

During its first year of operation, Plumbley Oil Company spent $11,000,000 in pre-production costs on various wells. Of this amount, $4,000,000 is associated with unsuccessful wells; $6,000,000 is associated with wells expected to be commercially successful; and $1,000,000 is associated with wells that have not yet been proven successful or unsuccessful. Revenues of $25,000,000 were generated from the production and sale of oil extracted from the commercially successful wells. This oil represents 30% of proved reserves from the commercially successful wells. Production costs for the year totalled $12,000,000. No inventory of oil is held by Plumbley.

	Successful Efforts	Full Cost
Revenues	$25,000,000	$25,000,000
Production costs	12,000,000	12,000,000
Development costs	5,800,000[a]	3,000,000[b]
Income before taxes	$ 7,200,000	$10,000,000

Supporting Computations for Development Costs:

Successful efforts	=	$4,000,000 + $6,000,000 × 30%	=	$5,800,000[a]
Full cost	=	$10,000,000 × 30%		=	$3,000,000[b]

Under full cost accounting, the assets will be higher by $2,800,000. This represents the 70% of the $4,000,000 dry hole costs that have not yet been written off to expense.

total assets and accumulated income under full cost will always be above those firms using successful efforts, all else equal.

After many years of activity, when the level of development activities becomes more uniform from year to year, the two methods will provide similar measures of income and development costs if the unit prices of inputs such as labor and other items necessary for development remain constant. Of course, increasing costs will also make those firms using successful efforts appear less profitable, even when there is no real growth for firms using successful efforts or full cost methods.

Given the effects full cost has on the balance sheet and income statement, it is probably no surprise that small oil and gas producers, sometimes referred to as "wildcatters," use the full cost method most frequently. Larger oil and gas companies are not affected as much by the use of full cost since the amounts of their exploration and development costs are small in comparison to their total assets. In addition, there are some who speculate that the large oil and gas companies prefer to report lower incomes to avoid Congressional scrutiny. Some historical perspective on the oil and gas controversy is provided in Appendix 10.1.

SUMMARY

Accounting conventions allow all costs necessary to bring an asset to productive use to be capitalized, as long as those costs are expected to generate future benefits. However, special problems arise whenever an asset is self-constructed or when a company incurs internal costs of installation and rearrangement related to the acquisition of plant assets. In these cases, the full costs of the internal activities not just the marginal costs associated with the particular efforts to bring the asset into productive use, should be capitalized. When self-construction entails significant costs during construction, a significant period of time, and the company has interest bearing debt outstanding over the construction period, interest costs that could have been avoided by using the capital tied up in construction to repay debt are also capitalized.

Assets acquired in nonmonetary exchanges are recorded at the fair market value of the asset surrendered. However, this is limited to cases in which fair value is readily determinable and consideration is not in the form of a similar asset. Similar asset exchanges are recorded at book values except where the fair value of the asset acquired is less than the book value of the asset surrendered.

Costs incurred following the acquisition of plant assets include: normal maintenance, which is charged to expense as incurred, and other expenditures that may increase the efficiency, quality, or useful life of plant assets. These latter costs are capitalized and matched against future revenues generated by the use of the plant asset.

Firms in the extractive industries account for the costs of exploration and development under either the successful efforts or full cost method. Both methods capitalize development costs up to the point where a well proves either dry or commercially viable. If a well proves dry, the development costs are immediately charged to expense under successful efforts. Under full cost, the cost of dry holes is capitalized and amortized to future periods as revenues from successful wells are recognized.

Appendix 10.1—The Oil and Gas Controversy

In response to pressure from the federal government to develop more useful reporting standards for the oil and gas industry, the FASB studied the issue of whether both the successful efforts and full cost methods should continue to exist within GAAP. In 1977, the FASB issued *Statement of Financial Accounting Standards No. 19*, "Financial Accounting and Reporting by Oil and Gas Producing Companies." In this pronouncement, the FASB endorsed the use of the successful efforts approach and banned the use of full cost.

Eventually, political pressure forced the FASB to rescind this Standard and return to the previous position that allowed both the successful efforts and full cost methods to co-exist. This Standard would have had significantly greater effects on the small wildcat firms than on the large, integrated oil companies. Protesting that successful efforts would have deleterious effects on their financial statements, small oil and gas firms feared they would be unable to raise new capital for exploration and development. Given that the Standard was proposed at a time when public policy supported an increase in domestic oil production, the appeal of the small producers met with considerable support.

Before examining this controversy more closely, it is important to appreciate the economic and political forces at work during this time. In the early 1970s, the United States faced an oil embargo. Long lines of vehicles formed at gas pumps, and other forms of rationing were effected. As a result, oil prices rose dramatically and domestic oil companies reported large profits. However, consumers could not acquire sufficient quantities of gasoline to support their activities.

Concerned about the activities of large oil companies, Congress sought to place various controls on their behavior in an effort to boost domestic production and increase availability of gasoline. An excess oil profits tax was one control specifically designed to impose costs on the oil companies and to redistribute their profits to society through the federal government. When government officials became frustrated by their inability to determine the underlying economic condition of large oil companies from published financial statement data, Congress instructed the Department of Energy (DOE) to take up the issue of reporting requirements for firms in this industry. DOE passed the task to the SEC, and the FASB undertook its efforts at that time.

The SEC did not see the problem as being an issue of how oil and gas companies matched development costs to revenues recognized under the traditional point-of-sale method. Instead, it took the position that the value of oil and gas companies resulted from their ability to identify the lowest cost sources of oil and gas resources and to extract them successfully. Consistent with this view, the SEC completely revised the reporting requirements for oil and gas producers. Focusing on the value of proved reserves, or on present values of future cash flows, the SEC's *reserve recognition accounting (RRA)* rejected the historical cost approach to reporting in favor of measurements based extensively on forecasts of future prices, costs, production schedules, and discount rates. Needless to say, such dependency on forecasts presented problems in verification and objectivity.

Because of the contrast between the SEC and the FASB approaches, the SEC did not support SFAS No. 19 when it was passed. The SEC viewed the changes the FASB offered as inadequate relative to the nature of the problem as presented by Congress. However, the process of developing the RRA system took several years. During the five years the controversy regarding oil and gas accounting raged between the FASB and the SEC, the underlying structure of the market for oil and gas changed dramatically. The ability of the oil exporting nations to maintain a cartel to set oil prices waned. As production increased, the prices of crude oil fell; and as consumption of oil and gas in the United States fell dramatically, the excess demand disappeared. In addition, oil and gas companies found new technologies to extract oil more effectively. As the public furor over the behavior of the oil and gas industry disappeared, Congress no longer had as keen an interest in regulating the oil and gas firms.

After all of their efforts to assess the state of financial reporting for oil and gas producers and to develop alternatives, the FASB backed away from requiring successful efforts, and the SEC abandoned its requirement for RRA as infeasible. The final outgrowth of these efforts was the adoption of *Statement of Financial Accounting Standards No. 69,* "Disclosures About Oil and Gas Activities." While SFAS No. 69 requires many of the disclosures incorporated in the RRA approach, this information is relegated to unaudited disclosures in the notes.

In particular, SFAS No. 69 requires the following disclosures by oil and gas producing companies:

1. A reconciliation of changes in the proved reserves during the year
2. Capitalized costs relating to oil and gas production
3. Results of oil and gas producing activities
4. Costs incurred in oil and gas property acquisition, exploration, and development
5. A standardized measure of the present value of future cash flows relating to proven reserves.[6]

---

[6] "Disclosures About Oil and Gas Activities," *Statement of Financial Accounting Standards No. 69* (Stamford, CT: FASB, 1979).

What is learned from the oil and gas controversy? One lesson is that the FASB's appeal to improved matching as a basis for supporting successful efforts was not sufficient motivation to outweigh the political opposition that formed. Also, an understanding of the interrelationships among economic events and the demands for financial information are necessary to identify properly users' needs and to construct alternative disclosure policies that can address those needs. Fortunately for the FASB, user interest in the issue of oil and gas reporting waned with changes in the economy. This prevented a major showdown among the FASB, SEC, and Congress—a showdown the FASB would have likely lost.

QUESTIONS

1. What determines a firm's *capital intensity*?
2. What are the characteristics of assets classified as *property*, *plant*, and *equipment*?
3. How does the fact that assets classified as property, plant, and equipment are held for use, rather than sale, affect their valuation?
4. How do the characteristics of markets for assets classified as property, plant, and equipment affect their valuation?
5. How is land held as an investment classified in the financial statements?
6. How is an option on land accounted for upon (a) acquisition, (b) exercise, and (c) lapse without exercise?
7. Why is it necessary to capitalize the cost of some land improvements separately from the cost of the land?
8. How should a firm account for the cost of plant rearrangement to improve efficiency?
9. How is the cost of assets acquired in a *lump-sum purchase* allocated to the individual assets acquired?
10. Where did the practice of interest capitalization begin? For what purpose was it originally intended?
11. What assets qualify for interest capitalization?
12. What does the calculation of capitalized interest specified by FASB Statement No. 34 attempt to approximate?
13. What disclosures are required for firms capitalizing interest cost?
14. Why is it necessary to have special accounting rules governing *nonmonetary exchanges*?
15. Which nonmonetary exchanges are not valued at fair value? Why?
16. Describe the accounting treatment for an exchange of similar productive assets with boot.
17. What is the basic principle in deciding whether to capitalize or expense expenditures made after the initial acquisition of a productive asset?
18. Briefly describe the differences between *full cost accounting* and *successful efforts accounting* in the oil and gas industry?

19. Why do smaller firms in the oil and gas industry tend to use the full cost accounting method?

20. (Appendix) Why did the FASB reconsider its decision to eliminate the full cost method from GAAP?

EXERCISES

10-1.   *Costs to be capitalized*

ABN Enterprises is currently expanding its Midwest manufacturing operations. During the process of selecting a site for a new production facility, options were purchased on three suitable tracts of land. One of these sites was selected, and ABN entered into a fixed-price contract with Dobb Construction to construct the factory building. Construction was in process at the end of the year. In addition to the construction cost, ABN made various expenditures associated with bringing the new facility into use. All expenditures associated with the expansion project have been recorded in a temporary account, itemized below.

REQUIRED:

For each of the expenditures listed below, determine whether the item should be: (A) capitalized in the Land account, (B) capitalized in the Land Improvements account, (C) capitalized in the Buildings account, or (D) charged to period expense.

1. Cost of option exercised on selected site.
2. Cost of unexercised options on alternative production sites.
3. Legal expenses related to land purchase.
4. Title transfer fee on land purchased.
5. Real estate sales commission paid.
6. Closing costs on land purchase.
7. Cost of delinquent property taxes on land purchased, paid by ABN.
8. Cost of demolishing existing structures on land purchased to prepare for construction.
9. Cost of excavation prior to construction.
10. Architecture fees.
11. Cost of building permits.
12. Progress payments made to Dobb Construction.
13. Cost of special assessment by county for sewers, curb and gutter.
14. Cost of fencing production facility, required by local ordinance.
15. Cost of installing underground electrical service to factory building.
16. Landscaping expense.
17. Cost of property tax for the current year.
18. Interest on loan obtained to finance construction of factory building.
19. Cost of personal liability insurance during construction.
20. Cost of promotional expense associated with ground breaking ceremony.

10-2.   *Costs to be capitalized*

Lane Company is in the process of modernizing its production facilities. Company records show the following expenditures related to this activity:

Cost of replacing existing heating plant	$ 60,000
Cleaning, painting, and minor repairs to production facilities	11,000
Cost of rearranging production facility layout to increase efficiency	30,000
Purchase of new machinery	160,000
Freight-in on new machinery	1,100
In-transit insurance on new machinery	400
Installation of new machinery	6,000
Inspection, cleaning, and adjustment of existing machinery	3,000
Cost of trial production run on new equipment	7,000
Allocated factory overhead expense for the period covering modernization	14,000
Interest cost on short-term loan obtained to finance new machinery purchase	2,000
Loss of revenues during period of modernization	42,000

REQUIRED:

Prepare an itemized schedule of the amounts that should be capitalized in the Buildings and in the Machinery and Equipment accounts.

10-3. *Interest capitalization*

On November 14, 1994, Matthew Co. began construction of a new company office building. It was expected that the building would be ready for use in March 1996. Weighted average accumulated expenditures related to this project during 1995 were $3,000,000. Matthew had the following debt outstanding during 1993:

(a) Construction loan of $2,000,000 to finance the office building construction. The loan, which carries 14% interest, was taken out on December 1, 1994, and matures on March 31, 1996.

(b) Eight-year Debenture bonds—12% bonds issued December 1, 1989, with interest payable annually on December 31; book value $4,000,000.

(c) Long-term loan of $2,000,000, which carries 13% interest, taken out on June 2, 1992, and matures on June 2, 2002.

REQUIRED:

Compute the amount of interest to be capitalized for 1995.

10-4. *Interest capitalization*

On July 1, 1994, Bluefin Resorts began work on a new dry-docking facility. Construction was expected to take one year. Upon completion, slip spaces in the facility will be leased to corporate clients for winter boat storage. Bluefin contracted with various local suppliers and tradespeople for products and services related to this project and recorded the following expenditures for construction in process during the 1994 fiscal year, ending December 31:

Balance of construction in process as of:

August 1, 1994	$ 70,000
September 1, 1994	106,000
October 1, 1994	138,000
November 1, 1994	206,000
December 1, 1994	224,000

To help support payments to suppliers and tradespeople, Bluefin acquired a secured construction loan of $60,000 on August 1, 1994. On October 1, 1994, Bluefin arranged and received from the same lender an additional loan of $60,000 to support construction payments. Both borrowings bear 14% interest and are payable in full 60 days after completion of construction. Bluefin's only other outstanding debt during this period was a 20-year first mortgage bond of $1,200,000, dated June 1, 1986, bearing a 12% rate of interest.

REQUIRED:

Compute the amount of interest to be capitalized for 1994.

10-5.   *Joint cost of purchase*

On June 6, 1995, Whight Furniture agreed to purchase the land, building, and all inventory of the financially distressed Furniture World Company for $712,000. Independent appraisals of the land and building by a local real estate firm indicate that the land is valued at $105,000 and the building is valued at $255,000. Whight's purchasing manager has determined that the Furniture World inventory has a current wholesale value of $390,000 and a current retail value of $520,000.

REQUIRED:

Determine the appropriate amounts that Whight should record for the land, building, and inventory, respectively.

10-6.   *Costs incidental to purchase*

Bundy Co. recently acquired a parcel of land and an existing warehouse on the land for $756,000. This price included a real estate sales commission fee of $21,600 and payment of the current year property tax assessment of $14,400 as required by state law. Independent appraisals of the land and warehouse indicate that the land is valued at $330,000 and that the warehouse is valued at $420,000.

REQUIRED:

Determine the appropriate amounts that Bundy should record for the land and for the warehouse, respectively.

10-7.   *Building acquired for stock*

Big Blue Corp. purchased a parcel of land and a building adjacent to its corporate headquarters to be used for a new employee fitness center. Independent appraisal by a local real estate firm indicated that the land was valued at $190,000 and that the building was valued at $360,000. In exchange for the land and building, Big Blue gave 10,000 shares of its $10 par value common stock held in treasury. The treasury shares given by Big Blue had been purchased for $52 per share.

REQUIRED:

Determine the appropriate amounts that Big Blue should record for the land and for the building, respectively, under the following assumptions:
1. Big Blue is a privately held corporation, and there is no active market for its stock.
2. Big Blue stock is actively traded on an established stock exchange, and the common shares given for the land and building had a fair market value of $54 per share on the date of exchange.

10-8.   *Exchange of similar productive assets*

On June 6, 1995, Morton Company and Dean Company, two local real estate developers, agreed to exchange parcels of undeveloped land suitable for similar uses. Morton had originally purchased its parcel of land for $86,000 on May 12,

1988, and an independent appraisal indicated a market value of $149,000 for the parcel on the date of exchange. Dean had originally purchased its parcel of land for $137,000 on March 3, 1992, and an independent appraisal indicated a market value of $146,000 for the parcel on the date of exchange.

REQUIRED:

Prepare the journal entries necessary to record this transaction for both Morton and Dean companies.

10-9.   *Exchange of similar productive assets*

ANF Manufacturing, a local toy producer, exchanged a computerized injection molding machine for a similar machine owned by Mega Ordnance, Unlimited. The machine given by ANF had a net book value of $128,000 (originally cost was $160,000) and a fair market value of $112,000 on the date of exchange. The machine given by Mega had been self-constructed several years ago at a cost of $116,000 and had a net book value of $92,800 and a fair market value of $111,000 on the date of exchange.

REQUIRED:

Prepare the journal entries necessary to record this transaction for both ANF and Mega companies.

10-10.   *Exchange of similar productive assets with boot*

Sigma Airlines and Alpha Charter entered into an agreement to exchange similar passenger aircraft. The plane given by Sigma was an ultra-quiet airliner better suited for Alpha's luxury charters, and the plane given by Alpha was more fuel-efficient and better suited for Sigma's multiple-stop routes. The airliner given by Sigma had originally been purchased for $2,900,000 and had a net book value of $2,200,000 and fair market value of $2,400,000 on the date of exchange. In addition to the plane, Sigma paid Alpha $200,000 cash. The airliner given by Alpha had a net book value of $2,800,000 (original cost was $3,600,000) and a fair market value of $2,600,000 on the date of exchange.

REQUIRED:

Prepare the journal entries necessary to record this transaction for both Sigma and Alpha companies.

10-11.   *Exchange of similar productive assets with boot*

Hard Times Fitness Spa traded a four-year old Universal weight machine to Flex Club International for a similar, newer Nautilus machine. The machine given by Hard Times had originally been purchased for $18,000 (accumulated depreciation was $3,000 at the date of exchange) and had a fair market value of $12,000 at the date of exchange. In addition to the machine, Hard Times paid Flex $3,000 cash. The Nautilus machine given by Flex had originally cost $17,000 (accumulated depreciation of $4,000 at date of exchange) and had a fair market value of $15,000 at date of exchange.

REQUIRED:

Prepare the journal entries necessary to record this transaction for both Hard Times and Flex companies.

10-12.   *Exchange of dissimilar assets*

Dr. Cutter, a plastic surgeon, traded a painting that had hung in her waiting room for a facial-modeling software system owned by Dr. Rose. The painting given by Dr. Cutter was an unsigned abstract thought to be a Pollock. Pollock was known to have cut up several of his larger works and occasionally use the pieces as payment to local merchants. Dr. Cutter had purchased the painting at an estate sale for $3,400. Dr. Rose, who is an avid aficionado of modern art, believes that if the painting were documented as a Pollock, it would bring as much as $300,000 at auction. The facial-modeling software given by Dr. Rose was a system the doctor had designed and developed over a number of years at a cost to date of $8,200. Although there are other similar software packages available, Dr. Cutter believes that because of the unique qualities of the system developed by Dr. Rose it could well become the industry standard. Dr. Cutter believes the copyrights to the system carry a conservative market value of $280,000.

REQUIRED:

Prepare the journal entries necessary to record this transaction for both Dr. Cutter and Dr. Rose.

10-13. *Exchange of dissimilar assets with boot*

Thompson Paper exchanged a three-year old delivery truck for an office computer system owned by Orin Company. The truck given by Thompson had a net book value of $22,300 (original cost was $36,000) and a fair market value of $24,000 on the date of exchange. The computer system given by Orin had originally cost $31,000 (accumulated depreciation of $9,000 at date of exchange) and had a current fair value of $19,500. In addition to the computer system, Orin gave Thompson $4,500 cash.

REQUIRED:

Prepare the necessary journal entries to record this transaction for both Thompson and Orin companies.

PROBLEMS

10-1. *Acquisition of assets: Incidental costs*

Below are transactions related to Nelson Farms, a large Midwest soybean producer:
(a) On September 2, 1995, Nelson exercised rights under purchase options and acquired two separate plots of land for $300,000 cash each. Plot A will be put into production the following spring, and Plot B will be held fallow for speculation and possible future expansion. Nelson had paid $5,000 for each of the purchase options. In addition, Nelson paid a real estate sales commission fee of 3% of purchase price on both plots. Independent appraisals indicated a value of $324,000 for Plot A and a value of $336,000 for Plot B.
(b) On October 4, 1995, Nelson paid a local nursery $4,000 cash to plant a windbreak of hardwood trees along the northwest corner of Plot A. Also on this date, Nelson paid $6,000 cash to have both Plots A and B graded to improve water drainage. In the past, Nelson has usually found it necessary to grade production acreage every nine years.
(c) On October 13, 1995, Nelson purchased a combine from Agrotec Company for $260,000. Although Agrotec offers a 2% discount of sales price for payment at time of purchase, due to liquidity constraints Nelson instead agreed to pay Agrotec in full 90 days from the date of purchase. The note signed by Nelson was for $265,300, which included charges of $1,200 for dealer preparation, $1,100 for delivery, $400 for in-transit insurance, and $2,600 for sales tax. Title was transferred to Nelson at the date of purchase.

(d) On December 16, 1995, Nelson paid property tax of $4,900 on Plot A and $4,600 on Plot B.

REQUIRED:

Prepare journal entries on Nelson Farms' books to record the above transactions.

10-2. *Costs to be capitalized*

Presented below are various transactions of the Tidd Company, a manufacturer of sporting equipment:

(a) On April 1, 1995, Tidd paid $296,000 cash for several new rubber molding machines. The price paid reflects a 2% discount in purchase price for cash payment and includes a $2,000 charge for a one-year service contract that covers normal maintenance and minor repair.

(b) Also on April 1, 1995, due to the age of its production facility, Tidd engaged a local engineering firm to perform a structural analysis of its facility prior to the installation of the new machinery, for $1,000. On April 19, 1995, Tidd received and paid cash for the engineering firm's report. The analysis revealed that the existing floor trusses were badly deteriorated and required replacement to operate safely machinery typically used in light manufacturing.

(c) On May 1, 1995, Tidd engaged Dunrite Construction to perform the required structural work on its production facility. For immediate cash payment, Dunrite agreed to do the work for $280,000. The price represented a substantial savings for Tidd. The work was expected to take six months to complete. To support the payment made to Dunrite, Tidd acquired a six-month construction loan of $280,000, dated May 1, 1995, bearing 11% interest.

(d) On August 14, 1995, Tidd paid $16,000 cash to an electrical contractor for changes made in the location of lighting and outlet fixtures in its production facility. The changes to the production facility were necessitated by rearrangement of plant layout required to accommodate the new machinery.

(e) On August 18, 1995, Tidd paid $11,000 cash for the installation of concrete bases for the new machinery and $2,100 cash for delivery of the new machinery. The delivery charge included a $700 holding penalty for storing the machinery while the structural repairs were in progress.

(f) On August 24, 1995, Tidd incurred an expense of $29,000 for labor ($2,600) and materials ($26,400) during a trial production run on the new machinery.

(g) On September 1, 1995, Tidd paid $53,000 cash for the installation of a new security system in the production facility. The old system, which was dismantled and discarded, had been installed for $37,000 on January 12, 1985, and had a net book value of $1,000 on the date of removal.

REQUIRED:

Prepare the journal entries necessary to record the above transactions on Tidd's books.

10-3. *Self-constructed assets*

On February 1, 1995, Viking Pattern began construction of a new conveyor system for its production facility. Prior to this undertaking, Viking had determined that a similar conveyor system could be purchased for $235,500, including installation from a local firm. The management of Viking Pattern, however, believed that they could construct the conveyor themselves at a substantial savings. During construction, which was completed on June 1, 1995, Viking had recorded the following items in the construction in process account:

Engineering expense	$ 12,000
Materials	103,000
Assembly labor	26,000
Drive motors	46,000
Freight-in and in-transit insurance on the drive motors	2,000
Testing and final adjustment	3,000
Allocated factory overhead	22,000
Removal of old system	13,000
Interest expense	9,500
Gain on self-construction	16,000

The following additional information is available:

(a) Engineering expense is based on a $40 per hour rate normally assigned to outside projects.

(b) Materials expense was based on current replacement cost of materials used from existing inventories. Book value of the materials used was $86,000.

(c) Assembly labor expense was based on actual hours worked by production employees on the conveyor system during slack periods. These workers would otherwise have been idle during slack periods.

(d) Factory overhead expense, which is 70% fixed expense, is assigned on the basis of production labor cost.

(e) Interest expense was calculated on the basis of Viking's implicit cost of capital. Viking is financed totally with equity capital.

(f) The gain on self-construction to be recognized is based on the difference between the cost of purchasing a similar conveyor system and the costs Viking incurred during self-construction.

REQUIRED:

Determine the appropriate cost Viking should record for the new conveyor system.

10-4.   *Interest capitalization*

On February 1, 1995, Buffet Company engaged Crystal Ships to build an 80-passenger day cruiser to be used in Buffet's entertainment and travel business operating out of Key West, Florida. The contract price for the day-tripper was $1,080,000. Pursuant to the contract, Buffet made the following progress payments to Crystal:

March 1, 1995	$180,000
July 1, 1995	200,000
October 1, 1995	220,000
March 1, 1996	240,000

The $240,000 balance due on the contract was paid on July 1, 1996, the date that Buffet took possession of the ship. Due to an unexpectedly slow tourist season, the day cruiser was not placed into service until September 1, 1996. To help support the progress payments, Buffet Company issued five-year bonds on December 31, 1995, the last day of its 1995 fiscal year. The bonds had a book value of $600,000 and paid 12% interest annually. Buffet's only other debt outstanding during this period was a 20-year first mortgage note with a book value of $3,000,000, dated June 4, 1989. The mortgage note carried 13% interest.

REQUIRED:

Determine the amount of interest Buffet should capitalize for 1996.

10-5.   *Interest capitalization*

Gatorworld Incorporated began construction of a petting zoo addition to their amphibious reptile theme park on August 1, 1995. Construction of the addition took seven months. Company records show the following construction in process balances for the 1995 fiscal year, which ended December 31, 1995:

August 31,	$210,000
September 30,	440,000
October 31,	544,000
November 30,	762,000
December 31,	890,000

To help finance construction costs, Gatorworld acquired a construction loan of $420,000 on July 1, 1995. The loan was due in full on July 1, 1996, and carried a 14% interest rate. Gatorworld had other debt outstanding during 1995 as follows:

(a) 15-year first mortgage bond, acquired 10/1/86; book value of $3,000,000; 16% annual interest

(b) 5-year debenture bonds issued 7/30/95; book value of $2,400,000; 12% annual interest

(c) 5-year debenture bonds issued 7/1/89 and retired 7/1/95; book value of $2,000,000; 13% annual interest

REQUIRED:

Determine the amount of interest Gatorworld should capitalize for 1995.

10-6.   *Exchange of assets*

John Waxman, the owner of Buff-Brite Car Wash, agreed to trade the car wash to Tremain Car Care Centers for a condominium in Florida and stock owned by Tremain. In the exchange which took place on June 6, 1994, Buff-Brite gave Tremain land originally purchased for $80,000, a building with a net book value of $48,000 (original cost was $160,000), and equipment with a net book value of $36,000 (original cost was $96,000) on the date of exchange. Independent appraisals of the land and building indicated a fair market value of $130,000 for the land and a fair market value of $210,000 for the building on the date of exchange. Due to the age of the equipment, a fair market value for the equipment could not be established.

The condominium given by Tremain had been originally purchased for $190,000 (net book value was $145,000) and had an independently appraised fair market value of $208,000 on the date of exchange. The stock given by Tremain had been purchased for investment purposes on July 5, 1990, for $168,000. On the date of exchange, the stock, which is actively traded on a major exchange, had a market value of $152,000.

REQUIRED:

Prepare the journal entries necessary to record this transaction for both Buff-Brite and Tremain companies.

10-7.   *Exchange of assets with boot*

On May 22, 1994, Rapid Transport traded a two-year old truck for a similar three-year old truck owned by ESP Parcel. The truck given by Rapid had a fair market value of $12,000, and accumulated depreciation of $6,200 on the date of exchange. Rapid correctly recognized a gain of $400 on the exchange. The truck given by ESP had originally been purchased for $15,800 and had a fair market value of $10,500 on the date of exchange. In addition to the truck, ESP gave Rapid $1,500 cash. ESP correctly recognized a loss of $1,200 on the exchange.

REQUIRED:

Reproduce the necessary journal entries that both Rapid Transport and ESP Parcel would have made to record this transaction.

10-8. *Exchange of assets with boot*

Bassin Company and Nelson Company, two large construction firms, agreed to exchange heavy excavation equipment on April 4, 1994. The machine given by Bassin had originally been purchased for $315,000 (net book value was $235,000 on date of exchange) and had a fair market value of $280,000 on the date of exchange. In addition to the machine, Bassin gave Nelson $225,000 cash. The machine given by Nelson had a net book value of $435,000 (original cost was $575,000) and a fair market value of $505,000 on the date of exchange.

REQUIRED:

Prepare the journal entries necessary to record this transaction for both Bassin and Nelson companies in both of the following situations:
1. The cash given by Bassin is considered a minor portion of the total consideration given.
2. The cash given by Bassin is considered a major portion of the total consideration given.

10-9. *Full cost vs. successful efforts accounting*

Carter Oil and Gas began operations on January 1, 1994, and has a fiscal year ending December 31. Selected year-end information on operations is presented below:

Parcel No	Exploration Cost	Acquisition Cost	Development Cost	Proven Reserves (Barrels)	Production Cost	Revenues
1994:						
1	$40,000	$2,000,000	$ 500,000	——	——	——
2	40,000	——	400,000	——	——	——
3	40,000	6,200,000	1,800,000	1,600,000	5,600,000	8,800,000
1995:						
1	——	——	——	——	——	——
2	——	4,600,000	1,600,000	900,000	8,400,000	13,200,000
3	——	——	——	800,000	11,200,000	17,600,000
4	50,000	2,200,000	900,000	——	——	——
5	50,000	4,000,000	1,200,000	——	——	——
1996:						
2	——	——	——	300,000	8,400,000	13,200,000
3	——	——	——	——	11,200,000	17,600,000
4	——	——	——	——	——	——
5	——	——	1,100,000	——	——	——

The following additional information is also available:

1994: Carter began exploration for oil on three parcels of land. Total exploration costs of $120,000 were incurred and assigned equally to the three parcels. Parcels 1 and 3 were purchased prior to exploration and development; extraction rights on Parcel 2 had not been acquired by year-end. Proven reserves of 2,000,000 barrels of oil were discovered on Parcel 3, 20% of which were extracted and sold during the year. The commercial viability of Parcels 1 and 2 was unknown at year-end.

1995: It was determined that Parcel 1 would not prove commercially viable, and operations on that parcel were stopped. Proven reserves of 1,500,000 barrels were discovered on Parcel 2, 40% of which were extracted and sold during the year. An additional 40% of the proved reserves on Parcel 3 were extracted and sold. Parcels 4 and 5 were purchased, and exploration and development efforts begun. The commercial viability of Parcels 4 and 5 was unknown at year-end.

1996: The remaining 40% of proved reserves on Parcel 3 and an additional 40% of proved reserves on Parcel 2 were extracted and sold during the year. It was determined that Parcel 4 would not prove commercially viable, and operations on that parcel were stopped. The commercial viability of Parcel 5 was unknown at year-end.

REQUIRED:

1. Determine Carter's income before tax for the years 1994, 1995, and 1996 under successful efforts accounting.
2. Repeat part (1) using full cost accounting.

10-10. *Full cost vs. successful efforts accounting*

Anderson Oil was organized on January 1, 1995, to search for and extract crude oil in Iowa. Information on company operations is provided below:

Parcel A: Parcel A was purchased for $720,000 in 1995. Cash expenditures for development during 1995 were $680,000. Efforts to find oil proved unsuccessful, and operations on this parcel were stopped during 1995.

Parcel B: Proven reserves of 1,400,000 barrels were discovered on Parcel B. Of these proven reserves, 350,000 barrels were extracted and sold during 1995; 630,000 barrels were extracted and sold during 1996; and the remaining oil was extracted and sold during 1997. Production costs were $14 per barrel extracted in 1995, $15 per barrel extracted in 1996, and $16 per barrel extracted in 1997. Selling prices per barrel of oil were $27 in 1995, $28 in 1996, and $30 in 1997. Development costs of $860,000 were paid in cash in 1995. Drilling rights on Parcel B were obtained in early 1995 under a royalty agreement in which Anderson was required to pay $3 per barrel of oil extracted from Parcel B, payable annually on December 31.

Parcel C: Parcel C was acquired on the last day of 1996 for $2,400,000 cash. Development costs of $1,700,000 were paid in cash during 1997. The commercial viability of Parcel C was unknown at the end of 1995.

Cash expenditures for exploration costs were $140,000 during 1995 and $80,000 during 1996.

REQUIRED:

1. Determine income before tax for the years 1995, 1996, and 1997 using successful efforts accounting.
2. Repeat part (1) using full cost accounting.

BALTIMORE GAS AND ELECTRIC COMPANY

The following information is taken from the 1990 annual report to shareholders of Baltimore Gas and Electric Company (BG&E). All assets are in $ thousands.

Income Statement Information:	1990
Depreciation expense	$170,586
Allowance for equity funds used during construction	27,086
Allowance for borrowed funds used during construction	26,266

	At December 31,	
Balance Sheet Information:	1990	1989
Investments and other assets		
Nuclear decommissioning trust fund	$ 21,335	$ 12,313
Utility Plant		
Plant in service		
Electric	$4,230,881	$4,034,444
Gas	496,603	471,740
Common	410,538	308,492
Total plant in service	$5,138,022	$4,814,676
Accumulated depreciation	(1,694,166)	(1,561,329)
Net plant in service	$3,443,856	$3,253,347
Plant held for future use	17,614	10,583
Construction work in progress	861,734	704,931
Nuclear fuel (net of amortization)	189,895	175,559
Net utility plant	$4,513,099	$4,144,420

Statement of Cash Flow Information:	1990
Cash Flows from Investing Activities	
Utility construction expenditures	$535,316
Nuclear fuel expenditures	20,519
Nuclear decommissioning trust fund	8,108

Information from notes to consolidated financial statements:

Note 1. Significant Accounting Policies

Nature of Business

BG&E and subsidiaries (collectively, the Company) is primarily an electric and gas utility serving a territory which encompasses Baltimore City and all or part of nine central Maryland counties.

Utility Plant and Depreciation

Utility plant in service is stated at original cost, which includes material, labor, construction overhead costs, and, where appropriate, an allowance for funds used during construction. Construction work in progress, plant held for future use, and nuclear fuel are stated at cost.

Additions to utility plant and replacements of units of property are capitalized to utility plant accounts. The original cost of plant retired is removed from utility plant, and such cost, plus removal cost, less salvage value, is charged to the accumulated provision for depreciation. Maintenance and repairs of property and replacements of items of property determined to be less than a unit of property are charged to maintenance expense.

Depreciation is generally computed using composite straight-line rates, applied to the average investment in classes of depreciable property. The composite depreciation rates by class of depreciable property are 2.80% for the Calvert Cliffs Nuclear Power Plant, 2.75% for the Brandon Shores Power Plant, 3.26% for other electric plant, 3.12% for gas plant, and 4.02% for common plant other than vehicles. Vehicles are depreciated based on their estimated useful lives.

Nuclear decommissioning costs are accrued by and recovered through a sinking fund methodology. In its December 1990 rate order, the Maryland Commission granted BG&E additional revenue to provide for an increase in its nuclear decommissioning accrual in order to accumulate a reserve of $275 million in 1989 dollars by the end of Calvert Cliffs' service life. The total decommissioning reserve of $52,026,000 and $41,135,000 at December 31, 1990 and 1989, respectively, is included in accumulated depreciation in the Consolidated Balance Sheets.

BG&E is required by regulations of the Nuclear Regulatory Commission (NRC) to provide financial assurance that decommissioning funds in an amount at least equal to an NRC-prescribed minimum level will be accumulated over the remaining service life of the Calvert Cliffs plant. Accordingly, BG&E has established a tax-qualified decommissioning trust to which a portion of decommissioning costs accrued have been contributed.

Allowance for Funds Used During Construction

The allowance for funds used during construction (AFC) is an accounting procedure whereby the cost of funds used to finance utility construction projects is capitalized as part of utility plant on the balance sheet and is credited as a noncash item on the income statement. The cost of borrowed and equity funds is segregated between net interest charges and other income, respectively. BG&E recovers the capitalized AFC and a return thereon after the related utility plant is placed in service and included in depreciable assets and rate base. AFC does not represent taxable income, and the depreciation of capitalized AFC is not a tax-deductible expense.

Nuclear Fuel

Nuclear fuel expenditures are capitalized and amortized as a component of actual fuel costs based on the energy produced over the life of the fuel. Fees for the future disposal of spent fuel are paid quarterly to the Department of Energy and are accrued based on the kilowatt-hours of electricity generated. Nuclear fuel expenses are subject to recovery through the electric fuel rate.

Investment

Marketable securities are stated at the lower of aggregate cost or market value, and other securities are stated at cost. Where appropriate, cost reflects amortization of premium and discount computed on a straight-line basis. Gains and losses on the sale of investment securities are recognized upon realization on a specific identification basis.

REQUIRED:

Prepare a schedule that explains the changes in the balances in utility plant and the nuclear decommissioning trust fund from December 31, 1989 to December 31, 1990 in as much detail as possible. State any assumptions you make.

PPG INDUSTRIES, INC.

CASE 10.2

The following financial statements are taken from the 1991 annual report of PPG Industries, Inc., a diversified industrial concern.

Balance Sheet as of December 31, 1991 and 1990 (Millions)

ASSETS	1991	1990
Current assets		
Cash and cash equivalents	$ 37.6	$ 59.3
Receivables (See Note 4)	1,057.9	1,069.3
Inventories (See Note 4)	875.3	945.1
Other	202.5	143.2
Total current assets	2,173.3	2,216.9
Property (See Note 4)	6,212.4	5,995.0
Less accumulated depreciation	3,029.2	2,739.9
Property—net	3,183.2	3,255.1
Investments	193.1	173.2
Other assets	506.6	463.0
Total	$6,056.2	$6,108.2

LIABILITIES AND EQUITY:

Current liabilities		
Short-term debt and current portion of long-term debt (See Note 5)	$ 404.9	$ 426.7
Accounts payable and accrued liabilities (See Note 4)	915.1	1,015.7
Income taxes (See Note 7)	15.0	23.0
Obligations under capital leases (See Note 8)	5.5	5.1
Total current liabilities	1,340.5	1,470.5
Long-term debt (See Note 5)	1,124.2	1,148.6
Obligations under capital leases (See Note 8)	39.0	37.6
Deferred income taxes (See Note 7)	475.6	460.9
Accrued pensions (See Note 9)	106.4	96.4
Provision for maintenance and repairs (Note 2)	NA	26.9
Other	240.5	251.4
Minority interest	75.5	69.4
Total liabilities	$3,401.7	$3,561.7
Shareholders' equity (See Note 6)		
Common stock	$ 242.1	$ 242.1
Additional paid-in capital	229.5	226.6
Treasury stock, at cost	−1,186.0	−1,183.3
Retained earnings	3,501.1	3,397.7
Unearned compensation	−218.6	-234.4
Minimum pension liability adjustment	−2.3	NA
Currency translation adjustment	88.7	97.8
Total shareholders' equity	2,654.5	2,546.5
Total	$6,056.2	$6,108.2

Statement of Earnings
For the Years Ended December 31, 1991, 1990, and 1989 (Millions)

	1991	1990	1989
Net sales	$5,672.6	$6,021.4	$5,734.1
Cost of sales	3,676.1	3,742.7	3,608.9
Gross profit	$1,996.5	$2,278.7	$2,125.2
Other expenses			
Selling, general and administrative	858.5	832.9	764.0
Depreciation	351.2	323.5	292.3
Research and development—net (See Note 14)	220.4	217.9	232.6
Interest	153.4	150.6	127.4
Business divestitures and realignments (See Note 3)	84.3	−.3	−28.1
Other charges	91.1	83.9	91.4
Total other expenses	1,758.9	1,608.5	1,479.6
Other earnings (See Note 13)	115.9	108.5	111.1
Earnings before income taxes and minority interest	353.5	778.7	756.7
Income taxes (See Note 7)	146.7	292.1	283.5
Minority interest	5.4	11.8	8.0
Earnings before cumulative effect of change in method of accounting	201.4	474.8	465.2
Cumulative effect on prior years (to Dec. 31, 1990) of change in method of accounting for major repairs to glass and fiber glass melting facilities, net of income taxes (See Note 2)	74.8	NA	NA
Net earnings	$ 276.2	$ 474.8	$ 465.2
Earnings per share:			
Earnings before cumulative effect of change in method of accounting	$1.90	$4.43	$4.18
Cumulative effect of change in method of accounting	0.70	NA	NA
Earnings per share	$2.60	$4.43	$4.18
Average shares outstanding	106.2	107.2	111.3

The accompanying notes to the financial statements are an integral part of this statement.

Notes to the financial statements (in part):

1. **Summary of Accounting Policies-**

    Property   Property is recorded at cost. We compute depreciation by the straight-line method based on the estimated useful lives of depreciable assets. Additional expense is recorded when facilities or equipment are subject to abnormal economic conditions or obsolescence. Significant improvements that add to productive capacity or extend the lives of properties are capitalized. Costs for repairs and maintenance are charged to expense as incurred. When property is retired or otherwise disposed of, the cost and related depreciation are removed from the accounts and any related gains or losses are included in income.

    Income taxes   Deferred taxes on income are provided for timing differences in the recognition of income and expense items for financial and tax purposes in accordance with Accounting Principles Board Opinion No. 11.

Reclassification   Certain amounts in the 1990 and 1989 financial statements have been reclassified to be consistent with the 1991 presentation.

2. Change in Method of Accounting

Effective Jan. 1, 1991, the Company adopted the capital method of accounting for the cost of rebuilding glass and fiber glass melting facilities. Under this method, costs are capitalized when incurred and depreciated over the estimated useful lives of the rebuilt facilities. In the past, the Company established a liability for the estimated cost of major repairs to its glass and fiber glass melting facilities through charges against earnings prior to the major repairs. It has become increasingly more difficult to estimate the costs of future repairs due to greater variability in the nature of and in the period between each major repair as a result of our continual efforts to modify and enhance our glass and fiber glass making processes. The change to the capital method for these costs was made because it does not require estimating the cost of, nor the period over which future repairs should be accrued and, as a result, provides for a better matching of expenses with revenue. The change in method also achieves an accounting treatment consistent with that of most of our major competitors.

The cumulative effect on retained earnings, net of tax, at Jan. 1, 1991, of changing to the capital method was $75 million and has been included in 1991 net earnings. The effect of the accounting change on 1991 net earnings, exclusive of the cumulative effect on retained earnings, and the pro forma effect on 1990 and 1989 net earnings, was not material.

4.

	December 31	
(Millions)	1991	1990
Property		
Land and land improvements	$ 281.8	$ 274.3
Buildings	1,164.1	1,120.9
Machinery and equipment	4,397.1	4,136.4
Other	237.9	226.4
Construction in progress	131.5	237.0
Total	$6,212.4	$5,995.0
Accounts payable and accrued liabilities		
Trade creditors	$ 520.4	$ 537.8
Accrued payroll	158.1	197.8
Maintenance and repairs	–	32.4
Business realignments	47.1	50.4
Other	189.5	197.3
Total	$ 915.1	$1,015.7

REQUIRED:

1. Describe, in your own words, PPG's old and new methods of accounting for the cost of rebuilding glass and fiber glass melting facilities. How has the accounting change described in Note 2 affected the timing of expense recognition for these costs? Which approach is more conservative?

2. Assume PPG faces a 34% marginal tax rate and that for tax purposes, the costs of rebuilding glass and fiber glass melting facilities are capitalized and depreciated. Prepare the journal entry that was made by PPG to record the change. Ignore the tax effects of the change.

3. Evaluate PPG management's statement that the accounting change provides for a better matching of expenses with revenue and speculate on other possible reasons for the change.

CASE 10.3 PENNZOIL COMPANY

The following income statement is taken from the 1988 annual report of Pennzoil Company:

PENNZOIL COMPANY
Consolidated Statement of Income
(Dollar amounts expressed in thousands except per share amounts)
Year Ended December 31,

	1988	1987	1986
Revenues			
Net sales	$2,088,412	$1,786,498	$1,782,177
Other income, net	185,488	49,804	139,046
	2,273,900	1,836,302	1,921,223
Costs and Expenses			
Cost of sales	1,341,896	1,109,570	1,001,658
Selling, general and administrative expenses	295,311	219,551	228,762
Depreciation, depletion and amortization	203,046	201,897	227,375
Exploration expenses	76,415	64,671	144,858
Taxes, other than income	38,703	36,396	52,166
Provisions for losses and gains on disposition and write-downs of assets (Note 9)	489,300	–	–
Interest charges	150,508	157,759	165,303
Interest capitalized	(23,619)	(38,957)	(37,274)
Income (Loss) Before Income Tax, Equity in Proven Properties, Inc. and Extraordinary Items	(297,660)	85,415	138,375
Income tax (benefit)	(123,999)	24,812	39,393
Equity (loss) in net income of Proven Properties Inc.	(13,299)	(15,089)	(76,312)
Income (Loss) Before Extraordinary Items	(186,960)	45,514	22,670
Extraordinary Items (Note 8)	1,662,402	–	(23,098)
Net Income (Loss)	1,475,442	45,514	(428)
Preference common stock dividends	15,690	15,690	15,690
Earnings (Loss) Available for Common Stock	$1,459,752	$ 29,824	$ (16,118)
Earnings (Loss) Per Share			
Before extraordinary items	$ (5.22)	$ .72	$ .17
Extraordinary items	42.80	–	(.56)
Total	$37.58	$ .72	$ (.39)
Dividends Per Common Share	$ 2.60	$2.20	$2.20

Information from the notes to the 1988 Pennzoil annual report.

1. (In Part): Summary of Significant Accounting Policies

Oil and Gas Producing Activities and Depreciation, Depletion, and Amortization

Effective June 30, 1988 Pennzoil changed its method of accounting for oil and gas operations from the full cost method to the successful efforts method. In September 1988, Pennzoil filed an amendment to its 1987 Annual Report on Form 10-K which reflected the restatement of the financial statements pursuant to this accounting change. Pennzoil's management concluded that the successful efforts method more appropriately reflects the mature nature of Pennzoil's oil and gas operations and enables investors and others to better compare Pennzoil to similar oil and gas companies, the majority of which follow the successful efforts method.

Under the successful efforts method, lease acquisition costs are capitalized. Significant unproved properties are reviewed periodically on a property-by-property basis to determine if there has been impairment of the carrying value, with any such impairment charged to exploration expense currently. All other unproved properties are generally aggregated and a portion of such costs estimated to be nonproductive, based on historical experience, is amortized on an average holding period basis.

Exploratory drilling costs are capitalized pending determination of proved reserves. If proved reserves are not discovered, the exploratory drilling costs are expensed. Other exploration costs are also expensed. All development costs are capitalized. Provision for depreciation, depletion and amortization is determined on a field-by-field basis using the unit-of-production method. The carrying amounts of proven properties are reviewed periodically and an impairment reserve is provided as conditions warrant.

The change in Pennzoil's accounting method increased 1988 net income by $44,354,000 or $1.14 per share, and 1987 net income by $2,136,000, or $.05 per share. The change decreased 1986 net income by $44,469,000, or $1.07 per share. As of December 31, 1987, retained earnings were reduced by $301,584,000 as a result of the accounting change.

Sulphur properties are generally depreciated and depleted on the unit-of-production method, except assets having an estimated life less than the estimated life of the mineral deposits, which are depreciated on the straight-line method.

All other properties are depreciated on straight-line or accelerated methods in amounts calculated to allocate the cost of properties over their estimated useful lives.

REQUIRED:

1. Explain how the change to the successful efforts accounting reduced retained earnings as of December 31, 1987 by $301,584,000 while net income for 1987 and 1988 were increased by $2,136,000 and $44,354,000, respectively.
2. Explain why there is no cumulative effect of the accounting change shown on the 1988 income statement for Pennzoil.
3. According to management, "the successful efforts method more appropriately reflects the mature nature of Pennzoil's oil and gas operations." Why?

CHAPTER 11

Property, Plant, and Equipment: Depreciation, Depletion, and Disposal

Chapter 10 dealt with accounting for the acquisition of productive assets. After productive assets are acquired and put into service, several events and transactions must still be recorded in the accounts. This chapter deals with recording those events and transactions occurring subsequent to acquisition: use of the assets, decreases in their value, and their disposal.

As productive assets are used, whatever productive capability they possess is consumed. For instance, a delivery truck may have the productive capability to travel 100,000 miles or a coal mine may have the productive capability to yield 5,000,000 tons of low sulfur coal. As the assets are used and their productive capability is effectively consumed, that usage is recorded as *depreciation* for plant and equipment and *depletion* for natural resources such as oil and gas drilling rights. The matching principle requires that the costs of productive assets not be recognized as expenses as they are incurred but rather allocated to expense by matching them with the revenues generated from their use. Depreciation and depletion involve any one of a number of rational and systematic calculations that recognize the cost of the asset, less any residual value, as expense over the asset's economic life. The effect of depreciation and depletion is to reduce the asset's *net book value*, or cost, less any accumulated depreciation recorded to date.

On occasion, a company will determine that the net book value of a particular asset exceeds the amount that can be realized through the use or sale of the asset. Such cases are known as *impairments* and are usually accompanied by an adjustment of the asset's net book value and recognition of a loss.

Property, plant, and equipment are disposed of in a variety of ways. Methods of *disposal* including sale, abandonment, and involuntary conversions such as casualty losses or condemnations. We examine the nature of and accounting treatment for these transactions in this chapter. We begin with a discussion of the nature of depreciation, a term which has several meanings.

THE NATURE OF DEPRECIATION

The English language is sometimes frustratingly imprecise. Depreciation is one of those terms that has several meanings, all related but with subtle and important differences. In its economic definition, depreciation represents a decline in value from use or the mere passage of time. Buyers of new cars become familiar with this concept of depreciation as they watch the market value of their cars fall over time, sometimes at an alarming rate. While the accounting concept of depreciation is related to the decline in value, there is an important difference.

While economists view the purpose of depreciation as recognition of a decline in the value of assets, accountants define **depreciation** as a cost allocation process. It is a direct consequence of the use of historical costs for valuation purposes and the principle of matching costs with revenues. It is not an attempt to measure the decline in economic value of the assets used in the firm's operating activities. In accounting for the depreciation of productive assets, firms use an estimate of the assets' fair values at the end of their estimated useful lives but generally ignore fair values at other points in time.

For example, assume that office equipment is acquired at the beginning of the year at a cost of $10,000. It is expected to provide service for five years and then have no value. At the end of the first year, the estimated market value of the equipment is $9,000. During its five-year useful life, the office equipment will make a contribution, directly or indirectly, to the firm's revenues. Traditional historical cost depreciation matches a portion of the $10,000 acquisition cost with the revenues generated each year. The amount to be allocated depends on the depreciation method chosen; but if straight-line depreciation is used, the charge to expense would be $2,000 ($10,000 ÷ 5).

Alternatively, if the goal of reporting depreciation were to capture the change in the asset's economic value as a measure of the cost of its use during the period, the charge to income would be only $1,000 ($10,000 - $9,000). While depreciation methods based on current market values have been proposed from time to time, generally accepted accounting principles (GAAP) still require that depreciation be computed on the basis of historical costs.

Why is depreciation measured using a historical cost allocation process? First, productive assets are held for use, rather than sale, and therefore, if there is no intent to sell the asset, information on market values may be irrelevant. However, ignoring market values might lead managers to use assets inappropriately. For instance, suppose a firm has a small building in a prime urban location where real estate values have escalated sharply in recent years. Ignoring the market value of this building might lead the firm to continue to own and operate the building when it could be sold for a much higher value to a real estate developer. Therefore, market values are indeed relevant even when the asset is intended to be held for use rather than for sale.

Why, then, don't we base our depreciation calculations on market values? In Chapter 10, it was noted that characteristics of productive assets and the markets in which they are traded raise concerns about the reliability of market prices for valuation purposes. These same concerns raise questions about the reliability of any depreciation methods based on changes in those market prices. As we have seen in Chapter 2, information in a firm's financial statements must be reliable. If the valuation of productive assets and the calculation of depreciation expense were based upon market prices, the lack of well-defined market prices would add an element of subjectivity to the financial statements and would give auditors difficulties in verifying amounts reported in the financial statements.

As a consequence of using historical costs for the valuation of productive assets and the calculation of depreciation, financial statements are not likely to be the best source of information about current market values of property, plant, and equipment. When productive assets are used as collateral to secure loans, lenders will be interested in the market values of these assets. However, the firm's financial statements will offer no information on this. What we observe here is the classic trade-off between relevance and reliability in financial statements. Because it is based on an easily verified amount, historical cost depreciation is less subjective than the economic concept of depreciation based on market values. However, it does not provide information to financial statement users about the economic cost of using productive assets over time.

DEPRECIATION METHODS

The authoritative literature has had surprisingly little to say about the calculation of depreciation. ARB No. 43 defines **depreciation accounting** as follows:

> The cost of a productive facility is one of the costs of the services it renders during its useful economic life. Generally accepted accounting principles require that this cost be spread over the expected useful life of the facility in such a way as to allocate it as equitably as possible to the periods during which services are obtained from the use of the facility. This procedure is known as depreciation accounting, a system of accounting which aims to distribute the cost or other basic value of tangible capital assets, less salvage value (if any), over the estimated useful life of the unit (which may be a group of assets) in a systematic and rational manner. It is a process of allocation, not of valuation.[1]

Over the years, a number of "systematic and rational" methods have been developed that achieve the objectives of this definition. Generally, acceptable depreciation methods can be classified in three basic alternatives:

1. Straight-line method
2. Accelerated methods
   (a) sum-of-the-years'-digits (SYD) method
   (b) declining balance methods
3. Methods based on usage

---

[1] "Restatement and Revision of Accounting Research Bulletins," *Accounting Research Bulletin No. 43* (New York: AICPA, 1953), ch. 9C, para. 5.

Straight-line depreciation implicitly assumes that the asset is utilized equally during each period of its life to contribute to revenues. Therefore, a constant cost is allocated to each year of the asset's useful life. Accelerated methods implicitly assume that the asset's pattern of usage is higher in the early years of its life than in the later years. For instance, this pattern of usage might apply if the asset is more efficient in the early years of its useful life. Thus, a larger portion of the cost is allocated to the early years than to the later years. Another justification sometimes offered for accelerated depreciation methods is that maintenance costs frequently increase as assets age. Use of accelerated methods allow total costs (depreciation plus maintenance) to remain relatively constant. Methods based on usage attempt to allocate costs based on the relationship between total usage expected from the asset and the actual usage in each period of the asset's life. Usage can be measured by input measures, such as hours of usage or by output measures, such as units of production.

In all these approaches, the actual calculation of periodic depreciation charges depends on three factors:

1. The asset's estimated economic useful life
2. The asset's capitalized cost
3. An estimate of the asset's value at the end of its useful life (commonly referred to as *salvage value*).

A distinction needs to be made between an asset's economic life and its physical life. Productive assets, if well-maintained, can have lengthy physical lives. A manual typewriter built in 1949 may function satisfactorily in 1994 at the task it was designed to perform in 1949. However, the task (and, hence, the machine) may have been rendered obsolete by technological advances. In 1994, word processing equipment is able to perform all the tasks of manual typewriters of 1949 and so much more. Thus, while the typewriter may continue to have a physical existence, its economic life has long since passed.

A relationship exists between the estimated salvage value of an asset and its estimated useful life. Some firms have an operating policy of acquiring new equipment, utilizing it in production for a short period, then selling the used equipment well before it has become valueless. For example, some trucking firms have a policy of selling used cabs and trailers after they are just a few years old. At the time of resale, these trucks have considerable value. Other trucking operations purchase these used assets and generate revenue from their use for many years. While the cabs and trailers are clearly capable of being used for a longer period than the original owner holds them, that firm has decided that the optimal holding period is somewhat shorter. Thus, the economic useful life of an asset used in depreciation calculations may be a shorter period than the period over which the asset is capable of providing service. To allocate properly the costs of the trucks in this situation, the useful life should reflect the disposition policy of the firm, not the actual period over which the assets are capable of providing service. In addition, estimates of salvage value should reflect the assets' estimated liquidation value at the expected point of sale. Through this process, the cost of the assets consumed over their economic useful lives—i.e, their original costs less salvage values—are matched with the revenues they helped generate.

Other factors also affect useful lives and salvage value estimates. Maintenance policies will influence the physical life of plant assets. Firms make decisions regarding the trade-off between loss of productive capacity due to equipment failure and the cost of routine maintenance. Different firms may have different policies regarding maintenance, and these differences are reflected in estimates of both salvage value and useful life. In addition, the nature of the asset will also have a considerable impact on these estimates. Assets that are highly specialized may have little salvage value relative to generalized assets. This problem is particularly acute in the high technology industries where a change in the production technology may leave a firm with worthless assets virtually overnight unless modification is possible.

Leasehold improvements are typically depreciated over their useful lives or the lives of the leases to which they pertain, whichever is shorter. A particular improvement to a leased retail facility might be expected to provide service for 10 years, but if the lease expires in 5 years and the firm will not be able to relocate any of the improvements to a new facility, then the remaining term of the lease determines the improvements' economic useful lives.

For companies with considerable experience in producing their products or services, estimates of useful lives and salvage values will likely come from their historical experience. Other sources of information are available from trade and industry sources. One tempting source of information regarding useful lives is the Tax Code. However, for tax purposes, firms are allowed to allocate the cost of plant assets as a reduction of taxable income based on several different methods including the Modified Accelerated Cost Recovery System (MACRS). Under MACRS, assets are written-off over a period (the *recovery period*), which is typically shorter than the assets' estimated useful lives. This faster write-off provides for deductions and, hence, tax savings sooner rather than later. These shorter recovery periods under MACRS may not be used as useful lives for financial reporting purposes. In fact, for most firms, depreciation for tax purposes is recognized over different periods and with different methods than depreciation for financial reporting purposes.

Once estimates of useful life and salvage value are determined, the difference between the assets' capitalized acquisition costs and their salvage values must be allocated over the assets' lives. The difference between cost and salvage value is called the **depreciable base** for the property. How this allocation is accomplished is determined by the depreciation method chosen. The basic methods are discussed in more detail below.

Straight-Line Depreciation

The most widely used method of depreciation for financial reporting purposes is **straight-line depreciation**.[2] Under this method, the depreciable base is allocated uniformly over the asset's life. Assume that Vouvray Incorporated has acquired a wine press on January 1, 1995, for a cost of $20,000. The press has a five-year useful life and a salvage value of $2,000. Exhibit 11.1 demonstrates

---

[2] Of 600 firms surveyed in the 1990 edition of *Accounting Trends & Techniques*, over 90% of them reported using the straight-line method for at least some portion of their productive assets.

EXHIBIT 11.1
Vouvray
Corporation—
Example of Straight-
Line Depreciation

VOUVRAY CORPORATION
Example of Straight-Line Depreciation

Purchase price of the wine press	=	$20,000
Salvage value	=	(2,000)
Depreciable base	=	$18,000

Life = 5 years

Year	Rate	Depreciable Base	Annual Depreciation	Net Book Value At Year-End
1995	1/5	$18,000	$3,600	$16,400
1996	1/5	18,000	3,600	12,800
1997	1/5	18,000	3,600	9,200
1998	1/5	18,000	3,600	5,600
1999	1/5	18,000	3,600	2,000

the pattern of depreciation and residual book value for the wine press using the straight-line method. Each year, Vouvray would make a journal entry of the following form to accrue the depreciation expense:

December 31, 1995:
Depreciation expense   3,600
    Accumulated depreciation   3,600
To record depreciation on the wine press on December 31 of each year.

Under all methods of depreciation, the annual charge to expense is not recorded as a direct reduction of the asset. Rather, the periodic depreciation charges are recorded in a valuation allowance (contra-asset) account. The difference between the asset's original acquisition cost and the accumulated depreciation is referred to as its **net book value** (**NBV**). By comparing the balance in accumulated depreciation with the assets' original cost, the financial statement reader can determine what portion of the asset's cost has been recognized as expense to date.

Accelerated Deprecation Methods

Accelerated depreciation methods are so named because they result in more depreciation expense early in the asset's life than does the straight-line method. The two most common accelerated methods are sum-of-the-years'-digits (SYD) and declining balance (DB) depreciation.

Sum-of-the-Years'-Digits Method   SYD derives its name from the components of its ratio. The numerator is the number of years of service remaining at the beginning of the period, and the denominator is the sum of the sequence of integers representing the years of life in the asset.[3] For example, an asset

---

[3] For an asset with a useful life of n years, the sum of digits 1 through n is $n(n + 1) \div 2$.

with a three-year life would have a SYD of 6(3 + 2 + 1). Over the life of the asset, the ratios used to compute the annual depreciation would be 3/6 for the first year, 2/6 for the second year, and 1/6 for the third year. Since the denominator is the sum of the digits that appear in the numerator of the asset's life, the ratios must sum to 1 over the asset's entire life. Exhibit 11.2 demonstrates the depreciation pattern and effect on net book value for the wine press acquired by Vouvray Corporation.

Declining Balance Method   An alternative accelerated method is the **declining balance method**. Under the declining balance method, a constant depreciation rate, which is some multiple of the straight-line rate, is applied to the declining net book value of the asset each year. The higher the multiple selected, the more accelerated the resulting write-off will be. For example, an asset that has a four-year life will be depreciated at a rate 25% (1/4 of its cost) each year under the straight-line method. If the **200% declining balance method** (also known as *double declining balance*) is used, a depreciation rate of 50% (200% of the straight-line rate) will be applied each year. If the **150% declining balance** method is used, a depreciation rate of 37.5% (150% of the straight line rate) will be applied each year. Once the appropriate annual rate has been determined, each year's depreciation is determined by applying this rate to the asset's net book value at the beginning of the period. Under this approach, salvage value is not removed from the capitalized cost prior to computing the depreciation. Instead, a "stopping rule," which yields a net book value equal to the asset's salvage value at the end of its useful life, is applied. One particularly simple stopping rule, illustrated in Exhibit 11.3 for the asset acquired by Vouvray Corporation, simply sets the depreciation expense in the final year of the asset's life equal to the amount necessary to yield a net book value equal to the asset's salvage value. Another common stopping rule, not illustrated here,

VOUVRAY CORPORATION				
Example of Sum-of-the-Years'-Digits Depreciation				
Purchase price	=		$20,000	
Salvage value	=		(2,000)	
Depreciable base	=		$18,000	
Life = 5 years				
Sum-of-the-Years'-Digits	=		5 + 4 + 3 + 2 + 1 = 15	

Year	Rate	Depreciable Base	Annual Depreciation	Net Book Value At Year-End
1995	5/15	$18,000	$6,000	$14,000
1996	4/15	18,000	4,800	9,200
1997	3/15	18,000	3,600	5,600
1998	2/15	18,000	2,400	3,200
1999	1/15	18,000	1,200	2,000

EXHIBIT 11.2
Vouvray Corporation—Example of Sum-of-the-Years'-Digits Depreciation

EXHIBIT 11.3
Vouvray
Corporation—
Example of 200%
Declining Balance
Depreciation

VOUVRAY CORPORATION
Example of 200% Declining Balance Depreciation

Purchase price	=	$20,000
Salvage value	=	(2,000)
Life = 5 years		
Rate = 200% of the straight-line rate	=	2 × 20% = 40%

Year	Rate	Depreciable Base	Annual Depreciation	Net Book Value At Year-End
1995	40%	$20,000	$8,000	$12,000
1996	40%	12,000	4,800	7,200
1997	40%	7,200	2,880	4,320
1998	40%	4,320	1,728	2,592
1999	40%	2,592	592[a]	2,000

[a]Depreciation in the final year is equal to the amount which will yield a net book value equal to the salvage value of the asset at the end of its useful life.

is to switch to straight-line depreciation when this method, applied to the asset's remaining net book value and its remaining useful life, yields a higher depreciation amount.

Compare the pattern of depreciation expense produced by the accelerated methods in Exhibits 11.2 and 11.3 to verify that they are, in fact, accelerated relative to the straight-line method applied to the same asset in Exhibit 11.1. Also notice that over the entire useful life of the asset, the same cumulative total of depreciation expense is recognized regardless of method. Thus, the depreciation method selected merely changes the amount of cost allocated to expense in particular periods, but it does not change the total amount allocated over all periods.

Methods Based on Usage

When the use of an asset can be measured in standardized input or output units, depreciation can be calculated on this basis. Usage is commonly measured in terms of the number of units of product produced (an output measure) or the number of machine hours utilized (an input measure) in the period. When depreciation is calculated on the basis of usage (known as the **units-of-production method**), the useful life of the asset is estimated in terms of units rather than years. When the asset produces a single type of product, the total production over the asset's life would be a reasonable basis for allocation. When many different products are produced on the same equipment, machine hours might be a more useful allocation basis since it may take twice as long to produce one product as another.

Once the useful life of the asset (in units) has been estimated, the depreciable base is spread over the total expected number of units to obtain a per unit depreciation charge. As the asset is used in each period, the depreciation expense for the period is computed by multiplying the annual usage times the per unit rate. Exhibit 11.4 demonstrates the application of this method to the wine press acquired by Vouvray Corporation, assuming that the expected total production from the press over its useful life is 100,000 barrels and that actual production was 40,000 barrels in the first year of use and 15,000 barrels for each of the next four years. The pattern of depreciation charges when a usage method is employed may be either accelerated or decelerated relative to straight-line, depending on the actual pattern of usage.

ACCOUNTING CHANGES INVOLVING DEPRECIATION

Given the number of alternative ways of computing depreciation and the need to estimate useful lives and residual values, accounting changes involving depreciation calculations (changes in principle and changes in estimate) are relatively common. We will consider both kinds of changes briefly.

Changes in Estimates of Salvage Value or Useful Life

When new information indicates that the estimate of the salvage value and/or the useful life of an asset is not correct, these parameters of the depreciation computation should be revised. As discussed in Chapter 3, a change of this type is a change in estimate rather than a change in accounting principle. Changes in estimate are handled prospectively, and no restatement of prior period financial statements or retroactive adjustment is made. Instead, the asset's remaining net book value is used to compute a new depreciation schedule based on the revised life and salvage value. Only future depreciation charges are affected. For example, assume that Vouvray determined at the

---

VOUVRAY CORPORATION
Example of Units-of-Production Depreciation

Purchase price	=		$20,000	
Salvage value	=		(2,000)	
Depreciable base	=		$18,000	
Life = 100,000 units				
Per unit depreciation	=		$18,000 ÷ 100,000 = $0.18	
Actual production	=		40,000 in Year 1 and 15,000 in each of the next 4 years.	

Year	Rate Unit	Usage	Annual Depreciation	Net Book Value At Year-End
1995	$0.18	40,000	$7,200	$12,800
1996	0.18	15,000	2,700	10,100
1997	0.18	15,000	2,700	7,400
1998	0.18	15,000	2,700	4,700
1999	0.18	15,000	2,700	2,000

EXHIBIT 11.4
Vouvray Corporation— Example of Units-of-Production Depreciation

beginning of 1997 that the wine press, which had been depreciated on a straight-line basis, would last another 5 years and have no salvage value at the end of its life. This would result in a new depreciation charge which spreads the remaining book value of the asset, $12,800, over a new useful life of 5 years. The result is a revised annual depreciation charge of $2,560 per year.

Changes in Depreciation Methods

When a firm switches from one depreciation method to another, it makes a change in accounting principle. As discussed in Chapter 5, changes in accounting principle are only permitted when the new method is somehow preferable to the old one. As a firm's business changes, the technology used in its operations may change. The pattern of usage of newly acquired productive assets may be different than that of older assets. As a consequence, management may decide that the formerly used depreciation method is no longer appropriate.

A change in principle of this type is handled retroactively by means of a cumulative adjustment to income, net of applicable income tax effects, in the year of the change. Restatement of the financial statements of prior periods to reflect the new depreciation method is not permitted. For example, assume that Vouvray Corporation elected to switch from SYD to straight-line depreciation for the wine press, effective January 1, 1997. The net book value of the wine press at the beginning of 1997 under SYD from Exhibit 11.2 was $9,200. Under straight-line depreciation, as shown in Exhibit 11.1, it would have been $12,800. The difference between these balances, $3,600, represents the pre-tax cumulative effect of the change in accounting principle from accelerated to straight-line depreciation. In other words, the cumulative difference between the amount of depreciation expense actually recorded under SYD and the amount that would have been recorded under straight-line is $3,600. Thus, Vouvray would use the following journal entry to adjust the balance in accumulated depreciation to make it appear that straight-line depreciation had always been in effect:

January 1, 1997:
Accumulated depreciation	3,600	
Cumulative effect of change in accounting for depreciation		3,600

To record the switch from sum-of-the-years'-digits depreciation to straight-line depreciation on January 1, 1997.

Depreciation for 1997 would be computed on the new, straight-line method. As part of the required disclosures, pro forma effects of the switch on prior years—i.e., as if the new method had been used in prior years—would be disclosed along with the effect on the current year. Tax effects would be included. In particular, assuming Vouvray had a 35% tax rate, it would record the cumulative effect in the income statement at its net of tax amount, $2,340.

Effects of the Choice of Depreciation Methods

Having shown that firms can choose from a number of alternative depreciation methods, it is important to understand the implications of the choice.

Exhibits 11.5 and 11.6 provide a comparison of the financial statement effects of straight-line and SYD depreciation in a very simple setting. In Exhibit 11.5, a no-growth situation is examined. The firm in this case has annual capital expenditures of $60 million. All of the productive assets are assumed to have estimated useful lives of three years. At the end of Year 3 and thereafter, the firm has reached a steady state in which assets are acquired to replace the assets being retired. As we can see in Exhibit 11.5, by comparing the amounts calculated under straight-line depreciation with those calculated under SYD depreciation, in Year 3 and thereafter, there is no difference between the two methods in the annual depreciation expense. However, because of the differences in the first two years, accumulated depreciation is higher under SYD, which would imply lower total assets and stockholders' equity as well.

In Exhibit 11.6, we consider growth in capital expenditures. While the capital expenditures in Year 1 are the same as in Exhibit 11.5, thereafter they increase by $6 million each year in Exhibit 11.6. In this scenario of growth, the firm always reports higher depreciation expense under SYD depreciation. This implies that total assets and stockholders' equity will be lower under SYD than under straight-line and that the difference will increase each year.

In summary, the magnitude of the effect of choosing one depreciation method over another depends on firms' rates of growth. Firms in a state of no growth will report approximately the same depreciation expense under the

Comparison of Straight-Line and Sum-of-the-Years'-Digits Depreciation No-Growth Case				
	YEAR 1	YEAR 2	YEAR 3	YEAR 4
Capital expenditures	$60	$ 60	$ 60	$ 60
Plant assets, at cost	60	120	180	180
Straight-line depreciation:				
Asset acquired in:				
Year 1	20	20	20	
Year 2		20	20	20
Year 3			20	20
Year 4				20
Depreciation expense	20	40	60	60
Accumulated depreciation	20	60	120	120
Plant assets, at NBV	40	60	60	60
SYD depreciation:				
Asset acquired in:				
Year 1	30	20	10	
Year 2		30	20	10
Year 3			30	20
Year 4				30
Depreciation expense	30	50	60	60
Accumulated depreciation	30	80	140	140
Plant assets, at NBV	30	40	40	40

EXHIBIT 11.5

Comparison of Straight-Line and Sum-of-the-Years'-Digits Depreciation— No-Growth Case

EXHIBIT 11.6

Comparison
of Straight-Line
and Sum-of-the-
Years'-Digits
Depreciation—
Growth Case

Comparison of Straight-Line and Sum-of-the-Years'-Digits Depreciation
Growth Case

	YEAR 1	YEAR 2	YEAR 3	YEAR 4
Capital expenditures	$60	$ 66	$ 72	$ 78
Plant assets, at cost	60	126	198	216
Straight-line depreciation:				
Asset acquired in:				
Year 1	20	20	20	
Year 2		22	22	22
Year 3			24	24
Year 4				26
Depreciation expense	20	42	66	72
Accumulated depreciation	20	62	128	140
Plant assets, at NBV	40	64	70	76
SYD depreciation:				
Asset acquired in:				
Year 1	30	20	10	
Year 2		33	22	11
Year 3			36	24
Year 4				39
Depreciation expense	30	53	68	74
Accumulated depreciation	30	83	151	165
Plant assets, at NBV	30	43	47	51

straight-line method as they would report under accelerated methods. While their total assets and stockholders' equity will be lower under an accelerated method than under straight-line, these differences will remain constant as long as the firms do not grow. Growing firms will always report higher depreciation expense under an accelerated method than under straight-line, and their assets and stockholders' equity will be lower by an increasing amount each year.

We have observed that several depreciation methods are generally acceptable and that they can produce quite different cost allocations. How do firms select a depreciation method? Depreciation calculations, like any cost allocation scheme, are inherently arbitrary. While management may believe one allocation scheme is more appropriate than another, it is not possible to identify one method that is unambiguously correct. Firms adopt a new depreciation method "to better match expenses with revenues," but just how the new method achieves this better matching is rarely described. While it is not fully understood why firms would prefer one accounting method to another, we can conclude that growing firms will prefer straight-line depreciation to the accelerated methods if they are concerned about reporting higher net income, assets, and stockholders' equity. Of course, since the choice of a depreciation method for financial reporting purposes has no effect on cash flows, it is difficult to see how reporting higher net income, assets, and stockholders' equity in this way would be beneficial unless the choice affects some contracts, which are written in terms of these accounting variables. For instance, firms with restrictive debt covenants requiring that they maintain ratios of debt to equity with a value no greater than 1.2 (i.e., the book value of debt cannot exceed the book value of equity by more than 20 percent) are likely to prefer accounting methods such as straight-line depreciation that result in increased stockholders' equity relative to accelerated methods.

SPECIALIZED DEPRECIATION METHODS

Companies with large numbers of productive assets have developed several depreciation techniques that greatly reduce the clerical burden of accounting for depreciation. In general, these shortcut methods reduce the bookkeeping costs of recognizing depreciation for each of many assets by calculating or approximating the total depreciation for a group of assets. Thus, instead of one depreciation calculation for each of 500 assets, the firm makes one calculation for the entire group of 500 assets with obvious savings of clerical effort and expense. These methods are known as inventory depreciation methods, retirement and replacement methods, and composite or group depreciation methods.

Inventory Depreciation

Inventory depreciation may be applied to an asset group consisting of many small items such as hand tools. When the sum of these items is material, but the value of an individual item is not, depreciation is determined through a process similar to that used to determine cost of goods sold for inventory. During the period, any purchases of new tools are capitalized; and at the end of the year, a physical inventory is taken and the units are valued. The valuation is often based on an appraisal, which is why this method is often referred to as the **appraisal method** of determining depreciation. The sum of the beginning balance and the purchases is then compared to the ending value, with the difference charged to depreciation expense. As a result, when an appraisal is used to value the units on hand at the end of the period, the resulting asset value represents an estimate of the market value of this class of property, plant, and equipment.

Retirement and Replacement Methods

Retirement and replacement methods are also applied to groups of items that are of small value individually, but are significant in aggregate. Railroad ties and utility poles are examples of the kinds of assets to which these methods might be applied. When these approaches are used, charges to depreciation expense are determined when the items that make up the group are either individually retired or replaced.

In the **retirement method**, the original cost of the asset is charged to depreciation expense when it is retired from service, less any proceeds from disposition at retirement. When new items are purchased, their costs are capitalized. There is no periodic allocation of the cost of these items. Rather, the entire cost is written off to expense at retirement. There is also no gain or loss recognition at retirement, since the difference between acquisition cost and selling price at disposition is charged to depreciation expense.

The **replacement method** recognizes depreciation expense when the items are replaced. The charge to depreciation is the difference between the purchase price of the replacement asset and the salvage value of the old asset. The value of the old asset remains on the financial records. Again, no gain or loss recognition occurs at replacement under this method.

When applied to individual assets, these methods obviously fail the "systematic and rational" test for depreciation methods. However, when applied to a large group of assets with individual items being retired and/or replaced on a regular basis, the results of these methods will provide a reasonable approximation of item by item depreciation at a fraction of the cost. If the number of items in the group remains relatively constant, retirement and replacement policies are stable over time, and prices of the items in inventory remain stable, these methods provide a measure of depreciation expense that approximates a straight-line approach to depreciating each individual item. If any of these conditions are not met, the depreciation charges under the inventory and retirement methods are analogous to a first-in, first-out calculation of cost of goods sold because the older ("first-in") costs of the units retired are charged to expense. Under the replacement method, the valuation is closer to a last-in, first-out approach because the cost of replacement units ("last-in") is expensed, leaving the old historical costs of units replaced still on the books. This is analogous to the cost of old LIFO inventory layers.

Group and Composite Depreciation Methods

Even when items in inventory are individually large, it may be convenient to treat large numbers of items as a single group for purposes of depreciation computation. For instance, a firm with a large fleet of delivery trucks or a firm with a large stock of office furniture and equipment would find it convenient to apply a single depreciation calculation to a group of assets rather than attempt to recognize depreciation on each item individually. This process is referred to as either **group depreciation** when the items are similar in nature (e.g., trucks) or **composite depreciation** when the items are dissimilar (e.g., manufacturing equipment), but the calculations involved are the same. Group and composite depreciation methods differ from the inventory, replacement, and retirement methods in that they allocate the historical acquisition cost of plant assets to periods using a systematic method. Unlike the individual asset methods, which use information on each asset's life and salvage values, group and composite methods use weighted averages in determining the rates at which cost is allocated to periods.

Let us consider an example that illustrates group and/or composite depreciation. Assume that a company has three types of items, which compose a single composite group, as follows:

	Estimated Useful Life	Acquisition Costs
Category A	10 years	$100,000
Category B	5 years	$ 60,000
Category C	4 years	$ 40,000

A weighted average rate of depreciation to be taken on the composite group will be determined by calculating the ratio of the amount of depreciation on the straight-line basis to the total acquisition cost of the assets. The computation would appear as follows:

			Straight-line
Category A	$100,000 ÷ 10 years	=	$10,000
Category B	60,000 ÷ 5 years	=	12,000
Category C	40,000 ÷ 4 years	=	10,000
Totals	$200,000	=	$32,000

Composite Rate = $32,000 ÷ $200,000 = .16

Assuming no new assets were purchased and no old assets were disposed of, the depreciation charge for the year would be determined by multiplying the value of the assets by the weighted average rate. In this example, the expense would be $32,000 ($200,000 × .16). When new assets within the categories that make up the composite group are purchased, the acquisition cost of the assets is simply added to the previous total; and a new depreciation amount is determined by multiplying the new total value by the same composite rate. For instance, assume that new assets are purchased in each category over the next fiscal year in the following amounts: $20,000 of Category A items, $10,000 of Category B items, and $3,000 of Category C items, for a total of $33,000. Depreciation charges for the year would be $37,280 ($233,000 × .16).

When the relative amounts of assets in each category change significantly, it may be necessary to reestimate the composite depreciation rate. In the example above, the change in the mix of assets among the categories due to new purchases is not significant enough to warrant recalculation. However, if the items in category C had amounted to $140,000, this would have had enough significant effect to warrant a recalculation. In addition, if the asset groups are redefined, the composite rate will have to be recomputed.

Since depreciation records are not kept on individual assets, it is not possible to identify a particular asset's net book value at any date after initial acquisition. Therefore, the disposal of assets from the composite group is handled without gain or loss recognition. As assets within the composite group are disposed of, the asset's original cost is removed from the property, plant, and equipment account; and any difference between the original cost and the proceeds from the sale of the old asset is removed from accumulated depreciation. Of course, any proceeds from the sale are also recorded. In this fashion, gains and losses on disposition are not recognized in the period of the disposition but are effectively deferred. For example, assume that items in Category A, with an original purchase price of $12,000, were retired by sale for $3,000 cash on June 14, 1993. The entry made to record this disposition would appear this way:

June 14, 1993:

Cash	3,000	
Accumulated depreciation	9,000	
Property, plant, and equipment		12,000

To record the sale of assets accounted for under composite
depreciation on June 14.

To summarize, these specialized depreciation methods are shortcuts whose primary attribute is their computational convenience. They should be viewed as approximation techniques that work acceptably well under general conditions to provide a depreciation amount that does not differ materially from the amount derived under more precise (and far more costly) methods. The accounting profession has learned that the benefits of more precise depreciation calculations can easily be outweighed by their costs.

DISPOSALS OF PROPERTY, PLANT, AND EQUIPMENT

Items of property, plant, and equipment may be disposed of in a variety of ways. We have already seen the accounting treatment of sales of assets and nonmonetary exchanges involving productive assets. Other types of disposals, examined here, include *abandonments* and a category known as *involuntary conversions*, which includes such transactions as casualty losses and condemnation proceedings. In general, accounting for disposals is the same, regardless of the type of disposal. At disposal, the asset's original cost and its balance in accumulated depreciation (which should reflect depreciation to the date of disposal) are removed from the accounts, and a gain or loss is recognized for the difference between the proceeds from disposal (if any) and the asset's net book value.[4]

When used assets are disposed of by sale, the company will receive something of value in exchange for the used asset. Assuming that cash is received, the sale will generate either a gain or loss based on the comparison of the asset's net book value at the point of sale with the selling price. When nonmonetary assets are exchanged, the determination of gain or loss depends on the character of the assets, as discussed in Chapter 10. The special rules for sales of real estate are discussed in Appendix 11.1.

The costs of disposal are usually expensed as incurred. In cases where the disposal costs are substantial, they may be accrued over the economic life of the asset to be disposed of. For instance, electric utilities face the prospect of "decommissioning" nuclear power plants at the ends of their useful lives. Since utilities cannot just walk away from their nuclear power plants at the end of the plants' economic lives, they estimate the costs of deactivating and rendering the plants safe. Decommissioning entails very large costs, which most utilities accrue over their plants' lives.

---

[4] Certain regulated companies (utilities) typically do not recognize a gain or loss on disposals of plant and equipment.

Abandonments

In the case of **abandonments**, firms essentially walk away from their assets and typically recover nothing. For instance, a railroad might abandon a right of way that it no longer finds profitable to operate. The assets abandoned may or may not have any net book value remaining. In either case, recording the abandonment results in removing the accumulated depreciation associated with the asset from the contra asset account and reducing the value of the gross property, plant, and equipment by the asset's original capitalized value. For fully depreciated assets, these effects will be equal. For example, assume that Barton Corporation disposed of a old truck by abandonment on July 11, 1993. The truck originally cost $15,000 and was fully depreciated. Barton would make the following journal entry to record the abandonment:

July 11, 1993:

Accumulated depreciation (vehicles)	15,000	
Vehicles		15,000

To record the abandonment of the fully depreciated truck on July 11.

To determine the net book value of any asset subject to disposal, it is important to compute any amortization or depreciation on the asset up to the date of sale. The purpose is to insure that the costs of using the asset in production are matched against the periodic revenues from operations, while the gain or loss on sale is computed based on the proper measure of remaining book value. In this way, income from operations is determined without including gains or losses on sales of property, plant, and equipment, which are not routine operating transactions for most corporations.

If the abandoned asset had a remaining net book value at retirement, then a loss will be recorded. Using the Barton example, assume that the accumulated depreciation on the vehicle was only $12,000 at abandonment. Barton would make the following entry:

July 11, 1993:

Accumulated depreciation (vehicles)	12,000	
Loss on abandonment of vehicles	3,000	
Vehicles		15,000

To record the abandonment of the truck on July 11.

Involuntary Conversions

Involuntary conversion refers to cases when company's assets are liquidated due to circumstances beyond its control. For example, a building might be involuntarily converted to an insurance claim as a result of fire or other casualty damage. Land held by a firm might be expropriated by the government under a right of eminent domain to allow for a freeway expansion or other public project. When this occurs, the real estate is involuntarily converted into a settlement from the government.

Accounting for these types of disposals is fundamentally the same as the examples above. For instance, when a governmental unit condemns real estate and orders it cleared for new roadways, the government must compensate the owner of the real estate. Gain or loss on the involuntary conversion is determined by comparing the compensation received to the real estate's net book value at the date of conversion. In the case of natural disasters, firms can acquire insurance to cover some or all of the losses that would otherwise arise. If insurance policies provide for payment when the loss occurs, gains or losses on the involuntary conversion are computed by comparing the value of the insurance proceeds to the net book value of the assets destroyed. Since insurance policies often provide coverage at replacement cost, it is possible that a gain will occur if replacement cost exceeds the asset's current net book value. Other insurance policies include coinsurance provisions to provide an incentive for adequate coverage to be maintained. Coinsurance is discussed in Appendix 11.2.

In any case, recording the involuntary conversion would match the asset's net book value against the proceeds from any insurance settlement and determine the gain or loss to be recorded. In some cases, involuntary conversions will meet the definition of an extraordinary item, as discussed in Chapter 3, and require the special disclosures associated with these events. However, this determination would depend on the unusual and infrequent nature of the conversion.

ASSET IMPAIRMENTS

Firms will occasionally write down productive assets below their original costs when the assets' values have been deemed permanently impaired. **Asset impairment** is defined as "the inability to recover fully the carrying amount of assets over their estimated useful lives."[5] Recognizing an asset impairment is analogous to applying the lower-of-cost-or-market value rule to inventories or marketable securities; however, there are significant differences. As we have seen, productive assets are held for use rather than for sale and the market values of these assets are inherently more subjective than the market values of other assets. As a consequence, unlike inventories and marketable securities, temporary situations when the net realizable value of a productive asset falls below its book value are ignored. However, when it appears that the asset's net realizable value has fallen below book value permanently and by a material amount, then the firm must record the impairment by writing off the difference between book value and net realizable value and recording a loss.

Although the FASB is currently considering the issue, there is no authoritative guidance on when it is and is not appropriate to record an asset impairment. The FASB added this topic to its active agenda in 1988 and released a discussion memorandum on the issue in 1990. Some observers are concerned that this lack of guidance has allowed some firms to record write-downs of questionable validity at management's discretion. Some firms have taken large

---

[5] "An analysis of the issues related to Accounting for the Impairment of Long-Lived Assets and Identifiable Intangibles," *Discussion Memorandum* (Norwalk, CT: FASB, December 7, 1990), para. 7.

asset write-downs in years of poor operating performance, a practice known as taking a "big bath." These write-downs, which frequently are associated with a change in the firm's management, have the effect of increasing the probability of future profitability for the firm by reducing future depreciation charges. The FASB is likely to seek ways of reducing the amount of management's discretion in the decision to record an asset impairment.

DEPLETION OF NATURAL RESOURCES

Firms involved in the extraction of natural resources such as timber, coal, oil, gas, gold, and other minerals account for the cost of their properties in a similar fashion. Upon acquisition of the property or the rights to extract natural resources from the property, the costs of the property or property rights are capitalized. As the natural resources are extracted from the property, the capitalized costs are systematically written off to expense as depletion. **Depletion** is the process of matching the costs of natural resource properties or property rights with the revenues recognized from the production and sale of the commodities. This approach is referred to as **cost based depletion** since it allocates only the original cost of the properties or property rights to periods in which revenues are recognized.

For financial reporting purposes, the most common means for determining depletion each period is the **units-of-production method**. For example, suppose Western Petroleum Products, Inc. paid $10 million for the drilling rights on property with estimated recoverable oil reserves of 5 million barrels. This yields a depletion cost of $2.00 per barrel of oil. If 150,000 barrels are extracted in the first year of production, depletion of $300,000 would be recognized. If Western Petroleum purchased the land in order to acquire the drilling rights, then the salvage value of the land would be subtracted from the acquisition price to determine the basis for the computation of depletion.

Depletion is measured differently for financial reporting purposes than for tax purposes. For tax purposes, a method called **percentage depletion** is allowed. Under the percentage depletion computation, the depletion expense for tax purposes is determined by multiplying total revenues generated from the sale of the commodity being extracted by a fixed percentage. Over the life of the extraction project, the total amount of depletion expense under this approach will typically far exceed the cost of the original property rights. This provides a tax incentive for exploration and development of natural resources by lowering the effective tax rate for firms in the extractive industries. While this public policy motivation of the tax law may serve the country well, it is not an appropriate basis for determining depletion expense for financial reporting. For financial reporting, cost based depletion is the only acceptable approach.

DISCLOSURES RELATED TO PROPERTY, PLANT, AND EQUIPMENT

At the beginning of Chapter 10, The Dow Chemical Company's balance sheet presentation of property, plant, and equipment was presented in Exhibit 10.1.

In addition, typical disclosures in the annual report to shareholders will include a statement of accounting policies used for valuation of property, plant, and equipment in the first note to the financial statements. If the company does not provide detailed information on the face of its balance sheet regarding the amount of property, plant, and equipment by major classification, this information is provided in a note on noncurrent assets. Exhibit 11.7 presents these disclosures for Raytheon Company, from its 1990 report to shareholders. Notice that the note describes the range of useful lives and methods used in the computation of depreciation.

For companies subject to SEC requirements, there are additional disclosure requirements contained in the 10-K reports regarding property, plant, and equipment. Supporting schedules that disclose the additions and retirements by class of asset are required for both the original cost and the accumulated depreciation accounts.

EXHIBIT 11.7

Raytheon Company— Disclosures Regarding Property, Plant, and Equipment

RAYTHEON COMPANY
Disclosures Regarding Property, Plant, and Equipment
1990 Annual Report

Note A: Accounting Policies

Property, plant, and equipment

Property, plant, and equipment are stated at cost. Betterments and major renewals are capitalized and included in property, plant, and equipment accounts, while expenditures for maintenance and repairs and minor renewals are charged to expense. When assets are retired or otherwise disposed of, the assets and related allowances for depreciation and amortization are eliminated from the accounts and any resulting gain or loss is reflected in income.

Provisions for depreciation are computed generally on the sum-of-the-years'-digits method, except for certain operations which use the straight-line or declining balance method. Depreciation provisions are based on estimated useful lives: buildings—20 to 45 years; machinery and equipment including production tooling—3 to 18 years; equipment leased to others—5 to 10 years. Leasehold improvements are amortized over the lesser of the remaining life of the lease or the estimated useful life of the improvement.

Note E: Property, Plant and Equipment

Property, plant, and equipment consist of the following at December 31 (in thousands):

	1990	1989
Land	$ 47,892	$ 47,871
Buildings and leasehold improvements	877,908	787,968
Machinery and equipment	2,512,663	2,293,489
Equipment leased to others	46,400	47,730
	3,484,863	3,177,058
Less accumulated depreciation and amortization	1,952,782	1,720,762
	$1,532,081	$1,456,296

SUMMARY

Depreciation of plant assets can be accomplished based on an analysis of individual assets or by analysis of groups of assets. In the case of individual assets, typical allocation methods include straight-line, sum-of-the-years'-digits, declining balance, and units-of-production methods. In all these methods, the process is conceptually simple. A salvage value is estimated, along with asset's useful life, and the original acquisition value is reduced to the salvage value over the asset's life. Sum-of-the-years'-digits and declining balance methods create larger expenses in the early years of an asset's life and smaller charges in the later years, relative to straight-line depreciation.

When individual asset depreciation is used, disposal of the assets generally results in the recognition of gain or loss from sale or abandonment. In some cases, the cost of tracking each individual item exceeds the benefits. Therefore, groups of assets are treated as a unit. Depending on the nature and size of the groups, firms may select alternative methods from those of inventory, replacement, retirement, and group or composite. In these methods, individual items are not identified; and disposal will generally not result in recognition of gain or loss.

The concept of gain or loss recognition for involuntary conversions is identical to that of other disposals. The only unique characteristic of these disposals is that insurance proceeds are often involved.

Cost based depletion is used for financial reporting purposes. In cost based depletion, periodic amortization is accomplished using a method similar to units-of-production depreciation. Cost based depletion differs from the percentage depletion method used for tax purposes in that cost based depletion limits the total expense over the life of the project to the original cost, while percentage depletion is based on a percentage of revenues recognized for tax purposes.

Appendix 11.1—
Sales of Real Estate

Real estate sales transactions are contractually complex. The seller may find it difficult to determine the appropriate point for recognition of a gain or loss under the general guidelines outlined in Chapter 4. To provide more specific guidance in accounting for real estate sales transactions, the FASB issued SFAS No. 66 in 1982.[6] SFAS No. 66 recognizes two broad classes of real estate sales transactions: retail land sales and all other sales of real estate. Retail land sales were discussed in Chapter 4. In this Appendix, we discuss other sales of real estate. Sales of real estate held for use, rather than for sale, fall under these rules.

The general conditions applying to sales other than retail land sales are that gain or loss shall be recognized at the time of sale (called the *full accrual method*) only when the amount of revenue to be collected can be reasonably determined and the seller's obligations under the contract are substantially complete. In particular, SFAS No. 66 imposes four tests to determine whether the full accrual method should be applied:

1. The sale has been consummated—i.e., a closing has taken place.
2. The buyer's initial and continuing investments are adequate to demonstrate a commitment to pay for the property.
3. The seller's receivable is not subject to future subordination—i.e., no other claims can become senior to it.
4. The seller has transferred the usual risks and rewards of ownership and does not have any substantial continuing involvement with the property.[7]

If any of these tests are not met, then the seller will not account for the transaction under the full accrual method. If the sale has not yet been consummated, the property and any related debt remain on the seller's books; and any amounts already received are accounted for as deposits. If the buyer's commitment to pay has not been established, the seller will account for the sale under the *installment method* and recognize any gains on the sale as the installments are collected. If the seller's receivable is subject to future subordi-

---

[6] "Accounting for Sales of Real Estate," *Statement of Financial Accounting Standards No. 66* (Stamford, CT: FASB, 1982).

[7] *Ibid.*, para 5.

nation, the seller will account for the transaction under the *cost recovery method* and only recognize a gain after full recovery of the property's cost. If the seller will continue to have involvement with the property after the date of sale such that the risks and rewards of ownership have not been transferred to the buyer, then the transaction is accounted for according to the nature of the seller's continuing involvement. For instance, suppose the seller is obligated to repurchase the property at a future date at a prespecified price. In such cases, the transaction is not viewed as a sale at all but rather as a *financing agreement*.

Appendix 11.2— Coinsurance

Some insurance policies include coinsurance clauses to create incentives for the owner of the asset to carry sufficient coverage. A **coinsurance clause** states a particular level of coverage, relative to the asset's fair value at the time of the loss, must be in force before the insurance company is required to pay the full value of its policy. For example, assume that an insurance company writes a policy with a face value of $100,000 and has a coinsurance clause requiring the owner of the asset to carry insurance equal to at least 80% of the asset's fair value at the time of the loss. Also assume that the value of the asset at the initiation of the policy was $150,000. Given these facts, the ratio of insurance to value is only 67% at the initiation of the policy. If a fire damaged the property immediately after the policy went into force, the insurance company would not be required to pay the full amount of the loss since the owner did not carry enough insurance to meet the coinsurance provision. Had the owner purchased $120,000 of insurance, the coinsurance requirement would have been met and the insurance company would be required to pay the full amount of the loss.

Insurance contracts with coinsurance clauses provide three possible outcomes in the event of a loss:

1. Payment of the entire face value of the policy if the loss exceeds the face value and the coinsurance clause is satisfied
2. Payment of the actual loss if the loss is less than the face value of the policy and the coinsurance clause is satisfied
3. Payment under the coinsurance provision of a portion of the loss up to a maximum of the face value of the policy.

When the coinsurance clause is not satisfied, the determination of the amounts recoverable from the insurance company is based on the extent to which the coinsurance requirement has been met.

For example, assume a policy with a face value of $100,000 and a coinsurance clause of 80% is taken out on an asset with a value of $150,000. A fire immediately occurs, resulting in a loss of $108,000 in the fair value of the property. The amount of the loss that can be recovered depends on the ratio of the total dollar value of all insurance on the property divided by the total dollar value of insurance required under the coinsurance provision. In this example, the dollar value of the insurance is $100,000, and the coinsurance clause required $120,000 ($150,000 × 80%). The ratio of these amounts is 10/12 ($100,000 ÷ $120,000). The insurance company will cover only 10/12th of the loss up to a maximum of the face value. In this case, the face value is $100,000 and 10/12th of the loss is $90,000. Since the loss under the coinsurance provision is lower, the company pays this amount.

In contrast, suppose the loss had been complete. The coinsurance provision would result in a covered loss of $125,000 ($150,000 × 10/12). Since this exceeds the face value of the policy, only the face value of $100,000 would be paid.

QUESTIONS

1. Economists regard *depreciation* as a decline in the value of an asset. How does the accounting concept of depreciation differ from the economic concept of depreciation?

2. A lending officer at a commercial bank is looking for information on the value of certain productive assets that a firm has pledged as collateral for a loan. How relevant are the amounts reported in the firm's financial statements for this purpose? Explain your answer.

3. What are the attributes of a depreciation method that qualifies under generally accepted accounting procedures?

4. What is the most popular depreciation method used for financial reporting purposes?

5. Regardless of method, what three factors are needed to calculate depreciation expense for an individual asset?

6. How could two firms use different estimated economic lives for the same asset?

7. Are the recovery periods specified under the Modified Accelerated Cost Recovery System acceptable for use as estimated useful lives in depreciation calculations made for financial reporting purposes?

8. What is the *depreciable base* of an asset?

9. Why are depreciation charges recorded in a separate accumulated depreciation account rather than as a direct reduction of the asset?

10. What makes a particular depreciation method accelerated?

11. Why is a *stopping rule* necessary with the declining balance depreciation methods?

12. What is a necessary condition for applying the *unit-of-production method*?

13. Explain how a revision in the estimate of an asset's useful life would affect the calculation of depreciation.

14. Explain how a change in depreciation method would be reflected in a firm's financial statements.

15. In choosing between straight-line and accelerated depreciation methods, explain the importance of the rate of growth in productive assets in determining the financial statement effects of the choice.

16. If a rapidly growing firm is concerned about certain restrictive debt covenants that place constraints on its maximum debt to equity ratio, would management likely prefer the use of straight-line or accelerated depreciation?

17. What is the purpose of specialized depreciation methods such as the *inventory* or *replacement method*?

18. Explain why the *retirement method* is analogous to the FIFO method, while the replacement method is analogous to LIFO.

19. When is it necessary to recompute a weighted average depreciation rate for use in the *group depreciation method*?

20. What is an *involuntary conversion* and is it accounted for any differently than other asset disposals?

21. Under what conditions will a firm report a loss on the *abandonment* of an asset?

22. When is it necessary to record the *impairment* of a productive asset's value?

23. (Appendix 11.2) What is the purpose of *coinsurance clauses* in insurance policies? How do they typically operate?

EXERCISES

11-1.   *Depreciation calculations*

Viking Paint purchased a new blending machine for $12,000 on December 31, 1993. Based on past experience with machines of this type, Viking expects the machine will have a useful life of four years and no salvage value at retirement. Viking's fiscal year-end is on December 31.

REQUIRED:

Prepare the necessary journal entries to record depreciation expense for the machine on December 31, 1994 and December 31, 1995 under each of the following methods:
1. Straight-line
2. Sum-of-the-years'-digits
3. Double declining balance

11-2.   *Depreciation calculations*

Pluto Corporation, which manufactures economy cars and light trucks, purchased a new robotic welding machine for $675,000 on January 2, 1994. Pluto expects that the welding machine will have a useful life of five years and a salvage value of $45,000 at retirement. Pluto's engineering department has estimated that total production from the machine will be 525,000 frame-units over its useful life. Actual frame-units produced were 115,000 during 1994 and 119,000 during 1995. Pluto's fiscal year-end is December 31.

REQUIRED:

Prepare the necessary journal entries to record depreciation expense for the machine on December 31, 1994 and December 31, 1995 under each of the following methods:
1. Straight-line
2. Sum-of-the-years'-digits
3. 150% declining balance
4. Units-of-production

11-3.   *Depreciation calculations*

On January 1, 1994, Albatross Airlines purchased a used airliner for $3,410,000. Independent appraisal indicated a fair value of $3,657,500 on the date of purchase. The airliner was immediately put into service. Albatross expected that the airliner would have a useful life of three years during which time 10,500 flight-hours would be logged. Salvage value at retirement is expected to be $1,100,000. Actual flight-hours logged were 3,640 during 1994, 3,485 during 1995, and 3,675 during 1996. Albatross' fiscal year-end is December 31.

REQUIRED:

Prepare the necessary journal entries to record depreciation expense for the airliner on December 31, 1995, and December 31, 1996 under each of the following methods:
1. Straight-line
2. Sum-of-the-years'-digits
3. 150% declining balance (last year depreciation taken to equate net book and salvage values)
4. Units-of-production

11-4.   *Depreciation calculations*

Andrews Company purchased a new delivery truck for $26,800 on December 31, 1993. Company policy is to retire delivery vehicles after five years of service. During the truck's useful life, Andrews expects 90,000 business miles to be logged on the vehicle. At retirement, the vehicle is expected to have a trade-in value of $3,400. Actual business miles logged on the delivery truck were as follows:

Year	Business Miles
1994	16,200
1995	16,650
1996	17,550
1997	17,100
1998	15,300

REQUIRED:

Assume Andrews fiscal year-end is December 31. Prepare the necessary journal entries to record depreciation expense for the delivery truck on December 31, 1994, and December 31, 1995, under each of the following methods:

1. Straight-line
2. Sum-of-the-years'-digits
3. Double declining balance (last year depreciation taken to equate net book and salvage values)
4. Units-of-production

11-5.   *Depreciation calculations*

On August 1, 1994, Matthews' Muscle Shop purchased a new multi-station rowing machine for $31,200. The machine is expected to have a useful life of three years and a salvage value of $6,000 at retirement. Matthews' fiscal year-end is December 31.

REQUIRED:

Prepare the necessary journal entries to record depreciation expense for the rowing machine on December 31, 1994, December 31, 1996, and July 31, 1997, under each of the following methods:

1. Straight-line
2. Sum-of-the-years'-digits
3. 150% declining balance (last year depreciation taken to equate net book and salvage values)

11-6.   *Retirement/replacement system*

Nellie's Diaper Service began 1994 with a stock of 60,000 diapers purchased at a cost of $24,000. During the cleaning process, diapers that show noticeable wear or staining are placed in storage bins and are periodically sold to a recycling firm for $.04 each. New diapers are purchased in bulk as needed. The following transactions related to Nellie's stock of diapers occurred in the first half of 1994:
(a) February 4: 40,000 diapers purchased at $.43 each.
(b) March 1: 30,000 diapers recycled at $.04 each.
(c) April 3: 20,000 diapers purchased at $.44 each.
(d) April 30: 40,000 diapers recycled at $.04 each.

REQUIRED:

Assume all transactions are for cash. Prepare the necessary journal entries to record the above transactions under each of the following assumptions:

1. Nellie's uses the retirement method to account for the cost of diapers.
2. Nellie's uses the replacement method to account for the cost of diapers.

11-7.   *Group/composite depreciation*

Reedem & Wheap, an accounting firm that specializes in the preparation of individual tax returns, acquired the following office equipment on January 1, 1993:
(a) Electronic calculators were purchased for $42,000; estimated useful life is six years; estimated salvage value is $6,000.
(b) Word processing equipment was purchased for $68,000; estimated useful life is five years; estimated salvage value is $8,000.
(c) Copy machines were purchased for $70,000; estimated useful life is three years; estimated salvage value is $16,000.

REQUIRED:

Compute the rate of depreciation per year to be applied to this office equipment under the group/composite method.

11-8.   *Change in estimate*

On January 1, 1985, Regal Stoneworks purchased six diamond-tipped saw blades used to cut slab marble for $140,000. At that time, Regal had estimated that the saw blades would have a useful life of 16 years and a combined salvage value of $2,400 at retirement. Inspection of the saw blades on January 3, 1994, revealed that the blades would only last another four years. This change in useful life is not expected to affect salvage value at retirement. Regal's fiscal year-end is December 31.

REQUIRED:

Assume that Regal uses straight-line depreciation for all assets. Prepare the necessary journal entries to record the change in estimated life on January 3, 1994, and depreciation expense for the saw blades on December 31, 1994.

11-9.   *Change in estimate*

Larson Machine Tool purchased its present production facility on January 2, 1982, for $796,000. At that time, the useful life of the building was expected to be 20 years and resale value at retirement was expected to be $40,000. Structural analysis on February 2, 1994, indicated an additional useful life of 16 years for the building. Resale value on the new retirement date was expected to be $72,000. Larson's fiscal year-end is December 31.

REQUIRED:

Assume that Larson uses straight-line depreciation for all assets. Prepare the necessary journal entries to record the changes in estimated life and resale value on February 2, 1994, and depreciation expense for the building on December 31, 1994.

11-10.   *Change in depreciation method*

On January 2, 1991, Andrews Landscaping purchased a new delivery truck for $26,700. The estimated useful life of the truck was six years and trade-in value at retirement was expected to be $3,600. On January 1, 1994, Andrews elected to change from sum-of-the-years'-digits to straight-line depreciation for the delivery truck.

REQUIRED:

1. Prepare the necessary journal entries to record the change in depreciation method on January 1, 1994.
2. Repeat part (1) assuming that the change in depreciation method was from 150% declining balance to straight-line.

11-11.   *Depletion*

Canyon Oil acquired the rights to search for and extract oil on Parcel C on October 7, 1993. The agreement required an immediate payment of $729,000 and a payment of $1.40 per barrel extracted payable at the end of each year of operation on the parcel. In addition, the agreement requires that Canyon seal all wells and restore the property to pre-drilling condition within six months of the cessation of extraction operations. Canyon has determined that the present value cost of restoration is $76,950.

On February 14, 1994, Canyon discovered proven reserves of 810,000 barrels of oil on Parcel C. It is expected that 223,000 barrels will be extracted during 1994, 282,000 during 1995, and 305,000 during 1996.

REQUIRED:

Determine the depletion expense that Canyon should recognize for Parcel C in each of the years 1993, 1994, 1995, and 1996.

11-12. *Asset disposals, impairments*

Nelson Company had the following transactions related to property, plant, and equipment during 1995:

(a)   September 1: Due to excess capacity, a machine is sold for $4,600. The machine had been purchased at a cost of $11,680 on January 2, 1989. At that time, the useful life of the machine was expected to be seven years and salvage value was expected to be $1,600. Nelson had been recognizing the cost of this machine under the straight-line method.

(b)   October 1: A machine is sold at the end of its estimated useful life for $1,600. The machine had been purchased for $9,880 on October 1, 1991. At that time, salvage value at retirement was expected to be $1,400. Nelson had been recognizing the cost of this machine under the straight-line method.

(c)   November 21: A truck that had been purchased on March 3, 1988 for $16,800 was abandoned. At the date of purchase, Nelson expected that the truck would have a useful life of six years and a salvage value of $2,200 at retirement. Nelson had been recognizing the cost of the truck under the double-declining balance method.

(b)   December 31: Nelson determined that, due to poor maintenance, a machine had been permanently impaired. The machine had been purchased for $38,000 on January 2, 1989. At that time, Nelson expected that the machine would have a useful life of ten years. Accumulated depreciation of $19,200 (including expense for the current year) has been recorded for the machine under the straight-line method. Estimated net realizable value on December 31, is $8,000.

REQUIRED:

Assume all transactions are for cash and that Nelson's fiscal year-end is December 31. Prepare the necessary journal entries to record the above transactions.

11-13. *Involuntary conversion, coinsurance, Appendix 11.2*

On November 23, 1995, Seaside Resort in Key West, Florida, was completely destroyed by hurricane Sharon. Buffet Company, which owns and operates Seaside, had developed the resort complex in early 1995 at a cost of $2,800,000. Independent appraisal on November 1, 1995, indicated a fair value of $2,500,000 for the resort complex. The insurance policy on the resort, which covers such disasters, has a face value of $2,750,000 and contains an 80% coinsurance clause.

REQUIRED:

1. Determine the amount recoverable by Buffet under the insurance policy.
2. Repeat part (1) assuming that the face value of the policy is $2,100,000.
3. Repeat part (1) assuming that the face value of the policy is $1,500,000 and that the loss in fair value to Seaside is $1,600,000.

PROBLEMS

11-1. *Depreciation calculations*

On July 1, 1993, Beam Company purchased a new forklift for $17,500. Although the seller offers a 2% discount for cash payment, due to liquidity constraints Beam chose not to take the discount. Freight-in charges of $300 and in-transit insurance cost of $150 on the forklift were prepaid on the date of purchase. Beam expected that the forklift would have a useful life of six years and a salvage value of $3,600 at retirement.

On January 1, 1996, due to environmental considerations, Beam replaced the original diesel engine on the forklift with an electric drive motor. The electric motor was purchased for $6,400 and installed at an additional cost of $800. The price paid by Beam for the electric motor included an $1,100 trade-in allowance on the diesel engine. At the time of replacement, Beam estimated that the forklift would have a useful life of five years from the date of replacement and a salvage value at retirement of $3,900. Beam's fiscal year-end is December 31.

REQUIRED:

Prepare the necessary journal entries to record depreciation expense for the forklift on December 31, 1993, December 31, 1994, and December 31, 1996, under each of the following methods:
1. Straight-line
2. 150% declining-balance
3. Sum-of-the-years'-digits

11-2. *Exchange of assets, depreciation calculations*

On October 1, 1995, Red Baron Flight Schools exchanged a twin-engine aircraft for a newer version of the same aircraft owned by ESP Parcel. The aircraft given by Red Baron had been purchased used for $144,000 on January 2, 1994, and had a fair value of $128,000 on the date of exchange. Red Baron had been recording depreciation expense on the aircraft using the sum-of-the-years'-digits method over an estimated three-year useful life and an expected trade-in value of $80,000 at retirement. In addition to the aircraft, Red Baron gave ESP $32,000 cash. The aircraft given by ESP had been purchased new for $195,000 and had a fair value of $160,000 on the date of exchange. Red Baron's fiscal year-end is December 31.

REQUIRED:

1. Prepare the necessary journal entries to record the exchange on October 31, 1995.
2. Repeat part (1) assuming that Red Baron had been using the straight-line method to record depreciation expense for the old aircraft.

11-3. *Group/composite depreciation*

Benny's Bodywork, which owns and operates three auto-body repair shops, began operations on July 1, 1993. On that date, Benny's made the following investment in machinery and equipment:

Item	Cost	Estimated Salvage	Estimated Life
Air compressors	$305,000	$55,000	10 yrs.
Paint sprayers	110,000	4,000	5 yrs.
Buffers	135,000	31,000	4 yrs.
Sanders	260,000	54,000	5 yrs.

On January 1, 1994, Benny's acquired the following additional machinery and equipment:

Item	Cost	Estimated Salvage
Air compressors	$35,000	$6,300
Paint sprayers	12,000	500
Buffers	16,000	3,700
Sanders	27,000	5,600

On May 4, 1995, Benny's sold the following machinery and equipment for cash:

Item	Cost	Estimated Salvage	Selling Price
Air compressors	$42,000	$7,500	$8,400
Paint sprayers	19,000	800	200
Sanders	31,000	6,200	7,000

REQUIRED:

1. Assume Benny's fiscal year-end is December 31. Prepare the necessary journal entries to record depreciation expense for machinery and equipment on December 31, 1993, December 31, 1994, and December 31, 1995, using the composite method.
2. Prepare the necessary journal entries to record the retirement of machinery and equipment on May 4, 1995.

11-4. *Asset acquisitions and retirements*

Ferguson Company, which manufactures ceramic plumbing fixtures, was organized on November 12, 1992, and began operations on January 2, 1993. The following information relates to Ferguson's investment in plant, property, and equipment:

Property and Plant

The land and building that house Ferguson's original production facility were purchased for $350,000 on December 30, 1992. Independent appraisal had indicated fair values of $111,000 for the land and $259,000 for the building on the date of purchase.

On October 1, 1993, Ferguson contracted with Nelson Construction to construct an additional production facility on the existing site for a total cost of $930,000. Construction was expected to take nine months. The contract called for progress payments of $300,000, $150,000, and $120,000 on the first of the month for the last three months of 1993. During 1994, progress payments of $120,000 were made on January 1, and March 1. The balance was paid on June 30, when construction was completed. No new debt was acquired to finance construction. Ferguson's weighted average annual interest rate on debt outstanding during the construction period was 12%.

Equipment

Ferguson's investment in equipment, all of which was purchased on January 1, 1993, is classified into four categories:

Equipment Type	Cost
Molding machinery	$283,500
Glazing and buffing machines	162,000
Kiln ovens	324,000
Small equipment	40,500

Transactions related to equipment during 1994 were as follows:

(a) On February 2, a glazing machine that had been purchased for $27,000 was sold for $12,000. Also on this date, buffing equipment was acquired for $9,000 cash.

(b) On May 3, small equipment that had been purchased for $16,400 was traded in on similar new equipment that cost $18,350. The price of the new small equipment included a trade-in allowance of $3,350 on the old equipment. Ferguson uses the replacement method to record small equipment expense.

(c) On June 30, Ferguson exchanged two of its molding machines for similar, newer machines. The machines given by Ferguson had been purchased for $94,500 (net book value was $60,500 on date of exchange) and had a fair value of $70,400 on June 30. In addition to the molding machines, Ferguson paid $4,600 cash. The machines received by Ferguson had a fair value of $75,000 on the date of exchange.

REQUIRED:

Prepare an itemized schedule showing changes in property, plant, and equipment for Ferguson Company during 1994 using the following format:

Description	Balance on 12/31/93	Additions	Retirements	Balance on 12/31/94

11-5. *Depreciation calculations*

Refer to the information given in Problem 11-4 for Ferguson Company. In addition, the following information related to depreciation expense on Ferguson's investment in property, plant, and equipment is also available:

(a) Depreciation expense for the original production facility is recorded using the straight-line method over an estimated useful life of 20 years and an expected salvage value of $83,000 at retirement.

(b) Depreciation expense for the new production facility will be recorded using the straight-line method over an estimated useful life of 25 years and an expected salvage value of $90,000 at retirement.

(c) Depreciation expense for the molding machines is recorded using the sum-of-the-years'-digits method over an estimated useful life of six years. Salvage value was expected to be 10% of original cost. The estimated salvage of the molding machines received on June 30 is equal to the estimated salvage value on the machines exchanged.

(d) Depreciation expense for the glazing and buffing machines is recorded using the composite method and a weighted average depreciation rate of 18%. Due to rapid obsolescence, negligible salvage value is expected for these assets.

(e) Depreciation expense for the kiln ovens is recorded using the 150% declining-balance method over an estimated useful life of 15 years and a expected salvage value of $33,900 at retirement.

(f) Depreciation expense for the small equipment is recorded using the replacement method.

REQUIRED:

Prepare an itemized schedule of changes in accumulated depreciation for Ferguson Company during 1994 using the following format:

Description	Balance on 12/31/93	Additions	Retirements	Balance on 12/31/94

11-6. *Changes in depreciation method*

Viking Pattern, a small tool and die manufacturer, recently made significant expenditures for production machinery. On January 1, 1989, Viking purchased a high-precision lathe for $33,600. The lathe was expected to have a useful life of six years and a salvage value of $4,200 at retirement. On October 1, 1990, Viking purchased a welding machine for $16,320. The welding machine was expected to have a useful life of four years and a salvage value of $2,240 at retirement. Viking's policy is to use an accelerated depreciation method to record machine expense in the early years of an asset's useful life and then switch to straight-line in the year in which this method, when applied to the asset's remaining net book value over its remaining life, yields a higher depreciation charge. All changes in depreciation method are recorded as of January 1, the first day of Viking's fiscal year.

REQUIRED:

1. Prepare the necessary journal entries to record the changes in depreciation method for the lathe and the welder, assuming that depreciation expense is initially recorded using the sum-of-the-years'-digits method.
2. Repeat part (1) assuming that depreciation expense is initially recorded using the 150% declining-balance method.

11-7. *Change in depreciation method*

Scudder Company purchased a new delivery truck for $17,500 on July 1, 1992. At that time, Scudder expected that the truck would have a useful life of five years and a trade-in value of $2,650 at retirement. Depreciation expense on the truck was determined using the sum-of-the-years'-digits method. On January 1, 1995, Scudder elected to switch to straight-line depreciation on the truck. Also at this time, Scudder determined that the estimated useful life of the truck would be six rather than five years. Scudder's fiscal year-end is December 31.

REQUIRED:

1. Prepare the necessary journal entries to record the change in depreciation method on January 1, 1995, and to record depreciation expense for the truck on December 31, 1995. Round all numbers to the nearest dollar.
2. Repeat part (1) assuming that depreciation expense for the truck had initially been recorded using the double declining balance method.

11-8. *Asset disposals*

The records of Hardtimes, Unlimited, a large logging company operating in northern Minnesota, reveal the following transactions related to property, plant, and equipment during 1994:

(a) On June 1, logging operations that began in 1989 on a tract of land owned by the state of Minnesota were discontinued. Hardtimes had constructed several buildings used for storage and housing on this tract at a cost of $86,400 on June 30, 1989. The buildings, which were being depreciated over an estimated six-year life (zero salvage value) using the straight-line method, were abandoned when logging operations were discontinued.

(b) On July 14, a tract of timber that Hardtimes had purchased for $400,000 on January 3, 1992, was expropriated by the state of Minnesota under the Wildlife Habitat Act. At the date of expropriation, Hardtimes had extracted 964,000 of the estimated 1,600,000 board-feet of lumber on the tract. Resale value for the tract of timber upon completion of logging had originally been estimated at $80,000. Hardtimes received $200,000 from the state of Minnesota on the date of expropriation.

(c) On September 1, Hardtimes received payment from its insurer for damage to equipment that occurred during a fire on August 2. The damage amounted to a loss of $310,000 in the fair value of the equipment. The equipment had a net book of $420,000 (original cost was $580,000) and a fair value of $375,000 on the date of the fire. The insurance policy on the equipment had a face value of $250,000 and contained an 85% coinsurance clause.

(d) On October 1, it was discovered that insect infestation had destroyed 400,000 board-feet of lumber on a tract of timber that had been purchased for $270,000 on April 4, 1991. Of the estimated 1,800,000 board-feet of lumber on this tract, 950,000 board-feet had been extracted as of October 1, 1994. Market prices for this type of lumber, which have been stable for several years, were $.18 per board-foot on October 1, 1994. Hardtimes had expected zero resale value for this tract of timber.

REQUIRED:

Assume Hardtimes' fiscal year-end is December 31. Prepare the necessary journal entries to record the above transactions.

CASE 11.1

ROHM AND HAAS COMPANY

Balance Sheet Information

	1989	1988
	\$ MILLIONS	
Total current assets	\$1,001	\$1,032
Investments in and advances to unconsolidated subsidiaries and affiliates	107	100
Land, buildings and equipment, net	1,148	935
Other assets, net	189	175
	\$2,455	\$2,242

SUMMARY OF SIGNIFICANT ACCOUNTING POLICIES

Land, Buildings and Equipment and Related Depreciation

Land, buildings and equipment are carried at cost. Assets are depreciated over their estimated useful lives. Effective January 1, 1989, the company changed its method of depreciation for newly acquired buildings and equipment to the straight-line method. Buildings and equipment acquired before that date continue to be depreciated principally by accelerated methods. Maintenance and repairs are charged to earnings; replacements and betterments are capitalized.

The cost and related accumulated depreciation of buildings and equipment are removed from the accounts upon retirement or other disposition; any resulting profit or loss is reflected in earnings.

NOTES TO CONSOLIDATED FINANCIAL STATEMENTS

Note 12: Land, Buildings and Equipment, Net

(Millions of dollars)	1989	1988
Land	\$ 16	\$ 19
Buildings and improvements	403	365
Machinery and equipment	1,640	1,407
Capitalized interest cost	88	68
Construction	249	203
	2,396	2,062
Less accumulated depreciation	1,248	1,127
Total	\$1,148	\$ 935

The principal lives (in years) used in determining depreciation rates of various assets are: buildings and improvements (10–50); machinery and equipment (5–20); automobiles, trucks and tank cars (3–10); furniture and fixtures, laboratory equipment and other assets (5–10).

Effective January 1, 1989, the company changed its method of depreciation for newly acquired buildings and equipment to the straight-line method. The change had no cumulative effect on prior years' earnings but did increase net earnings by \$9 million, or \$.14 per share in 1989.

At December 31, 1989, the gross book values of assets depreciated by accelerated methods totaled $1,449 million and assets depreciated by the straight-line method totaled $682 million.

In 1989, 1988 and 1987, respectively, interest costs of $20 million, $16 million and $11 million were capitalized and added to the gross book value of land, buildings and equipment. Amortization of such capitalized costs included in depreciation expense was $8 million in 1989, $7 million in 1988 and $5 million in 1987.

REQUIRED:

1. Explain why the change in depreciation method did not have a cumulative effect on prior years' earnings but did increase net earnings by $9 million.
2. Under what circumstances would a change in depreciation method be expected to have a cumulative effect on prior years' earnings?
3. From the information provided, calculate the approximate overall rate of interest used in the interest capitalization calculation.
4. From the information provided, determine what transactions have caused the gross book value of land, buildings, and equipment to increase from $2,062 million at December 31, 1988, to $2,396 million at December 31, 1989.

JACKPOT ENTERPRISES, INC.

CASE 11.2

Jackpot is engaged in the gaming industry and generates revenues from route operations and, beginning in 1990, from casino operations. Gaming route operations involve the installation, operation, and servicing of gaming machines owned by Jackpot that are located in leased or licensed space primarily in retail stores, bars, and restaurants throughout Nevada. Casino operations began on November 1, 1989. The following information is taken from the firm's 1992 annual report.

Excerpts from management's discussion and analysis:

Depreciation expense in the 1992 period increased by approximately $.7 million over the 1991 period. The increase in depreciation expense in the 1992 period was primarily attributable to the costs associated with the purchase of gaming machines and related equipment for placement at new locations and for the replacement of certain machines and equipment at existing locations. In line with management's policy of upgrading gaming equipment whenever it is determined that newer equipment will provide greater player appeal and better economies to Jackpot, Jackpot replaced approximately 50% of its gaming machines at existing locations during fiscal 1990 and 1991.

Jackpot increased the number of machines in operation on its gaming routes by 471 during 1991 and 267 in 1990. Of the 471 machines placed in operation in 1991, 290 were the result of the machines in operation from the acquisition of a business. Of the $9.2 million in additional revenue from gaming route operations, approximately $8.0 million was generated from revenues from additional machines, including those of the business from date of acquisition, placed in operation in 1991. With respect to many of the new locations, Jackpot experiences disproportionate costs and expenses as a percentage of revenue earned from such locations during the beginning months of operations. The remaining increase in route operation revenues was primarily the result of increased play from existing machines in operation net of lost machine play from terminated locations.

The percentage increase in depreciation expense in relation to total operating costs was primarily attributable to the costs associated with the purchase of gaming machines and related equipment for placement at new locations and for the replacement of certain machines and equipment at existing locations as explained above. The percentage increase in depreciation was also affected by the full year of operations at the Nugget and the Owl Club. In addition, depreciation was increased on a comparative basis as a result of a reduction by Jackpot in the estimated useful life of the gaming machines purchased after December 31, 1989 (see Note 1 of Notes to Consolidated Financial Statements herein). As a result of the above, depreciation increased by approximately $1.0 million in 1991.

Net cash used by investing activities in 1992 was approximately $5.0 million which was the result of cash used for the purchase of approximately $2.0 million of equipment, the advance of approximately $.7 million to location operators, the deposit into escrow of approximately $.3 million towards the purchase of a substantial portion of the northern Nevada gaming route operation of Bally Gaming, Inc. and the purchase of approximately $3.4 million of location lease rights, net of approximately $1.4 million of cash generated from the net sales of temporary investments, including those reserved for gaming acquisitions.

JACKPOT ENTERPRISES, INC. AND SUBSIDIARIES
Consolidated Balance Sheets
June 30, 1992 and 1991
(Dollars in Thousands)

ASSETS	1992	1991
Current assets:		
Cash and cash equivalents	$ 8,734	$ 6,285
Temporary investments	3,299	1,028
Cash equivalents and temporary investments, at cost which approximates market, reserved for gaming acquisitions	5,926	9,383
Prepaid expenses	2,914	1,443
Deferred Federal income tax	437	NA
Other current assets	1,068	2,249
Total current assets	22,378	20,388
Property and equipment, at cost:		
Land and buildings	2,820	2,820
Gaming equipment	19,420	18,996
Other equipment	2,769	2,744
Leasehold improvements	720	701
	25,729	25,261
Less accumulated depreciation	9,648	7,221
	$16,081	$18,040
Lease acquisition costs and other intangible assets, net of accumulated amortization of $8,717 and $6,891	$ 8,570	$ 7,030
Goodwill, net of accumulated amortization of $1,768 and $1,574	5,862	6,056
Lease and other security deposits	2,730	2,748
Other non-current assets, net	7,388	8,401
Total assets	$63,009	$62,663

LIABILITIES AND STOCKHOLDERS' EQUITY	1992	1991
Current liabilities:		
Current portion of long-term debt	$ 3	$ 158
Accounts payable	642	503
Accrued interest	436	458
Other current liabilities	3,191	2,698
Total current liabilities	4,272	3,817
Long-term debt, less current portion	573	935
8.75% convertible subordinated debentures due 2014	29,921	31,421
Deferred Federal income tax	NA	253
Accrued rent	2,737	2,914
Other liabilities	2,455	2,199
Total liabilities	$39,958	$41,539
Commitments and contingencies		
Stockholders' equity:		
Preferred stock–authorized 1,000,000 shares of $1 par value; none issued	NA	NA
Common Stock–authorized 15,000,000 shares of $.01 par value; 5,608,528 and 5,237,820 shares issued	$ 56	$ 52
Additional paid-in capital	20,719	16,250
Retained earnings	2,606	4,822
Less 26,666 shares of common stock in treasury in 1992, at cost	–330	NA
Total stockholders' equity	23,051	21,124
Total liabilities and stockholders' equity	$63,009	$62,663

JACKPOT ENTERPRISES, INC. AND SUBSIDIARIES
Consolidated Statement of Income
Years Ended June 30, 1992, 1991, and 1990
(Dollars in Thousands, except per share data)

	1992	1991	1990
Revenues:			
Route operations	$56,847	$49,146	$39,893
Casino operations	5,886	5,577	1,467
Service fees from related party	NA	NA	67
Totals	$62,733	54,723	41,427
Costs and expenses:			
Route operations	39,850	35,101	27,794
Casino operations	4,952	4,898	1,377
Amortization	2,133	1,931	1,470
Depreciation	3,560	2,861	1,814
General and administrative	5,428	5,527	4,746
Totals	55,923	50,318	37,201
Operating income	6,810	4,405	4,226
Other income (expense):			
Interest and other income	745	1,258	2,728
Interest expense	–2,806	–3,154	–3,152
South Dakota investments:			
Write-down of investments to estimated recoverable value	NA	–606	NA
Loss from equity investees	–92	–247	NA
Other expense	–349	NA	NA
Totals	–2,502	–2,749	–424
Income before income tax and extraordinary gain	4,308	1,656	3,802
Provision (credit) for Federal income tax:			
Current	1,928	556	1,335
Deferred	-464	–195	–388
Totals	1,464	361	947
Income before extraordinary gain	2,844	1,295	2,855
Extraordinary gain from repurchase of 8.75% convertible subordinated debentures, net of income tax	204	366	NA
Net income	$ 3,048	$ 1,661	$ 2,855
Earnings per share:			
Income before extraordinary gain	$.50	$.23	$.50
Extraordinary gain	.04	.07	NA
Net income	$.54	$.30	$.50

See Notes to Consolidated Financial Statements.

NOTES TO CONSOLIDATED FINANCIAL STATEMENTS

Note 1—Significant accounting policies (in part):

Depreciation of property and equipment:-For financial statement purposes, depreciation is provided using the straight-line method for property and equipment, including property held for rental. Estimated useful lives, limited as to leasehold improvements by the term of the lease, range as follows:

Buildings	30 to 40 years
Gaming equipment	4 to 7 years
Other equipment	3 to 7 years
Leasehold improvements	1 to 21 years

As a result of Jackpot's evaluation of changes in gaming technology and its adoption of a policy whereby it intends to replace economically productive gaming machines whenever it is projected that newer gaming machines will significantly increase revenues, Jackpot reduced the estimated useful life of gaming machines purchased after December 31, 1989 to a range of 4 to 6 years and changed the estimated useful lives of certain other equipment. Gaming machines are included in gaming equipment in the accompanying consolidated balance sheets. The estimated useful life of gaming machines purchased prior to the change in estimate ranged from 5 to 7 years. The change in estimate decreased income before extraordinary gain and net income by approximately $128,000 and $90,000, or $.02 per share, for the years ended June 30, 1992 and 1991, respectively, and had no material effect on income before extraordinary gain and net income for the year ended June 30, 1990.

REQUIRED:

1. Note that Jackpot's change in the estimated useful lives of gaming machines is the result of a change in the firm's policy concerning when to replace the machines. This suggests that other firms may be depreciating the same machines over different estimated useful lives. What is the nature of depreciation that would allow two different firms to depreciate identical assets over different useful lives?

2. From the information provided, determine and explain in as much detail as possible what transactions occurred in fiscal 1992 that affected the balances in the various property and equipment accounts.

3. Suppose Jackpot had not made the change in estimate of the useful lives of gaming equipment. What balances in the fiscal 1992 financial statements would differ? By how much? Assume Jackpot's effective tax rate is 34 percent in all years.

CHAPTER 12

Intangible Assets

Intangible assets are those that have no physical existence and no contractual claims to cash such as receivables. Like property, plant, and equipment, intangible assets embody future benefits that are generally consumed in the generation of revenues from goods and services in future periods. Lack of physical existence does not imply that these types of assets cannot be identified. **Identifiable assets** are those that can be separated and transferred by sale without requiring the sale of the company as a whole. For example, patents, copyrights, and trademarks, which are identifiable by examination of documents representing the legal right embodied in them, represent future benefits through the government's granting of an exclusive right to use a brand name, product, literary work, or artistic work.

Intangible assets also arise from efforts by corporations to acquire knowledge (obtain information) that their competitors do not have. This knowledge can be embodied in such physical assets as technical manuals, special product formulas, or engineering or design drawings, each of which is identifiable. However, informational advantages are often difficult to identify specifically, thereby giving rise to a nonidentifiable intangible asset called *goodwill*. Goodwill may also arise from other factors that provide companies an ability to create unique markets for their goods or services such as exceptional abilities to undertake market research to improve the positioning of products, an ability to use distribution channels better to deliver goods to the marketplace, or exceptional managerial talent.

Accounting for intangible assets requires an understanding of the circumstances in which the costs to obtain an intangible asset can be recorded as an asset, the means by which this cost is matched to the future revenues generated from the consumption of the intangible asset, and final disposition of the asset. This chapter begins with an overview of accounting for intangibles and then turns to a discussion of selected types of specific intangible assets that provide examples of this general structure.

THE SIGNIFICANCE OF INTANGIBLE ASSETS

In light of the increased activity in corporate takeovers over the past 20 years, intangible assets have become a significant part of many balance sheets. In 1986, Honeywell acquired an operating segment of Sperry Corporation called the Sperry Aerospace Group. Exhibit 12.1 is an excerpt from the 1988 Honeywell Annual Report that describes the results of this acquisition. Out of a purchase price of over $1.0 billion, $587.8 million was attributable to intangible assets alone. Given the importance of technological know-how and specialized product information in the aerospace industry, it is not surprising that an acquisition of this nature would contain such a large portion of intangible assets.

THE CHARACTER OF INTANGIBLE ASSETS

Intangible assets are often associated with the ownership or control of information. For example, a *patent* is an embodiment of knowledge into a government granted, exclusive right to use the information the patent represents. More generically, drawings embody the knowledge that a firm has regarding particular technologies for the design or production of a product. In general, it

---

Valuation of Intangibles
Acquisition of Sperry Aerospace by Honeywell, Inc.

On December 30, 1986, Honeywell acquired the Sperry Aerospace Group, a leading supplier of avionics systems and related equipment, and purchased related assets in certain foreign locations in 1987. The aggregate cost for these acquisitions was $1,029.0.

The acquisition has been accounted for as a purchase for financial reporting purposes. The purchase price has been allocated to the net assets acquired, including intangible assets, based on their fair values at the acquisition date as established by an appraisal in 1987. Following is the final valuation of net assets acquired:

Receivables	$ 131.9
Inventories	166.6
Property	224.6
Intangible assets	587.8
Other assets	52.1
	1,163.0
Notes payable	25.0
Payables and accruals	106.7
Long-term debt	2.3
	134.0
Net assets	$1,029.0

EXHIBIT 12.1

Valuation of Intangibles—Acquisition of Sperry Aerospace by Honeywell, Inc.

is much more difficult to design a contract that transfers ownership of information not embodied in physical assets than it is to transfer physical assets. Since it is not possible to prevent the seller from "remembering" the information sold, the difficulty arises due to the buyer's inability to prevent the seller from continuing to enjoy the benefits of the information transferred. Informational assets that a company can protect may be the driving force behind its profitability; and, therefore, these assets have considerable private value to the corporation. However, if the information becomes widely available, these same assets lose their value.

As a consequence of both the difficulty of selling intangibles in individual exchanges and the desire of most companies to retain intangibles to realize future operating profits, the sale of intangibles as individual assets is much less common than the sale of other physical assets such as property, plant, and equipment. The lack of individual asset exchanges for intangibles also makes it more difficult to assess the future benefits an intangible represents. Without exchanges for similar types of property rights and because they depend more on single users' assessments, an intangible asset's future benefits and the probability of these benefits materializing are difficult to measure. There are no market prices that reflect the aggregate beliefs of all traders to use for comparison.

When an exchange of informational assets does take place, the buyer clearly has an interest in not paying more for the information than the value of the future benefits to be derived from its use. For this reason, the exchange price in a purchase of an intangible is believed to represent a reasonably objective basis for asserting that the costs incurred in the purchase represent the value of the probable future benefits acquired. Since probable future benefits are acquired, an asset is recorded.

In the case of internally developed intangibles, costs are incurred in an attempt to develop information that is valuable to the company. Not all costs will develop valuable information. A wide difference of opinion exists as to:

- The sources of future benefits
- The probability of the benefits materializing

Without an ability to observe other transactions in which similar informational assets are exchanged, the assessment of the value of the existing future benefits, if any, is made even more difficult. As a result, a dichotomy exists in accounting for externally purchased and internally developed intangible assets.

ACCOUNTING FOR INTANGIBLE ASSETS — GENERAL RULES

For purposes of financial reporting, the accounting treatment applied to intangible assets depends on three primary characteristics:

1. Identifiability of the intangible. Identifiability refers to the ability to separate the intangible asset from the entity as a whole such that it could be transferred by sale without a need to transfer the ownership of the entire entity.

2. The manner in which the intangible is obtained. The key distinction here is between internally generated intangibles and those purchased from external parties.

3. The expected number of future periods to benefit from the utilization of the intangible asset. Some intangibles may have indefinite lives, while others have only limited periods of economic usefulness. For intangibles with specific legal lives, their economic lives may still be shorter than their legal lives.

Internally Generated Intangibles

When companies incur costs that might ultimately result in the generation of an intangible asset, the treatment of these costs depends on whether the intangible is expected to be identifiable or nonidentifiable. APB No. 17 explicitly requires that all costs incurred to maintain or develop nonidentifiable intangible assets must be charged to expense in the period the costs are incurred. Since a nonidentifiable intangible cannot be transferred independently from the transfer of the corporation as a whole, the decision not to allow recognition of such assets is consistent with the uncertainties of assessing the existence of future benefits relating to this asset and the probability that these benefits will materialize.

The prohibition on recognition of internally generated nonidentifiable assets does not extend automatically to internally generated identifiable intangibles. In general, if costs are incurred internally to develop an intangible asset and if the future benefits generated from the incurring of these costs are probable, then these costs may be capitalized as an intangible asset, as opposed to being treated as a period cost.

Because of the practical difficulty associated with assessing the nature and probability of realization related to an intangible asset's future benefits, several specific regulations restrict the degree of managerial discretion in the recognition of internally generated intangible assets. These specific guidelines, which are applicable to both research and development costs and software development costs, are discussed later in this chapter to illustrate the types of problems that arise in assessing the nature of future benefits associated with intangible assets and the probability of their materializing and the manner in which accounting regulators dealt with these issues.

Externally Acquired Intangibles

When an intangible is acquired through an arm's-length exchange, APB No. 17 requires that the asset be capitalized at its purchase price. Since identifiable intangible assets can be transferred individually, their value when acquired in an exchange is determined by the selling price. Nonidentifiable assets can only be transferred by sale of the organization and must have their value inferred from the purchase price by subtracting the fair value of all other identifiable assets and liabilities acquired. If the acquisition of intangibles arises from non-monetary exchanges, the rules for these exchanges, discussed in Chapter 10, are employed to establish the value of the intangible.

Recognizing the Consumption of Intangible Assets

As with property, plant, and equipment, the cost of most intangible assets is assumed to be consumed over some economic life through their conversion into goods and services to generate revenue or matched to the selling prices of the intangibles if they are disposed of by sale. Some intangible assets may not have their value consumed over time. Consequently, it could be argued that they have an indefinite life. For example, the formula for Coca-Cola is an intangible asset that Coke has kept secret for many years. With the success of this product, the formula is likely to be more valuable now than it was when it was first developed; and it may have indefinite value as long as Coke can prevent others from duplicating it.

Prior to the adoption of APB No. 17, it was common practice not to amortize intangibles such as goodwill if they were deemed to have an indefinite life. As of November 1, 1970, the effective date of APB No. 17, the cost of all intangible assets acquired after that date must be recognized as an expense systematically over a period reflecting the economic life of the intangible, not to exceed 40 years. The process of allocating the cost of intangible assets to periods is called **amortization**. Computation of the amount of amortization to be charged to expense each period is to be based on a straight-line method, unless it can be demonstrated that some other approach is superior.[1] Typically, intangibles are assumed to have zero salvage value. Intangibles acquired prior to November 1, 1970, which are demonstrated to have an indefinite life, can continue to be carried without amortization.

In the event that an intangible asset is disposed of by sale, a gain or loss will be recognized based on the difference between the selling price of the intangible and the net book value (original cost less accumulated amortization) at the point of sale. Recall that only identifiable intangibles can be separately transferred by sale.

EXAMPLES OF ACCOUNTING AND REPORTING FOR COMMON INTANGIBLE ASSETS

Given the wide variety of firm-specific characteristics that might give rise to an intangible asset, it is not possible to discuss all forms of intangibles here. Some common examples of identifiable intangible assets include:

- Patents
- Copyrights
- Trademarks and brand names
- Licenses
- Initial franchise costs paid by the franchisee
- Organizational costs

The only commonly reported nonidentifiable asset is goodwill. Each of these is examined in more detail below.

---

[1] "Intangible Assets," *Accounting Principles Board Opinion No. 17* (APB: August, 1970), para. 30.

Patents

A **patent** is an exclusive right, granted by the U.S. Government, to use a process or produce a product. A patent has a legal life of 17 years. When the process or product that is patented is developed internally, the development costs typically fall in the category of research and development, which is reviewed later in the text. Other costs of obtaining a patent include the legal fees of patent attorneys who undertake research to determine the validity of the patent application and develop the necessary documents to support the registration. Costs associated with registration of a patent can be capitalized. However, companies often forgo this alternative due to lack of materiality.

When purchased from a third party, the patent's cost is capitalized at acquisition. The capitalized value can include any costs associated with the acquisition, such as attorneys fees. For example, assume that on August 1, 1994, Oppenheim Industries acquired a patent from Josters Enterprises by exchanging 100 shares of its $1 par common stock, which had a market value of $60,000 on that date. In addition, Oppenheim incurred legal fees to negotiate the transfer in the amount of $3,000, which was paid in cash. Oppenheim would make the following entry to record the acquisition:

```
August 1, 1994:
Patents                                              63,000
    Common stock                                                100
    Additional paid-in capital                                59,900
    Cash                                                       3,000
To record the exchange of stock for the patent from Josters.
```

After the original value of the patent is determined, it is necessary to assess the number of future periods over which the benefits of the patent will accrue. Since the legal life of the patent is 17 years, the economic life cannot exceed this period. However, it may be much shorter. Patents for products in high technology fields can be replaced by a new generation of products within a few years or even months. The determination of the economic life of a patent will depend on knowledge about the product or process and the industry in which it is used.

Continuing the Oppenheim example, assume the patent acquired by Oppenheim has an expected economic life of 60 months from the date of acquisition. Oppenheim has a fiscal year-end at December 31. As a result, at December 31, 1994, the company would record amortization of $5,250 ($63,000 ÷ 60 months × 5 months). Oppenheim would make the following entry to record amortization of the patent for 1994:

```
December 31, 1994:
Amortization expense                                 5,250
    Accumulated amortization                                  5,250
To record amortization from August 1 to December 31, 1990.[2]
```

---

[2] The credit in the above entry is often charged directly against the intangible asset without using the accumulated amortization valuation allowance.

Copyrights

Similar to a patent, a **copyright** is granted for the right to reproduce and sell artistic or literary works instead of products or production processes. The government grants a copyright for the life of the creator plus 50 years. The valuation and amortization of a copyright follows the same basic procedures as a patent. While the economic life of a copyright may well extend beyond 40 years, APB No. 17 arbitrarily imposes a maximum life of 40 years.

Trademarks and Brand Names

Trademarks and **brand** or **trade names** represent words or symbols that are used to identify a product specifically. Trademarks can be registered with the U.S. Patent Office for a period of 20 years and are renewable as long as the trademark is in continuous use. Legally, the life of a trademark is indefinite; but in a world of constantly changing products, its economic life is likely to be limited.

If firms develop trademarks internally, costs are incurred to develop and then to register them. Generally, the costs incurred to develop a trade or brand name include the costs of design of logos (corporate identification symbols), marketing research, and advertising. Due to the difficulty of linking costs with the actual generation of future benefits, these types of costs are treated as expense when incurred.

Costs to register a brand name or trademark can be capitalized in the same fashion as the costs to register a patent. The costs incurred to acquire a brand name or trademark by purchase from a third party should be capitalized as an intangible asset when the exchange is recorded. If litigation to defend the use of brand names or trademarks is successful, these costs can also be capitalized, using the same basic rules as applied to patents. Trademarks and brand names are registered indefinitely, but any cost capitalized when the trademark or brand name is created must be amortized over a period not to exceed 40 years.

Corporations also develop corporate identification symbols, or corporate logos, but the costs associated with these efforts are generally included in organization costs, which are discussed later.

Licenses

A **license** provides a legal right to use some resource. Licenses are commonly used to allow one company to manufacture and sell a product that requires the use of a patented process owned by another company. The patent holder will usually issue a license to the manufacturing firm to use the patented process in return for a fixed payment, a royalty, or both.

If a fixed payment is involved, the payment is in return for the right to use the patent for several years. Thus, the payment represents the value of an intangible asset, the license, that will be used to produce revenues over several future periods. This type of payment should be capitalized and amortized over the life of the license.

Royalty payments are generally tied directly to the manufacture or sale of the manufactured product. If tied to sale, they are a period cost recognized at the point of sale but are not subject to capitalization. If the royalties are due on manufacture, the royalty costs should be capitalized into the cost of the inventory and matched against revenue when the inventory is sold.

Initial Franchise Fees

The reporting of initial franchise fees by the franchisor was discussed in Chapter 4. Here the question is how the franchisee should account for initial franchise fees that the franchise agreement requires be paid at the inception of the agreement. When an initial payment is made to the franchisor, the franchisee must identify the nature of the payment. In most franchise arrangements, the franchisee will be paying for both tangible and intangible assets. The tangible assets include inventory and equipment and often the building in which the franchisee will operate. These tangible assets should be recorded at their fair value. When the initial fees are in excess of the fair value of tangible assets acquired, the excess is recorded as an intangible asset called *franchising fees*.

Franchise fees should be amortized over the life of the franchise agreement or the expected economic life of the franchise, whichever is shorter. In no case can the amortization extend beyond 40 years.

Litigation Costs and Intangible Assets

Many of the legal rights that represent the real source of value for intangible assets must be protected by periodic litigation against those who would infringe on these rights. For example, receiving a patent does not automatically imply that no other person or entity will use the patented process or produce the product. To enforce patent rights requires that holders litigate their rights in court. In fact, many times patents are found to be invalid as a result of court cases.

When litigation is undertaken to enforce the rights under patents or other intangible assets, the costs associated with a successful defense can be capitalized as an addition to the carrying value of the patent. The logic behind this treatment stems from the observation that successful defense of the rights increases their value in use. As a result, incurring litigation costs to assert the underlying rights successfully is a cost that may benefit future periods and can be represented as an asset. However, there are limits on the capitalization of litigation costs. Care must be taken to insure that the recorded value of the intangible does not exceed reasonable estimates of the costs recoverable from future revenues.

When capitalized, litigation costs must be amortized over the remaining useful life of the intangible; but even the useful life may be changed by successful litigation. If a patent defense is unsuccessful, the litigation costs should be charged to expense. It is also possible that any remaining value for the intangible should be written off, or the useful life reduced, since an unsuccessful defense may indicate that the patent itself was invalid or that it was not effective against the competitor's new technology or products.

While capitalization of litigation costs is acceptable, many companies simply charge these costs to expense as incurred for three reasons:

1. It is hard to determine whether these costs actually increase the value of the legal right embodied in a patent, copyright, or other intangible.
2. The costs are often immaterial in relation to reported income for the periods involved.
3. Litigation of this form can continue for many years before resolution, resulting in a need to capitalize litigation costs well before the outcome of the litigation is known.

If capitalization of litigation costs is undertaken for ongoing litigation and the defense of the rights turns out to be unsuccessful, all costs capitalized during litigation must be immediately charged to expense.

Organizational Costs

When a corporation begins operations, it must prepare a set of articles of incorporation and file these with the Secretary of State in the state the business is registered. This process is costly and requires legal and other technical assistance, such as that of lawyers and accountants, in the process of forming the business. In addition, there are other costs to forming a corporation such as those to develop a corporate logo. These costs are incurred to create the corporation and to benefit its entire life. As such, they can be capitalized and recorded as **organizational costs**. While such costs have an indeterminate life, they must be amortized over a period of up to 40 years, for costs incurred after November 1, 1970. Since the Internal Revenue Code allows amortization over not less than five years, many companies elect this time line for financial statement purposes as well.[3]

How far does the concept of organizational costs extend? Some corporations have actually capitalized losses in the early years of operations under the argument that start-up losses of this type are a necessary part of beginning a corporation and should be part of the organizational costs spread over years of future profitability. This position is an extension of the same guidelines that are used to identify costs to be included in inventory or costs that can be capitalized when new property, plant, and equipment are acquired. Recall that when new property, plant, and equipment is acquired, all costs necessary to bring the asset to productive use can be capitalized and charged to expense in future periods as the asset generates revenue through use in production. Such costs include any costs of pilot production activity prior to starting production for sale (less any salvage value of the products produced in the pilot runs). The logical extension of this argument to the creation of a new business is that any losses incurred in the "start-up" phase of operations should be capitalized

---

[3] Shorter amortization periods for tax purposes accelerate the tax savings. Use of the same amortization period for both book and tax purposes is often done for convenience as there is no requirement that these amortization periods be equivalent.

as an asset, as long as the principal business operations of the firm have not yet begun.

The implication of the above argument was that instead of charging various costs incurred in the creation of a viable business to income in the period incurred, costs such as general and administrative costs incurred prior to starting the principal operations should be capitalized as part of the organizational costs of the corporation. However, the counterargument is that the future benefit of such costs is highly uncertain and that capitalization of such costs may be misleading to users in that it signals "probable" future benefits, whose existence is not reflective of the economic reality of the risks associated with a start-up business.

To clarify the accounting and reporting for start-up enterprises, the FASB released SFAS No. 7, "Accounting and Reporting by Development Stage Enterprises," in June, 1975. A **development stage enterprise** is a business whose planned principal operations have not commenced (e.g., is still in the start-up phase) or whose planned principal operations have commenced, but there has been no significant revenue therefrom.[4] Enterprises that qualify as being in the development stage are required to use the same accounting principles and produce the same financial reports as ongoing business enterprises.

This requirement implies that revenue and expense recognition are no different for start-up companies than they are for any ongoing business. As such, this rules out the ability to capitalize development stage losses as part of the organizational costs of the enterprise. However, the special disclosure requirements for these types of enterprises help financial statement users identify such items as losses incurred in the development stage. These reporting requirements are:

1. Cumulative net losses should be reported in stockholders' equity under the descriptive caption, "deficit accumulated during the development stage."[5]
2. The income statement should contain information on the cumulative revenues and expenses recognized during the development stage.

3. The cash flow statement should provide information on cumulative cash flows from operations, investing, and financing activity during the development stage.
4. The statement of stockholders' equity should disclose each of the following from inception of the enterprise:
    (a) The date and number of securities issued for every sale of equity securities,
    (b) The dollar amount per unit of equity security issued, and
    (c) For each noncash exchange of equity securities, the nature of the consideration given and the basis for assigning dollar amounts.

When an enterprise passes out of the development stage, the requirement that cumulative amounts be disclosed is dropped. Any prior period results presented for comparative purposes will not include the cumulative amounts.

---

[4] "Accounting and Reporting by Development Stage Enterprises," *Statement of Financial Accounting Standards No. 7* (Stamford, CT: FASB, June, 1975), para. 8.

[5] *Ibid.*, para. 11.

Deferred Charges

Deferred charges include all items that do not seem to fit readily into other categories. Costs that often fall in this category include: bond issue costs; long-term, prepaid assets such as rents or insurance; miscellaneous long-term receivables that might arise from the sale of property, plant, or equipment; and often times many of the small dollar amounts for the intangible assets discussed above when these items are not individually significant enough to warrant separate disclosure in the balance sheet. To the extent that any of these items are intangible assets, the general rules for amortization over a life of not more than 40 years applies.

Goodwill

Goodwill reflects the fact that the sum of the values of the individual, identifiable assets in place is less than the value of the whole. Goodwill is a nonidentifiable asset because it cannot be separated and sold individually. It is transferred only when the assets that give rise to it are sold as a unit. Due to its relatively unique status as an intangible that is only reported following the purchase of a business as a unit, an understanding of goodwill and the underlying source of its value will require more development than the discussion of the preceding intangible assets. The discussion of goodwill that follows focuses first on an economic interpretation of goodwill, then turns to methods of estimation, and finally addresses the valuation of goodwill for financial reporting purposes.

Goodwill—An Economic Interpretation

Economically, goodwill represents the present value of future economic rents a company is expected to earn. An **economic rent** is the difference between the expected earnings level and the earnings level required to provide equity investors with a return sufficient to compensate them for the inherent risks of the business, called the **required return**. The earnings level required to provide a sufficient return is called the **normal**, or **required**, **earnings**. Normal earnings for a period can be estimated by multiplying the required rate of return demanded by investors by the amount of capital invested at the start of the period. When a company has a competitive advantage that results in expected earnings exceeding the normal earnings, it is said to be producing economic rents.

For example, assume that New Ventures Incorporated has identified a new, not presently available product it believes will have considerable demand. New Ventures is the only company that has determined how to organize a production facility to produce this product. To begin operations will require an investment of $200,000, which must be maintained as long as production continues. The company expects to receive a net cash inflow (cash collections from sales less cash payments for materials, labor, and other costs) of $25,000 per year indefinitely (referred to as a *perpetuity* of $25,000 per year). Based on the risks involved in the industry in which the product falls, the required rate of return for this investment is 10%.

Given these facts, the expected earnings in this example is $25,000 per year, indefinitely. The normal earnings are $20,000, determined by multiplying the required rate of return, 10%, by the investment at the beginning of each period, $200,000. The economic rent is $5,000 per year, into perpetuity. To determine the amount of economic goodwill present in this example, the $5,000 perpetuity would be discounted at 10%. Goodwill is $50,000 [$5,000 ÷ .10].

In this example, valuing the goodwill at $50,000 implies that if New Ventures started the business by investing $200,000 in a subsidiary, it could sell the subsidiary to other investors for $250,000 after beginning operations. This price provides the new investors with a return of exactly 10% per year on their investment, and New Ventures would benefit by the value of the goodwill it created by starting the company. In addition, since the goodwill arises from a perpetuity, it will also never decline in value.

Sources of Economic Rents   Perhaps the primary source of economic rents is differential access to, and skill in employing, information. When one company is able to obtain better information regarding market demands, develop more efficient manufacturing processes by seeing new and different ways to accomplish production, or even develop new technologies for innovative products, these informational advantages create opportunities for companies to earn economic rents. High-level corporate executives spend much time trying to identify new areas of opportunity for their organizations. Clearly, the identification of and ability to utilize these types of opportunities to the corporation's advantage depends heavily on the talents of the people who work for the firm.

Other major sources of economic rents can come from *economies of scale*. An economy of scale exists when the marginal cost of each additional unit produced is lower than the one before. In these situations, the lowest cost of production can be accomplished by having one company produce all of the supply. However, this also places the producer in the position of monopolist, which may result in consumers paying higher prices. Generally, when economies of scale are significant, government regulation or oversight is used to control the pricing of the goods or services. The utility industry is an excellent example of this type of situation. The goal of regulation in these situations is to reduce the amount of economic rents that could be earned if the utilities were unregulated.

There are other factors that influence the size of economic rents. Import/export regulations alter the competitive status of U.S. firms compared to their foreign counterparts. Sometimes events that alter the ability of competitors to continue in operation can alter the size of economic rents earned by others in the industry. Whatever the conditions, the present value of expected rents represents the economic concept of goodwill.

Estimating Goodwill   The economic definition of goodwill is heavily dependent on expectations of future earnings and future normal earnings. When estimates of goodwill must be made, these expectations must be quantified. Many different approaches have been developed for estimating the amount of goodwill a company has developed. Two basic approaches are presented here: **excess earnings** and **price-earnings multiplier**. The excess earnings approach attempts to estimate directly the value of goodwill. The price-earnings multiplier approach determines goodwill indirectly as a residual value.

The excess earnings approach requires estimates of expected future earnings and required earnings for all periods in which it is anticipated that expected future earnings will exceed the required earnings of the firm. Often these estimates come from the company's historical performance, and it is assumed that the average performance over the past several years will be repeated in the future. For example, assume that Trest Corporation is being sold. Trest had averaged profits of $100,000 a year over the past five years. The average fair value of Trest's identifiable net assets over this period is estimated at $900,000.[6] The required rate of return for similar risk investments is estimated to be 8%. In this situation, Trest's excess earnings will be computed as:

$$\$100,000 - (\$900,000 \times 8\%) = \$28,000$$

Once an estimate of the average annual excess earnings is computed, an estimate of how many years into the future this will continue must be made. For Trest, assume the excess earnings will continue for five years. To estimate the amount of goodwill, multiply the number of years by the excess earnings, resulting in goodwill of $140,000 ($28,000 per year × 5 years). Alternatively, the excess earnings for five years might be discounted using the present value of an annuity of $1 for 5 periods at 8%. This computation yields $111,796 ($28,000 × 3.9927).

The approach described above can be refined to depend more on estimates of future earnings than on replication of past patterns, but one thing is clear. Estimates of goodwill from this approach can vary widely due to changes in any of the assumptions regarding expected future earnings, the required rate of return, or the fair value of assets that must be available to generate the earnings in each period. Since these variables are determined by professional judgment, there is little external evidence that can be used to assess the reliability of the judgments employed.

The price-earnings multiplier approach uses a different tactic to develop an estimate of goodwill. Under this approach, the first step is to estimate a total value for the company, including any goodwill, then subtract the net fair value of all identifiable assets and liabilities. What remains is the value of goodwill. To utilize this approach, a measure of sustainable future earnings is multiplied by a price-earnings multiplier to obtain an estimate of the company's total value. **Sustainable future earnings** is the average annual earnings that would be expected from the company, assuming that it maintained its present size. In the Trest example, if the company has been of stable size over the past 5 years, the $100,000 average earnings over that time might be used as an estimate of the company's sustainable income.

The price-earnings multiplier is computed from the ratio of price per share to sustainable earnings per share (price per share ÷ sustainable earnings per share) for other firms in the same industry as the company for which the goodwill computation is being undertaken. The price-earnings multiplier will incorporate the effects of growth and the required rate of return for firms in

---

[6] Note that the value of net identifiable assets refers to all identifiable assets including cash, receivables, inventory, property, etc., not just the value of identifiable intangible assets.

the industry. For industries with higher required rates of return, the price-earnings multiplier will be lower. For industries exhibiting high growth opportunities, the price-earnings multiplier will be higher. Suppose the price-earnings multiplier for Trest was determined to be 11.0. This implies that the value of the equity of Trest is $1,100,000 ($100,000 × 11.0). In turn, if the fair value of the net assets required to generate the income of $100,000 per year were $900,000, a total equity value of $1,100,000 implies goodwill of $200,000.

As with the excess earnings approach, the price-earnings multiplier approach also requires many assumptions and judgments to produce an estimate. It is particularly sensitive to small variations in the multiplier. Ultimately, these approaches are employed to obtain a ballpark estimate that will provide a decision maker with useful information of the price which might be offered to purchase a corporation.

Accounting for Internally Developed Goodwill   Since goodwill is a non-identifiable intangible and APB Opinion No. 17 does not permit recording any amount associated with internally generated nonidentifiable assets, internally generated goodwill cannot be recorded as an asset. However, we are now in a position to understand better the logic of this ruling. A significant portion of people's effort in corporations is devoted to creating competitive advantages. On the surface, it might seem reasonable to expect firms to capitalize those costs they can identify as being related to the creation of goodwill. This procedure would not violate the historical cost approach to valuing assets. However, it is very difficult to determine which activities are actually related to generation of economic rents and which are necessary to maintain a normal earnings level. Even when existing efforts can be identified as relating to the creation of economic rents, such as strategic planning efforts, it is not clear how to determine if such efforts are successful. Since the available means for developing an internal estimate of the value of goodwill are subject to a great degree of volatility depending on what assumptions are chosen, there is simply no reliable means to ascertain the existence or value of goodwill for financial reporting. With these observations in mind, it is not surprising that the APB decided not to allow recording of internally generated goodwill.

Accounting for Purchased Goodwill—At Acquisition   In contrast to the problem of valuing internally generated goodwill, when one company purchases another, the value for the goodwill present in the acquired corporation can be established based on the price paid in the transaction.[7] The process used to develop this valuation generally proceeds as follows:

---

[7] This situation differs from the lump sum asset acquisition problem discussed in Chapter 10 in the scope of the exchange. In the lump sum asset acquisition of Chapter 10, a few assets were purchased for a single price, but the assets are not any more valuable as a unit than they would be if purchased individually. There is little or no synergy to acquiring the assets as a unit. As a result, the prices of the individual assets when added together are not materially different from the price of the bundle. When the asset bundle is purchased to acquire a material synergistic effect, as in the case of a corporate takeover, the value of the bundle materially exceeds the sum of the values of the individual assets that make up the bundle. This implies goodwill. When the synergy is material enough to warrant recording goodwill as a separate asset is a matter of professional judgment.

1. All identifiable assets acquired are identified.
2. All liabilities assumed by the purchaser are identified.
3. Fair values are developed for all identifiable assets and liabilities assumed.
4. The purchase price is compared to the fair value of the net identifiable assets (fair value of identifiable assets – the fair value of liabilities assumed). If the purchase price exceeds the fair value of the net identifiable assets, the difference is goodwill. If the purchase price is less than the fair value of the net identifiable assets, the difference is **negative goodwill** or **badwill**.

Exhibit 12.2 contains an example of the valuation of goodwill for the acquisition of Deck, Inc. by Gray Corporation. Gray acquired all of the assets and assumed all of the liabilities of Deck, Inc. on January 1, 1994, in exchange of $375,000 cash. On that date the following information was available:

	Book Value	Market Value
Current assets	$ 10,000	$ 12,000
Plant and equipment	400,000	350,000
Patents	0	38,000
	$410,000	$400,000
Current liabilities	$ 15,000	$ 15,000
Long-term debt	70,000	85,000
	$ 85,000	$100,000

Gray would begin the process by searching for all identifiable assets Deck may have had at the date of the acquisition. This search would identify such assets as product formulae, engineering designs, and others that Deck may not have recorded as assets under GAAP. Based on the information in the example, Deck appears to have had a patent with no book value at the time of the acquisition but with a market value of $38,000. If this patent was developed internally, it may have existed as an unrecorded identifiable, intangible asset prior to the acquisition.

Gray would also seek to identify all the liabilities assumed in the acquisition, although Deck would have likely recorded these at some value prior to the acquisition. Following these steps, fair values will be assigned to all identifiable assets and liabilities. Fair value estimates come from various forms of analysis. Identifiable noncurrent assets such as property, plant, and equipment are often appraised by experts. Receivables are typically valued at net realizable value. Inventory is evaluated using information on expected selling prices, selling expenses, and normal profit to arrive at a realizable value less normal profit. Liabilities are typically valued using present value techniques. The results of all this effort are the fair values indicated earlier for the identifiable assets and liabilities assumed. Exhibit 12.2 defines the value for goodwill present in the acquisition by subtracting the fair value of the net identifiable assets from the purchase price. This yields $75,000 for goodwill. Gray's journal entry to record the acquisition is also included in Exhibit 12.2.

| EXHIBIT 12.2
Determination
of Goodwill—
Gray Corporation
Acquisition of
Deck, Inc.

Determination of Goodwill
Gray Corporation Acquisition of Deck, Inc.

Fair market value of consideration paid to Deck		$375,000
Less: Net fair market value of identifiable assets:		
Current assets	$ 12,000	
Plant and equipment	350,000	
Patents	38,000	
Current liabilities	(15,000)	
Long-term debt	(85,000)	(300,000)
Goodwill		$ 75,000
Journal entry of Gray to record the exchange:		
Current assets	12,000	
Plant and equipment	350,000	
Patents	38,000	
Goodwill	75,000	
Current liabilities		15,000
Long-term debt		85,000
Cash		375,000

Given the allocation process described above, it is possible for the analysis to yield negative goodwill. Negative goodwill cannot be explained economically. From an economic perspective, negative goodwill arises only when the future expected earnings of the corporation are below that which shareholders require as a minimum earnings level, given the risks inherent in the company's operations. In turn, the existence of negative goodwill suggests that the corporation's assets should be liquidated, its liabilities paid, and the remainder distributed to the shareholders. However, this assumes that all the fair values assigned to the identifiable assets and liabilities assumed are without possible error. Since these values are themselves estimates, they are subject to unknown errors. When those errors happen to result in a significant overstatement of the value of the net identifiable assets, negative goodwill can result.

In recognition of this problem, APB No. 16 requires that when negative goodwill is encountered, the recorded value of certain identifiable assets should be reduced from their estimated fair market value in an attempt to eliminate negative goodwill.[8] The assets that are subject to this adjustment are the noncurrent assets acquired, with the exception of noncurrent investments in marketable securities. When there are several assets in this category, the negative goodwill is allocated among them. In practice, this allocation is based on the relative fair market values of each asset category.

This allocation process is exemplified in the acquisition of Equinox, Inc. by Gray Corporation in Exhibit 12.3. Gray acquired all of the assets and assumed all of the liabilities of Equinox on April 1, 1994, for $1,400,000 cash. An analy-

---

[8] "Business Combinations," *Accounting Principles Board Opinion No. 16* (APB, August, 1970), para. 9.

sis of the book and market values of the identifiable assets and assumed liabilities of Equinox at that date revealed the following:

	Book Value	Market Value
Current assets	$ 290,000	$ 400,000
Land	100,000	300,000
Building and equipment	1,000,000	2,200,000
Investments in marketable securities	110,000	100,000
	$1,500,000	$3,000,000
Current liabilities	$ 200,000	$ 300,000
Long-term debt	700,000	800,000
	$ 900,000	$1,100,000

EXHIBIT 12.3
Allocation of
Negative Goodwill—
Gray Corporation
Acquisition of
Equinox, Inc.

Allocation of Negative Goodwill
Gray Corporation Acquisition of Equinox, Inc.

Computation of Goodwill:

Fair market value of consideration given to Equinox		$1,400,000
Less: Net fair market value of identifiable assets:		
Current assets	$ 400,000	
Land	300,000	
Building and equipment	2,200,000	
Investments in marketable securities	100,000	
Current liabilities	(300,000)	
Long-term debt	(800,000)	(1,900,000)
Goodwill		$ (500,000)

Allocation of Negative Goodwill:

Assets	Estimated Fair Market Value	Percent of Total	Allocation of Negative Goodwill	Adjusted Value
Land	$ 300,000	12.0%	$ (60,000)	$ 240,000
Building and equipment	2,200,000	88.0%	(440,000)	1,760,000
Total	$2,500,000	100.0%	$(500,000)	$2,000,000

Journal entry of Gray to record the exchange:

Current assets	400,000	
Land	240,000	
Building and equipment	1,760,000	
Investments in marketable securities	100,000	
Current liabilities		300,000
Long-term debt		800,000
Cash		1,400,000

Negative goodwill, as computed in Exhibit 12.3, is $500,000. This negative goodwill is then allocated to the asset categories "land" and "building and equipment," based on the original fair value estimates of $300,000 for land and $2,200,000 for building and equipment. As a result, the fair value for land is reduced by 12% of the negative goodwill, or $60,000. The fair value of building and equipment was reduced by 88% of the negative goodwill, or $440,000. Gray's journal entry to record the acquisition is presented at the bottom of Exhibit 12.3.

The logic behind the allocation of negative goodwill recognizes the likely source of the measurement error in market values for identifiable assets that would give rise to a computation of negative goodwill. Current assets such as cash, receivables, and inventory are generally the easiest assets for which to obtain estimates of market values, as are investments in marketable securities. By the application of discounting procedures, fair market values for liabilities are also relatively easy to acquire. It is more difficult to obtain good estimates of fair market value for noncurrent productive assets. Thus, these estimates are the ones most subject to error in measurement. The rules regarding the allocation of negative goodwill recognize this fact by only reducing the recorded values of those assets where the market value estimates are most suspect.[9]

Accounting for Purchased Goodwill—Post-Acquisition   When purchased goodwill is recorded in an acquisition, it must be amortized over a period not to exceed 40 years.[10] While selection of this maximum period is arbitrary, it is supported on the belief that goodwill will expire at some point in time and 40 years seems to provide a liberal limit on how soon that may occur. Frequently, the amortization period chosen is considerably less than 40 years. In some acquisitions, the process the buyer uses to set the offer price will be used to assess the likely period over which the rents existing at the time of the acquisition are to be realized. Consequently, if the buyer forecasts rents to last for eight years, the goodwill implied in the purchase price will be amortized over eight years to match the purchaser's expectations at the time the original acquisition occurred. Of course, goodwill acquired prior to November 1, 1970, is not required to be amortized.[11]

Research and Development Costs

SFAS No. 2 defines **research** as the planned search or critical investigation aimed at discovery of new knowledge with the hope that such knowledge will be useful in developing a new product or service, or a new process or technique, or in bringing about a significant improvement to an existing product

---

[9] *Ibid.* If the negative goodwill were larger than the sum of the fair market values of the noncurrent assets (excluding investments in marketable securities), then the noncurrent assets would be reduced to a carrying value of zero, and the negative goodwill that remains would be recorded as a deferred credit.

[10] This includes any negative goodwill recorded as a deferred credit at the time of the acquisition.

[11] *Accounting Principles Board Opinion No. 17, op. cit.*, para. 33.

or process.[12] **Development** is defined as the translation of research findings or other knowledge into a plan or design for a new product or process or for a significant improvement to an existing product or process whether intended for sale or use.[13]

Economic Forces Leading Up to SFAS No. 2 Prior to the issuance of SFAS No. 2 regarding the treatment of research and development (R&D) costs, companies had the option of charging the cost of all R&D activities to expense in the period incurred or capitalizing the portion of these costs that were deemed to provide probable future benefits. When a reasonable link exists between incurring of R&D costs and generation of future revenues, capitalization of costs incurred in the current period, with amortization to expense in the future periods in which revenues will be generated as an outgrowth of the research and development effort, would provide better matching than charging the costs to expense as incurred.

The freedom to choose provided corporate managers with an ability to communicate the extent to which the firms' R&D efforts were proving successful by carefully choosing the amount and types of R&D expenditures to capitalize as an asset. However, given the difficulties of predicting the existence of future benefits at the time many R&D costs are incurred, the freedom to capitalize also provided opportunities for managers to manipulate reported income.

Prior to SFAS No. 2, auditors had to pass judgment on the fairness of financial statements that included R&D assets without a readily verifiable, nonsubjective means to evaluate management representations regarding the amount of R&D cost to be capitalized in a particular period. SFAS No. 2 responded to this problem by mandating that R&D costs not performed on a contract basis be charged to expense in the period incurred. While corporations clearly undertake R&D activities with the expectation of generating future benefits that will recoup these costs and generate profits, the link between incurrence of cost and eventual benefit is deemed too tenuous to support treatment of these costs as an intangible asset. SFAS No. 2 affected a relatively small set of companies that had elected to capitalize R&D costs prior to the effective date of this standard. The vast majority of companies involved in R&D were already treating costs incurred as an expense of the period.

Accounting for Research and Development Costs SFAS No. 2 provides specific guidance as to the classification of activities as part of research and development. Exhibit 12.4 provides some examples of activities that would and would not be classified as research and development.

Research and development expenditures include two categories of costs:

---

[12] "Accounting for Research and Development Costs," *Statement of Financial Accounting Standards No. 2* (FASB, October, 1974), para. 8(a).

[13] *Statement of Financial Accounting Standards No. 2, op. cit.*, para., 8(b).

Classification of Activities as R&D or Non-R&D	
RESEARCH AND DEVELOPMENT	**NON-RESEARCH AND DEVELOPMENT**
a. Laboratory research aimed at discovery of new knowledge.	a. Engineering follow-through in an early phase of production.
b. Searching for applications of new research findings or other knowledge.	b. Quality control during commercial production, including routine testing of products.
c. Conceptual formulation and design of possible product or process alternatives.	c. Trouble shooting in connection with breakdowns during commercial production.
d. Testing in search for or evaluation of product or process alternatives.	d. Routine, ongoing efforts to refine, enrich, or otherwise improve upon the qualities of an existing product.
e. Modification of the formulation or design of a product or process.	e. Adaptation of an existing capability to a particular requirement or customer's need as part of a continuing commercial activity.
f. Design, construction, and testing of pre-production prototypes and models.	f. Seasonal or other periodic design changes to existing products.
g. Design of tools, jigs, molds, and dies involving new technology.	
h. Design, construction, and operation of a pilot plant that is not of a scale economically feasible to the enterprise for commercial production.	
i. Engineering activity required to advance the design of a product to the point that it meets specific functional and economic requirements and is ready for manufacture.	

EXHIBIT 12.4

Classification of Activities as R&D or Non-R&D

1. Costs incurred during the period that provide no reliably estimated future benefit
2. Costs that provide future benefit either for future research and development activities or through alternative uses

Costs in the first category would include salaries and wages, minor expenditures for supplies, and other similar costs. Costs in the second category would include items of property, plant, and equipment or other intangible assets such as patents that must be acquired to support the research and development effort.

Periodic costs such as wages, salaries, utility costs, materials, etc., are treated as part of research and development expense in the period they are incurred. If inventories of materials are significant, they should be accounted for in the same fashion as ordinary inventories, except that the expense should be part of research and development expense, not cost of sales. In addition to the direct costs incurred for R&D activity, it is also appropriate to allocate a portion of the overhead, or indirect, costs of the company's operations to R&D and include this in the research and development expense for the period. An example of these allocable costs would include supervisory salaries where supervisors spend part of their time overseeing both production and R&D activities. Electricity, power, light, insurance, and other costs are treated in the same way.

Costs incurred to acquire assets with future benefits should be capitalized. These costs are then matched against revenues through depreciation or amortization, but the expense should be recognized as part of research and development expense. If the asset is useful only in future research and development efforts, the useful life of the asset should be determined with reference only to this activity. If the asset has alternative future uses, such as a building that is used to house research and development activity but could be used for other activities as well, the useful life of the asset should be determined with reference to the alternative use as well.

Research and development expense should be disclosed for each period that an income statement is presented, either on the face of the income statement or in the notes. If R&D expense is particularly important to a firm's operations, the company may elect to disclose the amount for the period as a line item in the income statement. An example of such disclosure of R&D expenses for Eaton Corporation is presented in Exhibit 12.5.

Research and development expenses are obviously an important part of Eaton's operations. These expenses represent an average of 36.8% of pre-tax profits over the three years presented. When R&D expense is not individually significant, it is often included in selling and administrative expense with note disclosure of material individual R&D expenses.

Costs for Development of Computer Software

A computer program is an example of an identifiable intangible asset. Computer programs are developed for both internal use by corporations and for external sale by software development companies. Software can also be developed to be sold as part of another product. For example, a computerized manufacturing system requires programs to direct the flow of activity on a mechanized assembly line. Software development costs are categorized along two dimensions:

1. Whether the software is developed internally or purchased externally
2. Whether the development is solely for internal use or part of a product to be sold to customers

EXHIBIT 12.5

Eaton Corporation—
Disclosure of
Research and
Development
Expense as a
Separate Item

EATON CORPORATION
Disclosure of Research and Development Expense as a Separate Item

	1986	1985	1984
		(in millions)	
Net Sales	$3,811.6	$3,674.5	$3,509.8
Costs and expenses:			
Cost of products sold	2,870.5	2,703.2	2,526.5
Selling and administrative expenses	497.6	482.2	465.0
Research and development expenses	134.1	123.6	112.6
Provision for exiting businesses	74.7	0	0
	$3,576.9	$3,309.0	$3,104.1
Income from operations	$ 234.7	$ 365.5	$ 405.7

Internally Developed Software for Internal Use   When companies develop software for their own internal use, there is generally a specific goal or purpose for the development effort. The result of the development effort creates an identifiable asset in the form of programs, which could conceivably be sold separately if the company elected to do so. Whether costs of this type fall under the category of research and development costs is subject to debate. SFAS No. 2 includes activities such as "modification of the formulation or design of a product or process" as R&D activities. However, the efforts to develop computer software have been segregated from the definition of research and development effort, particularly in applications where the major investment that a firm makes to provide its service is in the form of software development.

For example, companies that specialize in servicing mortgage portfolios expend considerable resources to develop specialized software to track information on each mortgage they service. These companies may have little in the way of other noncurrent assets. In these situations, companies have treated software development as separate from R&D and capitalized these costs. If capitalized, they must be amortized under the same rules as any intangible asset.

Externally Acquired Software for Internal Use   A company will often elect to acquire software for internal use by purchasing it from a third party, instead of incurring the cost to develop it internally. Since this software is an identifiable asset and acquired in an exchange, the costs can be capitalized and amortized to future periods based on the useful life of the software.

Internally Developed Software for Sales to Customers   SFAS No. 86 addresses the issue of accounting for software development when the purpose is to provide goods or services, which are represented by the output of this development effort, to customers. In the preceding discussion on research and development activity, the general rule was to expense R&D as incurred. The definition of R&D activity focused primarily on the process of developing new technologies. Costs incurred after the new technology was in place, such as quality control or engineering follow-through, were not considered R&D costs; and these were either charged to expense, capitalized as an asset, or capitalized as part of the cost of inventory, depending on the nature of the cost incurred.

The rules for accounting for software development costs represent a refinement of the rules developed for research and development expenditures, with some significant differences. Software development is broken down into three distinct time periods:

1. Development prior to having a technologically feasible product or process (the research and development phase)
2. Development done after technological feasibility has been established to bring the product or process to a state of marketability to the customer (the cost capitalization phase)
3. Development done to provide customer service or maintenance of the product or process after it has become available to the customer (the production and distribution phase)

Technological feasibility implies that all planning, design, coding, and testing activities necessary to establish that the product can be produced to meet its performance requirements are completed.[14]

The minimum requirements necessary to satisfy these general characteristics depend on whether the software development process includes a detailed product design or just a prototype. If a prototype is developed, the prototype must represent a fully functioning version with all major functions expected of the software included. In the case of a detailed product design, the following conditions must be met:

1. The product design must be complete and the enterprise must demonstrate the existence of the necessary skills, hardware, and software technology to produce the product.
2. The detail program design and its consistency with the product design have been documented.
3. The detailed program design must be reviewed for high-risk development issues, and any uncertainties identified must have been resolved through coding and testing.

Costs incurred in Stage 1 are considered research and development costs and accounted for under SFAS No. 2. Costs in Stage 2 are capitalized and amortized over the future periods in which revenues are anticipated. Costs in Stage 3 are period costs, which are charged to expense as incurred.

The general process of software development is depicted in Exhibit 12.6. Determining when software is at a point of technological feasibility is a very difficult, but crucial, judgment. In Exhibit 12.6, the critical event is denoted as the development of the detailed program or prototype that generally embodies the technology and, if successful, will render the project feasible.

All costs incurred prior to the establishment of a technologically feasible software product must be charged to expense as incurred under the requirements of SFAS No. 2 relating to research and development expenditures. Costs incurred after this point to obtain production masters, including final coding and testing costs, should be capitalized until the product is made available to customers. Capitalized costs during this period would include an allocation of overhead for supervision and other indirect costs. Costs incurred for maintenance and customer support following the sales of the initial product are to be treated as period expenses.[15]

Amortization of the capitalized cost of software is to be based on the larger of:

---

[14] "Accounting for the Costs of Computer Software to be Sold, Leased, or Otherwise Marketed," *Statement of Financial Accounting Standard No. 86* (FASB, August 1985), para. 4.

[15] An exception exists when the software is part of a larger product or process being developed. Costs of software development must be charged to expense until all the research and development efforts on any component of the larger product or process is completed. This implies that when the starting point of the larger product is a software package, and that software is fully developed prior to the completion of the research and development efforts on other parts of the product, no software development cost can be capitalized.

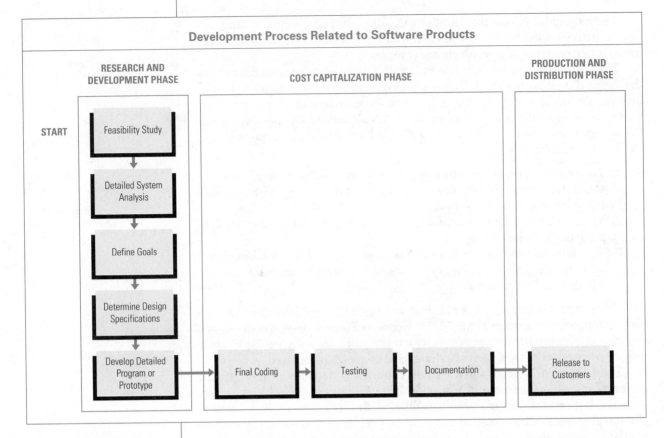

EXHIBIT 12.6

Development Process Related to Software Products

1. The ratio of current gross revenues to the total of current and future estimated revenues
2. Straight-line amortization

Amortization is to begin when the product is generally available for release to customers. For example, assume Datadisaster, Inc. had capitalized $600,000 of software development costs. Current period revenues from this project were $200,000 and future estimated revenues are $2,300,000. The amortization based on the percentage of revenues would be $48,000 [($200,000 ÷ $2,500,000) × $600,000]. If the product had an estimated useful life of only three years, straight-line amortization would be $200,000. In this situation, the straight-line method yields the larger amortization and would be required.

Purchased Software for Resale or Incorporation into Saleable Products
When software is acquired from third parties for the purpose of resale, the costs should be treated as inventory costs. When software is acquired from third parties for the purpose of modification or incorporation into a product that is ultimately sold, the treatment of the costs depends on the status of the research and development effort on the product for which the software is to become part. If *all* the research and development efforts on the larger product

or process are complete, the software cost should be capitalized. If all research and development is not complete, the software costs should be charged to expense unless part of the costs are incurred for software that has an alternative future use. When an alternative use exists, the cost of the software allocated to this use can be capitalized.

Software Development Costs and the Net Realizable Value Test Once the capitalized value of the software development costs is determined, regardless of how it is acquired, the carrying value of the intangible asset is subject to a net realizable value test. If, at any time, the carrying value of the unamortized software costs exceeds the estimated net realizable value from future revenues, the asset should be immediately reduced to net realizable value and the adjustment charged to expense for the period. Net realizable value is the estimated future gross revenues from the product reduced by the estimated costs of completing and disposing of the product. Those costs include the cost of maintenance and customer service.

Disclosure of Software Development Costs Companies that have significant amounts of software development cost typically disclose the unamortized computer software costs at each balance sheet date and the total amount of software development cost charged to expense. Those costs that are treated as research and development costs are to be disclosed in accordance with the requirements of SFAS No. 2. Exhibit 12.7 presents an example of the disclo-

EXHIBIT 12.7
Datacopy
Corporation—
Disclosures Relating
to Software
Development Costs

DATACOPY CORPORATION
Disclosures Relating to Software Development Costs

	1986	1985
Balance Sheet:		
Noncurrent Assets—Software development costs	$1,099,317	$382,004

Note 4. Software Development Costs

In 1985, the Company adopted Financial Accounting Standards Board Statement No. 86, "Accounting for the Costs of Computer Software to be Sold, Leased, or Otherwise Marketed" (FASB Statement No. 86). In accordance with FASB Statement No. 86, the Company capitalizes certain costs incurred internally in creating computer software modules. Costs incurred prior to the onset of development and production of software modules are charged to expense. At the time production of the software modules commences, the module is considered to be a working model under FASB Statement No. 86. Thereafter, software development costs are capitalized until the module is available for general release. At the time the module performs the primary functions described in the original specifications, contains the convenience features required for it to be usable in a production environment, and is completely documented. Amortization is provided on the basis of units shipped to total anticipated units shipped: however, the annual amortization expense, at a minimum, will not be less than 20% of the capitalized cost.

Capitalized costs consist of salaries and an allocation of indirect costs and amounted to $800,526 in 1986 and $396,293 in 1985. Amortization of these costs amounted to $83,213 and $14,289 in 1986 and 1985, respectively. Costs incurred to improve and support existing modules are charged to expense as incurred.

sures relating to software development costs for Datacopy Corporation, for the first year that SFAS No. 86 was employed.

In this example, Datacopy has described its development process in a manner consistent with the process embodied in SFAS No. 86. In addition, note that the amortization is based on numbers of units, instead of selling price, but is never less than 20% of the capitalized cost. Given that the amortization requirements allow the use of this form of amortization only when it results in larger amounts than straight-line, the reference to 20% of the capitalized costs implies that the software has a five-year life. Finally, note that the company has provided full disclosure of the activity in the "software development costs" asset account. From this information, users can easily recreate the activity as follows:

Beginning Balance	$ 382,004
Additions: Capitalized Costs	800,526
Deductions: Amortization	(83,213)
Ending Balance	$1,099,317

SUMMARY

Intangible assets are assets with no physical existence, but they provide future benefits to the company. Identifiable intangible assets are those that can be separated from a group of assets and transferred independently. The only nonidentifiable asset that is ever recorded in the financial statements is goodwill.

Intangible assets may be generated internally or acquired externally. Costs incurred to develop nonidentifiable intangibles internally are never capitalized as assets. Costs incurred to develop internal identifiable intangibles are often charged to expense in the period incurred, but they may be capitalized if the costs do not fall into the category of research and development costs. Externally acquired intangibles are capitalized at their purchase price. Exhibit 12.8 lists the major features associated with accounting for intangible assets.

Matching the cost of intangible assets against the revenues they help to generate is accomplished through periodic amortization. APB No. 17 sets a maximum amortization period of 40 years for any intangible acquired after November 1, 1970, but actual amortization periods are to reflect the economic life of the intangible if this is less than 40 years. Since many intangibles arise from specific legal provisions, or by contract, the legal life may provide a maximum amortization period much shorter then 40 years. Straight-line amortization, assuming no salvage value, is the preferred and most common method of accomplishing matching.

QUESTIONS

1. What is unique about an *intangible asset*?
2. Distinguish between *identifiable* and *nonidentifiable* intangible assets and give examples of each.

Summary of Intangible Assets

TYPES OF INTANGIBLES	INTERNALLY DEVELOPED	EXTERNALLY ACQUIRED
Patents Legal Life = 17 years	Cost of development treated as R&D costs. Cost of registration may be capitalized.	Purchase price is capitalized.
Copyrights Legal Life = 50 years and beyond	Cost of development may be recorded as an asset. Cost of registration may be capitalized.	Purchase price is capitalized.
Trademarks Legal Life = Indefinite	Cost of development treated as R&D. Cost of registration may be capitalized.	Purchase price is capitalized.
Licenses Legal Life = Set by contract	n/a	Payment of licensing fees may be capitalized if they related to several periods.
Franchise Fees Legal Life = Set by contract	n/a	Initial fees in excess of the value of all other identifiable assets received may be capitalized.
Organization Costs	Costs may be capitalized	n/a
Goodwill	Costs are never capitalized	Recorded as the difference between the purchase price of a group of assets and the net fair value of the identifiable assets acquired.
Research and Development Costs	Capitalized only when R&D is undertaken for another party pursuant to a contract.	When various identifiable intangibles, such as drawings, etc., are produced by the R&D effort of another party, the acquisition price of these assets may be capitalized.
Software Development Costs	For internally applied software, all non-R&D costs may be capitalized. Development costs for software held for sale alone, or as part of another product, only costs incurred after the technological feasibility of the product has been proven can be capitalized.	Externally acquired software may be capitalized at the purchase price if it is incorporated into a product on which all other R&D efforts are complete or if the software is to be used internally. If the software is to be resold as is, the costs are part of inventory.

EXHIBIT 12.8

Summary of
Intangible Assets

3. Why is there a difference in the accounting and reporting for externally developed intangible assets and internally developed intangible assets?

4. What are *patents*? How do they differ from *copyrights*?

5. What is the legal life of a patent? Why is the legal life different from the economic life?

6. What are the general rules for *amortization* of intangibles?

7. How are litigation costs to defend the legal rights under any intangible accounted for?

8. In a franchise arrangement, what two types of fees are typically paid by the franchisee? How is each type of fee accounted for?

9. If you were asked to estimate the value of a corporation, how might you go about valuing its tangible assets, identifiable intangible assets, liabilities, and unidentifiable intangible asset?

10. Provide three examples of expenditures that might be included in organizational costs.

11. What does the concept of *goodwill* represent?

12. Can a company capitalize an estimate of its internally generated goodwill? Why or why not?

13. What circumstances allow goodwill to be recorded?   How is goodwill handled after it is recorded?

14. What are research and development costs and how are they reported in the financial statements?

15. If research and development efforts result in a patent, are the costs capitalized as part of the value of the patent? Why or why not?

16. How might research and development costs create an economic benefit for a corporation? Why is this economic benefit ignored for accounting purposes? How does this treatment relate to the definition of an asset in SFAC No. 6?

17. When software is purchased from a third party, under what conditions can the cost be capitalized? When can it not be capitalized?

18. What is a *development stage enterprise* and how is it different from any other business entity?

EXERCISES

12-1.   *Trademarks: Amortization*

Wall Company bought a trademark from Black Corporation on June 1, 1990, for $112,000. An independent consultant estimated that the remaining useful life is 50 years. Its unamortized cost on Black's accounting records was $56,000. Wall decided to write off the trademark over the maximum period allowed.

REQUIRED:

Prepare the journal entry to record the amortization of the trademark as of December 31, 1993.

12-2.   *Patents: Acquisition and amortization*

During 1994, Kay Company incurred $102,000 of research and development costs in its laboratory to develop a patent that was granted on July 1, 1994. Legal fees and other costs associated with the registration of the patent totalled $20,500. The economic life of the patent is estimated at 10 years. Kay wishes to use the maximum allowable life to amortize the cost of the patent.

REQUIRED:

Prepare journal entries to account for the costs involved in developing and obtaining the patent, along with the amortization of any capitalized value as of December 31, 1994.

12-3. *Trademarks: Legal costs and amortization*

On January 1, 1994, Vick Company purchased a trademark for $400,000, having an estimated useful life of five years. In January, 2000, Vick paid $60,000 for legal fees in a successful defense of the trademark. As a result of the successful defense, Vick estimated the remaining life at January, 2000, to be eight years.

REQUIRED:

Prepare a schedule showing the amortization of the trademark over its entire life.

12-4. *Organizational costs: Capitalization*

Plaza Company was organized late in 1993 and began operations on January 1, 1994. Plaza is engaged in conducting market research studies on behalf of manufacturers. Prior to starting operations, the following costs were incurred:

Attorney's fees in connection with organization of Plaza	$4,000
Improvements to leased offices prior to occupancy	7,000
Meetings of incorporators, state filing fees, and other organizational expenses	5,000

REQUIRED:

Describe how Plaza should account for each of these costs and prepare journal entries necessary to record the activity.

12-5. *Research and development: Classification of costs*

Korn Company incurred the following costs during 1993:

Modification to the formulation of a chemical product	$135,000
Trouble-shooting in connection with breakdowns during commercial production	150,000
Design of tools, jigs, molds, and dies involving new technology	170,000
Seasonal or other periodic design changes to existing products	185,000
Laboratory research aimed at discovery of new technology	215,000

REQUIRED:

Prepare a schedule setting forth which of the above costs would be included in research and development expense for Korn Company. Include an explanation of why such a classification is appropriate.

12-6. *Research and development: Classification of costs*

During 1994, Mason Corporation incurred the following costs:

Research and development services performed by Lee Corp. for Mason	$300,000
Testing and evaluation of new products	250,000
Laboratory research aimed at discovery of new knowledge	370,000

REQUIRED:

For each of the costs described above, provide a rational for its inclusion or exclusion from research and development expense for Mason.

12-7.   *Research and development: Classification of cost with fixed assets*

Ward Company began operations on January 1, 1993. During the year, the company incurred research and development costs as follows:

Equipment acquired for use in various research and development projects	$975,000
Materials purchased	200,000
Compensation costs for personnel	500,000
Outside consulting fees	150,000
Indirect costs allocable to research and development	250,000

The equipment purchased is exclusively for research and development and is expected to be in use for five years. At the end of the year, a physical inventory of materials indicated that $43,000 of materials remained.

REQUIRED:

Prepare a schedule to compute the amount Ward should report as research and development expense for 1993.

12-8.   *Development stage enterprises*

Towne Systems Corporation was a development stage enterprise from October 10, 1992 (inception) to December 31, 1994. The year ended December 31, 1995, is the first year in which Towne is an established operating enterprise. The following are among the costs incurred by Towne:

	10/1/92 to 12/31/94	1/1/95 to 12/31/95
Leasehold improvements, equipment and furniture	$1,000,000	$150,000
Security deposits	60,000	15,000
Research and development	750,000	450,000
Laboratory operations	175,000	275,000
General and administrative	250,000	400,000

REQUIRED:

How would Towne report each of these costs in its financial statements?

12-9.   *Software development costs: Capitalization vs. expense*

Miccom, Incorporated is a company that specializes in the development and sale of computer software. During the year, it incurred the following costs:

Feasibility study for new product	$230,000
Programmer's fees for development of a prototype program	30,000
Costs of final coding and testing of new products released in the year	140,000
Development aimed at product upgrades	176,000
Customer service	198,000
General overhead costs	340,000

Miccom amortizes capitalized software development costs over three years and estimates that 30% of its overhead relates to customer service, 45% to development of new products, and 25% to the preparation of proven products for sale. During the year, Miccom reported revenues of $1,430,000.

REQUIRED:

Prepare the income statement of Miccom for the year.

12-10. *Software development: Acquisition of software from vendors for integration into other products*

Datasearcher's is in the business of developing new computer software applications for computer controlled manufacturing facilities. During 1994, Datasearcher's found it necessary to acquire certain software packages from other companies to use as part of a larger computer control program. The first software package was purchased for $100,000 at the beginning of the development project prior to the point at which a detailed program design had been developed. The second software package was purchased for $76,000, during the final stages of preparation for sale to customers. This software package was offered as an add-on to the main system for customers who wanted a more extensive control program. Datasearcher's released the product on September 1, 1994, and earned revenues of $1,400,000 during 1994 on the product. Estimates that the final product will generate $5,600,000 over the next four years as follows:

1995	$3,600,000
1996	1,000,000
1997	800,000
1998	200,000

REQUIRED:

Prepare the journal entries that Datasearcher's would use to record all activities related to the purchased software during 1994.

12-11. *Goodwill: Computation at acquisition, no differentials*

Keil Corporation purchased all of the assets and liabilities of Havre Company for $300,000. The net fair market values of the assets acquired was $275,000.

REQUIRED:

Compute the goodwill recorded by Keil in the acquisition.

12-12. *Goodwill: Computation at acquisition, book-market differentials*

Jest Company acquired all the assets and liabilities of Regents Corporation on June 15, 1994, by paying $800,000. On the date of the acquisition, the fair market values of the identifiable assets and liabilities appeared as follows:

Current assets	$ 200,000
Land	300,000
Plant	600,000
Equipment	400,000
	$1,500,000
Current liabilities	$ 100,000
Long-term debt	300,000
	$ 400,000

REQUIRED:

Prepare the journal entry made by Jest to record the acquisition.

12-13. *Franchise fees: Capitalization vs. expense*

Gentry Enterprises operates a franchise in the cities located in the Southwest. In January, 1994, Gentry purchased several new franchises. The initial costs associated with these franchises was $300,000. Gentry is an exclusive franchisee, and the franchise contracts are all 15 years in duration, with the option for renewal for an additional 10 years at the franchisee's request.

All Gentry's franchise agreements call for an annual franchise fee of 5% of revenues from the franchise. Gentry generated $6,700,000 in franchise revenues for 1994. In addition, Gentry estimates that the economic life of the franchises are only about eight years.

REQUIRED:

Prepare journal entries to record the activities relating to franchises for Gentry during 1994.

PROBLEMS

12-1. *Various intangibles: Recording activity, balance sheet presentation, effects of expensing research and development*

The following transactions occurred during 1995 for Fast Sell, Inc.:
(a) Paid $24,000 in legal costs for organizing the company on February 1.
(b) Purchased a trademark for $54,000 on March 1.
(c) Paid an initial franchise fee of $120,000 on July 1. No tangible assets were included in this fee.
(d) Over the year, the company engaged in activity classified as research and development and incurred costs of $21,000.
(e) Paid $5,000 of continuing fees relating to the franchise agreement on December 31.

The trademark had an estimated economic life of five years; the franchise cost was amortized over ten years; and organization costs were amortized over the maximum period allowable. Reported income before taxes for the year was $342,000.

REQUIRED:

1. Prepare the necessary journal entries for 1995 under GAAP.
2. Prepare the Intangible Assets section of the balance sheet as of December 31, 1995.
3. Suppose the company had capitalized the research and development costs and elected to amortize them over the next seven years. How would this effect reported pre-tax income for 1995?
4. Discuss some of the problems that arise in matching of research and development costs incurred in the current period to future revenues.

12-2. *Accounting for research and development activities*

Clinton Corporation is involved in the development and manufacture of specialized plastic resins for many uses. As part of its operations, it engages in research and development activities. The following transactions occurred during 1995:

(a) February 15: Purchased land and a building to house the research and development (R&D) operations. Payment was in the form of a cash down payment of $50,000 and a note due in five years for the $150,000 balance. The note contained a face interest rate of 3%, but the market rate of interest for similar loans was 12% at the time the sale was consummated. Face interest is paid annually on the anniversary of the sale. The land and building were appraised at $50,000 and $150,000, respectively. The building is assumed to have a remaining life of 30 years and no salvage value.

(b) June 1: Paid legal fees and registration fees of $750 for a patent on a new resin. Clinton determined that the cost to develop this patent was $40,000 based on the time records kept by the research personnel who worked on this project over the past two years. These costs were originally charged to research and development expense.

(c) July 1: Purchased equipment for $30,000 on account to be used in the R&D activities. After the acquisition, Clinton modified the equipment to be useable in the research and development effort. Without modification the equipment would have had a useful life of ten years with no salvage value. However, the modifications limited the usefulness of the asset to the research and development project for which it was employed. This project has an uncertain future.

(d) December 31: Paid the following costs for R&D:

Materials	$103,000
Labor	255,000
Overhead (not including depreciation)	497,500

The company depreciated its buildings by the straight-line method and depreciated machinery and equipment by the sum-of-the-years'-digits method. The patent is being amortized over five years.

REQUIRED:

1. How much will Clinton report as research and development expense for 1995?
2. Speculate on why you think current GAAP will not allow Clinton to capitalize the research and development costs associated with the development of the new patent:
   (a) When those costs were being incurred
   (b) Retroactively after the effort has proven the existence of a future benefit in the form of a patentable product
3. What assets would Clinton report in its balance sheet as a result of the above transactions and how would these be presented?

12-3. *Research and development activities: development stage enterprises*

The Thomas Company is in the process of developing a revolutionary new product. A new division of the company was formed to develop, manufacture, and market this new product. As of year-end (December 31, 1995), the new product has not been manufactured for resale; however, a prototype unit was built and is in operation.

Throughout 1995 the new division incurred certain costs. These costs include design and engineering studies, prototype manufacturing costs, administrative expenses (including salaries of administrative personnel), and market research costs. In addition, approximately $500,000 in equipment, with an estimated useful life of ten years, was purchased for use in developing and manufacturing the new product. Approximately $200,000 of this equipment was built specifically for the design development of the new product. The remaining $300,000 of equipment was used to manufacture the pre-production prototype and will be used to manufacture the new product once it is in commercial production.

REQUIRED:

1. What is the definition of "research" and "development" costs as applied in SFAS No. 2?
2. How should Thomas account for the various costs described above in its 1995 financial statements?
3. Is this a development stage enterprise? Why or why not?

12-4.   *Research and development costs: identification and allocation of costs*

Erich Corporation has a history of developing its own product ideas through intensive research efforts. As part of its major manufacturing facilities, it maintains a laboratory, which is used for both research into new products and quality control testing for production of its current products. The lab covers about 15% of the square footage in the facility. The following information is available relating to the operations of the laboratory for the year.

(a) At the beginning of the year, the lab had an inventory of supplies valued at $120,000. During the year, an additional $430,000 of supplies were purchased, and at year-end only $62,000 of supplies remained. Erich estimates that 80% of its lab supplies are used in research activity and 20% in quality control.

(b) Salaries for personnel in the lab amounted to $780,000 for the year. Based on the time allocation of personnel, about 65% of the paid hours are spent on research, while 35% are spent in quality control.

(c) Equipment, originally purchased three years ago at a price of $320,000, is used in the lab. The equipment had an estimated life of five years. In the current year, additional equipment worth $210,000 was purchased. The new equipment is expected to last seven years. Normally, Erich uses the straight-line method of depreciation for fixed assets.

(d) Utility costs such as electric, gas, and water are not separately billed for the lab. During the year, Erich was billed for a total of $576,000 in utility costs.

(e) Erich reported other overhead for the lab and plant at $2,971,000. Erich allocates overhead to production facilities based on the amount of space allocated to each production line.

(f) The company also paid executive salaries of $538,000 for the year. The executives have only a tangential association with the research and development activities.

REQUIRED:

Prepare a schedule to determine how much Erich should report as research and development expense for the year.

12-5.   *Various intangibles: Correction of existing financial statements*

Bush Corporation was incorporated on January 3, 1993. The corporation's financial statements for its first year's operations were not examined by a CPA. You have been engaged to examine the financial statements for the year ended December 31, 1994, and your examination is substantially completed. The corporation's trial balance appears below.

Bush Corporation
Trial Balance
December 31, 1994

Cash	$ 36,000	
Accounts receivable	42,500	
Allowance for doubtful accounts		$ 500
Inventories	38,500	
Machinery	75,000	
Equipment	29,000	
Accumulated depreciation		10,000
Patents	85,000	
Leasehold improvements	26,000	
Prepaid expenses	10,500	
Organization costs	29,000	
Goodwill	24,000	
Delta license	50,000	
Gamma license	24,000	
Accounts payable		147,500
Unearned revenue		12,500
Capital stock		300,000
Retained Earnings, January 1, 1994	27,000	
Sales		668,500
Cost of goods sold	454,000	
Selling and general expenses	173,000	
Interest expense	3,500	
Extraordinary losses	12,000	
Total	$1,139,000	$1,139,000

The following information relates to accounts that may yet require adjustment.

(a) New patents were acquired by Bush for its manufacturing process on January 2, 1993, at a cost of $68,000. An additional $17,000 was spent in December 1994 to improve machinery covered by the patents and charged to the Patents account. Depreciation on fixed assets has been recorded for 1994 in accordance with Bush's practice, which provides for a full year's depreciation for property on hand at June 30 and no depreciation otherwise. Bush uses the straight-line method for all depreciation and amortization and amortizes its patents over their legal lives.

(b) On January 3, 1993, Bush purchased a licensing agreement from Delta Company (referred to as the Delta license). The terms of this agreement indicate that the license is for an unlimited period of time. The balance in the Delta license account includes its purchase price of $48,000 and expenses of $2,000 related to the acquisition. On January 1, 1994, Bush purchased a second license from Gamma Corporation, which has a life expectancy of ten years. The balance in the Gamma license account includes its $23,000 purchase price and $1,000 in acquisition expenses. In late December, 1994, an explosion caused a permanent 60% reduction in the expected revenue-producing value of the Gamma license.

(c) The balance in the Goodwill account includes (1) $8,000 paid December 30, 1993, for an advertising program it is estimated will assist in increasing Bush's sales over a period of four years following the disbursement, and (2) legal expenses of $16,000 incurred for Bush's incorporation on January 3, 1993.

(d) The balance in the Organization Costs account properly includes costs incurred during the organizational period. The corporation has elected to amortize these costs over a five-year period.

REQUIRED:

Prepare an analysis of each asset in the trial balance that requires any adjustment due to the information provided above. For each adjustment, explain the rationale on which you base the adjustment in terms of applicable GAAP.

(AICPA adapted)

12-6. *Various intangibles: Recording acquisition and subsequent activity*

Tully Corporation has been in business for several years. The following information was available regarding activities of Tully during 1993:

(a) On January 1, 1995, Tully signed an agreement to operate as a franchisee of Rapid Copy Service, Inc. for an initial franchise fee of $85,000. Of this amount, $25,000 was paid when the agreement was signed, and the balance is payable in four annual payments of $15,000 each beginning on January 1, 1996. The agreement provides that the down payment is not refundable and that no future services are required of the franchiser with respect to the initial fees. The present value of the future payments for the initial fees is $43,700, at a rate of 14%, which represents the market rate for loans of this type. The agreement also calls for an annual payment of 5% of revenues from the franchise. Tully's revenues for 1995 amount to $900,000. The franchise agreement has a life of ten years, but is renewable at the option of the franchisee for a second ten-year period. Tully estimates that the economic life of the franchise is only seven years.

(b) Tully incurred $78,000 of experimental and development costs in its laboratory to develop a patent that was granted on January 2, 1995. Legal fees and other costs associated with registration of the patent totalled $16,400. Tully estimates the useful life of the patent to be eight years.

(c) A trademark was purchased from Walton Company for $50,000 on July 1, 1993. Expenditures for successful litigation in defense of the trademark paid at the culmination of the trial on August 1, 1995, totalled $12,000. Tully was originally amortizing the trademark over ten years but, as a result of the successful litigation, estimates that the remaining useful life to be 15 years.

REQUIRED:

1. Prepare the journal entries necessary to record all the activities described relating to Tully's 1995 fiscal year.

2. Prepare a schedule showing the Intangible Asset section of Tully's December 31, 1995, financial statement.

12-7. *Negative goodwill and other intangibles: Recorded in business acquisition, amortization*

On January 1, 1994, Cort International has acquired the assets and liabilities of Newcor Corporation by issuing 10,000 shares of its $2 par common stock for all of the assets and liabilities of Newcor. Cort's common stock traded at a price of

$36 per share at the time of the acquisition. In addition, Cort paid legal fees to negotiate the acquisition in the amount of $34,000.

At the time of the acquisition, the following information was available regarding the assets and liabilities of Newcor.

	Book Value	Market Value
Cash	$ 15,000	$ 15,000
Inventory	112,000	154,000
Other current assets	5,000	5,000
Land	75,000	150,000
Plant and equipment	600,000	450,000
(Accum. depreciation)	(120,000)	
Licenses	11,000	62,000
	$ 698,000	836,000
Current liabilities	$ 57,000	$ 57,000
Long-term debt	300,000	270,000
	$ 357,000	$327,000

The licenses of Newcor relate to manufacturing processes that were acquired under licensing arrangements with other companies and expire in five years. Newcor amortizes goodwill over the maximum allowable life.

REQUIRED:

1. Prepare a schedule to compute the goodwill Cort will record as a result of this acquisition.
2. Prepare the journal entry to record the acquisition.
3. Prepare the journal entries to amortize goodwill and the licenses during the year following the acquisition.

12-8. *Goodwill and organizational costs: treatment in a business combination*

On June 30, 1994, Beacon Manufacturing acquired all of the assets and liabilities of Obermyer, Inc. by paying $2,000,000. At the time of the acquisition, the following information was available regarding the assets and liabilities of Obermyer:

	Book Value	Market Value
Cash	$ 150,000	$ 150,000
Marketable securities	200,000	225,000
Accounts receivable	400,000	385,000
Inventory	711,000	918,000
Land	210,000	430,000
Plant and equipment	1,489,000	1,200,000
(Accum. depreciation)	(378,000)	
Organizational costs	17,000	0
	$2,799,000	$3,308,000
Current liabilities	$ 540,000	$ 570,000
Long-term debt	1,000,000	1,100,000
	$1,540,000	$1,670,000

The organizational costs were being amortized over a remaining life of ten years. Goodwill is amortized over a 20-year life.

REQUIRED:

1. Prepare a schedule to compute the goodwill recorded in the acquisition.
2. Prepare the journal entry to record the acquisition.
3. Prepare the journal entries to amortize any intangibles for the fiscal year ending December 31, 1994.

12-9. *Goodwill: Estimation of value preacquisition*

Questor Corporation is considering the acquisition of Mesa Products. Questor has obtained the following information regarding Mesa:

Net income for the past four years:

| 1992 | $500,000 | 1994 | $630,000 |
| 1993 | 570,000 | 1995 | 550,000 |

Information on the estimates of market value of Mesa's assets and liabilities are as follows:

	Market Value
Cash	$ 90,000
Receivables	750,000
Inventory	300,000
Land	150,000
Buildings	800,000
Equipment	2,600,000
Current liabilities	140,000
Long-term debt	1,000,000

Questor estimates that Mesa has few growth opportunities for the future on its own but can sustain an income level equal to the average income over the last four years, with one exception. In 1993, Mesa suffered an extraordinary loss in the amount of $120,000, which is included in the income figures above but is not expected to recur. Questor has also estimated that the required rate of return from any investment in Mesa is 15%.

REQUIRED:

1. Compute the excess earnings of Mesa.
2. Assuming the excess earnings would continue forever, how much goodwill would you estimate Mesa has? Given this estimate, what price would you set for Mesa?
3. Assume Questor has determined that a price-earnings multiple for the valuation of Mesa's equity should be 7.4. What does this imply as a purchase price for Mesa? Prepare a schedule to determine the implied amount of goodwill in this purchase price.
4. Assuming Questor ends up paying a price equal to the net fair market value of the identifiable assets plus goodwill equal to four years' excess earnings, prepare the journal entry to record the acquisition.

12-10. *Goodwill and patents: Valuation in a business combination, subsequent amortization*

Barker Enterprises acquired Yetta Manufacturing on August 30, 1995, by paying $890,000. On the date of the acquisition, the following information was available regarding the book and market value of Yetta's identifiable assets:

	Book Value	Market Value
Cash	$ 5,000	$ 5,000
Receivables	50,000	45,000
Inventory	115,000	165,000
Land	60,000	190,000
Buildings	200,000	150,000
Equipment	400,000	438,000
(Accum. depreciation)	(190,000)	
Long-term investments	43,000	45,000
Patents	0	22,000
	$683,000	$1,060,000
Current liabilities	$177,000	$ 177,000
	$177,000	$ 177,000

Patents had a remaining life of six years as of the date of the acquisition. Buildings had a remaining life of 15 years, and equipment had an average remaining life of five years as of August 30, 1995. The long-term investments held by Yetta were all marketable debt securities.

REQUIRED:

1. Prepare a schedule to determine any goodwill recorded in this acquisition along with the values to be placed on the identifiable assets and liabilities acquired.
2. Prepare the journal entry to record the acquisition.
3. Prepare the journal entries to record the depreciation and amortization on the acquired assets at December 31, 1995.

12-11. *Software development costs by software manufacturers: Treatment of costs as assets or expenses*

Barrow Systems is a computer software company. In 1993, the firm incurred the following costs in the process of designing, developing, and producing a new generation of computer games, which it expects to begin marketing in 1994:

Marketing feasibility study costs	$ 70,000
Systems planning and design costs	200,000
Programming costs	320,000
Prototype development costs	80,000
Production of product masters	600,000
Testing	400,000
Production	210,000

The feasibility study, planning and design, and programming all occurred prior to the completion of the working prototype. Fox estimates total revenues over the four-year life of the product will be $15 million, with $3 million in revenues expected in 1994.

REQUIRED:

1. Classify each of the costs indicated above as one of the following:
   (a) Costs charged to expense of the period
   (b) Costs to be capitalized as an intangible asset
   (c) Costs to be capitalized as inventory
2. Explain the rationale for treating some costs incurred in (1) as an expense of the period while other costs are capitalized as an intangible asset.
3. Develop a schedule to determine the amortization of any costs identified as relating to an intangible asset for 1994, assuming the expected revenues are achieved.
4. Suppose the costs described above were incurred by the company to develop software that would be used to control its own manufacturing process, without any external use. How would this change the classification you proposed in (1) above?

SCIENTIFIC MICRO SYSTEMS, INC.

The following information is an excerpt from the financial statements for Scientific Micro Systems, Inc., for the year ended December 31, 1986.

BALANCE SHEET:	1986	1985
Total current assets	$30,108,000	$22,380,000
Note receivable and deposits	–	369,000
Property, plant, and capitalized software, at cost less accumulated depreciation and amortization	6,402,000	5,199,000
Purchased technology, less accumulated amortization of $1,957,000 and $1,286,000	1,398,000	2,069,000
Goodwill and other intangible assets, less accumulated amortization of $1,201,000 and $796,000	3,684,000	4,089,000
Total Assets	$41,592,000	$34,106,000

INCOME STATEMENT:	1986
Net sales	$65,273,000
Cost of goods sold	46,458,000
Gross profit on sales	$18,815,000
Less—other costs and expenses	
Research, development, and engineering	4,841,000
Selling, general, and administrative	9,030,000
Interest and other expense (income)	(34,000)
Amortization of goodwill and purchased technology	1,076,000
Income (loss) before provision for taxes	$3,902,000

Notes:

Significant Accounting Policies—Intangible Assets

The excess of the Company's investment in acquired business over the fair value of net assets acquired (goodwill) is being amortized on a straight-line basis over its estimated useful life, twelve years.

Technology acquired in connection with a business acquisition is being amortized on a straight-line basis over its estimated useful life, five years.

REQUIRED:

1. What percentage of total assets do the intangible assets of Micro represent for the two years presented? What percentage of income before taxes does the amortization of intangibles represent for 1986?
2. Speculate on what the asset Purchased Technology might mean? In what way does this asset represent an intangible asset? Is it identifiable? Is it separable?
3. Do you think the company that Micro purchased to obtain the purchased technology had it recorded as an asset? Why or why not?
4. What does the asset Goodwill represent?
5. Do you think the company that Micro purchased had recorded this goodwill on its books? Why or why not?
6. Prepare the journal entry to record the amortization of each of the two intangible assets.

CASE 12.2

GENERAL CINEMA CORPORATION

Over the years, General Cinema has acquired several companies, which own the rights to various beverage franchises. In the financial statements for the year ended October 31, 1986, General Cinema reported the following information:

BALANCE SHEET:	1986	1985
Intangibles, principally beverage franchises	$54,479	$51,887

Notes:

Significant Accounting Policies—Intangibles

Intangibles acquired prior to fiscal 1971 are not amortized because management considers their value to be of a permanent nature. Intangibles resulting from acquisitions subsequent to fiscal 1970 in the amount of $26,063,643 are amortized on a straight-line basis, over 40 years. The amortization amounted to $723,000 in 1986, $662,000 in 1985, and $270,000 in 1984.

REQUIRED:

1. What is a beverage franchise and why does it represent an intangible asset?
2. How might General Cinema have determined the value of such franchises? (Hint: The company reported no goodwill on its books as a result of the acquisitions).
3. Prepare the journal entry to amortize the franchises for 1986.
4. Assuming no franchises were sold during 1986, how much did General Cinema pay for new franchises purchased during 1986? Prepare the entry the company would use to record these acquisitions.
5. What is the carrying value of the franchises that are not being amortized?
6. Is the decision by General Cinema to not amortize these franchises consistent with generally accepted accounting principles? If so, under what circumstances could this be done?

CASE 12.3

BECTON, DICKINSON, AND COMPANY

Becton, Dickinson is a pharmaceutical company that distributes a wide range of hospital products. In the company's annual report to shareholders dated September 30, 1986, the following information was included regarding intangible assets.

BALANCE SHEET:	1986	1985
	(dollars in thousands)	
Intangibles		
Patents	$116,595	$ 5,248
Goodwill	31,642	18,749
Other Information:		
Amortization of intangibles	6,897	2,477

Notes:

Intangibles include goodwill, which represents costs in excess of net assets of companies acquired, and patents. Patents and goodwill are being amortized over periods, ranging from ten to forty years, using the straight-line method.

REQUIRED:

1. What is a patent? From where does it derive its economic value?
2. From the information provided, is it likely that Becton, Dickinson acquired patents in 1986 as individual assets? Why or why not?
3. Is it possible to amortize a patent over 40 years? What restrictions exist on the amortization periods for patents?
4. Can goodwill be amortized over 40 years?
5. How much did the company pay to acquire the patents and goodwill purchased in 1986, assuming no patents nor any portion of goodwill was sold during 1986?
6. Is it possible to determine how much was paid for patents and goodwill separately? If yes, do so. If your answer is no, what additional data would you need?

NORTEK INCORPORATED

CASE 12.4

Excerpts from Nortek, Incorporated's December 31, 1986 financial statements follow:

	1986	1985
	(dollars in thousands)	
Goodwill less accumulated amortization of $6,551,000 and $3,929,000	$134,487	$78,434

Notes:

The Company has classified as goodwill the cost in excess of fair value (including tax attributes) of the net assets of companies acquired in purchase transactions. Goodwill is being amortized on a straight-line method over 40 years. Amortization charged to the consolidated statement of operations amounted to $2,837,000, $1,670,000, and $1,254,000 for 1986, 1985, and 1984, respectively.

REQUIRED:

1. What does the phrase "cost in excess of fair value of the net assets of companies acquired in purchase transactions" mean? What does it have to do with goodwill?
2. Prepare the journal entry to record the amortization of goodwill for Nortek in 1986.
3. Analyze the changes in the accumulated amortization account for Nortek. How do you interpret what you found?
4. How much new goodwill did Nortek acquire in 1986? (Your answer depends on (3) above).

5. Given your answer in (4) and the knowledge that Nortek amortizes goodwill over 40 years, how do you explain the increase in amortization of $1,167,000 during 1986?

CASE 12.5

BRYANT AND COHEN STEEL

Bryant and Cohen Steel Incorporated (BCSI) is a fabricator of specialty metal products located in Illinois. In order to remain competitive in the industry, BCSI has undertaken a major renovation of one of its production plants. Part of the renovation was to install a computer guided manufacturing process, which coordinates the work of several operations within the plant. Since BCSI is a specialty fabricator, it needs to be able to develop new software to control the production process when a new type of fabrication process is required. As a result, it has decided to maintain an in-house staff of computer programmers to address this task.

When BCSI acquired the equipment and computers at the time of the initial installation, it also purchased baseline software that was developed to control the production process for the basic lines of products BCSI most often produces. The cost of the original installation of all equipment was $147.0 million, broken down as follows (dollars in millions):

Production equipment	$ 98.0
Computer equipment	43.0
Software costs	6.0
Total	$147.0

Since that original installation, BCSI has spent an additional $3.2 million in costs related to development of software in the current year. Software development occurs in two basic ways. Most often, modifications are made to the existing software to insert a control module that will add some special feature to a typical series of manufacturing steps. The original software was prepared to facilitate these types of minor modifications to suit specific customer needs. In other cases, customers approach BCSI for entirely new fabricated products that cannot be produced using the existing software. In these situations, totally new software must be developed to control the production process. Generally, BCSI expects the customer to purchase the specialized products over a long period of time and does not price out the full cost of program development in the price quotes for the initial quantities ordered. In some cases, where the customer indicates that the purchase is likely to be a one-time order, the full cost of the programs is charged out. Even in these situations, BCSI has often found that the customer will return for future purchases, or that the programs can be modified for other specialty orders that arise, thereby reducing the software development costs for later specialty orders.

BCSI has established a policy of capitalizing all software development cost associated with specialty projects and charging all software development related to modification of the initial software to expense. The result of this policy was to capitalize $1.9 million of software development cost in the current period, in addition to the $6.0 million paid for the production software related to the initial installation of the new production facility.

REQUIRED:

1. Setting aside any specific accounting standard relating to computer software, do the costs BCSI incur related to development of software to control the manufacturing process create an asset? Why or why not?
2. Assuming that the response to (1) above was that these costs do represent an asset, is the asset tangible or intangible? Identifiable or nonidentifiable? What difference would these classifications make in your treatment of these costs?
3. In the case of BCSI, what type of classification of assets might be affected if the software development costs were capitalized?
4. How does the development of software for internal use differ, if at all, from the development of software for sale to consumers?
5. Do the policies of BCSI regarding software development costs conform to current GAAP?

PART 4

Valuation and Representation of
Liabilities and Equity

Long-Term Notes and Bonds Payable

In the Financial Review section of its 1973 annual report, the management of United Brands Company included the following statement:

> United Brands took several steps during 1973 to strengthen its financial structure and to provide funds for major expansions of facilities.

One of the steps taken was described as follows:

> In March 1973, the Company consummated an exchange of $75 million of a new series of 9.125% subordinated debentures for $125 million of outstanding 5.50% convertible subordinated debentures. The exchange had the effect of reducing the Company's debt by $50 million, as well as eliminating approximately 50% of the potential dilution of the Company's capital stock by conversion of debt. No sinking fund payments will now be required on the remaining 5.50% debentures until 1989.

This same transaction was described in more detail in the financial statements (Note 10—Long-Term Debt) as follows:

> In March 1973, the Company accepted $125,000,000 aggregate principal amount of its 5.50% convertible subordinated debentures due 1994 tendered under an exchange offer, issued $74,918,000 of 9.125% subordinated debentures due 1998 and paid $12,582,000 in cash realizing a gain of $38,800,000.

On the surface, this transaction appears to be quite a good deal for United Brands. The apparent benefits include:

1. Reduction of long-term debt by $50 million
2. A reported gain of $38,800,000
3. Elimination of sinking fund payments until 1989
4. Extension of the debt's maturity date from 1994 to 1998

Our objectives in this chapter are to study the terminology and the economics of long-term debt, as well as the prescribed accounting treatment, so we can understand just what United Brands has accomplished here. After reading the above descriptions of the transaction, you may not even understand the nature of it. In simpler terms, United Brands exchanged some new bonds with a face value of $74,918,000 and an interest rate of 9.125% plus $12,582,000 in cash for some old bonds with a face value of $125,000,000 and an interest rate of 5.50%. But why? Was this really such a good deal for United Brands? Why did the bondholders ever agree to the exchange? And just what is a convertible subordinated debenture? These are the kinds of questions we address in this chapter.

We will argue that generally accepted accounting principles, as applied to long-term debt, do not always capture the economic reality of transactions. As evidence, we will examine the United Brands' debt exchange described above. Despite the fact that, as indicated in its annual report, United Brands seems rather proud of itself over this transaction, we will make a case that the company is actually worse off as a consequence. In fact, in a Forbes magazine article, Abraham Briloff, the well-known accounting critic, described the transaction rather uncharitably as "just so much fiscal masturbation!"[1] We shall see why. First, we need to describe various long-term debt instruments and the transactions involving them.

NOTES AND BONDS AND THEIR TRANSACTIONS

The terms **notes** and **bonds** are often used interchangeably. Both terms refer to a formal document that serves as evidence of the borrower's indebtedness. A note is any promissory note signed by a borrower. Bonds can be thought of as a particular class of notes, usually with maturities of ten years or longer, issued in borrowing transactions by corporations and units of government to investors at large in a **public offering** or to particular investors in a **private placement**. This chapter deals with transactions related to long-term notes and bonds payable. Other types of long-term obligations such as those resulting from certain lease transactions are discussed in Chapter 17.

Long-term notes and bonds payable can arise in a variety of different transactions. Here are three examples:

1. Ajax Corp. borrows $50,000 cash on a five-year term loan from a commercial bank.
2. Benton Co. issues mortgage bonds with a face value of $100,000,000 due in 25 years in a public offering and receives $98,000,000 in cash.
3. Carter, Inc. purchases a piece of machinery and, in connection with the purchase, issues a promissory note calling for payments to the vendor of $1,500 per month for five years. (This type of obligation that calls for periodic payments of some constant amount is known as an *installment note.*)

---

[1] "Now You See It…," *Forbes* (April 15, 1973), p. 42.

In each of these cases, the firm has borrowed an amount that is due, at least in part, more than 12 months in the future. Certainly, there are differences in the three cases. One obvious difference is the source of the borrowed funds—a commercial bank for Ajax, investors in corporate bonds for Benton, and an equipment vendor for Carter. Another difference is the timing of the payments to repay the amount borrowed plus interest. However, these differences are matters of form, rather than matters of substance, and essentially the same accounting procedures would be applied to each of these three long-term borrowing transactions.

When a firm borrows long-term, it typically agrees to repay the amount borrowed plus some amount of interest over a period of time greater than one year. It may also make other promises to lessen the lender's risk. These promises might be pledging assets as collateral or agreeing not to take on additional debt or pay excessive amounts out as dividends. Such promises made by the borrower are known as **restrictive debt covenants**. Sometimes the debt is retired (paid back) before it matures (becomes due). Other times the original contract between borrower and lender is altered or restructured by mutual consent. These are the types of basic transactions we need to understand; and once we understand them, we will examine their prescribed accounting procedures. We begin by examining the nature of the relationships that typically exist between borrower and lender in these long-term borrowing transactions and, in the process, introducing some new terminology.

TYPICAL FEATURES OF DEBT CONTRACTS

The general purpose of **debt contracts** (also known as *bond indentures* in the case of bonds) is to state very explicitly the rights and obligations of the parties. Some provisions of the contract simply define the basic borrowing/lending transaction. That is, the contract will identify the borrower and lender, define payment amounts and due dates, and state a rate of interest. Other provisions of debt contracts are designed to lessen the lenders' risks by restricting the range of activities available to borrowers, thereby increasing the probability of repayment.

Basic Terms

On May 21, 1991, The Hertz Corporation announced an issue of senior subordinated notes in *The Wall Street Journal*. The announcement is reproduced in Exhibit 13.1. The **principal amount** or **face value** of this note issue is $100 million. That is the amount The Hertz Corporation agrees to pay to the noteholders at the notes' **maturity date**, May 15, 1998, or 7 years after their issuance in 1991. Notes such as these that all mature on a particular date are called **term notes**. Sometimes, portions of a particular issue of notes or bonds will mature at different times. Such bonds are known as **serial bonds**. The **stated rate of interest** (sometimes called the *coupon rate*) is 9.5% The stated rate determines the amounts of the periodic payments Hertz is obligated to make. Most notes of this type offer semiannual interest payments. In this case, Hertz will pay

*This announcement is neither an offer to sell nor a solicitation of an offer to buy these securities.
The offer is made only by the Prospectus and the related Prospectus Supplement.*

May 21, 1991

$100,000,000

The Hertz Corporation

9¹/₂% Senior Subordinated Notes due May 15, 1998

Price 99.095%

*Copies of the Prospectus and the related Prospectus Supplement may be obtained in any State
in which this announcement is circulated where the undersigned
may legally offer these securities in such State.*

Lehman Brothers

Source: The Wall
Street Journal *(May
21, 1991)*

out $4,750,000 (9.5% × $100,000,000 × 1/2) every six months for 7 years on May 15 and November 15. Thus, The Hertz Corporation is promising to pay noteholders $100,000,000 at the maturity date of May 15, 1998, plus 14 payments of $4,750,000 during the 7 years the notes are outstanding for a grand total of $166,500,000.

Notice that the announcement also specifies a price for the notes of "99.095%." The 99.095% figure applies to face value. Thus, if all the notes were sold on May 21, 1991, the gross proceeds from the note issue were 99.095% of $100,000,000, or $99,095,000. Since Hertz must pay fees to the underwriters of the note issue (the firm listed at the bottom of the announcement in Exhibit 13.1), the net proceeds to Hertz will be even less. The pricing of notes and bonds will be discussed more fully in a following section.

To summarize, ignoring the cost of issuing the notes, the following calculation describes the amounts borrowed and the amounts to be repaid by The Hertz Corporation in the transaction described in Exhibit 13.1:

Amount borrowed:	
$100,000,000 × 99.095%	$ 99,095,000
Amount to be repaid:	
Principal	100,000,000
Interest (14 × $4,750,000)	66,500,000
Total	166,500,000
Difference	$ 67,405,000

By issuing these notes, Hertz is borrowing $99,095,000 and promising to pay back a total of $166,500,000. The difference between the amount borrowed and the amount to be repaid represents the cost of using the borrowed funds over the seven-year period the notes are expected to be outstanding. As we shall see, this is the total amount Hertz will recognize as interest expense over the period the notes are outstanding.

Call Provision

Today, virtually all notes and bonds are issued with a call provision in the contract. These **call provisions** allow the issuer a means of retiring the notes and bonds before their regular maturity dates at prespecified prices. They also allow the issuer a relatively inexpensive way of refinancing the debt if interest rates decline. If bonds are **callable**, the issuer may demand that they be surrendered prior to their maturity date. In exchange, the issuer will pay a call price specified in the contract. These call prices, usually stated in terms of a percentage of face value, typically reflect a **call premium**. That is, the issuer is required to pay an amount in excess of face value to call the bonds in for early retirement. For instance, bonds callable at 102 would require payment of 102% of their face value to be retired early. As the time to maturity decreases, the call premium usually decreases.

Security Agreements

Debt contracts will often require a **lien** on particular assets to secure the long-term indebtedness. A lien provision gives the lender the right to keep the assets if the borrower defaults. That is, the lender may foreclose and take title to the assets. Thus, a lien provision lessens the risk of the transaction for the lender.

Perhaps the best known type of lien is a **mortgage** on real estate. If the debt contract includes a mortgage, then particular parcels of real estate are pledged as collateral to secure the loan. For instance, in its 1990 annual report, El Paso Electric Company, a major electric utility in the southwest, listed nine separate "First Mortgage Bonds" and two "Second Mortgage Bonds." In the notes to its financial statements, El Paso Electric Company revealed that, "Substantially all of the Company's utility plant is subject to liens under the First and Second Mortgage Indentures." An **indenture** is the contract that exists between the borrower and its lenders. Thus, in the very unlikely event that El Paso Electric Company defaults on any of its First or Second Mortgage Bonds, bondholders have a certain amount of protection.

When assets are pledged as collateral to secure bonds, such bonds are known as **collateral trust bonds**. For example, the rolling stock of railroads (locomotives and cars) and the flight equipment of airlines are commonly financed by a particular type of collateral trust bonds known as **equipment trust certificates**. In such an arrangement, the assets financed by the equipment trust certificates are pledged as collateral on the loan. This arrangement is similar to the consumer automobile loan. Upon final satisfaction of the indebtedness, the railroad or airline (or consumer) will have clear title to the assets in question.

The amount of protection afforded by these security agreements depends on the value of the assets pledged as collateral at the time of the borrower's default. If the assets pledged as collateral are highly specialized equipment, for instance, then they may have relatively little value on the open market. The borrower's financial distress may, in fact, imply that the assets pledged as collateral have been unable to earn an adequate return and, therefore, may not be worth enough to secure the loan adequately.

Bonds for which the debt contract does not specify particular assets pledged as security for the loan are known as **debentures**. Investors in debentures will only have recourse to the corporation's general assets, not to any particular assets. Because debentures have no security agreement to protect lenders, the contract usually contains certain restrictions on the borrowing firm's activities to lessen the risk of the loan. Some of these restrictive covenants to protect the lender are discussed below.

Covenants to Protect the Lender

The debt contract will often contain clauses that impose certain restrictions on the borrower's activities. These *restrictive debt covenants* are designed to protect the lender by preventing the borrowing firm from taking certain actions that might increase the probability of default. Thus, the role of these restrictive debt covenants is to lessen the risk of the loan. Numerous types of restrictive covenants can be found in firms' debt contracts. We will examine only a few.

Restrictions on Additional Borrowing   As a firm borrows additional funds, it increases its fixed commitments. That is, additional borrowing implies additional future required payments for principal and interest. As these commitments mount, the probability of the firm being unable to meet them all increases. Thus, if a firm is allowed to take on additional debt, the risk of default on existing debts will increase. Therefore, debt contracts commonly restrict the amount of additional debt a borrowing firm may incur.

These restrictions are often stated in terms of a maximum allowable ratio of debt to equity. For example, a firm's debt covenant might preclude it from any additional borrowing if it would cause the ratio of indebtedness to net worth to exceed 200%. Sometimes the limitation on additional borrowing is stated in terms of a minimum required times interest earned ratio (usually defined as income before income taxes and interest expense divided by interest expense). Whether the limitation is expressed in terms of a maximum debt to equity ratio or a minimum required times interest earned ratio, the effect is to put a cap on the firm's borrowing, thus protecting existing creditors.

Restrictions on the Payment of Dividends   One way to insure that sufficient cash is available to repay long-term indebtedness is to prevent the borrowing firm from paying dividends in excess of some amount. For instance, the restriction might state that the firm may not pay dividends in excess of 50% of its net income after the date of the borrowing. These restrictions on the payment of dividends are discussed further in Chapter 15.

Restrictions on Acquisitions and Dispositions   A firm's riskiness can be changed dramatically through a merger with another firm or as a result of the firm's disposal of certain assets. These changes in the firm's riskiness will, in turn, affect the riskiness of its securities. To prevent such risk shifts from occurring, bond indentures sometimes restrict or prohibit merger activity and dispositions of certain of the firm's assets.

The Role of Accounting in Debt Covenants   Restrictions on additional borrowing and on the payment of dividends are often stated in terms of values found in the firm's financial statements, (e.g., debt, stockholders' equity, and net income). Obviously, the borrower must provide financial statements to the lender or lender's representative so that compliance with the contract can be assessed. Exactly how these financial statement values are determined is often not stated or, rather, imprecisely stated as "determined according to generally accepted accounting principles." As a consequence, a firm's choice of particular accounting principles determines, in part, the terms of its debt contracts and may have some real economic consequences. For instance, suppose a rapidly growing firm faces a restriction on additional borrowing stated as a maximum ratio of debt to equity of 150%. Any acceptable accounting method (such as straight-line depreciation) that, relative to its alternatives (such as accelerated depreciation), tends to report higher income for the growing firm will tend to produce higher equity and a lower ratio of debt to equity. This, in turn, will give the firm more freedom to assume additional debt. Recent research into the choice of accounting methods from available alternatives suggests that these choices may be influenced by how close a firm comes to violating the constraints imposed by its restrictive debt covenants.[2]

Sinking Fund Requirements

A **sinking fund** is one earmarked for the retirement of a particular bond issue. If the debt contract contains a sinking fund requirement, then the borrower is essentially required to retire some portion of the bond issue each year. The existence of a sinking fund makes it less likely that the borrower will default and, thus, lessens the risk of the bond issue to the lender.

For instance, the First Mortgage Bonds of El Paso Electric described earlier have a sinking fund requirement described in the notes to its 1990 financial statements, in part, as follows:

> The First Mortgage Indenture securing its First Mortgage Bonds provides for sinking funds. The Company is required to make annual payments to a trustee equivalent to 1%, $1,115,000 at December 31, 1990, of the greatest aggregate principal amount of such series outstanding prior to a specified date.

The requirement to establish and make payments to a sinking fund is a way of formally accumulating and earmarking funds for debt retirement.

Subordinated Bonds

As we saw with United Brands, firms issue bonds and notes that are described as **subordinated bonds** or **junior bonds**. Holders of these bonds have a claim that is subordinated, or junior, to the claims of other creditors should the borrower declare bankruptcy. That is, if the borrowing firm goes bankrupt, the claims of holders of subordinated bonds will only be honored, if at all, after the claims of senior creditors have been satisfied in full. Thus, subordinated debt is a riskier investment than senior debt and will typically carry a higher rate of interest. The notes issued by The Hertz Corporation in Exhibit 13.1 were described as "senior subordinated notes." While this sounds contradictory (How can they be both senior and subordinated?), this description is meant to imply that these notes have a senior claim among the class of subordinated notes.

Why are subordinated bonds issued? As we have already seen, lenders often protect their investments by restricting a firm from taking on additional debt. Such restrictions may have a rather severe effect on the borrowing firm and may prevent it from attracting the capital needed to grow and prosper. Instead of prohibiting additional borrowing, lenders can allow the firm to issue subordinated debt, which gives them some protection. The protection comes from the senior bondholders' higher rank in the "pecking order" of creditors in the event of bankruptcy.

---

[2] See, for instance, R. Holthausen, and R. Leftwich, "The Economic Consequences of Accounting Choice: Implications of Costly Contracting and Monitoring," *Journal of Accounting and Economics* (1983), pp. 75-117.

Conversion Features

Another common feature is the right to exchange the debt securities for a pre-specified number of shares of common or, occasionally, preferred stock. Convertible bonds are attractive because they allow investors to participate in the growth in value of a company's stock while protecting them from the risks of decreases in the stock's value. The convertible feature is also attractive to issuing corporations because they will carry a lower rate of interest than similar bonds without the conversion feature. Moreover, if the company is successful, the bondholders will elect to convert their bond holdings to stock, and the debt will not have to be repaid.

To illustrate some of the basic issues with regard to convertible bonds, consider the following example. Ballantine Corp. issues convertible bonds on January 1, 1993. Each $1,000 bond is convertible into 40 shares of Ballantine Corp. common stock. The current market value of Ballantine stock is $15. The bonds are also callable at 104.

The conversion rate of exchange is one, $1,000 bond to 40 shares of common stock. This is often expressed as a conversion price. In this case, the bonds are said to be convertible at $25 per share ($1,000 ÷ 40 shares). At the current market price of Ballantine common stock, $15, investors have no incentive to convert their bonds because they would be converting a $1,000 bond into stock worth $600 (40 shares × $15). The conversion feature will only become valuable to the bondholders if the market price of Ballantine common stock rises. In fact, since these bonds are also callable and if the price of Ballantine common stock rises high enough, Ballantine can effectively force conversion by calling the bonds. Suppose the price of Ballantine common stock doubles to $30 per share and management calls the convertible bonds. At that point, the holders of the convertible bonds have a choice: to accept the call price of 104% of face value, or $1,040 per bond; or to convert the bond into 40 shares of common stock worth $30 apiece, or $1,200 in total. Only those investors who are not paying attention will fail to convert their bonds into stock.

Recall that United Brands had some 5.5% convertible subordinated debentures involved in its exchange of debt securities described at the beginning of this chapter. Debentures are unsecured bonds—that is, no United Brands' assets are pledged as collateral. Subordinated implies that the holders of these bonds will have a claim that is junior to that of other creditors should United Brands go bankrupt. The conversion feature of these bonds allows conversion at $55. That is, one, $1,000 convertible subordinated debenture can be converted into approximately 18.18 shares of United Brands' common stock. At the time, management stated that one advantage of the debt exchange was that it eliminated "approximately 50% of the potential dilution of the Company's capital stock by conversion of debt." However, the market value of United Brands' common stock at the time of the debt exchange was only $9.50. Conversion was, therefore, hardly imminent.

PRICING OF NOTES AND BONDS

What determines the interest rate a firm pays when it borrows long-term? Why were The Hertz Corporation bonds described in Exhibit 13.1 priced to sell at 99.095% of their face value? As we shall see, the answers to these questions are closely related. Interest rates on long-term notes and bonds are determined in the capital markets and are based on the risks investors perceive. Investors provide the capital that firms require by investing in their equity securities (common stock and preferred stock) and debt securities (notes and bonds). In general, investors evaluate investments in terms of risk and require additional compensation (in the form of a higher rate of return) for risky securities. That is, the higher the risk of a particular investment, the higher the return investors require. This basic relationship between investment risk and return holds for all investments.

The rate of interest firms pay also depends on general economic conditions nationally and globally. Such factors as the rate of inflation, growth in Gross Domestic Product, and a nation's balance of payments will all have an effect on interest rates. As these general economic conditions change, so will the interest rates a firm is required to pay on its debt. For instance, as we see in Exhibit 13.2, the 1990 annual report of Owens-Corning Fiberglas Corporation

OWENS-CORNING FIBERGLAS CORPORATION Long-Term Debt as Reported in the 1990 Annual Report		
10. LONG-TERM DEBT		
(In millions of dollars)	**1990**	**1989**
Unsecured credit facility due in 1994, variable	$ 208	$ 128
Unsecured credit facility, payable in Canadian dollars, due in 1994, variable	191	184
Senior subordinated debentures due in 2001, 11.75%	240	300
Junior subordinated discount debentures due in 2006 (net of unamortized discount of $20 million in 1990 and $71 million in 1989)	189	263
Notes due through 2007, 4.75% to 14.25%, payable in foreign currencies	113	115
Debentures due in 2010, 12% subject to annual sinking fund requirements of $4 million	51	62
Bonds, payable in Deutsche marks, due in 2000, 7.25% (see Note 18)	50	50
Debentures, payable in Canadian dollars, due in1991, 10%	30	30
Industrial revenue bonds, expiring from 1993 through 2012, at rates from 5.75% to 10.25%	22	26
Debentures due in 2000, 9.5%, subject to annual sinking fund requirements of $3 million	21	25
Bonds, payable in Swiss francs, due in 2000, 5.375%	10	8
Extendible notes due in 2005, 9.50% through 1990, 11.15% through 1993	8	100
Note due through 1999, 8.5%		24
	1,133	1,315
Less: Current portion	(47)	(114)
Total long-term debt	$1,086	$1,201

EXHIBIT 13.2
Owens-Corning Fiberglas Corporation—Long-Term Debt as Reported in the 1990 Annual Report

listed various components of long-term debt with interest rates ranging from 4.75% to 14.25%. Has the riskiness of Owens-Corning Fiberglas Corporation's debt really varied that much in recent years? Not very likely. Rather, interest rates in general have changed with changes in economic conditions.

Numerous factors contribute to the risk of a corporation's notes or bonds. We will discuss only a few of them here. First, a firm may not be able to make the payments called for under the debt contract. This default risk depends, in turn, on the inherent volatility of the firm's business and its susceptibility to business fluctuations caused by industry-wide and economy-wide factors. Second, the maturity date of the bond or note is also a factor in determining its risk. The longer a bond or note is outstanding, the higher is the probability that the firm will default or that interest rates will fluctuate widely.

To illustrate the relationship between interest rates and bond prices, we will consider two examples. First, we will examine a **zero coupon bond**. This is a particularly simple debt security. A company that borrows by issuing zero coupon bonds promises to pay the face value of the bonds at their maturity date, nothing more. No promise is made to pay interest over the time the bonds are outstanding. Thus, these bonds carry a coupon rate of zero. Second, we will consider the more common and more complicated example of coupon bonds—i.e., bonds with a non-zero coupon rate. While the coupon payments add some complexity to the analysis, it will become apparent that regardless of the bond's form, the same basic relationship between interest rates and bond prices holds.

Zero Coupon Bonds

To illustrate the pricing of zero coupon bonds, consider the following example. On January 1 of Year 1, Xerxes Corp. issues $100 million (face value) of zero coupon bonds due in 10 years. The proceeds from this bond issue are $32.2 million.

Would any rational lender accept a zero rate of return? Of course not. Even if the investment carried absolutely no risk, investors would have no incentive to invest in a security offering a zero rate of return. So, how can investors earn a positive rate of return on an investment that is apparently offering a zero rate of interest? If investors buy the bonds for less than their face value of $100 million and receive $100 million at maturity, they will earn a positive rate of return. Therefore, the only way these bonds can offer a positive rate of return is if they sell for less than face value. Whenever a bond is issued for less than its face value, it is said to be issued at a *discount*. Zero coupon bonds are always issued at a discount.

Since investors were only willing to pay $32.2 million for these bonds, we can conclude that they were unwilling to accept the stated rate of return, zero. What rate of return did they demand? That is, what is the *effective interest rate* on these zero coupon bonds? The price paid for these bonds represents investors' consensus calculation of the present value (at the effective rate of interest) of the amounts they will receive if they hold the bonds to maturity. Thus, the effective interest rate is that rate which will set the present value of the amounts to be repaid equal to the amount borrowed. In this present value calculation, the present value ($32.2 million, the amount borrowed) and the future value ($100 million, the amount due in 10 years) are known. What is needed is an interest rate that will set the amount borrowed equal to the present value of the amount to be repaid at maturity. That is, assuming annual compounding of interest:

$$\$32.2 \text{ million} = \$100 \text{ million} \times (PV, n=10, r=?)$$

Solving for the PV factor,

$$(PV, n=10, r=?) = .3220$$

By referring to Table 1 at the end of the book and scanning across the row for 10 periods until we find a factor equal to .3220, it is apparent that a 10-period factor of .3220 implies an effective rate of 12%. Thus, under the terms of these bonds, Xerxes Corp. is borrowing $32.2 million at an effective interest rate of 12% with principal and interest payments due at maturity.

We can verify that 12% is the effective interest rate on these bonds by constructing an amortization table. The basic format of an amortization table for zero coupon bonds is shown in Exhibit 13.3.

In the simplest terms, interest on any obligation is the difference between the amount borrowed and the amount to be repaid. Xerxes borrowed $32.2 million and is obligated to repay $100 million after 10 years. Thus, the total interest cost on these bonds is $67.8 million. By the nature of the contract here, no payments of principal or interest are due until the maturity date of the bonds. Despite the fact that principal and interest are repaid in one lump sum,

XERXES CORP.
Amortization Table for Zero Coupon Bonds

(1) DATE	(2) 12% INTEREST	(3) PAYMENT	(4) CHANGE IN BALANCE	(5) BALANCE
1/ 1/X1				$32,200,000
12/31/X1	$ 3,864,000	0	$ 3,864,000	36,064,000
12/31/X2	4,327,680	0	4,327,680	40,391,680
12/31/X3	4,847,002	0	4,847,002	45,238,682
12/31/X4	5,428,642	0	5,428,642	50,667,323
12/31/X5	6,080,079	0	6,080,079	56,747,402
12/31/X6	6,809,688	0	6,809,688	63,557,090
12/31/X7	7,626,851	0	7,626,851	71,183,941
12/31/X8	8,542,073	0	8,542,073	79,726,014
12/31/X9	9,567,122	0	9,567,122	89,293,136
12/31/Y0	10,706,864*	($100,000,000)	$(89,293,136)	0
Total	$67,800,000			

*Includes rounding error.

EXHIBIT 13.3
Xerxes Corp.—
Amortization Table
for Zero Coupon
Bonds

an interest cost can be calculated for each year the zero coupon bonds are outstanding as shown in the amortization table.

Interest on the zero coupon bonds is calculated by applying the effective interest rate of 12% to the outstanding liability balance. Thus, in Year 1, $32,200,000 is outstanding for a year at 12% interest, resulting in interest cost of $3,864,000. Since none of this interest cost is paid during the year, this amount is added to the liability balance, resulting in a balance of $36,064,000 at the start of Year 2. Each year, the interest cost is determined by applying the 12% effective interest rate to the previous liability balance in Column 5. Since the liability grows to exactly $100 million after 10 years, the amount due, we have confirmed that 12% is indeed the effective interest rate in this case.

Suppose a single investor purchased the entire $100 million offering of zero coupon bonds and, after holding them for five years, decided to sell them. A transaction of this type is said to take place in the *secondary market*. That is, it only involves investors, not the issuer of the bonds, Xerxes Corp. How much will investors in the secondary market be willing to pay for these bonds, which are now due in five years? Just as before, the price investors are willing to pay for the bonds represents investors' consensus calculation of the present value (at their required rate of interest) of the amounts they will receive if they hold the bonds to maturity. If 12% is still the required rate of interest, the price of the bonds in the secondary market can be calculated as follows:

$$\text{Price} = \$100,000,000 \times (PV, n{=}10, r{=}12\%) = \$56,747,402$$

Notice that this is the same amount as shown on the amortization table for 12/31/X5. Thus, the balance shown in the amortization table for any date is the present value (at that date) of the remaining payment(s) at the original effective interest rate of 12%.

After five years, investors may require a rate of return that is something other than 12%. This can occur for a variety of reasons such as changes in the riskiness of Xerxes Corp. or changes in general economic factors that influence interest rates. Regardless of the causes, the price of the bonds can be determined as before. Merely calculate the present value of the bonds at the new required rate of interest. If investors demand a 15% rate of interest on these bonds at 12/31/X5, the price of the bonds in the secondary market will be:

$$\text{Price} = \$100,000,000 \times (PV, n{=}10, r{=}15\%) = \$49,717,674$$

If investors demand a 10% rate of interest on these bonds at 12/31/X5, the price of the bonds in the secondary market will be:

$$\text{Price} = \$100,000,000 \times (PV, n{=}10, r{=}10\%) = \$62,092,132$$

By comparing these prices with the price at a 12% rate of interest, we can observe the inverse relationship that exists between the price of bonds and interest rates. That is, if the required interest rate falls from 12% to 10%, the price of the bonds rises from $56,747,402 to $62,092,132. Likewise, if the required interest rate rises from 12% to 15%, the price of the bonds will fall from $56,747,402 to $49,717,674. This relationship reflects the fact that the price of the bonds is just the present value of the future payments, and present values decrease as interest rates increase.

Coupon Bonds

The same general relationship we have just illustrated applies to ordinary coupon bonds. Consider the following example. Yellow Corp. issues $10 million (face value) bonds due in five years with a stated rate of 12% per year compounded semiannually. Suppose the proceeds from the issuance of these bonds amount to $9,297,642.

Since the proceeds are less than face value, as was the case with the zero coupon bonds discussed earlier, these bonds are said to be issued at a discount. Why didn't investors pay face value for the bonds? Apparently, they were not willing to accept a 12% rate of return on these bonds. By paying less than face value, investors are able to earn a rate of return in excess of the stated rate. We can demonstrate that the effective interest rate on these bonds is 14% per year compounded semiannually (7% every six months). The effective rate is the rate that will discount the future cash payments back to a present value equal to the proceeds from the bond issue. When issuing these bonds, Yellow Corp. is making two promises: to pay $10 million in five years and to pay $600,000 ($10,000,000 × .06) every six months for five years. If 14% is the effective rate of interest, then the present value of these two promises at 14% will be equal to the proceeds from the issuance of the bonds.

Face value:	$10,000,000	×	(PV, n=10, r=7%)	=	$5,083,493
Coupons:	$ 600,000	×	(PVA, n=10, r=7%)	=	4,214,149
Total					$9,297,642

Since this is exactly equal to the proceeds, 14% per year compounded semiannually is the effective interest rate. Notice that when semiannual compounding is in effect, the rate per period is one-half the annual rate and the number of periods is twice the years to maturity.

Once again, an amortization table will indicate clearly that 14% compounded semiannually is indeed the effective interest rate on these bonds. The amortization table for these bonds, included in Exhibit 13.4, is only slightly more complicated than that used for zero coupon bonds. First, the relevant period is six months, rather than one year, and, second, the semiannual coupon payments must be taken into account.

Interest is computed each period by applying the effective interest rate to the outstanding liability balance. Initially, Yellow Corp. has a liability equal to the amount borrowed, $9,297,642. Interest at 7% per six-month period for the first six months amounts to $650,835. At the end of the first six-month period, a coupon payment of $600,000 is due and payable. Since the $600,000 payment does not cover the interest cost of $650,835, the liability balance will increase by the difference. This pattern continues until the maturity date when the liability balance equals the face value (the amount due to be repaid) of $10 mil-

EXHIBIT 13.4
Yellow Corp.—
Coupon Bond
Amortization Table

	YELLOW CORP. Coupon Bond Amortization Table			
(1) DATE	(2) 7% INTEREST	(3) PAYMENT	(4) CHANGE IN BALANCE	(5) BALANCE
1/ 1/X1				$ 9,297,642
6/30/X1	$ 650,835	$(600,000)	$50,835	9,348,477
12/31/X1	654,393	(600,000)	54,393	9,402,870
6/30/X2	658,201	(600,000)	58,201	9,461,071
12/31/X2	662,275	(600,000)	62,275	9,523,346
6/30/X3	666,634	(600,000)	66,634	9,589,980
12/31/X3	671,299	(600,000)	71,299	9,661,279
6/30/X4	676,290	(600,000)	76,290	9,737,569
12/31/X4	681,630	(600,000)	81,630	9,819,198
6/30/X5	687,344	(600,000)	87,344	9,906,542
12/31/X5	693,458	(600,000)	93,458	10,000,000
Total*	$6,702,358			

*Total adjusted for rounding difference.

lion. Had we been using the incorrect effective interest rate in this amortization table, the liability balance at maturity would not equal the face value of the bonds.

The interest cost has two components in this case. First, there is the stream of 10 coupon payments of $600,000 for a total of $6,000,000. Second, there is the difference between the amount borrowed, $9,297,642, and the amount due and payable at maturity, $10,000,000. This amount, $702,358, is known as the *bond discount*. Thus, the total interest cost in this case is $6,000,000 plus $702,358, or $6,702,358. Notice that this is the amount shown as the total interest cost on the amortization table.

The key point to bear in mind here is that the price of the bonds is determined by the relationship between the interest rate the bonds offer (the coupon rate) and the interest rate the investors demand (the effective rate). These bonds offered 12% compounded semiannually, while investors demanded 14%. The inevitable result was that the bonds were priced at a discount. This is the same situation as we saw earlier for the zero coupon bonds. In that case, the bonds offered 0% and investors demanded 12%, resulting again in the bonds being priced at a discount.

This is also the same situation we observed in the announcement of The Hertz Corporation senior subordinated notes offering in Exhibit 13.1. Recall that these notes, offering an interest rate of 9.5%, were priced at 99.095% of face value. Thus, the price of the entire $100 million issue will be .99095 × $100,000,000 = $99,095,000. The reason for this discount is precisely the same as we have already observed—investors demanded a higher rate of interest than that offered by the bonds. Ordinarily, coupon bonds will carry a coupon rate that is estimated to be the rate investors will demand. However, in the short time between setting the coupon rate and bringing the bonds to market, market conditions can change and result in an adjustment in the pricing of the bonds, as we observe with the Hertz offering.

Bonds also may be issued at a *premium*—i.e., the proceeds are greater than face value. This will occur when the rate of interest the bonds offer is higher than that demanded by investors. The amortization table is similar to what we have already illustrated. When bonds are issued at a premium, the coupon payments are greater than the interest cost; and the liability balance gradually decreases from the amount borrowed to the face value.

Suppose the Yellow Corp. bonds described above were issued for an amount that offered investors a 10% effective interest rate, compounded semi-annually. These bonds will sell for $10,772,174, calculated as follows:

Face value:	$10,000,000	×	$(PV, n=10, r=5\%)$	=	$ 6,139,133
Coupons:	$ 600,000	×	$(PVA, n=10, r=5\%)$	=	4,633,041
Total					$10,772,174

A properly constructed amortization table will show the liability balance decreasing from $10,772,174, the amount borrowed, to $10,000,000, the amount due at maturity, over the five years the bonds are outstanding.

The relationship between the interest rate the bonds offer (the coupon rate) and the interest rate the investors demand (the effective rate) also affects the pricing of coupon bonds at dates subsequent to their issuance. If the rate of interest investors demand changes subsequent to the issuance of bonds, the price of the bonds in the secondary market will be affected. If interest rates rise, the rate the bonds offer will be less attractive to investors; and the bonds will be priced at a discount. If the interest rate falls, the rate of interest offered by the bonds will be more attractive to investors, and the bonds will sell at a premium—i.e., above their face value.

This relationship helps explain part of the United Brands' situation described at the beginning of the chapter. Recall that United Brands exchanged some new bonds with a face value of $74,918,000 and an interest rate of 9.125% plus $12,582,000 in cash for old bonds with a face value of $125,000,000 and an interest rate of 5.50%. If we assume for the moment that the new 9.125% bonds were issued at face value, then investors accepted new bonds plus cash worth $87,500,000 ($74,918,000 + $12,582,000) for their old bonds, which carried a face value of $125,000,000. But why? As you can see from the two interest rates here, the rate of interest on United Brands' long-term debt has risen rather sharply from 5.50% to 9.125%. We have already observed that when interest rates rise, the market price of bonds in the secondary market falls. Thus, the market value of the old United Brands' 5.50% bonds must have been no greater than $87,500,000 for the bondholders to agree to the exchange. In fact, the market value of the old bonds was only about $76,000,000 due to the rise in interest rates. United Brands offered a premium above market value as an inducement for bondholders to agree to the exchange.

The market value of bonds on any date is the present value of the payments the bonds offer at the rate of interest the investors demand. Thus, replacing its old debt, which had a market value of $76,000,000, with cash and new debt worth $87,500,000 would seem to make United Brands decidedly worse off in terms of market values (i.e., the present value of its obligations) despite the fact that the transaction, we are told, produced a gain of $38,800,000 on the firm's income statement. How can a firm that has just *increased* the present value of its long-term obligations report a *gain* as a result of the transaction? We will come back to this point later in discussing accounting for debt extinguishments. For now, we only need to observe that the gain is computed in terms of book values, while the real economic effects of the transaction are computed in terms of market values.

ACCOUNTING FOR ISSUANCE OF AND INTEREST ON LONG-TERM NOTE AND BONDS PAYABLE

Accounting for the issuance of long-term debt and recognition of interest expense are governed primarily by APB Opinion No. 21, issued in 1971.[3] The basic principle states that the liability is initially recorded at its present value, and interest is recognized by the effective interest method. The accounting treatment of the debt depends somewhat on whether the long-term notes or bonds payable were issued in exchange for cash or in exchange for property, goods, or services. We consider these two cases separately below.

Note or Bond Issued in Exchange for Cash

APB Opinion No. 21 states that when a note or bond is issued in exchange for cash, "it is presumed to have a present value at issuance measured by the cash proceeds exchanged." As we saw above, the price of bonds (and, hence, the proceeds from their issuance) depends on the relationship between the stated rate of interest and the rate of interest demanded by the investor(s) acquiring the bonds.[4] If the stated rate equals the rate investors demand, the bonds are said to be issued at par value or face value. If the stated rate is less than (more than) the rate investors demand, the bonds are issued at a discount (premium). Regardless of whether the bonds are issued at face value, a discount, or a premium, the basic accounting treatment is the same in each case. Initially, a liability is recorded at an amount equal to the amount borrowed, and interest is recognized under the effective interest rate method. We will illustrate all three of these cases with the following example bond issue. On June 30, 1995, Schooner Systems, Inc. issued bonds with a face value of $100,000, a stated rate of interest of 12% per year compounded semiannually, and a maturity date of June 30, 1998. Interest is payable each December 31 and June 30.

While a three-year maturity is somewhat unrealistic for bonds, it simplifies the illustrations without any loss of generality.

---

[3] "Interest on Receivables and Payables," *Accounting Principles Board Opinion No. 21* (New York: AICPA, 1971).

[4] If the reasons for this relationship between interest rates and the price of bonds are not well understood, students are advised to return to the previous section on the pricing of bonds before proceeding further.

Bonds Issued at Face Value   If these bonds are priced to yield 12% compounded semiannually, the gross proceeds from the issue will be equal to the face value of the bonds, or $100,000 in this case. Schooner's journal entry to record this bond issue is as follows:

June 30, 1995:
Cash   100,000
   Bonds payable   100,000
To record issuance of bonds payable at face value.

When the stated rate is equal to the effective rate, as it is here, the interest expense will be exactly equal to the interest payments. The amortization table in Exhibit 13.5 illustrates that interest expense each six-month period is computed at 6% (one-half of the annual rate, compounded semiannually) times the liability balance. The liability balance does not change over time because the amount paid every six months is precisely equal to the interest expense. Therefore, the interest expense is also constant over time. Every six months, Schooner's journal entry to record interest expense and the coupon payment will be made as follows:

December 31, 1995:
Interest expense   6,000
   Cash   6,000
To record interest expense and interest paid on
  December 31, 1995.

Suppose that Schooner Systems' year-end is November 30. In this case, Schooner will need to make an accrual entry every year-end to record five months of interest expense (July through November) that has accrued but has not yet been paid, as follows:

November 31, 1995:
Interest expense   5,000
   Accrued interest payable   5,000
To accrue interest payable at fiscal year-end.

SCHOONER SYSTEMS, INC. Amortization Table for 3-Year Bonds Issues at Par				
(1)	**(2)**	**(3)**	**(4)**	**(5)**
	6% INTEREST	**INTEREST**		
DATE	**EXPENSE**	**PAID**	**AMORTIZATION**	**BALANCE**
6/30/95				$100,000
12/31/95	$6,000	$(6,000)	0	100,000
6/30/96	6,000	(6,000)	0	100,000
12/31/96	6,000	(6,000)	0	100,000
6/30/97	6,000	(6,000)	0	100,000
12/31/97	6,000	(6,000)	0	100,000
6/30/98	6,000	(6,000)	0	100,000

EXHIBIT 13.5
Schooner Systems, Inc.—Amortization Table for 3-Year Bonds Issued at Par

Schooner's entry to record the December 31 interest expense and payment in such a case (assuming no reversing entry was made) will appear as follows:

December 31, 1995:
Interest expense	1,000	
Accrued interest payable	5,000	
Cash		6,000

To record interest paid on December 31, 1995.

Bonds Issued at a Discount   Suppose these bonds offering a 12% rate of interest compounded semiannually are priced to yield 14%. How do you squeeze 14% out of bonds offering 12%? Simply price them at a discount—i.e., below face value. The proceeds from the bond issue can be calculated as follows:

Face value:	$100,000	×	(PV, n=6 , r=7%)	=	$66,634
Coupons:	$ 6,000	×	(PVA, n=6, r=7%)	=	28,599
Total					$95,233

Since this amount is less than the face value of the bonds, Schooner would record the issuance with a contra-liability account, discount on bonds payable, as follows:

June 30, 1995:
Cash	95,233	
Discount on bonds payable	4,767	
Bonds payable		100,000

To record bonds payable issued at a discount.

Notice that the net liability for bonds payable is precisely equal to the amount borrowed, as before.

Bonds payable	$100,000
Less: Discount on bonds payable	(4,767)
Net bonds payable	$ 95,233

The amortization table in Exhibit 13.6 provides the information we need to record interest expense and the semiannual coupon payments. The entries will not be identical every period in this case because the interest expense is increasing over time. Why? The interest expense is computed by applying a fixed rate of 7% per semiannual period to the liability balance. The liability balance is growing (or, equivalently, the discount is being amortized) because the coupon payments of $6,000 do not cover the interest cost each period. Applying a constant interest rate to an increasing liability balance yields an increasing amount of interest expense. Schooner would make the following journal entry to record the interest expense and coupon payment for the first six-month period ended December 31, 1995:

EXHIBIT 13.6
Schooner Systems,
Inc.—Amortization
Table for 3-Year
Bonds Issued at a
Discount

SCHOONER SYSTEMS, INC.
Amortization Table for 3-Year Bonds Issues at a Discount

(1) DATE	(2) 7% INTEREST EXPENSE	(3) INTEREST PAID	(4) AMORTIZATION	(5) BALANCE
6/30/95				$ 95,233
12/31/95	$6,666	$(6,000)	$666	95,899
6/30/96	6,713	(6,000)	713	96,612
12/31/96	6,763	(6,000)	763	97,375
6/30/97	6,816	(6,000)	816	98,191
12/31/97	6,873	(6,000)	873	99,064
6/30/98	6,936	(6,000)	936	100,000

December 31, 1995:

Interest expense	6,666	
Cash		6,000
Discount on bonds payable		666

To record interest expense and interest paid at December 31, 1995.

If appropriate entries with amounts taken from the amortization table above are recorded for each of the subsequent six-month periods, the Discount on bonds payable account will have a balance of zero on June 30, 1998.

If Schooner's year-end is November 30, the following accrual entry will be necessary on November 30, 1995:

November 30, 1995:

Interest expense	5,555	
Discount on bonds payable		555
Accrued interest payable		5,000

To accrue interest expense at fiscal year-end.

These amounts all correspond to five-sixths of the amounts for the first six-month period.

Bonds Issued at a Premium   Suppose these bonds offering a 12% rate of interest compounded semiannually are priced to yield only 10%. How do you get only 10% out of bonds offering 12%? Price them at a premium. The proceeds from the bond issue can be calculated as before.

Face value:	$100,000	×	$(PV, n=6, r=5\%)$	=	$ 74,622
Coupons:	$6,000	×	$(PVA, n=6, r=5\%)$	=	30,454
Total					$105,076

Since this amount is now greater than the face value of the bonds, Schooner would record the issuance with a separate valuation account, usually known as Premium on bonds payable, as follows:

June 30, 1995:

Cash	105,076	
Premium on bonds payable		5,076
Bonds payable		100,000

To record bonds payable issued at a premium.

The result of this entry is to record the liability at $105,076, an amount equal to the amount borrowed.

Interest expense is recognized, once again, under the effective interest method. The appropriate amortization table appears in Exhibit 13.7. This amortization table shows the interest expense is decreasing over time. Why? The liability balance is decreasing (or, equivalently, the premium is being amortized) because the coupon payments of $6,000 more than cover the interest cost each period. Applying a constant interest rate to an decreasing liability balance yields a decreasing amount of interest expense. Schooner would make the following journal entry to record the interest expense and coupon payment for the six-month period ended December 31, 1995:

December 31, 1995:

Interest expense	5,254	
Premium on bonds payable	746	
Cash		6,000

To record interest expense and interest paid on
December 31, 1995.

If appropriate entries with amounts taken from the amortization table in Exhibit 13.7 are recorded for each of the subsequent six-month periods, the premium on bonds payable account will have a balance of zero on June 30, 1998.

If Schooner's year-end is November 30, the following accrual entry will be necessary on November 30, 1995:

November 30, 1995:

Interest expense	4,378	
Premium on bonds payable	622	
Accrued interest payable		5,000

To accrue interest expense at fiscal year-end.

EXHIBIT 13.7

Schooner Systems, Inc.—Amortization Table for 3-Year Bonds Issued at a Premium

SCHOONER SYSTEMS, INC.
Amortization Table for 3-Year Bonds Issued at a Premium

(1) DATE	(2) 5% INTEREST EXPENSE	(3) INTEREST PAID	(4) AMORTIZATION	(5) BALANCE
6/30/95				$105,076
12/31/95	$5,254	$(6,000)	$(746)	104,330
6/30/96	5,216	(6,000)	(784)	103,546
12/31/96	5,177	(6,000)	(823)	102,723
6/30/97	5,136	(6,000)	(864)	101,859
12/31/97	5,093	(6,000)	(907)	100,952
6/30/98	5,048	(6,000)	(952)	100,000

An alternative method of recognizing interest expense, known as **straight-line amortization**, is sometimes employed when the amount of discount or premium is so small that the amount of interest expense will not differ materially from that computed under the effective interest method. This method's only virtue is its simplicity. Under this method, the total amount of discount or premium is amortized in a straight-line calculation (i.e., a constant amount each period) yielding a constant amount of interest expense each period.

All of the entries to record interest expense for the Schooner System, Inc. bonds issued at a discount would appear as follows under straight-line amortization:

December 31, 1995:

Interest expense	6,794.50**	
Discount on bonds payable		794.50*
Cash		6,000.00

To record interest expense based upon straight-line amortization of discount.

* $4,767 ÷ 6 periods = $794.50 per period
** $6,000.00 + $794.50 = $6,794.50

All the entries to record interest expense for the Schooner System, Inc. bonds issued at a premium would appear as follows under straight-line amortization:

December 31, 1995:

Interest expense	5,154**	
Premium on bonds payable	846*	
Cash		6,000

To record interest expense based upon straight-line amortization of premium.

* $5,076 ÷ 6 periods = $846 per period
** $6,000 − $846 = $5,154

Bonds Issued Between Interest Payment Dates   The Schooner Systems, Inc. examples employed to illustrate the basic accounting for notes and bonds issued in exchange for cash all assumed the bonds were issued on a date with exactly six months before the first interest payment date. That, of course, is not always the case. Any delays in their issuance will result in the first interest period being shorter than the others. However, the bondholder will receive a full coupon payment at the end of the first period, even though the bonds have not been outstanding for a full six months. Unless some adjustment is made, the issuer will have to pay for interest costs that apply to a period prior to the issuance of the bonds.

To compensate, it is standard practice to price the bonds at an amount that includes accrued interest from a date that is exactly six months prior to the first interest payment date. Recall The Hertz Corporation senior subordinated notes described in Exhibit 13.1. These notes, which pay interest every May 15 and November 15, were issued on May 21, 1991. Thus, an investor buying the bonds on the day they were issued will receive the first semiannual interest payment after holding the bonds for six days less than six months. Therefore, the price paid for the notes would include six days interest (May 15 to May 21).

To illustrate the accounting issues involved when bonds are issued between interest payment dates, let us rework the Schooner Systems, Inc. example slightly by delaying their issuance by 15 days as follows. On July 15, 1995, Schooner Systems, Inc. issued bonds with a face value of $100,000, a stated rate of interest of 12% per year compounded semiannually, and a maturity date of June 30, 1998. Interest is payable each December 31 and June 30, and the bonds are priced to include interest from June 30, 1995.

If the bonds are priced to yield 12% (i.e., they are issued at face value), then investors will pay a total of $100,000 plus 15 days interest on $100,000 at 12% compounded semiannually. Using a 360-day year to simplify the calculation, the 15 days of accrued interest amounts to $100,000 $\times$ .06 $\times$ 15 $\div$ 180 = $500. Thus, the total proceeds will amount to $100,500. Schooner would use standard accounting practice and record this $500 as a *credit* to interest expense, as follows:

July 15, 1995:		
Cash	100,500	
Bonds payable		100,000
Interest expense		500
To record issuance of bonds between interest payment dates.		

At the end of the first six-month interest period, Schooner can record the interest expense and coupon payment in the usual way:

December 31, 1995:		
Interest expense	6,000	
Cash		6,000
To record interest expense for the first six months.		

After these two entries, the balance in interest expense is $5,500, precisely the amount that should be there for bonds that have been outstanding 15 days less than six months.

The logic of this practice is the same as that behind reversing entries. The objective is to avoid overstating interest expense by an amount that has been paid but does not apply to this period.

Debt Issue Costs   Another issue we have overlooked to this point is the cost of issuing debt. These costs can be substantial, particularly in the case of public offerings. In such cases, the debt issuance costs will include fees paid to underwriters, attorneys, accountants, and the SEC. The treatment of these costs, as specified in APB Opinion No. 21, is to record them as a deferred charge and amortize them in the same manner as any discount or premium over the time to maturity of the debt.[5] However, the FASB stated in *Statement of Financial Accounting Concepts No. 3* that debt issue costs effectively reduce the amount borrowed and, thereby, increase the effective rate of interest. Therefore, this line of reasoning would suggest that debt issue costs be accounted for in the

---

[5] *Accounting Principles Board Opinion No. 21, op. cit.*, para. 16.

same manner as a discount on bonds payable. However, *Statements of Financial Accounting Concepts*, while designed to help in the formulation of generally accepted accounting principles (GAAP), are not themselves an integral part of GAAP. Therefore, treatment of debt issuance costs as a deferred charge, as prescribed by APB Opinion No. 21, is the only method consistent with current GAAP.

Note or Bond Issued in a Noncash Transaction

When a note is issued in exchange for property, goods, or services, the obligation's present value is somewhat less obvious than when the note is exchanged for cash. The reason: The value of property, goods, and services is often less readily determinable than the value of cash. Therefore, while the note's face value is presumed to represent the value of the obligation, that is not the case if:

1. Interest is not stated
2. The stated interest rate is unreasonable, or
3. The stated face amount of the note is materially different from the current cash sales price for the same or similar items or from the market value of the note at the date of the transaction."[6]

In any of these situations exist, the note will be recorded at "the fair value of the property, goods, or services or an amount which reasonably approximates the market value of the note, whichever is more reasonably determinable."[7]

The treatment of notes issued in noncash exchanges is designed to recognize the substance of the transactions rather than their form. Financing is costly. Therefore, if a note fails to mention a rate of interest or mentions one that looks suspicious given current market conditions, interest at an appropriate rate will be *imputed* to the note in the following manner. When the fair value of the property, goods, or services or the market value of the note is readily determinable, interest will be imputed at the effective rate—i.e., the rate that will yield a present value of the obligation equal to the fair value of the property, goods, or services received or the market value of the note, whichever is more determinable. If neither is determinable, then interest is imputed at a rate that would apply to comparable financing obtained elsewhere. To illustrate these concepts, consider the following example. On July 31, 1995, Fancy Fashions Corp. takes advantage of a dealer's offer of 0% (free!) financing for a limited time and acquires a truck with a price of $23,000. Fancy Fashions pays $5,000 cash and signs a note calling for payments of $500 per month for 36 months. Shortly after taking delivery, management of Fancy Fashions finds that they could have acquired a virtually identical truck from another dealer for a cash price of $18,830.

The truck's fair value in this case appears to be $18,830 rather than the $23,000 amount, which Fancy Fashions agreed to pay. This fair value amount would be used to record the truck's cost, and the present value of the install-

---

[6] *Ibid.*, para. 16.

[7] *Ibid.*

ment note would be determined by taking the asset's fair value less the amount of the cash down payment. Thus, Fancy Fashions' journal entry to record the purchase of the truck and the issuance of the note is as follows:

July 31, 1995:

Truck	18,830	
Discount on notes payable	4,170	
Cash		5,000
Installment notes payable		18,000

To record issuance of installment note for purchase of truck.

The effect of this treatment is to split the total of $23,000, which Fancy Fashions has agreed to pay, into $18,830 that applies to the truck's cost and $4,170 that applies to the cost of financing the transaction (i.e., the interest cost). This total amount of interest cost will be recognized as interest expense each period by the effective interest rate method. To apply this method, we first must determine the rate that is implicit in this transaction. This is the rate that, when applied to the monthly payments, will yield a present value equal to the amount financed ($13,830), which is calculated as the truck's fair value ($18,830) minus the cash down payment ($5,000).

$$\$500 \times (PVA, n=36, r=?) = \$13,830$$

We can solve this equation for the present value factor and then refer to the present value table for annuities (Table 2) at the end of the book to find what interest rate is implied by a 36-period factor of this value. Alternatively, a financial calculator will solve the problem more directly.

$$(PVA, n=36, r=?) = \$13,830 \div \$500 = 27.660$$

Referring to Table 2 at the end of the book, this value for a 36-period annuity factor implies an interest rate of 1.5% per period. This is the rate used in recognizing interest expense each month. For the first month, interest expense is calculated at $207.45 ($13,830 × 1.50%). To record the first month's interest and payment, Fancy Fashions would make the following journal entry:

August 31, 1995:

Interest expense	207.45*	
Installment notes payable	500.00	
Cash		500.00
Discount on notes payable		207.45

To record the first installment due August 31.

*($18,000 − $4,170) × 1.50% = $207.45

The interest expense each period is calculated by applying the effective rate to the outstanding loan balance.

Notice that an interest rate of 1.5% per month has been imputed to this note despite the fact that it was advertised as being interest-free. Thus, accountants tend to view low-rate financing "deals" such as this one (and those offered with increased frequency by automobile manufacturers) as adjustments of the price of the asset purchased. In other words, Fancy Fashions did not buy a $23,000 truck and finance it at 0%. Rather, it bought a $18,830 truck and financed it at 1.5% per month, or 18% per year.

If neither the truck's fair value nor the note's market value is readily determinable, interest will be imputed at a rate that would apply to comparable financing obtained elsewhere. Suppose that neither the fair value of the truck nor the market value of the note signed by Fancy Fashions is determinable and that it is estimated that comparable financing would cost the firm 2.0% per month. If so, then the truck's cost and the note's present value are determined as follows:

PV of note: $500 × (PVA, n=36, r=2.0%) =		$12,744
Cash down payment		5,000
Cost of truck		$17,744

Fancy Fashions' journal entry to record the transaction is as follows:

July 31, 1995:

Truck	17,744	
Discount on notes payable	5,256	
Cash		5,000
Installment notes payable		18,000
To record issuance of installment note to purchase truck.		

Since the imputed rate of interest is higher in this second example, more of the total $23,000 cost has been allocated to interest and less to the cost of the truck than in the previous example. Fancy Fashions would record the first month's interest expense and loan payment as follows:

August 31, 1995:

Interest expense	254.88*	
Installment notes payable	500.00	
Cash		500.00
Discount on notes payable		254.88
To record the first installment due August 31.		

*($18,000 − $5,256) × 2% = $254.88

DEBT EXTINGUISHMENT

How do firms extinguish their debt obligations? The most obvious way to extinguish debts is to repay them either at or before the maturity date. In addition, firms may treat debt as extinguished when they have formally set aside funds to make the principal and interest payments in a transaction known as *in-substance defeasance*.

Debt Extinguishment at Maturity

When long-term debt is repaid at maturity, there are no troublesome accounting issues with which to deal. The accounting procedures already illustrated for long-term debt issuance and interest cost will ensure that, regardless of whether the debt was originally issued at a premium or discount, the liability balance at the obligation's maturity will equal the amount due. To see this, simply look at each of the amortization tables illustrated and notice how the ending balance is equal to the debt's face value. Therefore, the journal entry to record the debt extinguishment will simply involve a debit to the long-term debt account and a credit to cash for the amount paid at maturity.

Debt Extinguishment Prior to Maturity

Long-term debt is sometimes retired before the originally scheduled maturity date. Debt instruments usually include a call provision that allows the issuer to retire debt before maturity. Call provisions prevent the issuer from being "locked in" at an unfavorable interest rate.

In an earlier example, the Yellow Corp. bonds issued on 1/1/X1 at an effective rate of 14% compounded semiannually. Suppose that by 12/31/X2, the interest rate on these bonds in the secondary market has fallen to 10% and that the bonds are callable at 102. Does it make economic sense for Yellow Corp. to retire these bonds early?

Intuitively, it would seem that if Yellow Corp. can replace 14% debt with 10% debt, it will be better off. We can answer this question more precisely by finding the present value of the remaining obligations of the old bond issue at the new prevailing rate of interest, the rate at which the firm would have to borrow to retire the old bonds. This present value can be calculated as:

Face value:	$10,000,000	×	$(PV, n=6, r=5\%)$	=	$ 7,462,154
Coupons:	$ 600,000	×	$(PVA, n=6, r=5\%)$	=	3,045,415
Total					$10,507,569

Thus, Yellow Corp. has an opportunity to retire outstanding debt with a present value of $10,507,569 by paying only $10,200,000. It will clearly be better off to retire the debt early.

Curiously enough, despite the fact that the firm is better off as a result of the transaction, the early debt retirement will result in a loss on the financial statements. Referring to Exhibit 13.4, the bonds' book value on 12/31/X2 is $9,522,714 (principal amount of $10,000,000 and unamortized discount of $477,286). To retire them early will require a cash payment of $10,200,000, the call price. Yellow Corp. would make the following journal entry to record the early retirement of this debt:

December 31, Year 2:

Bonds payable	10,000,000	
Extraordinary item: loss on debt retirement	677,286	
Cash		10,200,000
Discount on bonds payable		477,286
To record early extinguishment of debt.		

Under the requirements of SFAS No. 4, this loss, if material, would appear on Yellow Corp.'s income statement in Year X2 as an extraordinary item, net of any income tax effects.[8]

How can the financial statements show a loss on the transaction when we have already seen that the firm is better off as a result? The problem is caused by the fact that the financial statements ignore the changes in interest rates that have occurred since the bonds were issued. That is, on 12/31/X2, the bonds are carried on the firm's books at their present value at the original interest rate of 14%, not the current rate of 10%. By ignoring changes in interest rates, financial statements can produce these results, which run counter to intuition. On the other hand, this practice of carrying long-term liabilities at their present value at the historical interest rate is entirely consistent with the historical cost principle. Under historical cost accounting, the cost of goods and services is measured at costs actually incurred; and changes in asset values due to changes in cost are ignored.

The initial example in this chapter illustrates a case in which the early retirement of debt produced a gain on the income statement but did not benefit the company. From the financial statements of United Brands, Exhibit 13.8 shows a reconstruction of the approximate financial statement effects of the decision to exchange new bonds with a face value of $74,918,000 and an interest rate of 9.125% plus $12,582,000 in cash for old bonds with a face value of $125,000,000 and an interest rate of 5.50%. United Brands' journal entry to

UNITED BRANDS COMPANY Approximate Financial Statement Effects of the 1973 Debt Exchange	
Old bonds retired:	
Face value	$125,000,000
Less discount	(3,018,000)
Book value	121,982,000
Exchanged for	
New bonds issued:	
Face value	74,918,000
Less discount	(4,985,000)
Book value	69,933,000
Cash:	12,582,000
Total consideration	82,515,000
Gain before taxes and underwriters' fees	39,467,000
Underwriters' fees (paid in cash)	667,000
Gain on exchange (before tax effects)	$ 38,800,000

EXHIBIT 13.8
United Brands Company— Approximate Financial Statement Effects of the 1973 Debt Exchange

---

[8] "Reporting Gains and Losses from Extinguishment of Debt," *Statement of Financial Accounting Standards No. 4* (Stamford, CT: FASB, 1975), para. 8.

record the transaction must have looked something like the following (000s omitted):

1973:

5.50% Convertible subordinated debentures payable	125,000	
Discount on 9.125% subordinated debentures payable	4,985	
9.125% Subordinated debentures payable		74,918
Discount on 5.50% convertible subordinated debentures payable		3,018
Cash		13,249
Extraordinary item—gain on debt exchange		38,800

To record debt refinancing by United Brands.

Now let us address the more fundamental question of whether the transaction makes any economic sense. A transaction of this type makes economic sense if it results in a reduction of the present value of the firm's indebtedness. Other aspects of the transaction such as the reduction in the debt's book value and reduction of the potential for conversion of bonds into stock certainly have some value but are less important than the change in the present value of United Brands' debt. Did the firm reduce the present value of its long-term obligations by exchanging the old 5.50% convertible subordinated debentures due in 1994 for the lesser amount of 9.125% subordinated debentures due in 1998 plus cash?

As we have already seen, when new debt is issued, it is recorded at the obligation's present value at the effective rate of interest. Thus, United Brands incurred a new obligation with a present value of $69,933,000 and paid $12,582,000 in cash for total consideration of $82,515,000. We need to compare this with the present value of the old 5.50% convertible subordinated debentures at the current effective rate of interest. Since the new 9.125% debentures were issued at a discount, their effective interest rate was actually greater than 9.125%. To solve for the effective rate, we need to solve for an interest rate that will result in the sum of the present values of the remaining principal and interest payments on the 9.125% debentures equal to $69,933,000. Remember: The transaction took place in 1973, and these bonds are due in 1998. That is 25 years or 50, six-month interest periods from the date of issuance.

Principal:	$74,918,000	×	$(PV, n=50, r=?)$	=	PV of principal
Coupons:	$ 3,418,134*	×	$(PVA, n=50, r=?)$	=	PV of coupons
Total PV					$69,933,000

*$74,918,000 × 9.125% ÷ 2 = $3,418,134

This problem is difficult to solve. An approximation can be obtained using tables and a trial-and-error technique, but a financial calculator or personal computer can better solve the problem. The effective interest rate turns out to be approximately 9.845% per year compounded semiannually, or 4.9225% every six months. We can now use this rate to find the present value of the old bonds at the new rate of interest. Remember: The transaction took place in 1973, and the old bonds are due in 1994. That is 21 years or 42, six-month interest periods from the date of the transaction.

Principal:	$125,000,000	×	$(PV, n=42, r=4.9225\%)$	=	$16,611,328
Coupons:	$ 3,437,500*	×	$(PVA, n=42, r=4.9225\%)$	=	60,550,689
Total PV					$77,162,017

*$125,000,000 × 5.50% ÷ 2 = $3,437,500

United Brands eliminated debt with a present value of $77,162,017 by taking on new debt with a present value of $69,933,000 and paying cash of $12,582,000. Thus, it is are actually worse off as a result of the transaction by more than $5 million.

Present value of new debt plus cash paid	$82,515,000
Present value of old debt	77,162,017
Worse off by	$ 5,352,983

Why, then, did United Brands do it? We can only speculate in answering that question. Did United Brands' management succumb to the temptation of reporting a $38,800,000 gain in 1973? As *Forbes* pointed out, United Brands was not a particularly profitable firm, averaging a profit margin of only 0.4% in the five years prior to this transaction.[9] Perhaps management thought it could convince financial statement readers that the company was more profitable by recognizing a gain on this debt exchange. Although GAAP now require that such gains be prominently reported as extraordinary items, that was not the case in 1973. Perhaps the action was motivated by restrictive debt covenants and the desire to reduce the ratio of debt to equity. Management may have also been interested in bolstering the price of the stock. However, research has shown that the stock market does not react naively to any event or transaction that increases a firm's net income.[10] Whatever the explanation, the point remains that the accounting treatment for long-term debt allows firms to report gains from transactions that actually make them worse off as a result.

Debt Defeasance

SFAS No. 76 allows firms another way to remove debt from their financial statements, without technically retiring it, known as **in-substance defeasance**. Actually, SFAS No. 76 was a response to a practice that a number of prominent firms have followed: placing certain assets in a trust that is earmarked for making principal and interest payments on a particular debt issue. Thus, the debt is provided for without actually being retired. The 1985 annual report of Fluor Corporation provides an example of in-substance defeasance:

---

[9] *Forbes, ibid.*

[10] For instance, Kaplan and Roll have concluded in a similar context that while "earnings manipulation may be fun, its profitability is doubtful." R. Kaplan and R. Roll, "Investor Evaluation of Accounting Information: Some Empirical Evidence," *Journal of Business* (April 1972), p. 244.

In October 1985, the company completed an "in-substance defeasance on $63,090,000 of 14% Eurodollar notes then outstanding by placing in an irrevocable trust $72,870,000 of U.S. government securities to be used solely for satisfying scheduled payments of both interest and principal on the notes, which will be called in September 1986. The notes and U.S. government securities have been excluded from the Consolidated Balance Sheet at October 31, 1985. The premium on early extinguishment of the notes is included in the extraordinary item..."

What is the motivation for a transaction that takes $72,870,000 of U.S. government securities to get rid of $63,090,000 of debt? Defeasance is often a less expensive way of "retiring" debt than the more traditional alternatives of a call or exchange offer. Calls are only feasible when the debt contract contains a call provision and the call period has begun. Moreover, calls require payment of a call premium, which may entail considerable expense. As we have seen in the United Brands' debt exchange, exchange offers also usually entail a premium when the debt securities are publicly held to induce bondholders to make the exchange.

How are such transactions accounted for? SFAS No. 76 states that debt may be considered extinguished if:

> The borrower irrevocably places cash or other assets in a trust to be used solely for satisfying scheduled payments of both interest and principal of a specific obligation and the possibility that the debtor will be required to make future payments with respect to that debt is remote.[11]

The assets placed into the trust, if not cash, must be essentially risk-free; and their cash flows must approximately coincide with the required debt service payments. When a trust is created to service the debt, the firm may remove the obligation from its balance sheet as if it had been retired. Any gain or loss on the transaction, computed as illustrated above, will be reported on the income statement as an extraordinary item.

TROUBLED DEBT RESTRUCTURINGS

When a borrower is in financial difficulty, the lender will sometimes agree to grant certain concessions (or a court will order such concessions) and modify the terms of the original debt agreement. The alternative to such an agreement may be the borrower's bankruptcy, which could be more costly for the lender. Thus, the lender needs to decide whether more of the obligation can be recovered through a debt restructuring or in bankruptcy court.

The accounting profession calls these events **troubled debt restructurings**, and their treatment in the borrower's financial statements depends on the nature of the concessions granted by the lender. The FASB recognizes two general types of troubled debt restructurings:

---

[11] "Extinguishment of Debt," *Statement of Financial Accounting Standards No. 76* (Stamford, CT: FASB, 1983), para. 3.

1. A full settlement achieved by a transfer of assets or grant of equity interest
2. A modification of the terms of the loan agreement.[12]

Full Settlements

If the lender agrees to accept a transfer of assets or a grant of an equity interest in full settlement of the debt, the borrower will recognize a gain as an extraordinary item equal to the difference between the debt's carrying value (book value plus any accrued interest) and the fair value of the assets transferred or equity interest transferred. For instance, consider the following situation:

> Blue Corp. has a $100,000, 10% note payable to National Bank. The note is due on 12/31/95, and interest payments are due on 12/31 of each year. On 12/31/93, the bank agrees to accept inventory with a book value of $75,000 and a market value of $90,000 in full settlement of the obligation.

First, Blue Corp. would recognize a gain on the realization of the fair value of its inventory.

December 31, 1993:

Inventory	15,000	
Gain on realization of inventory		15,000

To record the gain on realization of inventory.

Next, Blue Corp. would record the use of inventory to settle its obligation to the bank. Assuming it has already accrued interest for the year, Blue Corp. would make the following necessary entry:

December 31, 1993:

Note payable	100,000	
Accrued interest payable	10,000	
Inventory		90,000
Gain on debt restructuring		20,000

To record full settlement of note to bank by transfer of assets.

Modification of Terms

A more common type of troubled debt restructuring is known as a **modification of terms**. Any forgiveness of payments or extension of due dates falls into this category. Under troubled debt restructurings of this type, the borrower will typically not recognize any gain unless the total amount to be repaid under the modified agreement is less than the debt's carrying value. For example, consider the following case. Blue Corp. has a $100,000, 10% note payable to National Bank. The note is due on 12/31/95, and interest payments are due on 12/31 of each year. On 12/31/93, the bank agrees to forgive the interest payment due that day.

---

[12] "Accounting by Debtors and Creditors for Troubled Debt Restructurings," *Statement of Financial Accounting Standards No. 15* (Stamford, CT: FASB, 1977), para. 5.

In this case, the total amount to be repaid under the modified agreement is not less than the debt's carrying value, assuming that interest for the year ended December 31, 1993, has already been recorded.

Book value of the note	$100,000
Accrued interest	10,000
Carrying value	$110,000
Principal amount	$100,000
Interest payment due 12/31/94	10,000
Interest payment due 12/31/95	10,000
Total amount to be repaid	$120,000

Therefore, no gain would be recognized under GAAP, even though it is obvious that Blue Corp. is better off by $10,000 as a result of the transaction.

However, Blue Corp. will probably make the following (optional) entry to record the debt restructuring:

December 31, 1993:
Accrued interest payable	10,000	
Notes payable		10,000
To record modification of terms of loan agreement.		

This will leave the note payable on the books at $110,000. The purpose of this entry is to remove the amount of interest, which has already been accrued but has just been forgiven, from the current liability classification, Accrued Interest. It is not permissible to credit interest expense by the $10,000 just forgiven since that would recognize a gain on the transaction.

Interest for 1994 and 1995 will total $20,000. It must be recognized by the effective interest rate method. However, since the original terms of the loan contract have been altered, a new effective interest rate must be computed.

Principal:	$100,000	×	$(PV, n=2, r=?)$	=	PV of principal
Interest:	$ 10,000	×	$(PVA, n=2, r=?)$	=	PV of interest
Total present value					$110,000

Using a financial calculator, we obtain an effective interest rate of 4.65%. Blue Corp. will use this rate to recognize interest expense for the remaining two years. An amortization table for the loan, as modified, appears in Exhibit 13.9.

Blue Corp's entries for 1994 and 1995 would be recorded as follows:

December 31, 1994:
Interest expense	5,115	
Notes payable	4,885	
Cash		10,000
To record interest on restructured note payable for 1994.		

	BLUE CORP. Loan Amortization Table Under Modified Loan Agreement			
(1) DATE	(2) 4.65% INTEREST EXPENSE	(3) INTEREST PAID	(4) AMORTIZATION	(5) BALANCE
12/31/93				$110,000
12/31/94	$5,115	$(10,000)	$(4,885)	105,115
12/31/95	4,885	(10,000)	(5,115)	100,000

EXHIBIT 13.9

Blue Corp.—Loan Amortization Table Under Modified Loan Agreement

December 31, 1995:
Interest expense   4,885
Notes payable   5,115
   Cash   10,000
To record interest on restructured note payable for 1995.

Notice that only $10,000 of interest expense is recognized over the two remaining years of the loan, even though a total of $20,000 is to be paid out. Effectively, the $10,000 gain from the debt restructuring is being recognized as a reduction of interest expense over the remaining life of the loan.

To illustrate a more extreme case, suppose that on December 31, 1993, the bank agrees to forgive all three of the remaining interest payments. In this case, the carrying value ($110,000) exceeds the total amount to be repaid ($100,000), and Blue Corp. would recognize a gain of $10,000 as an extraordinary item.[13] Blue Corp.'s entry to record the transaction would be as follows.

December 31, 1993:
Accrued interest payable   10,000
   Extraordinary item: gain on debt restructuring   10,000
To record gain on troubled debt restructuring by modification of terms.

This will leave the liability on the books at $100,000, the total amount due in two years' time. Notice that the liability is no longer stated at its present value. Obviously, since all remaining interest payments have been forgiven, Blue Corp. does not need to record any interest expense over the remaining year the loan is outstanding.

Please note that Blue Corp. is better off by a larger amount than this reported gain would indicate. The actual benefit of the debt restructuring can be computed as follows:

12/31/93 Interest forgiven	$10,000
12/31/94 Interest forgiven 10,000 (PV, $n=1$, $r=10\%$)	9,091
12/31/95 Interest forgiven 10,000 (PV, $n=2$, $r=10\%$)	8,264
Actual gain	$27,355

[13] Under SFAS No. 15, the corresponding gain the lender recognized is to be treated as an ordinary item.

Suffice it to say that when troubled debt restructurings occur, the borrower's financial statements in the year of the transaction will typically understate the benefit received from the change in the loan agreement.

Why did the FASB opt for a method that does not recognize the debtor's gains from modifications of the terms of debt agreements? Remember: In formulating accounting principles, many different constituencies have an interest in the accounting treatment prescribed for particular events. In the case of troubled debt restructurings, commercial banks and other lenders to corporate America intensely lobbied the FASB. Essentially, their argument was that if every modification of terms was recognized as a gain by borrowers and a loss by lenders, it could have serious repercussions for the banking industry, which, in turn, would have an adverse impact on the entire U.S. economy. The FASB apparently found this argument convincing.

INNOVATIVE FINANCIAL INSTRUMENTS

Over the last decade, a bewildering array of new financial instruments has appeared. No longer do firms merely issue bonds and common and preferred stock. These days, firms engage in interest rate swaps, issue put and call options on their stock or on interest rates or: foreign currency contracts, issue securities where the amount payable is linked to the price of some commodity, issue interest rate caps and floors, and issue financial guarantees, among many others. What is the motivation behind these innovative transactions, and what are the innovative financial instruments that result from them?

In most cases, the motivation for these innovative financial instruments is risk management. Companies are exposed to a variety of risks because of price fluctuations. For example, a bank issuing a fixed-rate, 30-year mortgage is exposed to risk if interest rates change significantly over the 30 years that its return will be fixed. Companies engaged in import and export activities are exposed to risks if exchange rates fluctuate. Most of the innovative financial instruments issued in recent years can be viewed as a means of allowing firms to manage their risks by transferring them to other firms or individuals.

For instance, a firm that has **floating rate debt**, or debt with a rate that varies or "floats" with some general measure of interest rates such as banks' prime lending rate, is exposed to considerable risk should interest rates increase and the firm's interest costs rise. One way a firm can manage this risk is to enter into an **interest rate swap**. In such a swap, a bank or other financial intermediary arranges for the firm with the floating rate debt to swap or exchange its obligation to pay interest at a floating rate with another firm's obligation to pay interest at a fixed rate. Effectively, after an interest rate swap, floating rate debt is converted to fixed rate (and, thereby, less risky) debt.

Some critics allege that another motivation, which has nothing to do with risk management, exists for these innovative financial instruments. It is alleged that firms use some of these financial instruments to achieve **off-balance sheet financing**. That is, it keeps the firms' obligations from being reported as balance sheet liabilities. There is no question that currently many of these financial instruments expose firms to risks of loss that are either not recognized at all, or not recognized in full, in the financial statements. Thus, to the extent that firms can issue these innovative financial instruments for valuable consideration and not be required to report them on their balance sheets, they have achieved off-balance sheet financing.

The FASB added a project on financial instruments and off-balance sheet financing to its agenda in 1986. Given the complexity of the issues, the Board decided the best course of action was to focus first on ways to improve financial statement disclosures about innovative financial instruments rather than try to tackle the more difficult issues of how to account for transactions involving them. The result of this first stage of the project was *Statement of Financial Accounting Standards No. 105*, "Disclosure of Information about Financial Instruments with Off-Balance Sheet Risk and Financial Instruments with Concentrations of Credit Risk," issued in 1990. SFAS No. 105 defines a **financial instrument** this way:

> A financial instrument is cash, evidence of an ownership interest in an entity, or a contract that both:
>
> 1. Imposes on one entity a contractual obligation (a) to deliver cash or another financial instrument to a second entity or (b) to exchange financial instruments on potentially favorable terms with the second entity
>
> 2. Conveys to the second entity a contractual right (a) to receive cash or another financial instrument from the first entity or (b) to exchange other financial instruments on potentially favorable terms with the first entity.[14]

Firms that issue financial instruments are exposed to the **risk of accounting loss**, or a loss that may have to be recognized in the financial statements if:

1. Another party to the contract fails to perform (*credit risk*)
2. Future changes in market prices make the financial instrument less valuable (*market risk*), or
3. There is a theft or physical loss.

If a financial instrument exposes a firm to the risk of accounting loss that exceeds the amount of obligation recognized on the firm's balance sheet, the instrument is said to have **off-balance sheet risk**. For instance, a manufacturing firm may guarantee a key supplier's obligation to insure that the supplier can provide a continuing supply of some necessary components for the manufacturing firm's products. Under GAAP, the obligation resulting from this guarantee would not be reported on the manufacturing firm's balance sheet and would, therefore, entail off-balance sheet risk.

Whenever a financial instrument entails off-balance sheet risk, the following disclosures are required:

1. The face or contract amount
2. The nature and terms, including
   (a) Credit and market risk
   (b) Cash requirements
   (c) How the instrument is accounted for

----

[14] "Disclosure of Information about Financial Instruments with Off-Balance Sheet Risk and Financial Instruments with Concentrations of Credit Risk," *Statement of Financial Accounting Standards No. 105* (Norwalk, CT: FASB, 1990), para. 6.

If a financial instrument has off-balance sheet credit risk, the following disclosures are also required:

1. The amount of loss incurred if another party to the contract failed completely to perform and the collateral, if any, proved to be of no value
2. The firm's policy of requiring collateral to secure financial instruments subject to credit risk and the nature of that collateral

The FASB's financial instruments project is ongoing. The Board has already issued a draft of a new statement that would require disclosure of the market values of financial instruments where it is practicable to do so. Discussion continues on how to distinguish between debt and equity instruments and how to measure and recognize financial instruments in the financial statements. Accounting standards will likely proliferate in this area. Stay alert for future developments.

SUMMARY

Long-term notes and bonds are priced in the capital markets at the present value of the future cash flows they offer investors. When investors deem the rates offered by the securities are inadequate, given the risk involved in the securities and current market conditions, the notes or bonds will be issued at a discount. If the notes or bonds offer returns in excess of those investors demand, they will be issued at a premium.

A firm issuing long-term notes or bonds for cash initially records the liability at the amount borrowed. Interest is recognized by the effective interest rate method, which amortizes any discount or premium over the term to maturity. Debt issue costs are deferred and amortized over the time to maturity of the debt. Most firms show the deferred debt issue costs as an asset (deferred charge). When notes or bonds are issued in a noncash transaction and if the stated rate is unreasonable given current market conditions, interest must be imputed to the note at a rate different from the stated rate.

When debt is extinguished early, either through retirement or defeasance, the resulting gain or loss may not fully capture the economic reality of the transaction. That is, a firm may report losses when it is better off as a result of the transaction or it may report gains when it is worse off. If gains or losses from debt extinguishments are material, they are reported as extraordinary items.

Troubled debt restructurings may occur as full settlements or modifications of terms. While debtors will typically recognize gains from full settlements, they will only recognize gains from modifications of terms when the total amount to be repaid (not the present value of that amount) under the modified loan agreement is less than the debt's carrying value.

Financial instruments may expose a firm to off-balance sheet risk if the potential accounting loss from the obligation exceeds the amount of the obligation, if any, reported on the firm's balance sheet. If so, certain disclosures are required.

QUESTIONS

1. Distinguish between a *private placement* and a *public offering* of bonds.
2. Define the following terms related to long-term bonds:
    (a) Bond indenture
    (b) Face value
    (c) Term notes (or bonds)
    (d) Serial bonds
    (e) Coupon rate or stated rate of interest
3. Why do many notes and bonds contain a *call provision*?
4. Distinguish between a *debenture* and a *mortgage* bond.
5. Why do *restrictive debt covenants* sometimes include restrictions on additional borrowing?
6. Explain how the existence of restrictive debt covenants might influence a firm's choice of accounting methods.
7. What is the purpose of a *sinking fund*?
8. Explain how *subordinated debt* differs from *senior debt* and why firms issue subordinated debt.
9. Why are some bonds issued at a *discount*? at a *premium*?
10. Explain how and why the price of bonds changes as interest rates change.
11. If a bond is priced at 98 percent of face value, what is the relationship between the stated rate of interest and the effective rate?
12. As discount on bonds payable is amortized, is the net liability for bonds payable increasing or decreasing? Explain.
13. For the issuer of a bond, does the amount of amortization using the effective interest method increase or decrease each year if the bond was sold at a discount? at a premium? Why?
14. When bonds are sold at a premium, is the amount recognized as interest expense each period greater than, less than, or the same as the amount paid out for interest? Explain.
15. When bonds are sold at a discount, is the amount recognized as interest expense each period greater than, less than, or the same as the amount paid out for interest? Explain.
16. When bonds are sold at face value, is the amount recognized as interest expense each period greater than, less than, or the same as the amount paid out for interest? Explain.
17. When will the price of bonds include accrued interest? Why?
18. How are bond issuance costs accounted for?
19. When is it necessary to impute an interest rate in a bond transaction? Why?
20. Explain why a gain on the extinguishment of debt is most likely to occur when interest rates have increased.
21. What is meant by *in-substance defeasance* of debt?
22. What are the two types of *troubled debt restructurings*? Briefly describe the accounting for each.
23. How do some innovative financial securities contribute to *off-balance sheet financing*?

EXERCISES

13-1.   *Bonds issued at a premium*

On July 1, 1995, Carson, Inc. issued 5,000 of its 10%, $1,000 bonds. The bonds were priced at 102 and were issued through an underwriter to whom Carr paid bond issue costs of $100,000.

REQUIRED:

Calculate the proceeds from the issuance of the bonds and prepare a journal entry to record the transaction.

13-2.   *Early retirement of bonds*

On June 30, 1995, Letterman Company had the following bonds payable outstanding: face value, $10,000,000; maturity date, June 30, 1995; stated rate, 8% compounded semiannually; interest payment dates, June 30 and December 31. On June 30, 1995, the balances in the bond discount and deferred bond issue costs accounts were $350,000 and $100,000, respectively. Letterman acquired all of these bonds at 94 on June 30, 1995, and retired them.

REQUIRED:

Calculate the gain on extinguishment of debt and prepare a journal entry to record the transaction.

13-3.   *Bonds issued at a discount*

On April 1, 1995, Hall, Inc., issued 400 of its 10%, $1,000 bonds payable priced at 97 plus accrued interest. The bonds are dated January 1, 1995, and mature on January 1, 2005. Interest is payable semiannually on January 1 and July 1.

REQUIRED:

1. Calculate the proceeds from the issuance of bonds and prepare a journal entry to record the transaction.
2. Prepare a journal entry to record interest on July 1, 1995. Hall amortizes bond discount using the straight-line method.

13-4.   *Pricing of bonds*

On January 1, 1995, Lenno Company issued 10-year bonds with a face value of $10,000,000 and a stated interest rate of 8% per year, payable semiannually July 1 and January 1.

REQUIRED:

1. Calculate the proceeds from the bonds assuming they were priced to yield 10%.
2. Calculate the proceeds from the bonds assuming they were priced to yield 6%.

13-5.   *Effective interest method*

On January 1, 1995, Costas Corp. issued $25,000,000 face amount of bonds, with interest to be paid semiannually at a 10% annual rate. The bonds mature on December 31, 2004, and were priced to yield 8%.

Required:

1. Calculate the proceeds from the issuance of the bonds and prepare a journal entry to record the issuance.
2. Calculate the interest expense to be recognized for the year ended December 31, 1995.

13-6.   *Zero coupon bonds*

On April 1, 1995, Goldberg, Inc. issued zero coupon bonds with a face value of $50,000,000. The bonds mature on March 31, 2010, and were priced to yield a 6% annual rate, compounded semiannually.

Required:

1. Calculate the proceeds from the issuance of the bonds and prepare a journal entry to record the issuance.
2. Calculate the interest expense to be recognized for the year ended December 31, 1995.

13-7.   *Early retirement of debt*

Limbaugh, Inc., issued $5,000,000 face amount of 10% bonds with interest payable on January 1 and July 1. The bonds were called in at 103 on July 1, 1995, and retired. Unamortized bond discount amounted to $250,000 at July 1, 1995. Limbaugh's income tax rate is 34% for 1995.

Required:

Show how the early retirement of debt would be shown on Limbaugh, Inc.'s 1995 income statement.

13-8.   *Issuance of bonds*

On October 1, 1995, Rivera, Inc., issued at 101, plus accrued interest, 400 of its 10%, $1,000 bonds. The bonds are dated July 1, 1995, and mature on July 1, 2005. Interest is payable semiannually on January 1 and July 1.

Required:

Calculate the proceeds from the issuance of bonds and prepare a journal entry to record the transaction.

13-9.   *Early retirement of bonds*

On February 1, 1995, Gifford Corp. issued 12%, $20,000,000 face amount, 10-year bonds for $22,340,000 plus accrued interest. The bonds are dated November 1, 1994, and interest is payable on May 1 and November 1. Gifford reacquired all of these bonds at 102 on May 1, 1999, and retired them. Unamortized bond premium on that date was $1,560,000. Gifford's tax rate is 34%.

Required:

Calculate the net gain or loss on the retirement of debt and prepare a journal entry to record the transaction.

13-10.   *Troubled debt restructuring*

On April 1, 1995, First Commercial Bank agreed to accept a building appraised at $600,000 in full settlement of a $700,000 note issued by Henry's Hardware Co. The note carries a 12% annual interest rate with interest payable every December 31. The last interest payment occurred on December 31, 1994; and interest has not been accrued since then. The building was carried on Henry's books at its cost of $800,000 less accumulated depreciation of $250,000. Ignore taxes.

REQUIRED:

Prepare all journal entries to record this transaction on the books of Henry's Hardware Co.

13-11. *Troubled debt restructuring*

In response to the financial difficulties of Betty's Boutique, Inc., the Bank of Last Resort agreed to modify the terms of its loan to Betty's. The payments for $10,000 of principal amount and $1,000 of interest due today have been postponed for one year. Betty's agrees to pay the $11,000, originally due today, plus an additional $1,100 in interest in one year.

REQUIRED:

Prepare all journal entries to record this transaction on the books of Betty's Boutique, Inc.

PROBLEMS

13-1.   *Convertible bonds*

Refer to the 1992 Allegheny Ludlum annual report included in Chapter 1. Find the reference in the notes to the financial statements to the convertible subordinated debentures issued in March 1992.

REQUIRED:

1. If all $100 million of convertible subordinate debentures are converted, how many additional shares of common stock will be issued?
2. Suppose the debentures had been issued with a conversion price of $50. Would they likely have carried a higher or lower interest rate? Explain your answer.

13-2.   *Pricing of bonds: effective interest method*

On January 1, 1995, the Clinton Company sold its 10% bonds that had a face value of $5,000,000. Interest is payable at June 30 and December 31 each year. The bonds mature on December 31, 1997. The bonds were sold to yield a rate of 8% per year, compounded semiannually.

REQUIRED:

1. Calculate the proceeds from the issuance of the bonds.
2. Prepare an amortization schedule for the bonds using the effective interest method.

13-3.   *Early retirement of bonds*

On December 1, 1995, the Reagan Company issued its 7%, $12,000,000 face value bonds, due November 1, 1998, for $12,175,000, plus accrued interest. Interest is payable on November 1 and May 1. On July 1, 1997, Reagan reacquired the bonds at 98, plus accrued interest. Reagan appropriately uses the straight-line method for the amortization of bond premium because the results do not materially differ from using the interest method.

REQUIRED:

Prepare a schedule to compute the gain or loss on this early extinguishment of debt. Show supporting computations in good form. Ignore income taxes.

13-4.   *Issuance of note: extinguishment of debt*

On October 1, 1995, Carter Corp. issued a long-term note and received $101,930 in cash. The terms of the note are as follows:

Face value	$100,000
Maturity date	September 30, 2000
Interest payment dates	March 30, September 30
Stated annual rate of interest	10.5%
Effective annual rate	10.0%
Call price	103

Note: All interest rates are annual rates, compounded semiannually. Carter uses the effective interest rate method.

REQUIRED:

1. Prepare a journal entry to record the issuance of the note.
2. Calculate interest expense for the fiscal years ended December 31, 1995 and 1996.
3. Suppose the note is called for redemption on April 1, 1999. Prepare a journal entry to record the extinguishment of the debt.

13-5.   *Troubled debt restructuring: modification of terms*

Ford Technology Inc. (FTI) borrowed $500,000 from First National Bank & Trust of Denver on September 1, 1995. The loan is to be repaid in 12 equal quarterly installments of $50,231 for an effective rate of 12% per year, compounded quarterly. The installment payments are due November 30, February 28, May 31, and August 31, each year through August 31, 1998.

FTI makes the first five payments as scheduled; but on February 28, 1997, FTI is in financial distress and is unable to make the payment due that day. The bank forgives the payment due that day and FTI agrees to make all remaining payments as scheduled.

REQUIRED:

1. Calculate the carrying value of FTI's obligation to First National Bank & Trust of Denver on February 28, 1997, the date the loan agreement is modified.
2. Prepare a journal entry to record the troubled debt restructuring in FTI's accounts on that date.
3. Prepare a journal entry to record the quarterly payment made by FTI on May 31, 1995.

13-6.   *Issuance of note for noncash asset: troubled debt restructuring*

On May 1, 1995, Nixon Builders, Inc. purchased some machinery from Southwest Supply Corp. by issuing a three-year, $100,000 note with interest stated at 6% per year, payable on April 30 of each year. While the fair market value of the machinery is not determinable, the firm estimates that the firm's annual cost of borrowing over three years is 12%.

REQUIRED:

1. Prepare a journal entry to record the purchase of the machinery and issuance of the note on May 1, 1995.
2. Prepare a journal entry to record the interest expense for the year ended April 30, 1996, and the payment on that date.
3. On April 30, 1997, Nixon Builders is unable to make the payment due on that date. Southwest Supply Corp. agrees to forgive the interest payment due that day, and Nixon Builders agrees to make all remaining payments as scheduled. Prepare any journal entries necessary for Nixon to record the troubled debt restructuring, interest expense for the year ended April 30, 1998, and final payment of the note and interest.

13-7. *Issuance: retirement of bonds*

On December 1, 1995, Johnson Electric Power Co. issued the following bonds. Note: all interest rates are annual rates compounded semiannually.

Face value:	$5,000,000
Maturity:	November 30, 2020
Stated interest rate:	9.625%
Interest payment dates:	May 31, November 30
Effective rate:	10%

REQUIRED:

1. Calculate the proceeds from this bond issue and show how the issuance of bonds would be recorded.
2. Calculate interest expense to be recognized for the year ended December 31, 1995.
3. Determine the net book value of these bonds on December 1, 1998.
4. Assume the bonds are called at 101 on December 1, 1998. Show how the early retirement of the bonds would be recorded.

13-8. *Zero coupon bonds*

On July 1, 1995, Kennedy Corporation (KC) issued $750 million of zero coupon notes due July 1, 2005. These notes were priced at 25.245% of face value to yield 14.25% to maturity, compounded semiannually.

REQUIRED:

State how the issuance of these notes would affect the amounts reported on the:
1. Balance sheet at December 31, 1995
2. Income statement for the year ended December 31, 1995
3. Statement of cash flows for the year ended December 31, 1995. Note: KC reports cash flows from operating activities in the indirect format.

13-9. *Bond issuance: in-substance defeasance*

On July 1, 1995, Eisenhower Corp. issued the following bonds:

Face value	$5,000,000
Maturity date	June 30, 2005
Stated interest rate	8%
Effective interest rate	10%

Note: All interest rates are annual rates, compounded semiannually.

1. Calculate the proceeds from issuance of the bonds and prepare a journal entry to record the transaction.
2. Calculate interest expense for the year ended December 31, 1995.
3. On July 1, 2000, Eisenhower Corp. undertakes an in-substance defeasance by buying U.S. government securities at a cost of $4.5 million and placing them irrevocably into a trust for the sole purpose of making the principal and interest payments on the 8% bonds issued five years earlier. The cash flows generated by these government securities are adequate to meet the payments due on the 8% bonds. Prepare a journal entry to record the transaction.

HUMANA INC.

The following information is taken from the 1988 annual report of Humana Inc.:

	1988	1987	1986
	(dollars in thousands)		
Income before extraordinary item and cumulative effect of a change in accounting principle	$227,040	$182,839	$54,452
Extraordinary loss on early extinguishment of debt, net of income tax of $9,597 (Note 6)	(16,133)	–	–
Cumulative effect on prior years of a change in accounting principle for retirement plan actuarial gains, net of income tax of $9,645	16,214	–	–
Net income	$227,121)	$182,839	$54,452

Note 6 (In Part): Long-Term Debt

A summary of long-term debt follows ($000):

	1988	1987
Senior collateral debt, 6% to 15% (rates, generally fixed, average 10.4%), payable in periodic installments through 2007	$ 227,787	$ 258,951
Other senior debt, 8.3% to 13.8% (rates, generally fixed, average 12%), payable in periodic installments through 2013	443,540	577,941
Commercial paper, 8.3% composite effective rate	369,689	191,933
Subordinated debt, 5% to 9.5% (rates, all fixed, average 9.3%), payable in periodic installments through 1999	2,282	64,267
8% convertible subordinated debentures, payable in annual installments from 1994 to 2009, conversion price of $37.80 per share	200,000	200,000
	1,243,298	1,293,092
Amounts due within one year	32,680	55,626
Long-term debt	$1,210,618	$1,237,466

During the first quarter of 1988, the Company retired approximately $160 million of certain long-term debt with an average interest rate of 15% primarily through issuance of commercial paper. In order to limit the Company's exposure to future increases in interest rates on the commercial paper, the Company entered into agreements under which interest rates will approximate 8%. The first agreement, in the amount of $110 million, expires in 1997, while the remaining $50 million will expire in 1993.

Borrowings under the commercial paper programs are classified as long-term debt due to the credit available under the three revolving credit agreements discussed below and the Company's intention to refinance these borrowings on a long-term basis.

REQUIRED:

1. Prepare a schedule that explains the change in the balance in long-term debt from December 31, 1987, to December 31, 1988. State clearly any assumptions you make in your analysis.
2. Calculate the extent to which Humana Inc. is better or worse off as a result of the $160 million debt refinancing.

CASE 13.2

BAKER HUGHES INCORPORATED

	1988	1987
	($000)	
Total current liabilities	$610,171	$683,502
Long-term debt (Note 6)	440,007	460,767
Deferred income taxes	73,373	73,407
Other long-term liabilities	21,485	28,350
Minority interest	11,002	27,086

NOTES TO CONSOLIDATED FINANCIAL STATEMENTS

6 (In Part): Indebtedness:

Long-term debt at September 30, 1988 and 1987 consisted of the following:

(In Thousands of Dollars)	1988	1987
Commercial paper		$ 4,475
Zero Coupon Guaranteed Notes due 1992 with an effective interest rate of 14.48%, net of unamortized discount of $37,616 ($49,026 in 1987)	$ 61,419	57,695
6.00% Debentures due 2002 with an effective interest rate of 14.66%, net of unamortized discount of $113,910 ($116,573 in 1987)	111,090	108,427
4.125% Swiss Franc 200 million Bonds due 1996 (principal and interest payments hedged through a currency swap at an effective interest rate of 7.82%)	103,177	102,503
9% Debentures due November 1, 2008	36,459	47,375
9.5% Convertible Subordinated Debentures due December 15, 2006 convertible into common stock at $58.91 per share	99,171	99,125
Convertible Subordinated Debentures due through 1994 with an interest rate at September 30, 1988 of prime on $1,308 and LIBOR 022 -5/8 % on $9,724 (see Note 8)	11,032	9,711
Other indebtedness with an average interest rate of 8.9% at September 30, 1988	17,659	31,456
Total long-term debt	$440,007	$460,767

Redemption of the Zero Coupon Notes due 1992 and the 6% Debentures due 2002 may be made at the option of the Company, in whole or in part, at any time at par plus accrued interest. Furthermore, the Zero Coupon Notes due 1992 may be redeemed prior to maturity at prices (expressed as a percentage of principal amount) of 57.16% at September 30, 1988 and scaling upward over time to 86.95% (in each case together with accrued amortization of original issue discount) in the event of certain changes affecting United States or Netherlands Antilles taxation.

The 9% Debentures due November 1, 2008 have a $2,400,000 per annum sinking fund requirement beginning November 1, 1989 and may be redeemed by paying a premium which decreases proportionally from 4.8% at November 1, 1988 until it is eliminated in 2003. The 9.5% Debentures due December 15, 2006 have a $5,000,000 per annum sinking fund requirement beginning December 15, 1992 and may be redeemed by paying a premium which decreases proportionally from 3.45% at December 15, 1988 until it is eliminated in 1992. Optional payments, not to exceed the amounts of the mandatory sinking funds requirements, may be made in addition to the mandatory payments. During 1988, the Company repurchased $11,060,000 of its 9% Debentures due 2008 and $7,685,000 principal amount of its Zero Coupon Guaranteed Notes due 1992. The net gain on these transactions was not significant.

The provisions of the notes, debentures, bonds and unsecured credit agreements have an effect on the ability of the Company to, without prior written consent, among other things, incur borrowings, sell certain assets, pay cash dividends, acquire other businesses and purchase the Company's capital stock. At September 30, 1988, the Company could pay dividends and purchase the Company's common stock up to an amount not exceeding $83,961,000.

At September 30, 1988, long-term debt was due in aggregate annual installments of $10,384,000; $4,489,000; $3,027,000; $64,254,000; and $7,934,000 in each of the five years in the period ending September 30, 1993.

During 1988 and 1987, the maximum aggregate short-term borrowings outstanding at any month-end were $62,396,000 and $104,847,000, respectively; the average aggregate short-term borrowings outstanding based on quarter-end balances were $47,110,000 and $63,660,000, respectively; and the weighted average interest rates were 16.6% and 22.6%, respectively. The average interest rates on short-term borrowings outstanding at September 30, 1988 and 1987 were 15.5% and 17.6%, respectively. Throughout the year and at September 30, 1988, substantially all of the Company's short-term borrowings were outside of the United States and denominated in currencies other than the U.S. dollar. A significant portion of such borrowings were in high inflation rate countries in Latin America where such borrowings are incurred as a hedge of a net asset position.

REQUIRED:

1. Prepare a schedule explaining why the balance of Zero Coupon Guaranteed Notes due 1992 increased to $ 61,419,000 at September 30, 1988, from $57,695,000 at September 30, 1987.
2. Prepare a schedule explaining why the balance of 6.00% Debentures due 2002 increased to $111,090,000 at September 30, 1988, from $108,427,000 at September 30, 1987.
3. Calculate the approximate total interest expense on long-term debt for fiscal 1988.
4. What is "The purpose of the provisions of the notes, debentures, bonds and unsecured credit agreements that have an effect on the ability of the Company to, without prior written consent, among other things, incur borrowings, sell certain assets, pay cash dividends, acquire other businesses and purchase the Company's capital stock"?

CHAPTER 14

Stockholders' Equity: Capital Formation

Stockholders' equity represents the value of resources provided by investors who hold a residual claim on the corporate entity's cash flows and assets. In general, equity claims differ from those of debt holders in several important ways. In the event of a corporate liquidation, where all assets are either sold or distributed to various claimants, equity holders usually do not receive any distributions unless all debt claims are fully satisfied. In addition, debt holders have a right to demand payment of obligations at specific times; and should the corporation be unable to pay these obligations when due, debt holders can force the company into bankruptcy. Equity holders usually do not have the right to demand payments from the corporation. While debt holders have first claim to payments of obligations, they also have an upper limit on how much cash they can receive. There already exists at least one class of equity investors whose potential cash flows from the corporation have unlimited upside potential.

A corporation's equity claims need not be represented by a single type of security. Exhibit 14.1 is an excerpt of the stockholders' equity accounts of James River Corporation. James River discloses the existence of at least three different types of equity claims:

1. Redeemable preferred stock
2. Nonredeemable preferred stock
3. Common stock

In this and the following chapters, we seek to understand why different classes of equity securities arise and how these differences reflect themselves in the corporations' financial reports. In addition, other stockholders' equity accounts exist for additional paid-in capital and retained earnings. We also seek to understand what these accounts represent and how transactions and events during the period are reflected in the reported amounts.

EXHIBIT 14.1
James River
Corporation—
Stockholders' Equity
Accounts

JAMES RIVER CORPORATION
Stockholders' Equity Accounts
As of April 24, 1988 and April 26, 1987
(dollars in millions)

	1988	1987
Preferred stock		
Redeemable preferred stock	$ 4,918	$ 8,235
Nonredeemable preferred stock	300,000	100,000
Common stock, $.10 par value; shares outstanding, 1988—81,193,394 and 1987—82,353,560	8,119	8,235
Additional paid-in capital	1,229,507	1,260,720
Retained earnings	639,851	478,243

In general, accounting for activities relating to stockholders' equity can be broken down into two basic categories:

1. **Capital formation**, which relates to raising new equity capital
2. **Corporate distributions**, which relate to the distribution of corporate assets or additional equity claims to shareholders

This chapter addresses issues that arise in the capital formation process, while Chapter 15 takes up issues relating to corporate distributions. In addition, a few miscellaneous issues that do not fall readily into either of these two basic categories are discussed at the end of Chapter 15.

AN OVERVIEW OF THE BASIC REPORTING CATEGORIES FOR STOCKHOLDERS' EQUITY

As currently constructed, the value of stockholders' equity reported in corporate financial statements can be broken down into three major categories:

1. Contributed capital
2. Retained earnings
3. Other special valuation accounts

Contributed capital is the amount of equity capital corporations raise through sale of their equity securities. *Retained earnings* represents the corporations' accumulated earnings that have been reinvested in additional assets instead of distributed to shareholders as dividends.

In general, accounting practices in the United States stipulate that companies must report the effects of all events and transactions as part of income unless they involve:

1. The issuance or repurchase of equity, or
2. Distributions to shareholders under their rights as equity holders

This has resulted in a fairly simple breakdown of stockholders' equity for presentation in the balance sheet.

However, in recent years, several accounting pronouncements have created special equity accounts that accumulate the effects of certain events and transactions, which are excluded from net income for other reasons. These include situations where the aggregate market value of a noncurrent portfolio of marketable debt securities being held to maturity is below the aggregate cost of the portfolio (discussed in Chapter 16) and situations in which minimum liability requirements relating to obligations under defined benefit pension plans are required (discussed in Chapter 18). In addition, when foreign subsidiaries are consolidated with U.S. parent corporations, the effects of translating the financial statements of the foreign subsidiaries into U.S. dollar equivalents may result in a *cumulative translation gain or loss*. Understanding the nature and purpose of these other special equity accounts requires an examination of the types of transactions that spawn them. Equity accounts relating to long-term investments and the minimum liability under defined benefit pensions plans will be covered later. The topic of foreign currency translation is beyond the scope of this text and will not be covered.

Exhibit 14.2 presents an excerpt from Allegheny Ludlum's balance sheet as it appeared in the 1992 report to shareholders. An examination of this disclosure indicates that the company did not have any of the other equity valuation allowances relating to long-term investments, foreign operations, etc., to report in either of the two years presented. In addition, while the company has two classes of equity shares authorized, it appears that the preferred stock has not been issued.

Contributed Capital

Contributed capital can be further subdivided into two components:

1. Legal capital
2. Additional paid-in capital

Legal capital is the minimum amount exchanged for the shares issued. Historically, legal capital could not be distributed to shareholders as divi-

---

ALLEGHENY LUDLUM CORPORATION AND SUBSIDIARIES
Presentation of Shareholders' Equity
(dollars in thousands)

	1992	1991
SHAREHOLDERS' EQUITY		
Preferred stock, par value $1: authorized—50,000,000 shares; issued—none		
Common stock, par value $.10: authorized—100,000,000 shares; issued—33,862,433 shares	$ 3,386	$ 3,386
Additional capital	164,262	164,194
Retained earnings (after adoption of FAS No. 106 in 1992)	113,169	220,544
Common stock in treasury at cost—994,294 and 1,002,661 shares	(23,873)	(23,635)
Total Shareholders' Equity	$256,944	$364,489

EXHIBIT 14.2
Allegheny Ludlum Corporation and Subsidiaries— Presentation of Shareholders' Equity

dends unless the corporations were liquidated. Legal capital is represented by the par, or stated value, of the equity securities issued. **Additional paid-in capital** (also referred to as *paid-in surplus*, *capital in excess of par*, and several other descriptive titles) represents amounts contributed to the corporation in excess of the legal capital of the shares issued. Referring again to Exhibit 14.2, Allegheny Ludlum reported $3.386 million of common stock at par and $164.262 million for additional paid-in capital for 1992.

Retained Earnings

Retained earnings is the corporation's accumulated net income that has not been distributed to shareholders via dividends or other capital transactions. The distinction between contributed capital and retained earnings was important in the past when corporation law sometimes placed a maximum limit on the size of corporation distributions to shareholders based on the balance in retained earnings. Current corporation laws have made this distinction less important. We will take up this issue in more detail in Chapter 15. Referring to Exhibit 14.2, Allegheny Ludlum reported a balance in retained earnings of $113.169 million at the end of 1992.

Treasury Stock

When corporations repurchase their shares from investors, they can elect to retire the shares or place them in the status of treasury stock. *Retirement* of stock converts previously issued and outstanding shares to the status of unissued stock, similar to shares that have never been issued. **Treasury stock** represents the value of shares that have been issued, and repurchased, but not retired by the corporation.

Since the purchase of treasury stock requires corporations to distribute assets to former shareholders to acquire the stock, it is a form of corporate distribution and is discussed in detail in Chapter 15. How corporations present treasury stock in their balance sheets varies slightly, depending on the preferences of managers regarding the form of the balance sheet and the legal status of the shares held in treasury, which is dictated by state law. Treasury stock can be disclosed as a reduction of contributed capital, similar to the effects of retirement of stock, or it can be represented as a reduction of total stockholders' equity. The latter treatment is based on the premise that treasury stock represents a reduction of equity through a distribution to shareholders, regardless of whether the distribution is related to contributed capital or retained earnings.

Allegheny Ludlum elected to disclose the value of treasury shares as a reduction in total stockholders' equity. Referring to Exhibit 14.2, the reduction of stockholders' equity for treasury stock is reported as $23.873 million at the end of 1992.

CORPORATIONS AND STATE CORPORATION LAWS

The formation, governance, and activities of corporations are ultimately controlled by state corporation laws. Each state is free to adopt whatever legislation it deems appropriate to regulate this activity. State corporation laws vary but generally set forth the following:

1. How a corporation is started
2. The existence and maintenance of legal capital
3. The ability of corporations to make corporate distributions to shareholders
4. How and when corporations can sell or repurchase their securities
5. The types of equity securities that can be created

All states require a corporation to file a formal document with the state where the corporation is to be located. This document, called the **articles of incorporation**, sets forth basic rules regarding the conduct of the corporation's business, the corporation's location of legal residence, the names of the major parties involved in the formation, and the types of securities that the corporation can legally issue as equity claims.

The formation of a corporation creates a legal "person," responsible for its own acts, separate and distinct from the individuals who invest in the company through the purchase of shares. Because they are separate and distinct from their corporation, shareholders are granted **limited liability**. Limited liability implies that if the corporation is unable to pay its bills, then its creditors cannot demand the shareholders to pay them out of their own pockets.

SEPARATION OF OWNERSHIP AND CONTROL—THE ROLE OF LIMITED LIABILITY

Limited liability encourages the separation of ownership and control of corporations. **Separation of ownership and control** refers to the ability to hire professional managers to run corporations without requiring day-to-day supervision by shareholders. To appreciate how limited liability encourages separation of ownership and control, consider the following example. You own a business but find that your time is too valuable in other areas to run the day-to-day operations of the company. If limited liability were not available and you were to hire a manager to run the company, each time the manager entered into a loan agreement with the bank or other creditor, you would be *personally* liable for repayment as the owner of the company. Because of this economic exposure, you would be less likely to hire a manager, and/or you would need to monitor the manager more carefully than if you had limited liability for the manager's actions.

The benefits of limited liability can be substantial when large amounts of capital need to be raised from many individuals, all of whom hold a relatively small stake in the company and do not want to be exposed to personal risk for corporate failure. The corporate form of business mitigates some of the need for shareholders' monitoring and facilitates the movement of equity capital from one sector of the economy to the other by providing limited liability.

The separation of ownership and control does not imply that shareholders can ignore corporate governance altogether. All corporations are required to have a governing body, called the **board of directors**, that is elected by shareholders who hold equity securities that carry voting rights. Under corporation laws, the board has sole responsibility for certain actions such as hiring and compensating executives, declaring dividends, and certain other matters regarding the determination of the overall direction of corporate activity. Other forms of stockholder governance include:

1. The requirement that an annual meeting of the shareholders be held to conduct business reserved for shareholders alone
2. The creation of incentives for managers to perform well in directions that shareholders believe are important
3. The production of annual financial reports to provide information regarding corporate performance to investors

TYPES OF EQUITY SECURITIES

Equity securities come in a variety of forms, and each class of equity claims may have different rights. Any allocation of shareholder rights that is acceptable under the laws of the state where the corporation is domiciled can be accomplished by issuing different classes of equity securities. The most pervasive issues that underlie the issuance of multiple classes of equity claims are twofold:

1. The allocation of the residual claim on the corporation's cash flows and assets
2. The allocation of voting rights

While all corporations must have at least one class of equity, voting common stock, they may issue several different classes of common stock. Each class may have a different right to share in dividends or to vote on issues brought before the shareholders. When multiple classes of common stock are created, each class is commonly labeled with a letter (e.g., Class A common or Class B common). To understand some of the reasons for creating multiple classes of common stock, consider a corporation that has grown from a small family business. The descendants of the original founder wish to maintain continued control over the company, but they also wish to issue common shares to provide managers with incentives in the form of stock options or just to raise new equity capital from third-party investors. The creation of a nonvoting class of common stock (call it Class B common), which will share equally in dividends, would provide a means to raise additional equity capital while retaining voting control of the company.

Considerable research has been done on the valuation of the shares of companies using this dual-class common equity structure. As you might expect, the evidence suggests that the nonvoting shares sell at a discount relative to the voting shares. This result is consistent with the intuition that having a say in corporate governance via the right to vote is a valuable feature of share ownership.

The example above is not meant to be comprehensive. A large number of reasons exist for the creation of multiple classes of equity securities. Whatever the reason, allocations of corporate distributions and voting rights are the two basic features of equity ownership that vary across equity classes. Creating multiple classes of common stock is only one way to distribute the rights of the equity holders. It is also possible for corporations to issue preferred stock as an alternative to multiple classes of common stock. The one characteristic that distinguishes common and preferred stock is the rights of the holders upon liquidation of the corporation. All common shareholders rank last in their rights to any distributions at liquidation. That is, preferred shareholders rank above any common shareholder.

Preferred Stock

Corporations can issue stock that grants its holders preference in receipt of cash upon liquidation. This type of equity security is called **preferred stock,** a claim that ranks above common shares in the event of liquidation and usually has a prior claim to any dividends distributed during a period. Under common law, preferred shareholders are assumed to have voting rights similar to the common shareholders unless otherwise specified.

Preferred stocks contain provisions that define the rights of the preferred shareholders. The more typical of these include:

1. A *nonvoting* provision (although it is possible for preferred stockholders to have superior voting rights to those of the common shareholders).
2. A *liquidation value* representing a specific maximum amount to which each preferred shareholder is entitled in the event the corporation liquidates.
3. A *call price* representing a price at which the corporation can force the preferred shareholder to sell the preferred shares back to the company. Call price provisions are generally not exercisable for a period of a few years after issue.
4. A *cumulative dividend* provision stipulating that if dividends are not declared in one period, they accumulate and must be paid in a later period before dividends on lower-level securities, such as common shares, can be declared.
5. A *convertibility* provision allowing preferred shareholders to convert their holdings to common shares in a pre-specified proportion.
6. A *participation* provision allowing the preferred shareholders to participate with common shareholders in dividend distributions in excess of the preference dividend on the preferred shares, based on a predetermined ratio.

Why Are Multiple Types of Equity Securities Issued?

Since different types of equity securities create different types of claims to the corporation's future cash flows or different rights to influence the nature of future operations, each type of security represents a different set of risks and rewards for investors. For example, the inclusion of a provision for cumulative dividends or convertibility in a preferred stock will generally reduce the risk of preferred stock compared to similar instruments without these provisions. Due to the nature of the liquidation preference, preferred stocks are generally less risky than common stock in the same corporation.

The differences in risk and ability to control the corporation's operations, embedded in different equity securities, induce different incentives for different investor groups. In our earlier discussion of multiple class common stock, retention of voting control was the major reason for creation of a second class of common stock. Exhibit 14.3 describes a situation Kaiser Steel experienced during the 1980s. That situation motivated the creation of a special class of preferred shares. The firm, being in financial difficulty, was able to find new management who believed changes could be made that would stabilize the firm. However, the new managers wanted to benefit from their efforts if they were successful by holding the firm's common equity. While the existing shareholders were willing to let the new managers try to revive the company, they also did not want to trade away all their claims on the company's future value. In particular, the existing shareholders wanted some means to dislodge the incoming managers if they proved unsuccessful. The compromise solution was the creation of a special class of preferred stock with special rights as described in Exhibit 14.3.

Some forms of equity security have been created for reasons that appear related principally to financial reporting advantages. In the late 1970s and early 1980s, the issuance frequency of a special form of preferred stock, referred to as

EXHIBIT 14.3 Kaiser Steel Creation of a Special Class of Preferred Stock	**KAISER STEEL** **Creation of a Special Class of Preferred Stock**
	In the 1980s, Kaiser Steel was reorganized as part of an acquisition of the company by J.A. Frates (an Oklahoma businessperson). In the acquisition, the old voting common shareholders of Kaiser exchanged all their common stock for a new form of preferred stock. This preferred stock had several peculiar characteristics. Under the terms of the stock issue, if Kaiser failed to pay the preferred stock dividend over any consecutive two-year period, the preferred shareholders would be given the right to vote and could replace the board of directors and managers of the company. Other provisions required monies to be set aside to repurchase the preferred stock on an annual basis. What purpose did this serve?
	Kaiser had been a major steel manufacturer during the 1950s and 1960s. More recently, the company had experienced a financial decline. Mr. Frates offered to purchase all of Kaiser's common stock by exchanging it for the special class of preferred stock that was created for the sole purpose of removing all the previous common shareholders from their status as voting residual claimants. Apparently, Mr. Frates believed that Kaiser could be brought out of its difficulties, or liquidated, in a profitable way. However, he did not want to share these potential benefits with all the other common shareholders by leaving them in place as voting common shareholders.
	On the other hand, the outside shareholders were not going to give up their voting power for nothing. In this case, the cost to Mr. Frates of obtaining full voting control was to make the old common shareholders new equity claim on the company's cash flow a higher ranking claim than it would have been as a common stock claim. This allowed greater protection for the old common shareholders since the new management (now controlled by Mr. Frates) could not declare any common dividends or make any liquidation distributions to common shareholders before all the preferred stockholders were paid in full. It also appears that the provision regarding reinstatement of voting power was necessary to provide sufficient incentive for these common shareholders to sell out. This suggests that while the former common shareholders were willing to give Mr. Frates some time to pull Kaiser out of its difficulties, they were not willing to forgo receipt of cash flows for more than two years before taking back control of the company.

mandatorily redeemable preferred stock, increased substantially. Mandatorily redeemable preferred stock had rights similar to those for standard preferred shares, expect that the corporation set a date on which all such shares must be retired. This gave the preferred shares many of the same attributes as bonds. What distinguished the mandatorily redeemable preferred stock from a bond was principally investors' rights in the event of liquidation. As with other preferred stocks, the holders of the mandatorily redeemable preferred would rank below the debt holders in the event of liquidation.

Corporations that issued this form of equity classified the capital contributed as equity capital and increased stockholders' equity accordingly. This classification was a hotly debated issue in accounting and financial reporting. Many accountants and members of the SEC viewed the economic substance of mandatorily redeemable preferred as equivalent to debt and wanted it classified in the long-term debt section of the balance sheet, not as part of stockholders' equity. Proponents of this view noted that the companies that were issuing these types of securities typically did not face a significant probability of bankruptcy. Also, the proponents claimed that the use of this security was simply a ruse to improve debt to equity ratios, while making commitments of future cash flows that were essentially equivalent to those of debt obligations.

The SEC resolved this debate in 1982 when it required all firms issuing mandatorily redeemable preferred stock to classify the value of this contribution outside of the stockholders' equity section. Therefore this amount was formally removed from the computation of total stockholders' equity. Subsequent to this ruling, the issuance of this type of preferred stock has virtually come to a halt, which strongly suggests that its popularity did not lie in any risk-sharing feature of the security but, rather, its effect on various financial ratios.

CAPITAL FORMATION

A corporation generates equity capital for new investment in one of two ways:

1. Re-investing earnings generated during the current period
2. Selling equity claims

Capital Formation—Reinvested Earnings

The most common source of new capital is reinvested earnings. Whenever companies generate profits from selling their goods and services, the managers and board of directors must decide what to do with the additional resources provided by profits. These resources can be reinvested in the corporations by purchasing new inventory, plant assets, or other assets, or by paying off liabilities and reducing the total outstanding debt. Alternatively, the resources can be distributed to shareholders through any of several means, the most common being a dividend payment.

The difference between raising equity capital via reinvestment of earnings compared to new share issues is that the costs of raising capital are reduced since no new securities need be printed, no registration costs exist, and no attorney's or accountant's fees need be incurred. This makes internally generated capital the most popular source of equity capital for many companies.

Capital Formation—Sale of New Securities

The alternative to internally generated equity is the sale of new securities. Equity securities can be issued in either public or private markets. For public markets, which are regulated by the SEC, equity securities are bought and sold in two different submarkets, either primary markets or secondary markets.

The Primary Market   The **primary market** consists of all new issuances of securities by public corporations. The active players in this market include the issuing corporation, corporate underwriters, brokers and dealers who make up the syndicate used to distribute the new issue, and investors who ultimately purchase the shares. An **underwriter** is a party who takes primary responsibility for lining up purchasers for the shares and insuring that all the registration requirements of the Securities and Exchange Commission are met. These registration requirements are primarily informational filings that must be made available to all potential investors. Included in this packet of information are audited financial statements.

To identify potential investors who will purchase the shares, underwriters typically put together a syndicate of brokers and security dealers who are paid commissions to find investors. Ultimately, the shares are sold to investors who pay the underwriter the issue price of the stock. The underwriters then remit to the issuing corporation the amount raised from the sale, less the commissions the underwriters retain. In some instances, corporations settle the commissions by allowing the underwriters to retain a certain percentage of the shares in the issue instead of directly paying cash.

If the sale of new securities is to be made to a large number of investors, underwriters are typically used because they provide access to a large network of brokers and dealers who can assist in the placement of the new issue. However, underwriters are not required to bring a new equity issue to market; and corporations may avoid underwriters' fees by bringing the share issue directly to the market.

In some cases, the corporation may issue all of the shares of the new issue to a single investor or to a small group of investors. These types of transactions are referred to as *private placements*. Private placements may involve an underwriter or consultant who performs the service of finding individual investors with sufficient capital to absorb such a purchase, but this is not necessary. If the shares are not to be resold for a period of time, private placements do not require extensive filing with the SEC. Consequently, transactions costs for private placements are generally lower due to decreased registration costs and possibly lower placement fees.

The Secondary Market   The **secondary market** is a market for resale. Investors wishing to buy or sell an existing security can enter the secondary market to acquire or dispose of the security of interest. To execute an exchange in the secondary market, investors pay commissions to brokerage firms who have the right to execute trades in the market were the security trades. For example, if shares of Du Pont Corporation are to be sold, these shares are traded on the New York Stock Exchange. Only brokers with a seat on this exchange can trade shares there, and a fee is charged to perform this service. Corporations generally are not active in the secondary market for their own shares. However, on occasion corporations may wish to acquire some of their outstanding shares for retirement or to be held as treasury stock. In addition, corporations can resell their treasury stock in this market.

Transactions Costs

Corporations must bear many costs to bring a new issue to the market. These costs include legal fees, accounting fees, underwriting fees, and other out-of-pocket expenses. These transactions costs, generically referred to as **issue costs**, reduce the net cash generated from the sale of the securities. When corporations incur brokerage costs in the secondary market, these transactions costs are also related to exchanges between the corporations and their shareholders. In either case, transactions costs of this nature should not be charged to expense. Rather, they should be reflected only as a reduction in the value of the capital invested by stockholders.

Other Methods for Issuing Shares

There are other means by which new shares can be issued. Public corporations may attempt to raise capital from existing shareholders by using a rights offering. A **stock right** is a contract that allows the holder to purchase shares of stock at a fixed price over a given period of time. If corporations wish to raise capital from existing shareholders, they can issue rights to each existing shareholder, entitling the holder to purchase additional shares. If the investors exercise these rights, new equity capital is created from the proceeds that the investors must pay (along with the surrender of the right) to acquire additional shares.

Nonpublicly traded corporations often utilize stock subscriptions as a means to issue new shares. A **stock subscription** is a contract to purchase a specified number of shares at a specified price, with the contract to be executed at some future point. These contracts are popular with start-up corporations that seek investors to purchase shares after official operations have begun. While investors may be unwilling to provide capital immediately, or not until the corporation is actually functioning, they may be willing to commit to purchase shares when, and if, this occurs.

Corporations may also issue new equity securities when investors decide to convert other securities into equity by exercising the conversion rights in securities such as stock rights, warrants, convertible debt, or employee stock options. While the issue of employee stock options is left to later chapters where a wide range of employee incentive arrangements are discussed, the effect of the issuance and conversion of other convertible securities is addressed later in this chapter.

Accounting for Stock Issues

The current accounting treatment afforded the issuance of equity securities has its roots in the history of corporation law and the presumption that capital transactions shall be excluded from the determination of net income (codified in ARB No. 43). Early legislation governing the corporate form of business sought to protect creditors by establishing the concept of par (or stated) value. **Par value** indicated the minimum amount of capital that had to be contributed to the company to purchase a share of stock. In addition, par value represented the legal capital of the firm; and corporation law generally did not allow companies to distribute dividends if there was insufficient capital to absorb the effects of the dividend without using the legal capital. In some states, the dividend limitation was extended to requiring sufficient amounts of retained earnings to absorb the effects of the dividend before it could be paid. This requirement preserved both legal capital and additional paid-in capital for the creditors' benefit.

The legal distinction between legal capital, contributed capital, and retained earnings was transferred to the financial statement presentation of contributed capital. This provided financial statement users with information on the relationship among legal capital (par), total contributed capital (par plus additional paid-in capital), and retained earnings. The purpose of this disclosure related directly to the corporations' ability to make distributions to shareholders. Whenever new shares, common or preferred, are issued, the proceeds received for the shares are allocated between legal capital (par or stated value) and an account representing any excess over par value paid for the shares, called **additional paid-in capital**.

For example, assume that on March 24, 1995, Hatteris Corporation sold 1,000,000 shares of its $2 par value common stock for $5. The net proceeds of the sale are $5,000,000 (1,000,000 × $5). Of this total, $2,000,000 (1,000,000 × $2) is allocated to par value, and the balance of $3,000,000 is additional paid-in capital. Hatteris would make the following journal entry to record this transaction:

March 24, 1995:		
Cash	5,000,000	
Common stock—$2 Par		2,000,000
Additional paid-in capital on common		3,000,000
To record the issuance of 1,000,000 shares of $2 par		
common stock at a price of $5/share.		

In states that require par or stated value, shares generally may not be sold for less than par value. However, when such a sale is allowed, the purchaser is contingently liable for the deficit should any creditor seek to collect a claim against the corporation and the corporation had insufficient funds to pay it.[1]

When the articles of incorporation are filed, corporations are free to set par value at any amount. Par value can also be changed after the articles are originally filed by filing an amendment to the articles of incorporation. The par value set by most corporations is a minimal amount (typically anywhere from

---

[1] The contingent liability is subject to the statute of limitations, which typically runs no longer than seven years from the original purchase of the stock.

one cent to one dollar). Consequently, there are no longer cases where the sale of stock need occur at less than par value. In addition, many states have adopted no-par statutes. Under no-par statutes, there is no legal capital, and the entire amount raised from the sale of shares is entered into a common stock account. Assuming that Hatteris was in a no-par state, the issuance of 1,000,000 no-par shares for $5 per share would be recorded as follows:

March 24, 1995:

Cash	5,000,000	
Common stock—no-par		5,000,000
To record the issuance of 1,000,000 shares of no-par		
common stock at a price of $5/share.		

Issuance of Preferred Stock

Corporations may issue preferred stock with a par value, stated value, or without par. In most cases, the dividend on preferred shares is set so that when a new issue is brought to market it sells for par or stated value. This eliminates any need for additional paid-in capital accounts relating to preferred shares. The total number of preferred shares a company can issue is set forth in the articles of incorporation and represents the number of shares authorized.

When preferred stock is issued, the corporation typically allocates proceeds between an account representing the par (or stated) value of the preferred and additional paid-in capital on preferred stock. Variations in reporting practices do exist. For example, some companies report the value of preferred stock at its original issue price without separating the par value from additional paid-in capital. These variations stem from differences in individual state corporation laws regarding the legal treatment of additional paid-in capital from preferred stock, as well as the lack of material variations between the issue price and par or stated value in most preferred stock issues.

Accounting for Issue Costs

Issue costs associated with the sale of new equity securities are a cost of raising capital. Since the effects of capital transactions should not affect income, the appropriate treatment of these costs is to reduce additional paid-in capital by an amount equal to these costs. When corporations use the primary market to sell their shares, the incorporation of the issue costs into additional paid-in capital occurs naturally by recording only the net proceeds from the issue.

For example, assume that on April 1, 1996, Bardo Corporation issues 10,000,000 shares of $1 par common stock for $12 per share. The issue is handled by Investors' Specialists, an underwriter. Investors' Specialists takes a commission of 5% out of the proceeds. In this situation, the underwriter will collect the proceeds of the sale of the stock from the ultimate purchasers, an amount equal to $120,000,000. Out of these proceeds, the underwriter will remit only $114,000,000 ($120,000,000 × 95%) to Bardo Corporation. This amount is net of the commission of $6,000,000, which represents the issue costs. If Bardo makes the following entry, it will have implicitly removed the issue costs from the additional paid-in capital:

April 1, 1996:

Cash	114,000,000	
Common stock at par		10,000,000
Additional paid-in capital		104,000,000

To record the issuance of 10,000,000 shares of $1
par common stock.

In the above entry, the $6,000,000 of underwriter's fees implicitly reduces the amount recorded as additional paid-in capital. Other issue costs, such as attorney's fees or accounting fees, can be charged directly against the additional paid-in capital account.

In some cases, underwriters may accept shares of stock in lieu of cash as compensation for their efforts. For example, assume that instead of accepting a commission in the above example, Investors' Specialists agreed to accept 500,000 shares of stock. In this case, Bardo would receive cash of $12 per share for only 9,500,000 shares, for total proceeds of $114,000,000. Bardo's entry to record the issuance would be identical to the one above.

Nonmonetary Exchanges Involving Stock

Cash is not the only asset a corporation might receive in exchange for its stock. Property, plant, and equipment or even shares of another corporation might be exchanged. Human labor might also be exchanged for shares. When shares are issued in exchange for services (labor), state laws require that the services must have been already performed. Consequently, the shares will represent compensation for services rendered in lieu of cash. It is illegal to issue stock in exchange for future services.

Regardless of the type of noncash consideration exchanged for the shares, the rules for nonmonetary exchanges control the valuation placed on the shares issued. In nonmonetary exchanges, the value of both the items involved in the exchange is based on the value of the item with the more readily ascertainable market value.[2] Suppose that Little Corporation exchanged 10,000 shares of no-par stock for a piece of equipment on October 12, 1994. To record this exchange, Little's first step would be to determine a fair value for the equipment. This value could be established by a direct appraisal of the value of the equipment or imputed through a determination of the value of the 10,000 shares of stock. Whichever estimate of fair value is judged to be more reliable should be used.

Assume that Little Corporation shares are publicly traded at $5 per share. Little's journal entry to record the exchange, based on this value, would appear as:

October 12, 1994:

Equipment	50,000	
Common stock—no-par		50,000

To record the issuance of 10,000 shares of no-par stock in
exchange for equipment.

---

[2] A special problem arises when a nonmonetary exchange occurs between the corporation and its promoters. Promoters are the parties who initially form the corporation and sponsor its early distribution of shares. Since these parties are considered related parties, the value of nonmonetary assets contributed by promoters is recorded at its historical cost basis to the promoter.

Nonmonetary Exchanges and Watered Stock   Nonmonetary exchanges always create problems in valuation. How can the market value of a given asset be ascertained? There are many ways to support an estimate of market price. Information on the selling prices of similar assets may be used, discounted cash flow techniques may be appropriate, or even the use of price level adjusted historical costs might provide a basis for estimation of market value. The development of the estimate is often left to a professional appraiser whose business is to estimate assets' market values.

The market value estimate may be purposefully inflated to make the value of the asset contributed to the firm appear higher and, thus, support the purchase of more shares at any given price. When these situations occur, the stock issued is known as **watered stock** because the valuation of the shares has no firm support. If it can be shown that watered stock was issued, state law will hold the purchaser liable to the corporation for any inflation in the value of the assets contributed, regardless of whether the purchaser continues to hold the shares or sells them. Again, the statute of limitations restricts the time period for which this liability exists.

Capital Formation Through a Rights Offering

In issues of stock rights, corporations distribute rights to purchase shares to their existing shareholders. Generally, the price at which the shares can be purchased must be close to the existing market price when the rights are issued. However, corporation laws do recognize that corporations may pass on some of the savings in issue costs in the form of exercise prices, which are slightly below the current market price. This provides an inducement to shareholders receiving the rights to exercise them. In turn, it increases the likelihood that corporations will obtain the capital they require. Rights can be issued on any type of security, but they are usually convertible into common stock.

Stock rights are generally short-duration securities that expire in a matter of a few weeks from their original issue. They can be sold by the shareholder who receives the right in the original distribution. Stock rights distributions do not directly generate any inflow of resources to the corporation. As a result, no journal entry is made to record an offering of stock rights. When rights are exercised, the exercise price represents the selling price of the shares, which is allocated between par or stated value and additional paid-in capital as required.

As part of what is called a "takeover defense," rights have been used more extensively in recent years. Corporations have issued long-lived rights, which are not exercisable unless some other group attempts to purchase control of the corporation, through share purchases in the secondary market. In many cases, the rights are issued to acquire convertible preferred stock or common stock at a price well below the prevailing market price at the date the stock is purchased. Since these rights are only activated when some other group attempts a takeover, it makes the cost of a takeover more expensive. This additional cost comes from the need to purchase a controlling interest in both the currently outstanding shares and the shares issued as holders convert the rights to purchase shares very cheaply. This may make the takeover too expensive and leaves the company protected.

While the economic purpose of long-term rights is substantially different than the short-term variety, accounting for their issuance is identical. From an accounting and reporting perspective, the important feature of rights issues is that the corporation receives no compensation at the date the rights are issued. Consequently, no exchange of significance to the valuation of stockholders' equity is deemed to have occurred at issue. It will be necessary to incorporate note disclosure, indicating the existence of outstanding long-term rights, so that users are aware of the convertible claim's existence.

Issuing Stock Through the Use of Stock Subscriptions

Many corporations are too small to sell major share issues through organized exchanges. These firms, and those corporations that are just in the formation stage, often use stock subscriptions. As earlier defined, *stock subscription* is a contract to purchase a given number of shares at a given price. It provides corporations with the legal right to collect money from subscribers, and obligates the companies to issue stock when payments are made. In the simplest of cases, the subscription is paid in full at one time, and the shares are issued at payment.

Whether corporations will make any journal entries to record the signing of the subscription contracts depends on the likelihood of collection under the contracts. If collection of the proceeds is reasonably assured, corporations will record receivables at the time the contracts are signed. If collection is highly questionable, no entries will be created.

For example, assume Minot Corp. has entered into a subscription agreement on January 12, 1995, with Bill Willis for the purchase of 10,000 shares of stock at $3 per share. The stock has a $2 par value and collection is reasonably assured. At the time the subscription contract is entered into, Minot records a receivable for the purchase price as follows:

January 12, 1993:		
Subscriptions receivable	30,000	
Subscribed stock at par		20,000
Additional paid-in capital on common		10,000
To record the receipt of a subscription contract for 10,000		
shares of $2 par common stock to be sold at $3/share.		

The additional paid-in capital adjustment is recorded at the time the subscription contract is signed, not at the date the shares are issued. The subscribed stock account is an equity account that represents the commitment of the corporation to issue shares. For nonpublic companies, the subscription receivable can be classified as an asset or a contra-equity account. If the receivable is classified as an asset, the classification as current or noncurrent depends only on how long a period will pass before payment is expected. The classification of the receivable as a contra-equity account is designed to prevent overstatement of equity and assets prior to the actual collection of the proceeds required to obtain the shares. For publicly listed corporations, the SEC requires that subscription receivables be classified as a contra-equity account; and many practitioners transfer that requirement to their nonpublicly listed clients.

Assume that on February 1, 1995, Bill Willis paid the balance of the subscription receivable and the shares were issued. Minot's following two entries capture these events:

February 1, 1995:

Cash	30,000	
Subscriptions receivable		30,000
To record the payment of the subscription contract.		
Subscribed stock at par	20,000	
Common stock—$1 par		20,000
To record the issuance of the shares under the subscription contract.		

In some cases, the collection of proceeds occurs in installments. When installment payments are used, there are two typical, different contractual arrangements regarding the issuance of shares:

1. Shares are issued in proportion to the cash paid.
2. No shares are issued until all cash is paid.

Under the second arrangement, failure to pay all amounts due can result in either a refund of installment payments made to date and nonissuance of shares or forfeiture of all installment payments made to date and nonissuance of shares.

Using the previous example, assume that Bill Willis agreed to make two payments of $15,000 each on January 22, 1995 and February 1, 1995. Further assume that Bill makes the first payment but defaults on the second. The journal entries to record the subscription contract will be unaffected by the need for installments as long as their collection was likely when the agreement was originated. In all of the cases described above, Minot would record receipt of the first installment payment as follows:

January 22, 1995:

Cash	15,000	
Subscriptions receivable		15,000
To record the receipt of the first installment.		

The following entries reflect the treatment of the remaining events under the alternatives:

Shares issued in proportion to cash paid
   January 22, 1995:

Subscribed stock	10,000	
Common stock at par		10,000
To record the issuance of shares after the first installment payment.		

   February 1, 1995:

Subscribed stock	10,000	
Additional paid-in capital on common	5,000	
Subscriptions receivable		15,000
To record default on the second installment.		

Refund of previous installments
    February 1, 1995:

Subscribed stock	20,000	
Additional paid-in capital on common	10,000	
Subscriptions receivable		15,000
Cash		15,000

To record default on the second installment and refund of first installment.

Forfeiture of previous installments
    February 1, 1995:

Subscribed stock	20,000	
Additional paid-in capital		5,000
Subscriptions receivable		15,000

To record default on the second installment and forfeiture of first installment.

Capital Formation—Donated Capital

Donated capital arises from the contribution of assets to corporations without a commensurate issuance of equity claims. On occasion, shareholders may donate assets to corporations. However, the more common situations arise from inducements provided by local governments to encourage corporations to locate facilities in particular areas. Donations of land or other assets for this purpose are recorded as increases to the related asset accounts, based on the fair value of the contributed asset and a credit to additional paid-in capital from donations.

Capital Formation From Issuance of Warrants

A *stock warrant* is a security that allows the holder to purchase a pre-determined number of shares of stock at a given price for a set period of time. While similar to stock rights, warrants differ in two fundamental ways:

1. The duration of these securities is much longer, sometimes several years.
2. Corporations generally issue warrants in exchange for consideration.

When warrants are issued for consideration, a journal entry is necessary to record the asset received and the addition to contributed capital. For example, assume that on May 10, 1994, Kaylite Corporation issued 5,000 warrants to purchase its $2 par common stock for $5. Each warrant entitled the holder to purchase one share of common stock. The warrants were issued for $20,000 and expire three years from the date of issue. Kaylite would record this transaction as follows:

March 10, 1994:

Cash	20,000	
Additional paid-in capital from outstanding warrants		20,000

To record the issuance of 5,000 warrants.

The purchaser may elect to exercise the warrants, let them lapse, or sell them to another investor. Any warrant that allows an investor to purchase shares at less than the current market price at the latest exercise date of the warrant will be exercised, since the investor can immediately sell the shares for a higher price. Warrants whose exercise price is always above the market price will never be exercised. If the warrants are exercised, the holder of the warrants must surrender these securities and pay $5 per share for the 5,000 shares to be exchanged. Suppose the warrants were exercised at maturity, Kaylite's journal entry to record this transaction would appear as follows:

```
May 10, 1997:
Cash                                                        25,000
Additional paid-in capital from outstanding warrants        20,000
    Common stock at par                                              10,000
    Additional paid-in capital on common                             35,000
To record the exercise of all warrants and issuance of stock.
```

In the event that the warrants expire, the monies originally paid for the warrants become a permanent part of additional paid-in capital. Kaylite's journal entry to reflect this might appear as follows:

```
May 10, 1997:
Additional paid-in capital from outstanding warrants        20,000
    Additional paid-in capital from expired warrants                 20,000
To record the expiration of outstanding warrants.
```

Capital Formation—Issuance of Compound Securities

At times corporations may issue several securities as a bundle, referred to as a **compound security**. A typical example of this is the issuance of bonds with detachable warrants. In such an issue, the purchaser receives a bond with a face value and face interest rate that set forth the future cash flows to be received and a set of warrants that allow the purchaser to acquire equity securities also. Since part of this bundle is equity and part is debt, it is appropriate to allocate a portion of the purchase price to each separate element of the package. This allocation is accomplished using the relative fair values of the two securities.[3]

For example, assume that bonds with a face value of $100,000 were sold on January 12, 1993, along with warrants for 10,000 shares of common stock (warrants for 100 shares of common went with each $1,000 face value bond). The total proceeds of the issue were $120,000. The market value of the bond was $98,000, and the market value of a warrant was $2 each ($20,000 for all the warrants). The warrants expire on January 12, 1995. The proceeds will be allocated as follows:

$$\text{To Debt:} \quad [\$98,000 \div (\$98,000 + \$20,000)] \times (\$120,000) = \$99,661$$

$$\text{To Warrants:} \quad [\$20,000 \div (\$98,000 + \$20,000)] \times (\$120,000) = \$20,339$$

---

[3] Note that this allocation process for bundled securities is identical to the allocation of value when assets are acquired for a lump-sum (excluding the acquisition of goodwill) as discussed in Chapter 10.

The total proceeds in this example are not equal to the sum of the market values of the two securities. This situation arises because the measures of the relative market values may come from sources that are not necessarily contemporaneous with the sale of the compound security. If trading prices for each security are used, market trades in these securities may not occur for some time after the initial issue. If new information arrives in the market over the interim period, the underlying market values may be changing without any trading to allow us to observe the price changes. Alternatively, the allocation may be done on the basis of estimated values for the securities (appraisals done by an expert in valuation), but even here the estimates may be acquired prior to issuance and not reflect the actual price paid for the bundle.

Once the allocation of the proceeds has taken place, the following journal entry would be used to record the issuance of the joint securities (assuming issuance on an interest payment date and without issue costs):

January 12, 1993:		
Cash	120,000	
Discount on bonds payable	339	
Bonds payable		100,000
Additional paid-in capital from outstanding warrants		20,339
To record the issuance of the bonds and warrants.		

Given the discount of $339, an effective interest rate on the bonds would have to be computed, and the interest expense would be recorded in the future using this effective rate. The additional paid-in capital from outstanding warrants would be treated identically to amounts that arise from the straight sale of warrants.

Accounting for Convertible Securities

Corporations often issue debt that is convertible into some form of equity claim or preferred stock that is convertible into a common stock claim. When convertible debt is issued, the price paid for the security is partly due to the value of the underlying debt claim and partly due to the underlying equity claim represented by the conversion feature. In the case of a convertible debt security, it is conceptually possible to determine the value of the conversion feature independent of the value of the underlying debt security. This would require subtracting an estimate of the present value of the promised cash flows under the terms of the debt security from the total proceeds of the convertible debt issue.

For example, assume convertible bonds with a face value of $100,000, paying interest at 10% semiannually, were issued for $110,000. Bonds with the same face interest rate and risk level as these without the conversion feature were selling at $98,000. The difference, $12,000, represents the value of the equity conversion option and could be recorded in the equity section of the balance sheet. However, generally accepted accounting principles do not allow this type of treatment when the compound security cannot be broken down into separate parts. In this case, the conversion option cannot be traded separately from the debt security. Consequently, the entire value of the debt issue must be recorded as a liability when the debt is issued.

Convertible Debt

Owners of convertible debt generally have little incentive to exercise the conversion feature prior to the maturity of the debt or to take advantage of the last opportunity to exercise, whichever comes first. The debt's market value will reflect the ability to convert into equity; and when the equity value is high, the debt will trade at higher prices. By not converting, convertible debt holders keep their options open. If equity prices fall, investors can rely on the cash flows as debt holders instead of having to rely on cash flows to equity as the only source of value.

Corporate management may wish to force conversion of a convertible bond if possible. The corporate managers' motivation for this may be to reduce the burden of interest payments to facilitate short-term cash flow management or to reduce the corporations' leverage position due to debt covenant restrictions or other operating considerations. In general, there are no means for corporate management to trigger conversion of debt unless the debt is also callable. A call feature allows management to accelerate the maturity of the debt. If the call is executed at a time when the value of the equity into which the debt can be converted is larger than the debt's call price, debt holders will convert. This is one of the economic advantages of placing call prices in convertible securities.

Regardless of its timing, the conversion of debt into equity can be accounted for by two alternative methods: book value or market value. The book value method transfers the remaining book value of all the debt-related accounts (bond payable, premium or discount, unamortized issue costs, and any interest payable) into the contributed capital accounts. No gain or loss is recorded. This approach is the most commonly used. Recording the exchange in this fashion focuses on the equity portion of the transaction and seeks to avoid effects on income due to the issuance of equity.

The market value method revalues the debt to market value and recognizes any gain or loss in the revaluation before transferring the new value in the debt accounts to contributed capital. This method treats the debt's liquidation as an early extinguishment, recognizing any gain or loss, and then an issuance of equity replaces the revalued debt. Any gain or loss under the market value method must be reported as an extraordinary item.

The following example amplifies the procedures for recording the conversion of a convertible debt. Madrona Inc. has outstanding $2,000,000 of face value, 6%, convertible debt. Associated with this debt is a remaining issue discount of $230,000 and unamortized issue costs of $50,000 as of January 1, 1995. Interest is paid on March 1 and September 1 of each year. The bonds mature on March 1, 2000. Each $1,000 face value bond is convertible into 20 shares of $5 par common stock. Assume that on January 1, 1995, bondholders converted $500,000 of these bonds into common stock. On January 1, 1995, the stock was trading at $125 per share, but the bonds were never traded on an organized exchange. How should this transaction be recorded?

Under either method of reporting this conversion, Madrona would first need to ascertain the net book value of the bonds converted, along with the proportionate share of any unamortized issue costs relating to the converted bonds. In this example, only 25% ($500,000 ÷ $2,000,000) of the bonds are converted, so only 25% of the accrued interest payable, discount, and deferred issue costs would be included in the determination of the carrying value of the bond, as follows:

Par value of bonds converted	$500,000
Share of deferred issue costs .25 × $50,000	(12,500)
Share of accrued interest $500,000 × .06 × 4/12	10,000
Share of unamortized bond discount .25 × $230,00	(57,500)
Net carrying value	$440,000

In addition, Madrona would need to determine the number of common shares to be issued and the associated par value of these shares:

Number of Bonds Being Converted:

($500,000 total face value) ÷ ($1,000 face value per bond) = 500 bonds being converted

Number of Shares Being Issued:

(500 bonds converted) × (20 common shares per bond) = 10,000 common shares being issued

Par Value of Shares Being Issued:

($5 par) × (10,000 shares) = $50,000 of total par value

Given the above computations, Madrona's journal entry to record the conversion under each of the two methods would appear as follows:

January 1, 1995:

	Cost Method		Market Value Method	
Bonds payable	500,000		500,000	
Accrued interest payable	10,000		10,000	
Extraordinary loss on early retirement by conversion	n/a		810,000	
Deferred issue costs		12,500		12,500
Discount on bonds payable		57,500		57,500
Common stock at par		50,000		50,000
Additional paid-in capital on common		390,000		1,200,000

To record the conversion of 500 bonds into 10,000 shares of common.

To apply the market value method in the above example, the market value of the bonds must be inferred from the market value of the shares into which the bonds are converted since no trading price for the debt was observable. Consequently, the market value of the bonds was determined as follows:

Market Value of Shares Being Issued:

$125 per share of market value × 10,000 shares issued = $1,250,000 of total market value

Debt can be convertible into other forms of equity besides common stock. For instance, debt might be convertible into preferred shares. The accounting rules for recording such conversions are the same as those discussed above. The only difference is that the company is giving up a preferred stock claim in return for retiring the debt; and the issuance of this claim, instead of a common stock claim, is recorded.

Convertible Preferred Stock

When convertible preferred stock is originally issued, the entire proceeds are recorded in the contributed capital accounts relating to preferred stock, even though some portion of this value may arise from the ability to convert it into common stock in the future. When an actual conversion takes place, it is recorded by transferring the amounts originally recorded in the preferred stock contributed capital accounts into the common stock contributed capital accounts. No gain or loss may be recorded since this conversion involves the issuance and retirement of equity claims only, and these exchanges cannot affect net income.

For example, assume that Damron Corporation issued 10,000 shares of $5 par, convertible, 10%, preferred shares. The initial offering price was $8 per share. The preferred is convertible into two shares of $1 par common stock per share of preferred. Preferred shareholders converted 2,500 of the preferred shares into common stock on May 3, 1993.

The carrying value of the preferred shares would include $12,500 of par value ($5 par × 2,500 shares), plus $7,500 of paid in capital in excess of par ($8 issue price − $5 par) × (2,500 shares), or a total of $20,000. Damron will issue two shares of common for each share of preferred, so 5,000 shares of common must be issued (2 × 2,500 preferred shares). Since 5,000 shares of common are issued and the value attached to these shares is the $20,000 carrying value of the preferred converted, $5,000 must be added to the common stock at par account ($1 par × 5,000 shares) and the remainder of $15,000 added to the additional paid-in capital in excess of par on common. Damron's journal entry would appear as follows:

May 3, 1993:		
Preferred stock at par	12,500	
Additional paid-in capital on preferred	7,500	
Common stock at par		5,000
Additional paid-in capital on common		15,000
To record the conversion of 2,500 preferred shares into common stock.		

CHANGES IN STATE CORPORATION LAWS AND THEIR IMPLICATION FOR STOCKHOLDERS' EQUITY

The reporting format that separates contributed capital and retained earnings and further divides contributed capital into par or stated value and additional paid-in capital is governed by historical relationships and outdated notions that distributions to shareholders are somehow limited to the amounts reported as retained earnings. In the 1980s, many states altered their corporation laws and adopted various versions of the Model Business Corporations Act (MBCA) to regulate corporate activity. The MBCA not only eliminates the concept of par or stated value, but it also eliminates retained earnings as a focal point for limiting distributions to shareholders. In many states that have adopted these new restrictions, the limitations on distributions to shareholders are twofold:

1. That the company remain solvent, usually described as having current assets exceed current liabilities
2. That the distribution be limited to the amount by which the fair value of assets exceeds the liabilities

Taken literally, these requirements allow distributions regardless of the size of retained earnings or the nature of the contributed capital, so long as they do not violate any other contractual limitations such as restrictions imposed by debt covenants.[4] Even in states where par or stated value has not been completely eliminated, defining the maximum distribution a corporation could make based on the fair value of assets basically destroys any consequence to par or stated values.

In many states where these requirements have been adopted, the law is written so that the limitation on the size of any distribution to shareholders is determined based on financial statements prepared on the basis of either:

1. Accounting practices or principles that are reasonable under the circumstances
2. Fair value

If (1) above is applied, it may appear that there is still a role for the separation of contributed capital and retained earnings in limiting corporate distributions to shareholders as accounting practices or principles generally maintain this distinction. However, the alternative use of fair value all but eliminates any need to retain the focus on retained earnings since a distribution will be legal so long as the fair value of assets exceeds the fair value of liabilities subsequent to the distribution. This requirement makes moot the distinction between types of capital.

Many states impose additional requirements based on the nature of the proposed distribution (i.e., whether the distribution is a dividend, treasury stock purchase, or partial liquidation). However, very few states have regulations that depend on the archaic notion of distinguishing between contributed capital and retained earnings or between legal capital and additional paid-in capital. Since distinguishing legal capital from additional paid-in capital has lost most of its legal content, the current approach to accounting for capital formation via stock issues may be abandoned in the near future.

---

[4] Debt covenants were discussed in Chapter 13. They represent contractual limitations on managerial actions and are enforceable in all states. The remainder of this discussion focuses only on the minimum limitations on corporate distributions imposed by state laws.

FINANCIAL REPORTING REQUIREMENTS

Generally accepted accounting principles currently require that disclosure related to stockholders' equity include the amounts of contributed capital, by type of security, on the face of the balance sheet. Most companies elect to report a single balance for additional paid-in capital. The single balance sums all the individual additional paid-in capital accounts from common stock, preferred stock, warrants, donated capital, etc. The only other explicit reporting requirement for stockholders' equity is that disclosure of changes in the separate accounts comprising stockholders' equity be provided, if material. Most companies accomplish this by producing a statement of changes in stockholders' equity, which provides a reconciliation of each stockholders' equity account and the activity therein over the year. Exhibit 14.4 presents the Statement of Shareholders' Equity reported by Allegheny Ludlum Corporation, which uses this format for disclosure.

| EXHIBIT 14.4

Allegheny Ludlum Corporation— Statement of Shareholders' Equity

ALLEGHENY LUDLUM CORPORATION
Statement of Shareholders' Equity
1992 Annual Report to Shareholders

Note 6—Shareholders' Equity

(thousands of dollars)	COMMON STOCK	ADDITIONAL CAPITAL	RETAINED EARNINGS	TREASURY SHARES
Balance at December 31, 1989	$2,258	$165,317	$168,117	$ (6,370)
Net income			68,936	
Dividends on common stock at $.86 per share			(28,623)	
3-for-2 stock split	1,128	(1,129)	(2)	
Exercise of stock options		(22)	(14)	111
Purchase of 742,850 treasury shares at cost				(17,441)
Balance at December 30, 1990	3,386	164,166	208,414	(23,700)
Net income			41,110	
Dividends on common stock at $.88 per share			(28,960)	
Employee stock plans		28	(20)	1,329
Purchase of 57,600 treasury shares at cost				(1,264)
Balance at December 29, 1991	3,386	164,194	220,544	(23,635)
Net loss			(78,374)	
Dividends on common stock at $.88 per share			(28,960)	
Employee stock plans		68	(41)	1,607
Purchase of 61,600 treasury shares at cost				(1,845)
Balance January 3, 1993	$3,386	$164,262	$113,169	$(23,873)

Other companies elect to incorporate this disclosure in a variety of places within their financial statements. Exhibit 14.5 displays Honeywell, Incorporated's note disclosures associated with the 1988 annual report, a portion of which was presented in Exhibit 14.2. Honeywell provided a reconciliation of activity in the cumulative translation gain account in one note, the contributed capital and treasury stock accounts in a second note, and retained earnings in a third note. However, the sum of the information provided in this fashion meets current disclosure requirements.

REPORTING CAPITAL FORMATION ACTIVITIES IN THE CASH FLOW STATEMENT

Whenever any equity security is issued in exchange for cash, the cash inflow is classified as a financing cash flow for purposes of classification and reporting in the cash flow statement. Issuance of different types of equity securities, if material, should preferably be disclosed separately. Transaction costs that are paid in the process of raising equity capital should be reported as a reduction in the cash inflow from the equity issue. Thus, the net cash inflow is reported in the financing activities section of the cash flow statement.

Issuance of stock in exchange for noncash assets or the conversion of convertible debt or preferred stock are noncash transactions. Consequently, these events do not give rise to a cash flow that is reported on the face of the cash flow statement. However, disclosure of these exchanges is required as a significant noncash transaction either as a side-bar to the cash flow statement or in the notes to the financial statements.

SUMMARY

This chapter began with a review of the current structure of financial reporting for stockholders' equity. In particular, four major sections of stockholders' equity were identified: contributed capital, retained earnings, treasury stock, and other valuation accounts. The motivation for this format is deeply rooted in the origins of corporation law. This format's major focus is providing information to investors regarding limitations on corporate distributions that historically were linked to the existence of retained earnings in some cases.

Contributed capital arises from the issuance of equity securities. While many forms of equity securities may exist, two basic categories of equity are preferred and common stock. Preferred stock provides holders with preferences in claims to dividends and to corporate distributions in the event of liquidation. Contributed capital is reported as two components: legal capital or par (stated) value and additional paid-in capital. Legal capital, or par value, represents the minimum price that can be paid for newly issued shares as well as the capital that corporation law has historically required to be maintained following any corporate distribution. When new shares are issued, the proceeds from the share issue are allocated between the par or stated value and additional paid-in capital based on these legal capital requirements.

EXHIBIT 14.5

Honeywell,
Incorporated—
Selected Note
Disclosures on
Stockholders' Equity

HONEYWELL, INCORPORATED
Selected Note Disclosures on Stockholders' Equity
Annual Report to Shareholders for Fiscal 1988

4. Foreign Currency Translation

Foreign currency assets and liabilities are generally translated into U.S. dollars using the exchange rates in effect at the statement of financial position date. Results of operations are generally translated using the average exchange rates throughout the period. The effects of exchange rate fluctuations on translation of assets and liabilities are reported as accumulated foreign currency translation in stockholders' equity. Following is a summary of the changes in accumulated foreign currency translation:

	1988	1987
Balance January 1	$120.3	$ 14.7
Translation adjustments	(19.9)	105.6
Balance December 31	$100.4	$120.3

Gains and losses from foreign currency transactions are included in net income. Foreign currency exchanges gains or losses, net of income taxes, were not material in any year.

17. Capital Stock

	COMMON STOCK	ADDITIONAL PAID-IN CAPITAL	TREASURY STOCK
Balance January 1, 1986	$71.1	$675.7	$ (99.8)
Purchase of treasury stock—2,308,700 shares			(170.4)
Issued upon conversion of debentures—820,193 treasury shares		(9.2)	58.3
Issued for employee stock plans—1,385,666 treasury shares		(2.7)	84.3
36,765 shares cancelled			
Balance December 31, 1986	71.1	663.8	(127.6)
Purchase of treasury stock—4,283,000 shares			(323.1)
Issued for employee stock plans—1,214,504 treasury shares		(15.0)	92.3
38,820 shares cancelled	(0.1)		
Balance December 31, 1987	71.0	648.8	(358.4)
Purchase of treasury stock—448,758 shares			(31.5)
Issued for employee stock plans—1,052,470 treasury shares		(13.9)	75.3
3,882 shares cancelled			
Balance December 31, 1988	$71.0	$634.9	$(314.6)

18. Retained Earnings

	1988	1987	1986
Balance January 1	$1,763.6	$1,599.2	$2,087.4
Net income (loss)	(434.9)	253.7	(398.1)
Dividends			
1988—2.10 per share	(89.1)		
1987—2.025 per share		(89.3)	
1986—2.00 per share			(90.1)
Balance December 31	$1,239.6	$1,763.6	$1,599.2

Included in consolidated retained earnings are undistributed earnings of companies owned 20 to 50 percent, which are accounted for using the equity method, amounting to $99.4 at December 31, 1988.

Accounting for exchanges between corporations and their shareholders (in the role of shareholders) is guided by the principle that reported income should not be affected by these types of exchanges. As a result, issue costs that are incurred during the issuance of new equity securities are not charged to expense. Rather, they represent a reduction in the net amount of capital raised by the issue. Consequently, recording issuance costs results in a reduction of additional paid-in capital.

Other means of issuing new equity capital include the use of stock subscriptions, stock rights offerings, stock warrant offerings, and the conversion of compound securities such as convertible preferred stock or convertible debt. Each of these transactions has special requirements, but all of them ultimately are reflected in changes to the legal capital and additional paid-in capital accounts reported as part of stockholders' equity.

Disclosure requirements relating to stockholders' equity are not extensive. Companies may use various formats to provide information to users on the events and transactions that altered the balances in each of the stockholders' equity accounts.

Finally, changes in state corporation laws have made the distinctions, upon which the current financial reporting structure for stockholders' equity was founded, obsolete. The notion that a company needs retained earnings to support a distribution of assets to shareholders is no longer accurate in general. Legal capital is a concept that is slowly disappearing from corporation law. Replacing these concepts is the notion that corporations should be allowed to make distributions of assets as long as:

1. The company does not become insolvent as a result of the distribution.
2. The fair value of assets exceeds the fair value of liabilities.
3. The distribution does not violate any other contractual limitation the company has committed to.

QUESTIONS

1. To what does the term *legal capital* refer?
2. What are the *articles of incorporation* and what role to they have in controlling a corporation's functioning?
3. How does the concept of *separation of ownership and control* relate to a corporation?
4. Why is the separation of ownership and control so important?
5. What is an equity security? What basic types of equity securities exist?
6. What is a call provision and what securities might be subject to such a provision?
7. Why is there a demand for so many forms of equity?
8. What are the rights of preferred shareholders to dividends when the shares are noncumulative? Cumulative?
9. What are *issue costs* and how are they accounted for?
10. What is a *stock right*? What is a *stock warrant*? Compare and contrast the characteristics of a stock right with those of a stock warrant.
11. What is *donated capital* and how is it valued?

12. What is a conversion privilege and how does it work?

13. How does the current market price of a convertible preferred stock or bond affect the recording of its conversion into common stock?

EXERCISES

14-1. *Common stock issue*

Landy Corporation was organized on January 2, 1993, with authorized capital of 100,000 shares of $10 par value common stock. During 1993, Landy had the following transactions:

(a) January 2: Issued 20,000 shares at $12 per share.

(b) April 23: Issued 1,000 shares for legal services when the market price was $14 per share.

REQUIRED:

Prepare journal entries to record the activities described above and prepare the Contributed Capital section of Landy's balance sheet at the end of 1993.

14-2. *Common stock: watered stock*

On June 15, 1992, Masters Corporation issued 10,000 shares of its $2 par common stock to William Dasher in exchange for land, building, and equipment. Mr. Dasher contended that the assets were valued at $1,200,000. Masters' shares are not traded on a public exchange. Several months later, it was discovered that the assets contributed by Mr. Dasher were actually only worth $900,000 at the time of the original exchange.

REQUIRED:

1. Prepare a journal entry to record the original exchange assuming the market value of the assets was $1,200,000.

2. How will the later discovery of the true value of the assets affect the financial statements of the company, if at all?

14-3. *Stock issues: preferred, common, subscriptions*

The Amlin Corporation was incorporated on January, 1991, with the following authorized capitalization:

(a) 20,000 shares of common stock, no par value, stated value $40 per share, and

(b) 5,000 shares of 5% cumulative preferred stock, par value $10 per share.

During 1991, Amlin issued 12,000 shares of common stock for a total of $600,000 and 3,000 shares of preferred stock at $16 per share. In addition, on December 20, 1991, subscriptions for 1,000 shares of preferred stock were taken at a purchase price of $16. These subscribed shares were paid for on January 2, 1992.

REQUIRED:

1. Prepare the journal entries for the contributed capital transactions during 1991 along with the contributed capital section of Amlin's December 31, 1991, balance sheet.

2. What effect would the payment of the subscriptions on January 2, 1992, have on the contributed capital accounts?

14-4. *Convertible preferred: issuance*

On July 1, 1993, Hart Corporation issued 1,000 shares of its $10 par common and 2,000 shares of its $10 par convertible preferred stock for a lump sum of

$40,000. At this date Hart's common stock was selling for $18 per share and the convertible preferred stock for $13.50 per share.

REQUIRED:

How would Hart record the issuance of these securities?

14-5.   *Convertible preferred: issue and conversion*

On October 1, 1993, Nastel Inc., issued 20,000 shares of its no-par, $1 noncumulative, convertible preferred stock for $250,000. On March 15, 1994, 10,000 shares of the preferred stock along with any claim to dividends were converted into shares of Nastel's $2 par common stock at the rate of three shares of common for each preferred share. No dividends had been declared on the preferred stock since it was issued.

REQUIRED:

Prepare a journal entry to record both the issuance of the preferred stock on October 1, 1993 and the conversion of the preferred shares on March 15, 1994.

14-6.   *Shares issued for nonmonetary assets*

The December 31, 1992, condensed balance sheet of Dunn Services, a proprietorship, follows:

Current assets	$140,000
Equipment (net)	130,000
	$270,000
Liabilities	$ 70,000
John Dunn, Capital	200,000
	$270,000

Fair values at December 31, 1992, are as follows:

Current assets	$160,000
Equipment	210,000
Liabilities	70,000

On January 2, 1993, Inco Corporation purchased the assets of Dunn Services and assumed its liabilities in exchange for 5,000 shares of Inco's $10 par value common stock.

REQUIRED:

1. Prepare the journal entry necessary to record this issuance of common stock.
2. Would your answer change if Mr. Dunn owned all of Inco Corporation's stock?

14-7.   *Stock rights: issuance, conversion, expiration*

To raise additional capital, Cheapshot, Inc. issued 100,000 stock rights to its existing shareholders. Each right allows the holder to acquire two shares of common stock at a price of $42 per share. Current market price of Cheapshot is $44 per share on a national exchange. The rights expire eight months after issue. During the eight months, 70,000 rights were exercised when the market price of the share was $45. The remainder were unexercised at the end of their life.

REQUIRED:

Prepare the journal entries necessary to record the activity described above.

14-8.   *Convertible preferred stock: issuance and conversion*

During 1993 Bradley Corporation issued for $110 per share, 5,000 shares of $100 par value convertible preferred stock. One share of preferred stock can be converted into three shares of Bradley's $25 par value common stock at the option of the preferred shareholder. On December 31, 1994, all of the preferred stock was converted into common stock. The market value of the common stock at the conversion date was $40 per share.

REQUIRED:

How would Bradley record this conversion?

14-9.   *Debt with detachable warrants*

Makepeace Corporation issued $100,000 of face value debt with detachable warrants for total proceeds of $110,000. With each $1,000 face value bond, five warrants were attached. Each warrant allows the holder to acquire one share of Makepeace's $10 par common stock for $22. The market price of the common stock at this time was $25 per share. After the issuance, the bond traded without the warrant at a price of 80. Warrants were traded at a price of $5 each.

REQUIRED:

Prepare the journal entry necessary to record the issuance of the debt and warrants.

14-10.   *Conversion of warrants*

Assume that 100 of the warrants issued in Exercise 14-9 are actually converted into common stock.

REQUIRED:

1. Prepare the journal entry necessary to record this conversion.
2. If the remaining warrants lapse, how would Makepeace reflect this in its financial statements?

14-11.   *Convertible bonds: recording conversion*

Packer Industries issued 4,000, 8%, convertible bonds on January 1, 1986, at 93. Each bond has a face value of $1,000 and is convertible into five shares of Packer's $12 par common stock anytime after January 1, 1991. The bonds pay interest on June 30 and December 31, and they mature on December 31, 2005. On January 1, 1992, holders of 1,500 of the bonds elected to convert. Packer uses the straight-line method to amortize any discount or premium on debt issues.

REQUIRED:

Prepare the journal entry to record the conversion using the book value method.

14-12.   *Convertible bonds: recording conversion*

On June 30, 1994, the holders of 1,000 of Mindano Corporation's convertible bonds elected to exchange the bonds for stock. The bonds had a face value of $1,000,000 and a remaining unamortized issue premium of $120,000 on June 30th. The debt has a face interest rate of 10% and pays interest on January 1 and July 1. In addition, unamortized issue costs relating to the bonds amounted to $23,000 on the date of conversion. Each $1,000 bond is convertible into ten shares of $1 par common stock. The market value of the stock issued in this conversion was $1,375,000. The market value of the bonds is uncertain since they were never traded in an open market.

REQUIRED:

Prepare a journal entry to record the conversion of the bonds under both the book value and market value methods.

PROBLEMS

14-1. *Various share issues: subscriptions*

Mezzinee Corporation began operations on January 1, 1993. The following transactions occurred during the company's first year of operations:

(a) January 1, 1993: Issued 50,000 shares of $5 preferred stock with a par value of $60, for $61.50 per share. The preferred stock is noncumulative, nonparticipating, with a call price of $64 per share and a liquidation value of $70 per share.

(b) February 1, 1993: Issued 300,000 shares of no-par common stock for $5,250,000. The no-par stock had a stated value of $5 per share.

(c) April 1, 1993: Subscriptions to 15,200 shares of common stock are received at a price of $22 per share. The subscription contracts call for the issuance of stock only after full payment. If full payment is not made, any installments are forfeited; and no obligation to issue shares exists. The subscribers to the stock paid 25% of the purchase price when the subscription contracts were signed.

(d) May 31, 1993: Full payment was received for 10,500 shares of the subscribed stock. The remaining subscriptions lapsed without being paid.

REQUIRED:

1. Prepare the journal entries necessary to record the transactions described above.
2. How do the risks and rewards of the preferred shareholders of Mezzinee compare to those of the common shareholders, given the terms indicated? How would the risks and rewards of the preferred shareholders be affected if the stock were cumulative rather than noncumulative? What if it were participating instead of nonparticipating?

14-2. *Essay on categories of stockholders' equity*

A corporation's capital (stockholders' equity) is a very important part of its statement of financial position.

REQUIRED:

Identify and discuss the general categories of capital (stockholders' equity) for a corporation. Be sure to enumerate specific sources included in each general category.

(AICPA adapted)

14-3. *Preferred stock conversion—stock rights: presentation of stockholders' equity*

Carr Corporation had the following stockholders' equity account balances at December 31, 1993:

Preferred stock	$1,800,000
Additional paid-in capital from preferred stock	90,000
Common stock	5,150,000
Additional paid-in capital from common stock	3,502,000
Retained earnings	4,000,000
Treasury common stock	(270,000)

Transactions during 1994 and other information relating to the stockholders' equity accounts were as follows:

(a) Carr's preferred and common shares are traded on the Over-The-Counter market. At December 31, 1993, Carr had 100,000 authorized shares of $100 par, 10%, callable at $110, noncumulative, convertible preferred stock; and 3,000,000 authorized shares of no-par common stock with a stated value of $5 per share. All of the common shares were originally issued for $8.40 a share. Each preferred share was convertible into three shares of common stock anytime on or after January 1, 1993.

(b) On January 1, 1994, Carr called all of the preferred shares. At that time, half of the preferred stockholders chose to convert their shares to common and half elected to tender the preferred shares to the company. To satisfy the need to issue common shares under the conversion feature, shares of new common stock were issued.

(c) On September 1, 1994, 250,000 stock rights were issued to the common stockholders, permitting the purchase of one new share of common stock in exchange for one right and $11 cash. On September 25, 1994, 210,000 stock rights were exercised when the market price of Carr's common stock was $13 per share. Carr issued new shares to settle the transaction. The remaining 40,000 rights were not exercised and expired.

REQUIRED:

1. Prepare the journal entries Carr would use to record the above activities.
2. Prepare the Stockholders' Equity section of Carr's balance sheet at December 31, 1994, assuming that Carr reported income of $500,000 and declared no dividends during 1994.
3. Discuss the factors that might have led Carr to call the preferred stock.

14-4.   *Multiple choice questions*

Problem 14-4 consists of the following four multiple choice questions:

1. On February 1, 1992, authorized common stock was sold on a subscription basis at a price in excess of par value, and 20% of the subscription price was collected. On May 1, 1992, the remaining 80% of the subscription price was collected. Additional paid-in capital would increase on

	February 1, 1992	May 1, 1992
(a)	No	Yes
(b)	No	No
(c)	Yes	No
(d)	Yes	Yes

2. The issuance of shares of preferred stock to shareholders
   (a) Increases preferred stock outstanding
   (b) Has *no* effect on preferred stock outstanding
   (c) Increases preferred stock authorized
   (d) Decreases preferred stock authorized

3. A company issued rights to its existing seven shareholders to purchase shares of common stock. When the rights are exercised, additional paid-in capital would be credited if the purchase price
   (a) Exceeded the par value
   (b) Was the same as the par value
   (c) Was the same as the par value, but less than the market value at the date of exercise
   (d) Was less than the par value

4. A company issued rights to its existing shareholders to purchase, for $30 per share, unissued shares of $15 par value common stock. When the rights lapse
   (a) No entry will be made
   (b) Additional paid-in capital will be debited
   (c) Additional paid-in capital will be credited
   (d) Stock rights outstanding will be debited
   (AICPA adapted)

14-5.   *Variety of stock issues: motivation for conversions*

Brandywine Enterprises entered into the following capital stock exchanges during 1993, the first year of its existence:
   (a) Issued 40,000 shares of $1 par value common stock at $12 per share.
   (b) Issued 1,000 shares of $22 par value, 8% preferred stock at $25 per share. The preferred is convertible into two shares of $1 par common stock at the option of the holder.
   (c) Issued in a joint sale 3,000 shares of the preferred stock and 15,000 shares of common stock for a lump sum of $291,000. Immediately after the sale, the market values of the preferred stock and common stock were $24.50 and $12.25, respectively.
   (d) Issued 2,000 shares of preferred stock for land with an estimated fair market value of $50,000.
   (e) Received 1,000 shares of common stock as a donation from a stockholder. The shares had a market value on the date of the contribution of $13 per share and had been purchased by the shareholder for $12 per share. The contributor had purchased the shares in the original issue of 40,000 shares offered by the company and owned only the 1,000 shares prior to making the contribution. Brandywine retired the shares.
   (f) Received subscriptions to 12,000 shares of common stock at a price of $15 per share. The subscribers paid 30% of the purchase price at the signing of the subscription agreement. The balance will not be paid until the next fiscal year.

Brandywine had 100,000 shares of common and 50,000 shares of preferred stock authorized.

REQUIRED:

1. Prepare the journal entries necessary to record the above transactions.
2. Assuming that Brandywine's ending retained earnings balance was $100,000, prepare the Stockholders' Equity section of the company's balance sheet.
3. Assuming that all of the preferred shareholders selected to convert their shares to common when the market value of common was $15 per share, what journal entry would Brandywine make to record the conversion?
4. Discuss the factors that might have led the investors in Brandywine to convert their preferred stock into common shares.
5. Discuss some of the reasons why Brandywine might have elected to use stock subscriptions to raise new equity capital instead of an underwritten public offering in the primary market.

14-6.   *Warrants and convertible debt*

Merganser Companies entered into the following exchanges regarding its capital stock during the current period:
   (a) Issued 100,000 shares of $6, no-par, preferred stock for $68 per share. The stock is noncumulative, nonparticipating, and convertible into six shares of

$1 par common stock for each preferred share. The stock is callable at $70 per share and has a liquidation value of $75 per share.

(b) Issued bonds with a face value of $4,000,000 along with detachable warrants. Each $1,000 bond had a warrant for two shares of $1 par common stock. The bonds were estimated to have a market value of $990 at the date of issue, and each warrant was expected to have a value of $120. The proceeds from the joint issue amounted to $4,432,000.

(c) Bonds with a face value of $2,300,000 issued several years ago were converted into 92,000 shares of $1 par common stock. At the time of the conversion, the bonds had a book value of $2,265,000 and accrued interest of $105,000. In addition, debt issuance costs of $32,000 were still unamortized at the date of conversion. The common stock was traded on a national exchange at a price of $30 per share on the date of the conversion. Merganser uses the market value method of recording bond conversions.

(d) Half of the preferred stock issued at the beginning of the current year was converted into common. The conversion was satisfied by issuing new shares of common stock. The remaining preferred stock was then called and retired for cash.

(e) Three thousand (3,000) of the warrants issued with the bonds above were exercised. Each warrant calls for a payment of $80 to obtain two shares of common stock. The remainder of the warrants were allowed to lapse.

REQUIRED:

1. Prepare the journal entries required for all of the transactions described above.
2. Does the conversion feature in a bond make it more or less valuable? Explain.

14-7. *Convertible bonds: accounting for conversion using alternative approaches*

Corvette Enterprises issued 5,000, 8.25% convertible bonds on January 1, 1993. The market rate of interest was 9% on the date of issue. Each $1,000 face value bond is convertible into nine shares of Corvette's $22 par common stock anytime after January 1, 1995. The bonds pay interest on July 1 and January 1, and mature on January 1, 1998. Underwriter fees associated with the issue were $125,000. Corvette uses the straight-line method to amortize issue costs and bond discounts or premiums. On April 2, 1995, holders of 2,100 bonds elected to convert. The bonds were selling at 102 on the date of conversion.

REQUIRED:

1. Prepare the journal entries necessary to record the conversion of the bonds under both the book value and market value methods.
2. What factors do you believe would be important in management's decision regarding the choice of accounting method (book or market method) to apply to the conversion?

14-8. *Variety of capital formation transactions*

Nelson Company was organized on January 1, 1994, and entered into the following capital stock exchanges during its first year of operations:

(a) January 20: Nelson issued 400,000 shares of $12 par common stock for $27.25 per share. In lieu of cash, the underwriters agreed to accept 16,000 of the common shares issued. In addition, Nelson incurred legal fees of $74,000 related to the issue.

(b) February 3: Nelson issued bonds with a face value of $800,000 along with detachable warrants. Each $1,000 bond had a warrant for three shares of

$12 par common stock. The bonds were estimated to have a market value of $820,000 at the date of issue, and each warrant was expected to have a value $84. Total proceeds from the issue were $891,200. Issue costs of $32,000 were paid on the date of issue.

(c) March 6: Nelson Company received title to 90 acres of land from the State of Minnesota. The land was donated by the State for use as a production site. The land had a carrying value of $409,000 and an estimated market value of $1,216,000 as of March 1, 1994.

REQUIRED:

Prepare the journal entries necessary to record the above transactions.

14-9.   *Warrants and convertible preferred stock*

Andrews, Incorporated, entered into the following capital transactions during 1995:

(a) June 1: Andrews issued 10,000 warrants to purchase its $1 par common stock for $18. Each warrant entitles the holder to purchase five shares of common stock. The warrants were issued at a price of $35 per warrant. Legal expenses related to the issue amounted to $26,000 and were paid on the date of issue.

(b) July 9: Andrews exchanged 3,000 shares of its $100 par convertible pre-ferred stock for land owned by Jabba Investments. Each share of preferred stock is convertible into three shares of Andrews' $1 par common stock. The market price of Andrews' common stock was $32 per share on the date of exchange, and the land had an estimated fair value of $339,000.

(c) September 10: Jabba Investments elected to convert the preferred shares acquired on July 9. Andrews' common stock had a market price of $42 per share on September 9, and $41 on September 11.

(d) December 30: Eight thousand (8,000) of the common stock warrants were exercised. The remainder of the warrants were allowed to lapse.

REQUIRED:

Prepare the journal entries necessary to record the above transactions.

14-10. *Subscription contracts: variation of terms*

On February 2, 1994, Maximand Incorporated received subscriptions to 40,000 shares of $12 par common stock at a price of $22 per share. The subscription contract required payment of 30% of the contract price at date of subscription and the balance on June 2, 1994. Collection was reasonably assured at the time the contracts were signed. On June 2, 1994, payment in full was received on subscriptions for 35,000 shares. The remainder of the subscription contracts were in default.

REQUIRED:

Prepare the journal entries necessary to record the above transactions under the following contractual arrangements:

(a) Shares are issued in proportion to the cash paid.

(b) No shares are issued until all cash is paid. All installments made are for-feited on default.

(c) No shares are issued until all cash is paid. Installments made are refunded on default.

(d) Repeat part (a) assuming legal costs of $40,000 were incurred in preparing the subscription and were paid on February 2, 1994.

HAMMERMILL CORPORATION (A)

Presented below is the Liabilities and Shareholders' Equity section of Hammermill Corporation's 1981 Annual Report to Shareholders, along with some selected note disclosure regarding preferred stocks.

LIABILITIES AND SHAREHOLDERS' OWNERSHIP (dollars in thousands)	1981 (at 1/2/82)	1980 (at 12/28/80)
Current liabilities		
Accounts payable and accrued expenses	$127,493	$115,048
Short-term borrowings	–	17,821
Current portion of long-term obligations	6,192	7,530
Federal and state income taxes	3,115	3,597
Total current liabilities	136,800	143,996
Long-term obligations, less current maturities	247,013	179,976
Deferred items		
Deferred income taxes	74,593	56,944
Unamortized pension and other items	8,443	9,152
Total deferred items	83,036	66,096
Preferred stock		
Cumulative preferred stock, $100 par value		
4 1/2% series	–	136
4 1/4% series, redeemable at $103 per share	279	279
Second cumulative preferred stock, $1 par value		
$7 Series B (liquidating and redemption value, $25,000)	25,000	–
Preferred stock subject to mandatory redemption	25,279	415
$5 Series A (liquidating value, $7,615)	76	83
Preferred stock subject to mandatory redemption	76	83
Common stock and other shareholders' ownership		
Common stock, $1.25 par value	10,887	10,246
Capital in excess of par value	85,246	67,690
Retained earnings	285,176	253,493
	381,309	331,429
Less: treasury stock	(31,166)	(37)
	350,143	331,392
	$842,347	$721,958

Cumulative Preferred Stock

A summary of the cumulative preferred stock outstanding is as follows:

Cumulative preferred stock	1981	1980
Authorized: 12,875 shares		
Shares issued and outstanding		
4 1/2% series	–	1,359
4 1/4% series	2,785	2,785

The 4 1/4% series is subject to mandatory redemption; the 4 1/2% series was redeemed during 1981. Liquidating value of the 4 1/4% series is $100 per share. Annual sinking fund redemption requirements are 300 shares. The requirements of the series for the next five years have been fulfilled.

Second Cumulative Preferred Stock

A summary of the second cumulative preferred stock outstanding is as follows:

Second cumulative preferred stock	1981	1980
Authorized: 1,486,149 shares		
Shares issued and outstanding		
$5, Series A	76,147	83,312
$7, Series B	500,000	–

Liquidating value of the Series A stock is $100 per share (total $7,615,000) and of the Series B stock is $50 per share (total $25,000,000). Series A is convertible into common stock at $38 per share. Series A is redeemable at the option of the company at $100 per share. Series B is subject to mandatory annual redemption at $50 per share commencing in 1987 and may be redeemed at the option of the company at prices decreasing from $57 per share. Mandatory redemption amounts will be $1,923,000 per year in 1987 through 1999. The change in Series A shares outstanding resulted from conversions.

REQUIRED:

1. How many shares of common stock had the company issued on December 31, 1980 and 1981, respectively?
2. How were the balances in each of the preferred stock accounts in the equity section determined? Comment on the reasonableness of the presentation of the preferred shares in the equity section.
3. In reviewing the notes regarding the Cumulative Preferred Stock, the company indicates that these shares are subject to a mandatory redemption. What is a mandatory redemption? How are preferred shares subject to mandatory redemption any different than a bond?

HAMMERMILL CORPORATION (B)

CASE 14.2

The following disclosure was contained in the footnote regarding common stock in Hammermill Corporation's 1981 Annual Report to the Shareholders. Hammermill set a par value for its common stock of $1.25 per share.

Common Stock

A summary of the common stock outstanding is as follows:

Common stock	1981	1980
Authorized: 14,959,955 shares		
Shares issued and outstanding	7,832,262	8,183,646

The company has reserved 749,750 shares of common stock for conversion of the 5% convertible debentures; 200,387 shares are reserved for the conversion of second cumulative preferred stock; 544,212 shares are reserved for stock options; and 139,733 shares are contingently issuable in connection with acquisition agreements and employment agreements.

The changes in common stock and capital in excess of par value were as follows:

(thousands of dollars)	Common Stock Shares	Amount	Capital in Excess of Par Value
Restated Balance, December 31, 1978	$7,777,368	$ 9,722	$55,059
Employee stock options exercised	27,415	34	385
Conversion of preferred stock	2,182	3	(2)
Balance, December 30, 1979	7,806,965	9,759	55,442
Employee stock options exercised	53,577	67	1,087
Conversion of preferred stock	4,472	6	(4)
Stock issued for acquisitions	331,453	414	11,165
Balance, December 28, 1980	8,196,467	10,246	67,690
Employee stock options exercised	58,314	73	1,191
Conversion of preferred stock	18,840	24	(16)
Conversion of debentures	250	–	10
Stock issued for acquisition	388,994	486	15,074
Stock issued by pooled company	9,985	12	140
Payment of timberland acquisition obligations	36,933	46	1,157
Balance, January 3, 1982	$8,709,783	$10,887	$85,246

In February 1982, 400,000 shares of stock were issued in exchange for $13,354,000 of 8.07% notes payable. The aggregate value of the stock issued was $9,760.

REQUIRED:

1. In the discussion from the first paragraph of the note, the company indicates that it has "reserved" several hundred thousand shares of common stock. What does this mean? What effect does it have on the company's ability to issue more stock?
2. The date of the financial statement is January 2, 1982. However, in the last paragraph, the company discusses an exchange of stock for notes that occurred in February, 1982. Prepare the journal entry to record the exchange described. Assume that the exchange took place on February 1, 1982, and that the book value of the notes at the time of the exchange was 13,500,000, not including accrued interest since the last payment date of December 31, 1981. Use both the market value and book value approaches.

3. In Hammermill's reconciliation of its contributed capital from common stock for 1981, the company indicates that debentures were converted. These are not the bonds converted in February of 1982. Assuming that Hammermill used the book value method to record this conversion, what was the carrying value of the bonds that were converted prior to the exchange? Assuming that each bond had a face value of $1,000 and that they were originally issued at face value. If the remaining unamortized issue costs on the converted bonds equaled $10,000, how many shares of common stock were issued for each bond?

4. During 1981, Hammermill reports the results of conversion of the Series A preferred stock into common stock. By reference to the information regarding the Series A preferred stock in Hammermill Corporation Case 14.1, determine both the conversion rate used and the journal entry to record the conversion of the preferred into common for the year.

JAMES RIVER CORPORATION

CASE 14.3

James River Corporation, an integrated manufacturer of paper, film, and plastic products, serves the following strategic markets: Hygienics, Communications, Food and Consumer Packaging, Food and Beverage Service, and Specialty Industrial and Packaging. Primary products include: towel and tissue products such as Northern bathroom tissues; paper products such as Dixie disposable cups and dishware; and packaging for cereal boxes, snack foods, and other consumer products. In its 1988 Annual Report, James River included the following Statement of Changes in Capital Accounts:

	1988	1987	1986
Redeemable Preferred Stock			
Balance at beginning of fiscal year	$ 6,898	$ 8,879	$ 96,838)
Conversion of Series I Preferred Stock			(11,414)
Redemption of Series H Preferred Stock			$(76,000)
Preferred stock sinking fund requirements	(1,980)	(1,981)	(545)
Balance at end of fiscal year	$ 4,918	$ 6,898	$ 8,879
Non-Redeemable Preferred Stock			
Balance at beginning of fiscal year	$100,000		
Issuance of Series K Preferred Stock		$100,000	
Issuance of Series L Preferred Stock	200,000		
Balance at end of fiscal year	$300,000	$100,000	

Common Shareholders' Equity	1988	1987	1986
Common Stock:			
Balance at beginning of fiscal year	$ 8,235	$ 5,167	$ 2,905
Issuance of common stock in connection with acquisitions		3,048	58
Conversion of subordinate notes			433
Conversion of Series I Preferred Stock			38
Exercise of stock options and awards	21	20	11
Three-for-two split			1,722
Common shares repurchased	(137)		
Balance at end of fiscal year	$ 8,119	$8,235	$ 5,167
Additional Paid-In Capital:			
Balance at beginning of fiscal year	$1,260,720	$ 399,695	$309,788
Issuance of common stock in connection with acquisitions		864,920	20,647
Conversion of subordinate debentures			57,318
Conversion of Series I Preferred Stock			11,376
Exercise of stock options and awards	2,036	3,435	785
Three-for-two split			(1,722)
Common shares repurchased	(28,289)		
Stock issue costs and other	(4,960)	(7,330)	1,503
Balance at end of fiscal year	$1,229,507	$1,260,720	$399,695

In addition, in the notes to the financial statements, James River included the following information.

Preferred Stock

The Company is authorized to issue up to five million preferred shares having a par value of $10 per share. The preferred shares are issuable in series with varying dividend rates, redemption rights, conversion terms, sinking fund provisions, liquidation rights, and voting rights. Preferred stock outstanding at the end of fiscal 1988, 1987, and 1986 consisted of the following:

(in thousands)	1988	1987	1986
Series C, $100 liquidation value per share	$ 804	$ 1,111	$1,419
Series D, $100 liquidation value per share	2,680	2,920	3,160
Series E, $100 liquidation value per share	1,434	2,867	4,300
Series K, $50 liquidation value per share	100,000	100,000	–
Series L, $200 liquidation value per share	200,000	–	–
Total redeemable and non-redeemable preferred stock	$304,918	$106,898	$8,879

Mandatory annual redemption payments of $2 million, $.5 million, $.4 million, $.2 million, and $.2 million in fiscal 1989, 1990, 1991, 1992, and 1993, respectively, are required.

Redeemable Preferred Stock

Series C Cumulative Participating Preferred Stock

Mandatory dividends of $4.00 per share per annum are payable semiannually on the Series C Cumulative Participating Preferred Stock ("Series C") and participating dividends up to a maximum of $6.00 per share are payable annually based on the earnings of a certain subsidiary of the Company. In fiscal 1988, 1987, and 1986, only mandatory dividend payments were required. Annual sinking fund payments of $307,200 are required until the Series C is fully redeemed.

Series D Cumulative Preferred Stock

The Series D Cumulative Preferred Stock ("Series D") has an annual dividend rate of $8.75 per share, payable quarterly. The Series D is redeemable, in whole or in part, at a per share price declining from $104.15 at April 24, 1988 to $100 in December 1996 and thereafter, plus dividends earned but unpaid to the date of redemption. Quarterly sinking fund payments of $60,000 are required until December 1997 when a final payment of $400,000 is due.

Series E Cumulative Preferred Stock

The Series E Cumulative Preferred Stock ("Series E") has an annual dividend rate of $8.75 per share, payable quarterly. The Series E is redeemable, in whole or in part, at a per share price of $100, plus dividends earned but unpaid to the date of redemption. The final sinking fund payment of $1,433,400 is required in December, 1988.

Series H Preferred Stock

On April 25, 1986, the Company effectively redeemed all 760,000 of the then outstanding shares of its Series H Preferred Stock at a price of $100.73 per share plus accrued dividends to the redemption date. The effect on earnings per common share for fiscal 1986 was not material.

Series I $5.85 Cumulative Convertible Preferred Stock

The Series I Cumulative Convertible Preferred Stock ("Series I"), having a liquidation value of $45 per share, was convertible into common stock at $20 per share. On August 8, 1985, the 253,649 then outstanding shares of Series I were converted into 570,709 shares of common stock.

Non-Redeemable Preferred Stock

Series J Cumulative Convertible Preferred Stock

On March 31, 1986, the Company redeemed all 200 of the then outstanding shares of its Series J Cumulative Convertible Preferred Stock, $10 par value, which had been issued to a trust in December, 1985.

Series K $3.375 Cumulative Convertible Exchangeable Preferred Stock

On November 4, 1986, two million shares of Series K $3.375 Cumulative Convertible Exchangeable Preferred Stock were issued at a price of $50 per share. The Series K is convertible at the option of the holder at any time into James River common stock at a conversion price of $40.75 per share, subject to adjustment under certain conditions. The Series K is not redeemable prior to November 1, 1988, unless the closing price of the James River common stock has equalled or exceeded 150% of the then effective conversion price per share for at least 20 trading days within 30 consecutive trading days ending within five trading days prior to the date notice of redemption is given. With respect to redemptions in that event prior to November 1, 1988, and to redemptions thereafter, the Series K is redeemable, in whole or in part, at the option of James River at redemption prices declining from $53.04 per share at April 24, 1988 to $50 per share on November 1, 1996 and thereafter. Beginning November 1, 1988, the Series K is exchangeable in whole, at the option of James River, on any dividend payment date for James River's 6.75% Convertible Subordinate Debentures due November 1, 2016 ("6.75% Debentures") at the rate of $50 principal amounts of 6.75% Debentures for each share. The 6.75% Debentures, if issued, will be convertible at the option of the holder at any time, unless previously redeemed, into James River common stock on the same terms as the preferred shares.

Series L $14.00 Cumulative Convertible Exchangeable Preferred Stock

On September 29, 1987, James River issued one million shares of Series L $14.00 Cumulative Convertible Exchangeable Preferred Stock. The Series L is convertible at the option of the holder at any time into James River common stock at a rate of five shares of common for each share of Series L, subject to adjustment under certain conditions. The Series L is not redeemable prior to October 1, 1989. With respect to redemptions thereafter, the Series L is redeemable, in whole or in part, at the option of James River at redemption prices declining from $211.20 on October 1, 1989 to $200 per share on October 1, 1997 and thereafter. Beginning October 1, 1989, the Series L is exchangeable in whole, at the option of James River, on any dividend payment date for James River's 7% Convertible Subordinate Debentures due October 1, 2017 ("7% Debentures") at the rate of $200 principal amount of 7% Debentures for each preferred share. The 7% Debentures, if issued, will be convertible at the option of the holder at any time, unless previously redeemed, into James River common stock on the same terms as the preferred shares.

Common Stock

The Company is authorized to issue 150 million common shares, each with a par value of $.10. Common shares of the Company were reserved for issuance as follows:

Stock options granted or available for grant	3,574,741	3,773,692
Conversion of Series K	2,453,988	2,453,988
Conversion of Series L	5,000,000	–
Total reserved shares	11,028,729	6,227,680

REQUIRED:

1. What is a mandatory redemption feature and how do preferred stocks with this feature differ from those that only have a call provision?

2. James River has several classes of preferred stock. Identify the major differences among the various classes of stock and indicate whether you believe the differences increase or decrease the risks of ownership.

3. James River issued the Series C preferred stock to acquire stock in a corporation that became a subsidiary of James River. Assume that the subsidiary was privately held by a small group of shareholders prior to that acquisition. Speculate on the reason that terms such as those present in the Series C stock may have arisen in such a situation.

4. Each of the preferred shares has a liquidation value. What does the liquidation value represent?

5. All preferred stock issued by James River has a par value of $10. The common stock has a par value of $.10. What does par value represent and how is it determined?

6. Utilizing the information from the financial statements, prepare the journal entries that James River used to record the issuance of the Series K and Series L preferred stocks in 1987 and 1988, respectively. In addition, prepare the journal entry James River used to record the issuance of common stock issued in connection with acquisitions for 1987, assuming that the acquisition was recorded as a debit to investments and that all the stock issue costs and other are related to these acquisitions. How did the par value of the shares issued in these exchanges affect the manner in which James River recorded the issuances?

7. In 1986, James River recorded the conversion of subordinate notes. Assuming the conversion occurred on the day following the payment of interest on the notes and that the company used the market value method, what was the market value of the debt at the date it was converted? How would any gain or loss from the conversion be reflected in the financial statements? Assuming that the conversion was recorded using the book value method, what was the total book value of the debt immediately prior to conversion? How would any gain or loss from conversion using the book value method be reflected in the financial statements?

8. Prepare the journal entry James River used to record the conversion of the Series I Preferred Stock in 1986.

9. Assume that on November 1, 1988, James River exercised its option to convert the Series K preferred stock into 6.75% Debentures. Prepare the journal entry to record this conversion.

10. If the conversion described in (9) were to occur, how would it affect the rights of the Series K preferred shareholders? Would the conversion be likely to increase or decrease the value of the investment held by Series K shareholders? Why might James River elect to exercise this option?

11. In the note on common stock, James River indicates that it has reserved common shares. What does this mean and why is it necessary?

12. The Company indicates that it has 150 million shares of common stock authorized. What does the term *authorized* mean? How many shares does the company actually have outstanding at the end of 1988?

CHAPTER 15

Stockholders' Equity: Corporate Distributions

Chapter 14 provided a general overview of the financial statement presentation of stockholders' equity and a detailed discussion of accounting and reporting for activities involving capital formation. This chapter addresses accounting and reporting for various forms of corporate distributions. In addition, a variety of special topics relating to stockholders' equity such as reporting appropriations of retained earnings, prior period adjustments, and quasi-reorganizations are discussed at the end of this chapter.

A **corporate distribution** involves the distribution of:

1. The company's assets to its shareholders through the declaration of dividends or the repurchase of stock
2. Additional shares of the corporation in the form of stock splits or stock dividends

Corporate distributions can have a significant impact on the balance sheet of a corporation. For example, Roberts, Samson, and Dugan discussed the effects when Holiday Corporation paid a special dividend of $65 per share to its shareholders.[1] As a result of this dividend, the book value of Holiday's total stockholders' equity went from a *surplus* of approximately $639 million to a *deficit* of approximately $770 million. The total cash outflow amounted to over $1.4 billion.

Clearly, this corporate distribution had a major effect on Holiday's financial statements. How can a corporation create such a massive deficit, not just in the balance of retained earnings, but in total stockholders' equity? If you were a debtholder of Holiday, wouldn't you be concerned about the compa-

---

[1] Michael Roberts, William Samson, and Michael Dugan, "The Stockholders' Equity Section: Form Without Substance?", *Accounting Horizons* (December 1990), pp. 35-46.

ny's continuing ability to pay interest and principal on its debts, given such a large distribution of cash? Would you be able to do anything to stop such distributions? As a debtholder, would the financial statement presentation of stockholders' equity be useful to you in determining Holiday's ability, or that of other corporations, to undertake distributions of this nature? These questions will be answered by examining the variety of corporate distributions that may arise and the accounting and reporting requirements related to each.

DISTRIBUTIONS OF CASH TO SHAREHOLDERS

During the life of a corporation, corporate managers and boards of directors often find it useful to distribute a portion of the corporation's cash to shareholders. These distributions come in one of two forms: share repurchases or declaration and payment of cash dividends.

Share repurchases are exchanges between shareholders and the corporation in which the corporation purchases the investors' shares. When a corporation acquires its own shares, these shares must either be retired or placed in treasury. Corporate share repurchases distribute cash only to those shareholders who sell stock back to the company. Share repurchases must be authorized by the board of directors.

Cash dividends represent periodic distributions of cash to shareholders based on a per share rate. Cash dividends are distributed pro-rata to all shareholders. Cash dividends are paid only when the board of directors authorizes the distribution by declaring a dividend. In both share repurchases and cash dividends, cash is transferred from the corporation to shareholders, thereby reducing the corporation's assets as well as the book value of stockholders' equity.

Corporate Share Repurchases

Managerial motivations to distribute cash vary. Share repurchases are undertaken for many reasons, including:

1. To provide shares to satisfy the needs of various convertible securities such as options, convertible bonds, or convertible preferred stock without having to increase the total number of outstanding shares by issuing previously unissued shares.
2. To remove a specific group of shareholders from ownership, sometimes called a *targeted share repurchase*.
3. To affect the relative percentage of the corporation managers hold and, thereby, increase their ownership rights.

Regardless of the motivations, corporations that acquire shares of their own stock do not record these shares as an asset since shares acquired in these exchanges do not provide a future benefit that will materialize in revenues or income. By definition, exchanges between corporations and their shareholders are not income-producing transactions. Shares acquired in a repurchase are economically no different than shares that have been authorized but unissued.

Corporations must decide whether to *retire* shares acquired in a repurchase or to treat them as *treasury stock*. When shares are retired, they reassume the status of authorized, but unissued, shares. When shares are placed in treasury, they are considered issued, but not outstanding shares. Shares placed in treasury cannot receive dividends. However, some state corporation laws do distinguish between treasury shares and unissued stock on some dimensions. Treasury shares may be exempt from certain legal limitations on the issuance of authorized, but previously unissued, common shares. The broad adoption of the Model Business Corporation Act (MBCA) has effectively eliminated legal differences between shares placed in treasury and those that are in the unissued category in many states. However, even in these states, corporations usually retain the designation of treasury shares for financial reporting purposes instead of treating all repurchased shares as retired.

Recording Share Repurchases—Retired Stock

When shares are repurchased with cash and retired, the exchange is recorded by:

1. Reducing the contributed capital accounts by the dollar amount that represents the historical price at which the shares were originally issued
2. Reducing the cash balance
3. Making adjustments to other additional paid-in capital accounts or retained earnings as necessary

When retired shares are acquired at prices below their original issue price, the difference represents an addition to additional paid-in capital. When the acquisition price is above the historical issue price, the difference represents a reduction in stockholders' equity, which may affect additional paid-in capital and/or retained earnings.

Retirement at Prices Below the Historical Issue Price   Assume that Brightwell Industries originally issued 10,000 shares of $1 par common stock at $6 per share on January 1, 1991. On June 12, 1995, Brightwell repurchased 4,000 of these shares at $4.50 per share and retired the stock. In this situation, the retired shares are repurchased at a price below the historical issue price. For completeness, Brightwell's journal entry to record the original issuance of the stock would have appeared as follows:

January 1, 1991:		
Cash	60,000	
Common stock at par		10,000
Additional paid-in capital		50,000
To record the issuance of $1 par common stock at $6 per share.		

Brightwell's journal entry to record the repurchase and retirement would appear as:

June 12, 1995:

Common stock at par	4,000	
Additional paid-in capital	20,000	
Additional paid-in capital—retired stock		6,000
Cash		18,000

To record the repurchase and retirement of 4,000 shares of
common stock.

In the above entry, common stock at par is reduced by the par value of the retired shares; the existing additional paid-in capital is reduced by the original issue premium [($6 – $1) × (4,000 shares)]; and cash is reduced by the total purchase price of $18,000. In addition, a new contributed capital account entitled additional paid-in capital—retired stock was created. In this example, the credit to this new capital account represents the difference between the historical price of the retired shares when first issued and the repurchase price. Since the shares were repurchased at a price below the historical issue price, a permanent addition to contributed capital is created when the shares are retired. No gain is recognized on share repurchases. To aid in tracking the effects of share retirements through the various equity accounts, Panel A of Exhibit 15.1 demonstrates the effects of the above journal entries on the equity account balances.

For reporting purposes, corporations do not segregate the sources of additional paid-in capital. In this example, the additional paid-in capital from the original issue of shares would be added to the additional paid-in capital created from the retirement and reported as a single amount in the financial statements. Given the amounts above, the total additional paid-in capital account will have a balance of $36,000. Of this balance, $30,000 arose from the original issue of the

EXHIBIT 15.1
The Brightwell
Industries
Example—Tracking
the Effects of Share
Retirements
Through Various
Equity Accounts

Tracking the Effects of Share Retirements Through Various Equity Accounts
The Brightwell Industries Example

Panel A: Using Separate Additional Paid-In Capital (APIC) Accounts

Common Stock at Par		APIC from Issuance		
	60,000		50,000	Original Issuance of Stock
4,000		20,000		Retirement
56,000			30,000	Balance

	APIC from Retirements		
			Original Issuance of Stock
	6,000		Retirement
	6,000		Balance

Total APIC from all sources = $30,000 + $6,000 = $36,000

Panel B: Using a Single Aggregated Additional Paid-In Capital (APIC) Account

Common Stock at Par		APIC from Issuance	
	60,000		50,000
4,000		14,000	
56,000			36,000

remaining 6,000 outstanding shares; $6,000, from the fact that 4,000 retired shares were originally issued for $24,000 but were retired for only $18,000.

The Segregation of Additional Paid-in Capital by Source   The segregation of additional paid-in capital by source is similar to a set of subsidiary accounts to the additional paid-in capital control account. Generally accepted accounting principles, as delineated by ARB No. 43 and APB Opinion No. 5, indicate a preference for retaining this level of detail in the additional paid-in capital accounts. However, APB Opinion No. 5 also acknowledges that state corporation laws may specify treatments other than those preferred by GAAP and that these should be deemed acceptable. Since state corporation laws generally do not require segregation, many corporations do not maintain sufficiently detailed records to identify additional paid-in capital by source. If Brightwell did not segregate its additional paid-in capital by source when the repurchased shares were retired, it would have made the following journal entry instead of the one above:

June 12, 1995:		
Common stock at par	4,000	
Additional paid-in capital	14,000	
Cash		18,000
To record the repurchase and retirement of 4,000 shares of common stock.		

In this entry, the net change in total additional paid-in capital resulting from the retirement is charged to additional paid-in capital, without identifying the type of exchange. As a result, the total contributed capital is $36,000, just as it was previously. However, there are no subsidiary ledger accounts tracking various sources of contributed capital in excess of par value. Panel B of Exhibit 15.1 demonstrates how these events would be captured in the underlying accounts using a single, aggregate additional paid-in capital account.

In the remainder of this chapter, we adopt a policy of segregating each type of additional paid-in capital based on the nature of the exchanges that gave rise to the capital contribution. Consequently, paid-in capital from issuance of common stock is segregated from paid-in capital from retirement of common stock, treasury stock transactions, or any other form of exchange. While this approach is the preferred method under GAAP, practice varies considerably in this regard. Therefore, it is not possible to generalize how a particular company may have recorded similar exchanges to those presented here.

Retirement at Prices Above the Historical Issue Price   When the repurchase price exceeds the original issue price, the excess is first treated as a reduction of any additional paid-in capital created from similar past transactions. Then, any remainder is treated as a reduction of retained earnings.[2] For

---

[2] Some states would allow the excess to be charged against the balance of the additional paid-in capital on common stock if the adjustment would not result in a deficit in the balance of additional paid-in capital on common. If the excess is larger than the existing balance of additional paid-in capital, retained earnings must be charged for the difference.

example, assume that after the previous retirement of shares, Brightwell retires an additional 2,000 shares of common stock at a price of $10 per share on October 5, 1996. Based on the activity relating to common stock up to the date of this retirement of 2,000 shares, Brightwell had the following balances in various additional paid-in capital accounts:

Additional paid-in capital from original issue	$30,000
Additional paid-in capital from retired stock	6,000
Total additional paid-in capital	$36,000

Brightwell would use the following journal entry to record the retirement of the additional 2,000 shares:

```
October 5, 1996:
Common stock at par                              2,000
Additional paid-in capital                      10,000
Additional paid-in capital—retired stock         6,000
Retained earnings                                2,000
  Cash                                                      20,000
To record the repurchase and retirement of 2,000 shares of
  common stock.
```

In the above entry, the adjustments to additional paid-in capital proceed in the following sequence:

1. Remove the original issue premium from additional paid-in capital on original issue of common stock (the account labeled additional paid-in capital in this example).
2. Reduce the additional paid-in capital from other similar transactions up to the point where the balance is equal to zero (the account labeled additional paid-in capital—retired stock).
3. Any additional charges are recorded by reducing retained earnings.

This sequence is preferred by GAAP and explains the amounts entered in the above entry. Additional paid-in capital is reduced by the original issue premium based on the historical selling price of $6 per share and a par value of $1 [($6 − $1) × (2,000 shares) = $10,000]. The adjustment to additional paid-in capital—retired stock arises from the earlier retirement of 4,000 shares at a price below the historical issue price and can be offset to absorb the deficit in the current retirement, but only to the point where the balance in the account is reduced to zero. After reducing the additional paid-in capital—retired stock to zero, retained earnings are reduced by the residual of $2,000 to account fully for the decline in stockholders' equity due to the distribution of $20,000 cash to the shareholders. Exhibit 15.2 tracks the effects of this retirement into Brightwell's underlying account balances using separate accounts for each type of additional paid-in capital.

Share Repurchases—Treasury Stock

When corporations elect not to retire shares that have been repurchased, these shares are carried in treasury. Shares held in treasury can be valued by using either the repurchase price (**cost method**) or the par value of the shares (**par value method**), if a par value exists. While the cost method is more often used, both methods are acceptable under GAAP. Regardless of which method is used, the balance in the treasury stock account always represents a reduction of stockholders' equity (i.e., treasury stock is a contra-equity account).

To compare the treatment of treasury stock under the cost method to its treatment under the par value method, consider the following sequence of events. Tary Corporation originally issued 10,000 shares of $50 par common stock for $52 a share. The following entry was made to record this sale on November 1, 1992:

November 1, 1992:		
Cash	520,000	
Common stock at par		500,000
Additional paid-in capital		20,000

The company entered into the following treasury stock transactions:

- On March 1, 1994, repurchased 100 shares for the treasury at $45 per share.

- On April 1, 1994, repurchased 100 more shares for the treasury at $60 per share.

- On May 1, 1994, sold 100 shares out of treasury for $55 per share.

- On June 1, 1994, sold 100 shares out of treasury for $45 per share.

Tracking the Effects of Share Retirements Through Various Equity Accounts
Using Separate APIC Accounts
The Brightwell Industries Example Continued

Common Stock at Par		APIC from Issuance		
	60,000		50,000	Original Issuance of Stock
4,000		20,000		1995 Retirement
	56,000		30,000	Balance
2,000		10,000		1996 Retirement
	54,000		20,000	Balance

APIC from Retirements		Retained Earnings*		
	0		0	Original Issuance of Stock
	6,000		0	1995 Retirement
	6,000		0	Balance
6,000		2,000		1996 Retirement
	0		2,000	Balance

*Other effects on retained earnings such as accumulation of earnings or dividend distributions are suppressed in this example to highlight the effects of share retirements on retained earnings.

EXHIBIT 15.2

The Brightwell Industries Example Continued—Tracking the Effects of Share Retirements Through Various Equity Accounts—Using Separate APIC Accounts

The Cost Method of Accounting for Treasury Stock

Under the cost method, recording the acquisition of shares increases the balance in the treasury stock account and decreases cash in the amount of the purchase price. Tary Corporation's journal entries to record the acquisitions of treasury shares would appear as follows under the cost method:

March 1, 1994:

Treasury stock	4,500	
Cash		4,500

To record the repurchase of 100 shares of treasury stock at $45 per share.

April 1, 1994:

Treasury stock	6,000	
Cash		6,000

To record the repurchase of 100 shares of treasury stock at $60 per share.

When treasury stock is reissued, any difference between the stock's carrying value and the reissue price must be accounted for through adjustments to additional paid-in capital or retained earnings. Carrying value of the treasury shares issued can be determined though the use of a first-in, first-out, or weighted average cost flow assumption, or by specific identification since each stock certificate has a unique identification number. As with the retirement of stock, tracing the adjustments related to treasury share reissues through the additional paid-in capital and retained earnings accounts depends primarily on state corporation laws and the materiality of the effects, as well as the level of detail in the records maintained by the corporation regarding the sources of additional paid-in capital.

Consider the resale of 100 shares of treasury stock for $55 per share on May 1, 1994. Using the first-in, first-out method, the shares' carrying value would be $45 per share. Alternatively, a weighted average approach would assign cost of $52.50 per share $\{[(100 \times \$45) + (100 \times \$60)]/200\}$. For this discussion, first-in, first-out will be used. Having assigned a cost of $4,500 to the shares, the sale of the shares for $5,500 implies an increase in additional paid-in capital. Tary's journal entry, assuming it uses a separate additional paid-in capital account, to record the sale of the treasury stock would appear as follows:

May 1, 1994:

Cash	5,500	
Treasury stock		4,500
Additional paid-in capital—treasury stock		1,000

To record the reissue of 100 shares of treasury stock for $55 per share, purchased at $45 per share.

On June 1, 1994, Tary sells the remaining treasury shares for $45, or a total selling price of $4,500. Since these shares would have a total carrying value of $6,000, the issuance of these shares must result in a decline in the additional paid-in capital accounts. The decline in additional paid-in capital will be reflected first in the removal of all additional paid-in capital from other treasury stock transactions and then in the removal of the amount of additional

669

paid-in capital created from the original issuance of the shares. If the balances in these accounts are insufficient to absorb the difference between carrying value and the resale price of the treasury stock, Tary would charge the remainder to retained earnings as follows:

June 1, 1994:		
Cash	4,500	
Additional paid-in capital—treasury stock	1,000	
Additional paid-in capital	200	
Retained earnings	300	
Treasury stock		6,000

To record the reissue of 100 shares of treasury stock for $45 per share, purchased at $60 per share.

Exhibit 15.3 traces each of these journal entries into the underlying equity accounts, using a separate account for each type of additional paid-in capital created.

EXHIBIT 15.3

The Tary Corporation Example—Tracking the Effects of the Cost Method of Accounting for Treasury Stock Transactions

Tracking the Effects of the Cost Method of Accounting for Treasury Stock Transactions Through the Equity Accounts Using Separate APIC Accounts
The Tary Corporation Example

Common Stock at Par		APIC from Issuance		
	500,000		20,000	Original Issuance of Stock
	0		0	First Treasury Purchase
	0		0	Second Treasury Purchase
	0		0	First Treasury Sale
		200		Second Treasury Sale
	500,000		19,800	Balance

Treasury Stock		APIC—Treasury Stock		
	0		0	Original Issuance of Stock
4,500			0	First Treasury Purchase
6,000			0	Second Treasury Purchase
	4,500		1,000	First Treasury Sale
	6,000	1,000	0	Second Treasury Sale
	0		0	Balance

Retained Earnings*			
	0		Original Issuance of Stock
	0		First Treasury Purchase
	0		Second Treasury Purchase
	0		First Treasury Sale
300			Second Treasury Sale
300			Balance

*Other effects on retained earnings such as accumulation of earnings or dividend distributions are suppressed in this example to highlight the effects of share retirements on retained earnings.

The Par Value Method of Accounting for Treasury Stock

Under the par value method, treasury shares are valued at their par value, not at the price paid to acquire them. This implies that adjustments for the difference between the repurchase price and the par value of the shares must occur at reacquisition. When treasury shares valued under the par value method are reissued, treasury stock is reduced for the par value of the shares sold; and the difference between the resale price and par value is treated as an adjustment to additional paid-in capital.

The allocation of the difference between the repurchase price and the par value of treasury shares follows the same guidelines as indicated earlier for share retirements. The original amount of additional paid-in capital created when the treasury shares were originally issued must be removed. Any additional adjustments will be reflected in additional paid-in capital—treasury stock and/or retained earnings. Exhibit 15.4 traces the activity.

Consider Tary Corporation's first repurchase of 100 shares of common stock on March 1, 1994. The par value of the shares acquired was $5,000 ($50

EXHIBIT 15.4

The Tary Corporation Example—Tracking the Effects of the Par Value Method of Accounting for Treasury Stock Transactions

**Tracking the Effects of the Par Value Method of Accounting for Treasury Stock Transactions Through the Equity Accounts Using Separate APIC Accounts
The Tary Corporation Example**

Common Stock at Par		APIC from Issuance		
	500,000		20,000	Original Issuance of Stock
	0	200		First Treasury Purchase
	0	200		Second Treasury Purchase
	0		0	First Treasury Sale
			0	Second Treasury Sale
	500,000		19,600	Balance

Treasury Stock		APIC—Treasury Stock		
	0		0	Original Issuance of Stock
5,000			700	First Treasury Purchase
5,000		700		Second Treasury Purchase
	5,000		500	First Treasury Sale
	5,000	500		Second Treasury Sale
	0		0	Balance

Retained Earnings*		
	0	Original Issuance of Stock
	0	First Treasury Purchase
100		Second Treasury Purchase
	0	First Treasury Sale
	0	Second Treasury Sale
100		Balance

*Other effects on retained earnings such as accumulation of earnings or dividend distributions are suppressed in this example to highlight the effects of share retirements on retained earnings.

per share × 100 shares), and the original additional paid-in capital created when these shares were issued was $200 ($2 per share × 100 shares). The shares were repurchased for $45. Under the par value approach, the treasury stock account will increase by the par value of the shares reacquired. The additional paid-in capital from the original issuance of the shares will be removed. Cash will decrease by the purchase price. The difference between the shares' historical issue price and the repurchase price represents a net increase in additional paid-in capital arising from treasury stock transactions. Tary's journal entry to record the treasury stock purchase using the par value method would appear as follows:

March 1, 1994:

Treasury stock	5,000	
Additional paid-in capital	200	
Additional paid-in capital—treasury stock		700
Cash		4,500

To record the repurchase of 100 shares of treasury stock at $45 per share.

On April 1, 1994, when Tary repurchases another 100 shares for $60 per share, the company would record an increase in the treasury stock of $5,000 for the par value of the shares and would reduce the additional paid-in capital by $200 for the original issue premium on the common stock. However, the difference between the repurchase price of $6,000 and the original issue price of the stock, $5,200 would require adjustments to additional paid-in capital—treasury stock and retained earnings in order to absorb the entire differential as follows:

April 1, 1994:

Treasury stock	5,000	
Additional paid-in capital	200	
Additional paid-in capital—treasury stock	700	
Retained earnings	100	
Cash		6,000

To record the repurchase of 100 shares of treasury stock at $60 per share.

When the treasury shares are reissued, the treasury stock account is reduced by the par value of the shares issued, cash is increased by the issue price, and the difference is recorded as additional paid-in capital—treasury stock.[3] The following journal entries show how Tary would handle the resale of the shares:

May 1, 1994:

Cash	5,500	
Treasury stock		5,000
Additional paid-in capital—treasury stock		500

To record the reissuance of 100 shares of treasury stock at $55 per share.

---

[3] Note that no cost flow assumption is necessary under the par value method, since all shares are carried at par value regardless of their acquisition price.

June 1, 1994:

Cash	4,500	
Additional paid-in capital—treasury stock	500	
Treasury stock		5,000

To record the reissuance of 100 shares of treasury stock at $45
  per share.

Panel B of Exhibit 15.3 demonstrates how these journal entries affect the underlying equity account balances. Note the differences between the par value and cost methods are particularly related to the effects on the APIC from issuance and retained earnings.

Retirement of Shares Carried in Treasury

At some point after the acquisition of treasury stock, managers may elect to retire the shares. Retirement of treasury shares carried on the cost method is recorded by removing the balance in the treasury stock account, reducing the legal capital accounts for the par or stated value of the shares, and making appropriate adjustments to additional paid-in capital or retained earnings in the same fashion as if the shares had been purchased at the time of retirement. For example, assume that in the Tary Corporation example discussed earlier, the first 100 shares of treasury stock purchased at $45 were retired on April 15, 1997. Tary would make the following entry if the treasury shares were recorded using the cost method:

April 15, 1997:

Common stock at par	5,000	
Additional paid-in capital	200	
Treasury stock		4,500
Additional paid-in capital—retired stock		700

To record the retirement of the treasury shares originally issued at
  $52 per share and repurchased at $45 per share.

Under the par value method, retirement simply requires a debit to the common stock at par and a credit to the treasury stock account for the par value.

Issuance of Treasury Shares in Exchange for Convertible Securities

Corporate managers often acquire treasury shares to be used when the option to convert other securities is exercised. When this situation arises, the carrying value of the treasury shares must be removed from the treasury stock account; and any differences between the carrying value and the value received in exchange for the treasury shares should be treated as an adjustment to additional paid-in capital.

For example, assume that Rege Industries had a convertible bond with a face value of $100,000, which was issued at face value without issue costs several years ago. On July 1, 1996, immediately after an interest payment date, the bond was converted into 50,000 shares of $1 par common stock. The conversion was satisfied by the issuance of 50,000 treasury shares with a cost of

$75,000. The bond's market value immediately prior to conversion was $103,000. Using the book value method of recording this conversion, $100,000 would be the assigned value to the treasury shares being issued. Rege's journal entry would appear as:

July 1, 1996:

Bonds payable	100,000	
Treasury stock		75,000
Additional paid-in capital		25,000

To record the conversion of the bonds using the book value method.

If the market value method had been used to record the conversion, the value attributed to the treasury shares being issued would be $103,000. Rege's journal entry to record the conversion would appear as follows:

July 1, 1996:

Bonds payable	100,000	
Loss on conversion of bonds	3,000	
Treasury stock		75,000
Additional paid-in capital		28,000

To record the conversion of the bonds using the market value method.

Cash Distributions—Corporate Dividends

Some corporations pay dividends, but many do not. Since the reinvestment of earnings is one of the cheapest forms of new equity capital formation, companies that have a great need for new equity capital generally do not pay dividends. Start-up companies, or smaller companies intensively involved in research and development efforts, usually conserve their available cash by electing not to pay dividends to shareholders.

Larger, more established companies generally do pay regular cash dividends to shareholders. The quarterly dividend is the most common. Corporate managers use the declaration of dividends to communicate their beliefs about the company's future prospects. Managers have a wealth of private information about the prospects for the company; dividend decisions can convey part of this information. Consequently, increases in quarterly dividends generally communicate good news about the company's future prospects.

Why use dividends to convey information about the future? Why not announce the specific plans to shareholders? In Chapter 1, we concluded that signals used to convey information are often preferable to specific information that competitors could use. Therefore, it may not be in the shareholders' best interest to make specific information about future plans public. For example, if the company plans to utilize a new production process to reduce significantly the cost of one of its primary products, announcing these plans too early may erode, or eliminate, the company's ability to take advantage of the opportunity. An increase in cash dividends prior to the realization of the increased profits resulting from the new production process can effectively *signal* shareholders that future profits are expected to rise, without explicitly indicating how this will happen.

Will firms with low or flat expected profits increase their dividend in response to the dividend increase by companies with good future prospects? Firms with low or flat expected profits will often find it too costly to increase their dividends to mimic firms with growing profits. Also, since future realizations can be compared with management's decision to increase dividends, investors can determine after the fact whether a dividend increase may have been motivated by honest beliefs about future profits or by attempts to mimic other companies. Managers' reputations may be damaged if they are not able to deliver the improved profits signaled by the dividend increase.

This signaling feature of dividends largely explains the pattern of corporate dividends. Most corporations attempt to maintain the same dividend from quarter to quarter (assuming the dividends are paid quarterly), unless they plan a permanent change in the dividend level. Changes in the dividend for corporations paying regular dividends serve as a particularly strong signal about the company's future prospects. Of course, corporations that pay dividends sporadically establish no pattern from which to judge changes in the dividend level.

Even corporations maintaining a stable dividend pattern may generate excess cash in a particularly good year. These corporations may decide to distribute the excess cash to shareholders in the form of a one-time increased dividend. When such distributions are made, corporations clearly indicate the distribution's nature to avoid having investors misinterpret the dividend increase as a "permanent" increase.

Financial statements do not provide information on increases or decreases in dividends in a timely manner. Financial reporting focuses on capturing the effects of dividend distributions on the components of stockholders' equity; it does not inform investors about changes in dividend policies. However, the effects of dividend distributions on the corporation's assets and equity structure are reported in the financial statements. Consequently, the financial reports serve as a means to audit the effects of dividend activities, even though they are not the primary source of information about dividend policy changes.

The Legal Mechanics of a Dividend

When a corporation issues a dividend, it follows several stages in the process. First, the board of directors must declare a dividend. The date on which this occurs is called the *date of declaration*. A dividend declaration formally commits the corporation to the distribution. A board cannot rescind a dividend announcement. It can only be reversed by a vote of the shareholders. As a result, when the board declares a cash dividend, a legal liability for distribution of cash is created and recorded on the date of declaration.[4]

---

[4] Note that this differs from the investors' recording of a dividend receivable discussed in Chapter 6. Investors are not entitled to receive a dividend unless they hold the shares on the ex dividend date. As a result, the company has entered into a liability to distribute cash to some shareholders, but the specific identity of the recipients and right to collect will not be determined until the ex dividend date.

At some specified date following the date of declaration (the ex dividend date), the shareholders who will actually receive the cash distribution are deter-- mined. Finally, the cash is actually paid out on the *date of distribution* to the shareholders who held the stock at the close of business on the ex dividend date.

Recording a Cash Dividend

Assume that Beta Corporation had 200,000 shares of stock issued and out- standing on July 1, 1993, at which time it declared a $1.25 dividend per share, payable on July 31, to the shareholders of record on July 15, 1993. Beta would make the following journal entries to record this dividend:[5]

July 1, 1993:

Retained earnings	250,000	
Dividends payable		250,000

To record the declaration of the $1.25/share cash dividend.

July 31, 1993:

Dividends payable	250,000	
Cash		250,000

To record the actual distribution of the cash dividend.

Corporate Distributions of Noncash Assets

The board of directors can elect to distribute assets other than cash to the shareholders. When noncash assets are used in exchange for share repurchas- es or are distributed in the form of a dividend, any gain or loss resulting from a difference in the book value of the asset distributed and its fair value at the date of declaration must be recognized as a gain or loss.[6]

One example of this type of distribution is a **property dividend**, in which noncash assets are distributed. A classic example of a property dividend dis- tribution occurred when the Federal government forced Du Pont Corporation to divest itself of holdings in General Motors as a reaction to antitrust proceed- ings many years ago. Du Pont determined that the easiest way to divest of the General Motors' shares was to distribute them as a property dividend to its own shareholders.

Recording a property dividend is similar to recording a cash dividend except:

1. The asset being distributed is adjusted to fair value with any gain or loss recognized at the date of declaration
2. The liability for the property dividend is linked to a specific asset

---

[5] The debit in this entry may be to a nominal account titled dividends. If this approach is uti- lized, the dividends account must be closed to retained earnings at the end of the period along with other nominal accounts.

[6] The requirement to recognize gain or loss provides comparability between firms that sell the property first, then distribute the cash to the shareholders and those that simply distribute the asset directly. In addition, the ability to recognize gain or loss depends on the reliability of fair value estimates. When fair value estimates are not deemed to be reliable, the asset will be distrib- uted at historical cost.

For example, assume Delta Corporation has declared a property dividend in shares of Gamma Company. The shares of Gamma are carried at a cost of $100,000 and currently have a market value of $130,000. The dividend was declared on August 1, 1994, distributable on November 1, to shareholders of record on September 1, 1994. Delta's journal entries to record this activity would appear as follows:

August 1, 1994:

Marketable securities	30,000	
Gain on marketable securities		30,000
To revalue the marketable securities being distributed as a property dividend to fair market value.		

Retained earnings	130,000	
Property dividend distributable		130,000
To record the liability for the property dividend.		

November 1, 1994:

Property dividend distributable	130,000	
Marketable securities		130,000
To record the distribution of the Gamma stock as a property dividend.		

If Delta Corporation had an October 31 fiscal year-end, it would have reported the obligation for the distribution of the property dividend as a current liability.

Preferred Stock Dividends

Preferred dividends must be declared along with, or prior to, the declaration of common dividends. Preferred stock dividends are often cumulative. This provision requires that if the preferred dividend is not declared in one period, then it must be declared and paid in later periods prior to the declaration of any common stock dividends. An undeclared preferred stock dividend is not a liability even if the dividends are cumulative. However, the existence of dividends in arrears on cumulative preferred does restrict the corporation's ability to make dividend distributions to common shareholders.

In some cases, preferred stock participates with common stock when the dividends declared exceed some contractually defined level. This contractual agreement, known as a **participation provision**, defines the level of declared dividends at which preferred shareholders begin to participate. A participation provision only becomes effective after the stated dividend on preferred is distributed. In addition, only the stated dividend on the preferred stock is typically subject to an accumulation clause in the preferred stock agreement.

Generally, before the participation provision is applicable, dividends sufficient to provide common shareholders with a percentage return on par value equal to that of the stated dividend on preferred must be distributed to common. Any dividends above this level are then shared between the preferred and common shareholders in relation to their total par values. The preferred stock agreement defines the specific relationship and may state a maximum level of participation.

Blegen Corporation has 90,000 shares of $10 par common stock outstanding and 1,000 shares of $100 par, 5% participating preferred stock. In this example, the total par value of the common stock is $900,000, and the total par value of the preferred stock is $100,000. Consequently, the common stock represents 90% [$900,000/($100,000 + $900,000)] of the total par value of all stock; preferred, 10%. Blegen's board of directors declares a total dividend of $125,000 for the year. The allocation of these dividends would be as follows:

	Preferred	Common
5% stated dividend to preferred $100 par × 1,000 shares × 5%	$ 5,000	
5% dividend on common $10 par × 90,000 shares × 5%		$ 45,000
Participation dividend $75,000 ($125,000 − $5,000 − $45,000)		
Preferred: $75,000 × 10%	7,500	
Common: $75,000 × 90%		67,500
Total dividends to be distributed	$12,500	$112,500

The journal entry to record the declaration and distribution of the dividend would be identical in form to those for common stock dividends discussed previously.

Limitations on Corporate Asset Distributions

Historically, by creating the concept of legal capital, state corporation laws originally sought to protect creditors. The notion was that any distribution of corporate assets could not occur if it would reduce total capital below the corporation's legal capital. Over the years, the concept of legal capital has been largely displaced by other legal restrictions on corporate distributions, which were discussed in Chapter 14.

In addition to state corporation laws, many debtholders also protect themselves from excessive asset distributions to equity investors by including limits on the size and nature of corporate asset distributions in lending agreements. These limitations are called *debt covenant restrictions* and were introduced in the discussion of corporate debt in Chapter 13. Since debt covenants are negotiated between a corporation and a particular lender, they can take any form that does not conflict with state statute. Effective debt covenants can protect the debtholder from shareholder distributions that would unduly increase the risks of default on the outstanding debt.

Typically, these contractual restrictions allow corporations to make asset distributions only to the extent that they do not exceed:

1. Earnings recorded after the signing of the debt agreement, plus
2. The proceeds of any new equity issues after the signing of the debt agreement, plus
3. A lump-sum amount referred to as the "dip."

The **dip**, or the amount of capital existing when the debt agreement is entered into, can be used to support corporate distribution in the future.

With the exception of the dip, these restrictions "lock up" the book value of equity existing at the time the debt agreement is signed. Any distributions for the purchase of stock (regardless of whether it is retired or placed in treasury) or for dividends reduces the available pool for supporting additional distributions. The pool of resources available at any time to support a distribution is referred to as the **unrestricted retained earnings**. This term appears to refer specifically to retained earnings. However, its use grows out of the fact that most firms subject to debt covenants create the ability to make corporate distributions by recording earnings following the signing of the debt contract. These earnings are obviously part of retained earnings.

If it undertakes an asset distribution that violates the debt covenant, the company is in technical default. **Technical default** means that a specific term in the contract is violated, not that the company cannot make payments for interest and principal. (Failure to make required payments would be an *actual* default.) In a technical default, the debtholder can take any of several actions, none of which are good for the debtor corporation:

1. Call the debt (demand immediate payment).
2. Renegotiate the debt (agree to waive default in exchange for better terms such as a higher interest rate).
3. Force the company into bankruptcy (if the company is also insolvent).

These restrictions, which exist in both publicly traded debt and debt obtained from private sources such as banks, provide a control mechanism over the debtor's actions and relieve the creditor of constant monitoring. The debtor corporation's management can conduct business as usual, as long as the debt covenants are not violated. Note that in these contracts, the covenant restrictions relate to the value of accounting numbers (such as earnings), which themselves are under the control of managers to the extent that managers select both the transactions to enter into and the accounting principles that govern the representation of those events in the financial statements.

Liquidating Dividends

The term **liquidating dividend**, as it pertains to the corporation issuing the stock, has a variety of meanings depending on the circumstances. In the classic approach to reporting stockholders' equity, where contributed capital and retained earnings are kept strictly separated, a liquidating dividend occurs when the balance in retained earnings is insufficient to absorb the full dividend distribution. In this case, retained earnings absorb the dividend until it is exhausted. The excess dividend represents a return of contributed capital and is charged against additional paid-in capital.

Since state corporation laws generally separate only legal capital (par value) from all other sources of capital, a liquidating dividend under most states' laws does not occur until the dividend exceeds the value of total stockholders' equity reduced by the value of any legal capital. In some states, a liquidating dividend occurs when the distribution results in the fair value of assets falling below the fair value of liabilities plus the value of legal capital. In such states, dividends are recorded as reductions in retained earnings, regardless of whether the result is a deficit or surplus.[7] Consequently, a lawyer may not describe a dividend that distributes part of additional paid-in capital as a liquidating dividend, but an accountant would. Since capturing the consequences of these distributions in the financial statements is linked to legal concepts embodied in state law, an attorney's advice is central to accounting for corporate asset distributions.

CORPORATE DISTRIBUTIONS—SHARE ISSUES

On occasion, corporate managers seek to alter the number of outstanding shares without raising new capital. This can be accomplished through the declaration of a *stock split* or a *stock dividend*. While the recording of these two events is different, the economic features of both are similar. Both distributions are declared by the board of directors. In each case, shareholders receive additional shares of stock in direct proportion to their holdings on the date of record. Generally, stock dividends are used when a corporation wishes to increase the number of outstanding shares by a small percentage, while a stock split is used to make large changes in the number of outstanding shares. In addition, a stock split can be used to reduce the total number of shares outstanding, which is not possible with a stock dividend.

The effects of stock distributions are not fully understood. If the act of distributing additional shares did not provide investors any new information, share prices should respond to a stock split or dividend by changing in inverse proportion to the number of shares issued. For example, a stock trading at $10 per share before a 2-for-1 stock split, which will distribute one new share for each one held prior to the split, should trade at $5 after the split if no new information is learned about the company's future prospects. If the split (or dividend) communicates information to investors about future prospects, the price in this example may change to a price above or below $5.

Stock splits, which have a significant effect on the number of outstanding shares, may be motivated by managers' desire to have the corporation's shares trade within a certain price range per share. This preference is motivated by the existence of transactions cost such as brokerage fees, which are larger for small-sized trades than for large-sized trades. An investor with $1,000 to invest can only purchase 10 shares if the price is $100; but that investor can purchase 100 shares if the price is $10. Brokerage fees on a 100-share trade might be 3%, while a 10-share trade might carry a brokerage fee of 5%. By reducing the price per share, managers may be able to attract more small investors and, thus, increase the demand for the corporation's stocks. In today's marketplace, with the proliferation of mutual funds that combine the purchasing power of many small investors, this motivation does not appear to be a likely explanation for splits in general, but it may explain some of these decisions.

---

[7] This is essentially what occurred in the Holiday Corporation example referred to at the opening of this chapter.

Companies that are unable to distribute cash dividends or those that want an alternative to an increase in cash dividends often use stock dividends. When stock dividends are distributed, they tend to increase the number of outstanding shares by a small fraction such as 5% or 10%. Some managers view stock dividends as a means to communicate to investors that while additional cash dividends cannot be paid now, the future is good and the investors should receive something to represent this potential. If distributed while the normal level of quarterly cash dividends per share is held constant, the stock dividend actually increases the total cash dividend payout. This has an effect similar to the increase of the cash dividend per share in the absence of the stock dividend. It signals investors of increased future profitability.

Recording Stock Dividends

Stock dividends are declared and distributed in the same fashion as cash dividends. However, when a stock dividend is declared, the corporation has no liability to record because no obligation to distribute assets of the corporation exists. Instead, it has committed to distribute additional shares of stock without compensation.

The process of recording a stock dividend does require that retained earnings be decreased when the dividend is declared, just as it would occur for a cash dividend. The amount of the decrease depends on the dividend's size. Dividends for 20% to 25% or less of the total outstanding shares may be treated as **small stock dividends**. Recording the effects of small stock dividends requires that the amount charged to retained earnings equal the market value of the shares issued. Dividends for more than 20% to 25% of the outstanding shares are **large stock dividends**. Recording large stock dividends requires that an amount equal to the par value of the shares issued be removed from retained earnings. Dividends in the 20% to 25% range can be classified as either large or small, depending on the accountant's judgment.

For example, assume that Jester Incorporated has 400,000 shares of $2 par common stock outstanding. On May 1, 1994, Jester declared a 10% stock dividend, distributable on May 31, 1994, to the shareholders of record on May 15, 1994. Following the announcement of the dividend, the stock traded at $5 per share. This is a small stock dividend, which requires that the market value of the shares issued, $200,000 ($5 per share × 400,000 shares × 10%), be charged to retained earnings. This amount will be distributed to the contributed capital accounts, based on the par value, $2, of the shares issued. Jester's entries to record the activity are as follows:

May 1, 1994:

Retained earnings	200,000	
Stock dividends distributable		200,000

To record the declaration of the small stock dividend.

May 31, 1994:

Stock dividends distributable	200,000	
Common stock at par		80,000
Additional paid-in capital		120,000

To record the distribution of the stock dividend.

Stock dividend distributable is an equity account that exists only from the date of declaration to the date of distribution.

If Jester Incorporated had declared a 50% stock dividend, it would constitute a large stock dividend. Following the announcement of the 50% stock dividend, the market value per share of Jester stock probably would trade at a price below $5 per share since it traded at this price following the announcement of a 10% dividend in the previous example. However, market value of the shares is not relevant in recording large stock dividends. The amount removed from retained earnings represents only the required addition to legal capital indicated by the fact that additional shares will be outstanding. Jester's journal entry to record this stock dividend would appear as follows:[8]

May 1, 1994:

Retained earnings	400,000	
Stock dividends distributable		400,000

To record the declaration of the 50% stock dividend at par
value ($2 per share × 400,000 shares × 50%).

May 31, 1994:

Stock dividends distributable	400,000	
Common stock at par		400,000

To record the distribution of the stock dividend.

Recording Stock Splits

In a traditional stock split, the corporation would simply alter the par value of the shares in inverse proportion to the split. For example, a company that declared a 2-for-1 split with 1,000,000 shares of $2 par common stock would also alter the par value of common to $1 per share. As a result, the total legal capital before and after the split is $2,000,000. In a reverse split, such as a 1-for-2 split, the opposite would occur. The par value would double to $4, and there would be only 500,000 shares outstanding following the split. No journal entry is necessary to record this.[9]

When the corporation does not elect to change the par or stated value of its stock, it may report the effects of the stock splits in several ways. The available treatments depend on whether the split is a normal split (which increases the total number of shares outstanding) or a reverse split (which decreases the total number of shares outstanding). In a normal split, two alternative approaches are available. The first approach transfers an amount equal to the par value of the newly issued shares from additional paid-in capital into the legal capital account. The second approach records a similar transfer from retained earnings instead of additional paid-in capital. The latter approach is identical in nature to the treatment of a large stock dividend and is more consistent with the guidelines established in ARB No. 43.

---

[8] Note that if a company had no-par stock with no stated value, there would be no journal entry to record a large stock dividend since there is no requirement to capitalize any portion of retained earnings to meet legal capital requirements.

[9] No formal journal entry is required with no par stock either. In any case, it is possible that a memo entry is placed into the general ledger to indicate the existence and timing of the split.

In a reverse split, only one approach is available. Since the legal capital is reduced by the reduction in the total number of shares outstanding, a transfer is recorded from the legal capital account into additional paid-in capital.

For example, assume that the equity section of Balsa Corporation appeared as follows:

Common stock, $3 par, 1,500,000 shares outstanding	$ 4,500,000
Additional paid-in capital	20,000,000
Retained earnings	15,500,000
Total stockholders' equity	$40,000,000

On October 9, 1993, Balsa declared a 3-for-1 stock split without changing its par value. Balsa will issue two additional shares of common stock for each share of stock currently held. Consequently, there is an increase of $9,000,000 ($3 par × 3,000,000 shares issued) required for the legal capital account. Balsa's journal entries to record this event appear as follows:

October 9, 1993:

Additional paid-in capital	9,000,000	
Common stock at par		9,000,000
To record the effect of the stock split as a transfer of additional paid-in capital.		

or

Retained earnings	9,000,000	
Common stock at par		9,000,000
To record the effect of the stock split as a transfer from retained earnings.		

The choice between the above methods may be influenced by state corporation laws, and an attorney should be consulted to review the manner in which the split should be recorded.

Retroactive Effects of Split on the Reporting of Stockholders' Equity

When a split is declared, regardless of how it is accounted for within the stockholders' equity accounts, it affects the total number of shares outstanding. In most states, when a split occurs, the number of issued and outstanding shares, as well as any effect on treasury shares, is affected retroactively. Therefore, all previous periods presented on the financial statements are adjusted to reflect share numbers as post-split shares.

Assume that Kat Industries had the following information in its financial statements for 1994:

Common stock, $1 par, authorized 10,000,000 shares; issued 2,000,000; 1,700,000 outstanding	$ 2,000,000
Additional paid-in capital	8,000,000
Retained earnings	12,000,000
Treasury stock (300,000 shares at cost)	(4,000,000)
Total stockholders' equity	$18,000,000

On January 1, 1995, the company declared a 2-for-1 split, distributing another 2,000,000 shares and cutting its par value in half. Assuming there were no treasury stock transactions for the year, at the end of 1995, Kat would present the following information in the comparative equity sections for 1994 and 1995:

	1995	1994
Common stock, $.50 par, authorized 10,000,000 shares, issued 4,000,000; 3,400,000 outstanding	$ 2,000,000	$ 2,000,000
Additional paid-in capital	8,000,000	8,000,000
Retained earnings	17,000,000	12,000,000
Treasury stock (600,000 shares at cost)	(4,000,000)	(4,000,000)
Total stockholders' equity	$23,000,000	$18,000,000

In this disclosure, Kat has altered the representations regarding the number of shares issued and outstanding, as well as the number of shares in treasury for 1991 due to the effects of the split in 1995.

REPORTING CORPORATE DISTRIBUTIONS IN THE CASH FLOW STATEMENT

All cash outflows for repurchase of shares, regardless of their classification as retired shares or treasury stock following reacquisition, are classified as financing cash outflows. While all cash outflows for the purchases of stock during the year may be combined into a single category of cash outflows, these outflows cannot be netted against inflows from other stock issues. Cash paid out in the form of dividends is also a financing cash outflow. Generally, corporations include all dividends paid as a single item in financing cash outflows.

Share distributions do not give rise to any cash flow. As a result, they are not reported in the cash flow statement. Since all stock dividends and splits must be disclosed either in the financial statements or notes regarding equity for the period, these items are typically not included in a list of noncash transactions for the period when preparing a reconciliation for the cash flow statement.

Distributions of noncash assets as property dividends also do not give rise to a cash flow and are, thus, excluded from the cash flow statement. However, these events are typically included in a listing of significant noncash transactions provided as additional disclosure for the cash flow statement. The difference between these events and the share distributions is that share distributions only affect the equity section of the balance sheet by rearrangement of various equity accounts. Property dividends alter both the equity and asset positions of the firm and, therefore, warrant additional attention in the note disclosures.

MISCELLANEOUS EQUITY EFFECTS

Three additional events that result in changes to the equity section of the balance sheet are: appropriations of retained earnings, prior period adjustments, and quasi-reorganizations. These events are discussed in the remainder of the chapter.

Appropriations of Retained Earnings

At any time, the board of directors may restrict the ability of retained earnings to support corporate distributions. These restrictions may simply reflect existing legal limitations, or they may exceed the legal limitations.

Appropriated retained earnings represents an amount of stockholders' equity that is set aside and cannot be used to support corporate distributions. Created by specific act of the board of directors, it is recorded by crediting a special equity account called appropriated retained earnings and debiting retained earnings. Appropriation of retained earnings can be reversed by a vote of the board. When the board elects to remove the appropriation, the balance in appropriated retained earnings is returned to the retained earnings account. Appropriations are very rare.

Prior Period Adjustments

As applied in the United States, GAAP have typically required that all events and transactions affecting income through changes in assets and liabilities be reported in the income statement. While a few special circumstances such as foreign currency translation are an exception to this rule, the exceptions are rare. As a result, very few events give rise to direct charges against retained earnings. Some of these events were investigated in the discussion on corporate distributions, but they were all non-income-producing events. Another situation that gives rise to direct charges against retained earnings are **prior period adjustments**. These represent changes that must be made to the beginning balance of retained earnings because the consequences of an event are traceable to periods prior to the current period.

Prior period adjustments are limited to two classes of events:

1. Adjustments specifically identified for this treatment that arise due to a specific accounting standard
2. Error corrections

While the treatment of specific accounting standards is discussed as appropriate throughout the text, error corrections deserve special attention.

Errors that generate prior period adjustments arise when GAAP are not correctly applied in one period and this is discovered in a later period. Errors can result from miscalculations or failure to collect and appropriately utilize available information at the time the judgment was made. An example of a miscalculation would be an error in computing depreciation expense for a particular year.

An error made due to a failure to collect available information may relate to a decision regarding accrual of a contingent liability. Suppose an accountant had to decide whether to accrue a liability for a loss from litigation in progress. Further assume that at the balance sheet date a court had entered a judgment against the company, but the accountant did nothing to discover this event. Based on the information at the accountant's disposal, no accrual was made. In this case, the failure to collect relevant information, which was available at the balance sheet date, led to an error in the financial statements. When discovered in a later period, this error requires a prior period adjustment.

An important difference exists between an error caused by the failure to collect sufficient information to form a judgment and judgment regarding a future event that turns out to be incorrect. For example, in reviewing the facts surrounding litigation at any particular date, an accountant determines that a liability should not be accrued. However, the court later decides against the company. The court's judgment does not imply that the accountant's initial decision was in error. Rather, it implies that new developments occurred and other facts became available *after* the accountant made the initial decision not to accrue the liability.

Correction of an error requires restatement of all prior periods to which the error relates. The extent to which a particular set of financial statements will be affected depends on how much comparative data is supplied along with the current year's financial statements. If single-year statements are produced, the error correction will appear as an adjustment to the opening balance of retained earnings, similar to the following:

Retained earnings, beginning balance as reported	$1,500,000
Adjustment for error in prior period	(200,000)
Adjusted beginning balance of retained earnings	$1,300,000
Net income	400,000
Dividends	(50,000)
Retained earnings, ending balance	$1,650,000

When several years of comparative data are presented and the period in which the error occurred is among those presented, restatement of all periods is required. This eliminates the need for an adjustment to beginning retained earnings in the current year since this balance will be correct. If the error relates to a period prior to the earliest year presented, the prior period adjustment will appear as an adjustment to the earliest reported retained earnings balance. In addition, note disclosure that describes the reason for the restatement and the effect it had on earnings per share for each period presented must be provided.

Quasi-Reorganizations

A formal **corporate reorganization** occurs through an action of a bankruptcy court, which restructures the liability and equity claims of a corporation filing for legal reorganization. Courts have the power to alter the claims on the firm. When a corporation is reorganized under the bankruptcy statutes and released from bankruptcy to function on its own, the corporation basically receives a legal fresh start with a new set of equity and debt claimants.

On the other hand, a **quasi-reorganization** does not involve the court system. A quasi-reorganization is an accounting treatment designed to provide a corporation with a "fresh start" as far as its financial statements are concerned, regardless of whether any legal reorganization has occurred. It does not require any actual corporate reorganization, but it is most common following a series of actions management takes to turn a company around. These actions often include selling major segments of the company's business and various transactions such as early debt retirements, which change the company's liability and equity structure. The important distinction is that these actions are not taken under the protection of the courts.

Conceptually, a quasi-reorganization is undertaken to revalue assets and liabilities to market value, restructure the equity section to eliminate any deficits in retained earnings, and give the balance sheet the appearance of a company that is just beginning operations. Quasi-reorganizations are only to be effected when a company has suffered several periods of operating losses, which have caused a deficit in retained earnings, but has turned the corner and is entering a period of sustained profitability. Generally, to turn a company's fortunes around so dramatically requires that management take actions that would fall under the category of a corporate restructuring. However, this is technically not necessary.

Some limits are imposed in implementing a quasi-reorganization. While revaluation of assets and liabilities to market is undertaken, a limit is imposed to prevent corporations from writing up net assets. That is, assets can be written up, but only to the extent that other assets are written down or liabilities are also increased. In many cases, this limitation is not binding because market values for assets are often below book values. Once the assets and liabilities have been revalued, the deficit balance in retained earnings is removed and transferred into the contributed capital accounts. At this point, it may be necessary to alter the par or stated value of the common shares to avoid a deficit in the additional paid-in capital account. Existing debtholders may need to approve any quasi-reorganization if debt covenants limit the application of this accounting treatment. Also, approval of the shareholders may be required, depending on state corporation law.

Assume Redink Corporation reported the following balance sheet as of December 31, 1993, along with information on market values:

	Book Value	Market Value
Current assets	$ 200,000	$210,000
Property, plant, and equipment	800,000	350,000
Accumulated depreciation	$(300,000)	
Total assets	$ 700,000	
Liabilities	$ 490,000	400,000
Common stock at par ($50 par)	260,000	
Additional paid-in capital	20,000	
Retained earnings (deficit)	(70,000)	
Total equities	$ 700,000	

Further assume that Redink executes a quasi-reorganization by altering its par value to $10 per share. Redink's journal entries to effect the quasi-reorganization would appear as follows:

```
December 31, 1993:
Current assets                              10,000
Accumulated depreciation                   300,000
Liabilities                                 90,000
Retained earnings                           50,000
  Property, plant, and equipment                        450,000
To record the revaluation of assets and liabilities.

Common stock at par                        208,000
  Additional paid-in capital                             88,000
  Retained earnings                                     120,000
To record the reorganization of the equity accounts and the
 reduction in legal capital arising from the change in par value.
```

As a result of the quasi-reorganization, Redink would have the following balances to report in its balance sheet:

Current assets	$210,000
Property, plant, and equipment	350,000
Total assets	$560,000
Liabilities	$400,000
Common stock at par ($10 par)	52,000
Additional paid-in capital	108,000
Retained earnings (12/31/93)	–
Total equities	$560,000

The retained earnings balance in this disclosure would be dated as of the date of the quasi-reorganization. The date of the quasi-reorganization should be disclosed for a period of at least seven years following the reorganization.

While comparative balance sheets from periods prior to the reorganization can be presented, they must appear as they originally were produced.[10]

SUMMARY

The primary focus of this chapter was on corporate distributions to shareholders. Corporate distributions fall into two main categories: distributions of corporate assets and distribution of shares without compensation. Corporate asset distributions are in the form of share repurchases or dividends. Corporate share repurchases are generally accomplished when the corporation exchanges cash for shares of its stock held by an investor. The reacquired shares may be retired, or they may be placed in treasury. If the shares are retired, the original issue price of the retired shares is removed from the contributed capital accounts. The difference between the cash paid to repurchase the shares and the amount of contributed capital raised when the shares were originally issued may be absorbed into the additional paid-in capital account or into a combination of additional paid-in capital and retained earnings.

When repurchased shares are placed in treasury, two approaches can be used to value the treasury stock: the cost method and the par value method. Under the cost method, treasury shares are valued at their repurchase price until they are resold or retired. If resale occurs, costs are assigned to shares on the basis of one of three cost flow assumptions: specific identification, first-in, first-out, or weighted average. Recording the treasury stock issue requires reducing the treasury stock account for the cost of the shares and recording the difference between their cost and the resale value as an adjustment to additional paid-in capital, or a combination of additional paid-in capital and retained earnings. Treasury shares can also be issued in the exercise of other convertible securities, in which case the value acquired in exchange for the treasury stock is determined with reference to the value of the consideration received in the conversion.

Under the par value method, all treasury shares are carried at par value. Additional paid-in capital is reduced for the amount of the original issue premium. The difference between the cost to repurchase the shares and the contributed capital generated from their original issue is treated as an adjustment to additional paid-in capital, or a combination of additional paid-in capital and retained earnings at the time the shares are acquired. When treasury shares recorded on the par value method are reissued, the treasury stock account is reduced by the par value of the shares, and any difference between the proceeds of the sale and par value are added to additional paid-in capital.

Dividends are corporate distributions declared by the board of directors and may be payable in cash or other assets of the corporation. When dividends are satisfied by noncash assets, they are referred to as property dividends. The declaration of cash or property dividends creates a liability for the

---

[10] With the recent completion of the project on reporting for entities in legal reorganization, the AcSEC has determined that the quasi-reorganization approach is not available for firms emerging from bankruptcy.

corporation at the date the dividend is declared. The accounting records recognize this liability by reducing retained earnings. This liability is liquidated at the date the dividend is distributed.

Corporate distributions of assets to shareholders is limited by state corporation law and by contractual limitations known as debt covenants. Most state corporation laws and debt covenants define the amount of corporate equity that can be distributed to shareholders in terms other than the balance of retained earnings. As a result, the distinction between contributed capital and retained earnings as a signal regarding the ability to distribute assets to shareholders is virtually useless.

Corporations will, on occasion, elect to distribute additional shares of stock to shareholders without compensation. These distributions take the form of stock dividends or stock splits. When stock dividends are declared, retained earnings must be reduced to increase the corporation's legal capital sufficiently to cover the par value of the new shares issued as a dividend. This is the only adjustment necessary for large stock dividends. For small stock dividends, those in which the distribution is 20% or less of the total outstanding shares, retained earnings must be reduced by the market value of the shares issued, not just the par value. When the stock distribution is in the form of a stock split, there may or may not be an inverse change in the par value per share of the stock to be distributed. If there is, no journal entry is required since the total legal capital before and after the split is equal. If the par value is unchanged, either retained earnings or additional paid-in capital must be reduced for the par value of the shares issued to maintain the legal capital at the total par value of the shares issued.

Miscellaneous activity in the stockholders' equity accounts includes appropriations of retained earnings, prior period adjustments, and quasi-reorganizations. Appropriations represent actions by the board of directors to restrict the availability of balances in stockholders' equity to support corporate distributions. Prior period adjustments are limited generally to error corrections and are reported as an adjustment to the beginning retained earnings in the earliest year presented in the financial statements, only when the error relates to periods before that date. If the error relates to years presented for comparative purposes, all years affected must be restated.

A quasi-reorganization is a reformulation of a corporation's balance sheet and provides the corporation with a fresh start. Fundamentally, the execution of a quasi-reorganization requires that assets and liabilities be revalued to market value, with a limit on the write up of certain assets such that the write ups cannot exceed the sum of the write downs to other assets or write ups in liabilities (no net gain recognition). In addition, the stockholders' equity section is reorganized to eliminate any deficit in retained earnings and to transfer all equity capital into the contributed capital accounts.

QUESTIONS

1. Identify two broad classes of *corporate distributions*. Within each class indicate two specific ways a corporation could undertake each class of distribution.

2. What is a *share repurchase* and why is it used?

3. Compare and contrast a share repurchase with a *cash dividend*.

4. When a corporate share repurchase is undertaken, what two alternative classifications may the corporation elect as a treatment for the reacquired shares?

5. Describe in words how the retirement of repurchased shares will affect the corporation's balance sheet. Under what circumstances can retained earnings be affected by a retirement?

6. Given the current status of state corporation laws and contractual limitations on corporate distributions, what significance is there, if any, of the manner in which additional paid-in capital and retained earnings are affected by retirements of common stock?

7. What is *treasury stock*?

8. What alternative methods are available for recording treasury stock transactions? How do they differ?

9. Why is treasury stock generally reported as a stockholders' equity account and not as an asset of the corporation?

10. Describe how changes in dividend levels may provide a signal to investors about the future prospects for a corporation.

11. What is the *date of declaration*, the *date of record*, and the *date of payment*, and how do they relate to the recording of cash dividends?

12. When noncash assets are distributed, how is the difference between the fair value of the asset at the date of distribution and its historical cost treated?

13. How are preferred stock dividends different from common stock dividends? How are they similar?

14. How does a *participation provision* work?

15. What are the possible sources of limitations on corporate distributions?

16. What is *unrestricted retained earnings*, and how is it computed?

17. What is *technical default* and what effect does it have?

18. Why might the concept of a *liquidating dividend* differ from corporation to corporation?

19. Define a *stock dividend* and a *stock split*. How are stock dividends and stock splits similar?

20. What is the difference between a *small* and a *large stock dividend*? How does the accounting for these different types of stock dividends differ?

21. How many ways can the effect of a 2-for-1 split be accomplished? Would all these methods have the same effect on the financial statements?

22. What is a *quasi-reorganization* and why would a company elect to undertake one?

23. What is the effect of *appropriated retained earnings*?

24. When is a *prior period adjustment* required? How is it reported in the financial statements?

EXERCISES

15-1.   *Purchase and retirement of shares*

Charles Corporation issued 100,000 shares of $2 par common stock for $9 per share in 1990. During 1992, the company repurchased and retired 10,000 shares of the $2 par common stock by paying $10 per share. In 1993, Charles repurchased and retired an additional 5,000 shares by paying $7 per share.

REQUIRED:

1. Prepare journal entries to record each share repurchase.
2. How would the entries be altered if the exchanges happened in opposite order?

15-2.   *Effect of retirement on additional paid-in capital: alternative approaches*

Bateman Corporation retired 25,000 shares of $1 par common stock, which was originally issued for $10 per share by paying $12 per share. Immediately prior to the retirement, Bateman reported the following balances in stockholders' equity:

Common stock at par, 1,000,000 shares authorized:	
140,000 issued and outstanding	$ 140,000
Additional paid-in capital	1,260,000
Retained earnings	300,000
Total stockholders' equity	$1,700,000

REQUIRED:

Prepare the stockholders' equity section immediately following the retirement of the shares assuming:
1. That only the historical issue price of the stock is removed from the contributed capital accounts.
2. That additional paid-in capital is used to absorb any required adjustments without reference to the original issue price of the shares.

15-3.   *Retirement of shares for less than original issue price*

The stockholders' equity section of Kern Corporation's balance sheet at December 31, 1994, was as follows:

Common stock, $10 par; authorized 1,000,000 shares;	
issued and outstanding 900,000 shares	$ 9,000,000
Additional paid-in capital	2,700,000
Retained earnings	1,300,000
Total stockholders' equity	$13,000,000

All outstanding shares of common stock were issued in 1983 for $13 per share. On January 2, 1995, Kern acquired 100,000 shares of its stock at $12 per share and retired them.

REQUIRED:

Prepare the stockholders' equity section of Kern Corporation's balance sheet immediately following the retirement.

15-4.   *Treasury stock transactions: purchase and resale*

Cox Corporation was organized on January 1, 1993, at which date it issued 100,000 shares of $10 par common stock at $15 per share. On January 10, 1995, Cox purchased 6,000 shares of its common stock at $12 per share. On December 31, 1995, Cox sold 4,000 treasury shares at $8 per share. Cox uses the cost method of accounting for treasury shares.

REQUIRED:

Prepare the journal entries necessary to record the treasury stock transactions described above, assuming these represent all the treasury stock transactions entered into by Cox and the company uses the approach recommended by GAAP.

15-5.   *Share issue and treasury stock transactions: par versus cost methods*

Victor Corporation was organized on January 2, 1994, with 100,000 authorized shares of $1 par value common stock. During 1994, Victor had the following capital transactions:

(a)   January 5: Issued 75,000 shares at $14 per share
(b)   September 1: Purchased 5,000 shares for treasury at $11 per share.
(c)   December 27: Issued 2,000 shares of treasury stock at $10 per share.

REQUIRED:

Prepare journal entries for these transactions using both the par value method and the cost method of accounting for treasury stock and the approach recommended by GAAP.

15-6.   *Stock dividend distributed in the form of treasury shares*

Sigma Corporation had the following stockholders' equity balances at the end of 1993:

Common stock, $2 par, 10,000,000 shares authorized; 1,500,000 shares issued; 1,300,000 shares outstanding	$ 3,000,000
Additional paid-in capital	7,800,000
Treasury stock (200,000 shares at cost)	(2,000,000)
Retained earnings	6,000,000
Total stockholders' equity	$14,800,000

All of Sigma's outstanding common stock was issued in a single offering when the company was started several years ago.

On January 2, 1994, Sigma declared a 10% stock dividend, distributable on January 31, 1994. The stock dividend was to be distributed in the form of treasury shares. Treasury shares are not eligible to participate in the stock dividend under state law in the state that Sigma is incorporated. The market value of Sigma's stock on January 2, 1994, was $12 per share.

REQUIRED:

Prepare the journal entries necessary to record the declaration and distribution of the stock dividend.

15-7.   *Treasury stock transactions and effects on retained earnings: cost method*

Cox Corporation was organized on January 1, 1995, at which date it issued 100,000 shares of $10 par common stock at $15 per share. During the period

January 1, 1993 through December 31, 1995, Cox reported net income of $450,000 and paid cash dividends of $230,000. On January 10, 1995, Cox purchased 6,000 shares of treasury stock at $14 per share. On December 31, 1995, Cox sold 4,000 shares of treasury stock at a price of $8 per share. Cox uses the cost method of accounting for treasury stock.

REQUIRED:

Prepare the statement of changes in retained earnings for Cox Corporation as of December 31, 1995, assuming Cox accounts for the treasury stock exchanges using the method preferred by GAAP.

15-8. *Treasury stock transactions: issuance of treasury stock in conversions using the par value method*

Branden Corporation was organized on January 1, 1990, at which date it issued 200,000 shares of $.01 par common stock at $60 per share. On March 15, 1994, Branden purchased 4,000 shares of its common stock at $70 per share. On July 23, 1996, Branden purchased an additional 10,000 shares of common stock at $72 per share. On December 31, 1990, Branden issued 12,000 shares of treasury stock to satisfy the conversion of 6,000 shares of its convertible preferred stock. The preferred stock had been issued at its par value of $50 per share several years ago. Branden uses the par value method of accounting for treasury stock.

REQUIRED:

Prepare the journal entries to record the purchase of the treasury stock and its reissuance in exchange for the preferred stock.

15-9. *Treasury stock transactions: issuance of treasury stock in conversions using the cost value method*

Use the information in Exercise 15-8.

REQUIRED:

1. How would the journal entries have appeared on Branden's financial records if it had used the cost method of accounting for treasury stock and assumed that the first shares purchased are the first issued?
2. What effect would using an average cost method of assigning value to the shares issued have had on the recording of the conversion?

15-10. *Preferred stock: issuance and repurchase under a call option*

Micor Corporation issued 200 shares of $100 par, 10%, preferred stock callable at 105 in 1978. In 1993, Micor exercised its call option, demanding redemption of all 200 shares. The shares were originally issued at 101. All dividends were paid to the date of the call, and Micor has had no other preferred stock transactions.

REQUIRED:

Prepare the journal entry to record the issuance and redemption of the preferred shares.

15-11. *Preferred stock: redemption under a call option*

The stockholders' equity section of Meza Mining and Drilling appeared as follows on December 31, 1993:

Common stock, no par, 10,000,000 shares; authorized; 3,000,000 issued	$15,000,000
Preferred stock, $10 par, 6%, noncumulative, callable at $12; 1,000,000 shares authorized; 150,000 shares issued and outstanding	1,500,000
Additional paid-in capital on preferred	300,000
Retained earnings	22,200,000
Total stockholders' equity	$39,000,000

On January 1, 1994 Meza called half of the preferred shares.

REQUIRED:

Prepare the journal entry to record the redemption of the preferred shares under the call provision.

15-12. *Cash dividends*

Scarpia Incorporated had 40,000 shares of $1 par common stock outstanding. It has always paid a dividend of $.50 per share semiannually by declaring the dividend on June 1 and December 1, payable on July 1 and January 1, to the shareholders of record on June 15 and December 15 of each year. Due to unexpectedly high earnings for the year, Scarpia not only declared its normal semiannual dividends in 1994, but it also declared a special dividend of $1.75 per share. The special dividend was declared on December 27, 1994, payable on January 25, 1995, to the shareholders of record on January 11, 1995.

REQUIRED:

Prepare all journal entries necessary to record the activity relating to the dividends for 1994.

15-13. *Cash dividends: preferred and common*

Alpha Corporation began operations on July 1, 1994, by issuing 10,000 shares of $10 par common stock for $350,000 and 2,000 shares of no par, $100 stated value, 8% preferred stock for $223,000. On February 1, 1995, Alpha issued an additional 2,000 shares of common stock for $80,000. On June 1, 1995, Alpha declared dividends on the preferred stock and an additional $1.00 per share dividend on common. Both dividends were payable on June 30, 1995, to shareholders of record on June 15. Net income for the year was $92,000.

REQUIRED:

Prepare the journal entries to record the declaration and distribution of the dividend.

15-14. *Dividends: allocation to preferred and common with dividends in arrears*

Culture Corporation had the following classes of stock outstanding as of December 31, 1995:

> Common stock, $20 par, 20,000 shares outstanding
>
> Preferred stock, 6%, $100 par, cumulative and participating, 1,000 shares outstanding

Dividends on the preferred stock have been in arrears for 1993 and 1994. On December 31, 1995, a total cash dividend of $90,000 was declared.

REQUIRED:

What are the amounts of dividends payable to both the common and preferred stock?

(AICPA adapted)

15-15. *Property dividends: distribution of securities*

On March 1, 1993, Lucia Corporation declared a property dividend consisting of two shares of Mongo Corporation stock and one share of Ming Corporation stock. The dividend was to be distributed on March 31, 1993. At the time the dividend was declared, the stock had the following values:

	Book Value	Market Value
Mongo Corporation	$23 per share	$20 per share
Ming Corporation	$10 per share	$12 per share

Lucia has 50,000 shares of its own common stock outstanding.

REQUIRED:

Prepare all journal entries to record the property dividend.

15-16. *Property dividend: distribution of inventory*

Bruno Breweries has recently decided to discontinue production of its light beer. Instead of attempting to sell the beer, the company has declared a property dividend to its shareholders to distribute the remaining cases of beer. Bruno carried the inventory at a cost of $1,975,000; but at retail prices, it would have sold for $2,500,000. Bruno declared the dividend on December 1, 1993, distributable on January 1, 1994.

REQUIRED:

Prepare the journal entries to record all the effects of the property dividend in 1993 and 1994.

15-17. *Stock dividends*

On December 31, 1994, Case Inc., had 300,000 shares of no-par stock issued and outstanding. Case declared a 10% stock dividend on July 1, 1995, distributable on August 1. At the date of the declaration, Case shares traded for $15 per share on a national exchange. By August 1, the price had fallen to $14 per share.

REQUIRED:

How should Case record the effect of the stock dividend?

15-18. *Stock dividends*

On December 31, 1994, the stockholders' equity section of Bergen Corporation appeared as follows:

Common stock, par value $10, authorized 30,000 shares; issued and outstanding 9,000 shares	$ 90,000
Additional paid-in capital	116,000
Retained earnings	146,000
Total stockholders' equity	$352,000

On March 1, 1995, Bergen declared a 15% stock dividend distributable on March 31. The market price of Bergen stock was $16 per share at that time. During 1993, the company reported a net loss of $32,000.

REQUIRED:

Prepare the journal entries necessary to record the stock dividend and the statement of changes in retained earnings for 1995 assuming all activity is indicated.

15-19. *Stock dividends*

On February 1, 1994, Omega Corporation had 1,340,000 shares of its $1 par common stock outstanding. On that date, Omega declared a 40% stock dividend, distributable on March 1 to shareholders of record on February 15. The market price of Omega's stock as of various dates was as follows:

2/01/94	$43 per share
2/15/94	$31 per share
3/01/94	$33 per share

REQUIRED:

Prepare the journal entries necessary to record the declaration and distribution of the stock dividend.

15-20. *Stock splits*

On July 11, 1994, Bart Corporation had 200,000 shares of $5 par common stock outstanding. The market price of the shares at that time was $12 per share. On the same date, Bart declared a 2-for-1 stock split. Immediately before the split, the company reported additional paid-in capital of $450,000 and retained earnings of $1,230,000.

REQUIRED:

Compute how much Bart will report in additional paid-in capital and retained earnings under each of the following scenarios:
1. Bart reduces the par value of common to $2.50 a share after the split.
2. Bart does not change par value and accounts for the split as a large stock dividend.
3. Bart does not change par value and adjusts other contributed capital accounts to record the dividend.

15-21. *Reverse stock splits*

On November 10, 1993, Boulevard Corporation split its common stock 1-for-4 in a reverse split. The market value was $20 per share prior to the split. Before the split, Boulevard had 200,000 shares of $12 par common stock outstanding, which were originally issued for $50 per share.

REQUIRED:

Determine the balances of each contributed capital account for Boulevard under the following assumptions:
1. Boulevard elects to alter the par value in inverse proportion to the split.
2. Boulevard elects to leave the par value of common at $12 per share.

15-22. *Liquidating dividends*

On January 1, 1995, the board of directors of Blake Mining Company declared a cash dividend of $800,000, payable on February 10 to the shareholders of record on January 18. The dividend is permissible under state law in Blake's state of incorporation. Selected data from Blake's December 31, 1994, balance sheet were as follows:

Common stock	$1,000,000
Additional paid-in capital	300,000
Retained earnings	600,000
Total stockholders' equity	$1,900,000

REQUIRED:

1. How much of the dividend would be considered a liquidating dividend under current financial accounting guidelines?
2. Prepare the journal entry to record the activity related to this dividend.

15-23. *Dividend restrictions: bond covenants*

Beta Corporation began the year with the following stockholders' equity balances:

Common stock, par value $1, authorized 1,000,000 shares; issued and outstanding 600,000 shares	$ 600,000
Additional paid-in capital	2,400,000
Retained earnings	2,300,000
Total stockholders' equity	$5,300,000

On this date, Beta issued bonds with a restriction on the size of any corporate distribution of assets to shareholders. Beta cannot declare dividends or purchase treasury shares in an amount that would exceed earnings from the date of the bond issue plus $1,000,000. During the year, Beta acquired 120,000 shares of treasury stock at $6 per share. Beta accounted for the treasury stock using the cost method. Net income for the year was $210,000.

REQUIRED:

1. Compute the maximum cash dividend that Beta could declare at the end of the year.
2. How would this amount be affected if Beta's board of directors voted to appropriate an amount of retained earnings equal to the beginning balance of retained earnings plus the cost of the treasury stock to acknowledge the effects of the debt covenant on retained earnings available to support dividends?

15-24. *Dividend restrictions: bond covenants*

Blanc Manufacturing began the year with the following stockholders' equity balances:

Common stock, no-par, $5 stated value; 200,000 shares authorized; 90,000 shares issued and outstanding	$ 450,000
Additional paid-in capital	750,000
Retained earnings	1,300,000
Total stockholders' equity	$2,500,000

On this date, Blanc issued bonds with a restriction on the size of any corporate distribution of assets to shareholders. Beta cannot declare dividends or purchase treasury shares in an amount that would exceed earnings from the date of the bond issue plus the proceeds of any new equity issues, plus $200,000. During the year, the company issued 5,000 shares of new common stock at $17 per share, purchased 7,000 shares of treasury stock at $12 per share, reported income of $70,000, and declared cash dividends in the amount of $50,000.

REQUIRED:

How much of the retained earnings balance at the end of the year is restricted?

15-25. *Quasi-reorganizations*

Reformation Technologies Incorporated (RTI) has elected to undertake a quasi-reorganization due to several years of poor operating performance. The equity section of RTI immediately prior to the reorganization appeared as follows:

Common stock, $10 par, 1,000,000 shares authorized; 270,000 shares issued and outstanding	$2,700,000
Additional paid-in capital	3,200,000
Retained earnings	(2,400,000)
Total stockholders' equity	$3,500,000

An investigation of the relationship between book and market values for the assets and liabilities of RTI revealed the following:

	Book Value	Market Value
Inventory	$ 340,000	$ 375,000
Property, plant, and equipment	4,200,000	2,100,000
Accumulated depreciation	(1,200,000)	–
Bonds payable	1,750,000	1,825,000

REQUIRED:

Prepare the entries necessary to effect the quasi-reorganization assuming that RTI reduces its par value to $1 per share on the common stock.

15-26. *Quasi-reorganizations*

Delta Industries underwent a quasi-reorganization at the end of the previous fiscal year. Delta's equity section at the end of the current year appeared as follows:

Common stock, no-par, 10,000,000 shares authorized; 5,200,000 shares issued and outstanding	$126,493,000
Retained earnings	2,400,000
Total stockholders' equity	$128,893,000

To effect the reorganization, Delta wrote down its inventories and plant and equipment by $60,000 and $245,000, respectively. Prior to the reorganization, Delta's common stock had a par value of $5 per share. No new shares were issued during the current year.

REQUIRED:

Prepare the stockholders' equity section of Delta as it would have appeared prior to the quasi-reorganization.

PROBLEMS

15-1. *Share transactions in common and preferred: issuance and retirement*

The Natchez Corporation reported the following in its stockholders' equity section on December 31, 1992:

Common stock, $2 par, 100,000 shares authorized;	
40,000 shares issued and outstanding	$ 80,000
Additional paid-in capital on common	120,000
Preferred stock, $10 par, 8% nonparticipating, noncumulative, callable at 105; 10,000 shares authorized, issued, and outstanding	100,000
Additional paid-in capital on preferred	5,600
Retained earnings	55,000

The following capital transactions occurred during 1993:

(a) Issued 9,200 shares of common stock at $14 per share.
(b) Purchased and retired 500 shares of the preferred stock at $52 per share.
(c) Called the remaining preferred shares and retired those not in treasury.

REQUIRED:

1. Prepare the journal entries to record the transactions described above.
2. Prepare the stockholders' equity section of the company's balance sheet at the end of the period assuming net income was $100,000 and no dividends were declared.

15-2. *Various equity transactions: share issues, dividends, treasury stock transactions*

Baustic Company had the following balances in its stockholders' equity accounts on December 31, 1994:

Common stock, $10 par	$ 400,000
Additional paid-in capital on common	342,000
Preferred stock, 10%, $50 par	300,000
Additional paid-in capital on preferred	75,000
Retained earnings	75,000
Treasury stock (2,000 shares at cost)	(50,000)
Total stockholders' equity	$1,142,000

The following transactions occurred during 1995:

(a) Cash dividends on the preferred stock were declared and paid. The preferred is noncumulative and has a call price of $52 per share.
(b) Dividends of $1 per share were declared on January 1 and December 1, 1995 for common stock. The January dividend was paid on February 15, 1995, but the December dividend will not be paid until January 15, 1996.
(c) On August 15, 1994, 7,500 new common shares were issued at $33 per share.
(d) On November 12, 1994, the treasury shares were sold for $63,000.
(e) Net income for the year was $83,000.

REQUIRED:

1. Prepare the journal entries necessary to record the transactions affecting stockholders' equity in 1994.
2. Prepare a statement of changes in retained earnings for 1994.

15-3. *Redemption of preferred, retirement of treasury stock, and rights issues*

Carr Corporation had the following stockholders' equity account balances at December 31, 1994:

Preferred stock	$1,800,000
Additional paid-in capital from preferred stock	90,000
Common stock	5,150,000
Additional paid-in capital from common stock	3,502,000
Retained earnings	4,000,000
Treasury common stock	(270,000)

Transactions during 1995 and other information relating to the stockholders' equity accounts were as follows:

(a) Carr's preferred and common shares are traded on the Over-the-Counter market. At December 31, 1994, Carr had 100,000 authorized shares of $100 par, 10%, callable at 110, noncumulative, convertible preferred stock; and 3,000,000 authorized shares of no-par common stock with a stated value of $5 per share. All of the common shares were originally issued for $8.40 a share. Each preferred share was convertible into three shares of common stock anytime on or after January 1, 1995. Treasury stock represents 30,000 shares of stock purchased at $9 a share. Carr uses the cost method of valuing treasury stock.

(b) On January 1, 1995, Carr called all of the preferred shares. At that time, half of the preferred stockholders chose to convert their shares to common and half elected to tender the preferred shares to the company. To satisfy the need to issue common shares under the conversion feature, 18,000 shares of treasury stock were reissued. All remaining common shares issued in the conversion were previously unissued shares.

(c) On July 1, 1995, Carr formally retired all of the remaining shares of its treasury common stock and had them revert to an unissued basis.

(d) On September 1, 1995, 250,000 stock rights were issued to the common stockholders permitting the purchase of one new share of common stock in exchange for one right and $11 cash. On September 25, 210,000 stock rights were exercised when the market price of Carr's common stock was $13 per share. Carr issued new shares to settle the transaction. The remaining 40,000 rights were not exercised and expired.

REQUIRED:

1. Prepare the journal entries Carr would use to record the above activities.
2. Prepare the stockholders' equity section of Carr's balance sheet at December 31, 1995, assuming that Carr reported income of $500,000 and declared no dividends during 1995.

15-4. *Various equity transactions and their effects on retained earnings*

Madison Corporation's capital structure is as follows:

	December 31,	
	1995	1994
Outstanding shares of:		
Common stock	336,000	300,000
Preferred stock (nonconvertible)	10,000	10,000

The following information was available regarding activities during 1995:

(a) On September 1, 1995, Madison sold 36,000 additional shares of common stock.

(b) During 1995, Madison paid dividends of $3 per share on its nonconvertible preferred stock.

(c) Warrants to purchase 20,000 shares of common stock at $38 per share were attached to the preferred stock at the time it was issued. The warrants, which expire on December 31, 1995, were all converted on June 1, 1995, when the market price was $43 per share.

(d) Income for 1995 was $400,000, and the retained earnings balance on January 1, 1993 was $8,100,000.

(e) On November 15, 1995, Madison purchased 50,000 shares of treasury stock at a price of $40 per share. Madison uses the cost method of accounting for treasury stock.

(f) Common dividends of $1 per share were declared on February 28, May 31, August 30, and November 30, respectively. Each dividend was payable in cash on the last day of the month following the declaration.

(g) On December 31, 1995, Madison declared a 15% stock dividend. The market value of the stock on that date was $45 per share.

REQUIRED:

1. Prepare all journal entries for activities that affect the retained earnings of Madison in 1995.

2. Prepare a statement of retained earnings that Madison would report for 1995.

15-5. *Treasury stock transactions, recreation of entries from balance sheet data*

Beef Corporation's stockholders' equity section appeared as follows on December 31, 1994:

Beef Corporation
Stockholders' Equity
December 31, 1994

Common stock, $1 par value; authorized 3,000,000 shares; issued 1,500,000 shares; outstanding 1,400,000 shares	$ 1,400,000
Additional paid-in capital:	
From original issue	14,000,000
From treasury stock	200,000
Total paid-in capital	15,600,000
Unappropriated retained earnings	8,100,000
Total stockholders' equity	$23,700,000

All of the outstanding common stock and treasury stock were originally issued in 1990 for $11 per share. The treasury stock is common stock reacquired on March 31, 1992. This represents the only treasury stock transaction Beef has ever entered into prior to the current year. Beef uses the par value method of accounting for treasury stock. During 1995, the following events or transactions occurred relating to Beef's stockholders' equity:

(a) February 12, 1995: Issued 400,000 shares of common stock for $12.50 per share. Of these shares, 100,000 represented shares held in treasury; and the rest were previously unissued shares.

(b) September 20, 1995: Beef's president retired. Beef purchased from the retiring president 100,000 shares of Beef's common stock for $17 per share, which was equal to market value on this date. This stock was cancelled.

(c) Beef reported income for the period of $2,100,000 and declared no dividends.

REQUIRED:

1. Based on the information provided, how much did Beef pay for the treasury stock acquired in March of 1992?

2. Prepare journal entries to record the activities during 1995.
3. Prepare comparative stockholders' equity sections as they would appear on December 31, 1994 and 1995, respectively.

15-6.   *Purchase, sale, and retirement of treasury shares*

Makepeace, Inc. had 1,000,000 shares of its no-par, $5 stated value common stock outstanding at the beginning of the year. All of these shares were originally issued at a price of $75 per share. The following events occurred in the treasury stock account during the period (in chronological order). Prior to the current period, Makepeace had not acquired any treasury shares.

(a)   Purchased 250,000 shares of its common stock from a dissident shareholder for $125 per share.
(b)   Sold 75,000 shares at $105 per share.
(c)   Sold an additional 60,000 shares at $130 per share.
(d)   Purchased another 15,000 shares at $123 per share.
(e)   Sold 120,000 shares at $127 per share.
(f)   Retired the remaining shares.

REQUIRED:

Prepare all journal entries to record these events under both the par value and cost methods of accounting for treasury stock. (Makepeace uses the first-in, first-out method of valuing treasury shares sold.)

15-7.   *Preferred treasury stock, splits, and stock dividends*

At the beginning of 1994, Majestic Corporation had 10,000 shares of $100 par preferred stock and 50,000 shares of no-par common stock outstanding. The preferred stock requires a $8 dividend and is cumulative. It was originally issued at par value. The common was originally issued at $34 per share. No dividends of any kind have been declared since January of 1992. Majestic had a beginning retained earnings balance of $200,000 and income of $600,000 for 1994. During 1994, the following events took place:

(a)   The company purchased 3,000 shares of preferred stock as treasury stock for $104 per share on February 14. Majestic uses the par value method of accounting for treasury stock and has had no previous treasury stock transactions.
(b)   On February 28, the company declared a cash dividend on common of $.10 per share along with the dividend on preferred plus all dividends in arrears. The dividends were distributed on March 31.
(c)   On June 22, the company sold 2,000 of the treasury shares for $106 per share.
(d)   Due to the rapid increase in the market price of the company's common stock, a 2-for-1 stock split was effected in the form of a 100% stock dividend declared on September 30, and distributed on November 30. The market value of the common stock at that time was $84 per share.
(e)   On December 15, a 10% stock dividend was declared, distributable on December 31. The market price per share of common on that date was $45.

REQUIRED:

1. Prepare all journal entries necessary to record the activities during 1994.
2. Prepare a statement of changes in retained earnings for 1994.

15-8.   *Treasury stock: comparison of par and cost methods*

Craft Company began operations on January 1, 1996. It has 50,000 shares of $10 par value common stock authorized and issued 30,000 shares for $11 per share on that date. On August 15, 1996, Craft purchased 1,000 shares of treasury stock for $12 per share. On September 14, 1996, Craft sold 500 shares of the treasury stock for $14 per share. Craft reported income for 1993 of $300,000 and declared no dividends.

REQUIRED:

1. Prepare the journal entries Craft would use to record the treasury stock transactions using both the cost and par value methods.
2. Prepare the stockholders' equity section of Craft's balance sheet at December 31, 1996, under both the cost and par value methods. What alternative ways exist for disclosing the effect of the treasury stock transactions?
3. What significant differences do you think result from the use of the cost or par value methods? Discuss.

15-9.   *Treasury stock, appropriations, and reverse stock splits*

Micro Breweries had the following balances in its stockholders' equity accounts on January 1, 1996:

Common stock, no-par; 12,300 shares issued and outstanding	$ 701,100
Retained earnings	412,540
Total stockholders' equity	$1,113,640

All of the company's common stock had been issued at the same price when the company was formed. The following transactions occurred during 1996:

(a) A property dividend was declared and distributed. The dividend was 1, six-pack of the company's new premium beer for each share of stock. At the time of the distribution, the market value of a six-pack was $4.70. The cost to manufacture the beer was only $1.80 per six-pack.
(b) Treasury stock consisting of 1,800 shares was purchased for $76 per share after the property dividend was distributed. Micro uses the cost method to account for treasury stock.
(c) A journal entry was made to restrict retained earnings by the cost of the treasury stock via the appropriation of retained earnings in an amount equal to the purchase price of the treasury shares.
(d) The treasury stock was retired and the appropriation of retained earnings was reversed.
(e) A 1-for-3 reverse stock split was effected at the end of the year. Net income for the period was $98,000.

REQUIRED:

1. Prepare journal entries to record the above events.
2. Prepare the stockholders' equity section of the balance sheet for Micro Breweries as of December 31, 1996.

15-10.   *Participating preferred, dividends, stock splits*

Montroy Corporation has provided the following information on its outstanding shares:

	$10 Par Common	$7.50, $100 par, Preferred
Authorized	10,000,000	2,000,000
Issued	6,230,000	370,000
Outstanding	5,685,000	370,000

(a) Cash dividends of $14,000,000 are declared and paid. The preferred stock was cumulative and fully participating. Preferred dividends were one year in arrears.

(b) Cash dividends were declared to the preferred shareholders. The preferred stock was noncumulative and nonparticipating. A $2 per share dividend was declared and paid on common stock.

(c) Cash dividends were declared and paid to the preferred shareholders. The preferred stock was cumulative and nonparticipating. Dividends for the preceding two years had not been declared. A 150% stock dividend was declared on common stock when the market price per share was $45.

(d) A 3-for-2 stock split was declared on common stock. The split was effected by adjustment of the par value of the common.

(e) Cash dividends were declared to the preferred stockholders. The preferred stock is noncumulative and nonparticipating. A property dividend payable in the shares of Mitchell Corporation was declared on the common shares. At the time of the declaration, the Mitchell stock had a market value of $2,300,000 and was being carried in the current portfolio of marketable equity securities at cost of $2,700,000. The current portfolio had an aggregate market value that exceeded cost at the time of the dividend.

(f) Cash dividends were declared to the preferred stockholders. The preferred stock is noncumulative and nonparticipating. A 12% stock dividend was declared and distributed to the common shareholders when the market value of the common shares was $15 per share.

REQUIRED:

For each of the independent situations above, prepare the appropriate journal entries and show supporting computations.

15-11. *Large stock dividend, cash dividends, treasury stock, and appropriations*

Presented below is the stockholders' equity section of Danube Corporation's balance sheet as of December 31, 1994:

Common stock, $1 par value; authorized 5,000,000; shares; issued 2,600,000 shares; outstanding 2,400,000 shares	$ 2,400,000
Additional paid-in capital on common stock	16,500,000
Treasury stock (200,000 shares at cost)	(3,600,000)
Unappropriated retained earnings	89,100,000
Total stockholders' equity	$104,400,000

All of the issued common shares were originally sold in a single offering when the corporation was formed. The treasury shares were purchased in a single acquisition. The following information relates to activities during 1995:

(a) February 12: The company declared a 30% stock dividend that was distributed on March 15. Treasury shares do not participate in stock dividends under state corporation law.

(b) April 15: The company declared a cash dividend of $.20 per share, payable on May 15, to the holders of record on April 30.

(c) June 22: The board of directors voted to appropriate $1,200,000 of retained earnings for a building program.

(d) September 20: Danube's president retired. The company purchased 100,000 shares of Danube's common stock from the president at price of $13 per share. The shares were retired.

(e) Earnings for 1993 were $3,000,000, not including the effects of an error correction that related to income reported in 1992. The error related to the accrual of deferred compensation, which resulted in an excess charge to expense of $140,000 for 1992.

REQUIRED:

1. Prepare all journal entries necessary to record the events during 1995 assuming Danube pays no taxes.
2. Prepare a statement of changes in retained earnings for the year assuming that only the 1995 financial statements will be issued without comparative prior years.
    (AICPA adapted)

15-12. *Issuance of compound securities, error correction, splits, dividends*

Mansard Incorporated had the following balances reported in its balance sheet at January 1, 1993:

Preferred stock, $70 par, 12%, mandatorily redeemable	$ 7,000,000
Common stock, $2 par; 1,000,000 shares authorized; 150,000 shares issued and outstanding	300,000
Additional paid-in capital on common	8,200,000
Retained earnings	12,700,000
Total stockholders' equity	$28,200,000

The following events occurred in 1993:
(a) On January 1, 1993, the company sold 50,000 shares of preferred stock and 200,000 shares of common stock for a lump sum of $11,250,000. The preferred stock was selling at $95 at the time and the common at $34. Issuance costs of $150,000 were incurred to place this issue with a large institutional investor.
(b) The company declared a 2-for-1 stock split on June 1, 1993. The par value of the shares was not changed, and the company elected to adjust other contributed capital accounts to effect the split.
(c) On July 11, 1993, an error was discovered in the ending balance of the allowance for doubtful accounts as of December 31, 1992. The error resulted in an understatement of the allowance by $75,000.
(d) On August 1, 1993, a 10% stock dividend was declared, distributable on August 31, 1993. The preferred stock dividends for the year were declared and paid on the same dates.
(e) When the preferred stock dividends were paid, half of the preferred stock was redeemed under the mandatory redemption feature. The redemption took place at par value.
(f) On December 31, the company appropriated $1,000,000 for contingencies. Net income for the year was $3,690,000.

REQUIRED:

Prepare all journal entries necessary to record the above events.

PEPSICO INCORPORATED

The following information was excerpted from the Annual Report to Shareholders of Pepsico, Inc. for 1982 as it related to an error in Pepsico's financial statements:

In December, 1982, Pepsico completed a review of financial irregularities in company owned foreign bottling operations, primarily in Mexico and the Philippines. As a result of this review, steps have been taken to correct these irregularities, prevent their recurrence, and terminate the individuals responsible.

The investigation, conducted by a task force that included special legal counsel and independent accountants, revealed that managers of these subsidiaries, working in collusion, falsified documents and evaded internal controls to overstate profits and thereby improve the apparent performance of their operations.

These irregularities caused an overstatement of assets, and understatement of liabilities, and an overstatement of net income for the period of January 1, 1978 through September 4, 1982, aggregating $92.1 million or 6.6 percent of net income. These adjustments were without tax benefit. As a result of the irregularities, the financial statements for the years 1978 through 1982 have been restated. A reconciliation of previously reported net income and net income per share to restated amounts is shown in the table below. The impact of the restatement on revenues was not significant. Interim financial data for previously reported quarters has also been restated.

PEPSICO INCORPORATED
Changes in Net Income and Net Income per share
(dollars in thousands)

	1981	1980	1979	1978
Income before extraordinary charge as previously reported	$333,456	$291,752	$264,855	$225,769
Decrease in net income from restatement	35,972	31,047	14,466	2,555
Income before extraordinary charge as restated	297,484	260,705	250,389	223,214
Extraordinary charge	–	17,762	–	–
Net Income	$297,484	$242,943	$250,389	$223,214
Income per share before extraordinary charge as previously reported	$ 3.61	$ 3.20	$ 2.85	$ 2.43
Decrease in income per share resulting from restatement	.39	.34	.15	.03
Restated income per share before extraordinary charge	3.22	2.86	2.70	2.40
Extraordinary charge	–	.19	–	–
Net Income per share	$ 3.22	$ 2.67	$ 2.70	$ 2.40

REQUIRED:

1. Given the description of the events that led Pepsico to make the changes discussed, do you believe that event should have been recorded as an error correction? Ignoring the requirements of GAAP, what other ways might Pepsico have used to adjust for the discovery?

2. How much of an effect did the error correction have on net income in each year (1978–1982, inclusive), both in dollar terms and as a percent of income prior to correction?

3. What changes would have occurred to Pepsico's financial statements (not the notes) as a result of the error corrections reported above. (Respond to this question in general terms, not specific account adjustments.)

4. How would Pepsico have recorded the effect of the error correction if it only presented its financial statements for 1982 without comparative years? How would it have presented the correction if only 1981 and 1982 financial statements were presented?

5. What likely effect would the release of the financial statements containing the error disclosure have on the share price of Pepsico's stock? Do you believe that the financial statements would have been the most timely source of information on the events surrounding the error?

6. Speculate on the relative importance of the error reported by Pepsico and an alternative error that is simply a miscalculation of depreciation expense for a single year. How much effect would the "information" regarding these two types of errors have for investors?

CASE 15.2   UNITED BRANDS COMPANY

In 1983, United Brands undertook a quasi-reorganization as described in the notes to its financial statements, which are presented below. In addition, the Company also altered its fiscal year-end from June 30 to March 31. This alteration resulted in the presentation of financial statements for a nine-month period instead of the normal twelve-month period.

Note 2 - Restructuring and Quasi-Reorganization

The Company has developed a strategic business plan which encompasses a significant restructuring of its banana operations, continuation of the improvement of its meat business which commenced in 1982 with a program of plant closings, and asset redeployment programs including the divestiture of certain operating units.

Restructuring

At March 31, 1983, the Company provided $120 million as a special charge against earnings, principally for the restructuring of the banana business of United Fruit Company. The program to restructure the banana business is being undertaken in order to better match the Company's supplies of bananas with selected profitable markets and to mitigate the future impact of the external factors which have adversely affected operating results. The program includes scaling back production in certain locations, reducing long-term commitments to purchase bananas and realigning transportation and distribution to match revised marketing objectives. The provision consists principally of estimates of losses on disposal of assets, severance costs, contract and lease termination payments and costs of operations during the phase-out period.

During 1982, the Company provided $19.1 million as a special charge against earnings for the closing or expected closing of several high labor cost meat packing facilities of its subsidiary John Morrell & Co.

Quasi-Reorganization

In conjunction with the restructuring and asset redeployment programs, the Company, with approval of the Board of Directors, revalued its balance sheet at March 31, 1983, to fair value in accordance with accounting principles applicable to quasi-reorganizations. Management utilized the expertise of investment bankers, actuaries, and outside appraisers in conducting the revaluation.

The principal adjustments to fair value included a $70 million net increase in the carrying value of certain operations which the company expects to divest; the revaluation of LIFO inventories resulting in an increase of $36 million; the revaluation of subordinated debt resulting in additional debt discount of $52 million; the recording of $40 million of unfunded pension and other employee benefit liabilities; and revaluation of intangibles resulting in a reduction of $271 million. Management has given consideration to the carrying values of the Company's remaining assets and liabilities and believes they approximate fair value. The fair value adjustments to the balance sheet resulted in a net charge to retained earnings of $174 million. The accumulated deficit in retained earnings at March 31, 1983 was then transferred to capital surplus.

Financial statements for United Brands at March 31, 1983 are presented on the following pages.

REQUIRED:

1. Based on the information provided on the effects of the quasi-reorganization, prepare the journal entry that United Brands would have used to record the reorganization. Any adjustments you find necessary but are not specifically described may be charged to other assets or other liabilities to balance the journal entry.

2. Based on the results of your entry in (1), prepare the entry to record the issuance of common stock, which is indicated by the increase in the capital stock at par.

3. Recast the balance sheet of United Brands as of March 31, 1983, to reverse the effects of the quasi-reorganization.

4. What effect did the reorganization have on the following ratios:
   (a) Debt to total equity
   (b) Funded debt to total equity
   (c) Current ratio
   (d) Quick ratio

5. What effects might the reorganization have on dividend payments and on debt covenant restrictions relating to the declaration of dividends?

6. Based on the information provided regarding the preferred stock dividends for 1982 and 1983, along with the balance sheet information regarding the amount of shareholders' equity relating to the preferred stocks, would you expect that United paid out all of the accumulating dividends on preferred stock in 1983? Why or why not?

7. If the company's assertion that all assets and liabilities have been restated to fair value is correct, what would you estimate United Brands' trading price per share of common stock would be immediately after the quasi-reorganization?
8. United describes a gain in the income statement from the exchange of capital stock for debt. What underlying event must have occurred to create this income statement effect, and how did United account for the exchange? (Provide a descriptive answer; specific numbers are not available in the data.)
9. Speculate on why you think the company undertook this accounting reorganization. Do you think this type of accounting treatment is useful or detrimental to the users of financial statements? Why or why not?

UNITED BRANDS
Consolidated Statement of Income

(in thousands except per share amounts)	NINE MONTHS ENDED MARCH 31, 1983	YEAR ENDED JUNE 30, 1982
Net sales	$2,406,328	$3,972,506
Operating costs and expenses:		
Cost of sales	2,237,605	3,650,541
Selling, general, and administrative	180,476	244,470
Depreciation	28,015	38,442
Operating income (loss)	(39,768)	39,053
Interest expense	(30,116)	(48,343)
Gain on exchange of capital stock for debt	–	9,499
Other income and expense, net	9,599	13,841
Income (loss) before restructuring and taxes	(60,285)	14,050
Provision for restructuring	(120,000)	(19,100)
Income (loss) before taxes	(180,285)	(5,050)
Income taxes	13,000	7,800
Net income (loss)	$ (167,285)	$ 2,750
Net income (loss) per common share		
Primary	$ (13.82)	$ .06
Fully diluted	(13.82)	.06

UNITED BRANDS COMPANY AND SUBSIDIARY COMPANIES
Consolidated Statement of Income and Retained in the Business

(in thousands except per share amounts)	NINE MONTHS ENDED MARCH 31, 1983	YEAR ENDED JUNE 30, 1982
Income retained in business at beginning of period	$144,752	$148,348
Net income (loss)	(167,285)	2,750
Dividends declared		
Preferred	(1,563)	(2,092)
Common ($.05 and $.40 per share)	(611)	(4,254)
	(24,707)	144,752
Quasi-reorganization adjustments		
Revaluation adjustments, net	(174,174)	–
Transfer to capital surplus	198,881	–
Income retained in business at end of period	–	$144,752

UNITED BRANDS COMPANY AND SUBSIDIARY COMPANIES
Consolidated Balance Sheet
(in thousands)

ASSETS	NINE MONTHS ENDED MARCH 31, 1983	YEAR ENDED JUNE 30, 1982
Current Assets		
Cash and equivalents	$ 50,829	$ 40,413
Trade receivables, less allowances of $6,815 in 1983 and $5,511 in 1982	189,561	180,355
Other receivables	44,362	43,952
Inventories	257,004	251,837
Prepaid expenses	12,741	11,822
Income tax benefit	24,361	–
Investment held for sale	107,500	–
Total current assets	686,358	528,379
Investments and long-term receivables	29,565	60,315
Property, plant, and equipment, net	332,617	362,740
Intangibles	43,000	313,828
Total assets	$1,091,540	$1,265,262

LIABILITIES AND SHAREHOLDERS' EQUITY		
Current Liabilities		
Notes payable	$ 220,505	$ 75,670
Long-term debt payable within one year	5,578	6,284
Accounts payable	151,757	152,757
Accrued liabilities	114,923	90,534
Accrued and deferred income taxes	9,987	23,673
Total current liabilities	502,750	348,918
Long-term debt	141,030	227,017
Accrued pension and other employee benefits	143,411	100,568
Other liabilities and deferred income taxes	79,734	20,511
Total liabilities	866,925	697,014
Shareholders' Equity		
$3.00 Cumulative convertible preferred stock	2,464	2,481
$1.20 Cumulative convertible preferred stock	29,606	29,606
$3.20 Cumulative convertible preferred stock	6,061	6,130
Capital stock, $1 par value	12,218	12,215
Capital surplus	174,266	373,064
Income retained in business	–	144,752
Total shareholders' equity	224,615	568,248
Total liabilities and shareholders' equity	$1,091,540	$1,265,262

TONKA CORPORATION CASE

Presented below is the stockholders' equity section of Tonka Corporation's 1982 balance sheet along with excerpts from the note disclosure regarding the acquisition of treasury stock.

Stockholders' Equity—Note D

Common Stock—par value $.66$_{2/3}$ a share:

Authorized—4,000,000 shares

Issued—1,672,796 shares	$ 1,115,198	$ 1,115,198
Additional paid-in capital	8,682,622	8,682,622
Retained Earnings	44,285,238	47,376,095
Foreign currency translation adjustment	(867,134)	–
	$53,215,924	$57,173,915
Less cost of treasury stock in		
treasury: 1982-600,000 shares	(20,821,741)	–
Total Stockholders' Equity	$32,394,183)	$57,173,915

During January 1982, the Company completed a tender offer to purchase 600,000 shares of its Common Stock for $34.50 a share plus fees and expenses. Under the terms of the offer, the Company paid $20,822,000 to purchase these shares, which are being held as treasury shares. The amount of retained earnings available for distribution to stockholders is reduced by the $20,822,000 cost of Common Stock in treasury.

REQUIRED:

1. Speculate on the motivation that might have led to Tonka's decision to repurchase the 600,000 shares.
2. Based on the information provided, what entry did Tonka make to record the purchase of the treasury shares under the cost method?
3. If Tonka had elected to use the par value method, how would the stockholders' equity section have appeared, assuming all of Tonka's outstanding common stock was originally issued at the same time?
4. How would Tonka's equity section have appeared if the Company had retired these shares instead of placing them in treasury? (Assume all shares were originally issued at the same time.)
5. Suppose that Tonka resold 40,000 shares at a price of $50 per share. Prepare the journal entry Tonka would use to record this event, given that it uses the cost method of accounting for treasury stock. How would your response change if the shares resold for only $30 per share?
6. How would the entries prepared in (5) change if Tonka had originally used the par value method of accounting for treasury shares?

BORG WARNER

Presented on the following pages are the income statement and balance sheet of Borg Warner Corporation for the year ending 1985, along with selected information contained in the notes to the financial statements.

REQUIRED:

1. Examine the transactions listed in the Capital Stock footnote relating to the conversion of the preferred stock to common. Assume that all the preferred stock was originally issued for $6.30 per share. Further assume that Borg Warner uses the cost method of accounting for common shares held as treasury shares and that the following represents the average cost per share held in treasury at each date indicated:

    2,365,392 shares at January 1, 1983 were carried at $12.50 per share.
    1,235,914 shares at January 1, 1984 were carried at $10.00 per share.
    2,833,742 shares at January 1, 1985 were carried at $19.37 per share.

   Given the information provided above, and that contained in the excerpted financial statements, respond to the following questions regarding the preferred stock:
   (a) What journal entry would have been used to record the original issuance of the 46,181 shares of preferred stock outstanding on January 1, 1983?
   (b) What is the conversion ratio under which preferred shares can be converted into common shares?
   (c) How would the repurchase of the preferred stock have been recorded in 1983 and 1985?
   (d) Assuming that the conversion of the preferred occurred on the first day of the year, how would Borg Warner have recorded the conversions of preferred to common in 1983 and 1984?
   (e) Why might investors elect to convert their preferred shares into common shares? Why might management want this to occur? How can management force such a conversion, if at all?

2. Assuming that the treasury shares purchased in 1983, 1984, and 1985 were acquired at $4.80, $20.15, and $21.61, respectively, prepare the journal entries necessary to record Borg Warner's treasury stock purchases in each year. How would these cash flows be reported in the cash flow statement? If the company had sold the treasury stock originally purchased for $21.61 at a price of $20, summarize the alternative effects this might have on the balance of additional paid-in capital under all of the acceptable alternative accounting treatments you can develop.

3. In 1984, Borg Warner had the holders of some of its convertible notes elect to exchange these for common stock. Did Borg-Warner appear to use the book value or market value method for recording this conversion? How can you tell? What journal entry was made at the time of this conversion, assuming that the company used the book value method and there was no interest payable on the date of the conversion?

4. In 1984, Borg Warner also exchanged common shares for debt with a book value of $6,000,000. How did the company record this retirement in exchange for shares? How would this transaction be reported in the cash flow statement?

BORG WARNER
Statement of Earnings
Year Ended December 31

(millions of dollars except per share data)	1985	1984	1983
Sales and Other Income:			
Net sales	$3,330.1	$3,302.7	$2,946.8
Other income	12.6	24.4	17.4
	3,342.7	3,327.1	2,964.2
Costs and Expenses:			
Cost of sales	2,520.9	2,481.2	2,202.3
Depreciation	107.2	101.2	97.0
Selling, general and administrative expenses	404.9	388.0	383.9
Interest expense and finance charges	38.5	36.5	38.7
Minority interests	1.8	4.9	5.5
Provision for income taxes	107.1	129.3	92.5
	$3,180.4	$3,141.1	$2,819.9
Net Earnings:			
Consolidated operation	$ 162.3	$ 186.0	$ 144.3
Financial services companies (net of $56 million unusual provision in 1985)	(16.2)	28.3	37.4
Investment in affiliates (including $25 million gain on Echlin sale in 1985)	33.6	(7.5)	7.2
Continuing operations	179.7	206.8	188.9
Discontinued operations	(1.2)	(.7)	(6.3)
Net earnings	$ 178.5	$ 206.1	$ 182.6
Earnings Per Common Share:			
Continuing operations	$ 2.02	$ 2.29	$ 2.10
Discontinued operations	(1.0)	(.01)	(.07)
Net earnings	$ 2.01	$ 2.28	$ 2.03

BORG WARNER
Balance Sheet
(millions of dollars)

ASSETS	1985	1984
Current Assets:		
Cash	$ 25.1	$ 39.9
Marketable securities	89.8	81.9
Receivables	364.1	353.2
Inventories	261.2	245.1
Other current assets	75.0	58.1
Total current assets	815.2	778.2
Investments and advances	746.0	715.1
Property, plant and equipment	917.4	823.2
Other assets and deferred charges	173.8	165.6
Investment in discontinued operations	170.2	164.1
	$2,822.6	$2,646.2

LIABILITIES AND SHAREHOLDERS' EQUITY		
Current Liabilities:		
Notes payable	$ 88.7	$ 72.6
Accounts payable and accrued expenses	467.2	462.3
Income taxes	46.6	39.2
Total current liabilities	602.5	574.1
Warranties and other liabilities	118.5	109.1
Deferred income	33.3	35.2
Deferred income taxes	132.3	114.6
Long-term debt	263.9	192.9
Minority shareholders' interest in consolidated subsidiaries	19.6	24.9
Shareholders' Equity		
Capital stock:		
Preferred stock, liquidation preference $2.9 million in 1985 and 1984	.2	.2
Common stock, 91,824,968 shares issued in 1985 and 1984	229.6	229.6
Capital in excess of par value	151.5	151.3
Retained earnings	1,461.5	1,365.1
Currency translation adjustment	(85.0)	(95.9)
	1,757.8	1,650.3
Less treasury common stock at cost	105.3	54.9
Total shareholders' equity	$2,822.6	$2,646.2

BORG WARNER

CAPITAL STOCK (number of shares)	ISSUED	IN TREASURY
Capital stock activity is detailed below:		
Preferred stock no-par value $4.50 cumulative convertible. Series A authorized 25,000,000		
Balance January 1, 1983	46,181	
Conversions to common shares	(13,523)	
Repurchases ($98 thousand)	(433)	
Balance December 31, 1983	32,225	
Conversions to common shares	(2,902)	
Repurchased ($32 thousand)	(159)	
Balance December 31, 1984	29,164	
Conversions to common shares	(158)	
Repurchases ($32 thousand)	(150)	
Balance December 31, 1985	28,856	
Common stock $2.50 par value authorized 250,000,000		
Balance January 1, 1983	85,906,616	2,365,392
Conversions from preferred shares		(135,230)
Purchases of Treasury shares		240,774
Conversions of adjustable rate convertible notes	737,576	
Shares issued under employee benefit plans	57,052	(489,213)
Shares issued under stock options plans		(610,643)
Shares issued as stock incentive rights under stock option plans		(135,166)
Balance December 31, 1983	86,701,244	1,235,914
Conversions from preferred shares	27,250	(1,770)
Purchases of Treasury shares		2,590,973
Conversions of adjustable rate convertible notes	4,525,317	
Exchange of $6.0 million in debt	314,144	
Shares issued under employee benefit plans	257,013	(486,152)
Shares issued under stock option plans		(455,194)
Shares issued as stock incentive rights under stock options plans		(40,329)
Shares awarded		(9,700)
Balance December 31, 1984	91,824,968	2,833,742
Conversions from preferred shares		(1,580)
Purchases of Treasury shares		3,068,572
Shares issued under employee benefit plans		(592,019)
Shares issued under stock option plans		(199,264)
Shares issued as stock incentive rights under stock option plans		(26,636)
Balance December 31, 1985	91,824,968	5,082,815

BORG WARNER
Capital in Excess of Par Value and Retained Earnings
(millions of dollars)

CAPITAL IN EXCESS OF PAR VALUE	1985	1984	1983
Capital in excess of par value for the years ended December 31 is summarized as follows:			
Capital in excess of par value at January 1	$ 151.3	$ 106.4	$ 101.4
Transfer to common stock to effect two-for-one stock split	–	–	(107.5)
Conversions of adjustable rate convertible notes	–	33.9	5.8
Exchange of $6.0 million debt for equity	–	5.2	–
Excess of proceeds over cost of shares issued under employee investment plans	1.3	6.9	5.6
Excess of cost over proceeds on shares issued under stock option plans	(1.7)	(3.1)	(3.0)
Excess of market price over cost on shares issued as stock incentive rights under stock option plans	.1	.4	1.7
Tax benefits arising from exercise of non-qualified stock options	.5	1.6	2.4
Capitalization of retained earnings	–	–	100.0
Capital in excess of par value at December 31	$ 151.5	$ 151.3	$ 106.4

RETAINED EARNINGS			
Retained earnings for the years ended December 31 are summarized as follows:			
Retained earnings at January 1	$1,365.1	$1,235.3	$1,220.3
Net earnings	178.5	206.1	182.6
	1,543.6	1,441.4	1,402.9
Deduction from retained earnings: Dividends declared:			
Preferred stock ($4.50 per share)	.1	.1	.2
Common stock ($.93 per share in 1985, $.86 per share in 1984 and $.78 per share in 1983)	82.0	76.2	65.7
Excess of cost over stated value on conversion and retirement of preferred stock	–	–	1.7
Capitalization of retained earnings	–	–	100.0
	82.1	76.3	167.6
Retained earnings at December 31	$1,461.5	$1,365.1	$1,235.3

CASE 15.5

FEDERATED DEPARTMENT STORES

The following pages provide excerpts from the 1986 annual report to shareholders of Federated Department Stores. Federated owned and operated a number of major department stores throughout the United States under various names. Federated has a fiscal year-end of January 31.

FEDERATED DEPARTMENT STORES
Balance Sheet
(dollars in thousands)

ASSETS	1986	1985
Current Assets:		
Cash	$ 101,097	$ 54,270
Accounts receivable	1,554,402	1,607,012
Merchandise inventories	1,405,992	1,320,097
Supplies and prepaids	42,508	43,448
Total current assets	3,103,999	3,024,827
Property and equipment (net)	2,451,629	2,249,624
Other assets	132,110	79,192
Total assets	$5,687,738	$5,353,643

LIABILITIES AND SHAREHOLDERS' EQUITY	1986	1985
Current Liabilities:		
Notes payable and long-term debt due within one year	$ 240,053	$ 42,749
Accounts payable and accrued liabilities	1,249,149	1,125,626
Income taxes	119,149	320,748
Total current liabilities	1,608,351	1,489,123
Deferred income taxes	420,042	186,091
Deferred compensation	204,890	189,648
Long-term debt	791,901	781,513
Shareholders' Equity:		
Preferred stock	–	–
Common stock	118,876	62,196
Capital in excess of par on common	25,597	98,506
Retained earnings	2,538,612	2,569,404
Treasury stock at cost	(20,531)	(22,838)
Total shareholders' equity	2,662,554	2,707,268
Total liabilities and shareholders' equity	$5,687,738	$5,353,643

Note 13. Shareholders' Equity (dollars in millions)

The authorized shares of the company consist of 5.0 million preferred shares, no par value, with none issued, and 200.0 million common shares, par value $1.25 per share with 95.1 million shares issued in 1986 and 99.5 million shares issued in 1985 and 1984. The company increased the authorized shares of common stock from 100.0 million to 200.0 million on May 29, 1986. Common shares outstanding at year end totalled 93.3 million in 1986, 97.6 million in 1985, and 97.3 million in 1984.

FEDERATED DEPARTMENT STORES

	1986	1985	1984
Common stock–par value			
Balance at beginning of year	$ 62.2	$ 62.2	$ 62.2
Retirements	(2.7)	–	–
2-for-1 stock split	59.4	–	–
Balance at end of year	118.9	62.2	62.2
Capital in excess of par value			
Balance at beginning of year	98.5	$ 102.4	105.5
Net change from treasury stock	(9.1)	(3.9)	(3.1)
Retirement of common stock	(4.4)	–	–
2-for-1 split	(59.4)	–	–
Balance at end of year	$ 25.6	$ 98.5	$ 102.4
Retained earnings			
Balance at beginning of year	2,569.4	2,406.7	2,194.1
Net income	287.6	286.6	329.3
Cash dividends	(129.5)	(123.9)	(116.7)
Retirement of common stock	(188.9)	–	–
Balance at end of year	$2,538.6	2,569.4	2,406.7
Less treasury stock			
Balance at beginning of year	22.8	27.2	28.4
Additions	23.1	18.3	12.9
Deductions	(25.4)	(22.7)	(14.1)
Balance at end of year	20.5	22.8	27.2
Total shareholders' equity	$2,662.6	$2,707.3	$2,544.1

During 1986 the company's Board of Directors authorized the repurchase of up to 10 million shares (20 million shares post-split) of its common stock. As of January 31, 1987, 2.2 million shares (4.4 million shares post-split) had been repurchased and retired. The company recorded the entire purchase price as the cost of the shares.

On January 23, 1986, the company declared a dividend of one preferred stock purchase right (one-half right post-split) on each outstanding share of common stock. Under certain conditions, each full right may be exercised to purchase one-hundredth of a share of a new series of preferred stock at an exercise price of $250 per one-hundredth share, subject to adjustment. The rights may only be exercised after a public announcement that a party acquired or obtained the right to acquire 20% or more of the outstanding shares of the company's stock. The rights, which do not have voting rights, expire on February 5, 1996, and may be redeemed by the company at a price of $.05 per right at any time prior to 10 days (or such longer period as the Board of Directors may determine) after the acquisition of 20% of the company's common stock.

REQUIRED:

1. Federated reports that it repurchased and retired 2.2 million shares of common stock in 1986:
   (a) What was the price per share of the stock when purchased?
   (b) What was the historical issue price of these shares?
   (c) Recreate the journal entry Federated used to record the retirement.

2. Federated reports the effects of a 2-for-1 stock split in 1986.
   (a) What journal entry, if any, did Federated use to record the split?
   (b) Is there anything unusual about the way the split was accounted for?
   (c) What other alternatives might Federated have used to effect the 2-for-1 split? How would the equity section of Federated's balance sheet appear under each of these alternatives?
   (d) How many shares of common stock were actually outstanding at the end of 1985 and 1984 (prior to the split)?
3. Federated uses the cost method of accounting for treasury stock.
   (a) How much cash did Federated distribute to shareholders via treasury stock acquisitions in each of the three years presented?
   (b) How much cash did Federated generate from the reissue of treasury shares in each of the three years presented?
   (c) How would the repurchase of treasury shares affect the unrestricted retained earnings of Federated under a typical debt covenant? Why?
   (d) Assume that you wished to recast the stockholders' equity accounts at the end of 1986 from the use of the cost method of accounting for treasury stock to the par value method. Further assume that all the shares in the treasury were originally issued for $3.30 per share. Prepare the restated stockholders' equity section.
4. Federated reports the payment of cash dividends in each year presented.
   (a) Assuming that Federated declares quarterly dividends on February 1, May 1, August 1, and November 1 of each year, payable on the last day of the month to shareholders of record on the 15th of each month, and that each quarterly dividend is exactly one-fourth of the total dividends paid during the fiscal year, prepare the journal entries to record the quarterly dividends for 1985 and 1986.
   (b) Compute the ratio of cash dividends to net income (the dividend payout ratio) for each of the three years presented. Did the stock split appear to have any effect on the total amount of cash Federated was distributing in the form of dividends?
   (c) Estimate the average actual annual dividend per common share outstanding for 1984, 1985, and 1986, before the split. Assume that the stock split occurred on the last day of 1986. How does the dividend per share change, if at all, over this period?
5. In the notes, Federated discusses a special dividend issued on January 23, 1986. Assuming this dividend was issued on all outstanding shares as of that date and there was no change in the number of outstanding shares between January 23, 1986, and January 31, 1986, respond to the following:
   (a) What entry was used to record this dividend?
   (b) Assuming that all the rights were exercised, approximately how many shares of preferred stock would be issued and how much cash would Federated generate as a result?
   (c) Prepare the journal entry implied by the information in (b).
   (d) Suppose the company elected to redeem the rights instead of having them exercised. How much cash would the company need to pay? Speculate on how this transaction might be accounted for.
   (e) Speculate on the motivation Federated might have had to issue a dividend of this type and explain how this dividend would accomplish the goal you speculate Federated might have had in issuing it.

PART 5

Advanced Topics

CHAPTER 16

Noncurrent Investments

Noncurrent investments are nonproducing assets acquired with the intent to hold them for periods in excess of one year. A **nonproducing asset** is not used directly in the production of a product or service. Noncurrent investments could include such assets as land purchased for speculation, bonds or notes of another company, equity securities of another company, and bond sinking fund balances. The level of long-term investments varies considerably across firms.

Investments in various types of marketable debt or equity securities are a central feature of the balance sheet in industries such as insurance and banking where large portfolios of securities are purchased and held for the long run to provide an investment return as part of the normal course of business. For manufacturing firms, long-term investments are more likely to arise from one company's desire to secure influence over another. For example, a manufacturer may wish to carry an equity interest in a major supplier to strengthen the degree of control over its inputs.

This chapter focuses on accounting and financial reporting by investors for long-term investments. A common thread that weaves through the accounting for these investments is the application of the historical cost approach. For some types of investments, the historical cost approach is applied without adjustment. In some cases, the historical cost approach is used to define the amounts reported as part of net income for the period, but adjustments are made in the balance sheet to reflect differences between the historical cost and current market values of investment assets. In other cases, where the investor obtains significant influence over the investee by virtue of the purchase of voting stock, the very definition of historical cost is altered by expanding slightly the definition of the accounting entity.

IMPORTANT ATTRIBUTES OF INVESTMENT ASSETS

Before examining the accounting for the various types of investments, it is first necessary to define a variety of classification attributes such as:

1. The current/noncurrent classification decision (applicable to all investments)
2. The marketable/nonmarketable nature of the investment assets (applicable to all investments)
3. The nature of any influence the investor has over the investee (of importance only to investments in equity securities)
4. The investor's ability and intent to hold the investments to maturity (important only for investments in debt securities)

Determining these attributes dictates the type of valuation approach used to account for each type of investment, based on the guidelines in SFAS No. 115, "Accounting for Certain Investments in Debt and Equity Securities."

Current or Noncurrent

The classification of investments as current or noncurrent depends on management's intent regarding liquidation. A **current investment** is held as a short-term investment and is expected to be liquidated within one year or the next operating cycle, whichever is longer. Such investments are typically composed of highly liquid marketable debt or equity securities, which are referred to as *trading securities*. As discussed in Chapter 6, these investments are presented at market value in the balance sheet, with any unrealized gain or loss recognized as part of income from operations for the period. The use of market value and the recognition of unrealized gains and losses are dictated by the short-term nature of these investments and the natural sensitivity that such investments have to fluctuation in market value since they are to be liquidated in the short term. An investment classified as current at the end of one year need not be actually liquidated during the next fiscal year. However, management must intend to hold the investment for sale in order for it to be classified as current.

An investment is classified as noncurrent when the investor's intent is to hold the asset beyond the next year or operating cycle. Because the investor's plan is to hold a long-term investment, a debate arises over the appropriateness of using the asset's market value in the balance sheet. Even greater debate exists over whether the unrealized gains and losses from such investments should be recognized in income for the period since management's investment strategy is taking a long-term perspective, which is not necessarily influenced by short-term fluctuations in the investments' prices.

Marketable or Nonmarketable

A **marketable investment** is one that is traded in well-organized markets with regularly quoted prices. Noncurrent investments not in the form of securities (or commodity contracts) are generally considered to be nonmarketable. Consequently, when a company purchases land for possible future expansion or sale, the land would be classified as a long-term, nonmarketable, investment.

Noncurrent investments in securities may be characterized as being marketable or nonmarketable. A **marketable security** is traded in organized markets, which include the New York, London, or Tokyo stock exchanges, the New York Exchange Bonds, the Over-the-Counter market, or the Chicago Board of Options Exchange. In these markets, many buyers and sellers trade actively and provide information, which is generally judged to be reliable, on the market value of securities.

However, even when securities are traded on such exchanges, a reliable measure of market value may be difficult to determine. Smaller corporations often have their shares traded on a local over-the-counter market. In some cases, the activity in these markets is very light, with trades occurring only infrequently (such as once a month). Whether these types of markets provide a reliable measure of "market value" is a matter of professional judgment. The point is that not all price quotes for traded securities are equally reliable.

When a corporation is privately held, its shares are not traded on any exchange. When one corporation purchases the stock in, or loans money to, another privately held corporation, the investment should be considered nonmarketable. A similar classification would be appropriate for notes or loans to companies whose equity securities are publicly traded if the debt security itself is not publicly traded. Classifying these securities as nonmarketable does not mean they have no value. Rather, it means there is no readily available, reliable market price to be observed. Nonmarketable investments in equity securities are valued using the cost method; and both dividends and realized gains and losses are reflected in income for the period. On the other hand, nonmarketable debt securities are valued at amortized cost; and interest income is determined using effective interest amortization.

The Influence of the Investor Over the Investee

When an investor acquires a small equity interest in an investee (the company issuing the securities), the size of investment usually precludes the investor from exerting significant influence over the investee's operations. The investor's economic benefit is well-represented by the dividends and price appreciation of the stock. Therefore, income from such investments is measured by dividends, plus any effect of market value fluctuations.[1]

---

[1] There is still a debate about when the effects of fluctuations in market prices should be recognized. Gains and losses could be recognized only at the point-of-sale, or whenever market value changes. In either case, the underlying notion is that income should be measured in response to dividends and market fluctuations.

In some cases, however, the investor's interest becomes large enough to exert significant influence over the investee's management. Dividends the investor receives during such periods are no longer a sound basis for measuring income because the investor may have influenced the investee's dividend policy to such degree that these distributions are no longer arm's-length exchanges. To exert such influence, the investor must generally control a significant portion of the investee's equity. When this type of economic influence exists, an alternative approach to recognizing income from an investment, called the equity method, must be applied.

APB Opinion No. 18 sets forth general guidelines for determining when significant influence exists. **Significant influence** is deemed to exist whenever the investor controls 20% or more of the investee's outstanding voting stock. The FASB has broadened this general guideline with Interpretation No. 35, which requires an overall evaluation of the relationship between the investor and investee, instead of a narrow application of the 20% criterion.

When a third party holds a majority interest in the investee, even an interest as large as 20% might lack significant influence. In these situations, the investor holding a 20% interest would have little effective influence over the investee's operations due to the direct control of the majority owner. In such situations, the cost method is appropriate.

On the other hand, there are cases where holding 5% of the outstanding shares might imply significant influence if the remainder of the shares are very widely dispersed. For example, an investor holding a block of 5% may influence the election of one or more board members. Depending on the size of the board, this situation might qualify as one in which the investor has significant influence over the investee. In the final analysis, professional judgment must be applied to determine whether significant influence exists. The guidelines set forth by the APB and FASB provide only broad assistance in making this judgment.

If significant influence exists, a special valuation method is used to determine the carrying value of and the income derived from the equity investment on a periodic basis. This method is commonly referred to as the **equity method**.[2]

Ability and Intent to Hold to Maturity

When an investor holds a marketable debt security, the valuation and income recognition process applied to such investment depends on the investor's ability and intent to hold the security to maturity. The investor's ability to hold such securities to maturity must be evaluated based on the facts and circumstances present at each balance sheet date. A past history of holding similar investments to maturity, combined with a current liquidity position that suggests cash flows from operations or other investment assets will be sufficient to meet all maturing obligations, would be adequate evidence of ability to

---

[2] When the ownership percentage of the investor exceeds 50%, the equity method is required if the investor produces stand-alone financial statements; *and* consolidated statements that represent the combined operations of the investor (parent) and investee (subsidiary) are also required by GAAP.

hold to maturity. Intent is unobservable; it can only be determined by management's indication of its plans for using such investments.

When both the ability and intent to hold to maturity are present, investments in debt securities can be valued at amortized cost with interest income recognized under the effective interest method. If either the ability or intent to hold to maturity is not present, these investments are combined with the noncurrent investments in marketable equity securities and presented in the balance sheet at market value. However, for these securities, unrealized gains and losses are not recognized in income for the periods in which they arise. Exhibit 16.1 presents a classification diagram that demonstrates the various attributes of investments in relation to how they are presented in the balance sheet and influence reported income.

ACCOUNTING FOR NONCURRENT INVESTMENTS WITHOUT SIGNIFICANT INFLUENCE

Regardless of its type, the acquisition of any investment asset is recorded at cost, based on the purchase price plus any transactions costs incurred to acquire it. This approach is the same as that employed for other assets. For example, the acquisition of a parcel of land for $100,000 cash plus commissions of 6% would result in an increase in investments of $106,000 and a decrease in cash of a similar amount. The acquisition of shares of common stock would be similarly recorded. For example, assume that on April 12, 1993, Becon Corporation purchases 10,000 shares of DuPont common stock at

EXHIBIT 16.1

Graphical Representation of Choice of Accounting Method for Investments

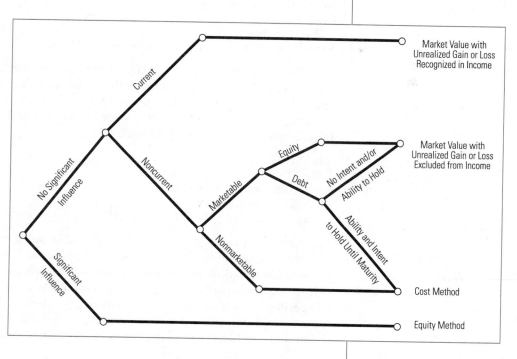

$720,000 (which includes brokerage fees of $15,000). Becon's entry to record this acquisition would appear as follows:

```
April 12, 1993:
Noncurrent investments                                    720,000
    Cash                                                              720,000
To record the acquisition of 10,000 shares of DuPont common at
  $70.50 per share, plus brokerage fees of $15,000.
```

Equity Investments Without Significant Influence—The Cost Method

When nonmarketable equity securities are acquired and the investor does not exert significant influence, accounting for these investments is governed by the cost method. The investor recognizes income when dividends are earned, assuming the investor holds the securities on the ex dividend date. For example, assume that Deed, Inc. owns a 10% interest in Mica Corporation. Mica declares a dividend of $10,000 on June 1, 1993, payable on July 1, 1993. The ex dividend date is June 15, 1993. Deed would make the following entry:

```
June 15, 1993:
Dividends receivable                                      1,000
    Income (loss) from investments                                  1,000
To record the dividend receivable arising form Mica's declaration
  of a dividend.
```

When the dividend is actually received, Deed would make the following entry:

```
July 1, 1993:
Cash                                                      1,000
    Dividends receivable                                            1,000
To record the cash received from the dividend of Mica.
```

When a security is sold, a realized gain or loss will be recognized at the time of sale. For example, suppose that following the dividend, on July 31, 1993, Deed elected to sell 1,000 shares of Mica for cash of $14 per share. Deed had originally purchased the Mica shares at $17 per share. Deed would make the following entry to record the realized loss:

```
July 31, 1993:
Cash                                                     14,000
Income (loss) from investments                           3,000
    Noncurrent investments                                         17,000
To record the sale of 1,000 shares of Mica Corporation stock.
```

Noncurrent investments must be reduced in value and any loss immediately recognized in income, when a permanent decline (or impairment) of value is identified. A permanent decline occurs whenever there is evidence that the equity security's value has declined below its historical cost and that this decline is not temporary. A permanent price decline should be immediately recognized in income as a realized loss, and the historical cost of the security should be reduced to an estimate of its permanent value. However, permanent declines in market value for noncurrent, nonmarketable investments are often difficult to identify, because there are no observable market prices to indicate that any decline has occurred.

Liquidating Dividends Under the Cost Method

When the cost method is used to value investments in equity securities, a special problem arises when dividends declared by the investee represent a return of the investor's original investment. From the investor's standpoint, the receipt of such dividends is not income but, rather, a return of the original investment. When this occurs, the dividend is referred to as a *liquidating dividend*. This terminology is somewhat unfortunate because "liquidating dividend" in this situation does not have the same implication as when the corporation issuing the dividend refers to a liquidating dividend.

To see the difference, consider the following example. On January 1, 1994, Baird Corporation purchased a 5% interest in Numero Company for $100,000. At the time of this purchase, Numero reported the following balances in its stockholders' equity accounts:

Common stock, no-par	$ 500,000
Retained earnings	1,500,000
Total stockholders' equity	$2,000,000

Suppose that on the day following the stock's acquisition, Numero declared a dividend of $200,000, of which Baird's 5% interest would be $10,000. Numero has reported no earnings following Baird's purchase of its stock. From Baird's perspective, the dividend represents a return of part of the assets Numero held when Baird determined that Numero's shares were worth $100,000. As a result, the dividend represents a return of part of Baird's investment, which is the essence of a liquidating dividend, not a distribution of earnings recorded by Numero following the investment by Baird. However, from Numero's perspective, the dividend is a distribution of assets that were accumulated by not distributing dividends equal to the amount of earnings in prior periods. As a result, the dividend is not liquidating part of Numero's contributed capital and, thus, is not a liquidating dividend from Numero's point of view.

For purposes of applying the cost method, an investor is deemed to receive a liquidating dividend whenever the dividend's effect is to reduce the investee's book value of stockholders' equity below its stated level on the date the investor acquired the interest. Recording a liquidating dividend requires that the historical cost of the investment be reduced by the amount of the liquidating dividend.

For example, assume that Kind Inc., purchased a 5% interest in Portny Company for $4,000 on January 1, 1993. At that time, Portny had a total book value of equity in the amount of $80,000. During the next year, Portny reported income of $40,000, but declared dividends of $50,000 on December 15, 1993. The ex dividend date was December 31, 1993. Of the dividends declared, $40,000 is deemed to be a distribution of the income for the period, but $10,000 is a reduction in the book value of Portny's equity below the amount of capital present at the time Kind acquired its interest.

This is a liquidating dividend to Kind since Portny not only distributes all of the income it earned since Kind acquired its interest, but it also distributed part of Portny's equity that was present at the time of Kind's initial investment. Since Kind owned a 5% interest in Portny, Kind would be entitled to receive a dividend of $2,500 (5% × $50,000), of which $2,000 represents a dividend out of Portny's current earnings (5% × $40,000) and $500 represents a liquidating dividend. Kind would prepare a journal entry of the following form to record the declaration of this dividend:

December 31, 1993:		
Dividends receivable	2,500	
Dividend income		2,000
Investment in Portny		500

To record the dividend of $2,500 from Portny, of which $500 is in the form of a liquidating dividend.

Since recording the effects of the liquidating dividend permanently reduces the carrying value (historical cost) of the investment in Portny shares, if Kind were to sell its 5% interest in Portny for $6,000 on January 21, 1994, Kind's entry to record the disposition would appear as:

January 21, 1994:		
Cash	6,000	
Investment in Portny		3,500
Gain on the sale of investments		2,500

To record the sale of the shares of Portny.

Note that in the entry, the cost of the Portny shares is the original cost of $4,000 reduced by the effect of the liquidating dividend, $500.

The Cost Method of Accounting For Debt Securities

When a corporation purchases notes or bonds as an investment and either the debt securities are nonmarketable or it has the ability and intent to hold the marketable debt securities to maturity, the cost method is applied. Under the cost method as applied to debt securities, any difference between the debt's maturity value and the purchase price must be amortized to income over the time to maturity of the debt. When the purchase price is in excess of (below) the maturity value, a purchase premium (discount) exists. Amortization of the premium or discount is calculated using the effective interest amortization process, and it should be included in the determination of income from these investments for each period the investments are held.

The purchase price at acquisition is recorded as the asset's value. For example, assume that on July 1, 1993, Investor, Inc. purchased a bond issued by Backdrop Company for $105,242. The bond had a face value of $100,000, pays interest semiannually on January 1 and July 1, at a face rate of 10% per year. The bond will mature three years from the date of purchase. The yield to maturity on this bond is 8%, which is the interest rate that will make the present value of the bond's future cash flows equal $105,242. Investor's journal entry to record this event would appear as follows:

July 1, 1993:

Investment in bonds	105,242	
Cash		105,242

To record the acquisition of the bonds of Backdrop.

In this example, Investor purchased the bonds at a premium above the face value of $5,242. Given the above information, Exhibit 16.2 presents the amortization schedule for the investment in bonds using the effective interest method. Investor's journal entries to record the interest income over the life of the bond would appear as follows:

December 31, 1993:

Interest receivable	5,000	
Investment in bonds		790
Income (loss) from investments		4,210

To accrue interest for the last six months of 1993.

July 1, 1994:

Cash	5,000	
Investment in bonds		822
Income (loss) from investments		4,178

To record interest for the first six months of 1994.

December 31, 1994:

Interest receivable	5,000	
Investment in bonds		855
Income (loss) from investments		4,145

To accrue interest for the last six months of 1994.

EXHIBIT 16.2

Effective Interest Amortization of Investor's Interest in Backdrop's Bonds

Effective Interest Amortization of a Bond Investment

Facts: Initial price = $105,242
     Compounding Period = Semiannual
     Interest Rate = 8%
     Life = 3 Years

(1) Date	(2) Investment in Bonds	(3) Interest Revenue (2) × 4%	(4) Face Interest	(5) Amortization of Premium (4) − (3)
12/31/93	$105,242	$4,210	$5,000	$790
7/01/94	104,452	4,178	5,000	822
12/31/94	103,630	4,145	5,000	855
7/01/95	102,775	4,111	5,000	889
12/31/95	101,886	4,075	5,000	925
7/01/96	100,961	4,038	5,000	962

July 1, 1995:

Cash	5,000	
Investment in bonds		889
Income (loss) from investments		4,111

To record interest for the first six months of 1995.

December 31, 1995:

Interest receivable	5,000	
Investment in bonds		925
Income (loss) from investments		4,075

To accrue interest for the last six months of 1995.

July 1, 1996:

Cash	105,000	
Investment in bonds		100,962
Income (loss) from investments		4,038

To record the maturity of the bond.

Debt Investments Purchased Between Interest Payment Dates   When a bond or note is purchased between interest payment dates, the purchaser must pay the face interest accrued on the bond to the seller, in addition to the price of the bond. When this occurs, the amortization of the investment discount or premium will proceed as in Exhibit 16.2, but the total purchase price must first be broken down into portions representing the accrued interest and the investment.

Assume that Banker, Inc. purchased a $50,000 bond by paying $52,000 plus accrued interest on April 15, 1993. Interest on the bond is at a face rate of 12%, payable on January 31 and July 31 each year. Interest accruing at the face rate from January 31 to April 15 would be $1,250 [($50,000 × 12%) ÷ 12 months] × [2 1/2 months]. The following journal entry would record Banker's acquisition:

April 15, 1993:

Investment in bonds	52,000	
Interest receivable	1,250	
Cash		53,250

To record the payment for the investment in bonds and the
accrued interest, which will be paid by the issuer at the next
interest payment date.

At this point, an amortization schedule based on an original value for the investment of $52,000 can be established to amortize the purchase premium and determine periodic interest revenue for Banker, Inc.

Recording Realized Gains and Losses from Sale   When debt securities carried on the cost method are sold during the accounting period, interest income is accrued up to the point of the sale; and any gain or loss from the sale is recognized in the income of the period. When the interest revenue is accrued, any purchase premium or discount will be amortized up to the date of the sale as well.

For example, assume that instead of holding the bond in Exhibit 16.2 to maturity, Investor, Inc. elected to sell it in the open market for $101,000 plus accrued interest on November 30, 1993. Investor would need to record interest revenue from July 1 up to the point of the sale as follows:

November 30, 1993:

Interest receivable	4,167	
Investment in bonds		713
Income (loss) from investments		3,454

To accrue interest up to the sale.

The interest receivable represents 5 months of interest at the face rate of 10% per year {[($50,000 × 10%) ÷ 12] × 5}, or 5/6ths of the amount that would have been recorded on December 31 ($4,145 × 5/6). The amortization of the purchase premium is determined as the difference between the interest revenue and the receivable.

To record the sale, along with the loss on disposition, Investor would record the following entry:

November 30, 1993:

Cash	105,167	
Income (loss) from investments	1,034	
Investment in bonds		102,034
Interest receivable		4,167

To record the sale of bonds plus accrued interest.

Investments in Debt Securities and Permanent Declines in Value   While less frequent than those for equity securities, permanent declines in the value of debt still may arise. Debt has a fixed set of cash payments promised by the issuer to the investor in the form of interest payments and payment of the face value at maturity. While the market value of the debt is affected by fluctuations in interest rates, which may occur due to changes in the riskiness of the bond, the interpretation of such changes in market value as temporary or permanent are more complex. If the investor holds the bonds to maturity and the issuer does not default, the investor will recover the initial investment in the bonds plus interest at the rate implied by the bond's price when it was first acquired. Consequently, declines in a bond's market value are only permanent if they reflect substantial increases in the likelihood that the issuer will default. Such cases exist when the issuer defaults on the debt or declares bankruptcy, and the likelihood of receiving full payment of the interest and face value of the debt is significantly in doubt.

If such a situation does arise, the investor must treat the decline in value as a permanent decline and recognize it as a realized loss by writing down the investment in bonds accordingly. When this situation arises, interest should not be accrued on the investment unless payment of the interest is reasonably assured. If the debt instrument on which a permanent decline has been recorded is sold, a gain or loss will be determined by comparing the selling price to the security's adjusted book value.

Investments in Marketable Equity Securities and Debt Securities Not Being Held to Maturity

Subsequent to the acquisition of these types of securities, their effects on reported income for the period will be determined using the cost method, as described earlier for equity and debt securities. However, the valuation of these investments in the investor's balance sheet will be based on market value, with the difference between the aggregate cost and aggregate market value of the portfolio reported as a contra-asset. Along with the contra-asset, an offsetting contra-equity account will be recorded as part of shareholders' equity. Because this approach uses the cost method in presentation of the income statement and the market value method for purposes of balance sheet construction, it is sometimes referred to as the **two-statement approach**.

Exhibit 16.3 provides an abbreviated balance sheet that portrays the presentation of these items. The unrealized gains of $20, which have arisen by the balance sheet date, reflect the fact that the portfolio's cost is below market value on that date by $20. Recording the unrealized gains increases total assets by $20, and this is also reflected by an increase in total equity of $20. However, the unrealized gains would not be reported in the income statement for the year. This is why they are not part of the ending retained earnings balance.

During any accounting period, some of the securities in the portfolio may be sold. At the time of sale, the realized gain or loss is determined by matching the historical cost (including any adjustments for permanent declines) to the selling price of the securities. The realized gain or loss is recognized as a component of income reported for the period. At the next balance sheet date, any change in the difference between the then existing book and market values of the portfolio will be recorded as an adjustment to the contra-asset account and the equity allowance account, simultaneously.

To see how this process evolves, consider the following example. At the end of 1994, Manor Corporation had a portfolio of noncurrent marketable securities that was acquired during the year. Prior to 1994, Manor had not invested in marketable securities which were to be held long-term. At December 31, 1994, the cost and market values of the securities in the noncurrent portfolio appeared as follows:

	Cost	Market
Security A	$12,000	$17,000
Security B	43,000	22,000
Security C	20,000	31,000
Security D	15,000	15,000
Total	$90,000	$85,000

All differences between cost and market are deemed to be temporary.

During 1994, Manor had used the cost method of accounting for each individual security in the portfolio. Securities A, B, and C are equities, and Security D is a bond. The bond was purchased at face value. Suppose the dividends declared and paid during 1993 amounted to $10,000 and the interest income, accrued but unpaid at year-end, was $2,000. The following entries are how Manor would record this information:

Various dates over the year:

Investment income	10,000	
Cash		10,000

To record the declaration and payment of dividends received from investments.

December 31, 1994:

Interest receivable	2,000	
Investment income		2,000

To accrue interest income on bonds carried as long-term investments not held to maturity.

EXHIBIT 16.3

Balance Sheet Presentation of Noncurrent Investments in Marketable Securities Not Held to Maturity

Balance Sheet Presentation of Noncurrent Investments in Marketable Securities Not Held to Maturity

ASSETS	
Current assets	
Cash	$ 100
Receivables	150
Inventory	175
Total current assets	425
Property, plant, and equipment	700
Accumulated depreciation	(200)
	500
Investments	200
Allowance for unrealized gains and (losses)	20
	220
Total assets	$1,145

LIABILITIES AND EQUITY	
Current liabilities	
Accounts payable	$ 70
Taxes payable	40
Accrued expenses	120
Total current liabilities	230
Long-term debt	300
Deferred taxes	100
Stockholders' equity	
Common stock	40
Additional paid-in capital	280
Retained earnings	175
Unrealized gains and losses on noncurrent marketable securities	20
Total stockholders' equity	515
Total liabilities and stockholders' equity	$1,145

Based on the detailed information provided above on each security in the portfolio, it can be determined that the portfolio's market value is $5,000 below carrying value as of the balance sheet date. Manor must report a valuation allowance as a contra-asset account to the noncurrent marketable security portfolio in the amount of $5,000. If the portfolio were classified as current, this allowance would result in a recognized loss of $5,000 included in reported income for the period. However, since the portfolio is noncurrent, no loss is recognized as part of reported income. Instead, Manor debits the loss to a special stockholders' equity account as follows:

December 31, 1994:

Equity allowance for unrealized loss on noncurrent marketable securities	5,000	
Allowance for adjustment to market value for noncurrent marketable securities		5,000

To record the allowance for the temporary decline in market value below book value of the noncurrent marketable securities portfolio.

A Comparison of Gross and Net Unrealized Gain or Loss   The net unrealized gain or loss is determined by the difference between the portfolio's total carrying value and its total market value. Unrealized gains and losses can also be measured at the individual security level. Security B has an unrealized loss of $21,000. Securities A and C both have unrealized gains of $11,000 and $5,000, respectively. The gross unrealized gain in the portfolio is determined by summing all the unrealized gains on securities whose market values are above cost at the individual level. The gross unrealized loss is similarly measured using only securities with individual unrealized losses. In this example, the gross unrealized gain would be $16,000, and the gross unrealized loss is $21,000. When the gross unrealized gains are netted against the gross unrealized losses, the total is the net unrealized loss. Gross unrealized gains and losses are not accounted for separately in the financial statements, but note disclosure of their amounts is required.

Recording Activity in Subsequent Periods   In 1995, Manor will record any income from dividends or interest earned using the cost method. If any security is sold from the portfolio, the realized gain or loss will be computed by comparing the security's historical cost carrying value to its selling price. None of these activities require an adjustment to the contra-asset or equity allowance account until the end of the period. For example, assume that Manor earned dividends of $5,000 and interest of $7,000 in 1995, all of which was collected in cash. In addition, it sold the investment in Security A for $15,000 on October 1, 1995, and purchased a new investment in Security E for $18,000 on November 1, 1995. Manor would use the following entries to record this activity:

Various dates throughout the year:

Cash	12,000	
Investment income		5,000
Investment income		7,000

To record the interest and dividend income for the year.

October 1, 1995:

Cash	15,000	
Investment income		3,000
Noncurrent investments		12,000

To record the sale of the investment in Security A.

November 1, 1995:

Noncurrent investments	18,000	
Cash		18,000

To record the purchase of Security E.

At the end of the next accounting period, an examination of the cost and market values of the securities in the portfolio reflect the following:

	Cost	Market
Security B	$43,000	$35,000
Security C	20,000	29,000
Security D	15,000	15,000
Security E	18,000	19,000
Total	$96,000	$98,000

All differences between cost and market are deemed to be temporary.

Based on this information, the portfolio's market value now exceeds cost by $2,000. In order to reflect this change in status in the financial statements, the contra-asset account must be changed from a credit of $5,000 (existing balance) to a debit of $2,000 (the desired balance). A similar change must be made for the equity valuation allowance. Manor's entry to accomplish that change would appear as follows:

December 31, 1995:

Allowance for adjustment to market value for noncurrent marketable securities	7,000	
Equity allowance for unrealized gain or loss on noncurrent marketable equity securities		7,000

To adjust the contra-asset and equity allowance accounts to reflect the current status of the market value of the portfolio relative to cost.

Transfers of Securities Between Current and Noncurrent Portfolios

Management can transfer a security between current and noncurrent portfolios. When this occurs, the transfer is made at the current market value of the security being transferred. Any unrealized gain or loss arising from the revaluation of the security to current market value is recognized immediately in the income statement of the period in which the transfer occurred. This procedure is designed to avoid creating an incentive for firms to transfer securities with unrealized losses into the noncurrent portfolio to avoid loss recognition in the income statement.

For example, assume that Griffin Corporation held an investment in Bascomb Corporation as a noncurrent marketable equity security. The cost of the investment was $50,000, and the current market value on December 31, 1995 was only $43,000. If Griffin elected to reclassify this investment as current, the following entry would be required:

```
December 31, 1995:
Loss on permanent decline in marketable securities          7,000
Current investments                                        43,000
    Noncurrent marketable securities                               50,000
To record the transfer of the Bascomb stock to current status
 and recognize a realized loss due to market value being below
 cost at the time of transfer.
```

Disclosure Requirements for Noncurrent Marketable Securities

Disclosure requirements for noncurrent investments in marketable securities include all of the following, measured as of the balance sheet date:

1. The aggregate market value and cost (or amortized cost) basis by major type of security
2. The gross unrealized losses by type of security
3. The gross unrealized gains by type of security

In addition, for each period an income statement is presented, the following must be disclosed:

1. The proceeds from the sales of all securities in the held-for-sale portfolio, along with the gross realized gains and/or losses on those sales
2. The basis on which cost was assigned to securities disposed of (first-in, first-out, weighted average, etc.)
3. The gross gains and/or losses arising from the transfer of any security between the trading, held-for-sale, and held-to-maturity portfolios
4. An explanation for any transfer of securities out of the held-to-maturity portfolio
5. The change in the valuation allowances included in the equity section of the balance sheet arising from the valuation of the noncurrent portfolio

For debt securities classified in the hold-to-maturity portfolio, additional information on their maturities structure must be provided. Also, aggregate market value and amortized cost must be disclosed for all maturities within one year, one to five years, five to ten years, and after ten years.

A Political Perspective on Accounting for Investments Without Significant Influence

The current state of financial reporting for investments in marketable securities, when the investor has no significant influence, has been achieved only after several decades of debate. In fact, the procedures discussed above are very new, going into effect with fiscal years starting after December 31, 1993. Prior to this new standard, a different approach was used. This earlier approach treated all noncurrent investments in debt securities in the fashion described for debt securities for which an investor has the ability and intent to hold to maturity. Marketable equity securities were accounted separately, using what was referred to as the *lower-of-cost-or-market* (LCM) approach, which was established by SFAS No. 12.

The lower-of-cost-or-market approach was applied to both the current and noncurrent portfolios of marketable equity securities. Under this approach, the difference between aggregate cost and aggregate market value is only recognized when market is below cost. Another way of saying this is that LCM recognized unrealized net losses but not unrealized net gains. The lower-of-cost-or-market concept is one we have seen before in the valuation of inventory.[2]

The unrealized losses in the current portfolio were charged to income, while unrealized losses in the noncurrent portfolio were charged to an equity allowance. The treatment of these unrealized losses was similar to the treatment of both unrealized gains and losses under the new standard.

The evolutionary development of these financial reporting standards is replete with examples of the economic and political forces that demonstrate in a microcosm many of the forces that work in all standard-setting areas. Before turning our attention to the forces behind the most recent alteration of reporting standards, let us first review and appreciate how SFAS No. 12 was first crafted.

SFAS No. 12 represents an interesting example of a situation where the FASB deviated from principles espoused in the conceptual framework in response to a cost/benefit trade-off. The FASB ultimately determined that imposing the requirement to carry marketable equity securities at full market value, and to recognize all unrealized gains and losses, would create costs for some firms that outweighed the benefits to users. To some, SFAS No. 12 represents an example where political pressures shaped accounting standards. We prefer to recognize it as a case where the FASB's social welfare function, as discussed in Chapter 2, lead to a particular trade-off that is not defensible solely on the tenets found in the conceptual framework. Horngren summarized the nature of the outside forces impinging on both the FASB and its predecessor, the Accounting Principles Board (APB).[3]

Following three years of deliberations, the APB originally planned to issue an exposure draft on marketable equity securities. It had narrowed its preferences to either flowthrough (valuation of the investments at full market value with all gains and losses recognized) or the spread of gains and losses over several years. (This method recognizes a fraction of the gain or loss arising due to changes in market value each year over several years.) Both of these methods reduce managers' ability to control the recognition of income from investments in marketable equity securities through their decisions regarding when to sell the investments. Consequently, reported income would likely have been more volatile under these methods than under the strict use of the cost method.

---

[2] Note that the LCM approach used in SFAS No. 12 was applied only at the portfolio level. The interested reader might note that the LCM methods applicable for inventory could be applied at any level of aggregation. Applying this approach only at the portfolio level compared to the individual security level significantly reduced the likelihood that losses would need to be recognized.

[3] Charles Horngren, "The Marketing of Accounting Standards," *Journal of Accountancy* (October 1973), p. 63.

In September 1971, an exposure draft was issued favoring the flowthrough method. The insurance industry, for which investments in marketable equity securities are very significant, bitterly opposed the method and persuaded the Securities and Exchange Commission (SEC) to oppose flowthrough. As a result, the APB reconsidered the topic in October and changed its preferences to either a two-statement approach (different valuation approach for the balance sheet than that used for the income statement) or spreading. The APB voted for the two-statement approach, although there was also strong support for spreading. In December, the APB was informed that fire and casualty insurers also opposed the spreading method; and the SEC would not impose any solution on an industry that opposed it so adamantly.

The APB then discussed either a two-statement approach or modification of current practice whereby companies would use market values in the balance sheet, realized gains and losses in the income statement, and unrealized gains and losses in stockholders' equity. However, the fire and casualty insurers also vigorously opposed the two-statement method.

As Horngren put it, "The APB's feasible alternatives changed in response to the likelihood of acceptability."[4] As the APB passed the job of standard setting to the FASB, it presented the SEC with a summary of its deliberations in March, 1972. The report did not contain any preferred solution.

Consequently, in 1974, when the FASB picked up the topic of marketable securities, it clearly faced a dilemma. The Dow Jones Industrial Average at the time had fallen by approximately one-third since 1972. With the cost method currently in use at the time, the losses this precipitous drop had caused were not being recognized unless investors liquidated their positions, which the insurance industry was generally not doing. The FASB believed that it needed a way to reflect the effects of the decreased values of these equity security investments, without running afoul of the insurance industry and the SEC. The earlier exposure draft and deliberations of the APB had exhausted all the theoretically sound alternatives. What the FASB was forced to do was develop a workable political compromise.

The conceptual framework embodied in the *Statements of Financial Accounting Concepts* did not exist when SFAS No. 12 was being framed. While SFAS No. 12 is inconsistent with the conceptual framework (as it was eventually defined), as well as with other areas of accounting where LCM concepts are applied, it represented the FASB's effort to balance two competing needs. The Board wanted to reflect the declines in market prices of stock held as investments without creating an unacceptable effect on the financial statements of an important economic sector, the insurance industry. The conceptual framework would have been of little help to the FASB in 1974.

Accounting theory, as delineated in the conceptual framework, dictates the valuation of marketable equity securities using market prices to provide the most relevant and reliable presentation of the economic value of such assets. Alteration of the measurement and reporting system for insurance companies would have changed the interpretation of balance sheet and income measures in an industry where regulations regarding minimum levels

---

[4] *Ibid.*

of equity are determined by groups other than the accounting standard setters. In turn, this has potential economic consequences that this sector of the
economy sought to avoid. The FASB's job is to decide when the negative
effects such changes in the measurement rules may have on some subset of
society will outweigh the benefits to other parts of society. In the case of SFAS
No. 12, the result is difficult to defend on the basis of other accounting standards or the conceptual framework. However, it is easy to understand in the
larger context of conflicting economic priorities.

The decade of the 1980s brought with it the large number of savings and
loan scandals, as well as a general weakness in the financial strength of many
banking institutions. In addition, there was a general failure in the low-grade
bond market (sometimes referred to as the junk bond market). Billions of dollars had been raised by corporations in the junk bond market to finance takeovers in the 1980s only to find that there were insufficient cash flows to repay
the bonds in the late 1980s and early 1990s. Many savings and loans tried to
cover their losses from investments in junk bonds by holding on to them and
using the cost method to value them in their balance sheets. This was consistent with GAAP at the time since debt securities were explicitly exempted
from the application of SFAS No. 12. Of course, the firms that had issued these
bonds eventually defaulted; and the bonds often became virtually worthless.
However, the use of the cost method as opposed to the market value approach
delayed the recognition of these events for some years.

After much of the S&L crisis ended, Douglas Breeden, who was head of
the SEC in the late 1980s and early 1990s, publicly endorsed the concept of full
market value as a means to head off similar problems that might arise in the
future. Note that this strong vocal support for the application of full market
value represented a change in emphasis, if not complete change in heart, compared to the SEC's reaction when the FASB was crafting SFAS No. 12. This
strong SEC support for converting to a full market value approach for all
investments in marketable securities reopened this whole issue. However,
even the SEC's strong position did not prevail. Members of the insurance and
financial institutions industries argued that:

1. For firms that have the capability to hold debt securities to maturity,
   short-term fluctuations in market value should not enter into measures
   of earnings because they are unimportant to the investor's long-run
   strategy and would only make earnings less informative or useful for
   investors.
2. For the noncurrent portfolio in general, a similar argument could be
   made to mitigate the need to recognize fluctuations in market value in
   income. However, disclosure of such via an equity valuation allowance
   would be acceptable.

It seemed likely that managers in these industries really did not want any
change in the reporting practices regarding investments. Also, it was clear that
with the SEC's support, the best that could be hoped for was to mitigate the
degree to which market value would influence income under certain circumstances. In the end, the FASB has supported the compromise position of the
insurance and banking industries; and the SEC has retreated from its original

demands in the face of this political pressure. Just as the conceptual framework would not have helped in 1974, it had little effect in resolving this debate in 1992.

THE EQUITY METHOD OF ACCOUNTING FOR INVESTMENTS WITH SIGNIFICANT INFLUENCE

When an investor has significant influence over the investee, the cost method is deemed inappropriate as a basis for valuation and income realization. The investor's ability to influence the investee's operations suggests that the investor directly affects the amount of profit or loss the investee reports by influencing corporate decisions. As a result, dividends are not an appropriate representation of income from the investee since the investor may be able to influence the investee's dividend policy. In addition, the market value of the investee's shares may depend on the investor's continued influence and involvement, making observed market value a questionable basis for valuation of the investor's shares.

As a result of significant influence, accountants have adopted an extended definition of the accounting entity. Under this extended definition, dividends declared by the investee and received by the investor are not income to the investor. Instead, the income from the investment reported by the investor depends on the investor's ownership interest in the investee's reported income. Dividends issued by the investee represent a liquidation of the investor's underlying claim on the investee's assets. Using this approach, the investor's investment account will increase as the investee's net equity increases and decrease if the investee's net equity decreases.

For example, assume that Bain Company purchased a 30% interest in McKnight Corporation on January 1, 1995, by paying $300,000 cash at a time when the total book value of equity for McKnight Corporation was reported at $1,000,000. Given these facts, Bain Company has purchased the interest at book value (30% × $1,000,000). Bain records this acquisition as follows:

```
January 1, 1995:
Investments                                          300,000
   Cash                                                        300,000
To record the purchase of McKnight stock.
```

If McKnight reported income for 1993 of $100,000, Bain would record income from its investment in McKnight of $30,000 (30% × $100,000) by preparing the following journal entry.[5]

```
December 31, 1995:
Investments                                           30,000
   Equity in earnings of McKnight                              30,000
To record the equity accrual associated with the income
   reported by the 30% investee.
```

---

[5] Conversely, if McKnight has reported a loss, Bain would report a loss from the investment equal to 30% of the total loss McKnight reported.

If McKnight declares a dividend, Bain reports the effect of this dividend as a reduction of the carrying value of the investment in McKnight on the ex dividend date. This makes sense because Bain had previously increased its investment in McKnight and reported the increase as income, when McKnight first reported the income that is now being distributed as a dividend. Assume that McKnight Corporation declared dividends in the amount of $50,000 on January 1, 1996. The ex dividend date was January 15, 1996. Bain would recognize a dividend receivable for 30% of the dividend, or $15,000, using the following entry:[6]

January 15, 1996:		
Dividends receivable	15,000	
Investment in McKnight		15,000
To record the declaration of the dividend by McKnight.		

Applying the Equity Method to Mid-Period Acquisitions

When an investor purchases an investment during the accounting period and accounts for it on the equity method, the purchase price is still recorded as the investment's original value. The investment's value still increases as the investee reports income and decreases with the declaration of dividends. However, the increase associated with the equity method accrual will only include the investor's share of the income of the investee *after* the date of the acquisition.

For example, assume Hagger Incorporated acquires 25% of Dutchwell Industries at book value of $200,000 on July 1, 1993. Dutchwell (the investee) reports income of $50,000 for all of 1993. Of this amount, $30,000 was earned from July 1, 1993 to December 31, 1993. Hagger (the investor) has a calendar year fiscal period. At December 31, 1993, Hagger will increase the investment account by 25% of the income reported by Dutchwell from July 1, 1993 through December 31, 1993, or $7,500.

Applying the Equity Method When the Purchase Price Is Not Equal to Book Value

In the previous discussion, the original purchase price paid by the investor was exactly equal to the book value of the investee's equity at the date of the acquisition, multiplied by the investor's acquired interest. This will not generally be the case. Normally, the purchase price will differ substantially from the value implied by the underlying book value of the investee's equity. Two factors contribute to this difference:

1. The book value of identifiable assets and liabilities are not generally equal to their market values.
2. The investor may be paying for goodwill that the investee has developed.

The valuation of goodwill was discussed in Chapter 12, along with the definition of an identifiable asset or liability. What is unique to the situations

---

[6] When the dividend is actually paid, the receivable would be removed and the cash receipt recorded.

of interest in this chapter is that the investor is only acquiring a proportionate interest in the investee's net assets, not a 100% interest. Consequently, the price the investor pays for the interest acquired will include a portion of any difference between the current book and market values for identifiable assets and liabilities as well as goodwill. The equity method requires that these differences, if material, be identified at the time of the acquisition and amortized over future periods to determine the investor's income from the investment.

Special computations are required to identify and trace the portion of the purchase price of any investment under the equity method to the material differences between book and market values for identifiable assets and to determine any goodwill arising in the acquisition. Consider the following example. On January 1, 1995, Buyup purchased a 40% interest in Seller for $510,000 cash at a time when the book value of Seller's equity was $900,000. Since Buyup acquired a 40% interest, Buyup's share of the book value of Seller's equity is $360,000 (40% × $900,000). The difference between the purchase price of $510,000 and the interest in Seller's book value of $360,000 represents a purchase premium of $150,000. A *purchase premium* exists whenever the price paid for the shares exceeds the underlying percentage interest in the investee's book value of equity. When the purchase price is below the underlying interest in the investee's book value of equity, the difference is referred to as a *purchase discount*.

The next stage in the allocation of the purchase price is to determine the difference between the fair value and the investee's book value for all identifiable assets and liabilities. Suppose that the following information was available regarding the assets and liabilities of Seller as of January 1, 1995:

Asset or Liability	Market Value	Book Value
Inventory	$ 240,000	$ 80,000
Equipment	600,000	650,000
Bonds Payable	$(200,000)	$(190,000)
	$ 640,000	$ 540,000

From this information, it is possible to discern why Buyup was willing to pay more than book value for its interest in Seller. The $150,000 premium is traceable partly to the fact that the book values of Seller's identifiable assets and liabilities did not reflect their current market values. In fact, the market value of the net identifiable assets (assets minus liabilities) is $100,000 higher ($640,000 − $540,000) than their book values. Since Buyup only acquired a 40% interest in these assets, its share of this difference between market and book values is only $40,000. This implies that of the $150,000 premium, $40,000 relates to differences between market and book values for Seller's net identifiable assets. The remainder must then be attributable to nonidentifiable assets, which are represented by goodwill of $110,000.

The distribution of excess schedule presented in Exhibit 16.4 shows this allocation process. This schedule traces the allocation of the purchase price, first to the book value of Seller's underlying assets and liabilities via the book value of Seller's equity, then to differences between book and market value for

EXHIBIT 16.4

Distribution of
Excess Schedule
Applicable to Buyup
Corporation's
Acquisition of 40%
Interest in
Seller, Inc.

Distribution of Excess Schedule Applicable to Buyup Corporation's Acquisition of 40% Interest in Seller, Inc.

Value of Original Investment				$ 510,000

Book Value of Investee's Equity	×	Investor's % Ownership		
$900,000	×	40%	=	$(360,000)
Purchase premium or (discount)				$ 150,000

Differentials Between Market Value and Book Value for Identifiable Assets and Liabilities:

Asset or Liability	Market Value	−	Book Value	= Difference	×	Investor's % Ownership	
Inventory	$240,000	−	$ 80,000	= $160,000	×	40%	$ 64,000
Equipment	600,000	−	650,000	= (50,000)	×	40%	(20,000)
Bonds payable	(200,000)	−	(190,000)	= (10,000)	×	40%	(4,000)
	$640,000		$540,000	= $100,000	×	40%	$ 40,000
Goodwill [purchase premium or (discount) − market adjustments]							$ 110,000

identifiable assets and liabilities, and finally arriving at a valuation for any goodwill implied by the purchase price.

While the differences between market and book values of the investee's identifiable assets and liabilities at acquisition influence the purchase price, they are not reflected in the investee's financial records. Buyup will make a journal entry to record the investment at $510,000, but Seller will make no entry. Over time, the benefits embodied in the investee's assets, and the obligations represented by the liabilities, will translate into income for the investee. The inventory will be sold by Seller, the equipment depreciated, and the bonds matured and retired.

When the investor does not purchase the investee's shares at a price equal to the book value of the stock, the investor must amortize all the differences between book and market values implicit in the purchase price. This includes the difference on inventory, equipment, bonds, and goodwill. The timing of the amortization is dictated by the underlying assets and liabilities for which a difference exists.

Exhibit 16.5 demonstrates the determination of the equity in earnings accrual assuming that:

1. Seller reported income of $200,000 for the first year following the acquisition
2. All the inventory was sold during the year
3. Equipment had an average remaining life of 5 years
4. The bonds mature in 4 years
5. Goodwill is amortized over 10 years

EXHIBIT 16.5
Equity Method
Accrual— Buyup
Corporation's
40% Investment in
Seller, Inc.

EQUITY METHOD ACCRUAL
Buyup Corporation's 40% Investment in Seller, Inc.

Determination of the Equity in Earnings Accrual:

Step 1: Investor's percentage of investee's reported income: $200,000 × 40% $ 80,000

Step 2: Amortization of investor's differences between market and book
         values for all assets and liabilities

Inventory	$64,000)	×	100%	$(64,000)
Equipment	(20,000)	×	1/5	4,000
Bonds payable	(4,000)	×	1/4	1,000
Goodwill	110,000	×	1/10	(11,000)
Net equity in earnings accrual				$ 10,000

In the equity accrual computation, the adjustments capture the effect of amortizing the differences between market and book values on income. To appreciate fully why these adjustments are necessary before the investor can record the equity method accrual, focus only on the inventory differential for the moment. When the inventory is sold by Seller, Seller will realize the inventory's full market value as revenue and match the book value against it as cost of sales. Using the data for market and book values from the distribution of excess schedule in Exhibit 16.4, this will result in a profit of $160,000. Under the equity method, Buyup would normally record 40% of this amount as the equity in earnings accrual in the absence of any adjustments. Buyup's share is $64,000.

However, when Buyup purchased the 40% interest, Seller's previous shareholders insisted that the purchase price reflect the full fair market value of the inventory as it existed on the date of the acquisition. Buyup actually paid a premium over book value of $64,000, which reflects the additional value in the inventory. From Buyup's viewpoint, the sale of the inventory generated no profit. Instead, the sale simply recaptured the value placed on the inventory at the date of the acquisition. By subtracting the investor's percentage share of the difference between market and book values of inventory at acquisition, in the amount of $64,000, from the basic equity accrual of $64,000, Buyup recognizes no income on these sales.

Similar logic is applicable to each of the other adjustments. Equipment in this example has a market value below book value. Consequently, the depreciation computed by the investee is larger than the depreciation that would be taken if market value were used.

To adjust for this difference, the investor adds back an amount to the equity in earnings accrual to represent the depreciation adjustment. When bonds have a market value above book value, it implies the existence of an additional premium on the bonds. Premiums are amortized over the life of the bond. In this example, straight-line amortization is used. Amortization of a bond premium would normally reduce interest expense. As a result, the investor increases the equity accrual for this amortization. Finally, the goodwill in this example is being amortized over a ten-year period. The net result of these effects is an equity in earnings accrual of $10,000. Buyup's journal entry to record this appears as follows:

December 31, 1993:
Investment in Seller   10,000
   Equity in earnings   10,000
To record the equity accrual for 1995 from the investment in
  Seller.

Over time, the differences between market and book values which existed at the date of the acquisition will be systematically amortized through income and removed from the investment account. When the last of this amortization has occurred, the investment account will represent the investor's interest in the book value of the investee's equity. This relationship will continue for the remainder of the investment's life.

If the investment is acquired during the investor's fiscal year, only the income and dividends from the date of the acquisition to year-end enter into the equity method journal entries. When the purchase price is not equal to book value, the amortization of the differentials must still be included, but only for the part of the year from the acquisition to year-end.

Disposition of Investments Carried on the Equity Method

When an investment carried on the equity method is sold, any gain or loss is computed based on the difference between the selling price and the existing book value of the investment at the time of the sale. An accrual will be necessary to record the investee's equity in earnings up to the date of the sale. When only a portion of the investment is disposed of, the investment account should be reduced by the proportion of the investment sold. For example, if Portion Incorporated held 30% of Datron Inc. and elected to sell 10% of Datron, Portion would be selling one-third of its investment (10% ÷ 30%). This would require that one-third of the value in the investment account be removed and matched against the selling price in determining gain or loss. If, as a result of such a sale, Portion no longer has significant influence over Datron, the remaining investment should be accounted for on the cost method. The cost basis of the investment will be determined by the remaining carrying value of the investment. The Appendix to this chapter discusses the switch from the equity to the cost method in more detail.

Loans and Advances to Equity Method Investees

When an investor makes a loan or advance to an investee, the investor adds the amount of the loan or advance to the investment account to reflect the total amount invested in the investee. The loan or advance is not subject to amortization and will not alter the determination of the investor's percentage ownership for purposes of determining the equity method accrual.

In some cases, losses suffered by the investee will be so large in amount that if the investor recognized a percentage of the loss, it would offset the sum of the remaining investment in stock plus any advances or loans to the investee. When this occurs, the investor should reduce the net investment to zero and stop applying the equity method. The only exception to this requirement is that if the investor has guaranteed the investee's obligations, or is otherwise committed to provide future financial support, the equity method is continued. However, the credit balance in the investment account is classified as a deferred credit.[7]

Disclosure Requirements Under the Equity Method

The disclosure requirements pertain to information that the investor must include in its financial statements regarding the identity, financial position, and results of investee's operations. In all cases, the name of each investee, the percentage ownership in each investee, the amount by which the carrying value of the investment exceeds the investor's interest in the underlying book value of the investee's equity, and the investor's accounting policies regarding how this difference is treated must be disclosed.[8]

Additional disclosures are required under various circumstances. If the investee's stock is publicly traded, the market value of the shares must be disclosed. If the investments are material, in the aggregate, to the investor's financial position, summarized information regarding the financial position and results of operations for all investees as a whole should be presented in the notes to the financial statements. Exhibit 16.6 presents an example of the disclosure provided by Lee Enterprises regarding various investments it carried on the equity method.

OTHER INVESTMENTS

On occasion, companies use other types of assets as investments. When companies invest in land, precious metals, or other types of assets, the historical cost approach to accounting requires that the assets be carried at original cost, unless a permanent decline in value has occurred. When permanent declines can be identified, the assets should be reduced to their market values and the losses realized. When such assets are disposed of, gains and losses are recognized as the difference between the asset's selling price and carrying value.

Cash Surrender Value of Life Insurance

Many businesses acquire life insurance on their key executive officers. Should one of these key people unexpectedly die, life insurance provides cash flow to aid in managing the firm during the transition. Insurance comes in many forms. Some policies, called term insurance policies, offer death benefits only. Other types of life insurance provide an investment vehicle, as well as death

---

[7] "The Equity Method of Accounting for Investments in Common Stock," *Accounting Principles Board Opinion No. 18* (March 1971), para. 19(i).

[8] *Ibid.*, para. 20(a).

LEE ENTERPRISES
Note Disclosures on Long-Term Investments Accounted for on the Equity Method
1992 Annual Report to Shareholders

Note 3. Investment in Associated Companies

The Company has an effective 50% ownership interest in two newspaper publishing companies operating at Lincoln, Nebraska (Journal-Star Printing Co.) and Madison, Wisconsin (Madison Newspapers, Inc.) and two direct marketing ventures, Quality Information Systems and Consumer Power Marketing. The Company had until September 25, 1991 (see Note 2) a 42% interest in New Mexico Broadcasting Company, Inc., operators of KRQE-TV, Albuquerque, New Mexico and KBIM-TV, Roswell, New Mexico; and until September 14, 1990 (see Note 2) a 50% ownership interest in NAPP Systems, Inc.

Summarized financial information of the associated companies is as follows:

Combined Associates	1992	1991	1990
	(In Thousands)		
Assets			
Current assets	$37,076	$34,247	$ 35,624
Investments and other assets	7,261	6,603	9,512
Property and equipment, net	9,007	8,461	13,365
	$53,344	$49,311	$ 58,501
Liabilities and Stockholders' Equity			
Current liabilities	$14,705	$14,173	$ 15,845
Long-term debt	1,119	66	6,506
Deferred items	1,689	1,585	1,752
Stockholders' Equity	35,831	33,487	34,398
	$53,344	$49,311	$ 58,501
Revenue	$85,568	$91,583	$163,843
Operating Income	25,499	21,170	40,376
New Income	16,599	13,133	26,631

Receivables from associated companies consist of dividends. Certain information relating to Company investments in these associated companies is as follows:

	1992	1991	1990
	(In Thousands)		
Share of:			
Stockholders' equity	$17,872	$16,703	$17,020
Undistributed earnings	16,543	15,346	12,485

benefits, and are known as whole life, universal life, and others.

For term policies, the annual premium represents the full cost of the benefits provided during that period. The paid premium should be recorded as a prepaid expense and amortized over the coverage period, which is usually one year. When life insurance also accrues some form of investment value over time, such as a cash surrender value, the premium for any period is for both the cost of the death benefit and for the buildup of investment value.

As the cash surrender value of the life insurance increases from year to year, the increase is recorded as an addition to the asset Cash Surrender Value of Life Insurance and a credit to the insurance expense of the period. In this manner, the expense for the period represents the outflow for the premium less the increase in the underlying investment asset also represented by the policy.

Cash surrender value also provides collateral for loans obtained from insurance companies. When a loan is obtained based on the cash surrender value of the policy, the loan should be reported as a reduction of the asset, not reported as part of the liabilities. This offset is applicable as long as the policy is in force because the insurance company always has direct prior claim on any cash payments from the policy to satisfy the loan.

Cash surrender value of life insurance is a noncurrent asset unless the policy has been cancelled and the company is awaiting distribution of the policy's cash value. Generally, these amounts are not material; and the cash surrender value of life insurance is lumped together with several other miscellaneous assets as part of other assets in the balance sheet. Exhibit 16.7 provides an example of the balance sheet classification and disclosure of cash surrender value for Hyde Athletic Industries, Inc.

SUMMARY

This chapter has explored the accounting treatments afforded various types of noncurrent investments that might be undertaken in the normal course of business. Noncurrent investments in assets that are nonmarketable, and for which the investor has no significant influence on the investee, are accounted for using the cost method. Only securities and precious metals traded on public exchanges are deemed to be marketable investments. If no significant influence exists, and the assets acquired are marketable, different accounting methods are employed, depending on the type of investment asset.

When investors have the ability and intent to hold marketable debt securities to maturity, they should account for the securities by using the cost method, or effective interest amortization. If investors lack the ability or intent to hold a marketable debt security to maturity, they use a two-statement approach. For the income statement, the cost method is applied; but for the balance sheet, market value is used. This two-statement approach is accomplished via the use of an equity valuation allowance that reports the net unre-

		1989	1988
HYDE ATHLETIC INDUSTRIES, INC.			
Balance Sheet Presentation of Cash Surrender Value of Life Insurance			
Other assets			
Cash surrender value of life insurance net of policy loans (1989 and 1988, $34,085 and $32,915)		$7,345	$4,997

EXHIBIT 16.7

Hyde Athletic Industries, Inc.— Balance Sheet Presentation of Cash Surrender Value of Life Insurance

alized gain or loss in the noncurrent portfolio in the shareholders' equity section of the balance sheet. The two-statement approach is also applied to all noncurrent investments in marketable equity securities if the investor lacks significant influence.

When investors acquire significant influence over investees by virtue of the acquisition of an equity interest, they must use the equity method of accounting for investments. When an investment is accounted for using the equity method, no-lower-of-cost-or-market rule is applicable.

Cash surrender value of key executive life insurance policies also forms another type of corporate investment. When insurance plans provide a cash surrender value, the increase in the cash surrender value each period is recorded as an increase in the asset and a decrease in the insurance expense of the period.

Appendix 16.1— Accounting for the Change from the Cost Method to/from the Equity Method of Accounting for Noncurrent Investments in Common Stocks

If ownership of an investment in common stock reaches a level where the holder of an investment previously carried under the cost method acquires significant influence, the valuation basis for the investment must be converted to the equity method. The change to the equity method is a change in accounting principle, which requires retroactive restatement. To record the effect of this switch, all previous periods must be restated to the equity method, even though the investor did not have significant influence during these earlier periods. The restatement requires going back to the original acquisition and preparing a distribution of excess schedule for that acquisition along with a recomputation of the equity in earnings to be reported for each prior period.

When an investor disposes of a large enough portion of the ownership interest to lose significant influence, a portion of the investment's carrying value is matched against the selling price of the interest, and gain or loss is recorded. The remaining investment is switched from the equity method to the cost method. In accounting for the change from the equity method to the cost method, the investment's carrying value under the equity method becomes the new cost basis. From this point on the cost method is applied.

Assume that on January 1, 1992, Tor Corp. purchased 10,000 shares of Tee Company's 100,000 shares of outstanding common stock for $8,400. The book value of Tee's net worth on this date was $80,000. Tor uses the maximum allowable period to amortize all intangibles. On January 1, 1994, Tor purchased an additional 15,000 shares of Tee Company stock for $15,050. This acquisition gave Tor significant influence over Tee's operations. The book value of Tee's equity on January 1, 1994, was $83,000. It was determined that $2,000 of the differential between Tor's purchase price and its claim on book value at January 1, 1994, was attributable to undervalued depreciable assets with an estimated remaining life of 10 years at January 1, 1994. On January 1, 1996, Tor sold 8,000 shares of Tee's common stock for $10,000.

Additional information:

	Income	Dividends
1992	$2,000	$1,000
1993	5,000	3,000
1994	6,000	4,000
1995	8,000	5,000

During the period from January 1, 1992 to January 1, 1994, Tor would have applied the cost method. Assuming that the common stock does not qualify as a marketable equity security, the only journal entries Tor would have made during this two-year period would appear as follows:

```
January 1, 1992:
Investments                                           8,400
   Cash                                                        8,400
To record the acquisition of Tee Company stock.

Various dates in 1992:
Dividends receivable                                   100
   Dividend income                                             100
To record the dividends declared by Tee Company,
   ($2,000 × 10%).

Various dates in 1993:
Dividends receivable                                   300
   Dividend income                                             300
To record the dividends declared by Tee Company,
   ($3,000 × 10%).
```

When Tor acquired the additional interest on January 1, 1994, Tor's investment in Tee went from a 10% share to a 25% share. This requires a change to the equity method. To compute the retroactive adjustment necessary to record this change in accounting principle, it is necessary to compute the balance that would have been in the investment account if the equity method had originally been used to account for Tor's 10% interest.

Under the equity method, a determination must first be made regarding the effect of any differences between market and book values of Tee's assets and liabilities at the time Tor acquired its original 10% interest. Given the data in the example, Exhibit 16.8 presents the distribution of excess schedule produced for the original 10% interest.

The $400 of goodwill in Exhibit 16.8 must be amortized over not more than 40 years. Assuming the maximum amortization period is chosen, the amortization will be $10 per year. In addition, under the equity method, the investor recognizes income as a percentage share of the investee's reported

| EXHIBIT 16.8

Distribution of
Excess Schedule—
Acquisition of
Interest in Tee Corp.

**Distribution of Excess Schedule
Acquisition of Interest in Tee Corp.
January 1, 1992**

Consideration	$ 8,400
Book value of equity in Tee (80,000 × .10)	(8,000)
Excess of purchase price over book value	$ 400
Fair market value adjustments:	
None	0
Goodwill	$ 400

income. Dividends are not income, but a conversion of the investment asset into a cash asset. Had Tor used the equity method during 1992 and 1993, it would have recorded the following journal entries:

January 1, 1992:

Investments	8,400	
Cash		8,400

To record the acquisition of Tee Company stock.

Various dates in 1992:

Dividends receivable	100	
Investments		100

To record the declaration of dividends by Tee Company.

December 31, 1992:

Investments	190	
Equity in earnings		190

To accrue the equity in earnings of Tee under the equity method,
  including amortization of goodwill in the amount of $10,
  ($2,000 × 10% − 400 ÷ 40).

Various dates in 1993:

Dividends receivable	300	
Investments		300

To record the declaration of dividends by Tee Company.

December 31, 1993:

Investments	490	
Equity in earnings		490

To accrue the equity in earnings of Tee under the equity method,
  including amortization of goodwill in the amount of $10,
  ($5,000 × 10% − 400 ÷ 40).

    Under the cost method, the value of the investment would be $8,400 on January 1, 1994. Under the equity method, the investment balance would have been $8,680 ($8,400 − $100 + $190 − $300 + $490). The difference of $280 is treated as a prior period adjustment. Tor's journal entry on January 1, 1994, to record this adjustment would appear as follows:

January 1, 1994:

Investments	280	
Retained earnings		280

To record the prior period adjustment arising from the retroactive restatement of the investment in Tee to the equity method.

In addition to the prior period adjustment on January 1, 1994, a second acquisition has occurred and must be accounted for. Tor's acquisition of the shares is recorded as follows:

January 1, 1990:

Investments	15,050	
Cash		15,050

To record the acquisition of an additional 15% interest in Tee Company.

Various dates in 1994:

Dividends receivable	1,000	
Investments		1,000

To record the dividend declaration of Tee Company, ($4,000 × 25%).

A distribution of excess schedule for the portion of the investment purchased at January 1, 1994, must also be prepared. Exhibit 16.9 presents this computation. In the second acquisition, both goodwill and a fair market value adjustment exist. Both must be amortized—the goodwill over not more than 40 years and the asset adjustment over the remaining life of the depreciable assets (10 years). Tor's journal entries for 1994 and 1995, under the equity method, are:

December 31, 1994:

Investments	1,275	
Equity in earnings		1,275

To record the equity method accrual, based on Tor's 25% interest in Tee's reported earnings less amortization of goodwill from the 1992 purchase, and amortization of both the fair market value adjustment and goodwill from the 1994 acquisition, ($6,000 × 25% − 400 ÷ 40 − 2,000 ÷ 10 − 600 ÷ 40).

EXHIBIT 16.9
Distribution of
Excess Schedule—
Acquisition of Tee
Corporation

Distribution of Excess Schedule
Acquisition of Tee Corporation
January 1, 1994

Consideration	$ 15,050
Interest in book value of equity: (83,000 × .15)	(12,450)
Excess of purchase price over book value	$ 2,600
Fair market value adjustments:	
Depreciable assets	(2,000)
Goodwill	$ 600

Various dates in 1995:
Dividends receivable   1,250
   Investments   1,250
To record the dividend declaration of Tee Company,
  ($5,000 × 25%).

December 31, 1995:
Investments   1,775
  Equity in earnings   1,775
To record the equity method accrual, based on Tor's 25%
interest in Tee's reported earnings less amortization of
goodwill from the 1992 purchase, and amortization of both the
fair market value adjustment and goodwill from the 1994
acquisition, ($8,000 × 25% − 400 ÷ 40 − 2,000 ÷
10 − 600 ÷ 40).

Changes From the Equity Method to the Cost Method

At the end of 1995, the balance in the investment account would be $24,530 under the equity method. When Tor sells 8,000 shares on January 1, 1996, it is disposing of 32% (8,000 shares out of a total of 25,000 shares) of its investment. This results in a remaining interest in Tee of only 17%, which requires a change back to the cost basis. This change is also a change in accounting principle, but it is accounted for on a prospective basis. When changing from the equity method to the cost method, no retroactive adjustment is required. The old equity basis value becomes the new cost basis for the remaining shares.

To determine how much of the carrying value of the investment account should be matched against the selling price of $10,000, a cost flow assumption is necessary. Assume that Tor uses the average cost method of identifying the cost of the shares sold. This implies that since 32% of the shares were sold, 32% of the cost of the investment should be matched against the selling price. Under this assumption the cost of the shares sold is $7,850 ($24,530 × 32%). Tor would use the following entry to record the sale:

January 1, 1996:
Cash   10,000
  Investments   7,850
  Gain on the sale of securities   2,150
To record the sale of 8,000 shares of Tee Company.

After the sale, the balance in the investment account would be $16,680 ($24,530 − $7,850). This represents the new cost basis for the remaining 17,000 shares.

An Observation on the Use of FIFO Methods of Assigning Costs to Shares Sold An alternative to the average cost method of determining the cost of the shares sold is the first-in, first-out method. Under FIFO, the first shares purchased are considered to be the first shares sold. The first 10,000 shares were part of the January 1, 1992, acquisition. To determine the basis under the equity method for these shares requires a separate computation of the activity following the January 1, 1994, acquisition.

At January 1, 1994, the original 10,000 shares were valued at $8,680 under the equity method. Activity relating to this 10% interest during 1994 and 1995 would have appeared as follows:

Balance on January 1, 1994	$8,680
Equity in earnings:	
10% × $6,000 − 400 ÷ 40	590
10% × $8,000 − 400 ÷ 40	790
Dividends:	
10% × $4,000	(400)
10% × $5,000	(500)
Ending Balance on December 31, 1995	$9,160

Since 8,000 of the initial 10,000 shares were sold on January 1, 1996, 80% of the value of these shares should be matched against revenue under the FIFO approach. In this case, the cost to be matched against the revenue of $10,000 would be $7,328, instead of the $7,850 that was matched under the average cost method.

From the computations above, it is clear why most firms choose the average cost method. Computing the value of shares on a FIFO basis requires many computations that are not necessary under normal circumstances. Also, a complete reconstruction of costs may not be possible.

QUESTIONS

1. In general, how does the historical cost method of accounting for any type of investment determine income and value the asset in the balance sheet?
2. What does the term *significant influence* refer to, and what does the existence of significant influence imply?
3. What is a realized gain or loss?
4. What is a recognized gain or loss? How does it differ, if at all, from a realized gain or loss?
5. What are gross unrealized gains or losses? How are they different from a net unrealized gain or loss?
6. In general, what is the significance of an investment security being *marketable*? Are all marketable investment securities treated similarly? Why or why not?
7. What are the differences between the cost and *equity method* of accounting for investments in common stock? Do they have anything in common?
8. When an investor acquires another company's common stock that is to be carried on the equity method, name at least two possible causes for the purchase price to exceed the investor's interest in the underlying book value of the investee's equity.
9. When the purchase price of common stock exceeds the underlying book value of the shares under the equity method, and the difference is attributable to undervalued land, equipment, and inventory, as well as residual goodwill, how will these differences affect the income reported by the investee and investor in future periods?
10. When an investment carried on the equity method is sold, how should the gain or loss be determined?
11. If an investor who held 40% of the investee's common stock sold part of the investment so that after the sale the investor held only 10% and lost significant influence,

how would the gain or loss on sale be determined and how would the conversion from the equity method to the cost method be accomplished?

12. How is the effective interest method applied to account for long-term investments in bonds?

13. How does the ability and intent to hold an investment security to maturity affect the manner in which the investment in accounted for? Why?

14. How can an executive life insurance policy be an investment?

15. When an executive life insurance has a cash surrender value, describe how the expense related to such an insurance policy should be computed.

16. When an investor acquires a 10% interest that is originally accounted for on the cost method and later acquires another 30% interest so that the equity method must be employed, how is the change from the cost method to the equity method accounted for?

EXERCISES

16-1. *Equity securities using the cost method*

On July 1, 1994, Wedmar Corporation purchased 10,000 shares of Sawtech for $13 per share. Wedmar has a fiscal year-end of December 31. Sawtech is a small, privately owned corporation that acts as a supplier to Wedmar. Sawtech has 200,000 shares outstanding and is not publicly traded. On December 15, 1994, Sawtech declared a dividend of $1.25 per share to be paid on January 15, 1995. The ex dividend date was December 30, 1994.

REQUIRED:

1. Prepare the journal entries made by Wedmar to record the activity associated with the investment in Sawtech.
2. What asset balances will be reported on Wedmar's December 31, 1994, balance sheet associated with its investment in Sawtech?

16-2. *Equity securities using the cost method*

On January 1, 1995, Mason Corporation purchased a 12% interest in Diamond Company by paying $340,000. Diamond Company shares are not traded on any major exchange. Mason does not have significant influence as a result of the acquisition, but it has classified the investment as noncurrent. During 1995 and 1996, Diamond declared and paid dividends totalling $70,000 and $120,000, respectively. Income for the same two years was $90,000 and $200,000. On January 1, 1996, Mason sold the shares of Diamond for $320,000.

REQUIRED:

Prepare the journal entries made by Mason to record the activity associated with the investment in Diamond.

16-3. *Equity securities: comparing cost, market, and equity methods*

On June 1, 1994, Goete, Inc. purchased 5,000 shares of Mundane Industries for $102,000, as a long-term investment. At the time of the purchase, Mundane had the following equity accounts:

Common stock (100,000 shares, no par)	$1,100,000
Retained earnings	900,000
Total stockholders' equity	$2,000,000

Both companies have a fiscal year ending on May 31. At the time of the acquisition, the fair value of Mundane's identifiable assets was equal to book value. Any goodwill is amortized over the maximum allowable period.

During the period June 1, 1994 to May 31, 1995, Mundane incurred a loss from operations of $100,000. On May 31, 1995, Mundane declared a dividend of $2 per share payable on June 30, 1996. The date of record for this dividend was January 15, 1996.

REQUIRED:

1. Prepare all journal entries of Goete necessary to record the activity relating to its investment in Mundane assuming that Mundane's shares are not marketable.
2. Describe in words how the financial statement effects you journalized in (1) would be changed if Mundane's shares were marketable and had a market value of $22.00 per share at May 31, 1995.
3. Prepare all journal entries required to record the activity relating to the investment in Mundane assuming the Goete has significant influence as a result of the acquisition.

16-4.   *Equity securities: simple equity method*

On January 1, 1995, Mace Company acquired a 25% interest in Blake Corporation, which gave Mace significant influence over Blake's operations. Mace purchased Blake's stock for $650,000, which represented 25% of Blake's book value of equity at the time of the acquisition. During 1995 and 1996, Blake reported income of $220,000 and $170,000, respectively. Blake paid dividends of $100,000 in each year.

REQUIRED:

Prepare the journal entries made by Mace to account for its investment in Blake during 1995 and 1996.

16-5.   *Equity securities: simple equity method with income and loss*

Dart Incorporated acquired a 30% interest in Kennebunk Imports on September 1, 1994, for $750,000. Both companies have a August 30 fiscal year-end. Kennebunk's equity section at the time of the acquisition appeared as follows:

Common stock ($10 par)	$1,500,000
Additional paid-in capital	200,000
Retained earnings	800,000
Total stockholders' equity	$2,500,000

During the next two years, Kennebunk reported a loss of $50,000 and income of $120,000, respectively. Kennebunk declared and paid dividends in the amounts of $30,000 and $50,000, respectively.

REQUIRED:

Prepare the journal entries made by Dart to account for its investment in Kennebunk during 1994 and 1995.

16-6.   *Equity securities: equity and cost method, disposition*

On January 1, 1996, Bart Company acquired as a long-term investment for $700,000 a 20% common stock interest in Hall Company when the fair value of Hall's net assets equal to book value was $3,500,000. Bart can exercise significant influence over operating and financing policies of Hall. For the year ended December 31, 1996, Hall reported net income of $360,000 and declared and paid cash dividends of $100,000. On December 31, 1996, Bart sold Hall's stock for $810,000.

REQUIRED:

1. How much, and what type of, income will Bart report for 1996?
2. If Bart did not have significant influence, how much income would it report for 1996?

16-7.   *Equity method: working backward to infer purchase price and book value of investee's equity at acquisition*

On January 1, 1994, Miller Company purchased 25% of Wall Company's common stock at a price equal to book value. Miller appropriately uses the equity method to account for the investment. At the end of 1994, Miller reported a balance in the investment account of $190,000. During 1994, Wall reported income of $120,000. Wall declared and paid dividends in 1994 of $48,000.

REQUIRED:

1. How much did Miller pay for its investment in Wall?
2. What was the book value of Wall at the time of the acquisition?

16-8.   *Equity method: income measurement with differentials*

Martin Industries acquired a 25% interest in Sade Mills for $400,000 on January 1, 1995. At the time of the acquisition, Sade reported a total book value of equity in the amount of $1,000,000. Any excess of the purchase price over the interest in book value is treated as goodwill. Goodwill is amortized over the maximum allowable period. During 1995, Sade reported income of $120,000 and declared no dividends.

REQUIRED:

1. Prepare a schedule to determine the amount of goodwill purchased by Martin.
2. Prepare a schedule to compute the equity in earnings accrual for Martin at December 31, 1995.

16-9.   *Equity method: allocation of purchase price*

Lake Corporation purchased a 30% interest in Trident Company for $1,400,000 on July 1, 1994. Both companies have June 30 fiscal year-ends. At the time of the acquisition, Trident reported a book value of equity in the amount of $4,000,000. Inventory and land carried on Trident's books were determined to be undervalued by $50,000 and $200,000, respectively, at the date of the acquisition. Trident values inventory using the first-in, first-out method. Any goodwill arising in the acquisition is to be amortized over 10 years.

REQUIRED:

Prepare a distribution of excess schedule for this acquisition.

16-10.   *Marketable securities held for sale: adjustment to market at year-end*

During 1994, Garr Company purchased marketable securities as a long-term investment held for sale. None of the securities were sold during 1994. At December 31, 1994, the following information was available:

Security	Cost	Market
A	$245,000	$230,000
B	180,000	182,000

REQUIRED:

What adjustments, if any, would be required at December 31, 1994?

16-11. *Marketable securities held for sale: subsequent years*

Referring to the information in Exercise 16-10, assume that Garr Company sold Security A during 1995 for $233,000 but held on to Security B. At the end of 1995, the market value of Security B was $186,000.

REQUIRED:

1. Prepare the journal entry to record the sale of Security A.
2. What adjustments, if any, would be required at December 31, 1995?

16-12. *Marketable equity securities: unrealized gains and losses*

During 1994, Rex Company purchased marketable equity securities as a long-term investment. The cost and market values at December 31, 1994, were as follows:

Security		Cost	Market
A	100 shares	$ 2,800	$ 3,400
B	1,000 shares	17,000	15,300
C	2,000 shares	31,500	29,500

Rex sold 1,000 shares of Company B stock on January 31, 1995, for $15 per share, incurring brokerage fees of $1,500.

REQUIRED:

1. What is the gross unrealized loss at December 31, 1994?
2. What is the gross unrealized gain at December 31, 1994?
3. What adjustments, if any, will Rex make regarding the valuation of marketable equity securities on December 31, 1994, assuming all price declines are considered temporary?
4. Assume the decline in value for the stock of Company C is permanent. How would this change your response in (1)?
5. Prepare the journal entry to record the sale of Company B's stock.

16-13. *Marketable securities: transfers between current and noncurrent*

On December 31, 1994, Ball Company purchased marketable securities as a long-term investment. At the end of 1994, the following data were available regarding these investments:

Security	Cost	Market
A	$39,000	$36,000
B	50,000	55,000
C	96,000	85,000

On December 31, 1994, Ball is considering reclassification of Security C as a current investment.

REQUIRED:

1. Prior to the reclassification, what are the gross unrealized gain and loss as of December 31, 1994?

2. Assuming Ball does not reclassify Security C as current, what amount must be established for the allowance for adjustment to market value on December 31, 1994?
3. Assuming Ball does reclassify Security C, prepare the journal entry to record the reclassification.
4. Following the reclassification of Security C, what amounts would the allowances for adjustment to market value have for both the current and noncurrent portfolios?
5. What conditions should exist before Ball is allowed to reclassify Security C?

16-14. *Multiple choice questions*

Exercise 16-14 consists of the following five multiple choice questions:

1. The market price of the common stock of an investee company increased during the year. How will the investor's investment account be affected by the increase in market price of that common stock under each of the following accounting methods?

	Cost Method	Equity Method
(a)	No effect	No effect
(b)	No effect	Increase
(c)	Increase	No effect
(d)	Increase	Increase

2. An investor uses the cost method to account for investments in common stock. Dividends in excess of the investor's share of the investee's earnings subsequent to the date of investment
   (a) Do not affect the investment account
   (b) Decrease the investment account
   (c) Increase the investment account
   (d) Increase investment income

3. How will the investor's investment account be affected by the investor's share of the earnings of the investee after the date of acquisition under each of the following accounting methods?

	Cost Method	Equity Method
(a)	No effect	No effect
(b)	No effect	Increase
(c)	Increase	No effect
(d)	Increase	Increase

4. An investor uses the equity method to account for its 30% investment in an investee's common stock. Amortization of the investor's share of the excess of fair market value over book value of depreciable assets at the date of the purchase should be reported in the investor's income statement as part of
   (a) Other expense
   (b) Depreciation expense
   (c) Equity in earnings of investee
   (d) Amortization of goodwill

5. Cash dividends declared out of current earnings are distributed to an investor. How will the investor's investment account be affected by those dividends under each of the following accounting methods?

	Cost Method	Equity Method
(a)	No effect	No effect
(b)	No effect	Decrease
(c)	Decrease	No effect
(d)	Decrease	Decrease

16-15. *Debt securities: cost versus market*

On June 1, 1994, Lance Manufacturing acquired $100,000 face value, 13% bonds of Kinnard Mining Incorporated by paying $115,826. The bonds pay interest on May 31 and November 30. The bonds mature five years from the date of purchase and have an effective yield of 9%. Lance has a December 31 fiscal year-end. The bonds traded at 98 and 110 (plus accrued interest) on December 31, 1994 and 1995, respectively. Lance sold the bonds for $112,000 (plus accrued interest) on October 15, 1996.

REQUIRED:

1. Assuming Lance classified these bonds as investments held for sale, prepare all journal entries necessary to account for this investment over its life. Round all computations to the nearest whole dollar.
2. Assuming Lance had the ability and intent to hold these bonds to maturity, discuss the changes which would occur in your response to (1) above.

16-16. *Debt securities: intent and ability to hold to maturity*

On May 1, 1994, 3D Corporation acquired $300,000 of face value, 8% bonds of Brainerd Manufacturing for $281,342 plus accrued interest. The bonds mature on January 31, 1996, and pay interest on January 31 and July 31 each year. The yield to maturity on these bonds was 12%. 3D considers the bonds a long-term investment and has the ability and intent to hold this investment to maturity.

REQUIRED:

1. Prepare the journal entry to record the purchase of the bonds.
2. Prepare an amortization schedule to compute the amortization of the purchase discount over the life of the bond (round to nearest dollar).
3. Prepare the journal entry that 3D will make to record the maturity of the bonds and the final interest payment (3D has a fiscal year-end of December 31).
4. Suppose that 3D did not have the ability to hold the bond to maturity but intended to try. If the market value of the bond at December 31, 1994, had been $298,000, what effect would this have on the financial statements?

16-17. *Life insurance*

On January 1, 1995, Gaul Inc., purchased a $1,000,000 ordinary life insurance policy on its president. The premium for the first three years of the policy was paid at inception in the amount of $60,000. At the end of 1995, the cash surrender value of the policy was $8,000.

REQUIRED:

Prepare the journal entries associated with the executive life insurance policy for 1995.

PROBLEMS

16-1. *Market value accounting—use of the contra asset/equity valuation allowance*

The portfolio of marketable equity securities of Ariel Aeronautics had the following activities from January 1, 1994 to January 1, 1996:

Date	Security	Shares	Sale or Purchase	Price
01/01/94	A	1,000	purchase	$18
01/01/94	B	1,000	purchase	20
03/30/94	C	1,000	purchase	35
10/31/94	A	2,000	purchase	24
10/31/94	C	2,000	purchase	27
01/01/96	D	1,000	purchase	10
06/30/95	A	1,500	sale	32

Year-End Market Prices:

Security	12/31/94	12/31/95	12/31/96
A	$24	$30	$32
B	19	15	18
C	30	20	24
D	8	9	15

REQUIRED:

1. Compute gross unrealized gains and losses for the portfolio for 1994, 1995, and 1996.
2. Make any necessary journal entries for a valuation allowance.
3. Record the entry for the sale of Security A.

16-2. *Variety of noncurrent investments*

Majestic Enterprises began fiscal 1994 with the following portfolio of noncurrent investments:

(a) Land purchased for speculation at a price of $120,000. Current market value is estimated at $180,000.

(b) Common stock of Baker Enterprises: 22,000 shares purchased at $19 per share, representing only 2% of the outstanding stock. Current market price of the shares was $22 per share on December 31, 1993.

(c) Common stock of Yeast Manufacturing: 50,000 shares purchased at $43 per share, representing 15% of the outstanding stock. Majestic does not exercise significant influence over Yeast. Yeast's shares traded at $35 per share on December 31, 1993.

(d) Bonds of Kernal Corp.: $300,000 face value, 10% bonds purchased for $304,000. Current carrying value is $302,000. The bonds mature in two years and pay interest on June 30 and December 31 each year. Majestic uses straight-line amortization since it does not result in a material difference when compared to the effective interest method.

Dividends from the investments in stock in 1994 were as follows:

Baker	$1.00 per share
Yeast	.50 per share

At the end of 1994, the following information was available regarding market values for the investments:

Baker	$25 per share
Yeast	$30 per share
Kernal	$340,000
Land	$220,000

In addition, the decline in value of the Yeast Company stock has been characterized as permanent.

REQUIRED:

1. Prepare the balance sheet presentation of the noncurrent investment account as of December 31, 1993.
2. Prepare a schedule to determine the income from investments.
3. Prepare the balance sheet presentation of the noncurrent investment accounts as of December 31, 1994.
4. Prepare the note disclosures regarding investments in noncurrent marketable securities to be included at December 31, 1994.

16-3. *Equity investments: cost, market value, and equity method*

On December 31, 1994, Lee Inc. reported as long-term investments the following marketable equity securities:

Dale Corp., 5,000 shares of common (1% interest)	$125,000
Ewing Corp., 10,000 shares of common (2%)	160,000
Fox Corp., 25,000 shares (10%)	700,000
Marketable equity securities at cost	$985,000
Allowance for adjustment to market value for noncurrent marketable securities	(50,000)
Marketable securities at market	$935,000

(a) On May 1, 1995, Dale issued a 10% stock dividend when the market price of its stock was $24.
(b) On November 1, 1995, Dale paid a cash dividend of $0.75 per share.
(c) On August 5, 1995, Ewing issued to all shareholders stock rights on the basis of one right per share. The rights entitle the holder to one share of common stock at $13. Market prices at the date of issue were $13.50 for the stock (ex rights) and $1.50 per right. The rights expire on March 5, 1996. On December 31, 1995, the rights traded at $1.00 each and the share price was unchanged.
(d) On July 1, 1994, Lee paid $1,520,000 for 50,000 shares of Dye Company, which represents a 20% interest. Lee does have significant influence over Dye as a result of the purchase. The fair value of all Dye's assets equaled book value with the exception of equipment, which had a ten-year life and was overvalued by $100,000. Lee amortizes goodwill over 20 years. At the time of the acquisition, Dye's book value of equity was $5,200,000.
(e) Market prices per share of the common stocks held as investments as of December 31, 1995 were as follows:

Dale Corp.	$23 per share
Ewing Corp.	14 per share
Fox Corp.	29 per share
Dye Corp.	27 per share

(f) Dye reported net income and paid dividends during 1990 as follows:

	Income	Dividends
Six months ended June 30, 1990	$200,000	None
Six months 6/30/90 – 12/31/90	370,000	$1.30/share

REQUIRED:

1. Prepare a distribution of excess schedule for the acquisition of Dye Corporation.
2. Prepare a schedule to compute Lee's equity in Dye's earnings for 1995.
3. Prepare schedules to determine the effects of the stock dividend and rights offerings of Dale and Ewing, respectively.
4. Prepare an analysis of the comparison of the cost and market values of marketable securities, indicating the gross unrealized gain and the gross unrealized loss at the end of 1995.
5. Prepare any journal entries necessitated by the analysis in (4).
   (AICPA adapted)

16-4.   *Equity and debt investments: market value and equity method*

On June 30, 1994, Bushy Company made three investments. Bushy purchased 1% of the outstanding stock of Bagot Inc. for $250,000, and 5,000 of the 12,500 outstanding common shares of Green Inc. for $450,000. In addition, Bushy paid $81,683 for a $100,000, 8% coupon bond in Aumerle Company. The bond was priced to yield 12%, and $4,000 interest had accrued on the bond at the time of purchase. Interest is accrued and paid semiannually, and the bond matures on December 31, 2002. All these securities are traded on a major exchange, and the bonds were held for sale as part of the noncurrent portfolio.

During 1995, Bagot's stock price declined 30% as the result of a product liability suit against the company. Bushy's management believes that the stock is unlikely to recover its value. Earnings and dividend information for Bagot and Green follows. Both companies declare and pay dividends at the end of the year. On June 30, 1994 Green had income of $75,000.

		1994	1995	1996
Bagot:	Net income	$1,250,000	$ (750,000)	$ (50,000)
	Dividend	1,000,000	500,000	0
Green:	Net income	150,000	120,000	160,000
	Dividend	50,000	50,000	50,000

On January 1, 1996, Bushy sold the bond for $80,307. On June 30, 1996, Bushy sold its interest in Green for $800,000. At the time of the sale, Green had income of $90,000. On December 31, 1996, Bushy sold its Bagot stock for $120,000. Information on the market value of these investments at the end of 1994 and 1995 were as follows:

	1994	1995
Bagot	$240,000	$140,000
Green	500,000	540,000
Aumerle	79,200	80,307

REQUIRED:

1. Present a schedule reconciling Bushy's investment in Green from purchase date to sale date.

2. Present an amortization schedule up to the date of sale for the Aumerle bond.

3. Present the journal entries for the purchase, maintenance, and sale of Bushy's long-term investments.

4. Prepare any entries necessary at the end of each year to recognize the difference between book and market values for these investments.

16-5.   *Essay on investments*

Presented below are four unrelated situations involving marketable securities:

Situation I

A noncurrent portfolio with an aggregate market value in excess of cost includes one particular security whose market value has declined to less than one-half of its original cost. The decline is considered to be other than temporary.

Situation II

A marketable security, whose market value is currently less than cost, is classified as noncurrent but is to be reclassified as current.

Situation III

A company's noncurrent portfolio of marketable securities consists of the common stock of one company. At the end of the prior year, the market value of the security was 50% of its original cost, and this effect was properly reflected in a valuation allowance account. However, at the end of the current year, the security's market value has appreciated to twice its original cost. The security is still considered noncurrent at year-end.

REQUIRED:

Evaluate the effect upon classification, carrying value, and income for each of the above situations.

(AICPA adapted)

16-6.   *Essay on investments in equity securities*

Walker Company has a noncurrent marketable securities portfolio. Walker does not own more than 5% of any class of securities in the portfolio. At the beginning of the year, the aggregate market value of the portfolio exceeded its cost. Cash dividends on these securities were received during the year. None of the securities in the portfolio were sold during the year. At year-end, the aggregate cost of the portfolio exceeded its market value. The decline was considered temporary.

During the year, Walker purchased for cash a 35% interest in Sipe Company. Cash dividends on this investment were received during the year, and the earnings of Sipe after the acquisition date were reported by Sipe to Walker.

REQUIRED:

1. Describe how Walker should report on its balance sheet and income statement the effects of its investments in the noncurrent marketable securities portfolio. Why?

2. Describe how Walker should report on its balance sheet and income statement the effects of its investment in Sipe. Why?

(AICPA adapted)

16-7.   *Equity method: multiple periods, sale of partial interest*

Valstead Company acquired a 30% interest in Jepp, Inc. for $2,400,000 on January 1, 1994. On the date of the acquisition, Jepp reported the following equity balances:

Common stock ($2 par)	$2,000,000
APIC	500,000
Retained earnings	3,000,000
Total equity	$5,500,000

Further investigation revealed that, with the exception of the following items, book value approximated market values for the identifiable assets and liabilities:

Asset or Liability	Market Value	−	Book Value	=	Difference
Inventory	$ 400,000	−	$200,000	=	$ 200,000
Land	$1,200,000	−	150,000	=	1,050,000
Patents	350,000	−	0	=	350,000
	$1,950,000		$350,000	=	$1,600,000

Jepp accounts for inventory on a first-in, first-out basis, and the patents have a remaining life of three years. Any goodwill is amortized over 30 years.
Jepp reported the following amounts for income and dividends during the period 1994–1997:

	Income	Dividends
1994	$300,000	$100,000
1995	400,000	100,000
1996	(200,000)	50,000
1997	700,000	50,000

Jepp sold the land that was on the books at the date of the acquisition in 1996.

REQUIRED:

1. Prepare a schedule to determine the equity in earnings accrual made by Valstead at the end of each of the four years, 1994–1997.
2. Prepare an analysis of the changes in the investment in Jepp account over the period 1994 to 1997.
3. Assume that on January 1, 1998, Valstead sold a 25% interest in Jepp for $3,000,000. During 1998, Jepp reported income of $800,000 and declared dividends of $100,000. Prepare the entries Valstead would use to record this activity in 1998, assuming Jepp's shares are not used on any exchange.

16-8.   *Equity method: multiple periods*

On September 30, 1994, Peto Inc. purchased 40% of the outstanding stock of Poins Inc. when Poins had total stockholders' equity of $3,450,000, including $120,000 in 1994 net income and $40,000 in 1994 dividends.
The purchase price reflected the underlying book value of the equity with the exception of inventory and equipment. The inventory's book value exceeded its $550,000 market value by $50,000. All the inventory was sold before the end of the year. The equipment's book value exceeded its $1,200,000 market value by $400,000. This equipment had a remaining life of five years.
The following income and dividend information was reported by Poins in 1994, 1995, and 1996:

	Income	Dividends
1994	$150,000	$50,000
1995	200,000	60,000
1996	460,000	70,000

On December 31, 1995, Peto sold 25% of its original investment for $350,000. On December 31, 1996, Peto sold its remaining interest in Poins for $1,300,000.

REQUIRED:

1. Determine the price Peto paid for the investment in Poins and prepare a schedule of the distribution of excess.
2. Prepare a schedule to determine the equity in earnings accrual Peto made for 1994, 1995, and 1996.
3. Determine the book value Peto assigned to the portion of the investment sold in 1995 and the remaining portion sold in 1996.
4. Prepare journal entries to record all activity in the investment in Poins account from October 1, 1994 to December 31, 1996. Assume dividends are declared and paid on the last day of each year.

16-9. *Equity method: multiple periods, sale of investment*

Palomino Company acquired a 25% interest in Franco Enterprises for $3,200,000 on June 1, 1994. On the date of the acquisition, Franco reported the following equity balances:

Common stock (1,000,000 shares of no-par)		$5,000,000
Retained earnings		
Beginning balance	$3,000,000	
Income 1/1/94 – 6/1/94	900,000	
Dividends 1/1/94 – 6/1/94	(300,000)	3,600,000
Total equity		$8,600,000

Further investigation revealed that, with the exception of the following items, book value approximated market values for the identifiable assets and liabilities:

Asset or Liability	Market Value	–	Book Value	=	Difference
Equipment	$ 3,200,000	–	$ 2,300,000	=	$ 900,000
Bonds	(1,200,000)	–	(1,700,000)	=	500,000
	$ 2,000,000	–	$ 600,000	=	$1,400,000

The equipment has an average remaining life of four years, and the bonds mature on June 30, 1997. Palamino amortizes goodwill over 20 years. Palamino held its investment in Franco until September 31, 1996, when it sold the entire investment for $7,000,000. Franco reported the following amounts for income and dividends during the remainder of 1994, all of 1995, and up to September 30, 1996:

	Income	Dividends
6/1/94 – 12/31/94	$1,200,000	$ 400,000
1/1/95 – 12/31/95	2,600,000	900,000
1/1/96 – 9/30/96	1,900,000	1,000,000

REQUIRED:

1. Prepare a schedule to determine the equity in earnings accrual Palamino made for 1994, 1995, and 1996.
2. Prepare journal entries for Palamino to record all activity in the investment in Franco account from June 1, 1994 through September 30, 1996.

16-10. *Noncurrent portfolio of marketable equity securities: multiple years*

Mopsadorcas Corp. maintains a long-term investment portfolio. The following is a summary of the activity in the portfolio during 1994, 1995, and 1996.

| Security | Per Share Transaction Description | Date | Market Values | | |
			12/31/94	12/31/95	12/31/96
A	buy 200 for $25	6/30/94	$28	$16	$22
B	buy 400 for $60	2/3/94	70	55	48
C	buy 200 for $100	4/5/94	98	52	60
A	sell 200 for $22	12/31/95			
C	sell 100 for $55	4/4/95			
D	buy 400 for $16	2/7/95	15	14	20

Other Activity:

1995:

Company A declared and paid a $.50 per share dividend.
Company B declared a 20% stock dividend.
Company C split 2-for-1 on March 31.
Company D paid a $.10 per share dividend.

1996:

Company A declared and paid a $.50 per share dividend.
Company B declared a 20% stock dividend.
Company C declared and paid a $.50 per share dividend.
Company D repurchased 40% of its outstanding stock in the open market.

REQUIRED:

1. Prepare a worksheet for each of the three years to determine the aggregate book and market values of the portfolio.
2. Prepare journal entries to account for the activity in the portfolio in 1995 and 1996. Assume all dividends are declared and paid in the same year.

16-11. *Equity method: year of acquisition*

Bowen, Inc. acquired a 40% interest in Jordan Corporation on May 1, 1994. Both companies have an April 30 fiscal year-end. Bowen paid $1,500,000 in cash for the interest in Jordan. On the date of the acquisition, Jordan reported the following equity balances:

Common stock (no-par)	$1,000,000
Retained earnings	4,000,000
Total equity	$5,000,000

Further investigation revealed that, with the exception of the following items, book value approximated market values for the identifiable assets and liabilities:

Asset or Liability	Market Value	–	Book Value	=	Difference
Equipment	$400,000	–	$2,200,000	=	$(1,800,000)

The equipment has a remaining useful life of 10 years. Jordan reported income of $600,000 for fiscal 1994-1995 and declared no dividends.

REQUIRED:

1. Prepare a distribution of excess schedule to compute the goodwill acquired by Bowen.
2. Prepare a schedule to determine the equity in earnings accrual made by Bowen on April 30, 1995.

16-12. *Debt securities: ability and intent to hold to maturity*

On December 31, 1995 York Company made the following bond investments:
(a) One Bedford Company $100,000 face value, 6% coupon bond maturing December 31, 2005, paying interest annually,
(b) Three Gloucester Inc. $100,000 face value, 12% coupon bonds maturing June 30, 2000, paying interest semiannually.

At the time of purchase, the bonds were considered comparable in risk to securities yielding a 10% return.

During 1995, the Gloucester bond was downgraded, resulting in an increase in its expected yield to 11.5%. York sold the bond with six months' interest accrued on December 31, 1995. The sale price reflected a 11% yield. The Bedford bond was sold with six months' interest accrued on June 30, 1996, for $90,834.

REQUIRED:

1. Prepare a schedule setting forth the amortization of any premium or discount and the determination of interest income over the life of the bond investments, assuming they were held to maturity.
2. Prepare journal entries to account for the actual activity in the bond accounts, including their purchase and sale. Ignore entries for the receipt of interest. Assume that the company has the ability and intent to hold the bonds to maturity.

16-13. *Debt securities and life insurance*

On December 31, 1994, Quince Inc. acquired five, $100,000 face value, 10% coupon bonds in Flute Company when the bonds were priced to yield 7%. The bonds mature on June 30, 1996, and pay interest semiannually.

Every December 31, Quince pays the $50,000 annual premium on the life insurance policy of its company president, Nick Bottom. The cash surrender value of the policy was as follows:

December 31, 1994	$ 73,000
December 31, 1995	84,000
December 31, 1996	95,000
December 31, 1997	110,000

On December 31, 1995, Quince borrowed $60,000 against the cash surrender value of the insurance policy at 6% interest, compounded monthly. Principal and all interest are due on December 31, 1997. Quince used all the cash to acquire land from Starveling Development Inc.

During 1994, the land was reappraised at $40,000. Quince sold the land for $42,500 and repaid the loan in full on February 1, 1997.

REQUIRED:

1. Present an amortization schedule for the bond.
2. Prepare journal entries relating to the acquisition of the bond, interest, and collection at maturity assuming interest payments correspond to accruals. Quince has the intent and ability to hold the bonds to maturity.
3. Present all journal entries necessary to account for the insurance policy and the related loan from December 31, 1994 through December 31, 1996.
4. Present the necessary journal entries to record activity in the land account from the purchase through the sale.

16-14. *Appendix: installment acquisitions and conversion from cost to equity*

On August 1, 1998, Costard Corp. purchased 25,000 of the 200,000 outstanding shares of Moth, Inc. for $20 per share. The net book value of Moth on the purchase date was $3,600,000, and the book value of assets and liabilities equaled their market values with the following exceptions:

Account	Market Over Book Value
Fixed assets	$100,000
Inventory	50,000
Land	100,000
Total	$250,000

The inventory was sold during 1998. The fixed assets had a remaining useful life of five years as of August 1. Costard uses the maximum allowable period to amortize all intangibles.

The Moth stock is not considered marketable, and Costard was not deemed to have significant influence after the purchase of the shares.

On January 1, 2000, Costard purchased another 25,000 shares of the Moth stock for $27 per share. On this date, the net book value of Moth was $5,025,000, and the book value of assets equaled their market values with the following exceptions:

Account	Market Over Book Value
Fixed assets	$ 40,000
Land	200,000
Total	$240,000

The assets had a remaining useful life of three years as of January 1. Costard is presumed to have significant influence in Moth's operations after the latest purchase of Moth stock.

The following information summarizes the activity of Moth, Inc.:

	Income	Dividend
1/1/98 – 7/31/98	$500,000	$100,000
8/1/98 – 12/31/98	220,000	100,000
1999	625,000	220,000
2000	750,000	250,000

Moth declares two equal dividends per year on 6/30 and 12/31. Dividends are paid one month after declaration.

REQUIRED:

1. Provide the journal entries for the initial purchase of Moth stock and the entries necessary to account for the investment during the period in which Costard does not have significant influence in Moth's operations.
2. Provide the journal entries necessary to account for the January 1, 2000, purchase of Moth stock and any adjustment for the change from the cost method to the equity method of accounting for the investment. Present distribution of excess schedules for both purchases along with a schedule reconciling the book value of the investment before and after the change in accounting method.
3. Provide the journal entries necessary to account for the activity in the investment account after the January 1, 2000, purchase. Support the entries with a schedule of amortization of excess purchase price.
4. Make a case to support the treatment of the excess market value over book value relating to land in applying the equity method on the investment in Moth.

16-15. *Appendix: equity method and the sale of interest and conversion to cost*

On January 1, 1999, Thaisa Corp. purchased 5,000 of the 20,000 outstanding common stock of Marina Corp. for $40 per share. The stock is not considered readily marketable. The book value of Marina's equity at the time of the purchase was $35 per share. The book values of assets and liabilities are considered equal to their market values at the time of purchase, with the following exceptions:

	Book Value – Market Value
Fixed assets (5-year life)	$50,000
Bond liability (maturity 12/31/08)	$30,000

Thaisa uses the maximum allowable time to amortize intangibles.
On December 31, 2000, Thaisa sold all but 1,000 shares of its Marina stock for $140,000. After the sale, Thaisa no longer has significant influence in Marina's operations. The following information summarizes the activity of Marina Corp.:

Year	Net Income	Dividend
1999	$70,000	$10,000
2000	50,000	10,000
2001	90,000	10,000
2002	40,000	5,000

Marina declares its dividend on the last day of each year and pays it on January 15.

REQUIRED:

1. Present a distribution of excess schedule for the purchase of Marina shares. Record the journal entry.
2. Present the journal entries to account for the investment during the period in which the equity method is used. Include supporting worksheets for the income accrual amounts.
3. Present the journal entry to record the sale of 3,000 shares of Marina Corp. stock. Support this entry with a worksheet that gives the computation of the book value of these shares.
4. Present the journal entries to account for the remaining investment in Marina after the sale of stock. What is the status of the Investment in Marina account at December 31, 2002?

LEE ENTERPRISES

Lee Enterprises, Incorporated reported the following information in its financial statements at September 30, 1982:

		September 30,	
	1982	1981	1980
Balance sheet			
Investments, associated companies	$18,128,000	$18,429,000	$16,638,000
Income statement			
Operating revenue:			
Equity in net income	$ 3,074,000	$ 3,841,000	$ 2,945,000

Note 1. Significant Accounting Policies

Investments in the common stock of associated companies are reported at cost plus the Company's share of undistributed earnings since the acquisition, less amortization of goodwill.

Note 2. Investment in Associated Companies

The Company has an effective 50% ownership interest in NAPP Systems (USA) Inc., a manufacturer of specialized graphic products, and three newspaper publishing companies operating at Lincoln, Nebraska (Journal-Star Printing Co.), Madison, Wisconsin (Madison Newspapers, Inc.), and Bismarck, North Dakota (Bismarck Tribune Company).

Summarized financial information of these companies is as follows:

ASSETS	1982	1981	1980
Current assets	$ 31,826,000	$ 27,604,000	$31,768,000
Investments and other assets	2,980,000	2,782,000	1,605,000
Property and equipment, net	26,222,000	27,924,000	29,585,000
	$ 61,028,000	$ 58,310,000	$62,958,000

LIABILITIES AND STOCKHOLDERS' EQUITY	1982	1981	1980
Current liabilities	$ 24,877,000	$ 20,789,000	$20,051,000
Long-term debt	3,966,000	4,238,000	13,237,000
Deferred items	3,414,000	4,077,000	4,223,000
Stockholders' equity	28,771,000	29,206,000	25,447,000
	$ 61,028,000	$ 58,310,000	$62,958,000
Revenue	$105,316,000	$110,835,000	$99,524,000
Operating income	11,547,000	17,432,000	10,930,000
Net income	6,319,000	8,620,000	6,093,000

Certain information relating to Company investments in these associated companies is as follows:

Share of:

Stockholders' equity	$ 14,511,000	$ 14,703,000	$12,805,000
Undistributed earnings	11,316,000	11,617,000	9,826,000
Net income	3,074,000	4,217,000	2,945,000

REQUIRED:

1. Briefly describe the process Lee Enterprises goes through to determine the equity in earnings of associated companies reported in its income statement, along with the valuation of the investment account.

2. How much goodwill amortization is included in the figure Lee reports as equity in net income for 1981 of $4,217,000 and 1982 of $3,074,000?

3. How must unamortized goodwill be contained in the value of the investment account at September 30, 1981 and 1982?

4. Given your response to (2) and (3), what appears to be the amortization period chosen by Lee for goodwill? Does this meet the requirements of APB No. 18?

5. How much cash did Lee receive from these investments during 1981 and 1982? How would Lee report these cash flows in its cash flow statement?

6. If Lee had used the cost method, instead of the equity method, for these investments in 1981 and 1982, how much difference would there have been in income before taxes? (Assume that none of the investees issued or repurchased any stock during 1981 or 1982.)

INTERCO INCORPORATED

CASE 16.2

Interco Incorporated, included the following disclosures regarding its noncurrent marketable equity security portfolio in its financial statements of February 28, 1982:

Note 1: Significant Accounting Policies

Marketable Investment Securities (in part)

Marketable equity securities (preferred stocks) are carried at the lower of cost or market. A valuation allowance, representing the excess of cost over market of these equity securities, is included in stockholders' equity.

Note 5. Marketable Investment Securities

Marketable investment securities consist of the following:

	1982	1981
Marketable equity securities, at cost	$ 3,586,000	$ 3,586,000
Less valuation allowance	247,000	754,000
Marketable equity securities, at market	3,339,000	2,832,000
Bonds, at cost	11,093,000	11,466,000
	$14,432,000	$14,298,000

The portfolio of marketable equity securities includes gross unrealized gains of $525,000 and unrealized losses of $772,000 at February 28, 1982. Net realized losses on the sale of securities, after applicable taxes, included in the determination of net earnings amounted to $90,000 for fiscal 1981. There were no realized gains or losses in fiscal 1982.

While the financial statements included in the 1982 annual report were prepared prior to the recent changes in accounting for marketable securities, you may assume for purposes of this case that management had both the intent and ability to hold the bonds to maturity. Consequently, they would not be included in the marketable securities portfolio for purposes of recognizing any unrealized gains or losses.

REQUIRED:

1. What differences exist in the treatment of noncurrent marketable securities relative to current marketable securities?
2. Prepare the journal entry Interco must have made to record the changes in the valuation allowance for noncurrent marketable securities in 1982.
3. How much money did Interco generate by the sale of securities during 1982? Assuming that all the bonds in the bond portfolio were originally purchased at face value, prepare the journal entry to record the sale of bonds during 1982.
4. Instead of the assumption in (3), assume that no new bonds were purchased and no old bonds matured or were sold during 1982. How might you explain to someone why the cost of the bonds declined?

CASE 16.3

TWIN DISC, INCORPORATED

Twin Disc, Incorporated reported the following information regarding its investment in an affiliate as part of its 1989 annual report. Twin Disc has a June 30 fiscal year-end.

	1989	1988
Balance Sheet (dollars in thousands)		
Noncurrent assets:		
Investment in affiliate	$7,021	$7,051
Income Statement (dollars in thousands)		
Equity in earnings of affiliate	$ 689	310

Note A: Significant Accounting Policies

The Company's 25% ownership of Niigata Converter Company, Ltd. is stated at cost, adjusted for its equity in undistributed earnings since acquisition and the effects of foreign currency translation.

Note E: Investment in Affiliate

Undistributed earnings of the affiliate included in consolidated retained earnings approximated $3,311,000 and $2,928,000 at June 30, 1989 and 1988, respectively. Following is a summary of condensed unaudited financial information pertaining to Niigata Converter Company, Ltd. (dollars in thousands):

	1989	1988
Current assets	$ 74,455	$ 68,633
Other assets	23,263	22,269
	$ 97,718	$ 90,902
Current liabilities	$ 66,390	$ 59,383
Other liabilities	3,244	3,317
Shareholders' equity	28,084	28,202
	$ 97,718	$ 90,902
Net sales	$124,464	$100,955
Gross profit on sales	20,192	14,936
Net earnings	2,757	1,238

REQUIRED:

1. Assuming that Niigata had no other events that affected its shareholders' equity other than reported income and dividends during 1989, prepare the journal entries Twin Disc would use to record activity relating to its investment in Niigata.
2. Twin Disc indicates that its investment in Niigata is carried at cost, with adjustments for equity in undistributed earnings. What does this imply about the relationship between the original purchase price of the investment in Niigata as it related to the book value of assets at that time? Are there any assumptions you need to make to respond to this question?

CASE 16.4

SCOPE INDUSTRIES

In its 1989 annual report, Scope Industries included the following information regarding investments in noncurrent marketable securities:

	1989	1988
Marketable securities, at lower of cost or market: (Market $24,213,725 in 1989 and cost $19,017,544 in 1988—Note 3)	$14,242,634	$18,075,460

Note 1: Significant Accounting Policies

The noncurrent portfolio of marketable securities is stated at the lower of aggregate cost or market at the balance sheet date and consists of common and preferred stocks, bonds, and U.S. Treasury obligations. Dividend and interest income are accrued when earned.

Realized gains or losses are determined on the specific identification method and are reflected in income. Unrealized losses on noncurrent marketable securities are recorded directly in a separate shareowners' equity account except those unrealized losses which are deemed to be other than temporary, which losses are reflected in income.

Note 3: Marketable Securities

Included in Investment and Other Income (Loss) are recognized losses and gains on marketable securities. Net losses of $1,966,867 and $5,347,315 were recognized in 1989 and 1988, respectively. Net gains of $2,742,005 were recognized in 1987. The recorded losses and gains were from sales of marketable securities and from recognized but unrealized losses of $2,463,591 and $4,084,421 in 1989 and 1988, respectively, on securities whose decline in value was deemed to be other than temporary.

At June 30, 1989, gross unrealized gains and losses (other than the above mentioned unrealized losses) on marketable securities were as follows:

Gross unrealized gains	$10,131,790
Gross unrealized losses	(160,699)

At the time Scope prepared these financial statements, GAAP only required that net unrealized losses be recognized by use of an equity valuation allowance.

REQUIRED:

1. Scope indicates that dividend and interest income are accrued as earned. When are dividends earned? When is interest earned?
2. What is the *specific identification method* and how does it work?
3. Scope indicates that the noncurrent portfolio consists of common and preferred stocks, bonds, and treasury securities. When reporting these investments, can all of these securities be lumped into a single portfolio? Explain.
4. What is the difference between a realized gain or loss and an unrealized gain or loss?
5. What is the difference between a recognized gain or loss and an unrecognized gain or loss? Describe the relationship between gains and losses that are realized/unrealized and those that are recognized/unrecognized.
6. Prepare journal entries to record the unrealized losses that were deemed to be other than temporary in 1988 and 1989.
7. If Scope were to have applied the current accounting requirements to the noncurrent portfolio of marketable securities, what journal entry would have been required at the end of 1989? What amount would appear in Scope's equity section in 1988 and 1989 relating to the net unrealized gain or loss on the noncurrent marketable security portfolio?
8. Assume that at the end of fiscal 1989, Scope elected to transfer all the securities in the noncurrent portfolio to the current portfolio. What journal entry would be necessary to record this transfer? Explain why you prepared the entry that you did.

Accounting for Leases

A **lease** is a contract that transfers property rights between the owner of an asset (called the *lessor*) to another party (called the *lessee*) without immediately transferring title to the asset. A **property right** is a legal right to benefit in some way from an asset. For example, the right to the use of equipment for a limited period of time is a property right. The right to sell an asset is another property right. In general, leases transfer some of these property rights (typically for the use of an asset) from the lessor to the lessee.

Typically, the lessee pays for these rights by making periodic payments, referred to as **lease payments**, to the lessor. Lease payments can take many forms. Some are predetermined and fixed at the beginning of the lease. Others are contingent on future events such as the level of sales the lessee generates. In addition, some lease payments (fixed or contingent) are cancellable at the request of either the lessee or the lessor.

While lease contracts can range from very simple contracts, such as the daily rental of tools from your local rental outlet, to very complex arrangements, such as long-term lease arrangements for real estate, all leases have three features in common:

1. Ownership of the asset, which is the subject of the lease, remains with the lessor over the term of the lease.
2. Some property rights are transferred from the lessor to the lessee.
3. The lease payments act as a means of financing the acquisition of the property rights transferred in the lease.

Leasing activity within the United States varies considerably by industry. The commercial and rental real estate markets depend primarily on leasing to generate revenues from the ownership of these types of real estate. The airline industry depends heavily on leasing from aircraft manufacturers (or their leasing subsidiaries) to finance the acquisition of aircraft. In fact, many manufacturers of industrial equipment have wholly owned leasing subsidiaries that arrange leases for customers of the manufacturing parent.

In many cases, a lease emerges as a result of a three-party agreement. For example, a manufacturer sells an asset to a bank, who then acts as the lessor of the asset, and enters into a lease with a lessee who wishes to acquire the use of the asset. The bank acts as a financier in the transaction between the manufacturer and the ultimate customer, but it assumes the risks of ownership of the asset since it purchased the asset from the manufacturer. Of course, banks only become involved in these types of arrangements when the manufacturer and the ultimate lessee are identified. Banks do not generally buy assets and then seek lessees, but financial institutions play an important role in leasing activity as financiers. Later in the chapter, we will see that these types of transactions actually represent a special type of leasing activity.

OVERVIEW OF FINANCIAL REPORTING FOR LEASE ACTIVITY

As noted above, all leases transfer some amount of property rights from the lessor to the lessee over the lease term in return for periodic lease payments. If we consider the property rights transferred in a particular lease as a percentage of all the property rights the asset represents, we can place leases on a continuum like that shown in Exhibit 17.1.

At one end of the continuum are leases of very short duration relative to the underlying economic life of the asset transferred. The lessee usually makes a single payment at the end of the lease term. An example of these leases might be a day's use of a special drill rented from the local rental outlet. At the other end of the spectrum are leases in which virtually all the asset's property rights are transferred from the lessor to the lessee over the lease term. Leases of this type might be for specialized equipment, under terms that ultimately transfer title to and all property rights in the asset from the lessor to the lessee at the end of the lease. Between these endpoints are other types of lease arrangements. For example, a lease of real estate for a year transfers more property

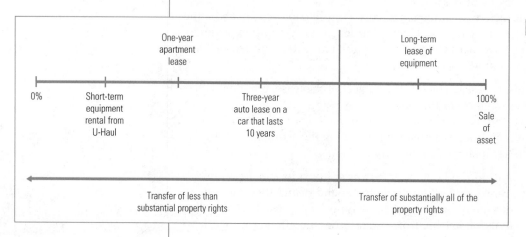

EXHIBIT 17.1

Classification of Lease Along a Continuum Representing the Percentage of Property Rights Transferred from Lessor to Lessee

rights to the lessor than a one-day lease of equipment, but it is less than a multiyear lease of equipment. The point is that all leases transfer property rights.

For financial accounting purposes, we convert this continuum into a dichotomy that characterizes leases as either *capital* or *operating*. A **capital lease** transfers substantially all the asset's property rights to the lessee over the life of the lease. Any lease that does not accomplish this is an operating lease. With capital leases, the lessor accounts for them as a sale; the lessee, as a purchase.

Since all leases transfer some property rights, the identification of leases in which substantially all property rights are transferred is somewhat arbitrary. However, the purpose of this classification is to distinguish between leases that have the substance of a sale and those that are in substance not a sale. Such an arbitrary dichotomy of the continuum is represented in Exhibit 17.1 by the vertical line at 90%. This cutoff suggests that all leases that transfer 90% of the asset's property rights through the lease are in substance a sale and should be accounted for as a capital lease.

For a lessee, classifying the lease as capital or operating is the only determination needed for accounting purposes. For a lessor, the classification scheme is a bit more complicated. The lessor first determines whether a lease is capital or operating. For capital leases, the lessor must classify each lease as either *sales-type* lease or *direct financing*. The classification of leases for both the lessee and the lessor is captured in Exhibit 17.2.

A sales-type lease arises when the lessor is a dealer or manufacturer of the asset being leased. When a sale is accomplished using a lease, the lessor recognizes revenue on the sale and matches the asset's manufacturing cost by a charge to cost of goods sold. A direct financing lease involves no dealer or manufacturer's profit or loss. A bank purchasing equipment from a manufacturer and then immediately leasing it to a lessee is an example of a direct financing lease. The bank obtains a return on its investment in the asset with the lessee's payments that both recoup the asset's cost and provide a profit for the bank. Alternatively, we could consider the lease payments as containing an "implicit" amount of interest that the bank charges for financing the lessee's purchase of the asset via a capital lease.

To develop a more complete understanding of how identifying a capital lease relates to the transfers or risks of ownership in the leased asset, the discussion in the remainder of this chapter begins by examining the real motivations for leasing. Following this, financial reporting for lessees and lessors is examined.

Purchases of Assets With and Without Financing

If a company wishes to assume all the risks and enjoy all the rewards of ownership associated with an asset, it will purchase the asset. When a purchase is

EXHIBIT 17.2

Classification of Leases for Financial Reporting Purposes

Classification of Leases for Financial Reporting Purposes		
Substance of Transactions	**Lessee**	**Lessor**
Sale	Capital Lease	Sales-Type Lease or Direct Financing Lease
Lease	Operating Lease	Operating Lease

made without using any financing, the purchaser generally obtains uncondi-tional rights to the asset. For example, if a company purchases an auto for cash, it can allow corporate personnel to drive it, or sell it, or even strip it down and sell it for parts. In recording the acquisition of the vehicle, the company would increase the asset property, plant, and equipment and decrease its cash.

A company may also obtain financing to acquire the car. However, to obtain financing, it may have to give up some property rights. Generally, the lender will require a lien on the auto. This prevents the company from selling the car without the lender's approval. In addition, the lender may require the company to insure the vehicle and may place other limits on the vehicle's use. While these situations represent limitations on the property rights during the life of the financing, they are not so serious as to alter the accounting for such an acquisition. The company would record the purchase and financing by increasing its assets and liabilities.

Leasing—A Contrast to the Purchase of Assets

Unlike purchases of assets, leases generally represent situations in which the purchaser of the property rights (the lessee) does not seek to obtain all of the rights, or to bear all the risks, of ownership. The many reasons for this can be divided into two major motivations: issues of taxation and issues of risk sharing.

Over the years, the tax law has provided many investment tax incentives, which generally benefit the title holder of the asset. When a company in a high tax bracket owns an asset that a company in a low tax bracket wants to use, a lease provides a means for the company in the high tax bracket to retain cer-tain tax advantages that go with the title. The low tax bracket company then benefits through a lease payment that would be lower than one required to purchase the asset, since the seller need not give up tax benefits to engage in the sale. Since the Tax Code is constantly changing, we will not discuss specif-ic tax benefits of leasing here. However, these types of situations, called *tax-arbitrage* situations, have significantly influenced the design of lease instru-ments at various times. However, while tax effects may influence the lease's structure, the classification of the lease as capital or operating for financial reporting purposes does not depend on its tax effects.

Risk sharing is probably the major motivation for entering into lease agreements. Leases allow an asset's property rights to be divided and trans-ferred individually. Thus, the risks of ownership can be allocated among sev-eral parties, each with a different means of benefiting from using some facet of the asset. To make this more concrete, consider the following example.

Buy Rite Menswear is a retail distributor of mens' clothing. It requires retail space for its shops. The company does not have any particular skill at managing large retail malls where its stores are located. In addition, the com-pany does not maintain an information network that would provide sufficient information to assess the relative risks of real estate ownership in the 200 or so communities in which it has stores.

Property Management, Inc. builds and operates large retail malls in the Midwest. The company has more than 50 years of experience managing retail outlets and buying and selling commercial real estate in the Midwest. When Buy Rite enters a new location, it has two options: to build a mall itself in which to locate or to lease space from companies like Property Management. Obviously, Buy Rite does not require an entire mall to conduct its individual business, but it does seek the locational advantage of being part of a retail complex. The lease allows the complex's owner to divide the mall into smaller units, or individual stores, for transfer to users. Of course, the complex could be sold as condominium units where each of the retailers owns his or her own store space. Why is this alternative very rarely used?

Buy Rite is interested in acquiring the use of space for only a brief period of time. It is not interested in assuming the risks associated with fluctuation in real estate values, which it would face if forced to purchase a location. It would be inefficient for Buy Rite to become as well informed about local real estate markets as Property Management is. As a result of the informational asymmetry between the parties, leasing provides an optimal means for Buy Rite to bear only the risks it has the ability to affect (the profitable operation of a retail mens' clothing store) and leave Property Management with the risks it can better bear.

Leases Versus Purchases—The Clash of Substance and Form

No clear economic basis exists for deciding when the substance of a lease is a sale and when it is not. Since they represent a sale of some property rights, all leases could be considered capital leases. However, all leases do not transfer substantially all of the rights and risks of ownership. As discussed above, the classification of a lease as capital depends on the interpretation of what constitutes a transfer of "*substantially all* of the property rights." In SFAS No. 13, the FASB provided specific guidance as to how this concept should be operationalized. We will examine these criteria in more detail after first discussing important terminology in the lease contract.

THE LEASE CONTRACT

Ultimately, a judgment must be rendered regarding the extent to which the risks and responsibilities of ownership will transfer from the lessor to the lessee over the life of the lease. A careful examination of the lease contract provides the basis for determining what rights and responsibilities are actually transferred.

The date a lease begins is called the **inception of the lease**. For legal purposes, a lease typically begins when the parties sign it. For accounting purposes, the inception of the lease is also the date of the lease agreement or the date of the commitment to enter into a lease if it is earlier.[1] A lease commitment must be in writing to constitute the inception of the lease; and all the principal provisions, such as the determination of the lease payments, must be included.

Leases may run for several periods. The **lease term** is defined as the period covered by the fixed noncancelable portion of the lease.[2] Many leases will

---

[1] "Inception of the Lease," *Statement of Financial Accounting Standards No. 23* (Stamford, CT: FASB), para. 6.

[2] "Accounting for Leases," *Statements of Financial Accounting Standards No. 13* (Stamford, CT: FASB), para. 5(f).

contain **renewal options**. Whether the term covered by the renewal option is included in the definition of the original lease term will depend on the nature of the renewal. Renewal options often exist where the terms are not specified but are subject to some form of arbitration. In other cases, the lease may allow the lessee to renew without an increase in the lease payment. When the renewal option provides for lease payments below those typically demanded in the marketplace, the renewal option is called a **bargain renewal option**.[3] For accounting purposes, the lease term includes the initial fixed noncancelable term plus the term covered by any bargain renewal options. Note that to identify a bargain renewal option requires judgment as to what lease payments would be demanded in the marketplace at the point of renewal and that this judgment must be made at the inception of the lease, not at the renewal point.

Lease payments generally fall into one of three categories: minimum lease payments, contingent lease payments, or executory costs. **Minimum lease payments** include those the lessee has committed to make, regardless of other conditions.[4] These payments represent the smallest amounts the lessee must pay, regardless of the level of sales or profitability achieved. In contrast, **contingent lease payments** are those the lessee will make only if certain conditions occur. For example, a retailer renting space in a shopping mall may be required to pay rent in the amount of $1,000 a month plus 3% of gross revenues. The fixed payment of $1,000 per month is part of the minimum lease payments, while the 3% of gross revenues is a contingent payment due only when sales are known.

Executory costs are those the lessee pays the lessor for maintenance or protection of the asset. In many cases, the lessor will require the lessee to maintain the asset or provide insurance on it. In other cases, the lease may require the lessee to pay the lessor for these services because the lessor has better technical abilities or more economies of scale in servicing many lessees. In many cases where the lessor bears these costs, remuneration is incorporated into the minimum lease payment, which may be adjusted for estimates of these future costs. It should also be noted that asset maintenance and protection are responsibilities of ownership. Specifying which party is responsible for these items also provides information on what ownership responsibilities are being transferred in the lease.

Another characteristic that may be found in a lease is a **purchase option**, which provides the lessee an opportunity to acquire full title to the asset at a specific time. The purchase option may indicate that the price is to be determined based on the property's market value as of the option date, or it may provide for the sale of the asset at a fixed price set in the lease. If the fixed price is substantially less than the asset's expected market value at the date the option can be exercised, the purchase option is called a **bargain purchase option**.[5] Again, note that a bargain purchase option requires a judgment, made at the inception of the lease, as to the asset's market value at the point when the purchase option can first be exercised.

---

[3] *Ibid.*, para. 5(e).

[4] *Ibid.*, para. 5(j).

[5] *Ibid.*, para. 5(d).

In leases where the lessor transfers responsibility for the asset's maintenance to the lessee, the lessor may require that the lease contain a **guaranteed residual**, which is a value the lessee insures the asset to have at the end of the lease. If the lessor sells the asset at the end of the lease and realizes less than the guaranteed residual amount, the lessee must make up the difference. Including this term in the lease gives the lessee an incentive to maintain the asset in good condition. Deterioration of the asset beyond that anticipated in normal use would require an additional payment to the lessor. Guaranteed residual payments are included as part of the minimum lease payments.

When the lessor retains title to the asset at the end of the lease, the asset's estimated residual value less any of the lessee's guaranteed residual represents the **unguaranteed residual**. The estimated residual value must be determined at the inception of the lease. The unguaranteed residual represents an amount the lessor expects to receive. However, this amount is not assured because the actual residual will depend on current market prices at the end of the lease; and the lessor cannot control them.

Finally, the lessee may or may not have the right to **sublease**, or to lease to another party the use of the asset now under the original lessee's control. **Sublease rentals** refer to the rent payments made to the original lessee under the terms of a sublease. In many cases, the ability to sublease is restricted or eliminated by the terms of the original lease between the original lessor and lessee.

ACCOUNTING BY THE LESSEE

Statement of Financial Accounting Standard No. 13, as amended, defines the rules for determining whether a lease is a capital lease or an operating lease for both lessees and lessors. From the lessee's perspective, a lease is classified as a capital lease if it meets any of the following four criteria:[6]

1. The lease transfers ownership of the asset to the lessee at the end of the lease term.
2. The lease contains a bargain purchase option under which the lessee can obtain title to the leased asset.
3. The lease term is equal to 75% or more of the estimated economic life of the leased property.
4. The present value of the minimum lease payments required under the terms of the lease, measured at the beginning of the lease term, equals or exceeds 90% of the fair market value of the leased asset at inception.

Criteria 3 and 4 are not applicable to leases for assets that begin in the last 25% of the asset's useful life. Thus, a lease for a 7-year-old car that has an expected life of 8 years is not subject to the tests indicated in Criterion 3 or 4. In addition, leases of land alone are evaluated using only the first two criteria since land is generally believed to have an indefinite service life. When a single lease covers both land and other assets such as a building, two possible treatments exist depending on how valuable the land is in comparison to the sum of

---

[6] *Ibid.*, para. 7.

the market values of the assets being transferred in the lease. If the fair value of the land is less than 10% of the total market value of all assets transferred, the lease is evaluated as a lease of depreciable assets and any of the four criteria are applicable. If the land represents more than 10% of the fair value of assets transferred, the lease must be split into two separate leases for accounting purposes. The portion covering land is evaluated using the first two criteria and the portion covering the depreciable assets is evaluated using all four criteria.

It is possible to see how the concept of transferring "substantially all" of the property rights in a lease is embodied within each of these four criteria. In the first criteria, the transfer of title results in a complete transfer of ownership via the lease. This transaction is virtually identical in economic terms to purchasing the asset and using it as collateral on a loan. The second criteria presumes the acquisition of complete ownership through the rational exercise of a bargain purchase option.

In Criteria 3 and 4, obtaining ultimate ownership is not a requirement. In Criterion 3, "substantially all" of the property rights is equated to acquiring 75% or more of the asset's useful life. Here, property rights are equated to years of economic benefits to be derived from the asset. In Criterion 4, "substantially all" of the property rights is determined by comparing the implicit price the lessor is paying via the present value of the lease payments to the price of complete ownership. If the lessor is paying 90% or more of the price of complete ownership, the presumption is that "substantially all" of the property rights in the form of economic benefit must be transferred over the lease term.

Determination of the Interest Rate for Discounting

Criterion 4 obviously requires discounting of the minimum lease payments (exclusive of any executory costs) to determine if the lessee should classify the lease as capital or operating. More generally, to determine the amount that the lessee will record for the value of the asset acquired under a capital lease and the liability for future lease payments, present value techniques are required. To compute a discounted value, an interest rate is chosen. The interest rate to be used in this computation is generally the lessee's incremental borrowing rate, unless the lessee knows the lessor's implicit interest rate and this rate is lower than the lessee's incremental borrowing rate.

The lessee's **incremental borrowing rate** is determined by reference to that interest rate the *lessee* would have paid on a loan to finance the asset's acquisition had the lessee not used leasing to acquire use of the asset. The **implicit interest rate** is determined by setting the *lessor's* future cash flows under the lease agreement equal to the leased asset's current fair value.

For example, assume Lessor Corporation leases equipment to Lessee Corporation for a five-year period. At the inception of the lease, the equipment could be purchased for a cash price of $57,211. Minimum lease payments are $10,000 per year, due at the beginning of each year. At the end of the lease term, the equipment reverts to Lessor; and the expected fair value at that time is $25,000. The implicit interest rate (equivalent to the internal rate of return to the lessor from the lease) is determined by solving the following present value computation:

$10,000 (1.0 + Present Value of an Ordinary Annuity of $1 at *i*% for 4 periods) + $25,000 (Present Value of $1 at *i*% in 5 periods) = $57,211

Recall that most leases require payments at the beginning of each period, not at the end. As a result, the first payment occurs at the inception of the lease and, therefore, is not discounted. This explains adding the value of 1.0 to the present value of an ordinary annuity to obtain the discount factor for the annual minimum lease payment. The lessor also expects a lump sum of $25,000 from the asset's sale at the end of the lease. This amount, even though the lessee does not pay it (this is an unguaranteed residual), is part of the lessor's cash flows and, thus, enters the computation of the implicit rate.

Solving for the interest rate is a trial-and-error process, which is typically accomplished by using a computer or financial calculator. In the example above, the implicit rate would be 10%. If Lessee could borrow funds at less than 10%, it would use its marginal borrowing rate to discount the minimum lease payments in applying Criterion 4. If Lessee's marginal borrowing rate was above 10%, the implicit rate would be used as long as Lessee could determine it. The reason for this requirement is that the lower the interest rate used, the higher the present value of the minimum lease payments. The higher the present value, the more likely the lease will be classified as a capital lease. Consequently, when uncertainty exists as to what interest rate is appropriate, the lower one is used to err on the side of classifying the lease as a capital lease.

As you can see from the example, determining the lessor's implicit rate requires knowledge of three items:

1. The asset's cash selling price at the inception of the lease
2. The minimum lease payments
3. Any unguaranteed residual value to the lessor

The lessee is typically informed of Items 1 and 2, but the lessee may not know Item 3. If the lessor's unguaranteed residual is unknown, the implicit rate cannot be determined; and the lessee must use its incremental borrowing rate to discount the minimum lease payments.

One last observation regarding the determination and application of the implicit rate needs to be made. The determination of the implicit rate depends on all cash flows that the lessor is expected to receive over the life of the lease, whether paid by the lessee or generated from the asset's terminal unguaranteed value. Since the unguaranteed residual is *not* part of the minimum lease payments, the lessee does *not* include these cash flows in determining the discounted value of the minimum lease payments. As a result, the present value of the lessor's cash flows under the lease will not equal the present value of the lessee's cash flows when an unguaranteed residual exists, even if both use the same implicit interest rate.

The Role of Professional Judgment in Evaluating Leases

It may appear that the criteria for identifying a capital lease are relatively straightforward and easy to apply, requiring little, if any, professional judgment. This is not the case. Only Criterion 1 is clear-cut. If the contract stipulates that the asset belongs to the lessee at the end of the lease, the lease is a capital lease. Here, no professional judgment is required. However, information sufficient to make an informed judgment in employing the other criteria must be developed.

In Criterion 2, a determination of what constitutes a bargain purchase must be made. This requires estimating the asset's *expected* fair market value at the date the option can be exercised and comparing the price under the purchase option to this expected fair value.

The concept of a bargain purchase is that the asset will be acquired at below market value. However, in this case, it is not a question of comparing a purchase price to a currently observable market price. Rather, the comparison is between the option exercise price and a *future* market price, which is not currently observable. Even appraisals of the asset's current value can vary widely. Projecting market values three, five, or sometimes ten years into the future is subject to substantial differences in estimates.

Two issues of judgment are immediately involved:

1. Different individuals will have different beliefs about the future market value.
2. Different individuals will disagree on how far below their forecast of market value the exercise price must be to constitute a bargain.

The presence of these judgmental factors implies that there will be differences of opinions regarding the existence of a bargain purchase option across professionals. This is a natural state of affairs.

In cases where the option exercise price is set at a nominal amount such as $1.00, the presumption is that the purchase option is a bargain purchase since the asset's scrap value is typically worth more than $1.00. However, when this is not the case, it may be difficult to develop sufficient evidence and then judge whether any significant option price is a bargain.

In Criterion 3, the asset's *expected* economic life is also a judgment that may be difficult to determine with accuracy. This makes the criterion difficult to employ in many cases where the lease is more than annual but less than many years in duration. Of course, the last criterion requires judgment, because the discount rate and the asset's current fair market value must be estimated.

Application of the Criteria for Identifying Capital Leases for the Lessee

Assume ABC Co. entered into a lease for equipment on December 31, 1993. The equipment had a fair market value of $600,000 and a useful life of 15 years. ABC agreed to pay $100,000 per year for 10 years under the lease, with each payment due on December 31. The first payment was due on the date the lease was signed. The lease payments do not contain any executory costs, and no guaranteed residual was included in the lease agreement. ABC has a marginal borrowing rate of 16% and does not know the lessor's implicit rate. Is this a capital lease?

It fails Criterion 1 since no mention is made of transfer of title. It fails Criterion 2 since there is no bargain purchase. It also fails Criterion 3 since the life of the lease is only 10 years, and 75% of the useful life would be 11.25

years. However, it meets Criterion 4. The present value of the minimum lease payments can be computed as:

Present value of first payment (1 × $100,000)	=	$100,000
Present value of remaining payments at 16% (using the present value of an ordinary annuity) (4.607 × $100,000)	=	460,700
Total discounted value		$560,700

Since 90% of $600,000 is $540,000, the present value of the minimum lease payments exceeds 90% of the leased asset's current fair market value. Thus, it is a capital lease.

Note again, in determining the present value of the minimum lease payments, the first payment is not discounted. This is commonly the case with leases as the first payment is often due at the inception of the lease and, thus, is not discounted.

Recording a Capital Lease by the Lessee at Inception

When a lease is determined to be a capital lease, the lessee must record an asset and an obligation under the capital lease. Using the data from the ABC Co. example above, this journal entry would appear as follows:

December 31, 1993:

Property, plant, and equipment	560,700	
Obligation under capital lease		560,700
To record the asset acquired and obligation incurred at inception of the lease.		

The dollar amount used in this entry is the discounted value of the minimum lease payments. In general, this amount is determined by excluding any payments for executory costs but including any guaranteed residual in the lease, both of which are zero in this example. The term of the lease will include any bargain renewal periods, or periods in which a failure to renew will impose a penalty of such sufficient size that the lessee will renew the lease.

The inception of a capital lease itself does not cause any cash flows. While an initial lease payment is usually due at inception, this need not be the case. The lessee's recording of the inception of a capital lease is considered a noncash transaction, which must be reported in the notes to the cash flow statement but is not part of cash flows from operating, investing, or financing activities.

Recording Activity Relating to the Capital Lease Obligation

The lessee typically makes the first lease payment at the date of inception, although this is not necessary.[7] When the first payment is made at inception,

---

[7] When the first lease payment does not occur at inception, it will be discounted to determine the present value of the minimum lease payments (the value of the obligation under capital leases). When it is made, the payment will be first applied to interest accruing from inception to the first lease payment, with the balance applied to reducing the obligation under capital leases, as is demonstrated for the later lease payments in the example.

recording the first payment reduces the obligation under capital leases by the value of the entire payment since no implicit interest is computed on a payment made at inception. In the case of ABC Co., the entry to record the payment would appear as follows:

December 31, 1993:
Obligation under capital lease   100,000
   Cash   100,000
To record the lease payment at inception of the lease.

From this point on, activity will relate to accrual of interest expense on the lease obligation and recording the minimum lease payments as repayment of interest and principal on the obligation. Using the information available at the inception of the lease, an amortization schedule for the liability can be computed. The amortization schedule for the liability depends on the interest rate selected and on the size and timing of the minimum lease payments under the lease. Exhibit 17.3 presents an amortization schedule for the lease obligation ABC Co. entered into on December 31, 1993.

The amortization schedule in Exhibit 17.3 begins with the present value of the obligation at inception. The first payment is fully applied to the principal of the obligation and results in a liability of $460,700 to be reported in the balance sheet at December 31, 1993. The ending liability in column (5) carries over to the beginning liability of the next year in column (1). Interest accrues on the beginning liability at 16% until December 31, at which time the lease payment covers the accrued interest, with any excess applied against the principal. For 1994, the interest is $73,712 (16% × $460,700]. With a lease payment of $100,000, the principal reduction is $26,288. This leaves an ending balance of $434,412. Note that this represents the present value of the remaining minimum lease payments discounted at 16%.

ABC CO.
Amortization Schedule for the Capital Lease Liability

Interest Rate = 16%

Year	(1) Liability at Beginning of Year	(2) Lease Payment	(3) Interest Portion	(4) Principal Portion	(5) Liability at End of Year
1993	$560,700	$100,000	$ 0	$100,000	$460,700
1994	460,700	100,000	73,712	26,288	434,412
1995	434,412	100,000	69,506	30,494	403,918
1996	403,918	100,000	64,627	35,373	368,545
1997	368,545	100,000	58,967	41,033	327,512
1998	327,512	100,000	52,402	47,598	279,914
1999	279,914	100,000	44,786	55,214	224,700
2000	224,700	100,000	35,952	64,048	160,652
2001	160,652	100,000	25,704	74,296	86,356
2002	86,356	100,000	13,644	86,356	0

EXHIBIT 17.3
ABC Co.—Amortization Schedule for the Capital Lease Liability

ABC's journal entry to record the activity relating to the capital lease obligation in 1994 would appear as follows:

December 31, 1994:

Obligation under capital lease	26,288	
Interest expense	73,712	
Cash		100,000

To record the interest expense and principal reduction relating to the minimum lease payment for 1994.

ABC would make an entry similar to that above for each year from 1995 through 2002 to record interest expense and principal reduction from the minimum lease payments. The interest on the capital lease obligation is subject to accrual should the accounting period not coincide with the timing of the lease payments. In addition, any payments for executory costs or for contingent lease payments would be directly charged to expense during the period. As with interest expense, these costs are subject to accrual at year-end.

As the lessee actually disburses cash to make the minimum lease payments, the portion allocated to the reduction of principal is identified as a financing cash outflow in the cash flow statement. The portion allocated to interest is an operating cash flow. This includes the initial lease payment that may arise at the inception of the lease, although in that case the entire payment is a reduction of principal and identified as a financing cash flow.

Recording Activity Relating to the Asset Acquired by Capital Lease

Recording activity relating to an asset acquired under a capital lease will depend on the nature of the asset acquired. In the example above, ABC acquired equipment that should be depreciated by the same depreciation methods used for similar equipment acquired by purchase. If the asset acquired were an intangible asset, it would be included with this category of assets in the balance sheet; and periodic amortization of the recorded value would be appropriate using the guidelines discussed in Chapter 12.

When a lease meets either Criterion 1 or 2, the depreciation period will be the asset's useful life. If Criterion 3 or 4 is the basis for capitalization, the depreciation period should be limited to the lease term. If a guaranteed residual exists, the asset's salvage value should be set equal to the guaranteed residual. This will result in the asset's value and the obligation under capital lease (including accrued interest) being equated at the end of the lease term. As a result, if the asset is sold for an amount equal to or more than the guaranteed residual, the lessee will record no gain or loss at expiration of the lease since removing the residual asset value will also remove the remaining lease obligation and accrued interest.

In the case of ABC Co., the lease qualified as a capital lease under Criterion 4 and, therefore, will have an amortization life equal to the lease term of 10 years. Using straight-line amortization, the annual charge will be $56,070. ABC's journal entry to record the depreciation for 1994 would appear as follows:

December 31, 1994:

Depreciation expense	56,070	
Accumulated depreciation		56,070

To record depreciation for 1994 on the equipment acquired under
 capital lease.

Each year, ABC will make entries to record the depreciation expense on
the asset similar to that above.

The Treatment of Guaranteed Residuals

Suppose the Margaux Corporation enters into a three-year lease to acquire the
use of equipment on December 31, 1993. The lease requires annual lease payments of $200,000 at the beginning of each lease year and guarantees the resid-
ual value of the leased asset at $70,000 at the end of the lease term. The lease is
a capital lease, and the lessor's implicit rate (which is known by Margaux and
is below Margaux's incremental borrowing rate) is 8%. How will the guaranteed residual be handled in recording the capital lease?

First, the initial obligation under capital lease will include the discounted value
of the three lease payments and the guaranteed residual. Using the 8% interest rate,
the present value of the minimum lease payments is computed as follows:

12/31/93	$200,000 × 1.0000	=	$200,000
12/31/94	200,000 × 0.9259	=	185,180
12/31/95	200,000 × 0.8573	=	171,460
12/31/96	70,000 × 0.7938	=	55,566
Totals	$670,000		$612,206

The amortization schedule for the obligation would contain the following
interest and principal payments:

Year	Liability at Beginning of Year	Lease Payment	Interest Portion	Principal Portion	Liability at End of Year
1993	$612,206	$200,000	$ 0	$200,000	$412,206
1994	412,206	200,000	32,976	167,024	245,182
1995	245,182	200,000	19,615	180,385	64,797
1996	64,797	0	5,203*	0	70,000

*Amount adjusted due to rounding in compound interest computations

At the end of the lease term, Margaux will have accrued interest payable
of $5,203; and the remaining balance in the capital lease obligation will be
$64,797, for a total liability of $70,000. At the same time, the property, plant,
and equipment would also have a net book value of $70,000 as the guaranteed
residual would have been used as the salvage value for depreciating the
equipment acquired under capital lease. If the lessor sold the asset for a value
at or above the guaranteed residual, Margaux would retire the asset and
remaining liability without any gain or loss as follows:

December 31, 1993:

Obligation under capital lease	64,797	
Accrued interest payable	5,203	
Accumulated depreciation	542,206	
Property, plant, and equipment		612,206

To record the termination of the lease when the no payment is
required under the guaranteed residual.

In the event that the asset sold for less than the guaranteed residual, Margaux would be required to make up any shortfall. This would be recorded as a cash outflow and a loss to Margaux at December 31, 1993. For example, suppose the asset sold for only $45,000 at the end of the lease. Margaux would be required to pay an additional $25,000 to the lessor. Margaux's journal entry to record this would appear as follows:

December 31, 1993:

Loss on disposition of equipment	25,000	
Obligation under capital lease	64,797	
Accrued interest payable	5,203	
Accumulated depreciation	542,206	
Property, plant, and equipment		612,206
Cash		25,000

To record the termination of the lease when payment is
required under the guaranteed residual.

Recording an Operating Lease by the Lessee

Should a lease fail all the tests for capitalization, it will be treated as an operating lease. The costs associated with operating leases are treated as period expenses, but they are subject to accrual at the end of the fiscal year. Assuming the lease in the ABC Co. example discussed earlier was operating instead of capital, the entry for the payment at inception would appear as:

December 31, 1993:

Prepaid rent	100,000	
Cash		100,000

To record the prepayment of the first year's lease expense.

At the end of 1994, the prepaid rent must be charged to expense of the period and the second lease payment recorded. ABC would record these events as follows:

December 31, 1994:

Rent expense	100,000	
Prepaid rent		100,000

To amortize the prepaid rent expense accrued in 1993.

December 31, 1994:

Prepaid rent	100,000	
Cash		100,000

To record prepayment of second year's lease expense.

If payments under an operating lease are not uniform, Technical Bulletin 85-3 requires that the periodic expense should reflect an equal amount of lease expense each period.[8] The expense is determined by spreading the total minimum lease payments over the lease term on a straight-line basis. This implies that if annual rental fees are rising, the lessee will accrue expense at an amount larger than the minimum lease payment. In turn, this requires the creation of a liability that will be reduced in future years when the payments begin to exceed the expense. If lease payments are higher in the early periods of the lease, a prepaid asset will be used to accumulate the difference between the payment and the periodic expense.

Capital Versus Operating Leases—Effects on Lessee's Financial Statements

When a lease is classified as a capital lease, the lessee's balance sheet will reflect an asset and a liability that would not appear if the lease were classified as operating. The lessee's income statement will reflect both depreciation and interest expense over the term of a capital lease instead of rent expense that would be reported under an operating lease. How do these differences affect the impression a reader gets from examining the financial statements?

Using the ABC Co. example discussed earlier, ABC's balance sheet would report a significantly higher level of debt under the capital lease, compared to the operating lease alternative. In turn, this would result in a much higher ratio of the book value of debt to the book value of equity (leverage ratio). Since higher leverage is generally a signal of higher risk, classifying the lease as capital would appear nonadvantageous to ABC. Given a choice, ABC's management would probably prefer that their lease activity not be classified as capital lease activity.

However, caution must be used in reaching this conclusion. While it is true that the decision to classify a lease as capital, rather than operating, will result in a higher leverage ratio for the lessee, management may use the financial reports to inform investors about the nature of the company's leases. If investors know about the existence of leasing activity, they will develop expectations regarding the amount of leasing a company is involved in. For some companies, this estimate may be too low; for others, too high. Companies for which the estimate is too high have an incentive to disclose information on leasing activity to correct the investors' estimation error. Once this happens, only companies for which investors originally underestimated the effects of leasing will have no disclosures. In turn, investors will revise their beliefs about the company's level of leasing activity. Ultimately, disclosure may occur solely due to managerial self-interest.

The history of leasing disclosures, and particularly the capitalization of leases, suggests that corporate managements fought hard to avoid requirements for capitalization. From this we can conclude that while there may be occasions where managerial self-interest might drive disclosure, other forces must have been at work in the area of leasing to restrict disclosure.

The fact that financial reporting requirements adopted by the FASB treat leases as capital or operating reduces the possible information that could be

---

[8] "Accounting for Operating Leases with Schedule Rent Increases," *FASB Technical Bulletin No. 85-3* (November 1985), para. 2–3.

conveyed to investors. The principle of full disclosure suggests that in addition to the categorization of leases as capital and operating for financial statement purposes, additional information is needed. This is the basis for the extensive note disclosure requirements for lessees that will be discussed shortly.

As for the effects on income, the pattern of reported expenses for ABC under each alternative is displayed in Exhibit 17.4. The computations reveal that while the components of expense are different, the impact on annual reported income of classifying a lease as capital instead of operating is not as dramatic as the balance sheet consequences. The extent to which the differences between annual income and the balance sheet consequences differ is affected by the depreciation method chosen and the pattern of lease payments. Accelerated depreciation methods, and/or a pattern of lease payments that has smaller payments early in the lease and larger ones later, will result in a greater disparity between expenses reported under each type of lease in its early years.

In summary, the information contained in, and the interpretation of, financial statements for firms that are extensively involved in leasing as a lessee requires significant familiarity with the financial reporting requirements relating to capital and operating leases. Naive use of summary measures such as leverage ratios can lead to inappropriate comparisons between firms heavily involved in long-term operating leases and others having significant capital leases. While financial reporting requirements dichotomize leases into only two categories, the economic factors at play may make some firms extensively using operating lease much closer to those using capital leases than other firms with operating leases.

Disclosure Requirements for the Lessee

When a lessee prepares its financial statements, several disclosure requirements must be met for both capital and operating leases. These requirements

EXHIBIT 17.4
ABC Co.— Comparison of Expense Recognition Under Capital and Operating Leases for the Lessee

ABC CO.
Comparison of Expense Recognition Under Capital and Operating Leases for the Lessee

	CAPITAL LEASE ALTERNATIVE			OPERATING LEASE ALTERNATIVE
Year	Interest	Depreciation	Total	Rent
1994	$ 73,712	$ 56,070	$ 129,782	$ 100,000
1995	69,506	56,070	125,576	100,000
1996	64,624	56,070	120,694	100,000
1997	58,967	56,070	115,037	100,000
1998	52,402	56,070	108,472	100,000
1999	44,786	56,070	100,856	100,000
2000	35,952	56,070	92,022	100,000
2001	25,704	56,070	81,774	100,000
2002	13,644	56,070	69,714	100,000
2003	0	56,070	56,070	100,000
Total	$439,300	$560,700	$1,000,000	$1,000,000

include a general description of the lessee's leasing arrangements with special attention to:

1. The method of determining any contingent rental payments
2. The existence and terms of any renewal or purchase options
3. Any restrictions placed on the company as a result of the leases such as dividend restrictions or debt limits.

The financial statements must report separately the obligation under capital leases as well as the assets held under capital leases (net of any accumulated amortization or depreciation). These balances should not be included with other liabilities or assets.

In addition, the following data must be presented:[9]

1. The gross dollar investment in assets held under capital leases, by major classification.
2. A summary of the total minimum lease payments under capital leases for each of the next five years and the total minimum lease payments for periods beyond five years. The total is to be reduced by any executory costs and imputed interest to reconcile to the balance sheet lease obligation at the end of each reported period.
3. The total minimum sublease rentals, if any, for both capital and operating leases, individually.
4. The total contingent rentals for all periods represented in the income statement, as well as the rental expense for each period under all operating leases. Rental expense should be divided into minimum rentals, contingent rentals, and sublease rentals.
5. A summary of the minimum rental payments under all operating leases for each of the next five years.

Exhibit 17.5 is an excerpt from the Albertson's, Inc. annual report dated February 1, 1990, covering its disclosures relating to leases. Note that the disclosures are actually in three basic parts:

1. Information on the asset side of the balance sheet regarding assets acquired under capital lease and their depreciation (amortization)
2. Information on liabilities recorded on the liability side of the balance sheet relating to capital lease obligations and minimum lease payments
3. Information on the expenses reported under operating leases

Albertson's also reports the present value of the minimum rental payments under operating leases, as if these were treated as capital leases. This is not required, but it can be useful to financial statement users. For users who treat all leases with minimum required lease payments as a form of long-term debt, they can simply add the reported present value of the minimum rental payments, $341,000,000, to the liabilities reported in the balance sheet of Albertson's and then recompute debt-to-equity ratios with the new amount for debt. Without this information, users could attempt to discount the reported minimum rentals; but given the large amount that will occur after 1994

---

[9] SFAS No. 13, *op. cit.*, para. 16.

ALBERTSON'S, INC.
Lease Disclosures for the Lessee

The company leases a portion of its real estate. The typical lease period is 25 to 30 years and most leases contain renewal options. Exercise of such options is dependent on the level of business conducted at the location. In addition, the company leases certain equipment. Some leases contain contingent rental provisions based on sales volume at retail units or miles travelled for trucks.

Assets under capital leases are capitalized using interest rates appropriate at the inception of each lease. Contingent rentals associated with capital leases were $3,115,000 in 1989, $3,036,000 in 1988, and $2,417,000 in 1987. Following is an analysis of the company's assets under capital lease (in thousands):

	February 1, 1990	February 2, 1989	January 28, 1988
Real Estate	$141,980	$144,523	$140,466
Equipment	1,745	3,614	3,684
	$143,725	$148,137	$144,150
Accumulated Amortization	$ 66,113	$ 63,717	$ 57,910

Future minimum lease payments for assets under capital leases at February 1, 1990 are as follows (in thousands):

	Real Estate	Equipment	Total
1990	$ 16,422	$501	$ 16,923
1991	16,216	344	16,560
1992	16,041	100	16,141
1993	15,778	36	15,814
1994	15,591	7	15,598
Remainder	141,113		141,113
Total minimum obligations	221,161	988	222,149
Less executory costs	(128)		(128)
Net minimum obligations	221,033	988	222,021
Less interest	(109,760)	(190)	(109,950)
Present value of net minimum obligations	111,273	798	112,071
Less current portion	(4,740)	(382)	(5,122)
Long-term obligations at February 1, 1990	$106,533	$416	$106,949

Capital lease obligations terminated in 1989 amounted to $3,296,000. Capital lease obligations incurred amounted to $3,482,000 in 1989, $5,094,000 in 1988, and $7,494,000 in 1987. These transactions are considered noncash items and, accordingly, are not reflected in the consolidated cash flows.

Minimum obligations have not been reduced by minimum capital sublease rentals of $8,129,000 receivable in the future under noncancellable capital subleases. Executory costs include such items as property taxes and insurance.

Rent expense under operation leases was as follows (in thousands):

	1989	1988	1987
Minimum rent	$55,653	$52,333	$48,545
Contingent rent	3,889	4,387	3,869
	59,542	56,720	52,414
Less sublease rent	(12,050)	(10,844)	(8,978)
	$47,942	$45,876	$43,436

EXHIBIT 17.5

Albertson's, Inc.—
Lease Disclosures
for the Lessee

ALBERTSON'S, INC.
Lease Disclosures for the Lessee (Continued)

Future minimum lease payments for all noncancellable operating leases and related subleases having a remaining term in excess of one year at February 1, 1990 are as follows (in thousands):

	Real Estate	Subleases
1990	$ 46,803	$ (4,919)
1991	47,526	(4,789)
1992	47,161	(4,280)
1993	46,623	(3,751)
1994	46,483	(3,353)
Remainder	651,116	(23,438)
Total minimum obligations (receivables)	$885,712	$(44,530)

The present value of minimum rental payments under operating leases, calculated using the incremental interest rates at the inception of the lease, is approximately $341,000,000 at February 1, 1990.

($651,116,000 as reported), it would be difficult to estimate a present value for these payments since we cannot determine how this lump sum is distributed over the years following 1994.

ACCOUNTING BY THE LESSOR

Lessors classify leases into one of three categories: sales-type leases, direct financing leases, or operating leases. Classifying a lease as a sales-type or direct financing lease implies that the essence of the transaction is a transfer of substantially all of the property rights in the asset from the lessor to the lessee. A lease is only an operating lease if it fails to meet the criteria for classification as a sales-type or direct financing lease.

When the lessor is a manufacturer or dealer who engages in both sales and leases of the asset and when the lease transfers substantially all of the property rights to the lessee, the lease is called a sales-type lease. Recording a sales-type lease requires the lessor to recognize revenue at the inception of the lease based on the present value of the future cash flows under the lease contract, including any unguaranteed residual. Since the lessor is a manufacturer/dealer, the asset being leased was previously carried as inventory. When the revenue is recognized, the lessor will charge the cost of the inventory to cost of sales. The lessor will also record interest income over the life of the lease.

In cases where a corporation is not a manufacturer or dealer of the leased asset but elects to lease assets previously used in its own production process, the lease may also be classified as a sales-type lease if gain or loss is implied by the lease terms and the lease meets all the other criteria of a capital lease for the lessor. The major difference here is that the lessor will record any income generated from the lease of this asset as a gain or loss on disposition since the asset is not an inventory item.

When the lessor is not a manufacturer/dealer, nor has it utilized the leased asset in its own production process, a lease that transfers substantially all of the property rights in the leased asset to the lessee is classified as a direct financing lease. The primary trait of a direct financing lease is that the lessor generates income under the lease solely from the implicit interest embedded in the lease payments. There is no dealer profit to record at the inception of the lease; and so, the lessor records no revenue (gain) at that time. At inception, the leased asset is removed from the lessor's financial records and a receivable of equal value is created.

Over the life of the lease, the lessor will record interest income, which represents the lessor's only source of profit in these leases. A bank entering into a capital lease of equipment by purchasing the equipment from a manufacturer and then immediately leasing it to a lessee, which was discussed earlier in the chapter, is a classic example of a direct financing lease.

Criteria for Identifying Sales-Type and Direct Financing Leases by the Lessor

To be classified as a capital lease, the lease must satisfy one of the same four criteria required for a capital lease for the lessee. In addition, both of the following two criteria must be met:

1. The collectibility of the minimum lease payments must be reasonably assured.
2. No important uncertainties regarding the future costs the lessor will incur can remain.

Recall from the discussion of revenue (gain) recognition in Chapters 4 and 5 that to recognize income, it must be earned and the seller must receive assets whose fair value can be readily determined. Criterion 1 relates to the determination of the value of the lease receivable. If collection is reasonably assured, an allowance for uncollectible lease payments can be used to recognize any potential losses from noncollection in a reliable manner. As a result, revenue (gain) can be recognized at the time of the exchange.

Criterion 2 requires that the lessor has substantially completed all performance required under the contract. Without substantial performance, revenue cannot be recognized. This criterion does not require that all performance be completed. However, a reliable estimate of any future cost the lessor will incur to complete the transaction should be possible.

The costs to be considered in applying Criterion 2 above do not include costs for insurance or taxes over the life of the lease. These costs are matched against the interest income recognized in each period. Rather, the costs considered here represent commitments such as warranties on the leased asset, installation costs, or other types of commitments regarding the asset's initial exchange. These types of costs should be accrued at the time the sale is recorded. For example, if the lessor in a sales-type lease commits to installing the asset and the installation costs can be reliably estimated, then these costs should be accrued as an expense at the inception of the lease and revenue recognized at that time, even if the installation occurs sometime later.

Given the presence of these two additional criteria, it is possible for a lease to be a capital lease for the lessee and an operating lease for the lessor. When this occurs, both companies will record the same asset. The lessor will continue to carry the asset at historical cost, and the lessee will capitalize the asset as well. It is also possible for the lessor to record a lease as a capital lease when the lessee does not if there are multiple lessees involved in the exchange, each one acquiring part of the use of the asset. In such a circumstance, no company records the asset.

Before recording a lease as a capital lease, the lessor must determine which of the two types of capital leases the contract represents. For either a sales-type or direct financing lease, the lessor must determine the interest rate that will equate the present value of the minimum lease payments (excluding any executory costs) plus any unguaranteed residual at the end of the lease to the asset's current fair market value. As discussed earlier, this determines the implicit interest rate in the lease. The lessor always uses the implicit rate to discount the cash flows under the lease.

Sales-Type Leases

Following the determination of the implicit rate in a sales-type lease, the lessor must determine the classification of the asset on the balance sheet prior to the lease. If the asset was inventory, then the lessor will recognize revenue along with a charge to cost of sales for the cost of the inventory. If the asset was other than inventory, the lessor should determine gain or loss.

Sale of Inventory   Assume that on December 31, 1994, Bordeau Company (the lessor) leased a machine that it manufactures to Delta Company (the lessee). The lease calls for three annual lease payments of $300,000 each, due at the beginning of each year. Delta pays all executory costs. At the end of the lease, the machine will belong to Delta; Bordeau will receive no residual value at the end of the lease. Bordeau normally sells this equipment for $820,660, which results in an implicit interest rate of 10% for the lease. The cost to manufacture the machine was $500,000. Since the asset represents the lessor's normal inventory, Bordeau's journal entries to record the sale and the lease appear as follows:

December 31, 1994:		
Minimum lease payments receivable	900,000	
Unearned interest on minimum lease receivables		79,340
Sales		820,660
To record the sale via a capital lease.		

December 31, 1994:		
Cost of sales	500,000	
Inventory		500,000
To relieve the inventory for the carrying value of the asset sold via the capital lease.		

In the first of these journal entries, the minimum lease payment receivable represents the gross value of the minimum lease payments plus any unguaranteed residual value from the asset at the end of the lease term. For Bordeau, this is simply the sum of the three minimum lease payments since ownership of the asset will transfer to Delta at the end of the lease.

The unearned interest on minimum lease receivables represents the portion of the future minimum lease payments and unguaranteed residual that are allocated to interest by discounting these future cash flows. The net difference between the minimum lease payments receivable and the unearned interest is referred to as the **net lease receivable** and is equal to the present value of the lessor's future cash flows under the terms of the lease. At inception, the lessor's net investment in the lease receivable is equivalent to the revenue generated from the sale, which is also equivalent to the current fair market value of the asset being leased.

If Bordeau were to prepare a balance sheet on December 31, 1994, after recording the sales-type lease (but before recording the receipt of the first lease payment), it would report the following as a receivable:

Minimum lease payments receivable	$900,000
Unearned interest	(79,340)
Net lease receivable	$820,660

Part of this balance would be reported as a current asset (the amounts to be collected within the next year), and the remainder would be classified as a noncurrent receivable.

By recording the sales revenue and cost of sales in this fashion, the accounting records treat this sales-type lease in two parts:

1. A sale of the property rights represented by the asset that requires immediate recognition of revenues and costs
2. A financing arrangement that gives rise to a long-term receivable

In that way, the accounting records treat these exchanges in the same manner as a sale of inventory on credit.

Sale of Other Assets   If Bordeau had decided to lease a piece of equipment it had previously used in its own production process and the lease qualified as a capital lease, how would the process of recording such a lease differ from that described above? Using the information relating to the lease by Bordeau, but assuming the leased asset was a piece of equipment that Bordeau had acquired some time ago for $600,000 and that accumulated depreciation of $140,000 had been accrued prior to the inception of the lease, the following entry would be appropriate:

December 31, 1994:		
Minimum lease payments receivable	900,000	
Accumulated depreciation	140,000	
Unearned interest on minimum lease receivables		79,340
Property, plant, and equipment		600,000
Gain on sale of property, plant, and equipment		360,660
To record the receivable, unearned interest, and gain on the sales-type lease.		

In this example, the leased asset is not the lessor's normal inventory, but a gain or loss was implied by comparing the present value of the minimum lease payments to the net book value of the leased asset prior to the exchange.

The recording process is basically the same as the sales-type lease example above, with an important exception. At inception, Bordeau recognizes no revenue, and cost of sales is not affected when it records the lease. Instead, the net receivable arising from the sale will be offset directly against the asset's carrying cost to determine a net gain or loss from the lease.

Accounting for Activity Relating to the Minimum Lease Payments Receivable After Inception

Following the recording of the actual sale, collections of the minimum lease payments will be recorded as a reduction of the receivable. Interest will be accrued as interest income based on the passage of time. Since Bordeau receives the first lease payment at the inception of the lease, it will record the payment, without any accrual of interest, in the following manner:

December 31, 1994:

Cash	300,000	
Minimum lease payments receivable		300,000

To record receipt of the first lease payment at inception.

As time passes, interest will be accrued on the net uncollected balance of the receivable. As the interest income is recognized, the unearned interest on minimum lease payments receivable will be reduced. If there are payments for executory costs or contingent lease payments, these revenues will be recognized when earned; and any costs incurred will be charged to expense in such a manner as to match them properly against the revenue recognized. Exhibit 17.6 presents the amortization schedule that Bordeau Company would use to recognize interest income over the remainder of the lease term. Bordeau's journal entries for each year would appear as follows:

December 31, 1995:

Cash	300,000	
Unearned interest on minimum lease payments receivable	52,060	
Interest income		52,060
Minimum lease payments receivable		300,000

To record receipt of the December 31, 1995, lease payment and recognize interest income for 1995.

EXHIBIT 17.6

Bordeau Company—
Schedule of Activity
Relating to a Capital
Lease from the
Lessor's Perspective

BORDEAU COMPANY
Schedule of Activity Relating to a Capital Lease from the Lessor's Perspective

Year	Lease Receivable Before Payment	Unearned Interest Before Payment	Minimum Lease Payment	Interest Portion	Principal Portion	Lease Receivable After Payment	Unearned Interest After Payment
1994	$900,000	$79,340	$300,000	$ 0	$300,000	$600,000	$79,340
1995	600,000	79,340	300,000	52,060	247,940	300,000	27,280
1996	300,000	27,280	300,000	27,280	272,720	0	0

December 31, 1996:

Cash	300,000	
Unearned interest in minimum lease payments receivable	27,280	
Interest income		27,280
Minimum lease payments receivable		300,000

To record receipt of the December 31, 1996, lease payment
and recognize interest income for 1996.

Direct Financing Leases

If, instead of manufacturing the asset leased to Delta, Bordeau Company had purchased it from another company for $820,660 immediately prior to entering into the lease, this lease would be a direct financing lease instead of a sales-type lease. Under a direct financing lease, no manufacturer's profit is recognized at the inception of the lease. Thus, no income effect is recorded. In a direct financing lease, the minimum lease payments receivable and unearned interest are determined in the same fashion as the sales-type lease. The lessor removes the leased asset from its books when the receivable and unearned interest are recorded as follows (using the information in the Bordeau example):

December 31, 1994:

Minimum lease payments receivable	900,000	
Unearned interest in minimum lease payments receivable		79,340
Property, plant, and equipment held for lease		820,660

To record the direct financing lease.

Note that in the entry above, the asset was carried as property, plant, and equipment held for lease. The purpose for using this account title is to remind you that in direct financing leases the assets under lease are not the lessor's typical inventory, nor are they the lessor's productive assets. This title describes a class of assets held for disposition that the lessor does not manufacture. If the lessor held such assets at a balance sheet date, they would probably be included under the caption of inventory for financial reporting purposes, since they are being held for sale via capital lease.

Accounting for Activity Relating to the Minimum Lease Payments Receivable After Inception   The journal entries used to recognize interest income and record the receipt of the minimum lease payments under a direct financing lease would be identical to those used in a sales-type lease. As a result, Bordeau would use the entries already provided in the sales-type lease example for the receipt of the first lease payment and those for the activity in 1995 and 1996 if the lease were a direct financing lease as well.

Accounting for Operating Leases by the Lessor

When it does not qualify for treatment as sales-type or direct financing, a lease is treated as an operating lease. In an operating lease, the lessor records lease revenue when the lease payment is earned. Any payments received for executory costs or contingent lease payments are recognized as revenue when earned. The lessor will charge to expense any costs associated with generating the lease revenues, as well as depreciation on the asset under lease.

Had the lease covering the transfer of the machine from Bordeau to Delta failed the tests for capitalization, Bordeau's entries to record the activity as an operating lease would have appeared as follows:

December 31, 1994:
| Cash | 300,000 | |
| Unearned rental income | | 300,000 |

To record receipt of the first rent payment covering 1995.

December 31, 1995:
| Unearned rental income | 300,000 | |
| Rental income | | 300,000 |

To recognize income from 1995 rental period.

| Cash | 300,000 | |
| Unearned rental income | | 300,000 |

To record receipt of the second rent payment covering 1996.

December 31, 1996:
| Unearned rental income | 300,000 | |
| Rental income | | 300,000 |

To recognize income from 1996 rental period.

| Cash | 300,000 | |
| Unearned rental income | | 300,000 |

To record receipt of the second rent payment covering 1997.

December 31, 1997:
| Unearned rental income | 300,000 | |
| Rental income | | 300,000 |

To recognize income from 1997 rental period.

In addition, since the lessor would still be carrying the leased asset as equipment on its books, Bordeau would continue to record depreciation expense on the equipment over the life of the lease.

Capital Versus Operating Leases—Effects on Lessor's Financial Statements

From the entries in the above examples of sales-type, direct financing, and operating leases, it is clear that these three different types of leases have different effects on the lessor's income statement and balance sheet. In both types of capital leases, the lessor removes one type of asset and replaces it with another. Typically, the leased asset is carried as a current asset, inventory, and is replaced with another asset, the net lease receivable, which is mostly noncurrent. For sales-type leases, the value of the net lease receivable differs from the value of the inventory by the amount of income or loss reported in the exchange. For a direct financing lease, the net lease receivable is of equal value to the inventory recorded prior to the lease.

When the lessor enters into an operating lease, the asset under lease is classified as a part of property, plant, and equipment and is depreciated. As a result, the effects of a capital and an operating lease on total current and total noncurrent assets are very similar. The balance sheet effects of operating and capital leases for lessors differ primarily by the subclass of asset recorded, capital leases generating receivables while operating leases result in recording of property, plant, and equipment.

The effect of capital leases on the lessor's income statement are more dramatic. Exhibit 17.7 demonstrates a comparison of the income effects under the three types of leases for Bordeau. To complete the table, depreciation on the asset under the operating lease was computed using straight-line depreciation with no salvage value. Note that the depreciable base differs under an operating lease in comparison to the sales-type and direct financing lease alternatives. This reflects the presence of the dealer's profit in the sales-type leases.

What you see in the comparison is a significant acceleration in the timing of income recognition for the lessor under a capital lease when compared to an operating lease. Even in the comparison of the direct financing lease and the operating lease (where the asset was acquired for the same cost under both cases), the interest income recognized under the direct financing lease is higher than the net effect of rental income and depreciation recorded under the operating lease in the early years of the lease term. This feature, combined with the improved balance sheet position of having a receivable recorded instead of the property, plant, and equipment, make classification of a lease as a capital lease more appealing to the lessor's managers than that of an operating lease.

Initial Direct Costs

Lessors face an additional problem in how to account for the costs of securing lease agreements with customers. Indirect costs such as advertising are always

EXHIBIT 17.7
Bordeau Company—
Comparison of
Pre-Tax Income for
Lessor Under Capital
and Operating
Leases

BORDEAU COMPANY
Comparison of Pre-Tax Income for Lessor Under Capital and Operating Leases

	SALES-TYPE LEASE			OPERATING LEASE		
Year	Gross Margin	Interest Income	Total	Rental Income	Depreciation Expense	Total
1994	$320,660	$ 0	$320,660	$ 0	$ 0	$ 0
1995	0	52,060	52,060	300,000	(166,667)	133,333
1996	0	27,280	27,280	300,000	(166,667)	133,333
1997	0	0	0	300,000	(166,666)	133,334

Depreciable Base for Equipment = $500,000

	DIRECT FINANCING LEASE			OPERATING LEASE		
Year	Gross Margin	Interest Income	Total	Rental Income	Depreciation Expense	Total
1994	$ 0	$ 0	$ 0	$ 0	$ 0	$ 0
1995	0	52,060	52,060	300,000	(273,553)	26,447
1996	0	27,280	27,280	300,000	(273,553)	26,447
1997	0	0	0	300,000	(273,554)	26,446

Depreciable Base for Equipment = $820,660

charged to expense as incurred. Costs that directly relate to completing lease agreements and increase as the volume of leasing transactions increase are referred to as **initial direct costs**. These costs include commissions, legal fees to write leases, and the cost of credit checks. Initial direct costs are matched against the revenues they generate. Since the pattern of revenue recognition differs for each type of lease, the exact method of accounting for initial direct costs depends on the type of lease.

In a sales-type lease, the sales revenue, equal to the present value of the minimum lease payments, is recorded when the lease is signed. Only interest income is deferred to later periods. Consequently, in a sales-type lease, the initial direct costs are charged to expense as incurred, thereby matching the costs and revenues. In an operating lease, the revenues are recorded on a straight-line basis over the lease term. Consequently, matching is achieved by capitalizing the initial direct costs and amortizing them on a straight-line basis over the lease term. For a direct financing lease, the interest income is recorded using the effective interest method. Thus, interest income is high in the early years of the lease when the net lease receivable value is high. It decreases over time as the net lease receivable decreases. To achieve the matching of revenues and expenses in a direct financing lease, the initial direct costs must be capitalized and amortized using the effective interest method in accordance with the requirements of SFAS No. 91.[10]

To demonstrate the process of amortization of the initial direct costs, consider the case of Able Company. Able incurred $910 of initial direct costs to complete a 3-year lease, entered into on January 1, 1994. Lease payments of $10,000 per year are due at the end of each year, and title to the asset passes to the lessee at the end of the lease. The leased equipment cost Able $24,860, and the lease is properly accounted for as a direct financing lease. As a result, Able would prepare the following journal entries at the inception of the lease:

January 1, 1994:

Minimum lease payments receivable	30,910	
Unearned interest income in minimum lease payments receivable		5,140
Equipment held for lease		24,860
Cash		910

To record the inception of the lease and capitalize the initial direct costs.

January 1, 1994:

Cash	10,000	
Minimum lease payments receivable		10,000

To record the receipt of the initial lease payment at inception.

The implicit interest rate in the lease, ignoring the initial direct costs, is 10%. Panel A of Exhibit 17.8 presents the amortization schedule for the lease payments at the implicit rate without consideration of the initial direct costs. Because Able incurred $910 of initial direct costs, its net lease receivable at

---

[10] "Accounting for Nonrefundable Fees and Costs Associated with Originating or Acquiring Loans and Initial Direct Costs of Leases," *Statement of Financial Accounting Standards No. 91* (Stamford, CT: FASB, December 1986).

inception increased to $25,770 ($30,910 – $5,140]. The interest rate that equates three annual payments of $10,000 each to a present value of $25,770 is only 8%. This becomes the new implicit rate Able will use to recognize interest income over the life of this lease. Using these facts, Able must create a new amortization schedule, which is presented in Panel B of Exhibit 17.8.

The amortization of the initial direct costs is determined by the difference between the amount of interest income reported in Panel A and Panel B. These amounts are set forth in Panel C. The journal entry Able would use to record the amortization of the unearned interest and the initial direct costs at the end of 1994 appears as follows:

December 31, 1994:
Unearned interest income in minimum lease payments
  receivable   2,490
    Interest income   2,060
    Minimum lease payments receivable   430
To record interest income and amortize the initial direct costs.

At the end of the lease term, the minimum lease payments receivable and the unearned interest income in minimum lease payments receivable will both fall to zero as a result of:

EXHIBIT 17.8

Treatment of Initial Direct Costs in Direct Financing Leases

Treatment of Initial Direct Costs in Direct Financing Leases

Panel A: Amortization Schedule Without Initial Direct Costs

Year	Net Investment at Beginning of Year	Payment	Interest	Principal Reduction	Net Investment at Year-End
1994	$24,860	$10,000	$2,490	$7,510	$17,350
1995	17,350	10,000	1,740	8,260	9,090
1996	9,090	10,000	910	9,090	0

Panel B: Amortization Schedule With Initial Direct Costs

Year	Net Investment at Beginning of Year	Payment	Interest	Principal Reduction	Net Investment at Year-End
1994	$25,770	$10,000	$2,060	$7,940	$17,830
1995	17,830	10,000	1,430	8,570	9,260
1996	9,260	10,000	740	9,260	0

Panel C: Amortization of Initial Direct Costs

Year	Interest Income at 10%		at 8%		Amortization
1994	$2,490	–	$2,060	=	$430
1995	1,740	–	1,430	=	310
1996	910	–	740	=	170
			Total		$910

1. The collections of lease payments
2. The amortization of the initial direct costs
3. The recognition of the interest income using the revised 8% implicit rate

Disclosure of Lease Activity by the Lessor

Lessors are required to provide a general description of all the leasing arrangements entered into. For leases that qualify as capital leases for the lessor, the following disclosures are required:[11]

1. The future minimum lease payments must be disclosed with deductions for any executory costs and any allowance for uncollectible minimum lease payments.
2. The unguaranteed residual values accruing to the lessor.
3. The amount of unearned income included in the minimum lease receivable.
4. A reconciliation of the future minimum lease payments for each of the next five years and in aggregate.
5. The amount of unearned income recognized in each period presented in the income statement to offset the initial direct costs in direct financing leases.
6. The total contingent rentals included in income for each period presented.

For leases classified as operating, the following disclosures are required:

1. The carrying amount of assets subject to operating leases by major classification, including the accumulated depreciation recorded.
2. A reconciliation of the future minimum lease payments under operating leases for the next five years.
3. Total contingent rentals included in income for each period presented.

Exhibit 17.9 presents the notes to the financial statements of McDonnell Douglas Corporation (MDC) for 1989 regarding its activities as a lessor. Notice that MDC combines receivables from capital leases and other notes in its disclosure of the future payments receivable. In particular, the sum of the column labeled principal payments and installments is $3,412 at December 31, 1989. This amount reconciles to the sum of the minimum lease payments (undiscounted) of $2,748 plus the value of the notes receivable $664 as of December 31, 1989. As a result, MDC has met all of the disclosure requirements listed above, as long as the minimum lease payments contain no executory costs and there are no contingent rentals.

Accounting for Sales-Type Leases Involving Real Estate

Recognition of the dealer profit present in sales-type leases that involve real estate is governed by the requirements of SFAS No. 66, "Accounting for Sales

---

[11] SFAS No. 13, *op. cit.*, para. 23.

of Real Estate," not SFAS No. 13. As discussed in Appendix 5.2, SFAS No. 66 sets forth a number of criteria that must be met to recognize the profit on a real estate sale at the time of the exchange. In general, to fully recognize any profit on such a transaction, the seller must be transferring ownership to the buyer without retaining any continuing interest in the property or incurring any continuing responsibility for development, and the terms of the exchange must require a sufficient down payment as well as sufficient periodic payments of any of the purchase price financed by the seller to reflect the normal terms of a third-party mortgage. While the application of SFAS No. 66 to leases of real estate is beyond the scope of this text, it should be noted that the treatment of leases for land alone are evaluated differently than leases of both land and buildings.

EXHIBIT 17.9

McDonnell Douglas Corporation— Disclosures of Lease Activity by the Lessor

MCDONNELL DOUGLAS CORPORATION
Disclosures of Lease Activity by the Lessor

Finance Receivables and Property on Lease

The net investment in finance and lease receivables and property on lease consists of the following:

December 31 (dollars in millions)	1989	1988
Sales type and direct financing leases:		
Minimum lease payments	$ 2,748	$2,174
Residual values ($83 guaranteed at December 31, 1989)	340	300
Unearned income	$(1,025)	(786)
Net investment	2,063	1,688
Notes receivable	664	529
	2,727	2,217
Allowance for doubtful accounts	(47)	(44)
	2,680	2,173
Investment in operating leases, net of accumulated depreciation of $296 in 1989, $285 in 1988	589	522
	3,269	2,695
Property held for sale or lease	4	18
	$ 3,273	$2,713

The aggregate amount of scheduled principal payments and installments to be received on notes and lease receivables and minimum rentals to be received under noncancellable operating leases consist of the following at December 31, 1989:

	Principal Payments and Installments	Minimum Rentals
1990	$ 588	$116
1991	479	98
1992	479	69
1993	466	49
1994	316	32
After 1994	$1,084	52

Sale-Leaseback Arrangements

Companies may find it more useful to convert from owning their assets to leasing them. This may occur because the company no longer wishes to bear all the risks of ownership and needs only the right to use the asset in production. The company may also have several good investment opportunities it wishes to exploit and needs all of the financial capital it can obtain. A sale-leaseback arrangement is often the solution to these situations.

A **sale-leaseback** is actually a series of contracts. A company finds a second party willing to buy an asset (usually for cash) it currently owns and then enters into a lease arrangement whereby it retains the use of the asset but passes ownership to the second party. Since the lease generally requires periodic payments, one typically due at inception, the net effect for the company seeking a sale-leaseback is to make more cash available today for other uses while retaining the right to use the productive assets necessary for operations. The discussion that follows deals with the sale-leaseback of non-real estate assets. Accounting for the sale-leaseback of real estate is not discussed.

When a sale-leaseback of non-real estate assets arises, the appropriate treatment for the lease portion of the transaction is determined by applying the same rules for any other lease situation.[12] However, any gain or loss on the sale portion of the exchange is not recognized. Instead, the gain or loss is deferred and recognized periodically over the life of the lease. The periodic recognition of the gain or loss from the original sale reflects the depreciation process used for the leased asset, if the lease is a capital lease, or the rate at which the gross lease receivable is collected over the life of the lease.

For example, if 10% of the asset value is depreciated in the first year of a capital lease, 10% of the profit or loss on the sale is recognized as well. If the lease is not a capital lease, 10% of the gross lease payments need to be collectible during the first year of the operating lease so 10% of the profit or loss from the original sale can be recognized in that first year.

Exceptions to the general requirement that gains or losses on the sale be deferred in a sale-leaseback arise when:

1. The asset's fair market value is below its carrying value at the date of the initial sale
2. Only a minor part of the asset's remaining use is covered by the leaseback
3. When more than a minor part, but less than substantially all, of the remaining use is covered by the leaseback, and the profit on the sale exceeds the present value of the minimum lease payments

When the asset's fair value at the date of the sale-leaseback transaction is below its existing book value, any loss implied by the difference must be immediately recognized. This is a form of lower-of-cost-or-market requirement applied at the date of the sale-leaseback exchange.

The second exception arises when the discounted value of the lease payments under the leaseback are less than 10% of the fair market value of the

---

[12] Accounting for a sale-leaseback of real estate is also influenced by the requirements of SFAS No. 66 related to the nonretail sale of real estate. This issue is beyond the scope of this text.

property under lease. In this situation, the lease portion of the exchange transfers only a minor portion of the asset's remaining property rights and the sale is treated independently of the leaseback. Note that the leaseback cannot qualify as a capital lease under these conditions. All gains or losses from the sale are immediately recognized.

The last exception covers those cases when the seller-lessee realizes a profit on the sale that is larger than the discounted value of the future minimum lease payments. This occurs when the lease is characterized as not transferring substantially all of the asset's property rights back to the seller-lessee. Thus, the present value of the minimum lease payments must exceed 10% of the fair market value of the asset under lease. However, the lease could not be characterized as a capital lease, or it would transfer substantially all of the property rights to the lessee over the lease term. Leases that fall in this category must be operating leases.

In this situation, if the profit from the initial sale exceeds the discounted value of the minimum lease payments in the leaseback arrangement, the excess profits are immediately recognized. The future minimum lease payments are discounted using the lessee's incremental borrowing rate or the implicit interest rate, if known and lower. The remainder of the profit on the sale will be recognized over the period of the lease.

Leveraged Leases

In a **leveraged lease**, the lessor finances a substantial part of the cost of acquiring the leased asset by raising debt from a third-party lender. In addition, the debt must be such that the lender has no recourse, in the event of default, against any assets of the lessor, except the lease payments generated from the lease of the asset in question.

The special problems that arise in accounting for a leveraged lease pertain only to the lessor. Unaffected by the use of such a financing arrangement, the lessee evaluates the lease as it does for any other lease. If the lessor enters into a sales-type lease, it accounts for the leveraged lease as it does for all sales-type leases. Also, the lessor records separately the debt undertaken to finance the lease. The special accounting rules are only applicable to direct financing leases that are arranged as leveraged leases. A complete treatment of the accounting for leveraged leases is beyond the scope of this text. The specific rules for leveraged leases are contained in SFAS No. 13, paragraphs 108–114. These rules are demonstrated in Appendix E of SFAS No. 13 for those who wish more in-depth discussion of this material.

SUMMARY

Leases are contracts that transfer property rights from the lessor to the lessee in exchange for periodic lease payments. When substantially all of the property rights are transferred over the lease term and the lessee commits to minimum noncancellable lease payments, the lessor sells the asset to the lessee in this transaction.

When the substance of the contract is a sale, the lease is classified as a *capital lease*. This implies that the accounting process will record the transaction as if the lessor sold the asset to the lessee and took a receivable in exchange. If the exchange is not classified as a capital lease, both the lessee and lessor treat the periodic lease payments as rent expense or rental income for the periods covered by the lease payments.

Motivations to use leasing include both the allocation of certain tax benefits and risk sharing. Those companies in higher tax brackets can obtain larger benefits. Parties with differential access to information regarding the value of the various property rights present in any asset can share the risks through leasing.

Accounting for the lessee requires the application of several criteria to determine if a lease qualifies as a capital lease. When a lease meets one of the four criteria discussed in the chapter, the lessee records an asset at the inception of the lease, along with the associated long-term liability for the obligation under capital lease. Both the asset and obligation are valued using the present value of the minimum lease payments the lessee commits to under the terms of the lease. After inception, interest is accrued on the obligation under capital leases; and each lease payment is allocated between payment of interest and a residual decrease in the remaining obligation. The asset is depreciated (or amortized) using methods common for the type of asset acquired.

For the lessor, a lease must meet two additional criteria to be a capital lease. In addition, capital leases are divided into two categories: *sales-type leases* and *direct financing leases*. Sales-type leases arise when a profit or loss is implicit in the transaction beyond the interest component present in all deferred payment plans. Direct financing leases are those capital leases in which the only profit to the lessor is the implicit interest that is part of the minimum lease payments in the contract.

Special problems arise in handling *unguaranteed residuals*, *initial direct costs*, *sale-leaseback* transactions, and *leveraged leases*. Each of these special areas was discussed in turn. In addition, the chapter explored the financial statement consequences of treating a lease as capital or operating for both the lessee and the lessor. For the lessee, the financial statement implications were higher book leverage ratios and most likely lower earnings in the early years of the lease term when a lease was treated as a capital lease rather than an operating lease. In turn, this led us to speculate that lessees would generally prefer to classify leases as operating rather than capital. For lessors, higher income in the early years of the lease, along with improved balance sheet disclosures from the presence of a receivable compared to property, plant, and equipment, made capital leases preferable.

QUESTIONS

1. Who is a *lessor*? A *lessee*?
2. Why is a company motivated to lease an asset?
3. What is a *bargain renewal option* and how does it relate to leasing?
4. What is a *bargain purchase option*?
5. How does a *contingent lease payment* differ from a *minimum lease payment*?
6. What are *executory costs* and who pays for them?
7. What is the conceptual difference between a *capital* and an *operating* lease?

8. How do the four criteria for determining a capital lease for the lessee fit into the conceptual difference between a capital and an operating lease?

9. How does the lessee determine the interest rate used to discount future lease payments?

10. For the lessee, what financial statement effects result from treating a lease as a capital lease instead of an operating lease?

11. What is the difference between a *sales-type lease* and a *direct financing lease*?

12. What effect do *initial direct costs* have under a sales-type lease versus a direct financing lease?

13. What is a *sale-leaseback*, and why might these types of transactions exist?

14. What happens to the gain or loss from the sale portion of a sale-leaseback? On what does your answer depend?

EXERCISES

17-1. *Operating leases—minimum and contingent rentals; executory costs*

Glen Apparel, Inc., leases and operates a retail store. The following information relates to the lease for the year ended December 31, 1995:

(a) The store lease, an operating lease, calls for fixed monthly rent of $1,500 the first day of each month and an additional rent equal to 6% of net sales over $300,000 per calendar year. Net sales for 1995 are $900,000.

(b) Additionally, Glen paid executory costs to the lessor for property taxes of $5,000 and insurance of $2,500.

REQUIRED:

Prepare the journal entries Glen Apparel would record relating to this lease for 1995, assuming the payment for any contingent rentals is not made until three months after the end of the fiscal year.

17-2. *Renewal options and lease terms; classifying a lease*

Kern Corporation entered into a 10-year lease for the rental of retail space. The annual rental includes a fixed fee of $120,000 per year, payable on the first day of the year, and an additional rental computed as 3% of revenues in excess of $600,000. In addition, Kern has two renewal options for 10 years each that stipulate the fixed rental is to decline by 50% at each renewal date (falling to $60,000 at the first renewal, and $30,000 at the second). The additional rental fee will decline to 2% of sales in excess of $600,000 with the first renewal and 1% of sales in excess of $600,000 at the second renewal. The renewal terms are considered very favorable to Kern and represent significantly lower rentals than are typical for the area.

Kern's marginal borrowing rate is 15%, and it does not know the implicit rate present in the lease. Kern estimates that of the annual rentals, $5,000 relates to the costs of property taxes and insurance, which the lessor supplies; and this is not expected to change over the life of the lease. Kern is responsible for normal maintenance on the property. The space has a useful life of 35 years.

REQUIRED:

1. What is the lease term of this lease for purposes of classifying it as capital or operating?

2. What are the minimum lease payments over the life of the lease?

3. Based on the information provided, which criteria for capitalization (if any) does this lease meet?

17-3. *Criteria for capitalization; discount rate differences*

On January 2, 1995, Rice Company entered into a 10-year, noncancellable lease as lessee, requiring annual payments of $100,000 payable at the beginning of each year. Rice's incremental borrowing rate is 14%, while the lessor's implicit interest rate, known to Rice, is 12%. The leased property has an estimated useful life of 12 years. The lessor retains ownership of the property at expiration of the lease. The property is estimated to have a fair market value on January 2, 1995, of $630,000.

REQUIRED:

1. Which of the criteria used to determine whether the lease is a capital lease to Rice are satisfied? Which ones are not?
2. Prepare the journal entry for Rice to account for the activity relating to the lease during 1996.

17-4. *Computation of expenses for the lessee in a capital lease*

On January 1, 1995, Vick Company as lessee signed a 10-year, noncancellable lease for a machine, stipulating annual payments of $20,000. Vick made the first payment on January 1, 1995, and appropriately treated this transaction as a capital lease. The 10 lease payments have a present value of $135,180 at January 1, 1995, based on implicit interest of 10%.

REQUIRED:

1. Prepare the amortization schedule for the life of the lease that Vick could use to prepare its journal entries for interest expense over the lease.
2. What entries would be appropriate for 2000, assuming Vick uses straight-line amortization of leased assets?

17-5. *Computing the implicit rate*

An office equipment representative has a machine for sale or lease. If you buy the machine, the cost is $7,596. If you lease the machine, you will have to sign a noncancellable lease and make 4 payments of $2,000 each. You will make the first payment on the first day of the lease. At the time of the last payment, you will receive title to the machine.

REQUIRED:

Compute the implicit interest rate in this lease.

17-6. *Lessee's classification of a lease*

East Company leased a new machine from North Company on May 1, 1994, under a lease with the following information:

Lease term	10 years
Annual rental payable at beginning of each lease year	$40,000
Useful life of machine	15 years
Incremental borrowing rate	14%
Fair market value of machine at inception	$270,000

East has the option to purchase the machine on May 1, 2004, by paying $50,000, which approximates the machine's expected fair value on the option exercise date.

REQUIRED:

Is this a capital lease or an operating lease? Why?

17-7.   *Operating and capital lease accounting for the lessee: journal entries and classification*

On January 1, 1994, Ott Company leased a new machine from Wolf with the following pertinent information:

Lease term	12 years
Annual rental payable at beginning of each year	$70,000
Useful life of machine	15 years
Incremental borrowing rate	12%
Implicit interest rate	14%

The lease contains no renewal options, but Ott has an option to purchase the machine for $10,000 at the end of the lease. The asset's expected market value at the end of the lease is $50,000.

REQUIRED:

1. Does this qualify as a capital lease? Why or why not?
2. Prepare the journal entries for 1994 to record the lease, assuming it is a capital lease with straight-line amortization of the leased asset.
3. Prepare the journal entries for 1994 under the assumption that the lease is an operating lease.
4. Prepare the journal entries that would be made in the year 2004, assuming the purchase option is exercised under both the capital lease treatment and the operating lease treatment.

17-8.   *Guaranteed residuals; comparison of capital and operating leases*

Day, Inc., leased a machine for a period of 8 years, contracting to pay $200,000 at inception of the lease term on December 31, 1994, and $200,000 annually on December 31 for the next seven years. At the end of the lease, Day guaranteed the value of the machine would be at least $400,000. The expected market value of 8-year-old equipment of this type was $750,000. Day used a discount rate of 12% to record the lease as a capital lease.

REQUIRED:

1. What should Day record as the value of the asset under capital lease at inception?
2. What should Day record as the obligation under capital leases?
3. If the asset is sold at the end of the lease for $340,000, how will this effect Day's financial statements?

17-9.   *Initial costs, executory costs, and lease payments in operating leases*

On January 1, 1994, Taft Company leased a warehouse to Green under an operating lease for 10 years at $40,000 per year, payable the first day of each lease year. Taft paid $18,000 to a real estate broker as a finder's fee. The warehouse is depreciated $10,000 per year. On January 1, 1994, Taft incurred insurance costs of $2,000 and property taxes of $5,500.

REQUIRED:

How should Taft reflect these activities in its 1994 financial statements?

17-10. *Accounting for the lessor; executory costs borne by lessor*

Grady Company purchased a machine on July 1, 1995, for $720,000. The machine is expected to have a10-year life, no residual value, and will be depreciated by the straight-line method. On the same date, the machine was leased to Lesch Company for a 3-year period at an annual rental of $125,000. Grady could have sold the machine for $860,000 instead of leasing it. Grady incurred maintenance and other executory costs of $15,000 in 1995 under the terms of the lease.

REQUIRED:

How should the effects of this lease be accounted for in Grady's balance sheet and income statement as of December 31, 1995?

17-11. *Classification of lease by lessor; comparison of income under alternatives*

Grey Company manufactures equipment that is sold or leased. On December 31, 1994, Grey leased equipment to Ray for a 5-year period expiring December 31, 1999, at which date ownership of the leased asset will be transferred to Ray. Equal payments under the lease are $40,000 and are due on December 31 of each year. Ray made the first payment on December 31, 1994. Collectibility of the remaining lease payments is reasonably assured, and Grey has no material cost uncertainties. The normal sales price of the equipment is $154,200, and the equipment cost Grey $120,000.

REQUIRED:

1. Is this lease a sales-type, direct financing, or operating lease? Why?
2. Prepare a schedule to demonstrate how Grey's income statement will reflect the effects of this lease over its life.

17-12. *Classification of a lease by the lessor; journal entries*

On August 1, 1994, Kern Company leased a machine to Night Company for a 6-year period, requiring payments of $10,000 at the beginning of each year. The machine cost Kern $44,934, which is the fair value at the lease date, and has a useful life of 7 years with no residual value. Kern also incurred $3,032 of initial direct costs in consummating the lease. The company has a calendar year fiscal period. Night recorded the lease as a capital lease. Kern has determined that the lease payments are reasonably collectible, and Kern estimates the insurance and taxes it must pay on the machine will amount to approximately $1,000 per year. These costs will be paid on the anniversary date of the lease for the upcoming year. Kern has no other responsibilities under the lease.

REQUIRED:

1. Is the lease a sales-type, direct financing, or operating lease? Why?
2. What is Kern's implicit interest rate?
3. What interest rate will be used to amortize the unearned revenue if the lease is a capital lease?
4. Prepare the journal entries for 1994.

17-13. *Sales-type leases; initial direct costs; profit recognition*

Fox Company, a dealer in machinery and equipment, leased equipment to Tiger, Inc., on July 1, 1994. The lease is appropriately accounted for as a sale by Fox and as a purchase by Tiger. The lease is for a 10-year period (the useful life of the asset) expiring June 30, 2004. Tiger made the first of 10 equal annual payments of $500,000 on July 1, 1994.

Fox had purchased the equipment for $2,675,000 on January 1, 1994, and established a list selling price of $3,375,000. In addition, Fox incurred $12,000 of commissions to its salespeople in consummating the lease.

REQUIRED:

1. Assuming that the present value at July 1, 1994, of the rent payments over the lease term discounted at 12% (the appropriate interest rate) was $3,165,000, what is the amount of profit on the sale and the amount of interest income Fox should record for the year ended December 31, 1994?
2. How will the initial direct cost be accounted for?

17-14. *Sale-leasebacks; income statement effects*

On January 1, 1994, Marsh Company sold an airplane with an estimated useful life of 10 years. At the same time, Marsh leased back the airplane for 9 years in a lease that qualifies as a capital lease. Pertinent data are:

Sales price	$5,194,614
Book value of airplane	1,000,000
Accumulated depreciation on airplane	3,000,000
Annual rentals under leaseback:	
Years 1-3	1,200,000
Years 4-9	600,000
Implicit interest rate	12%

Annual rentals are due on the first day of each year.

REQUIRED:

What effects does the sale-leaseback have on Marsh's 1994 income?

17-15. *Sale-leasebacks; journal entries*

On December 31, 1994, Pell, Inc., sold a machine to Flax and simultaneously leased it back for 3 years, paying $75,000 per year under the lease. The leaseback contains no bargain purchase option, and the asset reverts to Flex at the end of the lease. Pertinent information is as follows:

Sales price	$360,000
Carrying amount	315,000
Accumulated depreciation	85,000
Estimated remaining useful life	12 years
Present value of lease rentals at 10%	$205,165 (implicit rate of 10%)

REQUIRED:

What journal entries should Pell make during 1994 and 1995 relating to this sale-leaseback?

17-16. *Sale-leaseback; deferral of profit*

The following information pertains to equipment sold by Bard Co. to Kerr Co. on December 31, 1995:

Sales price	$300,000
Book value	100,000
Estimated remaining economic life	20 years

Simultaneously with the sale, Bard leased back the equipment for a period of 10 years. The present value of the minimum lease payments totalled $165,000.

REQUIRED:

How much of the profit on the sale should Bard defer at December 31, 1995?

PROBLEMS

17-1.   *Lessee accounting; classification and journalization*

Arcan Corporation is in the business of leasing heavy machinery. On July 1, 1994, Arcan entered into a lease with Roadbuilder's of America for used equipment. The terms of the lease are as follows:

Term:	10 years
Required lease payments:	$75,000 on July 1, each year
Guaranteed residual:	$150,000
Expected residual value:	$200,000

At the inception of the lease, the equipment was 5 years old and had a remaining useful life of 15 years. Arcan purchased the used equipment for the lease just prior to inception for $518,792. At the end of the lease, the equipment reverts to Arcan. Roadbuilder's is to perform all maintenance.

REQUIRED:

1. Assuming that Roadbuilder's has a marginal borrowing rate of 15% and does not know Arcan's implicit rate, apply each of the criteria for a capital lease and determine which of these is satisfied.
2. Using the 15% discount rate, how will Roadbuilder's record the effect of entering into this lease?
3. Prepare an amortization schedule for the lease obligation presenting the balance as of July 1 of each year during the lease term.
4. What entries will Roadbuilder make at the end of its fiscal year on December 31, 1994?
5. Assuming that the equipment is sold for $150,000 in the final year of the lease, prepare the journal entries Roadbuilder's would make in the year 2004.

17-2.   *Lessor accounting; compliment to Problem 17-1*

Use the information in Problem 17-1.

REQUIRED:

1. What additional criteria must be met before Arcan will be required to treat this lease as a capital lease? Is this a sales-type lease or a direct financing lease? Why?
2. Compute Arcan's implicit rate for the lease.
3. Prepare the journal entries that Arcan would record during 1994, assuming it has a fiscal year-end on December 31, 1994.
4. Prepare the journal entries Arcan would make in the year 2004, again assuming that the asset was sold for $150,000 at the end of the lease term.

17-3.   *Lessee accounting—multiple leases; classification; journalization*

On January 1, 1994, Borman Company, a lessee, entered into three noncancellable leases for brand new equipment: Lease J, Lease K, and Lease L. None of the three leases transfer ownership of the equipment to Borman at the end of the lease term. Borman has an incremental borrowing rate of 15%.
The following information is peculiar to each lease:
(a) Lease J does not contain a bargain purchase option; the lease term is for 5 years, which is 80% of the equipment's estimated economic life. Minimum lease payments are $50,000 per year, including executory costs of $3,000. The implicit interest rate in the lease is 13%.

(b) Lease K contains a bargain purchase option; the lease term is for 3 years, which is 50% of the equipment's estimated economic life. Minimum lease payments are $15,000 per year, and there are no executory costs. The bargain purchase option can be exercised at the end of the third year by paying $60,000. The implicit rate in the lease is 17%.

(c) Lease L does not contain a bargain purchase option; the lease term is for 5 years, which is 50% of the equipment's estimated economic life. Minimum lease payments are $30,000 per year. Borman does not know the implicit rate in this lease, but the estimated fair market value of the equipment is $125,000.

REQUIRED:

1. How should Borman Company classify each of the three leases above? Why?
2. What amount, if any, should Borman record as a liability at the inception of the lease for each of the three leases above?
3. Prepare all journal entries required to record the activity relating to these leases for 1994 and 1995.

17-4.   *Lessee accounting for capital leases—essay*

On January 1, 1997, Lani Company entered into a noncancellable lease for a machine to use in its manufacturing operations. The lease transfers ownership of the machine to Lani by the end of the lease term. The term of the lease is 8 years. The minimum lease payment made by Lani on January 1, 1993, was one of 8 annual payments. At the inception of the lease, the criteria established for classification as a capital lease by the lessee were met.

REQUIRED:

1. What is the theoretical basis for the accounting standard that requires the lessee to capitalize certain long-term leases? Do not discuss the specific criteria for classifying a specific lease as a capital lease.
2. How should Lani account for this lease at its inception and determine the amount to be recorded?
3. What expenses related to this lease will Lani incur during the first year of the lease, and how will they be determined?
4. How should Lani report the lease transaction on its December 31, 1997, balance sheet?

   (AICPA adapted)

17-5.   *Lessor and lessee accounting for the same lease; journalization*

On February 20, 1994, Riley, Inc., purchased a machine for $1,100,000 for the purpose of leasing it. The machine is expected to have a 10-year life, no residual value, and will be depreciated on the straight-line basis. The machine was leased to Sutter Company on March 1, 1994, for a 4-year period at an annual rental of $216,000. There is no provision for the lessee to renew the lease or purchase the machine at the expiration of the lease term. However, Sutter did guarantee the asset's residual value to be at least $500,000 at the end of the lease. Riley expects the asset to be worth $507,808 at the end of the lease. Riley paid $22,504 of commissions associated with negotiating the lease in February 1994. Sutter has an incremental borrowing rate of 12%, and Riley has not determined the implicit rate in the lease. In any case, Sutter does not know what Riley's implicit rate is.

REQUIRED:

Prepare the journal entries for Riley and Sutter to record the activity related to the lease in 1994.

17-6. *Lessor and lessee accounting for the same lease; determining annual lease payments under the lease; journalization at inception*

Dumont Corporation, a lessor of office machines, purchased a new machine for $500,000 on December 31, 1993, which was delivered the same day (by prior arrangement) to Finley Company, the lessee.

The following information relating to the lease transaction is available:

(a) The leased asset has an estimated useful life of 7 years, which coincides with the lease term.

(b) At the end of the lease term, the machine will revert to Dumont, at which time it is expected to have a residual value of $60,000 (none of which Finley guarantees).

(c) Dumont's implicit interest rate (on its net investment) is 12%, which Finley knows.

(d) Finley's incremental borrowing rate is 14% at December 31, 1993.

(e) Lease rental consists of 7 equal annual payments, the first of which Finley paid on December 31, 1993.

(f) Dumont appropriately accounted for the lease as a direct financing lease and Finley accounts for it as a capital lease. Both lessor and lessee are calendar-year corporations and depreciate all fixed assets on the straight-line basis.

REQUIRED:

1. Compute the annual rental under the lease (round all amounts to the nearest dollar).

2. Compute the amounts of the investment in capital leases and the unearned interest income that Dumont should disclose at the inception of the lease on December 31, 1993.

3. What expense should Finley record for the year ended December 31, 1993?

4. What entry will Dumont make at the end of the lease, assuming it sells the asset for $50,000 at that time?

(AICPA adapted)

17-7. *Accounting for leases by lessor and lessee—essay*

From the standpoint of the *lessee*, capital leases and operating leases are the two classifications of leases described in FASB pronouncements. From the standpoint of the *lessor*, sales-type leases and direct financing leases are two of the classifications of leases described in FASB pronouncements.

REQUIRED:

1. Describe how the lessee would account for a capital lease both at the inception of the lease and during the first year of the lease, assuming the lease transfers ownership of the property to the lessee by the end of the lease.

2. Describe how the lessee would account for an operating lease both at the inception of the lease and during the first year of the lease, assuming the lessee makes equal monthly payments at the beginning of each month of the lease. Describe the change in accounting, if any, when rental payments are not made on a straight-line basis.

3. Compare and contrast a sales-type lease with a direct financing lease as follows:
   (a) Investment in the capital lease
   (b) Amortization of unearned interest revenue
   (c) Manufacturer's or dealer's profit
   (AICPA adapted)

17-8. *Lessor accounting; indirect costs; journalization in multiple years·*

Basic Industries has entered into a lease on November 1, 1994, for equipment that it manufactured for sale. The lease provides for 10 annual lease payments at the beginning of each of the next 10 years in the amount of $200,000 per year. At the end of the 10-year term, title to the asset transfers to the lessee. Basic manufactured the equipment at a cost of $540,000 and normally sells the equipment for $1,202,370. The implicit rate in the lease is 12%. As part of the agreement, Basic will pay all personal property taxes and insurance on the equipment during the lease. These costs are estimated at $10,000 per year. Basic also incurred initial direct costs of $81,845 relating to the lease due to commissions and legal fees to negotiate the lease with the lessee. Basic has a calendar-year fiscal period. The executory costs are paid at the beginning of each lease year, and Basic paid $10,000 in both 1994 and 1995.

REQUIRED:

Prepare all journal entries Basic would make for fiscal years ending December 31, 1994, and December 31, 1995.

17-9. *Lessee accounting; renewal periods; purchase options; journal entries*

On January 2, 1992, Baker Company entered into a 3-year, noncancellable lease, as lessee, requiring annual payments of $90,000 payable at the beginning of each year. Baker's incremental borrowing rate is 14%, while the lessor's implicit interest rate, known to Baker, is 15%. The leased property has an estimated useful life of 7 years. At the end of the third year, Baker has the option to renew the lease for an additional two years at the terms or pay a termination penalty of $250,000. At the end of 5 years, Baker can purchase the asset for $3,000. The asset's fair market value in 5 years is estimated to be $50,000.

REQUIRED:

1. Prepare an amortization schedule that Baker could use to determine the interest portion of the minimum lease payments for each year of the lease.
2. Prepare the journal entries Baker would make to record the activity relating to this lease in 1992 and the entry to record the exercise of the bargain purchase at the end of the lease.

17-10. *Sales-type leases; implicit rate determination; unguaranteed residual; indirect costs*

Marko Industries manufactures equipment that it markets by direct sale and by entering into long-term lease arrangements. Marko entered into a lease of equipment that cost $412,340 to construct and normally sells for $709,087. The equipment has a useful life of 7 years and reverts to Marko at the end of the lease term. Terms of the lease are as follows:

Term	7 years
Annual lease payments	$130,000 at the beginning of each year
Executory cost	5,730 per year
Unguaranteed residual	$50,000 at end of Year 7
Initial indirect costs	$22,000

REQUIRED:

1. Determine the implicit interest rate in this lease.
2. Prepare a schedule to amortize the unearned interest present in this lease.

3. Prepare journal entries for the first year of the lease, assuming the inception of the lease occurs on the first day of Marko's fiscal year and the executory costs are paid in advance on that date.

4. Prepare journal entries for the last year of the lease, assuming that Marko sells the asset at the end of the lease for $65,000.

17-11. *Lessee and lessor accounting for the same lease; journal entries; comparison of the valuation of lessee liabilities and lessor net investment*

Makemoney Enterprises purchases assets that it then leases. Makemoney has entered into a lease with Hard Driver, Inc., for a fleet of trucks on January 1, 1994. Makemoney purchased the trucks immediately prior to entering the lease at a price of $1,842,593. The lease provides for 3 annual lease payments in the amount of $500,000 per year beginning at inception. Makemoney incurred initial direct costs of $48,859 to negotiate the leases. The trucks all have an expected useful life of 7 years.

At the end of the lease year term, the trucks revert to Makemoney. During the lease, the lessee pays for the licenses and insurance on the trucks. These costs are estimated to be $35,000 per year. Hard Driver has guaranteed a residual value for the trucks at $800,000. Makemoney estimates that the trucks will be worth approximately $1,000,000 at the end of the lease. Hard Driver has an incremental borrowing rate of 17% and does not know Makemoney's implicit rate.

REQUIRED:

1. Why is this a capital lease for Hard Driver?
2. Prepare Hard Driver's amortization schedule for the lease.
3. Prepare all of the journal entries Hard Driver would make over the life of the lease. Assume the asset's fair market value at the end of the lease exceeds the guaranteed amount.
4. What criteria would the lease have to meet to be a capital lease for Makemoney? What kind of capital lease would it be?
5. Assuming the lease is a capital lease for Makemoney, prepare an amortization schedule for the lessor.
6. Prepare all journal entries Makemoney would make over the life of the lease, assuming the trucks are retained by Makemoney at the end of the lease but their fair market value at that time is estimated to be $1,100,000.
7. What factors cause the net investment in the capital lease the lessor records differ from that the lessee records?

17-12. *Lessee accounting for lease of specialized equipment; capitalization; criteria; journal entries; bargain purchase option not exercised*

On January 1, 1994, Iras Data Systems entered into a lease agreement with Charmian Air Cargo for a computer. The terms of the lease are as follows:

Term:	4 years
Bargain renewal option:	Up to two years after lease expiration at 10% discount
Required lease payments:	$100,000 due yearly on January 1
Guaranteed residual (at end of 1999):	$50,000
Expected residual (at end of 1999):	$50,000

This computer cost Iras $354,500 to build and install. Iras has sold similar computers recently for $483,800, on average; but each system is designed to the customer's specifications, and Charmian's system is the most elaborate ever set up at Iras. These computers are expected to last about 8 years with normal use. Iras usually buys back the components and either restores them or sells them on the open market. Charmian has agreed to maintain the computer over the lease period and return it to Iras on the date of termination of the lease.

Iras incurred and paid $2,456 in credit investigation costs and legal fees in 1989 to set up the lease for Charmian. Iras also awarded a bonus of $3,000 in December of 1993 to the employee who signed Charmian to the lease.

Before entering into the lease agreement, Charmian's management had planned for the company to borrow the cash to purchase the computer. Charmian's bank had set up a $500,000 line of credit at 14% interest to finance the purchase. Ultimately, it was decided that the cash would be used instead to upgrade aircraft, if a favorable leasing arrangement could be made for the computer.

The computers are somewhat specialized to the air freight industry, and Iras is one of few suppliers. Thus, Charmian's controller does not consider the recent price data on such computers to be very reliable for the computation of a discount rate.

REQUIRED:

1. Apply each of the criteria for a capital lease and determine which is satisfied. Assuming the recent sales average is used in applying Criterion 4, discuss the pros and cons of using this value.
2. How will Charmian record the effect of entering into this lease?
3. Prepare an amortization schedule for the lease obligation presenting the balance as of January 1, 1994.
4. What entries will Charmian make at the end of the fiscal year on December 31, 1994?
5. Assuming Charmian exercised the bargain purchase option, what entry would Charmian record if Iras sold the components to a third party for $40,000 on December 31, 1999?
6. Speculate on what entry Charmian would make in the event that the bargain purchase option was not exercised and the computer is returned to Iras at the end of four years (assuming that any guaranteed residual value requirement existing at that time was met)?

17-13. *Lessor accounting for specialized asset leases; compliment to Problem 17-12*

Use the information in Problem 17-12.

REQUIRED:

1. What additional criteria must be met for Iras to treat this lease as a capital lease? Is this a sales-type lease or a direct financing lease?
2. Compute Iras' implicit rate for the lease.
3. Prepare a schedule allocating principal and interest payments over the life of the lease. Prepare the journal entries Iras will record for the period January 1, 1994 to December 31, 1994.
4. Assume the asset is sold at the end of the lease under the same terms as described in the previous problem. What are the journal entries for the termination of the lease and the transfer of the leased asset?

CASE 17.1

UAL, INC.

UAL, Inc., is a holding company for United Air Lines and several other subsidiaries. As is common in the airline industry, long-term leases are used to acquire flight equipment and other related assets. Presented below are the income statement, balance sheet, and the note regarding the leasing activity of UAL as they appeared in the company's 1981 financial statements.

Lease Obligations (note disclosure)

As of December 31, 1981, United leased 58 of its aircraft. The majority of these leases have terms of 15 years, and expiration dates range from 1982 through 2000. Under the terms of the leases for 48 of the aircraft, United has the right of first refusal to purchase (and, as to an additional five of the aircraft, UAL has agreed to purchase), at the end of the lease term, certain aircraft at fair market value and others at a percentage of cost. Majority owned subsidiaries of Westin operate several hotels (one of which is subleased to another hotel operator) under leases expiring from 1996 through 2007. Other leases include airport passenger terminal space, aircraft hangars and related maintenance facilities, cargo terminals, flight kitchens, other equipment, and automobiles.

Future minimum lease payments as of December 31, 1981 under capital leases and under noncancelable operating leases having initial or remaining lease terms of more than one year are shown below:

(in thousands)	Capital Leases	Operating Leases
Payable during:		
1982	$ 119,784	$ 57,043
1983	114,562	51,974
1984	107,079	47,797
1985	95,759	44,320
1986	86,170	41,692
After 1986	990,033	534,781
Total minimum lease payments	$1,513,387	$777,607
Imputed interest (at rates of 5.25% to 20.5%)	755,136	
Present value of minimum lease payments	758,251	
Less—current portion	46,853	
Long-term obligations under capital leases	$ 711,398	

Amounts charged to rent expense, net of minor amounts of sublease rentals, were $80,804,000 in 1981 and $74,705,000 in 1980.

In addition to the information contained in these disclosures, the following data was contained in UAL's funds statement for the year:

Increase in Obligations Under Capital Leases	$152,412,000
Additions to Leased Property Under Capital Leases	146,161,000
Reduction of Obligations Under Capital Leases	64,344,000

Statement of Consolidated Operations (in thousands)	1981	1980
Operating revenues:		
Airline		
Passenger	$3,937,912	$3,880,689
Cargo	346,690	331,204
Contract services	257,066	246,939
	4,541,668	4,458,832
Hotel	454,378	425,921
Business services	145,128	156,582
	5,141,174	5,041,335
Operating expenses:		
Operations	2,706,100	2,635,448
Aircraft fuels	1,346,205	1,342,529
Depreciation and amortization	315,509	305,102
Sales and advertising	618,487	527,328
General and administrative	232,884	213,019
	5,219,185	5,023,416
Earnings (loss) from operations	(78,011)	17,909
Other deductions (income):		
Interest expense	138,954	123,238
Interest capitalized	(22,736)	(17,492)
Temporary investment income	(26,989)	(29,079)
Gain on disposition of property	(8,044)	(47,717)
Other	(11,666)	(15,249)
	69,519	13,701
Earnings (loss) before income taxes	(147,530)	4,208
Income taxes before investment tax credits	(65,500)	6,400
Investment tax credits	(11,500)	(23,200)
	(77,000)	(16,800)
Net earnings (loss)	$ 70,530	$ 21,008
Net earnings (loss) per share	$ (2.40)	$ 0.70

Statement of Consolidated Financial Position (in thousands)	1981	1982
Current assets:		
Cash	$ 34,478	$ 24,910
Temporary investments	160,143	294,013
Receivables	593,222	607,775
Spare parts	113,885	143,274
Aircraft fuel and supplies	70,831	83,021
Prepaid expenses	54,831	59,537
	1,027,390	1,212,530
Operating property and equipment:		
Flight equipment	2,729,677	2,647,935
Advances on flight equipment purchase contracts	188,848	116,876
Other property and equipment	1,429,668	1,320,970
Less—accumulated depreciation and amortization	2,165,893	1,928,217
	2,182,300	2,157,564
Leased property under capital leases:		
Flight equipment	783,060	735,114
Other	176,482	151,817
Less—accumulated amortization	368,847	372,066
	590,695	514,865
Other assets:		
Receivables and investments	115,303	97,442
Intangibles of acquired companies	20,300	20,900
Other	39,789	38,157
	175,392	156,499
Total assets	$3,975,777	$4,041,458
Liabilities:		
Current liabilities:		
Commercial paper	$ 178,704	$ 152,192
Long-term debt maturing in one year	69,553	59,034
Current obligations under capital leases	46,853	46,213
Advance ticket sales and deposits	358,731	396,680
Accounts payable	357,474	356,500
Accrued salaries and wages	211,582	199,315
Accrued and deferred income taxes	22,005	23,409
Other accrued liabilities	244,933	197,017
	1,489,835	1,430,360
Long-term debt	469,948	546,317
Long-term obligations under capital leases	711,398	623,969
Deferred credits	196,909	264,737
Equity of others in hotel subsidiaries	7,222	5,800
Redeemable preferred stock	5,795	6,175
Preferred stock	2,646	2,675
Common stock	147,925	147,598
Additional capital invested	420,677	419,507
Retained earnings	525,540	596,438
Treasury stock	(2,118)	(2,118)
	1,094,670	1,164,100
Total liabilities and equity	$3,975,777	$4,041,458

REQUIRED:

1. Compute UAL's debt-to-equity ratio as reported (including the capital lease obligations) and by adjusting the balance sheet to remove the effects of the capitalization of the aircraft leases. How important do you believe the difference in debt-to-equity ratios is under the two approaches?

2. Given the information provided, prepare a journal entry to record the new capital leases UAL entered into during 1981. (Hint: You will have to decide why the increase in capital lease obligations of $152,412,000 is not equal to the increase in property under capital leases of $146,161,000 to make this entry. What other assets might UAL have received under a lease for aircraft that would be classified as a current asset?)

3. Prepare the journal entry to record the minimum lease payments for 1982 based on the data provided at the end of 1981, assuming all payments are made on December 31, 1982. Assuming that UAL reported a similar level of interest expense on its capital leases in 1981, what percentage of the total interest expense reported in UAL's income statement is related to lease activity?

4. What events during 1981 would result in the accumulated amortization of leased property under capital leases to decline from $372,066,000 to $368,847,000? Assume no leases were terminated prior to expiration.

5. In the supplemental information, UAL reports that the reduction of principal on capital lease obligations amounted to $64,344,000 in 1981. However, in the 1980 balance sheet, UAL reports a current portion of the lease obligation of only $46,213,000. Why do these amounts differ?

6. Based on your response to (3), (4), and (5), how do the income statement effects arising from UAL's capital leases compare with the cash flow effects during 1981?

THE PILLSBURY COMPANY

CASE 17.2

The following is an excerpt from the financial statement disclosures of Pillsbury Company's regarding its operations as a lessor for 1986.

Notes:

8. Investments as lessor

Restaurant subsidiaries lease buildings and land to franchisees. The building portions of the leases are direct financing leases, while the land portions are operating leases. Substantially all leases are for 15 to 20 years, provide for minimum and contingent rentals, and require the franchisee to pay executory costs.

Minimum future lease payments to be received during the fiscal years ending May 31:	Capital Leases	Operating Leases
	(in millions)	
1987	$ 29.7	$ 29.7
1988	30.2	28.9
1989	31.0	28.5
1990	31.0	27.0
1991	30.7	26.4
Later	307.3	275.0
	$459.9	$415.5

Net investment in direct financing leases at May 31:	1986	1985
	(in millions)	
Minimum lease payments receivable	$459.9	$ 420.9
Allowance for uncollectibles	(4.4)	(4.0)
Estimated unguaranteed residual value	3.8	3.8
Unearned amount representing interest	(261.4)	(226.9)
Net investment	$197.9	$ 193.8
Current portion included in receivables	(4.6)	(4.5)
Net investment in direct financing leases	$193.3	$ 189.3

	Year ended May 31		
Rental income:	1986	1985	1984
	(in millions)		
Minimum rental income (a)	$31.7	$26.6	$23.9
Contingent rental income	32.3	32.8	27.9
	$64.0	$59.4	$51.8

(a) Includes contingent rentals on both owned and leased property under direct financing and operating leases.

REQUIRED:

1. Based on the description of the assets covered by Pillsbury's activities as a lessor, what conditions must exist for the company to capitalize the building leases but not the real estate leases?
2. What does Pillsbury's statement regarding the fact that the capital leases are direct financing leases imply?
3. Using information contained in the note, how much of the minimum lease payment in 1987 will be treated as interest income?
4. Assume the following occurred during 1986:

Minimum lease payments for leases entered into prior to December 1, 1985	$29,900,000
Initial lease payments collected at inception for capital leases entered into in 1986	$10,000,000

Prepare the journal entries Pillsbury would use to record interest revenue on the capital leases, collections on the pre-existing capital leases, and the activity relating to the new capital leases for 1986.
5. Prepare the journal entry to record Pillsbury's rental income for 1986.

6. Based on your response to (4), how much impact did capitalization of the leases have on Pillsbury's income before taxes for 1986 compared to treating them as operating leases?

DAYTON HUDSON

Dayton Hudson Corporation is a Minnesota based company that owns several department store chains in the Midwest and West. The Target and Mervyn chains specialize in mass marketing of consumer goods in lower price ranges, while its Dayton's chain specializes in higher priced luxury goods. What follows is an excerpt from the Annual Report to Shareholders for 1985. After reviewing the information presented below, respond to the questions at the end of the case.

Note Disclosures:

Leases

For financial reporting, we classify leases as either operating or capital leases. Capital leases are recorded as assets on our Statements of Financial Position and we report interest expense and depreciation expense on the leases instead of rent expense. Operating leases are not capitalized and lease rentals are expenses. For tax purposes we deduct rent expense on all leases.

Many of our longer-term leases include options to renew, with renewal terms varying from five to 30 years. Certain leases also include options to purchase the property. In addition, we have capital leases on equipment with remaining terms ranging from one to five years.

The detail of leased property and equipment which we have capitalized in our Statements of Financial Position is:

	Feb. 1, 1986	Feb. 2, 1985
Land and buildings	$154,562	$146,754
Equipment	19,022	19,182
Accumulated depreciation	(58,905)	(51,203)
Total	$114,679	$114,733

If we were to capitalize the minimum lease payments for all of our operating leases with initial terms of over one year, the present value of these payments would be approximately $392,791 at February 1, 1986 and $359,839 at February 2, 1985. These present values were calculated using an average interest rate for each lease based on the year of inception. The weighted average interest rate used to calculate the 1985 present value was 13%, compared with 12% for 1984.

The impact of recording depreciation expense and interest expense rather than rent expense on the capital leases has been to decrease our net earnings by $1,792 in 1985, $1,672 in 1984, and $1,501 in 1983. Capital lease depreciation expense was $7,953 in 1985, $8,144 in 1984, and $7,736 in 1983.

Many of our store leases entitle the lessor to receive additional rent if sales of the leased stores exceed certain stipulated amounts. The additional rents are referred to as percentage rents because they are usually based on a percentage of sales over stated levels. Real estate taxes, insurance, and other executory costs may be included in our rental payment or charged in addition to the rent. In either case we have included these expenses in Occupancy Costs in our Results of Operations.

Composition of Rental Expense	1985	1984	1983
Minimum rentals on long-term operating leases	$ 77,378	$ 71,311	$66,319
Short-term rentals	9,944	12,044	13,844
Percentage Rents:			
Operating leases	20,299	20,157	18,158
Capital leases	1,250	1,523	1,565
Sublease income	(1,003)	(527)	(1,828)
Executory costs	(1,671)	(1,604)	(1,465)
Net Expense	$106,197	$102,904	$96,593

Future minimum lease payments which must be made under noncancelable lease agreements existing at the end of 1985 are:

	Operating Leases	Capital Leases
1986	$ 79,933	$ 22,043
1987	75,908	21,021
1988	72,334	19,805
1989	67,660	19,372
1990	63,845	19,328
After 1990	445,230	263,506
Total minimum lease payments (a)	$804,910	$365,075
Less: Interest		219,437
Executory costs		12,447
Capitalized lease obligations, including current portion of $5,042		$133,191

(a) Minimum lease payments have not been reduced by minimum sublease rentals due in the future under noncancelable subleases ($6,750 for operating leases, $12,650 for capital leases)

CONSOLIDATED RESULTS OF OPERATIONS

(thousands of dollars)	1985 52 Weeks Ended February 1, 1986	1984 53 Weeks Ended February 2, 1985	1983 52 Weeks Ended January 28, 1984
Revenues	$8,793,372	$8,009,030	$6,963,255
Costs and Expenses			
Cost of retail sales, buying and occupancy	6,278,260	5,709,483	4,924,887
Selling, pub., adm.	1,466,518	1,310,042	1,160,472
Depreciation	163,805	148,453	125,471
Rental expense	106,197	102,904	96,593
Interest expense, net	82,292	81,457	71,449
Interest and depreciation on capital leases	24,422	24,333	22,406
Taxes other than income taxes	146,304	136,239	111,307
Unusual expenses	—	16,777	—
	8,268,798	7,529,688	6,512,585
Earnings Before Income Taxes	524,574	479,342	450,670
Provision for Income Taxes			
Current	192,331	210,456	164,352
Deferred	48,623	9,540	40,861
Net Earnings	$ 283,620	$ 259,346	$ 245,457
Net Earnings Per Share	$ 2.92	$ 2.68	$ 2.54

CONSOLIDATED STATEMENTS OF FINANCIAL POSITION

(thousands of dollars)	February 1, 1986	February 2, 1985
ASSETS		
Current Assets		
Cash	$ 91,801	$ 59,462
Marketable securities	96,422	2,500
Accounts receivable (net of allowance for doubtful accounts of $34,672 and $26,520)	1,060,129	995,967
Merchandise inventories (net of accumulated LIFO provision of $164,124 and $149,408)	1,272,175	1,103,922
Other	28,034	19,267
	2,548,561	2,181,118
Property and Equipment		
Land	235,437	194,705
Buildings and Improvements	1,252,025	1,080,952
Fixtures and Equipment	895,327	761,416
Construction-in-progress	99,459	74,213
Accumulated depreciation	(750,363)	(620,328)
	1,731,885	1,490,958
Property Under Capital Lease, Net	114,679	114,733
Other	22,389	13,041
	$4,417,514	$3,799,850
LIABILITIES AND SHAREHOLDERS' INVESTMENT		
Current Liabilities		
Accounts payable (including outstanding drafts of $154,819 and $126,727)	$ 734,415	$ 611,490
Accrued liabilities	375,983	322,541
Income taxes payable	109,213	104,302
Current deferred income taxes	174,067	159,679
Current portion of capital lease obligations and long-term debt	24,753	10,356
	1,418,431	1,208,368
Capital Lease Obligations	128,149	125,197
Long-Term Debt	794,514	625,442
Deferred Income Taxes and Other	129,065	104,341
Shareholders' Investment		
Common stock	97,196	96,992
Additional paid-in capital	12,748	9,490
Retained earnings	1,837,411	1,630,020
	1,947,355	1,736,502
	$4,417,514	$3,799,850

REQUIRED:

1. Given the data in the case, what percentage of land and buildings and equipment are assets under capital lease? How does this change if the operating leases were capitalized? (Assume the discounted value of the operating lease payments equals the value of the assets under capitalization.) What does this tell you about the extent to which Dayton-Hudson relies on leasing as a means of obtaining assets? Given the nature of the business Dayton-Hudson operates, speculate about the company's motivation for its use of leasing.

2. How does Dayton-Hudson's capital lease activity compare in size to its operating lease activity? Given the data in the case, estimate the effect that capitalization of the operating leases would have on Dayton-Hudson's debt-to-equity and return-on-assets ratios. Do you think these effects are material? Why or why not?

3. What distinguishes capital from operating leases with regards to their representation in Dayton-Hudson's financial statements? Do you think this distinction should be made?

4. Explain why the weighted average interest rate used in discounting the operating leases changed from 1984 to 1985?

5. What is an executory cost?

6. Dayton-Hudson presents an analysis of rental expense for the period. Why are percentage rents that relate to capital leases listed in this reconciliation? Why are they not included in the minimum lease payments? What is sublease income and why is it deducted from rent expense? Why are executory costs deducted from rent expense? Do they represent income for the period?

7. Assume the minimum lease payment for 1986 has no executory costs included. How much of this payment is interest and how much is principal?

8. In your opinion, does Dayton-Hudson appear to be changing its reliance on leasing in any substantial way during 1986?

CHAPTER 18

Employee Compensation: Defined Benefit Pension Plans

When the issue of compensation is discussed, the focus is often on the hourly wage or salary paid directly to employees. However, the concept of employee compensation is broader than just an hourly wage or monthly salary; it embraces the total cost of obtaining the services of individuals, including health and welfare benefits, retirement costs, and incentive payments such as bonuses. In the next two chapters, we examine the various elements that make up employee compensation. We seek to develop an appreciation for the economic forces that result in the wide range of elements that are part of an employee compensation package, as well as an understanding of how these elements are reflected in financial statements.

Chapter 19 reviews the issues of incentive compensation, health and welfare benefits (for both active and retired employees), and defined contribution retirement plans, which can be used as both a means of providing incentives and retirement income. This chapter focuses solely on *defined benefit pension plans* whose primary purpose is to provide retirement income to covered employees. Defined benefit pension plans (also referred to as *defined benefit plans*) are complex agreements. Estimates of the future benefits beneficiaries will receive requires forecasts of many variables such as the workers' life spans, their projected length of employment with the sponsor, their projected retirement dates, and many others. To manage the costs of such plans, the sponsoring company must transform these forecasts of future benefits into measures of the present value of those future benefit streams. Generally, an *actuary* develops these estimates, on which accountants rely extensively to prepare the information regarding defined benefit plans for financial reporting.

This chapter is broken down into four parts. First, an overview of the structure of defined benefit plans is presented. Second, we explore the economic motivation to create retirement plans in general. Third, because the work of the actuary is so central to accounting and reporting for defined benefit pension plans, we examine the basic actuarial process. Finally, the process of accounting and reporting for defined benefit plans is discussed.

OVERVIEW OF THE STRUCTURE OF DEFINED BENEFIT PENSION PLANS

A **defined benefit pension plan** is an arrangement by the sponsoring corporation to provide retirement benefits to the employee-beneficiary. The agreement specifies a *benefit formula*, which is used to compute the final retirement benefits the employee receives. It does not necessarily guarantee that the corporation will ultimately make the payments.[1] The arrangement generally stipulates that a trust be created. A trust is that legal entity designed to manage resources placed in its care by the sponsor of the plan for the benefit of the beneficiaries, or those employees covered by the plan. The trust is managed by an individual, partnership, or another corporation. The funds an employer contributes to the trust are to be used exclusively for the payment of retirement benefits and/or the payment of trust expenses. However, the sponsoring corporation has discretion, within some broad limits, as to the size of the actual contributions.[2]

Once funds have been transferred to the trust, a trustee invests those funds and distributes the trust assets to beneficiaries. A **trustee** is a fiduciary, meaning someone who is charged with the responsibility to act in the best interests of another. Thus, the trustee of a pension plan undertakes safe, prudent investments in the best interests of the employee/beneficiary. If those investments are not prudent, the trustee may be legally liable for losses suffered.

If more than 100 workers are covered by a defined benefit pension plan, the terms of that plan must meet the requirements of federal regulations, as established in the **Employee Retirement Income Security Act (ERISA) of 1974**. These regulations affect many characteristics of defined benefit plans, as well as certain aspects of its administration such as the minimum amount of money the sponsor must contribute to the trust each year and the treatment of any additional contributions should the trust funds be depleted.

Several governmental organizations have split responsibilities for administration of ERISA. Annual financial filings are prepared for the Department of Labor, which, along with the IRS, oversees the minimum funding requirements. A new entity, called the **Pension Benefit Guarantee Corporation (PBGC)**, regulates the process by which defined benefit plans covered by ERISA can be terminated. Sponsors of plans not covered by the ERISA legisla-

---

[1] The ultimate payment of benefits will depend on the amount of funds placed into the pension trust, either by the company or through the intervention of the federal government (which is discussed later). The liability of the sponsoring corporation for benefits is an issue on which courts still vary considerably.

[2] The trust also has financial statements that capture the results of the activity of the trust. The guidelines for construction of financial reports for pension trusts are presented in SFAS No. 35, but are not covered in this text.

tion are affected by ERISA only to the extent that minimum funding requirements have become part of the Tax Code administered by the IRS.

Factors Influencing the Size of the Retirement Benefits

Several factors influence the amount of future cash to be paid out as benefits to covered employees in a defined benefit plan. These features can be broadly classified into two major groups: those that are part of the contract terms, and those that relate to characteristics of the employee population. The first group includes contractual terms such as the benefit formula which determines the amount of retirement benefit to be paid to retirees, whether retirement benefits are to be paid to a surviving spouse if the employee dies before the spouse, and the terms covering an employee's rights to benefits if they quit working for the employer before they retire. Perhaps the most influential of these factors in determining the amount of a retiree's benefits is the benefit formula. As the name implies, a benefit formula is a mathematical expression (function) that transforms variables such as length of employment, wage or salary level, and other factors defined in the contract into a monthly, or annual, retirement benefit to be paid to an individual employee. We will examine these formulae in more detail later in the chapter.

Contractual provisions, called vesting provisions, protect the rights of employees to collect retirement benefits even if they terminate their employment with the sponsor prior to retirement. Vesting provisions interact with other contract provisions to define the extent to which the sponsor will be obligated to pay retirement benefits accrued for service to the date of termination. All benefits accrued may not vest. These issues are also discussed later in the chapter.

The second group includes such features as the average life expectancy of the employee population and average age at retirement. The ultimate payment of benefits will depend on how long an employee (or covered spouse) lives following retirement. While the inputs to the benefit formula will be known with certainty at the date of retirement, these factors can only be estimated before that time.

The Function of the Actuary

Due to the complexity of these plans, both the company considering the adoption of a defined benefit plan, as well as the employees covered by the plan, will need help in assessing the costs of various terms that might be incorporated into the contract. Estimation of the costs of a pension plan is the job of an actuary. An **actuary** is an individual trained in the use and development of estimates relating to mortality and other attributes that influence the expected costs of any form of deferred benefit (such as life insurance or pension benefits). The actuary evaluates the employer's work force based on factors that might alter the **mortality rates** (likelihood that an employee will die at a given age), **turnover** (rate at which employees leave the employ of the company and are replaced by new workers) of the work force, and the *expected retirement age* of the employees. These estimates, called **actuarial assumptions**, along with the terms of the contract regarding matters such as the rate at which benefits accrue, the vesting provisions, etc., are used to obtain estimates of the cost of the plan.

The actuary establishes the pattern of contributions the sponsor should make to fund fully the pension plan over a given period of time. *Full funding* simply means that the assets in the pension trust are worth at least as much as the present value of the obligation for payment of future benefits. The actuary first translates the contract terms and status of the current work force into an estimate of the total future benefits to be paid. Then, the actuary develops a cash flow plan for the sponsoring firm to use in funding the pension trust. In fact, under ERISA, when the sponsor files its annual report with the Department of Labor, the actuary must sign a statement that the company has met all minimum funding requirements during the year. In this way, the consulting actuary is forced to accept responsibility for monitoring the sponsor's activity and notifying the government if the sponsor is not following the requirements.

THE ECONOMIC MOTIVATION FOR RETIREMENT PLANS

The primary purpose of any retirement plan is to act as a means for employees to defer a portion of their current compensation to periods following retirement. Why does this make economic sense? Given that, as a whole, people will prefer a dollar now to one promised anytime in the future, why would employees willingly give up part of their current income in exchange for a promise by the company to supply payments after retirement? Economic motivations for retirement plans are discussed in the following section.

Fundamental Forces

When employees implicitly give up a dollar of current wages to receive retirement benefits, the payments after retirement must be greater than one dollar to provide them a sufficient return and to make their investment in a retirement plan preferable to receipt of a dollar of current wage. However, individuals can always invest part of their current incomes for retirement on personal account. Given this, why would individuals wish to give up control of the funds that represent the source of retirement income payments to the company that employs them? The answer to this question lies in the additional benefits employees can enjoy by relinquishing responsibility for retirement income to the employer.

The Tax Motivation

While there are many sources of such advantages, probably the most important one is the ability to defer taxes. Corporations can create retirement plans in which their contributions to the retirement trust on behalf of the employees are not taxable income to the employees until the benefits are paid out following retirement.

While individuals who are not covered by formal retirement plans at their place of employment have some options for tax deferred retirement investing such as Individual Retirement Accounts (IRAs), these opportunities are very limited under the tax law of the United States. As a result, for individuals to set aside retirement funds on personal account may require that they use "after tax" dollars. That is, they must pay taxes on their income in the current period and set aside retirement monies out of what remains after current taxes are paid. It is true that the retirement income in these cases is not taxable, but individuals cannot benefit from deferring the tax consequences associated with the portion of current income used to fund the retirement benefits.

In addition to the personal tax benefits that employees can enjoy by having corporations set aside part of their current compensation for retirement, the corporation is also in a unique position to take advantage of this situation. Taxable corporations can take tax deductions for monies paid into a pension trust when contributions are made, even though the beneficiaries are not taxed until receipt of the benefits. The trust itself can be organized in such a way that it is not a taxable entity. This provides an acceleration of tax benefits to the corporation and deferral of tax costs to the employees. The government is economically subsidizing the use of corporate retirement programs. This economic subsidy can be shared between the corporation and its employees, providing a means for the employees to receive potentially even greater benefits. Congress clearly believes it is in the best interests of our society to provide a tax subsidy to encourage the creation of corporate-sponsored retirement plans, which effectively reduce the dependence of senior citizens on other forms of government subsidy.

Other Motivations

There are other potential advantages to corporate-sponsored plans. A corporate pension trust is much like a mutual fund in which the employees (past and present) are the investors. Private pension trusts represent one of the largest sources of investment capital in the country. As a result of their size, pension trusts may be able to take advantage of certain economies of scale. For example, they can buy and sell large blocks of shares to reduce the commissions paid to brokers for executing trades. Of course, individuals can form investment groups on private account to accomplish the same thing. However, the use of corporate-sponsored plans may be partially related to the fact that these types of arrangements are easier and less costly to administer since the investment "group" is already identified by employment with the sponsor.

Finally, even if there were no tax benefits or economies of scale in management of the investment funds, some employees would prefer to have a forced savings plan administered by their corporations as a means of disciplining themselves to save for retirement.

THE ACTUARIAL PROCESS—TURNING PROMISES INTO DOLLARS

This section develops an understanding of how contractual terms in the defined benefit program, actuarial assumptions, and other factors combine under the skills of an actuary to produce a funding pattern for the plan. In the past, accountants developed the estimates of the pension cost to recognize as expense in a particular period by employing any of a wide variety of actuarial approaches that are still used to determine funding patterns. Developing an appreciation for this process is central to a conceptual appreciation for why accountants have recently limited the measurement of periodic pension expense to only one actuarial approach to improve matching.

Details of the Design of Defined Benefit Plans

As indicated earlier, the most important, single element in all defined benefit plans is the determination of a benefit formula. Benefit formulas are typically of two types: unit credit formulas or "final pay" formulas. In a defined benefit pension plan that adopts a *unit credit formula* (which we will refer to as a **unit credit plan**), the employee is credited with a unit of service every time certain requirements are met. For example, a unit of service might mean working at least 100 days during a calendar year. The contract then stipulates how large a benefit is to be paid per unit of credited service. This type of arrangement is common for hourly employees and union contracts. These types of plans may or may not adjust the value of a unit credit for inflation. Most frequently, the value of a unit credit is altered when necessary by a change in the pension plan called an **amendment**. Amendments are nothing more than agreed upon changes in the original plan regarding the provision of pension benefits.

For defined benefit pension plans that adopt *final pay formulas* (which we will refer to as **final pay plans**), the agreement provides a formula that determines the pension benefit to be paid to a retired employee based on both:

1. The years of service provided by the employee
2. Some average of the wages or salary that the individual earned in the final years of employment with the company

For example, a pension contract could require that the monthly retirement benefit for an employee who has worked at least 25 years be determined as 2% of the employee's average annual salary over the five years immediately preceding retirement. In such a case, an employee with 25 years of service and an average salary of $40,000 per year over the 5 years prior to retirement would have a monthly pension benefit of $800 (.02 × $40,000). Since the retirement benefit is formally linked to final pay, these plans automatically adjust the benefit level for inflation to the extent that wages are increased as a result of inflation. Final pay plans are common for both managerial personnel and hourly workers.

In addition to providing a formula to compute the full monthly benefit, the agreement will also specify how quickly the rights to the full monthly benefit accrue and a minimum retirement age at which the beneficiary can begin to draw the benefits. In the previous example of a final pay plan, the contract terms suggest that full benefits only accrue after 25 years of service. A simple example of an agreement where the rate of accrual of the benefits meets this requirement would be one that accrues benefits at a uniform rate of 4% per year over the 25-year period. This means that an employee who reaches retirement age but has only 10 years of service and an average salary of $40,000 would only have accrued 40% of the retirement benefit at retirement. If this were the case, the employee would only receive a benefit of $320 per month (.40 × $800).

The rate at which benefits accumulate need not be uniform. In fact, defined benefit plans typically have lower accrual rates in an employee's early years of service than in his or her later years. An example of this type of accrual schedule appears below:

Years in the Plan	Benefit Accrual Rate		Percent of Total Accrued	
1–8	2.5%	×	8 years =	20%
9–20	3.0%	×	12 years =	36%
21–31	4.0%	×	11 years =	44%
			Total	100%

In this plan, an employee must be employed for 31 years to gain the full pension benefit. With a maximum retirement age of 65, this would mean that employees starting with the company after their 34th birthdays would never attain full benefits under the plan. ERISA has set requirements for how much variability can exist in the accrual rates present in a plan of this type. Some unregulated plans where all benefits accrue at one time after many years of service still exist. For example, the employee receives nothing until putting in 15 years of service, at which time he or she receives the rights to 100% of the benefits. Such terms were more prevalent prior to ERISA.

Another major element of a pension plan is the vesting provision, which, as earlier explained, entitles the employee to collect retirement benefits under the plan regardless of his or her continued employment with the company. For example, using the accrual provisions described in the table above, assume the terms of the pension contract call for vesting of all benefits over a 5-year period at the rate of 20% per year. At the end of the first year of credited service, an employee would have accrued 2.5% of the total benefit under the plan, but only 20% of this amount (or .5% of the full retirement benefit) would be vested.

Under the terms of this plan, an employee who works for the company four years and then quits would have accrued a benefit of 10% (4 years × 2.5% per year) of the full retirement benefit. However, by terminating employment, the employee will only be entitled to receive the vested portion of the accrued benefit as of the date of termination. The vested benefit portion is 80% (4 years × 20% per year) of the accrued benefit. If this plan were a final pay plan and stipulated the full retirement benefit to be computed as 40% of the average salary for 5 years prior to retirement, the employee's vested benefit in this example will be determined by taking the full retirement benefit computed using the average salary for the 5 years preceding termination and multiplying by the vested portion, which is 8% (80% of 10%).

Since vesting provisions protect employees from the loss of retirement benefits through termination, they allow the employee more freedom in deciding to stay with a company. Upon leaving the company, the employee need not give up all retirement benefits. On the other hand, built-in incentives influence an employee to remain with the company. For an employee with fewer years on the job, the percentage of his or her benefits that have vested is much less than 100% of the accrued benefits. For such an individual, termination may result in a significant loss of benefits.

In addition, since most plans use a sliding scale in accruing benefits (benefits accrue more rapidly in later years than in early ones), an employee who terminates employment and then works for another firm with a similar plan will resume accruing benefits under the new employer's plan at a much slower rate than he or she would have received from the old employer's plan. This also creates incentives for employees to stay on the job. Employers use this incentive to help retain experienced and competent people since turnover of these individuals can be very costly and disruptive. From this discussion, we can see one way of using a defined benefit plan to accomplish more than just providing retirement income. The terms of the plan also can be structured in such a way as to encourage employees to remain with the company and provide a steady source of labor.

The Actuarial Process

An actuary's primary job is to translate the promises embodied in the defined benefit plan's terms into estimates of the present value of the future expected benefits. The primary use of these estimates is to develop a funding pattern of contributions the company will make to the trust to provide sufficient capital to pay all future benefits. In addition, corporate managers seek estimates of the present value of the future expected benefits as a means to control costs and negotiate employee compensation packages, which might include changes in the retirement plan's terms.

Before computing a present value, an estimate of the future benefit streams the beneficiaries are expected to receive is necessary. To accomplish this, an actuary must make assumptions regarding life expectancy, salary increases, employee turnover, and other factors. These actuarial assumptions are input, along with other data on income, age, and benefit formula, to estimate the future benefit stream. After determining this stream of estimated benefits, the actuary discounts it by choosing an **actuarial discount rate**. The discounted amount represents the present value of the total benefits to the present work force. Another way to view this present value is that it represents the actuary's best estimate of the amount of money the company would need to set aside in the pension trust today to accumulate sufficient assets from the initial contribution and interest on the investments to pay all future benefits as they come due.

It is also important to realize that this amount is not likely to be immediately funded for several reasons. If a firm were to contribute this total amount at the inception of the plan, the Internal Revenue Code would not allow deduction of all this amount in one year. Instead, much of it would be spread over at least a 10-year period. In addition, very few companies would have sufficient cash available to make such a payment immediately upon the inception of the plan.

Assuming companies will not fund the entire present value of future benefits at the inception of the plan, an actuary is also responsible for developing a contribution pattern the firm will use to fund the pension trust with sufficient assets to pay the benefit claims of the retired employees. The development of a funding pattern will require an *allocation* of the present value of the future benefits across multiple time periods. This allocation process is accomplished by the choice of an **actuarial cost method**. Many such methods are available, and each creates a unique pattern of funding.

Determination of a Funding Pattern—Actuarial Cost Methods

The selection of an actuarial cost method involves trade-offs. From the company's viewpoint, there are various cash flow implications to the funding decision. If it has excess cash, the company may prefer to use it to fund the pension plan, at least up to the maximum amount that can be deducted for tax purposes in one year. On the other hand, if cash is tight, the company may prefer a slower funding process, which will not place additional strains on its cash flows. The employees would generally prefer more rapid funding of the trust, since this is the source of the assets that will eventually pay their benefits. However, even the employees are not likely to want the company to go broke in the short run funding the trust. An actuary can influence the rate of funding by the cost method selected. Because of the fiduciary duty to the beneficiaries of the pension trust to protect their benefits, an actuary generally prefers more rapid funding patterns to slower ones. This results in a preference for actuarial cost methods that will, on average, transfer more assets to the pension trust earlier.

The many actuarial cost methods are called by such names as entry age normal, aggregate, accrued benefit method, and frozen initial liability. To provide sufficient grasp of the effects of alternative actuarial cost methods and to lay a foundation for the accounting treatment of these plans, we focus on only two of the methods: the *projected accrued benefit cost method* and the *entry age normal cost method*. These two methods are chosen because the accrued benefit method is essentially the approach the FASB takes for purposes of accounting and financial reporting for defined benefit pension plans, and the entry age normal is a commonly used method that provides a dramatic difference in the funding pattern to compare to the accrued benefit approach. What follows is an example that demonstrates how the actuarial assumptions are first used to determine a pattern of expected future benefits. Then, these benefits are discounted to determine a present value. Finally, the two actuarial cost methods discussed above are utilized to determine and compare funding patterns.

Developing Actuarial Estimates

To understand how an actuary develops estimates and how the choice of actuarial cost method affects funding, take the following (relatively basic) fact situation:

> Mr. P is the sole employee covered by the pension plan of Darvelle Industries. Mr. P began working for Darvelle when he was 20 years of age. He is now 55. Darvelle just began its pension plan, so the inception of the plan coincides with Mr. P's 55th birthday. The plan requires that Mr. P retire at age 65 and that an annual pension benefit paid to Mr. P will be equal to 25% of his aver-

age annual income over the 5 years immediately preceding his retirement. Mr. P currently makes $40,000 per year. The plan also indicates that employees covered by the contract will enter the plan (first be eligible to participate) at their 25th birthday and that the benefits will accrue at the rate of 2.5% per year until age 65. Retroactive credit for services already rendered will be given to Mr. P for all years of employment after his 25th birthday, or 30 years of service at the inception of the plan. Benefits vest at the rate of 20% per year, resulting in full vesting after 5 years of credited service. For our purposes let us assume that Mr. P will live until age 80, dying on his birthday.

To project the size of the annual retirement payment to be made to Mr. P for the 15 years from his retirement (at age 65) to his death (at age 80), first we must estimate the five-year average expected salary immediately prior to retirement. To accomplish this, the actuary must make an assumption about Mr. P's future salary increases. Assume that Mr. P will receive increases at a rate of 5% annually. Normally, the actuary would also develop an estimate of the likelihood that Mr. P would leave the company before retirement and that he might die in any year between now and age 80. In this example, we assume that Mr. P will remain employed and that he will die for certain at age 80. While these simplifying assumptions will not alter the insights we gain regarding how the actuarial cost methods work, they will influence the dollar amounts we obtain. Dealing with these complexities requires considerable actuarial expertise.

Using the 5% increase and compounding it for the next 10 years provides an estimate of each year's annual salary. For the last 5 years, these estimates would appear as follows (estimates have been rounded for convenience):

Average Expected Salary Over the Last Five Years of Employment

Years to Retirement	Projected Salary
5	$ 51,100
4	53,600
3	56,300
2	59,100
1	62,000
Total	$282,100

Average salary: $282,100 ÷ 5 = $56,420

Full retirement benefit: $56,420 × 25% = $14,105 per year

Since Mr. P will have given 40 years of service at retirement, he will be entitled to 100% of the full retirement benefit.

The above computation indicates that the pension trust will need to pay $14,105 per year to Mr. P for 15 years (from age 65 to 80) as a retirement benefit. Having now the estimate of the future benefit stream that Darvelle expects to pay Mr. P, we can determine the value of the assets that need to be in the pension trust by the time Mr. P retires, assuming Darvelle wishes to have fully funded the pension obligation for Mr. P's benefits at that time.

To compute any present value, the actuary must choose a discount rate (interest rate). For actuarial purposes, this rate is often chosen to reflect the long-term investment return on high-quality investments such as those held in the portfolios of large insurance companies. Assume the actuary has chosen a discount rate of 8%. To evaluate the present value of the benefit stream when Mr. P retires at age 65, the actuary simply applies the present value factor for an annuity of $1 at 8% for 15 periods to the annual payment of $14,105. This yields a present value of $120,731.

If the pension trust had assets valued at $120,731 under its control at Mr. P's retirement and could invest them to earn exactly 8% per year, the fund assets would be sufficient (with the earnings each year) to pay Mr. P all 15 payments of $14,105 and have nothing left at the time Mr. P dies. The pattern of cash flows implied by this process is demonstrated in Exhibit 18.1. The $120,731 represents the amount that Darvelle would ideally like to have in the pension trust on the date of Mr. P's retirement. Notice that to estimate this amount, the actuary needed assumptions on mortality (Mr. P will die at 80), turnover (Mr. P will not leave the firm until retirement), future salary increases (5%), expected date of retirement (65), and an interest rate (8%). All these assumptions will be the source of possible differences between the predicted and actual results as time passes.

One way Darvelle could fund this obligation is to wait until Mr. P. retires, and then contribute $120,731 to the pension trust. This is called *terminal fund-*

| EXHIBIT 18.1
Example of Cash Flows in Pension Trust During Retirement

EXAMPLE OF CASH FLOWS IN PENSION TRUST DURING RETIREMENT
(Assumes all payments are made at year-end)

Mr. P's Age*	Beginning Assets in Pension Trust	Earnings at 8%	Pension Payment	Ending Assets in Pension Trust
65	$120,731	$9,658	($14,105)	$116,284
66	116,284	9,303	($14,105)	111,482
67	111,482	8,919	($14,105)	106,296
68	106,296	8,504	($14,105)	100,695
69	100,695	8,056	($14,105)	94,646
70	94,646	7,572	($14,105)	88,113
71	88,113	7,049	($14,105)	81,057
72	81,057	6,485	($14,105)	73,437
73	73,437	5,875	($14,105)	65,207
74	65,207	5,217	($14,105)	56,319
75	56,319	4,506	($14,105)	46,720
76	46,720	3,738	($14,105)	36,353
77	36,353	2,908	($14,105)	25,156
78	25,156	2,012	($14,105)	13,063
79	13,063	1,042	($14,105)	0

*Mr. P dies on his 80th birthday, so no payment is made when Mr. P is 80 years old.

ing. Terminal funding is not acceptable to the Internal Revenue Service for tax purposes, the Pension Benefit Guarantee Corporation or the actuary. The reason is that it fails to provide sufficient security to the beneficiaries regarding the accumulation of assets that will ultimately pay the retirement benefits. Another option would be to contribute $14,105 a year each year during Mr. P's retirement. This is called *pay as you go funding*, which is also not acceptable for the same reason.

Darvelle could also decide to fund fully the trust at the date of inception (although this would not be likely). To do so, Darvelle must determine the present value of the future benefits as of the inception of the plan (when Mr. P is 55) instead of the date of Mr. P's retirement (age 65). Using the assumed interest rate of 8%, this amount can be computed by discounting the $120,731 of present value at age 65 back to age 55 using the present value factor for $1 at 8 percent in 10 periods (.4632). The resulting present value of the future benefits to Mr. P as of the date of inception is $55,922.

If Darvelle placed this amount into the trust at the inception of the plan and if all of the actuarial estimates were correct, no additional money would be needed by the trust. The contribution of $55,922 at inception would earn 8% for each of the next 10 years, before any money is withdrawn to pay Mr. P's benefits. In 10 years, the pension trust would have $120,731, which is sufficient to pay the benefits. Exhibit 18.2 demonstrates this growth of assets in the trust.

As we have discussed previously, several factors make a lump-sum contribution of this type unlikely. Darvelle will need to develop a funding pattern that will systematically fund the $120,731 required at retirement. The $120,731 required to fund fully Mr. P's benefits at retirement will come partly from the

---

EXHIBIT 18.2

Example of Cash Flows in Pension Trust from Inception to Retirement

EXAMPLE OF CASH FLOWS IN PENSION TRUST FROM INCEPTION TO RETIREMENT
(Assumes the present value of all future benefits were funded at inception)

Mr. P's Age	Beginning Assets in Pension Trust	Earnings at 8%	Ending Assets in Pension Trust
55	$ 55,922	$4,474	$ 60,396
56	60,396	4,832	65,228
57	65,228	5,218	70,446
58	70,446	5,636	76,082
59	76,082	6,087	82,169
60	82,169	6,574	88,743
61	88,743	7,099	95,842
62	95,842	7,667	103,509
63	103,509	8,281	111,790
64	111,790	8,941	120,731
65	120,731		

Total earnings of the trust over 10 years = $64,809

contributions made by Darvelle and partly from the earnings of the trust on its investment of those contributions. The more rapidly the funding occurs, the more the trust can earn, and the less the company will have to contribute.

This can be verified by comparing the present value of the benefits at inception, $55,922, to the present value of the benefits at retirement, $120,731. If the company funds all the benefits at inception, it will only pay $55,922; and the earnings of the trust will make up the additional $64,809. (See Exhibit 18.2.) If the company waited until Mr. P retired, it would have to pay $120,731 into the trust because the trust had no earnings to contribute toward the payment of benefits.

The speed with which a plan is funded depends on the company's operating cash flows; investment opportunities; access to capital from sources such as banks, bond markets, and equity markets; and the minimum funding requirements embodied in the Tax Code. The selection of actuarial assumptions and an actuarial cost method will reflect discussions between the corporate sponsor and the actuary regarding the reasonableness of the assumptions and the company's preference for faster or slower funding alternatives.

A Comparison of Actuarial Cost Methods

Two alternative actuarial cost methods which are acceptable under both ERISA and the tax code are the projected benefit and entry age normal methods. These two are comparatively analyzed in the sections that follow.

The Projected Accrued Benefit Cost Method   Under the **projected accrued benefit cost method**, which bases the estimates of retirement benefits on future salary, the first step in developing a contribution pattern is to split the present value of the benefits at inception into two parts. One part relates to benefits accrued for service rendered prior to the date of inception, while the other relates to benefits that will accrue for service to be rendered between the date of inception and the date of retirement. This split is accomplished by determining what percentage of the future benefits has been awarded under the agreement for service rendered before the agreement was actually in effect. In Mr. P's case, he was given credit for the 30 years he had worked prior to the inception of the plan at an accrual rate of a constant 2.5% per year. Thus, Mr. P was given retroactive credit for 75% of his final retirement benefit. The remaining 25% will be accrued in future years.

The projected accrued benefit cost method identifies the 75% portion as the **prior service cost** at the inception of the plan. The value of the prior service costs at inception is simply 75% times the present value of all future benefits, $55,922, or $41,942. The remaining 25% represents the present value of the total future **normal costs**, which is the present value of the portion of the total cost of the plan allocated to each year after inception. Under the accrued benefit cost method, the annual allocation depends on the contractual rate at which employees accrue benefits. In this example, Mr. P will earn 2.5% of the retirement benefit each year, and the present value of this accrual is the normal cost for the year. Exhibit 18.3 demonstrates this computation for each of the remaining 10 years of Mr. P's employment.

EXHIBIT 18.3

Computation of
Future Normal Cost
Under the Projected
Accrued Benefit
Actuarial Cost
Method

**COMPUTATION OF FUTURE NORMAL COST UNDER THE
PROJECTED ACCRUED BENEFIT ACTUARIAL COST METHOD**
(Assumes contributions will be made at year-end)

Mr. P's Age	Value at Retirement of Benefit Accrued During Service Year*	Present Value Factor at 8%**	Normal Cost for Service Year
55	$3,018	.5002	$1,510
56	3,018	.5402	1,630
57	3,018	.5834	1,761
58	3,018	.6301	1,902
59	3,018	.6805	2,054
60	3,018	.7350	2,218
61	3,018	.7938	2,396
62	3,018	.8573	2,587
63	3,018	.9259	2,794
64	3,018	1.0000	3,018

*Present value of total projected benefits at retirement = $120,731
  Portion accrued annually = $120,731 × 2.5% = $3,018 per year
**Present value factors are all at 8%, but each consecutive factor discounts the future value by one
  less year.

As Exhibit 18.3 demonstrates, Mr. P is accruing 2.5% of the final retirement benefit in each year, but the effects of discounting are less and less important in determining the normal cost as retirement is approached. The fact that contributions to the pension trust will have less time to accrue interest means that the company must contribute higher dollar amounts if it waits to make a contribution.

If Darvelle makes a contribution to the pension plan at inception of $41,942 to cover the prior service costs at inception, makes annual contributions for normal cost as prescribed in Exhibit 18.3, and the trust earns a return of exactly 8% each year, then at the time Mr. P retires, the fund will have assets of $120,731, which will pay Mr. P's retirement benefits without further support from the company.

Of course, the company will usually not prefer to fund even the prior service costs at inception in a lump sum, for the same reasons that it would not fully fund the plan immediately. Assume that Darvelle elects to fund the prior service cost over a 10-year period. The prior service costs had a present value of $41,942 at inception. Assuming that Darvelle wishes to pay in equal annual installments, the amount of the annual payment for the past service cost can be computed by taking the principal amount of $41,942 and dividing by the present value factor for an annuity of $1 for 10 periods at 8% (6.7106). This computation would result in an annual payment of $6,250 per year at the end of each of the next 10 years. If this were the funding choice for the past service costs, Darvelle would need to contribute both the annual normal cost shown in Exhibit 18.3 plus $6,250 for each year to fund fully the plan at Mr. P's retirement. This would imply the funding pattern over the next 10 years, which appears in Exhibit 18.4.

The Entry Age Normal Cost Method   An alternative to the accrued benefit cost method is the **entry age normal cost method**. In this allocation method, the rates at which benefits accrue under the pension agreement are ignored in allocating the cost to specific years. Instead, the actuary takes the total present value of the benefits estimated to accrue at retirement and converts this amount into an annual annuity covering the period from Mr. P's hypothetical entry into the plan until his retirement. In our example, Mr. P's hypothetical entry date would be his 25th birthday. This would have been the date he would have entered the plan if it had been in existence.

To compute the value of the annuity that would fund the $120,731 required at retirement over a 40-year period (the number of years from Mr. P's hypothetical entry at age 25 to retirement at age 65), the actuary must divide the amount required ($120,731) by the present value of an annuity factor of $1 at 8% for 40 years. The required annuity would be $466 per year. Under the entry age normal cost method, the prior service cost at inception is defined as the amount required at the inception of the plan to make up for the annuity payments not made from age 25 to age 55 (the age of Mr. P at inception). Note that this amount is not just 30 years times $466. Since Darvelle could not make the annuity payments of $466 for the first 30 years, it has also lost the interest the trust could have earned on these contributions. For this reason, the equivalent amount required at inception to make up for the lost contributions must also make up for the lost interest. The actuary can compute

EXHIBIT 18.4

Funding Pattern Under Projected Accrued Benefit Actuarial Cost Method—10-Year Amortization of the Past Service Costs

FUNDING PATTERN UNDER PROJECTED ACCRUED BENEFIT ACTUARIAL COST METHOD
10-YEAR AMORTIZATION OF THE PAST SERVICE COSTS
(Assumes contributions will be made at year-end)

Mr. P's Age at Contribution	Normal Cost Component	+	Past Service Cost Component	=	Total Contribution	+	Trust Assets At Beginning Of Year	+	Earnings On Trust Assets	=	Trust Assets At End Of Year
55	$1,510		$6,250		$ 7,760		$ 0		$ 0		$ 7,760
56	1,631		6,250		7,881		7,760		621		16,262
57	1,761		6,250		8,011		16,262		1,301		25,574
58	1,902		6,250		8,152		25,574		2,046		35,772
59	2,054		6,250		8,304		35,772		2,862		46,938
60	2,218		6,250		8,468		46,938		3,755		59,161
61	2,396		6,250		8,646		59,161		4,733		72,540
62	2,587		6,250		8,837		72,540		5,803		87,180
63	2,794		6,250		9,044		87,180		6,975		103,199
64	3,018		6,250		9,268		103,199		8,264		120,731
Selected Totals					$84,371				$36,360		

this amount as the future value of an annuity of $466 at 8% for 30 years, which would be $52,790 ($466 × 113.283).

If Darvelle used this actuarial cost method, it would have a constant normal cost of $466 per year; and the past service cost of $52,790 would need to be allocated over some selected future period. If we use 10 years for the amortization of the past service cost to remain consistent with the previous example, the annual contribution to fund the past service cost would be $7,868 (computed by dividing the $52,790 by the factor for the present value of an annuity of $1 at 8% for 10 periods). Exhibit 18.5 demonstrates the funding pattern and value of trust assets accruing using the entry age normal cost method.

A Comparison of Funding Under the Alternative Cost Methods

Examining Exhibits 18.4 and 18.5 allows us to compare the funding pattern under the projected accrued benefit cost method to that of the entry age normal cost method. The important feature to note is that the entry age normal method will transfer assets to the pension trust more rapidly than the accrued benefit method. However, both smooth out the cash flow requirements considerably more than requiring immediate funding.

The accelerated funding under the entry age normal method results in a smaller drain on firm cash flows over the entire funding period since the trust is able to earn a larger portion of the total cost of the retirement benefits through investments. However, the smaller total contribution of the entry age normal approach is accomplished by placing a larger cash flow burden on the company in the short run. The overall cash savings, and the more rapid build up of assets in the trust, are attractive features of the entry age normal method. Actuaries and beneficiaries find the more rapid asset growth in the trust to be

EXHIBIT 18.5

Funding Pattern Under the Entry Age Normal Actuarial Cost Method— 10-Year Amortization of the Past Service Costs

FUNDING PATTERN UNDER THE ENTRY AGE NORMAL ACTUARIAL COST METHOD
10-YEAR AMORTIZATION OF THE PAST SERVICE COSTS
(Assumes contributions will be made at year-end)

Mr. P's Age at Contribution	Normal Cost Component	+	Past Service Cost Component	=	Total Contribution	+	Trust Assets At Beginning Of Year	+	Earnings On Trust Assets	=	Trust Assets At End Of Year
55	$466		$7,868		$ 8,334		$ 0		$ 0		$ 8,334
56	466		7,868		8,334		8,334		667		17,335
57	466		7,868		8,334		17,335		1,387		27,056
58	466		7,868		8,334		27,056		2,164		37,554
59	466		7,868		8,334		37,554		3,004		48,892
60	466		7,868		8,334		48,892		3,911		61,137
61	466		7,868		8,334		61,137		4,891		74,362
62	466		7,868		8,334		74,362		5,949		88,645
63	466		7,868		8,334		88,645		7,092		104,071
64	466		7,868		8,334		104,071		8,326		120,731
Selected Totals					$83,340				$37,391		

most important, and this is why the entry age normal method is one of the more popular actuarial cost methods for determining the funding pattern.

Deviations from Actuarial Expectations—The Creation of Actuarial Gains and Losses

So far we have assumed that:

1. The pension fund will earn exactly the predicted 8% rate of return
2. We know when Mr. P will die
3. We know Mr. P will continue to work for the company until retirement

In practice all these estimates prove incorrect to some degree. Differences between estimates and actual outcomes result in **actuarial gains or losses**. When the actual return on trust assets is below 8%, an actuarial loss occurs. Future contributions or earnings must make up for this shortfall. On the other hand, if mortality is higher than expected (beneficiaries die earlier than expected), this results in an actuarial gain. On average, we expect the actuarial gains and losses to be zero over time, but they occasionally become so large that changes must be made to the estimates and the funding pattern to adjust for these items.

Actuarial gains and losses are measured as of the valuation date. The valuation date is a point in time when the actuary re-assesses the current status of the plan and the reasonableness of the assumptions that are being used to determine the funding patterns. Valuation dates occur at regular intervals, typically annually. When any of the actuarial assumptions are changed on a valuation date, the effect these have on the actuarial liability for retirement benefits creates a gain (if the liability decreases) or loss (if the liability increases). In addition, the actual earnings on trust assets can be compared to the estimated earnings, with any difference being another source of actuarial gain (if actual exceeds expected earnings) or loss (if actual is less than expected earnings).

The presence of an actuarial gain or loss implies that the sponsoring firm will need to pay less (in the case of a gain) or more (in the case of a loss) money into the trust than was previously anticipated. Actuaries typically use a five-year averaging process to adjust the cash contributions for these gains and losses. Consequently, the annual contribution is not immediately increased or decreased by the full amount of the current year actuarial loss or gain. Instead, the current period contribution is adjusted based on the average actuarial gain or loss over the past five years. This process smooths the funding pattern and allows gains and losses to partially offset one another over the five-year horizon.

Vested Benefits

Another issue relating to defined benefit plans is the valuation of **vested benefits**. In the example above, Mr. P was always fully vested, meaning that all benefits he had accrued would be his regardless of any further employment with Darvelle. The vested benefits are typically measured using current salary levels, not projected salary levels. The vested benefit obligation reflects the cost of the pension benefits that employees may take with them upon termination.

If termination occurs, the benefits paid to the employee on retirement depend on the salary over the last five years of employment prior to departure.

If we assume that Mr. P has earned an average of $38,000 over the 5 years immediately prior to inception, then the vested benefit obligation would be computed as follows:

Vested Benefits = (Average Salary for Latest 5-Year Period) × (Total Benefits Accrued to Date) × (Percent of Accrued Benefits Which are Vested)

$38,000 × (25% × 75%) × 100% = $7,125 per year in benefits

Present Value at Age 65: $7,125 × 8.559 = $60,990

Present Value at Inception (Age 55): $60,990 × .4632 = $28,251

Thus, the vested benefit obligation would be $28,251, even though the obligation for accrued benefits was $41,942. In the above computation, the total benefits earned to date would be computed based on the full benefit that the plan allows (25% of average final pay) times the proportion of that benefit accrued for the years of service Mr. P has already provided (30 years × an accrual rate of 2.5% per year). Since all accrued benefits are immediately vested under the terms of the plan as described earlier, 100% is the appropriate percentage of accrued benefits that are vested.

Had the pension plan not called for immediate vesting, the vested benefit obligation in this example would be smaller and could be computed by multiplying by the percentage of the benefits actually vested. For example, suppose that only 80% of the benefits accrued were vested, the vested benefit obligation would be $22,600 (28,250 × .80).[3]

Accountants and actuaries often talk about the **unfunded vested benefit obligation**. This is simply the vested benefit obligation minus the value of the assets in the pension trust. This obligation has a particular economic significance. If all the employees of the company were to quit and go elsewhere, the vested benefit obligation would become the only obligation the company has under the pension plan. However, if the company terminated the plan, the employees would be entitled to all benefits accrued to date, based on their salaries to the date of termination of the plan. This termination liability, referred to as the **accumulated benefit obligation**, differs from the vested benefit obligation only by the amount of the benefits that are accrued but unvested at the time of the plan's termination. The **unfunded accumulated benefit obligation** is the difference between the accumulated benefit obligation and the value of the assets in the pension trust.

Contributory and Noncontributory Plans

One last feature to note before turning our attention to accounting and reporting for defined benefit plans is that of employee contributions to plans. Some

---

[3] Under current regulatory requirements, there is no plan that could delay full vesting beyond 7 years of employment. This implies that Mr. P, having already provided 30 years of service to the company at the inception of the plan, would have to be fully vested regardless of the specific provision of the plan as long as it was covered by ERISA or was a tax qualified plan.

defined benefit plans require that employees contribute monies toward their retirement benefits out of their wage or salary compensation each period. Other plans allow employees to make contributions in addition to those made by the plan to increase the size of the ultimate retirement benefits. When employees are required to, or allowed to, participate in this fashion, the plan is called **contributory**. When employees cannot participate, the plan is called **noncontributory**.

ACCOUNTING FOR DEFINED BENEFIT PLANS

The primary accounting issue for defined benefit pension plans is how to match the ultimate costs of the plan to revenue. A related issue is how to measure any asset or liability arising from a defined benefit plan. From the discussion of the economic motivations for retirement plans, it would seem reasonable to assert that the costs of retirement plans actually accrue during the working life of the employees covered by the plan. As a result, the application of the matching concept requires allocation of the costs of defined benefit pension plans over the service lives of the covered employees, providing that reliable estimates of the future costs can be obtained. The appropriate determination of the balance sheet asset or liability associated with these plans was a hotly contested issue when the current reporting standard was developed.

Historically, accountants simply borrowed allocation methods actuaries used to assign the costs of defined benefit pension plans to the periods covered by the expected service lives of employees. Note that actuaries never intended the allocation methods to satisfy the matching concept. In the 1960s the Accounting Principles Board, in Opinion No. 8 (APBO 8), addressed the issue of expense and liability recognition relating to defined benefit pension plans by defining standards for expense recognition that allowed a wide latitude for companies. According to APBO No. 8, pension expense would be determined by applying one of several acceptable actuarial cost methods, all of which required allocation of pension costs to all periods of service. Both of the methods examined previously would have been acceptable under this reporting standard.

Asset and liability recognition for the balance sheet was based on any differences between the periodic expense and the periodic contributions. This implies that over time, if the contributions were larger than the expense, a prepaid pension cost asset was recorded. On the other hand, if the accumulated contributions were less than the accumulated expense, an accrued pension cost liability was recorded. Under this reporting standard, a liability could accrue only if the cumulative pension expenses were more than the company's cumulative contributions to the trust. In short, liability recognition had little to do with the nature of any accrued benefit obligation under the pension contract.

In 1986, the Financial Accounting Standards Board issued Statement No. 87, "Employers Accounting for Pensions." This Standard changed the manner of accounting for defined benefit plans considerably and defined the first requirements for inclusion of a special pension liability in the balance sheet of sponsoring firms. This liability is directly related to an obligation for accrued benefits under the pension contract. SFAS No. 87 relies on measurement procedures common to the accrued benefit method discussed previously, but it develops an accounting method that is very different from the predecessor approach. To handle the transition from the old method to the new, a special transition process was adopted. The following presentation examines the accounting for defined benefit plans adopted after January 1, 1987 (under the new rules), then discusses the transition treatment for plans that existed prior to that date. The effects of the transitional treatments will be with us for many years. Thus, even though the transition occurred several years ago, it still has an impact on current reporting. In addition, the current reporting standards treat liability recognition for defined benefit plans separately from expense recognition. For this reason, expense recognition will be presented first, followed by a discussion of the additional requirements regarding the special liability recognition.

Pension Expense Recognition—Basic Components

Determining the sponsoring firm's periodic pension expense revolves around the valuation of the **projected benefit obligation**, which represents the present value of the projected benefits to be paid to current employees under the plan at retirement, but earned based on service rendered to date. This estimate is based on forecasts of final pay (for final pay related plans), along with any anticipated promotions that employees are likely to receive, and is adjusted for actuarial estimates of such factors as turnover and mortality. As a present value, the projected benefit obligation must be discounted by choosing a discount rate. Selection of this rate is accomplished by comparison with the implicit interest rate available from insurance companies selling annuity contracts that would provide similar retirement benefits.

The pension expense for a period will include the increase in the projected benefit obligation that results from the interest effect (called the **interest cost component**) and the service effect (called the **service cost component**). Note how similar this process is to the actuarial determination of the funding pattern in the projected accrued benefit cost method example discussed earlier. However, this is not the end of the process. The expense will be reduced by the **actual return (earnings)** on the trust assets for the period. The actual return (earnings) on trust assets is made up of the following:

1. Interest earned on interest bearing securities
2. Dividends earned on equity securities
3. Realized gains and losses from sales of assets
4. Unrealized gains and losses on assets held at the end of the period

The pension expense computation will always *begin* with these three components: the service cost component, the interest cost component, and a reduction for the actual earnings on trust assets. Other components of pension expense may arise under special circumstances.

Unrecognized Prior Service Cost

When a company adopts, or amends a pension plan, it usually gives its current employees credit for service rendered prior to amendment or inception of the plan. The **unrecognized prior service cost** is the present value of the increase in expected future benefits attributable to the retroactive grant of service credits at the creation or amendment of a defined benefit pension plan.

The motivation for granting retroactive credit is to generate goodwill with the current employee group in the hope of recovering those costs through increases in the group's future productivity.[4] As such, the cost of these benefits should not be charged to expense immediately but deferred and amortized over the future periods that the employees provide the increased productivity. This system of expense recognition better matches the costs of the pension plan to the revenues generated to pay for it. In this sense, the prior service cost is "unrecognized" until the amortization flows into the income statement through the pension expense. Hence, *unrecognized prior service cost* refers to the unamortized portion of this cost, which will be charged to pension expense in future periods. This amortization represents the fourth component of expense.

The amortization process used to expense the unrecognized prior service cost must be linked to those services rendered by the employees covered by the plan at the date of amendment or inception. On the date of inception (or amendment), the company expects a certain number of years of service from its work force. As each year passes, the total number of expected years of service from those employees present on the date of amendment or inception declines. The percentage represented by the ratio of the decrease in service years divided by the total number of years of expected service at the date of amendment or inception is used as the basis for amortization of the unrecognized prior service cost.

For example, assume that XYZ Company adopted a plan when it had five employees with expected service lives as follows:

Employee	Expected Service Life
A	10.0 years
B	8.0 years
C	6.0 years
D	5.5 years
E	0.5 years

The total expected number of service years is 30 years from all employees. After the first year of the plan, the total decrease in service years is 4.5 years. This represents 15.0% (4.5 ÷ 30) of the total service years of the employee group at inception, and this percentage of the unrecognized prior service cost at inception would be amortized during the first year.

Alternatively, straight-line amortization may be used. The average service life is determined by taking the total expected service years and dividing by

---

[4] This goodwill is a reputational benefit that the sponsor enjoys by voluntarily altering the terms of the plan retroactively. This can make employee groups comfortable with less specificity regarding the effects of such economic factors as inflation, wage changes, and others on the retirement benefit. Allowing more flexibility in the contract can save the sponsor considerable cost in implementing the plan, but only at the employees' risk since lack of specific contract language can be abused. Companies grant retroactive credit to convince current employees that tighter contractual restrictions are unnecessary since future changes in the agreement will be passed on to them as if they had always been in effect.

the number of employees. In this example, the average would be 6 years (30 ÷ 5), and the amortization of the unrecognized prior service cost would be one-sixth of the total for each of the next 6 years. The straight-line method is acceptable if it creates an equal or more rapid rate of amortization, and this method is by far the most popular approach in practice. In the following examples, this form of amortization will be used exclusively.

Basic Pension Expense Determination

The projected benefit obligation and the unrecognized prior service cost do not appear on the sponsoring firm's balance sheet. Thus, much of the data to determine the pension expense must be kept in memo records. To provide an easy way to track the information necessary, Exhibit 18.6 presents an approach to pension expense determination, along with the off-financial statement data for a hypothetical company called EMX Inc.

> EMX adopts a defined benefit plan on January 1, 1993. At that time, the actuary used a discount rate of 8% to project the benefit arising from retroactive credit of $300,000. The company intends to develop a portfolio of assets in the pension trust, which it believes can earn a return of 12%. During the first year, the actuary indicates that the service cost component should be $75,000; but because more rapid funding is preferred, the actuary chooses a different actuarial cost method for determining contributions. The contribution to the pension fund for the first year under this alternative funding approach was $200,000, and no benefits were paid during the first year. At inception, the average remaining service life of the employees was 5 years.

Immediately at inception, a projected benefit obligation is created for $300,000, and an unrecognized prior service cost is also created for the same amount. This amount is entered in the column Projected Benefit Obligation as a credit (numbers in parentheses indicate credits) and in the column headed Unrecognized Prior Service Cost as a debit. These adjustments are recorded in Exhibit 18.6. This event is an off-financial statement event in that it does not trigger asset/liability recognition by the sponsoring company, EMX. Also, note that the off-balance sheet information is organized around debit and credit adjustments just as if it were on a balance sheet.

The periodic pension expense is determined by adding the service cost component (which increases the projected benefit obligation), the interest cost component (which also increases the projected benefit obligation by 8% of the $300,000 beginning balance), the expected return on plan assets (which is zero in the first year because nothing is contributed to the trust until year-end), and the amortization of the unrecognized prior service cost over 5 years (which reduces the unrecognized prior service cost).[5]

---

[5] In all the examples used in this text, including the end-of-chapter exercises and problems, we assume that all payments to the trust and benefits paid out of the trust are made at year-end. This simplifies the computation of the interest cost component and the expected return on plan assets since no cash flows ocur over the period to change these balances. For example, if cash contributions were made to the trust on the first day of the year, expected earnings would need to incorporate this effect. Since adding this complexity does nothing to enhance our conceptual understanding of the issues, but does complicate the actual computations involved, we have elected to apply the more simplified assumptions here.

EMX, INC.
Pension Expense Determination
For Period Ending December 31, 1993

Assumptions for 1993:

1. Service Costs = $75,000
2. Discount Rate for Benefits = 8%
3. Expected Rate of Return on Plan Assets = 12%
4. Average Remaining Service Lives of Employees at 1/1 = 5 years
5. Actual Earnings on Pension Trust Assets for 1988 = 0
6. Unrecognized Prior Service Cost on 1/1 = $300,000
7. Projected Benefit Obligation at 1/1 = $300,000
8. Benefits Paid in 1993 = 0
9. Contribution to the Pension Trust, on last day of 1993 = $200,000.

	Financial Statement Effects			Off-Balance Sheet Memo Records		
	Pension Expense	Cash	Prepaid or (Accrued) Pension Cost	Projected Benefit Obligation	Plan Assets	Unrecognized Prior Service Cost
Balance 1/1/93				$(300,000)	$ 0	$300,000
1993 Activity:						
Service Cost Component	$ 75,000			(75,000)		
Interest Cost Component	24,000			(24,000)		
Actual Earnings	0				0	
Unrecognized Prior Service Cost Amortization	60,000					(60,000)
Funding		$(200,000)			200,000	
Net Change	$159,000	$(200,000)	$41,000	$ (99,000)	$200,000	$ (60,000)
Balance 12/31/93			$41,000	$(399,000)	$200,000	$240,000

EXHIBIT 18.6

EMX, Inc.—
Pension Expense
Determination

The actuary must supply the amount of the annual service cost. In this example, the actuary indicated a service cost of $75,000. When entered into the working paper, the service cost for the period increases both the expense (a debit) and the projected benefit obligation (a credit). A similar adjustment occurs for the interest component, which in this example, was $24,000.

The adjustment for the actual return on plan assets is handled differently. The actual return reduces the pension expense (a credit) and increases the plan assets (a debit). For the first year of this example, there is no return since no assets were invested at the beginning of the year. In addition, since no return was expected, the actual and expected return for the year are equal.

The amortization of the unrecognized prior service cost is first computed using the rules discussed earlier. In this example, the average service life of 5 years was used to amortize the $300,000 of unrecognized prior service cost at $60,000 per year. This amortization is entered into the working paper by reducing the unrecognized prior service cost (a credit) and increasing the pension expense (a debit). At this point, all the components of the pension expense totals $159,000. The actual contribution to the pension trust must be entered. This does not affect the expense recognition, but it does decrease cash (a credit) and increase the assets in the pension trust (a debit) by $200,000.

From the information in Exhibit 18.6, a journal entry can be formulated to record the pension expense relating to EMX's pension plan in 1993. The entry would appear as follows:

December 31, 1993:		
Pension expense	159,000	
Prepaid pension cost	41,000	
Cash		200,000

To record the pension expense accrual for 1993.

Note that because the funding pattern is based on a different allocation process than the expense determination, a balance sheet prepayment is necessary to reflect the fact that funding is occurring more rapidly than the pension cost expense is being recognized. Had the expense been less than the contribution, an accrued pension liability would have been recorded. Also, when the off-balance sheet items are added, the net is a debit of $41,000.

It is no accident that the off-balance sheet items reconcile to the balance sheet accrual. The pension expense is a summary number that represents all the changes in the off-balance sheet pension asset and liability accounts. The journal entry reflects the expense and funding pattern of the plan, and the net asset/liability effect of the pension plan is reflected in the balance sheet accrual.

In reconciling the off-balance sheet items to the balance sheet accrual, some terminology is useful. The difference between the projected benefit obligation and the market value of plan assets is referred to as the plan's **funded status**. The plan's funded status can always be reconciled to the balance sheet accrual by adjusting it for the deferred items. In the example presented in Exhibit 18.6, the following reconciliation could be prepared:

Projected benefit obligation	$(399,000)
Market value of plan assets	200,000
Funded status	$(199,000)
Unrecognized prior service cost	240,000
Prepaid pension costs	$ 41,000

When the projected benefit obligation is larger than the value of the plan assets, the plan is referred to as *underfunded*. Conversely, when the assets exceed the projected benefit obligation, the plan is referred to as *overfunded*.

Unrecognized Gains and Losses

In future years, EMX will continue the same process described above to compute its pension expense. Since the pension trust now has assets to invest, the expense will be reduced by the actual return on those assets. Over time, actual results will differ from expected results. Such differences were defined as actuarial gains and losses in our discussion of the actuarial process; but for accounting purposes, they are labelled **unrecognized gains and losses**. Unrecognized gains and losses do not affect pension expense in the period they arise.[6] Instead, they are deferred. At the beginning of each accounting period, a determination is made as to whether any portion of the cumulative unrecognized gain or loss should be recognized in the current period.

To evaluate the need for amortization of unrecognized gains or losses, the cumulative unrecognized gain or loss is compared to 10% of the larger of the projected benefit obligation or plans assets at the beginning of the year. If the cumulative unrecognized gain or loss is less than the 10% limit, no amortization is taken of any portion of the cumulative gain or loss. If the cumulative unrecognized gain or loss exceeds the 10% limit, the excess is amortized using the same process discussed for the unrecognized prior service cost. This process is called **corridor amortization** since the 10% limit defines a corridor in which no amortization will occur.[7] A demonstration of this follows in the 1994 and 1995 extensions of the EMX example.

> Assume that in 1994 EMX experienced an actual return on trust assets of $80,000 and that an actuarial revaluation of the mortality rates appropriate for EMX's work force reduced the projected benefit obligation by $92,000 at year-end (implying an increase in mortality rates). The service cost and contributions for 1994 are identical to those for 1993, and the trust paid $15,000 in retirement benefits during the year. In 1995, EMX earned $40,000 on trust assets, had a service cost of $75,000, contributed only $100,000, and paid $50,000 in retirement benefits.

In Exhibit 18.7, the existence of unrecognized gains and losses in 1994 requires an additional column to track the cumulative amount of these items. We would expect that the gains recorded this year will be offset against losses in the future so that, on average, the expected outcomes relating to earnings of the trust assets and other actuarial assumptions will be realized in the long run. However, when the cumulative balance of the unrecognized gain or loss gets too large, the likelihood that it will be offset by future events is small; and the expense recognition process can no longer ignore the existence of these unrecognized items.

A 10% corridor defines the measure of "largeness" used to determine when amortization is appropriate. When the beginning balance of the cumulative unrecognized gain or loss exceeds 10% of the larger of the beginning projected benefit obligation or the beginning balance of trust assets, amortization

---

[6] For completeness, a sponsor may recognize all gains and losses immediately in the period they occur. This policy must be applied to all gains and losses in all periods. Any change from this policy requires recognition as a change in accounting principle. The authors of this text are unaware of any major corporation that has adopted this option.

[7] In all the examples used in this text, the assets of the pension trust are valued at full market value. An alternative valuation method, called "market-related value," can be applied to determine pension expense. This method averages the unexpected gains and losses from earnings on plan assets over several years and values the assets at historical cost plus some percentage of the unrealized gains and losses. Market-related value cannot be used for the note disclosures regarding funded status or the application of the minimum liability requirements discussed later.

EMX, INC.
Pension Expense Determination
For Period Ending December 31, 1994

Assumptions for 1994:
1. Service Costs = $75,000
2. Discount Rate for Benefits = 8%
3. Expected Rate of Return on Plan Assets = 12%
4. Amortization of Prior Service Cost = $60,000
5. Actual Earnings on Pension Trust Assets for 1994 = $80,000
6. Gain on Actuarial Revaluation = $92,000
7. Benefits Paid in 1994 = $15,000
8. Contribution to the Pension Trust, on last day of 1994 = $200,000.

| | Journal Entry | | | Off-Balance Sheet Memo Records | | | |
	Pension Expense	Cash	Prepaid or (Accrued) Pension Cost	Projected Benefit Obligation	Plan Assets	Unrecognized Prior Service Cost	Unrecognized (Gains) and Losses
Balance 1/1/94			$41,000	$(399,000)	$200,000	$240,000	
1994 Activity:							
Service Cost	$ 75,000			(75,000)			
Interest Cost	31,920			(31,920)			
Actual Earnings	(80,000)				80,000		
Unrecognized Gain	56,000						$ (56,000)
Unrecognized Prior Service Cost Amortization	60,000					(60,000)	
Actuarial Revaluation				92,000			(92,000)
Funding		$(200,000)			200,000		
Benefit Payments				15,000	(15,000)		
Net Change	$142,920	$(200,000)	$57,080	$ 80	$265,000	$(60,000)	$(148,000)
Balance 12/31/94			$98,080	$(398,920)	$465,000	$180,000	$(148,000)

will be required. An actuarial gain or loss cannot affect pension expense in the year it occurs. The amortization is determined on the beginning balances, not current year activity. In 1994, EMX had no beginning unrecognized gain or loss carried over from previous years; and, thus, no amortization is required.

Completing Exhibit 18.7 for EMX in 1994 requires the same steps as in Exhibit 18.6 for 1993, with three important differences. First, the beginning balances in each of the balance sheet and off-balance sheet accounts are carried over from the ending balance in the previous period.

Second, when the return on plan assets is entered, the actual return is entered first into the expense column as a reduction (credit) and an increase in the trust assets (debit) of $80,000. The expected return was only $24,000 (12% times the beginning balance of trust assets of $200,000). In this case, the actual return exceeded the expected return, so an unrecognized gain arises for the

EXHIBIT 18.7
EMX, Inc.—
Pension Expense
Determination

difference of $56,000. This is entered as an increase in the expense (debit) and an increase to the unrecognized gain or loss column as a gain (credit).

In essence, this process reduces the pension expense by the *expected earnings on plan assets*, which is represented as the difference between the actual earnings and the unrecognized gain or loss. Thus, the expected earnings (actual earnings minus the unrecognized gain or loss) are included in pension expense.

Third, the unrecognized gain arising from the change in mortality rates and resulting in a reduction (debit) to the projected benefit obligation of $92,000 and an increase (credit) in the cumulative unrecognized gain of the same amount must be entered. At year-end, the cumulative unrecognized gain was $148,000. None of this unrecognized gain had any effect on the 1994 pension expense, but it may have an effect on the 1995 expense.

After completing the computations in Exhibit 18.7, EMX would make the following journal entry to record pension expense:

December 31, 1994:

Pension expense	142,920	
Prepaid pension cost	57,080	
Cash		200,000

To record the pension expense accrual for 1994.

As a result of this entry, the balance sheet item, prepaid pension cost, is increased to an ending balance of $98,080. Because of the effects of the revaluation and the rapid funding process EMX adopted, the pension plan, which had a larger projected benefit obligation than it had assets (a situation described as being underfunded) at the beginning of the year, has more assets than liabilities for projected benefits (described as being overfunded) at year-end.

The pension expense determination for 1995 is presented in Exhibit 18.8. Since an unrecognized gain or loss exists at the beginning of the period, it is necessary to use the corridor amortization rules to determine whether any portion of the unrecognized gain needs to be amortized to expense. The unrecognized gain at the beginning of the year is $148,000.

The plan assets at January 1, 1995, are $465,000, which is larger than the projected benefit obligation. Therefore, the corridor is defined as 10% of the plan assets, or $46,500. Since $148,000 exceeds $46,500, amortization must be recorded for 1995. The amortization is computed on the difference between the cumulative gain and the maximum corridor. In this example, the amortization will be based on the difference between $148,000 and $46,500, or $101,500.

The portion of this $101,500 to be recognized as expense will be determined by the average service life of the employees covered as of January 1, 1995. We will assume this is 7 years. As a result, the amortization of the unrecognized gain will decrease pension expense in 1995 by $14,500 ($101,500 ÷ 7). This amortization is entered into the working paper by a reduction (debit) in the unrecognized gain and a decrease (credit) in pension expense.

During 1995, EMX experiences an unrecognized loss due to the poor earnings of the pension trust assets, which fell below the expected return by $15,800. This unrecognized loss offsets part of the cumulative unrecognized gain that existed at the beginning of the period, but it does not affect the amortization of the beginning balance. The amortization simply reduces the beginning unrecognized gain even further.

EMX, INC.
Determination of Pension Expense
For Period Ending December 31, 1995

Assumptions for 1995:
1. Service Costs = $75,000
2. Discount Rate for Benefits = 8%
3. Expected Rate of Return on Plan Assets = 12%
4. Amortization of Prior Service Cost = $60,000
5. Actual Earnings on Pension Trust Assets for 1995 = $40,000
6. Benefits Paid in 1995 = $50,000
7. Contribution to the Pension Trust, on last day of 1995 = $100,000.

| | Financial Statement Effects | | | Off-Balance Sheet Memo Records | | | |
	Pension Expense	Cash	Prepaid or (Accrued) Pension Cost	Projected Benefit Obligation	Plan Assets	Unrecognized Prior Service Cost	Unrecognized (Gains) and Losses
Balance 1/1/95			$ 98,080	$(398,920)	$465,000	$180,000	$(148,000)
1995 Activity:							
Service Cost	$75,000			(75,000)			
Interest Cost	31,914			(31,914)			
Actual Earnings	(40,000)				40,000		
Unrecognized Loss	(15,800)						15,800
Unrecognized Prior Service Cost Amortization	60,000					(60,000)	
Unrecognized Gain Amortization	(14,500)						14,500
Funding		$(100,000)			100,000		
Benefit Payments				50,000	(50,000)		
Net Change	$96,614	$(100,000)	$ 3,386	$ (56,914)	$ 90,000	$ (60,000)	$ 30,300
Balance 12/31/95			$101,466	$(455,834)	$555,000	$120,000	$(117,700)

As an outgrowth of the computations in Exhibit 18.8, EMX would prepare the following journal entry to record pension expense for 1995:

December 31, 1995:

Pension expense	96,614	
Prepaid pension cost	3,386	
Cash		100,000

To record the pension expense accrual for 1995.

The amortization process indicated by the 1995 computations will continue until the cumulative unrecognized gain or loss falls below the corridor limits. As the projected benefit obligation and trust assets increase and the continued amortization of the cumulative gain reduces the size of the unrecognized gain, the unrecognized gain will decline to a point where amortization is no longer necessary, assuming no other large unrecognized gains occur in the future.

EXHIBIT 18.8

EMX, Inc.— Determination of Pension Expense

As the amortization of the unrecognized prior service cost is completed, amortization will stop; and no unrecognized prior service cost will remain. The only way for this item to reappear is if EMX amends the plan. If some portion of the cost of an amendment arises due to retroactive service credit, a new unrecognized prior service cost will arise. That amount will be added to the projected benefit obligation and will increase the unrecognized prior service cost. Amortization of this new unrecognized prior service cost will proceed as explained in the earlier example.

Transition Gains and Losses

For defined benefit plans existing when SFAS No. 87 went into effect (which was January 1, 1987 at the latest), some method of conforming the old measurement and reporting process to the new method described above had to be developed. Prior to SFAS No. 87, firms may have had a prepaid pension cost asset or an accrued pension cost liability on their books. SFAS No. 87 did not alter the size of this carryover asset or liability. Instead, the FASB simply required the creation of a balancing adjustment called a **transition gain/loss**.

When it first adopted SFAS No. 87, a firm started with three items:

1. The carryforward balance of the pension cost asset or liability on its balance sheet
2. The projected benefit obligation as of the date of adoption
3. The market value of plan assets as of the date of adoption

Under the expense determination process just presented, the off-balance sheet items (the projected benefit obligation minus the market value of plan assets) must reconcile to the balance sheet account.

For most firms, the net funded status of the plan (projected benefit obligation minus the market value of plan assets) was not equal to the balance sheet accrual. When this occurred, the firm recorded an adjusting item off-balance sheet to pick up the difference. If the funded status was above the balance sheet accrual (i.e., if the projected benefit obligation minus the market value of plan assets was less than the balance sheet accrual), the firm recorded a transition gain. If the funded status was smaller than that recorded in the financial statements, the firm recorded a transition loss.

For example, if a company had recorded a prepaid pension asset of $50 when it converted to SFAS No. 87, and the actuary indicated that the projected benefit obligation at that point was $200 with pension assets at a market value of $110, then the funded status at conversion would be a net obligation of $90, not an asset of $50. To adjust for the difference between the balance sheet asset of $50 and the off-balance sheet funded status of the plan, underfunded by $90, a transition loss of $140 was necessary. This loss would reconcile the off-balance sheet status of the plan to the on-balance sheet asset as follows:

Projected benefit obligation	$(200)
Plan assets at market value	110
Funded status	(90)
Transition loss	140
Balance sheet prepaid asset	$ 50

If the balance sheet accrual had been a liability of $150, then the company would have recorded a transition gain of $60 to adjust for conversion to SFAS No. 87.

Both transition losses and gains must be amortized to expense in the same fashion as unrecognized prior service cost (i.e., the average service life of the work force on the date of adoption of SFAS No. 87) or over a 15-year period at the sponsor's election. Once the transition item is fully amortized, it will never reappear. Many companies still have a portion of this transition item affecting the computation of pension expense.

Presented in Exhibit 18.9 is an example of the treatment of the unrecognized transition gain/loss for Delta Inc. in 1995. The assumptions are listed at the top of the working paper. The only effect a transition gain or loss has on pension expense recognition is through the annual amortization of this balance. In this example, the amortization of the transition gain is computed as $10,000 per year ($150,000 of unamortized transition gain at the beginning of 1995 divided by 15 years, which is the average service life of employees in the plan at the date Delta adopted SFAS No. 87). The amortization is entered in the working paper as a reduction (debit) of the transition gain and a reduction (credit) of the pension expense. All other computations are the same as the previous examples.

As a result of these computations Delta Inc. would prepare the following pension expense recognition entry on its books:

```
December 31, 1995:
Pension expense                                   161,250
  Accrued pension cost                                          11,250
  Cash                                                         150,000
To record the pension expense accrual for 1995.
```

In this situation, Delta has contributed into the plan an amount that is less than the expense to be recognized, which in turn resulted in an accrued pension cost liability. The classification of the prepaid pension cost or accrued pension cost liability depends on whether the excess funding (expense) will reverse itself within the next accounting period. If this will not occur, the asset/liability should be classified as a noncurrent item.

Note Disclosure Relating to Defined Benefit Pension Plans

For companies not affected by the minimum liability recognition rules to be discussed shortly, the note disclosure required by SFAS No. 87 reflects most of the off-balance sheet information contained within the working papers, which have been discussed previously. The notes must contain:

DELTA, INC.
Determination of Pension Expense with Transition Items
For Period Ending December 31, 1995

Assumptions for 1995:
1. Service Costs = $140,000
2. Discount Rate for Benefits = 8%
3. Expected Rate of Return on Plan Assets = 10%
4. Average Remaining Service Lives of Employees at Adoption of SFAS No. 87 = 15 years
5. Average Remaining Service Lives of Employees at 1/1/95 = 20 years
6. Actual Earnings on Pension Trust Assets for 1995 = Loss of $100,000
7. Remaining Transition Asset = $150,000
8. Actual Benefits Paid for 1995 = $70,000
9. Contribution to the Pension Trust, on last day of 1995 = $150,000.
10. Unrecognized Prior Service Cost from 1993 Amendment to the Plan = $300,000
11. Average Remaining Service Lives of Employees at Date of Amendment = 15 years

	Financial Statement Effects			Off-Balance Sheet Memo Records				
	Pension Expense	Cash	Prepaid or (Accrued) Expense	Projected Benefit Obligation	Plan Assets	Deferred Transition (Gain) Loss	Unrecognized Service Cost	Unrecognized Prior (Gains) Losses
Balance 1/1/95				$ (990,000)	$700,000	$(150,000)	$300,000	$140,000
1995 Activity:								
Service Cost	$140,000			$ (140,000)				
Interest	79,200			(79,200)				
Actual Earnings	100,000				(100,000)			
Unrecognized Gain	(170,000)							170,000
Amortization of Transition Gain	(10,000)					10,000		
Amortization of Unrecognized Prior Service Cost	20,000						(20,000)	
Amortization of Unrecognized Loss	2,050							(2,050)
Funding		$(150,000)			150,000			
Benefits Paid				70,000	$ (70,000)			
Net Change	$161,250	$(150,000)	$(11,250)	$ (149,200)	$ (20,000)	$ 10,000	$ (20,000)	$167,950
Balance 12/31/95			$(11,250)	$(1,139,200)	$680,000	$(140,000)	$280,000	$307,950

EXHIBIT 18.9
Delta, Inc.—
Determination of
Pension Expense
with Transition
Items

1. A description of the plan, employees covered, and funding policies
2. The discount rate used to determine the present value of the projected benefit obligation
3. The expected rate of return on trust investments
4. A reconciliation of the pension expense computation that clearly discloses the actual return on plan assets
5. A reconciliation of the funded status of the plan at year-end

The reconciliation of the pension expense for the period will appear as follows for the Delta Inc. example:

Pension expense components:

1. Service cost	$ 140,000
2. Interest cost	79,200
3. Actual loss on plan assets	100,000
4. Other (net)	(155,450)
Total pension expense	$ 163,750

The Other classification includes the effect of deferring the actuarial loss due to poor investment performance, the amortization of the transition gain, the amortization of the unrecognized prior service costs, and the amortization of the cumulative beginning unrecognized loss. The important issue is that the computation of the expense is based on expected returns, and the note reconciliation is focused on disclosing the actual return. This is partly due to the fact that the user already has been told what the expected rate of return on plan assets is. Thus, disclosing the actual return has the potential to be more informative.

The reconciliation of the funded status of the plan is simply a way of disclosing all of the off-balance sheet data, which provides the basis for expense computation. In addition, the projected benefit obligation is divided into subcomponents. The disclosure starts with the vested benefit obligation (which is based only on the portion of the accrued benefits that are portable and is computed using current, not future, salaries; adds the accumulated but unvested benefits to derive the accumulated benefit obligation (which measures the accrued benefits to date using current, not future, salaries); and finally adds the adjustment for future salaries, increasing the accumulated benefit obligation to the projected benefit obligation. The disclosure might appear as follows:

Reconciliation of balance sheet liability:

Vested benefit obligation	$ (400,000)
Accrued but nonvested benefits	(200,000)
Accumulated benefit obligation	$ (600,000)
Adjustment for future salaries	(539,200)
Projected benefit obligation	$(1,139,200)
Plan assets	680,000
Funded status	$ (459,200)
Deferred transition loss	(140,000)
Unrecognized prior service cost	280,000
Unrecognized gains and losses	307,950
Accrued pension cost	$ (11,250)

When a company supports several, separate defined benefit plans, the reconciliation of pension cost can be aggregated across all plans; but the reconciliation of the funded status cannot. The reconciliation of funded status is aggregated for two separate groups:

1. For all plans whose accumulated benefit obligation exceeds the value of plan assets
2. For all plans whose plan assets exceed the accumulated benefit obligation

The reason for this separation will be clearer after the following discussion on minimum liability recognition. Exhibit 18.10 presents an example of the disclosure required for such situations in part of the note disclosure for Ampco-Pittsburgh Corporation in 1989.

Minimum Liability Recognition

One aspect of accounting for defined benefit plans that has been debated at length is liability recognition. There is no common agreement on what measure of "liability" is appropriate to use in recording a pension obligation. Should the vested benefit obligation be the focus of liability recognition, or should it be the projected benefit obligation, or something else? A secondary issue involves whether the trust assets should be netted against the liability, or whether the assets should be recorded as separate corporate assets and the liability reflected at its gross amount.

By examining the pension expense determination process, we have observed that a balance sheet liability can arise when the accumulated contributions are below the accumulated pension expense recognized. The **minimum liability provision** requires that the smallest value reported in the sponsor's balance sheet be the unfunded accumulated benefit obligation. Plans that have trust assets in excess of the accumulated benefit obligation have no minimum liability to report. When they have an unfunded accumulated benefit obligation, firms employ special procedures to determine whether an adjustment to the balance sheet will be required. Before examining this adjustment process, let us first consider the debates that led the FASB to adopt this particular treatment.

Obtaining Consensus on a Definition of the Liability for Defined Benefit Plans

Arguments over the liability recognition issue stem primarily from the contingent nature of the pension obligation and the fact that the eventual future benefit to be paid is often dependent on salaries not yet paid. Differing views of the severity of the contingency result in different opinions regarding the appropriate amount to record in the corporation's financial statements. Those who take the most restrictive view argue that the entire pension cost estimation process is so fraught with error that no reliable estimate is possible and no liability should be recorded. At the other extreme are those who support recording the entire projected benefit obligation on the basis that they believe it is both reasonably estimable and payment for these costs is probable.

AMPCO-PITTSBURGH CORPORATION
Disclosure Relating to Defined Benefit Plans
December 31, 1989

The Corporation has non-contributory defined benefit pension plans covering substantially all of its employees. The benefits are based on either years of service or a percentage of compensation multiplied by years of service.

The Corporation's funding policy with respect to the Corporate-sponsored pension plans covered by the Employee Retirement Income Security Act of 1974 ("ERISA") is to fund each year's pension expense on a basis that satisfies the maximum amortization periods of ERISA, plus any additional amounts which the Corporation may determine to be appropriate.

The net pension credit related to continuing operations for all Corporate-sponsored pension plans consist of the following components (amounts in thousands):

	1989	1988	1987
Service Cost	$ 963	$ 898	$ 1,373
Interest Cost on Projected Benefit Obligation	6,424	6,242	7,451
Less Return on Plan Assets	$(8,384)	$(8,139)	$(9,037)
Net Amortization and Deferral	158	25	181
Net Pension Cost	$ (839)	$ (974)	$ (32)

The assumptions used in determination of the net pension credit are: discount rate of 10% in 1989 and 1988; 8.75% in 1987; rate of increases in compensation of zero to 5.5%; expected long-term rate of return on assets of 10%.

In 1987, certain pension obligations to retirees were settled through the purchase of non-participating annuity contracts resulting in reductions in operating costs and expenses of continuing operations of $7,438.

The reconciliation of the funded status for pension plans, in which assets exceeded accumulated benefit obligations including discontinued operations, is as follows:

	December 31, 1989	December 31, 1988
Actuarial present value of:		
Vested benefit obligation	$ 86,120	$51,990
Accumulated benefit obligation	$ 90,784	$53,906
Actuarial present value of projected benefit obligation	$ 93,505	$57,117
Plan assets at fair value	124,506	78,612
Plan assets in excess of projected benefit obligation	31,001	21,495
Unrecognized gain	(15,376)	(1,835)
Unrecognized transition asset net of amortization	(1,443)	(1,489)
Net pension asset recognized in the balance sheet in other noncurrent assets	$ 14,182	$18,171

The reconciliation of the funded status for pension plans, in which the accumulated benefit obligation exceeds assets, is as follows:

	December 31, 1988
Actuarial present value of:	
Vested benefit obligation	$ 34,133
Accumulated benefit obligation	$ 34,649
Actuarial present value of projected benefit obligation	$ 34,649
Plan assets at fair value	24,385
Projected benefit obligation in excess of plan assets	(10,264)
Unrecognized gain	(5,686)
Unrecognized transition obligation net of amortization	3,065
Net pension liability recognized in the balance sheet in other noncurrent liabilities	$(12,885)

All of the plan assets are in one merged trust and in 1989 certain of the plans were merged. This merger did not impact pension expense or defined benefits.

EXHIBIT 18.10

The FASB originally proposed reporting the projected benefit obligation, net of the pension assets, as a liability in the sponsor's financial statements.   In addition, it recommended recording the unrecognized service cost as an intangible asset, and the unrecognized gains and losses as a valuation allowance to the liability. This treatment would have resulted in placing all the off-balance sheet balances on the financial statement. Changes in these accounts would have directly affected the pension expense. In this way, the liability valuation process would have driven the expense recognition in an integrated way. Ultimately, this proposal was rejected.

Why did the FASB drop this proposal? There are several factors, the major reason being that the proposal was politically unpopular. It would have resulted in a major change in book leverage ratios for many firms that sponsor defined benefit plans that are underfunded relative to the projected benefit obligation. Since book leverage ratios are a common measure used in debt covenants and other contractual arrangements, a major change would have resulted in violations of these contractual covenants, seriously affecting their ability to continue operations.

In addition, recording the projected benefit obligation as a liability means basing the liability on salaries that are not yet earned. Since future unearned salaries are not considered a corporation's liability, how could a retirement benefit based on these salaries be a company's liability? Given the conceptual issue regarding future salaries and the political objections from the corporate sector, the FASB backed away from requiring this form of liability recognition.

Having discarded the projected benefit obligation, the only other candidates were the vested benefit and accumulated benefit obligations. Many firms argued for using the unfunded vested benefit obligation. The support for this comes from the legal requirement to pay vested benefits even upon termination of the employee and the fact that the unfunded vested benefit measure reflects the extent to which current trust assets are insufficient to pay these benefits. It was probably not a coincidence that a large number of corporations had fully funded all vested benefits at the time the FASB undertook consideration of this accounting rule. Thus, there were only a few industries that would have been significantly affected by requiring some balance sheet adjustment for the unfunded vested benefit obligation.

Another alternative was the accumulated benefit obligation, which received support because it is generally (with some adjustments) the measure of the termination liability under ERISA if the employer elects to terminate the plan. The FASB strongly believed that the basis for liability recognition should not be portability and, thus, rejected the vested benefit argument. The accumulated benefit measure was accepted because of its prominence under ERISA and because the only difference between this measure and the projected benefit measure is due to future salaries. By choosing this measure, the FASB diffused the major conceptual problem with the use of the projected benefit obligation as well. However, since this measure of the liability is not fundamentally related to the expense recognition process, the liability recognition process had to be grafted to the expense recognition process discussed previously. This grafting results in a requirement that some companies, in certain situations, must make additional adjustments to the balance sheet to meet the minimum liability requirements of SFAS No. 87.

The apparent indecision relating to liability recognition is echoed by the fact that while the minimum liability requirements for ongoing plans focus on the accumulated benefit measure, if a pension plan is taken over in an acquisition, the acquiring firm is required to record an obligation on its balance sheet for the unfunded projected benefit obligation, not the unfunded accumulated benefit obligation. The differences in treatment of the same obligation for continuing plans and other plans acquired in corporate takeovers points out the inconsistencies that developed due to the political nature of the final reporting standard.

Recording the Minimum Liability Adjustments

The minimum liability requirements are effective for all sponsoring firms whose accumulated benefit obligation is greater than the value of trust assets as of the end of their accounting periods. The requirement states that a company in this situation must adjust its balance sheet so that a liability at least equal to the unfunded accumulated benefits is recorded. The adjustment required to record this liability will depend, in part, on whether a prepaid pension cost asset or an accrued pension cost liability has already been recorded.

In recording the minimum liability, any previously recorded prepaid/ accrued pension cost is to be subsumed by the minimum liability. Thus, if a prepaid pension cost asset of $10 was recorded as a result of the pension expense recognition process, and the company had an unfunded accumulated benefit obligation of $30, the adjustment necessary to record the minimum liability would be $40 (a credit to the prepaid pension cost asset of $10 and a credit to the minimum liability of $30). If an accrued pension liability of $10 had existed, the adjustment would then be only $20 (a debit of $10 to the accrued liability and a credit of $30 to the minimum liability).

Of course, requiring a firm to record an additional liability necessitates adjustment elsewhere in the financial statements. The net adjustment to record the minimum liability will also result in an adjustment to assets or equity to obtain a balance sheet that still balances. The rules used to determine how the remainder of the journal entry will appear are very complicated and depend on the existence of any unrecognized prior service cost.

In situations where the company has an unrecognized prior service cost at year-end and must make an adjustment for the minimum liability, the company may record an intangible asset to offset the liability, but only up to the amount of the unrecognized prior service cost. In the prepaid pension cost asset example above, the net adjustment of $40 could be debited to an intangible asset if the company had unrecognized prior service cost of at least $40 at year-end. The journal entry to adjust for this minimum liability would appear as:

Intangible asset arising from unrecognized prior service cost	40	
Prepaid pension cost		10
Minimum liability for unfunded accumulated benefits		30

To record the adjustments for the minimum liability recognition relating to the defined benefit plan.

In situations where the unrecognized prior service costs are smaller than the adjustment necessary to record the minimum liability, an intangible is recorded equal to the unrecognized prior service costs. The balance must then be recorded (net of applicable taxes) in an equity valuation account established for the sole purpose of reporting this allowance. If we change the example above slightly and assume that the unrecognized prior service cost was only $15 at year-end, and ignore taxes, the following journal entry would record the adjustments for the minimum liability:

Intangible asset	15	
Allowance for accumulated benefit obligation	25	
Prepaid pension cost		10
Minimum liability for unfunded accumulated benefits		30

To record the minimum liability adjustment under the defined benefit plan.

In this journal entry, the allowance is an equity account similar in nature to the valuation allowance required for the noncurrent marketable securities portfolio when the aggregate market value of the portfolio falls below historical cost.

If a company finds that it no longer needs to record a minimum liability, the minimum liability, intangible, and equity valuation allowance are simply removed from the books; and the original prepaid or accrued pension cost is restored. A more extensive example of the minimum liability requirements follows. Liability Management Incorporated (LMI) faces the possibility of having to recognize a minimum liability in each of three years, 1991–1993. The funded status of LMI's pension plan at the end of each year, prior to the minimum liability recognition, is as follows:

	1991	1992	1993
Vested benefit obligation	$(1,000)	$(1,100)	$(1,450)
Accumulated/unvested benefit obligation	(150)	(100)	(50)
Accumulated benefit obligation	(1,150)	(1,200)	(1,600)
Obligation from projected salary	(350)	(352)	(53)
Projected benefit obligation	(1,500)	(1,552)	(1,653)
Plan assets at fair value	1,100	1,210	1,400
Funding status	$ 400	$ 342	$ 253
Unamortized transition loss	160	120	80
Unrecognized prior service cost	0	0	0
Unrecognized net (gain) or loss	280	22	123
Balance sheet prepaid or (accrual)	$ 40	$ 200	$ (50)

A minimum liability is to be recognized only when the assets in the plan (at fair value), plus or minus any balance sheet accrual, are less than the accumulated benefit obligation. For LMI this obligation is as follows:

	1991	1992	1993
Market value of assets	$ 1,100	$ 1,210	$ 1,400
Accumulated benefit obligation	$(1,150)	$(1,200)	$(1,600)
Net liability	$ (50)	$ (0)	$ (200)

This implies that LMI must record a liability of at least these amounts in each of the three years. However, the size of the adjustment necessary to record this liability will be reduced for any deferred pension cost liability already recognized or increased to offset any prepaid pension cost asset already recognized. For LMI, this results in the following adjustments:

	1991	1992	1993
Net liability	$50	0	$200
Balance sheet (accrual) or asset	40	0	(50)
Balance sheet adjustment	$90	0	$150

Once the size of the liability adjustment has been determined, we can determine the size of the intangible asset to be recorded as an offset to the liability. The intangible asset cannot exceed the sum of any unrecognized prior service cost plus the remaining unamortized transition loss (transition gains are ignored). In this example, there was no unrecognized prior service cost, but LMI did have a transition loss of $160 in 1991, $120 in 1992, and $80 in 1993. Notice that the amortization of the transition loss will systematically lower the maximum intangible that can be recognized, along with minimum liability.

Since the minimum liability adjustment in 1991 is $90 and the maximum intangible that LMI could record is $160, the minimum liability recognition requirement will result in the following journal entry:

December 31, 1991:

Intangible asset arising from unrecognized prior service cost	90	
Prepaid pension cost		40
Minimum liability for unfunded accumulated benefits		50

To record the adjustments for the minimum liability recognition relating to the defined benefit plan.

In the entry above, the balance in the prepaid pension cost account, which was the result of the journal entry made to record the pension expense for the period, is removed from the books; and only the minimum liability remains with the intangible asset. The adjustments in the above entry can only be determined after completing the expense recognition process and determining the prepaid/accrued pension cost account balance.

At the end of 1992, LMI will go through its normal expense recognition process. In addition, since the value of the plan assets exceeds the accumulated benefit obligation, no minimum liability is recorded. Thus, for 1992, LMI would reverse the entry made in 1991 and remove the minimum liability, the intangible asset, and restore the beginning prepaid pension cost. The ending balance of the prepaid pension cost asset would be $200, but no liability would be required.

During 1993, LMI would again record pension expense in its normal fashion. The result of recording the pension expense is reflected in the reconciliation presented previously. As a result, LMI is again in a situation where the minimum liability requirements must be met by adjusting the balance sheet. However, at this point, the liability adjustment is $150, after adjusting for the accrued pension obligation LMI has already recorded. The intangible at the end of 1992 cannot exceed the $80 of unamortized transition loss; and so to complete the recording of the minimum liability, an equity valuation account must be established for the difference of $120. LMI's entry to record the minimum liability would appear as follows:

December 31, 1993:

Intangible asset	80	
Equity allowance for accumulated benefit obligation	120	
Accrued pension cost		50
Minimum liability for unfunded accumulated benefits		150

To record the minimum liability adjustment under the defined benefit plan for 1993.

As in the previous example, the only pension liability in the final balance sheet is the minimum liability.

If LMI were to adopt an amendment to its plan that created an increase in the unrecognized prior service cost, this would correspondingly increase the maximum size of the intangible. Of course, such an amendment may also increase the accumulated benefit obligation. In this way, the ongoing events that alter the status of the plan at any point may also change the firm's minimum liability recognition requirement.

The minimum liability provisions of SFAS No. 87 must be applied on a plan-by-plan basis. If a company sponsors one plan that is overfunded and a second that is underfunded, it cannot offset the overfunding of one plan against the underfunded level of the second. Instead, a minimum liability must be recognized for the second plan. Exhibit 18.11 provides an example of

---

BF GOODRICH CORPORATION
Disclosures Regarding Funded Status and Minimum Liability
December 31, 1989

BF Goodrich and its subsidiaries have several contributory and non-contributory defined-benefit plans covering substantially all employees. Plans covering salaried employees generally provide benefit payments using a formula that is based on employee's compensation and length of service. Plans covering hourly employees generally provide benefit payments of stated amounts for each year of service.

The Company's general funding policy for pension plans is to contribute amounts sufficient to satisfy regulatory funding standards. Provisions of the Omnibus Budget Reconciliation Act of 1987 allow additional tax deductible contributions for underfunded U.S. plans. In January 1990, the Company, under these provisions, made cash contributions of $26.2 for the 1989 plan year, $18.8 of which was not required under ERISA. After giving effect to these contributions, cumulative contributions made by the Company have exceeded the ERISA minimum funding requirements by $26.5. Plan assets for these plans consist principally of corporate and government obligations and commingled funds invested in equities, debt, and real estate.

EXHIBIT 18.11
BF Goodrich Corporation—Disclosures Regarding Funded Status and Minimum Liability

EXHIBIT 18.11 |
Continued

BF GOODRICH CORPORATION
Disclosures Regarding Funded Status and Minimum Liability
December 31, 1989

The components of net periodic pension cost for the Company's defined benefit pension plans are as follows (dollars in millions):

	1989	1988	1987
Service Cost for Benefits Earned	$ 7.2	$ 7.4	$ 8.1
Interest Cost on Projected Benefit Obligation	46.6	45.7	40.9
Actual Return on Plan Assets	(55.0)	(51.9)	(15.7)
Net Amortization and Deferral	16.1	18.4	(16.6)
Net Pension Cost	$ 14.9	$ 19.6	$ 16.7

Curtailment losses of $1.5 for 1989 and $5.2 for 1988, which resulted from dispositions of business units classified as discontinued operations, are not reflected in net pension cost in the preceding table, but are included in "income (loss) from discontinued operations" in the Consolidated Statement of income.

The following table sets for the funded status (based principally on measurement dates of September 30, 1989 and 1988) of the Company's defined-benefit pension plans and amounts recognized in the Consolidated Balance Sheet at December 31, 1989, and 1988:

	1989	
	Plans with Assets Exceeding Accumulated Benefit Obligation	Plans with Accumulated Benefit Obligation Exceeding Assets
Actuarial value of accumulated benefit obligation:		
Vested	$ 43.2	$ 425.6
Non-vested	1.2	26.9
Accumulated benefit obligation	44.4	452.5
Plan assets at fair value	115.1	387.7
Plan assets in excess of (less than) accumulated benefit obligation	$ 70.7	$ (64.8)
Projected benefit obligation	$ 61.7	$ 507.5
Plan assets at fair value	115.1	387.7
Plan assets in excess of (less than) projected benefit obligation	$ 53.4	$(119.8)
Consisting of:		
Unrecognized transitional asset (liability)	$ 24.2	$ (72.2)
Unrecognized prior service cost	(.5)	(39.7)
Unrecognized net gain (loss)	18.5	(7.9)
Adjustment required to recognize minimum liability	-	64.8
Contribution made subsequent to measurement date	-	(1.3)
Prepaid (accrued) pension cost recognized in the balance sheet	11.2	(63.5)
Total	$ 53.4	$(119.8)

EXHIBIT 18.11

Continued

BF GOODRICH CORPORATION
Disclosures Regarding Funded Status and Minimum Liability
December 31, 1989

	1989	
	Plans with Assets Exceeding Accumulated Benefit Obligation	**Plans with Accumulated Benefit Obligation Exceeding Assets**
Actuarial value of accumulated benefit obligation:		
Vested	$38.0	$373.8
Non-vested	1.5	23.6
Accumulated benefit obligation	39.5	397.4
Plan assets at fair value	97.8	353.3
Plan assets in excess of (less than) accumulated benefit obligation	$58.3	$ (44.1)
Projected benefit obligation	$57.2	$439.1
Plan assets at fair value	97.8	353.3
Plan assets in excess of (less than) projected benefit obligation	$40.6	$ (85.8)
Consisting of:		
Unrecognized transitional asset (liability)	$25.9	$ (81.5)
Unrecognized prior service cost	(.5)	(.2)
Unrecognized net gain (loss)	9.1	(9.0)
Adjustment required to recognize minimum liability	-	-
Contribution made subsequent to measurement date	-	-
Prepaid (accrued) pension cost recognized in the balance sheet	6.1	(13.1)
Total	$40.6	$ (85.8)

Commencing in 1989, Statement of Financial Accounting Standards No. 87, "Employers Accounting for Pensions," requires recognition in the balance sheet of a minimum liability for underfunded plans. The minimum liability that must be recognized is equal to the excess of the accumulated benefit obligation over plan assets. A corresponding amount is recognized as either an intangible asset or a reduction of equity. Pursuant to this requirement, BF Goodrich had recorded, as of December 31, 1989, an additional liability of $64.8, and intangible pension asset of $63.1, and an equity reduction of $1.7.

General benefit improvements granted during 1989 in the Company's principal salary plan are reflected in the 1989 unrecognized prior service cost.

Major assumptions used in accounting for BF Goodrich's defined benefit pension plans are as follows:

	1989	1988	1987
Discount rate for obligations	9.25%	9.75%	10.00%
Rate of increase in compensation levels	6.00%	6.00%	6.00%
Expected long-term rate of return on plan assets	9.50%	9.50%	9.25%

the disclosures related to the BF Goodrich's pension plans as of December 31, 1989 and 1988, respectively. Notice that the adjustments for the minimum liability are applied only to those plans that have an unfunded accumulated benefit obligation. In addition, the adjustment was only required for 1989, not for 1988. This is due to the implementation of the minimum liability requirements in 1989 as discussed in BF Goodrich's note.

SUMMARY

This chapter has examined the issues in accounting and reporting for defined benefit pension plans. A relatively detailed overview of the actuarial process was provided to understand much of the terminology used in this area. As part of that discussion, the important components of a defined benefit plan contract such as the benefit formula, accrual provisions, and vesting provisions were identified. The role of governmental oversight in regulating these provisions was also briefly described. After reviewing the role of the actuary's calculations in determining a funding pattern for the pension plan, the discussion turned to the accounting treatment afforded defined benefit plans.

The projected benefit obligation was introduced, and its relationship to the expense recognition process was discussed. Expense recognition was found to consist of six possible components:

1. A service cost component
2. An interest cost component
3. A reduction for the expected return on trust assets
4. Amortization of unrecognized prior service costs
5. Amortization of unrecognized gains or losses (when necessary)
6. Amortization of transition gains or losses (when necessary)

From this process, a working paper was developed to track all activity related to accounting for the pension plan. This working paper not only allowed for greater ease of organization, but it also provided data necessary to prepare the required note disclosure.

Minimum liability recognition was discussed as an outgrowth of the FASB's perceived need for balance sheet recognition of the unfunded accumulated benefit obligation. Adjustments to a sponsoring firm's balance sheet for this minimum liability provision were examined.

QUESTIONS

1. Describe the *actuary's* main role as it relates to a *defined benefit plan*.
2. What is an *actuarial assumption*? Give examples.
3. What is an *actuarial cost method*?
4. What do actuaries mean when they speak of *prior service cost*?
5. How do the concepts of the *accrued benefit cost method, prior service cost*, and the *projected benefit obligation* fit together?

6. How does the actuarial concept of *normal cost* relate to the accounting concept of service cost?

7. What is an *actuarial gain or loss*, and how does it relate to the accounting concept of *unrecognized gains and losses*?

8. What are the components of pension expense for financial reporting purposes?

9. Describe the rule used to amortize unrecognized prior service costs.

10. What is *corridor amortization* and how does it work?

11. How is the *minimum liability* measured?

12. What basis is there for recording an intangible associated with the minimum liability, and what is the maximum amount of this intangible?

13. When recognizing the minimum liability, if the intangible asset is too small to offset all of the adjustment, how will the balance be recorded?

EXERCISES

18-1.   *Comparison of funding patterns under alternative cost methods*

ABC Company has just adopted a defined benefit pension plan. The actuary indicated that the past service cost of the plan under the entry age normal method is $500,000 and that the normal cost for the next year would be $100,000. Under the accrued benefit method, the past service cost is only $300,000; and the normal cost for next year will be $60,000. ABC wishes to fund the past service cost over a period of 20 years, and the actuary suggested an interest rate of 8% to determine the funding pattern.

REQUIRED:

Prepare an estimate of the contribution required under each of these alternative actuarial cost methods.

18-2.   *Basic expense determination*

ABC Corp. began 1994 with a fully funded projected benefit obligation of $2,400,000. ABC had no unrecognized prior service cost, no transition gain or loss, no unrecognized gains or losses, and no balance sheet accrual relating to prepaid/accrued pension cost. ABC uses a discount rate of 10% in determining the projected benefit obligation and has an expected rate of return on plan assets of 8%. The actuary has indicated that the service cost for 1994 will be $350,000. ABC contributed $450,000 on the last day of the year.

REQUIRED:

Assuming that ABC earned $206,000 on plan assets in 1994, had no other unrecognized gains or losses, and paid benefits in the amount of $430,000, determine the following:
1. Interest cost component
2. Expected return on plan assets
3. Pension expense
4. Prepaid/accrued pension cost
5. Ending projected benefit obligation
6. Ending value of plan assets

18-3.   *Basic expense determination*

ABC Corp. began 1995 with a projected benefit obligation of $800,000, pension trust asset of $700,000, and an accrued pension cost on its balance sheet of $100,000. ABC had no unrecognized prior service cost, no transition gain or loss, and no unrecognized gains or losses. ABC uses a discount rate of 10% in determining the projected benefit obligation and has an expected rate of return on plan assets of 10%. The actuary has indicated that the service cost for 1995 will be $30,000. ABC contributed $20,000 to the plan on the last day of 1995.

REQUIRED:

Assuming that ABC earned $50,000 on plan assets in 1995, had an actuarial revaluation that increased the ending projected benefit obligation by $50,000, and paid benefits on the last day of the year in the amount of $70,000, determine the following:
1. Interest cost component
2. Expected return on plan assets
3. Pension expense
4. Prepaid/accrued pension cost
5. Ending projected benefit obligation
6. Ending value of plan assets
7. Ending value of unrecognized gain or loss

18-4.   *Expense measurement with prior service cost*

The following information was extracted from Mymy Corporation's records regarding the ending balance of several items related to Mymy's defined benefit plan as of December 31, 1994:

Projected benefit obligation	$2,000,000
Value of trust assets	1,400,000
Unrecognized prior service cost	540,000
Balance sheet accrued pension cost	60,000
Discount rate for benefits	9%
Expected return on plan assets	10%
Average service lives of work force at inception of plan	8 years

Mymy had adopted this plan on January 1, 1992. During 1995, Mymy had service costs of $235,000, contributed $500,000 to the fund, paid benefits of $360,000, and earned $260,000 on its trust assets. Contributions and benefit payments occur on the last day of the year.

REQUIRED:

Determine the ending balances for the following items:
1. Pension expense
2. Prepaid/accrued pension cost
3. Unrecognized prior service cost

18-5.   *Determination of amortization periods for prior service cost*

Assume the unrecognized prior service cost at the inception of a pension plan was $1,000,000. The information relating to the service lives of employees at the date of the adoption of the plan is available.

Expected Years of Service	Number of Employees in Category
10	10
9	8
8	5
7	5
6	5
5	6
4	7
3	5
2	8
1	12

REQUIRED:

1. How would the determination of the pension expense and ending unrecognized prior service cost differ if you used an average service life or the proportionate reduction in total service years to amortize the unrecognized prior service cost?
2. When is the average service life appropriate?

18-6.   *Expense measurement with prior service cost and unrecognized gains*

The following information was extracted from Beta Corporation's records regarding the beginning balance of several items related to Beta's defined benefit plan:

Projected benefit obligation	$4,500,000
Value of trust assets	5,200,000
Unrecognized prior service cost	1,200,000
Unrecognized gain	200,000
Balance sheet prepaid pension cost	1,700,000
Discount rate for benefits	6%
Expected return on plan assets	8%
Average service lives of work force for amortization of unrecognized prior service cost	10 years

During the current year, Beta had service costs of $370,000 and earned $480,000 on its trust assets.

REQUIRED:

Determine the ending balances for the following items:

1. Pension expense
2. Unrecognized prior service cost
3. Unrecognized gain or loss

18-7.   *Corridor amortization*

At the beginning of the year, Deca Corp. had a projected benefit obligation of $1,200,000, trust assets of $600,000, and an unrecognized loss of $180,000. The average service life of the work force at the beginning of the year is estimated at 6 years.

REQUIRED:

1. Determine the size of the corridor used in deciding whether the unrecognized loss should be amortized.
2. Calculate the amortization to be recognized for the year.
3. Would your answer differ if Deca had reported an unrecognized gain of $100,000 during the year?

18-8.   *Transition gains and losses*

Apco Corporation has had a defined benefit pension plan for many years. As a result, in 1987 when Apco first employed the new pension reporting standard the FASB developed, it has a transition loss of $399,000. In 1987, the average service life of Apco's work force covered by the plan was 15 years.

In 1994 Apco collected the following information regarding other components of its pension expense:

Service cost	$35,000
Interest cost	55,000
Expected return on plan assets	42,000

Apco has no unrecognized prior service cost, and does not require any amortization of an unrecognized gain or loss.

REQUIRED:

1. Compute the pension expense of Apco, including the amortization of the transition loss.
2. What would the ending unamortized transition loss be on December 31, 1994?

18-9.   *Effect of various amortizations on pension expense*

Zeta Corporation reported the following information in the notes to its 1994 financial statements:

Projected benefit obligation	$2,750,000
Value of trust assets	2,435,000
Unrecognized prior service costs	980,000
Unrecognized loss	336,000
Transition gain	120,000

At the time Zeta converted to the current pension reporting standard on January 1, 1989, the expected average service life of its employees was 7 years. The unrecognized service cost arose from an amendment to the plan dated January 1, 1991, at which time the expected average service life had increased to 10 years. As of January 1, 1995, the expected average service life of Zeta's work force has again increased to 12 years.

REQUIRED:

Compute the amounts to be included in pension expense for 1995 relating to the amortization of unrecognized prior service costs, unrecognized losses, and the transition gain.

18-10.   *Minimum liability requirements*

After completing the determination of pension expense for the year, Heavydebt Inc. had recorded a prepaid pension cost of $67,000. At this point, Heavydebt is trying to determine what adjustments it must make, if any, to meet the minimum liability recognition rules for the accumulated pension obligation. Heavydebt has an accumulated benefit obligation in the amount of $1,200,000 and pension trust assets valued at only $920,000. Heavydebt has no transition item, but it does have an unrecognized prior service cost in the amount of $430,000.

REQUIRED:

Prepare the journal entry necessary to record the minimum liability required of Heavydebt.

18-11. *Minimum liability requirement with prior service costs*

Maco Corporation reports the following regarding the status of its defined benefit pension plan as of December 31, 1994, but before any adjustment for the minimum liability:

Vested benefit obligation	$225,000
Accumulated/unvested benefit obligation	425,000
Accumulated benefit obligation	750,000
Obligation from projected salary	225,000
Projected benefit obligation	975,000
Plan assets at fair value	600,000
Funding status	375,000
Unrecognized transition loss obligation at year-end	120,000
Unrecognized net (gain) or loss	170,000
Balance sheet prepaid or (accrual)	$ (85,000)

REQUIRED:

1. Prepare the journal entry necessary to record the minimum liability of Maco, ignoring taxes.
2. If the transition item had been a gain, instead of a loss, describe how that would have affected your computations?

18-12. *Minimum liability requirements without prior service costs*

In reconciling the data on its defined benefit plan, Kaiser Corporation discovered it was subject to the minimum liability recognition rules of SFAS No. 87. Kaiser has determined that it presently has an accrued pension cost on its books in the amount of $245,000, but the minimum liability required is $569,000. At the present time, Kaiser has no unrecognized prior service cost, but it does have an unamortized transition gain of $200,000.

REQUIRED:

Determine the journal entry Kaiser must make to record the minimum liability, ignoring taxes.

18-13. *Note disclosures*

Using the data in the following working paper for Decon Inc., prepare the footnote disclosure required relating to the reconciliation of pension expense for 1994.

Decon, Inc.
Workpaper to Determine Pension Expense
For Period Ending 12/31/94

	Financial Statement Effects				Off-Balance Sheet Memo Records			
	Pension Expense	Cash	Prepaid or (Accrued) Expense	Projected Benefit Obligation	Plan Assets	Deferred Transition (Gain) Loss	Unrecognized Prior Service Cost	Unrecognized (Gains) Losses
Bal. 1/1/94			$ 49,000	$(923,000)	$ 687,000	$100,000	$210,000	$ (25,000)
1994 Activity:								
Expense Components:								
Service Cost	$ 80,000			(80,000)				
Interest	92,300			(92,300)				
Earnings	(103,050)				$ 200,000			(96,950)
Amortization of Transition Liability	20,000					(20,000)		
Amortization of Unrecognized Prior Service Cost	30,000						(30,000)	
Funding		$(250,000)			250,000			
Benefits Paid				127,000	(127,000)			
Net Change	$ 119,250	$(250,000)	$130,750	$ (45,300)	$ 323,000	$ (20,000)	$ (30,000)	$ (96,950)
Bal. 12/31/94			$179,750	$(968,300)	$1,010,000	$ 80,000	$180,000	$(121,950)

18-14. *Note disclosures*

Use the data from the working paper for Exercise 18-13 and assume the accumulated benefit obligation is 60% of the projected benefit obligation and the vested benefits are 20% of the accumulated benefits.

REQUIRED:

Prepare the footnote disclosure required regarding the funded status of the plan at the end of 1994.

PROBLEMS

18-1. *Expense recognition*

Fisher Corp. adopted a defined benefit pension plan as of January 1, 1994. At that date, the projected benefit obligation was $1,400,000, which equalled the unrecognized prior service costs. The benefits are determined using a discount rate of 10%, but Fisher expects a return of 12% on trust assets. The unrecognized prior service cost is being amortized over 20 years. During 1994, several events occurred; and at year-end, Fisher had a projected benefit obligation of

$1,750,000, trust assets of $300,000, an unrecognized loss from an actuarial revaluation of $20,000, and an unrecognized prior service cost of $1,330,000. In 1995, the actuary indicated that the service cost for the year was $267,000. Actual earnings on trust assets amounted to $40,000. To date no benefits have been paid out of the pension trust. Fisher contributed $465,000 to the pension trust during the year.

REQUIRED:

Prepare a working paper to account for the 1995 activity relating to the determination of Fisher Corporation's pension expense.

18-2.   *Expense recognition with actuarial gains and losses*

At the beginning of 1993, Strawhaut Manufacturing reported the following information regarding the funded status of its pension plan:

Vested benefit obligation	$ (365,000)
Accumulated/unvested benefit obligation	(435,000)
Accumulated benefit obligation	$ (900,000)
Obligation from projected salary	(600,000)
Projected benefit obligation	$(1,500,000)
Plan assets at fair value	1,700,000
Funding status	$ 200,000
Unrecognized prior service cost	525,000
Unrecognized net (gain) or loss	(215,000)
Balance sheet prepaid or (accrual)	$ 510,000

Strawhaut was amortizing the unrecognized prior service cost over a remaining period of 5 years. The company uses a discount rate of 6% and has an expected rate of return on trust assets of 10%.

At the beginning of 1993, Strawhaut determined that the average service life of its employees was 8 years. During 1993, the service cost of the plan was $275,000, and the actual return on plan assets was $140,000. In addition, at the end of 1993, an actuarial revaluation was undertaken and resulted in an actuarial adjustment to the projected benefit obligation to increase this balance by $85,000. The trust paid out retirement benefits in the amount of $160,000 during 1993. During 1993, Strawhaut made no contributions due to the overfunded status of the plan at the beginning of the year.

REQUIRED:

Prepare a working paper to compute the pension expense of Strawhaut Manufacturing for 1993?

18-3.   *Actuarial gains and losses and amendments*

Precept, Inc. has sponsored a defined benefit pension plan for its hourly employees for many years. During 1993, Precept's actuary indicated that the service cost for the year was $582,000 and contributions to the plan would be $930,000. The trustee for the plan has indicated that benefits in the amount of $1,320,000 were paid at year-end and earnings on trust assets for the year were $832,000. Precept had an unamortized transition loss of $1,200,000 at the beginning of 1991 when it changed its reporting for defined benefit plans to the new requirements of SFAS No. 87. This loss was being amortized over a period of 8 years.

On July 1, 1992, Precept had adopted an amendment to increase the benefits for all employees covered under the plan. The effect of this amendment was to increase the projected benefit obligation by $1,500,000. The average remaining service lives of employees affected by the amendment on July 1, 1992, was 7.5 years.

At the beginning of 1993, Precept reported a projected benefit obligation of $8,100,000 with plan assets valued at $6,500,000. Precept uses 8.5% as a discount rate for the future benefits and expects a 9.2% return on plan assets. In addition, Precept had a cumulative unrecognized gain at January 1, 1993, of $576,000; and the average service lives of employees covered on January 1 was 7.2 years.

REQUIRED:

1. Reconstruct the beginning balances for the balance sheet and off-balance sheet items relating to the defined benefit plan.
2. Prepare a working paper to determine the Precept's pension expense.

18-4.   *Determining amortization periods, gains and losses and unrecognized prior service costs*

In 1994, Mandan, Inc. began a defined benefit pension plan. The unrecognized prior service cost at the inception of the plan was $300,000. At that time, the distribution of employees by years of expected remaining service was as follows:

Years of Remaining Service	Number of Employees
20	13
15	17
10	15
5	10

In 1994, the pension expense reported for financial statement purposes consisted of service cost of $34,000, interest cost of $42,000 (computed at an assumed rate of 14%), and the amortization of the unrecognized prior service costs. Mandan contributed $140,000 to the plan at year end.

When the mortality tables for workers in Mandan's industry significantly changed, an actuarial revaluation was undertaken at the end of 1994. This revaluation resulted in an actuarial loss of $57,000.

For 1995, the actuaries have indicated that the service cost component should be $45,000; and Mandan can expect a 10% return on plan assets invested. Mandan made a contribution of $140,000 at year-end and earned $18,900 on the pension assets during 1995. No benefits have been paid since the inception of the plan, and no employees were hired or fired during 1994 or 1995.

REQUIRED:

Prepare a schedule to determine the pension expense for 1995, along with the balances of the off-balance sheet pension accounts at the end of 1995.

18-5.   *Minimum liability recognition*

Microft Corporation has been accounting for its defined benefit pension plans using SFAS No. 87 for several years without the need to record an adjustment for the minimum liability provisions. At the end of 1994, Microft discovered that it had an unfunded accumulated benefit obligation in the amount of $260,000. At that same time, Microft had a remaining transition loss of $80,000, an unrecognized prior service cost from an amendment to its plan of $240,000, and an unrecognized gain of $32,000. Microft has recorded its pension expense for the year; and, as a result, currently shows an accrued pension cost on its balance sheet of $200,000.

REQUIRED:

Prepare the journal entry necessary for Microft's compliance with the minimum liability requirements of SFAS No. 87.

18-6.   *Expense and minimum liability interaction*

At the beginning of 1994, Shortcash, Inc. reported the following information regarding the funded status of its pension plan:

Vested benefit obligation	$ (300,000)
Accumulated/unvested benefit obligation	450,000
Accumulated benefit obligation	$ (750,000)
Obligation from projected salary	500,000
Projected benefit obligation	$(1,250,000)
Plan assets at fair value	300,000
Funding status	$ (950,000)
Unrecognized prior service cost	50,000
Unrecognized net (gain) or loss	800,000
Pension intangible	(50,000)
Allowance for the excess of the minimum liability over the pension intangible	(160,000)
Deferred taxes on excess	(140,000)
Balance sheet liability	$ (450,000)

By the end of 1994, the unfunded accumulated benefit obligation had risen to $575,000. In addition, the unrecognized prior service cost at December 31, 1994 had fallen to $40,000; and the unrecognized loss had risen to $860,000. Shortcash had not funded any of the pension expense for the period, and the expense was reported at $120,000. Shortcash has a 40% tax rate.

REQUIRED:

Prepare the journal entry necessary to adjust the minimum liability at the end of 1994.

18-7.   *Expense and minimum liability interaction*

Anderson, Inc., began a defined benefit pension plan on April 1, 1995. Anderson's fiscal year ends on September 30 each year. At the plan's inception, the unrecognized prior service cost was $500,000. The average service life of Anderson's employees at inception was 10 years. Anderson uses a discount rate of 8.8% to determine the present value of plan benefits. Service costs for the portion of the year that the plan existed were estimated at $102,500.

Anderson made three contributions to the pension trust during the remainder of fiscal 1995. Each was in the amount of $80,000; and they were made on April 1, July 1, and September 30. The plan paid no benefits during 1995, but the trust earned $12,300 on investments by year-end. Anderson expects the trust to earn a 9.2% rate of return on assets.

At the end of the fiscal year, the accumulated benefit obligation represented 70% of the projected benefit obligation.

REQUIRED:

Prepare all journal entries required to account for Anderson's defined benefit plan during fiscal 1995.

18-8.   *Expense determination and drafting of note disclosures*

Delta, Inc., converted to the new pension standard in 1987. It is now December 31, 1994, and the following information has been obtained regarding the activity in the pension plan for the year:

Service costs = $140,000

Discount rate for benefits = 8%

Expected rate of return on plan assets = 10%

Average remaining service lives of employees at adoption of SFAS No. 87 = 15 years

Average remaining service lives of employees at January 1, 1994 = 20 years

Actual earnings on pension trust assets for 1994 = (100,000) loss

Remaining transition gain on January 1, 1994 = $150,000

Actual benefits paid for 1994 (Paid on December 31) = $70,000

Effect of an actuarial revaluation on December 31 = Increase in the projected benefit obligation of $30,000

Contribution to the pension trust, on last day of 1994 = $150,000

Unrecognized prior service cost at January 1, 1994, arising from an amendment adopted on January 1, 1992 = $300,000

Average remaining service lives of employees at date of amendment = 15 years

At the beginning of 1994, Delta had a projected benefit obligation of $990,000 and plan assets of $700,000.

REQUIRED:

Prepare the pension expense computation for 1994 and any related schedules required in the notes, assuming 20% of the projected benefit obligation is vested and the accumulated benefit obligation is 50% of the projected benefit obligation.

18-9.   *Accounting for multiple plans*

Darvon Chemical Corporation has had separate defined benefit pension plans for its hourly and salaried workers for some time. At the end of 1995, after recording the pension expense for the year, Darvon discovered that for the first time the hourly plan had unfunded accumulated benefits, while the salaried plan was still significantly overfunded. Neither plan had any transition gain or loss remaining, nor were there any unrecognized prior service costs at the end of 1995. Information on the two plans is presented below:

	Salaried	Hourly
Accumulated benefit obligation	$ (800,000)	$(1,200,000)
Projected benefit obligation	$(1,700,000)	$(1,800,000)
Plan assets	1,500,000	750,000
Unrecognized losses	400,000	900,000

REQUIRED:

1. Can Darvon use the overfunded status of the salaried plan to offset the underfunded status of the hourly plan? Why or why not?
2. Prior to the recognition of any minimum liability, what was recorded on Darvon's balance sheet related to the defined benefit plans?
3. Make any journal entry necessary to apply the minimum liability recognition rules under SFAS No. 87. (Ignore taxes.)

PILLSBURY CORPORATION

Pillsbury was an independent corporation in the food and restaurant business prior to early 1989, when it was acquired by a British firm. Presented below is the note describing the retirement plans of Pillsbury Corporation as it appeared in the 1986 Annual Report of the Company.

Summary of Data from the Statement of Earnings: (in millions)

	1986	1985	1984
Earnings before taxes	$377.1	$340.2	$303.7
Taxes on income	169.0	148.4	133.9
Net earnings	$208.1	$191.8	$169.8
Net earnings per share	$ 4.77	$ 4.42	$ 3.91

Summary of Data from Balance Sheet: (in millions)

	1986	1985
Current assets:		
Cash and equivalents	$ 96.5	$ 59.7
Receivables	492.7	383.5
Inventories	490.2	432.8
Advances on purchases	30.0	18.7
Prepaid expenses	49.7	26.8
Total	1,159.1	921.5
Property, plant, and equipment:	1,763.2	1,403.0
Net investment in direct financing leases	193.3	189.3
Intangibles	421.6	163.2
Other assets	121.6	101.5
Total Assets	$3,658.8	$2,778.5
Current liabilities:	$1,135.5	$ 744.1
Long-term debt	972.9	647.7
Deferred taxes	202.5	192.4
Other deferrals	33.7	28.9
Common stock (no par)	325.2	324.9
Treasury stock	(24.4)	(23.3)
Retained earnings	1,050.4	916.5
Accumulated foreign currency translation	(37.0)	(52.7)
Total Liabilities and Equity	$3,658.8)	$2,778.5)

16. Retirement Plans

The Company and its subsidiaries have noncontributory defined benefit retirement plans covering substantially all salaried and full-time hourly employees. Benefits for salaried employees are based on final average compensation. The hourly plans include various monthly amounts for each year of credited service. Substantially all of the plans are funded by annual contributions to tax exempt trusts. The Company's funding policy is consistent with the funding requirements of federal law and regulations. Plan assets consist principally of listed equity securities and corporate obligations and U.S. government bonds.

In Fiscal 1986, the Company adopted Statement of Financial Accounting Standards No. 87, "Employer's Accounting for Pensions" (SFAS 87), retroactive to June 1, 1985. Pension cost and related disclosures are determined under the provisions of SFAS 87 for Fiscal 1986 and under the provisions of previous accounting principles for Fiscal 1985 and 1984. The effect of the change was to reduce pension expense in Fiscal 1986 by $12.4 million.

Net pension costs consists of the following:

	Year Ended May 31, 1986 (In millions)
Service costs-benefits earned during the year	$ 7.2
Interest cost on projected benefit obligation	23.9
Actual return on plan assets	$(96.3)
Deferred gain	66.8
Amortization of transition asset	(7.8)
Net pension credit	$ (6.2)

The company and its subsidiaries are also participants in multiemployer defined benefit pension plans covering a small number of hourly employees. The pension cost for multiemployer plans in Fiscal 1986 was $1.1 million.

At May 31, 1986, the weighted average discount rate and rate of increase in future compensation used in determining the actuarial present value of the projected benefit obligation were nine percent and six percent, respectively. The expected long-term rate of return on plan assets was ten percent.

The funded status of the plan and the amount recognized on the balance sheet are as follows:

	Year Ended May 31, 1986 (In millions)
Actuarial present value of benefit obligation:	
Vested benefits	$(202.2)
Nonvested benefits	(21.2)
Accumulated benefit obligation	$(223.4)
Effect of projected future compensation increases	(69.7)
Projected benefit obligation	$(293.1)
Plan assets at fair value	389.6
Plan assets in excess of projected benefit obligation	$ 96.5
Unrecognized prior service cost	.7
Unrecognized net gain	(18.5)
Unrecognized transition asset	(74.8)
Prepaid pension asset	$ 3.9

Pension expense for Fiscal 1985 and 1984 was $7.8 million and $13.2 million, respectively. The reduction in Fiscal 1985 pension expense is due primarily to a one percentage point increase in the rate of return assumption. The actuarial present value of accumulated plan benefits at May 31, 1985 was $181.5 million (of which $18.0 million was nonvested), compared with net assets available for benefits of $298.2 million. The assumed average rate of return used in determining the actuarial present value of benefits for Fiscal 1985 was nine percent, except for those benefits at May 31, 1985 which were matched to a dedicated bond portfolio yielding 15.25 percent.

REQUIRED:

1. What do the following terms mean with regard to Pillsbury:
   (a) Service cost
   (b) Interest cost on projected benefit obligation
   (c) Actual return on plan assets
   (d) Deferred gain
   (e) Projected benefit obligation
   (f) Vested benefits
   (g) Accumulated benefit obligation
   (h) Plan assets at fair value
   (i) Unrecognized prior service cost
   (j) Unrecognized transition asset
   (k) Noncontributory
   (l) Multiemployer plans

2. What does the statement that some benefits are based on "final average compensation" mean? What does it mean to say that hourly plans "include various monthly amounts for each year of credited service"? How are these plans different and how does this difference influence the accounting and reporting process?

3. What was the pre-tax effect on Pillsbury's reported income for 1986 of the change in accounting for pension costs? What would you estimate the after-tax effect was on net income and earnings per share. How does the growth in EPS from 1984–1985 compare with the growth from 1985-1986 with and without the change? Why do you think Pillsbury adopted SFAS No. 87?

4. Using the working paper format presented in this chapter, reconcile the activity relating to Pillsbury's defined benefit pension plans. Assume that the benefits paid out of the trust during 1986 amounted to $4.9 million. Recreate the journal entry that Pillsbury might have used to record the activity relating to the defined benefit plans on its books. How much cash did Pillsbury contribute to its pension trust during 1986?

5. How sensitive is your answer to (3) to the assumption that the benefit payments were $4.9 million? Without that knowledge, would it be possible to determine both the cash contributions and the amount of benefits that Pillsbury paid simultaneously?

6. Implicitly, what is the average real rate of interest that Pillsbury is using to discount future benefits? Does this seem reasonable? What does it imply about how the long-run rate of return should be interpreted?

7. Pillsbury discusses a "dedicated bond portfolio." What do you think this is and why can Pillsbury use a higher interest rate to discount benefits "matched" to this portfolio?

8. How much effect did the one percent change in discount rate between 1984 and 1985 have on pension expense in dollars? As a percent of expense from 1984? On EPS for 1985? Does the fact that Pillsbury elected a long-run expected rate of return of 10% (a one percent increase over 9% used previously) have the same implication for 1986?

9. Given the data, project the pension expense expected for 1987, assuming the service costs in 1987 are equal to those of 1986 and the amortization periods for all other items are the same.

DAYTON HUDSON CORPORATION

Dayton Hudson Corporation is in the business of retail clothing and dry goods. It operates several chain stores such as Target and Mervyn's as well as its own upscale set of department stores under the name of Daytons. Contained in the financial reports of the Dayton Hudson Corporation for fiscal year 1985 was the following information regarding the defined benefit pension plans the Company sponsored. All dollar amounts in the case are in thousands of dollars, except earnings per share figures.

Pension Plans

We have three defined benefit pension plans which cover all employees who meet certain requirements of age, length of service and hours worked per year. The benefits provided are based upon years of service and the employee's compensation during the last five years of employment.

Contributions to the pension plans, which are made solely by the Corporation, are determined by our outside actuarial firm. To compute net pension cost, our actuarial firm estimates the total benefits which will ultimately be paid to eligible employees and then allocates these costs to their service periods. Assumptions are made on the years the employees will work, their future salary increases, the number of employees who will earn the right to receive benefits under the plans, the rate at which to discount future pension benefits and the rate of return which will be earned on the plans' present assets and future contributions.

During 1985, we changed our method of accounting for pension costs to conform to the newly issued Statement of Financial Accounting Standards No. 87, "Employers' Accounting for Pensions." The change reduces our 1985 net pension cost by $13,385. Restatement of prior years is not permitted by the Statement.

The Statement requires employers with defined benefit pension plans to calculate pension costs using the unit credit actuarial cost method, which we adopted in 1983. Service cost under the unit credit method is computed by determining the increase in future pension benefits resulting from the current year's service and discounting these future cash flows to the present. Therefore, service cost will increase as employees age. The projected benefit obligation is the actuarial present value of all future benefit payments for services rendered to date, including an assumption as to future compensation levels.

DAYTON HUDSON CORPORATION
Note Disclosure Regarding Defined Benefit Pension Plans

Reconciliation of Funded Status to Accrued Pension Cost	Fair Market Value of Plan Assets (a)	Plus Projected Benefit Obligation	Plan Assets in Excess of Projected Benefit Obligation	Less		Accrued Pension Cost (f)
				Unrecognized Net Actuarial Gains	Unrecognized Transition Asset	
Balance January 1, 1985	$217,160	$(174,786)(b)	$42,374	$ –	$54,948	$(12,574)
Net pension cost (credit)						
Service cost		(8,641)				(8,641)
Interest cost		(16,605)				(16,605)
Assumed return on plan assets	20,630					20,630
Amortization					(7,958)	7,958
Net pension credit						3,342 (d)
Net actuarial gains	24,270	518		24,788		
Contributions	95					95(e)
Benefit payments	(15,204)	15,238				34
Balance December 31, 1985	$246,951	$(184,276)(c)	$62,675	$24,788	$46,990	$(9,103)

(a) Plan assets consist of equity securities, fixed income securities and insurance contracts.

(b) December 31, 1984 amounts are not the same as the January 1, 1985, balances due to the implementation of Statement No. 87. The December 31, 1984, projected benefit obligation was $217,283 with $185,379 in accumulated benefits, of which $174,148 was vested.

(c) Includes $161,131 of accumulated benefits, of which $152,941 is vested.

(d) Net pension cost for 1984 and 1983 was $7,364 and $11,155, respectively, compared with a net pension credit of $3,342 for 1985.

(e) The plans' 1984 contribution receivable of $95 was paid in 1985. No contributions were made in 1984 and 1983 contributions were $7,390. The plans' 1985 contribution receivable of $4,870 will be paid in 1986.

(f) This liability is included in Deferred Income Taxes and Other in the Statements of Financial Position.

Actuarial assumptions:	1985	1984	1983
Discount rate	9.5%	7.5%	7.0%
Expected long-term rate of return on plan assets	9.5%	7.5%	7.0%
Average assumed rate of compensation increase	6.9%	6.7%	6.5%
Average amortization period	6.9 years	10 years	20 years

The Statement also provides more guidance in the selection of the actuarial assumptions indicated in the following table. Previously, these assumptions were acceptable if, in the aggregate, pension results were reasonable. Now, each assumption is required to be analyzed individually and reviewed annually.

The period over which to amortize unrecognized pension costs and credits, including prior service costs (we have none) and actuarial gains and losses is based on the remaining service period for those employees expected to receive pension benefits. Actuarial gains and losses result when actual experience differs from that assumed or when actuarial assumptions are changed.

At January 1, 1985, our pension plans had an unrecognized net asset of $54,948. This transition asset is not recorded on our balance sheet, but is being amortized to net pension cost over 6.9 years, which is the average remaining service period of our employees.

During 1985 Dayton Hudson also reported pre-tax income from operations of $524,574, net income of $283,620, and net income per share of $2.92.

REQUIRED:

1. What is the unit credit actuarial cost method and how is it relevant to the determination of the annual pension cost?
2. What is the effect on pre-tax operating income from the change to the new accounting standard on a percentage basis? What would you estimate this to translate into as an effect on net income and earnings per share?
3. What did Dayton Hudson actually report as pension cost for the defined benefit plans in 1985? What was the cash flow out of the Company relating to the defined benefit pension plans for 1985?
4. What does the statement related to the actuarial assumptions, "Previously, these assumptions were acceptable if, in the aggregate, pension results were reasonable" mean to you?
5. Speculate on the effect the changes in actuarial assumptions in 1985 did to the amount of pension expense reported during the period compared to the assumptions in use in 1984.
6. Define each of the following items of pension expense and describe how Dayton Hudson computed each component:
   (a) service cost
   (b) interest cost
   (c) amortization
7. What is an "assumed return on plan assets"? What was the actual return on plan assets for 1985?
8. Speculate as to why the activity relating to benefit payments affected the accrued pension cost account. Prepare a journal entry that accounts for this event.
9. Prepare an estimate of the pension cost Dayton Hudson will report for 1986, using the data presented in the notes.
10. If Dayton Hudson had elected to apply the minimum liability provisions of SFAS No. 87 (these were optional until 1989), would the company have been required to record a minimum liability? Why or why not?
11. Would your response to (10) change if the pension trust had experienced an actual loss of $100 million on plan assets for the year instead of the return in (7)?
12. Describe the procedure used to obtain the estimated average service period of 6.9 years. Would this be the basis for amortization of any unrecognized gains or losses and any unrecognized prior service cost? Why or why not?

JAMES RIVER CORPORATION

James River Corporation is a manufacturer of paper and packaging products for industrial and consumer goods. In 1988, the company reported sales of $5,097,978,000, with earnings per share of $2.36 on a reported net income of $209,010,000. The Company reported a tax rate of approximately 45%. As part of its financial statements, James River included the following information on its retirement plans:

Note 6: Retirement Plans

The Company has a number of pension plans covering substantially all employees. These include plans which are administered by the Company, as well as union-administered multiemployer plans. James River's plan covering salaried employees is contributory and provides pension benefits based upon the employees career average compensation and years of service. Salaried employees are eligible to participate in the plan upon the completion of six months of service. Employee contributions are determined as .75% of each covered employee's earnings up to the Social Security taxable wage base, and 1.4% of earnings in excess thereof. Plans covering hourly employees (including multiemployer plans) are generally noncontributory and provide pension benefits based on stated amounts for each year of service. Employees covered under hourly plans are eligible to participate upon the completion of up to one year of service. Employees become fully vested in the Company-administered plans upon the completion of ten years of service. The funding policy for all Company-administered plans is to make at least the minimum annual contribution required by the Employee Retirement Income Security Act of 1974. Contributions to multiemployer plans are generally based on fixed rates set forth in negotiated labor contracts.

The components of net periodic pension cost in fiscal 1988 and 1987 were as follows:

(in thousands)	1988		1987	
Service cost—benefits earned during year		$ 23,462		$ 20,655
Interest accrued on projected benefit obligation		74,202		69,209
Return on plan assets:				
Actual	$(11,352)		$(126,804)	
Deferred	(78,522)	$(89,874)	40,984	$(85,820)
Net amortization and deferral		946		(1,759)
		8,736		2,285
Contributions to multiemployer plans		5,865		5,818
Total pension cost		$ 14,601		$ 8,103

Net amortization and deferrals consist of amortization of the net asset existing at the date of initial application of Statement of Financial Accounting Standards No. 87, "Employers Accounting for Pensions" ("SFAS 87") in fiscal 1986, and deferral and amortization of subsequent net gains and losses.

Pension expense and plan obligations are calculated using assumptions that are estimates of factors that will determine, among other things, the amount and timing of future benefit payments. Weighted average rate assumptions used in determining the fiscal 1988 and 1987 net pension cost were as follows:

	1988	1987
Discount rate	8.0%	8.7%
Rate of increase in future compensation levels	6.0%	6.7%
Long-term rate of return on plan assets	10.0%	10.7%

The following table sets forth the funded status of the Company-administered plans and the amounts recognized in the Company's balance sheet at April 24, 1988 and April 26, 1987, based on valuations as of January 31, 1988 and January 31, 1987, respectively. Benefit obligations at January 31, 1988 were determined using an assumed discount rate of 8.0% and an assumed rate of increase in future compensation levels of 6.0%.

	April 24, 1988	
	Assets Exceed Accumulated Benefits	Accumulated Benefits Exceed Assets
Actuarial present value of projected benefit obligation, based on employment service to date and current salary levels:		
Vested benefits	$(526,334)	$(359,270)
Nonvested benefits	(38,092)	(23,595)
Accumulated benefit obligation	$(564,426)	$(382,865)
Additional amounts related to projected salary increases	(265)	(29,580)
Projected benefit obligation	$(564,691)	$(412,445)
Plan assets at fair value (primarily equity securities, corporate bonds, and short-term investments)	596,005	313,349
Plan assets in excess (less than) projected benefit obligation	$ 31,314	$ (99,096)
Unrecognized net loss from past experience different from that assumed	49,226	78,549
Prior service cost not yet recognized	2,276	21,525
Unrecognized net asset at April 29, 1985, being recognized over 15 to 19 years	(2,403)	(31,085)
Net pension asset (liability) recognized in the consolidated balance sheet	$ 80,413	$ (30,107)

	April 26, 1987	
	Assets Exceed Accumulated Benefits	Accumulated Benefits Exceed Assets
Actuarial present value of projected benefit obligation, based on employment service to date and current salary levels:		
Vested benefits	$(617,394)	$(216,848)
Nonvested benefits	(47,902)	(19,021)
Accumulated benefit obligation	$(665,296)	$(235,869)
Additional amounts related to projected salary increases	(23,814)	(56)
Projected benefit obligation	$(689,110)	$(236,395)
Plan assets at fair value (primarily equity securities, corporate bonds, and short-term investments)	752,829	162,644
Plan assets in excess (less than) projected benefit obligation	$ 63,719	$ (73,751)
Unrecognized net loss from past experience different from that assumed	7,199	43,469
Prior service cost not yet recognized	4,231	3,945
Unrecognized net asset at April 29, 1985, being recognized over 15 to 19 years	(28,578)	(7,705)
Net pension asset (liability) recognized in the consolidated balance sheet	$ 46,571	$ (34,042)

SFAS 87 requires the recognition of a liability in the amount of the Company's unfunded accumulated benefit obligation, with an equal amount to be recognized as either an intangible asset or a reduction of equity, net of applicable deferred income taxes, no later than fiscal 1990. James River intends to adopt these provisions of SFAS 87 when so required. Based on the actuarial and plan asset information as of January 1988, James River would be required to record an additional liability of approximately $39.4 million. The actual impact upon adoption will depend on the funded status of the Company's pension plans at that date. The adoption of these provisions will have no impact on net income or cash flow.

REQUIRED:

1. What is a contributory plan and how does the one described by James River Corporation work? Provide an example. (Hint: You will need to invent some numbers to do this, but do not worry about the actual situation as much as the general process).
2. What similarities and differences exist between the hourly and salaried plans? How do these affect the accounting and financial reporting problems?
3. Without preparing a working paper, determine how much cash was contributed to the defined benefit pension trusts administered by the Company. What journal entry recorded this activity?
4. Does all of the pension cost of $14.6 million for both Company-sponsored and multiemployer plans get charged to expense in 1988? Why or why not?
5. How does James River determine the following amounts:
   (a) Service cost
   (b) Interest cost
   (c) Return on plan assets

Prepare computations of items (b) and (c) and develop an explanation for why the estimates you prepare do not agree totally with those in the note.

6. What is included in the amount reported as "net amortization and deferral?" Estimate each component of this amount separately from the data provided.

7. Given your estimates in (4), prepare a working paper to capture the total activity in James River's pension trusts for 1988. You will need to add the underfunded and overfunded plans. What other events must have taken place during 1988 to make sense out of your working paper?

8. Are the underfunded plans presented in the 1987 reconciliation the same underfunded plans as those in the 1988 reconciliation? How can you tell?

9. What is the minimum liability that James River discusses? How did the company arrive at the amount of $39.4 million? Why is there no income or cash flow effect of recording this additional liability? How is that possible?

10. If James River had applied the minimum liability provisions to both 1987 and 1988, how would the 1987 balance sheet have changed, and what journal entry would be required in 1988?

11. Given that James River has some plans that are overfunded and others that are underfunded, speculate on the effects this might have on the incentives of the covered employees in each type of plan to contribute their maximum effort to the Company?

12. Is James River required to split the reconciliation of the funded status of underfunded and overfunded plans for disclosure purposes, or did they simply choose this format in the interests of providing more complete information?

13. Given the interest rates reported by James River, can we infer that the company actually changed its assumptions during 1988? What does the relationship between the discount rate, compensation increase rate, and long-term rate of return on plan assets suggest to you about what James River is attempting to do with the choice of these rates?

Employee Compensation: Incentive Contribution Programs, Defined Contribution Pension Plans, and Other Employment Benefits

In Chapter 18, we explored the use of defined benefit pension plans to provide retirement income for employees. In that discussion, we noted that various terms in a defined benefit pension plan, such as the rate of benefit accrual and benefit vesting, are often designed to provide incentives for employees to remain with the company to maximize their retirement benefits. While characteristics such as these do represent "incentives," they are not linked directly to the corporation's profitability or share price performance.

Incentive compensation programs, as the term is used here, refer to specific compensation devices, such as employee stock options or bonus arrangements, that link the amount of reward an employee receives to achievement of some target goal such as raising share price. These types of programs have become an important part of compensation for corporation managers over the past 20 years. This chapter begins by examining the economic characteristics of these types of incentive compensation programs and then explores the accounting and financial reporting treatment of these plans.

In some cases, incentive compensation plans are linked with the provision of retirement benefits or savings plans for employees. Examples of these arrangements include:

1. Employee stock purchase plans, which allow employees to purchase shares of the employer stock at reduced prices
2. Employee stock ownership plans (or ESOPs), which grant employees shares of the employer's stock to sell for retirement income
3. Profit-sharing defined contribution retirement plans, which place monies into a trust on employees' behalf based on the achievement of profit targets for the period.

These plans are examined more closely after the discussion of incentive compensation programs, which do not have the retirement benefit characteristics.

Finally, this chapter examines the accounting and reporting requirements related to other employment benefits such as health and life insurance, day care benefits, dental plans, and other types of general benefits that employers provide their employees. Costs for these types of benefits represent a significant portion of corporations' total compensation cost. Of particular interest are the accounting and reporting for those benefits that extend beyond the employees' working lives into their retirement years.

WHY DO FIRMS NEED INCENTIVE COMPENSATION PROGRAMS FOR MANAGERS?

The separation of ownership and control of a corporation into shareholders and managers, respectively, means that those who have a claim on the company's profits (shareholders) are not the individuals who directly control the decisions (managers) that ultimately generate those profits. If all managers were naturally motivated to maximize a corporation's profits for the shareholders' benefit, they could be paid a flat salary in return for their agreement to work for the company each period. However, managers may not naturally expend as much effort in making the company successful as the shareholders would desire.

Shareholders hire managers to maximize the shareholders' investments. Shareholders are not generally involved in day-to-day decision making, so they may not observe the managers' effort or lack of effort to build shareholders' wealth. How do shareholders (owners) encourage managers to maximize their efforts on behalf of the shareholders?

One way to align more closely the managers' motivations with those of shareholders is to tie managers' compensation to the company's performance. Offering managers who are in a position to influence the firm's performance through their decisions more compensation when performance is good and less when it is bad will result in decisions that are more closely aligned with shareholders' best interests. This process is called "risk sharing" since the owner requires the manager to bear some risk as a means of creating an incentive for "better" decisions.

Of course, shareholders do not desire to overpay the manager. The total expected compensation that managers are offered from both a base salary and the incentive compensation program will depend on what alternative opportunities the managers may have for employment. In some cases, the other alternatives will pay so much that shareholders would not be willing to offer enough total compensation to obtain the managers' services. In any case, the potential rewards of the incentive compensation program are not just tacked onto a base salary that is already high enough to get the managers to work for the shareholders; the value of the incentive would be partially lost if the salary is too high. Instead, the existence of the incentive compensation program should result in lower salary in order to make the expected total compensation meet the level required to hire the managers.

Specific incentive arrangements are not always necessary because other economic forces are at work to motivate managers to attain a high level of performance. One of these factors is that managers may be concerned about their reputations in the marketplace. Managers with good reputations for success will be able to command greater pay in the marketplace. If managers are fired for not acting in the shareholders' best interest, their reputations may be harmed and they may find equivalent employment difficult to obtain. However, most firms find it useful to develop some form of incentive compensation package to encourage managerial behavior consistent with the shareholders' interests.

Incentive compensation arrangements also benefit companies by serving to attract those managers who are more confident about their ability to succeed with the company. For high-quality managers, the risk is potentially less than for other managers since they will be better able to meet the goals established in the incentive agreement. Thus, these arrangements not only help control managers after hiring, but they also find managers with high levels of ability in the first place.

Incentive compensation, then, is a natural means to deal with the fact that managers are human and are not likely to work to their full potential without some monetary reward as a source of motivation when their actions cannot be constantly observed.

FACTORS INFLUENCING THE FORMS OF INCENTIVE COMPENSATION

A successful incentive compensation program focuses on performance targets that:

1. May be affected by the managers' decisions, and
2. Are most likely to increase the corporation's value to the shareholders.

A common performance target is share price, since increasing the corporation's market value will generally be in the best interests of the shareholders. Programs that grant shares directly to managers or provide stock options that allow managers to purchase shares of stock at fixed prices are designed around the belief that this will tie managers' economic welfare directly to the shareholders' welfare and create proper incentives.

Does providing a manager with a direct ownership interest in the corporation always represent the best solution to the incentive problem? The answer is *no*. While offering managers ownership interest meets criteria (2), it does not always satisfy criteria (1). Providing an ownership interest to some managers may expose those managers to too much risk because the decisions under their control have little effect on share price. This may be due to the nature of the company's business or the manager's position in the company. For example, the value of a gold mining company will vary directly with the market price of gold. Since no company executive can control the market price of gold, the firm's share price will be highly volatile regardless of how well-managed the company might be. In such situations, giving managers ownership interests forces them to bear the risk of share price variation, which is beyond their control. Other performance targets may provide more information about the quality of managerial decisions and still be linked to share price. Reported accounting earnings, for example, will reflect the outcomes related to managerial decisions, and they are less sensitive to fluctuations in the economy, at least in the short run. As a result, incentive compensation plans that focus on net income targets as a measure of performance might work better for this type of corporation.

The manager's position in the corporation should influence the form of any incentive compensation program. Top executives of a corporation can substantially influence the setting of corporate strategies. These strategies are expected to translate into larger corporate profits and higher value for shareholders. When share prices of the company are very sensitive to the development and implementation of corporate strategies, linking the executives' total compensation to share price via a stock-based incentive compensation program is quite reasonable. However, for the sales manager who has little direct control over corporate profitability but is responsible for management of the sales force, an incentive compensation program that links the payment of a bonus to meeting annual sales goals may be a better incentive. Many of the factors that affect stock price are out of the sales manager's control; therefore, the use of shares as an incentive forces the sales manager to bear the risk of share price movements without the offsetting benefit of being able to influence these price movements.

The taxation of compensation or, more directly, the fact that the Internal Revenue Code taxes different forms of compensation differently provides an additional dimension to consider in the design of incentive compensation programs. Developing compensation contracts with particular features that minimize the total taxes the corporation and manager pay can be mutually beneficial. For example, a manager may prefer that compensation be in some deferred form if future tax rates may be smaller than present rates and/or the compensation is not needed for current consumption.

If the company can structure a transaction in such a way that it reduces the total taxes the manager and the company pay, then there will be more left for both after taxes. Even if the total taxes are not reduced, but just deferred, a benefit equal to the time value of the deferred tax payment will be realized.

As can be seen from even this brief discussion, determining the appropriate form for an incentive compensation program is not an easy task. It can differ for each manager and each company. This is one reason why so many forms of compensation exist to meet the needs of so many different situations. All incentive plans have common features:

1. They provide compensation contingent upon some future event
2. The presence of this contingent compensation, along with the fixed salary component of the employee's compensation, must be sufficient to lure qualified people into the firm, but not overpay them
3. The contingency represents the realization of some observable or measurable outcome that is believed to lead to higher value for the shareholders

In the end, the combination of risk sharing and tax reduction work in complicated ways to create many different forms of incentive compensation. We will investigate several forms of these plans to understand the accounting issues involved and how they do or do not relate to the underlying economic forces that contributed to the development of these plans.

ACCOUNTING FOR INCENTIVE COMPENSATION ARRANGEMENTS

From an accounting perspective, one goal of financial reports is to match the cost of labor to the revenues the company generates from using the labor inputs. In some cases, such as production-line employees, labor cost is treated as a product cost. In others, such as executive-level employment, labor cost is typically a period cost. In either case, when a company provides some form of incentive compensation, it may be difficult to evaluate the company's "cost" of the incentive plan for the current accounting period.

Determining how much compensation expense to recognize in a period arising from incentive plans is a difficult task. The economic force that is at work revolves around expected compensation. Actual compensation may differ from the expectation and may not be realized for several accounting periods. Should compensation expense be based on expectations? If so, how can reliable estimates of these expectations be acquired? If not, is matching being violated? If stock-based incentive plans are used, the ultimate payment of the compensation may not even come directly from the sponsoring corporation, but rather directly from the sponsor's shareholders. Does this imply that no compensation expense should be recognized by the corporation since the use of stock-based incentives imposes no direct liability for distribution of assets by the corporate sponsor?

There are no absolute right answers to these questions. Generally, accountants have tried to capture some measure of the total compensation paid to managers in the financial reports. This measure is based on the actual outcomes, not the amounts expected at the time the contract is entered into. For example, when a corporation awards shares to an employee without receiving payment for them, the stock's market value is generally treated as a measure of the compensation paid. When compensation is contingent on some future event, there may be accruals of estimated compensation prior to the final realization of the contingency. However, ultimately, the total compensation to be recognized will be determined when the event is realized.

PROGRAMS THAT ARE PRIMARILY INCENTIVE COMPENSATION PROGRAMS

Incentive compensation programs come in many forms such as stock option plans, stock appreciation rights, short-term bonus plans, and long-term bonus plans such as phantom stock plans and unit credit plans. Each of these is examined in this section of the chapter.

Stock Option Plans

In general, an *option* is a contract that allows the holder to purchase a share of stock for a stated fixed price (called the *exercise price*, or "strike" price). The option also specifies the period over which a share can be acquired, called the *exercise period*. The options of interest here are called **employee stock options**, which are generally granted only to specific individuals and cannot be traded.

The Structure of an Employee Stock Option   In most cases, employee stock options have an exercise period of several years (up to ten years is common). Employee stock options usually require that the recipient be employed by the corporation when the option is exercised. In addition, a minimum period of employment before the option can be exercised is stipulated. If the employee quits or is fired before the first date on which the option can be exercised, the option is said to *lapse* (become void or unusable).

Contract terms of this latter type are designed to make it costly for employees to depart from the company once they have received the option. A decision to leave would result in giving up the potential to benefit from any share price increases that occur before the exercise date of their options.

How Do Employee Stock Options Work?   Employee stock option plans allow corporations to tie their employees' wealth to the value of the corporation's shares. As was discussed previously, the manager will bear whatever risk is associated with the company's stock that is not under the manager's control. Many economic factors enter into the company's valuation, and no manager can control all these factors. For this reason, there will be times when the employee makes good decisions but the share price falls.

In general, this uncertainty makes the use of stock options more appropriate for those individuals who are planning the company's long-term strategy than for those working on an assembly line. Upper-level management makes decisions that will be most closely linked to share value, and this makes options an effective incentive tool for this group of employees.

Understandably, options are a popular way of compensating key executives of large corporations. In fact, many corporate executives find these incentives very desirable because they believe they can control the firm's future and increase share price significantly by their managerial skill. Stock options allow them to benefit from that skill without affecting the corporation's operating cash flow.

Accounting for Employee Stock Options—Important Dates   Several dates are important in accounting for stock options. The **date of inception** is the date the board of directors establishes the stock option plan. The **grant date** is the date on which options are actually assigned to specific individuals. The most important date for accounting purposes is the **measurement date**, which is defined in *Accounting Principles Board Opinion No. 25* as the date on which both of the following characteristics have been finally determined:

1. The exercise price
2. The number of options specific individuals will receive[1]

The grant date represents the earliest date that could be used as the measurement date under these provisions. However, the date of the grant may not be the measurement date if the exercise price of the option is not fixed on that date.

---

[1] "Accounting for Stock Issued to Employees," *Accounting Principles Board Opinion No. 25* (AICPA, October 1972), para. 10(b).

For accounting purposes, the measurement date represents the point when a final computation of the total compensation cost to be recognized in the financial statements is computed. Total compensation to be recognized under an option is determined by the difference between the market price of the shares and the exercise price of the option on the measurement date, times the number of shares under option. For example, if the market price per share at the measurement date was $10, the exercise price per share was $7, and there were 1,000 shares under option, the total compensation cost to be recognized from these options would be $3,000 ($10 − $7)(1,000 shares). Note that we have said nothing about the periods in which this total compensation should be charged to expense. All this computation determines is the total amount of compensation that the financial reports will ultimately recognize as expense related to these options.

Because the measurement date is the date on which the compensation cost related to the options is determined for accounting purposes, it is also the date on which the determination is made regarding whether the options are to be considered compensatory or noncompensatory *for financial reporting purposes*. An option contract must be **compensatory** for financial reporting purposes if the option's exercise price is significantly below the stock's market price on the measurement date. If the stock's market price is not significantly below the exercise price on the measurement date, it is may be classified as either compensatory or **noncompensatory** for financial reporting purposes.[2] Regardless of its classification, when the market price is at or below the exercise price at the measurement date, no compensation expense will be recognized in the financial statements. Small differences between the exercise price and the market price of the stock that reflect transactions costs present in issuing new shares are not considered significant and do not result in classification of the option as compensatory.

The terms *compensatory* and *noncompensatory* are not descriptive of the options' economic characteristics. At the grant date, all options have value and, thus, represent economic compensation to the manager at that time. Regardless of the option's exercise price there is always some possibility (albeit small in some cases) that the stock price will rise above the exercise price during the option's life. This makes the option valuable. However, because the option cannot be traded, the manager cannot translate the option's value into monies that could be spent on something else until the option can be exercised and the shares acquired can be sold in the marketplace. This option arrangement encourages the manager to take actions that increase the future share price in order to increase the option's value.

Accounting for Employee Stock Options—Noncompensatory Plans   For noncompensatory options, no journal entry is made to record any compensation either when the options are granted or at the measurement date if later. When

---

[2] A noncompensatory plan offers options equally to a large number of employees based on such factors as level of salary and does not discriminate on the basis of employment position. In addition, the exercise price must equal market at the date of the grant. These characteristics were established many years ago by the IRS code for tax purposes, and the term *noncompensatory* is derived from that source.

noncompensatory options are exercised, the proceeds from the exercise (determined by multiplying the exercise price times the number of shares acquired under option) are recorded as the total consideration for the shares issued.

The following example demonstrates the accounting procedures relating to a noncompensatory option. On January 1, 1995, ABC Company granted options for 1,000 shares, at $2 per share, to its employees. The options were exercisable anytime in the next four years. On January 1, 1995, the market value of ABC shares was $2 per share. On July 1, 1996, the employees exercised the options when the market price of ABC stock was $3 per share. In this case, the measurement date was January 1, 1995, since both the exercise price and individuals receiving the options were determined on that date. Since the exercise price was not below market on the measurement date, these options are classified as noncompensatory options. No journal entry would be required to record the issuance of the options.

When the options were exercised, the employees would pay the company $2,000 (1,000 shares × $2 per share), and this would reflect the entire proceeds from the share issue since the options were not assigned a value when they were issued. Assuming no-par stock was issued, the journal entry to record the share issue would appear as:

July 1, 1996:

Cash	2,000	
Common stock, no-par		2,000

To record the proceeds from the issuance of stock under the noncompensatory employee option program.

The employees in this example will benefit by the increase in the market price of the stock received. When sold, the stock price appreciation provides partial compensation for employment. Note that the employees need not exercise the options until the stock price has increased, thus limiting the risk they bear from investing in the company using options as opposed to purchasing shares in the open market.

Accounting for Employee Stock Options—Compensatory Plans   When an option plan is compensatory (options issued to targeted individuals) but the exercise price is equal to the market price on the measurement date, the plan is accounted for in the same fashion as a noncompensatory plan. When the exercise price in an option contract is significantly below the market price on the measurement date, compensation equal to the difference between the total market value and the total exercise price of the shares under option will be accrued at the measurement date. Any share price changes occurring after the measurement date are not relevant to the determination of compensation expense to be recognized in the financial statements, regardless of the effect these share price changes may have on the option's value.

Expense Recognition

The total compensation determined at the measurement date under a compensatory stock option may not be immediately charged to expense. If the option contract stipulates that the compensation under the option plan is for service to be rendered over the next two years, and this is supported by setting the option's first date of exercise two years after the grant, then the compensation must be spread over the next two years, not recognized immediately. The only case where the entire compensation would be immediately charged to expense occurs when the options are granted for past service and are immediately exercisable.

Assume that on May 1, 1993, Baker Corporation granted options to its CEO for 4,000 shares at an exercise price of $5 per share when the market price was $8 per share. The options had a five-year life. In this example, the grant date is the measurement date, and the total compensation on the measurement date is $12,000 [($8 − $5)(4,000 shares)]. Now, consider the following two examples. In the first case, assume the options are immediately exercisable. As a result, the total compensation of $12,000 would immediately be charged to expense. Since Baker issued options in generating this cost, the following journal entry would be appropriate:

May 1, 1993:
Compensation expense	12,000	
Additional paid-in capital from outstanding stock options		12,000
To record the total compensation as expense at the measurement date for the compensatory stock options.		

In the second case, assume the first date that the options can be exercised is May 1, 1995, or two years after the grant date. This implies that the total compensation will be earned over the next two years. Consequently, the total compensation should be recognized as expense over the next two years. The total compensation is assigned to each year using a straight-line amortization approach. As a result, only $6,000 of compensation will be recognized for each full year of service. Recording the effects of the compensatory options in this case requires a series of entries. At the measurement date, the total compensation is accrued; but no expense is recognized. This is accomplished as follows:

May 1, 1993:
Deferred compensation from stock options	12,000	
Additional paid-in capital from outstanding stock options		12,000
To accrue the total compensation under compensatory stock options at the measurement date.		

The deferred compensation account in the journal entry above is presented in Baker's balance sheet as a contra-equity account. As a result, the credit to additional paid-in capital on the measurement date is offset by the creation of the contra-equity account at the same point in time. As time passes, the deferred compensation is deemed to be earned by the employee, resulting in the amortization of the deferred compensation to expense. Assuming Baker has a December 31 year-end, at the end of 1993, the following entry would record the amortization of the deferred compensation:

December 31, 1993:
Compensation expense	3,500	
Deferred compensation from stock options		3,500
To amortize the deferred compensation for seven months from May 1 to December 31, 1993.		

Exhibit 19.1 presents Baker's equity section as it might appear at the end of 1993, following the incorporation of the above entries. The amortization would continue over 1994 ($6,000 of expense recognized) and 1995 (the balance of $2,500 of expense recognized) until the deferred compensation from stock options was fully amortized to expense. At May 1, 1995, the contra-equity account would have a balance of zero; and the additional paid-in capital from outstanding stock options would still have a balance of $12,000.

Recording the Exercise of Compensatory Options

Once an option is granted, the final resolution of the employee's right to convert the option into a share of stock will occur through one of three actions:

1. The employee will elect to exercise the option
2. The employee will allow the options to expire without exercise
3. The option will be cancelled (voided) for some other reason

If an employee elects to exercise the option, the corporation will issue shares in exchange for the cash representing the option's exercise price and the previous capital the company had recorded as the value of the paid-in capital from stock options. In the Baker Corporation example, assume the CEO remained in the employ of Baker for several years and elected to exercise the options on January 1, 1996. Baker's journal entry to record this exercise would appear as follows (regardless of whether there had been a two-year service requirement):

January 1, 1996:		
Cash	20,000	
Paid-in capital from outstanding stock options	12,000	
Common stock, no-par		32,000
To record the exercise of options for 4,000 shares at $5 per share and the transfer of the paid-in capital from the compensatory options.		

Recording Expiration of Compensatory Options

If the employee allowed the options to expire without exercise (referred to as allowing the options to **lapse**), a reclassification of the paid-in capital from

---

BAKER CORPORATION
Presentation of Paid-In Capital from Stock Options and Deferred Compensation

Stockholders' equity (December 31, 1993)	
Common stock, no-par; 800,000 shares authorized; 300,000 shares issued and outstanding	$300,000
Additional paid-in capital from outstanding stock options	12,000
Deferred compensation—stock options	(8,500)
Retained earnings	200,500
Total stockholders' equity	$504,000

EXHIBIT 19.1

Baker Corporation— Presentation of Paid-In Capital from Stock Options and Deferred Compensation

outstanding stock options to expired stock options would be appropriate. This adjustment would occur at the end of the life of the options, or May 1, 1998. Baker's journal entry to accomplish this would appear as follows:

```
May 1, 1998:
Paid-in capital from outstanding stock options            12,000
   Paid-in capital from expired stock options                          12,000
To record the expiration of the stock options.
```

Recording the Cancellation of Compensatory Options

Once an option is granted, the company cannot generally cancel it without offering the employee either the right to exercise prior to cancellation or some other form of substitute compensation. However, the employee's ability to exercise an option is generally dependent on employment with the company on the date of exercise. If an employee leaves the corporation without exercising an option, the option is cancelled.

For currently exercisable options, an employee who contemplates departing the corporation can decide whether to exercise the options or let them be cancelled in the event of departure. Cancellation of exercisable options in the event of departure results in a journal entry similar to the one above to record the lapse of options.

For options that require a minimum service period to obtain exercise rights and if the employee has not satisfied this requirement by the date of departure, the departure cancels the option. In addition, the cancellation implies that the compensation accrued at the measurement date and amortized over the minimum service period to obtain the right to exercise was never fully earned. For example, consider the second case in the Baker Corporation example discussed earlier. Suppose the CEO left the employ of Baker on April 1, 1994, prior to the date on which the right to exercise the options would have been earned. The options are no longer outstanding and no future compensation should be recognized.

What about the compensation recognized in 1993, or the amount that would otherwise have been recognized for the period from January 1 to April 1, 1994? When a termination of employment cancels an option plan before the first date of exercise, any compensation recognized in a prior period is reversed in the current period. This adjustment is treated as a revision of an accounting estimate. Based on the facts and circumstances at the end of 1993, the $3,500 of compensation expense was accrued as the best estimate of the cost of the compensatory option plan which could be matched against revenues. Since then new information (the CEO has departed) has become available, and the estimate must be revised. The estimate of total compensation under the option plan went from $12,000 to zero, and the accrued expense of $3,500 must be reversed in 1994. Since the CEO's departure occurs prior to the end of the accounting period for the 1994 fiscal year, no compensation expense will be recognized in 1994 relating to this plan. In addition, the value estimated for the options, which originally increased Baker's paid-in capital, must also be removed.

The following journal entry would record the adjustments as of the date the CEO departed:

April 1, 1994:

Paid-in capital from outstanding stock options	12,000	
Deferred compensation from stock options		8,500
Compensation expense		3,500

To record the effect of the employee termination and cancellation
of the options.

Measuring Compensation When Measurement Date Follows the Grant Date

To this point, the discussion of compensatory stock options has focused on cases where the measurement date and the grant date coincide. It is possible to grant an option that has no determined exercise price. For example, assume that on January 1, 1994, Brainerd Enterprises grants an option to its CEO for the purchase of 1,000 shares of stock. The exercise price for the options is set at 80% of the market value of the shares when the option is exercised if the exercise occurs prior to December 31, 1995, or $4 per share thereafter. In this case, the measurement date will be the earlier of the exercise date of the option or January 1, 1996. Since the final exercise price will be known by January 1, 1996, under the terms of the contract, this represents the latest possible measurement date.

When this situation arises, estimates of the total compensation under the option will be accrued over the time between the grant date and the measurement date based on information available at each balance sheet date. In the case of Brainerd, if we assume the options are not exercised by the end of 1994, an estimate of the total compensation under the option contract is obtained at December 31, 1994 by comparing the market value of the shares at that date to an estimated exercise price. The estimated exercise price would be 80% of the existing market value. If the ending market value of Brainerd's stock at December 31, 1994 was $3 per share, the estimated compensation would be $600 [$3 − (.8)($3)][1,000 shares]. Since the options are exercisable immediately, there is no deferred compensation; and the estimate of total compensation is accrued for 1994 as follows:

December 31, 1994:

Compensation expense	600	
Paid-in capital from outstanding stock options		600

To accrue the estimate of total compensation under the option plan.

If the options are not exercised at the end of 1995, the exercise price is fixed by the contract at $4. As a result, the requirements that identify the measurement date have been satisfied. Assume that the price at December 31, 1995 was $4.50 per share. As a result, the final total compensation at the measurement date is only $500 ([$4.50 − $4.00] × [1,000 shares]). An adjustment would be required as follows:

December 31, 1995:

Paid-in capital from outstanding stock options	100	
Compensation expense		100

To accrue the final compensation under the stock option plan.

If the options had actually been exercised prior to January 1, 1996, then the measurement date would be set at the date of exercise. The total compensation would be determined by comparing the stock's actual exercise price to its market value on the date of exercise and multiplying by the number of shares under option. Any difference between the estimated compensation already accrued and the actual compensation realized will be treated as an adjustment to compensation expense at the date of exercise. In situations such as this, the accounting records do report the actual benefit the employee earns by receiving the compensatory options.

If the CEO in the above example had been required to provide service for some period prior to earning the right to exercise the options, the process of estimating the total compensation based on the observed market price of the stock at each balance sheet date would still be applied. However, part of the total estimated compensation would have been deferred and part would have been charged to expense, based on the amortization process applied in the earlier examples of options where the grant date and the measurement date coincided.

Share Grants and Awards of Restricted Stock   Occasionally, corporations will simply award shares of stock to employees without receiving payment. In these situations, the shares' market value at the time of grant is recognized as the total compensation related to the share grant. If the grant restricts the employee's ability to sell the stock, then the total compensation should be attributed to the period from the date of the grant to the date the shares become unrestricted. For public corporations, if shares that are unregistered with the SEC are issued to an employee, they are restricted as to their resale for two years. This restriction does not prevent the sale of shares; rather, it restricts the number of such shares an employee may sell during any period. As a result, employees receiving restricted shares receive an asset similar to an option that cannot be exercised for a two-year period. Consequently, the compensation expense is recognized over the minimum holding period.

The General Tax Status of Employee Stock Options   Before turning our attention to other forms of incentive compensation programs, we will examine the tax treatment of option programs because it has significantly influenced the design of option programs. Changes in the tax treatment of option programs are partially responsible for the development of other forms of incentive compensation programs, which replaced or enhanced option programs when Tax Code changes made them less attractive. The taxation of income obtained from employee stock options is complex, and this discussion is not designed to develop specific expertise in this area.

Generally, taxes could be levied on income generated from holding stock options or the shares acquired thereunder when:

1. The option is received
2. The option is exercised
3. The shares acquired under the option are ultimately sold

Generally, employees who receive the options prefer the third choice because it defers the tax consequences as long as possible and the sale of the shares will generate the cash needed to pay the taxes.

If a stock option plan is offered to all employees without discrimination based on level of employment, the exercise prices are not significantly below the stock's market price at the grant date, and several other specific requirements are met, the options granted under this program will be considered **qualified stock options** for tax purposes. The taxes on income from qualified stock options for the employees covered are levied when the shares acquired under the options are ultimately sold. However, the sponsoring corporation receives no tax deduction for compensation expense under these plans.

For example, assume Jane Reynolds received options to purchase 15,000 shares of her employer's stock with an exercise price of $20 per share on January 1, 1993, when the market price per share was also $20. The option plan is a qualified plan for tax purposes. Jane exercised the options on June 1, 1994, when the market price per share was $23 and ultimately sold the shares on December 31, 1994, for $28 per share. Jane will not be required to pay any taxes on the difference between the market value of the shares and the exercise price on June 1, 1994, when she exercised the options. She will pay taxes on the difference between the selling price of the shares and her purchase price, or $8 per share ($28 − $20) when she sells the shares on December 31, 1994. The corporation that employs Jane will not receive any tax deduction for compensation related to these options.

Any option not meeting the requirements of a qualified plan may still be given special treatment as an **incentive stock option (ISO)**. An incentive stock option can be offered to specific groups of employees, but the option's exercise price must not be significantly below the stock's market price at the date of grant. Many other limitations in the Tax Code must also be met before an option can be defined as an ISO, but these limitations are not important to us here. The use of ISOs is limited to a maximum number of shares that can be placed under option, and this maximum is quite restrictive.[3] ISOs are given the same tax treatment as qualified option plans.

Options that are not qualified and do not meet the limitations required to be ISOs are called **nonqualified options**. The treatment of nonqualified options depends on the option's terms. In general, if the option's exercise price is not significantly below the market price at the date of grant, the employee will be required to include in taxable income an amount equal to the difference between the stock's market and exercise prices when the options are exercised. The sponsoring corporation will be allowed a tax deduction for compensation expense in an amount equal to the income the employee reported at the date of exercise. When eventually selling the shares, the employee must include in taxable income any gain or loss from the sale based on a comparison of the shares' selling price to their market price at the date of exercise.

For example, assume Jack Knowles received options for 100,000 shares of stock in Highboy Corporation at an exercise price equal to the then existing market price of $20 per share on January 1, 1993, which was also the measurement date. Jack exercised the options on December 1, 1993, when the market price was $23 per share. Jack sold the shares for $22 per share on February 15, 1994. In this case, Jack would include $300,000 ([$23 per share market value −

---

[3] For example, as this text goes to print, the maximum is only 100,000 shares.

$20 per share exercise price] × 100,000 shares) as taxable income in 1993. Jack would then have a tax basis in the shares of $2,300,000, the market value at the date of exercise. When Jack sold the shares in February 1994, he experienced a loss of $100,000 ($2,200,000 selling price − $2,300,000 tax carrying value) and may be allowed to offset this loss against taxable income in 1994.

Given these facts, Highboy Corporation would be allowed a tax deduction for compensation expense of $300,000 in 1993. However, no further deductions are available after the date of exercise. This presents an interesting situation for Highboy. For financial reporting purposes, this option plan was noncompensatory because the option's exercise price was equal to the shares' market value at the measurement date. As a result, no compensation expense is ever recorded in the financial reports for these options. However, the company does receive a tax benefit from the tax deduction referred to above. How should this tax benefit be disclosed in the financial statements?

Since this tax benefit arises from a transaction relating to the issuance of stock and no compensation expense was ever recognized from the options, the tax benefit is treated as a direct adjustment to additional paid-in capital. Assuming that Highboy's tax rate in the year the deduction arose was 30%, the tax benefit would be $90,000 ($300,000 deduction × 30% tax rate). Highboy would record this tax benefit as follows:

December 1, 1993:		
Taxes payable	90,000	
Paid-in capital from tax benefits of compensatory options		90,000
To record the tax benefits from the deduction relating to the		
options as contributed capital.		

Stock Appreciation Rights (SARs)

Prior to the mid-1970s, options could more easily qualify for preferential tax treatment similar to that now offered ISOs. Under more favorable tax treatment, employees often had incentives to hold on to shares acquired through the exercise of options for long periods following exercise. This enhanced the "incentive value" of the option plans because as long as managers held the shares, their own welfare was economically linked to that of the rest of the shareholders.

In the mid-1970s, the tax rules changed and recipients of options were commonly taxed when they exercised them. This created a problem for the employee who often had to sell the shares immediately to generate cash to pay the taxes. If the employee immediately sold the shares acquired under option, then the plan's incentive benefit was lost. As a result, an alternative form of incentive compensation program arose. This program paid participants in cash but linked the cash payments directly to the level of share price. These plans, called **stock appreciation rights (SARs)**, do not award any of the rights and privileges of share ownership (such as the right to vote) to recipients but do tie recipients' wealth to the share price performance of the sponsoring company.

Generally, an SAR promises to pay an amount in dollars, which is determined by the difference between the share price at the maturity of the SAR contract and a prespecified price (usually set at the market price at the date of the compensation contract). Many SARs also allow the participant to take the payment in cash, shares of stock, or a combination of both.

For example, assume the current share price of ABC Corp. is $5. In its simplest form, a stock appreciation right would promise to pay a key executive, in cash, the difference between the market price at the end of two years and $5. If the share price increased to $12 by that time, the executive would receive $7 for each SAR awarded. If ABC had awarded 10,000 SARs, the executive would receive $70,000 cash.

If the prespecified starting price is equal to the market value when the contract is entered into, no tax liability exists until the cash is paid. This has the advantage of only creating a tax liability for the executive when cash is available to pay it. In addition, there are usually several other important features of SAR contracts. The SAR is often open-ended in that the contract allows the employee to continue to benefit from share price appreciation after the end of the required employment period. This is accomplished by allowing the employee to choose when to "cash out" the plan, not requiring that settlement occur immediately after the end of the required employment period.

A significant drawback to this form of compensation is that a readily ascertainable market price is critical to use an SAR. While a privately held corporation might use a stock option, it would have difficulty using a SAR because a market price of its shares is not readily available. In addition, the cash flow implications for a growing company may be a consideration.

Accounting for SAR plans is similar to the accounting for a stock option when the exercise price is not set at the date of the grant. However, there are some important differences between these two types of plans. With an SAR plan, the corporate entity promises to commit its future resources, conditional on the movement of its share price. The corporation's, not its shareholders', resources are directly affected with an SAR. In an option, the future share price determines the total compensation the executive will receive. However, the corporation does not directly bear this cost. Rather, the shareholders do through the dilution of their ownership. Since the accounting entity of concern is the corporation, the stock option has different implications than the SAR for the corporation.

The company's obligation for future payment of cash is a contingent liability. In accounting for any contingency, issues regarding both the probability of incurring the actual liability for payment and the degree to which such a liability is estimable must be considered. The FASB has decided that obligations under SAR plans satisfy these two criteria because the current market value is a reasonable estimate of future market values, and the sponsor of the SAR plan generally intends to pay out some compensation under this type of incentive agreement.

As a result, the obligation for compensation under the terms of the agreement is determined periodically based on the observed market price at the end of each successive year and the requirements for continued service on the employee's part. During the periods prior to exercise, the compensation earned is accrued as a liability under the SAR. When the employee actually exercises the SAR, the obligation is liquidated by the payment of cash. Suppose a plan required employment for two years before payout. The difference between the market price at the end of Year 1 and the prespecified price would be used to estimate the total compensation under the contract. Since only one-half of the total required service has been rendered by the end of the first year of the program, one-half of any estimated compensation is accrued.

At the end of Year 2, the current market price of the shares is used to reestimate the total compensation. Since all of the required service is rendered, the SAR vests with the employee; and an accrual for the entire amount must be made. However, the portion of the accrual to be charged to expense in Year 2 will only be the amount that must be added to the Year 1 accrual to obtain the estimated ending balance.

If the market price falls, the liability will be decreased by actually reducing the current year's compensation expense. Changes in the market price result in a change in the estimate of the total compensation and flow through the compensation expense during the period.

Assume that ABC Corp. established an SAR plan on December 31, 1989, which entitled officers to receive cash for the difference between the market price of its shares and a preestablished price of $10. ABC granted its president 100,000 SARs, required an employment period of four years before exercise, and required that the president be employed by the company on the date of exercise. The president exercised the SARs on January 1, 1995. The market price of ABC's shares fluctuated as follows:

Date	Market Price
12/31/89	$10
12/31/90	14
12/31/91	8
12/31/92	12
12/31/93	15
12/31/94	18

As of the grant date, no compensation is realized on these SARs for two reasons:

1. No portion of the required service has been rendered.
2. The market price and the preestablished price are equal. (Compensation is only computed on the excess of market over the pre-established price.)

On December 31, 1990, the employee has rendered 25% (1 of 4 years) of the required service, and the market price exceeds the preestablished price by $4 per share ($14 − $10). The total compensation estimated at December 31, 1990, is $400,000 ($4 × 100,000). Of this amount, only 25% is "earned" based on service, so the accrual will be $100,000 (.25 × $400,000). ABC's journal entry will appear as:

December 31, 1990:
Compensation expense   100,000
   Liability under stock appreciation right plan   100,000
To record compensation expense accruing under the SAR plan.

By December 31, 1991, 50% of the required service is rendered; and the market price has changed. In fact, the market price has fallen below the set price. For this reason, we estimate that no compensation is now accrued under the plan. This means ABC must write off the liability recorded above and make an offset to the current period's compensation expense as follows:

December 31, 1991:
Liability under stock appreciation right plan   100,000
  Compensation expense   100,000
To record the adjustment to compensation expense accrued
  under the SAR plan by the end of 1991.

Thus, at the end of 1991, no accrued compensation exists on this plan, given our current information on market prices.

By December 31, 1992, the market price has risen to $12 a share; and the president has completed 75% of the required service. The total compensation under the SAR is estimated as $200,000 [($12 − $10) × 100,000], of which 75%, or $150,000, should be accrued to date. At the beginning of 1992, no accrual had been made, so ABC's entry to accrue a total liability of $150,000 would be:

December 31, 1992:
Compensation expense   150,000
  Liability under stock appreciation right plan   150,000
To accrue compensation under the SAR plan for 1992.

By the end of 1993, all service has been rendered, so the total compensation to be accrued is $500,000 [($15 − $10) × 100,000]. At the beginning of the year, ABC accrued $150,000 of this liability, so only $350,000 need be added using an entry that is identical in form to the one in 1992. In 1994, the share price rises to $18, indicating total compensation of $800,000. Since $500,000 was accrued by January 1, 1994, ABC need only add an additional $300,000 for 1994.

When the SARs are exercised on January 1, 1995, the liability is liquidated by paying cash. In this case, ABC's entry would appear as:

January 1, 1995:
Liability under stock appreciation right plan   800,000
  Cash   800,000
To record payment of the obligation accrued under the SAR
  plan.

If the president had quit prior to providing all the required service, ABC would have removed any compensation liability accrued to that date from its books; and its compensation expense of the period would have been reduced. Thus, changes in market price or employment are both treated as changes in accounting estimates and adjusted through the current period expense, not retroactively.

Bonus Programs, Phantom Stock, and Performance Unit Plans

Throughout the discussion of stock options and SAR plans, the focus of the incentive plans has been on the shares' market value. This is reasonable for top executives in large, publicly traded corporations, which are the predominate users of stock option programs. Small, privately held corporations generally do not use such plans for several reasons, including:

1. The closely held nature of their ownership often precludes the issuance of shares to "outsiders"
2. Since the market price of a share is not observable, there is no way to define a contract around that number

In addition, the desire to link managers' compensation to variables other than share price, due to the indirect effect their decisions may have on price, also makes option and SAR programs inappropriate for some managers. As a result, several alternative incentive compensation programs have arisen.

Annual Bonus Plans The most common form of incentive compensation is the annual bonus. Annual bonuses are typically awarded when an employee's annual evaluation indicates good performance along the dimensions the company and/or supervisors believe are most important. The determination of annual bonuses may be formalized in a contract or may be informally administered. An example of a formal contract would be one that pays the CEO a cash bonus of $50,000 if income before taxes and the bonus exceed $1,000,0000 for the year. In such a situation, a clear target triggers the contingent compensation. Accounting for these types of incentive arrangements requires that any bonus due at the end of a fiscal period should be accrued, regardless of whether it has been paid.

Long-Term Plans Longer-term bonus programs also exist. These set performance goals that are measured over several years and then compensate the manager based on the achievement of these targets. These plans can be structured in many ways. The discussion that follows examines a few of the more common forms of these plans.

Phantom Stock Plans **Phantom stock plans** award contingent compensation based on a formula that mimics the returns the corporation's common shareholders receive without actually issuing stock or a claim to stock in the company. Phantom stock plans reward managers for increases in such variables as book value per share (adjusted for such factors as stock splits, stock dividends, and cash dividends). Phantom stock plans are used in many situations where share price is not observable or where tying employees' wealth to stock prices would require that the employees bear too much risk.

The terms of these plans can be structured in many ways. Some plans will pay cash equal to the book value per share at some specified future date. Others will pay cash equal to the increase in book value per share over a pre-specified period. In any case, the essence of the agreement is that the employees' compensation is related to variables generally linked to increased equity value. Of course, such plans will only be acceptable to shareholders if the incentive to increase book value per share will also result in decisions that maximize the equity's value in general.

As was discussed in earlier chapters, some accounting choices that maximize the book value per share will not maximize the market value of equity. One example may be the LIFO/FIFO choice for inventory valuation. LIFO, by reducing the tax burden, may increase the company's market value but will reduce earnings and, thus, reduce the book value of equity. These types of conflicts must be considered in setting the targets used in compensation programs. In addition, managers may actually misrepresent information in the financial statements and make it appear that the performance targets have been met, when in fact they have not. While this type of fraud is rare, using accounting-based targets as performance goals does provide incentive to misrepresent.

Phantom stock plans are at least one step removed from directly linking the employees' wealth to the company's share price. If employees are very risk averse (do not like risk), awarding shares may place too much risk on them and they may not function well. In the extreme, it could result in emotional breakdowns, departure of the employees, or other types of failure to perform in a reasonable fashion.

The accounting process by which book value is determined is more stable and less subject to market fluctuation. For this reason, book value of equity may be a very good measure to use in contracting with a very risk averse employee so long as there is some relationship between high book value per share and high market value. In addition, the book value per share is more likely to be linked directly to the quality of the decisions the employee makes. Therefore, it is easier to evaluate the employee's performance.

Accounting for Phantom Stock Plans   Accounting for these types of agreements is conceptually similar to that for an SAR program, except the compensation is not linked to an observable variable like stock price. Unlike accounting for SARs, no authoritative pronouncement guides the accounting for most phantom stock plans. The accountant must exercise professional judgment in this area.

Compensation under a phantom stock plan is contingent on the occurrence of some future event. It is, thus, a contingent liability and should be accounted for under the terms of SFAS No. 5. If the obligation is probable and reasonably estimable, it should be accrued in advance of actually observing the event that triggers payment.

Consider a situation in which a manager is awarded 10,000 phantom shares. A cash payment will be computed for each phantom share based on the increase in the book value per share of common stock over a five-year period. Assume the company has never, and will not, pay any dividends. At the end of the first year, the book value per share of common has risen by $2 per share. Is there sufficient basis for recording a liability for the increase in book value during the first year of the arrangement? Is the obligation sufficiently probable of occurring at this point? Can it be reasonably estimated using the current book value per share?

Professionals will disagree in their answers to these questions. Generally, compensation is not accrued under these circumstances because of the material uncertainties that exist over the next four years. This may be mitigated by an assessment of the history of growth in book value per share and the accountant's assessment of the company's future earnings power. Both of these factors must be evaluated to assess the likelihood that the liability for payment will occur.

Even when no liability is recorded at the end of the first year, if the book value per share grew over the next three years such that at the end of Year four, the corporation had a very high probability of paying out on the phantom stock plan, there would likely be an accrual for this obligation. The point is that professional judgment in such situations is necessary.

Performance Unit Plans   **Performance unit plans** provide payment to the manager in the form of equal valued units, which are earned by accomplishing targets with multiple dimensions. For example, a performance unit plan might award cash for each performance unit earned. Participants might earn performance units by attaining such goals as growth in sales, cost per unit produced, or growth in earnings per share. A 6% sales growth might be worth 100 performance units, while an earnings per share growth of 6% might be worth 1,000 performance units. At the end of the period, the value of each performance unit is set by the compensation committee of the board of directors; and each participant is given his or her share of the total compensation.

Compensation in these plans may be in cash, in shares of stock, or in options to purchase shares of stock. In addition, the plans may be long-term (setting targets measured over several years) or short-term (annual). In the annual plans, compensation will be recognized in the year earned based on the fair value of the award (either the cash paid or stock awarded). Since the actual determination of the amounts to be awarded do not occur until after the end of the accounting period, an estimate must be accrued at year-end to charge the expense properly to the period in which the income earned from the employee's efforts was recorded.

Long-term performance unit plans are accounted for similarly to a phantom stock plan. However, in many cases, it is very difficult to estimate what value the compensation committee will place on a performance unit. This results in no accrual prior to the completion of the time period covered by the plan since the obligation for payment on the plan is not estimable until that point.

Other Long-Term Bonus Plans   Other types of simple long-term bonus plans also exist. Usually, these simple plans provide for payment of a cash bonus contingent on achieving some target. The target is chosen to reinforce a particular corporate strategic goal. For instance, a long-term bonus plan for a vice president of marketing may require that average growth in sales over a five-year period be 12% per year. If sales growth is less, no bonus is paid. In these situations, accrual of the bonus generally occurs when the conditions for its payment are met.

In the case of the marketing VP, it is not possible to state with certainty that a 12% average growth rate will occur until after the last year's sales figures are entered. It can be argued that no accrual should be made until the end of the bonus contract. On the other hand, if the contract had stated a sales level that should be achieved (such as achievement of $20 million of sales within the next five years), then as soon as the sales level is achieved, the bonus might be accrued even if it is not payable until the end of the five-year period. Once again, the use of professional judgment, guided by the requirements the profession has established for recognizing contingent liabilities, will be necessary to resolve the issue of what accrual should be made, if any, in the financial reports.

Note Disclosures for Incentive Compensation Programs

The choice between these various forms of incentive compensation arrangements will depend on the corporation's nature (publicly or privately held), the organization's strategic goals (i.e., if sales growth is the most important strategic goal, then performance plans targeted on this goal may be most important), the extent of owner management (more owner management reduces the need for incentive type arrangements), tax laws, and other factors. When incentive compensation plans are significant, the existence and status of these plans is usually described in the notes to the sponsoring corporation's financial statements. Note disclosure usually describes the plan, and, in option or share plans, reconciles the options or shares issued, cancelled, or exercised during the period.

JOINT INCENTIVE COMPENSATION PROGRAMS AND RETIREMENT/SAVING PLANS

There are several types of programs that represent a combination of incentive compensation and retirement (or general savings) plans. These include stock purchase programs, employee stock ownership plans (ESOPs), and profit-sharing defined contribution retirement plans. Each of these is examined in turn in the sections that follow.

Employee Stock Purchase Programs

Employee stock purchase programs allow employees to purchase shares of stock in the corporation through payroll deductions. These often combine features of a savings program and a corporate matching program to encourage employees to purchase shares of the corporation. Usually employees may set aside a portion of their current wages which are then matched by the company's proportionate contribution. The total proceeds are then used to buy shares that are placed in trust for the employees' benefit. The shares may be acquired from the company at prices slightly below current market value due to the company's ability to save issuance costs by selling directly to employees. The company generally reserves the right to repurchase the shares if employees retire or otherwise terminate participation in the plan.

The Tax Code generally allows individual participants to defer taxes on the employer's contributions in these plans. On the other hand, the employer is allowed a tax deduction for contributions to these plans as made. Thus, corporations have some added tax advantages. However, access to the wealth represented by the shares is limited to the point of termination or retirement in most cases. Thus, individuals must relinquish some financial flexibility to purchase shares in this type of plan.

The value of broad-based employee stock ownership plans lies mainly in the degree to which they create a common set of goals for all the company's employees since everyone is a potential shareholder. Usually, the size of the equity interest for any single individual is not large; but even a small amount of equity participation may increase the employee's commitment to the organization. Accounting for these plans simply requires that any contribution the employer makes for a period be charged to compensation expense in that period.

Employee Stock Ownership Plans (ESOPs)

Another form of share ownership plan that provides both performance incentives and savings/retirement features is an **employee stock ownership plan (ESOP)**. In these plans, a trust is established to acquire shares of the sponsoring corporation. The shares the trust acquires are allocated to individual participants over time, based on rules established when the ESOP is started. Usually, the allocation is based on the size of the employee's wages or salary as a percentage of the total wages and salaries of all participants. The stock issued to an ESOP may be the voting common stock of the company, or it may be a special class of stock created just for the ESOP.

A Description of a Basic ESOP   In the most basic form of an ESOP, the trust receives the corporation's contributions, which it then uses to purchase the shares necessary to meet the plan's requirements. These shares can be either purchased directly from the corporation or in the open market. When participation in an ESOP is available to virtually all employees, the plan qualifies for special tax treatment. Any contributions to the ESOP trust provide a tax deduction in the year the contributions are made. In addition, since the ESOP can purchase the shares directly from the corporation, the sponsor can simply contribute the required shares to the ESOP and take a tax deduction for the market value of the shares contributed.

Generally, employees cannot directly acquire the shares held in their account. Instead, if the ESOP benefit has vested when the employee leaves the company, the employee will receive the cash equivalent of the shares' market value at that date. Employees covered by tax qualified ESOPs are not taxed on the value of their interest until they receive cash payments from the trust, similar to the taxation of a defined benefit pension plan. To obtain the cash required to pay employees, the ESOP will sell the shares allocated to the employee either in the open market or back to the corporation. Because the shares are held on the employee's behalf, the employee's economic welfare is linked directly to the performance of the sponsor's share price. Because the ultimate benefit depends only on the sponsor's share price, this represents a very risky form of retirement benefit.

A Typical Leveraged ESOP   Historically, when many ESOPs were originally created, the trust borrowed a large amount of money from a bank or from the sponsor it used to purchase a large block of shares. ESOPs that borrow funds to acquire shares are referred to as **leveraged ESOPs** and are very popular. Due to restrictions of the Tax Code, ESOPs can hold cash for only a short period of time. Consequently, virtually all the ESOP's assets must be shares of the sponsoring corporation. An ESOP may hold shares that are not assigned to individual accounts, referred to as *unassigned shares*. With leveraged ESOPs, the shares the ESOP owns are not all assigned immediately to individuals because there are many more shares in the trust than the agreement requires.

Over time, the company will make contributions to the ESOP to allow the trust to repay the debt. The ESOP will also receive dividends on the shares the trust holds if the sponsor declares dividends on the shares. These dividends can be used to purchase additional shares or repay the debt of a leveraged ESOP. They may also be distributed to the employee/beneficiaries.

Bank borrowing to finance ESOP share purchases was motivated by the fact that the Tax Code allowed the banks to avoid paying taxes on interest income from loans to tax qualified ESOPs. As a result, sponsoring firms could create an ESOP, have the ESOP borrow funds from a bank, sell shares to the ESOP, and obtain the cash while ultimately paying much lower interest costs on the borrowed funds. The lender's tax advantages have been substantially altered by recent changes in the Tax Code. However, sponsors have found that ESOPs provide other benefits beyond the lower interest rates on borrowing that motivate their continued use.

Nontax Benefits of ESOPs   From the preceding discussion, it is clear that a major economic force in the creation of an ESOP is tax benefits. However, these plans also have some performance incentives since employee welfare does become linked to the sponsoring corporation's long-run performance. In addition, the corporation selects the ESOP's trustee. When the ESOP purchases voting stock, the trustee votes those shares at shareholder meetings. For this reason, some companies have been accused of using ESOPs as an anti-takeover device.

By creating an ESOP, placing a "management friendly" person in the position of the trustee, and then having the ESOP buy a large amount of the corporation's outstanding shares, the sponsoring firm's management can virtually assure themselves that no hostile takeover can be successful. This forces any potential acquirer of the sponsor to negotiate directly with the sponsoring firm's management to complete a successful acquisition. In turn, this puts managers in a position to "put their own interest first" before those of the shareholders. Whether these accusations are indeed true is unclear. However, this situation does point out the double-edged effect that ESOPs might have on different types of incentives.

Accounting and Reporting for ESOPs   From a financial reporting perspective, ESOPs present several problems. If the ESOP borrows money to acquire shares, should the debt be accounted for in the sponsoring firm's financial statements? In addition, when should the company record compensation expense, if any, related to the granting of shares to employees? How should the compensation be measured? The American Institute of Certified Public Accountants (AICPA) has published a *Statement of Position (SOP) No. 76-3* relating to ESOPs. In addition, several EITF consensus statements have dealt with specific issues regarding the reporting of activity related to ESOPs.

These statements require that the ESOP's debt should be recorded as a liability on the corporation's books, with an offset against the stockholders' equity section of the balance sheet. The liability and contra-equity account should be simultaneously reduced as the loan is repaid. Compensation expense is to be recorded when cash is transferred to the trust to pay for the debt. The portion of the contribution representing interest on the loan should be reported as interest expense, with the remainder classified as compensation expense.

Assume that Employee Shareholders, Inc., has adopted an ESOP on January 1, 1993. The ESOP acquired a $1,000,000 bank loan. The loan requires repayment of the principal over 3 years with interest of 10% on the unpaid balance. Loan payments occur on January 1 of each year. The ESOP uses the loan to purchase shares in the open market. Contributions to the ESOP (determined based on the maximum allowed as a tax deduction) over the next 3 years were made as follows on December 31st of each year:

Year	Contribution	Interest	Compensation
1993	$ 500,000	$100,000	$ 400,000
1994	400,000	60,000	340,000
1995	286,000	26,000	260,000
Total	$1,186,000	$186,000	$1,000,000

Given the information above, Employee Shareholders would record the following entries relating to the ESOP:

January 1, 1993:

Commitment to the employee stock ownership plan	1,000,000	
Employee stock ownership plan debt		1,000,000

To record the contra-equity account and liability associated with the employee stock ownership plan.[4]

December 31, 1993:

Compensation expense	400,000	
Interest expense	100,000	
Cash		500,000

To record the contribution to the ESOP.

January 1, 1994:

Employee stock ownership plan debt	400,000	
Commitment to the employee stock ownership plan		400,000

To reduce the contra-equity account and liability by the principal repayment.

Similar entries would be made at the end of 1994 and 1995 for compensation expense, except that the amounts would be $340,000 and $260,000, respectively. Interest expense of $60,000 and $26,000, respectively, would also be recognized in each year. On January 1, 1995 and 1996, the ESOP liability and contra-equity

---

[4] The liability recorded for the ESOP debt would typically be disclosed in the balance sheet as part of the current portion of long-term debt or as long-term debt, depending on the timing of the principal payment.

account would be reduced by the amount of the principal payment covered by the cash transferred from the ESOP to the bank. Had the ESOP not borrowed money, but waited to purchase shares with company contributions, the compensation expense would still be measured by the company's cash contribution to the ESOP. Of course, the sponsoring corporation would record no debt.

Under the accounting treatment discussed above, compensation expense is related to the ESOP's cash flows. In turn, these cash flows are designed to indicate the allocation of shares in the ESOP to specific participants, even though the participants do not own the shares directly. Unassigned shares do receive dividend distributions but are currently treated as unissued for purposes of the earnings per share computation.

A slight alteration in the accounting procedures discussed above is necessary when the funds for the ESOP are raised by having the company borrow money directly, then make a loan to the ESOP to purchase the shares. When the company borrows on its own, the liability is directly a debt of the company and is recorded like any other liability. When the company, in turn, loans money to the ESOP, a receivable is created and cash is reduced. The receivable should be classified as a contra-equity account.

Another issue arises with the declaration of dividends on shares the ESOP holds. Should the value of those dividends be considered as an ordinary dividend, or should they be charged to compensation expense based on the observation that the dividends are being paid on shares whose original value would be reported as compensation? The AICPA took the position that the dividends should be reported as an ordinary dividend, not as compensation expense.

Defined Contribution Pension Plans

In a **defined contribution pension plan**, a retirement plan, the sponsor agrees to make periodic contributions to a trust on the employees' behalf based on a contractual formula. The trustee invests the contributions on the employees' behalf. At retirement, the employees are entitled to payment of whatever monies have accumulated in their individual accounts within the plan. If the plan meets the requirements of the Tax Code for qualified status, the corporation can take tax deductions on the contributions when made, and employees are not taxed on the benefits until they are paid out from the trust. Unlike defined benefit pension plans, defined contribution plan sponsors make no promises regarding the magnitude of the retirement benefit employees will receive.

Salary-Based Plans   The contribution formula can be based on anything the parties agree is acceptable. Typically, the formula is based on a percentage of wages or salary, or it is linked to the company's profitability. Plans linked to profitability are referred to as **profit-sharing plans**. For plans where contributions are based on a percentage of salary or wages and cease when the employees retire, the pension expense to be recognized in any period is simply the amount the contract requires be contributed. At the balance sheet date, the contributions may not yet have been made and, therefore, an accrued liability will be necessary.

For example, assume that Beta Corporation has a defined contribution pension plan that calls for contributions of 9% of salary or wages up to a maximum wage or salary of $50,000. Qualifying wages and salaries for 1993 were $2,300,000. The pension expense for 1993 would be $207,000 ($2,300,000 × 9%). Further assume the company had contributed $190,000 to the pension trust on the employees' behalf as of December 31, 1993, with the balance to be contributed within 60 days of the end of the fiscal year. Beta's journal entry to record the activity relating to the defined benefit pension plan for 1993 would appear as follows:

December 31, 1993:		
Pension expense	207,000	
Accrued expenses		17,000
Cash		190,000

To record pension expense and cash contributions for the defined benefit pension plan.

Benefits under a defined contribution pension plan vest similarly to those under a defined benefit pension plan as discussed previously. Vesting may take place over several years, or it may occur at the point contributions are made to the trust. When an employee departs prior to full vesting of benefits in a defined contribution plan, the excess monies held in the trust are generally used to satisfy the current year's accruals for other employees. This reduces the amount of cash the sponsor must contribute to fund the currently accruing benefits of employees still covered by the plan.

Profit-Sharing Plans   When a defined contribution plan is structured as a profit-sharing plan, the only major difference is that the annual contributions are linked directly to reported accounting earnings. Whatever contribution is accrued under the plan for a particular year must be recognized as pension expense in that period, regardless of whether the contribution was actually made. As a result of the linkage of the contribution to accounting earnings, profit-sharing defined contribution plans provide performance incentives to covered employees. Assuming that higher earnings indicate greater share value, the profit-sharing plan provides an incentive for all participating employees to make decisions that will increase shareholder wealth.

One important feature of these plans is that they tend to be more long-run oriented. Since employees generally will not begin drawing from the trust for many years, and it is the total amount in the trust, not the annual contributions, that govern the size of any retirement benefits, employees may be more willing to make decisions that create larger long-run profits instead of maximizing year-to-year net income. In this regard, the corporation's long-term health may be enhanced.

Continuation of Contributions Beyond Retirement   Some defined contribution plans commit to making contributions even after the employee's retirement. When this occurs, a reasonable estimate of the size of these future payments should be made; and the obligation for their payment should be accrued over the employee's working life, instead of being charged to expense after the employee's retirement.

This accrual problem is more readily assessed when the plan is based on salary than on incentive payments such as a profit-sharing plan. Since profit-sharing plans require that income be reported prior to determination of any contributions, it is generally not reasonable to accrue contributions that will continue after retirement on this type of plan until the required income is actually reported. For salary-based plans, the continued contributions will be based on salary immediately prior to retirement. In this case, the future salary should be estimated; and a liability equal to the present value of those post-retirement contributions should be accrued over the employee's service life.

Excess Contributions by the Sponsor   Employers may contribute an amount in excess of the required contribution to a defined contribution plan. When this occurs, the pension trust has assets that are not allocated to specific employees. These assets can be invested, and returns on the assets are tax-exempt. Thus, a company with temporary excess cash may elect to over-contribute to its defined contribution plan and obtain tax-free returns on the investments. As a result, in later years, the company will not need to make as large a contribution.

When this occurs, the excess contribution is not treated as an expense of the period. Instead, the pension trust investments are carried as assets on the sponsoring firm's balance sheet. If the investments are in marketable securities, those securities are carried as part of the company's marketable securities portfolio. Only the required portion of the contribution is considered compensation. In future years when the excess contributions are assigned to plan participants, the assets' carrying value at that point will be treated as compensation; and the assets will be removed from the corporate balance sheet.

OTHER EMPLOYEE BENEFITS

Corporations often provide a wide array of benefits to their employees. These include paid vacation and sick leave programs, employee health insurance plans, provision for day care, legal aid plans, and a host of other programs. Accounting for compensated absences, such as vacation and sick leave programs, requires an identification of the periods to which the costs of such benefits should be attributed. Accounting for the other types of benefits mentioned above can be divided into two parts:

1. Accounting for costs incurred for active employees
2. Accounting for costs incurred on behalf of retired employees

Both of these are addressed in the last sections of the chapter, with special attention focused on accounting for other post-retirement benefits as defined by SFAS No. 106.

Vacation and Sick Pay Plans

Vacation and sick pay plans cover employees' absences and promise to pay the employees their normal wage or salary. Generally, these plans limit the number of vacation and sick days an employee may use in any 12-month period (usually a calendar year). Some plans of this type stipulate that unused vacation and sick pay will lapse at the end of the year and, thus, cannot be accumulated from year-to-year. Most plans allow some form of carryover for unused vacation and sick leave.

Accounting for plans that have lapsing provisions is quite straightforward. Salaries and wages paid during compensated absences of this type are simply charged to expense in the period paid. For plans that allow benefits to accrue over time, different rules exist for expense recognition and the valuation of the liability. SFAS No. 43 deals specifically with the rules for accrual of compensated absences. For a compensated absence to be subject to accrual, it must meet all of the following four conditions:[5]

1. The obligation of the employer must be related to the employee's right to receive future compensation for services rendered in the past. (The employee must have accrued the right to the benefit due to services already performed.)
2. The right to collect such benefits must accumulate or vest. This means that the benefits must carry forward from year-to-year or require payment at termination. Even when the contract does not stipulate accrual, if the employer's policy is to give credit informally for accrued leave, a liability should be recognized.
3. Payment of the compensation is probable.
4. The amount can be reasonably estimated.

The last two provisions relate to the standard tests for any contingent liability, which the obligation for payment of the benefits represents. In estimating the obligation, no guidance exists as to whether current wage levels should be used to estimate the size of the obligation or whether future wage levels should be incorporated. Since the liquidation of the obligation will depend on wage in existence when the compensated absence occurs, it would appear reasonable to attempt to incorporate future wage increases if these are estimable. In general, current wages are the most common basis for accrual of these benefits.

Other Benefits for Active Employees

When an employer provides health and life insurance to its current employees, the costs of such insurance policies should be charged to expense in the period the premium binds coverage. If an employer elects to self-insure, an accrued liability for future claims may be appropriate if such obligations meet the criteria for recognition as a contingent liability. Relatively few companies elect to self-insure for active employees; and when they do, there is rarely sufficient data to record a contingent liability.

---

[5] "Accounting for Compensated Absences," *Statement of Financial Accounting Standards No. 43* (FASB, November 1980), para. 6.

Other Post-Employment Benefits (OPEBs)

In addition to providing various forms of health and welfare benefits such as health insurance, life insurance, dental plans, day care services, and legal services during the period employees are employed, many companies also provide continuation of these benefits to employees following their retirement. When a single employer commits to providing these services for employees after retirement, SFAS No. 106 requires that the expected costs for these post-retirement benefits should be accrued during the employee's service life. The remainder of this chapter examines the process by which the expected post-retirement costs are estimated for these plans and how these costs are allocated to periods during the service life of the employees covered. The allocation process is very similar to that used for the assignment of costs related to defined benefit pension plans discussed in Chapter 18.

What Are the Unique Properties of OPEB Plans?   A typical OPEB provides cost reimbursement for health care costs following retirement for employees who have satisfied certain requirements. Generally, these requirements relate to a minimum number of years of service and a minimum retirement age. Unlike defined benefit pension plans, no specified rate at which benefits accrue is stipulated. If an individual retires prior to accumulating the minimum number of service years, no benefit is provided.

In many of these plans, the employee's ability to receive the benefit depends on employment with the sponsoring company until retirement. This implies that vesting of the benefit will not occur until the actual date of retirement, and then only to the extent that other conditions necessary to receive any benefits have been satisfied.

Another characteristic separates OPEBs from defined benefit pension plans. The Internal Revenue Code does not generally provide tax deductions for contributions that companies make to trusts created for the purpose of funding the ultimate payment of benefits.[6] As a result, other post-employment benefit plans are funded on a "pay-as-you-go" basis, where the current year's payments to retirees come directly from the corporation. These payments are tax deductible when made directly to the individual. Consequently, there is virtually no pre-funding of these benefits.

Finally, OPEB plans are often cancellable at the sponsor's discretion. Depending on the terms of the plan, cancellation may require that employees who are already retired at the time of cancellation continue to receive benefits, but any employee still working would be ineligible. Some plans allow for the cancellation of benefits to retired employees as well. Other plans are negotiated as part of a labor package with unions and cannot be cancelled without union approval.

Accounting for OPEBs   Prior to SFAS No. 106, the costs of OPEB plans were generally charged to expense when the payments were made to employees.

---

[6] The Tax Code does allow any earning from assets placed in a trust for the payment of these benefits to be untaxed, but the corporate contribution is not deductible when made.

This treatment was motivated by several observations. First, it was believed that the magnitude of these costs were small in aggregate. Second, the ability of a large number of companies to terminate the plan at will led many to believe that no real obligation for future benefits existed; thus, accrual of these costs would be inappropriate. Third, the lack of tax deductions for pre-funding suggested that firms would continue "pay-as-you-go" funding; and this attenuated the companies' desire to obtain accurate estimates of the future costs of OPEB plans.

Following the adoption of SFAS No. 87, which provided specific guidance in accounting for defined benefit pension plans, the FASB began an effort to standardize the financial reporting requirements for OPEBs. The FASB suggested that when companies intended to continue OPEB plans in the future, the going concern assumption could be used to motivate accrual of the future expected costs even if no formal legal liability existed at the balance sheet date. The FASB then sought inputs from industry regarding the size of these promised benefits. Many in industry and in the accounting profession were surprised at the magnitude of the present value estimates for the future benefits under existing OPEB plans. Some estimates of the total value of these benefits for all sponsoring companies were so large that they exceeded the market value of all shares traded on the NYSE! Armed with this revelation, OPEB plans became a major focus of attention, both for purposes of developing financial reporting requirements and for the general management and oversight of the programs that corporations were putting into place.

The Expected Post-Retirement Benefit Obligation (EPBO)   The starting point to determine the periodic expense to be recognized from an OPEB is the **expected post-retirement benefit obligation (EPBO)**. This amount is the actuarial present value, as of the valuation date, of the total post-retirement benefit payments for current and past employees. To determine this amount, an actuary must consider any estimated future cost increases that the sponsor will bear under the program's current terms and practices. If plans link the magnitude of the benefits to the employee's final pay, estimates of future compensation levels must also be incorporated. In addition, if the plans are integrated with public plans such as Medicare, expected changes in these public programs that would have significant impact on the employer's costs for the plan must be included. The actuary chooses a discount rate to determine the present value of the expected benefits. The discount rate should be selected by reference to interest rates available on high-quality investment securities.

In some ways, the EPBO is similar to the projected benefit obligation of a defined benefit pension plan, but conceptually it is quite different. The EPBO represents the present value of *all* expected future benefits to be paid. The projected benefit obligation is the present value of the expected future benefits to be paid, *which are accrued based on service provided to date*. Consequently, an actuary's estimate of EPBO does not depend on the number of years of service an employee has rendered, or needs to render, to be eligible for the benefit. Like the projected benefit obligation, the EPBO is computed using a number of forecasts regarding such characteristics as expected retirement age, mortality, final pay (when applicable), and others.

Consider Vesta Corporation, which has three current employees, one retiree, and a post-retirement health care plan. The plan requires that the employee be at least 56 years old to qualify and employed by the company at retirement to receive benefits. There is no minimum number of years of service an employee must provide to receive benefits. As of January 1, 1992, the company adopted the requirements of SFAS No. 106. The actuarial discount rate is set at 10%. Exhibit 19.2 displays the information the actuary compiled regarding the EPBO estimate by employee.

Examining Exhibit 19.2 reveals that Fred is currently age 25 and was hired by the company when he was 20. Terms of the plan require employees to be at least 56 to qualify, and employees are expected to retire at age 65. To determine the EPBO for Fred of $10,000, the actuary had to estimate the amount of benefits that are expected to be paid to Fred from his expected retirement at age 65 to his death. The actuary then had to discount this amount to January 1, 1992, using the discount rate and adjusted for the probability that Fred will actually remain in the employment of Vesta long enough to collect the benefits. (A turnover assumption must be developed.) The actuary performed similar analysis for Marcia and Rod. Since Agnes is already retired, the EPBO for her reflects the present value of future benefits to be paid from January 1, 1992, to her death. No adjustment for turnover is appropriate in her case.

The Accumulated Post-Retirement Benefit Obligation (APBO)   Following the determination of the EPBO, another measure of the obligation for future benefits must be ascertained. This measure is called the **accumulated post-retirement benefit obligation (APBO)**. The APBO is the actuarial present value, as of the valuation date, of the total post-retirement benefit payments attributable to service rendered to date. In effect, the APBO is a subset of the EPBO since in a case where 100% of all benefits are fully accrued, the APBO would equal the EPBO.

Accrual of benefits is deemed to occur uniformly over the period from the first date an employee begins work for the corporation up to the **full eligibility date**, or the date, under the plan's terms, an employee becomes eligible to

EXHIBIT 19.2
Vesta Corporation—
Information on the
Work Force and
EPBO as of
January 1, 1992

VESTA CORPORATION
Information on the Work Force and EPBO as of January 1, 1992

Employee	Status	Age	Minimum Age at Hiring	Minimum Age to Qualify	Expected Retirement	EPBO
Fred	Active	25	20	56	65	$ 10,000
Marcia	Active	40	25	56	65	25,000
Rod	Active	57	32	56	65	50,000
Agnes	Retired	66	37	56	-	30,000
Total						$115,000

receive benefits. For example, if the plan states that employees must provide 15 years of service to be eligible, the full eligibility date would be the 15th anniversary of employment. As a result, the accrual of benefits will be deemed to occur uniformly over the 15-year period. In the case of Vesta Corporation, the full eligibility date is the 56th birthday of the employee. In the case of Fred, Exhibit 19.2 suggests that his minimum service period to full eligibility is 36 years since he began employment at age 20 and must reach 56 to be eligible.

Exhibit 19.3 demonstrates how the APBO as of January 1, 1992, for Vesta Corporation could be computed from the EPBO information provided in Exhibit 19.2. The total years of service to date in column (2) is computed by comparing the age of the employee at hiring to the current age from Exhibit 19.2. Similarly, the required years of service in column (3) is the difference between the employee's age at hiring and 56, which is the minimum age for participation. The attribution percentage is the percentage of the required years of service already contributed, or the ratio of column (1) to column (2). Multiplying the EPBO by the attribution percentage gives the APBO at January 1, 1992, which is the valuation date in this example.

Changes in the APBO due to the effects of an additional year of service each employee provides, called the **service cost**, and interest on the beginning APBO, called the **interest cost**, will play a major role in determining the expense to be recorded relating to an OPEB. The APBO is not recognized as a liability on the sponsoring firm's balance sheet. Instead, it represents an "off-balance sheet" item, just as the projected benefit obligation for a defined benefit plan is an "off-balance sheet" item.

The Transition Obligation   When a company first adopts SFAS No. 106, a transition item similar to the one arising for defined benefit pension plans when SFAS No. 87 was adopted, is created. The transition obligation is determined by the difference between the APBO and the balance of any obligation already accrued in the sponsor's balance sheet relating to the OPEB liability. The transition item is another "off-balance sheet" item. The transition item for an OPEB is

EXHIBIT 19.3

Vesta Corporation— Computation of the APBO from Information on the EPBO as of January 1, 1992

			VESTA CORPORATION		
			Computation of the APBO from Information on the EPBO as of January 1, 1992		
Employee	(1) Years Employed	(2) Required Years of Service	(3) Attribution Percentage (1)/(2)	(4) EPBO	(5) APBO (3) × (4)
Fred	5	36	14%	$ 10,000	$ 1,400
Marcia	15	31	48%	25,000	12,000
Rod	25	24	100%	50,000	50,000
Agnes	n/a	n/a	100%	30,000	30,000
Total				$115,000	$93,400

generally an obligation equal to the APBO on the date SFAS No. 106 was adopted. In the case of Vesta Corporation, the transition obligation would be $93,400.[7]

Expense Recognition for OPEBs   The periodic expense to be recognized relating to an OPEB is referred to as the **net periodic post-retirement benefit cost**. It is composed of the following elements:

1. Service cost
2. + Interest cost
3. + Amortization of the transition obligation
4. + Amortization of unrecognized prior service cost
5. − Actual return on plan assets
6. +/− Amortization of cumulative unrecognized gain or loss

The actuary determines the OPEB's service cost, which represents the present value of the benefits attributed to an additional year of service. The interest cost is determined using the actuarial discount rate applied to the APBO's beginning balance. The transition obligation may be recognized at once or it may be amortized over the average service lives of the employees covered by the plan at the date SFAS No. 106 is adopted. If the average service life is less than 20 years, an amortization period of 20 years can be chosen.[8]

Unrecognized prior service cost occurs whenever an amendment to the OPEB plan alters the level of benefits to be provided. It is measured as the increase in the APBO arising from the amendment's effect. Conceptually, it is identical to the unrecognized prior service cost used in accounting for defined benefit pension plans. The unrecognized prior service cost is not recognized immediately as expense of the period in which the amendment occurs. Instead, it is deferred and amortized over the average remaining required years of service for employees covered by the plan at the date of the amendment.

Since the expense recognition process for OPEBs is modeled after that of defined benefit pension plans, the **actual return on plan assets** is treated as a reduction of period expenses. Any difference between the actual return and the expected return for the period is treated as an unrecognized gain or loss to be deferred. Consequently, the net periodic post-retirement benefit cost is actually reduced by the expected return on plan assets for the period. However, as noted earlier, very few of these plans are pre-funded. As a result, no assets exist in the plan and no return is expected. Nonetheless, should changes in the Tax Code emerge to encourage pre-funding of these plans, or should a corporation simply elect to take this route, the periodic expense can be affected by the return on plan assets.

---

[7] Corporations adopting SFAS No. 106 have the option of immediately recognizing the transition obligation on their balance sheet or electing the "off-balance sheet" deferral approach. If immediate recognition is elected, the amount is also treated as a cumulative effect of a change in accounting principle in the period of adoption. The examples in the text assume the deferral approach is elected.

[8] Under some circumstances, additional amortization of the transition obligation may be required if the cumulative expense as determined by SFAS No. 106 from the transition date would be smaller than the cumulative expense under the old pay-as-you-go system of expense recognition. Generally, this situation is not expected to arise and is not discussed here.

Unrecognized cumulative gain or loss arises due to changes in actuarial assumptions or differences between expected and actual returns on plan assets. It is subject to the same corridor amortization process as with defined benefit pension plans. In the case of OPEBs, the corridor is defined as 10% of the APBO.

Recognition of the Net Periodic Post-Retirement Benefit Cost—An Example

Continuing the Vesta Corporation example allows us to see how the basic expense recognition process for OPEBs functions. In particular, we will see how similar this process is to that used for defined benefit pension plans, once we redefine the measure of liability from the projected benefit obligation to the APBO used in OPEB accounting.

During the year, there were no changes in the actuarial assumptions of Vesta's plan. All active employees continued in that status for the entire year, and no new employees were added. The actuarial present value of the service cost for the year was $330 for Fred and $825 for Marcia. Note that since Rod has reached the age of full eligibility, no further service cost is incurred during the remainder of his years with the company. Payments to Agnes for benefits during the year amounted to $5,000.

Exhibit 19.4 tracks the changes in the APBO for 1992 and demonstrates the computation of the employees' average service life at adoption of SFAS No.

EXHIBIT 19.4
Roll Forward of the APBO

VESTA CORPORATION FOR 1992
Roll Forward of the APBO

Panel A: Roll forward of the APBO

Employee	Beginning APBO	Interest Accrual at 10%	Service Cost	Benefit Payments	Ending EPBO
Fred	$ 1,400	$ 140	$ 330	–	$ 1,870
Marcia	12,000	1,200	825	–	14,025
Rod	50,000	5,000	–	–	55,000
Agnes	30,000	3,000	–	(5,000)	28,000
Total	$93,400	$9,340	$1,155	$(5,000)	$98,895

Panel B: Computation of Average Service Life of Employee Group at Adoption of SFAS No. 106

Employee	Age at Adoption of 106	Expected Age at Retirement	Expected Years of Service
Fred	25	65	40
Marcia	40	65	25
Rod	57	65	8
Agnes	66	65	0
Total			73

Average Service Life = 73 ÷ 4 = 18.25 years.

106, which is used to amortize the transition obligation. The changes in the APBO related to service and interest are translated into adjustments to expense and the off-balance sheet amounts in Exhibit 19.5. In Exhibits 19.4 and 19.5, the interest accrual is based on the 10% discount rate times the beginning APBO (19.4 examines this at the individual level while 19.5 applies it to the aggregated amounts). In both Exhibits, benefit payments reduce the size of the APBO, and additional service costs increase it. As a result, an ending balance of the APBO for each employee can be determined as in Exhibit 19.4. Both the aggregate interest cost and service cost components are entered into the workpaper in Exhibit 19.5 as increases in the off-balance sheet APBO and increases in the expense to be recognized for the period. Benefit payments are also a cash outflow from the corporation for the period. Vesta does not fund the plan; so, there are no assets on which to earn a return. The expected return is, therefore, zero, as is the actual return. No additional adjustment is necessary for this component in Vesta's case.

Since this is Vesta's first year of application for SFAS No. 106, there was no beginning unrecognized cumulative gain or loss.

The last element of expense is the amortization of the transition obligation, which in this example is based on the 20-year election since the average ser-

EXHIBIT 19.5

Vesta Corporation—
Working Paper for
Tracking OPEB
Activity

VESTA CORPORATION
Working Paper for Tracking OPEB Activity

Item	Financial Statement Effects			Off-Balance Sheet Effects				
	OPEB Expense	Cash Payment	Accrued Asset or (Liability)	APBO	Plan Assets	Transition Obligation	Unrecognized Prior Service Cost	Unrecognized (Gain) or Loss
Opening Balance	$ n/a	$ n/a	$ 0	$(93,400)	$ 0	$93,400	$0	$0
Service Cost	1,155	–	–	(1,155)	–	–	–	–
Interest Cost	9,340	–	–	(9,340)	–	–	–	–
Actual Return	–	–	–	–	–	–	–	–
Unrecognized (gain)/loss	–	–	–	–	–	–	–	–
Amortization of Transition Obligation	4,670	–	–	–	–	(4,670)	–	–
Amortization of Prior Service Cost	–	–	–	–	–	–	–	–
Amortization of Unrecognized (gain)/loss	–	–	–	–	–	–	–	–
Contribution	–	5,000	–	–	5,000	–	–	–
Benefits	–	–	–	(5,000)	$(5,000)	–	–	–
Change	$15,165	$5,000	$10,165	$ 5,585	$ 0	$ (4,670)	$0	$0
Ending Balance			$10,165	$(98,895)	$ 0	$88,730	$0	$0

vice life of Vesta's employee population is less than 20 years. This amortization reduces the off-balance sheet transition item and increases expense for the period. Total expense amounts to $15,165. Vesta actually paid out $5,000 of benefits. As a result, the net balance of $10,165 represents a liability for accrued net periodic post-retirement benefit cost, which Vesta must record at the end of 1992. The journal entry Vesta would record appears as follows:

December 31, 1992:

Net periodic post-retirement benefit cost	15,613	
Cash		5,000
Accrued post-retirement benefit cost		10,613

At the beginning of the discussion regarding the financial reporting requirements for OPEBs, we noted a relationship exists between the EPBO and the APBO through the attribution percentage that reflects the extent to which employees accumulate benefits through continued service to the sponsor. Since this is always true, it should be possible to recreate the ending balance of the APBO for Vesta using information on the beginning EPBO, the discount rate, benefits paid, and attribution percentage as of December 31, 1992. Exhibit 19.6 presents this reconciliation.

Recall that the EPBO represents the actuarial present value of the total future expected benefits. It is not dependent on the extent to which the benefits are deemed to be accrued through service. As a result, in years where no

EXHIBIT 19.6

Vesta Corporation—
Reconciliation of
EPBO and APBO at
Year-End

VESTA CORPORATION
Reconciliation of EPBO and APBO at Year-End

Panel A: Roll Forward of the Beginning EPBO

Employee	Beginning EPBO	Interest Accrual at 10%	Benefit Payments	Ending EPBO
Fred	$ 10,000	$ 1,000	$ –	$ 11,000
Marcia	25,000	2,500	$ –	27,500
Rod	50,000	5,000	$ –	55,000
Agnes	30,000	3,000	(5,000)	28,000
Total	$115,000	$11,500	$(5,000)	$121,500

Panel B: Computing the Ending APBO from the Ending EPBO

	(1)	(2)	(3)	(4)	(5)
Employee	Years Employed	Required Years of Service	Attribution Percentage	EPBO	APBO
Fred	6	36	17%	$ 11,500	$ 1,870
Marcia	16	21	51%	27,500	14,025
Rod	26	24	100%	55,000	55,000
Agnes	n/a	n/a	100%	28,000	28,000
Total				$115,000	$98,895

changes are made in the actuarial assumptions, the EPBO grows only due to the effects of present value and declines only due to benefit payments actually made. The ending EPBO can be converted into the ending APBO by multiplying the ending EPBO by the attribution percentage for each employee, *as of year-end*. For Frank and Marcia, another year of service had increased the attribution percentage since both are younger than age 56. For Rod, another year does not change his attribution percentage since he is already over age 56.

Other Disclosures Regarding OPEBs   Note disclosures relating to OPEBs require the same basic details as those for defined benefit pension plans. A required description of the plan must include:

1. The nature of the plan
2. Employee groups covered
3. Types of benefits provided
4. Funding policy
5. Types of assets held
6. The nature and effects of any significant matters affecting comparability for the periods presented
7. Any modifications of the existing cost-sharing provisions of the plan
8. The existence and nature of any commitment to increase monetary benefits

In addition, schedules that present the components of net periodic cost and the reconciliation of the plan's funded status to the balance sheet accrual are also required. Components of net periodic cost must include, at a minimum, service cost, interest cost, actual return on plan assets, amortization of the transition obligation, and other items. The reconciliation of the funded status to the balance sheet accrual should contain information on the APBO broken down by benefits to retirees, fully eligible participants, and other active participants. In addition, the market value of plan assets, unrecognized transition obligation, unrecognized prior service cost, and unrecognized gain or loss should be reported.

Other disclosures are also required. These include:

1. The assumed health care cost trend rate(s) used to measure the expected cost of benefits covered by the plan for the next year and the ultimate trend, as well as when the long-term rates are expected to be achieved.
2. The weighted-average discount rate and rate of compensation increase used to forecast the APBO and the pre-tax rate of return on plan assets, along with the tax rate applicable to income from any assets placed in trust on the plan's behalf.
3. The effect of a one-percentage-point increase in the assumed health care cost trend rate on the measurement of the APBO and the aggregate service cost and interest cost components of the net periodic expense, holding all other assumptions constant.

Unlike defined benefit pension plans, no minimum liability requirement exists for OPEBs. The FASB proposed this in their original exposure draft but was unable to convince its constituents that a minimum liability provision was appropriate. Note that the minimum liability provision for defined benefit plans is related to the measure of termination liability imposed by federal regulation on these plans. No such regulation exists for OPEB plans.

SUMMARY

This chapter completed our examination of various types of compensation offered to employees beyond an hourly wage rate or monthly salary. This chapter focused on three major categories of compensation:

1. Incentive compensation programs that are primarily performance incentives
2. Joint incentive and savings/retirement plans
3. Other benefits offered to both existing and retired employees

The economic motivation for incentive compensation programs was discussed in the context of finding ways to overcome the fact that managers have private information regarding their efforts and would prefer not to expend that effort, all other things held constant. Linking a portion of the manager's compensation to outcomes that both the manager and the shareholders observe can be useful if the outcomes can be influenced by managerial effort and are related to increases in the company's value. Since many different observable outcomes could be the focus of incentive plans, the chapter examined the accounting and reporting issues related to incentive plans. Stock option and SAR plans, which focus directly on share price were first examined; and then the chapter turned to other forms of short- and long-term incentive plans that may focus on factors such as reported net income, book value per share, increases in sales, or a host of other factors.

Accounting for option plans requires that an estimate of the total compensation to be recognized in the financial statements be made at the measurement date. This compensation may be allocated to several periods if a minimum length of service is required before the employee can exercise the option. If no minimum service period is required, the total compensation is recognized immediately. In stock option plans, where the measurement date is later than the grant date, and for SAR plans, compensation prior to the final determination of the plan's results is accrued based on annual estimates of the total compensation under the plan. This is then amortized over the service period required in such plans.

Long-term bonus plans that do not focus on share price may also result in accrual of compensation expense over the plan's life. However, this decision depends on the evaluation of the contingent liability for payment of the ultimate incentive compensation. As a result, if the obligation for payment is not probable or cannot be reliably estimated, it will not be accrued prior to actual determination of the final benefit.

Incentive programs that also include savings/retirement features include stock purchase programs, ESOPs, and profit-sharing defined contribution pension plans. In the first two of these programs, providing share ownership to employees creates an incentive for higher performance in order to increase share price. For profit-sharing plans, the focus is typically on reported net income. Accounting for stock purchase programs and defined benefit pension plans requires the recognition of any contributions required by the company due to performance of the period as expense at the end of the period, regardless of whether the payments have been made. Accounting for ESOPs is similar, but special problems arise in leveraged ESOPs relating to the reporting of the obligation undertaken by the ESOP and the interest thereon.

Other employee benefits include a wide array of plans, but vacation and sick pay plans and other post-retirement benefit plans were of particular interest in this discussion. Vacation and sick pay that accumulates from period to period should generally be recognized as an expense in the period the employee provides the service that gives rise to the benefit. For other post-retirement benefits, the benefits are deemed to accrue during the employee's working life and should be charged to expense during this period. The process for accruing these benefits requires the use of actuarial estimates and attributes these costs to the years of service an employee renders up to the date of full eligibility for the benefits.

QUESTIONS

1. What does the term *incentive compensation* mean?
2. List several different forms of incentive compensation.
3. Why do shareholders willingly relinquish part of their ownership to managers through share ownership plans?
4. What is a *stock option*?
5. What is the difference between an *employee stock option* and a regular stock option?
6. What is a *measurement date*?
7. How do we determine whether a stock option is *compensatory* or *noncompensatory*, and what does this mean?
8. Does classifying an option as noncompensatory mean it is worthless? Explain.
9. What is a *stock appreciation right* and how does it differ from a stock option?
10. If you were offered a choice between a stock option plan and a stock appreciation rights plan, what factors might influence your decision regarding which to choose, assuming each offered compensation linked to the same number of shares?
11. What is meant by a *defined contribution plan*?
12. From a sponsor's point of view, how can a defined contribution retirement plan act as an incentive compensation mechanism?
13. Briefly describe what post-retirement health and welfare benefits are and the nature of the accounting controversy surrounding this form of compensation.

EXERCISES

19-1.   *Identification of important dates for option plans*

On March 28, 1994, Peco Corporation's board of directors voted to put in place a stock option plan for top executives. At this time, 100,000 shares of previously unissued, $2 par, common stock were set aside for use in this plan. On January 1, 1995, Mark Daytrim was hired as Chief Executive Officer of Peco and awarded options for 15,000 shares of Peco's common stock. The exercise price was to be determined one year later on January 1, 1996, if Mr. Daytrim was still with the company.

REQUIRED:

1. Define the date of adoption, the grant date, and the measurement date related to the stock option program described above.
2. Can you determine from the facts provided if this is a compensatory or non-compensatory plan? Why or why not?

19-2.   *Stock option plans*

On January 1, 1994, Baxter Corporation granted John Elliot, the president, an option to purchase 10,000 shares of Baxter's $20 par common stock at $30 per share. The option is intended as additional compensation over the next two years and is, therefore, not exercisable until January 1, 1996. The option can be converted for up to four years after the first date of exercise. The market price of Baxter's common stock was $35 per share on January 1, 1994, $37 per share on December 31, 1994, $40 per share on January 1, 1996, and $45 per share on December 31, 1996. Baxter has not exercised any of the options.

REQUIRED:

1. Determine the amount of the additional compensation expense that Baxter should report for 1994, 1995, and 1996.
2. What amounts would be reported in the equity section of Baxter Corporation relating to the stock options at the end of 1994, 1995, and 1996?

19-3.   *Stock option plans*

Compensatory stock options for 5,000 shares of $1 par common stock were granted to executives of Mesa Incorporated on October 1, 1993 with an exercise price of $12 per share. The market price on October 1 was $15 per share. The options were exercisable for two years beginning on January 1, 1995. On March 15, 1994, one of the executives covered by the plan departed from Mesa, and the company cancelled options covering 2,000 of the shares.

REQUIRED:

Prepare all journal entries required to account for the transactions relating to stock options in 1993 and 1994.

19-4.   *Stock option plans*

Megor Co. has a compensatory stock option plan that has resulted in $120,000 of compensation expense being recognized over the past three years. At the measurement date of the plan, 40,000 shares were put under option at $13 per share, when the market price was $16 per share. All of these options are now exercisable; and during the current year, options for 15,000 shares were exercised when the market price was $15 per share. The remaining options lapsed at year-end. Megor's common stock has a $1 par value.

REQUIRED:

Prepare a journal entry to record the exercise of the options for 15,000 shares and the lapse of the remaining options for 25,000 shares.

19-5.   *ESOPs*

In 1994, Sharewithus, Inc., adopted an employee stock ownership plan (ESOP). The plan calls for annual company contributions that will be used to purchase shares. In 1994, Sharewithus contributed $120,000 to the ESOP, which was used to purchase 15,000 shares of Sharewithus common stock at a price of $8 per share. Of the 15,000 shares purchased, only 7,500 were actually allocated to employees under the plan. The remainder were left unallocated.

REQUIRED:

Prepare the journal entry that Sharewithus would use to record the compensation expense under the ESOP.

19-6.   *Leveraged ESOPs*

Marcus Co. started an employee stock ownership plan by arranging a loan in the amount of $500,000 to the ESOP which purchased previously unissued shares of the corporation. The loan was made in 1993 by a local bank and is guaranteed by Marcus Co. Marcus immediately sold 100,000 shares of its $1 par common stock to the ESOP for $5 per share. None of the shares have been allocated to participants in the ESOP by the end of 1993. At year-end, Marcus had a contribution of $100,000 due to the ESOP, representing interest of $30,000 and principal repayment of $70,000 on the ESOP's loan.

REQUIRED:

Prepare the journal entries used to record this activity on the books of Marcus.

19-7.   *Accounting for stock appreciation rights*

On January 1, 1993, for past services, Diven Company granted Mary Allen, its president, 5,000 stock appreciation rights, which are exercisable immediately and expire three years after the date of the grant. On exercise, Allen is entitled to receive cash for the excess of the stock's market price on the exercise date over its market value on the grant date. Allen exercised all the rights on December 31, 1994. Share price data are as follows:

01/01/93	$25
12/31/93	30
12/31/94	40

REQUIRED:

How much compensation should Diven report as a result of the SARs in 1993 and 1994?

19-8.   *Accounting for stock appreciation rights*

EMX Corporation created an SAR program for its top three executives. Under the plan, each will receive cash compensation in the amount of the excess of the market price of EMX's common stock over a preset price of $15 per share at exercise. EMX granted 32,000 SARs under the plan on 1/1/94, all of which are immediately exercisable. Share price data over a three-year period was as follows:

01/01/94	$15
12/31/94	22
12/31/95	17
12/31/96	25

REQUIRED:

Assuming none of the SARs were exercised over this time period, compute the amount of the annual expense and ending liability for each of the three years.

19-9.   *Accounting for long-term bonus plans*

Magic Kettle Corporation has a long term incentive bonus plan for each of its three key executives. One of these is the vice president of marketing, Mr. Mark Frankel. In Frankel's plan, the incentive targets are growth in total sales and size of Magic Kettle's market share over a five-year period beginning in 1992 and ending in 1998. These goals are stated as the axes in the following matrix. Numbers in the matrix represent the percentage of the base bonus that will be awarded if that level of performance is achieved. The base bonus for this plan is $100,000.

| Market Share at End of 1998 | 10% | 15% | 20% |
Percent Growth in Sales			
15%	30	50	70
20%	60	80	100
25%	90	110	130

Assume that it is now the end of 1997 and you are involved in the audit of Magic Kettle Corporation. Until now your firm has decided that payments under this long-term bonus plan were not subject to accrual due to the uncertainties of obtaining the targets. However, as of the end of 1997, Magic Kettle currently has obtained an 18% market share and an average growth in sales over the past four years of 26%.

REQUIRED:

What, if any, accrual would be appropriate?

19-10.   *Recording activity on long-term bonus plans*

Use the data in Exercise 19-13 but assume you have made no accrual under the long-term plan.

REQUIRED:

1. What journal entry would you make at the end of 1998, assuming that the market share and growth rates remained constant?
2. How would this change if you had accrued a bonus of $88,000 at the end of 1997?

19-11.   *Accounting for defined contribution plans*

Frasco Corp. has a defined contribution plan that makes contributions to a pension trust on behalf of its employees. The contribution for each year is determined by a percentage of base salary up to a maximum of $50,000. Currently, the percentage is 5% of qualified base salary. This contribution is made until an employee reaches age 65 or quits, whichever comes first. Frasco has 20 employees who participate in the plan, and a distribution of their salaries is as follows:

Salary	No. of Employees
$80,000	1
60,000	2
40,000	4
35,000	3
25,000	10

REQUIRED:

Determine the expense Frasco should report for the year relating to this plan.

19-12. *Defined contribution; profit-sharing plans*

Cheap Air is a low-fare airline that specializes in flying between the United States and Japan. Cheap Air has decided to adopt a defined contribution pension plan that provides retirement benefits to some employees and acts as an incentive plan by linking contributions to the plan to income before taxes. The plan calls for contributions in the amount of 20% of income before taxes if this exceeds $200,000, and nothing otherwise. Allocation of this contribution across the five employees (A, B, C, D, and E) covered by the plan depends on the number of performance units they are awarded by the compensation committee of the board of directors at the end of the year.

Assume that Cheap Air had income before taxes of $325,000, and that the individuals, A, B, C, D, and E were awarded 4, 5, 2, 3, and 6 performance units respectively.

REQUIRED:

1. Determine the expense Cheap Air should recognize for the period.
2. How much would each employee have in his or her pension fund at the end of the year when the contribution was made?

19-13. *Defined contributions post-retirement*

Country Home has long had a policy of continuing contributions to its defined contribution plan for five years after retirement. The contributions were made at the same level as was contributed on behalf of the employee in the year prior to retirement. Country Home normally contributes 10% of salary on behalf of all covered individuals. A new executive officer, Cheryl Johnson, has been hired at a current salary of $120,000 per year. Country Home estimates that the cost of continuing contributions after Ms. Johnson's expected retirement age (which is 10 years away) will be $15,000 per year for each of the five years. Actuarial experts indicate that if the company were to fund these contributions over the remaining working life of Ms. Johnson, it would cost $3,600 per year for the next 10 years.

REQUIRED:

What expense should Country Home report in the current year relating to Ms. Johnson?

19-14. *OPEBs*

Kettle Industries has three employees who are covered by a post-retirement health and welfare benefit plan. The plan provides post-retirement health care benefits to employees who have completed 25 years of service and attained the age of 60. In addition, benefits are only provided if the employee was still in the employ of the company at the date of retirement, which is expected to be at age 65. The following information was provided on each employee as of the end of the current fiscal year:

Employee	Status	Age	Age at Hiring	EPBO
A	Active	32	24	$27,000
B	Active	62	36	55,000
C	Active	50	20	42,000

REQUIRED:

Compute the accumulated benefit obligation as of the end of the fiscal year for Kettle Industries.

19-15. *OPEBs*

Alcan Corporation reported the following information regarding its post-retirement health care plan as of January 1, 1993:

APBO	$1,200,000
Transition obligation	(700,000)
Unrecognized prior service cost	0
Unrecognized gain or (loss)	140,000
Accrued liability	$ 640,000

Alcan adopted SFAS No. 106 on January 1, 1992, and elected to amortize its transition obligation over 8 years. The company used a 12% discount rate in determining the above amounts. As of January 1, 1993, the estimated average service life of the employees in the plan was 7 years.

On July 1, 1993, the Company adopted an amendment to the plan that increased costs by $180,000. The average remaining service life of employees in the plan at the time of the amendment was 10 years, due to several layoffs in the first part of the year. Alcan does not prefund its obligation for these benefits and paid out $98,000 in cash during 1993 to retired employees for benefits under the plan. The service cost of the year was $130,000. No actuarial gains or losses were reported for 1993.

REQUIRED:

1. Prepare a working paper to track the changes in the APBO and other "off-balance sheet" amounts related to the post-retirement health care plan of Alcan.
2. Prepare a journal entry to record the expense the company should recognize for 1993.

19-16. *OPEBs*

Picnic Corporation adopted a post-retirement health care plan for its employees on January 1, 1994, subsequent to the implementation of SFAS No. 106. The plan provided credit for the previous service of employees already employed by Picnic, and the estimated present value of the accumulated benefits at inception of the plan was $200,000, using a 6% rate of interest. At the adoption, the average service life of employees covered by the plan was 25 years. No retired employees were included in the plan, and none retired in 1994. Consequently, no benefits were paid out in 1994. The plan, reevaluated by the actuaries on December 31, 1994, experienced an actuarial loss due to changes in the work force of $50,000 as of that date. For the year ended December 31, 1994, Picnic recognized an expense related to this plan of $60,000.

REQUIRED:

How much was the service cost component of the expense for 1994?

PROBLEMS

19-1. *Accounting for compensatory options*

On January 1, 1992, Holt, Inc., granted stock options to officers and key employees for the purchase of 20,000 shares of the company's $10 par common stock at $25 per share. The options were exercisable within a four-year period beginning January 1, 1994, by grantees still in the employ of the company, and expiring December 31, 1998. The market price of Holt's common stock was $33 per share on the date of the grant. Holt prepares a formal journal entry to record this award.

On April 1, 1993, 2,000 option shares were terminated when the employees resigned from the company. The market value of the common stock was $35 per share on this date.

On March 31, 1994, 12,000 option shares were exercised when the market price of common stock was $40 per share. The remaining options were allowed to lapse without exercise.

REQUIRED:

Prepare journal entries to record the activity relating to the stock options in 1992, 1993, 1994, and 1998.

19-2.   *Accounting for compensatory stock options*

When a compensatory stock option plan is authorized, current accounting pronouncements require that the measurement of all compensation to be accrued under the option plan take place on the measurement date. If the market price of the stock on the measurement date is equal to the exercise price in the option agreement, no compensation is recognized under the plan.

(AICPA adapted)

REQUIRED:

1. Discuss the criteria for determining the measurement date.
2. Does the situation described above, where no compensation is recorded, actually reflect the underlying economic facts of the situation?
3. Suggest an alternative measurement rule you believe may better capture the underlying economic cost of such plans.

19-3.   *Accounting for compensatory stock options*

Mazell, Inc. has adopted a stock option plan to provide incentives for its key executives. At the beginning of 1993, Mazell reported a balance in its deferred compensation account of $350,000, which is being amortized over a remaining service period of 2.5 years. This deferred compensation arose from options issued previously. The stock options outstanding account had a balance of $750,000, representing the value attached to 10,000 shares under outstanding stock options. During 1993, Mazell issued options to its employees for an additional 21,000 shares at an exercise price of $65 per share. At the time of the award, the market price was $72 per share. These options will not be exercisable for another 5 years. Of the options outstanding at the beginning of the year, 2,000 lapsed during 1993 and none were exercised.

REQUIRED:

Prepare journal entries to record the activity relating to the stock options in 1993.

19-4.   *Accounting for stock appreciation rights plans*

XLP Corp. established an SAR plan on December 31, 1992, which entitled officers to receive cash for the difference between the market price of its shares and a preestablished price of $75 per share. On this date, it granted its president 100,000 SARs, its Executive Vice President 50,000 SARs, and its Chief Financial Officer 75,000 SARs, provided that they meet a required employment period of two years before exercise and be employed by the company on the date the SARs are exercised. The SARs expire on 12/31/99.

The president exercised her SARs on April 15, 1995, when the market value of XLP common stock was $92 per share. Shortly thereafter, on July 1, 1995, XLP split its common shares 2-for-1; and the market price fell to $49 per share. The SARs plan is insulated against splits and stock dividends. Thus, the preset price in the SAR plan dropped to $37.50 per share; and each remaining participant was entitled to twice the number of SARs. On January 1, 1997, the CFO exercised his SARs; but the market price fell after this and the Executive Vice President elected not to exercise her SARs by the end of 1999.

The market price of XLP's shares fluctuated as follows:

Date	Market Price
12/31/92	$75
12/31/93	80
12/31/94	72
12/31/95	56
12/31/96	60
12/31/97	58
12/31/98	65

REQUIRED:

Prepare all journal entries for the period 1992–1999 as they relate to the SAR plan described above.

19-5. *Comparison of stock option plans and SAR plans*

Incentives, Inc. is considering two possible means of creating performance incentives for its top executives. One is to grant stock options exercisable at the current market price of the stock. The second is to create stock appreciation rights with a prespecified price equal to the current market price of the stock.

REQUIRED:

How would each plan be accounted for, and what are the significant differences in the nature of these alternatives that justify the different accounting treatments?

19-6. *Recording ESOP activity*

On April 1, 1992, Equitable Corporation instituted an employee stock ownership plan that covered all full-time employees. At the inception of the plan, the company guaranteed a bank loan for the ESOP in order to provide funds for the ESOP to purchase previously unissued shares of the corporation. The loan was for $2,000,000 at an interest rate of 12% per year on the unpaid balance. Loan payments, including interest and principal are due on April 1 of each year. On April 1 of 1993 and 1994, the company transferred $425,000 to the ESOP for payment of interest and reduction of principal. Equitable Corporation has a December 31 fiscal year-end.

REQUIRED:

Prepare the journal entries Equitable Corporation would use to record the activity relating to the ESOP.

19-7. *Accounting for ESOPs*

In establishing its employee stock ownership plan (ESOP), International Marketing Enterprises loaned $1,200,000 to the ESOP on March 15, 1992, to purchase

300,000 shares of its previously unissued no-par common stock. The loan carries an interest rate of 9% per year on the unpaid balance. International obtained these funds by issuing notes with a similar interest rate to investors. The note was to be repaid from contributions to the ESOP by the company over time with each payment due November 30. International has a November 30 year-end. The following information summarizes activity in the ESOP over the period from its inception to November 30, 1994:

Date	Contribution	Shares Assigned to Participants
11/30/92	200,000	10,000
11/30/93	400,000	75,000
11/30/94	500,000	125,000

REQUIRED:

1. Prepare the journal entries that International Marketing Enterprises would use to record the activity described above up to the end of the 1994 fiscal year.
2. How would the financial statements of International reflect the effects of the ESOP at the end of 1994?

19-8. *Accrual of vacation and sick pay*

Jewett and Sherman, Inc. has a policy of allowing some of its employees to accrue vacation and sick leave when it is not used during the year. A maximum of one week of vacation may be carried over, but sick days can accumulate up to 130 days. Each year employees receive two weeks (10 days) of vacation and an additional 7 sick days. When an employee covered by the policy quits or retires, the accumulated sick leave is paid as a severance to the individual but any accrued vacation days are forfeited.

At the beginning of 1994, employment records for the firm indicated the following information:

Individual	Base Pay	Accrued Vacation	Accrued Days of Sick Leave
A	$40,000	3 days	130 days
B	60,000	0 days	82 days
C	30,000	0 days	32 days
D	42,000	5 days	107 days
E	75,000	4 days	98 days

During the year, the following occurred:

Individual	Vacation Days Taken	Sick Days Taken
A	11 days	0 days
B	8 days	2 days
C	10 days	7 days
D	5 days	0 days
E	13 days	3 days

In addition, E left the employ of the company at the end of 1994. No raises were given during the year, but at December 31, 1994 each employee covered by this plan was given a 10% raise. Jewett and Sherman accrue vacation and sick pay on the basis of a 260 day working year.

Prepare the accrual which Jewett and Sherman will make for vacation and sick pay at December 31, 1994.

19-9. *Various incentive programs*

Sandy Bottom Barge Company has several types of incentive plans which are in place to reward its employees. Total direct wages and salaries of the company amounted to $2,376,000 for 1995. In addition, the following incentive agreements were in place.

(a) Stock options were given to several key employees. At the beginning of the year options for 15,000 shares at $5 a share were outstanding. These were issued several years ago when the market price of the stock was $8 per share. These options were immediately exercisable, and all of them were exercised during the current year when the market price was $12 per share. Additional options on 25,000 shares were issued at $9 a share on May 1, 1995. At the date of the grant the market price was $12 per share and the exercise price was set. These options will not be exercisable for 3 years.

(b) Sandy Bottom also has a defined contribution pension plan. The terms of the plan call for contributions of 10% of wages or salary up to a maximum of income of $50,000 per year, but only if net income before the cost of the plan exceeds $10,000,000. Sandy Bottom has income before compensation expense of $15,000,000. Qualifying wages for the plan amounted to $1,750,000.

(c) Sandy Bottom also has annual bonus arrangements for key executives. The Vice President of Marketing and the Vice President of Administration both receive a cash bonus linked to reported income. Each bonus is computed as 5% of income before taxes and consideration of any of the bonuses, up to a maximum of $100,000 per year.

The CEO was to receive a bonus payable in shares of stock, based on reported income before taxes and the CEO's bonus, but after consideration of all other compensation costs. The CEO is to receive shares under the following schedule:

Income	Shares
less than $1,000,000	0
$1,000,000–$5,000,000	1,000/$1,000,000 of income
$5,000,000–$10,000,000	1,200/$1,000,000 of income
$10,000,000 or more	1,500/$1,000,000 of income
	up to a maximum of 40,000 shares

At year-end, Sandy Bottom's common stock traded at $13 per share.

Prepare a schedule to determine total compensation expense for Sandy Bottom during 1995. Also prepare all journal entries necessary to record the activity described.

19-10. *Stock options and tax effects*

On January 1, 1993, Humboldt Co. granted its four vice presidents 5,000 common stock options apiece. The exercise price, $20 per share, was equal to the market price on that day. The options do not qualify for incentive stock option treatment for tax purposes, and the company does not offer the plan to other employee classes. The options are exercisable within a five-year period beginning on January 1, 1993. Humboldt has a 30% marginal tax rate.

The activity related to the options of each executive follows:

Name	Exercise Date	Price
Ambler	12/31/93	$22
Benoit	6/30/94	30
Chandler	6/30/94	30
Dahl	Lapsed	

REQUIRED:

1. Are these options compensatory or noncompensatory for financial accounting purposes? For taxation purposes? Why?
2. Present the journal entries necessary on the option grant date and the measurement date.
3. Present the journal entries necessary on the exercise dates. Assume the par value of common stock is zero.
4. Present the journal entries for the options that lapsed.

19-11. *Various compensation issues*

Lanza Corporation is currently closing its books at year-end, December 31, 1994. The trial balance on the next page shows all adjustments have been made with the exception of those relating to compensation and taxes.

The following information relates to Lanza's employee compensation:

(a) As of December 31, 1994, $141,345 was earned but not paid in 1994. Associated with this is $21,200 in payroll deductions for taxes and $6,500 in employer's portion of payroll tax.

(b) The company offers an employee stock purchase plan to all employees. Each year-end, employees may elect to use up to 5% of their current yearly gross wages to purchase stock in Lanza. The amount is deducted in equal installments from each monthly paycheck the following year. A matching amount is contributed on behalf of each employee at the same time. The total is subsequently submitted to a trustee who is responsible for purchasing the stock and holding it until the termination of employment.

Each year-end, the company books the entire amount of its future matching obligation as a debit to deferred compensation and a credit to payable to stock purchase plan trustee. Elections on December 31, 1993 and December 31, 1994 were $91,800 and $110,000, respectively. No enrolled employees terminated employment during 1994.

(c) On June 30, 1994, Lanza granted options on 10,000 shares of Lanza stock to one of its key employees. The options are exercisable at $20 per share as of December 31, 1992. On the grant date, the market price of Lanza stock was $25 per share.

(d) Lanza's existing stock option plan is compensatory. The options are exercisable at 90% of market value up to December 31, 1997 and at $22 per share thereafter. The options, 50,000 in all, were granted to company executives on December 31, 1992.

(e) Lanza has a profit-sharing plan in which 5% of net income before profit-sharing contribution and income tax, up to $100,000 annually, is contributed to an employee defined contribution pension plan.

REQUIRED:

Reproduce all adjusting journal entries for compensation necessary on December 31, 1994.

Lanza Corporation
Trial Balance
As of December 31, 1994

Account	Debits	Credits
Cash	$ 262,845	
Accounts receivable	450,000	
Inventory	550,000	
Deferred compensation– Stock options	50,000	
Deferred compensation– Stock purchase plan	7,650	
Other assets	4,770,000	
Cost of goods sold	3,600,000	
Compensation expense	1,693,655	
Other expense	900,000	
Accounts payable		650,000
Pension obligation		1,079,500
Payable to stock purchase plan trust		7,650
Other liabilities		450,000
Common stock—no-par		1,320,000
Paid in capital from outstanding stock options		27,000
Retained earnings		750,000
Sales revenue		8,000,000
Total	$12,284,150	$12,284,150

19-12. *OPEBs*

Precept, Inc. has sponsored a post-retirement health and welfare plan for its
hourly employees for many years. During 1993, Precept's actuary indicated that
the service cost for the year was $582,000 and payments for benefits for retired
employees was $930,000. Precept uses the pay-as-you-go approach to funding
benefits. Precept had an unamortized transition loss of $7,200,000 at the begin-
ning of 1992 when it adopted SFAS No. 106. This loss was being amortized over
a period of 8 years.

On July 1, 1993, Precept had adopted an amendment to increase the benefits for
all employees covered under the plan. The effect of this amendment was to
increase the accumulated benefit obligation by $1,500,000. The average remain-
ing service lives of employees affected by the amendment on July 1, 1993 was
7.5 years. This represented the first amendment to the plan since adopting
SFAS 106.

At the beginning of 1993, Precept reported an accumulated benefit obligation of
$8,100,000. Precept uses 8.5% as a discount rate. In addition, Precept had a
cumulative unrecognized gain at January 1, 1993 of $576,000, and the average
service lives of employees covered on that date was 7.2 years. No new actuarial
gain or loss was reported in 1993.

1. Reconstruct the beginning balances for the balance sheet and off-balance sheet items relating to the post-retirement benefit plan.
2. Complete the preparation of a working paper to determine the expense to be recognized by Precept for 1993.

19-13. *OPEBs*

In 1994, Mandan, Inc. began a post-retirement health care plan. The unrecognized prior service cost at the inception of the plan was $300,000. At that time, the distribution of employees by years of expected remaining service was as follows:

Years of Remaining Service	Number of Employees
20	13
15	17
10	15
5	10

In 1994, the expense reported for financial statement purposes consisted of service cost of $34,000, interest cost of $42,000 (computed at an assumed rate of 14%), and the amortization of the unrecognized prior service costs. Mandan paid no benefits in 1994.

As a result of a significant change in the mortality tables for workers in Mandan's industry, an actuarial revaluation was undertaken at the end of 1994. This revaluation resulted in an actuarial loss of $57,000.

For 1995, the actuaries have indicated that the service cost component should be $45,000. Mandan paid out $14,000 for benefits to retirees during 1995. No employees were hired or fired during 1994 or 1995.

REQUIRED:

Prepare a schedule to determine the expense for 1995 along with the required reconciliations for both the expense and off-balance sheet items for inclusion in the notes.

DAYTON HUDSON CORPORATION

Dayton Hudson Corporation sponsors both a stock option program and a performance unit plan. Information regarding the activity in the shareholders' equity and relating to these plans for the period 1983 through 1985 was contained in Dayton's 1985 financial statements and is reproduced below. Dayton has set the par value of common shares at $1.

CONSOLIDATED STATEMENTS OF SHAREHOLDERS' INVESTMENT

(thousands of dollars)	Total	Common Stock	Additional Paid-in Capital	Retained Earnings
Balance, January 29, 1983	$1,348,763	$48,238	$47,514	$1,253,111
Net earnings	245,457			245,457
Dividends declared	(60,425)			(60,425)
Stock option activity	6,384	240	6,144	
Two-for-one split	–	48,315	(48,315)	
Balance, January 28, 1984	1,540,179	96,793	5,343	1,438,143
Net earnings	259,346			259,346
Dividends declared	(67,369)			(67,369)
Stock option activity	4,346	199	4,147	
Balance, February 2, 1985	1,736,502	96,992	9,490	1,630,120
Net earnings	283,620			283,620
Dividends declared	(76,229)			(76,229)
Stock option activity	3,462	204	3,258	
Balance, February 1, 1986	1,947,355	97,196	12,748	1,837,511

Notes:

Stock Options and Performance Shares

We have two stock option plans for key employees. At present, no new grants can be made under either plan. Grants have included stock options, performance shares, or both. The options have included Incentive Stock Options, Non-Qualified Stock Options, or a combination of both. Twelve months after the grant date, 25% of any options granted become exercisable with another 25% after each succeeding 12 months. The options are cumulatively exercisable and expire no later than 10 years after the date of the grant. The performance shares pay cash and stock if certain selected performance goals are met at the end of a four-year period.

We record compensation expense on performance shares based on the current market price of our common stock and the extent to which the performance goals are being met. We recorded expense of $1,401, $1,207, and $1,808 in 1985, 1984, and 1983, respectively. When employees exercise options, the total option price is credited to Common Stock and Additional Paid-in Capital, and no expense is incurred.

The number of shares of unissued common stock reserved for future grants under all the plans was 1,265,347 at the end of 1985 and 1,575,841 at the end of 1984.

Option and Performance Shares Outstanding	Options		Shares Exercisable	Performance Shares
	Number of Shares	Price Per Share		
1983				
Beginning of year	1,397,708	1.99–27.13	679,116	206,152
Granted	285,380	33.88–37.34		
Cancelled	(29,621)	9.97–17.44		
Exercised	(348,642)	2.61–17.44		
1984				
Beginning of year	1,304,825	1.99–37.34	611,913	177,682
Granted	214,451	32.63–36.13		
Cancelled	(83,015)	12.36–36.44		
Exercised	(198,096)	1.99–35.94		
1985				
Beginning of year	1,238,165	4.52–37.34	689,192	134,109
Granted	340,761	39.94		
Cancelled	(34,121)	14.30–39.94		
Exercised	(186,656)	4.52–37.34		
End of year	1,358,149	7.13–39.94		100,109

REQUIRED:

1. Describe briefly what you think a performance share is and how Dayton Hudson awards these.
2. What journal entry did Dayton make for the compensation under the performance share plan in 1985?
3. How much potential dilution (as a percentage of total shares outstanding) do the shares under option represent?
4. Why is an option cancelled? Are the cancelled options likely to be exercisable?
5. Assume that during 1982 Dayton did not grant any shares under the option plan and that the average market price of Dayton Hudson stock was as follows over the period 1983-1986:

> 1983 = $36.00 per share
> 1984 = $35.25 per share
> 1985 = $41.00 per share

   Estimate how much compensation expense Dayton would report in its 1985 income statement relating to these options and prepare the journal entry to record these effects.
6. How do you reconcile the number of options exercised in each of the three years presented to the number of shares indicated as issued under options in the statement of stockholders' equity?
7. Why are the number of shares of common stock reserved for options at the end of 1985 less than the total number of shares under option?

DAYTON HUDSON CORPORATION

Dayton Hudson Corporation sponsors an employee stock ownership plan. In its 1985 financial statements, Dayton Hudson includes the following information in the notes to the statements regarding this plan. In addition, Dayton reports that cash dividends per share in 1985 were $.76.

Employee Stock Ownership Plan

We have an Employee Stock Ownership Plan to provide employees with an additional opportunity to own shares of our common stock. All contributions to the Plan are made by the Corporation. Cash contributions are used by the Plan Trustee to purchase Dayton Hudson common stock. All eligible employees share equally in that year's contribution. The annual contributions are made based upon the applicable tax laws in effect for the year to which the contribution related. We accrued a contribution of $3,937 for the plan year ended December 31, 1985. Our contribution accruals for the plan years ended December 31, 1984 and 1983 were $3,530 and $3,156, respectively. Our contributions are paid to the Plan the following year.

Assets and Equity of Employee Stock Ownership Plan	December 31, 1985	1984
Cash and equivalents	$ 240	$ 19
Dayton Hudson common stock at market value (cost: 1985–$7,024; 1984–$4,443)	8,716	4,095
Contribution receivable	3,937	3,530
Total assets and equity	$12,893	$7,644

REQUIRED:

1. From whom is the contribution receivable recorded by the ESOP collectible? How was this obligation recorded by the party responsible for payment?
2. Assume that ESOP uses the money collected on the receivable to purchase Dayton Hudson shares in the open market. What effect, if any, will the repurchase have on financial statements of Dayton Hudson?
3. From the information provided in the note, is the ESOP of Dayton Hudson a leveraged ESOP (i.e., is there a loan currently outstanding against the ESOP's assets)?
4. Assuming the ending market price of Dayton Hudson stock was $41 per share and the number of shares represented by the ending value of shares in the ESOP was constant over the year (i.e., all new shares were purchased on January 1 and held all year), how much was paid to the ESOP in dividends for the year? How did Dayton Hudson record the effects of these dividends?

BLUE HILL, INCORPORATED

Blue Hill, Incorporated has several different types of compensation plans for its key executives. These plans are designed to provide motivation to management to maximize share value for the owners. The following describes various parts of the plans in existence.

For Marta Chief, the CEO, the company has both a stock option plan and a long-term bonus plan linked to various performance targets. The stock option plan provides the following:

On January 1, 1993, Ms. Chief received options for 10,000 shares of the company's $2 par common stock. The provisions of the plan indicate that for 5,000 of the shares under option, the exercise price is set at 80% of the prevailing market price on the date of exercise, with a maximum price of $15 per share. For the remaining 5,000 shares under option, the exercise price is initially set at $10 per share but is adjusted if certain performance targets are accomplished.

These targets are:

1. If income before taxes and incentive compensation for 1993 exceeds $500,000, the exercise price is reduced by $2 per share.
2. If sales growth over the 1994–1997 period averages 20%, the exercise price is reduced by $2 per share.
3. If earnings per share at the end of 1995 is at least $1 per share, the exercise price will be reduced by $1 per share.

In any case, the minimum exercise price is limited to $7 per share. The options can be exercised at any time.

In addition to the stock option plan, Ms. Chief also participates in a cash bonus plan that was established on January 1, 1990. The plan pays a cash bonus equivalent to $250,000 times the percentage indicated in the following table, based on the accomplishment of sales growth and earnings per share growth over the seven-year period ending December 31, 1996. If the growth on either dimension falls short of the minimum indicated, no bonus is paid.

| Average 7-year sales growth | 20% | 25% | 30% | 35% |
Average 7-year EPS growth				
10%	50	70	90	110
15%	80	100	110	120
20%	100	110	120	130

In addition to the plan for Ms. Chief, Blue Hill has another incentive plan in existence for Mr. V. P. Makestuff, who is in charge of production for the company. Mr. Makestuff was awarded a "phantom stock" program on January 1, 1993. This program offers compensation to its participants equal to the change in the book value per share of common stock over the life of the plan. Mr. Makestuff was awarded 25,000 phantom shares on January 1, 1992 when the book value per share was $3. At the election of the participant, the compensation earned under the program can be in the form of cash or shares. If shares are elected, the number of shares to be awarded is determined by the number of shares that could be purchased with the earned compensation at the market price per share when the plan is cashed out. However, a maximum of 15,000 shares can be issued under the plan. The plan can be cashed out at the employee's election anytime after the end of one year.

It is now December 31, 1994, and you have been assigned the responsibility for determining the amount of compensation to be recognized by Blue Hill with respect to these plans. You have collected the following information:

(a) Blue Hill has always had 1,000,000 shares of stock outstanding. Whenever an option is exercised, the company repurchases shares in the open market sufficient to satisfy the option. The company has never declared a dividend. No compensation has been accrued in previous periods for Ms. Chief's performance plan, but otherwise appropriate entries have been made.

Per Share	Market Price	Book Value
January 1, 1993	$10	$3.48
January 1, 1994	12	4.00
December 31, 1994	16	

(b) Income before taxes and incentive compensation for 1993 was $520,000.
(c) Earnings per share growth over the period from 1990–94 has averaged 18% Earnings per share for 1994 without consideration of any compensation relating to the above plans is $0.80 per share. Sales growth over the 1990–94 time period has averaged 22%.

On July 1, 1994, Ms. Chief exercised the option for 5,000 shares of common stock whose exercise price was 80% of the then existing market price of $14 per share. Ms. Chief then sold these shares for $19 per share.

REQUIRED:

1. Is the phantom stock plan really a stock option plan that would fall under the requirements of APB No. 25, or is it a cash incentive plan that would not be covered? What are the issues to be decided in resolving this question?
2. Compute the amount of compensation that would be appropriate for each of the compensation plans discussed above. For the phantom stock plan, prepare computations under the assumption that it is a stock option plan and under the assumption that it is not.
3. Prepare the journal entries to record the activity relating to the compensation plans.
4. Why would a company use a phantom stock plan for the vice president of manufacturing and an option plan for the CEO? Why not use an option plan for both?

CHAPTER 20

Accounting for Income Taxes

Annual reports contain a variety of information regarding the effects of corporate income taxes on firms. Consider the data in the Allegheny Ludlum Corporation 1992 Annual Report (presented on pages 43 through 80 of this text). The company reported total income tax expense on continuing operations of $31,942 and $31,281 (in thousands) in 1992 and 1991, respectively. Income from continuing operations was $78,799 and $72,391, respectively. This is an average tax rate of approximately 40.5% for 1992 and 43.2% for 1991. In addition, in 1992 Allegheny also offset the cumulative effect of the accounting change resulting from adopting SFAS No. 106 with a tax benefit of $85,596. Clearly, income tax effects are both material and a pervasive part of the measurement of various components of income in the multiple-step income statement format.

In its 1991 and 1992 balance sheets, Allegheny reports a variety of different tax-related accounts. In 1992, Allegheny reports a noncurrent deferred tax asset of $21,586, a current deferred tax liability of $13,515, and a current liability for income taxes payable of $12,353. In 1991, the company had no deferred tax asset but reported both a current and noncurrent deferred tax liability of $19,531 and $63,250, respectively. In addition, it reported a current income tax payable at $2,734. The data suggest that in 1991, the total tax liabilities of $85,515 ($19,531 + $63,250 + $2,734) represented over 21% of total liabilities. The situation changes dramatically by 1992. If we net the tax-related assets against the tax-related liabilities, the 1992 net tax liability falls to only $4,282 ($13,515 + $12,353 - $21,586), which is only 0.7% of total liabilities.

Note 8 to the financial statements (partially reproduced in Exhibit 20.1) provides additional details about the components of income tax expense. The total tax expense is divided by source (federal and state) and by type (current and deferred). Total federal income tax expense on operating income was

ALLEGHENY LUDLUM CORPORATION
Excerpt from Note on Income Taxes
1992 Annual Report

Income taxes (credits) consist of the following:

(in thousands of dollars)	1992	1991	1990
Current:			
Federal	$28,442	$20,928	$29,259
State	8,755	6,432	5,655
Subtotal current expense	37,197	27,360	34,914
Deferred:			
Federal	$ (3,393)	$ (388)	$ 5,389
State	(1,862)	4,309	605
Subtotal deferred expense	(5,255)	3,921	5,994
Total income tax expense	$31,942	$31,281	$40,908

$25,049 for 1992 and $20,540 for 1991 (for an average tax rate of 31.8% and 28.4%, respectively), and total state income tax expense relating to operating income was $6,893 in 1992 and $10,741 in 1991 (for an average tax rate of 8.7% and 14.8%, respectively). Allegheny reports both a current and deferred income tax expense component. Current tax expense was $37,197 in 1992 and $27,360 in 1991, representing 116.5% of total tax expense in 1992 and 87.5% in 1991. The remainder is in deferred tax expense.

These disclosures raise a number of questions. What is the difference between the deferred and current portion of income tax expense? Why does the deferred component of income tax expense increase Allegheny's expense in 1991 and decrease it in 1992? How did Allegheny determine these deferred tax components? What relationship exists, if any, between the deferred tax portion of tax expense and the assets and liabilities labeled "deferred taxes" in the balance sheet? Why were the deferred tax balances reported in Allegheny's balance sheet so dramatically different in 1991 and 1992?

This chapter addresses these and other questions about reporting for income taxes. The chapter begins with an examination of the relationship between GAAP for financial reporting and accounting methods used for tax reporting. Understanding the relationship between these two measurement and reporting systems is the key to understanding the foundation of the problem in measuring and reporting tax amounts in the financial statements.

Following this discussion, several alternative conceptual approaches to reporting for income taxes are examined. The last major section of the chapter examines current U.S. reporting standards relating to income taxes.

THE RELATIONSHIP BETWEEN GAAP AND THE TAX CODE

In the United States, GAAP are designed as guidelines for the recognition of transactions and events in financial statements. As we have seen throughout this text, financial reports provide an important information channel for the aggregation and communication of the effects of a variety of events and transactions to outsiders. GAAP provide a basis for defining the measurement of *income before taxes* for financial reporting purposes (which we will refer to as **book income**).

The Tax Code is designed to raise revenue for a governmental unit by levying taxes on a statutory definition of income referred to as **taxable income**. The Tax Code is more concerned with issues of taxpayers' ability to pay and other social equity issues than it is with providing useful information to third parties who are interested in evaluating the corporation's performance or future cash flows. Consequently, the rules governing the recognition of transactions and events in the measurement of taxable income differ from GAAP.

Permanent and Temporary Differences

In general, the differences between the rules used to define book income and those used to define taxable income can be classified in one of two categories: permanent differences or temporary differences. A **permanent difference** is a difference between the book value and tax basis (also referred to as carrying values) of an asset or liability that arises because one of the two systems includes the effects of certain events or transactions the other does not.[1] For example, a corporation would include in its book income interest on state or local government bonds. However, the Federal Tax Code excludes this item as taxable income in any period.

A **temporary difference** is a difference in the book value and tax basis of an asset or liability that arises because of differences in the *timing* of the recognition given to certain events and transactions under the two systems. For example, assume Delta Corporation capitalized the purchase of a piece of equipment at $100,000 for both book and tax purposes at the beginning of 1992. Delta computes book depreciation using the straight-line method over 5 years with no salvage value, resulting in depreciation of $20,000 per year. The Tax Code allows depreciation to be computed on an accelerated basis, which results in depreciation deductions of $35,000, $25,000, $20,000, $15,000, and $5,000 over the 5-year life of the asset.

Given this difference in the timing of recognition for depreciation, Delta can map the pattern of temporary differences in the plant and equipment asset to which the depreciation relates. The temporary differences associated with plant and equipment at the end of each year appear as follows:

At End of Year	Book Basis	Tax Basis	Temporary Difference
1992	$80,000	$65,000	$15,000
1993	60,000	40,000	20,000
1994	40,000	20,000	20,000
1995	20,000	5,000	15,000
1996	0	0	0

---

[1] The definition of permanent differences proposed here deals with the differences between the regular income tax system and the financial accounting system. It ignores the alternative tax system, which defines taxable income with direct reference to book income. This is consistent with how the alternative tax system has been treated in accounting for income taxes under U.S. reporting standards. The effects of the alternative tax system are discussed later in the chapter.

If all other elements of book and taxable income were identical, the differences in depreciation expense would result in taxable income being lower than book income by $15,000 in 1992 and $5,000 in 1993. In 1994, both book and taxable income would be equal, but book income would be lower than taxable income in 1995 and 1996 by $5,000 and $15,000, respectively. Over the entire life of the asset, total depreciation charges would be $100,000 under either the book system or the tax system, but the timing of the expense recognition would be the different. As a result, the differences in the assets' book value and tax basis are only temporary.

Temporary Differences and Managerial Discretion

Temporary differences arise for various reasons. In some cases, the Tax Code simply defines a measurement system that differs from GAAP. For example, the Tax Code requires a corporation that generates revenue by renting property to recognize rental revenue for tax purposes when it is received, regardless of when it is earned for financial reporting purposes. As a result, if a renter pays the rental fees for three years in advance, the Tax Code requires the corporation to include the entire payment in taxable income in the year received. GAAP require the corporation to treat the payment as unearned revenue until the service is actually provided and the renter receives the use of the property. Corporate managers have no choice of accounting methods for either financial reporting or determination of taxable income in this case.

In other cases, such as the depreciation example cited above, managers can choose the accounting methods used for either book or tax purposes, or both. For financial reporting purposes, managers may choose from a variety of depreciation policies, from straight-line to several accelerated methods. Similar, albeit more limited, choices are available for tax purposes. For example, a corporation could choose to use straight-line depreciation for both book and tax purposes, thereby eliminating the existence of any temporary difference related to differences in depreciation policies for book and tax purposes. In general, managers choose policies for tax purposes that delay the payment of income taxes as long as possible. A corporation that is currently reporting taxable income can choose an accelerated depreciation policy for tax purposes to defer taxes by maximizing its tax deductions early, rather than later, in the life of the asset.

The choice of depreciation policies for financial reporting purposes is motivated by other concerns. For financial reporting, managers might choose straight-line depreciation to communicate to outsiders about the pattern of consumption for depreciable assets when the consumption pattern is uniform. Then, when the pattern is more rapid in the early life of the asset, managers may choose the accelerated methods. Alternatively, the manager's choice of the straight-line method may be motivated by their desire to report the largest amount of book income as soon as possible. Whatever the motivation, the point is that even if managers were free to select the same measurement rules for measuring book income as they do for determining taxable income, they would often not do so. These decisions give rise to temporary differences.

MEASURING INCOME TAX EFFECTS—A PROBLEM IN MATCHING

If the Tax Code used exactly the same measurement and reporting rules as GAAP used for financial reporting, book income and taxable income for each period would be identical. The effect of every event and transaction on income for each period would be the same under both systems. As a result, the currently payable taxes reported on a corporation's tax return would include the tax consequences of every event and transaction reported in the GAAP financial statements. A corporation could match the tax effects of all events and transactions in its financial statements with the income they create by reporting the current period taxes due on the tax return as tax expense.

If the only differences between book and tax income were from permanent differences, a corporation could still satisfy matching by reporting the current taxes due as tax expense because permanent differences never create any tax effect anyway. However, when temporary differences exist, there is a timing problem. The income effects of a variety of events and transactions appear in the GAAP financial statements in different periods than they appear in tax statements. Consequently, the income taxes due in any period reflect the effects of events and transactions reported in the financial statements in prior periods, the current period, and future periods. If a corporation uses the current taxes due as a measure of tax expense for the period, it will mismatch expense against income.

A reporting system that determines tax expense for any period based solely on the taxes due to the government is referred to as a **flowthrough system** of accounting for income taxes. The term *flowthrough* comes from the fact that this system makes no attempt to allocate tax consequences across periods based on when the effects of events and transactions appear in the financial statements. Instead, it lets the current taxes due "flowthrough" to the income statement as an expense.

Some countries, other than the United States, have adopted flowthrough as GAAP. West Germany, Belgium, and India use a version of flowthrough. However, since these countries have a high level of concurrence between their GAAP and tax rules, temporary differences are minimal. In the absence of temporary differences, flowthrough satisfies all notions of matching. A number of U.S. accountants also support the flowthrough approach due to the complexities of trying to determine the amount and timing of tax effects that will appear in tax returns in future periods.[2]

To appreciate more fully why the flowthrough method fails to provide adequate matching in situations where temporary differences exist, consider the following simplified example. Suppose GAAP required a corporation to report the effects of a sale as income in the year of the sale, but the Tax Code required a corporation to report these effects as taxable income in the next year when it collects the cash from the sale. Further assume that Base Corporation began operations in 1993 by having investors contribute $30,000 of capital to the company. Base used this capital to purchase an asset that it sold on credit, generating revenue of $50,000 and costs of $30,000 for a book income of

---

[2] For a more extensive discussion of the benefits of the flowthrough method, see the commentary of John Burton and Bob Sack in *Accounting Horizons* (June 1989), p. 110.

$20,000 in 1993. Base will collect the cash from the sale in 1994. The Tax Code requires corporations to pay income taxes at a 40% rate in all periods.

Exhibit 20.2 presents Base Corporation's comparative balance sheets and income statements under both GAAP and tax systems. Several notable features distinguish these comparative financial statements. First, the GAAP and tax-based financial statements can be reconciled by listing the effects of permanent and temporary differences. In this example, the only difference, a temporary difference, relates to the valuation of the liability for unearned income. GAAP value this liability at zero because all income from the sale is immediately recognized. However, the Tax Code values this liability at $20,000 since no income is recognized in 1993.

Second, the differences in balance sheet valuation are reflected in the differences in income for periods prior to the balance sheet date. In this example, Base Corporation has a difference in income between the GAAP and tax systems of $20,000, which represents the entire temporary difference relating to the unearned income liability. If Base had operated for several years, the differences between book value and tax basis for assets and liabilities would not be equal to the difference in book and tax income for 1993. However, they would be equal to the sum of all book and tax differences over the company's life.

Third, the temporary difference of $20,000 relating to the unearned income liability will reverse itself in future periods. In fact, at the end of 1993, this difference is expected to reverse in 1994. The term *reverse* simply implies that whatever the differences between book and tax income in prior periods that gave rise to the temporary difference, future differences in book and tax income will run in the opposite direction in aggregate. This characteristic defines a temporary difference.

EXHIBIT 20.2

Year-End Financial Statements for Base Corporation for Both Book and Tax Purposes Ignoring Taxes

Year-End Financial Statements for Base Corporation for Both Book and Tax Purposes Ignoring Taxes
December 31, 1993

BALANCE SHEETS:	BOOK	TAX
Assets		
Accounts receivable	$50,000	$50,000
Total assets	$50,000	$50,000
Liabilities and equity		
Unearned income	$ 0	$20,000
Contributed capital	30,000	30,000
Retained earnings	20,000	0
Total liabilities and equity	$50,000	$50,000

INCOME STATEMENTS:		
Revenues	$50,000	$ 0
Costs	30,000	0
Income before taxes	$20,000	$ 0

If the flowthrough method were applied in the Base Corporation example, income tax expense for 1993 would be zero, since no tax is due on the taxable income of zero reported in 1993. In 1994, the unearned income deferred under the tax system will become taxable when Base collects the cash. Book income for 1994 will be zero, assuming Base entered into no other transactions in that year. Since taxable income in 1994 will be $20,000, tax due in 1994 will be $8,000 ($20,000 × 40%). In turn, the tax expense reported in 1994 would be $8,000. In the end, Base Corporation would report net income (after tax) of $20,000 in 1993 and a net loss of $8,000 in 1994. Clearly, the loss in 1994 is simply the tax effects of the events and transactions reported as part of book income in 1993. Due to inappropriate matching of the tax effects to the recognition of the underlying events, this approach appears to overstate income in 1993 and understate income in 1994. How can Base rectify this?

Base can rectify the situation by attempting to accrue a liability for the expected future tax effects arising from the reversal of the existing temporary difference at December 31, 1993. This process is referred to as **interperiod tax allocation**. That is, it attempts to reallocate the actual tax cash flows from periods in which they are due to periods in which they match the book income effects of the events and transactions that gave rise to the tax consequences.

One possibility is to accrue an income tax liability for the future tax consequences of the reversing temporary differences. However, the tax consequences are not really a liability in the sense that they do not represent a contractual or legal obligation to make payment of assets. The obligation will not exist until Base collects the actual cash *and* the time arrives to file a tax return defining the legal obligation to pay. As a result, Base does not record the accrual of possible tax obligations as a liability for income taxes. Instead, it uses an account, deferred taxes, to accrue the tax effects of reversing temporary differences. Deferred tax accounts do not represent legal liabilities for payment. Rather, they reflect estimates of tax amounts that may arise when existing temporary differences reverse themselves.

Base Corporation could improve the matching of the tax effects with the income reported for purposes of financial reporting by accruing a liability for deferred taxes of $8,000 in 1993 and recording it as an expense of the period, as follows:

December 31, 1993:

Tax expense—deferred portion	8,000	
Deferred tax liability		8,000

To accrue the tax effects associated with the temporary differences recorded in book income in 1993.

By using this approach, Base attempts to measure the income tax expense for financial reporting purposes by forecasting the amount of tax liability that arises when the difference in the book and tax bases for unearned revenue at the end of 1993 reverses itself in 1994.

Exhibit 20.3 displays Base Corporation's updated GAAP and tax basis financial statements for 1993, after accounting for income taxes. It also provides a reconciliation of the net assets and net income under the two systems. Because the book system recognizes deferred tax items while the tax system

EXHIBIT 20.3

1993 Year-End
Financial Statements
for Base Corporation
for Both Book and
Tax Purposes
Including the Tax
Effects

1993 Year-End Financial Statements for Base Corporation for Both Book and Tax Purposes Including the Tax Effects
December 31, 1993

BALANCE SHEETS:	BOOK	TAX
Assets		
Accounts receivable	$50,000	$50,000
Total assets	$50,000	$50,000
Liabilities and equity		
Unearned income	$ 0	$20,000
Deferred tax liability	8,000	
Contributed capital	30,000	30,000
Retained earnings	12,000	0
Total liabilities and equity	$50,000	$50,000
Reconciliation of net assets:		
Net assets reported under GAAP	$42,000	
Net deferred tax liability	8,000	
Temporary difference on unearned income	(20,000)	
Net assets under tax system	$30,000	

INCOME STATEMENTS:		
Revenue	$50,000	$ 0
Costs	30,000	0
Income before taxes	20,000	0
Income taxes:		
Current	0	0
Deferred	8,000	0
Net income	$12,000	$ 0
Reconciliation of net income:		
GAAP net income	$12,000 ✓	
Deferred tax expense	8,000 ✓	
Temporary differences arising in 1993	(20,000) ✓	
Taxable income	$ 0 ✓	

does not, Base can reconcile the net assets under the two systems only by including the effect of deferred taxes along with the underlying temporary difference.

Having captured the expected future tax consequences of the reversing temporary difference in GAAP income for 1993, what happens in 1994? In 1994, the taxable income will be $20,000; and Base Corporation will need to accrue an actual liability for taxes payable of $8,000. However, at this point, the difference between book and tax bases for Base's assets and liabilities has disappeared. A deferred tax liability to be recognized no longer exists because the future tax effect at the end of 1993 has become the currently payable tax obligation in 1994. To record these two events, Base Corporation could make the following journal entry:

December 31, 1994:

Tax expense—current portion	8,000	
Deferred tax liability	8,000	
Tax expense—deferred portion		8,000
Income taxes payable		8,000

To record the obligation for taxes payable and the reversal of the temporary difference.

Exhibit 20.4 presents Base Corporation's ending book and tax balance sheet, assuming the corporation retains all cash collected from the sale and has not yet paid the tax liability for 1994. No differences remain between the book and tax value of equity as all temporary differences have disappeared and no permanent differences exist.

Further examination of the entry for 1994 reveals that the current portion of tax expense reflects the amount due on the 1994 tax return. The deferred tax effects represent a deferred tax benefit that reduces the total tax expense. In fact, the deferred tax benefit exactly offsets the current portion of tax expense. The total tax expense is zero. Recall that book income was also zero for 1994; therefore, the tax expense matches the book income for the period.

The process that Base Corporation employs for measuring and reporting deferred tax consequences is referred to as the **asset/liability approach** to deferred taxes. This approach captures the future tax consequences of existing temporary differences by forecasting future tax cash flows relating to the reversal of the temporary differences and then summing these forecasted cash flows into a total deferred tax asset or liability. Base Corporation had a deferred tax liability because the reversal of the temporary difference existing at December 31, 1993, would give rise to taxable income in future periods. Had this reversal given rise to a tax refund, Base would have reported a deferred tax asset.

Under the asset/liability approach, the deferred tax expense for any period is determined by the required change in the net deferred tax asset or liability from the beginning to the end of the period. Using the data for Base Corporation, a deferred tax liability of $8,000 is required at the end of 1993. Since the

1994 Year-End Balance Sheets for Base Corporation for Both Book and Tax Purposes Including the Tax Effects December 31, 1994		
	BOOK	**TAX**
Assets		
Cash	$50,000	$50,000
Total assets	$50,000	$50,000
Liabilities and equity		
Taxes payable	$ 8,000	$ 8,000
Contributed capital	30,000	30,000
Retained earnings	12,000	12,000
Total liabilities and equity	$50,000	$50,000

EXHIBIT 20.4
1994 Year-End Balance Sheets for Base Corporation for Both Book and Tax Purposes Including the Tax Effects

beginning deferred tax liability is zero (the company just began operations in 1993), the required change in the liability is also $8,000. Base reports this as an expense (the liability increased) for 1993. In 1994, the ending deferred tax liability is assessed at zero, requiring a decline of $8,000. Base records this amount as a deferred tax benefit (negative expense) in 1994.

The Allegheny Ludlum Corporation—A Reexamination

At the start of this chapter, a question was posed regarding the relationship between the deferred tax items in Allegheny's balance sheet and those in its income statement. It is now possible to see how this interrelationship worked for the company in its 1992 fiscal year.

We noted earlier that at the end of 1992, Allegheny reported a deferred tax asset of $21,586, a deferred tax liability of $13,515, and income taxes payable of $12,353. The income taxes payable liability represents the amount due to state and federal governments for taxes that appear on the current year's tax return. Netting the deferred tax liability and asset results in a net deferred asset of $8,071. This implies that Allegheny expected the future tax consequences of existing temporary differences to result in a net tax savings of $8,071 in future years.

At the end of 1991, the company reported two deferred tax liabilities of $19,531 and $63,250 for the current and noncurrent portions, respectively. This implies a net deferred tax liability of $82,781 at the beginning of 1992. If the beginning net deferred tax liability was $82,781 and the ending net deferred tax asset was $8,071, the total deferred tax expense for the period must have been a benefit of $90,852 ($82,781 + $8,071). Then why did Allegheny report the deferred tax portion of income tax expense as a benefit of only $5,255? What happened to the difference of $85,597?

The answers to these questions relate to the tax effects of the cumulative effect of the change in accounting principle. The company allocated tax costs of $85,596 to this effect, all of which is deferred taxes. (The apparent $1 difference is probably due to rounding.) In the end, we see that the total deferred tax expense reported in the income statement is equal to the change in the net deferred tax asset/liability for the period. However, Allegheny allocated the deferred tax expense across various income components; and determination of the net deferred tax asset/liability requires the accumulation of balance sheet deferred tax accounts from a variety of locations within the statement.

The Tax Code and Its Role in Accounting for Income Taxes

To identify the existence of temporary differences, which are the building blocks of interperiod tax allocation, you must be familiar with both the Tax Code and GAAP. At this point in your career, you probably have very limited exposure to the intricacies of the Tax Code. Even more, the Tax Code and GAAP are constantly changing. In fact, some previous events and transactions are no longer sources of temporary differences, while other new sources have arisen.

To understand the concepts involved in the measurement and reporting of income taxes in the financial statements, we need not invoke specific provisions of an existing Tax Code. We only need to understand how temporary differences, once identified, are used to determine the deferred tax amounts a company reports in its financial statements. As a result, we will not attempt to develop an intricate understanding of the Tax Code at this time. Instead, we will generally define various sources of temporary differences typical of Tax Codes, without reference to a specific Tax Code. If some specific aspect of the U.S. Federal Tax Code is of particular importance to our understanding of the valuation of deferred taxes, it will be developed in greater detail.

Alternative Approaches to the Flowthrough and Asset/Liability Approaches

While many U.S. corporations currently use the asset/liability approach and several other countries use flowthrough, other methods exist for handling the problem of temporary differences. Two other major approaches are the **deferral method** and the **net-of-tax method**.

The deferral method does not directly estimate the future tax cash flow consequences of existing temporary differences. Instead, it focuses on determining the deferred portion of income tax expense by applying existing tax rates to the differences between book and tax income of the current period that gives rise to the temporary differences.[3] If the Tax Code never changed and if tax rates were constant across all types of income (capital gains/losses and ordinary income) and all levels of income (flat-rate tax schemes), then no difference in the valuation of deferred tax components under the asset/liability approach and the deferral approach.

When tax rates change, the asset/liability approach responds immediately by revaluating existing deferred tax assets and liabilities. The deferral method only focuses on the current period differences between book and tax income to determine expense and then simply adjusts the ending asset/liability to reflect the current period's expense. Thus, it does not revalue deferred tax assets and liabilities immediately. In general, changes in Tax Codes over time can result in large differences between the amounts that corporations would report for deferred tax assets and liabilities under these two approaches.

Worldwide, more corporations use the deferral method to account for deferred taxes. The United States employed it under APB No. 11 prior to the release of SFAS Nos. 96 and 109 in the late 1980s and early 1990s. It is also currently used in Canada, Mexico, the United Kingdom, Australia, and Singapore. The International Accounting Standards Committee also recognizes the deferral method as acceptable.

The net-of-tax approach embeds the tax effects of temporary differences into the valuation of the assets and liabilities that cause the temporary difference. For example, the Base Corporation liability that caused the temporary

---

[3] When the deferral method is used, the differences between book income and taxable income for a period, which will reverse themselves in future periods or represent the reversal of earlier differences, are called *timing differences*. Conceptually, a timing difference and a temporary difference are similar. However, a timing difference focuses on the reconciliation of book and tax income, while a temporary difference focuses on the reconciliation of book and tax bases in assets and liabilities.

differences at the end of 1993 was the unearned income of $20,000. The tax effect of this temporary difference was $8,000. Base would have recorded no unearned income in its book balance sheet. The only asset or liability on the book balance sheet related to the sale that gave rise to the unearned income is the receivable of $50,000. Under the net-of-tax approach, the $8,000 deferred tax liability would be offset against the balance of accounts receivable, and the asset would be reported at $42,000 instead of reporting a deferred tax liability of $8,000. In its income statement, Base could have used a variety of possible disclosure approaches, including reporting the sales revenue net of the deferred tax effects (revenue would then have been only $42,000) or reporting a deferred tax expense as was done previously.

In the United States, corporations have used the net-of-tax approach in special circumstances. Under APB No. 11, corporations used the net-of-tax approach to value assets acquired in a business combination. However, the passage of SFAS No. 96 abolished this practice, and the approach is not commonly used elsewhere in the world.[4]

Additional Measurement Issues

In addition to the alternative conceptual approaches to accounting for deferred taxes, several other broad measurement issues deserve special attention. These relate to deciding:

1. Which temporary difference to include in the computation of deferred tax effects
2. Whether discounting the future tax consequences is appropriate
3. What tax rates to use

What Temporary Differences Should We Focus On?   Accountants have debated this question extensively. Many believe that all temporary differences should be included in the determination of the deferred tax assets and liabilities. This is the **comprehensive allocation approach**. Others favor including only those temporary differences that are likely to reverse themselves in the near term. This is the **partial allocation approach** because it focuses only on a subset of all the temporary differences.[5]

To appreciate the partial allocation approach, consider the pattern of temporary differences associated with depreciable assets for a company that is constantly expanding its fixed asset base. The temporary differences for each item of plant and equipment at the end of any year will reverse themselves over the rest of that asset's life. However, since the company adds new assets each year, the reversal of temporary differences on older assets is more than

---

[4] For a discussion of the merits of the net-of-tax approach, see the commentary of Phillip Defliese, *Accounting Horizons* (March 1991), p. 89.

[5] Note that the issue of whether partial or comprehensive allocation should be applied is independent of the decision to value the tax effects of the book and tax differences using the asset/liability, deferral, or net-of-tax approaches. The choice of comprehensive versus partial allocation determines which differences to focus on in applying the valuation rules but says nothing about which valuation rule is appropriate.

offset by the creation of temporary differences on new assets. At the level of total plant and equipment, the temporary differences never appear to reverse, which is a characteristic of a permanent difference.

Since the Tax Code relies on historical acquisition cost for determination of depreciation, a firm does not have to grow in terms of physical capacity to be in a situation where the total temporary difference on plant and equipment never appears to reverse. Under inflation, the cost of maintaining the same level of physical assets in place will accomplish the same thing, since the purchase of replacement assets will always be at higher prices than those in existence when the company purchased the original assets. Consequently, under reasonable assumptions about inflation, the total temporary differences driven by depreciation differences may never reverse or, at least, will not reverse for many years.

Proponents of partial allocation argue that companies should treat such situations as if the differences were permanent because the probability of reversal is low. In addition, the company's ability to estimate the future tax consequences of reversals, which will not occur in the foreseeable future, is also questionable.

SFAS Nos. 96 and 109 rejected the partial allocation approach in favor of the comprehensive approach to interperiod tax allocation. The comprehensive allocation approach had been applied previously under the deferral method in APBO No. 11 as well.[6] However, even SFAS No. 109 exempts certain selected temporary differences from inclusion in the determination of deferred tax assets and liabilities. The exemptions are highly specialized. For example, a company does not accrue a deferred tax liability for undistributed earnings in a foreign subsidiary if the investment is permanent. The undistributed earnings of a subsidiary create a temporary difference because, under the equity method used for GAAP purposes, the parent's percentage share of the subsidiary's reported income is included in income. However, for tax purposes, the parent uses the cost method.

Under the cost method, a company reports income only when it pays dividends. Consequently, the investment is valued differently for book and tax purposes, but this difference will eventually disappear if dividend distributions are larger than income in future periods. Foreign subsidiaries face additional tax complications due to the imposition of foreign income taxes and the ability of a U.S. parent corporation to use credits for those foreign taxes to offset the tax on future dividend distributions. If the investment is not expected to generate dividends in excess of earnings for many years, the reversals will not occur for some time and may be offset by tax credits when they do occur. As a result of all this complexity, the FASB exempted these temporary differences from consideration in accounting for deferred taxes.

These types of specialized exclusions require knowledge of the Tax Code that is beyond the scope of this text. For our purposes, all temporary differences will be included in the determination of deferred tax asset and liability amounts.

---

[6] Under APBO No. 11, a number of differences between book and tax income that could reverse themselves in later years were nonetheless treated as permanent differences. The number of these special cases was reduced dramatically by SFAS Nos. 96 and 109, but they are not fully eliminated.

Should Future Tax Effects Be Discounted?   Base Corporation did not determine the tax effects of temporary differences by discounting the future estimated tax cash flows and recording the present value of these net cash flows as a deferred tax asset or liability. Why not? Doesn't APBO No. 22 demand that any receivable or payable with cash flows extending beyond one year be discounted and reported at net present value?

SFAS Nos. 96 and 109 specifically preclude the application of discounting to the measurement of deferred tax assets and liabilities. The motivation for this is both pragmatic and conceptual. To apply discounting techniques, two estimates must be made. First, an estimate of the timing of the future tax cash flows arising from the current temporary differences on a year-by-year basis is needed. Second, a discount rate must be selected. Each of these poses particular problems.

Estimating the timing of the future tax cash flows that will arise from the reversal of the temporary differences depends on what future events will trigger the reversal. Let's use a depreciation example to see why this is true. Suppose that at the end of 1994, Baker Corporation had a temporary difference on a depreciable asset of $50,000. If Baker holds the asset until it is fully depreciated for both book and tax, this temporary difference will reverse itself over the next three years as follows:

1995	$25,000
1996	15,000
1997	10,000
Total	$50,000

If we apply a 40% tax rate to these reversals, the tax cash flows would be $10,000, $6,000, and $4,000 in 1995, 1996, and 1997, respectively. In discounting these future tax cash flows, Baker can determine the amount of the deferred tax liability it should report at the end of 1994.

However, what if Baker plans to generate reversal of these temporary differences by selling the asset at the beginning of 1995? This would result in reversal of the full $50,000 of temporary differences at the time of the sale. (The gain from the sale will be $50,000 larger for tax purposes than for book purposes.) Applying the 40% tax rate to this scenario would yield tax cash flows of $20,000, $0, and $0 for 1995, 1996, and 1997, respectively. Discounting these cash flows yields a much different present value than in the previous scenario. Note that these two scenarios yield the same estimate of total future tax cash flows (undiscounted) because the tax rate is constant under the two alternatives.

Use of discounting requires management to forecast the timing of the reversal of current temporary differences. Since the timing is driven by decisions that management has not made yet, auditors have difficulty in determining whether the timing of the reversals is based on management's unbiased forecast or its desire to minimize the amount of current deferred tax expense by pushing tax cash flows as far into the future as possible. The difficulty of making these forecasts, combined with the potential for manipulation, contributes to the pragmatic decision to disallow discounting.

In addition, selecting a discount rate is also problematic. How should a discount rate be chosen? Should a risk-free rate be used? Should an estimate of the cost of capital be selected for this purpose? If an estimate is to be developed, how do we ensure that management generates an unbiased estimate of whatever rate is selected? Because these issues are not clear-cut, they also contributed to the FASB's decision to forego discounting of deferred tax assets and liabilities.

In addition to the practical problems of implementing discounting procedures under the asset/liability approach, discounting was not used under the deferral approach, which preceded SFAS No. 96, because it made little sense. Under the deferral approach, a company did not measure deferred tax expense for a period by making an estimate of what the future tax consequences of existing timing differences (differences between book and tax income for the period) would be. Instead, the company focused on what its tax expense would have been if all its revenues, expenses, gains, and losses reported in book income had also been reported for tax purposes in the current year. The tax effect was a current period measure, and applying a discount factor to this estimate appeared inconsistent. Consequently, the history of deferred tax reporting never embraced discounting; and this historical precedent meant that accountants had little experience with applying the concept of discounting to deferred tax liabilities. We cannot determine how much effect this history may have had, but it is worth acknowledging that the issue of discounting had been avoided to a great extent by the adoption of the deferral method.[7]

What Tax Rates Should be Employed?   This choice is not independent of the approach a company selects to account for deferred taxes. If the company uses the deferral approach, it automatically implies that the answer to this question is the current period's tax rates. However, this is not true for the net-of-tax or asset/liability methods.

Determining the deferred tax asset or liability balance at the end of an accounting period depends critically on the company's selection of a tax rate to apply to the temporary differences. A variety of alternative approaches have been suggested to determine this rate under the asset/liability approach. One alternative is to apply the current year's effective marginal tax rate. This approach essentially presumes that this marginal tax rate will be constant over the period that the temporary differences will reverse.

When first introduced in SFAS No. 96, the liability method assumed that the company would have no future income for book purposes. As a result, the tax rate assigned to a particular temporary difference depended on the timing of the reversal and the application of the graduated tax rate scheduled on a year-by-year basis. For example, if the Tax Code taxes the first $100,000 of income in any year at 20% and taxes any additional income at 35%, the reversal of the existing temporary differences would be scheduled over future

---

[7] For a concise discussion of the debate on discounting, see James O. Stepp, "Deferred Taxes: The Discounting Controversy," *The Journal of Accountancy* (November 1985), pp. 98-109.

years. The first $100,000 of reversals in any year would have a tax rate of 20%; any amounts about this level, a tax rate of 35%. The problem with this approach is that it requires scheduling of the reversal of current temporary differences, which is problematic for reasons discussed earlier.

SFAS No. 109 requires judgment in selecting tax rates. For example, if existing circumstances support a company's judgment that future levels of taxable income will result in the application of the maximum marginal income tax rates and if existing tax law does not include provisions for changes in these rates in future years, then the company should apply the maximum marginal tax rate to all existing temporary differences.

The FASB limited the application of tax rates to those in the current Tax Code. If the current Code requires a change in rates in future years, the company should take this into account in valuing the deferred tax asset/liability. For example, if the current Tax Code at the end of 1994 calls for a tax rate decrease in 1997, then the company's accountant would value any reversing temporary differences occurring after 1996 by the rates scheduled to take effect after 1996. However, if the current Tax Code has no such provision but the accountant believes Congress will change the rates in the future, the accountant cannot use this belief to value the deferred tax asset/liability. This approach eliminates management's ability to manipulate the deferred tax balances by predicting future Tax Code changes, which cannot be effectively audited.

ACCOUNTING AND REPORTING FOR INCOME TAXES: APPLICATION OF SFAS 109

Exhibit 20.5 describes the general stages required in measuring the deferred tax amounts a corporation must report in its financial statements under existing U.S. GAAP. These general steps assume that the corporation has no unused tax credit carryforwards or net operating loss carryforwards. These features of the U.S. Tax Code are examined in greater detail later.

EXHIBIT 20.5 Steps in the Measurement of Deferred Tax Assets and Liabilities	**Steps in the Measurement of Deferred Tax Assets and Liabilities**
	1. Identify all differences between the book value and tax basis of assets, liabilities, and equities (when necessary).
	2. Determine whether the differences between book value and tax basis are the result of temporary or permanent differences.
	3. Sum all temporary differences into a single total, referred to as the net temporary difference.
	4. If the maximum marginal tax rate is expected to be constant, multiply this rate by the net temporary difference to determine the net deferred tax asset or liability to record in the balance sheet. If the future marginal tax rates are not constant, assess the timing of the reversals of the existing temporary differences through a scheduling exercise and assign the tax rates for each future period assigned.
	5. Determine the change in the net deferred tax asset or liability from the beginning of the period to the end of the period and record this change as an adjustment to the deferred tax asset or liability and the deferred tax portion of tax expense for the period.

These general steps focus on the measurement of the net deferred tax asset or liability. Classification of deferred tax balances as current or noncurrent is discussed later in the chapter, along with problems with the allocation of taxes across components of net income such as Allegheny's reported cumulative effect of the change in accounting principle.

Estimation of Deferred Tax Liabilities When Marginal Tax Rates Are Constant

The steps in Exhibit 20.5 are relatively straightforward for a firm that expects taxable income sufficient to require payment of taxes at the maximum marginal tax rate. However, the firm should review the current tax law to ascertain whether it specifies any changes that will alter the definition of a temporary difference or the rate at which it will be taxed in the future.

The following example follows this process through a two-year period, 1994 and 1995, for Klein Corporation.

Klein Corporation began operations in 1994 and, therefore, had no book-to-tax differences at the beginning of the year. An analysis of Klein Corporation's book and tax bases of its assets and liabilities as of the end of 1994 yields the information in Exhibit 20.6. Upon careful examination, we discover that the differences arose from the following events:

1. The difference in receivables arose because Klein uses the allowance method of accounting for bad debts for book purposes but must use the direct write-off method for tax purposes.
2. The difference in interest receivable arose because Klein purchased investments on which the interest is tax-exempt. Klein received no interest in 1994, but it did accrue interest receivable for financial accounting purposes in the year.
3. The difference in accrued expenses arose because for tax purposes Klein deducted expenses, which it will not recognize in its financial statements until later.

The book-to-tax differences described in Items 1 and 3 above are temporary. They will reverse in future periods. Item (2) is permanent, this income is permanently excluded from taxable income and will never appear on the company's tax return. The reconciliation of the value of "net assets under GAAP" and "net assets under tax" highlights the existing differences and groups them into net permanent differences (limited to the interest receivable difference) and net temporary differences (the net of the receivables and accrued expense differences).

The interpretation of the two temporary differences is somewhat different. Because the company included a provision for bad debts in its GAAP income, which was larger than the expense allowed on the tax return, the reversal of this difference will result in lower future taxes when Klein actually writes off uncollectible accounts. This temporary difference gives rise to an estimated future tax benefit. The fact that Klein deducted an expense for tax purposes but not for GAAP purposes reflects the opposite situation. Here, a tax benefit is created in the current year that will result in a higher taxable income in

EXHIBIT 20.6

Klein Corporation—
Book and Tax
Balance Sheets
Excluding Tax
Effects for 1994

KLEIN CORPORATION
Book and Tax Balance Sheets Excluding Tax Effects for 1994

	TAX	BOOK
Assets:		
Receivables	$ 75	$ 70
Interest receivable	–	7
Other assets	630	630
Total assets	$705	$707
Liabilities and equity (ignoring taxes)		
Accrued expenses	40	30
Other liabilities	190	190
Equity	475	487
	$705	$707

RECONCILIATION OF BOOK AND TAX AMOUNTS:	
Net assets under GAAP	$487
Permanent differences:	
Accrued interest	(7)
Temporary differences:	
Receivables	5
Liabilities	(10)
Net assets under tax	$475

future years when the temporary difference reverses. This gives rise to an expected future tax liability. Because the temporary difference relating to the liability is larger than that relating to the benefit, the net temporary differences will give rise to a deferred tax liability.

If we assume Klein has a 40% tax rate and expect this to be constant for all future periods, the net deferred tax liability at the end of 1994 is determined by applying the 40% tax rate to the net temporary differences. In this example, the ending net deferred tax liability would be $2, ($5 × 40%). Since Klein had no beginning deferred tax asset or liability, the change in the liability is an increase of $2, representing the deferred tax expense for the period.

A complete determination of tax expense requires an assessment of both the current and deferred portions of tax expense. Exhibit 20.7 presents Klein's simplified income statement for both book and tax purposes. Given the taxable income of $20 and a 40% tax rate, the current portion of tax expense would be $8 ($20 × 40%). Klein's journal entry to record the tax expense for the period would appear as follows:

```
December 31, 1994:
Current portion of tax expense                    8
Deferred portion of tax expense                   2
   Taxes payable                                           8
   Deferred tax liability                                  2
To accrue the tax expense for 1994.
```

KLEIN CORPORATION Book and Tax Income Statement for 1994		
INCOME STATEMENT:	**TAX**	**BOOK**
Revenues	$95	$102
Bad debt expense	5	10
Other expenses	70	60
Taxable (pre-tax) income	$20	$ 32

Taxes due = $20 × 40% = $8.

RECONCILIATION OF BOOK AND TAX AMOUNTS:	
GAAP income	$32
Permanent differences	(7)
Temporary differences	
Bad debt expense	5
Other expenses	(10)
Taxable income	$20

EXHIBIT 20.7
Klein Corporation—
Book and Tax
Income Statement
for 1994

After determining its taxes due and its deferred portion of tax expense, Klein can incorporate these amounts into its analysis of the tax and book balance sheets. The results of these adjustments are presented in Exhibit 20.8. Notice that a complete reconciliation of book and tax balance sheets requires the inclusion of the permanent and temporary differences *and* consideration of the net deferred tax asset or liability, even though only the temporary differences drive the deferred tax balances.

Balance Sheet Classification of Deferred Tax Balances

Under SFAS No. 109, classifying the deferred tax assets/liabilities as either current or noncurrent depends on the classification of the underlying assets or liabilities that give rise to the temporary differences that drive the deferred tax amounts. Klein's temporary differences arise from a current asset (net receivables) and a current liability (accrued expenses). As a result, Klein would classify the total net deferred tax liability of $2 as a current liability. If the assets and liabilities from which the temporary differences arise were both noncurrent, Klein's net liability would be noncurrent.

Special problems arise when some of the temporary differences relate to current assets or liabilities and others relate to noncurrent assets or liabilities. Suppose, for example, that Klein's net receivables were current but the accrued expense was a noncurrent liability. The temporary differences would be grouped by current and noncurrent source assets and liabilities as follows:

EXHIBIT 20.8

Klein Corporation—
Book and Tax
Balance Sheets
Including Tax Effects
for 1994

KLEIN CORPORATION
Book and Tax Balance Sheets Including Tax Effects for 1994

BALANCE SHEETS:	TAX	BOOK
Receivables	$ 75	$ 70
Interest receivable	–	7
Other assets	630	630
Assets	$705	$707
Liabilities and equity (ignoring taxes)		
Accrued expenses	40	30
Taxes payable	8	8
Deferred tax liability	–	2
Other liabilities	190	190
Equity	467	477
	$705	$707

RECONCILIATION OF BOOK AND TAX AMOUNTS
 (incorporating tax effects):

Balance sheet focus:	
Net assets under GAAP	$477
Net deferred tax liability	2
Permanent differences:	
Accrued interest	(7)
Temporary differences:	
Receivables	5
Liabilities	(10)
Net assets under tax	$467

Current receivables	$ 5	×	40%	=	$ 2 asset	
Noncurrent accrued expenses	$(10)	×	40%	=	$(4) liability	

In this case, Klein's *net* deferred tax balance sheet position is still a liability of $2; but for financial reporting purposes, Klein must report a current deferred tax asset of $2 and a noncurrent deferred tax liability of $4 on its balance sheet.

While the linkage between the classification of the asset or liability that gave rise to the temporary difference and the classification of the deferred tax asset or liability is crucial in applying SFAS No. 109, this is not the only way a corporation can determine the classification of deferred tax balances. Another alternative is to forecast the timing of the reversals of existing temporary differences and to classify as current the tax effects of those reversals scheduled to occur in the next fiscal year. The corporation would then classify as noncurrent any tax effects from reversals of temporary differences in years after the next fiscal year.

This was the method SFAS No. 96 required when it was first adopted. However, SFAS No. 106 abandoned it as part of a move away from the use of scheduling as a basis for measurement of the deferred tax amounts and because determining which temporary reversals would arise in any future period is subject to considerable judgment.

The Articulation of Income Statement and Balance Sheet Differences

The difference in the tax and book bases of net assets (which is the same thing as the difference in the tax and book bases of equity) is determined principally by the accumulated differences between tax and book income over all prior periods. During Klein's first year of operations, 1994, difference between book and tax income was $12 (book income > taxable income). At year-end, the net difference in the book and tax basis of equity (ignoring taxes) was also $12 (book equity > tax equity). This is a direct function of the fundamental accounting identity.

We can further break down these total differences by specific asset or liability. For example, the differences in revenues can be traced to the difference in the interest receivable; the differences in bad debt expense, to the differences in receivables; and the difference in other expenses, to the accrued expense liability. Consequently, the corporation can trace the level of temporary differences by taking the beginning differences in the book and tax bases of assets and liabilities and adjusting for any differences reflected in the current period comparison of book and tax income.

The articulation (interrelationship) between the balance sheet reconciliation of book and tax differences in asset and liability values and the income statement reconciliation of book and tax income is a useful tool to ensure that the corporation properly includes every temporary difference in determining its deferred tax asset and liability balances.

The Klein Corporation Example Continued

Exhibit 20.9 provides Klein Corporation's results of operations and its balance sheet for 1995, before consideration of the income tax effects arising for 1995. Klein reported taxable income for 1995 as $30. Given the constant tax rate of 40%, the taxes due for 1995 will be $12. This also represents Klein's current portion of tax expense for the year.

The reconciliation of the taxable and book income for 1995 provides all the information necessary to update the temporary differences on which the deferred tax assets or liabilities at the end of 1995 will depend. In turn, the change in the net deferred tax asset or liability during 1995 will determine the deferred portion of income tax expense.

Klein had additional temporary differences relating to bad debt expense in 1995. This implies that the write-offs were less than the provision for bad debts for 1995, just as they were in 1994. In addition, Klein accrued more interest on its tax-free investment, which is a permanent difference; and the difference in the accrued expenses reversed itself during 1995 (book expense was

EXHIBIT 20.9

Klein Corporation—
Book and Tax
Income Statement,
Balance Sheets, and
Reconciliation
Excluding Tax
Accruals for 1995

KLEIN CORPORATION
Book and Tax Income Statements, Balance Sheets, and Reconciliation
Excluding Tax Accruals for 1995
December 31, 1995

INCOME STATEMENT:	TAX	BOOK
Revenues	$122	$133
Bad debt expense	7	12
Other expenses	85	75
Taxable (pre-tax) income	30	46
Taxes due = $30 × 40% = $12		

BALANCE SHEETS:		
Receivables	$ 95	$ 85
Interest receivable	–	18
Other assets	700	720
Assets	$795	$823
Liabilities and equity		
Accrued expenses	50	50
Deferred taxes	–	2
Other liabilities	248	248
Equity	497	523
	$795	$823

RECONCILIATION OF BOOK AND TAX AMOUNTS:	
Income statement focus:	
GAAP income	$ 46
Permanent differences	(11)
Temporary differences	
Bad debt expense	5
Depreciation expense	(20)
Other expenses	10
Taxable income	$ 30
Balance sheet focus:	
Net assets under GAAP	$523
Net deferred tax liability—beginning balance	2
Permanent differences	
Accrued interest	(18)
Temporary differences	
Receivables	10
Other assets	(20)
Net assets under tax	$497

higher than tax expense). Since Klein has elected to depreciate newly acquired assets more rapidly for tax purposes than for book purposes, a new temporary difference has also arisen. This gives rise to a temporary difference at the end of 1995 of $20 on other assets.

By using the reconciliation of the tax and book value of equity as of the end of 1994 and the reconciliation of book and tax income in 1995, Klein can compute the deferred tax balances. This reconciliation would be accomplished as follows:

Temporary Differences	As of December 31, 1994	Activity During 1995	As of December 31, 1995
Receivables	$ 5	$ 5	$ 10
Accrued expenses	(10)	10	0
Other assets	0	(20)	(20)
	$ (5)	$ (5)	$(10)

Once Klein has identified the temporary differences as of the end of the current fiscal year, it must determine:

1. The net deferred tax asset or liability at the end of 1995 to determine the deferred tax portion of tax expense
2. The breakdown of the net deferred tax asset or liability into its current and noncurrent components, if necessary

The net deferred tax asset or liability will be determined by the net temporary differences of $(10). This net temporary difference implies that the ending net deferred tax balance sheet amount will be a liability. Using the 40% tax rate, Klein's liability is estimated to be $4.

Given that the net deferred tax liability at the end of 1994 was $2, Klein must increase its net deferred tax liability by an additional $2 in 1995 to achieve the desired ending balance of $4. Klein's journal entry to record the tax accrual for 1995 would appear as follows:

```
December 31, 1995:
Current portion of tax expense              12
Deferred portion of tax expense              2
   Taxes payable                                      12
   Deferred tax liability                               2
To accrue the tax expense for 1995.
```

For purposes of balance sheet classification, Klein must divide its net deferred tax liability of $4 into current and noncurrent components. This would be accomplished as follows:

Current receivables	$ 10	×	40%	=	$ 4 asset
Noncurrent other assets	$(20)	×	40%	=	$(8) liability
Net	$(10)	×	40%	=	$(4) liability

Klein's formal income statement and balance sheet in 1995 are presented in Exhibit 20.10. The reconciliation of the book and tax balance of equity at the end of 1995, including tax effects, would appear as follows:

EXHIBIT 20.10

Klein Corporation—
Income Statement
for Fiscal Years
Ended December
31, 1995 and 1994
and Balance Sheets
as of December 31,
1995 and 1994

KLEIN CORPORATION
Income Statement
For Fiscal Years Ended December 31, 1995 and 1994

	1995		1994	
Revenues		$133		$102
Expenses				
Bad debts		12		10
Other		75		60
Income before taxes		46		32
Tax expense				
Current portion	$12		$ 8	
Deferred portion	2	14	2	10
Net income		$ 32		$ 22

KLEIN CORPORATION
Balance Sheet
December 31, 1995 and 1994

	1995	1994
Assets		
Current		
Receivables	$ 85	$ 70
Deferred taxes	4	–
Accrued interest receivable	18	7
	107	77
Noncurrent		
Other	720	630
Total assets	$827	$707
Liabilities and equity		
Current		
Accrued expenses	$ 50	$ 30
Taxes payable	20	8
Noncurrent		
Other	240	190
Deferred taxes	8	2
Equity		
Common stock—no par	455	455
Retained earnings	54	22
Total liabilities and equity	$827	$707

Balance sheet focus:

Net assets under GAAP	$(509)	(reported in balance sheet)
Net deferred tax liability— ending balance	4	(reported in balance sheet)
Permanent differences:		
Accrued interest	(18)	[$(7) in 1994 + $(11) in 1995]
Temporary differences:		
Receivables	10	($5 in 1994 + $5 in 1995)
Other assets	(20)	[$(20) in 1995]
Net assets under tax	$485	($497 in Exhibit 20.9 − $12 of taxes payable in 1995)

While full reconciliation of book and tax equity values is always possible, this is not necessary for purposes of accounting for deferred taxes. All that is required is a running (cumulative) total of book-to-taxable income adjustments in each period that give rise to the temporary differences in the book and tax bases for the underlying assets and liabilities. Given the beginning balance of the temporary differences, by asset or liability, and the current period changes to the total temporary differences that are revealed by reconciling taxable and pre-tax book income, the ending temporary differences will be revealed. The corporation then uses these ending differences, along with future tax rates, to determine its net deferred tax asset or liability at the end of the period. Once the corporation determines its ending net deferred tax asset or liability, the deferred tax portion of tax expense represents the change in its net deferred tax asset or liability for the period.

In working through the Klein Corporation example, simplified assumptions regarding the Tax Code made it possible to see how the asset/liability approach to deferred tax valuation works at a conceptual level. In particular, our assumption of a constant Tax Code with constant rates applied to all components of income is unrealistic. Tax codes often apply different tax rates to different events. For example, the U.S. Tax Code has at times treated capital gains from the sale of assets differently than gains that were part of ordinary income. These types of differences complicate the assignment of tax rates to temporary differences if the event that triggers the reversal of the temporary difference also triggers different tax rates.

Whenever the tax effects of reversing temporary differences are sensitive to the timing of those reversals, the corporation must incorporate an analysis of the timing of those reversals into its determination of deferred tax amounts. This process is generally referred to as **scheduling** of the reversals for existing temporary differences. Under SFAS No. 109, scheduling is only required if:

1. The tax rates applied to or tax treatment of existing temporary differences are scheduled to change based on the existing Tax Code
2. The company will probably not pay taxes at the maximum marginal tax rate
3. The expiration of certain tax credits or net operating loss carryforwards present problems with realization of these tax benefits (This item will be discussed more fully in the next section.)

Net Operating Losses and the Carryback/Carryforward Provisions

The Tax Code defines the concept of an operating loss for tax purposes by setting forth criteria for what types of revenue, expense, gain, and/or loss must be included in its computation. When the sum of these items results in a loss for the period, the company has no tax liability for the period.[8] However, the company does not automatically receive a tax refund.

The Tax Code allows the corporation to use the operating loss to offset taxable income for the three years prior to the year in which it recognized the loss for tax purposes to obtain a refund of taxes paid on the income of those prior periods. This provision is referred to as the **operating loss carryback** (or just *carryback*) provision in the Tax Code. If a company elects to use the carryback provision, it must carry back any operating loss to the third year prior to the year of the loss and then apply it by moving forward in time.

Suppose a company reported taxable income of $20,000, $25,000, and $40,000 in Years 1, 2, and 3, respectively. The company had a 30% tax rate in Years 1 and 2 and a 40% rate in Year 3. In Year 4, the company records an operating loss for tax purposes of $55,000. To determine the refund it will receive from any carryback, the company must first apply the $55,000 loss to reduce taxable income in Year 1 (the year three years prior to the year of the loss). Since income in this year was only $20,000, the loss offsets all of the taxable income originally reported in Year 1. The application continues for Years 2 and 3 until the loss has been completely offset as shown in Exhibit 20.11.

As a result of the carryback process, the company's tax refund will recoup all of the taxes in Years 1 and 2 and taxes on the difference between $30,000 and $40,000 of taxable income in Year 3. The total amount of the refund would be $17,500.[9] If the company did not have three previous years of activity, it would first apply the carryback to the earliest tax year.

If the operating loss had exceeded the company's total taxable income over the preceding three years, the company can carry the remaining loss *forward* and use it to reduce taxable income in future periods. This is referred to as an **operating loss carryforward**. At present, losses can be carried forward for a maximum of 15 years. If they do not provide a tax benefit by sheltering otherwise taxable income in that time period, they expire unused. Corporations can choose not to apply any carryback of losses and can elect only to carryforward losses, but they rarely use this option.

Recognition of the Benefits of Net Operating Losses in Financial Statements

When a corporation incurs a net operating loss for tax purposes, the tax benefits may arise in one of two ways:

---

[8] When a net operating loss exists under the regular U.S. Tax Code, the corporation may still have to pay taxes under the alternative tax system discussed later in the chapter.

[9] The company would obviously have preferred to apply the loss first to the Year 3 taxable income. This would have resulted in a larger refund due to the higher tax rate in this year. However, the Tax Code requires the company to carry the loss back three years and then roll it forward to the extent not fully utilized.

Example of the Application of the Tax Loss Carryback Provision

	YEAR			
	1	2	3	4
Taxable income	$ 20,000	$ 25,000	$ 40,000	
Tax loss	–	–	–	$(55,000)
Loss carryback	(55,000) ←			
Adjusted taxable income	$(35,000)			
Carryback rollforward	35,000 →	(35,000)		
Adjusted taxable income	$ 0	$(10,000)		
Carryback rollforward		10,000 →	(10,000)	
Adjusted taxable income		$ 0	$ 30,000	
Computation of tax refund:				
Reduction in taxable				
Income from loss	$ 20,000	$ 25,000	$ 10,000	
Carryback				
Tax rate	x 30%	x 30%	x 40%	
Refund of taxes paid	$ 6,000	$ 7,500	$ 4,000	

Total refund from carryback = $6,000 + $7,500 + $4,000 = $17,500

EXHIBIT 20.11

Example of the Application of the Tax Loss Carryback Provision

1. The corporation may obtain a refund of previous taxes if it elects to apply the carryback provisions of the Tax Code
2. The corporation's future taxable income will be sheltered from tax because of the offset from a net operating loss carryforward

The corporation immediately recognizes any refund generated by a carryback as a tax refund receivable in its balance sheet and as a related tax benefit in the current portion of income tax expense as reported in its income statement. The recognition of benefits from any net operating loss carryforward depends on the existence of other temporary differences and an assessment of the probability that the loss carryforward benefit will be realized.

NOL Carryforwards When No Other Temporary Differences Exist   When a net operating loss generates a carryforward, the carryforward creates a probable future benefit *if* the corporation is likely to use the carryforward to save taxes in future periods. To examine how this future benefit is reflected in the financial statements, if at all, consider first the situation in which no other temporary differences exist. In this setting, taxable income is equivalent to book income less permanent differences and no deferred tax amounts exist, exclusive of any recorded carryforward benefit. Under these conditions, the corporation may record a deferred tax asset equal in value to the realizable tax benefits arising from the expected application of the carryforward to future taxable income. The measurement of the deferred tax asset will depend on estimates of the future tax savings that will be generated from the application of the carryforward.

For example, assume Diecast Corporation has no temporary differences and has reported income for both financial reporting and tax purposes totalling $140,000 over the immediately preceding three-year period, 1990-1992. Diecast has a constant 20% tax rate. Consequently, the taxes it paid over this three-year period amounted to $28,000. In 1993, the company reports a net operating loss for tax purposes of $300,000. The loss was the result of a strike during the year, which resulted in lost sales. Such an event is not likely to recur in the foreseeable future. Consequently, Diecast believes that any operating loss carryforward will be fully realized in future periods. These benefits are expected to accrue at the 20% tax rate the company has experienced in the past.

In 1993, Diecast elects to carry back the operating loss to recoup previously paid taxes. As a result, it can obtain a $28,000 refund by applying $140,000 of the loss to the income reported during 1990–1992. This leaves a tax loss carryforward of $160,000 to be used in the future. The deferred tax benefit arising from this loss carryforward will be $32,000, ($160,000 × 20%). Since Diecast has no other temporary differences, the tax expense for 1993 will reflect only the refund and future deferred tax benefit of the operating loss. In 1993, Diecast would prepare the following journal entry to record the tax effects of the period:

December 31, 1993:		
Tax refund receivable	28,000	
Deferred tax asset	32,000	
Tax expense (benefit)—current portion		28,000
Tax expense (benefit)—deferred portion		32,000

To record the recognized benefit of the realized operating loss
reported for tax purposes in 1993.

The corporation must classify the deferred tax asset created by the NOL carryforward as either current or noncurrent in its balance sheet, yet this does not relate to a temporary difference in the company's particular asset or liability. When it cannot associate a temporary difference such as the carryforward benefit with a particular asset or liability, the company classifies it as current or noncurrent based on the expected timing of the reversal. If evidence suggests that this carryforward will be fully or partially utilized in 1994, then the company can classify all or a portion of the deferred tax asset as a current asset. If it expects none of the carryforward benefit to be realized in 1994, the company will classify the entire balance as noncurrent.

Considerable controversy has arisen over the recognition of deferred tax assets, particularly those associated with NOL carryforwards. Because recognition of NOL carryforward benefits as a deferred tax asset requires the forecasting of earnings in future periods, some accountants believe it is inherently beyond the scope of the historical cost accounting system. Therefore, these benefits should not be recognized until they are actually used. Others would recognize these benefits prior to their actual use only in exceptional circumstances where the realization was assured beyond a reasonable doubt. Still others would relax the criteria for recognition even further, allowing recognition so long as there was reasonable likelihood that the benefits would be realized in future periods.

Practitioners' viewpoints vary greatly on the relationship between the level of uncertainty surrounding the eventual realization of any NOL carryforward benefits and the recognition of a deferred tax asset. SFAS No. 109 has taken the approach that the expected future tax benefits of an NOL should be recognized in full. However, in cases where sufficient evidence suggests that the full benefit may not be realized, an allowance shall be established to reflect the effects of this uncertainty.

NOL Carryforwards and Their Effect on Subsequent Years   Assume that in 1994 Diecast reports income of $270,000 for both financial reporting and tax purposes. At this time, the company will use the remaining NOL carryforward for tax purposes to reduce taxable income in 1994 from $270,000 to $110,000. At a 20% tax rate, the currently payable taxes in 1994 would be $22,000. In addition, Diecast will have used up all of the deferred tax asset, which represented the benefits of the carryforward prior to its actual application. To reflect these effects, Diecast would make the following journal entry at the end of 1994:

December 31, 1994:

Tax expense—current portion	22,000	
Tax expense—deferred portion	32,000	
Taxes payable		22,000
Deferred tax asset		32,000

To record the recognized benefit of the realized operating loss
reported for tax purposes in 1994.

In accounting for the NOL carryforward benefit, Diecast matches the tax benefit of the loss against income for the year it incurs the loss but does not reduce the total tax expense in the year it applies the loss on its tax return. This system works well as long as the estimates of future tax benefits to be realized are reliable. If the company's ability to ultimately utilize the carryforward benefit is questionable, a naive application of the above process allows the corporation to "front-end load" the benefit of an NOL that may never actually be realized. This is why the company must take additional steps should the realization of the NOL carryforward benefits be unassured.

If Diecast had not recognized any portion of the deferred tax benefit from the NOL carryforward in 1994, tax expense in 1994 would be zero and tax expense in 1995 would be $22,000. It would report no deferred tax items since there are no other temporary differences. In this example, nonrecognition of the NOL carryforward benefit is essentially an application of the flowthrough method of accounting for deferred taxes.

NOL Carryforwards and Other Temporary Differences—An Integration
In most cases, reporting an NOL for tax purposes occurs at the same time that other temporary differences exist. If tax rates are expected to be constant in the future, the integration of the effects of ordinary temporary differences and the effects of the operating loss carryforward requires that the company first apply the tax loss carryforward to reduce any existing deferred tax liability to zero before it can recognize any deferred tax asset.

Integrating NOLs With Other Temporary Differences in the Loss Year

During 1994, Sedon reported income before taxes for financial reporting purposes of $100,000. It had temporary differences relating to accelerated depreciation on new assets purchased during 1994 that resulted in an NOL for tax purposes of $250,000. Assume that at the end of 1993, Sedon had no deferred tax assets or liabilities on its books. Sedon had reported income for both book and tax purposes of $220,000 over the previous three years.

The difference between book and tax income for 1994 is explained by the existence of the depreciation difference of $350,000. This difference is the only source of temporary differences in the tax and book bases of assets and liabilities at the end of 1994. Sedon pays taxes at a constant rate of 35% and elects to carry back the NOL for tax purposes. Exhibit 20.12 displays the reconciliation of Sedon's book and tax income for 1994 in Panel A, along with a reconciliation of the temporary differences at the beginning and end of the year in Panel B.

Panel C indicates that only $220,000 of the operating loss in 1994 can be applied to the previous years' taxable income to generate a tax refund, and the amount of the refund will be $77,000. This represents the current portion of tax expense (benefit) for 1994. In turn, this leaves an NOL carryforward for tax purposes of $30,000 ($250,000 – $220,000).

EXHIBIT 20.12

Sedon Corporation—Integration of NOL Carryforward Benefits With Other Temporary Differences—Fiscal Year 1994

SEDON CORPORATION
Integration of NOL Carryforward Benefits With Other Temporary Differences
Fiscal Year 1994

Panel A: Reconciliation of Book and Tax Income for 1994

Pre-tax book income	$ 100,000
Depreciation differences	(350,000)
Taxable income (loss)	$(250,000)

Panel B: Reconciliation of Ending Temporary Differences

Temporary differences on plant and equipment at January 1, 1994:	$ 0
Temporary differences due to differences in depreciation for 1994:	350,000
Temporary difference on plant and equipment at December 31, 1994:	$ 350,000

Panel C: Determination of Carryback Benefit

Taxable income 1991–1993	$ 220,000
Carryback (taxable income from from Panel A)	(250,000)
Unused carryforward	$ (30,000)
Tax refund = current portion of tax expense = $220,000 × 35% =	$ 77,000

Panel D: Determination of Net Deferred Tax Asset/Liability at December 31, 1994

	Temporary Difference	Tax Rate	Deferred Tax Amount
Plant and equipment, December 31, 1994	$350,000	35%	$ 122,500
NOL carryforward	(30,000)	35%	(10,500)
Total	$320,000	35%	$ 112,000
Deferred tax expense = $112,000 – 0 = $112,000			

When other temporary differences exist, a company must first apply an NOL carryforward for tax purposes to reduce any deferred tax liability that arises from other temporary differences. In Sedon's case, this implies that it must apply the net operating loss carryforward to reduce any temporary differences arising from the use of different depreciation methods for book and tax. Panel D demonstrates how Sedon uses the NOL carryforward to reduce the deferred tax effects of the temporary differences arising from depreciation. The result is that the deferred tax liability at the end of 1994 will be $112,000.

If Sedon had no operating loss in the current period, it would have reported a net deferred tax liability of $122,500, based on net temporary differences of $350,000 on plant and equipment as of December 31, 1994. The benefit of the loss in 1994 is reflected in two ways:

1. A current portion of tax expense, which reflects the benefit of the refund from the carryback
2. A reduced deferred tax portion of tax expense from the benefit of reducing the net temporary differences by the carryforward amount

Sedon's journal entry to capture these effects would appear as:

December 31, 1994:		
Tax refund receivable	77,000	
Tax expense—deferred portion	112,000	
Tax expense (benefit)—current portion		77,000
Deferred tax liability		112,000
To accrue the tax expense for 1994.		

Sedon would classify all of the deferred tax liability in the above entry as noncurrent since the underlying asset that gives rise to the net liability is noncurrent and the carryforward benefit reduces this cost. Sedon would not record the carryforward benefit as a separate asset unless all of the deferred tax liability has been eliminated. Note also that the total tax expense for 1994 is $35,000.

Integrating NOL Carryforwards and Other Temporary Differences in Subsequent Years   Assume that in 1995 Sedon reports income before taxes of $150,000 for financial reporting purposes. Sedon's temporary differences increase to $450,000 relating to plant and equipment due to an additional book-to-tax income difference of $100,000 in 1995. Given this book-to-tax difference in income, taxable income for 1995 would be $50,000. These facts are summarized in Panels A and B of Exhibit 20.13.

Panel C demonstrates how Sedon applies the NOL carryforward of $30,000 to reduce the taxes due in 1995. The result is a tax payable of only $7,000. Note that the taxes payable for 1995 would have been $17,500 if no NOL carryforward existed. Panel D presents the computation of the ending net deferred tax liability, which is now based solely on the existing temporary difference related to depreciation since the NOL has been completely used up. The ending deferred tax liability must be $157,500. To achieve the desired ending balance in the deferred tax liability in the financial statements, an increase of $45,500 is required. This represents the deferred portion of tax expense for 1995. Sedon's journal entry to record these events is as follows:

EXHIBIT 20.13

Sedon Corporation—
Integration of NOL
Carryforward
Benefits With Other
Temporary
Differences—Fiscal
Year 1995

SEDON CORPORATION
Integration of NOL Carryforward Benefits With Other Temporary Differences
Fiscal Year 1995

Panel A: Reconciliation of Book and Tax Income for 1995

Pre-tax book income	$ 150,000
Depreciation differences	(100,000)
Taxable income	$ (50,000)

Panel B: Reconciliation of Ending Temporary Differences

Temporary differences on plant and equipment at January 1, 1995:	$ 350,000
Temporary differences due to differences in depreciation for 1995:	100,000
Temporary difference on plant and equipment at December 31, 1995:	$ 450,000

Panel C: Determination of Carryforward Benefit

Taxable income for 1995, pre-carryforward	$ 50,000
Carryforward	(30,000)
Taxable income for 1995, after carryforward	$ 20,000
Tax payable = current portion of tax expense = $20,000 × 35% =	$ 7,000

Panel D: Determination of Net Deferred Tax Asset/Liability at December 31, 1995

	Temporary Difference	Tax Rate	Deferred Tax Amount
Plant and equipment, December 31, 1995	$450,000	35%	$ 157,500
Deferred tax expense = $157,500 – $112,000 = $45,500			$ 45,500

December 31, 1995:

Tax expense—current portion	7,000	
Tax expense—deferred portion	45,500	
Taxes payable		7,000
Deferred tax liability		45,500
To accrue tax expense for 1995.		

Sedon will again classify the total deferred tax liability as a noncurrent liability since the plant and equipment to which it relates is a noncurrent asset. Note that Sedon's total income tax expense is $52,500.

Tax Credits and Tax Credit Carryforwards

At various times, Congress has created special tax credits as incentives for corporations to undertake certain activities. One of the most popular tax credits over the past three decades has been the investment tax credit. Other credits include credits for income taxes paid to foreign governments and credits that arise from research and development efforts. All these credits have certain common characteristics. A **tax credit** is a dollar amount that a company can use to directly reduce the taxes payable for a period. Unlike a tax deduction, which reduces the amount of taxable income, tax credits directly reduce taxes due.

In many cases, corporations immediately use tax credits in the year they arise to reduce current taxes payable. However, there are limits on how much of these credits can be used in any period. If the entire credit is not used, the corporation may carry it forward or backward, depending on the specific rules of the current Tax Code. If carried backward, the tax credit generates a refund that reduces the current portion of tax expense in the year the credit arises. If the credit is carried forward, the corporation first applies it to reduce any existing deferred tax liabilities and may record any excess as a deferred tax asset if realization is reasonably assured. If realization is not reasonably assured, then the corporation applies the same procedures described below for evaluating the carrying value of a deferred tax asset.

The Alternative Minimum Tax System

Throughout the preceding discussions, we have occasionally noted that the U.S. Tax Code is actually composed of two parallel tax systems: the ordinary tax system and an alternative minimum tax system. The alternative minimum tax system attempts to achieve greater equity in the payment of taxes across taxpayers. Some corporations end up reporting zero taxable income (or a tax loss) in periods when book income is very high due to the variety of tax advantages for these companies. Accelerated depreciation, specialized tax credits, special depletion allowances in the extractive industries, and a host of other tax benefits in the regular tax system create these advantages.

Congress placed these tax benefits into the Code to provide tax incentives for certain activity by corporations that were already bearing their fair share of taxes. They were not designed to provide "tax loopholes" for profitable firms to avoid taxes completely. In an effort to ensure that profitable firms did not escape taxation completely, Congress enacted the alternative system. Basically, the alternative system requires a separate computation of taxable income and determination of tax. If the tax due under the regular system is higher than that due under the alternative system, the tax is paid under the regular system. If the alternative system tax is larger, tax is paid under this system. Any difference between the taxes paid under the alternative system and the taxes that would have been paid under the regular system represents a tax credit that a corporation can carry forward or backward.

Under SFAS No. 109, if a company is required to pay taxes under the alternative system, the current portion of tax expense is the amount due. Deferred tax amounts are based on the temporary differences that arise under the regular system, regardless of how the current period taxes are determined. However, a company that generates an alternative tax credit carryforward may apply it to reduce existing deferred tax liabilities or to recognize a deferred tax asset if realization of the credit is probable. As a result of this approach, the only consequence the alternative tax system has on reporting for income taxes is when it is actually used to determine taxes due. When the alternative system is used, a company applies any carryforward credit created in the same fashion as any other credit.

Deferred Tax Assets—A More Detailed Examination

Throughout the discussion above, three different settings that give rise to a deferred tax asset have been considered:

1. Ordinary temporary differences
2. Recognition of temporary differences arising from NOL carryforward benefits
3. Recognition of temporary differences arising from tax credit carryforwards

Whenever deferred tax assets arise due to any of these temporary differences, the company must determine the likelihood that the recognized benefits will be fully realized in future periods. √

If it is "more likely than not" that some portion of the deferred tax benefit will not be realized, a valuation allowance is required.[10] Clearly this analysis is subjective. The purpose of this requirement is to avoid recognition of an asset in situations where reasonable professional judgment would suggest that the full benefit of the carryforward is not likely to occur, given the company's prospect of creating sufficient future taxable income to utilize the benefit.

While judgment of the context in which the deferred tax asset arises is essential, SFAS No. 109 provides some guidance to factors that might influence the need for an allowance. Such an allowance is not required if:

1. The reversals of existing temporary differences are sufficient to absorb the effects of any deductible temporary differences or carryforwards over their remaining life, or
2. Future taxable income sufficient to absorb the net deductible amount is likely.

Situation 1 arises whenever a net deferred tax liability exists. Recall that a net deferred tax liability is the total deferred tax amount arising from both current and noncurrent deferred tax assets or liabilities. A net liability implies that any current or noncurrent deferred tax asset is smaller than its noncurrent or current deferred tax liability counterpart, respectively. A net deferred tax liability can only arise if the net temporary differences (including the carryforward benefits) will give rise to net taxable amounts in future periods.

In general, the only time a corporation needs to consider an allowance is when it has recorded a net deferred tax asset. In these cases, the future reversing temporary differences are not sufficient to absorb the deductible amounts that give rise to the net deferred tax asset. If the corporation expects its future taxable income will provide a basis for realization, no allowance will be required even when it records a net deferred tax asset.

What evidence might support the need for an allowance? SFAS No. 109 sets forth partial guidance on what it refers to as "tangible, negative evidence" that will usually support the accrual of an allowance.[11] These conditions include:

---

[10] "Accounting for Income Taxes," *Statement of Financial Accounting Standards No. 109* (Stamford, CT: FASB, 1992), para. 17(e).

[11] *Ibid.*, para. 23.

1. A history of unused NOL carryforwards expiring,
2. The presence of expected continuing losses in the immediate future years,
3. Unsettled circumstances (such as outstanding lawsuits) that, if unfavorably resolved, would adversely affect realization, or
4. A carryforward period so short as to limit realization under current conditions.

These conditions are examples of what the FASB believed were important contextual considerations to support a need for an allowance. They are not meant to be all-inclusive or deterministic.

Even when tangible, negative evidence is present, it is still possible to conclude that no allowance is required. If contravening positive evidence outweighs the negative evidence present in the above list, the corporation can overturn the negative evidence and avoid recognition of an allowance. The following types of positive evidence support realization:

1. The existing sales backlog will produce sufficient income to ensure realization of the entire deferred tax asset,
2. The entity's assets have appreciated values above their tax basis sufficient to realize the deferred tax benefit if these assets were liquidated, or
3. The entity has a strong earnings history, and the loss appears to be an aberration rather than a continuing condition.

In the final analysis, the corporation must use professional judgment in assessing the likelihood that it will use the NOL carryforward benefits.

If an allowance is deemed necessary, the corporation creates it by charging the deferred portion of tax expense and crediting the allowance for estimated unrealized tax benefits. For example, if we use the information in the Diecast example on NOLs discussed earlier, Diecast recorded the following entry on its books to record the benefits of an NOL carryforward in the year it arose (Diecast had no other temporary differences):

December 31, 1993:		
Tax refund receivable	28,000	
Deferred tax asset	32,000	
Tax expense (benefit)—current portion		28,000
Tax expense (benefit)—deferred portion		32,000
To record the recognized benefit of the realized operating loss		
reported for tax purposes in 1993.		

Had there been evidence to support the position that some or all of this carryforward benefit was more likely than not to go unrealized, Diecast would have been required to establish an allowance account. Assume that due to future income projections, $10,000 of the carryforward benefit was more likely than not to go unrealized. Diecast would have made the following entry in place of the one above:

December 31, 1993:		
Tax refund receivable	28,000	
Deferred tax asset	32,000	
Tax expense (benefit)—current portion		28,000
Tax expense (benefit)—deferred portion		22,000
Allowance for unrealized tax benefits		10,000
To record the recognized benefit of the realized operating loss		
reported for tax purposes in 1993.		

The above entry reduces the extent of the realized benefit by $10,000 and establishes this as the balance in the valuation allowance, which Diecast reports in its balance sheet as an offset to the deferred tax asset. As time passes, the allowance may rise or fall, depending on whatever new information becomes available about the likely realization of any remaining benefit. Any changes in the allowance are directly reflected in the deferred tax portion of income tax expense.

The Scheduling Exercise

In all of the examples discussed thus far, the timing of the reversals of existing temporary differences has been unimportant. This is due to the assumptions that maximum marginal tax rates will remain constant and that any NOL carryforwards will not expire before all current temporary differences reverse. If either of these assumptions are not applicable, the company will find the timing of future reversals to be of material importance in determining deferred tax items in its income statement and balance sheet.

For example, assume that Pinder Corporation has net temporary differences of $100,000 at the end of 1994. The currently enacted Tax Code sets the maximum marginal tax rates for 1994 at 20%, but they will rise to 30% after 1996. What tax rates should Pinder apply to the net temporary differences to determine its net deferred tax liability at the end of 1994? The answer depends on when Pinder expects the tax cash flows arising from the reversal of the $100,000 net temporary difference to occur. If Pinder anticipates the flows to occur in 1995 or 1996, then it would apply the current tax rate of 20%. If it does not expect the flows to occur until after 1996, then Pinder would apply the currently enacted rate for the post-1996 period of 30%. If $30,000 reverse in 1995 and 1996, with the remainder after 1996, Pinder would apply a weighted average rate of 27%, (20% $\times$ .3 + 30% $\times$ .7]. To achieve the ultimate answer to the question, Pinder should prepare a schedule that sets forth the timing of the reversal of currently existing temporary differences.

Scheduling may also be required when assessing the need for an allowance relating to a deferred tax asset. If a deferred tax asset relating to an NOL carryforward has been created, a corporation must determine the likelihood that it will be fully utilized before the end of the carryforward period. In turn, this requires an assessment of the timing of expected future income and the timing of the reversals of other temporary differences that the NOL carryforward might offset. Only income expected to arise, or reversals of other temporary differences during the carryforward period, can provide support for the likely realization of the carryforward benefits.

The process of scheduling the reversing of temporary differences requires the corporation to assess what events will occur in the future to trigger reversal and when these events will occur. For example, assume that Kelgain Corporation has existing temporary differences relating to three areas: plant and equipment, accrued compensation cost, and accrued other expenses at the end of 1994. The amounts were as follows:

Temporary Differences:	
Plant and equipment	$ 500,000
Accrued compensation	(400,000)
Other expenses	200,000
Net temporary differences	$ 300,000

Suppose an examination of these differences, combined with an assessment of how they will reverse and how the Tax Code will treat these reversals, yielded the schedule in Panel A of Exhibit 20.14. In preparing this schedule, the following expectations are built-in:

1. Plant and equipment assets will be depreciated for one year; then, they will be sold, triggering the entire temporary difference remaining at sale.
2. Compensation differences will only reverse after a key executive retires, which is expected to occur in five years.
3. Other expenses will reverse in the next year.

The projections indicate that most of the reversals will arise in 1995 and 1996, with the exception of the compensation temporary difference, which reverses in 1999.

The schedule implies that taxable income in 1995 and 1996 will be above book income, assuming Kelgain creates no new temporary differences in these years. The net reversals in 1995 and 1996 are commonly referred to as net taxable amounts. It also implies that taxable income will be below book income in 1996, because the compensation temporary difference arose from treating the cost as an expense for book purposes in periods prior to the end of 1994. However, the costs will not be allowed as a tax deduction until 1999. The reversal in 1999 is commonly referred to as a net deductible amount.

Armed with this schedule of reversals, Kelgain can assess the effects of changing tax rates or other horizon issues such as NOL expiration dates on the deferred tax assets and liabilities. Undertaking such an analysis requires integration of this schedule with other data.

For example, if the tax rates in 1995 and 1996 will be 40%, but are currently scheduled to decline to 20% in all years after 1996, how will Kelgain apply the tax rates to this schedule? One approach would be to assume that future taxable income will always be positive and of sufficient size to absorb the net deductible amount in 1999. Then, Kelgain can apply tax rates of 40% to the scheduled reversals in 1995 and 1996 and a rate of 20% to the reversal in 1999, yielding a total deferred tax liability of $200,000 [($300,000 + $400,000) × 40% − $400,000 × 20%].

EXHIBIT 20.14

Kelgain
Corporation—
Scheduling of the
Timing for the
Reversal of Current
Temporary
Differences

KELGAIN CORPORATION
Scheduling of the Timing for the Reversal of Current Temporary Differences

Panel A: Timing of Reversals	1995	1996	1997	1998	1999	Total
Plant and equipment	$100,000	$400,000	–	–	–	$500,000
Compensation	–	–	–	–	$(400,000)	(400,000)
Other expenses	200,000	–	–	–	–	200,000
Subtotal	$300,000	$400,000	–	–	$(400,000)	$300,000

Panel B: Application of NOL Carryback Under a No Book Income Assumption						
Subtotal	$300,000	$400,000	–	–	$(400,000)	$300,000
Carryback	–	(400,000)			400,000	–
Adjusted balance	$300,000	$ 0	–	–	$ 0	$300,000
Tax rate	× 40%					
Deferred tax	$120,000					

An alternative approach might be to assume that Kelgain will have no book income in any future period. Then, the $400,000 net deductible amount in 1999 will give rise to a net operating loss for tax purposes of $(400,000). Kelgain could then carry back this loss three years and use it to offset the net taxable amount scheduled to arise in 1996. Ultimately, this sequence of events would result in a total deferred tax liability of only $120,000 [(300,000 + 400,000 – 400,000) × 40%]. This process is mapped out in Panel B of Exhibit 20.14.

Which of these two approaches, or a myriad of others, should Kelgain use? There is no "right" answer to this question: The practitioner must use judgment to decide which of the alternative scenarios appears more likely. If Kelgain has consistently had sufficient taxable income to satisfy the first set of assumptions and if the firm expects no changes in its operating environment that would lead to reduced future taxable income, then the first approach would be more appropriate. If Kelgain is just breaking even in terms of taxable income and does not expect this to change in the next few years, the later set of assumptions would provide more reliable estimates.

In situations like these, management may try to convince the auditor that the second scenario is more reasonable. Tax expense would be lower and net income would be higher in the current period. Management may be trying to manipulate earnings, and the accountant should compare this position with management's position in other areas, such as its internal budgets for the coming periods, for consistency.

In the final analysis, scheduling the reversal of currently existing temporary differences can be an important tool for assessing the appropriate valuation of deferred tax assets and liabilities. Performing the scheduling task requires a working knowledge of the Tax Code and of management's plans for the future, which affect the timing of the realization of the tax effects related to reversing temporary differences.

Effects of Changes in Tax Laws

From time to time, tax laws will change, and both tax rates and tax treatments afforded different transactions are altered. When these changes affect the timing of the temporary differences or the tax benefit/liability they represent, the corporation must compute the effect of these changes and disclose it as a separate portion of the current period's tax expense. The effect of a change in the Tax Code will be computed as of the date the new tax rules go into effect, regardless of whether this occurs at the beginning of an accounting period or at some interim point in time.

Exhibit 20.15 is an excerpt from the Allegheny Ludlum Annual Report to Shareholders in 1991, which disclosed the effect of a change in state tax laws and how this was handled. Note that Allegheny made the adjustment to the deferred tax liability as of August 4, 1991 and this resulted in a significant increase in the net deferred tax liability and the deferred tax expense for the third quarter of $3.2 million.

Disclosure Requirements for Deferred Taxes—The Income Statement

Most of the disclosures relating to deferred tax balances that appear in the income statement have been integrated into our previous discussion. The corporation must disclose the composition of the tax expense for the period on either the face of its income statement or in the notes thereto.   The following components are required disclosures:

1. Current tax expense or benefit
2. Deferred tax expense exclusive of No. 6
3. Investment tax credits
4. Government grants when recognized as a reduction of income taxes
5. Benefits of operating loss carryforwards
6. Adjustments to the deferred tax assets/liabilities arising from changes in the tax law

The current tax expense or benefit relates to the amounts due or refundable from the corporation's tax return for the period. However, it excludes any interest or penalties for tax deficiencies. These items are not part of tax expense.

ALLEGHENY LUDLUM CORPORATION
Example of the Effect of Changes in Tax Codes

Note 7: Income Taxes

On August 4, 1991, Pennsylvania increased its Corporate Net Income Tax rate from 8.5% to 12.25%, retroactive to January 1, 1991. The liability method of accounting for income taxes requires the effect of a tax rate increase on current and accumulated deferred income taxes to be reflected in the period in which the rate increase was enacted. Accordingly, in the third quarter, the Company recorded an additional tax expense of approximately $3.2 million, or $.10 per share. The required adjustment to prior year's accumulated deferred income tax liabilities represented $2.7 million of the total adjustment.

EXHIBIT 20.15
Allegheny Ludlum Corporation— Example of the Effect of Changes in Tax Codes

Disclosure Requirements for Deferred Taxes—The Balance Sheet

As indicated previously, corporations that use a classified balance sheet must divide the ending net deferred tax asset/liability into a current and noncurrent portion. Corporations should disclose only one net current deferred tax asset/liability and one net noncurrent deferred tax asset/liability. The only exception to this is when deferred tax assets and liabilities arise from different tax jurisdictions, such as state and federal income tax codes. State and federal deferred tax assets or liabilities cannot be netted, but they can be combined. For example, if a corporation has a current deferred tax liability for federal purposes and a current deferred tax asset for state purposes, it cannot net these against one another. It must report each separately. However, if both state and federal codes gave rise to current deferred tax liabilities, the corporation can combine these into a single balance in its statement of financial position.

The corporation would also report an obligation for current taxes payable or a tax refund receivable in its balance sheet. These amounts would appear in the current liability or current asset section, respectively.

Disclosure Requirements for Deferred Taxes—Note Disclosures

Several requirements exist regarding information that a corporation must include in its notes to the financial statements. The corporation must reconcile the reported amount of tax expense attributable to income from continuing operations to the amount of tax that would result from the application of domestic federal statutory income tax rates to income from continuing operations. This reconciliation can be performed in dollars or in percentages of income, with each significant source of difference disclosed separately. Statutory rates for this disclosure are the regular tax rates. Nonpublic enterprises may forego the numerical reconciliation, but they must still provide a description of significant reconciling items.

For financial reporting and tax purposes, the corporation must disclose the amount and timing of any net operating loss carryforwards. In addition, the corporation should provide a description of all significant temporary differences.

Exhibit 20.16 presents the reconciliation of statutory and effective tax rates Allegheny Ludlum presented in its 1992 Annual Report, along with the breakdown of the deferred tax expense by major sources of temporary differences. Note that the major difference in tax rates stems from state income taxes, which the corporation must pay in addition to the federal taxes.

With regard to the effect of temporary differences, the major factors arise from different depreciation methods, different rules for capitalization of inventoriable costs, and different rules for the recognition of certain types of compensation and other postretirement benefits (which was new in 1992). Note that the pattern of deferred tax balances relating to property, plant, and equipment has grown in 1992, which is consistent with the intuition behind the arguments favoring partial allocation that these differences never reverse in aggregate.

It is interesting to note that if fiscal 1990 had been included in this comparison, we would have seen the deferred tax liability relating to property, plant,

| EXHIBIT 20.16
Reconciliation of
Effective and
Statutory Rates and
a Descriptions of
Temporary
Differences

ALLEGHENY LUDLUM CORPORATION
Reconciliation of Effective and Statutory Rates and a Description of Temporary Differences
Annual Report to Shareholders for 1992

The following is a reconciliation of the statutory federal income tax rate to the actual effective income tax rate:

Percent of Pretax Income	1992	1991	1990
Federal tax rate	34.0%	34.0%	34.0%
Increase (decrease) in taxes resulting from:			
State and local income taxes, net of federal tax benefit	5.8	9.8	3.8
Other	0.7	(0.6)	(0.6)
	40.5%	43.2%	37.2%

Deferred tax assets and/or liabilities result from temporary differences in the recognition of income and expense for financial and income tax reporting purposes, and differences between the fair value of assets acquired in business combinations accounting for as purchases and their tax bases. They represent future tax benefits or costs to be recognized when those temporary differences reverse. The categories of assets and liabilities which have resulted in differences in the timing of the recognition of income and/or expense are as follows:

Deferred Tax Assets (in thousands of dollars)	1992	1991
Postretirement benefits other than pensions	$ 89,976	–
Deferred compensation and other benefit plans	40,813	$ 41,981
Other items	11,709	7,013
Total deferred tax assets	$142,498	$ 48,994

Deferred Tax Liabilities (in thousands of dollars)	1992	1991
Depreciation	$ 97,086	$ 96,768
Inventory valuation—net	29,788	30,085
Other items	7,553	4,922
Total deferred tax liabilities	$134,427	$131,775
Net deferred tax asset (liability)	$ 8,071	$ (82,781)

and equipment actually fall in that year. This feature is interesting because one of the commonly cited arguments in support of partial allocation is that some temporary differences, such as those relating to depreciation, never reverse in aggregate. This example suggests this is not always true. The pattern of the deferred compensation effects suggests a partial reversal of the total temporary difference in 1992 as the deferred tax asset amount related to this temporary difference falls slightly from 1991 to 1992. The other items can be similarly analyzed.

The other major effect on deferred taxes arises from the adoption of SFAS No. 106 on other post-retirement benefits. The U.S. Tax Code only allows a tax deduction for these costs as paid. Under SFAS No. 106, companies must accrue the present value of the expected costs over the working life of the employees covered. When Allegheny adopted SFAS No. 106, the company elected to recognize the entire liability for benefits accrued in earlier periods immediately. This is what gave rise to the cumulative loss on the change in accounting principle, and it also gave rise to a large deferred tax benefit of $89,976 by the end of 1992.

Since Allegheny reports a net deferred tax asset and makes no mention of an allowance associated with this asset, the company must believe that the realization of this benefit is more likely than not to occur. Given the sizeable deferred tax liabilities that will give rise to net taxable amounts in the future and the fact that Allegheny has a substantial history of profitable operations that require payment of taxes at the maximum marginal tax rates, the lack of an allowance appears appropriate.

A Historical Perspective on Accounting for Deferred Taxes in the United States

APBO No. 11, issued in 1967, was the first authoritative pronouncement governing accounting for income taxes. This Opinion required the application of the deferral method in a fairly comprehensive fashion. In 1987, the FASB issued SFAS No. 96, which constituted a major revision of the existing practices regarding accounting for income taxes. This new standard shifted accounting for income taxes to the asset/liability approach. Originally, SFAS No. 96 was to be effective for fiscal years beginning after December 15, 1988. However, since it was so controversial, SFAS No. 96's implementation was delayed twice. Then, the FASB issued a revised standard, SFAS No. 109, to replace sections of SFAS No. 96 as originally implemented. Why was APBO No. 11 deemed to be inadequate? Why was SFAS No. 96 so controversial? These are the questions we explore below.

APBO No. 11 was originally constructed in the 1960s. The prevailing philosophy then was to let accounting focus on the measurement of revenue and expense items and to let the balance sheet valuation process occur as an outgrowth of the definitions of revenue and expense. In the early 1970s, the FASB replaced the APB and began its conceptual framework project, which produced the Statements of Accounting Concepts discussed in Chapter 2. This conceptual framework redirected the focus of accounting measurement from revenue and expense measurement, per se, to valuation of assets and liabilities where revenues and expenses arise as the valuation of the assets and liabilities change over time. Following the development of the conceptual framework, the FASB revisited many of the standards the APB had written and completely redefined the measurement principles therein. One major example was the change in accounting for defined benefit pension plans, which we discussed in Chapter 18.

The FASB's concerted attempts to redirect the focus of accounting measurement to asset and liability valuation eventually and directly conflicted with the use of the comprehensive deferral approach to deferred taxes. This conflict motivated the FASB to seek a method of accounting for deferred taxes that was more consistent with the asset/liability valuation approach established in the conceptual framework. The FASB's motivation to revise the standard on deferred tax accounting was not driven by public outcry from users of financial statements regarding the inadequacy of the methods employed under APBO

No. 11. Instead, the pressure to revise APBO No. 11 was principally internal to the FASB and related to its desire to obtain consistency across standards.

Regarding the controversy SFAS No. 96 created, several root causes for this reaction existed. First, No. 96 was considerably more complex in its implementation than SFAS No. 109, which has been the focus of our analysis. SFAS No. 96 required that the pattern of future reversals for all temporary differences be scheduled out—no exceptions. It also required that in computing the net ending deferred tax asset or liability, the company must assume that it will report zero book income in all future periods. This implies that the difference between tax and book income in any future period will be driven by the timing of the reversals of existing temporary differences. The zero book income assumption also meant that the company must estimate the tax effects of the reversing differences using the existing graduated corporate tax rates, which are lower for low levels of income, than for higher levels of income instead of applying the maximum marginal tax rates.

SFAS No. 96 was also very conservative in its recognition of deferred tax assets. When reversing differences gave rise to a forecasted net operating loss in a future period, the company had to apply the rules for carryback and carryforward to determine its realization. If the forecasted loss could not be carried back to a period when a refund of previously paid taxes could be obtained, the company could not recognize a deferred tax asset. If a net operating loss carryforward was actually created due to an operating loss in the current period, the company could use it to reduce net taxable amounts that would otherwise give rise to a deferred tax liability. However, the company could never recognize an asset to reflect a future benefit from this loss in excess of existing net taxable amounts.

Because the zero book income assumption was simply not realistic, many practitioners complained that the results of applying SFAS No. 96 were meaningless; and basing an estimate of future tax consequences on this assumption was pointless. In addition, practitioners were very concerned that the cost of implementing the requirement to schedule the reversals of all temporary differences far exceeded the benefits. Scheduling future reversals depends critically on management's future actions. Obtaining unbiased estimates of the timing of these reversals was of concern to many practitioners. Since some temporary differences take many years to reverse (sometimes as long as 40 years or more), many believed that the standard was overly fixated on the form of measurement and not sufficiently flexible to allow professional judgment about the overall reasonableness of the deferred tax accruals.

SFAS No. 109 is a compromise. It eliminates the need for extensive scheduling in many applications. It allows for the application of maximum marginal tax rates to all temporary differences if, in the opinion of the professional, this is a reasonable expectation in light of the circumstances. It also relaxes the requirements for recognition of deferred tax assets so that NOL carryforward benefits can be recognized fully if, in the judgment of the professional, the circumstances indicated that this is a reasonable expectation in light of the circumstances. Overall, the changes considerably simplify the application of the asset/liability method without losing the fundamental concept behind its implementation.

Intraperiod Tax Allocation

Up to this point, the discussion has focused on determining income tax expense for situations where the only activities reported in the financial statements arise from normal operations. When events and transactions occur that result in reporting for discontinued segments, extraordinary items, cumulative effects of accounting changes, or capital transactions such as a prior period adjustment, the company must separate the tax consequences of these events from the income taxes associated with income from continuing operations. The identification of, and rules regarding the reporting for, these items were discussed in Chapter 3 (for items found in the income statement) and in Chapters 14 and 15 (for items related to the equity section).

In these earlier discussions, we noted that a company must report these items net of applicable taxes but we refrained from a discussion of how a company should identify those tax effects. The present discussion resolves that question. The process of allocating the total income taxes for a period among these various components of income is called *intraperiod tax allocation*, since it relates to the allocation of the total tax expense (benefit) for a period across different components of income, not across different periods.

The steps in the intraperiod tax allocation process are described in Exhibit 20.17. To understand how these steps are employed, consider the example of Pace Corporation. Pace reported income from continuing operations before taxes of $500,000 and a pre-tax extraordinary loss of $120,000 for financial reporting purposes. For tax purposes, net taxable income was only $200,000, of which $300,000 related to continuing operations and $100,000 related to the extraordinary loss. A reconciliation of this information is provided in Panel A

EXHIBIT 20.17 |
Steps for Intraperiod
Tax Allocation

Steps for Intraperiod Tax Allocation

Step 1: Determine the total tax expense for the period.

Step 2: Determine the tax expense associated with income from continuing operations as if this were the only category.

Step 3: Subtract the tax expense for income from continuing operations from the total tax expense for the period to determine the tax effects to allocate among all other categories.

Step 4: For the remaining categories, group all items of loss together. Determine how much the current period's total taxes would be increased if these losses did not exist (the marginal tax benefit of the losses). This computation yields the total tax savings from all loss categories. If more than one loss category exists, the marginal benefit of each loss individually must be determined as well. The sum of the individual tax benefits may not equal the total marginal benefit computed above. If this occurs, the total marginal tax benefit is allocated across the loss category based on the ratio of the individual tax savings of each item to the sum of the individual tax savings.

Step 5: The tax expense allocated to the gain categories is the difference between the sum of the tax effects allocated to income from continuing operations plus the loss categories and the total tax expense. If there are multiple gain categories, the allocation of the total tax effects for all gains is again accomplished based on the ratio of the tax effects of each individual gain to the total of all the individual tax effects.

of Exhibit 20.18. Based on this information, Pace would compute its tax bill for the year as $90,000.

Examination of Panel A reveals that temporary differences of $200,000 were created during the year due to differences in the book and tax revenues and expenses that are part of income from continuing operations. Reversals of temporary differences existing at the beginning of the year, in the amount of $20,000, related to the extraordinary loss recorded in the year. A reconciliation of the net temporary differences at the beginning and end of the year, along with the associated deferred tax amounts, is presented in Panel B of Exhibit 20.18. At the beginning of the year, Pace reported a net deferred tax liability of $9,000, reflecting future temporary differences of $20,000 at a 45% tax rate. The year-end net deferred tax asset or liability would be based on the future tax consequences of the temporary differences of $200,000. Using the 45% tax rate, the ending deferred tax liability would be $90,000. This implies that the total deferred portion of tax expense for the year would be $81,000, the change in the liability.

As a result of these computations, total tax expense for the period would be $171,000 ($90,000 + $81,000). These computations complete Step 1 as set forth in Exhibit 20.17. Pace must allocate this total expense between income from continuing operations and the extraordinary loss.

In Step 2 of the intraperiod allocation process, Pace assesses the tax expense that would have resulted if the only items in its financial statement and the tax return were those events and transactions classified as part of income from continuing operations. To compute the current portion of tax expense on income from continuing operations, Pace multiplies the taxable income associated with income from continuing operations by the tax rate as follows:

PACE CORPORATION
Intraperiod Tax Allocation

Panel A: Reconciliation of Book and Tax Income

Panel A: Reconciliation of Book and Tax Income	Continuing Operations	Extraordinary Items	Total
Pre-tax book income	$ 500,000	$(120,000)	$ 380,000
Reconciling items relating to temporary differences	$(200,000)	20,000	(180,000)
Taxable income	$ 300,000	$(100,000)	$ 200,000
Taxes payable = current portion of tax expense = $200,000 × 45% = $90,000			

Panel B: Reconciliation of Changes in Net Temporary Differences and Deferred Taxes	Temporary Differences	Tax Rate	Deferred Tax Amount
Beginning net temporary differences	$ 20,000	45%	$ 9,000
Additions to net temporary differences in current year	180,000	45%	81,000
Ending net temporary differences	$200,000	45%	$90,000

EXHIBIT 20.18
Pace Corporation—Intraperiod Tax Allocation

Income from continuing operations	$ 500,000
Temporary differences	(200,000)
Taxable income without extraordinary item	$ 300,000
Tax rate	× 45%
Currently payable taxes without extraordinary loss	$ 135,000

If the extraordinary loss had not occurred, the temporary differences at the end of the year would have amounted to $220,000 since the $20,000 of temporary differences associated with the extraordinary loss would not have reversed. Pace's net deferred tax liability would then be $99,000, and its deferred portion of tax expense relating to continuing operations would be $90,000 ($99,000 – $9,000). Pace's total tax expense for the year associated with income from continuing operations is $225,000 ($135,000 current + $90,000 deferred).

Since the total tax expense computed above was $171,000 and the tax expense related to continuing operations is $225,000, the difference is the amount of the taxes Pace will allocate to the other categories. In this case, only one other category exists, the extraordinary loss. As a result, the tax benefit of the extraordinary loss is $54,000 ($225,000 – $171,000). Pace would report the following in its income statement for the year:

Income from continuing operations		$500,000
Income taxes:		
Currently payable	$135,000	
Deferred	90,000	225,000
Net income before extraordinary items		$275,000
Extraordinary loss:		
(Net of income tax benefits of $54,000)		(66,000)
Net income		$209,000

In the Pace example, only one category of events that require intraperiod tax allocation existed. Consequently, Steps 4 and 5 of Exhibit 20.17 were not required. In some cases, there may be multiple extraordinary losses or a mixture of losses and gains from such events and discontinuation of business segments, prior period adjustments, etc. In such cases, a company must sum all the loss categories and compute the total tax benefit of all the losses as Pace did for the extraordinary loss. If gain categories exist, the tax effects allocated to the gain categories (in total) will be determined as the amount of taxes necessary to reconcile the total tax effects and those already determined for continuing operations and the loss categories.

For example, assume Black Corporation had determined its total tax expense for the period was $200,000. In addition, the tax effects associated with income from continuing operations was $180,000, and the tax benefits of the loss categories had been assessed at $50,000. Black would assign the gain categories an allocation of $70,000 of tax expense so that the total tax expense equalled the amounts it allocated to each category ($180,000 - $50,000 + $70,000 = $200,000).

Allocation of the total tax effects of the gain or loss categories to the individual items within that category requires an analysis of the marginal effect of each item within the category on total tax expense. For example, continuing with Black Corporation, assume the loss category represents two extraordinary losses. Evaluated alone, the marginal tax savings of Loss A was $27,000, while the marginal benefit of Loss B was $33,000. Thus, the sum of the two marginal effects alone is a tax savings of $60,000. However, Loss A represents 45.0% of the sum ($27,000 ÷ $60,000), while Loss B represents 55.0% ($33,000 ÷ $60,000). To allocate the $50,000 of loss benefit from the two losses considered simultaneously, Black should allocate 45.0% ($22,500) to Loss A and 55.0% ($27,500) to Loss B.

The reason that the sum of the individual tax benefits does not equal the tax benefit of the sum of the two losses may lie in various differences in treatment the Tax Code affords the two exchanges if they occur individually or jointly. More commonly, the benefit will differ whenever the company's marginal tax rate changes with the level of taxable income. Either loss alone may not put the company into a lower tax bracket, but the two simultaneously may result in a lower overall tax rate.

INCOME TAX EFFECTS AND THE CASH FLOW STATEMENT

Under the requirements of SFAS No. 95, a company must classify all tax cash flows as operating cash flows. If the company uses the direct method to present cash flows from operations, it must disclose the cash payments for income taxes as a line item. Obviously, the actual cash payments for income taxes exclude all deferred tax items.

If the company uses the indirect method, it must treat all deferred tax components of tax expense as an adjustment to income to convert it to cash flows from operations. The change in the income tax payable liability will also be a reconciling item to convert income to cash flows from operations. Note that because the deferred tax portion of tax expense is itself added back to income as a reconciling item, any changes in the current portion of deferred tax assets or liabilities is *not* a reconciling item in converting income to cash flows from operations. The effect on income of changes in the current asset or liability balance of deferred taxes is already subsumed in the determination of the deferred tax portion of tax expense.

SUMMARY

This chapter has addressed many issues in the area of accounting and reporting for income taxes. It began by exploring differences between the Tax Code and GAAP regarding the recognition of events and transactions. This led to a distinction between permanent and temporary differences. Permanent and temporary differences refer to the existence of a difference between the book and tax bases of nontax assets and liabilities. Permanent differences represent differences that will never reverse themselves in future periods, while temporary differences are those that will eventually be driven to zero by reversals in future periods.

Several alternative approaches to accounting for deferred taxes were reviewed, including flowthrough, deferral, asset/liability, and net-of-tax. Other measurement issues gave rise to consideration of a partial versus comprehensive inclusion of temporary differences, the role of discounting, and the selection of tax rates to estimate deferred tax effects. The central distinction between flowthrough and other methods is that flowthrough measures tax expense based on the amounts due on the tax return for the period. As a result, it fails to match tax costs to the events and transactions reflected in the financial statements for the period unless the Tax Code uses the same measurement principles as GAAP. SFAS No. 109 has selected the asset/liability valuation approach, applied on a comprehensive basis, using currently enacted tax rates and no discounting.

The result of interperiod tax allocation was to report tax expense (benefit) for a period using two components: a current portion of tax expense (benefit) and a deferred portion of tax expense (benefit). The determination of the current portion of tax expense (benefit) depends on the amount of taxes due for the current period from the corporation's tax return. The amount of the deferred tax portion of tax expense (benefit) is determined by the change in the net deferred tax asset or liability over the period.

Determining the future tax effects of reversing temporary differences may require scheduling the pattern of reversals in future periods based on information available at the balance sheet date. Scheduling is required whenever tax rates are scheduled to change or the availability of reversing temporary differences to offset NOL or tax credit carryforwards is at issue.

Once the net deferred tax asset/liability has been determined, it must be further divided into current and noncurrent components. Current deferred tax balances arise because the temporary differences that create the deferred tax balance relate to current assets or liabilities or are expected to reverse in the next fiscal year if they cannot be specifically identified with a particular asset or liability (such as an NOL carryforward).

Finally, the chapter also examined how the total tax expense (benefit) identified with a particular period is allocated across various components of income. This process is referred to as intraperiod tax allocation. Basically, this process depends on the computation of the effects each component of income will have on tax expense (benefit) for the period, once the tax expense (benefit) related to income from continuing operations has been determined individually.

QUESTIONS

1. Why is accounting for deferred taxes an issue?
2. Why don't companies simply use the same rules for determining income for financial reporting and tax purposes?

3. What is the difference between the caption "currently payable income taxes" and "liability for deferred income taxes"?

4. What is a *temporary difference*?

5. What is a *permanent difference*?

6. Develop an example of a temporary difference that would give rise to a deferred tax liability. What assumptions must you make to recognize the deferred tax liability for financial reporting purposes?

7. Develop an example of a temporary difference that would give rise to a deferred tax asset. What assumptions must you make to recognize the deferred tax asset for financial reporting purposes?

8. How do the tax regulations regarding the treatment of net operating losses affect the computation of deferred taxes?

9. How is the classification as to the current or noncurrent status of any deferred tax asset/liability determined?

10. How should a company disclose the tax expense for a period on the face of its income statement?

11. What information regarding income taxes should a company provide in its notes to the financial statements?

12. What is the difference between *interperiod tax allocation* and *intraperiod tax allocation*?

13. Assess the disclosure requirements for income taxes from the perspective of providing information regarding the timing and amounts of future cash flows relating to taxes.

14. Compare and contrast the *deferral*, *asset/liability*, and *net-of-tax* approaches to the treatment of temporary differences.

15. What role does discounting play in the determination of deferred tax assets and liabilities? Provide a justification for this treatment of interest effects.

16. What is the difference between *partial* and *comprehensive allocation*? How would you describe the system employed under SFAS No. 109?

EXERCISES

20-1.   *Reconstruction of temporary differences from reconciliation of book and tax income*

Karas Corporation has operated profitably since its inception in 1993. The company was started by issuing stock in exchange for $2,000,000 of cash. The reconciliation between book and tax income for each of the years 1993–1995 is presented below:

Historical Results:	1993	1994	1995
Book income	$200,000	$ 900,000	$1,945,000
Temporary differences:			
Depreciation	(70,000)	$(200,000)	(440,000)
Compensation	60,000	70,000	(30,000)
Goodwill amortization	0	20,000	15,000
Taxable income	$190,000	$ 790,000	$1,490,000
Tax paid (30%)	$ 57,000	$ 237,000	$ 447,000

The company has paid no dividends, and future tax rates are expected to be constant at 30%.

REQUIRED:

Prepare a reconciliation of the book and tax bases in net assets at the end of each year presented.

20-2.   *Computation, classification, and journalization—constant tax rates*

Makedo Company reported a net temporary difference of $80,000 relating to property, plant, and equipment at the end of 1994, the first year of its operations. Makedo has a 40% tax rate in the current year and paid taxes of $6,000. The Tax Code calls for a constant future tax rate of 40%.

REQUIRED:

1. Compute the ending deferred tax liability and deferred tax expense for Makedo.
2. Prepare the journal entry that Makedo will use to record all of the tax effects in 1994.
3. How will Makedo classify the deferred tax asset/liability on its balance sheet?

20-3.   *Computation of deferred tax amounts—constant tax rate*

At the end of 1994, Basic, Inc. has the following schedule of temporary differences:

	Book Basis	Tax Basis
Property, plant, and equipment	$250,000	$230,000
Allowance for uncollectible accounts	(23,000)	0

Basic had reported taxable income in 1994 of $16,000 and paid taxes of $4,500. Basic has a constant future tax rate of 40%. At the beginning of the year, Basic reported a net deferred tax of $2,500.

REQUIRED:

Compute Basic's deferred tax amounts for expense and balance sheet presentation at the end of 1994.

20-4.   *Reconciliation of book-to-tax differences; computation of tax amounts—multiple sources of differences; constant tax rates)*

Spannel Corp. has been in business for several years. At the beginning of the year, the company prepared the following analysis of differences between the book and tax values of assets and liabilities:

Asset/Liability	Book Basis	Tax Basis	Type
Goodwill	$ 300,000	$1,200,000	Perm.
PPE	4,500,000	3,600,000	Temp.
Accrued comp.	(700,000)	0	Temp.
Unearned revenue	(150,000)	0	Temp.

At the end of the current year, Spannel performed a reconciliation of its book and tax income, which appears as follows:

Book income	$1,400,000
Goodwill amortization	100,000
Depreciation	(250,000)
Accrued compensation	(70,000)
Unearned income	50,000
Taxable income	$1,230,000

At year-end, the only items classified as current on which differences existed were the unearned income (in total) and half of the deferred compensation. Spannel faces a constant tax rate of 35% for the present and future years.

REQUIRED:

1. Prepare a schedule to determine the net temporary difference between the book and tax bases of assets and liabilities for Spannel at year-end.
2. Compute Spannel's net deferred tax liability and deferred tax expense for the current year.
3. How will Spannel report the deferred tax balance sheet items?

20-5. *Computation of amounts—changing tax rates*

At the end of 1994, Dectron, Inc. has the following schedule of reversing temporary differences over the next five years:

Year	Depreciation	Warranty Costs	Employee Compensation
1995	5,000	(3,000)	0
1996	10,000	(2,000)	0
1997	15,000	0	0
1998	20,000	0	0
1999	0	0	(30,000)

The depreciation differences result from having taken larger depreciation deductions in prior periods for tax purposes than for book purposes. Warranty costs are accrued for financial reporting purposes, and Dectron expects these to result in deductible expenses for tax purposes over the next two years. The temporary difference relating to employee compensation arose from the use of compensatory stock options, which are first exercisable in 1999. Dectron faces the following tax rates for the current and future periods:

1994–1996	20%
1997–1998	30%
1999	35%

REQUIRED:

1. Prepare a computation of the ending net deferred tax liability for 1994, assuming that future income will be sufficient to absorb any net deductible amounts scheduled in future years.
2. Prepare a computation of the ending deferred tax liability for 1994, assuming that future book income will be zero.
3. Explain the reasons for the differences between the results of Requirements 1 and 2.

20-6.   *Computation of tax amounts—changing tax rates; reconstruction of current year taxable income*

Moredread started operations on January 1, 1994. During 1994, the company reported book income of $125,000. Income for federal tax purposes in 1994 was $65,000. Temporary differences between book and tax income are created by using different depreciation methods for book and tax. Book and tax depreciation over the lives of Moredread's fixed assets are estimated as follows:

	1994	1995	1996	1997	1998
Book	90,000	90,000	90,000	90,000	90,000
Tax	150,000	200,000	67,000	33,000	0

In addition, the federal tax rates on corporate income are scheduled as follows:

1994–1995	45%
1996–1997	30%
1998	25%

Moredread has no other differences between book and tax income.

REQUIRED:

Compute the tax expense for Moredread along with the balance sheet amounts that would be reported at the end of the year assuming:
1. Moredread has not paid any portion of its current tax during the year.
2. The Company is expected to generate sufficient book income to absorb any net deductible amounts from depreciation in the year they arise.

20-7.   *Computation and classification of deferred tax amounts—changing tax rates; scheduling; effects of assumptions about future book income*

Dox Inc., began 1994 with a net deferred tax liability of $46,000. Dox faces tax rates in the current and following year of 40%, but this will decline to only 25% after next year. Dox prepared the following schedule of reversing temporary differences at the end of the current year:

	1995	1996	1997	1998	1999
Depreciation	$(7,000)	$(10,000)	$30,000	$50,000	$ 70,000
Compensation		(20,000)			(20,000)

Dox reported taxable income in 1994 and in the previous two years of $10,000 per year.

REQUIRED:

1. Assuming that Dox is expected to report book income in all future periods sufficient to absorb any net deductible amounts created by the temporary differences, determine the net deferred tax asset/liability to be reported at the end of 1994 and the deferred tax expense for the period.
2. Based on only the information in the problem, how would you divide the net deferred tax asset/liability in Requirement 1 into its current and noncurrent components and why?
3. Suppose you discover that Dox is not likely to have any book income for several years due to changes in market conditions. Without doing any specific computations, how might this fact influence the computation of the deferred tax balance at the end of 1994?

20-8.   *NOL effects—no other temporary differences; conditions for full benefit recognition*

Travell Corporation has operated successfully for many years. In the current year, it suffered a net operating loss for tax purposes of $500,000. In the preceding three years, the company reported total taxable income of only $300,000. Travell has no temporary differences.

REQUIRED:

1. Assuming Travell has a constant tax rate of 40% and wished to report the maximum possible benefit from this loss, how would the company report the effects of the operating loss in its income statement and balance sheet?
2. What conditions would have to exist for you, as an auditor, to conclude that the treatment in Requirement 1 is appropriate under GAAP?

20-9.   *NOL effects—first year of operations; other temporary differences; deferred tax amounts with and without the NOL effects*

Frost Industries has reported a net operating loss for tax purposes of $50,000 in 1994, the first year of its operations. It reported book income at $20,000, with the difference being explained by temporary differences on property, plant, and equipment of $(80,000) and on the allowance for uncollectible accounts of $10,000. Receivables for Frost are either collected within 6 months of their due date or written off as uncollectible. Depreciable assets have a 10-year life. Tax rates are expected to be constant at 30% for all periods.

REQUIRED:

1. In the absence of the tax loss carryforward, what amounts would Frost report in its income statement and balance sheet relating to deferred taxes at the end of 1994?
2. How will the incorporation of any benefits from the operating loss carryforward change the amount of the net deferred tax asset/liability reported at the end of 1994?
3. How do you think the incorporation of the operating loss carryforward benefit might affect the separation of the net deferred tax asset/liability into its current and noncurrent components?

20-10.   *NOL effects; other temporary differences; years subsequent to loss*

At the beginning of 1995, Seacort Corporation had net temporary differences relating to noncurrent assets of $800,000 (book basis was above tax basis) and an operating loss carryforward of $1,000,000. The company faces a constant tax rate of 50% for all years. Seacort expects all temporary differences on noncurrent assets to reverse within the carryforward period. In addition, Seacort does not anticipate the excess of the carryforward over the other temporary differences in 1995.

During 1995, a reconciliation of book and taxable income (exclusive of any operating loss carryforward) showed the following:

Book income	$ 540,000
Temporary differences	(200,000)
Taxable income	$ 340,000

REQUIRED:

1. Assuming that at the end of 1994, it was more likely than not that Seacort would realize the full benefit of the operating loss carryforward, prepare an

analysis of the beginning balance, changes in, and ending balance of any deferred tax asset or liability that Seacort would report in 1995.

2. Assuming that at the end of 1994, an allowance was established for the possible lack of realization of 10% of the remaining operating loss carryforward. By year-end, the allowance was deemed to be unnecessary. Prepare the journal entry to record all income tax related activity for 1995. (Show supporting computations.)

20-11. *Tax credit carryforwards; other temporary differences*

At the beginning of 1995, Scott Industries reported a net deferred tax asset of $200,000 arising from net temporary differences on long-term liabilities (accrued costs of other postretirement benefits) and property, plant, and equipment of $800,000 at a tax rate of 25%. During 1995, Scott reported the following reconciliation of book and tax income under the regular tax system:

Book income	$ 100,000
Temporary differences:	
Depreciation	(120,000)
OPEBs	20,000
Taxable income	$ 0

While no taxable income existed under the regular tax system, taxes of $20,000 were required under the alternative tax system. Scott received a tax credit of $20,000, which it elected to carryforward. Scott has historically reported taxable income in excess of $700,000 per year and expects to return to that level of profitability next year. A strike in 1995 was the major reason for the low level of profitability for the year.

REQUIRED:

Prepare the journal entry Scott will use to record the income tax effects in 1995. (Show all supporting computations.)

20-12. *Effect of legislative changes in the Tax Code*

At the beginning of 1995, Gamma-Hydra Corporation reported a net deferred tax liability of $151,875. This was based on net temporary differences arising on noncurrent assets and liabilities of $337,500 and the then existing corporate tax rate of 45%. On July 1, 1995, Congress enacted changes to the existing Tax Code that immediately reduced the corporate tax rate to 30% for all income after that date.

An analysis of book and tax income for the periods from January 1, 1995 to June 30, 1995, and July 1, 1995 to December 31, 1995, reveal the following:

	1/1/95–6/30/95	7/1/95–12/31/95
Book income	$600,000	$400,000
Temporary differences	(37,500)	(50,000)
Taxable income	$562,500	$350,000

Gamma-Hydra has always paid taxes and expects to continue to be profitable in the future.

REQUIRED:

1. Prepare the section of the income statement starting with income before taxes and ending with net income for Gamma-Hydra in 1995, assuming that

the company elects to disclose all components of income tax expense on the face of its financial statements.

2. Prepare all journal entries necessary to record activity relating to income taxes for the year, assuming the company makes estimated tax payments to the government during the year as follows:

April 1	$100,000
July 1	100,000
October 1	75,000

Hint: When an estimated tax payment is made, you can treat it as a debit to current tax expense and make an adjustment at year-end for any remaining current tax expense.

20-13. *Intraperiod tax allocation*

Western Company reported an extraordinary pre-tax loss from flood damage for 1995 of $300,000, along with income from continuing operations of $380,000. Western has no temporary or permanent differences. The corporate Tax Code applies a tax rate of 25% on the first $100,000 of taxable income and 40% on amounts above $100,000. In addition, the Tax Code does not distinguish between income or loss from continuing operations and the effects of events that are classified as extraordinary for financial accounting purposes.

REQUIRED:

Prepare the section of Western's income statement for 1995, beginning with income from continuing operations before taxes and ending with net income.

20-14. *Intraperiod tax allocation*

Blackridge Corporation began 1994 with a noncurrent deferred tax liability of $300,000, based on temporary differences relating to property, plant, and equipment of $1,000,000 and a constant tax rate of 30%. During 1994, the Company reported pre-tax income from continuing operations of $250,000 (for book purposes) and a gain from the sale of a discontinued operation of $100,000 (for book purposes). The sale of the discontinued segment occurred on the first day of the year.

The sale of the segment accelerated the reversal of $70,000 worth of temporary differences that would otherwise not have occurred. Due to special characteristics of the Tax Code, the gain from sale was partially taxed at a lower rate, 15%. Only $50,000 of the taxable gain was eligible for this treatment.

A reconciliation of book and tax income for the year, broken down by component of book income, appeared as follows:

	Ordinary	Discontinued	Total
Book income	$ 250,000	$100,000	$350,000
Depreciation differences	(100,000)	70,000	(30,000)
Taxable income	$ 150,000	$170,000	$320,000
		Taxed at regular rates	$270,000
		Taxed at special rates	50,000
		Total	$320,000

REQUIRED:

Prepare the section of Western's income statement for 1995, beginning with income from continuing operations before taxes and ending with net income.

PROBLEMS

20-1. *Comparison of the deferral and asset/liability approaches—one source of temporary differences; changing tax rates over time; multiple years*

The only differences between the book and tax bases of assets, liabilities, and equities for Demon Corporation are due to depreciation. Demon began operations on January 1, 1994, and reported taxable income for 1994 of $120,000. The tax rate for 1994 is 25%, and the tax rate for all years beyond 1994 is presently scheduled at 30%. At the end of 1989, Demon had prepared the following analysis of its depreciable assets and the future depreciation charges for both book and tax purposes:

	Book basis	$1,200,000
	Tax basis	900,000

Depreciation	1995	1996	1997	Total
Book	$400,000	$400,000	$400,000	$1,200,000
Tax	450,000	300,000	150,000	900,000

Demon was expected to be sufficiently profitable to absorb any net deductible amounts arising in future periods in the years they occur. Assume Demon had no new temporary differences arising during the years 1995–1997 and that the company reported taxable income of $150,000 in each of these future years.

REQUIRED:

1. Prepare a schedule that would reconcile book and tax income for each year, 1994–1997, and a separate schedule that would determine the net temporary differences at the end of each year.
2. Prepare the journal entries that Demon would use to record all activity relating to income taxes in each year 1994–1997, applying the asset/liability approach.
3. Prepare a schedule that compares the results in Requirement 2 with the amounts that would be reported using the deferral approach, assuming that the current year's tax rate is applied to the differences between book and tax income to compute deferred tax expense under this approach.
4. Explain why there is a balance in the deferred tax balance sheet account at the end of 1997 under the deferral approach but not under the asset/liability approach.

20-2. *Computation and journalization of tax effects—multiple sources of temporary differences; alternative assumptions about future book income; multiple years*

Assume Cantrell had the following schedule of reversing temporary differences relating to depreciation and deferred compensation at the end of 1994:

	1995	1996	1997	1998
Depreciation	$(10,000)	$0	$10,000	$20,000
Compensation	0	0	0	(15,000)

Cantrell started operations in 1994 and reported taxable income of $5,000. Tax rates for Cantrell are as follows:

1994–1995	45%
1996	30%
1997–1998	25%

Assume Cantrell is expected to have sufficient book income to absorb any net deductible amounts that will arise due to the reversal of existing temporary differences unless otherwise indicated.

REQUIRED:

1. How would Cantrell compute the deferred taxes amounts for 1994?
2. If the reversing difference on depreciation for 1998 were $50,000, how would that change the deferred tax effects for 1994?
3. How would your answer to Requirements 1 and 2 change if there were evidence that Cantrell will report zero book income for the next several years?
4. Assuming there are no new temporary differences in 1995, other than those already scheduled in Requirement 2, and that taxable income in 1995 was $80,000, how would Cantrell compute the 1995 deferred tax balances?

20-3. *Reconstruction of temporary differences from book-to-tax income reconciliations; graduated tax rates; changing tax rates; comparison of the asset/liability approach with the net-of-tax approach*

DFT, Incorporated began operations on January 1, 1994. A reconciliation of book and taxable income for the years 1994, 1995, and 1996 are provided below. Tax rates for 1994–1996 were 20% on the first $100,000 of income and 45% thereafter. Tax rates for 1997 and beyond are 35% on all income.

Historical Results	1994	1995	1996
Book income	$200,000	$270,000	$435,000
Temporary differences			
Depreciation	(90,000)	(120,000)	(150,000)
Permanent differences	0	(20,000)	(15,000)
Taxable income	$110,000	$130,000	$270,000
Tax paid	$ 24,500	$ 33,500	$ 96,500

An analysis of the future temporary differences relating to depreciation at the end of 1996 revealed the following schedule of book and tax depreciation expenses in the future periods:

	1997	1998	1999	2000	Total
Book	$320,000	$250,000	$210,000	$210,000	$990,000
Tax	360,000	200,000	70,000	0	630,000
Net	$ (40,000)	$ 50,000	$140,000	$210,000	$360,000

Assume that on January 1, 1996, DFT reported the following deferred tax accounts on its balance sheet:

Noncurrent deferred tax liability	(91,000)
Net beginning deferred tax liability	$(91,000)

Unless otherwise indicated, assume that DFT expects to pay taxes in all future periods at the maximum marginal tax rate.

REQUIRED:

1. Explain the relationship, if any, between the differences in depreciation expense for book and tax in the years 1994–1996 and the size of the temporary difference between the book and tax basis in property, plant, and equipment at the end of 1996.
2. Given the facts above, what should DFT report as the balance in the deferred tax liability at December 31, 1996?
3. How should DFT report tax expense in the income statement? Prepare the journal entry to record tax expense.
4. How would the balance sheet disclosure differ if the tax effects of temporary differences were determined in the fashion you used in Requirements 2 and 3 but the net-of-tax approach was used for reporting?
5. How would your response to Requirements 2 and 3 change if there was evidence that DFT would not generate sufficient income in future years to be taxed at the maximum marginal tax rates? **Hint:** This question does not seek a specific computation; however, you may use supporting computations to aid in communicating your response.

20-4. *Continuation of Problem 20-3 to additional years*

Using the information in Problem 20-3, assume that in 1997, DFT reported an operating loss for both book and tax purposes. The reconciliation of book and tax income for 1997 is as follows:

Book loss	$(700,000)
Temporary differences	
Depreciation	(140,000)
Permanent differences	(25,000)
Taxable loss	$(865,000)

In addition, DFT prepared the following schedule of future reversals of existing temporary differences as of December 31, 1997:

	1998	1999	2000	Total
Net	$(100,000)	$360,000	$240,000	500,000

In addition, the company elected to apply as much of the operating loss as possible as a carryback to obtain a refund of previously paid taxes. The loss was due to unusual circumstances that should not recur. The company expects to pay taxes at the maximum marginal rate in all future periods. In 1998, DFT reported the following reconciliation of book and tax income, without regard to the benefit of any operating loss carryforwards:

Book income	$625,000
Temporary differences	
Depreciation	(160,000)
Permanent differences	(15,000)
Taxable income	$450,000

In addition, DFT prepared the following schedule of future temporary differences as of December 31, 1998:

	1999	2000	2001	Total
Net	$(200,000)	$410,000	$450,000	$660,000

REQUIRED:

1. Provide an explanation for the continuing apparent growth in the size of DFT's net temporary difference over the years. How does this phenomenon relate to the arguments that favor partial allocation?
2. Prepare all supporting computations necessary to compute the income tax expense and deferred tax assets or liabilities for 1997 and 1998. You may assume that DFT reported only a noncurrent deferred tax liability of $132,000 as of January 1, 1997.
3. Prepare journal entries to record the effect of income taxes on the results of operation and balance sheets for 1997 and 1998. Explain how the deferred tax amounts will be classified into any current and noncurrent components.
4. Prepare the section of DFT's income statements for 1997 and 1998, beginning with income from continuing operations.
5. In 1997, the statutory tax rate was 35%. Prepare a schedule that reconciles DFT's effective tax rate (reported tax expense divided by reported pre-tax income) to the statutory rate by setting forth each source of difference between these two rates and their marginal effect.

20-5.   *Computation of income tax expense—follows reversals over several years*

Shepard Labs began operations in the current year, 1994. The company reported taxable income of $90,000 for the year and book income of $250,000. The total net temporary differences of $160,000 were scheduled to create the following pattern of reversals in future years:

1995	$ (30,000)
1996	50,000
1997	70,000
1998	(100,000)
1999	60,000
2000	60,000
2001	50,000

Shepard Labs faces a constant tax rate of 30% in all periods.

REQUIRED:

1. Assume Shepard Labs reports book income of $100,000 per year for each of the years 1995–2001 and has no new temporary differences to arise outside of the reversal of those existing at the end of 1994. Prepare the tax expense computation for the current year and for each of the next seven years.
2. Prepare a graph that plots the behavior of the net deferred tax asset/liability over the seven-year period, along with the balance of the net temporary differences at the end of each year.

20-6.   *Computation and reporting effects of legislative change in tax rates*

Using the information in Problem 20-5, assume that on the last day of 1997, Congress changed the tax rate from 30% to 40%.

REQUIRED:

How would Shepard Labs report the effects of this change in tax law in its financial statements?

20-7. *Computations and journal entries—follows reversals over several years*

Mal-Mut Industries has been in operation for several years. At the beginning of 1994, Mal-Mut had a net deferred tax liability of $200,000 recorded on its books, all of which was classified as a noncurrent liability. In the past two years, it has reported taxable income of $300,000 each year. Tax rates for Mal-Mut are currently 30% for the current year and the next two years. After that, tax rates are scheduled to increase to 45%. During the current year, Mal-Mut reported taxable income of $400,000 and prepared the following schedule of future reversals of the existing net temporary difference:

1995	$ 100,000
1996	120,000
1997	(240,000)
1998	200,000
1999	360,000

Assume that at the end of 1994 and 1995, Mal-mut is expected to report sufficient book income in 1997 to absorb the net deductible amount scheduled to arise in that period. However, actual results in 1994 and 1995 create no book income in either year. At the end of 1995, the expectation is that there will be no book income for 1996–1999. Further assume that no new temporary differences are created over the 1995-1999 period.

REQUIRED:

1. Prepare computations of the deferred portion of tax expense and the deferred tax balance sheet amounts Mal-Mut reported for the current year and years 1995–1999.
2. Prepare the journal entries that Mat-Mut would make each period.

20-8. *NOL effects in the presence of other temporary differences; recognition of carry-forward benefit in year of loss*

Losers, Incorporated has operated profitably for several years. However, in Year 5, the company reported a net operating loss for tax purposes. Schedules that reconcile the differences between book and tax income for each year of the company's existence are as follows:

Historical Results	Year 1	Years 2–4	Year 5
Book income	$300,000	$1,400,000	$(2,085,000)
Temporary differences			
Depreciation	(90,000)	(300,000)	(120,000)
Compensation	80,000	150,000	0
Permanent differences	0	(20,000)	(15,000)
Taxable income	$290,000	$1,230,000	$(2,220,000)
Tax paid (30%)	$ 87,000	$ 369,000	n/a

The company has elected to apply the operating loss as a carryback to obtain a refund of previous taxes. Loser expects to return to profitability and pay taxes in future periods at the 30% constant rate, which is currently legislated to exist in all future years.

REQUIRED:

1. Construct a schedule that will determine the temporary differences in existence at the beginning of Year 5, by source. Determine the net deferred tax asset/liability as of January 1, Year 5.
2. Assuming it is likely that any operating loss carryforward will be realized, prepare the journal entries to record the income tax effects relating to Loser's results of operations and balance sheet for Year 5.
3. Suppose there was evidence to suggest that Loser was more likely than not to be incapable of fully utilizing any carryforward benefit. In particular, an analysis of future income opportunities for Loser suggests that taxable income over the carryforward period is only anticipated to total $500,000. How will this alter your response to Requirement 2?

20-9.   *NOL effects in years subsequent to the loss with other temporary differences*

Baker Corporation has operated for several years. At the beginning of 1996, the company reported the following reconciliation of book and tax differences in assets and liabilities:

	Book Basis	Tax Basis
Property, plant, and equipment	$7,800,000	$7,400,000
Accrued compensation	80,000	0

In 1995, Baker reported a net operating loss for tax purposes, part of which it carried back to obtain a refund of previously paid taxes. The remainder, $750,000, was carried forward to be applied against future taxable income. In 1996 and 1997, Baker reported the following reconciliation of book and tax incomes (without regard to any carryforward benefit):

	1996	1997
Book income	$730,000	$1,070,000
Temporary differences		
Depreciation	(150,000)	(280,000)
Compensation	50,000	70,000
Permanent differences	(30,000)	(50,000)
Taxable income	$600,000	$810,000

Baker faces a 40% tax rate in all years.

REQUIRED:

1. Prepare a schedule to determine the magnitude of all temporary differences, by source, at the end of 1996 and 1997.
2. Assuming Baker accrued the full benefit of the tax loss carryforward in 1995, prepare the journal entries to record all tax effects for 1996 and 1997, assuming the accrued compensation is classified as a noncurrent liability.
3. Suppose Baker had been unsure of the full utilization of the operating loss carryforward at the end of 1995 and had established an allowance for possible nonrealization of the loss in the amount of $50,000. At the end of 1996, this uncertainty had been resolved and the entire loss carryforward was expected to be realized. Prepare the journal entries to record all tax effects for 1996 and 1997, assuming the accrued compensation liability is classified as a current asset.

20-10. *Intraperiod tax allocation—deferred taxes on equity valuation allowances*

Comajor Corporation reports a net operating loss of $100,000 from continuing operations in 1994, which is the first year of operations. It also has an extraordinary item, a discontinued segment, and an equity valuation allowance for unrealized losses on noncurrent marketable securities. The extraordinary item is a gain of $370,000; the discontinued segment results in an additional loss of $120,000; and the ending equity valuation allowance was $60,000. All income is taxed at a rate of 30% in all periods. Comajor reports the following total temporary differences:

Depreciation	$ 80,000
Unrealized loss on equity securities	(60,000)
Total temporary differences	$ 20,000
Tax rate	30%
Deferred tax liability (12/31/94)	$ 6,000

Focusing only on the transactions and events included in income from continuing operations, Comajor would have had the following temporary differences:

Depreciation	$ 140,000
Loss carryforward	(100,000)
Net temporary differences	$ 40,000
Tax rate	30%
Deferred tax liability	$ 12,000

The increased temporary difference on depreciation arises due to accelerated depreciation on assets that were disposed of during the year. Of the $60,000 increase, $20,000 was associated with assets disposed of with the discontinued segment and $60,000 was associated with the extraordinary item.

REQUIRED:

How should Comajor report the tax effects for 1994?

MITRON CORPORATION

Mitron Corporation has operated profitably since its inception in 1990. In 1994, the company reported a net operating loss for tax purposes. A summary of the reconciliation between book and tax income for each of the years 1990-1994 is presented below:

Historical Results	1990	1991–1993	1994
Book income	$200,000	$900,000	$(1,945,000)
Temporary differences:			
Depreciation	(70,000)	(200,000)	(40,000)
Compensation	60,000	70,000	0
Goodwill amortization	0	(20,000)	(15,000)
Taxable income	$190,000	$750,000	$(2,000,000)
Tax paid (30%)	$ 57,000	$225,000	n/a

On December 31, 1994, Mitron prepared the following analysis of the temporary differences and the timing of its reversals based on the items currently reported in its financial statements:

	1995	1996	1997	1998
Depreciation	$(50,000)	$90,000	$110,000	$160,000
Compensation	0	0	(130,000)	0

Corporate tax rates are scheduled at 30% for all years prior to 1997. After 1996, the corporate tax rates will be 45%. At December 31, 1993, Mitron's temporary differences were scheduled to occur prior to 1997. Tax laws governing operating loss carrybacks and carryforwards allow a three-year carryback and a 15-year carryforward. Mitron decided to carry back the maximum amount of loss to recover previously paid taxes.

During 1995 and 1996, Mitron reported the following reconciliations between book and tax income:

	1995	1996
Book income	$1,220,000	$1,070,000
Temporary differences:		
Depreciation	(100,000)	(150,000)
Compensation	20,000	30,000
Goodwill amortization	(40,000)	(50,000)
Taxable income	$1,100,000	$ 900,000

At the end of each year, Mitron reported the following schedule of reversing temporary differences:

At the end of 1995	1996	1997	1998
Depreciation	$(10,000)	$ 190,000	$230,000
Compensation	0	(130,000)	(20,000)

At the end of 1996	1997	1998	1999	2000
Depreciation	$ 90,000	$240,000	$210,000	$ 20,000
Compensation	(130,000)	(20,000)		(30,000)

On December 31, 1998, Congress passed a new tax act that increased the tax rate for corporations to 50%. Mitron is incorporated in a state that has no corporate income tax.

The company classified the entire balance of the accrued compensation liability, which is the source of the compensation temporary difference as a noncurrent liability in 1994 and 1995, but reclassified $130,000 of this amount to a current liability at the end of 1996.

REQUIRED:

1. Speculate on the kinds of events that would have given rise to the reconciling items between book and tax income and the changes in these differences over the periods discussed.
2. Prepare schedules to compute the deferred tax amounts that Mitron would report under existing GAAP in each of the years 1994, 1995, and 1996, respectively. You may assume that realization of the benefits of any operating loss carryforward are more likely than not to occur. You may also assume that the actual taxable income that arose in 1995 and 1996 was equivalent to the forecasted levels as of the end of 1994 and 1995, respectively.
3. Prepare Mitron's financial statement disclosures relating to deferred taxes in each of the years presented. Include the balance sheet disclosure, income statement disclosures, and any note disclosures (including a reconciliation of the statutory tax rate to the effective rate).
4. If Mitron used the deferral method of interperiod tax allocation, what would be the deferred tax portion of the provision for taxes in each of the three years presented? You may assume that any carryforward benefit is recognized in full in the year of the loss using current year tax rates.
5. Evaluate the usefulness of deferred tax reporting and compare the benefits and limitations of the liability and comprehensive methods of tax allocation as they apply to Mitron.

ALLIED PRODUCTS CORPORATION

Allied Products Corporation (Allied Products) manufactures and markets products for specific market niches primarily within three core businesses: agricultural equipment, transportation/industrial products, and materials technology. Agricultural equipment includes farm tractors, implements, and related equipment. Transportation/industrial products and services include prototype tooling and production dies used to produce automotive parts, stamped metal automotive body panels, metal forming presses, trailer chassis, replacement parts for work-over oil rigs, drill distribution, and oil and gas well stimulation services. In its materials technology business, Allied Products manufactures insulating materials and specialty products for the electrical, electronic, and defense industries and custom compounds thermoplastic resins. Allied Products also has a wholly-owned consolidated finance subsidiary that provides retail financing for farm equipment and industrial machinery. Additionally, the company has minority equity interests in two affiliated companies, the investments in which were written off in 1989.

Allied Products adopted the requirements of SFAS No. 96 related to accounting for income taxes in 1988. Recall that SFAS No. 96 was replaced by SFAS No. 109 in 1993. One of the major differences between SFAS Nos. 96 and 109 is the manner in which tax loss carryforwards and tax credit carryforwards are recognized. Under SFAS No. 96, tax loss (credit) carryforwards could only be recognized when they were used to offset the effects of net taxable amounts arising from the reversal of other temporary differences. Under SFAS No. 109, all tax loss (credit) carryforwards are recognized; and when it is more likely than not that some portion of these benefits will not be realized, a valuation allowance is used to reduce any deferred tax asset by the portion of the benefits that are expected to expire unused.

The following pages contain selected excerpts from Allied Products' 10-K filing for 1989.

**ALLIED PRODUCTS CORPORATION AND CONSOLIDATED SUBSIDIARIES
CONSOLIDATED BALANCE SHEETS
December 31, 1988 and 1989**

	December 31, 1988	December 31, 1989
ASSETS		
Current Assets:		
Cash and marketable securities	$ 7,878,000	$ 8,169,000
Notes and accounts receivable, less allowances of $3,348,000 and $2,870,000, respectively	186,042,000	177,365,000
Inventories -		
Raw materials	53,168,000	44,756,000
Work in process	46,309,000	64,933,000
Finished goods	55,282,000	62,929,000
	154,759,000	172,618,000
Prepaid expenses	1,683,000	960,000
Total current assets	350,362,000	359,112,000
Other Assets:		
Investment in affiliated companies	413,000	–
Notes receivable, due after one year	18,532,000	20,447,000
Deferred charges	35,912,000	34,025,000
Other (includes cash of $2,448,000 and $1,571,000 restricted for capital expenditures as of December 31, 1988 and 1989, respectively)	10,430,000	7,059,000
	65,287,000	61,531,000
Plant and Equipment, at cost:		
Land	2,973,000	2,968,000
Buildings and improvements	30,534,000	33,472,000
Machinery and equipment	77,358,000	84,130,000
	110,765,000	120,570,000
Less - Accumulated depreciation	45,174,000	54,165,000
	65,591,000	66,405,000
	$481,240,000	$487,048,000

	December 31, 1988	1989
LIABILITIES AND SHAREHOLDERS' INVESTMENT		
Current Liabilities:		
Notes payable to banks	$ 8,000,000	$ –
Current portion of long-term debt	28,610,000	18,714,000
Accounts payable	76,859,000	57,484,000
Accrued expenses—		
Salaries, wages, etc.	8,414,000	9,672,000
Taxes, other than income taxes	4,020,000	4,011,000
Interest	1,210,000	3,144,000
Other, including insurance, warranty, pensions, etc.	26,334,000	31,704,000
Accrued income taxes	833,000	545,000
Total current liabilities	154,280,000	125,274,000
Long-term debt, less current portion shown above	152,971,000	215,001,000
Deferred credits and other long-term liabilities	18,677,000	17,097,000
Redeemable preferred stock: $10.81 Series C Cumulative Preferred Stock; stated value $100 per share; authorized and issued 150,000 shares at December 31, 1988 and 1989 (liquidation value of $100 per share; $15,000,000 in the aggregate at December 31, 1988 and 1989)	15,000,000	15,000,000
Shareholders' investment:		
Preferred stock—		
Series B Variable Rate Cumulative Preferred Stock, stated value $50 per share; authorized 350,000 shares; issued and outstanding 306,000 shares at December 31, 1988 and 1989 (liquidation value of $50 per share, $15,300,000 in the aggregate at December 31, 1988 and 1989)	15,300,000	15,300,000
Undesignated—authorized 1,500,000 shares at December 31, 1988 and 1989; none issued	–	–
Common stock, par value $5 per share; authorized 25,000,000 shares; issued 5,012,646 shares at December 31, 1988 and 1989	25,063,000	25,063,000
Additional paid-in capital	53,793,000	53,058,000
Retained earnings	46,156,000	21,255,000
	140,312,000	114,676,000
	$481,240,000	$487,048,000

ALLIED PRODUCTS CORPORATION AND CONSOLIDATED SUBSIDIARIES
CONSOLIDATED STATEMENTS OF INCOME (LOSS)
For the Years Ended December 31, 1987, 1988 and 1989

	Year Ended December 31,		
	1987	1988	1989
Net sales	$496,878,000	$577,515,000	$564,614,000
Cost of products sold	419,203,000	480,064,000	474,313,000
Gross profit	77,675,000	97,451,000	90,301,000
Selling and administrative expenses	64,656,000	70,776,000	75,992,000
	13,019,000	26,675,000	14,309,000
Other costs and expenses—			
Interest expense	16,567,000	18,834,000	24,532,000
Other (income) expense, net	(1,912,000)	1,024,000	59,000
Provision for writedown of inventory to net realizable value and other consolidation costs	–	–	10,000,000
	14,655,000	19,858,000	34,591,000
Income (loss) before income taxes	(1,636,000)	6,817,000	(20,282,000)
Provision for income taxes	–	276,000	–
Income (loss) before cumulative effect of a change in accounting principle	(1,636,000)	6,541,000	(20,282,000)
Cumulative effect on prior years of changing to a different method of accruing for certain dealer costs	–	–	(2,141,000)
Net income (loss)	$ (1,636,000)	$ 6,541,000	$(22,423,000)

NOTES TO CONSOLIDATED FINANCIAL STATEMENTS

1. Summary of Significant Accounting Policies: Accounting Changes

In 1989, the Company changed its method of costing a certain portion of its inventory within the Agricultural Equipment Group from the last-in, first-out (LIFO) method which does not exceed market to the lower of first-in, first-out (FIFO) cost or market. In recent years, the cost of these inventories has stabilized. The adoption of this accounting change had the effect of decreasing the net loss in 1987 by $35,000 ($.01 per common share), increasing net income in 1988 by $1,089,000 ($.21 per common share) and no effect on the net loss in 1989. The change more accurately reflects the financial position of the Company. Previously issued consolidated financial statements and related notes to consolidated financial statements have been restated to reflect the effects of changes associated with this accounting change.

Also in 1989, the Company changed its method of recognizing expenses associated with certain dealer costs within the Agricultural Equipment Group. The new method better matches expenses with revenue recognition. This change resulted in a one-time charge to income of $2,141,000 ($.43 per common share) and is reflected in the accompanying Consolidated Statements of Income (Loss) as "Cumulative effect on prior years of changing to a different method of accruing for certain dealer costs."

Income Taxes

During 1988, the Company adopted SFAS No. 96—Accounting for Income Taxes—on a retroactive basis. Income taxes are provided on income for financial reporting purposes, after adjustment for income and expense items that will never enter into the computation of taxes payable.

Investment tax credits were accounted for as a reduction of the provision for income taxes during the year the applicable assets were placed in service or when realized.

3. *Income Taxes:*

The Company recorded no credit for income taxes in 1987 and 1989 as the Company had no tax loss carrybacks available to reduce the pre-tax loss of those years. During 1988, the Company recorded a tax provision of $2,756,000. Offsetting a major portion of this provision was the utilization of net operating loss carryforwards of $2,480,000 resulting in a net tax provision of $276,000. In future years, the Company will utilize its tax loss carryforwards to reduce taxes payable.

The reconciliation of the differences between the effective income tax rate and the Federal statutory rate is shown below:

	Year Ended December 31, 1988	
	Amount (In thousands of dollars)	Percent Pre-Tax Income
Provision for income taxes at the federal statutory rate	$ 2,318	34%
Utilization of net operating loss carryforward	(2,480)	(36)
Permanent book over tax difference on acquired assets	392	5
Effect of companies on the equity basis	131	2
Other, net	(85)	(1)
Provision for income taxes	$ 276	4%

The Company's consolidated Federal income tax returns through 1985 have been examined by the Internal Revenue Service. All items were resolved with no detriment to the Company.

At December 31, 1989, the Company has available net operating loss carryforwards of up to $246,785,000 (of which $214,747,000 results from the Company's acquisitions of Xonics, Cooper, White Farm, Lilliston and Verson) which expire between 1991 and 2004 and investment tax credit carryforwards of $2,829,000 (which expire between 1990 and 2001) including up to $1,737,000 resulting from these acquisitions. Net operating loss carryforwards include $39,089,000 of net loss carryforwards which may be utilized only against income, if any, of certain former subsidiaries of Xonics which currently are not actively engaged in a business.

In responding to the following questions, you may assume that the corporate tax rate Allied would use in all computations of deferred tax effects is constant at 34%.

REQUIRED:

1. Examine the reconciliation of the difference between the effective income tax rate and the federal statutory rate provided in Note 3, then respond to the following:
   (a) Explain how Allied derived the $2,318 figure.
   (b) What does the caption "Permanent book over tax difference on acquired assets" mean to you relative to the computation of tax expense for Allied? Are these amounts increasing or decreasing taxable income relative to book income?
   (c) Assume the Tax Code measures taxable income from investments using the cost method, while GAAP requires the use of the equity method. Explain what implication this would have on your interpretation of the amounts under the caption "Effect of companies on the equity basis."
   (d) Assume the category of "Other, net" reflects the consequences of other temporary differences. In the absence of the tax loss and tax credit carryforwards, what effect would these temporary differences have had on taxable income relative to book income? Give some examples of temporary differences that might create this effect.

2. If Allied had been able to employ the guidelines of SFAS No. 109 on accounting for operating loss and tax credit carryforward benefits in 1989, how would the total assets, liabilities, and shareholders' investment have changed? What would have happened to the company's leverage ratio. (You may assume that all benefits are more likely than not to be realized for this analysis.)

3. Based on the information in the case, does it seem likely that Allied will recognize the entire benefits of the operating loss carryforwards? What factors enter into your analysis? What implication would this have for your response to Requirement 2, if any?

4. How were the total tax effects accounted for in 1989 (as reported by Allied) allocated between income from continuing operations and the cumulative effect of the change in accounting principle? Was this in accordance with the requirements of GAAP? Why or why not? (The intraperiod tax allocation rules under SFAS No. 96 are identical to those discussed in the chapter.)

5. Assume that Allied used the indirect method to prepare its cash flow statement for each year presented. What adjustments, if any, were required in the cash flow statement to arrive at cash flows from operations?

6. If you were the CEO of Allied when the FASB adopted the requirements of SFAS No. 109 and you had the option of adopting these requirements before they were mandatory, would you adopt No. 109 early? Why or why not?

HONEYWELL INC.

At the end of 1988, Honeywell, Inc. operated in four major business areas: home and building automation and control, industrial automation and control, space and aviation systems, and defense and marine systems. Home and building automation and control were essentially involved in climate control and security systems for private residential and office buildings. Industrial automation and control were principally involved in data recording and systems for the control of manufacturing operations. Space and aviation systems were involved in flight controls for commercial and military aircraft, along with spacecraft controls; and defense and marine systems were principally engaged in development of weapons systems for the government.

Honeywell adopted the requirements of SFAS No. 96 for accounting for income taxes as of January 1, 1988. It had previously employed the comprehensive deferral method of accounting for income taxes. Selected excerpts from Honeywell's 1988 financial reports follow:

Dollars and Shares in Millions Except Per Share Amounts	1988	1987	1986	1985	1984	1983
RESULTS OF OPERATIONS						
Sales	$7,148.3	$6,688.4	$5,386.9	$5,000.3	$4,544.1	$4,247.3
Cost of sales	5,426.3	4,783.2	3,851.0	3,500.3	3,149.3	2,958.5
Research and development	323.4	289.8	246.7	242.1	218.7	208.0
Selling, general and administrative	1,275.3	1,100.2	985.4	875.9	776.8	721.7
Discontinuance of product lines	150.8					
Gain on sale of real estate	(33.7)					
Nonrecurring items			219.4			
Interest—net	216.9	112.3	57.0	55.4	31.7	45.2
Equity income	(9.8)	(8.5)	(12.4)	(9.9)	(7.7)	(1.8)
	7,349.2	6,277.0	5,347.1	4,663.8	4,168.8	3,931.6
Income (loss) from continuing operations before income taxes	(200.9)	411.4	39.8	336.5	375.3	315.7
Provision for income taxes[1]	234.0	157.7	26.9	116.9	91.0	110.1
Income (loss) from continuing operation[2]	$ (434.9)	$ 253.7	$ 12.9	$ 219.6	$ 284.3	$ 205.6
Income (loss) from discontinued operations net of income taxes			(3.3)	55.8	25.3	25.6
Provision for (loss) on disposal of discontinued operations net of income taxes			(407.7)	6.2	(70.6)	
Net income (loss)[2]	$ (434.9)	$ 253.7	$ (398.1)	$ 281.6	$ 239.0	$ 231.2
EARNINGS (LOSS) PER COMMON SHARE						
Continuing operations[1,2]	$ (10.22)	$ 5.75	$ .28	$ 4.80	$ 6.06	$ 4.48
Discontinued operations			(.07)	1.22	.54	.55
Provision for (loss) on disposal of discontinued operations			(9.04)	.14	(1.50)	
Net income (loss)[2]	$ (10.22)	$ 5.75	$ (8.83)	$ 6.16	$ 5.10	$ 5.03
CASH DIVIDENDS PER COMMON SHARE	$ 2.10	$ 2.025	$ 2.00	$ 1.95	$ 1.90	$ 1.80
FINANCIAL POSITION						
Working capital						
Current assets	$2,763.6	$2,790.7	$2,169.5	$2,406.4	$2,357.4	$2,042.9
Current liabilities	2,394.0	2,124.7	2,249.3	1,229.8	1,217.3	1,043.3
	$ 369.6	$ 666.0	$ (79.8)	$1,176.6	$1,140.1	$ 999.6
Capitalization						
Short-term debt	$ 314.8	$ 751.4	$ 881.2	$ 230.4	$ 253.4	$ 161.7
Long-term debt	800.7	762.1	672.0	712.7	821.6	842.4
Total debt	1,115.5	1,513.5	1,553.2	943.1	1,075.0	1,004.1
Stockholders' equity	1,731.3	2,245.3	2,221.2	2,566.9	2,380.9	2,313.7
	$2,846.8	$3,758.8	$3,774.4	$3,510.0	$3,455.9	$3,317.8

Statement of Financial Position

ASSETS (dollars in millions)	1988	1987
CURRENT ASSETS		
Cash and temporary cash investments	$ 180.4	$ 405.1
Receivables	1,310.2	1,286.4
Inventories	1,134.5	1,099.2
Deferred income taxes	138.5	
	2,763.6	2,790.7
INVESTMENTS AND ADVANCES	237.6	252.6
PROPERTY, PLANT AND EQUIPMENT		
Property, plant and equipment	2,540.4	2,518.4
Less accumulated depreciation	1,181.7	1,068 2
	1,358.7	1,450.2
OTHER ASSETS		
Long-term receivables	68.5	141.0
Goodwill	118.0	84.6
Patents, licenses and trademarks	203.1	225.9
Software and other intangibles	275.6	299.0
Other	64.0	88.7
Net assets of discontinued operations		69.6
TOTAL ASSETS	$5,089.1	$5,402.3

LIABILITIES AND STOCKHOLDERS' EQUITY	1988	1987
CURRENT LIABILITIES		
Short-term debt	$ 314.8	$ 751.4
Accounts payable	284.6	251.3
Customer advances	63.9	58.5
Income taxes	316.9	163.1
Accrued compensation and benefit costs	383.7	331.6
Accrued interest	153.3	29.6
Other accrued liabilities	876.8	539.2
	2,394.0	2,124.7
LONG-TERM DEBT	800.7	762.1
OTHER LIABILITIES	125.9	183.2
DEFERRED INCOME TAXES	37.2	87.0
STOCKHOLDERS' EQUITY		
Common stock—$1.50 par value; Authorized—130,000,000 shares; Issued—1988—47,343,325 shares; 1987—47,347,207 shares	71.0	71.0
Additional paid-in capital	634.9	648.8
Retained earnings	1,239.6	1,763.6
Treasury stock—1988—4,215,626 shares; 1987—4,819,338 shares	(314.6)	(358.4)
Accumulated foreign currency translation	100.4	120.3
	1,731.3	2,245.3
TOTAL LIABILITIES AND STOCKHOLDERS' EQUITY	$5,089.1	$5,402 3

5. Nonrecurring Items

In 1986 Honeywell announced plans to realign its operations and to focus on its core businesses. As a result of the implementation of these plans, Honeywell recorded nonrecurring charges of $219.4, reducing income from continuing operations $134.4 ($2.98 per share) during the fourth quarter of 1986.

Charges resulting from business reorganizations, plant consolidations and relocation, termination of operations and revaluation of goodwill amounted to $165.4, reducing income from continuing operations $107.1 ($2.37 per share).

Termination costs related to a work force reduction of 3,200 employees amounted to $54.0, reducing income from continuing operations $27.3 ($0.61 per share).

6. Discontinued Product Lines

In 1988 Honeywell sold Training and Control Systems Division, a provider of electronic simulation-based military training systems, for $114.0. The sale price is subject to contingent contractual adjustments. Also sold in 1988 were a protection services subsidiary in the U.K. for $51.9, and the water management systems business of a U.S. subsidiary for $13.5.

In 1988 Honeywell announced its intention to sell its Electro Optics semiconductor operations located in Colorado Springs, Colo. These planned sales reflect Honeywell's resolve to continue focusing on core businesses where it has a competitive advantage. The income statement pretax loss of $150.8 on discontinuance of product lines includes the profits on the sale of product lines in 1988 and provisions for the anticipated losses on disposition of the other product lines currently held for sale.

7. Income Taxes

In 1988 Honeywell adopted Financial Accounting Standard No. 96 (FAS 96), "Accounting for Income Taxes," and elected not to restate prior years. The cumulative effect of this change to January 1, 1988 was not significant and has been included in 1988 tax expense. Had this change in accounting not been made, net income would have been approximately $20.0 more than reported in the 1988 consolidated income statement .

The components of income from continuing operations before income taxes consist of the following:

	1988	1987	1986
Domestic	$(393.6)	$254.4	$(14.3)
Foreign	193.7	157.9	52.4
Intercompany eliminations	(1.0)	(0.9)	1.7
	$(200.9)	$411.4	$ 39.8

The provision for income tax on that income is as follows:

	1988	1987	1986
Current Tax Expense			
United States	$ 285.4	$ 68.9	$ 53.2
Foreign	90.5	63.5	31.3
State and local	46.4	10.4	11.1
Total current	422.3	142.8	95.6
Deferred Tax Expense			
United States	(182.0)	9.6	(57.3)
Foreign	2.6	1.0	(4.3)
State and local	(8.9)	4.3	(7.1)
Total deferred	(188.3)	14.9	(68.7)
Total Provision for Income Taxes	$ 234.0	$157.7	$ 26.9

The U.S. current tax expense shown above is after reductions of $31.6 in 1988 reflecting the use of a tax capital loss carryforward, and of $4.6 in 1986 due to the use of U.S. tax credits.

Taxes paid were $185.5 in 1988, $92.5 in 1987 and $49.2 in 1986.

Deferred income taxes are provided for the temporary differences between the financial reporting basis and the tax basis of Honeywell's assets and liabilities.

Significant temporary differences and their effects on deferred tax expense are:

	1988	1987	1986
Excess of tax over book depreciation	$ 8.7	$24.2	$ (2.1)
Long-term contracts installment sales, and sale/leasebacks deferred for tax purposes	(121.3)	3.8	10.1
Nonrecurring items	10.1	50.0	(75.3)
Employee benefits	(25.2)	(31.2)	
Asset valuation reserves	(27.2)	(14.6)	
Miscellaneous accruals	(29.5)	(19.8)	4.3
Restructuring reserves	(38.1)		
Losses on discontinuance of product lines	(64.3)		
Changes in unrecorded tax benefits related to future deductions	163.1		
Interest	(38.5)		
State and local	(8.9)	4.3	(7.1)
Other	(17.2)	(1.8)	1.4
Total	$(188.3)	$14.9	$(68.7)

The provision for income taxes differs from the amount computed using U.S. statutory rates as follows:

	1988	1987	1986
Taxes on income at U.S. federal statutory rates	$ (68.3)	$164.6	$18.3
U.S. tax credits			(4.6)
State taxes	24.7	8.8	2.2
Variation in tax rates on foreign income	26.0	(5.9)	1.2
Foreign withholding taxes and additional taxes on foreign dividends	44.4		
Equity income	(3.3)	(3.2)	(6.3)
Revaluation of goodwill	(3.0)		17.5
Capital loss carryforward	(31.6)		
Adjustments to effective tax rates used in recording tax assets and liabilities	(87.2)		
Unrecorded tax benefit related to future tax deductions	146.0		
Other	5.9	(6.6)	(1.4)
Provision for income taxes	$234.0	$157.7	$26.9

In 1988 certain adjustments to current and deferred income tax liabilities were necessitated by recent court decisions and legislation. The provision for income taxes includes the net effect of these adjustments to the extent that deferred tax assets could not be recognized under FAS 96. Additionally, in 1988 Honeywell recorded $113 of interest expense relating to disputed tax issues in prior years.

Provision has not been made for U.S. or additional foreign taxes on $316.4 of undistributed earnings of international subsidiaries as those earnings are considered to be permanently reinvested in the operations of those subsidiaries. It is not practicable to estimate the amount of tax that might be payable on the eventual remittance of such earnings. On remittance, certain foreign countries impose withholding taxes. The amount of withholding tax that would be payable on remittance of the entire amount of such undistributed earnings would approximate $27.9.

Foreign tax credits of $47.7 are available through 1993 to offset U.S. taxes on foreign source income, subject to certain annual limitations.

Operating loss, alternative minimum tax loss and capital loss carryforwards at December 31, 1988, for financial reporting purposes were $429.3, $69.2 and $65.3 respectively.

Operating loss carryforwards expire in 2004 to 2006; alternative minimum tax loss carryforwards expire in 2006 to 2022; and capital loss carryforwards expire in 1992 to 1993.

Foreign subsidiaries had financial reporting and tax operating loss carryforwards of $32.2 and $14.3, respectively.

REQUIRED:

1. Based on the information provided in Note 7, what were the maximum marginal corporate tax rates for Honeywell in 1986, 1987, and 1988, respectively? Explain how you arrived at your conclusion.

2. Honeywell reports that the effects of adopting the asset/liability method for valuation of deferred tax balances in 1988 was not significant. What conditions must have existed for this to be the case?

3. Examine the breakdown of the provision for taxes into its current and deferred components provided in Note 7. Provide a rationale for why it is possible to have current tax expense and a deferred tax benefit in the same year (1986) and both current and deferred tax expense in the next year (1987). How is it possible to report an operating loss of over $200 million dollars and still have current taxable income as Honeywell reported in 1988?

4. Examine the schedule of significant temporary differences and their effects on deferred tax expense as provided in Note 7, then respond to the following:

   (a) Assume the nonrecurring item listed in the schedule refers to the information in Note 5. How much of the tax effect of the nonrecurring items discussed in Note 5 arose from Honeywell's ability to deduct a portion of these costs from its tax return in 1986? Given the nature of these items, provide a general description of the relationship between the recognition of these costs for book and tax purposes over the 1986–1988 period.

   (b) Assuming the pattern of effects reported for long-term contracts, installment sales, and sale/leasebacks are primarily driven by the use of the installment method for tax and full accrual for book purposes, what does the pattern of tax effects for these temporary differences tell you about what is going on with these transactions over the 1986–1988 time period? Are these effects increasing or decreasing taxable income relative to book income?

   (c) Briefly explain why employee benefits might be a source of temporary differences. Elsewhere in the financial report, Honeywell indicates that it adopted the requirements of SFAS No. 87 relating to defined benefit pension plans in 1987. Is there any reason why this might have contributed to the rise in deferred taxes indicated in the post-1987 time period?

   (d) Speculate on why an asset valuation reserve or the restructuring reserves might generate deferred tax effects? Are these items causing book income to be above or below taxable income for each year in the 1986–1988 time frame?

   (e) What does the information provided on depreciation differences suggest about the growth in Honeywell's depreciable asset base over the three years presented? What does this imply about the reversal of these differences in aggregate for Honeywell?

   (f) Why might losses recorded at the time a decision is made to discontinue a product line, as described in Note 6, give rise to deferred tax effects? Are these effects for Honeywell creating a deferred tax asset or liability?

5. In a portion of Note 7, Honeywell indicates that it has the following types of loss and credit carryforwards at December 31, 1989:

Operating loss carryforward	$429.3
Capital loss carryforward	65.3

None of these have been recognized for financial reporting purposes as of December 31, 1989. Using a federal tax rate of 34%, and ignoring state tax effects, how would Honeywell's balance sheet at December 31, 1988, have changed if it had recognized the full benefit of all these carryforwards? If you were Honeywell's auditor and wished to evaluate the firm's ability to recover these benefits in accordance with the requirements of SFAS No. 109, what information from the case would be useful in arriving at your decision regarding the need for an allowance? (Note that Honeywell could not have availed itself of the requirements of SFAS No. 109 in 1988.)

6. How will the income tax effects for 1987 and 1988 be reflected in Honeywell's cash flow statement, assuming it prepares this statement using the indirect method? Where will Honeywell include the tax effects of the discontinued segment in its cash flow statement for 1986?

PART 6

Recapitulation

The Cash Flow Statement

Cash flows is the term used to describe various transactions causing cash to move into and out of a business during a period. Cash inflows or receipts include: amounts collected from customers; amounts realized on the sale of property, plant, and equipment; and amounts obtained by issuing debt and equity securities. Cash outflows or expenditures include: amounts paid to employees and suppliers; amounts paid to acquire plant and equipment; and amounts paid as dividends to stockholders.

Analysis of firms' cash flows—how cash is obtained and how it is spent—is an important activity for managers as well as existing and potential investors and lenders. Managers need to know the source of cash to meet obligations as they arise. If the business's day-to-day operations will not provide enough cash so the firm can pay its debts, then the firm will need to obtain external financing or consider the sale of certain assets to raise the necessary cash. Lenders are concerned with how their loans will be repaid. Investors need to know whether a firm is likely to have enough cash to pay dividends. The **cash flow statement** is designed to provide useful information about a firm's cash flows by describing how cash was obtained and how it was spent.

As firms have increased the amount and number of transactions financed by various forms of debt, analysis of firms' cash flows has become increasingly important. Subsequently, the demand for better information about a firm's cash flows has increased. One transaction that has increasingly focused attention on firms' cash flows is the **leveraged buy-out (LBO)**. In an LBO, investors buy the corporation's stock using a relatively small amount of their own money and a relatively large amount of borrowed money. Very often, the assets of the company acquired secure the debt. With an LBO, the firm experiences an enormous increase in debt ("leverage"). For example, Kohlberg, Kravis, and Roberts acquired RJR Nabisco for $25 billion in 1989, adding approximately $23 billion in debt to the firm's balance sheet in the process. Needless to say, such an increase in leverage requires close attention to the firm's cash flows, which it uses to make interest and principal payments on the debt.

The accounting profession has focused on providing financial statement users with information about firms' funds flows—i.e., how firms obtain and spend their funds. **Funds** is a more general term than cash and can be defined in many ways, including either cash or, more commonly, *working capital*. APBO No. 3, issued in 1963, was the first authoritative pronouncement covering these "funds statements." Opinion No. 3 recommended, but did not require, the inclusion of a supplementary funds statement, the statement of source and application of funds.[1] From 1971 to 1988 and under APBO No. 19, firms had to include a funds statement, with a recommended title of "Statement of Changes in Financial Position," whenever they prepared a full set of financial statements.[2] Despite the change in title, the objective of the required statement of changes in financial position was the same as that of the optional statement of source and application of funds: to provide information on how firms obtained and spent their funds during a period.

For a number of reasons, the statement of changes in financial position was probably never as useful a financial statement as the accounting policy makers had intended. First, APBO No. 19 permitted several definitions of funds, including cash, cash and marketable securities, quick assets (cash, marketable securities, and receivables), and working capital (current assets minus current liabilities). This hindered comparisons of funds flows among firms. Second, the format of the statement was so flexible that it created confusion and further hindered comparisons.

Over the period that a statement of changes in financial position (SCFP) was required, more and more firms recognized that the most useful definition of funds was, in fact, cash. By the mid 1980s, a majority of firms were probably preparing SCFPs with funds defined as cash. According to the American Institute of Certified Public Accountants' 1986 edition of *Accounting Trends and Techniques*, in 1982, 58 percent of the 600 firms surveyed presented their SCFPs with funds defined as working capital, and 42 percent defined funds as cash. By 1985, only 37 percent of the 600 firms surveyed used the working capital definition of funds, and 63 percent defined funds as cash.

The Financial Accounting Standards Board (FASB) recognized these problems with the SCFP and trends in financial reporting practice. In November 1987, the FASB responded to recommendations of such prestigious organizations as the Financial Executives Institute by issuing *Statement of Financial Accounting Standards No. 95*, "Statement of Cash Flows." SFAS No. 95 requires that for fiscal years ending after July 15, 1988, firms provide a new funds statement, now called the cash flow statement, in lieu of a statement of changes in financial position. This chapter takes a close look at this newest financial state-

---

[1] "The Statement of Source and Application of Funds," *Accounting Principles Board Opinion No. 3* (New York: AICPA, 1963), para. 8.

[2] "Reporting Changes in Financial Position," *Accounting Principles Board Opinion No. 19* (New York: AICPA, 1971), para. 7.

ment—the definitions of items included in the statement, its format, and techniques for its preparation.

By considering the cash flow statement in the final chapter in the text, we do not imply that it is an afterthought or is of less importance than other information presented. Rather, by placing it at the end, we can consider the cash flow implications of topics considered throughout the text. Not only will this chapter provide a thorough examination of the cash flow statement, it will also serve as a review of many of the topics considered in the previous chapters.

OVERVIEW OF THE CASH FLOW STATEMENT

The FASB has long recognized the need to provide information about cash flows in the financial statements. *Statement of Financial Accounting Concepts No. 1*, published in 1978, states that:

> Financial reporting should provide information to help investors, creditors, and others assess the amounts, timing, and uncertainty of prospective net cash inflows to the related enterprise.[3]

The cash flow statement, as subsequently defined by the FASB, helps individuals assess future cash flows by providing information about past cash flows. Although financial statements are used to help resolve uncertainty about future events, they are fundamentally historical records of events and transactions that have occurred.

The purpose of a cash flow statement, as the FASB espoused in SFAS No. 95, is a straightforward enough matter:

> The primary purpose of a statement of cash flows is to provide relevant information about the cash receipts and cash payments of an enterprise during a period.[4]

The Board maintains that this information, used in conjunction with the rest of the financial statements, will help financial statement users make the following assessments about a firm:

1. Its ability to generate positive future net cash flows
2. Its ability to meet its obligations and pay dividends and its need for external financing
3. Reasons for any differences between net income and related cash receipts and expenditures
4. The effects of both cash and noncash investing and financing transactions during the period.[5]

---

[3] "Objectives of Financial Reporting by Business Enterprises," *Statement of Financial Accounting Concepts No. 1* (Stamford, CT: FASB, 1978), para. 37.

[4] "Statement of Cash Flows," *Statement of Financial Accounting Standards No. 95* (Stamford, CT: FASB, 1987), para. 4.

[5] *Ibid.*, para. 5.

Notice that despite its title, the cash flow statement also provides information about certain **noncash transactions**.

SFAS No. 95 imposes some structure on the format of the cash flow statement. First, the statement must explain the change during the period in the balance of a firm's cash and its assets that are deemed to be essentially equivalent to cash. These **cash equivalents** are very liquid, short-term investments that a firm typically makes to earn a return on otherwise idle cash balances. To qualify as cash equivalents for the purposes of a cash flow statement, these investments must be readily convertible into a known amount of cash *and* have a maturity date of three months or less from the date of investment.[6] U.S. Treasury bills and commercial paper (short-term promissory notes of corporations) are examples of securities that may qualify as cash equivalents.

Absent any noncash investing and financing transactions, a cash flow statement is essentially nothing more than a summary of cash receipts and cash expenditures. SFAS No. 95 requires a firm to classify these receipts and expenditures as the result of one of three mutually exclusive types of transactions: investing activities, financing activities, and operating activities.

Let us review a cash flow statement presented in accordance with the provisions of SFAS No. 95. Exhibit 21.1 contains Ajax Corp.'s cash flow statement, along with a required schedule that reconciles net income to net cash provided by operating activities. We will be deriving the statement and reconciliation schedule later in the chapter. For now, we will use it simply to illustrate some of the essential features of the statement.

As you can see, Ajax's cash flow statement classifies cash receipts and expenditures into three categories: cash flows from operating activities, cash flows from investing activities, and cash flows from financing activities. SFAS No. 95 also requires disclosure of any material noncash investing and financing activities in connection with the cash flow statement. Ajax apparently did not enter into any of these transactions during the year. Had it done so, Ajax would have included in these noncash investing and financing activities items such as:

> Converting debt to equity; acquiring assets by assuming directly related liabilities, such as purchasing a building by incurring a mortgage to the seller; obtaining an asset by entering into a capital lease; and exchanging noncash assets or liabilities for other noncash assets or liabilities.[7]

Let us examine the essential characteristics of each type of cash flow activity.

Operating Activities

Operating activities are those directly involved in providing goods and services to customers. According to the FASB, activities that are neither investing nor financing are, by default, operating activities. As a general rule,

> Cash flows from operating activities are generally the cash effects of transactions and other events which enter into the determination of net income.[8]

---

[6] *Ibid.*, para. 7.

[7] *Ibid.*, para. 32.

[8] *Ibid.*, para. 21.

EXHIBIT 21.1
Ajax Corp.—
Cash Flow
Statement for
the Year Ended
December 31, 1995

AJAX CORP.
Cash Flow Statement for the Year Ended December 31, 1995
($000s)

Cash flows from operating activities:	
Collections from customers	$23,370
Paid for interest	(90)
Paid to suppliers	(15,090)
Paid to employees	(5,390)
Paid for taxes	(1,000)
Net cash provided by operating activities	1,800
Cash flows from investing activities:	
Proceeds from sale of fixed assets	875
Paid to purchase fixed assets	(2,000)
Net cash used for investing activities	(1,125)
Cash flows from financing activities:	
Proceeds from short-term borrowing	250
Paid to retire short-term notes payable	(100)
Paid for cash dividends	(600)
Paid to retire long-term debt	(75)
Net cash used for financing activities	(525)
Net increase in cash	$ 150

AJAX CORP.
Reconciliation of Net Income to Net Cash Provided by Operating Activities
For the Year Ended December 31, 1995
($000s)

Net income		$1,625
Less:	Gain on sale of fixed assets	(40)
	Increase in accounts receivable	(130)
	Increase in inventory	(230)
Plus:	Depreciation	150
	Increase in accounts payable	180
	Increase in wages payable	115
	Increase in taxes payable	130
Net cash provided by operating activities		$1,800

Noncash operating activities include the purchase and sale of goods and services on account. Ajax's operating cash flows represent amounts received from customers and amounts paid for various expense items.

Investing Activities

Firms invest in a wide variety of assets, including productive assets such as machinery and equipment, real estate, debt or equity securities, and loans to individuals or other firms. A firm classifies any cash paid or received in connection with the acquisition or disposal of these investment assets on its cash flow statement as a cash flow from **investing activities**. Noncash investing activities include acquiring the stock of another corporation by issuing shares of stock. Ajax's investing activities all relate to the purchase and sale of fixed assets.

Firms are also sometimes said to "invest" in such assets as inventory and accounts receivable in connection with their operations. However, for the purposes of SFAS No. 95, these activities are viewed as operating activities.

Financing Activities

Firms obtain financing from owners and lenders. Any cash paid to or received from owners (including dividends) or from lenders in connection with borrowing transactions (except interest) is viewed as a cash flow from **financing activities**. Noncash financing transactions include financing the use of assets through a capital lease transaction. Ajax's financing activities include borrowing and repayment of borrowings and payment of dividends.

Both dividends and interest can be viewed as providing a return for those individuals and organizations supplying a firm's financing. However, under SFAS No. 95, only dividends are viewed as a financing activity, while interest payments are viewed instead as an operating activity. Why do firms classify these two similar kinds of transactions differently on their cash flow statements? The Board was interested in classifying the cash consequences of items that are included in the determination of net income as operating items. Therefore, since GAAP recognize interest but not dividends as an expense, the FASB decided to classify the payment of interest as an operating activity.

Direct Vs. Indirect Method

Perhaps the most controversial part of SFAS No. 95's requirements are those provisions dealing with how to present the cash flows from operating activities. In fact, based in large part on the rules for presenting operating cash flows, three of the seven FASB members voted against SFAS No. 95, leaving only the barest of majorities in favor of the standard. Let us examine this controversy for a moment.

The now superseded APBO No. 19 required firms to present funds provided or used by operations on their statements of changes in financial position (SCFP) in either of two formats known as the direct and indirect methods. Under the **direct method**, firms provide a list of operating sources and uses of funds, ending in a net source or use of funds. (Cash flows from operating activities are presented in the direct format in Ajax Corp.'s cash flow statement in Exhibit 21.1.) Under the **indirect method** and to reconcile net income with net source or use of funds from operations, firms make a series of adjustments to net income to arrive at the net source or use of funds from operations. The reconciliation of net income to net cash provided by operating activities, also contained in Exhibit 21.1, presents net cash provided by operating activities in the indirect format.

Notice that while both approaches yield the same total, they do not provide the same level of detail. The direct approach provides information about which transactions generated cash inflows from operating activities ("collections from customers") and which transactions generated cash outflows from operating transactions ("paid for interest," etc.). The reconciliation approach of the indirect method only provides the net inflow or outflow of cash from operating activities. On the other hand, the indirect calculation permits a reconciliation of net operating cash flow with net income. The direct method does not. Since most firms have traditionally used (and still use) the indirect approach, their SCFPs were less informative than they might have been because they lacked the detailed information about operating cash inflows and outflows.

The prevalence of the indirect method in connection with the old statements of changes in financial position has led to much confusion. For instance, notice how depreciation is added to net income on the reconciliation schedule in Exhibit 21.1. The indirect presentation leads many users of financial statements to conclude that depreciation is a "source of funds" since it is a positive quantity on the statement. For instance, consider the following quote from the business press:

> Cash flow will fatten whenever capital spending—a main user of cash—decreases and depreciation—a big cash booster—increases.[9]

Of course, depreciation is not a source of funds at all. When a firm records depreciation as an expense, it receives no cash. Rather, it adds depreciation back on the reconciliation because depreciation is an expense it subtracted to derive net income. However, depreciation does not require any use of the firm's funds in the same period. Because this confusion exists over the indirect method, many (including three members of the Board) hoped that the FASB would require the direct method.

Instead, the FASB opted for a compromise position. It prefers that firms use the direct method. However, if a firm uses the direct method in its cash flow statement, it must also use the indirect method to reconcile net income to net cash flow provided by operating activities, as shown in Exhibit 21.1. The fact that firms can (and most do) present their operating cash flows by the indirect method means that some financial statement readers are probably still confused by what the calculation shows. We make an effort to clear this confusion in the next section.

Before turning to the preparation of the statement, let us stop for a moment and ask ourselves just what Ajax's cash flow statement tells us. During the year ended December 31, 1995, Ajax had a net cash inflow of $1,800,000 from operating activities. That is, it collected $1,800,000 more from its customers than it paid for various operating costs. This net cash provided by operating activities was enough to pay a net $1,125,000 for investing activities and a net $525,000 for financing activities and to increase the firm's cash balance by $150,000. Ajax appears to be in a healthy situation. It has financed

---

[9] Leah J. Nathans, "Why 'Cash Flow' Might Still be Magic Words," *Business Week* (December 25, 1989), p. 114.

its operating and investing activities, paid $600,000 in dividends, and repaid $75,000 in long-term debt with only a relatively modest increase of $150,000 in short-term debt. However, notice that Ajax's cash outflows from investing activities have been reduced by the $875,000 received from the sale of certain fixed assets.

PREPARING THE CASH FLOW STATEMENT

The procedures used in preparing the cash flow statement depend on the information the preparer has available. We will consider two examples that differ in the amount and type of information provided. In the first example, the information consists of beginning and ending balance sheets, a statement of income and retained earnings, and a summary of cash receipts and expenditures. In the second and more difficult example, the cash flow statement must be prepared without the summary of cash receipts and expenditures.

Preparing the Cash Flow Statement: A Simple Example

To illustrate the preparation of a cash flow statement and to discuss some format issues with concrete examples, let us begin with the fairly straightforward example of Ajax Corp., whose balance sheets and statement of income and retained earnings are shown in Exhibits 21.2 and 21.3, respectively.

The Direct Method   We will begin by preparing a cash flow statement with net cash flows from operating activities presented by the direct method.

Step 1: Identify Cash Receipts and Expenditures   At the most basic level, preparing a cash flow statement is nothing more than reviewing the firm's cash receipts and expenditures during the period and classifying them as cash flows from operating activities, investing activities, or financing activities. Therefore, let us begin with a list of cash receipts and expenditures aggregated by type of transaction (receipt or expenditure). A summary of this type would be prepared by reviewing the activity for the year in Ajax's cash accounts and is contained in Exhibit 21.4.

Step 2: Classify Cash transactions as Operating, Investing, or Financing Activities   Ajax's summary of cash receipts and expenditures is a primitive cash flow statement in that it shows sources and uses of cash. However, it can be far more informative if we classify the cash receipts and expenditures according to type. As we have seen, SFAS No. 95's classification scheme requires that cash transactions be classified into three mutually exclusive sets: operating activities, investing activities, or financing activities.

Recall that cash flows from operating activities are generally the cash effects of transactions and other events that enter into the determination of net income. Therefore, the following receipts and expenditures from the above summary appear properly classified as *operating activities*:

EXHIBIT 21.2
Ajax Corp.—
Balance Sheets

AJAX CORP.
Balance Sheets
($000s)

	DECEMBER 31,	
ASSETS:	**1995**	**1994**
Cash	$ 400	$ 250
Accounts receivable, net	2,750	2,620
Inventories	4,565	4,335
Total current assets	$ 7,715	$ 7,205
Fixed assets, at cost	10,350	9,225
Less: Accum. depreciation	2,100	1,990
Net fixed assets	$ 8,250	$ 7,235
Total assets	$15,965	$14,440
LIABILITIES & EQUITY:		
Notes payable	$ 250	$ 100
Accounts payable to suppliers	1,820	1,640
Accrued wages payable	225	110
Taxes payable	350	220
Total current liabilities	$ 2,645	$ 2,070
Long-term debt	5,050	5,125
Common stock	2,200	2,200
Additional paid-in capital	3,400	3,400
Retained earnings	2,670	1,645
Total stockholders' equity	$ 8,270	$ 7,245
Total liabilities & equity	$15,965	$14,440

EXHIBIT 21.3
Ajax Corp.—
Statement of
Income and
Retained Earnings
for the Year Ended
December 31, 1995

AJAX CORP.
Statement of Income and Retained Earnings
For the Year Ended December 31, 1995
($000s)

Net sales		$23,500
Cost of goods sold	$14,050	
S,G,A expenses	6,495	
Depreciation	150	
Interest expense	90	$20,785
Gain on sale of fixed assets		40
Income before taxes		$ 2,755
Income taxes		1,130
Net income		$ 1,625
Cash dividends		600
Increase in retained earnings		$ 1,025

EXHIBIT 21.4

Ajax Corp.— Summary of Cash Receipts and Expenditures for the Year Ended December 31, 1995

AJAX CORP.
Summary of Cash Receipts and Expenditures
For the Year Ended December 31, 1995
($000s)

Cash Receipts:	
Collections from customers	$23,370
Proceeds from short-term borrowing	250
Proceeds from sale of fixed assets	875
Total cash receipts	24,495
Cash Expenditures:	
Paid to purchase fixed assets	$ 2,000
Paid for interest	90
Paid to retire short-term notes payable	100
Paid for cash dividends	600
Paid to suppliers	15,090
Paid to employees	5,390
Paid for taxes	1,000
Paid to retire long-term debt	75
Total cash expenditures	24,345
Increase in Cash Balance	$ 150

Operating receipts:	
Collections from customers	$23,370
Operating expenditures:	
Paid for interest	90
Paid to suppliers	15,090
Paid to employees	5,390
Paid for taxes	1,000

According to Statement No. 95, investments include loans, debt and equity instruments, property, plant, and equipment, and other productive assets. Therefore, the cash flows from Ajax's investing activities include:

Investing receipts:	
Proceeds from sale of fixed assets	$ 875
Investing expenditures:	
Paid to purchase fixed assets	2,000

Financing activities involve transactions with the owners of the firm and transactions that involve borrowing and repaying (or otherwise settling) obligations. Ajax's cash transactions of this type include the following:

Financing receipts:

Proceeds from short-term borrowing	$250

Financing expenditures:

Paid to retire short-term notes payable	100
Paid for cash dividends	600
Paid to retire long-term debt	75

Step 3: Prepare the Cash Flow Statement   We can now put these amounts into a cash flow statement with the results shown earlier in Exhibit 21.1. The cash flow statement we have just prepared uses the direct method to present net cash provided by operating activities. That is, the operating sources and uses of cash are explicitly listed. An acceptable alternative is the indirect method, which adjusts net income to derive net cash provided by operating activities. We present this approach next.

The Indirect Method   When a firm uses the direct method, it must also provide a schedule that reconciles net income to net cash flow from operating activities. This schedule must show the indirect method of calculating net cash provided by operating activities. Moreover, a firm must also disclose information about all noncash investing and financing activities in connection with the cash flow statement. Our approach so far satisfies neither of these requirements.

Since we must disclose the noncash investing and financing transactions, we need a way to identify them. Reviewing the year's activity in the asset, liability, and stockholders' equity accounts would reveal such transactions. However, we can accomplish the same goal indirectly by seeing if the transactions we are already aware of explain the changes in the balances on Ajax's balance sheet. One convenient mechanism for this purpose is the transactions analysis worksheet presented in Exhibit 21.5. As we shall see, this worksheet also helps us prepare the required schedule that reconciles net income to net cash flow from operating activities.

The worksheet presents the balances presented on the firm's balance sheet in columnar form, with beginning balances on the top line and ending balances on the bottom. Each line reflects the effects of a particular transaction or type of transaction in the aggregate. These transactions were identified from the firm's summary of cash receipts and expenditures and its statement of income and retained earnings already presented. If these known transactions explain all the changes observed on the balance sheet, then we need not worry about noncash investing and financing transactions.

Let us examine each line on the worksheet in some detail to understand it completely. A few general observations are in order. Since all revenues, expenses, gains, and losses are closed to retained earnings at year-end, for the purposes of the worksheet, we simplify the procedure somewhat by bypassing these temporary accounts and recording such transactions as direct increases and decreases of retained earnings. (We do not imply that the firm recorded them in this fashion.) Refer to the worksheet as we review the way each trans-

AJAX CORP.
Transactions Analysis Worksheet
For the Year Ended December 31, 1995
($000s)

	Cash	Accts. Rec.	Inv.	Net Fixed Assets	Notes Pay.	Accts. Pay.	Wages Pay.	Taxes Pay.	LTD	Common Stock	APIC	Ret'd Earn.
Balance 12/31/94	250	2,620	4,335	7,235	100	1,640	110	220	5,125	2,200	3,400	1,645
Collections	23,370	(23,370)										
Borrow short-term	250				250							
Sale of fixed assets	875			(835)								40
Fixed assets acq'd.	(2,000)			2,000								
Interest	(90)											(90)
Repay notes payable	(100)				(100)							
Cash dividends	(600)											(600)
Payments to suppl.	(15,090)					(15,090)						
Payments to empl.	(5,390)						(5,390)					
Payments for taxes	(1,000)							(1,000)				
LTD repaid	(75)								(75)			
Net sales		23,500										23,500
Cost of goods sold			(14,050)									(14,050)
SGA expenses						990	5,505					(6,495)
Depreciation				(150)								(150)
Income tax expense								1,130				(1,130)
Inventory purchases			14,280			14,280						
Balance 12/31/95	400	2,750	4,565	8,250	250	1,820	225	350	5,050	2,200	3,400	2,670

EXHIBIT 21.5

Ajax Corp.—
Transactions
Analysis Worksheet
for the Year Ended
December 31, 1995

action is recorded. We need to provide explanations for the changes in all balances. Therefore, our worksheet is not complete until all columns total to the ending balances we observe on the December 31, 1995 balance sheet. Moreover, each line on the worksheet is analogous to a journal entry in that it preserves the *fundamental accounting identity* that assets equal the sum of liabilities and stockholders' equity. That is, if a particular transaction increases assets, then liabilities and/or stockholders' equity must increase by the same aggregate amount.

The first transactions entered on the worksheet are the cash receipts and expenditures.

Collections: All of Ajax's sales are on account; therefore, all amounts collected from customers are collections on account. The effect of these collections was to increase Ajax's cash balance and decrease its accounts receivable balance.

Short-term borrowing: Short-term borrowing transactions increase the firm's cash balance and also increase its notes payable liability, here by $250,000.

Sale of fixed assets: The sale of fixed assets generated proceeds of $875,000. From the income statement, we observe that the transaction produced a gain of $40,000. That is, the proceeds from the sale exceeded the net book value of the assets sold by this amount; and the worksheet reflects the gain as an increase in retained earnings. If the proceeds were $875,000 and this amount reflects a gain of $40,000, the net book value of the assets sold must have been $835,000; and the worksheet reflects this decrease in net fixed assets. By concentrating on the net fixed assets balance rather than the gross amount and accumulated depreciation separately, we avoid the necessity of separately determining and recording the historical cost and accumulated depreciation of the assets sold.

Fixed assets acquired: The summary of cash receipts and expenditures showed a $2,000,000 expenditure for the acquisition of fixed assets. Therefore, our worksheet reflects this transaction as a reduction of the firm's cash balance and a corresponding increase in net fixed assets.

Interest: The payment for interest and amount of interest expense shown on the firm's income statement are both $90,000. Therefore, we reflect the interest payment and expense together on the worksheet as reductions of cash and retained earnings. Please note that, in general, the amount of interest paid need not equal the amount shown as interest expense. (The expense is recognized on the accrual basis and, therefore, is an expense of the period in which it is incurred, regardless of when it is paid.)

Repay notes payable: When Ajax repays its liabilities, the firm's cash balance decreases as does its liability balance. Our worksheet reflects the $100,000 repayment of notes payable accordingly.

Cash dividends: Cash dividends represent a distribution of the corporation's cash to the stockholders, reducing both cash and retained earnings by $600,000 in this case.

Payments to suppliers: As many firms do, Ajax records all obligations to suppliers as accounts payable before making payment. Therefore, the actual payments totalling $15,090,000 reduce the firm's cash balance and accounts payable by this amount.

Payments to employees: The payments to employees of $5,390,000 reduce the firm's cash balance and the firm's liability to its employees, shown on the balance sheet as accrued wages payable. Since a liability of $110,000 existed at the start of the year, we can conclude that only $5,280,000 of the wages paid were earned in 1995. Moreover, since there is a liability for wages payable of $225,000 at year-end, it follows that Ajax has not paid all of the wages earned in 1995 and included as wage expense on the 1995 income statement.

Payments for taxes: Ajax paid a total of $1,000,000 for taxes in 1995, reducing the firm's cash balance and its liability for taxes payable by that amount.

Long-term debt (LTD) repaid: This payment is handled in a manner consistent with other payments of existing obligations. Both the cash balance and the liability balance decrease by $75,000.

Having recorded all of the cash receipts and expenditures on our worksheet, we can turn to the transactions summarized on the firm's statement of income and retained earnings (Exhibit 21.3). Some of these items—e.g., the interest expense, the gain on the sale of fixed assets, and the dividends—have already been recorded and we need to be careful, therefore, to avoid recording them twice.

Net sales: Since Ajax's sales are all on account, the net sales for the year of $23,500,000 increased the accounts receivable and the retained earnings balances by that amount.

Cost of goods sold: Cost of goods sold represents the cost of the products Ajax sold to its customers during the year. Therefore, inventory is reduced by $14,050,000, representing the cost of the items delivered to customers. The corresponding expense is shown as a reduction of retained earnings in the same amount.

Selling, general, and administrative (SGA) expenses: Ajax classifies all wage expense in this income statement category. Therefore, the $6,495,000 expense amount includes wage expense. As we observed above in recording the payments to employees, the $5,390,000 paid to employees included $110,000 earned but unpaid at the end of 1994 and $5,280,000 earned this year. However, note the liability for wages payable in the amount of $225,000 at December 31, 1995. It follows that the employees earned this amount, in addition to the $5,280,000 they were paid for wages earned this year, for a total wage expense of $5,505,000. If the total SGA expense is $6,495,000 and $5,505,000 of this amount represents wage expense, then all other expense categories amount to $990,000 ($6,495,000 − 5,505,000). This represents the cost of goods and services consumed during the period in the firm's selling, general, and administrative functions. Ajax records all nonwage costs as accounts payable. Therefore, the effect of the SGA expense on our worksheet is to increase accounts payable by $990,000, increase wages payable by $5,505,000, and reduce retained earnings by the total amount of the expense, $6,495,000.

Depreciation: Depreciation expense represents the fixed asset cost allocated to expense in 1995. Thus, we show it on the worksheet as a reduction of the net fixed assets balance and a reduction of retained earnings for the amount of expense recognized for the year, $150,000.

Income tax expense: The firm records its tax obligations in the taxes payable liability. The expense for the year of $1,130,000 represents the amount of tax obligations incurred this year. Therefore, we show the tax expense as an increase in taxes payable and a corresponding decrease in retained earnings.

That concludes the transactions summarized on both the summary of cash receipts and expenditures and the statement of income and retained earnings. If no other transactions had occurred, we should find that all columns total to the ending balances observed on the December 31, 1995, balance sheet. That is not the case here.

Inventory purchases: The totals of the inventory column and the accounts payable column are below their respective ending balances by $14,280,000. Apparently, another transaction occurred, which increased inventory and accounts payable by this amount. That must represent the cost of inventory purchased on account, and we show this final transaction on the worksheet accordingly.

Now our worksheet is complete. First, let us examine our worksheet to determine if any noncash transactions occurred that require disclosure in connection with our cash flow statement. We did uncover one noncash transaction of which we were previously unaware—namely, the purchase of $14,280,000 of inventory on account. This, however, is a noncash operating transaction, and SFAS No. 95 only requires disclosure of noncash investing and financing transactions. Therefore, we need not concern ourselves with any disclosures of noncash investing and financing activities.

We can use the worksheet to prepare our schedule that reconciles net income to net cash flows from operating activities. While a worksheet such as this is not essential for this purpose, it helps us understand the reconciliation. In a schedule that reconciles net income to net cash flows from operating activities, there are two types of reconciling items. First, because income is recognized on the accrual basis, we need to reconcile between the amount of revenues and expenses recognized and the corresponding cash receipts and expenditures. Second, the income statement may include gains and losses resulting from certain nonoperating, or investing and financing, activities such as gains or losses from the sale of facilities or from the retirement of long-term debt. Since these are not operating items, they should not be included in our calculation of net cash provided by operating activities.

First, let us observe our worksheet to determine what caused any differences between revenues and expenses and the corresponding cash receipts and expenditures.

By focusing on the accounts receivable column of our worksheet, we can observe the difference between the revenue amount of $23,500,000 shown on the income statement and the corresponding cash collections amount of $23,370,000 we have already observed. Because Ajax earned more revenue than it collected, the balance in accounts receivable increased by $130,000, from $2,620,000 at the start of the year to $2,750,000 at year-end. Had Ajax collected more revenue than it earned, we would have observed the balance in accounts receivable decreasing instead of increasing. Thus, the difference between the amount of revenue earned and the amount of cash collected from customers can be "explained" or reconciled by the change in accounts receivable. In other words, since the receivable balance increased by $130,000, we know Ajax collected $23,370,000 ($130,000 less than the revenue earned of $23,500,000). The reconciliation of revenues and collections would appear as follows:

Net sales	$23,500,000
Less: Increase in accounts receivable	(130,000)
Collections from customers	$23,370,000

Let us aggregate the cost of goods sold of $14,050,000 and selling, general, and administrative expense of $6,495,000 into total operating expenses of $20,545,000. Likewise, let us aggregate payments to suppliers of $15,090,000 and payments to employees of $5,390,000 into total payments for operating expenses of $20,480,000. This aggregation is necessary since the accounts payable balance relates to both items.

How can we reconcile the difference of $65,000 between these two amounts? Since the inventory balance increased by $230,000, from $4,335,000 to $4,565,000, we know that Ajax purchased $230,000 *more* inventory ($14,280,000) than it sold ($14,050,000). Likewise, by examining the accounts payable column of our worksheet and observing that the balance has increased by $180,000, from $1,640,000 to $1,820,000, we know that Ajax paid $180,000 *less* than the sum of the inventory purchased ($14,280,000) and the nonwage SGA expense incurred ($990,000), or $15,090,000. Finally, by examining the wages payable column of our worksheet and observing that the balance has increased by $115,000, from $110,000 to $225,000, we know that Ajax has paid $115,000 *less* to employees than the $5,505,000 it recognized as wage expense for the year, or $5,390,000. Thus, the difference between operating expenses and the amount paid for operating expenses can be reconciled as follows:

Total operating expenses	($20,545,000)
Less: Increase in inventory	(230,000)
Plus: Increase in accounts payable	180,000
Increase in wages payable	115,000
Total payments for operating expenses	($20,480,000)

Since interest expense and interest paid are exactly the same amounts, no reconciling items are needed. We can reconcile the difference between tax expense ($1,130,000) and taxes paid ($1,000,000) by examining the taxes payable column on our worksheet. Because Ajax paid less than the tax obligation incurred for the year, the liability for taxes payable increased by $130,000, from $220,000 to $350,000. Thus, the increase in taxes payable is the reconciling item between tax expense and tax paid, as follows:

Tax expense	($1,130,000)
Plus: Increase in taxes payable	130,000
Payments for taxes	($1,000,000)

Two other items require reconciliation between Ajax's income statement and cash flow statement. First, certain expenses, such as depreciation and amortization of the previously incurred costs of leased assets and intangible assets, require no cash payment whatsoever in the current period. Thus, the $150,000 of depreciation expense on Ajax's income statement is a reconciling item in its entirety. Second, any gains or losses from nonoperating items are reconciling items since we are attempting to reconcile to the net cash provided by *operating* activities. Thus, the $40,000 gain from the sale of fixed assets on Ajax's income statement is also a reconciling item in its entirety.

All of these reconciling items are summarized in Exhibit 21.6, which is more elaborate than the reconciliation in Exhibit 21.1. Rather than show the reconciling items as adjustments to a particular revenue or expense to obtain a particular cash receipt or expenditure as in Exhibit 21.6, it is more common to show them as adjustments to net income to obtain net cash provided by operating activities as in Exhibit 21.1. Thus, the only real difference between the direct and indirect methods of presenting net cash flows from operating activities is the treatment of reconciling items. If the reconciling items are treated as adjustments to net income, then the resulting net cash flows from operating activities will be presented in the indirect format. If, however, the reconciling items are treated as adjustments to the components of net income—particular revenues and expenses, gains and losses—then the resulting net cash flows from operating activities will be presented in the direct format.

If a cash flow statement is prepared with net cash provided by operating activities presented by the indirect method, the reconciliation we have just prepared will substitute for the direct listing of operating cash flows; and the statement will appear as shown in Exhibit 21.7.

For a rather simple and straightforward situation, this has been a rather lengthy examination of the preparation of a cash flow statement. We introduced a worksheet technique that was probably not necessary, given the case's simple nature. When we turn next to a more comprehensive example, the worksheet will be considerably more useful. Make sure you are comfortable with the approach taken in this simple case before proceeding further.

Preparing the Cash Flow Statement: A Comprehensive Example

Superior Products Corp. has provided the following information: income statement (Exhibit 21.8) and statement of stockholders' equity (Exhibit 21.9) for the year ended December 31, 1995; balance sheets as of December 31, 1995

EXHIBIT 21.6
Ajax Corp.—
Reconciliation
Between the
Income Statement
and Cash Flows
from Operating
Activities for the
Year Ended
December 31, 1995

AJAX CORP.
Reconciliation Between the Income Statement and Cash Flows from Operating Activities
For the Year Ended December 31, 1995
($000s)

Income Statement Items:		Reconciling Items:		Operating Cash Flows:	
Net sales	$23,500	Increase in accounts receivable	$(130)	Collections from customers	$ 23,370
		Increase in inventory	(230)		
Cost of goods sold	(14,050)	Increase in accounts payable	180	Payments to suppliers	(15,090)
SGA expenses	(6,495)	Increase in wages payable	115	Payments to employees	(5,390)
Total operating expenses	(20,545)		(65)	Payments for operating exp.	(20,480)
Interest expense	(90)			Interest paid	(90)
Tax expense	(1,130)	Increase in taxes payable	130	Taxes paid	(1,000)
Depreciation expense	(150)	Depreciation expense	150		0
Gain on sale of fixed assets	40	Gain on sale of fixed assets	(40)		0
Net income	$ 1,625	Net reconciling items	$ 175	Net cash flows from operating activities	$ 1,800

EXHIBIT 21.7
Ajax Corp.—
Cash Flow
Statement for
the Year Ended
December 31, 1995
(Indirect Method)

AJAX CORP.
Cash Flow Statement
For the Year Ended December 31, 1995
(Indirect Method)
($000s)

Cash flows from operating activities:	
Net income	$1,625
Less: Gain on sale of fixed assets	(40)
Increase in accounts receivable	(130)
Increase in inventory	(230)
Plus: Depreciation	150
Increase in accounts payable	180
Increase in wages payable	115
Increase in taxes payable	130
Net cash provided by operating activities	$1,800
Cash flows from investing activities:	
Proceeds from sale of fixed assets	875
Paid to purchase fixed assets	(2,000)
Net cash used for investing activities	(1,125)
Cash flows from financing activities:	
Proceeds from short-term borrowing	250
Paid to retire short-term notes payable	(100)
Paid for cash dividends	(600)
Paid to retire long-term debt	(75)
Net cash used for financing activities	(525)
Net increase in cash	$ 150

and 1994 (Exhibit 21.10); and additional information relevant to the task of preparing a cash flow statement, presented below.

Additional information:
1. Depreciation of property, plant, and equipment: Depreciation of $5,672 is included in selling, general, and administrative expenses on the 1995 income statement.
2. Amortization of intangible assets: Amortization of intangible assets in the amount of $245 is included in selling, general, and administrative expenses on the 1995 income statement.
3. Capital leases: Certain equipment (primarily delivery trucks) are acquired under long-term lease contracts, which are accounted for as capital leases. Amortization of leased equipment in the amount of $808 is included in selling, general, and administrative expenses on the 1995 income statement.
4. **Sale of Davenport facility:** On March 19, 1995, the company sold the Davenport, Iowa facility, which had a net book value of $4,865 at the date of sale. This sale produced a gain of $7,003, which is included in other income on the 1995 income statement.

SUPERIOR PRODUCTS CORP. AND SUBSIDIARIES
Income Statement
For the Year Ended December 31, 1995
($000s)

Revenues	$115,053
Less: Provision for doubtful accounts	(2,301)
Net revenues	112,752
Costs and expenses:	
Cost of goods sold	68,233
Selling, general, and administrative	37,498
	105,731
Operating income	7,021
Other income and (expense):	
Interest expense	(3,226)
Other income, net	6,959
	3,733
Income before taxes	10,754
Taxes on income	1,826
Net income	$ 8,928

EXHIBIT 21.8
Superior Products Corp. and Subsidiaries— Income Statement for the Year Ended December 31, 1995

SUPERIOR PRODUCTS CORP. AND SUBSIDIARIES
Statement of Stockholders' Equity
For the Year Ended December 31, 1995
($000s)

	CAPITAL STOCK	RETAINED EARNINGS	TREASURY STOCK
Balance, 12/31/94	$19,621	$18,356	$(1,090)
Net income		8,928	
Stock dividend	5,406	(5,406)	
Cash dividend		(5,899)	
Purchase treasury stock			(119)
Balance, 12/31/95	$25,027	$15,979	$(1,209)

EXHIBIT 21.9
Superior Products Corp. and Subsidiaries— Statement of Stockholders' Equity for the Year Ended December 31, 1995

EXHIBIT 21.10

Superior Products
Corp. and
Subsidiaries—
Balance Sheets

SUPERIOR PRODUCTS CORP. AND SUBSIDIARIES
Balance Sheets
($000s)

	DECEMBER 31,	
ASSETS:	**1995**	**1994**
Cash and marketable securities	$ 1,457	$ 1,023
Accounts receivable	13,035	12,224
Less: Allowance for doubtful accounts	(521)	(489)
Net accounts receivable	12,514	11,735
Inventories	21,320	18,209
Prepaid expenses	256	317
Total current assets	35,547	31,284
Property, plant, and equipment	73,975	78,245
Less: Accumulated depreciation	(35,055)	(36,882)
Net property, plant, and equipment	38,920	41,363
Equipment held under capital leases	21,021	14,996
Less: Accumulated amortization	(4,560)	(3,752)
Net equipment held under capital leases	16,461	11,244
Investments, at cost	8,234	7,015
Intangible assets, net	3,174	2,025
TOTAL ASSETS	$102,336	$92,931

LIABILITIES & EQUITY:		
Notes payable	$ 0	$ 505
Current portion of long-term debt	1,240	1,456
Trade accounts payable	11,750	10,496
Accrued expenses	2,478	2,103
Income taxes payable	312	254
Total current liabilities	15,780	14,814
Long-term debt	41,067	37,013
Deferred taxes	5,692	4,217
Stockholders' equity		
Capital stock (20 million shares authorized)	25,027	19,621
Retained earnings	15,979	18,356
Less: Treasury stock, at cost	(1,209)	(1,090)
	39,797	36,887
TOTAL LIABILITIES AND EQUITY	$102,336	$92,931

5. **Long-term debt:** The company's long-term debt consists of the following amounts:

	December 31, 1995	December 31, 1994
10.5% Bonds, due 2001	$30,000	$30,000
Less: Unamortized discount	(1,486)	(1,762)
	28,514	28,238
Term loan payable	2,025	4,323
Capital lease obligations	11,768	5,908
Total long-term debt	42,307	38,469
Less: Current portion	(1,240)	(1,456)
Long-term debt, net of amounts currently due	$41,067	$37,013

6. **Taxes on income:** The primary difference between the company's taxable income and its income before taxes is attributable to its use of accelerated depreciation methods for federal income tax purposes and the straight-line method for financial reporting purposes.

7. **Other income, net:** Other income, net, on the 1995 income statement consists of the following amounts:

Gain on the sale of Davenport facility	$7,003
Miscellaneous other, net	(44)
Other income, net	$6,959

8. **Investment in Backwater Plumbing:** In 1995, the company acquired a 10 percent interest in Backwater Plumbing Corp. for $1,219 in cash. The investment is carried at cost, which is approximately equal to market value at December 31, 1995.

9. **Acquisition of patents:** In 1995, the company acquired certain patents from Sutol Development Corp. at a cost of $1,394.

10. **Miscellaneous:** All purchases and sales are made on account. All acquisitions of property, plant, and equipment, if any, except those involving capital leases, were for cash. The balances for prepaid expenses and accrued expenses do not include any amounts for interest. All retirements of short-term and long-term debt were for cash.

Our task is to prepare a cash flow statement for Superior Products Corp. with net cash provided by operating activities presented by the direct method and a separate schedule that reconciles net income to net cash provided by operating activities. In this example, no summary of cash receipts and expenditures is provided. Therefore, we will derive the cash transactions by using the transactions analysis worksheet, which is contained in Exhibit 21.11.

Using the information provided in the income statement and the additional information, we will use the transactions analysis worksheet in Exhibit 21.11

EXHIBIT 21.11

Superior Products
Corp.—Transactions
Analysis Worksheet

SUPERIOR PRODUCTS CORP.
Transactions Analysis Worksheet
1995
($000s)

	Cash	A/R	Inv. Purch.	Ppd. Exp.	Net PPE	Leased Assets	Invest.	Intang.	N/P	C/LTD	A/P	Accd. Expenses	T/P	LTD	Def. Tax.	C. Stk.	Ret. Earn.	T Stk.
12/31/94	1,023	11,735	18,209	317	41,363	11,244	7,015	2,025	505	1,456	10,496	2,103	254	37,013	4,217	19,621	18,356	(1,090)
Revenues, net		112,752															112,752	
CGS			(68,233)														(68,233)	
SGA					(5,672)	(808)		(245)				30,773					(37,498)	
Interest expense	(2,950)													276			(3,226)	
Sale of facil.	11,868				(4,865)												7,003	
Other expenses											44						(44)	
Tax expense													351		1,475		(1,826)	
Stock dividend																5,406	(5,406)	
Cash dividend	(5,899)																(5,899)	
Purch. T. stock	(119)																	(119)
Investment	(1,219)						1,219											
Acq patents	(1,394)							1,394										
Collections	111,973	(111,973)																
Inv. purch.	71,344		71,344								71,344							
Pay sup. & emp	(100,471)			(61)							(70,134)	(30,398)						
Incr. PPE	(8,094)				8,094													
Incr. leased eq.						6,025								6,025				
Decr. N/P	(505)								(505)									
Taxes paid	(293)												(293)					
Decr. LTD	(2,463)									(216)				(2,247)				
12/31/95	1,457	12,514	21,320	256	38,920	16,461	8,234	3,174	0	1,240	11,750	2,478	312	41,067	5,692	25,027	15,979	(1,209)

to explain the changes we observe in the asset, liability, and stockholders' equity balances between the two balance sheet dates. Some of these changes will be the result of cash transactions we will need to include on our cash flow statement. Some may be the result of noncash financing and investing activities we will need to disclose in connection with our cash flow statement. Let us turn to the worksheet and observe the process by which these transactions are identified.

The worksheet is set up as before. One column is provided for each asset, liability, and stockholders' equity amount shown on the balance sheet, except that assets with related contra-account balances—e.g., accounts receivable and the allowance for doubtful accounts—are shown net. This shortcut will actually make completion of the worksheet easier since there will be fewer balances whose changes need to be explained. Balances at the start of the period, December 31, 1994, are inserted across the top of the worksheet, while balances at the end of the period, December 31, 1995, are inserted across the bottom. We start with the information contained on the income statement to explain changes in the balances. Refer to Exhibit 21.11 as we discuss each line of the worksheet.

Revenues, net: Since all sales are on account, the firm's net revenues of $112,752,000 increased the net accounts receivable balance and increased retained earnings. As before, we do not use separate columns on the worksheet for revenues and expenses since Superior closes these temporary accounts to retained earnings at year-end.

Cost of goods sold (CGS): Superior sold goods costing $68,233,000 during the year. This implies that goods costing this amount were removed from inventory, and Superior recognized their cost as an expense of the period, reducing retained earnings.

Selling, general, and administrative expenses (SGA): This category of expenses totals $37,498,000 and includes numerous items, including depreciation of $5,672,000, amortization of leased assets of $808,000, and amortization of intangibles of $245,000. These three items are shown on the worksheet as reductions of the net assets to which they relate. After accounting for these three items $30,773,000 of SGA expense still remains to be recorded. These items could have had any or all of the following effects: reduce cash, reduce prepaid expenses, increase accounts payable, and increase accrued expenses. Since we cannot determine the effect on each of these items without a detailed analysis of the account balances, we will arbitrarily show the entire $30,773,000 as an increase in accrued expenses. While this is almost certainly not the way these items were originally recorded, we will still be able to determine the amount of cash paid to suppliers and employees with this procedure as we show below.

Interest expense: The information Superior provided about its long-term debt shows that the unamortized bond discount decreased by $276,000 during the year without any corresponding reduction in the principal amount outstanding. Therefore, it seems certain that of the $3,226,000 of the total interest expense shown on the income statement, $276,000 represents the amortization of bond discount and the remainder, or $2,950,000, was paid in cash. Thus, our worksheet shows cash decreasing by $2,950,000, long-term debt increasing by $276,000 as the discount is amortized, and retained earnings decreasing by the total amount of $3,226,000.

Sale of facilities: The "other income, net" category includes the gain of $7,003,000 on the sale of the Davenport facility and miscellaneous other expenses of $44,000. The additional information provides the net book value of the Davenport assets sold at $4,865,000. Since the sale produced a gain, we know that the proceeds from the sale were greater than net book value by the amount of the gain, or $11,868,000 in total. Therefore, our worksheet shows cash increasing by this amount, net property, plant, and equipment decreasing by the net book value of the Davenport facilities sold, and retained earnings increasing by the amount of the gain.

Other expenses: The $44,000 of other expenses included in "other income, net" is shown as an increase in accounts payable and a decrease in retained earnings. We do not know for certain that these items increased accounts payable. However, handling this item in this manner, we will still be able to determine the total amount of cash paid to suppliers and employees.✓

Tax expense: The income statement shows tax expense of $1,826,000. Notice on the balance sheet that the deferred tax liability has increased by $1,475,000. This implies that $351,000 of the income tax expense ($1,826,000 – $1,475,000) was payable currently and $1,475,000 of the income tax expense has been deferred and is payable in a future period.

We have now recorded all of the items summarized on Superior's income statement. Let us next turn to the items included in its statement of stockholders' equity and the additional information not already recorded in the transactions analysis worksheet.

Stock dividend: The stock dividend reduces Superior's retained earnings and increases its capital stock by $5,406,000.

Cash dividend: The cash dividend reduces Superior's retained earnings and cash balances by $5,899,000.

Purchase treasury stock (T stock): The balance in treasury stock is shown on the worksheet as a negative component of stockholders' equity. By purchasing treasury stock for $119,000 during the year, Superior reduced both its cash and stockholders' equity balances by that amount.

Investment: Superior's investment in Backwater Plumbing reduced the firm's cash balance and increased its investments by $1,219,000.

Acquisition of patents: Superior's acquisition of patents from Sutol Development decreased its cash balance and increased its intangible assets balance by $1,394,000.

Now that we have recorded all of the information provided in the worksheet, we must determine what other transactions have apparently taken place. This is accomplished by examining each column and determining what additional activity is required to yield the ending balances at December 31, 1995.

Collections: To arrive at the ending balance of $12,514,000 in net accounts receivable, we need to record a transaction that will reduce the balance by $111,973,000. The net accounts receivable balance is reduced by collections on account. Since Superior collects cash from customers, the cash balance increases by the same amount.

Inventory purchases (Inv. Purch.): To arrive at the ending inventory balance of $21,320,000, a transaction that increases inventory by $71,344,000 is required. This must represent the cost of inventory purchased during the year. Since Superior purchases on account, accounts payable increase by the same amount.

Payments to suppliers and employees: The amount paid to suppliers and employees can be determined as the composite effect on prepaid expenses, accounts payable, and accrued expenses. The individual changes necessary to derive these three accounts' ending balances have no real significance because they depend on the way we have recorded items previously. For instance, the fact that we need to reduce prepaid expenses by $61,000 to derive the ending balance of $256,000 is due to the fact that none of the SGA or other expenses were shown on the worksheet previously as reducing the prepaid expense balance. If some of the SGA expense had been recorded as a reduction of prepaid expense, rather than as an increase in accrued expense, the amounts needed to explain the changes in both prepaid expenses and accrued expenses would differ; but the total effect would not change. So, regardless of how we handled SGA and other expenses earlier, the total payments to suppliers and employees must agree with the total of $100,471,000 shown on the worksheet. You may want to convince yourself of this by changing the way SGA expenses were handled earlier and seeing that the resulting payment amount is not affected.

Increase property, plant, and equipment (PPE): After depreciation and the sale of the Davenport facilities have been recorded, we need to increase the net PPE by $8,094,000 to derive the ending balance of $38,920,000. This must represent the cost of PPE acquired during the year for cash.

Increase in leased equipment: After amortization for the year has been recorded, we can infer that leased equipment has increased by $6,025,000, apparently as the result of additional capital lease transactions. These transactions increase Superior's capital lease obligations (which are included in long-term debt) by the same amount.

Decrease notes payable (N/P): The $505,000 notes payable balance has disappeared, apparently because it was repaid in full.

Taxes paid (T/P): After increasing taxes payable by the amount of the current year's tax expense, which is currently due, the balance needs to decrease by $293,000 to yield the ending balance of $312,000. This must represent the taxes paid during the year.

Decrease long-term debt (LTD): Long-term debt has been reduced by $2,247,000 (noncurrent portion) and $216,000 (current portion) for a total of $2,463,000. This represents the amount of long-term debt retired during the year.

At last, the worksheet is complete. Our interest is primarily on the transactions summarized in the cash column. All that remains is to classify these cash transactions as either operating activities, investing activities, or financing activities and to put them in the appropriate format for a cash flow statement. Based on the definitions the FASB provided, the cash transactions we have identified for Superior Products Corp. would probably be classified as shown in Exhibit 21.12 (under the direct method).

Since disclosure of the effects of noncash investing and financing activities is required in connection with the cash flow statement, Superior would have to disclose the following transactions that we identified in completing our worksheet:

Noncash investing and financing activities:

Assets acquired in capital lease transactions $6,025

Moreover, since our cash flow statement presents net cash provided by operating activities by the direct method, SFAS No. 95 also requires a reconcil-

EXHIBIT 21.12

Superior Products Corp.— Cash Flow Statement for the Year Ended December 31, 1995 (Direct Method)

SUPERIOR PRODUCTS CORP.
Cash Flow Statement
For the Year Ended December 31, 1995
(Direct Method)
($000s)

Cash flows from operating activities:	
Collections from customers	$111,973
Payments to suppliers and employees	(100,471)
Payments for interest	(2,950)
Payments for taxes	(293)
Net cash provided by operating activities	8,259
Cash flows from investing activities:	
Sale of Davenport facility	11,868
Increase property, plant, and equipment	(8,094)
Acquire investment	(1,219)
Acquire patents	(1,394)
Net cash provided by investing activities	1,161
Cash flows from financing activities:	
Repay notes payable	(505)
Cash dividends	(5,899)
Repay long-term debt	(2,463)
Purchase treasury stock	(119)
Net cash used for financing activities	(8,986)
Increase in cash balance	434
Beginning cash balance	1,023
Ending cash balance	$ 1,457

iation of net income to net cash provided by operations. By referring to the transactions analysis worksheet in Exhibit 21.11 and a summary of the reconciling items in Exhibit 21.13, you should be able to see how the reconciliation in Exhibit 21. 14 is prepared.

If a complete cash flow statement is prepared with net cash provided by operations presented by the indirect method, the result would appear as shown in Exhibit 21.15. Once again, disclosure of the noncash investing and financing activities is required under this format as well.

OTHER CASH FLOW ISSUES

Several additional issues need to be discussed before our treatment of the cash flow statement is complete.

Required Disclosures

If a firm elects to present its cash flows from operating activities in the preferred direct format, SFAS No. 95 requires that the operating cash flows should be broken down, at a minimum, into the following categories:

1. Cash collected from customers, including lessees, licensees, and the like
2. Interest and dividends received
3. Other operating cash receipts, if any
4. Cash paid to employees and other suppliers of goods or services, including suppliers of insurance, advertising, and the like
5. Interest paid
6. Income taxes paid
7. Other operating cash payments, if any

Firms are encouraged to report in even more detail if it is feasible and meaningful to do so.

If a firm elects to present its cash flows from operating activities in the indirect format, SFAS No. 95 requires that the reconciliation between net income and net cash flows from operating activities report all major classes of reconciling items. At a minimum, separate reporting of the changes in receivables, inventory, and payables pertaining to operating activities is required. In addition, disclosure of the amounts of interest and income taxes paid during the period must be required, even if the indirect format is used.

Gross and Net Cash Flows

In general, amounts reported on the cash flow statement are to be reported gross rather than net. For instance, if a firm sold plant and equipment for $25,000 in cash and spent $95,000 on new plant and equipment, it should report both of these transactions as cash flows from investing activities rather than the net amount of $70,000.

Some items are reported net because the amounts involved are relatively large, turnover is quick, and the items mature in a relatively short period.

EXHIBIT 21.13
Superior Products
Corp.—
Reconciliation
Between the
Income Statement
and Cash Flows
from Operating
Activities for the
Year Ended
December 31, 1995

SUPERIOR PRODUCTS CORP.
Reconciliation Between the Income Statement and Cash Flows from Operating Activities
For the Year Ended December 31, 1995
($000s)

Income Statement Items:		Reconciling Items:		Operating Cash Flows:	
Net revenues	$112,752	Increase in accounts receivable	(779)	Collections from customers	$111,973
		Depreciation	5,672		
		Amortization of leased assets	808		
		Amortization of intangibles	245		
		Increase in inventory	(3,111)		
Cost of goods sold	(68,233)	Decrease prepaid expenses	61		
SGA expenses	(37,498)	Increase in accounts payable	1,254		
Other expenses	(44)	Increase in accrued expenses	375		
Total operating expenses	(105,775)		5,304	Pay suppliers & employees	(100,471)
Interest expense	(3,226)	Amortization of bond discount	276	Interest paid	(2,950)
Gain on sale of facilities	7,003	Gain on sale of facilities	(7,003)		
		Deferred taxes	1,475		
		Increase in taxes payable	58		
Tax expense	(1,826)		1,533	Taxes paid	(293)
Net income	$ 8,928	Net reconciling items	$ (669)	Net cash flows from operating activities	$ 8,259

SUPERIOR PRODUCTS CORP.
Reconciliation of Net Income to Net Cash Provided by Operations
For the Year Ended December 31, 1995
($000s)

Net income	$ 8,928
Add: Depreciation	5,672
Amortization of leased assets	808
Amortization of intangibles	245
Amortization of bond discount	276
Deferred taxes	1,475
Decrease in prepaid expenses	61
Increase in accounts payable	1,254
Increase in accrued expenses	375
Increase in taxes payable	58
Less: Gain on sale of Davenport facility	(7,003)
Increase in accounts receivable	(779)
Increase in inventory	(3,111)
Net cash provided by operating activities	$ 8,259

EXHIBIT 21.14

Superior Products Corp.—Reconciliation of Net Income to Net Cash Provided by Operations for the Year Ended December 31, 1995

Thus, transactions involving investments, loans receivable, and debt are reported on a net basis if the original maturity of the item is three months or less. In some cases, a firm will receive or pay cash on behalf of a customer. Demand deposit accounts at banks or other financial institutions are a good example. In such cases, the FASB decided that net changes in these items can be reported on the cash flow statement without impairing the usefulness of the statement.

Business Combinations

When a firm acquires another firm in a business combination, the entire cost of the acquisition is treated as a cash outflow from investing activities. Some of the assets acquired (and some of the liabilities assumed) may be current items such as receivables, inventory, prepaid items, accounts payable, and accrued expenses. Thus, balances in these accounts will change as a result of an investing activity as well as the more typical operating activities. If the cash flows from operating activities are presented in the indirect format, we need to be careful to exclude the changes in current assets and liabilities resulting from the business combination in our reconciliation.

For example, suppose Parent Co. acquired Daughter, Inc. during the year. One of the asset categories acquired was Daughter's receivable balances. In figuring its cash flows from operating activities, Parent should adjust its net income by the change in its receivable balances net of receivables of Daughter acquired. Otherwise, the cash flows for these items will be counted twice: once as an operating activity and once as an investing activity. For this reason, you may observe financial statements in which the changes in receivables, invento-

SUPERIOR PRODUCTS CORP.
Cash Flow Statement
For the Year Ended December 31, 1995
(Indirect Method)
($000s)

Cash flows from operating activities:	
Net income	$ 8,928
Add: Depreciation	5,672
Amortization of leased assets	808
Amortization of intangibles	245
Amortization of bond discount	276
Deferred taxes	1,475
Decrease in prepaid expenses	61
Increase in accounts payable	1,254
Increase in accrued expenses	375
Increase in taxes payable	58
Less: Gain on sale of Davenport facility	(7,003)
Increase in accounts receivable	(779)
Increase in inventory	(3,111)
Net cash provided by operating activities	$ 8,259
Cash flows from investing activities:	
Sale of Davenport facility	11,868
Increase property, plant, and equipment	(8,094)
Acquire investment	(1,219)
Acquire patents	(1,394)
Net cash provided by investing activities	1,161
Cash flows from financing activities:	
Repay notes payable	(505)
Cash dividends	(5,899)
Repay long-term debt	(2,463)
Purchase treasury stock	(119)
Net cash used for financing activities	(8,986)
Increase in cash balance	434
Beginning cash balance	1,023
Ending cash balance	$ 1,457

non-oi

ry, and the like reported on the cash flow statement do not agree with the differences between the beginning and ending balances reported on the balance sheets. The changes reported as adjustments to net income on the cash flow statement are the result of only operating activities while the balance sheets will reflect all activities.

SUMMARY

As the FASB stated in SFAS No. 95, "The primary purpose of a cash flow statement is to provide relevant information about the cash receipts and cash payments of an enterprise during a period." This information is relevant to a variety of financial statement users, including managers, investors, and lenders. In the cash flow statement, "cash" is defined as cash and cash equivalents. Cash equivalents are investments that can be readily converted into a known amount of cash and that mature in three months or less. Cash flows are presented in the statement in one of three mutually exclusive categories: operating, investing, or financing activities. Firms must also disclose noncash investing and financing activities, either in the cash flow statement or in the accompanying notes. Cash flows from operating activities may be presented under either the direct or indirect method, although direct presentation is encouraged. If a firm uses the direct presentation of operating cash flows, it must also provide the indirect method in a separate supporting reconciliation schedule. The method used to prepare the cash flow statement will depend on the information available to the preparer. A worksheet approach such as that illustrated in this chapter is a convenient method, particularly as the complexity of the situation increases.

QUESTIONS

1. What is a *cash equivalent*?

2. Under what circumstances may a firm report the net amount of related cash receipts and expenditures rather than the gross amounts?

3. How does a firm classify cash receipts and expenditures on its cash flow statement?

4. What is a *noncash investing activity*? How would a firm handle this item on its cash flow statement?

5. What is a *noncash financing activity*? How would a firm handle this item on its cash flow statement?

6. How are the following terms defined with regard to the cash flow statement?

   (a) Operating activities

   (b) Investing activities

   (c) Financing activities

7. Briefly explain the difference between the *direct method* and the *indirect method* of presenting net cash provided by operating activities.

8. When must a firm include a schedule that reconciles net income with net cash provided by operations in connection with its cash flow statement?

9. Indicate whether the following items (a–t), which would appear on a firm's cash flow statement, should be classified as (1) cash flows from operating activities, (2) cash flows from investing activities, (3) cash flows from financing activities, or (4) noncash investing and financing activities.

   (a) Proceeds from issuance of common stock

   (b) Payment for the purchase of XYZ Corp., net of cash acquired

   (c) Common stock issued upon conversion of long-term debt

   (d) Dividends received from affiliates

   (e) Cash paid to settle product liability lawsuit

(f) Proceeds from sale of facility

(g) Principal payments under capital lease obligations

(h) Dividends paid

(i) Interest paid, net of amount capitalized

(j) Cash received from customers

(k) Interest received

(l) Payment received on note for sale of plant

(m) Proceeds from issuance of long-term debt

(n) Capital lease obligation incurred

(o) Expenditures for property, plant, and equipment

(p) Cash paid to suppliers and employees

(q) Insurance proceeds received

(r) Net borrowings under line-of-credit agreement

(s) Income taxes paid

(t) Liabilities assumed in connection with the acquisition of XYZ Corp.

10. Briefly explain how the following transaction would be presented on a cash flow statement.

Giga, Inc. invests $100,000 cash in U.S. Treasury bills due in 90 days.

EXERCISES

21-1. *Reconciling net income to net cash provided by operating activities*

Power Products Co. has calculated its net cash provided by operating activities under the direct method as follows:

Collections from customers	$ 14,605
Paid to suppliers and employees	(11,729)
Paid for taxes	(697)
Paid for interest	(116)
Net cash provided by operations	$ 2,063

Its income statement for the year ended December 31, 1995 appears as follows:

Power Products Corp.
Income Statement
For the Year Ended December 31, 1995

Sales	$14,720
Cost of goods sold	(8,605)
Selling, general, and administrative expenses	(3,101)
Depreciation	(592)
Interest expense	(114)
Income before taxes	$ 2,308
Income tax expense	(740)
Net income	$ 1,568

Balances in relevant asset and liability accounts are as follows:

	12/31/95	12/31/94
Accounts receivable	$1,220	$1,105
Inventories	745	687
Accounts payable	410	375
Taxes payable	185	142
Accrued interest	10	12

REQUIRED:

Prepare a schedule that reconciles net income to net cash provided by operating activities.

21-2. *Net cash provided by operating activities: direct and indirect*

Ross Motors, Inc. presents the following 1995 income statement and selected balance sheet information:

Ross Motors, Inc.
Income Statement
For the Year Ended December 31, 1995

Sales	$1,520,000
Cost of goods sold	1,312,000
Gross income	208,000
Depreciation expense	7,000
Other operating expense	176,000
Income before taxes	25,000
Income tax expense	8,000
Net income	$ 17,000

Ross Motors, Inc.
Selected Balance Sheet Information

	December 31, 1995	1994
Accounts receivable	$127,000	$109,000
Inventories	164,000	153,000
Prepaid insurance	2,000	4,000
Accounts payable	94,000	87,000
Accrued wages payable	6,000	7,000
Taxes payable	2,000	3,000

REQUIRED:

Calculate net cash provided by operations for Ross Motors, Inc. for the year ended December 31, 1995, under both the direct and indirect methods.

21-3. *Balance sheet; determining net cash provided by operating activities*

The following information is available for B&C Industries, Inc.

B&C Industries, Inc.
Balance Sheet
December 31, 1995

Cash	$ 10,000	Payables	$ 40,000
Receivables	40,000	Stockholders' equity	120,000
Inventory	60,000		
Plant & equipment	50,000		
	$160,000		$160,000

B&C Industries, Inc.
Income Statement
For the Year Ended December 31, 1995

Sales	$400,000
Cost of goods sold	240,000
Gross profit	160,000
Depreciation expense	5,000
Other operating expenses	135,000
Net income	$ 20,000

B&C Industries, Inc.
Cash Flow Statement
For the Year Ended December 31, 1995

Cash flows from operating activities:	
Collections from customers	$380,000
Payments to suppliers and employees	(375,000)
Net cash flows from operating activities	5,000
Cash flows from investing activities:	
Purchase of plant and equipment	(11,000)
Net cash flows from investing activities	(11,000)
Cash flows from financing activities:	
Dividends	(18,000)
Net cash flows from financing activities	(18,000)
Decrease in cash balance	$ 24,000

REQUIRED:

1. Prepare a balance sheet as of the start of the period, December 31, 1994.
2. Prepare a schedule that reconciles net income to net cash provided by operating activities for the year ended December 31, 1995.

J

21-4. *Cash flow statement: direct and indirect methods*

The beginning and ending balance sheets for Morgan Corp. appear as follows:

Morgan Corp.
Balance Sheets

	December 31,	
	1995	1994
Cash	$ 100	$ 150
Accounts receivable	650	540
Merchandise inventory	800	720
Prepaid rent	145	155
Property, plant, and equipment	1,500	1,800
Total assets	$3,195	$3,365
Accounts payable	$ 225	$ 255
Wages payable	110	145
Interest payable	60	65
Notes payable	500	400
Paid-in capital	1,000	800
Retained earnings	1,300	1,700
Total liabilities & equity	$3,195	$3,365

During the year, the following cash transactions took place:
(a) Cash collected from customers, $4,200
(b) Cash borrowed from bank, $250
(c) Cash paid in by owners, $200
(d) Cash paid to suppliers, $2,400
(e) Cash paid to employees, $1,200
(f) Cash paid for rent, $500
(g) Cash paid to the bank: $150, principal; $75, interest
(h) Cash dividends paid, $375

REQUIRED:

1. Prepare an income statement for the year ended December 31, 1995.
2. Prepare a cash flow statement (direct method) for the year ended December 31, 1995.
3. Prepare a schedule that reconciles net income to net cash provided by operations for the year ended December 31, 1995.

21-5. *Cash flow statement: direct method*

The following transactions took place in the first year of operations of Acme Wholesale, Inc., a paper products wholesaler.
(a) Acme's owners paid in a total of $50,000 cash to start the business on January 2, 1995.
(b) Space in an industrial park was leased. Monthly rent of $1,500 was paid on the first day of each month.
(c) A delivery truck was purchased at a cost of $12,000 cash.
(d) Inventory purchases for the year amounted to $210,000. All purchases were made on account.
(e) During the year, the firm's sales amounted to $294,000, all on account. The cost of goods sold was $186,000.

(f)   Employees earned $35,000 during the year.

(g)   An insurance policy covering the business against casualties was taken out on July 1, 1995. A 12-month premium of $7,500 was paid in full on that date.

(h)   Payments totalling $185,000 were made to suppliers of inventory.

(i)   Employees were paid a total of $32,000.

(j)   A total of $282,000 was collected from the firm's customers. Any remaining balances are expected to be paid in full.

(k)   Depreciation on the delivery truck was computed to be $2,400.

(l)   Other operating expenses amounted to $13,700 and were paid in cash.

(m)   The owners of the business withdrew $14,000 cash from the company.

REQUIRED:

Prepare a cash flow statement for Acme Wholesale, Inc. for the year ended December 31, 1995, in accordance with generally accepted accounting principles. Present cash provided by operating activities by the direct method.

21-6.   *Schedule to reconcile net income with cash provided by operations*

Refer to the transactions in Exercise 21-5 for Acme Wholesale, Inc.

REQUIRED:

1.   Calculate the ending balances for accounts receivable, inventory, prepaid expenses, and accounts payable.

2.   Prepare a schedule that reconciles net income with net cash provided by operations.

21-7.   *Cash flow statement: direct method*

The following is a list of transactions for Club Corp. for the year ended December 31, 1995. (In $000):

(a)   Proceeds from issuance of common stock, $1,500

(b)   Payment for the purchase of XYZ Corp., net of cash acquired, $2,775

(c)   Common stock issued upon conversion of $500 million of long-term debt, par value $125

(d)   Dividends received from affiliates, $60

(e)   Cash paid to settle product liability lawsuit, $90

(f)   Proceeds from sale of facility, $1,800

(g)   Principal payments under capital lease obligations, $375

(h)   Dividends paid, $600

(i)   Interest paid, net of amount capitalized, $660

(j)   Cash received from customers, $41,550

(k)   Interest received, $165

(l)   Payment received on note for sale of plant, $450

(m)   Proceeds from issuance of long-term debt, $1,200

(n)   Capital lease obligation incurred, $850

(o)   Expenditures for property, plant, and equipment, $3,000

(p)   Cash paid to suppliers and employees, $36,000

(q)   Insurance proceeds received, $45

(r)   Net borrowings under line of credit agreement, $900

(s)   Income taxes paid, $975

(t)   Liabilities assumed in connection with the acquisition of XYZ Corp, $1,890

REQUIRED:

Prepare a cash flow statement in accordance with generally accepted accounting principles.

PROBLEMS

21-1. *Cash flow statement: direct and indirect methods*

Green, Inc. provided the following balance sheets and income statement:

Green, Inc.
Balance Sheets
($000s)

	December 31,	
	1995	1994
Cash	$ 150	$ 100
Accounts receivable	225	200
Inventory	525	450
Total current assets	900	750
Fixed assets	1,200	1,000
Less: Accumulated depreciation	(350)	(200)
Net fixed assets	850	800
Investments	500	750
Total assets	$2,250	$2,300
Accounts payable	350	300
Accrued expenses	40	25
Total current liabilities	390	325
Bonds payable	1,000	1,150
Owners' equity	860	825
Total liabilities and equity	$2,250	$2,300

Green, Inc.
Income Statement and Statement of Owners' Equity
For the Year Ended December 31, 1995
($000s)

Sales revenue		$1,480
Cost of goods sold	$900	
Depreciation	150	
Selling and administrative expenses	300	1,350
Operating income		130
Loss on sale of investments		(50)
Net income		80
Less: Dividends		(45)
Increase in owners' equity		$ 35

REQUIRED:

1. Prepare a cash flow statement for Green, Inc. in accordance with generally accepted accounting principles. Present cash flows from operating activities in the direct approach.
2. Provide a separate schedule that reconciles net income with net cash provided by operating activities.

21-2. *Cash flow statement: direct and indirect methods*

Carbon Products, Inc. provides the following information:

Carbon Products, Inc.
Balance Sheets

	December 31, 1995	December 31, 1994
Cash	$ 1,820	$ 1,025
Accounts receivable	14,990	13,240
Less: Allow. for doubtful accts.	(745)	(620)
Net receivables	14,245	12,620
Inventories	16,105	14,445
Prepaid expenses	277	294
Total current assets	32,447	28,384
Property, plant, equipment	50,986	45,004
Less: Accumulated depreciation	(15,520)	(12,060)
Net prop., plant, equip.	35,466	32,944
Total assets	$67,913	$61,328
Notes payable	$ 7,300	$ 5,600
Accounts payable	10,539	8,870
Accrued expenses	298	482
Taxes payable	1,683	1,040
Total current liabilities	19,820	15,992
Mortgage payable	33,409	35,521
Stockholders' equity	14,684	9,815
Total liabilities and equity	$67,913	$61,328

Carbon Products Inc.
Income Statement
For the Year Ended December 31, 1995

Sales		$164,273
Less: Provision for bad debts		(3,285)
Net sales		160,988
Expenses:		
Cost of sales	(125,792)	
Depreciation expense	(3,460)	
Selling and admin. expenses	(17,938)	
Interest expense	(3,670)	(150,860)
Income before taxes		10,128
Income tax expense		(3,875)
Net income		6,253
Less: Cash dividends		(1,384)
Increase in stockholders' equity		$ 4,869

REQUIRED:

1. Prepare a cash flow statement for Carbon Products, Inc. in accordance with generally accepted accounting principles. Present cash flows from operating activities in the direct approach.
2. Provide a separate schedule that reconciles net income with net cash provided by operating activities.

21-3. *Cash flow statement: direct and indirect methods*

Kirk Corporation's balance sheets as of December 31, 1995 and 1994 and its income statement for the year ended December 31, 1995 appear as follows:

Kirk Corporation
Balance Sheets
($000s)

	December 31, 1995	December 31, 1994
Cash	$ 265	$ 250
Receivables	390	410
Inventory	350	370
Total current assets	$1,005	$1,030
Plant and equipment	1,750	1,250
Less: Accumulated depreciation	(450)	(290)
Net plant and equipment	1,300	960
Investments	300	175
Intangible assets	30	35
Total assets	$2,635	$2,200
Accounts payable	$ 110	$ 140
Accrued expenses	45	65
Dividends payable	5	20
Total current liabilities	$ 160	$ 225
Notes payable	725	600
Common stock	1,000	850
Retained earnings	750	525
Total liabilities and equity	$2,635	$2,200

Kirk Corporation
Income Statement
For the Year Ended December 31, 1995
($000s)

Sales		$4,320
Cost of goods sold	$2,460	
Depreciation and amortization	205	
Selling, general, and administrative expense	1,390	4,055
Operating income		$ 265
Gain on sale of equipment		15
Net income		$ 280

Additional information (000s):

(a) Depreciation of plant and equipment amounted to $200 in 1986. Amortization of intangibles amounted to $5.

(b) Equipment costing $200 with accumulated depreciation of $40 was sold for $175 cash.

(c) A new plant was purchased for $700 cash.

(d) An investment in Spock Enterprises was acquired at a cost of $150 by issuing stock.

(e) The board of directors declared dividends of $55 during the year.

(f) New long-term notes payable of $125 were issued to help finance the cost of the new plant.

REQUIRED:

1. Prepare a cash flow statement for Kirk Corporation in accordance with generally accepted accounting principles. Present cash flows from operating activities in the direct approach.

2. Provide a separate schedule that reconciles net income with net cash provided by operating activities.

21-4. *Cash flow statement: direct and indirect methods*

Madison Manufacturing Co. provided the following information:

Madison Manufacturing Co.
Balance Sheets
($000s)

	December 31,	
	1995	1994
Cash	$ 2,858	$ 700
Receivables	13,750	10,780
Less: Allowances	(650)	(580)
Net receivables	13,100	10,200
Inventories	9,100	8,500
Prepaid expenses	350	300
Total current assets	$25,408	$19,700
Property, plant, equipment	17,500	15,300
Accumulated depreciation	(3,500)	(4,600)
Net prop., plant, equip.	14,000	10,700
Total assets	$39,408	$30,400
Notes payable—banks	$ –	$ 7,200
Accounts payable	4,800	4,600
Accrued expenses	400	400
Total current liabilities	$ 5,200	$12,200
Long-term debt	12,590	8,200
Common stock ($5 par)	9,450	4,000
Additional paid-in capital	7,740	1,400
Retained earnings	4,428	4,600
Total equity	$21,618	$10,000
Total liabilities & equity	$39,408	$30,400)

Madison Manufacturing Co.
Income Statement
For the Year Ended December 31, 1995
($000s)

Sales	$13,820
Less: Provision for doubtful accounts	(1,220)
Net sales	12,600
Cost of goods sold	6,940
Selling and general expense	810
Depreciation expense	1,460
Interest expense	790
Income taxes	1,300
Net income	$ 1,300

Madison Manufacturing Co.
Statement of Changes in Stockholders' Equity
($000s)

	Capital Stock	Additional Paid-in Capital	Retained Earnings
Balance, 12/31/94	$4,000	$1,400	$4,600
Net income			1,300
Cash dividends			(672)
Stock dividends (5%)	200	600	(800)
Conversion of bonds	250	740	
Sale of stock	5,000	5,000	
Balance, 12/31/95	$9,450	$7,740	$4,428

REQUIRED:

1. Prepare a cash flow statement for Madison Manufacturing Co. in accordance with generally accepted accounting principles. Present cash flows from operating activities in the direct approach.
2. Provide a separate schedule that reconciles net income with net cash provided by operating activities.

21-5. *Cash flow statement: direct and indirect methods*

Compact Devices provides the following information:

Compact Devices, Inc.
Balance Sheets
($000s)

	December 31, 1995	December 31, 1994
Cash	$ 305	$ 245
Accounts receivable, net	2,895	2,061
Inventories	2,430	1,942
Prepaid expenses	52	29
Total current assets	5,682	4,277
Property, plant, equipment @ cost	5,390	4,108
Less: Accumulated depreciation	(1,953)	(1,635)
Net property, plant, equipment	3,437	2,473
Other assets	202	228
Total assets	$9,321	$6,978
Notes payable	$ 0	$ 55
Current portion of long-term debt	155	120
Accounts payable	2,541	1,951
Accrued expenses	52	43
Income taxes payable	74	78
Total current liabilities	2,822	2,247
Long-term debt	2,750	1,880
Deferred income taxes	412	320
Common stock	555	375
Additional paid-in capital	1,013	721
Retained earnings	1,809	1,483
Less: Shares held in the treasury	(40)	(48)
Total stockholders equity	3,337	2,531
Total liabilities and equities	$9,321	$6,978

Compact Devices, Inc.
Income Statement
For the Year Ended December 31, 1995
($000s)

Net revenues		$8,184
Cost of goods sold	$5,125	
Selling and administrative expense	894	
Depreciation and amortization expense	520	
Interest expense	319	6,858
Income before taxes		$1,326
Income tax expense		447
Net income		$ 879

Compact Devices, Inc.
Statement of Stockholders' Equity
($000s)

	Common Stock	Additional Paid-in Capital	Retained Earnings	Treasury Shares
Balance, 12/31/94	$375	$ 721	$1,483	$(48)
Net income	879			
Net sales of treasury shares	8			
Cash dividends	(443)			
Stock dividends	45	65	(110)	
Issuance of new common shares	135	227		
Balance, 12/31/95	$555	$1,013	$1,809	$(40)

Note:

Depreciation and amortization expense consists of the following:

Depreciation of plant and equipment	$494
Amortization of intangibles	26
Total	$520

REQUIRED:

1. Prepare a cash flow statement for Compact Devices Inc. in accordance with generally accepted accounting principles. Present cash flows from operating activities in the direct approach.
2. Provide a separate schedule that reconciles net income with net cash provided by operating activities.

21-6. *Cash flow statement: direct method*

Balance sheets for the years ended December 31, 1994 and 1995 and income statement for the year ended December 31, 1995 for Ballantine Corp. appear as follows:

Ballantine Corp.
Balance Sheets
($000s)

	December 31,	
	1995	1994
Cash	$ 1,670	$ 1,205
Accounts receivable, net	54,231	47,812
Inventories	61,098	50,228
Prepaid expenses	521	427
Total current assets	117,520	99,672
Land	25,094	25,094
Buildings	74,216	68,440
Equipment	67,091	48,004
Total	166,401	141,538
Less: Accumulated depreciation	(74,012)	(56,712)
	92,389	84,826
Equipment held under capital lease	24,310	
Less: Accumulated amortization	(4,210)	
	20,100	
Other assets	11,045	12,940
Total assets	$241,054	$197,438
Notes payable	$ 2,401	$ 4,096
Current portion of long-term debt	5,420	5,300
Accounts payable	39,945	31,091
Accrued expenses	420	308
Taxes payable	5,095	4,505
Total current liabilities	53,281	45,300
Long-term debt	52,360	54,021
Capital lease obligations	22,775	
Deferred income taxes	16,333	12,056
Capital stock	48,191	43,498
Retained earnings	51,095	45,103
Less: Treasury stock	(2,981)	(2,540)
Total stockholders' equity	96,305	86,061
Total liabilities and equity	$241,054	$197,438

Ballantine Corp.
Income Statement
For the Year Ended December 31, 1995
($000s)

Net sales	$448,885
Cost of goods sold	(278,950)
Selling and administrative expenses	(104,220)
Depreciation and amortization	(29,847)
Interest expense	(6,503)
Other income (expense)	1,209
Income before taxes	30,574
Income tax expense	(14,362)
Net income	$ 16,212

Ballantine Corp.
Statement of Stockholders' Equity
For the Year Ended December 31, 1995
($000s)

	Capital Stock	Retained Earnings	Treasury Stock
Balance, 12/31/94	$43,498	$45,103	$(2,540)
Net income		16,212	
Purchase of treasury stock			(441)
Cash dividends		(10,220)	
Issuance of stock	4,693		
Balance, 12/31/95	$48,191	$51,095	$(2,981)

Notes to financial statements:

1. Depreciation and amortization expense includes the following amounts:

Depreciation of buildings & equipment	$23,742
Amortization of equipment held under capital lease	4,210
Amortization of intangible assets	1,895
Total depreciation and amortization	$29,847

2. Long-term debt consists of the following:

	12/31/95	12/31/94
Zero coupon bonds, $40,000 face value, due 2005	$20,032	$19,611
Mortgage payable	34,410	39,710
Term loan	3,338	–
Total	$57,780	$59,321
Less: Amount currently due	5,420	5,300
Net long-term debt	$52,360	$54,021

REQUIRED:

1. Prepare a cash flow statement for Ballantine Corp. in accordance with generally accepted accounting principles. Present cash flows from operating activities in the direct approach.
2. Provide a separate schedule that reconciles net income with net cash provided by operating activities.

FREDERICK'S OF HOLLYWOOD, INC.

The following information is taken from the 1990 annual report of Frederick's of Hollywood, Inc., a specialty retailing and mail order business.

Income Statement
For the Year Ended September 1, 1990

Net sales	$98,573,000
Costs and expenses:	
Cost of goods sold, buying and occupancy costs	52,335,000
Selling, general and administrative expenses	39,198,000
	91,533,000
Operating profit	7,040,000
Other income (expense):	
Interest income	171,000
Miscellaneous	(131,000)
	40,000
Earnings before income taxes	7,080,000
Income taxes	2,838,000
Net earnings	$ 4,242,000
Net earnings per share	$ .75

Statement of Cash Flows (in part)
For the Year Ended September 1, 1990

Cash flows from operating activities:	
Net income	$4,242,000
Adjustments to reconcile net income to	
net cash provided by operating activities:	
Depreciation and amortization	2,620,000
Loss on sale of fixed assets	89,000
Changes in assets and liabilities	
Accounts receivable	(249,000)
Merchandise inventories	(3,136,000)
Prepaid expenses	316,000
Other assets	32,000
Accounts payable and accrued expenses	893,000
Income taxes payable	(185,000)
Deferred income taxes	351,000
Net cash provided by operating activities	$4,973,000

REQUIRED:

Prepare the "cash flows from operating activities" section of the cash flow statement for Frederick's of Hollywood, Inc. in the direct format. State clearly any assumptions you make in your analysis.

CASE 21.2

STRUCTURAL STEEL SERVICE CORP.

Structural Steel Service Corp. is a manufacturer of fabricated structural steel and completed its first six months of operations on April 30, 1993. Balance sheet and income statement for the firm appear as follows:

STRUCTURAL STEEL SERVICE CORP.
BALANCE SHEET
APRIL 30, 1993

ASSETS:

Current Assets	
Cash	$ 12,768
Accounts receivable, less allowance for doubtful accounts of $10,000	1,995,672
Notes receivable	2,208
Inventories (Notes 2, 3, and 5)	1,008,580
Prepaid expenses	53,054
Total current assets	3,072,282
Property and Equipment, at cost (Notes 2 and 5)	
Building	898,904
Furniture and fixtures	17,298
Machinery and equipment	1,231,222
Trucks and automobiles	123,358
Total cost	2,270,782
Less: Accumulated depreciation	148,072
Net property and equipment	2,122,710
Other Assets	
Organizational costs, net of accumulated amortization of $362	3,258
Software, net of accumulated amortization of $150	3,000
Net other assets	6,258
Total Assets	$5,201,250

LIABILITIES AND STOCKHOLDERS' EQUITY:

Current Liabilities	
Note payable (Note 2)	$ 529,316
Current portion of long-term debt	176,320
Bank overdraft	16,502
Accounts payable	975,160
Accrued expenses	80,336
Total current liabilities	1,777,634
Long-Term Debt, exclusive of current portion included above (Note 5)	3,013,840
Commitments and Contingencies (Note 6)	
Stockholders' Equity	
Common stock, par value $2.00 per share,	
1,000,000 shares authorized,	
300,000 shares issued and outstanding	600,000
Accumulated deficit	(190,224)
Total stockholders' equity	409,776
Total Liabilities and Stockholders' Equity	$5,201,250

Structural Steel Service Corp.
Statement of Operations
From November 1, 1992 (Date of Inception) to April 30, 1993

Sales	$6,939,062
Cost of Sales	5,980,560
Gross profit	958,502
Operating Expenses	1,034,958
Operating loss	(76,456)
Other Income (Expense), including interest expense of $146,976	(113,768)
Loss before provision for income taxes	(190,224)
Provision for Income Taxes	–
Net Loss	$(190,224)

Structural Steel Service Corp.
Statement of Stockholders' Equity
From November 1, 1992 (Date of Inception) to April 30, 1993

	Common Stock	Accumulated Deficit
Balance, November 1, 1992	$ –	$ –
Sale of 300,000 shares of common stock	600,000	–
Net loss		(190,224)
Balance, April 30, 1993	$600,000	$(190,224)

Structural Steel Service Corp.
Notes to Financial Statements
From November 1, 1992 (Date of Inception) to April 30, 1993

1. SUMMARY OF SIGNIFICANT ACCOUNTING POLICIES

Inventories: Inventories are stated at the lower of cost (first-in, first-out) or market.

Property and Equipment: Property, plant, and equipment are stated at cost. Depreciation is computed using various methods over the estimated useful lives of the assets ranging from three to thirty-one and one-half years.

Revenue Recognition: Revenue is recognized as product is produced according to contractual agreement.

Computer Software: Computer software is stated at cost. Amortization is computed using the straight-line method over an estimated life of five years.

2. NOTE PAYABLE

The Company has a credit line of up to $1,600,000 payable on demand with First National Bank. Interest accrues at one and one-half percent over the prime rate. The credit line is secured by inventory, accounts receivable, equipment and intangible assets. The credit line is guaranteed by the assets of Modern Steel Fabricators, Inc. and the officers of Burroughs Bar Stock, Inc. As of April 30, 1993, the company has utilized $529,316 of the available line of credit.

3. INVENTORIES

Inventories consist of:

Raw materials	$ 948,580
Small tools and fasteners	60,000
Total inventories	$1,008,580

4. PROVISION FOR INCOME TAXES

Under the provisions of the Internal Revenue Code, the Company has, at April 30, 1993, $190,224 of net operating loss carryforwards, which can be offset against future taxable income. These carryforwards expire on April 30, 2008.

5. LONG-TERM DEBT

Long-term debt consists of the following:

10% note payable to Burroughs Bar Stock, Inc., payable in monthly installments of $30,000 with a balloon payment of $1,440,000 at October, 1995. This note is secured by inventory, accounts receivable, and equipment.	$1,916,160
Unsecured officer notes at 8% per annum due on demand after April 30, 1994.	1,274,000
	3,190,160
Less: Amounts due within one year	176,320
	$3,013,840

The total amount of long-term debt maturing in subsequent years is as follows:

Year Ended April 30,	Amount
1994	$ 176,320
1995	1,468,784
1996	1,545,056
	$3,190,160

6. COMMITMENTS AND CONTINGENCIES

Consulting Fees: The Company has a three-year commitment with two consultants for assistance in the management of the Company. The compensation of the consultants is set at $62,400 each, per year.

Leases: The Company leases certain buildings, automobiles, and automotive equipment under noncancellable operating leases. The amount of the rent expense charged to operations for the six months ended April 30, 1993 was $176,208. Future minimum lease payments under noncancellable leases are as follows:

Year Ended April 30,	Amount
1994	$357,028
1995	193,040
1996	20,176
1997	9,224
	$579,468

Structural Steel Service Corp.
Schedules of Supplementary Information
From November 1, 1992 (Date of Inception) to April 30, 1993

COST OF SALES:

Materials	$4,447,718
Wages	533,672
Payroll taxes	55,866
Insurance	44,412
Union expense	21,394
Contract labor	857,080
Supplies	20,418
Total cost of sales	$5,980,560

OPERATING EXPENSES:

Salaries	$ 184,322
Payroll tax expense	19,628
Professional services	149,086
Fuel oil	23,696
Repairs and maintenance	73,830
Utilities	22,530
Office supplies	22,818
Postage and freight	3,782
Computer expense	3,016
Telephone	14,454
Collection expense	680
Advertising	3,564
Dues and subscriptions	17,356
Licenses and fees	1,198
Printing	4,082
Insurance	13,314
Travel and entertainment	37,038
Truck and automobile expenses	42,312
Lease and car rental	7,136
Equipment rental	155,562
Depreciation	148,072
Amortization	512
Miscellaneous	512
Bad debt expense	10,000
Employee benefits	76,458
Total operating expenses	$1,034,958

OTHER INCOME (EXPENSE):

Rental income	$ 29,360
Interest income	3,848
Interest expense	(146,976)
Total other income (expense)	$(113,768)

REQUIRED:

1. Prepare a cash flow statement for Structural Steel Service Corp. for the six months ended April 30, 1993, in accordance with generally accepted accounting principles. Present cash flows from operating activities in the direct approach.
2. Provide a separate schedule that reconciles net income with net cash provided by operating activities.

PART 7

Appendices

A Review of the Accounting Process

In this Appendix, we briefly review some details of the accrual accounting process. This review reacquaints you with material typically covered in introductory accounting courses: the double-entry bookkeeping system, including routine entries to record normal business transactions; adjusting entries to implement full accrual accounting and to correct errors; and reversing entries, which are optional but often very helpful in ensuring that particular items of revenue and expense are not double-counted or neglected altogether. This Appendix also introduces you to the various devices such as journals, ledgers, and trial balances for storing and processing accounting data. While firms' accounting systems differ greatly in terms of particular details, the basic structure described in this Appendix should provide a good foundation for understanding the systems of most business enterprises.

AN OVERVIEW OF THE ACCOUNTING PROCESS

Exhibit A.1 provides a summary of the procedures typically involved in the accounting process for most firms. We describe the process as it applies to a manual system—i.e., one not based to any significant degree on automated procedures. While automated accounting systems are more available and less expensive now than they were a few years ago, manual systems are still used. In an automated system, a computer performs some of the procedures described; and some of the books and documents described will only exist as files within the computer system rather than in more tangible form. Aside from these obvious differences between manual and automated accounting systems, their operations are quite comparable. Please be aware, however, that

An Overview of the Accounting Process		
ACTIVITY	**HOW OFTEN?**	**BOOKS, DOCUMENTS**
1. Record transactions	As they occur	Journals
2. Update account balances	Periodically	Ledger
3. List account balances	Whenever financial statements are to be prepared	Trial balance
4. Make and record adjustments	As necessary	Journals, ledger
5. List adjusted account balances	Whenever financial statements are to be prepared	Adjusted trial balance
6. Prepare income statement	As required	Adjusted trial balance
7. Record closing entries	After income statement has been prepared	Journals, ledger
8. Prepare balance sheet	As required	Post-closing trial balance
9. Record reversing entries	Optional	Journal, ledger

EXHIBIT A.1

An Overview of the Accounting Process

when we refer to "documents" and "books," we may well be referring to the electronic variety rather than paper.

The accounting process begins as transactions occur. For instance, a firm acquires goods and services from various suppliers; makes sales to customers; pays cash to employees, vendors, taxing authorities, and other creditors and collects cash from customers; and obtains cash by borrowing from banks and other lenders and by issuing ownership shares to existing and new owners. In a purely manual system, the firm creates or has evidence of each transaction by one or more documents. It documents cash disbursements by entries in a checkbook, canceled checks, and periodic bank statements; cash receipts, by cash receipt reports, deposit tickets, and bank statements. These documents, in turn, are the basis for entries into the firm's accounting system.

The effects of transactions enter a firm's accounting system in several stages. First, as transactions occur, a firm records them in its journals, or books of original entry, as debits and credits to the appropriate accounts. Accountants have taken the noun, *journal*, and turned it into a verb by calling the activity of recording transactions in the journals as "**journalizing** the transactions."

As we shall see, firms typically employ several types of journals in their accounting systems. Some special-purpose journals are designed for only a particular type of recurring transaction such as sales or purchases, while the general journal handles transactions occurring less frequently and any necessary adjusting entries. Periodically, journal entries are summarized and account balances are updated to reflect the effects of the journal entries. A firm maintains its account balances in the **general ledger**, which is a cumulative record of all transactions organized by account. The particular accounts maintained in a firm's general ledger are listed in the **chart of accounts**, essentially an index to the general ledger.

The process of updating the account balances in the general ledger is known as "**posting** the journal entries to the ledger." How often the journal entries are posted to the ledger depends on the information needs of the firm's management. In smaller, owner-managed firms, management usually knows what is happening without frequent reference to the accounting system (and the financial statements and reports derived from it). In these firms, managers may find that monthly posting of entries to the ledger is perfectly adequate for their needs. In large, decentralized firms, managers rely on the accounting system much more heavily to evaluate the firm's performance and usually post daily entries to update account balances and to permit more frequent preparation of financial statements. Automated systems permit continuous posting.

Journalizing transactions and periodically updating the account balances by posting the journal entries to the ledger are fairly continuous activities. Whenever a firm's management wants to prepare financial statements (typically at fixed, regular intervals), the routine activities of journalizing and posting will be interrupted somewhat to allow for statement preparation. The preparation of financial statements typically begins with preparation of a **trial balance**, or listing of all ledger accounts and their balances. Account balances are examined for obvious bookkeeping errors such as an out-of-balance condition and to determine if any adjusting entries are necessary.

Adjusting entries are necessary for a number of reasons. First, they are required to enter certain events into the accounting system, even though no formal transaction has taken place. Often these events are attributable to the mere passage of time. For instance, depreciation of any plant and equipment needs to be recorded each accounting period, but no transaction with an outside party triggers the recording of depreciation. Second, to recognize revenues and expenses properly in the accounts under the accrual basis of accounting, certain account balances must be adjusted to recognize revenue as earned and to match the appropriate expenses with revenues. The following adjusting entries may be needed:

1. If revenue has been earned but not yet received, an adjustment for accrued revenue is necessary.
2. If revenue has been received but not yet earned, an adjustment for unearned revenue may be needed, depending on how it was originally recorded.
3. When expenses that have not yet been paid need to be matched with revenue, an adjustment for accrued expenses is necessary.
4. If costs have been incurred but should be matched with future revenues, an adjustment to prepaid expenses may be necessary, depending on how they were originally recorded when incurred.
5. Adjusting entries are also needed to correct bookkeeping errors that have been made in recording events and transactions during the current period. For instance, suppose a collection on account from a particular customer was mistakenly credited to notes receivable. While the trial balance would not be out of balance, the balance in accounts receivable would be too high and the balance in notes receivable too low. An adjustment with a debit to notes receivable and a credit to accounts receivable would correct the error.

Once all adjustments have been recorded in the journals and posted to the ledger, the firm customarily prepares another trial balance, called the **adjusted**

trial balance, which reflects the adjustments. This allows the firm's accountants to double-check the balances before they prepare the financial statements. If the adjusted trial balance requires no further adjustments, then the accountants can immediately prepare the financial statements.

To prepare financial statements from the account balances shown in the adjusted trial balance, the accountants identify the appropriate statement for each account balance and then aggregate account balances and insert the totals in the proper format. In a manual system, these procedures can be streamlined with a worksheet using a technique similar to that illustrated later in this Appendix.

Certain account balances reflect flow variables, or activity for the period. These balances must be added to or subtracted from the balances in the accounts that contain the related stock variables—i.e., the cumulative effect of all transactions to date. For instance, most accounting systems use separate, temporary revenue and expense accounts to record flow variables (changes) for a particular period and to facilitate the preparation of the income statement. All of the flows described by balances in revenue and expense accounts pertain to a particular stock variable captured by the balance in the firm's retained earnings account. To reflect all activity to date (and in order for the balance sheet to balance), stock variables (e.g., retained earnings) must be updated by the amounts of all related flow variables for the period (e.g., revenues and expenses). Accountants call this process "**closing** the books," and it requires closing entries. The effect of closing entries involving revenues, expenses, gains, and losses is to update retained earnings by the amount of any income or loss for the period and to leave the temporary revenue and expense accounts with zero balances before the next accounting period's activity is recorded.

To ensure that all necessary closing entries have been recorded and posted properly, a firm's accountants may wish to prepare yet another trial balance, which is called the **post-closing trial balance**. All the temporary accounts should have zero balances. Another optional step in the closing process is to prepare **reversing entries** ("reversals"), which are designed to prevent double-counting of or no recording of certain revenues and expenses. As we shall see, while reversing entries are certainly not the only way to accomplish this, they are often the most convenient technique.

In the rest of this Appendix, we elaborate on the various steps in this process and provide examples and illustrations. By the end of the Appendix, you will have a reasonably good, if rather general, understanding of the operation of most accounting systems. However, it bears repeating that each accounting system will have its own idiosyncrasies; and no intermediate accounting text can provide comprehensive descriptions of all the variations you will encounter.

PROCESSING EVENTS AND TRANSACTIONS

We begin our discussion of the accounting process by first considering the kinds of events and transactions that a firm records in its accounts. Accountants use the term **recognition** to describe the process of formally recording items in a firm's accounts as assets, liabilities, owners' equity, revenues, expenses, gains, or losses. As we shall see, it is difficult to formulate a concise and useful statement of the criteria for accounting recognition. *Statement of Financial Accounting Concepts No. 5* offers the following broad criteria for accounting recognition.

1. The item meets the definition of an element of financial statements: asset, liability, owners' equity, revenue, expense, gain, or loss.
2. The information about the item is relevant—i.e., it is capable of making a difference in user decisions.
3. The item's relevant attribute is measurable with sufficient reliability.
4. The information is reliable: representationally faithful, verifiable, and neutral.[1]

So broad, these criteria are of little use in trying to answer the question: What events and transactions does a firm record in its accounts?

Recordable events are those that change the amounts of a firm's assets, liabilities, or owners' equity. According to SFAS No. 5, these changes are of two types:

1. Inflows and outflows
2. Changes in amount while assets are held or liabilities are owed resulting from either changes in utility or changes in price.[2]

Let us consider each type of change.

Inflows and outflows are typically the result of transactions between the firm and other parties. Most of these transactions involve exchanges of valuable goods and services—i.e., both inflows and outflows. For instance, employees provide labor services to a firm in exchange for cash and other employment benefits. The firm provides its customers with goods and services in exchange for the customers' cash or promise to pay cash at a later date. A relatively few transactions do not involve exchanges but, rather, inflows or outflows only. For instance, a firm may make charitable contributions or owners' may contribute goods or services to the firm. Routine transactions involving inflows and outflows are recorded as they occur.

Changes in the amounts of assets while they are held or in the amounts of liabilities while they are owed usually do not occur as the result of a transaction but, rather, as the result of some other event or merely the passage of time. For instance, the usefulness of plant and equipment (i.e., its service potential) declines as the assets are used. The market value of a portfolio of marketable securities may rise or fall as a consequence of general economic conditions. Since these events are not the result of transactions, recording them in the accounts usually requires an adjusting entry. Moreover, many regularly occurring, significant economic events are not afforded any accounting recognition, usually because of measurability problems or questions about the

[1] "Recognition and Measurement in Financial Statements of Business Enterprises," *Statement of Financial Accounting Concepts No. 5* (Stamford, CT: FASB, 1984), para. 63.

[2] *Ibid.*, para. 89.

verifiability of the amounts involved. For instance, in October of 1987, the Dow Jones Industrial Average closed down over 500 points on a single day. While this was certainly a significant economic event for the world economy, relatively few firms outside of the securities industry formally recorded any effects of the event in their accounts.

Documentation

As most transactions occur, **source documents** are created and provide evidence of the transaction. The basis for recording the transactions in the accounts, source documents are of many types and exist in both paper and electronic forms. Let us examine the kinds of documents associated with several ordinary types of transactions.

As customers check out at the local grocery store, their purchases are typically recorded at a cash register. Even basic, "no-frills" cash registers create two paper tapes: one that the customer receives as a receipt and the second that the machine stores to record the sales it processes by the end of the day. More advanced point-of-sale equipment is connected to the firm's computers and records the day's sales electronically.

As a firm orders goods from its suppliers, several documents typically will be created. First, the firm sends a purchase order to the supplier and retains a copy for its files. When the goods are received, the firm will prepare a receiving report, which can be compared to the purchase order to ensure that the correct merchandise has been received. These documents are then forwarded to the accounting department and become the basis for the journal entries to record the purchases.

Transactions could conceivably be recorded without all this documentation. However, without adequate documentation, the information in the accounting system would lack verifiability. Audits of financial statements would be impossible if a firm did not maintain documentation to serve as evidence of the transactions. The only way auditors can determine if transactions have been accounted for properly is to examine the evidence contained in the **audit trail** provided by the documentation the firm maintains. Thus, in addition to ensuring transactions are recorded properly in the accounts, documentation is necessary for ex post verification of the amounts recorded in connection with an audit of the financial statements.

Journal Entries

The mechanism for recording events and transactions in the accounts begins with the **journal entry**. Journal entries are based on the double-entry bookkeeping system with the debit/credit convention first documented by Fra Luca Pacioli in the fifteenth century. The accounting structure for a particular firm is determined by its **chart of accounts**, which consists of a list of all the accounts a firm uses to record the effects of events and transactions. In most accounting systems, accounts are identified by an account name and an account number. A simple chart of accounts for Carter Corporation is found in Exhibit A.2.

CARTER CORPORATION
Chart of Accounts

NO.	NAME	NO.	NAME
100	Cash	270	Additional paid-in capital
110	Notes receivable	280	Retained earnings
115	Accrued interest receivable	300	Sales revenue
120	Accounts receivable	310	Interest revenue
128	Deposits with suppliers	400	Purchases
129	Allowance for doubtful accounts	405	Cost of goods sold
130	Inventories	410	Salary expense—sales
140	Prepaid expenses	415	Salary expense—administration
150	Furniture and fixtures	420	Advertising expense
151	Accumulated depreciation	425	Travel and entertainment expense
200	Notes payable—banks	430	Rent expense
210	Accounts payable	435	Insurance expense
215	Customer deposits	440	Depreciation expense
220	Income taxes payable	445	Bad debt expense
230	Accrued expenses	450	Interest expense
250	Notes payable—long-term	455	Income tax expense
260	Common stock	460	Other expenses

Carter Corporation follows the convention of assigning account numbers from 100 to 199 to the asset accounts, 200 to 299 to the liability and stockholders' equity accounts, 300 to 399 to revenues, and 400 to 499 to expenses. While Carter Corporation does not maintain separate accounts for gains and losses, these would also be typically incorporated into a chart of accounts. Carter's chart of accounts is included for illustrative purposes only. Please note that other firms' charts of accounts will likely differ substantially due to the different kinds of events and transactions affecting their account balances as well as the different information needs and preferences of management.

Strictly speaking, unless you are familiar with a firm's chart of accounts, you cannot prepare an appropriate journal entry to record an event or transaction. One could easily propose a debit or credit to an account that does not exist. Nevertheless, in the problems and exercises at the end of this Appendix and the chapters throughout the text, we ask you to make appropriate journal entries without first specifying the firm's chart of accounts. You are asked to think in terms of a generic chart of accounts and, unless the problem specifies otherwise, to assume that the accounts you require to record the entry are included in the firm's chart of accounts.

Journal entries consist of a series of debits and credits to various accounts. The terms **debit** and **credit** are used to describe the effects of transactions on account balances. Increases in asset balances, decreases in liability balances, and decreases in owners' equity balances (including expenses) are recorded as debits (abbreviated, rather mysteriously, as *Dr.*). Decreases in assets, increases in liabilities, and increases in owners' equity (including revenues) are recorded as credits (abbreviated *Cr.*). The double-entry bookkeeping system ensures that the **fundamental accounting identity** (Assets = Liabilities + Owners' Equity) is always maintained. That is, for each journal entry, the total amount of debits equals the total amount of credits.

Each account in a firm's chart of accounts can be illustrated with a T-account. In T-account form, debits are conventionally shown on the left of the "T," while credits are shown on the right. In this context, debit and credit can be viewed as synonymous with left and right, respectively. Exhibit A.3 summarizes the mechanics of journal entries with T-accounts. To ensure that the mechanics of journal entries are understood, let us examine a few routine business transactions, the journal entries to record them in the accounts, and the resulting effect on the T-accounts.

An examination of the daily cash register tapes reveals that Abe's Groceries, Inc. had sales of $5,245, today, all for cash. The journal entry to record this would be as follows:

Today's date:		
Cash	5,245	
Sales revenue		5,245

In T-account form, the effects of the sales transaction would appear as follows:

Abe's Groceries pays a supplier $4,292 in cash for merchandise purchased previously on account. Abe's journal entry to record this transaction would appear as follows:

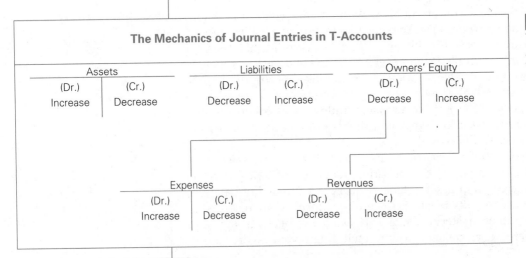

The Mechanics of Journal Entries in T-Accounts

Assets		Liabilities		Owners' Equity	
(Dr.)	(Cr.)	(Dr.)	(Cr.)	(Dr.)	(Cr.)
Increase	Decrease	Decrease	Increase	Decrease	Increase

Expenses		Revenues	
(Dr.)	(Cr.)	(Dr.)	(Cr.)
Increase	Decrease	Decrease	Increase

EXHIBIT A.3

The Mechanics of Journal Entries in T-Accounts

Accounts payable	4,292	
Cash		4,292

In T-account form, the effects of the payment on account would appear as follows:

Cash	Accounts Payable
4,292	4,292

Abe's Groceries receives a bill for $795 from its electric utility covering the previous month's electric service. Since the electricity has already been consumed, Abe's would recognize this amount as an expense with the following journal entry:

Utility expense	795	
Accounts payable		795

After this entry has been recorded, the T-accounts would appear as follows:

Utility Expense	Accounts Payable
795	795

Notice that each of these journal entries is symmetric. That is, the total amount of debits equals the total amount of credits. In this way, Abe's assets will equal its sum of liabilities and owners' equity.

Types of Journals

Most firms use several journals to record events and transactions. Although only one journal is necessary, recording frequently occurring transactions in a general-purpose journal is tedious and inconvenient. The process can be streamlined considerably by using special-purpose journals that are designed for particular types of transactions only—e.g., sales, purchases, cash receipts, and cash disbursements. However, a firm will also need a general-purpose journal to record transactions that do not occur often enough to warrant a special-purpose journal. Let us examine how some special-purpose and general-purpose journals might appear. Bear in mind that these are only samples of the many formats likely to be encountered in use.

Journals for Recurring Transactions   The objective of special-purpose journals is to facilitate the recording of recurring transactions by not requiring repetitive entries of the same account names and numbers in the journal. Rather, the account names and numbers of the affected accounts are printed as column headings in the special-purpose journal. One simply records the journal entry by entering the date, identifying information, and debit and credit amounts in the appropriate columns. Moreover, the columnar form of these journals makes it easy to total the columns. Then, only the totals, rather than the individual entries, are posted to the ledger. Let us examine some examples of special-purpose journals Carter Corporation uses.

Cash Receipts Journal   Carter Corporation's cash receipts journal is shown in Exhibit A.4. The first three columns contain the date of the transaction, the identity of the payor, and the amount received, respectively. Since cash receipts always involve a debit to the cash balance, the amount inserted in column 3 represents the amount of the debit to cash.

Most of Carter's cash receipts are from customers who have made purchases on account. Therefore, columns 4 and 5 are designed to accommodate this usual source of cash received. Carter uses the convention of assigning a three-digit account prefix to identify the type of account (e.g., account no. 120 identifies accounts receivable—trade) and a five-digit suffix to identify a particular subaccount or customer (e.g., Baltimore Mfg. Co. is customer 20456). Thus, to record a credit to accounts receivable in its cash receipts journal, Carter only needs to enter an account number and an amount.

If other accounts receive a credit, columns 6–8 are used to enter the account number, account name, and amount. For instance, the July 2 receipt from John A. Williams Corp. represents a deposit from a customer rather than a payment on account. Therefore, account 215-91732 (customer deposits from John A. Williams Corp.) is credited.

When the cash receipts entries are posted to the ledger, totals for the debit to cash and credit to accounts receivable can be used rather than the individ-

EXHIBIT A.4
Carter Corporation—
Cash Receipts
Journal

CARTER CORPORATION
Cash Receipts Journal

| | | | | | CREDIT | | |
| DATE | RECEIVED FROM | DEBIT AMOUNT | ACCOUNTS RECEIVABLE | | OTHER | | |
			ACCT. NO.	AMOUNT	ACCT. NO.	NAME	AMOUNT
(1)	(2)	(3)	(4)	(5)	(6)	(7)	(8)
Jul. 1	Baltimore Mfg. Co.	439.45	120-20456	439.45			
Jul. 1	York Products Corp.	820.92	120-93710	820.92			
Jul. 1	Columbia Plumbing Co.	1,309.25	120-23058	1,309.25			
Jul. 2	John A. Williams Corp.	48.23			215-91732	Customer deposits	48.23
Jul. 2	Midwest Supply Co.	742.90	120-57290	742.90			
Jul. 2	Bill Johnston	125.00			125-34502	Due from employees	125.00
Jul. 2	St. Paul Brokerage	2,054.11	120-76380	2,054.11			
Jul. 3	Madison Metals	1,834.90	120-55293	1,834.90			
Jul. 3	Toledo Electrical	590.34	120-80328	590.34			
Jul. 3	Rogers Systems, Inc,	1,000.00			110-83067	Notes receivable	1,000.00
Jul. 3	Total	8,965.10		7,791.87			1,173.23

ual entry amounts. However, each of the items in the other columns will have to be entered separately.

Cash Disbursements Journal   Carter Corporation's cash disbursements journal is shown in Exhibit A.5. The first four columns contain the date of the transaction, the check number, the identity of the payee, and the amount paid, respectively. Since cash disbursements always involve a credit to the cash balance, the amount inserted in column 4 represents the amount of the credit to cash.

Most of Carter's cash disbursements are made to suppliers for purchases on account. Therefore, columns 5 and 6 are designed to accommodate this usual debit to accounts payable. Thus, to record a debit to accounts payable in its cash disbursements journal, Carter only needs to enter an account number and an amount in columns 5 and 6.

If other accounts receive a debit, columns 7–9 are used to enter the account number, account name, and amount. For instance, the July 1 payment to the Internal Revenue Service represents a payment of taxes payable rather than accounts payable. Therefore, account 220-10001 (Taxes payable to the IRS) is debited.

Once again, since totals only can be used to update the account balances, a considerable reduction of clerical effort results.

Sales Journal   Carter Corporation's sales journal is shown in Exhibit A.6. The first four columns contain the date of the transaction, the invoice number,

EXHIBIT A.5

Carter Corporation—
Cash Disbursements
Journal

CARTER CORPORATION
Cash Disbursements Journal

				DEBIT				
				ACCOUNTS PAYABLE		OTHER		
DATE	CK. NO.	PAID TO	CREDIT AMOUNT	ACCT. NO.	AMOUNT	ACCT. NO.	ACCT. NAME	AMOUNT
(1)	(2)	(3)	(4)	(5)	(6)	(7)	(8)	(9)
Jul. 1	34091	Washington Automotive	490.37	210-94209	490.37			
Jul. 1	34092	Internal Revenue Service	2,045.55			220-10001	Taxes payable	2,045.55
Jul. 1	34093	Adams Manufacturing Co.	593.00	210-03491	593.00			
Jul. 1	34094	Jefferson Industries	1,650.45	210-42854	1,650.45			
Jul. 2	34095	Jackson Service Corp.	839.88	210-40358	839.88			
Jul. 2	34096	Madison National Bank	3,000.00			200-58032	Notes payable—s/t	3,000.00
Jul. 2	34096	Madison National Bank	360.00			205-58032	Accrued interest pay	360.00
Jul. 2	34097	Monroe Gas Company	256.71	210-59230	256.71			
Jul. 2	34098	Cleveland Electric Co.	781.36	210-29400	781.36			
Jul. 2	34099	Grant Advertising	4,550.00	210-34110	4,550.00			
Jul. 2		Total	14,567.32		9,161.77			5,405.55

CARTER CORPORATION
Sales Journal

| | | | | DEBIT | | | | |
| | | | | ACCOUNTS RECEIVABLE | | OTHER | | |
DATE	INV. NO.	CUSTOMER NAME	CREDIT AMOUNT	ACCT. NO.	AMOUNT	ACCT. NO.	ACCT. NAME	AMOUNT
(1)	(2)	(3)	(4)	(5)	(6)	(7)	(8)	(9)
Jul. 1	24956	Columbia Plumbing Co.	265.90	120-23058	265.90			
Jul. 1	24957	Princeton Products	125.45			100-10001	Cash—First Bank	125.45
Jul. 1	24958	Baltimore Mfg. Co.	2,375.00	120-20456	2,375.00			
Jul. 1	24959	St. Paul Brokerage	3,495.35	120-76380	3,495.35			
Jul. 2	24960	Cornell Crafts, Inc.	675.81			110-25820	Notes receivable	675.81
Jul. 2	24961	Madison Metals	4,350.00	120-55293	3,480.00	215-55293	Customer deposits	870.00
Jul. 3	24962	Toledo Electrical	645.73	120-80328	645.73			
Jul. 3	24963	Brown Products, Inc.	833.57	120-26529	833.57			
Jul. 3	24964	Rogers Systems, Inc.	1,341.82			110-83067	Notes receivable	1,341.82
Jul. 3		Total	14,108.63		11,095.55			3,013.08

EXHIBIT A.6

Carter Corporation—
Sales Journal

the identity of the customer, and the amount of the transaction, respectively. Since sales transactions always involve a credit to the revenue balance, the amount inserted in column 4 represents the amount of the credit to revenue.

Most of Carter's sales are made on account. Therefore, columns 5 and 6 are designed to accommodate this usual debit to accounts receivable. Thus, to record a debit to accounts receivable in its sales journal, Carter only needs to enter an account number and an amount in columns 5 and 6.

If other accounts receive a debit, columns 7–9 are used to enter the account number, account name, and amount. For instance, the July 2 sale to Madison Metals (invoice no. 24961) involves both a debit to accounts receivable for $3,480.00 and a debit to customer deposits for $870.00. Apparently, when Madison Metals placed an order, it made an advance payment of $870.00, which can now be recognized as revenue. Thus, the total revenue of $4,350.00 recognized on this transaction consists of $870.00, which was received previously, and $3,480.00, which has not yet been received.

Purchases Journal   Carter Corporation's purchases journal is shown in Exhibit A.7. The first four columns contain the date of the transaction, the identity of the vendor, the purchase order number, and the amount of the transaction, respectively. Carter uses a periodic inventory system (see Chapter 9) and records all purchases with a debit to the temporary account purchases. Therefore, the amount inserted in column 4 represents the amount of the debit to purchases.

Most of Carter's purchases are made on account. Therefore, columns 5 and 6 are designed to accommodate this usual credit to accounts payable.

CARTER CORPORATION
Purchases Journal

| | | | | CREDIT | | | | |
| | | | | ACCOUNTS PAYABLE | | OTHER | | |
DATE	VENDOR	P.O. NO.	DEBIT AMOUNT	ACCT. NO.	AMOUNT	ACCT. NO.	ACCT. NAME	AMOUNT
(1)	(2)	(3)	(4)	(5)	(6)	(7)	(8)	(9)
Jul. 1	Jefferson Industries	56032	3,489.28	210-42854	3,489.28			
Jul. 1	Cincinnati Cleaning Co.	56033	517.82	210-28035	517.82			
Jul. 1	Minneapolis Merchants	56034	879.70	210-59005	879.70			
Jul. 1	Denver Drilling Supply	56035	2,595.00			200-33501	Notes payable	2,595.00
Jul. 2	Lincoln Corp.	56036	1,045.45	210-52945	1,045.45			
Jul. 2	Laramie Industries	56037	3,083.27	210-50732	2,466.62	128-50732	Deposits—suppliers	616.65
Jul. 2	Washington Automotive	56038	924.91	210-94209	924.91			
Jul. 3	Adams Manufacturing Co.	56039	1,731.84	210-03491	1,731.84			
Jul. 3	Reno Recreation Products	56040	5,025.33			100-10001	Cash—First Bank	5,025.33
Jul. 3	Total		19,292.60		11,055.62			8,236.98

EXHIBIT A.7

Carter Corporation—
Purchases Journal

Thus, to record a credit to accounts payable in its purchases journal, Carter only needs to enter an account number and an amount in columns 5 and 6.

If other accounts receive a credit, columns 7–9 are used to enter the account number, account name, and amount. For instance, the July 2 purchase from Laramie Industries (purchase order no. 56037) involves both a credit to accounts payable for $2,466.62 and a credit to deposits—suppliers for $616.65. Apparently, when it placed the order, Carter Corporation made an advance payment of $616.65, which can now be recognized as part of the cost of the goods purchased. Thus, the total amount of this purchase is $3,083.27, consisting of $616.65, which was paid previously, and $2,466.62, which has not yet been paid.

General Journal   Even though firms typically use special-purpose journals to record the vast majority of their transactions, they also need general-purpose journals to record some nonroutine journal entries. Most firms refer to these, appropriately enough, as the general journal. Entries in Carter Corporation's general journal are shown in Exhibit A.8.

Befitting its general-purpose role, the journal's format provides space for the date of the entry, account numbers, account names, and debit and credit amounts. A brief description of the entry is inserted immediately after the debit and credit amounts. Any event or transaction could conceivably be recorded in this general journal. However, its use is usually reserved to record those events and transactions for which no special-purpose journal exists.

CARTER CORPORATION
General Journal

DATE	NO.	ACCOUNT NAME	DEBIT	CREDIT
Jul. 1	100-00001	Cash—First National	45,000.00	
	260-00001	Common stock		15,000.00
	270-00001	Additional paid-in capital		30,000.00
		To record the issuance of 15,000 shares of $1 par value stock for $3 per share.		
Jul. 3	150-24045	Furniture and fixtures—showroom	12,500.00	
	100-20020	Cash—First Texas Bank		2,500.00
	250-64892	Notes payable—long-term		10,000.00
		To record purchase of new fixtures costing $12,500 for $2,500 in cash and $10,000 long-term note.		
Jul. 3	460-10010	Other expenses—bank service charges	35.45	
	100-10010	Cash—First National		35.45
		To record bank service charges for June.		

RECORDING AMOUNTS IN THE ACCOUNTS (POSTING)

Only after the firm posts all its journal entries and updates all its accounts can it determine current account balances and prepare financial statements. In this section, we examine this process in more detail and look at the books involved, general and subsidiary ledgers.

The General Ledger

A firm maintains its account balances and records the effects of all its journal entries in the general ledger. General ledgers are of various forms; but in a manual system, they often resemble a collection of T-accounts, one to a page. A page from Carter Corporation's general ledger showing its cash in bank account is illustrated in Exhibit A.9.

The debit and credit columns of the general ledger resemble the familiar T-account. Debit entries are recorded on the left; credit entries, on the right. To the left of the "T" are columns for the date, a reference to a particular journal where the entry was originally recorded, and a description. Carter Corporation's balance in Cash in Bank on July 1 was $12,456.13. As we have seen from our examinations of the firm's cash receipts and cash disbursements journals, considerable activity took place over the period of July 1–3. The total cash receipts of $8,965.10 over this period, as shown in the cash receipts journal in Exhibit A.4 have been posted as a debit to the account. The entry "CRJ" in the Reference column is merely a reference to the cash receipts journal as the source of the entry. The total cash disbursements of $14,567.32 over this peri-

EXHIBIT A.9

Carter Corporation—
Excerpts from the
General Journal—
Account 100-
10010–Cash (First
National Bank and
Trust)

CARTER CORPORATION
Excerpts from the General Journal
Account 100-10010—Cash (First National Bank and Trust)

DATE	REFERENCE	DESCRIPTION	DEBIT	CREDIT
Jul. 1		Balance forward	12,456.13	
Jul. 3	CRJ	Cash receipts, July 1–3	8,965.10	
Jul. 3	CDJ	Cash disbursements, July 1–3		14,567.32
Jul. 3	GJ	Bank service charges, June		35.45
		Total debits	21,421.23	
		Total credits		14,602.77
Jul. 3		Balance	6,818.46	

od, as shown in the cash disbursements journal in Exhibit A.5 have been post-ed as a credit to the account. The entry "CDJ" in the Reference column is merely a reference to the cash disbursements journal as the source of the entry. A third entry has been posted to the account to record bank service charges for the month of June. Presumably, in the June bank statement, Carter Corpora-tion was advised of these charges and made a journal entry in the general journal ("GJ") to record them. After all this activity, the firm had an ending cash balance of $6,818.46.

Subsidiary Ledgers

Some accounts in the general ledger are known as **control accounts**, which can be thought of as the total of a number of **subsidiary accounts** that apply to individual customers, vendors, items in inventory, etc. For instance, a firm needs to keep track of the amount each customer owes the firm. Therefore, a single accounts receivable account will not suffice. While the general ledger contains a single account called accounts receivable, it is supported by a sub-sidiary ledger that contains detailed records for each customer. The relation-ship between subsidiary accounts and control accounts is shown for Carter Corporation's accounts receivable—trade in Exhibit A.10. Accounts payable and inventory are also common control accounts supported by subsidiary accounts (and subsidiary ledgers).

As suggested by Exhibit A.10, the balance in the control account called accounts receivable—trade is actually the sum of the balances in individual customer accounts (the subsidiary accounts). For each customer, a ledger would be maintained showing entries for individual sales, collections on account, and any other activity. Thus, in Exhibit A.10, we observe that Carter Corporation has posted some of the individual transactions recorded in its sales and cash receipts journal to the individual customer accounts, while it has posted the total sales and collections on account to the control account. Ideally, Carter had the subsidiary and control accounts posted independently, or by different employees. If so, this provided a check on the system. Obvi-ously, at any point the total balances in the subsidiary accounts should equal

CARTER CORPORATION
Control Accounts and Subsidiary Accounts

Accounts Receivable—Trade
Control Accounts 120

7/1 Balance	42,782.25	7/3	7,791.87
7/3 SJ	11,095.55		
7/3 Balance	46,085.93		

Baltimore Mfg. Co. Acct. 120-20456		Columbia Plumbing Co. Acct. 120-23058		Brown Products, Inc. Acct. 120-26529	
1,026.78	439.45	1,309.25	1,309.25	1,455.95	
2,375.00		265.90		833.57	
2,962.33		265.90		2,289.52	

Madison Metals Acct. 120-55293		St. Paul Brokerage Acct. 120-76380		All Other Customer Accounts	
1,865.12	1,834.90	2,120.49	2,054.11	35,004.66	
3,480.00		3,495.35		645.73	2,154.16
3,510.22		3,561.73		33,496.23	

the control account balance. If not, an employee has made an error in posting or perhaps funds have been misappropriated.

THE UNADJUSTED TRIAL BALANCE

After posting is complete, the firm can then prepare its financial statements. Actual preparation of financial statements typically begins with the trial balance. A trial balance is simply a list of all the accounts and their current balances as recorded in the general ledger. A sample trial balance for Carter Corporation is contained in Exhibit A.11. For convenience, we will work with whole dollar amounts throughout the rest of this Appendix. Since Carter has not yet made adjusting entries, a trial balance such as that shown in Exhibit A.11 is frequently referred to as an **unadjusted trial balance**.

What is the purpose of the trial balance? First, a quick check of the totals of the debit and credit balances will reveal whether they are equal. If they do not equal, then one or more entries recorded during the period were in error. Second, an examination of the trial balance will help the accountant identify the need for any adjusting entries. For example, Carter's December 31, 1994, trial balance shows no balances for interest revenue, cost of goods sold, depreciation expense, bad debt expense, or interest expense. It is very unlikely that the proper balances for all of these accounts is zero. Rather, this points up the probable need for some adjusting entries.

CARTER CORPORATION
Trial Balance
December 31, 1994

NO.	NAME	DR.	CR.
100	Cash	1,245	
110	Notes receivable	2,650	
120	Accounts receivable	14,622	
129	Allowance for doubtful accounts		295
130	Inventories	22,173	
150	Furniture and fixtures	14,838	
151	Accumulated depreciation		3,267
200	Notes payable—banks		5,200
210	Accounts payable		8,403
250	Notes payable—long-term		12,240
260	Common stock		5,600
270	Additional paid-in capital		8,795
280	Retained earnings		10,471
300	Sales revenue		214,324
400	Purchases	155,216	
410	Salary expense—sales	23,197	
415	Salary expense—administration	16,203	
420	Advertising expense	1,743	
425	Travel and entertainment expense	872	
430	Rent expense	12,480	
435	Insurance expense	780	
450	Interest expense	2,140	
460	Other expenses	436	
	Total	268,595	268,595

Note: Accounts with zero balances are not shown.

ADJUSTING ENTRIES

Other than the routine entries made to record transactions, **adjusting entries** are those necessary under a double-entry, accrual accounting system. They are necessary for three general reasons. First, adjustments are necessary to apply the accrual basis of accounting. As discussed in Chapters 4 and 5, under the accrual basis, revenue is recognized when it is earned. Adjustments may be necessary to accrue revenue that has been earned but not yet collected or to defer the recognition of revenue that has been collected but not yet earned. Under the accrual basis, expenses are recognized by matching them with revenues. This implies that expenses may be recognized either before or after costs are actually incurred and paid. Thus, it may be necessary to accrue some expenses before they are incurred and to defer the recognition of expense on some costs that have already been incurred. Second, if a firm uses a periodic inventory system, it will need to make some adjusting entries to calculate cost of goods sold. Third, employees may have made errors in recording transactions, and adjustments are necessary to correct the errors. Finally, some expense items such as depreciation and amortization are based on the allocation of costs to many periods. These allocations will also require adjusting entries. Let us examine some examples of each type of situation requiring an adjustment and the appropriate entry. All of these examples relate to Carter Corporation's trial balance in Exhibit A.11.

Complying With the Accrual Basis of Accounting

Entries necessary to comply with the accrual basis of accounting are of several types. We shall examine one or more examples of each type.

Expenses Based on Allocations   As observed in examining Carter Corporation's unadjusted trial balance in Exhibit A.11, the firm recorded no depreciation expense for the year. We do observe that Carter lists furniture and fixtures on its trial balance, and these assets require depreciation expense. Without going into the details of the calculation, suppose Carter determines $1,275 is the necessary amount of depreciation expense for the year. To record this depreciation expense, Carter would make the following entry (with account numbers included for convenience):

Adjusting Entry No. 1:
Depreciation expense (440)   1,275
    Accumulated depreciation (151)   1,275
To record depreciation expense for the year.

Other expenses based on allocations include various types of amortization: those of intangibles, debt issuance costs, and assets acquired under capital leases, for example. All of these items are discussed in more detail in various chapters throughout the text.

Accrued Expenses   Accrued expenses represent costs recognized as expenses that have not yet been paid. Two types of adjustments are frequently necessary for accrued expenses: to accrue additional expenses and to adjust the balances of previously accrued expenses. Carter Corporation requires adjustments of each type.

Interest on the long-term notes payable is due every May 1 and November 1 in the amount of $765. No interest expense has been accrued for the period of November 1 – December 31, 1994. If $765 is the interest cost per six-month period, then the cost per month is $765 ÷ 6 = $127.50; and for two months, the appropriate amount is $127.50 × 2 = $255.00. To recognize this interest cost as an expense of the period ended December 31, 1994, and as an obligation on that date, Carter must make the following adjustment:

Adjusting Entry No. 2:
Interest expense (450)   255
    Accrued expenses (230)   255
To accrue interest expense on long-term debt for the period
    November 1–December 31, 1994.

We observed earlier that Carter included no income tax expense on the unadjusted trial balance. Suppose the firm calculates $55 is the amount of expense for the period that is soon due and payable. To accrue this income tax expense, Carter needs to make the following entry:

Adjusting Entry No. 3:
Income tax expense (455)   55
    Income taxes payable (220)   55
To accrue taxes payable.

Carter Corporation recognizes bad debt expense under the allowance method. This method, discussed more fully in Chapter 7, is necessary to match properly the bad debt expense with the related revenue. In short, this implies that Carter accrues bad debt expense on an estimated basis before it writes off accounts as uncollectible. Therefore, the balance in the allowance for doubtful accounts can be viewed as a kind of accrued expense. It is conventional to show the allowance for doubtful accounts on the asset side of the balance sheet as a contra account to (a reduction of) the accounts receivable rather than on the liability side. This is because the allowance for doubtful accounts is not an amount that will be paid out in the future. Rather, it represents an amount that is not expected to be collected in the future. The balance in the allowance for doubtful accounts should equal management's estimate of the amount of its existing receivables that will not be collected. Suppose Carter Corporation estimates it requires an allowance of $726. Since only $295 is the balance shown on the unadjusted trial balance, Carter must make the following adjustment:

Adjusting Entry No. 4:
Bad debt expense (445)   431
    Allowance for doubtful accounts (112)   431
To accrue bad debt expense.

Many other situations require expenses to be accrued based on estimates of future events, including warranty costs, pension costs, and the costs of other post-retirement benefits paid to employees. These situations, all covered in the text, will usually require adjustments.

Prepaid Expenses   Some businesses require payment in advance; and firms often need to make an adjustment for prepaid expenses. To illustrate, suppose Carter Corporation pays a $540 insurance premium on May 1 and charges this cost to insurance expense. However, the premium covers a policy period of 18 months. Therefore, the insurance coverage costs $540 ÷ 18 = $30 per month; and by December 31, 1994, only 8 months of coverage has been "consumed." This leaves 10 months or $300 of insurance coverage unexpired at year-end, which Carter should classify as an asset, prepaid insurance. To adjust:

Adjusting Entry No. 5:
Prepaid expenses (130)   300
    Insurance expense (435)   300
To recognize 10 months of prepaid insurance as an asset.

This entry reduces the amount of insurance expense recognized this period by the cost of the unexpired coverage.

Accrued Revenues   Under the accrual basis of accounting, revenue is recognized as it is earned even if collection has not yet occurred. Adjustments to accrue revenue are commonplace. Suppose Carter Corporation has a customer's note receivable of $2,400 that was received on November 1, 1994. Interest on the note amounts to $40 per month with the principal amount and all interest due at the note's maturity date, May 1, 1995. Carter has accrued no interest revenue for the two months it has held the note. To adjust:

Adjusting Entry No. 6:
Accrued interest receivable (115)	80	
Interest revenue (310)		80

To accrue interest revenue.

Deferred Revenues   In certain instances, a firm will receive cash from its customers in advance—i.e., before it delivers any goods or services to the customers. Under the accrual basis of accounting, the firm must exercise care to ensure the amount received is not recognized as revenue. While reviewing the accounting records to prepare the financial statements, Carter Corporation's accountant observed that a $500 customer deposit had been recognized as revenue. This is not consistent with the accrual basis of accounting since Carter Corporation has to do much more than take a customer's money to earn revenue. Until the revenue is earned, Carter should classify this amount as a customer deposit. Thus, sales revenue is overstated and customer deposits are understated by this amount. To adjust these balances, Carter must make the following adjustment:

Adjusting Entry No. 7:
Sales revenue (300)	500	
Customer deposits (240)		500

To reclassify customer deposit recorded as revenue.

Once the goods covered by the deposit are shipped to the customer, Carter Corporation can recognize the revenue.

Error Correction

As numerous transactions are recorded, errors are likely to be made. If detected prior to year-end, errors are corrected by making an adjusting entry. For instance, suppose a $250 payment received from Columbia Plumbing Co. (a customer) was recorded with a credit to accounts receivable when, in fact, it applied to the note receivable from the customer. Thus, as a consequence of this error, accounts receivable are understated and notes receivable are overstated by $250. To correct this error, Carter can make the following adjustment:

Adjusting Entry No. 8:
Accounts receivable (120)	250	
Notes receivable (110)		250

To correct payment applied to customer's account receivable in error.

Calculating Cost of Goods Sold Under a Periodic System

When a firm uses a periodic inventory system, it records purchases in a temporary account called, appropriately enough, purchases. The balance in the inventory account reflects the balance at the beginning of the period until the firm makes an entry to record the ending balance. To determine the ending balance, the firm takes a physical count of the inventory or uses some estimation procedure. While we elaborate on inventory issues in Chapters 8 and 9, we need to understand the adjusting entries necessary to determine the cost of goods sold.

Under a periodic inventory system, a firm determines cost of goods sold as follows:

	Beginning inventory
+	Purchases
-	Ending inventory
=	Cost of goods sold

Carter Corporation's trial balance shows a beginning inventory balance of $22,173 and a balance in purchases of $155,216. Now, suppose Carter determines that the ending inventory costs $23,144. Substituting these amounts into the above formula yields a cost of goods sold of $154,245. Carter must make adjustments to substitute the ending inventory balance for the beginning balance still carried in the inventory account and to calculate cost of goods sold. The following entries will accomplish these tasks:

Adjusting Entry No. 9:
| Cost of goods sold (405) | 22,173 | |
| Inventory (120) | | 22,173 |
To close beginning inventory to cost of goods sold.

Adjusting Entry No. 10:
| Inventory (120) | 23,144 | |
| Cost of goods sold(405) | | 23,144 |
To record ending inventory.

Adjusting Entry No. 11:
| Cost of goods sold (405) | 155,216 | |
| Purchases (400) | | 155,216 |
To close purchases to cost of goods sold.

Notice how the effect of these entries is as follows: entries (9) and (10) replace the beginning balance in inventories with the ending balance, and entry (11) closes the temporary account, purchases. The combined effect of the three entries (which can easily be consolidated into a single entry) is to leave the correct balance of $154,245 in cost of goods sold.

If a firm maintains a perpetual inventory system, these three adjusting entries are not required. Under such a system, the firm records inventory purchases as debits to inventories rather than as debits to a temporary account, purchases. Moreover, as it sells goods, the firm records entries with debits to cost of goods sold and credits to inventories. Thus, both the inventories and cost of goods sold will be correct without adjustment, except for the effects of any theft, spoilage, shrinkage, and/or other similar losses.

Summary of Adjusting Entries

The types of adjusting entries we have seen are as follows:

Entries to Comply with the Accrual Basis of Accounting
- Expenses Based on Allocations
- Accrued Expenses
- Deferred and Prepaid Expenses
- Accrued Revenues
- Deferred Revenues
- Error Correction
- Entries to Calculate Cost of Goods Sold under a Periodic System

THE ADJUSTED TRIAL BALANCE

The next step in preparing financial statements is an adjusted trial balance. The preparation procedure is the same as before, except adjusted account balances are used. We summarize the effects of the adjustments on Carter Corporation's general ledger account balances in Exhibit A.12 using T-accounts and show the resulting adjusted trial balance in Exhibit A.13.

With its adjusted trial balance completed, Carter Corporation can proceed to the preparation of its statements.

PREPARING FINANCIAL STATEMENTS AND CLOSING THE BOOKS

A firm can prepare its balance sheet and income statement directly from its adjusted trial balance. The income statement shown in Exhibit A.14 is just a formatted list of the revenue and expense account balances (account nos. 300–460) taken from Carter Corporation's adjusted trial balance in Exhibit A.13.

Before preparing the balance sheet, the firm closes its temporary revenue and expense accounts. Closing entries or "closing the books" accomplishes two things. First, the firm updates its retained earnings balance to reflect the results of operation for the current year. Second, the firm leaves its temporary revenue and expense accounts with a zero balance, which permits it to begin recording the revenues and expenses of the next accounting period. Closing entries usually take the following form. First, the firm closes all revenue and expense accounts to an income summary account. Then, it closes the income summary account to retained earnings. The use of an income summary account is not mandatory, but it is a convenient interim step. Carter Corporation's closing entries would appear as follows:

Closing Entry No. 1:		
Sales revenue	213,824	
Interest revenue	80	
Income summary		213,904
To close revenue accounts to income summary.		

CARTER CORPORATION
Summary of Adjusting Entries
(Note: Only affected accounts are shown)

Notes Receivable			Accounts Receivable			Allow. for Doubtful Accounts			Accrued Interest Receivable		
2,650			14,622					295	0		
	(8)	250	(8)	250			(4)	431	(6)	80	
2,400			14,872					726	80		

Inventories			Prepaid Expenses			Accumulated Depreciation			Income Taxes Payable		
22,173			0					3,267			0
	(9)	22,173	(5)	300			(1)	1,275		(3)	55
(10) 23,144			300					4,542			55
23,144											

Accrued Expenses			Customer Deposits			Sales Revenue			Interest Revenue		
		0			0			214,324			0
	(2)	255	(7)	500	(7)	500			(6)	80	
		255			500			213,824			80

Purchases			Cost of Goods Sold			Insurance Expense			Depreciation Expense		
155,216			0			780			0		
	(11)	155,216	(9)	22,173	(10) 23,144		(5)	300	(1)	1,275	
0			(11) 155,216			480			1,275		
			154,245								

Bad Debt Expense			Interest Expense			Income Tax Expense		
0			2,140			0		
(4)	431		(2)	255		(3)	55	
431			2,395			55		

(Numbers in parentheses refer to adjusting entry numbers in the text.)

Closing Entry No. 2:

Income summary	213,812	
Cost of goods sold		154,245
Salary expense—sales		23,197
Salary expense—administration		16,203
Advertising expense		1,743
Travel and entertainment expense		872
Rent expense		12,480
Insurance expense		480
Depreciation expense		1,275
Bad debt expense		431
Interest expense		2,395
Income tax expense		55
Other expenses		436
To close expense accounts to income summary.		

EXHIBIT A.12

Carter Corporation—
Summary of
Adjusting Entries

EXHIBIT A.13
Carter Corporation—
Adjusted Trial
Balance

CARTER CORPORATION
Adjusted Trial Balance
December 31, 1994

NO.	NAME	DR.	CR.
100	Cash	1,245	
110	Notes receivable	2,400	
115	Accrued interest receivable	80	
120	Accounts receivable	14,872	
129	Allowance for doubtful accounts		726
130	Inventories	23,144	
140	Prepaid expenses	300	
150	Furniture and fixtures	14,838	
151	Accumulated depreciation		4,542
200	Notes payable—banks		5,200
210	Accounts payable		8,403
215	Customer deposits		500
220	Income taxes payable		55
230	Accrued expenses		255
250	Notes payable—long-term		12,240
260	Common stock		5,600
270	Additional paid-in capital		8,795
280	Retained earnings		10,471
300	Sales revenue		213,824
310	Interest revenue		80
405	Cost of goods sold	154,245	
410	Salary expense—sales	23,197	
415	Salary expense—administration	16,203	
420	Advertising expense	1,743	
425	Travel and entertainment expense	872	
430	Rent expense	12,480	
435	Insurance expense	480	
440	Depreciation expense	1,275	
445	Bad debt expense	431	
450	Interest expense	2,395	
455	Income tax expense	55	
460	Other expenses	436	
	Total	270,691	270,691

Note: Accounts with zero balances are not shown.

Closing Entry No. 3:
Income summary
   Retained earnings
To close income summary to retained earnings.

After Carter makes and posts these closing entries to the appropriate accounts, its retained earnings balance will include the results of operations for the year. The ending retained earnings balance can be computed as follows:

CARTER CORPORATION
Income Statement
December 31, 1994

Sales revenue		$213,824
Interest revenue		80
Total revenue		213,904
Cost of goods sold	$154,245	
Salary expense—sales	23,197	
Salary expense—administration	16,203	
Advertising expense	1,743	
Travel and entertainment expense	872	
Rent expense	12,480	
Insurance expense	480	
Depreciation expense	1,275	
Bad debt expense	431	
Interest expense	2,395	
Income tax expense	55	
Other expenses	436	213,812
Net income		$ 92

Retained earnings, balance forward	10,471
Plus: Amount from income summary	92
Retained earnings, ending balance	10,563

If Carter places this balance for retained earnings and all other balances for the balance sheet accounts (accounts nos. 100 through 270) in a balance sheet format, the result will appear as in Exhibit A.15.

Had Carter Corporation declared any dividends this period, it would have recorded them in a temporary account and would have also made a closing entry. However, since dividends are regarded as a distribution of income rather than an expense, Carter would have closed them directly to retained earnings rather than through its income summary account.

THE POST-CLOSING TRIAL BALANCE

An optional step in the process is the preparation of a post-closing trial balance, which permits a final examination of the account balances to ensure that all necessary adjusting and closing entries have been made and posted properly. Carter Corporation's post-closing trial balance is included in Exhibit A.16. Note that none of the revenue and expense accounts are listed. This is appropriate since all of these accounts had zero balances after Carter posted the closing entries.

CARTER CORPORATION
Balance Sheet
December 31, 1994

ASSETS:

Cash		$ 1,245
Notes receivable		2,400
Accrued interest receivable		80
Accounts receivable	$14,872	
Less: Allowance for doubtful accounts	(726)	14,146
Inventories		23,144
Prepaid expenses		300
Total current assets		41,315
Furniture and fixtures	14,838	
Accumulated depreciation	(4,542)	10,296
TOTAL ASSETS		$51,611

LIABILITIES AND EQUITY:

Notes payable—banks		$ 5,200
Accounts payable		8,403
Customer deposits		500
Income taxes payable		55
Accrued expenses		255
Total current liabilities		14,413
Notes payable—long-term		12,240
Total liabilities		26,653
Common stock		5,600
Additional paid-in capital		8,795
Retained earnings		10,563
Total stockholders' equity		24,958
TOTAL LIABILITIES AND EQUITY		$51,611

REVERSING ENTRIES

A final (and optional) step is to make reversing journal entries. The objective of a reversing entry is to avoid a particular item of revenue or expense being recognized twice or not at all. Reversing entries are useful when the accounting system is automated. In many systems, the journal entries to record routine transactions are created automatically. For instance, Carter Corporation's computer might be programmed to record wage and salary expense at each payroll date. In fiscal periods when the year-end does not coincide with the last payroll date of the period, Carter would have to make an adjusting entry to accrue wage and salary expense for wages and salaries earned but unpaid at year-end. Because the automated accounting system will record the entire payroll as expense when it is paid after year-end, there is a risk that the

EXHIBIT A.16
Carter Corporation—
Post-Closing Trial
Balance—December
31, 1994

CARTER CORPORATION
Post-Closing Trial Balance
December 31, 1994

NO.	NAME	DR.	CR.
100	Cash	1,245	
110	Notes receivable	2,400	
115	Accrued interest receivable	80	
120	Accounts receivable	14,872	
129	Allowance for doubtful accounts		726
130	Inventories	23,144	
140	Prepaid expenses	300	
150	Furniture and fixtures	14,838	
151	Accumulated depreciation		4,542
200	Notes payable—banks		5,200
210	Accounts payable		8,403
215	Customer deposits		500
220	Income taxes payable		55
230	Accrued expenses		255
250	Notes payable—long-term		12,240
260	Common stock		5,600
270	Additional paid-in capital		8,795
280	Retained earnings		10,563
	Total	56,879	56,879

Note: Accounts with zero balances are not shown.

expense will be recognized twice—once in the period Carter makes the adjusting entry to accrue wage and salary expense and once in the period Carter actually pays the wages and salaries. In such cases, Carter could use a reversing entry (simply the reverse of the year-end adjusting entry to accrue wage and salary expense) to ensure that the expense is not recognized twice.

To see how reversing entries work, recall adjusting entry no. 6, which accrued $80 of interest revenue earned but not yet collected, as follows:

Adjusting Entry No. 6:
Accrued interest receivable   80
    Interest revenue   80

Recall that Carter received the note in question on November 1, 1994; it earned $40 interest per month, and the principal amount of $2,400 and all interest are due on May 1, 1995. Suppose Carter's bookkeeper makes the following journal entry when the note and interest are collected on May 1, 1995:

Cash   2,640
    Notes receivable   2,400
    Interest revenue   240

Essentially, the bookkeeper has forgotten the interest revenue that was accrued on December 31, 1994. This resulted in two months of interest revenue being double-counted: $80 was accrued at December 31, 1994, and is included again in the $240 of interest revenue recognized upon collection of the note.

To prevent this occurrence, Carter could have made a reversing entry after closing the temporary accounts in connection with the December 31, 1994 closing. A reversing entry is merely the opposite of the adjustment made to accrue interest revenue and would appear as follows:

Reversing Entry:

Interest revenue	80	
Accrued interest receivable		80

Since Carter has already closed the interest revenue account to retained earnings, this reversing entry will leave a debit balance of $80 in the interest revenue account and will eliminate the accrued interest receivable asset. When Carter collects the note and credits interest revenue for $240, the end result will be a credit balance of $160. This is equal to four months of interest at $40 per month, precisely the amount applicable to 1995. Look at the T-accounts that follow to see how the reversing entry avoids double-counting some of the interest revenue. Notice how after Carter makes the reversing entry and records the collection, the balance in interest revenue is $160, precisely the amount applicable to 1995.

Accrued Interest Receivable				Interest Revenue	
1/1	80			1/1	0
		Reverse 80	Reverse 80	Collect	240
6/1	0			6/1	160

Reversing entries are not mandatory. Carter could have avoided double-counting the $80 of interest revenue accrued in 1994 by making the following entry upon collection of the note and interest:

Cash	2,640	
Notes receivable		2,400
Interest revenue		160
Accrued interest receivable		80

This concludes the review of the accounting process. Once it closes temporary revenue and expense accounts and posts reversing entries (if any), Carter can now begin the process all over by recording the events and transactions of the new accounting period. This circular nature of the accounting process is captured by the name frequently used to describe it, "the accounting cycle."

USING A WORKSHEET TO PREPARE FINANCIAL STATEMENTS

The T-accounts used in this Appendix for recording adjusting entries are not a particularly efficient way to approach the problem of preparing financial statements. Exhibit A.17 contains a columnar worksheet that accomplishes this task very readily. No "generally accepted worksheet format" exists, and the work

EXHIBIT A.17

CARTER CORPORATION
Worksheet for the Preparation of Financial Statements

No.	Name	Trial Balance Dr.	Trial Balance Cr.	Adj. No.	Adjustments Dr.	Adjustments Cr.	Adjusted Trial Balance Dr.	Adjusted Trial Balance Cr.	Income Statement Dr.	Income Statement Cr.	Closing Entries Dr.	Closing Entries Cr.	Balance Sheet Dr.	Balance Sheet Cr.
100	Cash	1,245					1,245						1,245	
110	Notes receivable	2,650		8.		250	2,400						2,400	
115	Accrued interest receivable			6.	80		80						80	
120	Accounts receivable	14,622		8.	250		14,872						14,872	
129	Allowance for doubtful accounts		295	4.		431		726						726
130	Inventories	22,173		9. / 10.	23,144	22,173	23,144						23,144	
140	Prepaid expenses			5.	300		300						300	
150	Furniture and fixtures	14,838					14,838						14,838	
151	Accumulated depreciation		3,267	1.		1,275		4,542						4,542
200	Notes payable—banks		5,200					5,200						5,200
210	Accounts payable		8,403					8,403						8,403
215	Customer deposits			7.		500		500						500
220	Income taxes payable			3.		55		55						55
230	Accrued expenses			2.		255		255						255
250	Notes payable—long-term		12,240					12,240						12,240
260	Common stock		5,600					5,600						5,600
270	Additional paid-in capital		8,795					8,795						8,795
280	Retained earnings		10,471					10,471				92		10,563
300	Sales revenue		214,324	7.	500			213,824		213,824	213,824			
310	Interest revenue			6.		80		80		80	80			
400	Purchases	155,216		11.		155,216	0							
405	Cost of goods sold			9. / 10. / 11.	22,173 / 155,216	23,144	154,245		154,245			154,245		
410	Salary expense—sales	23,197					23,197		23,197			23,197		
415	Salary expense—administration	16,203					16,203		16,203			16,203		
420	Advertising expense	1,743					1,743		1,743			1,743		
425	Travel and entertainment expense	872					872		872			872		
430	Rent expense	12,480					12,480		12,480			12,480		
435	Insurance expense	780		5.		300	480		480			480		
440	Depreciation expense			1.	1,275		1,275		1,275			1,275		
445	Bad debt expense			4.	431		431		431			431		
450	Interest expense	2,140		2.	255		2,395		2,395			2,395		
455	Income tax expense			3.	55		55		55			55		
460	Other expenses	436					436		436			436		
	Total	268,595	268,595		203,679	203,679	270,691	270,691	213,812	213,904	213,904	213,904	56,879	56,879

sheet in Exhibit A.17 should be viewed as a sample of a particular approach, rather than as a prototype, to be used in all cases. If you are familiar with microcomputer spreadsheet software, you can readily see how such software could be used to create a worksheet template to automate the process. In fact, Exhibit A.17 was created in such a manner.

Operation of the worksheet is quite simple. Adjustments are made to the trial balance amounts, yielding the adjusted trial balance amounts. [Please note that the numbers (No.) under the Adjustments column refer to the adjusting entry numbers in the text.] The revenues and expense account balances are carried over to the Income Statement columns before being closed to retained earnings in the Closing Entries column. Notice that the Income Statement columns do not have the same totals. The total credits of $213,904 exceed the total debits of $213,812 by $92. This difference is the net income for the period that can be seen as a credit to retained earnings in the Closing Entries columns. The effect of the closing entries is to leave all of the income statement accounts with zero balances and to include the net income for the period in retained earnings. Preparation of the financial statements becomes just a matter of reformatting the amounts in the Income Statement and Balance Sheet columns of the worksheet.

SUMMARY

As transactions occur, one or more documents create evidence of each transaction. These documents are the basis for entries into a firm's accounting system. As transactions occur, the firm records them in its journals. Some special-purpose journals are designed to handle only particular types of recurring transactions such as sales or purchases, while the general journal handles transactions occurring less frequently and any necessary adjusting entries. Periodically, the firm summarizes journal entries and updates or "posts" account balances in its general ledger, which is a cumulative record of all transactions organized by account. The particular accounts a firm maintains in its general ledger are listed in the chart of accounts, essentially an index to the general ledger.

At regular intervals, management will interrupt the routine activities of journalizing and posting to allow for statement preparation. The preparation of financial statements typically begins with a trial balance, which is examined for obvious bookkeeping errors and to determine if any adjusting entries are necessary. Adjusting entries may be necessary to:

1. Enter certain events into the accounting system such as depreciation, even though no formal transaction has taken place
2. Apply properly the accrual basis of accounting
3. Correct bookkeeping errors that have been made in recording events and transactions during the current period.

Once the firm records all adjustments in the journals and posts them to the ledger, it must examine the adjusted trial balance to determine whether further adjustments are necessary.

The firm prepares financial statements from the adjusted trial balance. Before retained earnings will reflect the results of the current year's operations, the firm must close temporary accounts such as revenues, expenses, gains, losses, and dividends, leaving them with zero balances before the next accounting period's activity is recorded.

Optional steps in the process include preparation of a post-closing trial balance to ensure that all necessary closing entries have been recorded and posted properly and reversing entries to prevent certain revenues and expenses from being recorded twice or not at all.

PROBLEMS

A-1.   *Recording routine transactions*

REQUIRED:

Prepare journal entries to record the following events and transactions for Wilson Wrecking, Inc., which occurred on October 7, 1994.
(a) Wilson sends an invoice to a customer for services rendered in the amount of $14,245.
(b) Wilson receives a check for $5,720 from a customer representing payment in full on the customer's account.
(c) Wilson pays an invoice from its insurance agency in the amount of $12,600 for insurance coverage over the next 12 months.
(d) Wilson purchases a new truck at a cost of $37,525 for cash.
(e) Wilson receives a $5,000 check from a customer as an advance payment for work yet to be performed.

A-2.   *Recording routine transactions*

REQUIRED:

Prepare journal entries to record the following events and transactions for Consolidated Canneries, Inc., which took place on July 25, 1994.
(a) The firm borrows $20,000 on a 12% note payable due in 5 years.
(b) The firm sells some machinery that is no longer needed for $5,250. The original cost of the machinery was $20,000, and $14,600 of depreciation has been recorded to date.
(c) $4,200 is paid for principal and interest on a note payable that has been outstanding for 6 months. The note was issued in exchange for a $4,000 loan from Commercial Bank and Trust Co.
(d) The firm enters into a 1-year lease for some warehouse space. The lease calls for monthly payments of $4,000. As required by the lease contract, Consolidated pays the first and last month's rent at the signing of the lease.
(e) $2,398 is paid to a supplier in full settlement of an account payable balance in the same amount.

A-3.   *Recording routine transactions; special-purpose journals*

REQUIRED:

Prepare journal entries to record the following events and transactions of Texas Residential Electrical Equipment Co. (TREE Co.), which all took place on March

16, 1995. Indicate what special journal, if any, might be used to record each entry you propose.

(a) TREE Co. orders a new computer system from Business Electronics World to be delivered next week at a cost of $10,200.00, payable upon delivery.

(b) TREE Co. receives a shipment of circuit breakers it had ordered from Electric General Co. together with an invoice for $4,235.29.

(c) TREE Co. receives a payment on account for $310.35 from North Dallas Electrical Contractors Co.

(d) TREE Co. delivers an order to a construction site and bills the electrical contractor for $1,294.20.

(e) TREE Co. invests $120,000 in marketable securities.

A-4.   *Recording routine transactions; special-purpose journals*

Excerpts from the cash receipts journal of Reagan Corp. are below.

Reagan Corp.
Cash Receipts Journal

| | | | (Credit) | | | | |
| | | | Accounts Receivable | | Other | | |
Date	Received From	Debit Amount	Acct. No.	Amount	Acct. No.	Name	Amount
Jul. 1	Princeton Plumbing Co.	3,910.52	140-46074	3,910.52			
Jul. 2	John D. Warren Corp.	84.32			225-90623	Customer deposits	84.32
Jul. 3	Roberts Systems, Inc.	2,532.45			148-83067	Notes receivable	2,532.45

REQUIRED:

For each entry in the cash receipts journal:

1. Describe the transaction that has taken place.
2. Prepare a journal entry suitable for the firm's general journal to record it— i.e., as if the cash receipts journal did not exist.

A-5.   *Adjusting entries*

REQUIRED:

For each of the following items affecting Florida Fruit Co., prepare the necessary adjusting entry or entries at December 31, 1994, if any.

(a) Florida Fruit Co. has $50,000 in bonds payable outstanding. The bonds are due in the year 2011 and require a $6,000 annual interest payment on March 1 of each year.

(b) Depreciation of Florida Fruit Co.'s property, plant, and equipment is determined to be $24,565 for 1994.

(c) On November 1, 1994, the firm paid an insurance premium in the amount of $1,440. This payment provides insurance coverage for the 12 months starting on that date. The payment was charged to insurance expense.

(d) Florida Fruit Co. employees work Monday through Friday, and the weekly payroll amounts to $15,000, paid each Friday. Suppose December 31, 1994, occurs on a Thursday.

(e) Florida Fruit Co. uses a periodic inventory system. Its inventory balance at December 31, 1994, is determined to be $34,282. The balance in the inventory account, which reflects the balance at December 31, 1993, is $36,119; and the balance in the purchases account at December 31, 1994, is $633,619.

A-6.   *Reversing entries*

REQUIRED:

For each adjusting entry made in Exercise A-5, prepare any reversing entries you think are appropriate and indicate why.

A-7.   *Adjusting entries*

REQUIRED:

For each of the following items affecting Minnesota Milling Co., prepare the necessary adjusting entry or entries at December 31, 1994, if any.

(a) Twin Cities Steel Corp. is both a customer and a supplier of Minnesota Milling. A payment on account of $2,560 from Twin Cities Steel was credited to accounts payable rather than to accounts receivable.

(b) Minnesota Milling estimates its bad debt expense for 1994 to be $20,675.

(c) Minnesota Milling paid a $5,000 deposit to a supplier for certain returnable containers. This payment was charged to inventory purchases.

(d) Minnesota Milling received a $20,000 check from a customer representing an advance payment on a particular job. The payment was credited to revenue although work on the job has not yet begun.

(e) Minnesota Milling estimates that its income taxes for the fourth quarter of 1994, payable on January 15, 1995, are $12,783.

A-8.   *Reversing entries*

REQUIRED:

For each adjusting entry made in Exercise A-7, prepare any reversing entries you think are appropriate and indicate why.

A-9.   *Recording routine transactions; special-purpose journals*

Excerpts from the cash disbursements journal of New York Computer Corp. are below.

New York Computer Corp
Cash Disbursements Journal

| | | | | (Debit) | | | | |
| | | | | Accounts Payable | | Other | | |
Date	Ck. No.	Paid To	Credit Amount	Acct. No.	Amount	Acct. No.	Acct. Name	Amount
May 1	3721	Lincoln Appliance Corp.	904.73	215-49092	904.73			
May 2	3722	Internal Revenue Service	4,052.21			225-10001	Taxes payable	4,052.21
May 3	3726	Morris National Bank	6,000.00			205-58032	Notes payable	6,000.00
May 3	3726	Morris National Bank	300.00			245-58032	Accrued interest	300.00
May 4	3727	Monroe Equipment Company	4,250.00			155-56211	Purchase deposits	4,250.00

REQUIRED:

For each entry in the cash disbursements journal:

1. Describe the transaction that has taken place.
2. Prepare a journal entry suitable for the firm's general journal to record it—i.e., as if the cash receipts journal did not exist.

A-10.   *Adjusting entries; reversing entries*

REQUIRED:

For each of the following adjusting entries:

1. Explain what the entry accomplishes.
2. Describe a situation in which such an entry would be required.
3. Indicate whether a reversing entry would be appropriate and explain why.

(a) Notes payable	5,000	
Accounts payable		5,000
(b) Travel and entertainment expense	432	
Advertising expense		432
(c) Cost of goods sold	235,094	
Inventory	24,177	
Purchases		259,271
(d) Prepaid insurance	655	
Insurance expense		655
(e) Wage expense	3,295	
Accrued wages payable		3,295

A-11.   *Adjusting entries, reversing entries*

REQUIRED:

For each of the following adjusting entries:

1. Explain what the entry accomplishes.
2. Describe a situation in which such an entry would be required.
3. Indicate whether a reversing entry would be appropriate and explain why.

(a) Sales revenue	12,000	
Advances from customers		12,000
(b) Accrued interest receivable	1,050	
Interest revenue		1,050
(c) Machinery and equipment	2,568	
Maintenance expense		2,568
(d) Research and development expense	5,450	
Patents		5,450
(e) Bad debt expense	3,401	
Allowance for bad debts		3,401

A-12. *Closing entries*

The following account balances are taken from the December 31, 1994, adjusted trial balance of Western Wardrobe, Inc.

	Debit	Credit
Common stock		10,950
Additional paid-in capital		16,722
Retained earnings		12,095
Sales revenue		346,193
Interest revenue		260
Purchases	0	
Cost of goods sold	201,880	
Salary expense—sales	54,091	
Salary expense—administration	32,970	
Advertising expense	4,504	
Travel and entertainment expense	1,950	
Rent expense	35,670	
Insurance expense	1,266	
Depreciation expense	3,592	
Bad debt expense	1,375	
Interest expense	3,244	
Income tax expense	675	
Other expenses	1,410	

REQUIRED:

1. Prepare the entry necessary to close the revenue and expense accounts.
2. Prepare the stockholders' equity section of the December 31, 1994, balance sheet.

A-13. *Recording routine transactions*

REQUIRED:

Prepare journal entries to record the following events and transactions for Frank's Fastmart, Inc.

(a) At the end of the day, the store's cash register reveals the following transactions have taken place:

Cash sales	$12,651.25
Sales tax collected	942.49
Total cash collected	$13,593.74

(b) The weekly payroll was as follows:

Gross wages	$ 2,450.00
Amounts withheld:	
Federal income tax	686.00
Social security tax	184.00
Net pay	$ 1,580.00

Payroll taxes on the employer (these amounts are due at the end of the month and have not yet been paid):

Social security tax	$184.00
Unemployment tax	24.50
Total employer payroll taxes	$208.50

(c) The daily delivery from Bold Bakery was received together with an invoice for $256.85. This amount is due in 10 days and, therefore, has not yet been paid.

(d) Property taxes of $1,475 for the upcoming quarter are paid.

A-14. *Recording routine transactions*

REQUIRED:

Prepare journal entries to record the following events and transactions for Industrial Hardware, Inc. (IHI):

(a) A shipment of nuts and bolts is delivered to a customer together with an invoice for $931. The merchandise cost IHI $465.50.

(b) A saleswoman for the firm submitted the following expense report after an out-of-town trip:

Total travel and entertainment expenses	$ 904.62
Cash advance taken before trip	1,000.00
Amount owed to IHI	$ 95.38

(c) $500 is received from a customer as an advance payment on merchandise that IHI will have to special order.

(d) An invoice from Miller Manufacturing Co., one of IHI's suppliers, in the amount of $1,238.02 is paid.

A-15. *Adjusting entries; reversing entries*

On January 2, 1995, you begin the preparation of year-end financial statements for Southgate Industries, Inc. as of December 31, 1994. In your examination of the unadjusted trial balance as of that date and other company records, the following information comes to your attention:

(a) On December 31, 1994, the firm received a shipment of sub-assemblies from Northern Digital Co. together with an invoice for $14,523.55. Because most of the Accounting Department had gone home early to celebrate New Year's Eve, this purchase has not yet been recorded.

(b) Two shipments to customers scheduled for December 31, 1994, are still sitting on the loading dock on January 2, 1995. However, the invoices totalling $4,823.05 were mailed out on December 31 and were recorded (incorrectly) as 1994 sales.

(c) During early December, an employee received a $500 advance on his December 15 payroll because of a personal emergency. At the time, this amount was incorrectly charged to wage expense.

(d) On October 1, 1994, the firm paid an insurance premium of $2,880 covering the period October 1, 1994 to March 31, 1995. The entire $2,880 was charged to insurance expense.

(e) On November 31, 1994, the firm paid a $500 deposit for returnable containers to a supplier. This amount was charged to purchases.

REQUIRED:

For each item above:
1. Prepare the necessary journal entry (if any).
2. Prepare a suitable reversing entry, if appropriate. If no reversing entry is appropriate, explain why.

A-16.   *Adjusting entries; reversing entries*

You are engaged in the audit of the December 31, 1994, annual financial statements for Turbo Computer Systems, Inc. In your examination of the company records, the following information comes to your attention:

(a) In January, routine maintenance costing $4,259.93 was incorrectly charged to machinery and equipment. As a consequence, depreciation expense for 1994 is overstated by $426.

(b) On March 15, 1994, a $10,000 note issued March 16, 1993, and one year's interest of $1,200 was paid. The entire $1,200 was charged to interest expense for 1994. At December 31, 1993, interest expense on the note had been properly accrued and an appropriate reversing entry was prepared as of January 1, 1994.

(c) On July 1, 1994, the firm leased a fleet of automobiles for its sales staff. A required $15,000 security deposit was incorrectly charged to rent expense.

(d) On January 10, 1994 (the first payday for the year), the entire payroll of $14,356 was recognized as wage expense for 1994, even though $4,301 of that amount had already been properly accrued as wage expense for the year ended December 31, 1993, and no reversing entry had been made.

(e) On October 31, 1994, a 1-year subscription to the Schmead Data Corp. electronic information service costing $6,000 was charged to subscription expense.

REQUIRED:

For each item above:
1. Prepare the necessary journal entry (if any).
2. Prepare a suitable reversing entry, if appropriate. If no reversing entry is appropriate, explain why.

A-17.   *Special-purpose journals; adjusting entries*

You are the accounting manager for Crosstown Corp. and are reviewing the accounts prior to preparation of the annual financial statements as of December 31, 1994. During the last week of December, your regular bookkeeper was on vacation and his duties were performed by a temporary worker provided by Temporary Accounting Staff, Inc. Excerpts from the cash disbursements journal for this period are below.

Crosstown Corp.
Cash Disbursements Journal
(excerpts)

| | | | | (Debit) | | | | |
| | | | | Accounts Payable | | Other | | |
Date	Ck. No.	Paid To	Credit Amount	Acct. No.	Amount	Acct. No.	Acct. Name	Amount
Dec. 26	5732	Johnson Insurance Corp.	9,360.00			465-56091	Insurance expense	9,360.00
Dec. 27	5758	Dallas County Assessor	5,582.00	215-23904	5,582.00			
Dec. 27	5812	Delano Manufacturing Co.	755.34			275-25012	Machinery and eq.	755.34
Dec. 28	5836	Jack Hudson	500.00			495-40451	Travel and ent. exp.	500.00
Dec. 31	5879	Carver National Bank	1,800.00			475-18560	Interest expense	1,800.00

You have obtained the following additional information:

(a) Check no. 5732 represents a 6-month insurance premium covering the period December 15, 1994 through June 14, 1995.

(b) Check no. 5758 represents property taxes for the firm's Dallas office for 1995. No entry had been made to record the tax bill, which was received on December 15, 1994.

(c) Check no. 5812 represents payment in full of an invoice received from Delano Manufacturing Co. on November 30, 1994, for certain spare parts for Crosstown Corp.'s manufacturing equipment. Upon receipt of the invoice, it was correctly accounted for with a debit to Spare Parts Inventory and a credit to Accounts Payable.

(d) Check no. 5836 represents a travel advance to a district sales manager for a trip to be taken in the first week of January, 1995.

(e) Check no. 5879 represents interest for 18 months on a $10,000 note payable to Carver National Bank. Interest for 6 months had been properly accrued (but not reversed) as of December 31, 1993.

REQUIRED:

For each of the items in the journal, make any necessary adjusting entries.

A-18. *Special-purpose journals; adjusting entries*

You are engaged in the annual audit of Sonapanic Corp. as of December 31, 1994. During the course of your examination, you uncover several cash receipts that appear to have been recorded without proper review by the firm's controller who was ill for several days in December. Excerpts from the cash receipts journal for this period are below.

Sonapanic Corp.
Cash Receipts Journal
(excerpts)

| | | | (Credit) | | | | |
| | | | Accounts Receivable | | Other | | |
Date	Received From	Debit Amount	Acct. No.	Amount	Acct. No.	Name	Amount
Dec. 27	Baltimore Mfg. Co.	493.45	140-13391	493.45			
Dec. 27	James A. Salmonsen	109.52	140-46074	109.52			
Dec. 28	Clarke & Oates Agency	2,000.00			325-32670	Sales revenue	2,000.00
Dec. 28	Northeast Supply Co.	790.24	145-75920	790.24			
Dec. 28	Richardson Technology	5,325.44			148-83067	Notes receivable	5,325.44

You have obtained the following additional information:

(a) The December 27 receipt from Baltimore Mfg. Co. represented payment in full of the $450 note dated February 4, 1994, payable to Sonapanic Corp. plus accrued interest.

(b) The December 27 receipt from James A. Salmonsen represents a refund of a travel advance taken by Mr. Salmonsen (a regional sales executive) but not spent. The receipt was incorrectly credited to the account receivable from Salmonsen Bros. Co., a customer of Sonapanic.

(c) The $2,000 received form Clarke & Oates Agency on December 28 represents an advance payment for a custom telephone system ordered on the same date. Installation of the system is scheduled for January 28, 1995.

(d) The December 28 receipt from Northeast Supply Co. represents a refund of an amount overpaid by Sonapanic Corp. to Northeast, one of its suppliers. Northeast is also a customer of Sonapanic, and the receipt was incorrectly credited to its account receivable.

(e) The December 28 receipt from Richardson Technology represents payment in full of the $5,000 note dated June 16, 1994, payable to Sonapanic plus accrued interest.

REQUIRED:

For each of the items in the journal, make any necessary adjusting entries.

A-19. *Adjusting entries; calculation of cost of goods sold*

As controller for Basic Industrial Corp., you uncover the following items in the course of the year-end closing at December 31, 1994:

(a) An invoice for $309.25 was received from Texas Machinery & Equipment Co. on December 31, 1994, and a purchase for this amount was recorded. However, since the shipment did not arrive until January 3, this purchase should have properly been recorded in 1995.

(b) A machine purchased for $2,450.25 for use by the maintenance staff was incorrectly charged to inventory purchases.

(c) A shipment from Oklahoma Agricultural Technology arrived on December 29, 1994, and should have been recorded as a purchase for 1994. However, the invoice in the amount of $737.29 did not arrive until January 4, 1995, and, thus, no purchase was recorded until that date.

(d) A shipment from Minnesota Mfg. Co. arrived on December 29, 1994, and was returned the same day because of extensive damage. The invoice in the amount of $902.46 was received, but the bookkeeper did not process it since the shipment was returned immediately.

(e)   The year-end inventory was determined to be $29,335.50. This includes the shipment referred to in Item c.

The unadjusted trial balance shows the following account balances at December 31, 1994:

	Debit	Credit
Inventory	23,419.02	
Inventory purchases	147,827.75	
Purchase returns		9,630.17
Cost of goods sold	0.00	

REQUIRED:

Prepare any necessary adjusting entries for Basic Industrial Corp. at December 31, 1994.

A-20. *Closing entries; financial statement preparation*

An adjusted trial balance for Tennessee Bicycle Supply Co. at December 31, 1994, follows:

Tennessee Bicycle Supply Co.
Adjusted Trial Balance
December 31, 1994

Name	Debit	Credit
Cash	$ 3,261.90	
Notes receivable	6,288.00	
Accounts receivable	38,964.64	
Allowance for doubtful accounts		$ 1,902.12
Accrued interest receivable	209.60	
Inventories	60,637.28	
Prepaid expenses	786.00	
Furniture and fixtures	38,875.56	
Accumulated depreciation		11,900.04
Notes payable — short-term		13,624.00
Accounts payable		22,015.86
Income taxes payable		144.10
Accrued expenses		668.10
Customer deposits		1,310.00
Notes payable — long-term		32,068.80
Common stock		14,672.00
Additional paid-in capital		23,042.90
Retained earnings		27,434.02
Sales revenue		560,218.88
Interest revenue		209.60
Cost of goods sold	404,121.90	
Salary expense—sales	60,776.14	
Salary expense—administration	42,451.86	
Advertising expense	4,566.66	
Travel and entertainment expense	2,284.64	
Rent expense	32,697.60	
Insurance expense	1,257.60	
Depreciation expense	3,340.50	
Bad debt expense	1,129.22	
Interest expense	6,274.90	
Income tax expense	144.10	
Other expenses	1,142.32	
Total	$709,210.42	$709,210.42

REQUIRED:

1. Prepare an appropriate closing entry.
2. Prepare a balance sheet and income statement.

A-21. *Adjusting entries; financial statement preparation*

The following unadjusted trial balance has been prepared from the general ledger of Warm Springs Co. as of December 31, 1994:

	Debit	Credit
Cash	$ 1,345	
Accounts receivable	20,491	
Allowance for doubtful accounts		$ 156
Inventories	18,923	
Prepaid expenses		
Furniture and fixtures	16,429	
Accumulated depreciation		3,402
Notes payable—banks		2,500
Accounts payable		10,298
Income taxes payable		
Accrued expenses		
Notes payable—long-term		10,450
Common stock		9,235
Additional paid-in capital		12,765
Retained earnings		6,524
Sales revenue		72,129
Cost of goods sold	40,278	
Salary expense	14,451	
Advertising expense	2,056	
Travel and entertainment expense	1,056	
Rent expense	4,824	
Insurance expense	1,340	
Depreciation expense	2,845	
Bad debt expense		
Interest expense	1,548	
Income tax expense	452	
Other expenses	1,421	
Total	$127,459	$127,459

The following additional information is available:
(a) Bad debt expense for the year is estimated to amount to 1% of sales revenues.
(b) Rent of $402 for the month of January, 1995, was paid during the year and charged to rent expense.
(c) Salaries of $142 were earned during 1994; but, since the year-end did not coincide with a payday for all employees, these amounts were not paid as of December 31, 1994.
(d) A purchase of furniture in the amount of $547 was incorrectly charged to depreciation expense.
(e) Income tax expense of $115 is the appropriate amount for the fourth quarter. This amount has been neither accrued nor paid by December 31, 1994.

REQUIRED:

1. Prepare any adjusting entries necessary at December 31, 1994.
2. Using T-accounts or a worksheet, calculate the adjusted account balances at December 31, 1994, and prepare an adjusted trial balance.
3. Prepare a balance sheet as of December 31, 1994, and an income statement for the year then ended.
4. For any of the adjusting entries you proposed in Requirement 1, prepare any reversing entries you think would be appropriate and indicate why you think the reversing entry is necessary.

A-22. *Adjusting entries; financial statement preparation*

The following unadjusted trial balance has been prepared from the general ledger of Results, Inc. as of December 31, 1994:

	Debit	Credit
Cash	$ 458	
Notes receivable	1,475	
Accounts receivable	34,092	
Allowance for doubtful accounts	217	
Accrued interest receivable		
Inventories	28,766	
Prepaid expenses		
Furniture and fixtures	37,451	
Accumulated depreciation		$ 12,376
Notes payable—banks		5,000
Accounts payable		17,621
Income taxes payable		
Accrued expenses		
Notes payable—long-term		17,250
Common stock		17,773
Additional paid-in capital		16,451
Retained earnings		11,510
Sales revenue		128,158
Interest revenue		
Purchases	64,389	
Cost of goods sold		
Salary expense	23,791	
Advertising expense	4,095	
Travel and entertainment expense	6,590	
Rent expense	12,671	
Insurance expense	4,275	
Depreciation expense	4,810	
Bad debt expense		
Interest expense	1,705	
Income tax expense	1,109	
Other expenses	245	
Total	$226,139	$226,139

The following additional information is available:

(a) The notes receivable is a note of $1,475 received from a customer on July 1, 1994. The principal amount and all interest are due on June 30, 1995. The note bears interest at 18% per annum, and no interest revenue has been accrued to date.

(b) An ending allowance for doubtful accounts of $1,065 is deemed to be necessary at December 31, 1994.

(c) The ending inventories balance at December 31, 1994, is determined to be $29,463.

(d) Insurance premiums of $713, which provide coverage in 1995, were paid for and recognized as insurance expense for 1994.

(e) The $5,000 notes payable—banks was issued on October 1, 1994. The principal amount and all interest are due on April 1, 1995. The note bears interest at 16%, and no interest expense has been accrued to date. The $17,250 notes payable—long-term were issued in March of 1994 and require semiannual interest payments of $1,200 each March 1 and September 1. No interest expense for the last four months of 1994 has been accrued.

(f) Income tax expense has not been accrued for the fourth quarter of 1994. $136 is determined to be the appropriate amount for the fourth quarter and will be payable on January 15, 1995.

REQUIRED:

1. Prepare any adjusting entries necessary at December 31, 1994.
2. Using T-accounts or a worksheet, calculate the adjusted account balances at December 31, 1994, and prepare an adjusted trial balance.
3. Prepare a balance sheet as of December 31, 1994, and an income statement for the year then ended.
4. For any of the adjusting entries you proposed in Requirement 1, prepare any reversing entries you think would be appropriate and indicate why you think the reversing entry is necessary.

A-23.   *Comprehensive*

Kansas City Wholesale Equipment, Inc. provides the following post-closing trial balance at December 31, 1993:

	Debit	Credit
Cash	$ 782	
Notes receivable	1,823	
Accounts receivable	42,820	
Accrued interest receivable	125	
Inventories	30,519	
Prepaid insurance	456	
Furniture and fixtures	39,823	
Accumulated depreciation		$ 14,552
Notes payable—banks		15,000
Accounts payable		21,057
Income taxes payable		1,078
Accrued wages payable		206
Accrued interest payable		150
Notes payable—long-term		27,010
Common stock		10,025
Additional paid-in capital		7,905
Retained earnings		19,365
Sales revenue		
Interest revenue		
Purchases		
Cost of goods sold		
Wage expense		
Advertising expense		
Insurance expense		
Depreciation expense		
Interest expense		
Income tax expense		
Other expenses		
Total	$116,348	$116,348

During 1994, the following transactions took place:
(a)   The firm made sales, all on account, in the amount of $167,207.
(b)   The firm purchased inventory, all on account, in the amount of $92,840.
(c)   The firm purchased insurance coverage for cash in the amount of $1,356.
(d)   Wages of $46,025 were paid to employees during the year.
(e)   Furniture and fixtures costing $10,432 were purchased for cash.
(f)   A total of $91,665 was paid to the suppliers of inventory.
(g)   The $15,000 note payable, issued on December 1, 1993, at a 12% annual interest rate, due on June 1, 1994, was repaid on time including interest. The balance in accrued interest payable at December 31, 1993 applied to this note.

(h) As a result of a physical inventory, it was determined that goods costing $33,194 were in inventory on December 31, 1994.

(i) At December 31, 1994, it was determined that unexpired insurance coverage costing $1,450 still existed.

(j) Quarterly income tax payments totalling $8,056 were made during 1994.

(k) A total of $165,390 was collected on account from the firm's customers during 1994.

(l) On May 1, 1994, the firm received a check for $2,045 from a customer in full settlement of his note payable to the firm. The note was in the amount of $1,823 and $125 of accrued interest receivable had been recognized by December 31, 1993.

(m) Depreciation expense of $4,392 was recognized for the year.

(n) Furniture and fixtures acquired years ago at a cost of $3,855 and with accumulated depreciation of $2,095 recorded to date were sold for $1,500 cash on June 15, 1994.

(o) The firm computed its tax expense for 1994 to be $7,431.

(p) On October 1, 1994, the firm borrowed $20,000 from First National Bank & Trust of Kansas City. The debt is due in 5 years and carries an annual interest rate of 10% with interest payments due semiannually.

(q) December 31, 1994, did not coincide with the last payday of the year and, consequently, employees had earned $335 during 1994 but had not yet been paid by year-end.

(r) Advertising costs of $4,309 were incurred and paid in cash during the year.

(s) Other expenses of $2,011 were incurred and paid in cash during the year.

(t) Cash dividends of $3,500 were declared and paid during the year.

(u) On November 1, 1994, the firm received a $2,100 note, bearing interest at 12% per year, from a customer in lieu of payment on a past due account. The note was still outstanding at year-end.

REQUIRED:

1. Prepare all journal entries to record the 1994 transactions and any necessary adjustments.

2. Using T-accounts or any similar device, post the journal entries to the ledger accounts and prepare an adjusted trial balance at December 31, 1994.

3. Prepare a balance sheet at December 31, 1994, and an income statement for the year then ended.

Earnings Per Share

In a recent fiscal year, Pillsbury Company reported net income of $208.1 million. During the same period, General Mills, Incorporated reported net income of $183.5 million. Both companies are in the same industry. Would an investor who owned 100 shares in each company have been approximately as well off from the operations of these two corporations? This question can only be answered after incorporating differences in the capital structure (types of debt and equity claims) that each corporation has issued. This is the role of developing and reporting a separate measure of income referred to as **earnings per share (EPS)**.

CAPITAL STRUCTURE AND EARNINGS PER SHARE

Corporations that have only one class of common stock outstanding and no securities, which are not themselves common shares but can be converted into common shares, have a **simple capital structure**. When corporations issue any type of security that is convertible into common stock, the potential conversion of these securities into common shares represents a potential dilution of earnings per share. **Dilution** refers to situations where the issuance of additional common shares upon exercise of the conversion feature in another security would result in a reduction in the earnings per share figure. Securities that would cause dilution of earnings per share are called *dilutive securities*.

Corporations that issue an extensive array of convertible debt, convertible preferred stock, stock options, stock warrants, and other similar securities have a **complex capital structure**. However, if the potential dilution of earnings per share from considering all dilutive securities is less than 3% (e.g., earnings per share including the effects of these dilutive securities is greater than 97% of earnings per share without including the dilutive securities), the dilution is deemed to be immaterial and corporations have a simple capital structure for financial reporting purposes.

Corporations with simple capital structures report an earnings per share figure, referred to as **earnings per common share** or **simple earnings per share**. Corporations with complex capital structures report two earnings per share measures: **primary earnings per share (PEPS)** and **fully-diluted earnings per share (FDEPS)**. The differences between PEPS and FDEPS reflect the consequences of different assumptions used to adjust the earnings per share ratio for the effects of dilutive securities. The remainder of this Appendix examines how each of these earnings per share figures is computed.

Earnings Per Common Share

Earnings per common share is the ratio of earnings available to common shareholders divided by the average outstanding common shares over the accounting period for which earnings are reported. Earnings available to common shareholders is determined by subtracting any claims of the preferred shareholders on earnings for the period from reported income. If preferred shares have a cumulative dividend, the value of the dividend for the period is deducted from reported income regardless of whether it is paid. If the preferred dividends are noncumulative, net income is only reduced by the dividends actually paid during the period.

Computation of the weighted-average outstanding shares for the period requires an examination of the transactions that have affected the number of outstanding shares during the period. As with any weighted average, this computation weights the number of shares outstanding over any interval by the length of the interval. The number of shares outstanding is affected by new share issues, treasury share purchases or sales, as well as stock splits and stock dividends. The effects of stock splits and stock dividends are computed on a retroactive basis, as if they had occurred on the first day of the period.

To illustrate the process of computing the weighted-average number of shares outstanding, assume Layover Corporation has provided the following information regarding transactions in its common stock during the year:

1. On January 1, 1993, Layover had 150,000 shares of common stock issued and outstanding.
2. On April 30, 1993, Layover issued an additional 60,000 shares of common stock.
3. On July 1, 1993, Layover declared a 2-for-1 stock split, effective on July 31, 1993.
4. On December 1, 1993, Layover purchased 18,000 shares of treasury stock.

In addition, Layover reported net income of $640,000 for 1993 and declared and paid dividends on noncumulative preferred shares in the amount of $100,000. To compute the weighted-average number of shares to enter the earnings per common share computation, the effect of the 2-for-1 stock split at year-end must be retroactively applied to all transactions that preceded it during the year, as demonstrated in Exhibit B.1.

Note that this process weights the beginning balance by a value of 12/12ths, since these shares are effectively treated as being outstanding all year long, and doubles the shares because they were retroactively affected by the split. Similarly, the new shares issued as of April 30 are deemed to be outstanding for only 8 months of the year (8/12ths of the period) and also doubled for the retroactive effect of the split. Finally, the shares purchased on December 1 are post-split shares, which were withdrawn from circulation for only 1 month (1/12th) of the year.

Earnings Per Share Disclosures and Special Items

The discussion above focuses on how to compute the earnings per common share for corporations that have simple capital structures. For such public corporations, earnings per common share is all that is required as earnings per share disclosure. Of course, the effect of each component of net income must have its associated earnings per share effect. Thus, net income from continuing operations, each extraordinary item for the period, discontinued segment effects, and any cumulative effect of a change in accounting principle that are presented must each have an EPS effect disclosed. An example of the disclosures of earnings per common share for Clorox Corporation, which has a simple capital structure, is presented in Exhibit B.2.

When multiple components of income require EPS data, the EPS number for net income (or loss) is determined first. Then, each component reported between net income from continuing operations and net income is divided by the weighted-average number of shares to determine an EPS figure for each component. The EPS for net income from continuing operations is computed by adjusting the EPS for net income by the EPS effect of each of the components so that a summation of the EPS for net income (loss) from continuing operations and the EPS effect of each component total the EPS for net income (loss). This can be seen in Exhibit B.2 where Clorox presents EPS data for earnings from continuing operations ($2.63 for 1989), the effect of discontinued

EXHIBIT B.1

Layover
Corporation—Effects
of Stock Splits on
Weighted-Average
Share Computation

LAYOVER CORPORATION
Effects of Stock Splits on Weighted-Average Share Computation

	Shares Originally Outstanding		Effect of Split		Split Adjusted Shares		Months to Year-End		Weighted-Average Shares
Beginning Balance	150,000	×	2	=	300,000	×	12/12	=	300,000
Share Issue	60,000	×	2	=	120,000	×	8/12	=	80,000
Treasury Purchase	(18,000)	×	1	=	(18,000)	×	1/12	=	(1,500)
Totals					402,000				378,500

Earnings Per Share = Net Income Available to Common/Weighted-Average Shares
=$540,000/378,500 = $1.43

EXHIBIT B.2

Clorox Corporation—
Disclosure of
Earnings Per
Common Share for
Simple Capital
Structures

CLOROX CORPORATION
Disclosure of Earnings Per Common Share for Simple Capital Structures

(in thousands, except per share amounts)	1989	1988	1987
Net Earnings	$124,144	$132,570	$104,899
Earnings Per Common Share			
Continuing Operations	$2.63	$2.39	$1.93
Discontinued Operations	(.39)	.03	–
Total	$2.24	$2.36	$1.93
Weighted-Average Shares			
Outstanding	55,333	55,127	54,652

Notes to the Financial Statements:

Earnings Per Common Share

Earnings per common share are computed by dividing earnings after income taxes by the weighted-average number of common shares outstanding during each year adjusted for stock splits. The potential dilution from the exercise of stock options is not material.

operations (discontinued segments) (a loss of $0.39 for 1989), and net income ($2.24 for 1989) in such a fashion that the components sum to the total EPS for net income.

Simple EPS incorporates the concept of weighing the common shareholders' claims by the length of time the shares have been outstanding during the period. It incorporates the effects of preferred stock dividends, treasury stock exchanges, stock dividends, and stock splits as part of the computation. However, it does not incorporate the effects of any existing security that is convertible into common shares since the effects of this conversion must be immaterial to avoid the 3% dilution rule. Clorox describes its situation in exactly these terms in its note on significant accounting policies relating to earnings per common share as indicated in Exhibit B.2.

COMPLEX CAPITAL STRUCTURES AND DUAL PRESENTATION OF EPS DATA

Corporations having complex capital structures must use a different type of earnings per share disclosure, the **dual presentation**. Dual presentation refers to the two earnings per share numbers: primary earnings per share (PEPS) and fully-diluted earnings per share (FDEPS). A complex capital structure exists any time convertible securities have the potential to dilute earnings per common share more than 3%.

Dual Presentation

Dual presentation provides shareholders with some estimate of the potential dilution as if a portion of the convertible securities had been converted during the current year. The EPS computation for complex capital structures uses a series of pro-forma adjustments, which are computed by acting "as if" selected convertible securities were actually converted during the period.

The numerator of these EPS computations is based on the actual net income a firm reports for the period, adjusted for the effects on income that would have occurred if certain types of convertible securities had actually been converted. For example, if a convertible bond had actually been converted into common stock, the firm would not have recorded the interest expense on the debt. In addition, the tax benefits of the interest deduction would not have existed. In the pro-forma computations, the actual net income for the period is adjusted for the after-tax effect of removing the interest.

The denominator of the EPS computation is also affected. The number of additional shares that would be issued if the convertible security had been converted will be added to the denominator. In this way, one can think of the EPS computation as a forecast of what a firm's future EPS will be if next period's net income equals this period's reported net income and if the convertible securities were actually converted.

All EPS computations attempt to provide the most conservative estimate of the pro-forma effects of converting the various types of securities into shares of common stock. This implies that the EPS effects of such securities will only be included in the computation if they *reduce* EPS. Another way to say this is: Securities that can be converted into common stock will only be included in the EPS computation if they are dilutive. If the pro-forma conversion of a security into common stock would result in an *increase* in EPS, it is called *antidilutive* and is ignored.

Securities that can be converted into common stock are of many forms such as options, warrants, rights, stock performance plans, convertible debt, convertible preferred stock, and many others. Different rules are used to decide which of these securities are included in the pro-forma computation when PEPS is computed or when FDEPS is computed. PEPS focuses on providing a picture of the dilutive effect of those securities that are likely to be converted into common shares, while FDEPS is a broader measure of the total potential for current dilution. In this way, a range of potential dilutive effects is determined by reporting both primary and fully-diluted earnings per share.

Primary Earnings Per Share (PEPS)

The PEPS computation starts with simple EPS and then makes several adjustments for a select set of convertible securities. For a convertible security to be considered in the computation of PEPS, it must be classified as a **common stock equivalent**. A common stock equivalent is defined as:

> a security that is not, in form, a common stock but that usually contains provisions to enable the holder to become a common stockholder and that, because of its terms and circumstances under which it was issued, is in substance equivalent to a common stock.[1]

---

[1] "Earnings Per Share," *Accounting Principles Board Opinion No. 15* (New York: AICPA, May 1969), para. 25.

Two basic classifications of convertible securities must be considered in any computation of PEPS: stock options and warrants and convertible securities with individual yields (convertible bonds and preferred stock). Each classification has separate rules for determining whether the security qualifies as a common stock equivalent and will enter into the primary EPS computation. In all PEPS computations, if a convertible security has several different conversion rates over its life, the conversion rates used in the computations are the ones most favorable to the convertible security's holder within the next five years.

Stock Options and Warrants in PEPS

Stock options and warrants have value *only* because they are convertible into some other securities. Options and warrants that are convertible into common stock are always common stock equivalents because their value depends solely on the value of the underlying common stock. However, since some options and warrants are antidilutive, not all of them enter into primary EPS.

Necessary Conditions for Inclusion of Stock Options and Warrants in PEPS   In addition to being common stock equivalents, options and warrants must also pass several other tests for inclusion in primary EPS. These tests are:

1. The exercise price of the option or warrant must be below the market price of the stock for substantially all of one quarter.
2. The option or warrant must be exercisable within five years of the end of the fiscal period.[2]

Since primary EPS focuses on those convertible securities with the highest probability of conversion, these tests separate such options and warrants from all others.

Typical Treatment of Options and Warrants—The Treasury Stock Method   Once an option or warrant satisfies the above criteria and if it has a dilutive effect, it is incorporated into primary EPS by the **treasury stock method**. The treasury stock method refers to a series of computations that act as if the following transactions occurred during the period:

1. The investor holding the options or warrants presents them for conversion into common stock along with the exercise price required by the terms of the contract.
2. The company takes the proceeds from the exercise and purchases from the market as many shares of stock as possible to place in its treasury.
3. The company takes the shares purchased for the treasury and reissues them to the investor to satisfy part of the requirements of the option or warrant conversion.

---

[2] In addition to these individual tests, other special requirements are considered when the total number of shares under warrants and options exceed 20% of the outstanding shares. Since this is rarely violated, we ignore these special rules here.

4. The company issues previously unissued shares to make up any short-fall of shares that are required under the option or warrant contract but cannot be obtained from the repurchase of shares for the treasury out of the proceeds of the exercise.

Under the treasury stock method, the previously unissued shares issued in Stage 4 above are treated as an adjustment to the denominator of the EPS ratio. For purposes of computing PEPS, the purchase price assumed in Stage 2 is the average market price for the period under consideration.

When the average market price is above the exercise price, the treasury shares assumed repurchased in Stage 2 will be insufficient to meet all the demands for shares under the option. For example, if options exist for 1,000 shares at an exercise price of $10 when the market value of each share is $20, the proceeds from the exercise of the options of $10,000 will only purchase 500 shares at a market price of $20. Thus, the treasury shares used to satisfy the options would fall short of the total required by 500 shares.

This shortage is assumed to be made up from previously unissued shares in Stage 4. In the PEPS computation, these shares are treated as outstanding from the first date that the option qualified for inclusion in PEPS (i.e., the first date the option or warrant satisfied all of the criteria). Since this pro-forma computation increases the number of shares in the denominator of the EPS computation without affecting the income in the numerator, the EPS must be reduced (or diluted) by the inclusion of these options and warrants as long as the company reported net income. When a company reports a net loss, the net loss per share would actually be decreased by including the pro-forma effect of option and warrant conversions. This situation would make the effect of options and warrants antidilutive, and the company would report only simple earnings (loss) per share.

The effect of options and warrants whose exercise price is above the average market price is antidilutive and, therefore, ignored in the PEPS computation. To see why this is true, consider the following. When the average market price is below the exercise price, the proceeds from the exercise of the option would exceed the cash needed to repurchase the shares required under the option. For instance, if the exercise price of the options in the earlier example were $25, instead of the $10 presumed earlier, the total proceeds from exercise of options for 1,000 shares would be $25,000. With the market value per share at $20, only $20,000 would be necessary to repurchase sufficient shares at a market price of $20 to satisfy the share requirements under all of the options. This would still leave the company $5,000 of cash. Consequently, the company would have generated cash from the exercise of the option and not have any more shares outstanding. The extra cash would be available for investment or repayment of debt. In either case, it would increase income.

With these options or warrants, the denominator of the EPS computation would be unchanged; but the numerator would have to reflect the increased income from potential new investment. This would increase EPS or be anti-dilutive. No antidilutive option is included in the EPS computation; so, options and warrants whose exercise price is above the average market price for the period do not enter PEPS.

Treatment of Options and Warrants Exercised During the Period   The above discussion deals with options and warrants that are outstanding at the end of the period. What about options and warrants that are actually converted to common stock during the period? Consider the following specific example: Dynakin Corporation had 10,000 shares under option at an exercise price of $20 per share. Dynakin issued the options on April 1, 1993, and they were converted on July 1, 1993. Prior to the exercise of the options, Dynakin had 90,000 shares outstanding. The company reported net income of $110,000 for 1993, and no other share transactions occurred during the year.

On July 1, 1993, Dynakin would have increased the number of actual shares outstanding by 10,000 shares. At year-end, these newly issued shares would enter into the computation of the weighted-average shares outstanding included in simple EPS. Simple EPS for Dynakin would be [$110,000 ÷ (90,000 × 12 ÷ 12 + 10,000 × 6 ÷ 12)] or $1.16. No further adjustment is necessary to account for the shares issued at conversion.

However, the weighted-average shares outstanding included in simple EPS do not incorporate any adjustment for the dilutive effect that the options may have had prior to exercise. In this case, the specific period when the options may have had a dilutive effect was from April 1, 1993, to July 1, 1993. For options that have been converted during the period, if the average share price for the period prior to conversion was above the exercise price of the options, the dilutive effect of the options during the pre-exercise period must be included in PEPS. The adjustment for these options is computed using the treasury stock method, but the weighting of the share adjustment will be limited to the period the options were outstanding prior to conversion.

Suppose the average market price of Dynakin's stock for the period April 1, 1993 to July 1, 1993 was $15 per share. In this case, the exercise proceeds would more than cover the cost of purchasing the additional shares required under the option; and the effect of including the option would be antidilutive. As a result, no adjustment would be made for the pre-exercise period.[3] If the average market price of Dynakin's stock for the period was $32 per share, the exercise price is below the average market price; and the effect of including the option during the pre-exercise period will be dilutive. The computation of the share adjustment for the period prior to the actual conversion is demonstrated in Exhibit B.3 using the treasury stock method.

Convertible Securities With Individual Yields in PEPS

Convertible debt and preferred stock pose a special problem in computing primary EPS. Unlike options and warrants, these securities may have value for two reasons:

1. They are convertible into common stock, and the value of the common shares supports the value of the debt or preferred stock.
2. The securities offer an income stream that is not dependent on the value of the common stock.

---

[3] Note that it is not irrational for an investor to exercise the option just because the average market price over the pre-exercise period is below the exercise price. At the time of exercise, the market price may have been above the exercise price even though the average is not.

EXHIBIT B.3

Dynakin
Corporation—
Application of the
Treasury Stock
Method for Options
Exercised During the
Year

DYNAKIN CORPORATION
Application of the Treasury Stock Method for Options Exercised During the Year

Step 1: Determine the total proceeds from the exercise of the options:

10,000 options × $20 per share exercise price = $200,000 of total proceeds

Step 2: Determine the number of treasury shares that can be purchased with the proceeds of the option exercise using the average market price:

$200,000 ÷ $32 per share average market price = 6,250 shares

Step 3: Compute the number of previously unissued shares that must be issued in addition to the reissuance of the treasury shares to satisfy the demands of the option exercise:

10,000 total shares required − 6,250 treasury shares = 3,750 new shares

Step 4: Weight the newly issued shares by the period of time the option was outstanding up to the exercise date:

3,750 new shares × 3 months ÷ 12 months = 938 shares
(The option was outstanding from April 1 to July 1.)

Step 5: Compute the adjusted EPS by including the share adjustment in the denominator of the EPS ratio:

Net income ÷ weighted average shares for simple earnings per share + share adjustment for options

$110,000 ÷ (95,000 + 938) = $1.15 per share

Adjusted EPS of $1.15 < simple EPS of $1.16; the options are dilutive.

Convertible securities, whose value depends principally on the value of the underlying stock into which they can be converted, conceptually belong in primary EPS to the extent that they are dilutive and, therefore, should be classified as common stock equivalents. Convertible securities whose value is principally based on the income stream the security offers without the conversion feature are not common stock equivalents. How can one determine which category each convertible security falls into?

The Yield Test for Common Stock Equivalents   For securities of this type, it is possible to compute an effective yield at issuance. For a convertible bond, this yield reflects the yield to maturity on the bond as of the date of issuance. The yield to maturity on a newly issued bond is simply the interest rate that discounts the bond's future cash flows (interest and principal) back to the selling price of the debt at issue. For preferred stock, the effective yield is computed as the ratio of the annual dividend divided by the issue price of the preferred. When the effective yield is substantially below the yields on similar risk securities that are not convertible, the value of the security is supported more by the conversion feature than by the income stream it generates independent of the conversion potential. If the effective yield at issue is less than or equal to two-thirds of the average prevailing effective yield on Aa corporate bonds, the convertible debt or preferred stock is considered a common stock equivalent. This test is performed once when the security is issued. From that time on, the security will either be a common stock equivalent or it will never be. To be considered for inclusion in primary EPS, the security must be a common stock equivalent.

Time to First Conversion Test   In addition to being a common stock equivalent, convertible bonds or stock must also be convertible within five years of the balance sheet date to be included in PEPS. The reason for this restriction is the same as that for imposing the five-year limitation on options and warrants.

Determining the Dilutive Effect of Convertible Bonds and Stocks   Once a convertible bond or stock has satisfied the requirements for consideration in PEPS, the actual effect the security has on EPS will depend on whether it is dilutive or antidilutive. Only those securities that generate a dilutive effect on EPS will be included in PEPS.

To determine whether the effect of including a convertible security is dilutive, adjustments to both the denominator (the weighted-average shares outstanding) and the numerator (net income to common shareholders) of the EPS ratio must be computed. Each convertible bond or stock has a marginal EPS. Marginal EPS is the ratio of the income adjustment generated by a security divided by its share adjustment. When the marginal EPS for an individual security is below the EPS figure computed prior to including that security, the security is dilutive and will enter PEPS. If the marginal EPS is above the EPS computed prior to including the security, the effect of the security will be antidilutive and will be excluded from PEPS. Some caution is necessary when several securities that have both income and share adjustments are simultaneously considered for inclusion in PEPS. This situation will be covered later.

The income adjustment related to convertible bonds is the after-tax interest savings that would accrue if the bonds had been converted at the earliest point they met the tests for consideration in PEPS. For convertible preferred stock, the income adjustment is the current period's declared dividends (or accruing dividends if the preferred is cumulative and dividends for the current period are not declared). Since the corporation receives no tax deduction for payment of preferred dividends, the dividends are already in after-tax dollars.

Unlike options and warrants, when a convertible bond or stock is converted into common stock, the corporation receives no cash. As a result, it cannot take the proceeds from conversion and purchase treasury stock. Consequently, the share adjustments associated with convertible bonds and stock are computed assuming that all the shares required to be issued under the terms of the contract are previously unissued shares. As with options and warrants, the share adjustment is weighted by the period over which the convertible security qualified for consideration in PEPS.

Special Considerations When Multiple Dilutive Securities Exist   Consider the case of Prompt Corporation. Prompt computed its earnings per common share as $2 per share ($200,000 ÷ 100,000 shares). Prompt has two convertible debt issues that qualify as common stock equivalents. The marginal EPS for each security is as follows:

Security A = $1.99 ($19,900 ÷ 10,000 shares)

Security B = $0.50 ($20,000 ÷ 40,000 shares)

At first glance, it appears that both securities have a marginal EPS below the prior EPS and, thus, are dilutive. However, this observation ignores the fact that including Security B first will reduce the EPS below $1.99 and make the inclusion of Security A antidilutive. To see this, adjust the EPS computation to include Security B as follows:

$$(\$200,000 + \$20,000) \div (100,000 + 40,000) = \$1.57$$

If Security A were now included in the computation, the EPS figure would actually rise. Since the EPS computation reflects the maximum amount of dilution possible, Security A would be excluded from PEPS in this example.

The Prompt example demonstrates why it is important to rank, by marginal EPS effect, all the convertible securities that involve some form of income adjustment. This is also the reason that options and warrants are treated prior to the convertible debt and preferred stocks. These securities generally have only share adjustments to consider. Thus, they provide the maximum dilution of EPS prior to consideration of those securities that also have independent yields.

Fully-Diluted Earnings Per Share (FDEPS)

Once PEPS has been determined, a second computation may be necessary for FDEPS. Since FDEPS provides a broader based estimate of the effect of dilution than PEPS, the restrictions placed on securities to be included in this computation are fewer. In addition, a few measurement rules are also changed. This requires a reestimation of the adjustments required for options and warrants. One such measurement rule relates to the selection of the conversion rates used in the computations. PEPS uses the most favorable conversion rate within a five-year period following the balance sheet date, while FDEPS uses the most favorable rate within ten years following the balance sheet date.

There is no common stock equivalent for FDEPS. Generally, the only requirements for a security to enter fully-diluted EPS is that it be convertible within ten years of the balance sheet date and that the effect of including the pro-forma conversion of the security result in a dilution of EPS.

Stock Options and Warrants in FDEPS

All the options and warrants included in PEPS are included in FDEPS. However, the share adjustment must be determined using the higher of the average market price for the period (used in PEPS) or the ending market price. When the ending price is above the average, a recomputation of the share adjustment used in PEPS must be done. In addition, options and warrants that were not in PEPS because they were not exercisable within five years or because they were antidilutive using the average price may be included in FDEPS.

Convertible Securities With Independent Yields in FDEPS

For inclusion in FDEPS, no yield test applies. Thus, all of the convertible bonds and preferred stock that were included in PEPS may qualify for inclusion in

FDEPS. However, other convertible bonds or stocks may also be included; and these may have marginal yields below those included in PEPS. In some cases, this may result in exclusion of some of the securities included in PEPS since their effect on FDEPS is antidilutive. This situation is relatively unusual.

Treatment of these types of securities in FDEPS is identical to the treatment of similar securities in PEPS. Each will have an earnings adjustment and a share adjustment. To maximize dilution, they should be ranked from lowest to highest marginal EPS with each entering the computation in a stepwise fashion until the marginal EPS is higher than that obtained by including the previous convertible security.

EARNINGS PER SHARE: A COMPREHENSIVE EXAMPLE

Mason Corporation's capital structure is as follows:

	12/31/94	12/31/93
Outstanding shares of		
Common Stock	320,167	300,000
Nonconvertible Preferred Stock	10,000	10,000
8% Convertible Bonds (Face)	$1,000,000	$1,000,000
7% Convertible Bonds (Face)	$2,000,000	$2,000,000
5% Convertible Bonds (Face)	$1,200,000	0

The following additional information is available:

1. On April 30, 1994, Mason purchased 20,000 shares for its treasury at $29 per share.
2. On September 1, 1994, Mason sold 36,000 additional shares of common stock at $37 per share.
3. On December 1, 1994, Mason declared a 20% stock dividend to be distributed on January 1, 1995.
4. Net income for the year ended December 31, 1994 was $750,000.
5. During 1994, Mason paid dividends of $3 per share on the preferred stock and $1 per share on common stock.
6. The 8% bonds are convertible into 40 shares of common stock (after adjusting for the stock dividend) for each $1,000 bond. The Aa corporate yield at the time these bonds were issued was 10%; and they were issued at par value. The bonds are convertible at any time prior to maturity.
7. The 7% bonds have an effective yield of 6.0%, are convertible into 50 shares of common stock (after adjusting for the stock dividend) for each $1,000 bond, and were issued on January 1, 1989 at 110. The Aa corporate bond yield at the time of issue was 12%. The bonds are convertible any time after January 1, 1995. The bonds expire 10 years after the date of issue.

8. The 5% bonds are initially convertible into 5 shares of common stock for each $100 bond and were issued on May 31, 1994 at face value. After 2 years, the conversion rate increases to 8 shares of common per each $100 bond. The conversion rates were not protected for dilution due to stock splits and stock dividends. The Aa corporate bond yield on that date was 10%. The bonds are convertible any time after January 1, 1995.

9. Unexercised stock options to purchase 16,667 pre-stock dividend shares (20,000 shares of common stock after adjustment for the stock dividend) at $22.50 per share were outstanding at the beginning of 1994. On July 1, 1994, options for 4,167 pre-stock dividend shares were converted at a time when the market price of the stock was $30 per share. The average adjusted market price of Mason's common stock was $36 per share for each quarter and for the year ending December 31, 1994. The market price was $40 per share on December 31, 1994. The market price of Mason's stock was above the exercise price all year.

10. Warrants to purchase 30,000 shares of common stock (after adjustment for the stock split) at $38 per share were attached to the preferred stock when it was issued in 1989. The warrants, which expire on December 31, 1999, were outstanding at December 31, 1994. The market price of Mason's stock had exceeded the exercise price under the warrants for substantially all of three months during the last quarter of 1991. Since then the market price has consistently been below the exercise price.

11. Mason's effective tax rate was 40% for both 1993 and 1994.

The first step in determining the appropriate EPS figures Mason must report is to compute the weighted-average common shares outstanding and the related amount for simple EPS. Exhibit B.4 provides these computations. The next step is to identify all the common stock equivalents, since these must be considered in the computation of PEPS.

Stock Options and Warrants

All options and warrants are considered common stock equivalents. In addition, both meet the three-month test and both are convertible within five years. (Options were converted this year, and warrants expire within five years.) Thus, both the options and the warrants must be considered for inclusion in PEPS, separately. The options are dilutive and should be included. However, the warrants are antidilutive since the exercise price of $38 per share is above the average market price of $36 per share. The warrants are, therefore, excluded from PEPS.

Exhibits B.5 and B.6 present the computations of the share adjustments related to the dilutive options outstanding at year-end and those converted during the year, respectively. The total share adjustment relating to Mason's options is 6,563 shares. Including this effect in the EPS computation results in a reduction of EPS to $1.96 as demonstrated in Exhibit B.8.

MASON CORPORATION
Computation of Simple EPS

Computation of Weighted-Average Common Shares Outstanding

Shares Originally Outstanding		Effect of Stock Dividend		Dividend Adjusted Shares		Portion of Year Outstanding		Weighted-Average Shares
300,000	×	1.20	=	360,000	×	12/12	=	360,000
(20,000)	×	1.20	=	(24,000)	×	8/12	=	(16,000)
4,167	×	1.20	=	5,000	×	6/12	=	2,500
36,000	×	1.20	=	43,200	×	4/12	=	14,400
Totals				384,200				360,900

Computation of Income to Common Shareholders

Income for Simple EPS = Reported Net Income − Preferred Dividends

$750,000 − (10,000)($3) = $720,000

Computation of Simple EPS

Simple Earnings Per Share = $720,000 ÷ 360,900 = $2 per share

EXHIBIT B.5
Mason
Corporation—
Application of the
Treasury Stock
Method—Options
Outstanding at Year-
End—PEPS

MASON CORPORATION
Application of the Treasury Stock Method
Options Outstanding at Year-End—PEPS

Step 1: Determine the total proceeds from the exercise of the unexercised options:
15,000 options × $22.50 per share exercise price = $337,500 of total proceeds

Step 2: Determine the number of treasury shares that can be purchased with the proceeds of the option exercise using the average market price:
$337,500 ÷ $36 per share average market price = 9,375 shares

Step 3: Compute the number of previously unissued shares that must be issued in addition to the reissuance of the treasury shares to satisfy the demands of the option exercise:
15,000 total shares required − 9,375 treasury shares = 5,625 new shares

Step 4: Weight the newly issued shares by the period of time since the option first met the criteria for inclusion in PEPS:
5,625 new shares × 12 months ÷ 12 months = 5,625 shares

Convertible Debt

Effective Yield Test:

Convertible Debt	Effective Yield	Aa Corporate Yield
8% Convertible Bonds	8.0%	10%
7% Convertible Bonds	6.0%	12%
5% Convertible Bonds	5.0%	10%

Is 8.0% less than (2/3)(10%)? No, 8% bonds are not common stock equivalents.

Is 6.0% less than (2/3)(12%)? Yes, 7% bonds are common stock equivalents.

Is 5.0% less than (2/3)(10%)? Yes, 5% bonds are common stock equivalents.

Length of Time to First Date of Convertibility   Both bonds that qualify as a common stock equivalent are convertible within five years of December 31, 1990. Note that the 7% bonds were not convertible within five years of the year in which they were issued. Mason would have excluded these bonds from PEPS in 1993 for this reason, but it would not exclude them from the current year.

Test for Dilutive Effects   Exhibit B.7 demonstrates the computations of the income and share adjustments, along with the resulting marginal EPS for both convertible bonds that must be considered in the PEPS computation.

From the computation in Exhibit B.7, it is clear that the 5% debt will enter the computation first, followed by the 7% debt, assuming each results in a reduction in earnings per share. In Exhibit B.8, each convertible debt issue is included sequentially in the PEPS computation. In this example, both convertible debt issues are dilutive. However, if Mason's reported net income were

---

EXHIBIT B.6 |
Mason Corporation— Application of the Treasury Stock Method for Options Exercised During the Year—PEPS

MASON CORPORATION
Application of the Treasury Stock Method
For Options Exercised During the Year—PEPS

Step 1: Determine the total proceeds from the exercise of the converted options:
5,000 options × $22.50 per share exercise price = $122,500 of total proceeds

Step 2: Determine the number of treasury shares that can be purchased with the proceeds of the option exercise using the average market price:
$112,500 ÷ $36 per share average market price = 3,125 shares

Step 3: Compute the number of previously unissued shares that must be issued in addition to the reissuance of the treasury shares to satisfy the demands of the option exercise:
5,000 total shares required − 3,125 treasury shares = 1,875 new shares

Step 4: Weight the newly issued shares by the period of time the option was outstanding up to the exercise date:
1,875 new shares × 6 months ÷ 12 months = 938 shares

EXHIBIT B.7

Mason
Corporation—
Computation of
Marginal EPS for
Convertible Bonds—
PEPS

MASON CORPORATION
Computation of Marginal EPS for Convertible Bonds—PEPS

Computation of After-Tax Income Adjustment

7% Bonds: Interest Expense for 1990 = (.07)(2,000,000) − 200,000 ÷ 10 = $120,000
After-tax effect = (120,000)(1 − .40) = $72,000

5% Bonds: Interest Expense for 1990 = (.05)(1,200,000)(7 ÷ 12) = $35,000
After-tax effect = (35,000)(1 − .40) = $21,000

Computation of Share Adjustments

7% Debt: 2,000 bonds × 50 shares/bond = 100,000 shares
100,000 shares × 12 ÷ 12 = 100,000 share adjustment

5% Debt: 12,000 bonds × 8 shares/bond = 96,000 shares*
96,000 shares × 7 ÷ 12 = 56,000 share adjustment

* Note that 8 shares per bond is used for the 5% debt because it is the most favorable conversion
rate within the next five years.

Computation of Marginal EPS

7% Debt = 72,000 ÷ 100,000 = $0.72
5% Debt = 21,000 ÷ 56,000 = $0.38

EXHIBIT B.8

Mason
Corporation—
Schedule to
Compute Primary
Earnings Per Share
(PEPS)

MASON CORPORATION
Schedule to Compute Primary Earnings Per Share (PEPS)

	Shares	Income	Current EPS
Weighted-Average Shares	360,900	$720,000	$1.995
Options (add 6,563 shares)	367,463	720,000	1.959
5% Debt	423,463	741,000	1.750
7% Debt	523,463	813,000	1.553
Primary EPS			$1.55

$500,000 less than assumed in this example, the 7% debt would not enter into
the PEPS computation because it would be antidilutive. PEPS in that case
would only be $0.57 ($241,000 ÷ 423,463) prior to considering the 7% debt,
which has a marginal EPS of $0.72.

Fully-Diluted Earnings Per Share (FDEPS)

While the schedule in Exhibit B.8 completes the PEPS computation, it also
indicates that the degree of dilution from including securities that can be converted into common shares reduced EPS from $2 per share to only $1.55 per
share. This is a 23.5% reduction in EPS by just including the common stock
equivalents. Since this level of dilution already exceeds 3%, Mason has a complex capital structure and must use dual presentation of both PEPS and
FDEPS. The computation of FDEPS is summarized in Exhibit B.13. Each of the
adjustments in Exhibit B.13 is examined in more detail below.

Stock Options and Warrants   Since the year-end market price is above the average for the period, it is necessary to recompute the share adjustment for the options included in PEPS. In addition, the warrants now become dilutive because the ending market price is above the exercise price, even though the average was not. The new share adjustment for options outstanding at year-end, options exercised during the year, and warrants outstanding at year-end are demonstrated in Exhibits B.9, B.10, and B.11, respectively. The total share adjustment for all the options and warrants amounts to an additional 9,156 shares for FDEPS. This amount is entered in Exhibit B.13 as the adjustment to the denominator of the FDEPS computation.

Convertible Debt   Both issues of convertible debt included in PEPS must be considered for FDEPS. In addition, the 8% debt, which was not a common stock equivalent, may be included in FDEPS if its effect is dilutive and it is

---

EXHIBIT B.9

Mason Corporation— Application of the Treasury Stock Method—FDEPS— For Options Outstanding at Year-End

MASON CORPORATION
Application of the Treasury Stock Method—FDEPS
For Options Outstanding at Year-End

Step 1: Determine the total proceeds from the exercise of the unexercised options:
15,000 options × $22.50 per share exercise price = $337,500 of total proceeds

Step 2: Determine the number of treasury shares that can be purchased with the proceeds of the option exercise using the average market price:
$337,500 ÷ $40 per share ending market price = 8,438 shares

Step 3: Compute the number of previously unissued shares that must be issued in addition to the reissuance of the treasury shares to satisfy the demands of the option exercise:
15,000 total shares required − 8,438 treasury shares = 6,562 new shares

Step 4: Weight the newly issued shares by the period of time since the option first met the criteria for inclusion in PEPS:
6,562 new shares × 12 months ÷ 12 months = 6,562 share

EXHIBIT B.10

Mason Corporation— Application of the Treasury Stock Method For Options Exercised During the Year—FDEPS

MASON CORPORATION
Application of the Treasury Stock Method
For Options Exercised During the Year—FDEPS

Step 1: Determine the total proceeds from the exercise of the converted options:
5,000 options × $22.50 per share exercise price = $122,500 of total proceeds

Step 2: Determine the number of treasury shares that can be purchased with the proceeds of the option exercise using the average market price:
$112,500 ÷ $40 per share average market price = 2,813 shares

Step 3: Compute the number of previously unissued shares that must be issued in addition to the reissuance of the treasury shares to satisfy the demands of the option exercise:
5,000 total shares required − 2,813 treasury shares = 2,187 new shares

Step 4: Weight the newly issued shares by the period of time the option was outstanding up to the exercise date:
2,187 new shares × 6 months ÷ 12 months = 1,094 shares

convertible within ten years. The computations of the income and share adjustments, along with the marginal EPS for the 8% convertible debt, is demonstrated in Exhibit B.12.

Since the marginal EPS for the two convertible debt securities included in PEPS does not change in the FDEPS computation, the ranking of the convertible securities on the basis of their marginal EPS would appear as follows:

Security	Marginal EPS
5% Bond	$0.38
7% Bond	$0.72
8% Bond	$1.20

The order with which each security is placed into the FDEPS computation will be dictated by the ranking. As a result, in Exhibit B.13, the 5% bond is considered first, followed by the 7% bond, and finally the 8% bond. In this example, all of these securities are dilutive and all enter FDEPS.

MASON CORPORATION
Application of the Treasury Stock Method—FDEPS
Warrants Outstanding at Year-End

Step 1:   Determine the total proceeds from the exercise of the unexercised warrants:
30,000 warrants × $38 per share exercise price = $1,140,000 of total proceeds

Step 2:   Determine the number of treasury shares that can be purchased with the proceeds of the warrant exercise using the ending market price:
$1,140,000 ÷ $40 per share ending market price = 28,500 shares

Step 3:   Compute the number of previously unissued shares that must be issued in addition to the reissuance of the treasury shares to satisfy the demands of the warrant exercise:
30,000 total shares required − 28,500 treasury shares = 1,500 new shares

Step 4:   Weight the newly issued shares by the period of time since the option first met the criteria for inclusion in PEPS:
1,500 new shares × 12 months ÷ 12 months = 1,500 shares

MASON CORPORATION
Computation of Marginal EPS for Convertible Bonds—FDEPS

Income Adjustment Computation
Interest Expense for 1990 = (.08)(1,000,000) = $80,000
After-tax effect = (80,000)(1 − .40) = $48,000

Share Adjustment Computation
1,000 bonds × 40 shares/bond = 40,000 shares
40,000 shares × 12 ÷ 12 = 40,000 share adjustment

Marginal EPS Computation
$48,000 ÷ 40,000 = $1.20

EXHIBIT B.13

Mason Corporation— Computation of Fully-Diluted Earnings Per Share (FDEPS)

MASON CORPORATION
Computation of the Fully-Diluted Earnings Per Share (FDEPS)

	Shares	Income	Marginal EPS	Current EPS
Weighted-Average Shares	360,900	$720,000	n/a	$1.995
Options	370,056	720,000	n/a	1.946
5% Debt	426,056	741,000	$0.38	1.739
7% Debt	526,056	813,000	0.72	1.545
8% Debt	566,056	861,000	1.20	1.521
Fully-Diluted EPS				$1.52

SUMMARY

Earnings per share figures are designed to provide financial statement users with a quick means of comparing the earnings performance of different firms after controlling for differences in capital structure. Firms with simple capital structures have few, if any, securities that are convertible income common stock. Such companies present only a simple, or basic, EPS measure that represents the ratio of earnings available to common shareholders over the weighted-average common shares outstanding. Earnings available to common shareholders is computed by subtracting any preferred stock dividends from reported net income. The weighted-average share computations take into consideration any issuance or redemption of common stock over the period along with the effects of stock dividends and splits.

For firms with complex capital structures, dual presentation is required of both primary earnings per share (PEPS) and fully-diluted earnings per share (FDEPS). PEPS differs from basic EPS in that it incorporates the pro-forma effect of converting several types of convertible securities into common shares. For a convertible security to enter the computation of PEPS, it must meet the definition of common stock equivalent, be convertible within five years of the balance sheet date, and its effects on PEPS must be dilutive. Different classes of convertible securities are treated differently in the pro-forma computation of PEPS. Securities such as options and warrants generally have no effect on the numerator of the EPS computations while securities such as convertible bonds and preferred stocks affect both the weighted-average share computation and the definition of net income available to common shareholders.

FDEPS embraces a broader set of potentially dilutive securities than PEPS. To be considered for inclusion in FDEPS, a convertible security need only be convertible within ten years of the balance sheet date and have a dilutive effect when incorporated into FDEPS. The presentation of dual disclosure provides additional information on the effects of dilutive convertible securities that a single presentation of EPS cannot. Finally, EPS figures are required for each component of net income starting with net income from continuing operations and including each extraordinary gain or loss, results of discontinued operations, cumulative effects of changes in accounting principle, and finally net income.

PROBLEMS

B-1. *EPS calculations: simple, primary, and fully-diluted*

Information relating to the capital structure of Sharonne Inc. as of December 31, 1993 is as follows:

Outstanding shares of:

Common stock	300,000
8% cumulative preferred stock	100,000
10-year, 6% convertible bonds	$5,000,000

The following additional information is also available:

(a) Sharonne issued the $50 par, 8% cumulative preferred stock on June 30, 1992 for $51 per share. No dividends on preferred have been declared since the stock was issued.

(b) Sharonne issued the 10-year, 6% convertible bonds at par on January 1, 1990. Each $1,000 face value bond is convertible at any time prior to maturity into $12^{1}/_{2}$ shares of common stock. The bonds were not considered common stock equivalents at time of issue.

(c) On November 23, 1992, Sharonne granted options to purchase 60,000 shares of common stock at $60 per share. The options are exercisable at any time and expire on September 1, 1994. The options met the three-month test during the third quarter of 1993.

(d) On February 28, 1993, Sharonne sold 72,000 previously unissued shares of common stock for $79 per share. On the same date, it issued an additional 40,000 shares of preferred stock for $46 per share.

(e) On March 30, 1994, options on 30,000 common shares were exercised. The market price on the date of exercise was $86. The average market price for the first quarter of 1994 was $87.

(f) On June 1, 1994, Sharonne purchased 35,000 shares of common stock to be held in treasury.

(g) On June 15, 1994, Sharonne declared a 10% common stock dividend distributable on June 30, 1994. The conversion rates on Sharonne's outstanding stock options and convertible bonds are *not* protected from dilution due to stock dividends or splits.

(h) The remaining 30,000 options on common stock were exercised on August 30, 1994. The market price of common on the date of exercise was $84 per share. The average market price of common over the first three quarters of 1994 was $88. To satisfy the requirements of the options, Sharonne reissued 30,000 of the common shares placed in treasury on June 1. The remaining 5,000 common shares held in treasury were retired on September 1, 1994.

(i) Net income for the year ending December 31, 1994, was $2,145,000. Sharonne's effective tax rate is 30%.

(j) The average market price of Sharonne's common stock during 1994 was $87 per share. The market price of common on December 31, 1994 was $82.

Required:

Prepare the computations for simple, primary, and fully-diluted earnings per share for 1994 and indicate which amounts should be reported.

B-2. *EPS calculations: convertible bonds and preferred stock*

(a) On January 1, 1993, Weaver Industrials had 210,000 shares of $100 par, 4% cumulative, convertible preferred stock outstanding. Weaver issued all

210,000 preferred shares on August 3, 1991, for $21,840,000. The average yield on Aa Corporate bonds was 8% on August 3, 1991. Each preferred share is convertible at any time into 3 shares of $10 par common stock. On April 30, 1993, Weaver issued an additional 60,000 preferred shares at 103. On July 1, 1993, 90,000 of the preferred shares issued on August 3, 1991 were converted. All dividends required on preferred stock were declared and paid during 1993.

(b)   Weaver also had 5-year, 8% convertible bonds with a face value of $10,000,000 outstanding on January 1, 1993. Weaver issued the bonds at par on January 1, 1989. The bonds are considered common stock equivalents. Each $1,000 face value bond is convertible at any time into 22 shares of common stock.

(c)   On August 30, 1993, one-half of the bonds were converted.

(d)   Weaver began 1993 with 976,000 common shares outstanding. The average market price of Weaver common was $44 per share during 1993 and was $61 per share at year-end. Weaver reported net income of $5,964,000 and had an effective tax rate of 40% for 1993.

REQUIRED:

Prepare schedules to compute Weaver's primary and fully-diluted earnings per share for 1993. Be sure to indicate the size of any income or share adjustment necessary for each dilutive security and prepare all supporting computations for simple earnings per share.

B-3.   *EPS calculations: various stock transactions*

Victor Corporation was organized on January 2, 1994, with 1,000,000 authorized shares of $10 par common stock and 500,000 authorized shares of $50 par convertible preferred stock. During 1994, the following capital transactions took place:

(a)   January 3: Victor issued 100,000 shares of common stock at $26 per share.

(b)   January 5: Victor issued 60,000 shares of preferred stock at $40 per share. The preferred stock pays a 7% cumulative dividend, and each share is convertible at any time after January 1, 1996, into 2 shares of common stock. The yield on Aa corporate bonds was 12.5% on the date of issue and had risen to 14% on December 31, 1994.

(c)   February 1: Victor issued 70,000 shares of common stock at $28 per share.

(d)   March 1: Victor issued 4,000, 10-year, 6% bonds were issued to yield 8.5%. Each $1,000 face value bond was issued with 6 detachable warrants to purchase 1 share of common stock at any time for $25. The warrants, which expire on March 1, 1995, met the three-month test on June 1. The yield on Aa corporate bonds was 13% on the date the bonds were issued.

(e)   April 1: Victor declared a 10% common stock dividend distributable on May 1. The conversion rates on the convertible preferred stock and common stock warrants are subject to adjustment for the effects of stock dividends and splits.

(f)   April 30: Victor purchased 60,000 shares of common stock for $30 per share and placed them in treasury.

(g)   May 16: Victor declared a 2-for-1 common stock split.

(h)   June 30: Holders of 15,000 shares of preferred stock elected to convert their shares into common. Victor satisfied the conversion by reissuing treasury shares.

(i)   September 1: Victor issued 40,000 shares of common stock at $33 per share.

(j)   December 3: Victor declared the dividend on preferred stock and a $.50 per share dividend on common, payable on January 1, 1995.

Victor reported net income of $544,000 and had an effective tax rate of 30% for 1994. The average market price of Victor's common stock was $31 per share during 1994 and $39 at year-end.

REQUIRED:

Prepare the computations for simple, primary, and fully-diluted earnings per share for 1994 and indicate which amounts should be reported.

B-4.   *EPS calculations: simple, primary, fully-diluted*

Information relating to the capital structure of Perfect Tools as of December 31, 1993 is as follows:

$10 par common stock	$2,400,000
$100 par convertible preferred stock	4,500,000
10-year, 4% convertible bonds	8,000,000

Additional information relating to equity transactions during 1994 is as follows:

(a)   January 1: Options on 10,000 shares of common stock were exercised. The options were issued under an employee incentive plan, which granted each of the 6 division managers the option to purchase up to 2,000 shares of common stock per year over the 4-year period beginning January 3, 1992. The option exercise price was set at $51 per share, equal to the market price on the date of plan adoption. The market price of common stock was above the exercise price for substantially all of 1992.

(b)   March 1: Perfect Tools purchased 42,000 shares of common stock at $55 per share and placed them in treasury.

(c)   April 30: Perfect Tools issued an additional 30,000 shares of $100 par, convertible preferred stock at 103. Each preferred share pays a 6% noncumulative dividend and is convertible into 1.5 shares of common stock at any time. The preferred shares are considered common stock equivalents.

(d)   July 1: All of the 10-year, 4% bonds were converted. The bonds were issued at par on January 1, 1987, and were considered common stock equivalents. Each $1,000 face value bond was convertible into 20 shares of common stock.

(e)   August 1: Perfect Tools declared a 1-for-2 reverse common stock split. The conversion rate on the stock options was adjusted to reflect the effect of the stock split. The conversion rate on the preferred stock was *not* affected by the split.

(f)   September 2: Perfect Tools purchased and retired 21,000 shares of common stock at $74 per share. The treasury shares acquired on March 1 were retired on the same date.

(g)   December 31: Perfect Tools declared dividends on preferred, payable on January 15, 1994. The firm neither declared nor paid dividends on common stock prior to year-end.

(h)   Perfect Tools reported net income of $850,000 and had an effective tax rate of 40% for 1994. The average market price of Perfect Tool's common stock was $60 per share during 1994. The market price of common was $79 at year-end.

REQUIRED:

Prepare the computations for simple, primary, and fully-diluted earnings per share for 1994 and indicate which amounts should be reported.

B-5. *EPS calculations with and without dividends and preferred share retirements*

Checkers Pizza's capital structure is as follows:

	December 31,	
	1994	1993
Outstanding shares of:		
$1 par Common stock	4,162,000	4,162,000
Class A preferred stock	163,000	303,000
Class B preferred stock	284,000	284,000
8% convertible bonds (book value)	$18,612,000	$18,714,000

The following additional information is available:

(a) *Class A Preferred.* Checkers issued the $100 par, Class A preferred stock on June 6, 1990, at 98. Each Class A preferred share earns a 7% cumulative dividend and is callable at any time after December 31, 1992, at 102 plus accumulated dividends. Each Class A preferred share is convertible at any time after December 31, 1993, into 3 shares of common stock. The effective yield on Aa corporate bonds was 10.8% on June 6, 1990. On June 1, 1994, Checkers exercised its call option on 140,000 shares of Class A preferred stock.

(b) *Class B Preferred.* Checkers issued the $100 par, Class B preferred stock on January 9, 1986, at 104. Each Class B preferred share earns a 4% cumulative dividend and is fully participating. Each Class B preferred share is convertible at any time after January 1, 1989, into 3 shares of common stock. The effective yield on Aa corporate bonds was 6% on January 9, 1986.

(c) *8% Convertible Bonds.* Checkers issued 18,000, 12-year, 8% convertible bonds on January 1, 1989, at 106.8 to yield 7%. Checkers uses the straight-line method to amortize any issue premium or discount. Each $1,000 face value bond is convertible into common shares subject to the following schedule:

Effective Date	Conversion Rate Per Bond
January 1, 1991	30 shares
January 1, 1995	40 shares
January 1, 2000	50 shares

The bonds were considered common stock equivalents at the time of issue. Checkers neither declared nor paid dividends during 1994. Net income for the year was $13,900,000, and the effective tax rate was 40%.

REQUIRED:

1. Prepare schedules to compute Checkers' primary and fully-diluted earnings per share for 1994. Be sure to indicate the size of any income or share adjustment necessary for each dilutive security and prepare all supporting computations for simple earnings per share.

2. Repeat Requirement 1 assuming Checkers declared and paid cash dividends of $3,900,000 for 1994 and that there were no dividends in arrears at the beginning of 1994.

B-6. *EPS calculations: primary and fully-diluted*

Information relating to the capital structure of Monolith Computer as of January 1, 1993 is as follows:

Outstanding shares of:

$10 par common stock	330,000
$50 par convertible preferred stock	65,000
9% convertible bonds (book value)	$2,700,000
6% convertible bonds (book value)	$2,879,400

The following additional information is also available:
(a) Monolith issued $50 par, convertible preferred stock on April 16, 1990, for $51 per share. Each preferred share earns a 5% cumulative dividend and is convertible at any time after April 16, 1992, into 2 shares of $10 par common stock. The effective yield on Aa corporate bonds on April 16, 1990 was 7.2%.
(b) Monolith issued the 9%, 10-year, convertible bonds at par on January 1, 1991. Each $1,000 face value bond is convertible into common shares subject to the following schedule:

Effective Date	Conversion Rate Per Bond
January 1, 1994	25 shares
January 1, 2000	30 shares

The effective yield on Aa corporate bonds on January 1, 1991 was 14.1%.
(c) Monolith issued the 6%, 10-year, convertible bonds 93.3 to yield 7% on January 1, 1989. Each $1,000 face value bond (3,000 issued) is convertible into 22 shares of $10 par common stock at any time after January 1, 1992. The bonds are callable at face value plus accrued interest at any time after January 1, 1993. The effective yield on Aa corporate bonds was 10.8% on January 1, 1989. Monolith uses the straight-line method to amortize any issue discount or premium.
(d) Warrants to purchase 62,000 shares of common stock at $36 per share were outstanding on January 1, 1993. The warrants, which expire on January 1, 1996, were issued during 1992 and met the 3-month test in that year.
(e) On March 1, 1993, Monolith purchased 20,000 shares of common stock at $41 per share and placed them in treasury.
(f) On May 2, 1993, warrants for 30,000 shares of common stock were exercised. The market price of common was $43 per share on the exercise date. To satisfy the requirements of the warrant conversion, Monolith reissued the treasury shares acquired on March 1 and 10,000 previously unissued common shares.
(g) On June 1, 1993, Monolith declared a 2-for-1 common stock split. Only the conversion rate on the convertible preferred stock is protected from dilution due to stock dividends or splits. The conversion rates on all other convertible securities were *not* affected by the stock split.
(h) On September 2, 1993, Monolith elected to call and retire all of the 6% convertible bonds outstanding.
(i) On October 1, 1993, holders of 20,000 preferred shares elected to convert their shares into common stock.
(j) Monolith reported net income of $2,650,000 and had an effective tax rate of 30% for 1993. The average market price of Monolith common was $40 per share during 1993. The market price of common at year-end was $47 per share.

REQUIRED:

Prepare schedules to compute Monolith's primary and fully-diluted earnings per share for 1993. Be sure to indicate the size of any income or share adjustment necessary for each dilutive security and prepare all supporting computations for simple earnings per share.

Tables

EXHIBIT C.1
Financial Statement
Analysis—Summary
of Ratios

**Financial Statement Analysis
Summary of Ratios**

Liquidity:

Net working capital	=	Current assets − Current liabilities
Current ratio	=	Current assets/Current liabilities
Quick ratio	=	Quick assets/Current liabilities

Efficiency:

Accounts receivable turnover	=	Net credit sales/Net receivables
Days sales in receivables	=	365/Accounts receivable turnover
Inventory turnover	=	Cost of goods sold/Inventory
Days sales in inventory	=	365/Inventory turnover
Total asset turnover	=	Net revenues/Total assets

Capital structure:

Long-term debt/total assets	=	Long-term debt/Total assets
Total liabilities/total assets	=	Total liabilities/Total assets
Times interest earned	=	Operating income/Interest expense

Profitability:

Return on sales	=	Net income/Net revenues
Return on shareholders' equity	=	Net income/Shareholders' equity
Return on total assets	=	Net income/Total assets

DuPont Method:

$$\frac{\text{Net income}}{\text{Stockholders' equity}} = \frac{\text{Net sales}}{\text{Total assets}} \times \frac{\text{Total assets}}{\text{Stockholders' equity}} \times \frac{\text{Net income}}{\text{Net sales}}$$

EXHIBIT C.2—Present Value of $1

	1.00%	1.25%	1.50%	1.75%	2.00%	3.00%	4.00%	5.00%	6.00%	7.00%	8.00%	9.00%	10.00%	12.00%	14.00%	15.00%
1	0.9901	0.9877	0.9852	0.9828	0.9804	0.9709	0.9615	0.9524	0.9434	0.9346	0.9259	0.9174	0.9091	0.8929	0.8772	0.8696
2	0.9803	0.9755	0.9707	0.9659	0.9612	0.9426	0.9246	0.9070	0.8900	0.8734	0.8573	0.8417	0.8264	0.7972	0.7695	0.7561
3	0.9706	0.9634	0.9563	0.9493	0.9423	0.9151	0.8890	0.8638	0.8396	0.8163	0.7938	0.7722	0.7513	0.7118	0.6750	0.6575
4	0.9610	0.9515	0.9422	0.9330	0.9238	0.8885	0.8548	0.8227	0.7921	0.7629	0.7350	0.7084	0.6830	0.6355	0.5921	0.5718
5	0.9515	0.9398	0.9283	0.9169	0.9057	0.8626	0.8219	0.7835	0.7473	0.7130	0.6806	0.6499	0.6209	0.5674	0.5194	0.4972
6	0.9420	0.9282	0.9145	0.9011	0.8880	0.8375	0.7903	0.7462	0.7050	0.6663	0.6302	0.5963	0.5645	0.5066	0.4556	0.4323
7	0.9327	0.9167	0.9010	0.8856	0.8706	0.8131	0.7599	0.7107	0.6651	0.6227	0.5835	0.5470	0.5132	0.4523	0.3996	0.3759
8	0.9235	0.9054	0.8877	0.8704	0.8535	0.7894	0.7307	0.6768	0.6274	0.5820	0.5403	0.5019	0.4665	0.4039	0.3506	0.3269
9	0.9143	0.8942	0.8746	0.8554	0.8368	0.7664	0.7026	0.6446	0.5919	0.5439	0.5002	0.4604	0.4241	0.3606	0.3075	0.2843
10	0.9053	0.8832	0.8617	0.8407	0.8203	0.7441	0.6756	0.6139	0.5584	0.5083	0.4632	0.4224	0.3855	0.3220	0.2697	0.2472
11	0.8963	0.8723	0.8489	0.8263	0.8043	0.7224	0.6496	0.5847	0.5268	0.4751	0.4289	0.3875	0.3505	0.2875	0.2366	0.2149
12	0.8874	0.8615	0.8364	0.8121	0.7885	0.7014	0.6246	0.5568	0.4970	0.4440	0.3971	0.3555	0.3186	0.2567	0.2076	0.1869
13	0.8787	0.8509	0.8240	0.7981	0.7730	0.6810	0.6006	0.5303	0.4688	0.4150	0.3677	0.3262	0.2897	0.2292	0.1821	0.1625
14	0.8700	0.8404	0.8118	0.7844	0.7579	0.6611	0.5775	0.5051	0.4423	0.3878	0.3405	0.2992	0.2633	0.2046	0.1597	0.1413
15	0.8613	0.8300	0.7999	0.7709	0.7430	0.6419	0.5553	0.4810	0.4173	0.3624	0.3152	0.2745	0.2394	0.1827	0.1401	0.1229
16	0.8528	0.8197	0.7880	0.7576	0.7284	0.6232	0.5339	0.4581	0.3936	0.3387	0.2919	0.2519	0.2176	0.1631	0.1229	0.1069
17	0.8444	0.8096	0.7764	0.7446	0.7142	0.6050	0.5134	0.4363	0.3714	0.3166	0.2703	0.2311	0.1978	0.1456	0.1078	0.0929
18	0.8360	0.7996	0.7649	0.7318	0.7002	0.5874	0.4936	0.4155	0.3503	0.2959	0.2502	0.2120	0.1799	0.1300	0.0946	0.0808
19	0.8277	0.7898	0.7536	0.7192	0.6864	0.5703	0.4746	0.3957	0.3305	0.2765	0.2317	0.1945	0.1635	0.1161	0.0829	0.0703
20	0.8195	0.7800	0.7425	0.7068	0.6730	0.5537	0.4564	0.3769	0.3118	0.2584	0.2145	0.1784	0.1486	0.1037	0.0728	0.0611
21	0.8114	0.7704	0.7315	0.6947	0.6598	0.5375	0.4388	0.3589	0.2942	0.2415	0.1987	0.1637	0.1351	0.0926	0.0638	0.0531
22	0.8034	0.7609	0.7207	0.6827	0.6468	0.5219	0.4220	0.3418	0.2775	0.2257	0.1839	0.1502	0.1228	0.0826	0.0560	0.0462
23	0.7954	0.7515	0.7100	0.6710	0.6342	0.5067	0.4057	0.3256	0.2618	0.2109	0.1703	0.1378	0.1117	0.0738	0.0491	0.0402
24	0.7876	0.7422	0.6995	0.6594	0.6217	0.4919	0.3901	0.3101	0.2470	0.1971	0.1577	0.1264	0.1015	0.0659	0.0431	0.0349
25	0.7798	0.7330	0.6892	0.6481	0.6095	0.4776	0.3751	0.2953	0.2330	0.1842	0.1460	0.1160	0.0923	0.0588	0.0378	0.0304

EXHIBIT C.2—Present Value of $1

	1.00%	1.25%	1.50%	1.75%	2.00%	3.00%	4.00%	5.00%	6.00%	7.00%	8.00%	9.00%	10.00%	12.00%	14.00%	15.00%
26	0.7720	0.7240	0.6790	0.6369	0.5976	0.4637	0.3607	0.2812	0.2198	0.1722	0.1352	0.1064	0.0839	0.0525	0.0331	0.0264
27	0.7644	0.7150	0.6690	0.6260	0.5859	0.4502	0.3468	0.2678	0.2074	0.1609	0.1252	0.0976	0.0763	0.0469	0.0291	0.0230
28	0.7568	0.7062	0.6591	0.6152	0.5744	0.4371	0.3335	0.2551	0.1956	0.1504	0.1159	0.0895	0.0693	0.0419	0.0255	0.0200
29	0.7493	0.6975	0.6494	0.6046	0.5631	0.4243	0.3207	0.2429	0.1846	0.1406	0.1073	0.0822	0.0630	0.0374	0.0224	0.0174
30	0.7419	0.6889	0.6398	0.5942	0.5521	0.4120	0.3083	0.2314	0.1741	0.1314	0.0994	0.0754	0.0573	0.0334	0.0196	0.0151
31	0.7346	0.6804	0.6303	0.5840	0.5412	0.4000	0.2965	0.2204	0.1643	0.1228	0.0920	0.0691	0.0521	0.0298	0.0172	0.0131
32	0.7273	0.6720	0.6210	0.5740	0.5306	0.3883	0.2851	0.2099	0.1550	0.1147	0.0852	0.0634	0.0474	0.0266	0.0151	0.0114
33	0.7201	0.6637	0.6118	0.5641	0.5202	0.3770	0.2741	0.1999	0.1462	0.1072	0.0789	0.0582	0.0431	0.0238	0.0132	0.0099
34	0.7130	0.6555	0.6028	0.5544	0.5100	0.3660	0.2636	0.1904	0.1379	0.1002	0.0730	0.0534	0.0391	0.0212	0.0116	0.0086
35	0.7059	0.6474	0.5939	0.5449	0.5000	0.3554	0.2534	0.1813	0.1301	0.0937	0.0676	0.0490	0.0356	0.0189	0.0102	0.0075
36	0.6989	0.6394	0.5851	0.5355	0.4902	0.3450	0.2437	0.1727	0.1227	0.0875	0.0626	0.0449	0.0323	0.0169	0.0089	0.0065
37	0.6920	0.6315	0.5764	0.5263	0.4806	0.3350	0.2343	0.1644	0.1158	0.0818	0.0580	0.0412	0.0294	0.0151	0.0078	0.0057
38	0.6852	0.6237	0.5679	0.5172	0.4712	0.3252	0.2253	0.1566	0.1092	0.0765	0.0537	0.0378	0.0267	0.0135	0.0069	0.0049
39	0.6784	0.6160	0.5595	0.5083	0.4619	0.3158	0.2166	0.1491	0.1031	0.0715	0.0497	0.0347	0.0243	0.0120	0.0060	0.0043
40	0.6717	0.6084	0.5513	0.4996	0.4529	0.3066	0.2083	0.1420	0.0972	0.0668	0.0460	0.0318	0.0221	0.0107	0.0053	0.0037
41	0.6650	0.6009	0.5431	0.4910	0.4440	0.2976	0.2003	0.1353	0.0917	0.0624	0.0426	0.0292	0.0201	0.0096	0.0046	0.0032
42	0.6584	0.5935	0.5351	0.4826	0.4353	0.2890	0.1926	0.1288	0.0865	0.0583	0.0395	0.0268	0.0183	0.0086	0.0041	0.0028
43	0.6519	0.5862	0.5272	0.4743	0.4268	0.2805	0.1852	0.1227	0.0816	0.0545	0.0365	0.0246	0.0166	0.0076	0.0036	0.0025
44	0.6454	0.5789	0.5194	0.4661	0.4184	0.2724	0.1780	0.1169	0.0770	0.0509	0.0338	0.0226	0.0151	0.0068	0.0031	0.0021
45	0.6391	0.5718	0.5117	0.4581	0.4102	0.2644	0.1712	0.1113	0.0727	0.0476	0.0313	0.0207	0.0137	0.0061	0.0027	0.0019
46	0.6327	0.5647	0.5042	0.4502	0.4022	0.2567	0.1646	0.1060	0.0685	0.0445	0.0290	0.0190	0.0125	0.0054	0.0024	0.0016
47	0.6265	0.5577	0.4967	0.4425	0.3943	0.2493	0.1583	0.1009	0.0647	0.0416	0.0269	0.0174	0.0113	0.0049	0.0021	0.0014
48	0.6203	0.5509	0.4894	0.4349	0.3865	0.2420	0.1522	0.0961	0.0610	0.0389	0.0249	0.0160	0.0103	0.0043	0.0019	0.0012
49	0.6141	0.5441	0.4821	0.4274	0.3790	0.2350	0.1463	0.0916	0.0575	0.0363	0.0230	0.0147	0.0094	0.0039	0.0016	0.0011
50	0.6080	0.5373	0.4750	0.4200	0.3715	0.2281	0.1407	0.0872	0.0543	0.0339	0.0213	0.0134	0.0085	0.0035	0.0014	0.0009

EXHIBIT C.3—Present Value of an Annuity of $1

	1.00%	1.25%	1.50%	1.75%	2.00%	3.00%	4.00%	5.00%	6.00%	7.00%	8.00%	9.00%	10.00%	12.00%	14.00%	15.00%
1	0.9901	0.9877	0.9852	0.9828	0.9804	0.9709	0.9615	0.9524	0.9434	0.9346	0.9259	0.9174	0.9091	0.8929	0.8772	0.8696
2	1.9704	1.9631	1.9559	1.9487	1.9416	1.9135	1.8861	1.8594	1.8334	1.8080	1.7833	1.7591	1.7355	1.6901	1.6467	1.6257
3	2.9410	2.9265	2.9122	2.8980	2.8839	2.8286	2.7751	2.7232	2.6730	2.6243	2.5771	2.5313	2.4869	2.4018	2.3216	2.2832
4	3.9020	3.8781	3.8544	3.8309	3.8077	3.7171	3.6299	3.5460	3.4651	3.3872	3.3121	3.2397	3.1699	3.0373	2.9137	2.8850
5	4.8534	4.8178	4.7826	4.7479	4.7135	4.5797	4.4518	4.3295	4.2124	4.1002	3.9927	3.8897	3.7908	3.6048	3.4331	3.3522
6	5.7955	5.7460	5.6972	5.6490	5.6014	5.4172	5.2421	5.0757	4.9173	4.7665	4.6229	4.4859	4.3553	4.1114	3.8887	3.7845
7	6.7282	6.6627	6.5982	6.5346	6.4720	6.2303	6.0021	5.7864	5.5824	5.3893	5.2064	5.0330	4.8684	4.5638	4.2883	4.1604
8	7.6517	7.5681	7.4859	7.4051	7.3255	7.0197	6.7327	6.4632	6.2098	5.9713	5.7466	5.5348	5.3349	4.9676	4.6389	4.4873
9	8.5660	8.4623	8.3605	8.2605	8.1622	7.7861	7.4353	7.1078	6.8017	6.5152	6.2469	5.9952	5.7590	5.3282	4.9464	4.7716
10	9.4713	9.3455	9.2222	9.1012	8.9826	8.5302	8.1109	7.7217	7.3601	7.0236	6.7101	6.4177	6.1446	5.6502	5.2161	5.0188
11	10.3676	10.2178	10.0711	9.9275	9.7868	9.2526	8.7605	8.3064	7.8869	7.4987	7.1390	6.8052	6.4951	5.9377	5.4527	5.2337
12	11.2551	11.0793	10.9075	10.7395	10.5753	9.9540	9.3851	8.8633	8.3838	7.9427	7.5361	7.1607	6.8137	6.1944	5.6603	5.4206
13	12.1337	11.9302	11.7315	11.5376	11.3484	10.6350	9.9856	9.3936	8.8527	8.3577	7.9038	7.4869	7.1034	6.4235	5.8424	5.5831
14	13.0037	12.7706	12.5434	12.3220	12.1062	11.2961	10.5631	9.8986	9.2950	8.7455	8.2442	7.7862	7.3667	6.6282	6.0021	5.7245
15	13.8651	13.6005	13.3432	13.0929	12.8493	11.9379	11.1184	10.3797	9.7122	9.1079	8.5595	8.0607	7.6061	6.8109	6.1422	5.8474
16	14.7179	14.4203	14.1313	13.8505	13.5777	12.5611	11.6523	10.8378	10.1059	9.4466	8.8514	8.3126	7.8237	6.9740	6.2651	5.9542
17	15.5623	15.2299	14.9076	14.5951	14.2919	13.1661	12.1657	11.2741	10.4773	9.7632	9.1216	8.5436	8.0216	7.1196	6.3729	6.0472
18	16.3983	16.0295	15.6726	15.3269	14.9920	13.7535	12.6593	11.6896	10.8276	10.0591	9.3719	8.7556	8.2014	7.2497	6.4674	6.1280
19	17.2260	16.8193	16.4262	16.0461	15.6785	14.3238	13.1339	12.0853	11.1581	10.3356	9.6036	8.9501	8.3649	7.3658	6.5504	6.1982
20	18.0456	17.5993	17.1686	16.7529	16.3514	14.8775	13.5903	12.4622	11.4699	10.5940	9.8181	9.1285	8.5136	7.4694	6.6231	6.2593
21	18.8570	18.3697	17.9001	17.4475	17.0112	15.4150	14.0292	12.8212	11.7641	10.8355	10.0168	9.2922	8.6487	7.5620	6.6870	6.3125
22	19.6604	19.1306	18.6208	18.1303	17.6580	15.9369	14.4511	13.1630	12.0416	11.0612	10.2007	9.4424	8.7715	7.6446	6.7429	6.3587
23	20.4558	19.8820	19.3309	18.8012	18.2922	16.4436	14.8568	13.4886	12.3034	11.2722	10.3711	9.5802	8.8832	7.7184	6.7921	6.3988
24	21.2434	20.6242	20.0304	19.4607	18.9139	16.9355	15.2470	13.7986	12.5504	11.4693	10.5288	9.7066	8.9847	7.7843	6.8351	6.4338
25	22.0232	21.3573	20.7196	20.1088	19.5235	17.4131	15.6221	14.0939	12.7834	11.6536	10.6748	9.8226	9.0770	7.8431	6.8729	6.4641

EXHIBIT C.3—Present Value of an Annuity of $1

	1.00%	1.25%	1.50%	1.75%	2.00%	3.00%	4.00%	5.00%	6.00%	7.00%	8.00%	9.00%	10.00%	12.00%	14.00%	15.00%
26	22.7952	22.0813	21.3986	20.7457	20.1210	17.8768	15.9828	14.3752	13.0032	11.8258	10.8100	9.9290	9.1609	7.8957	6.9061	6.4906
27	23.5596	22.7963	22.0676	21.3717	20.7069	18.3270	16.3296	14.6430	13.2105	11.9867	10.9352	10.0266	9.2372	7.9426	6.9352	6.5135
28	24.3164	23.5025	22.7267	21.9870	21.2813	18.7641	16.6631	14.8981	13.4062	12.1371	11.0511	10.1161	9.3066	7.9844	6.9607	6.5335
29	25.0658	24.2000	23.3761	22.5916	21.8444	19.1885	16.9837	15.1411	13.5907	12.2777	11.1584	10.1983	9.3696	8.0218	6.9830	6.5509
30	25.8077	24.8889	24.0158	23.1858	22.3965	19.6004	17.2920	15.3725	13.7648	12.4090	11.2578	10.2737	9.4269	8.0552	7.0027	6.5660
31	26.5423	25.5693	24.6461	23.7699	22.9377	20.0004	17.5885	15.5928	13.9291	12.5318	11.3498	10.3428	9.4790	8.0850	7.0199	6.5791
32	27.2696	26.2413	25.2671	24.3439	23.4683	20.3888	17.8736	15.8027	14.0840	12.6466	11.4350	10.4062	9.5264	8.1116	7.0350	6.5905
33	27.9897	26.9050	25.8790	24.9080	23.9886	20.7658	18.1476	16.0025	14.2302	12.7538	11.5139	10.4644	9.5694	8.1354	7.0482	6.6005
34	28.7027	27.5605	26.4817	25.4624	24.4986	21.1318	18.4112	16.1929	14.3681	12.8540	11.5869	10.5178	9.6086	8.1566	7.0599	6.6091
35	29.4086	28.2079	27.0756	26.0073	24.9986	21.4872	18.6646	16.3742	14.4982	12.9477	11.6546	10.5668	9.6442	8.1755	7.0700	6.6166
36	30.1075	28.8473	27.6607	26.5428	25.4888	21.8323	18.9083	16.5469	14.6210	13.0352	11.7172	10.6118	9.6765	8.1924	7.0790	6.6231
37	30.7995	29.4788	28.2371	27.0690	25.9695	22.1672	19.1426	16.7113	14.7368	13.1170	11.7752	10.6530	9.7059	8.2075	7.0868	6.6288
38	31.4847	30.1025	28.8051	27.5863	26.4406	22.4925	19.3679	16.8679	14.8460	13.1935	11.8289	10.6908	9.7327	8.2210	7.0937	6.6338
39	32.1630	30.7185	29.3646	28.0946	26.9026	22.8082	19.5845	17.0170	14.9491	13.2649	11.8786	10.7255	9.7570	8.2330	7.0997	6.6380
40	32.8347	31.3269	29.9158	28.5942	27.3555	23.1148	19.7928	17.1591	15.0463	13.3317	11.9246	10.7574	9.7791	8.2438	7.1050	6.6418
41	33.4997	31.9278	30.4590	29.0852	27.7995	23.4124	19.9931	17.2944	15.1380	13.3941	11.9672	10.7866	9.7991	8.2534	7.1097	6.6450
42	34.1581	32.5213	30.9941	29.5678	28.2348	23.7014	20.1856	17.4232	15.2245	13.4524	12.0067	10.8134	9.8174	8.2619	7.1138	6.6478
43	34.8100	33.1075	31.5212	30.0421	28.6616	23.9819	20.3708	17.5459	15.3062	13.5070	12.0432	10.8380	9.8340	8.2696	7.1173	6.6503
44	35.4555	33.6864	32.0406	30.5082	29.0800	24.2543	20.5488	17.6628	15.3832	13.5579	12.0771	10.8605	9.8491	8.2764	7.1205	6.6524
45	36.0945	34.2582	32.5523	30.9663	29.4902	24.5187	20.7200	17.7741	15.4558	13.6055	12.1084	10.8812	9.8628	8.2825	7.1232	6.6543
46	36.7272	34.8229	33.0565	31.4165	29.8923	24.7754	20.8847	17.8801	15.5244	13.6500	12.1374	10.9002	9.8753	8.2880	7.1256	6.6559
47	37.3537	35.3806	33.5532	31.8589	30.2866	25.0247	21.0429	17.9810	15.5890	13.6916	12.1643	10.9176	9.8866	8.2928	7.1277	6.6573
48	37.9740	35.9315	34.0426	32.2938	30.6731	25.2667	21.1951	18.0772	15.6500	13.7305	12.1891	10.9336	9.8969	8.2972	7.1296	6.6585
49	38.5881	36.4755	34.5247	32.7212	31.0521	25.5017	21.3415	18.1687	15.7076	13.7668	12.2122	10.9482	9.9063	8.3010	7.1312	6.6596
50	39.1961	37.0129	34.9997	33.1412	31.4236	25.7298	21.4822	18.2559	15.7619	13.8007	12.2335	10.9617	9.9148	8.3045	7.1327	6.6605

EXHIBIT C.4—Future Value of $1

	1.00%	1.25%	1.50%	1.75%	2.00%	3.00%	4.00%	5.00%	6.00%	7.00%	8.00%	9.00%	10.00%	12.00%	14.00%	15.00%
1	1.0100	1.0125	1.0150	1.0175	1.0200	1.0300	1.0400	1.0500	1.0600	1.0700	1.0800	1.0900	1.1000	1.1200	1.1400	1.1500
2	1.0201	1.0252	1.0302	1.0353	1.0404	1.0609	1.0816	1.1025	1.1236	1.1449	1.1664	1.1881	1.2100	1.2544	1.2996	1.3225
3	1.0303	1.0380	1.0457	1.0534	1.0612	1.0927	1.1249	1.1576	1.1910	1.2250	1.2597	1.2950	1.3310	1.4049	1.4815	1.5209
4	1.0406	1.0509	1.0614	1.0719	1.0824	1.1255	1.1699	1.2155	1.2625	1.3108	1.3605	1.4116	1.4641	1.5735	1.6890	1.7490
5	1.0510	1.0641	1.0773	1.0906	1.1041	1.1593	1.2167	1.2763	1.3382	1.4026	1.4693	1.5386	1.6105	1.7623	1.9254	2.0114
6	1.0615	1.0774	1.0934	1.1097	1.1262	1.1941	1.2653	1.3401	1.4185	1.5007	1.5869	1.6771	1.7716	1.9738	2.1950	2.3131
7	1.0721	1.0909	1.1098	1.1291	1.1487	1.2299	1.3159	1.4071	1.5036	1.6058	1.7138	1.8280	1.9487	2.2107	2.5023	2.6600
8	1.0829	1.1045	1.1265	1.1489	1.1717	1.2668	1.3686	1.4775	1.5938	1.7182	1.8509	1.9926	2.1436	2.4760	2.8526	3.0590
9	1.0937	1.1183	1.1434	1.1690	1.1951	1.3048	1.4233	1.5513	1.6895	1.8385	1.9990	2.1719	2.3579	2.7731	3.2519	3.5179
10	1.1046	1.1323	1.1605	1.1894	1.2190	1.3439	1.4802	1.6289	1.7908	1.9672	2.1589	2.3674	2.5937	3.1058	3.7072	4.0456
11	1.1157	1.1464	1.1779	1.2103	1.2434	1.3842	1.5395	1.7103	1.8983	2.1049	2.3316	2.5804	2.8531	3.4785	4.2262	4.6524
12	1.1268	1.1608	1.1956	1.2314	1.2682	1.4258	1.6010	1.7959	2.0122	2.2522	2.5182	2.8127	3.1384	3.8960	4.8179	5.3503
13	1.1381	1.1753	1.2136	1.2530	1.2936	1.4685	1.6651	1.8856	2.1329	2.4098	2.7196	3.0658	3.4523	4.3635	5.4924	6.1528
14	1.1495	1.1900	1.2318	1.2749	1.3195	1.5126	1.7317	1.9799	2.2609	2.5785	2.9372	3.3417	3.7975	4.8871	6.2613	7.0757
15	1.1610	1.2048	1.2502	1.2972	1.3459	1.5580	1.8009	2.0789	2.3966	2.7590	3.1722	3.6425	4.1772	5.4736	7.1379	8.1371
16	1.1726	1.2199	1.2690	1.3199	1.3728	1.6047	1.8730	2.1829	2.5404	2.9522	3.4259	3.9703	4.5950	6.1304	8.1372	9.3576
17	1.1843	1.2351	1.2880	1.3430	1.4002	1.6528	1.9479	2.2920	2.6928	3.1588	3.7000	4.3276	5.0545	6.8660	9.2765	10.7613
18	1.1961	1.2506	1.3073	1.3665	1.4282	1.7024	2.0258	2.4066	2.8543	3.3799	3.9960	4.7171	5.5599	7.6900	10.5752	12.3755
19	1.2081	1.2662	1.3270	1.3904	1.4568	1.7535	2.1068	2.5270	3.0256	3.6165	4.3157	5.1417	6.1159	8.6128	12.0557	14.2318
20	1.2202	1.2820	1.3469	1.4148	1.4859	1.8061	2.1911	2.6533	3.2071	3.8697	4.6610	5.6044	6.7275	9.6463	13.7435	16.3665
21	1.2324	1.2981	1.3671	1.4395	1.5157	1.8603	2.2788	2.7860	3.3996	4.1406	5.0338	6.1088	7.4002	10.8038	15.6676	18.8215
22	1.2447	1.3143	1.3876	1.4647	1.5460	1.9161	2.3699	2.9253	3.6035	4.4304	5.4365	6.6586	8.1403	12.1003	17.8610	21.6447
23	1.2572	1.3307	1.4084	1.4904	1.5769	1.9736	2.4647	3.0715	3.8197	4.7405	5.8715	7.2579	8.9543	13.5523	20.3616	24.8915
24	1.2697	1.3474	1.4295	1.5164	1.6084	2.0328	2.5633	3.2251	4.0489	5.0724	6.3412	7.9111	9.8497	15.1786	23.2122	28.6252
25	1.2824	1.3642	1.4509	1.5430	1.6406	2.0938	2.6658	3.3864	4.2919	5.4274	6.8485	8.6231	10.8347	17.0001	26.4619	32.9190

EXHIBIT C.4—Future Value of $1

	1.00%	1.25%	1.50%	1.75%	2.00%	3.00%	4.00%	5.00%	6.00%	7.00%	8.00%	9.00%	10.00%	12.00%	14.00%	15.00%
26	1.2953	1.3812	1.4727	1.5700	1.6734	2.1566	2.7725	3.5557	4.5494	5.8074	7.3964	9.3992	11.9182	19.0401	30.1666	37.8568
27	1.3082	1.3985	1.4948	1.5975	1.7069	2.2213	2.8834	3.7335	4.8223	6.2139	7.9881	10.2451	13.1100	21.3249	34.3899	43.5353
28	1.3213	1.4160	1.5172	1.6254	1.7410	2.2879	2.9987	3.9201	5.1117	6.6488	8.6271	11.1671	14.4210	23.8839	39.2045	50.0656
29	1.3345	1.4337	1.5400	1.6539	1.7758	2.3566	3.1187	4.1161	5.4184	7.1143	9.3173	12.1722	15.8631	26.7499	44.6931	57.5755
30	1.3478	1.4516	1.5631	1.6828	1.8114	2.4273	3.2434	4.3219	5.7435	7.6123	10.0627	13.2677	17.4494	29.9599	50.9502	66.2118
31	1.3613	1.4698	1.5865	1.7122	1.8476	2.5001	3.3731	4.5380	6.0881	8.1451	10.8677	14.4618	19.1943	33.5551	58.0832	76.1435
32	1.3749	1.4881	1.6103	1.7422	1.8845	2.5751	3.5081	4.7649	6.4534	8.7153	11.7371	15.7633	21.1138	37.5817	66.2148	87.5651
33	1.3887	1.5067	1.6345	1.7727	1.9222	2.6523	3.6484	5.0032	6.8406	9.3253	12.6760	17.1820	23.2252	42.0915	75.4849	100.6998
34	1.4026	1.5256	1.6590	1.8037	1.9607	2.7319	3.7943	5.2533	7.2510	9.9781	13.6901	18.7284	25.5477	47.1425	86.0528	115.8048
35	1.4166	1.5446	1.6839	1.8353	1.9999	2.8139	3.9461	5.5160	7.6861	10.6766	14.7853	20.4140	28.1024	52.7996	98.1002	133.1755
36	1.4308	1.5639	1.7091	1.8674	2.0399	2.8983	4.1039	5.7918	8.1473	11.4239	15.9682	22.2512	30.9127	59.1356	111.8342	153.1519
37	1.4451	1.5835	1.7348	1.9001	2.0807	2.9852	4.2681	6.0814	8.6361	12.2236	17.2456	24.2538	34.0039	66.2318	127.4910	176.1246
38	1.4595	1.6033	1.7608	1.9333	2.1223	3.0748	4.4388	6.3855	9.1543	13.0793	18.6253	26.4367	37.4043	74.1797	145.3397	202.5433
39	1.4741	1.6233	1.7872	1.9672	2.1647	3.1670	4.6164	6.7048	9.7035	13.9948	20.1153	28.8160	41.1448	83.0812	165.6873	232.9248
40	1.4889	1.6436	1.8140	2.0016	2.2080	3.2620	4.8010	7.0400	10.2857	14.9745	21.7245	31.4094	45.2593	93.0510	188.8835	267.8635
41	1.5038	1.6642	1.8412	2.0366	2.2522	3.3599	4.9931	7.3920	10.9029	16.0227	23.4625	34.2363	49.7852	104.2171	215.3272	308.0431
42	1.5188	1.6850	1.8688	2.0723	2.2972	3.4607	5.1928	7.7616	11.5570	17.1443	25.3395	37.3175	54.7637	116.7231	245.4730	354.2495
43	1.5340	1.7060	1.8969	2.1085	2.3432	3.5645	5.4005	8.1497	12.2505	18.3444	27.3666	40.6761	60.2401	130.7299	279.8392	407.3870
44	1.5493	1.7274	1.9253	2.1454	2.3901	3.6715	5.6165	8.5572	12.9855	19.6285	29.5560	44.3370	66.2641	146.4175	319.0167	468.4950
45	1.5648	1.7489	1.9542	2.1830	2.4379	3.7816	5.8412	8.9850	13.7646	21.0025	31.9204	48.3273	72.8905	163.9876	363.6791	538.7693
46	1.5805	1.7708	1.9835	2.2212	2.4866	3.8950	6.0748	9.4343	14.5905	22.4726	34.4741	52.6767	80.1795	183.6661	414.5941	619.5847
47	1.5963	1.7929	2.0133	2.2600	2.5363	4.0119	6.3178	9.9060	15.4659	24.0457	37.2320	57.4176	88.1975	205.7061	472.6373	712.5224
48	1.6122	1.8154	2.0435	2.2996	2.5871	4.1323	6.5705	10.4013	16.3939	25.7289	40.2106	62.5852	97.0172	230.3908	538.8065	819.4007
49	1.6283	1.8380	2.0741	2.3398	2.6388	4.2562	6.8333	10.9213	17.3775	27.5299	43.4274	68.2179	106.7190	258.0377	614.2395	942.3108
50	1.6446	1.8610	2.1052	2.3808	2.6916	4.3839	7.1067	11.4674	18.4202	29.4570	46.9016	74.3575	117.3909	289.0022	700.2330	1083.6574

EXHIBIT C.5—Future Value of an Annuity of $1

	1.00%	1.25%	1.50%	1.75%	2.00%	3.00%	4.00%	5.00%	6.00%	7.00%	8.00%	9.00%	10.00%	12.00%	14.00%	15.00%
1	1.0000	1.0000	1.0000	1.0000	1.0000	1.0000	1.0000	1.0000	1.0000	1.0000	1.0000	1.0000	1.0000	1.0000	1.0000	1.0000
2	2.0100	2.0125	2.0150	2.0175	2.0200	2.0300	2.0400	2.0500	2.0600	2.0700	2.0800	2.0900	2.1000	2.1200	2.1400	2.1500
3	3.0301	3.0377	3.0452	3.0528	3.0604	3.0909	3.1216	3.1525	3.1836	3.2149	3.2464	3.2781	3.3100	3.3744	3.4396	3.4725
4	4.0604	4.0756	4.0909	4.1062	4.1216	4.1836	4.2465	4.3101	4.3746	4.4399	4.5061	4.5731	4.6410	4.7793	4.9211	4.9934
5	5.1010	5.1266	5.1523	5.1781	5.2040	5.3091	5.4163	5.5256	5.6371	5.7507	5.8666	5.9847	6.1051	6.3528	6.6101	6.7424
6	6.1520	6.1907	6.2296	6.2687	6.3081	6.4684	6.6330	6.8019	6.9753	7.1533	7.3359	7.5233	7.7156	8.1152	8.5355	8.7537
7	7.2135	7.2680	7.3230	7.3784	7.4343	7.6625	7.8983	8.1420	8.3938	8.6540	8.9228	9.2004	9.4872	10.0890	10.7305	11.0668
8	8.2857	8.3589	8.4328	8.5075	8.5830	8.8923	9.2142	9.5491	9.8975	10.2598	10.6366	11.0285	11.4359	12.2997	13.2328	13.7268
9	9.3685	9.4634	9.5593	9.6564	9.7546	10.1591	10.5828	11.0266	11.4913	11.9780	12.4876	13.0210	13.5795	14.7757	16.0853	16.7858
10	10.4622	10.5817	10.7027	10.8254	10.9497	11.4639	12.0061	12.5779	13.1808	13.8164	14.4866	15.1929	15.9374	17.5487	19.3373	20.3037
11	11.5668	11.7139	11.8633	12.0148	12.1687	12.8078	13.4864	14.2068	14.9716	15.7836	16.6455	17.5603	18.5312	20.6546	23.0445	24.3493
12	12.6825	12.8604	13.0412	13.2251	13.4121	14.1920	15.0258	15.9171	16.8699	17.8885	18.9771	20.1407	21.3843	24.1331	27.2707	29.0017
13	13.8093	14.0211	14.2368	14.4565	14.6803	15.6178	16.6268	17.7130	18.8821	20.1406	21.4953	22.9534	24.5227	28.0291	32.0887	34.3519
14	14.9474	15.1964	15.4504	15.7095	15.9739	17.0863	18.2919	19.5986	21.0151	22.5505	24.2149	26.0192	27.9750	32.3926	37.5811	40.5047
15	16.0969	16.3863	16.6821	16.9844	17.2934	18.5989	20.0236	21.5786	23.2760	25.1290	27.1521	29.3609	31.7725	37.2797	43.8424	47.5804
16	17.2579	17.5912	17.9324	18.2817	18.6393	20.1569	21.8245	23.6575	25.6725	27.8881	30.3243	33.0034	35.9497	42.7533	50.9804	55.7175
17	18.4304	18.8111	19.2014	19.6016	20.0121	21.7616	23.6975	25.8404	28.2129	30.8402	33.7502	36.9737	40.5447	48.8837	59.1176	65.0751
18	19.6147	20.0462	20.4894	20.9446	21.4123	23.4144	25.6454	28.1324	30.9057	33.9990	37.4502	41.3013	45.5992	55.7497	68.3941	75.8364
19	20.8109	21.2968	21.7967	22.3112	22.8406	25.1169	27.6712	30.5390	33.7600	37.3790	41.4463	46.0185	51.1591	63.4397	78.9692	88.2118
20	22.0190	22.5630	23.1237	23.7016	24.2974	26.8704	29.7781	33.0660	36.7856	40.9955	45.7620	51.1601	57.2750	72.0524	91.0249	102.4436
21	23.2392	23.8450	24.4705	25.1164	25.7833	28.6765	31.9692	35.7193	39.9927	44.8652	50.4229	56.7645	64.0025	81.6987	104.7684	118.8101
22	24.4716	25.1431	25.8376	26.5559	27.2990	30.5368	34.2480	38.5052	43.3923	49.0057	55.4568	62.8733	71.4027	92.5026	120.4360	137.6316
23	25.7163	26.4574	27.2251	28.0207	28.8450	32.4529	36.6179	41.4305	46.9958	53.4361	60.8933	69.5319	79.5430	104.6029	138.2970	159.2764
24	26.9735	27.7881	28.6335	29.5110	30.4219	34.4265	39.0826	44.5020	50.8156	58.1767	66.7648	76.7898	88.4973	118.1552	158.6586	184.1678
25	28.2432	29.1354	30.0630	31.0275	32.0303	36.4593	41.6459	47.7271	54.8645	63.2490	73.1059	84.7009	98.3471	133.3339	181.8708	212.7930

EXHIBIT C.5—Future Value of an Annuity of $1

	1.00%	1.25%	1.50%	1.75%	2.00%	3.00%	4.00%	5.00%	6.00%	7.00%	8.00%	9.00%	10.00%	12.00%	14.00%	15.00%
26	29.5256	30.4996	31.5140	32.5704	33.6709	38.5530	44.3117	51.1135	59.1564	68.6765	79.9544	93.3240	109.1818	150.3339	208.3327	245.7120
27	30.8209	31.8809	32.9867	34.1404	35.3443	40.7096	47.0842	54.6691	63.7058	74.4838	87.3508	102.7231	121.0999	169.3740	238.4993	283.5688
28	32.1291	33.2794	34.4815	35.7379	37.0512	42.9309	49.9676	58.4026	68.5281	80.6977	95.3388	112.9682	134.2099	190.6989	272.8892	327.1041
29	33.4504	34.6954	35.9987	37.3633	38.7922	45.2189	52.9663	62.3227	73.6398	87.3465	103.9659	124.1354	148.6309	214.5828	312.0937	377.1697
30	34.7849	36.1291	37.5387	39.0172	40.5681	47.5754	56.0849	66.4388	79.0582	94.4608	113.2832	136.3075	164.4940	241.3327	356.7868	434.7451
31	36.1327	37.5807	39.1018	40.7000	42.3794	50.0027	59.3283	70.7608	84.8017	102.0730	123.3459	149.5752	181.9434	271.2926	407.7370	500.9569
32	37.4941	39.0504	40.6883	42.4122	44.2270	52.5028	62.7015	75.2988	90.8898	110.2182	134.2135	164.0370	201.1378	304.8477	465.8202	577.1005
33	38.8690	40.5386	42.2986	44.1544	46.1116	55.0778	66.2095	80.0638	97.3432	118.9334	145.9506	179.8003	222.2515	342.4294	532.0350	664.6655
34	40.2577	42.0453	43.9331	45.9271	48.0338	57.7302	69.8579	85.0670	104.1838	128.2588	158.6267	196.9823	245.4767	384.5210	607.5199	765.3654
35	41.6603	43.5709	45.5921	47.7308	49.9945	60.4621	73.6522	90.3203	111.4348	138.2369	172.3168	215.7108	271.0244	431.6635	693.5727	881.1702
36	43.0769	45.1155	47.2760	49.5661	51.9944	63.2759	77.5983	95.8363	119.1209	148.9135	187.1021	236.1247	299.1268	484.4631	791.6729	1014.3457
37	44.5076	46.6794	48.9851	51.4335	54.0343	66.1742	81.7022	101.6281	127.2681	160.3374	203.0703	258.3759	330.0395	543.5987	903.5071	1167.4975
38	45.9527	48.2629	50.7199	53.3336	56.1149	69.1594	85.9703	107.7095	135.9042	172.5610	220.3159	282.6298	364.0434	609.8305	1030.9981	1343.6222
39	47.4123	49.8862	52.4807	55.2670	58.2372	72.2342	90.4091	114.0950	145.0585	185.6403	238.9412	309.0665	401.4478	684.0102	1176.3378	1546.1655
40	48.8864	51.4896	54.2679	57.2341	60.4020	75.4013	95.0255	120.7998	154.7620	199.6351	259.0565	337.8824	442.5926	767.0914	1342.0251	1779.0903
41	50.3752	53.1332	56.0819	59.2357	62.6100	78.6633	99.8265	127.8398	165.0477	214.6096	280.7810	369.2919	487.8518	860.1424	1530.9086	2046.9539
42	51.8790	54.7973	57.9231	61.2724	64.8622	82.0232	104.8196	135.2318	175.9505	230.6322	304.2435	403.5281	537.6370	964.3595	1746.2358	2354.9969
43	53.3978	56.4823	59.7920	63.3446	67.1595	85.4839	110.0124	142.9933	187.5076	247.7765	329.5830	440.8457	592.4007	1081.0826	1991.7088	2709.2465
44	54.9318	58.1883	61.6889	65.4532	69.5027	89.0484	115.4129	151.1430	199.7580	266.1209	356.9496	481.5218	652.6408	1211.8125	2271.5481	3116.6334
45	56.4811	59.9157	63.6142	67.5986	71.8927	92.7199	121.0294	159.7002	212.7435	285.7493	386.5056	525.8587	718.9048	1358.2300	2590.5648	3585.1285
46	58.0459	61.6646	65.5684	69.7816	74.3306	96.5015	126.8706	168.6852	226.5081	306.7518	418.4261	574.1860	791.7953	1522.2176	2954.2439	4123.8977
47	59.6263	63.4354	67.5519	72.0027	76.8172	100.3965	132.9454	178.1194	241.0986	329.2244	452.9002	626.8628	871.9749	1705.8838	3368.8380	4743.4824
48	61.2226	65.2284	69.5652	74.2628	79.3535	104.4084	139.2632	188.0254	256.5645	353.2701	490.1322	684.2804	960.1723	1911.5898	3841.4753	5456.0047
49	62.8348	67.0437	71.6087	76.5624	81.9406	108.5406	145.8337	198.4267	272.9584	378.9990	530.3427	746.8656	1057.1896	2141.9806	4380.2819	6275.4055
50	64.4632	68.8818	73.6828	78.9022	84.5794	112.7969	152.6671	209.3480	290.3359	406.5289	573.7702	815.0636	1163.9085	2400.0182	4994.5213	7217.7163

Glossary

The numbers in parentheses after the terms indicate the chapter where the term is first defined. Some of the definitions in this glossary are taken from specific accounting pronouncements. The appropriate footnote references appear in the chapter where the definition is originally given.

Abandonments (11): Situations in which firms walk away from their productive assets and typically recover nothing.

Absorption costing (8): A costing method where all costs, both fixed and variable, are treated as product costs.

Accounting (1): The process of designing and maintaining an information system that focuses on the flow of economic resources.

Accounts receivable (7): Rights to collect cash obtained in the exchange for the goods and service based on the terms of trade.

Accrual basis accounting (2): A system of financial reporting that attempts to record the financial effects of transactions and events that have cash consequences for the entity in the periods in which those transactions and events occur rather than in the periods in which cash is received or paid.

Accumulated benefit obligation (18): A measure of the sponsoring firm's liability for future benefit payments in a defined benefit plan that is based on current compensation levels and actual service to date.

Accumulated post-retirement benefit obligation (APBO) (19): The actuarial present value, as of the valuation date, of the total post-retirement benefit payments, other than pensions, attributable to service rendered to date.

Actuarial discount rate (18): The interest rate used to convert the estimated future pension benefit payments for the current workforce into a present value at a given valuation date.

Actuarial gains and losses (18): Differences between estimates made by actuaries and actual outcomes for defined benefit plans.

Actuary (18): An individual trained in the use and development of estimates relating to mortality and other attributes that influence the expected costs of insurance and retirement benefits.

Additional paid-in capital (14): Amounts contributed to the corporation in excess of the legal capital of the shares issued.

Additions (10): Expenditures to add components to existing assets.

Adjusted trial balance (Appx. A): A trial balance prepared after all adjustments have been recorded and posted.

Adjusting entries (Appx. A): Entries needed under accrual accounting made at the end of a period to bring the accounting records up to date.

Aggregation (1): The process of translating events and transactions into a common format and summarizing the total effect of all similarly coded events.

Allowance method (7): A method of accounting for uncollectible accounts in which the amount of bad debt losses expected is accrued based on expectations regarding future collections.

Amortization (13): A method of systematically recognizing a cost as expense, such as amortizing a discount or premium on bonds.

Annual report to shareholders (ARS) (1): General-use reports produced by entities engaged in business for profit.

Appropriated retained earnings (15): An amount of stockholders' equity that cannot be used to support general corporate distributions.

Asset impairment (11): The inability to recover fully the carrying amount of assets over their estimated useful lives.

Asset/liability approach (20): An approach that measures deferred tax expense as the change in the value of deferred tax assets and liabilities from one period to the next.

Assets (2): Probable future economic benefits obtained or controlled by an entity as a result of past transactions or events.

Assignee (7): The third party receiving the right to collection of the receivables.

Assignment of receivables (7): The transfer of a right to the cash collections from the receivables to a third party.

Assignor (7): The company assigning the receivable.

Asymmetric information (1): Any situation where different parties (i.e., managers and investors) have different access to information.

Auditor (1): An independent third party who examines the financial statements for conformity with agreed upon reporting standards to determine whether the statements present fairly the financial position, results of operations, and cash flows of the firm.

Audit trail (Appx. A): Documentation used to verify that the amounts recorded in the account records are correct.

Average costing (8): A cost flow assumption where both inventory and cost of goods sold are stated at an average cost figure.

Balance sheet (3): A financial statement that describes the firm's financial position at the close of business on a particular day.

Bank drafts (6): Commitments by banking institutions to advance funds on demand by the party to whom the draft was directed.

Bargain purchase option (17): An option to purchase leased assets at the end of the base term at a price that is expected to be below the asset's fair value.

Bargain renewal option (17): A renewal option that provides for lease payments below those typically demanded in the marketplace.

Board of directors (14): A governing body of a corporation elected by shareholders who hold equity securities that carry voting rights.

Bonds (13): A formal document that serves as evidence of the borrower's indebtedness.

Book income (20): Income before taxes for financial reporting purposes.

Boot (10): The dissimilar asset, debt, or equity that is part of an exchange of similar productive assets.

Call premium (13): The amount an issuer is required to pay in excess of face value to call the notes or bonds.

Call provisions (13): Bond provisions that allow the issuer a means of retiring the bonds before their regular maturity dates at prespecified prices.

Capital intensive (10): Firms that require a significant investment in plant and equipment.

Capital lease (17): A lease that transfers substantially all the asset's property rights to the lessee over the life of the lease.

Cash (6): An asset that includes petty cash, demand deposits, time deposits, undeposited checks, foreign currencies, bank drafts, and money orders.

Cash basis accounting (4): Revenues and expenses are recognized only at the point of cash receipts or disbursements.

Cash dividends (15): Periodic distributions of cash to shareholders based on a per share rate.

Cash equivalents (3): Very liquid, short-term investments typically made to earn a return on otherwise idle cash balances.

Cash flows (21): Any transactions that cause cash to move into and out of a business during a period.

Cash flow statement (21): A financial statement designed to provide useful information about a firm's cash flows by describing how cash was obtained and how it was spent.

Chart of accounts (Appx. A): A list of all accounts found in the general ledger.

Closing (Appx. A): The process of updating equity account balances by the amounts of all related revenues, expenses, gains, losses, and dividends.

Coinsurance clause (11): A feature of insurance policies that states a particular level of coverage, relative to the asset's fair value at the time of the loss, that must be in force before the insurance company is required to pay the full value of any claims.

Collateral trust bonds (13): Bonds that have certain assets pledged as collateral to secure them.

Comparability (2): The development of reporting and measurement procedures that are consistent across companies (cross-sectional).

Comparative balance sheets (3): A financial statement that shows balances at two or more points in time to permit comparison of the firm's financial position over time.

Compensating balance (6): The minimum balance that must be kept on deposit with the bank as part of a lending agreement.

Compensatory option (19): An option that is intended as compensation of employees; one that does not meet the definition of a noncompensatory option.

Completed contract method (5): A method of recognizing revenues on long-term contracts only at the completion of a project.

Complex capital structure (Appx. B): The capital structure of corporations that includes securities that may be converted or exercised into shares of common stock.

Composite depreciation (11): A depreciation method applied to groups of dissimilar items.

Compound security (14): An issue of several securities as a bundle.

Comprehensive income (2): Income measured by all changes in equity except those involving capital contributions or distributions to shareholders.

Conservatism (2): A bias in financial reporting favoring understatement of net assets and income.

Consignment (4): A transaction whereby the consignor delivers goods to the consignee, who agrees to attempt to sell the consignor's goods for a fee and to exercise a reasonable standard of care in protecting these goods from damage or loss.

Consistency (2): The use of reporting and measurement procedures that are consistent over time for a company.

Contingency (2): An existing condition, situation, or set of circumstances involving uncertainty as to possible gain or loss to an enterprise that will ultimately be resolved when one or more future events occur or fail to occur.

Contribution margin (4): Selling price less variable expenses.

Contributory pension plans (18): A pension plan in which employees are required or allowed to make contributions.

Control accounts (Appx. A): The account in the general ledger that contains the balance of all related accounts found in the subsidiary ledger.

Corporate reorganization (15): An action of a bankruptcy court that restructures the liability and equity claims of a corporation filing for legal reorganization.

Corridor amortization (18): A procedure applied to amortize cumulative pension gains or losses when they exceed 10% of the plan assets or projected benefit obligation, whichever is greater.

Cost based depletion (11): A process whereby the original cost of the properties or property rights are allocated to expense.

Cost recovery method (5): A method of recognizing revenues and expenses such that income is only recognized once the cost of the item sold has been fully recovered.

Credit (Appx. A): Decrease in assets, increase in liabilities and/or owner's equity.

Current assets (3): Cash and other assets that are reasonably expected to be realized in cash or sold or consumed during the normal operating cycle of the business.

Current investment (16): A short-term investment expected to be liquidated within one year or the next operating cycle, whichever is longer.

Current liabilities (3): Liabilities whose liquidation is reasonably expected to require the use of existing resources properly classified as current assets, or the creation of other current liabilities.

Date of declaration (6): The date the directors declare the dividend.

Date of distribution (6): The date when the dividend is actually distributed.

Debentures (13): Bonds for which the debt contract does not specify particular assets pledged as security for the loan.

Debit (Appx. A): Increase in asset balances, decrease in liability and/or owner's equity balances.

Decision usefulness (2): The ability or potential of information to influence a management decision.

Declining balance method (11): A depreciation method in which a constant depreciation rate is applied to the declining net book value of the asset each year.

Default risk (6): The likelihood that the issuing corporation will not be able to make all the promised cash payments at the scheduled dates.

Defined benefit pension plan (18): An arrangement by the sponsoring corporation to provide prespecified retirement benefits to the employee-beneficiary.

Defined contribution pension plan (19): A retirement plan in which the sponsor agrees to make periodic contributions to a trust on the employee's behalf based on a contractual formula.

Demand deposits (6): Amounts on deposit in financial institutions that are available on demand.

Depletion (11): The process of matching the costs of natural resource properties or property rights with the revenues recognized from the production and sale of the commodities.

Depreciation (11): A cost allocation process used to assign the costs of productive assets to the periods in which the assets are used.

Development stage enterprise (12): A business whose planned principal operations have not commenced or whose planned principal operations have commenced, but there has been no significant revenue therefrom.

Dilution (Appx. B): Situations in which the issuance of additional common shares upon exercise of the conversion feature in another security would result in a reduction in the earnings per share figure.

Direct financing leases (4): A long-term lease transaction where the lessor, other than a dealer or manufacturer, exchanges physical assets for financial assets; essentially an installment loan in disguise.

Direct method (21): A method of presenting the cash flows from operating activities on the cash flow statement in which firms list operating sources and uses of cash, ending in a net source or use of cash.

Direct write-off method (7): A treatment of the costs associated with uncollectible accounts as an expense at the time it proves to be uncollectible.

Discount on bonds (6): The excess of bonds' face value over their proceeds from issuance or current market value.

Distributions to owners (2): Decreases in net assets of a particular enterprise resulting from transferring assets, rendering services, or incurring liabilities by the enterprise to owners.

Dollar value LIFO (9): A technique, based on price indexes, widely used to allow firms to report inventory on a LIFO basis without having to maintain their inventory records on that basis.

Double extension method (9): A method used to determine a price index for use in applying dollar value LIFO that prices ending inventory twice, once at current prices and once at base period prices.

Earnings per share (Appx. B): A ratio that represents an allocation of earnings to each share of common stock.

Economic order quantity (8): An inventory model using estimates of order costs, carrying costs, stock-out costs, time required for production or order procurement and demand for inventory to determine an optimal inventory size for the firm.

Economic rent (12): The difference between the expected earnings level and the earnings level required to provide equity investors with a return sufficient to compensate them for the inherent risks of the business.

Employee stock options (19): A contract that allows the employee to purchase a share of stock for a stated fixed price over a specific period.

Employee stock ownership plan (ESOP) (19): A trust is established to acquire shares of the sponsoring corporation. The shares are allocated to individual participants over time, based on rules established when the ESOP is started.

Employee stock purchase programs (19): Programs that allow employees to purchase shares of stock in the corporation usually through payroll deductions.

Entry age normal cost method (18): An allocation method in which the total present value of the benefits estimated to accrue at retirement is converted into an annual annuity covering the period from entry into the pension plan to date of retirement.

Equity (2): The residual interest in the assets of an entity that remains after deducting liabilities.

Excess earnings approach (12): A method of determining goodwill that requires estimates of expected future earnings and required earnings for all periods in which it is anticipated that expected future earnings will exceed the required earnings of the firm.

Ex dividend date (6): The date on and after which the rights to the next dividend will not transfer to the purchaser of the stock.

Executory contracts (3): Contracts that have remaining obligations to be performed by one or more of the parties (i.e., lease contracts).

Executory costs (17): The costs the lessee pays the lessor for maintenance or protection of the asset.

Expected post-retirement benefit obligation (EPBO) (19): The actuarial present value, as of the valuation date, of the total post-retirement benefit payments for current and retired employees.

Expenses (2): Outflows or other using up of assets or incurrence of liabilities during a period from delivering or producing goods, rendering services, or carrying out other activities that constitute the entity's ongoing operations.

External reporting (1): The communication to individuals or groups outside an organization's boundaries.

Extraordinary items (3): An event or transaction that is both unusual in nature and infrequent in occurrence, and produces a material gain or loss.

Extraordinary repairs (10): Infrequent repairs that typically involve an attempt to restore productive capacity by rebuilding part or all of the asset.

Feedback value (2): The usefulness in understanding how a past outcome might alter a decision regarding a future action.

Final pay plans (18): A defined benefit plan feature in which the formula used to determine the pension benefit is based on both years of service and some average of the wages or salary earned over the final years of employment with the company.

Financial reporting (2): Process of communicating inside information about the past activities, current status, and future opportunities of an enterprise to interested outside parties.

Financing activities (3): A section of the cash flow statement reporting cash paid to or received from owners or paid to or received from lenders in connection with borrowing (except interest).

First-in, first-out (FIFO) (8): A cost flow assumption that assumes the costs flow through inventory in chronological order, i.e., the costs of units sold are assumed to be the costs of the units acquired earliest.

Floating rate debt (13): Debt with a rate that varies with some general measure of interest rates such as banks' prime rate.

Flowthrough method (20): A reporting system that determines tax expense for any period based solely on the taxes due to the government.

Flow variable (3): Changes in some quantity over a period of time.

FOB destination (8): A shipping term designating that legal title to goods changes when the goods are delivered by a common carrier to the buyer.

FOB shipping point (8): A shipping term designating that legal title to goods changes when the goods are delivered to a common carrier.

Franchise (4): A contract whereby the franchisor allows the franchisee to operate a business in exchange for the franchisee's promise to pay fees to the franchisor.

Full disclosure principle (2): Explanations necessary to avoid misleading users of financial statements that go beyond basic measurement and reporting items. Much of the information in the notes to the financial statements is present to meet this principle.

Full eligibility date (19): The date an employee becomes eligible to receive post-retirement benefits.

Fully diluted earnings per share (FDEPS) (Appx. B): A pro forma calculation of EPS based upon the assumption that all potentially dilutive securities are exercised or converted into additional shares of common stock.

Fundamental accounting identity (3): Assets equal liabilities plus owners' equity.

Gains and losses (2): Increases or decreases in equity from peripheral or incidental transactions of an entity and from all other transactions or events and circumstances affecting the entity during a period except those that result from revenues, expenses, investments by owners, or distributions to owners.

General ledger (Appx. A): A cumulative record of all transactions recorded by a firm organized by account.

Generally accepted accounting principles (GAAP) (2): Accounting and reporting methods with substantial authoritative support.

Goodwill (12): The excess of price paid to acquire an interest in a company over the fair value of the share of net assets acquired.

Gross profit method (9): A method used to estimate the cost of ending inventories based upon the relationship between selling price and cost.

Group depreciation (11): A depreciation method applied to groups of similar items.

Guaranteed residual (17): The residual value of a leased asset guaranteed by the lessee to the lessor.

Holdback (7): A percentage of the total factored receivables that is set aside to absorb the effect of bad debt losses, sales discounts, sales returns, etc.

Holding gains (losses) (9): Increases or decreases in the value of an asset that occur while the item is held by a firm.

Identifiable assets (12): Assets that are included on the balance sheet of an acquired company.

Implicit interest rate (17): The rate of interest that will equate an obligation's present value to the fair values of the consideration exchanged for it.

Improvements (10): Expenditures that increase the efficiency or quality of the output produced by an asset.

Incentive compensation programs (19): Specific compensation devices that link the amount of reward an employee receives to achievement of some target goal.

Incentive stock option (ISO) (19): An option not meeting the tax requirements of a qualified plan that may still receive special tax treatment if specific requirements are met.

Income statement (3): The financial report summarizing the results of a firm's operations over a particular period in terms of revenues, expenses, gains, and losses.

Incremental borrowing rate (17): The rate the lessee would have paid to finance the asset's acquisition had the lessee not used leasing to acquire use of the asset.

Indenture (13): The contract that exists between a borrower and its bondholders.

Indirect method (21): A method of presenting the cash flows from operating activities on the cash flow statement in which net income is reconciled with net source or use of cash.

Initial direct costs (17): Costs of completing lease agreements incurred by the lessor.

Initial franchise fee (4): The consideration paid by the franchisee to the franchisor for establishing the franchise relationship and providing some initial services.

Installment sales method (5): A method in which gross profit is recognized on a pro rata basis as installment payments are collected; used in some cases for tax reporting purposes but rarely used for financial reporting purposes.

In-substance defeasance (13): Risk-free assets are irrevocably placed into a trust to service debt; if the trust's cash flows are adequate, the debt is treated as if it were extinguished.

Intangible assets (12): Assets that have no physical existence and no contractual claims to cash such as receivables.

Interest bearing debt (6): A debt contract that explicitly calls for both periodic payments of interest and repayment of principal.

Interest rate swap (13): An arrangement where an intermediary arranges for the firm with floating rate debt to swap or exchange its obligation to pay interest at a floating rate with another firm's obligation to pay interest at a fixed rate.

Intraperiod tax allocation (3): The process of reporting the tax effects of special items with those special items rather than as a part of tax expense shown in the continuing operations section of an income statement.

Inventories (8): The aggregate of those items of tangible personal property that are held for sale in the ordinary course of business, are in the process of production for such sale, or are to be currently consumed either directly or indirectly in the production of goods or services.

Inventory depreciation (11): A depreciation method applied to an asset group consisting of many small items whereby depreciation is calculated in the same manner as cost of goods sold.

Inventory turnover ratio (8): A measure of how quickly inventory moves through the firm generally defined as cost of goods sold divided by inventory.

Investing activities (3): A section of the cash flow statement reporting cash flows from the acquisition or disposal of such items as investments in productive assets, debt or equity securities, and loans to individual or other firms.

Investments (3): An asset classification that generally reports investments in the securities of other firms with an expected holding period greater than one year.

Investments by owners (2): Increases in net assets of a particular enterprise resulting from transfers to it from other entities something of value to obtain or increase ownership in the entity.

Involuntary conversions (11): Liquidations of a firm's assets due to circumstances beyond its control, such as condemnations.

Journal entry (Appx. A): The mechanism for recording events and transactions in the accounts.

Just in time (JIT) (8): An inventory management technique whereby suppliers deliver inventory exactly when it is needed for production, thereby minimizing carrying costs.

Last-in, first-out (LIFO) (8): A cost flow assumption that assumes that costs flow in reverse chronological order, i.e., the costs of units sold are assumed to be the costs of the units acquired last.

Lease (17): A contract that transfers property rights between the owner of an asset and another party without immediately transferring title to the asset.

Lessee (4): Person or company making a series of payments as consideration for the use of an asset in a lease transaction.

Lessor (4): Person or company providing the use of an asset for a period of time specified by the lease contract.

Liability (2): Probable future sacrifices of economic benefits arising from present obligations of a particular entity to transfer assets or provide services to other entities in the future as a result of past transactions or events.

License (12): A legal right to use some resource.

Lien (13): A debt contract provision that gives the lender the right to keep assets pledged as collateral if the borrower defaults.

LIFO reserve (8): The difference between the LIFO value of inventory and its FIFO or current value.

LIFO retail (9): A method that allows retail firms to keep their records based on retail prices but permits them to use LIFO for financial reporting and tax purposes.

Line-of-credit (6): A commitment from a bank to make loans to the company on demand up to a prespecified maximum.

Link-chain method (9): A method to determine an annual price index for application of dollar value LIFO that is constructed each year as the product of previous years' indexes.

Liquidating dividends (15): Dividend distribution that exceeds the value of total stockholders' equity reduced by the value of any legal capital.

Liquidity (6): An enterprise's ability to generate sufficient cash to meet creditors' demands when obligations come due.

Loan origination fees (4): A charge by lenders at the beginning of the loan; also known as points.

Long-term debt (3): Liabilities that involve obligations due more than one operating cycle from the balance sheet date.

Lower-of-cost-or-market (LCM) rule (8): The valuation principle applied to inventory that requires it be written down whenever market value is below cost.

Markdowns (9): Reductions in prices of items below their original retail prices.

Marketable investment (16): An investment traded in well-organized markets with regularly quoted prices.

Market value (8): The cost of an asset if acquired today, i.e., the replacement cost of the inventory.

Mark-to-market approach (6): An approach whereby all securities are adjusted to current market value at the end of the period.

Markup (9): Increases in the prices of items above their original retail prices.

Matching principle (2): The accounting principle that requires that costs, which can be directly related to the generation of revenue, should be recognized as an expense at the point when the related revenue is recognized.

Materiality (2): A judgment whether a particular amount in the financial statements is great enough to affect user decisions.

Monetary exchanges (10): Exchanges in which the consideration given up to acquire an asset is cash or a cash equivalent.

Monetary unit assumption (2): The assumption that the attributes of an element will be measured in nominal monetary units.

Money orders (6): Negotiable instruments giving the payee the right to receive cash.

Mortgage (13): A lien on real estate.

Multiple-step income statement (3): An income statement that requires several calculations to derive net income, thereby providing a more detailed presentation of income statement information than the single-step format.

Net lease receivable (17): The net difference between the minimum lease payments receivable and the unearned interest.

Net realizable values (3): The net amount of cash that a particular asset is expected to generate.

Neutrality (2): An element of reliability; freedom from bias or error.

Noncompensatory options (19): For financial reporting purposes, an option that is not deemed to be given to employees as compensation for services rendered.

Noncontributory plan (18): A pension plan that does not permit employees to make contributions to the plan.

Noncurrent investments (16): Nonproducing assets businesses acquire with the intent to hold them for periods in excess of one year.

Non-interest bearing debt (6): A debt contract that contains only a promise to pay a lump sum at maturity of the debt.

Nonmonetary exchanges (10): Exchanges made with nonmonetary assets or equity claims as consideration.

Normal maintenance (10): Any recurring costs that are necessary to maintain the asset's normal working condition.

Notes receivable (7): Rights, granted in a formalized financial instrument called a promissory note, to collect cash.

Objectivity (3): The principle that amounts reported on the financial statements should be subject to independent verification.

Off balance-sheet financing (13): Any of a firm's obligations that are not required to be reported as balance sheet liabilities.

Off balance-sheet risk (13): Situations in which a financial instrument exposes a firm to the risk of accounting loss that exceeds the amount of obligation recognized on the firm's balance sheet.

Operating activities (3): A segment of the cash flow statement that reports activities involved in providing goods and services to customers.

Operating cycle (3): The average period required for acquisition of inventory (if any), sale of goods or services, collection of cash from customers, and payment of cash to suppliers.

Operating leases (4): Leases that do not transfer the risks and reward of ownership to the lessee; the lease payments are, in essence, rent.

Operating loss carryback (20): The use of an operating loss to offset taxable income in prior years.

Operating loss carryforward (20): The use of an operating loss to reduce taxable income in future periods.

Operating profit (9): An element of replacement cost income that occurs when a unit of inventory is sold for more than its cost to replace the unit.

Organizational costs (12): The costs incurred when a corporation begins operations, such as preparing and filing articles of incorporation, developing a corporate logo, and legal and technical assistance.

Overdraft (6): Checks written in excess of the available cash; accounted for as a temporary loan.

Owners' equity (3): The owners' claims on the assets of the firm.

Patent (12): An exclusive right, granted by the U.S. Government, to use a process or produce a product.

Percentage depletion (11): A depletion method used for tax purposes in which total revenues generated from the sale of the commodity being extracted are multiplied by a fixed percentage.

Percentage of completion method (5): A method of recognizing revenues on long-term contracts as work progresses.

Performance unit plans (19): Plans that provide payment to the manager in the form of equal valued units, which are earned by accomplishing targets with multiple dimensions.

Periodic inventory system (8): An inventory record keeping system where inventory quantities are determined periodically by means of a physical count.

Permanent differences (20): A difference between book and tax bases of an asset or liability that arises because one of the two systems includes certain transactions or events and the other does not.

Perpetual inventory system (8): An inventory record keeping system where inventory records are maintained perpetually so that, ideally, inventory quantities are determinable at any time.

Petty cash (6): Cash balances kept on hand at various locations to pay for minor expenditures.

Phantom stock plans (19): Plans that award contingent compensation based on a formula that mimics the returns the corporation's common shareholders receive without actually issuing stock or a claim to stock in the company.

Pledging of receivables (7): Receivables used to secure a loan.

Post-closing trial balance (Appx. A): A trial balance prepared after closing entries have been recorded and posted.

Posting (Appx. A): The process of updating the account balances in the ledger for transactions recorded in the journals.

Predictive value (2): The usefulness of information for predicting future events.

Preferred stock (14): An equity security that ranks above common shares in claims in the event of liquidation and usually has a prior claim to any dividends distributed during a period.

Premium on bonds (6): The excess of bonds' current market value or proceeds from issuance over their face value.

Price-earnings multiplier approach (12): A method of determining goodwill that estimates the total value for the company, including any goodwill, then subtracts the net fair value of all identifiable assets and liabilities.

Primary earnings per share (PEPS) (Appx. B): Earnings per share based on common stock and common stock equivalents outstanding.

Primary market (14): The market for all new issuances of securities by public corporations.

Prior period adjustments (15): Adjustments to the beginning balance of retained earnings for the consequences of an event traceable to periods prior to the current period.

Probable events (2): In determining how to report a contingent loss, future events giving rise to the loss that are likely to occur.

Product costs (8): Costs assigned directly to inventory.

Profit-sharing plans (19): Defined contribution pension plans based on profitability.

Projected accrued benefit cost method (18): A method that bases the estimates of retirement benefits on future salary.

Projected benefit obligation (18): The present value of the projected benefits to be paid to current employees under the plan at retirement, but earned based on service rendered to date.

Promissory note (7): A legal document executed by a borrower and a lender setting forth the rights and responsibilities of both parties, along with the timing of any cash flows for payment of interest and principal.

Property dividend (15): A type of corporate distribution in which noncash assets are distributed.

Property, plant and equipment (3): Assets held for use, rather than for sale.

Property right (17): A legal right to benefit from an asset.

Public good (1): A good that has more value to society as a whole than it does to any individual.

Purchase allowance (8): An adjustment to purchases when a reduction in the price of goods is allowed after the acquisition.

Purchase option (17): A lease provision that provides the lessee an opportunity to acquire full title to the asset at a specific time.

Purchase return (8): An accounting adjustment made when purchased goods are returned as defective or unsuitable.

Qualified stock options (19): A stock option plan offered to all employees without discrimination based on level of employment, the exercise prices are not significantly below the stock's market price at the grant date, and other specific requirements are met will be considered qualified for tax purposes.

Quasi-reorganization (15): An accounting treatment designed to provide a corporation with a fresh start as far as its financial statements are concerned, regardless of whether any legal reorganization has occurred.

Realization (2): The act of converting noncash resources and rights into cash.

Receivable (7): A contractual right to collect cash at some point in the future.

Recognition (2): The process of formally recording or incorporating an item into the financial statements.

Recourse (7): The factor's requirement that the company transferring receivables pay for any uncollectible accounts or otherwise compensate the factor in the event of noncollection.

Relevance (2): The ability of accounting information to make a difference in a decision.

Reliability (2): The ability for accounting information users to be able to depend on accounting information that faithfully represents the economic conditions or events it purports to represent.

Renewal options (17): A lease provision that allows the lessee to renew the lease without an increase in the lease payment.

Replacement method (11): A depreciation method applied to groups of items that are of small value individually, but are significant in aggregate. Depreciation expense is recognized when the items are replaced as the cost of new items acquired.

Replacements (10): Components of assets replaced to extend their life.

Representational faithfulness (2): An element of reliability that exists when financial reports accurately portray similar underlying economic events similarly and different events differently.

Required return (12): The earnings level required to provide equity investors with a return sufficient to compensate them for the inherent risks of the business.

Restrictive debt covenants (13): Promises made by the borrower to lessen the lender's risk.

Retail inventory method (9): A method that allows firms to track their inventories at retail values while providing reliable estimates of goods' costs for financial reporting purposes.

Retainages (5): An amount allowed under some long-term contracts where the buyer retains a portion of the contract price pending the occurrence of some event; also known as retentions.

Retained earnings (14): The corporation's accumulated net income that has not been distributed to shareholders via dividends or other capital transactions.

Retirement method (11): A depreciation method applied to groups of items that are of small value individually, but are significant in aggregate. The original cost of the asset is charged to depreciation expense when it is retired from service.

Revenues (2): Inflows or other enhancements of assets of an entity or settlements of its liabilities during a period from delivering or producing goods, rendering services, or other activities that constitute the entity's ongoing major or central operation.

Reversing entries (Appx. A): An optional step in the accounting cycle designed to prevent double-counting or no recording of certain revenues and expenses.

Sale-leaseback (17): A series of contracts where a company finds a second party willing to buy an asset it currently owns and then enters into a lease arrangement whereby it retains the use of the asset but passes ownership to the second party.

Sales on approval (4): Sales where goods are shipped to the potential buyer who has the right to return them if they are not satisfactory.

Sales-type leases (4): A long-term contract that transfers virtually all the risks and rewards of ownership from the manufacturer or dealer lessor to the lessee.

Secondary market (14): A market for resale of equity and debt instruments.

Self-constructed assets (10): Assets in which a company has used some of its own labor or capital resources to construct or install.

Separation of ownership and control (14): The ability to hire professional managers to run corporations without requiring day-to-day supervision by shareholders.

Serial bonds (13): Bonds that mature at different times.

Share repurchase (15): Exchanges between shareholders and the corporation in which the corporation purchases the investors' shares.

Short-term investments in marketable securities (6): An asset category that represents investments in debt or equity securities of other entities, where management's intent is to liquidate the investment within the next operating cycle.

Simple capital structure (Appx. B): The capital structure of a corporation that has only one class of common stock outstanding and no securities which are not themselves common shares, but can be converted into common shares.

Single-step format income statement (3): An income statement where income is determined in a single step by subtracting all expenses from revenues.

Sinking funds (3): Separate investment funds established by a debt contract to insure that the necessary funds for the repayment of debt are available as the debt instruments mature; typically classified in the investments section of the balance sheet.

Social welfare decisions (2): Choices that will impose costs on some members of society and bestow benefits on others.

Source documents (Appx. A): Evidence of the transaction.

Specific identification (8): Assigning the specific cost of each item in inventory when determining costs of goods sold and inventory balances.

Stated rate of interest (13): The rate of interest stated on the bonds, sometimes called the coupon rate.

Stock appreciation rights (19):   Plans that do not award any of the rights and privileges of share ownership to recipients but do tie recipients' wealth to the share price performance of the sponsoring company.

Stock dividends (6):   A distribution of additional shares by a corporation to its existing shareholders.

Stock options (6):   Securities created by one investor and sold to another giving a right to purchase or sell shares of stock in a specific corporation for a fixed price over a certain period.

Stock right (6):   A security issued by a corporation to its shareholders granting the opportunity to purchase shares at a fixed price for a limited period.

Stock splits (6):   A distribution of additional shares by a corporation to its existing shareholders.

Stock subscriptions (14):   A contract to purchase a specified number of shares at a specified price, with the contract to be executed at some future point.

Stock variable (3):   Describes some quantity at a point in time.

Straight-line depreciation (11):   A depreciation method where the depreciable base is allocated uniformly over the asset's life.

Sublease (17):   To lease to another party the use of the asset now under the original lessee's control.

Subordinated bonds (13):   Bonds whose holders have a claim that is subordinated to the claims of other creditors.

Subsidiary ledger (Appx. A):   A listing of all customer, vendor, etc., accounts; the total of all subsidiary ledger accounts must equal the balance shown in the related control account.

Sustainable future earnings (12):   The average annual earnings that would be expected from the company, assuming that it maintained its present size.

Taxable income (20):   A statutory definition of the income on which taxes are levied.

Tax credit (20):   An amount that a company can use to directly reduce the taxes payable for a period.

Technical default (15):   Any violation of a specific term of the debt covenant.

Temporary differences (20):   A difference between book and tax bases of an asset or liability that arises because of differences in the timing of the recognition given to certain events or transactions under the two systems.

Term notes (13):   Notes that all mature on a particular date.

Time deposits (6):   Amounts on deposit in savings accounts.

Timeliness (2):   The need for information users to receive information before making a decision; an element of relevance.

Trade account receivable (7):   An account receivable that arises from the sale of a company's usual goods and services in the normal course of business.

Trademarks (12):   Words or symbols that are used to identify a product specifically.

Trading securities (6):   Securities held for the short-term.

Treasury stock (14):   The value of shares that have been issued and repurchased but not retired by the corporation.

Trial balance (Appx. A):   A listing of all ledger accounts and their balances.

Troubled debt restructurings (13):   A transaction in which a lender agrees to grant certain concessions and modify the terms of the original debt agreement; used when a borrower is in financial difficulty.

Trustee (18):   A fiduciary charged with the responsibility to act in the best interests of another.

Understandability (2):   Ability of the user of financial information to determine the significance of the data to the decision at hand.

Underwriter (14):   A party who takes primary responsibility for lining up purchasers for the shares in a new issue and who insures that all the registration requirements of the SEC are met.

Unfunded accumulated benefit obligation (18):   The difference between the accumulated benefit obligation and the value of the assets in the pension trust.

Unfunded vested benefit obligation (18):   The vested benefit obligation minus the value of the assets in the pension trust.

Unit credit plan (18):   A defined benefit pension plan feature in which the employee is credited with a unit of service every time certain requirements are met.

Units of production method (11):   A method of depreciation or depletion based on the actual usage of the asset.

Unrecognized pension gains and losses (18):   The differences between actual results and expected results of a pension plan that are not reflected in the financial statements.

Unrecognized prior service cost (18):   The present value of the increase in expected future benefits attributable to the retroactive grant of service credits at the creation or amendment of a defined benefit pension plan that are not reflected in financial statements.

Unrestricted retained earnings (15):   The retained earnings balance available at any time to support a distribution.

Variable (or direct) costing (8):   A costing method where only the variable manufacturing costs are treated as product costs.

Verifiability (2):   Situations observed by different individuals who agree that the underlying economic event should be measured and reported in the same manner.

Vested benefits (18):   The pension benefits that employees may take with them upon termination.

Warrants (6):   Rights issued for consideration by a corporation that give the warrant holder the right to purchase shares at a fixed price over a certain period.

Index

INDEX OF REAL COMPANIES